"A true bible of Italian cooking."
—LIDIA BASTIANICH, from the Foreword

IN 1929, two years before *The Joy of Cooking* was published in America and two decades before *The Silver Spoon* in Italy, Ada Boni wrote *Il Talismano della Felicità*—the original must-have culinary bible for Italians. Cataloging all the flavors and traditions that define Italian cuisine, it quickly became the quintessential wedding gift: a talisman of luck for newlyweds beginning a new life. "There can be no true happiness," Boni wrote, "if such an essential part of our daily lives as eating is neglected."

The Talisman of Happiness became a national treasure, growing in length every time a new edition was published. In this landmark first English-language edition of the complete work, featuring nearly 1,700 recipes, American cooks can finally appreciate *The Talisman* in full. Carefully translated to preserve the spirit and warmth of the original, this new edition makes the richness of Italy's regional cooking accessible to all—and includes American measurements, delightful illustrations, and forewords by Lidia Bastianich and Katie Parla.

Boni wrote *The Talisman* for anyone longing for a taste of the traditional, and she included notes offering kitchen insights with the occasional bit of stern guidance. Whether you are a seasoned cook or are just beginning your culinary journey, *The Talisman* offers the gift of good luck alongside timeless recipes that embrace the true spirit of Italian cuisine: cooking to feed the body and nourish the soul.

The TALISMAN of HAPPINESS

First published in North America, October 2025 by Voracious / Little, Brown and Company
Hachette Book Group
1290 Avenue of the Americas, New York, NY 10104
voraciousbooks.com

Originally published as *Il Talismano della Felicità* in Italy by Editore Colombo, 1929

Elwin Street Productions Limited
10 Elwin Street, London E2 7BU
elwinstreet.com

Consultant Editor: Drew Smith

Editorial & Translation: Elena Battista, Mary Cadogan, Cecilia Gasparini, Anna Gatteschi, Kay Halsey, Clarissa Hyman, Cristina Rizzo, Jane Roe, Marina Silvello, Kate Slate, Ben Weinstein

Illustrations: Federico Bonfiglio
Design & Art Direction: Moira Clinch, Xinyu Wang
Cover & Endpaper Design: Nick Misani

ISBN 978-0-316-57799-1
LCCN 2025935021

Printed in Canada

10 9 8 7 6 5 4 3

THE MOST ICONIC
ITALIAN COOKBOOK
EVER WRITTEN

The TALISMAN of

1,680 RECIPES

Ada Boni

FOREWORDS BY

Lidia Bastianich

Katie Parla

VORACIOUS

LITTLE, BROWN AND COMPANY
NEW YORK BOSTON LONDON

CONTENTS

Forewords 6
Publisher's Introduction 8
Notes for Cooks 10
Notes on Ingredients 12

1 *CONDIMENTI, SALSE E SUGHI*
SAUCES 14
White Sauces 16
Cream Sauces 17
Egg Sauces 19
Classic Sauces 23
Quick Sauces 29
Ragus 32
Tomato Sauces 37
Fish Sauces 42
Special Sauces 44

2 *ANTIPASTI*
APPETIZERS 50
Jellies, Butters & Creams 52
Bruschetta, Canapés & Crostini 57
Sandwiches 61
Little Pastries & Plates 64
Choux & Puff Pastries 71
Hot Appetizers 75
Vol-au-vents 80

3 *BRODI E ZUPPE*
BROTHS & SOUPS 86
Broths 88
Cream Soups 96
Minestre 102
Stracciatelle 112
Minestrone 114
Fish Soups 121
Classic Soups 136

4 *PASTA, RISO, GNOCCHI E POLENTA*
PASTA, RICE, GNOCCHI & POLENTA 142
Dried Pasta 145
Fresh Egg Pasta 170
Baked Pasta 194
Rice 207
Gnocchi 227
Polenta 233

5 *FRITTURE*
FRIED DISHES 240
Batters 242
Fritti Misti 243
Fried Fish 245
Croquettes & Fagottini 246
Mostaccioli 253
Mozzarella 254
Skewers 256
Arancini & Supplì 259

6 *PIZZE, CALZONI E TORTE SALATE*
PIZZAS, CALZONES & PIES 262
Pizzas 264
Calzones 273
Pies 275

7 *UOVA* EGGS 292

- Frittate & Frittatine 294
- Omelets 305
- Poached Eggs 207
- Baked Eggs 309
- Fried Eggs 311
- Boiled Eggs 313
- Scrambled Eggs 318
- Soufflés 320

8 *PESCE E FRUTTI DI MARE* FISH & SEAFOOD 326

- Sea Fish 329
- River Fish 378
- Crustaceans 386
- Mollusks 399

9 *CARNE* MEAT 410

- Veal 412
- Beef 465
- Lamb 516
- Goat 538
- Pork 541

10 *POLLAME E SELVAGGINA* POULTRY & GAME 568

- Chicken 570
- Turkey 593
- Other Birds 600
- Furred Game 612

11 *ORTAGGI, LEGUMI E INSALATE* VEGETABLES, LEGUMES & SALADS 624

- Vegetables 626
- Legumes 709
- Salads 718
- Pickles 727

12 *FRUTTA E DOLCI* FRUIT & DESSERTS 734

- Sugar Basics 736
- Preserved Fruit 737
- Fillings & Icings 748
- Creams & Sauces 751
- Toppings 755
- Puddings 758
- Desserts with Fruit 764
- Egg Desserts 776
- Pastry Desserts 784
- Desserts with Yeast 796
- Sponge & Génoise Cakes 810
- Sweet Soufflés 826
- Chilled Desserts 829
- Ice Cream 839
- Cookies & Sweet Treats 848
- Fruit 878

RECIPE FINDER 888

INDEX 898

FOREWORDS

LIDIA BASTIANICH

In 1929, Ada Boni published a true bible of Italian cooking, *Il Talismano della Felicità*, or in English, *The Talisman of Happiness.*

A talisman is an object that is deemed to have magical properties, makes one feel calm and happy, and is a carrier of good luck. Ada Boni clearly concluded that the magic wand that makes Italians feel happy, blessed, and lucky is good Italian food that can be shared with family and friends.

Determined to be the magician who could wave that wand, she collected thousands of classic Italian recipes from throughout the country. And for the first time, the small country's 20 regions, which all have extensive but separate culinary cultures, were brought together in her magnum opus.

As a young girl in Italy, I recall how young brides looked forward to receiving this cookbook. They knew its recipes would help keep their family together and strong. I first saw the book when I was a child and I will never forget the indelible image on its cover: a farmworker wearing a straw hat while eating his pasta e fagioli with gusto. Over the years, for Italians and much of the rest of the world, food has become even more important as a way to connect and bring joy and nourishment to one another. That's why I am so delighted to see this masterful and historic document, this great recording of Italian culinary traditions, brought back to life. This new format makes me nostalgic for the past, but also gives me hope for the future because now *The Talisman of Happiness* will have a beloved place in American kitchens, too.

KATIE PARLA

The first time I held *Il Talismano della Felicità*, nearly 25 years ago, I was struck first by its heft, and next by its quiet authority. It was not flashy, with glossy photos and baroque language. Instead, the tone of its nearly 1,000 pages was measured, its organization exacting, its recipes clear-eyed and practical. And yet, flipping through the sauces—*salsa besciamella bastarda piccante, maionese alle acciughe, condimento alla carrettiera—and pastas–cannolicchi con fagioli freschi, spaghetti con capperi e olive, and fettuccine alla ciociara*— I realized I was in the presence of something extraordinary: a map of Italian domestic life written with deep care and cultural precision. As a cultural historian and author of cookbooks like *Food of the Italian South and Food of the Italian Islands*, I've spent my career exploring how food embodies identity, memory, and place. Ada Boni and her epic tome have been my beacon from day one.

Comprehensive, trustworthy, and endlessly usable, *Il Talismano* was the definitive Italian home cookbook of the 20th century. Through the pages of *Preziosa*, the food magazine Boni cofounded in 1915, she shaped an entire worldview, one where cooking, etiquette, household management, and womanhood were woven together into a kind of domestic code. In an era of war and upheaval, *Preziosa* offered structure and solace. It was there that Boni began to assemble the recipes and philosophies that would form the backbone of the book.

That early editorial experience shaped her voice: clear, instructive, generous. She didn't traffic in vague gestures or intuitive improvisation. These recipes don't merely describe how to cook; they communicate why, how, and for whom you're doing it. That's what makes *Il Talismano* so radical even now: it honors the domestic arts as real arts.

My own work centers on this same principle. I write about food not just as sustenance, but as a system of meaning—about how carbonara is a window into Roman identity, or how a forgotten pasta shape in Basilicata tells a story of migration and survival. Boni, nearly a century earlier, was building that archive from her Roman kitchen. She gave structure to the chaos of daily cooking, while still capturing the sensual, regional, and sometimes contradictory spirit of Italian cuisine.

To read *Il Talismano* today is to engage with a living text. The first-edition recipes have been joined by hundreds more to create this first English language version with nearly 2,000 recipes. In these pages, you'll find recipes that feel very much of their time—ham quenelles and veal galantines—but also those that remain vividly current, like *bucatini all'amatriciana and saltimbocca*. It is a book to cook from, yes, but also to learn from, to live with, to pass on.

Ada Boni never sought fame. Her legacy is woven into the fabric of Italian food culture quietly and indelibly. May this English edition bring her voice into your kitchen—and become stained, dog-eared, and cherished, as it should be.

PUBLISHER'S INTRODUCTION

"*Many of you, ladies, may know how to play the piano well or to sing with exquisite grace. Many of you may have prestigious degrees, may speak foreign languages or be pleasant writers or fine painters. Others of you may be master tennis or golf players, or know how to drive a luxurious automobile with a firm hand. But, alas, if you examine your conscience, I am certain that not all of you can honestly say that you know how to perfectly coddle an egg.*"

—Ada Boni

This is how Ada Boni began her first edition of *Il Talismano della Felicità*—perhaps the most important Italian cookbook ever published. Hers was the first comprehensive cookbook to catalog recipes gathered across the regions of Italy and designed explicitly for the use of the home cook. Without it, the rest of the world may never have come to know and embrace Italian food the way we do today.

Ada was a trailblazing writer and cook who believed that mastery of cooking and the domestic arts was the key to a good life. "There can be no true happiness," she wrote, "if such an essential part of our daily lives as eating is neglected."

When Ada was born in Rome in 1881, the city had only recently been named the capital of Italy. In fact, Italy itself was only formally unified twenty years earlier. While each region had its own unique food culture, a coherent national cuisine was only beginning to take shape. Ada's talent for cooking revealed itself in childhood, perhaps inspired by her uncle, a prominent chef named Adolfo Giaquinto. Later, she married a writer and artist named Enrico Boni, and in 1915, they launched a magazine dedicated to "home economics" called *Preziosa*. Ada was its chief editor.

This was a time of massive change and modernization in Italy as politics shifted, global conflicts emerged, and social and domestic practices evolved. Many well-to-do families no longer employed cooks, and women began to enter the workforce as industrialization took root. As lifestyles changed, and young people, especially newlyweds, moved to urban centers for professional opportunities, the recipes and food traditions that had been handed down from generation to generation needed to be gathered and written down if they were to be preserved and practiced.

That is where Ada came in. In *Preziosa*, she published recipes each month from all over Italy, and even opened a cooking school in Rome. Ada quickly amassed a recipe collection that eventually turned into *The Talisman of Happiness*—whose first edition contained a massive 882 dishes. Before *The Talisman*, other books had attempted to define Italian cooking, but no other book brought together the cuisines of each region so comprehensively, or in a way that addressed the home cook as its primary audience.

Extraordinarily comprehensive while remaining practical and family-friendly, the book became an instant classic—an essential wedding gift for couples creating a new life together. It became hugely influential as the go-to for how to cook just about everything. The iconic Italian-American culinary teacher and cookbook author Marcella Hazan credits *The Talisman* with teaching her to cook: it was her trusted source for recreating the flavors and dishes she treasured after moving to the United States.

The book has never been out of print in Italy. Over the years and across many editions, it grew more than double in size, with each edition adding and subtracting recipes based on trends and culinary movements. A much-abbreviated version of *The Talisman* was published in the United States in the 1950s, though it contained a small percentage of its recipes and veered far from the original text. Until now there has never been a full English translation of this seminal book.

One of the extraordinary things about *The Talisman of Happiness* is how from just a few ingredients we have so many recipes. From basic pantry items such as butter, oil, flour, eggs, tomatoes, anchovies, Parmesan, and more, Ada conjured one of the greatest cuisines in the world. There is not one recipe for minestrone; there are twelve—each offering a variation on the theme, accounting for seasonality of ingredients as well as versions specific to a time, person, or region. This is the Mediterranean diet as it really was, and is.

Ada's recipes are written in simple, everyday language, and punctuated by asides—she often includes tips, advice, variations, suggestions to reuse leftovers, ideas for presentation, and how to pair a dish with other recipes.

In many ways, *The Talisman* was the predecessor to the modern cookbook of today, with many of these rubrics still being championed by authors around the globe. Unlike modern cookbooks that spell out every last detail, *The Talisman of Happiness* reads like being in the kitchen with a grandmother telling you to add a knob of this and a glass of that. We might call it intuitive cooking today: the kind of cooking that tells a story on the plate by starting with what you have on hand. It is a style of cooking that creates abundance out of nothing. It challenges you to think about the "why" of a recipe, to be in tune with your senses and appetites, and to be fully present in the kitchen.

The Talisman of Happiness is a humble invitation into the kitchen and carries the glory of Italian food and spirit of hospitality on every page. Over the nearly 100 years that it has been in print, it has equally influenced and inspired renowned chefs, food television stars, legendary cookbook authors, and everyday home cooks who are drawn to Ada's clear voice and sound teachings. That is why, after all these decades, this book remains not only a priceless culinary and cultural artifact, but the mother of all other Italian cookbooks that followed.

NOTES FOR COOKS

ABOUT THIS EDITION

This first full English edition of *The Talisman of Happiness* has been translated and edited with the aim to preserve Ada's voice, style, and approach while keeping a balance of practicality, historic interest, and the book's original character. In some places, the text may come across as old-fashioned; in others, the style and ideas speak clearly to the present moment. As dishes were added and removed over the years, the language describing a certain technique could differ from recipe to recipe. We have embraced these quirks as part of *The Talisman*'s charm and history.

This edition features 1,680 recipes. In Italy, revised editions have included varying numbers of recipes. We opted not to include recipes for techniques that are obsolete, ingredients that are very little used today, or recipes not of Italian origin that were added in later printings. Similarly, we have excluded the original material on table etiquette and choosing wines, as these are so specific to a historic period in Italy that they would not be appropriate or useful today.

STRUCTURE

This new edition is structured in the same way as the original Italian edition, and generally follows the course of a classic Italian meal. There are 12 chapters, starting with 92 sauce recipes, moving on to 77 antipasti, 105 soups, and 167 recipes for pasta, rice, gnocchi, and polenta. There are 40 fried dishes and 33 pizzas, calzones, and pies. There are 64 egg recipes, then 170 recipes for fish and seafood. The meat section has a total of 288 dishes and poultry and game has 89. Vegetables, legumes, and salads comprise 251 recipes, and the book ends with 304 delicious desserts.

In each chapter, recipes are arranged by category and alphabetical order by Italian name. The recipe finder on page 888 provides a list of recipes, in English, in the order they appear. A traditional alphabetical index by ingredient begins on page 898.

INSTRUCTIONS

Ada's teaching methodology is visual, and a dish is "cooked" when it looks and smells "done." Just as cooking pasta "al dente" or seasoning a dish "to taste" involves trusting your intuition and preferences, this style of cooking is more about feel and following your own desires than adhering to an exact prescription. We heartily recommend reading a recipe at least once (if not two or three times) before beginning it to ensure you have a clear picture of what needs to happen, in what order, and when.

MEASUREMENTS

Specific measurements have been Americanized. Quantities may seem vague at first glance, but are actually quite emphatic. Descriptions like a trifle, a handful, half a glass, and a finger keep as close to the original text as possible. They are not only charming, but visual and expressive in the best Italian fashion.

Note that while "half a glass" may sound as specific as "1/2 cup," a glass is a measurement used when the exact quantity is not that important. There is no standard conversion for its volume, but you would do well to think of a small wine or water glass, and cook from the heart—"a sentimento" as some Italians would say. Anything with a quantity of less than 1 (teaspoon, tablespoon, ounce, item) has been added to the method rather than the ingredient list. Herbs, spices, and aromatics only list quantities if the amount to use is significant.

Quantities for sauces vary across recipes, so the precise amounts needed are listed in the ingredients. Where practical, a cross-reference is made to the original recipe—sometimes only for technique and methodology purposes, and sometimes for both the technique and the original quantities. Other cross-references link up important sauces with pastas, or dough basics with pizzas.

SERVING SIZES AND YIELDS

All recipes serve six as standard. When a recipe makes more or less, this has been indicated in the text or sub-heading.

EQUIPMENT

Ada wrote at a time when kitchens had none of the modern aids that we now take for granted. As such, a minimum of gadgetry is called for. For example, only the occasional recipe directs a cook to use a blender, but this can be a food processor or hand blender. The question of oven temperatures was simple: on or off, warm or hot.

COOKING TIMES AND TEMPERATURES

Cooking times are occasionally stated by Ada and may veer on the long side by modern standards due to changes in fashion, vegetable varieties, and animal husbandry. As ever, tune into your senses and intuition. Stovetop temperatures only became prevalent after Ada's time. She had only a flame. Similarly, her recipes predate oven thermometers, though the chart opposite approximates Ada's descriptions in the modern kitchen.

Oven Temperature Conversions		
Very hot	450°F	230°C
	425°F	220°C
Hot	400°F	200°C
Moderately hot	375°F	190°C
Moderate	350°F	180°C
	325°F	160°C
Cool	300°F	150°C
	275°F	140°C

NOTES ON INGREDIENTS

Alchermes is an herbal tonic found in Tuscany, Emilia-Romagna, and Sicily that is bright red (from the shells of the kermes beetle) and flavored with sugar, cinnamon, cloves, nutmeg, and vanilla.

Alcohol, or more specifically, pure alcohol (like Everclear) with a proof of as much as 90% alcohol by volume (ABV) was used in older editions. Vodka and grappa can substitute but are usually only half the strength.

Anchovies, or acciughe, are widely called for, whether fresh, oil-packed in tins, or salt-packed in jars (in which case they should be rinsed well before use).

Artichokes must have their tough outer leaves partially or completely removed, and the bristly choke removed as well. Ada often prefers just the hearts.

Beans, or fagioli, are mostly dried and need soaking and longer cooking (the timing depends on their age) with aromatics. The exception is lentils, which do not need soaking or cooking longer than 20 minutes. Fresh beans can be found in the market in summer.

Broccoli rabe, also called rapini or cime di rapa, is not to be confused with the chicories. Broccoletti are broccolini, which are different than rapini.

Butter is always unsalted and at room temperature, unless specified.

Carrots are a staple; Ada mentions yellow carrots for choice but traditional orange ones work as well across all recipes.

Chestnuts were once a country staple. After shelling, the skin surrounding the chestnut must be pricked or cut through before roasting or boiling, or they will burst. After roasting, the skin needs to be peeled away and discarded. You can often buy them skinned and already steamed.

Chicory has many names: torpedo-shaped endive, deep purple radicchio, escarole, and frisée all share a notable bitterness.

Chocolate is always dark as default.

Coppa, also called capocollo and capicola, is made from cured pork neck. When made with pig or boar's head, it's called coppa di testa.

Cotechino is a Northern Italian pork sausage seasoned with warm spices like cloves and nutmeg.

Cream is heavy cream unless specified.

Eggs are large unless specified.

Fish varies with the region. If the type of fish called for in a recipe is unavailable in your location, consider substituting a species with a similar texture. For example, if sustainably fished shark is hard to find, substitute with an equally meaty-textured, thick, steak-like fish such as swordfish; for thin and flaky turbot, substitute sole or flounder, and so forth.

Flour is all purpose except where specified; tipo 00 is extra fine and silky, and called for when making certain doughs, such as pizza and some pastas.

Gelatin and isinglass are called for in historic Italian recipes to make jellies. Isinglass is made from the dried swim bladders of large fish, a tradition dating back to Roman times, though it's difficult to source today. Instead, use sheet gelatin, which can be found online or purchased from professional restaurant supply sources. If you can't find sheet gelatin, use granulated gelatin, substituting 1 tbsp of granulated gelatin for every 3 gelatin sheets, following the instructions on the package to bloom and dissolve.

Guanciale is the cured cheek or jowl of the pig. It's usually covered with a coating of black pepper to differentiate it from pancetta and ventresca.

Lardo, the hard fat taken from the back of the pig—and not melted down into spreadable lard as it is in the US and UK—was the original cooking fat in areas where there were no olive trees. Sugna is fresh pork fat, similar to what Americans know as fatback. Cooked down in an earthenware pot, it becomes strutto, which was a staple for cooking and gives much flavor, but has fallen out of fashion for health reasons.

Lentils do not need soaking before cooking, unlike other pulses. Many say the best come from Abruzzo and Umbria, specifically from the town of Castelluccio.

Luganega is a long, thin, and coiled fresh sausage popular in the north, although historically from the south.

Marsala is a sweet Sicilian wine often used in cooking. Madeira is called for as an alternative but is from Portugal.

Milk is full-fat, but semi-skimmed is acceptable.

Mollica di pane is the white part only of a loaf of bread, soaked in water or vinegar, and squeezed dry. Most households would have their own variation.

Mostarda are candied fruits preserved in a mustardy syrup and typically served with boiled meats. Versions from Cremona are most renowned. Mantua is a variety made with apples or quince and honey, often found in Veneto, whereas in Sicily, mostarda is made with grapes and almonds.

Mushrooms are a staple, particularly dried mushrooms. The best are porcini but many others are commonly used. They need to be reconstituted before cooking to revive.

Olive oil, virgin or extra virgin, is very often unfiltered.

Pancetta is the same cut of pork belly as for bacon but is not smoked. Pancetta is sold as a flat slab and is a mainstay of soffritto, while arrotolata is rolled, often much fattier, seasoned with clove and pepper, and preferred for longer cooking applications.

Pangrattato refers to crispy breadcrumbs.

Parmesan Ada always bought her Parmesan as a wedge and grated it just prior to using. If using pre-grated Parmesan, make sure it is 100% Parmesan.

Pastry doughs include pasta frolla, a sweet dough similar to pie dough in the US, shortcrust in the UK, and pate brisée in France; and sfogliata, known as puff pastry in the US and pâte feuilletée in France.

Pork skin from the belly with a lining of fat is commonly used to add flavor to sauces and soups. It should be blanched first. It is a distant reality from commercial snack cousins that linguistically sound the same, like pork rinds, cracklings, or scratchings.

Prosciutto crudo is uncooked, cured ham from the back thigh of the pig that is usually aged for 9 to 18 months. It can be sold in a block or in thin slices. Prosciutto cotto is cooked ham that is often lightly cured with sugar, salt, and juniper, then steamed, pressed, and sold as a block or in slices.

Ragù has different meanings depending on the region where the recipe originates. In Bologna, it is a sauce cooked for less than two hours. In Naples, the cooking time is much longer, and the ragù is often made from a whole piece of meat, perhaps pork rather than veal or beef.

Semola or semolina is the ground durum wheat for making pasta. The finest grind is labelled 00.

Shellfish names can vary from region to region. Shrimp and prawns often share the same jargon even if they are not really the same. Scampi is sometimes used to mean trawler-caught whereas langoustine are caught in pots or creels. In the kitchen, they are usually interchangeable, depending on size. In Ada's day they would always be sold live, heads on.

Soffritto, the foundation of many sauces and dishes, is made from a dice of celery, carrot, and onion cooked in oil or butter. Battuto, from Tuscany, is similar, but may also include celery leaves and a red onion.

Tomatoes are a mainstay. Passata is uncooked, puréed tomatoes, usually without anything else. Tinned tomatoes are usually peeled and whole. Many recipes call for fresh tomatoes to be blanched—plunged briefly in boiling water for 10 to 20 seconds so they can be skinned and seeded before the flesh is cooked or served. Tomato purée, sometimes called concentrato di pomodoro, or just conserva, is made in the south with salt by leaving the tomatoes out in the sun to dry. A purée may equate to three or four times the strength of fresh passata. The size of a tomato is generally not specified in Ada's recipes; use your own good sense.

Truffles are either white or black. The white truffle, tartufo bianco, comes from around Alba in the Piedmont region, and is the most prized. They are used raw, often thinly sliced or grated over pasta or eggs. The black truffle, called tartufo nero or tartufo di Norcia, is usually cooked before using.

Tuna tinned in olive oil means preserved in a tin or a jar, and is commonly used in place of fresh (or water-packed).

Vanilla, either as a powder or liquid extract, gives a penetrating scent, used to perfume creams, sugar, liqueurs, and fruit syrup. A little of it is enough to impart an excellent fragrance. Vanilla pods can be split and infused into liquids or made into vanilla sugar by adding the pod(s) to a container of sugar, covering, and setting aside to perfume the sugar for weeks or months.

Vinegar is always red or white wine vinegar, unless otherwise specified, e.g. balsamic.

Zampone, similar to cotechino sausage, uses the front part of the pig, where the legs go for prosciutto, but the casing is the skin of the trotter. Traditionally, it took many hours to soak and cook but today it can be found vacuum packed and pre-cooked.

"Sauces are of fundamental importance to the art of cooking."

There are four main sauce groups to consider for the home cook: flour and butter, eggs and oil, hot savory sauces, and tomato sauces. These basic preparations complement and enrich most recipes. Sauces are of fundamental importance to the art of cooking.

The best known of all is the white sauce, or béchamel. It has many uses for fish and meats to baking and soufflés. The proportions of the components vary depending on the use for which the sauce is intended, whether binding other sauces or serving as it is. For anything that is to be cooked, like a croquette or a pie, the sauce should be made thicker, either by reducing the amount of milk or leaving it on the stove longer. Often it will be flavored with cheese, especially for gratins, or enriched with more eggs and mustard for grills.

Here are some suggestions for thickening a white sauce. Simply dissolve a little potato starch in cold water and pour it slowly into the sauce, stirring with a wooden spoon or, using a knife, mix a little butter with a little flour and add it, bit by bit, to the boiling sauce, stirring with a whisk until the sauce is thicker. You will need to boil the sauce for at least 5 minutes to remove the raw taste of the flour.

For making savory sauces, the culinary bases used by restaurant chefs should not be overlooked but at home we have no need to over-elaborate. We may still employ a few scraps of cheap meats, maybe a chicken and some vegetables to make some supportive broths. We talk more of this in the next chapter.

But a fish sauce on the other hand is swift and no trouble using bones, fish heads, onions, carrots, celery, salt, and a little butter. It only needs to simmer gently for about 20 minutes. This can be used as a quick-and-easy fish broth.

Finally, for tomato sauces, Italy has more than 300 varieties of tomato and as many ways to treat them! Often in recipes tomatoes need to be skinned and seeded. The easy way to do this is to plunge them into boiling water for 10 seconds or so. Lift them out and let them cool and you will see the skin is easily peeled in your hands. Cut the tomato in half or quarters and use the tip of the knife to slip out the seeds, and just use the outside shell of flesh.

CONDIMENTI, SALSE & SUGHI

1

SAUCES

WHITE SAUCES

All recipes yield 2 cups

SALSA BESCIAMELLA

Basic White Sauce

3½ tbsp butter
⅓ cup flour
2 cups milk
Nutmeg
Salt

Melt the butter in a saucepan over medium heat. Add the sifted flour and cook slowly for a few minutes, stirring continuously, and without letting it take on any color. Take the saucepan off the heat and add the warm milk to the butter and flour, mixing with a wooden spoon.

Put the saucepan back over very low heat, stir constantly until the sauce begins to boil. Season with salt and a grating of nutmeg. Cover and let the sauce cook and thicken for about 15 minutes, always over very low heat and stirring occasionally.

SALSA BESCIAMELLA ALLE CIPOLLE

White Sauce with Onions

14 oz onions
2 tbsp butter
Beef broth
Salt
2 tbsp cream

White sauce:
3 tbsp butter, ¼ cup flour,
2 cups milk

For all meats and fish.

Peel and finely chop the onions. Simmer for 10 minutes. Drain well. Melt 1½ tablespoons of the butter in another pan. Set over high heat and add the onions. Let them sauté gently, not quite enough to color, and add a glass of beef broth. When they are soft, pass them through a food mill or a blender to make a purée.

Make a white sauce *(as above)* using the ingredient amounts listed here. Add the onion purée and let them both cook over very low heat, covered.

Lastly add the cream and the remaining ½ tablespoon of butter and pour into a gravy boat or pitcher.

SALSA BESCIAMELLA BASTARDA PICCANTE

Spicy White Sauce

5½ tbsp butter
5 tbsp flour
2 egg yolks
Lemon
2 tsp mustard
Salt
Pepper

For game.

Melt half the butter over very low heat in a saucepan. Add the flour and cook slowly for a few minutes, stirring continuously. Bring 2 cups of water to a boil and add a little at a time, until the sauce has returned to a boil. Season with a little salt and a pinch of pepper, reduce the heat, and cook for 10 minutes.

Remove from the heat and add the beaten egg yolks, stirring constantly, and the rest of the butter, cut into small pieces. To serve add a few drops of lemon juice, the mustard, and stir one last time with a wooden spoon and pour into a gravy boat or pitcher.

CREAM SAUCES

All recipes yield 2 cups unless otherwise stated

SALSA VELLUTATA

Cream Sauce

3½ tbsp butter
Flour
2 cups chicken broth
Parsley
Salt

Melt the butter over medium heat in a saucepan and add ⅓ cup flour all at once, mixing thoroughly with a wooden spoon. Cook for about 10 minutes over very low heat, stirring occasionally until the flour has taken a slight pale-yellow color. At this point, add the broth a spoon at a time and keep stirring until the sauce has started boiling again, then add more broth and so on. Finally add some chopped parsley and salt. Simmer in all for about 20 minutes and then sieve.

SALSA VELLUTATA AI FUNGHETTI

Mushroom Cream Sauce

1 lb mushrooms
3½ tbsp butter
Wine
Salt
Pepper

Cream sauce:
3½ tbsp butter, ¼ cup flour, 2 cups chicken broth

Make the cream sauce *(as above)*, using 3½ tablespoons of butter, the flour, and the chicken broth. Meanwhile, clean the mushrooms and wash them thoroughly and quickly without letting them soak. Then dry them with a cloth and dice them finely. Heat 3½ tablespoons of butter in a pan, toss in the mushrooms, and cook over brisk heat for a few minutes until all their juices have disappeared.

Season with salt and pepper and wet them little by little with 7 tablespoons of wine, letting it evaporate. Then incorporate into the cream sauce and let the flavors mingle, stirring occasionally. As soon as the sauce is thickened, check its flavour and add, if necessary, a little salt and pepper. Remove from the heat and keep it warm in a bain-marie.

SALSA VELLUTATA ALLA CREMA DI LATTE

Double Cream Sauce

7 tbsp cream
2 tbsp butter
Salt

Cream sauce:
2 tbsp butter, ¼ cup flour, 1 cup chicken broth

For stuffed pastas, such as cappelletti, ravioli, and cannelloni.

Make a cream sauce *(as above)* using half the butter, the flour, and chicken broth listed here. For the last 10 minutes of cooking, add half the cream a little at a time, always stirring. When the sauce has thickened well, remove it from the heat and taste it. Add salt if you need it. Pour in the remaining cream and the rest of the butter in small pieces, always stirring.

SALSA VELLUTATA ALLE UOVA

Cream Sauce with Eggs

3 egg yolks
Nutmeg
2 tbsp butter
Pepper

Cream sauce:
2 tbsp butter, ¼ cup flour, 2 cups chicken broth

For asparagus, fennel, and boiled cardoons.

Make a cream sauce *(p17)* using the ingredient amounts listed here. When it is warm, take off the heat and strain it through a sieve.

Whisk the egg yolks into the warm sauce, stirring constantly. Add a pinch of pepper and a whisper of nutmeg.

Put the pan back on the heat and stir without interruption so it becomes thicker. Remove from the heat, add the butter in small pieces, check the flavour, and serve it straight away or keep it warm in a bain-marie.

SALSA VELLUTATA AL POMODORO

Creamy Tomato Sauce

MAKES 3⅓ CUPS

1 onion
Olive oil
1 carrot
Parsley
Basil
2¼ lb tomatoes
Salt
Pepper

Cream sauce:
3 tbsp butter, ¼ cup flour,
3 cups broth

For baked pasta and pies.

Make a cream sauce *(p17)* with the ingredient amounts listed here. Chop the onion and sweat in some oil with chopped carrot, parsley, and basil.

Wash and peel the tomatoes and purée them in a food mill or blender. Add this purée to the onions and simmer for 30 minutes. Season with salt and pepper. Then combine with the white sauce and leave to cook together for a few minutes.

EGG SAUCES

All recipes yield 1 cup unless otherwise stated

MAIONESE

Mayonnaise

2 egg yolks
Olive oil
Vinegar or lemon juice
Salt
Optional: white pepper

The success of a mayonnaise depends on three factors. The temperature: the eggs and bowl must be warm. Second, the proportions between the eggs and the oil must be respected — for each egg yolk, you need 7 tablespoons of oil. Lastly, the oil must be added drop by drop. Here I have described the classic process, which takes a long time, but using a blender can make an equally successful mayonnaise.

Break the egg yolks into a bowl and season them with salt and 1 teaspoon of vinegar, stirring to combine. If you like, add a pinch of white pepper. Use a wooden spoon and start stirring them, trying to keep them toward the center of the bowl without spreading them too much. Then drop by drop, very slowly, begin to add the oil to the egg yolks, stirring gently and regularly. It doesn't matter whether the movement is always in the same direction.

When the eggs have absorbed a couple of spoonfuls of oil, the sauce may thicken too much, in which case immediately add a few drops of vinegar or lemon juice to loosen and keep pouring the oil. When the mayonnaise is the right consistency it will coat the back of the spoon. If it is too dense, add a tablespoon of warm water.

ADA SAYS: *If, despite all best efforts, the mayonnaise does not take, put a fresh egg in another bowl and try again using the old sauce.*

SALSA MAIONESE ALLA MOSTARDA

Mustard and Cornichon Mayonnaise

1 cup mayonnaise *(as above)*
1 tbsp mustard
Parsley
White pepper
3 cornichons
Optional: capers, anchovy paste

Make the mayonnaise and at the last moment add the mustard, some chopped parsley, and a pinch of white pepper.

Put the cornichons and capers (if using) in a clean dry cloth to squeeze out any vinegar, then chop and add to the mix. A little anchovy paste can complete this sauce.

SALSA MAIONESE ALLE ACCIUGHE

Anchovy Mayonnaise

1 cup mayonnaise *(p19)*
3 pickled onions
6 anchovies
Salt
White pepper

A tasty variation.

Once you have made your mayonnaise, finely chop the pickled onions, bone and finely chop the anchovies. Add them to the mayonnaise and give it a grind of white pepper and salt.

SALSA MAIONESE CON AGLIO

Garlic Mayonnaise

1 cup mayonnaise *(p19)*
4 garlic cloves
Lemon
Salt
Pepper

Make a mayonnaise, but skip the vinegar. Finely chop the garlic cloves and combine them with the mayonnaise along with the lemon. Season with salt and pepper.

SALSA MAIONESE CON UOVA INTERE

Quick Whole-Egg Mayonnaise

1 large egg
Olive oil
White vinegar or lemon juice
Salt
White pepper

Whisk the whole egg with a hand mixer or blender. Season with a pinch of fine salt. Pour in a cup of oil little by little, adding two tablespoons of vinegar or lemon juice from time to time to stop it getting too thick. When all the oil has been added, season with a pinch of white pepper.

ADA SAYS: *To this you can add chopped hard-boiled eggs, cornichons, mustard, parsley, as you wish.*

SALSA MAIONESE TARTARA

Tartar Sauce

4 egg yolks
1 tsp mustard
Vinegar
Olive oil
Capers
Parsley
Salt
Pepper
Optional: 1 raw egg yolk

Since this sauce cannot have the stability of a mayonnaise made with raw egg yolks, it is good to prepare it at the last minute. If you need to prepare in advance, add a raw egg yolk to bind.

Hard-boil the egg yolks. Place them in a bowl, crush them with a wooden spoon, and work them into a smooth paste. Then add a pinch of salt, the mustard, a pinch of pepper, and a little spoonful of the vinegar. Stir with a wooden spoon until perfectly smooth. At this point, as with making a mayonnaise, begin to add the oil drop by drop into the bowl and keep on whisking as you go. If needed, add more of the vinegar, but in very small quantities. Once the sauce is finished, complete with the chopped capers and parsley.

SALSA MAIONESE TARTARA RAPIDA

Quick Tartar Sauce

2 hard-boiled egg yolks
8 anchovy fillets
2 raw egg yolks
1 tsp mustard
Olive oil
Vinegar

This variation is fast because you can do it in a blender and combines raw and cooked eggs for stability.

In a blender, mix the hard-boiled egg yolks, the anchovy fillets, raw egg yolks, mustard, and a few tablespoons of the oil. With the machine running, start pouring in the oil, a little at time, and adding a little vinegar from time to time. When the sauce is well whipped, pour it into a gravy boat or pitcher and serve.

ADA SAYS: *This goes well with smoked salmon cut into squares.*

SALSA MAIONESE VERDE

Green Mayonnaise

Spinach
6½ tbsp capers
6 cornichons
Salt
White pepper

Mayonnaise:
2 egg yolks, ½ glass olive oil,
2 tbsp vinegar

First make a mayonnaise *(p19)* using the egg yolks, olive oil, and vinegar listed here.

Rinse ½ cup of spinach and blanch until it wilts. After draining, squeeze well in your hands so that no traces of water remain. Chop finely. Also chop the capers and cornichons, mix them with spinach, and purée the mixture in a food mill or blender. Pour the purée into the mayonnaise. Add salt and white pepper. Mix well.

SALSA OLANDESE

Hollandaise Sauce

7 oz butter
1 tsp potato starch
Milk
2 egg yolks
Lemon
Salt
Pepper

For boiled eggs, vegetables, boiled fish, and poultry.

In a small deep saucepan, stir together 1 tablespoon of the butter, the potato starch, 3 tablespoons of milk, the egg yolks, and some salt. Set the saucepan over very moderate heat and whisk constantly until the mixture has become thick and creamy.

Cut the remaining butter into small pieces. Take the pan off the heat and add the first small piece of butter and keep beating so the eggs absorb the butter. Return to very low heat and repeat with more butter removing the pan from the heat and bringing it back immediately with very low heat, continually beating the sauce. Toward the end of the process, alternate the butter with a small amount of extra milk making sure each time everything is absorbed. Finish with lemon juice and pepper. If you don't need to serve it right away, keep warm over a bain-marie.

ADA SAYS: *If, despite all precautions, the sauce breaks, put it in another bowl to cool. Break an egg in another pan and add the cold sauce little by little, beating until the sauce is whipped again. Finally put the pan in a bain-marie with warm water and keep beating.*

SALSA OLANDESE ALL'ARANCIA

Orange Hollandaise

1 cup hollandaise *(p21)*
Orange
Salt
Pepper

A variation for duck, geese, and pigeon.

Once you've made the hollandaise, grate the orange zest and juice the orange. While the hollandaise is still warm or in a warm bain-marie, mix the juice and zest into the sauce and keep it warm until ready to serve.

SALSA OLANDESE ALLA CREMA

Cream Hollandaise

1 cup hollandaise *(p21)*
2 tbsp cream
Lemon
Salt
Pepper

A variation for steamed asparagus or fennel.

Once you've made the hollandaise, take it off the heat and stir in the cream. If the sauce starts to break up, quickly beat another egg and add half of it to the sauce. Finish with the lemon juice.

SALSA OLANDESE ALLA CREMA SEMPLIFICATA

Simple Cream Hollandaise

MAKES 2 CUPS

9 oz butter, cold
Flour
2 cups meat or fish broth, or milk
1 egg
2 tbsp heavy cream
Lemon

A variation for boiled meats and fish.

In a small saucepan, melt 1 tablespoon of butter over very low heat. Stir in a spoonful of flour, then stir in the broth slowly, a little at a time. When the mixture is smooth and thick, with no lumps, put the pan inside a bigger pan of water as a bain-marie and keep warm.

To complete the sauce, cut up the rest of the butter (it should be very cold) into small pieces. Break the egg and whisk to incorporate. Then add one piece of butter at a time making sure it is well absorbed before adding the next.

Finally take the pan out of the bain-marie, whip in the cream and squeeze in a few drops of lemon juice. Pour into a gravy boat.

SALSA OLANDESE MAGRA

Light Hollandaise

1 cup low-fat yogurt
1 tsp lemon juice
Tabasco
4 egg yolks
Salt

A variation for broccoli, cauliflower, and asparagus.

This sauce is cooked in a bain-marie. Bring a larger pan of water to a boil. In a smaller pan, mix the yogurt with the lemon juice and a few drops of Tabasco. Beat the egg yolks and salt and add them. Put the smaller pan in the larger pan and keep stirring until you have a smooth and thick sauce.

CLASSIC SAUCES

All sauces are prepared for 6 people

CONDIMENTO AL GORGONZOLA

Gorgonzola Sauce

3½ oz Gorgonzola
7 tbsp butter
1 cup heavy cream
2 tbsp Cognac

For pasta, risotto, and roast meats.

Chop the Gorgonzola and butter and put both in a pan with the cream. Splash with the Cognac. Place over very low heat and with a wooden spoon work the mixture for a few minutes until you have a smooth cream.

CONDIMENTO ALL'AMATRICIANA

Amatriciana Sauce

2¼ lb tomatoes
1 onion
3½ oz guanciale
1 tbsp lard
1 cup grated pecorino
Salt
Pepper

For long, dried pasta.

Wash, peel, seed, and cut the tomatoes in pieces. Finely chop the onion with the guanciale. In a pan, heat the lard and add the onion and guanciale. When it browns, but not too much, add the tomatoes, season with salt and plenty of pepper. Be careful because the guanciale is somewhat salty. Cook over a lively heat for a few minutes, until the tomato is cooked but not broken. Finish with plenty of grated pecorino.

CONDIMENTO ALLA CARBONARA

Carbonara Sauce

1 onion
7 oz pancetta
2 tbsp butter
Grated Parmesan or pecorino
White wine
4 eggs
Salt

For egg pasta and spaghetti.

Slice the onion thinly and cut the pancetta into pieces. In a small pan, heat the butter and brown the onion and pancetta until they color. Pour in half a glass of wine and let it evaporate, then remove the pan from the heat.

Put the eggs in a bowl. Beat them as for an omelet. Add ½ cup Parmesan. Pour in the pancetta and onions and mix everything well with a wooden spoon and salt lightly.

When the pasta has boiled, drain and mix in the sauce and let it cook for a few moments more.

ADA SAYS: *Carbonara must be made at the last minute and stirred into the freshly cooked and drained pasta to cook together for a final minute before serving.*

CONDIMENTO ALLA CARRETTIERA

Drover's Sauce

7 oz pancetta
1 tbsp lard or olive oil
1 cup grated pecorino
Salt
Pepper

For spaghetti.

Cut the pancetta into small cubes and put them in a pan with the lard or olive oil. Sauté until the meat has melted and taken on a beautiful golden color.

Pour the meat into a bowl, grate in the pecorino and a strong grind of pepper. Combine with freshly cooked and drained pasta and leave to cook a few moments longer in the heat of the pan.

ADA SAYS: *Like carbonara, this needs to be mixed with the pasta at the last minute.*

SALSA PICCANTE ALLA MOLLICA DI PANE

Spicy Bread Sauce

Parsley
Capers
Garlic
1 tbsp chopped cornichon
Onion
2 anchovies
2 oz crustless white bread
3 tbsp olive oil
1 tbsp vinegar
Salt
Pepper

This sauce is either pounded in a pestle and mortar or you can use an electric mixer.

With a pestle and mortar: Bring together a good fist of parsley, some capers, garlic, the cornichon and half a chopped onion. Wash and bone the anchovies and add to the mix. Pound gently to crush. Soak the bread in water and squeeze dry in your hands. Add to the mix and mash everything to a paste. Season with salt and pepper. Put this paste in a bowl and dilute it slowly with the oil, assembling it like a mayonnaise. Finally, complete it with a tablespoon of vinegar.

SALSA PICCANTE ALLA MOSTARDA

Mustard Sauce

1 hard-boiled egg
2 tbsp wine vinegar
6 tbsp olive oil
2 tbsp chopped parsley
6 pickled onions
1 tbsp mustard
Salt
Pepper

For boiled meats.

Crush the hard-boiled egg in a bowl and slowly drop in the vinegar and then the oil slowly, stirring constantly. Finish with the finely chopped parsley, salt, and pepper. Finely chop the pickled onions and add them. Lastly, add the mustard.

SALSA PICCANTE ALLE ACCIUGHE

Spicy Anchovy Sauce

6 anchovies
2 tbsp capers
Vinegar
Olive oil
1 tsp mustard
1 tbsp chopped parsley

For fish and boiled meats.

Wash and cut the anchovies into very small pieces, then chop them finely together with the capers.

In a bowl, combine one tablespoon of vinegar, three tablepoons of oil, and the chopped anchovies and capers. Mix thoroughly and finish with the mustard and parsley. Give a last stir so all the ingredients come together.

SALSA PICCANTE ALLE CIPOLLINE

Pickled Onion Sauce

4 tbsp wine vinegar
4 tbsp white wine
15 pickled onions
2 tbsp chopped parsley
3 egg yolks
12 tbsp (6 oz) butter, cold
Salt
White pepper

In a small saucepan, combine the vinegar and wine and set over moderate heat. Chop the pickled onions and add to the pan along with the parsley and a grind of pepper. Boil gently uncovered until the liquid is reduced by half. Remove from the heat, strain, and allow to cool.

Put the egg yolks in a heavy-bottomed saucepan and whisk them. Then add the cooled wine reduction, including the onions, gradually letting the eggs absorb the liquid. Put the pan over very low heat or, better still, in a bain-marie over very hot water. Start adding the cold butter one small piece at a time, beating continuously with a whisk.

Take care that the sauce does not boil or it will break up. Only when the sauce has absorbed all the butter, add salt and more chopped parsley. Serve lukewarm.

SALSA DI CAPPERI

Caper Sauce

Onion
3½ tbsp butter
1 anchovy fillet
2 tbsp capers
Parsley
Flour
Wine vinegar
7 tbsp broth
Optional: sugar

Chop half an onion and sweat in a small saucepan with half the butter. Wash, bone, and chop the salted anchovy and mash with a wooden ladle into the onion mix.

Add the capers, some chopped parsley, and a pinch of flour. Cook for a minute or two, stirring, and then wet with a finger of vinegar and the broth. Cook a little bit longer to have a sauce of the right consistency.

Finish with the rest of the butter, off the heat.

ADA SAYS: *You can also add some sugar to the sauce, but it is not necessary.*

SALSA DI MENTA

Mint Sauce

2 oz mint
Wine vinegar
2 tbsp sugar

For boiled lamb.

Wash and dry the fresh mint leaves. Coarsely chop and put them in a bowl with a small glass of vinegar, half a glass of water, and the sugar. Be sure the liquid covers the leaves. Let steep for 30 minutes, then pour into a gravy bowl.

SALSA PICCANTE ALLE PRUGNE

Spicy Prune Sauce

10 prunes
1 onion
2 tbsp butter
1 oz prosciutto
Wine vinegar
Bay leaf
Salt

For roast pork or pies.

Soak the prunes in warm water and pit them.

Dice the onion and sauté in the butter in a small saucepan over moderate heat. Shred the prosciutto and add to the onions. Pour in six tablespoons of vinegar and let it almost completely evaporate. Then add the prunes, enough water to cover, and the bay leaf. Simmer very slowly, covered, until soft. Purée in a food mill or blender.

SALSA PICCANTE ALL'UOVO SODO

Spicy Hard-Boiled Egg Sauce

1 hard-boiled egg yolk
1 tbsp wine vinegar
3 tbsp olive oil
2 tbsp chopped parsley
Salt
Pepper

For all vegetables, especially asparagus and potatoes.

In a bowl, crush the hard-boiled egg yolk with a fork and dissolve with the vinegar to make a paste. Then add the oil slowly in a drizzle, stirring constantly. Finish with the parsley and season with salt and pepper.

SALSA PICCANTE COL POMODORO

Spicy Tomato Sauce

2 pickled onions
1 large onion
Olive oil
White wine
7 oz tomatoes
Lemon
Salt
Pepper

For boiled chicken and beef.

Slice the onions—pickled and whole—very finely and warm through gently in a quarter glass of olive oil. When the onions start to glisten, add half a glass of white wine and cook, slowly, until the wine has all evaporated.

Blanch, peel, seed, and cut the tomatoes into pieces and add to the pan. Season with salt and pepper. Simmer over low heat, stirring occasionally until the mixture takes on the appearance of a purée.

Remove from the heat and pour in some more oil and stir well. Squeeze in some lemon juice.

SALSA PICCANTE DI RAFANO ALLA CREMA

Horseradish Sauce with Cream

1 tbsp fresh horseradish
Mustard
1 tbsp vinegar
1 tbsp sugar
Heavy cream
1 loaf of bread
Milk
Salt

For roast meats, especially beef, or even cold meat pies.

In a bowl, mix the horseradish and half a teaspoon of mustard together with the vinegar, sugar, salt, and half a cup of cream. Take off the crusts and soak some of the white part of the bread in milk, squeeze dry, and mix in well. Refrigerate until well chilled. Must be served very cold.

SALSA PIEMONTESE

Piedmont Sauce

1 cup meat broth *(p88)*
4 anchovies
Garlic
Parsley
1 hard-boiled egg yolk
1 tsp potato starch
1 white truffle
Olive oil
Lemon
White pepper

For roast meats.

In a saucepan, bring the broth to a boil. Wash, bone, and chop the anchovies. Mince some garlic. Add the anchovies, garlic, parsley, and hard-boiled egg yolk to the broth in the saucepan.

Dissolve the potato starch in a little cold water and add to the sauce. Boil until you get a thick sauce, which you will then complete with a small chopped white truffle, a few drops of oil, a little lemon juice, and a pinch of white pepper. This sauce is served hot.

SALSA RUSTICA

Traditional Tomato Sauce

6 tomatoes
2 garlic cloves
Parsley
Basil
Olive oil
Vinegar
Lemon zest
Salt
Pepper

For boiled meat.

Dip the tomatoes for a moment into boiling water to loosen their the skins. Peel them, cut them into wedges and remove the seeds.

Chop together the garlic, a good handful of parsley, and plenty of basil. Put the chopped tomatoes in a bowl and season with salt, pepper, plenty of oil, a little vinegar, and a little bit of lemon zest. Mix everything well, cover and keep in the fridge. Serve very cold.

ADA SAYS: *Prepare 5 or 6 hours in advance, or the night before.*

SALSA SAN BERNARDO

Almond and Chocolate Sauce

3½ oz blanched almonds
Olive oil
3 slices homemade or good sourdough bread
3 anchovies
1 orange
1 tsp sugar
1 tbsp grated chocolate
Vinegar

Toast the almonds in a skillet with little oil until they have taken on a rather dark brown color. Toast the bread. Chop the almonds and toasted bread together. Wash, bone, and finely chop the anchovies. Add to the mix. Add the orange juice.

Add the mixture to a saucepan. Add the sugar and chocolate. Add two fingers of vinegar and a finger of water. Melt everything over moderate heat. When it thickens, pass it through a sieve.

ADA SAYS: *This sweet-and-sour sauce serves as an accompaniment to pan-cooked vegetables, such as eggplant or fennel.*

QUICK SAUCES

SALSETTA RAPIDA AÏOLI

Quick Garlic Sauce

1 egg yolk
Olive oil
6 garlic cloves
Salt

For boiled or roast fish.

This sauce can be made both in a blender or with a pestle and mortar. For a blender: Put the egg in the jar. With the machine running, add a glass of oil a little at a time, as for making mayonnaise. At the end, add the garlic and some salt. If using a pestle and mortar, start by crushing the garlic and salt, then add the egg and drip in the oil.

SALSETTA RAPIDA ALLE ACCIUGHE

Quick Anchovy Sauce

2 anchovies
Parsley
1 garlic clove
Vinegar
White wine
Pepper

For meat, boiled fish, and vegetables, cooked and raw.

Wash and bone the anchovies. Pound in a pestle and mortar (or in a blender) with a little parsley, a pinch of pepper, and the garlic. Dilute with a finger of vinegar and a finger of white wine.

SALSETTA RAPIDA DI UOVA E ACCIUGHE

Quick Anchovy and Egg Sauce

2 hard-boiled eggs
Parsley
4 anchovy fillets
3 tbsp butter
Salt

For steamed vegetables.

Peel the boiled eggs and chop finely together with a little parsley, the anchovy fillets, and salt. Melt the butter in a small pan and, when it froths, pour the chopped mixture in, stirring carefully. Serve hot.

SALSETTA RAPIDA DI UOVA ALLA MOSTARDA

Quick Egg and Mustard Sauce

2 hard-boiled egg yolks
1 tbsp Dijon mustard
Olive oil
Vinegar
1 tbsp chopped parsley

For artichokes, asparagus, and cardoons.

In a bowl, crush the egg yolks together with the mustard. Then, like making a mayonnaise, add half a glass of oil one drop at a time, and keep whisking. Finish with a splash of vinegar and the parsley.

SALSETTA RAPIDA DI UOVA E LIMONI

Quick Lemon Sauce

6 eggs
Fish broth
3 lemons

This is excellent for boiled fish.

Beat the eggs with ¼ cup water and a few tablespoons of hot broth. Stir in the juice from the lemons, being careful not to form lumps.

SALSETTA RAPIDA PICCANTE DI CAPPERI

Quick Caper Sauce

1 onion
3½ tbsp butter
1 anchovy fillet
2 tbsp capers
Parsley
Flour
Vinegar
Broth
Optional: sugar

Excellent with pork.

Chop the onion and sweat in a small pan with half the butter. When the onions are translucent, add the anchovy, chopped small, and work it into the onions with a ladle. Add the capers, chopped parsley, and a pinch of flour. Cook for a minute or two, stirring, then wet with a finger of vinegar and a half glass of broth. Let it cook a little longer until it has the right consistency. You can also add a little sugar here. Take off the heat and add the remaining butter. Serve hot.

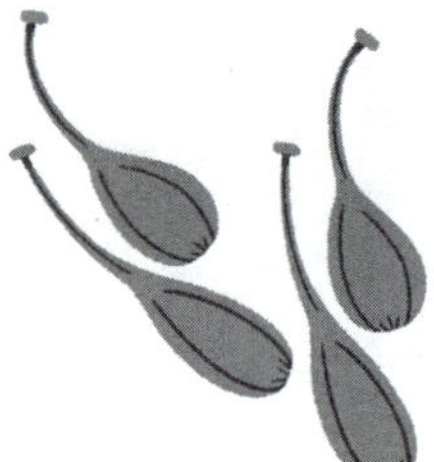

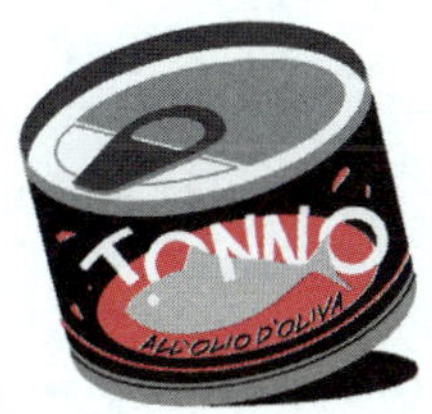

SALSETTA RAPIDA PICCANTE DI TONNO E ACCIUGHE

Quick Tuna and Anchovy Sauce

2 anchovies
2 oz tinned tuna in olive oil
1½ tbsp capers
Parsley
1 hard-boiled egg
Olive oil
1 lemon
Salt
Pepper

For boiled meats and fish.

Wash, bone, and finely chop the anchovies. Finely chop the tuna. In a bowl, combine the anchovies, tuna, capers, some parsley, and the hard-boiled egg. Add half a glass of oil, a drop at a time. Finish with the lemon juice. Season with salt and pepper. Mix well.

SALSETTA RAPIDA PICCANTE VERDE

Quick Spicy Green Sauce

2 anchovies
Parsley
Capers
Scallion
3 cornichons
Garlic
1 loaf of bread
Olive oil
Vinegar
Pepper

For meats and boiled fish, also for broccoli and cauliflower.

Wash, bone, and finely chop the anchovies. Chop the parsley, capers, scallion, and cornichons as finely as possible. Mince the garlic and add to the mix. Take a piece of the white part of the bread the size of an egg. Soak it and squeeze dry. Season with salt and pepper and chop everything to a mush.

Put all this in another bowl and pour in a medium glass of olive oil a little at a time like making mayonnaise. Finish with one tablespoon of vinegar.

RAGUS

RAGÙ ALLA BOLOGNESE

Ragu Bolognese

10 oz ground beef or a mix of veal and pork
3½ tbsp butter
3½ oz pork belly or pancetta
1 onion
1 carrot
1 celery stalk
Clove
200ml broth or milk
1 tsp tomato paste
Cream
White truffle
Salt
Pepper
Optional: chicken livers, chicken, pancetta, dried mushrooms, all cooked separately

For pasta, egg pasta, rice and casseroles.

Put the ground meat in a wide saucepan with half the butter. Then mince the pork belly and chop your vegetables—onion, carrot, and celery. Add the vegetables and clove to the beef and cook to brown. Add broth to cover and let it bubble down, then top up with more broth. Stir in the tomato paste and season with salt and pepper. Top up with enough water to cover the meats. Turn the flame right down and let it cook slowly.

At this point, if you are using any of the options (chicken livers, diced ham, dried mushrooms, all cooked separately) add them now and cook for the last 30 minutes.

To finish, add half a glass of cream and slices of white truffle.

ADA SAYS: *A Bolognese tradition often recommends using milk instead of broth.*

RAGÙ AL POMODORO

Tomato Ragu

3½ tbsp butter
Olive oil
10 oz lean ground beef
Red wine
1 lb tomatoes
Basil
Salt

For stuffed egg pastas and pasta bakes.

In a saucepan, heat the butter and oil over high heat. Add the ground beef and cook for a few minutes. Add salt and half a glass of wine a little at a time. Cover the pan and cook over low heat for 30 minutes.

Wash the tomatoes. Purée them in a food mill or blender. Add the tomato purée and a few basil leaves torn into pieces to the beef. Cover the pan again, bring to a boil, reduce the heat, and cook another 30 minutes to thicken the sauce.

RAGÙ CASALINGO CON SALSICCE E FUNGHI

Sausage and Mushroom Ragu

1 onion
1 carrot
1 celery stalk
Parsley
7 oz ground beef
Olive oil
3 sausages
Red wine
2 cups tomato passata
9 oz fresh mushrooms
Salt
Pepper

For stuffed egg pastas and pasta bakes.

Chop the onion, carrot, celery, and a handful of parsley. Put them and the ground beef in a pan with a glass of oil. Brown lightly. Remove the sausage casings and add to the pan. As the meats start to color, add half a glass of wine a little at a time, then finally the tomato passata and the salt and pepper. Cover and cook for 30 minutes.

Wash and slice the mushrooms. Add to the pan and let simmer another 30 minutes. If it gets too dry, top up with water.

RAGÙ CON FUNGHI SECCHI

Dried Mushroom Ragu

1 lb tomatoes
1 onion
1 carrot
1 celery stalk
10 oz ground beef
3½ tbsp butter
Olive oil
Red wine
2 oz dried mushrooms
Salt
Pepper

Wash, peel, and seed the tomatoes. Chop the onion, carrot, and celery. In a bowl, mix the ground beef with the onion, carrot, and celery so they all season each other.

Put everything in a saucepan with the butter and olive oil. Sauté over moderate heat until the beef is well colored, then add half a glass of wine. When the wine has evaporated, stir in the tomatoes and season with salt and pepper. Cover and cook over moderate heat for 20 minutes, stirring from time to time.

Soak the dried mushrooms in cold water. When they are reconstituted, rinse, and chop and add to the sauce. Continue cooking covered for another 30 minutes, stirring occasionally.

RAGÙ CON LE MANDORLE

Almond Ragu

1 onion
5 tbsp butter
3½ oz prosciutto
7 oz ground veal
White wine
3½ oz almonds
4 tsp heavy cream
Salt

For stuffed egg pastas and pasta bakes.

Finely chop the onion and sweat in the butter gently. Dice the prosciutto and mix with the ground veal and add to the pan. As soon as the onion glistens, start to pour a glass of wine into the mixture a little at a time. Salt moderately and let cook covered for 1 hour.

Chop the almonds and add them at the end with the cream. Let the flavors meld for a few minutes taking care that the cream does not disappear.

RAGÙ CON PROSCIUTTO

Prosciutto Ragu

1 oz dried mushrooms
3½ oz prosciutto
1 carrot
1 garlic clove
1 onion
Olive oil
9 oz ground beef
Red wine
1 lb tomatoes, peeled
Parsley
Nutmeg
Meat broth
Salt
Pepper

Soak the mushrooms in cold water for about 20 minutes, then drain, rinse, and chop them.

Finely chop the prosciutto, carrot, garlic, and the onion. Heat the oil in a pan and add the prosciutto, carrot, garlic, and onion. As the vegetables start to color, add the mushrooms and cook for a few minutes. Add the ground meat to the pan and let it brown well. Pour in half a glass of wine, a little at a time. As soon as it evaporates, add the chopped tomatoes and some parsley, stirring carefully. Season with a grating of nutmeg, a pinch of salt, and pepper. Cover and cook for 1 hour. If it gets too dry, add a little broth.

SUGO DI CARNE

Meat Sauce

2¼ lb beef, round or shank
9 oz lardo or prosciutto
Garlic
Olive oil or butter
Lard or prosciutto fat
Parsley
White wine
1 large or 2 small onions
1 carrot
1 or 2 celery stalks
Broth
Potato starch
Salt
Pepper

First, lard your meat: Cut a dozen pieces of lardo or prosciutto as big as your little finger. On a cutting board, mix some minced garlic with a pinch of salt and some pepper and rub the meat with this mixture. Make small incisions in the beef with a small knife and insert a piece of lardo or prosciutto fat. Having done this, tie the meat with a some string to keep it in shape. Put a little oil or butter and a mixture of lard or ham fat in a Dutch oven. Add a small piece of garlic and some parsley and as soon as the fats liquefy, add the beef and let it brown slowly. When it is a beautiful dark color, season with salt and pepper, moisten it with half a glass of dry wine, and continue to sauté until the wine evaporates. Now take the meat out of the pan and keep it warm.

Shred the onion, carrot, celery, and a bit of parsley. Put them in the same pot and brown them slowly until they wilt. Moisten from time to time with a spoonful of broth or boiling water.

When the vegetables are well cooked, return the meat to the pot, shallow-fry everything for another 10 minutes, turning the meat often. Add enough broth to cover the meat. Cover and reduce the heat, so that the meat will be cooked at the same time the sauce thickens—which will happen in a couple of hours.

Remove the meat from the pot. Spoon off all the fat that floats on the surface, then strain the sauce through cheesecloth or a cloth and a sieve into another pan. If you need to thicken it more, dissolve some potato starch in a little water or add to it a little flour and butter and let it simmer for another 10 minutes.

The meat here can be carved into slices and served with its sauce or used to make meatballs or a meatloaf.

◆ ADA SAYS: *To make a Madeira or Marsala sauce, use this meat sauce and when cooked through add a glass of either Madeira or Marsala and finish with a little extra butter browned in the pan.*

SUGO DI CARNE CON VINO ROSSO

Beef and Red Wine Sauce

Olive oil
2 or 3 garlic cloves
1¾ lb ground beef
1 carrot
1 onion
1 celery stalk
Red wine
Salt
Pepper

For all types of pasta. You can also use the meat for meatballs.

In a pan, heat half a glass of oil. Crush the garlic cloves, add to the pan, and let them color. Add the ground beef to brown, turning it as it cooks.

Chop the carrot, onion, and celery into small pieces and add to the pot. Add three glasses of red wine, cover, and cook over very low heat for 2½ hours. Check and add more wine or water if necessary, so that when you put the sauce on the table it will be sufficiently thickened.

Remove the meat from the pan. Purée the sauce in a food mill or a blender.

SUGO DI CARNE CON IL POMODORO

Beef and Tomato Sauce

2¼ lb boneless beef shank
Rendered lard or olive oil
1 onion
2 oz fatty prosciutto
1 garlic clove
Red wine
2¼ lb tomatoes (or 4 cups passata)
Salt
Pepper

For pasta, rice, and timbales.

Cut the meat into regular chunks. Put a spoon of lard or half a glass of olive oil in a pan. Chop the onion and sauté in the oil. When it starts to glisten, add chopped prosciutto, garlic, and, immediately after, the beef. Season with salt and pepper and brown the meat all over.

When it is a nice dark color, pour a glass of red wine into the saucepan, let it evaporate, then add the tomatoes. Cover and reduce the heat and let it cook gently for 2 hours. If it gets too dry add some water. The sauce should be thick and tasty.

SUGO DI CARNE IN UMIDO ALLA NAPOLETANA

Neapolitan Meat Sauce

2¼ lb tomatoes
1 onion
Basil
Parsley
1 lb pork loin
2 oz lardo or ham fat
3 tbsp lard
Red wine
Salt

For all kinds of pasta.

Wash the tomatoes, cut them into pieces. Dice the onion. Wash and chop the basil and parsley leaves. Put them all in one saucepan, add a pinch of salt and cook over low heat for about 30 minutes. Now pass everything through a sieve into a bowl or use a blender.

Tie the pork. Cut the lardo into small pieces. Salt the pork moderately, place in a saucepan, add the lardo and rendered lard, cover with water, and set over low heat to cook until all the water has evaporated. Add a glass of wine and when that evaporates, let the meat brown a few more minutes and add the tomato sauce. Cover and cook another 2 hours.

ADA SAYS: *To follow the Neapolitan style, this dish should be cooked in a clay pot on the stove.*

SUGO DI CARNE IN UMIDO CON FUNGHI

Meat and Mushroom Sauce

Olive oil
2 garlic cloves
1 lb 5 oz beef, round or shank
1 lb 5 oz pork loin
Red wine
6⅓ cups beef broth *(p88)*
Tomato paste
2 oz dried mushrooms
Salt
Pepper

For pasta, risotto, pies, and flans.

Place a pan that is big enough to take both meats on the heat. Add a glass of oil and the crushed the garlic. As soon as the garlic browns, remove it from the pan. Add the meats and brown over a high heat only for a few minutes, because browning for too long will make them dry. Season with salt and pepper, pour in a glass of red wine a little at a time, and let it evaporate.

In a separate pan, bring the beef broth to a boil. Stir in ¾ cup of tomato paste into it, then carefully lift your meats and put them in the broth. Cover and simmer over a low heat for 2½ hours.

Meanwhile, reconstitute the dried mushrooms in cold water for 20 minutes, then chop them up and add to the tomato and meats. Cook together for another 30 minutes.

TOMATO SAUCES

CONDIMENTO AI SETTE SAPORI

Tomato Sauce with Seven Flavors

1 lb tomatoes
Basil
Parsley
7 tbsp butter
7 oz mozzarella
Olive oil
Grated Parmesan
Salt
White pepper

For all types of short pasta such as orecchiette, penne, or rigatoni.

Wash the tomatoes, together with a handful of basil leaves, and the same amount of parsley. Chop coarsely and put in a bowl. Cut the butter and mozzarella into small pieces and mix in with half a glass of olive oil. Season with half a cup of Parmesan and white pepper. Stir regularly for about 30 minutes to macerate well.

SUGO DI POMODORO

Tomato Sauce

2¼ lb tomatoes
Olive oil
1 onion
1 carrot
1 celery stalk
Parsley
Basil
Salt
Pepper

For dried pasta, gnocchi, boiled rice, and meat.

Wash the tomatoes. Chop and put them in a saucepan with half a glass of oil. Dice the onion, carrot, and celery and add them to the pan. Add the parsley and some torn leaves of basil.

Cover the pan and simmer for 30 minutes. Take off the lid and cook for another 30 minutes to reduce. Finally, purée everything in a food mill or blender. Season with a little pepper.

SUGO DI POMODORO A CRUDO

Raw Tomato Sauce

2¼ lb tomatoes
Olive oil
Basil
Garlic
Salt
Pepper

A good sauce for summer dishes and cold pastas.

Wash the tomatoes. Cut into wedges and slide the seeds out. Cut in half again. Mix in a bowl with half a glass of olive oil and torn basil leaves. Crush and dice the garlic and season with salt and pepper. Mix well so everything is covered and let it marinate in its own juices for 30 minutes.

SUGO DI POMODORO AL BASILICO

Tomato and Basil Sauce

Basil
7 tbsp butter
2¼ lb tomatoes
1 cup heavy cream
Salt

For fresh and dried egg pasta.

Wash and dry a few basil leaves. Melt the butter in a saucepan, shred in the basil leaves, and simmer them gently for 10 minutes. Bring another pan of water to a boil and dunk the tomatoes in the boiling water for a few seconds to loosen the skin. Peel and chop. Add to the basil along with a little salt and simmer another 10 minutes. Add the cream and cook for a few more minutes to thicken.

SUGO DI POMODORO ALLA PIZZAIOLA

Pizzaiola Sauce

2 garlic cloves
Olive oil
2¼ lb tomatoes
Oregano
Parsley
Salt
Pepper

For all meats.

Crush and dice the garlic. In a saucepan, combine the garlic and half a glass of oil and set over heat. Peel the tomatoes and roughly chop. As soon as the garlic turns golden, add the tomatoes. Cook over strong heat. Season with salt and pepper and when the tomatoes are cooked, but not smashed, add the oregano and some chopped parsley. Finish with salt and pepper.

SUGO DI POMODORO ALL'ARRABBIATA

Arrabbiata Sauce

2 garlic cloves
2 or 3 chilis
Olive oil
2¼ lb tomatoes
Parsley
Salt

For penne and rigatoni.

Crush and dice the garlic, chop the chilis and put both in half a glass of oil in a pan to simmer. Let them fry for a few minutes while you chop the tomatoes. Add the tomatoes to the mix. Salt lightly. Cook over high heat for 15 minutes. Finish with chopped parsley.

SUGO DI POMODORO CON FUNGHETTI

Tomato Sauce with Mushrooms

1 onion
Olive oil
2¼ lb tomatoes
Basil
1 lb mushrooms
Garlic
Parsley
Salt

For gnocchi and egg pasta.

Dice the onion and put it in a saucepan to sweat in a glass of olive oil. Drop the tomatoes into boiling water for a few seconds, then peel and chop and add to the onions. Tear a few leaves of basil and add to the mix. Cover and cook over medium heat for 30 minutes.

Now prepare the mushrooms: Wash them quickly, take off the stems if they are woody, and cut into long slices, not too thin. Crush the garlic. Put it in a pan with half a glass of oil and let it brown. As soon as it turns golden, take it out and put the mushrooms in. Simmer for 10 minutes over medium heat. Salt and sprinkle with chopped parsley and pour everything into the pan with the tomatoes. Stir carefully, check for seasoning, and let the flavors combine for a few minutes.

SUGO DI POMODORO CON FUNGHI SECCHI

Tomato Sauce with Dried Mushrooms

2 oz dried mushrooms
2¼ lb tomatoes (or 4 cups passata)
2 garlic cloves
Olive oil
Parsley
Salt
Pepper

Let the mushrooms soak in cold water for 20 minutes, then wash them carefully and dice. If using fresh tomatoes, drop in boiling water to loosen the skin and then peel (or you can use passata).

Crush the garlic and warm it in a saucepan in half a glass of olive oil. As soon as it takes on some color, take it out and pour in the chopped tomatoes. Add some chopped parsley and the mushrooms. Season with salt and pepper. Cover and cook over moderate heat for 30 minutes.

SUGO DI POMODORO CON GLI AROMI

Tomato Sauce with Herbs

3½ tbsp butter
Olive oil
Onion
1 carrot
Bay leaf
Sage leaf
Rosemary
Parsley
2¼ lb tomatoes
1 cup broth
1 tsp potato starch
Marsala
Cayenne
Salt
Pepper

For beef and pork.

Melt the butter and a little oil in a saucepan over moderate heat. Dice half an onion and carrot, add to the pan, and sweat for 10 minutes. Add the bay leaf, sage, a little rosemary, and a few parsley leaves. Let them flavour the sauce, while you peel, seed, and finely chop the tomatoes. Add the tomatoes to the mix and cook for 10 minutes. As the tomatoes lose their moisture, top up with a cup of broth. Season with a little salt and pepper. Reduce the heat to very low and let it boil almost imperceptibly for another 10 minutes. Then pass the sauce through a sieve, collect it in another small saucepan, and put it back on the heat.

Dissolve the potato starch in some boiling water and add to the sauce. Add half a glass of Marsala and when the sauce has boiled again, add it little by little, mixing with a wooden spoon. As soon as the sauce is thickened, remove from the heat, cover, and keep it warm. Finish with a little cayenne pepper.

SUGO DI POMODORO CON PEPERONI E MELANZANE

Tomato Sauce with Peppers and Eggplant

2 yellow bell peppers
Garlic
Olive oil
5 large tomatoes
1 small eggplant
Black olives, pitted
Capers
Basil
6 anchovy fillets
Salt

For boiled meats and short dried pasta.

Firstly, roast your peppers whole in the oven for 30 minutes. As the skin colors and crinkles, take out and put in a plastic bag or a container. Leave for 20 minutes.

Crush the garlic and warm it in a pan with half a glass of olive oil. As soon as it colors, take it out. Dunk the tomatoes in boiling water for a few seconds to make them easier to peel. Cut in quarters, take out the seeds, and chop the flesh and add to the pan. Cut the eggplant, skin on, into cubes and add to the tomatoes. Leave to simmer until the eggplant is soft, about 12 minutes. Take the roast peppers out of their container and peel off the skin which should be easy now. Discard the seeds and core and slice lengthwise. Add to the pan along with a fist of olives, capers, chopped fresh basil leaves, and the anchovy fillets. Cover the pan and let it cook for a few more minutes, adding a few spoonfuls of water if necessary.

SUGO DI POMODORO CON SALSICCE

Tomato Sauce with Sausages

1½ oz dried mushrooms
6 sausages
Olive oil
2 garlic cloves
1 lb canned tomatoes, peeled
Salt
Pepper

For risottos and short dried pastas.

Soak the mushrooms in cold water for 20 minutes, then wash and cut in small pieces. Prick the sausages with a fork. Put them in a pan and cover with cold water. Simmer them over moderate heat and let the water evaporate so the sausages brown in their own fat.

Add oil and garlic to another saucepan and as they brown, pour in the tomatoes and cook over low heat for 10 minutes. Then add the mushrooms and sausages—if you like these can be chopped up. Add salt and cook for another 10 minutes, then finish with a grind of pepper.

SUGO DI POMODORO CON TONNO E FUNGHI

Tomato Sauce with Tuna and Mushrooms

1 oz dried mushrooms
Garlic
Olive oil
2¼ lb tomatoes, peeled
7 oz tinned tuna in olive oil
Parsley
Salt
Pepper

For steak and linguine.

Let the mushrooms soak in cold water for 20 minutes, then wash them and cut them into small pieces.

Crush the garlic and then brown in a saucepan in a medium glass of oil and take out. Pour in the tomatoes and immediately afterward the mushrooms. Season with salt and pepper, cover, and simmer over moderate heat for 30 minutes.

Break up the tuna, add to the mix, and simmer for a few minutes to thicken. Finish with chopped parsley.

SUGO DI POMODORO PICCANTE CON CIPOLLINE

Spicy Tomato Sauce with Cipollini Onions

1 large onion
6 borettane (pickled cipollini)
Olive oil
White wine
2¼ lb tomatoes
Lemon
Salt
Pepper

For boiled meats and cold pasta or rice dishes.

Dice the onion and the borettane. In a saucepan, warm them through in olive oil over low heat. When they are translucent, add half a glass of wine and cook gently until it has evaporated. Peel, seed, and cut the tomatoes into pieces and add them to the saucepan. Season with salt and pepper. Cook for 30 minutes over low heat, stirring occasionally until the mixture becomes a purée. Take off the heat and finish with some olive oil and a squeeze of lemon juice, if needed.

ADA SAYS: *Borettane are cipollini onions preserved in balsamic vinegar.*

SUGO DI POMODORO RAFFINATO

Refined Tomato Sauce

1¾ oz pancetta
3½ tbsp butter
2 small onions
1 carrot
1 celery stalk
Parsley
Wine
1 tbsp flour
2¼ lb tomatoes
Sugar
Basil
Salt
Pepper

For pasta, rice, and even gnocchi.

Cut the pancetta into strips and warm in the butter. Chop the onions and add to the pan as the fats start to run. Chop the carrot, celery, and parsley together on a cutting board and add to the pan.

Let everything brown well until the herbs have taken on a nice dark blond color, then add half a glass of wine slowly and stir from time to time. When the wine has evaporated, add the flour, mix in well, and cook for another 5 minutes.

While this is happening, put the tomatoes in boiling water for 10 seconds so the skins break open, then peel. Add to the pan. Season with salt and pepper and let simmer for 30 minutes stirring every now and then. If the sauce is a little sour, correct it with a trifle of sugar. Finish with a handful of chopped fresh basil leaves.

FISH SAUCES

CONDIMENTO ALLA MARINARA

Shellfish Sauce

Olive oil
2 garlic cloves
2¼ lb mussels
2¼ lb clams
Parsley
Salt
Pepper

For spaghetti and risotto.

Put half a glass of oil and the garlic cloves in a large pan. As soon as the garlic browns, add the mussels and clams. Increase the heat and shake well. As they open, mix in with their liquid. Throw away any that remain closed. Finish with chopped parsley, salt, and pepper.

CONDIMENTO ALLA MARINARA PICCANTE

Spicy Squid Sauce

2¼ lb baby squid
Olive oil
1 garlic clove
Parsley
Anchovy
1 or 2 chillies
White wine
Salt

For spaghetti and vermicelli.

Clean the squid. Remove the internal pen-shaped cartilage, rinse them thoroughly without cutting the ink sac, and dry them.

Put half a glass of oil in a pan with the crushed garlic clove. As soon as the garlic begins to brown slightly, add plenty of chopped parsley and, immediately after, the baby squid. Season with salt, a minced anchovy, and the chili and cook over high heat.

As it dries out, add a glass of white wine, and let it evaporate completely. Add a little water, reduce the heat, cover and leave to cook slowly. After about an hour, the squids should be cooked.

CONDIMENTO ALLA MARINARA RAFFINATO

Refined Shellfish Marinara Sauce

2¼ lb mussels
2¼ lb clams
Olive oil
2 garlic cloves
2¼ lb baby squid
White wine
Parsley
1 lb fresh shrimp, shell-on
Salt
Pepper

For pasta and risotto.

Scrub the mussels well and remove any beards. Wash them carefully. Wash the clams carefully, too.

Heat ¼ cup oil and the garlic in a large pan and as soon as the oil is hot, add the clams, cover the pan, and let cook over high heat, occasionally shaking the pan, until the clams open. Throw away any that remain closed. Take the clams out with a slotted spoon leaving their liquid and, if necessary, add some more oil and let it get hot again.

Put the mussels in the same pan, cover it, and shake it to let the mussels cook over high heat until they open completely. Take off the heat. Set the cooking liquid aside and after letting it rest, pour through a sieve into a bowl. Shell the mussels and clams.

Cut the squid into small pieces and season with salt and pepper. Warm half a glass of oil in a pan and when it is hot, add the squid pieces. Add a medium glass of wine and let it evaporate, then add the reserved cooking liquor from the clams and mussels; enough to cover the squid. Finally chop the parsley and add to the mix. Cover the pan and cook over low heat for about 30 minutes, stirring occasionally.

In another saucepan, heat half a glass of oil, add the shrimp, season with salt and pepper, and cook over high heat for about 10 minutes. As soon as the shrimp are cooked, shell them.

Finally, combine in a single container the mussels, clams, shrimp, and baby squid. Season them with their cooking juices and mix well.

CONDIMENTO CON LE SARDINE

Sardine Sauce

Olive oil
2 onions
1½ lb fresh sardines
6 anchovies
6 tbsp raisins
Saffron
6 tbsp pine nuts
Salt
Pepper

For dried pasta, in particular macaroni.

Put a glass of oil in a saucepan. Chop the onions well and sauté them until they take a nice golden color. Carefully clean and bone the sardines and add them to the pan. Stir vigorously with a wooden spoon, crushing the sardines with force so as to reduce them to a pulp.

Wash and bone the anchovies and melt with a few drops of oil in another pan for about 10 minutes, then add to the sardines.

Put the raisins in some warm water to plump up for 5 minutes. Add to the sardines. Finish the sauce with a pinch of saffron, salt, pepper, pine nuts, and the drained raisins. If the sauce is too dense, loosen with a little water. Then cover the pan and keep it warm.

SALSA VELLUTATA AL BRODO DI PESCE

Fish Sauce

MAKES 2 CUPS

5½ tbsp butter
5 anchovies
Capers
2 cornichons
Parsley
Salt

Cream sauce:
3½ tbsp butter, ⅓ cup flour, 2 cups fish broth

Make a cream sauce *(p17)* with the butter, flour and fish broth. Meanwhile, prepare an anchovy butter. Wash and bone the anchovy, chop into small pieces, and crush into the remaining 2 tablespoons butter with the blade of a knife.

Add this mix, one piece at a time, to the sauce. Take off the heat. Finish with a few chopped capers, cornichons, parsley, and salt.

SPECIAL SAUCES

BAGNA CAUDA

Bagna Cauda

14 tbsp (7 oz) butter
Olive oil
4 garlic cloves
12 anchovy fillets
Salt
Optional: truffle

A dip for cardoons, celery, fennel, radishes, etc., and also excellent with grilled steaks.

Put the butter and oil in a pan to warm. Finely chop the garlic. Sauté over very low heat so the garlic does not color. It must remain white.

Remove the pan from the heat, add the anchovy fillets, and let them melt, stirring with a wooden spoon. Season with a pinch of salt. At this point you could add white truffle in slices.

ADA SAYS: *Bagna cauda is a specialty of Piedmont from the 16th century. It must always be served warm.*

CONDIMENTO AL BURRO NERO

Brown Butter Sauce

7 tbsp butter
Wine vinegar
Salt

For poached eggs, boiled eggs, and boiled vegetables.

Put the butter in a pan and heat it until it has become the color of hazelnuts. Take the pan off the heat. In another small pan, combine two tablespoons of vinegar and a pinch of salt. Boil until it is reduced by half and then pour it into the butter, stirring carefully.

CONDIMENTO ALLA PAPALINA

Sauce for the Pope

7 tbsp butter
2 egg yolks
1 cup grated Parmesan
1 cup grated Gruyère
Milk
Salt

For dried pasta and boiled rice.

In a saucepan, melt the butter over very low heat. Once melted, transfer to a bowl and stir with a wooden spoon. Add the egg yolks, mix well, and then add both grated cheeses. Lastly add a little milk and a little extra salt.

ADA SAYS: *Named after Pope Pius XII; often served with fettucine as a lighter version than carbonara.*

CONDIMENTO ALLE NOCI

Walnut Sauce

3½ oz walnuts
7 tbsp butter
Sugar
Ground cinnamon
Salt

For fresh and egg pasta.

Toast the walnuts in a hot oven for a few minutes, and then take out and crush them coarsely in a tea towel. Cut the butter into pieces, place in a bowl, whip until creamy with a fork and, stirring constantly, add the crushed walnuts. Season with a little sugar, a trifle of cinnamon, and a pinch of salt.

CONDIMENTO AL MASCARPONE

Mascarpone Sauce

7 oz mascarpone
2 egg yolks
3½ oz ham
Grated Parmesan
7 tbsp butter
Salt

For egg pasta.

Melt the mascarpone in a bowl, using a few spoonfuls of hot water. Add the egg yolks, stirring with a wooden spoon. Cut the ham into small cubes and place in the bowl. Add half a cup of Parmesan. Finally, melt and pour in the butter and mix well. Season with salt.

CONDIMENTO AL PROSCIUTTO E PISELLI

Ham and Pea Sauce

1 onion
7 tbsp butter
2¼ lb fresh peas (or 14 oz frozen peas)
Milk
3½ oz ham
Salt

For egg pasta, ravioli, and risottos.

Chop the onion and put in a pan with the butter. Let it cook over low heat so the onion does not color. Put the peas in the same pan, add salt, and a glass of warm milk or water. Cover. Cut the ham into cubes and as soon as the peas are cooked, add the ham and cook for a few minutes, stirring well.

ADA SAYS: *Traditionally, this recipe uses prosciutto cotto, but you can also use prosciutto crudo.*

CONDIMENTO CON FUNGHETTI COLTIVATI

Mushroom Sauce

1 lb 5 oz mushrooms
Olive oil
1 garlic clove
White wine
Parsley
Salt
Pepper

For dried pasta, risotto, also roasted and boiled meats.

Wipe the mushrooms, wash them quickly, dry them carefully, check the stems for dirt, and cut them into slices.

Put half a glass of oil and the garlic in a large pan and as soon as the garlic begins to brown, add the mushrooms and cook over high heat for a few minutes. Then pour in half a glass of wine, reduce the heat, and continue to cook for another 10 minutes. Season with salt and pepper and a sprinkle of parsley.

CONDIMENTO CON FUNGHETTI E SPINACI

Mushroom and Spinach Sauce

7 oz mushrooms
Olive oil
2 lb 10 oz fresh spinach (or 1 lb 5 oz frozen)
5 tbsp butter
Chili
Cream
Salt
Optional: milk

For pasta shells and egg pasta.

Quickly wash the mushrooms, dry them carefully, check the stems, and cut into slices. In a pan, heat a glass of oil, add the mushrooms, cover, and cook for about 10 minutes, then salt them.

Rinse the fresh spinach thoroughly and cook it in a pan with just the water clinging to the leaves. Add salt and as soon as the leaves collapse, a couple of minutes, drain them. Squeeze them well to drain completely.

Add a good measure of butter to the warm pan and as soon as it melts, add the spinach and let sit. Blend with a little milk if you like.

Add the mushrooms, a chili, ¾ cup cream and mix well. Allow to simmer over low heat a few minutes; finally add the remaining butter in small pieces.

CONDIMENTO CON FUNGHI ALLA GENOVESE

Porcini Sauce Genoa Style

2¼ lb porcini
Olive oil
1 onion
2 garlic cloves
1 cup tomato passata
Parsley
Salt
Pepper

For tagliatelle and egg pasta.

Carefully wash the mushrooms, dry them immediately, and cut off the lower part of the stems. Cut into thick slices.

Heat half a glass of oil and the chopped onion in a pan. Let the onion fry very lightly, then add the chopped garlic and the mushrooms.

Let it develop flavour over moderate heat. Add the passata, season with salt and pepper and with finely chopped parsley. Cook for 30 minutes.

CONDIMENTO CON FUNGHI SECCHI E CREMA DI LATTE

Cream of Wild Mushrooms

2 oz dried wild mushrooms
3½ tbsp butter
1 cup heavy cream
Grated Parmesan
Salt
Pepper

For pasta and rice.

Let the mushrooms soak in cold water for about 20 minutes, then clean and wash them. Chop them finely and cook with the butter in a small saucepan with a little salt and water. Cover and cook 10 minutes over moderate heat. Add the cream and half a cup of Parmesan and a pinch of pepper.

CONDIMENTO CON LA RICOTTA

Ricotta Sauce

7 tbsp milk
1 egg yolk
1 lb ricotta
Grated Parmesan
Salt
Pepper

For egg pasta.

In a bowl, stir together the milk and the egg yolk. Add the ricotta and mix with a wooden spoon to make a cream. Lastly season with half a cup of Parmesan, a pinch of salt, and a pinch of black pepper.

CONDIMENTO CON LA RICOTTA E GLI SPINACI

Ricotta and Spinach Sauce

2 lb 10 oz fresh spinach
3½ tbsp butter
Milk
1 egg yolk
Grated Parmesan
14 oz ricotta
Salt

For pasta shells, rigatoni, and any short pasta, also boiled rice.

Wash the spinach leaves and cook them in a large pan until they collapse and then drain well.

Put the butter in the hot pan and let it melt, then return the spinach and let the flavors meld for a few minutes.

In a bowl, mix a little milk with the egg yolk, then add half a cup of Parmesan and the ricotta. Mix carefully and add to the spinach.

CONDIMENTO CON LA RICOTTA E LE SALSICCE

Ricotta and Sausage Sauce

14 oz ricotta
Grated Parmesan
1 egg yolk
3 sausages

For rigatoni, shells, and short pasta.

Pass the ricotta through a sieve into a bowl, season with a good pinch of salt, half a cup of Parmesan, and the egg yolk and mix everything with a wooden spoon.

Put the sausages in a skillet, prick them, cover them with a little water, and sauté. When the water is evaporated, brown them for a few minutes more in the fat. Take off the heat and let cool, then peel the casings off and mix in with the ricotta.

CONDIMENTO CON SALSICCE E UOVA

Sausage and Egg Sauce

Olive oil
6 fresh sausages, casings removed
White wine
Broth
4 eggs
Grated Parmesan
Salt

For pasta shells, farfalle, or fillings for pies.

Put half a glass of oil in a saucepan over medium heat. When it is hot but not too hot, add the sausage meat. Mash with a wooden spoon, wet with a little wine, and cook slowly adding a little broth if needed.

In another bowl, beat the eggs, as for an omelet, season with salt and some Parmesan and add them to the pan of sausages. Leave the saucepan over very low heat for a few moments until the eggs have set.

CRESCIONE IN PURÈ

Watercress Purée

2¼ lb watercress
Butter
Salt
Pepper

White sauce:
2 tbsp all-purpose flour, 2 tbsp butter, milk

Clean the watercress, freeing it from the leaves and the hardest stems, wash and blanch it for a few minutes in lightly salted boiling water. Then drain it and cool in cold water.

Squeeze the watercress dry and chop it finely, adding a few spoons of thick white sauce *(p16)* made with the ingredients here and a pinch of salt and a pinch of pepper.

Heat the purée in a saucepan and finish it with a piece of butter.

ADA SAYS: *Watercress purée goes very well with light meats, such as sweetbreads, turkey fillets, chicken, etc.*

PESTO ALLA GENOVESE

Pesto Genovese

2 garlic cloves
Basil
6 tbsp pine nuts
1 cup grated Parmesan or pecorino
Olive oil
Salt

Pesto can be used to season pasta - such as trenette - in which case it should be diluted with a little pasta cooking water. It can also be used to season vegetable soups and it should then be thinned with a little broth. If used to season boiled meats and fish, it should be thinned with a little vinegar.

Chop the garlic and a large handful of fresh basil with a pinch of salt to preserve the beautiful green of the leaves. Put them in a stone or wooden mortar and crush along with the pine nuts. Grate in the cheese and add, a little at a time, the olive oil, stirring carefully until the mixture is creamy, moderately salted.

ADA SAYS: *A blender simplifies the operation. All the ingredients go in at the same time and blend for some minutes.*

PESTO PICCANTE

Spicy Pesto

2 garlic cloves
Parsley
3 tbsp pine nuts
6 anchovy fillets
6 Gaeta olives, pitted
1½ tbsp capers
3 cornichons
2 hard-boiled eggs
2 egg yolks
Olive oil
Vinegar
Salt
White pepper

A seasoning for meat and fish, both boiled and roasted.

If you want to use the traditional system, chop the garlic, parsley, and pine nuts, transfer to a stone or wooden mortar and add—all cut into small pieces—the anchovy fillets, olives, capers, cornichons, and hard-boiled eggs. Pound well, then put everything into a bowl and with a whisk add the egg yolks little by little, the oil, and a glass of vinegar, seasoning all together with salt and white pepper.

If you want to use a blender, place the egg yolks in the jar first and with the machine running, pour the oil in little by little to make a basic mayonnaise. At this point, add the other ingredients already cut into small pieces: parsley, garlic, anchovy fillets, cornichons, pine nuts, capers, olives, boiled eggs. Finally, add salt and white pepper and vinegar so that the seasoning appears rather dense.

"A good antipasti selection should contain a variety of vegetables, and olives, cured meats, and seafood."

Here we bring together preparations that are commonly served before a meal as *antipasti*. A good antipasti selection should contain a variety of vegetables—both fresh and preserved—and olives, cured meats, and seafood.

We start with preparations for butters and creams which you can use for toasts, crostini, or to fill little pastries. These can be the base for more complex preparations or just to flavor a white sauce, or in some cases, to make jelly for decoration or a glaze.

Dried black olives can be used as an aperitif, prepared in the following way: Put them in a bowl, and pour boiling water over them; immediately drain the boiling water, so as not to boil them, and replace it with warm water to wash the olives well. Throw away this water too, and replace it with more lukewarm water. Leave the olives to soak for about half an hour so that they can revive.

When green olives are destined for a garnish, after having removed the stones, plunge them into a saucepan with boiling water and let them boil gently for 5 minutes. In this way they soften and lose the salt from their cure, making them sweeter.

We have an infinite number of different names for our more substantial appetizers. They almost always seem to come from the French—*bouchées*, *canapés*—or the English —*sandwiches*, *toasts*. However, while they are often similar, our Italian versions are rarely the same. The little pastries in this section can be made from store-bought pastry shells or you can make them yourself, using either puff or choux pastry.

More Italian are the *bruschetta* and *crostini*, which are slices of sandwich or black bread without crusts, toasted or fried in butter, on which you put a garnish of your choice. *Tramezzini* are Italian two-sided sandwiches with all four crusts removed, whipped butter, and your choice of filling, such as ham or chicken breast.

Red tomatoes of all kinds are found in markets all year round and lend themselves to numerous preparations. Among the peppers used as appetizers, the most sought after are round red peppers and long green ones. In summer, serve strips of roasted yellow and red peppers, seasoned with a strong, aromatic vinegar and a little olive oil. Cucumbers and celery, served raw, are also delightful fresh additions to any plate, while artichokes are equally welcome, whether served alone or as part of a more complex preparation.

The salamis of Fabriano, Felino, Milan, and Secondigliano; the *salamini alla cacciatora*; the *bondiole* and *culatello* from Emilia; the Roman *coralline*; the Venetian *luganiche*; *mortadella* from Bologna; and *soppressata* and *capocollo* from Abruzzo all offer a great variety of choice to your antipasti. All these cold cuts should be trimmed of their fat before being cut into thin and regular slices. Italian hams are rightly appreciated abroad, especially the prosciuttos prepared in San Daniele del Friuli and in Langhirano in Emilia. Indeed, in all the Italian regions you will find high-quality sweet and smoked hams.

Finally, vol-au-vents are literally a mouthful, made from puff pastry. Fillings can be as extravagant as artichokes with chicken livers or shrimp with truffle, but simpler concoctions can be just as good.

ANTIPASTI

APPETIZERS

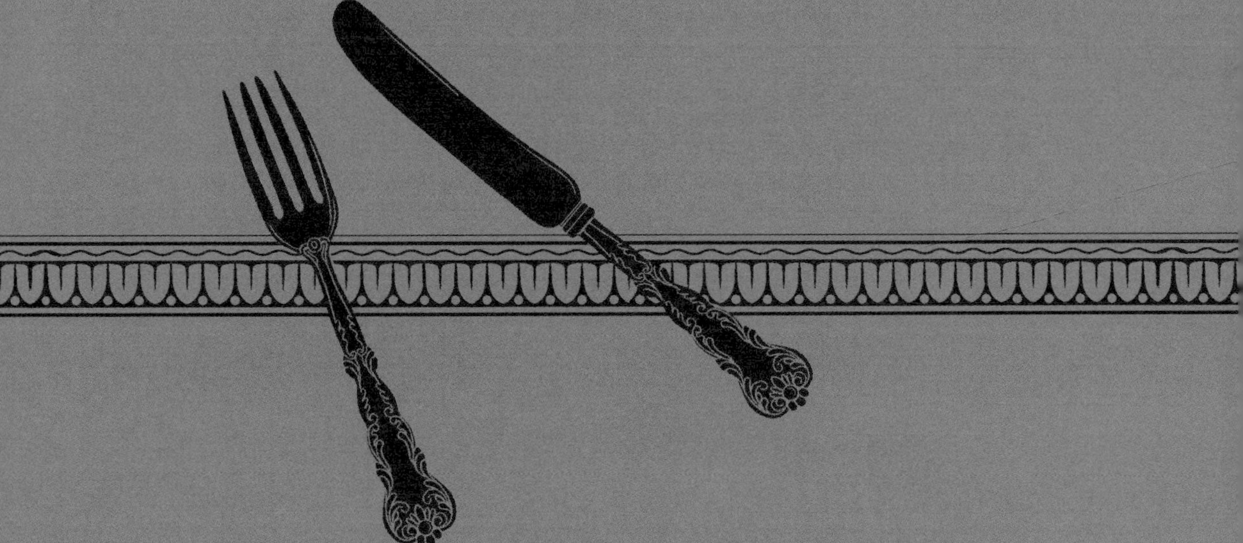

JELLIES, BUTTERS & CREAMS

TO USE JELLY

If you need to glaze a dish with jelly, bring the jelly to room temperature until it has reached a certain almost oil-like consistency. With the help of a small brush or spoon, apply a thin layer on top of the cold prepared dish and refrigerate until set. Then brush or spoon on a second layer. Keep in the refrigerator until ready to serve.

TO USE GELATIN BOUILLON

Commercially available bouillon cubes often contain gelatin allowing you to obtain a quick jelly that sets easily and in a short time. To make 2 cups of jelly: **Crumble one bouillon cube into 2 cups of cold water; bring the water to boil, stirring until the cube has completely dissolved.** *To improve the taste, you can add a few teaspoons of Marsala. Put the jelly in a mold and let it set in the fridge. This jelly has, it is true, neither the nutritional value nor the taste of jelly made with meat broth, but it is quick and therefore very useful in preparations.*

Jellies

GELATINA DI CARNE

Meat Jelly

MAKES 4½ CUPS

4¼ cups meat broth *(p88)*
2 egg whites
1 oz isinglass sheets, or gelatin
1 glass Marsala

This is the traditional way to make jelly using isinglass.

Make the meat broth as directed. Let the broth cool down, degrease it carefully, and then clarify it in the following way: Take two egg whites, place them in the bottom of a pot, pour the cold broth over it. Bring slowly to a boil for about 10 minutes over a very low heat; the egg whites will coagulate in the form of tiny flakes, and you will see the broth appear very clear. Let the broth rest with no heat for about 10 minutes. Wet a paper towel, wring it out, and use it to line a sieve set over a bowl. Ladle all the broth into the sieve.

Soak the isinglass sheets in cold water for 10 minutes in a small bowl. Pour 4¼ cups of the strained meat broth into a saucepan, add the isinglass sheets, place the pot over very heat, and let the mixture boil for about 2 minutes, stirring constantly. As soon as the jelly has cooled a little, add the Marsala.

GELATINA DI PESCE

Fish Jelly

MAKES ABOUT 6 CUPS

14 oz fish (hake or cod)
7 oz scraps of sole or other fish
2 onions
Parsley
1 oz isinglass sheets
2 egg whites
1 glass Marsala
Salt
Optional: 2 oz mushrooms

Put the well-gutted and washed fish, the trimmings, chopped onions, and parsley in a saucepan. If you have decided to use them, also add the washed mushrooms. Pour 12½ cups of water into the saucepan and cook over moderate heat for about 45 minutes.

Using a fine-mesh sieve, pour 6 cups of the resulting fish stock into a saucepan and let cool.

Calculate that 1 ounce of isinglass sheets are needed for every 6 cups of stock. Place the isinglass sheets in a small pan in cold water for a few minutes, then squeeze them with your hands and add them to the broth. Pour the egg whites into the broth and place the saucepan over low heat.

Bring the liquid to a simmer while gently whisking. Let boil over low heat for about 15 minutes and then strain the jelly through a sieve lined with a wet paper towel. As soon as the jelly has cooled a little, add the Marsala.

Butters

BURRO ALLA CAMPAGNOLA

Country Style Butter

7 tbsp butter
3 tbsp capers
1 oz cornichons
3 anchovy fillets
Parsley

Chop the butter into small cubes so it is easier to work. Add the capers. Dice the cornichons and the anchovies and work into the mix. Work with the back of a wooden spoon to a creamy paste. Chop the parsley finely. If you prefer an elegant smooth finish, pass through a mesh sieve.

ADA SAYS: *It is advisable to take your butter out of the fridge before you start so it is easier to work with.*

BURRO DI MONTPELLIER

Montpellier Butter

Spinach
Parsley
Chervil
Garlic
7 tbsp butter
1 hard-boiled egg yolk
1 fresh egg yolk
1 tsp capers
2 or 3 cornichons
4 anchovies
Olive oil
1 tsp white vinegar or tarragon vinegar
Mustard powder
Salt
Pepper

Take a handful of spinach leaves, some parsley and chervil; dip them in a pot of boiling water for a couple of minutes, drain and rinse under cold water, then squeeze dry.

With a mortar and pestle, crush the herbs with a small piece of garlic, the butter, the hard-boiled egg yolk, the fresh yolk, and the capers. Chop the cornichons and a couple of washed and boned anchovies. Season with a strong pinch of pepper.

When the mixture is reduced to a smooth paste, put it in a bowl and then, proceeding as for a mayonnaise, add a finger of olive oil, drop by drop, always mixing with a wooden spoon. Finally, add the vinegar and a pinch of mustard powder dissolved in a few drops of water.

BURRO D'ACCIUGHE

Anchovy Butter

2 oz anchovy fillets
9 tbsp butter

Wash the anchovies. Make sure to take out all the bones. Cut them into small pieces and mix in with the butter. Pound well and pass through a sieve.

BURRO DI DRAGONCELLO

Tarragon Butter

Tarragon leaves
9 tbsp butter

Bring a pan of water to a boil. Dip a handful of tarragon leaves briefly in the hot water, then rinse in cold water. Squeeze well and let dry before pounding in a pestle and mortar with the butter.

BURRO DI GAMBERETTI
Shrimp Butter

3½ oz shrimp
7 tbsp butter

Put a pan of cold water on the heat. Add the shrimp while still cold. As it comes to a boil, switch off the heat and let the shrimp cook in the hot water. Lift out with a slotted spoon, let cool, then shell them. Put them in a pestle and mortar. Chop the butter into small pieces and pound together and, if you prefer, pass them through a sieve.

BURRO DI SARDINE
Sardine Butter

3 tinned sardines in olive oil
7 tbsp butter

Slip a knife through the underside of the sardines and lift out the bones. Take off the heads so you are just left with the fillets. Mash with a fork and work in the butter.

Creams

CREMA DI PESCE
White Fish Cream

5 oz cooked white fish, boiled or cooked in butter
3½ tbsp butter

White sauce:
3 tbsp flour, 1½ tbsp butter, 1 cup milk

Prepare the white sauce *(p16)* using the flour, butter, and milk listed here. Let cool and then chill.

Make sure the fish has no bones. Pick any out and chop finely. Warm the butter in a pan, add 2 tablespoons of cold white sauce, and incorporate fully before finally folding in the fish.

CREMA DI POLLO
Chicken Cream

3½ oz chicken breast, roasted or poached
1½ tbsp butter

White sauce:
3 tbsp flour, 1½ tbsp butter, 1 cup milk

Prepare the white sauce *(p16)* using using the flour, butter, and milk listed here.

Dice the chicken. Warm the butter in a pan. Add the white sauce and stir well to amalgamate and only then fold in the chicken. Serve hot or cold.

CREMA DI PROSCIUTTO COTTO

Ham Cream

3½ oz ham
1½ tbsp butter

White sauce:
3 tbsp flour, 1½ tbsp butter,
1 cup milk

Prepare the white sauce *(p16)* using the ingredient amounts listed here.

Dice the ham well. Melt the butter in a pan and add 2 tablespoons of the white sauce, stir well. Add the ham and allow it to flavor the sauce for a few moments.

CREMA DI TARTUFI

Truffle Cream

1 oz black truffle
7 tbsp butter

White sauce:
3 tbsp flour, 1½ tbsp butter,
1 cup milk

Prepare the white sauce *(p16)* using the ingredient amounts listed here.

Dice the truffle. Melt the butter and add the truffle pieces. Then fold in 1 tablespoon of white sauce. Stir to get a smooth, speckled paste.

GORGONZOLA IN CREMA

Gorgonzola Cream

3½ oz Gorgonzola
7 tbsp butter
Salted crackers
Optional: cumin seeds

Take the rind off the Gorgonzola cheese and mix it with the butter. Fashion the mix into a ball and optionally sprinkle with cumin seeds. Put the cream in a crystal dish and refrigerate to chill before serving. Serve with salted crackers or biscuits.

PARMIGIANO IN CREMA

Parmesan Cream

1 cup cream
3½ oz grated Parmesan
5 oz Gruyère
5 oz Edam
White truffle

Whip the cream to soft peaks and gently mix in the Parmesan. Transfer to a small crystal dish. Smooth it well in the shape of a dome. Cut the Gruyère and Edam into sticks. Garnish from the top with a circle of alternating cheese sticks toward the base of the cream.

Sprinkle the top with grated white truffle and serve.

BRUSCHETTA, CANAPÉS & CROSTINI

All recipes make 12 portions unless otherwise stated

BRUSCHETTA CLASSICA

Classic Bruschetta

12 slices sandwich bread
Garlic
Olive oil
Salt

Set up a nice wood fire. Place the bread on the grill and let them toast over the embers. When toasted, rub the garlic over each slice and season with a little oil and a pinch of salt. Alternatively you can bake them in a hot oven. Serve immediately.

BRUSCHETTA CON POMODORO

Tomato Bruschetta

6 tomatoes
Olive oil
Basil
12 slices sandwich bread
Garlic
Salt

Wash and cut the tomatoes into strips, season with oil, salt, and a few leaves of basil. Put the slices of bread on a wire rack, toast them over an open fire—or in the hot oven. As soon as they are ready, rub a clove of garlic into each one and sprinkle with the tomato mix.

CANAPÈ ARLECCHINO

Harlequin Canapés

12 slices sandwich bread
7 tbsp butter
1 tbsp mustard
Black truffle
Cornichon
1 hard-boiled egg
Tongue

Cut the crusts off the bread and toast, so it is firm. Blend the butter with mustard. Spread on the toasts. Garnish with small pieces of chopped truffle, cornichon, strips of egg white and mashed yolk, and chopped tongue all arranged irregularly, but elegantly, alternating colours as much as possible.

ADA SAYS: *Canapès are one-centimetre-thick toasted and crustless bread slices that can be square, rectangle, circle, oval and triangle in shape; they are buttered and topped with various ingredients.*

CANAPÈ DI ACCIUGHE

Anchovy Canapés

12 slices sandwich bread
12 anchovy fillets
2 hard-boiled eggs

Anchovy butter:
7 tbsp butter, 2 oz anchovies

Prepare the anchovy butter *(p54)* using the amounts listed here Cut the bread into rectangles and spread with the anchovy butter.Wash the anchovies and then cut in two and again to make thin strips about ⅛ inch thick. With these strips make a grid over each piece of toast and place, alternating the colours, in each void of this grid a pinch of egg yolk and egg white. You can also pipe any remaining butter in a pastry bag with a nozzle and finish off the edges with a string of butter that will complete their elegance.

CANAPÈ DI GAMBERETTI

Shrimp Canapés

24 shrimp
Shrimp butter *(p55)*
3 hard-boiled eggs
1 loaf of bread

Wash the shrimp. Put them in a pan with boiling water, lightly salted. Let them cook for a few minutes, then drain, peel, and set aside. Make the shrimp butter.

Separate the egg whites from the yolks. Mash the yolks and finely chop the egg whites with a knife.

Cut out 12 round canapés from the bread and spread each with shrimp butter. On one side of the canapé, place the mashed egg yolk and on the other side, the chopped egg white.

In the middle, between the two colours, arrange a row of cooked and peeled shrimp, one leaning against the other.

CANAPÈ DI PROSCIUTTO

Ham and Jelly Canapés

Diced jelly *(p52)*
7 oz thick-sliced ham
3½ tbsp butter
2 bread slices

White sauce:
2 tbsp flour, 1 tbsp butter,
7 tbsp milk

Prepare the white sauce *(p16)*, using the ingredient amounts listed here. Refrigerate until cold. Prepare the jelly.

With a 2½-inch round pastry cutter, cut out disks of ham. Fold them into a half-moon shape and fix the top edge with a little bit of well-worked butter. Chop the ham trimmings and mix carefully with the butter in a bowl. Fold in the cold white sauce to incorporate. Spread on lightly toasted bread and finally place a half moon of ham on each canapé topped with a little piece of jelly.

◆ ADA SAYS: *The ham needs to be thick for the best results here.*

CROSTINI ALLA NAPOLETANA

Neapolitan Crostini

1 loaf of bread
Olive oil
10 oz mozzarella
12 anchovy fillets
7 oz tomatoes
Oregano
Pepper

From a loaf of sandwich bread, cut 12 rectangles the size of a playing card about ⅓ inch thick to make crostini.

Warm some oil in a pan and fry the crostini on one side only. In a new pan—ideally big enough to take all your crostini together or otherwise work in batches—set the crostini fried-side up and cover with a slice of mozzarella and an anchovy. Peel, slice, and seed the tomatos. Lay a slice on top with a pinch of pepper and a few leaves of oregano.

Drizzle on each toast a little oil and bake in a warm oven for 10 minutes until the mozzarella melts. Serve very hot.

CROSTINI DI FEGATINI DI POLLO

Chicken Liver Crostini

1 lb 5 oz chicken livers
Butter or oil for frying
Parsley
2 anchovies
Flour
1 or 2 tbsp broth
Lemon
1 loaf of bread
Pepper

Remove the gall from the livers and cut out any greenish bits with a knife. Chop the rest to a pulp. Warm some oil or butter in a pan and sauté the minced livers. Chop the parsley and add to the mix.

As soon as the livers are cooked, which happens almost immediately, add the anchovies. Season with a pinch of pepper—salt is not necessary due to anchovies—and sprinkle with half a teaspoon of flour. Wet with a little broth, add a little more, keep stirring, and then remove from the heat. Once away from the heat squeeze the juice out of half a lemon on to the livers.

From a loaf of sandwich bread, cut 12 rectangles the size of a playing card and ¼ inch thick to make crostini. Fry with a little oil or butter, and when they have taken on come colour, take the crostini out of the pan and cover with the liver mixture and arrange on a serving dish.

CROSTINI DI FEGATO DI MAIALE

Pork Liver Crostini

7 oz pork liver
Garlic clove
2 anchovies
2 pickled green chilies
Olive oil
1 loaf of bread
1 lemon
Salt
Pepper

Chop the pork liver on a cutting board with half a clove of garlic. Wash and bone the anchovies. Chop them too and add to the liver and do the same with the chili peppers.

Warm some oil in a pan and, when hot, add the liver mixture. Season with salt and pepper. Let it flavor a little, stirring, and then add a couple of spoons of water.

From a loaf of sandwich bread, cut 12 rectangles the size of a playing card and ¼ inch thick and either toast them or fry them. As soon as the liver is cooked, but not too much, spread the mixture on the crostini. Squeeze over the juice of a lemon and serve hot.

CROSTINI DI RICOTTA E SALSICCE

Ricotta and Sausage Crostini

7 oz ricotta
Milk
Grated Parmesan
3 sausages
1¾ oz Fontina or Gruyère
Bread
Oil for frying
Salt

Put the ricotta in a bowl along with a few tablespoons of milk. Season with salt and ¼ cup grated Parmesan. Then, stirring constantly with a wooden spoon, smooth it out into a cream.

Prick the sausages and cook them slowly in a little pan with a little water. When the water has evaporated, let the sausages brown in their own fat. Let cool, then peel them and chop the meat. Mix into the ricotta.

From a loaf of bread, cut 12 rectangles the size of a playing card to make crostini. Fry in oil, but on one side only. Oil a baking pan in which the crostini can all fit in one layer. Lay the crostini fried-side down. Spread the ricotta/sausage mix on the crostini and garnish with small sticks of Fontina or Gruyère. Bake in a warm oven for 10 minutes. Serve very hot.

GALLETTINE AL PEPE

Pepper Galettes

MAKES ABOUT 30

1½ cups flour
4 tbsp olive oil
2 eggs
2 tsp active-dry yeast
Butter, for greasing
1 egg
Salt
Pepper

Make a mound of the flour on a work surface and make a well in the centre. Add the oil, eggs, a spoonful of salt, plenty of freshly ground black pepper, and the yeast. Knead everything together like a pie dough. Let it rest for a while.

Roll out the dough to ¼ inch thick. With a 2-inch round pastry cutter, cut out disks and place on a lightly greased baking sheet. Gather the scraps and reroll to cut out more disks. When all the disks are on the baking sheet, brush them with a beaten egg and bake them in a preheated medium heat oven for 10 to 15 minutes and serve cold.

ADA SAYS: *These galettes lend themselves to tasty preparations for tea or buffets. Just pair them with some savory butter in the middle — such as anchovy, tuna, truffle — or a cream cheese.*

SANDWICHES

All recipes make 12 portions unless otherwise stated

SANDWICHES ALL'ARLECCHINO

Harlequin Sandwiches

7 oz roast chicken breast
Hearts of romaine
Tomato
2 oz Gruyère
1 hard-boiled egg
Mayonnaise
12 panini rolls
Salt
Pepper

Finely chop the chicken breast, the lettuce, tomato, Gruyère, and hard-boiled egg. Mix together in a bowl. Season with salt and a pinch of pepper. Gently work in 2 spoons of mayonnaise.

Cut the rolls open down the middle. Fill with the chicken mixture. Close the sandwiches by pressing lightly with your hand.

ADA SAYS: *If you don't want to eat sandwiches right away, keep them fresh like this: Take a towel, wet it, squeeze it, open it again, and line the inside of a larger container, so that the edges of the towel fall out. Line up the sandwiches inside and when you've got them all settled, fold the four edges of the towel inward to cover the sandwiches. Lightly weight them down with a plate until you need them. Or you can wrap in aluminum foil.*

SANDWICHES AL PROSCIUTTO

Prosciutto or Tongue Sandwiches

12 panini rolls
5 tbsp soft fresh cheese
5 tbsp butter
2 tbsp cream
7 oz sliced prosciutto or tongue
12 anchovy fillets

Split the rolls horizontally without going all the way through so the two sides are still connected. In a bowl, stir together, cheese, butter, and cream. Spread the mixture inside the rolls and lay in an anchovy fillet and a piece of prosciutto or tongue inside. Close the sandwiches up.

SANDWICHES PER GITE

Sandwiches with Anchovies and Ham

Anchovy butter *(p54)*
12 panini rolls
7 oz thinly sliced roast beef
2 oz sliced ham
2 hard-boiled eggs

First, make up the anchovy butter.

Split the rolls horizontally without going all the way through so the two sides are still connected. Spread the anchovy butter inside. Cover with slices of roast beef and ham. Chop the eggs into strips and set them on top and close the rolls up.

TARTINE AL RAFANO

Horseradish Tartine

3½ oz fresh horseradish
7 tbsp butter
12 slices black bread
2 cornichons
Capers

Finely grate the horseradish into a bowl. Cut the butter into cubes, add to the bowl, and work with a wooden spoon to soften and meld in the horseradish. Spread on the black bread. Cut the cornichons into wheels and garnish each slice with capers and cornichons.

TOAST ARLECCHINO

Harlequin Toast

MAKES 1

2 slices bread
Butter
Mustard
2 slices ham
2 thin slices Gruyère
1 marinated artichoke, halved
4 anchovy fillets
Tomato slices
Cornichons

This recipe can be easily scaled up to make as many toasts as you like. Lightly spread each slice of bread on one side with a little butter and a little mustard. Top with the ham, Gruyère, an artichoke half, a few anchovy fillets of anchovies, some tomato, and strips of cornichons.

Place the topped bread in a toaster oven (or under a broiler), which, as it heats up, will toast the bread and slightly melts the toppings, blending them well into a tasty and pleasant whole.

TOAST CON PETTI DI POLLO E FRITTATA

Grilled Chicken Frittata Sandwiches

MAKES 6

14 oz chicken breast
Flour
5 eggs
Breadcrumbs
7 tbsp butter
Grated Parmesan
Milk
12 slices sandwich bread
Salt

Split the chicken breast horizontally to make a total of 6 cutlets. Pound with the back of a knife to give them more of a sandwich shape. Dust with flour, then wipe through 2 beaten eggs well seasoned with salt and pepper, and lastly dredge in some breadcrumbs. Fry them in the butter taking care not to prolong the cooking too much.

Make 6 frittatine (mini omelets): In a bowl, vigorously beat the remaining 3 eggs, season with a little salt, ¼ cup grated Parmesan, and half a glass of milk. In a 6-inch skillet, melt 1 tablespoon butter and pour in 2 tablespoons of the beaten eggs, tilting the pan so that the mixture spreads out in all directions, then let it set. As soon as the omelet is firm, slide it on to a plate and continue making the rest of the omelets, using 1 tablespoon butter and 2 tablespoons of egg for each.

To assemble the sandwiches: Line up the slices of bread, butter one side and on half of them put a chicken breast and an omelet to cover. Then cover with another slice of bread pressing down so they are compact. Fry some oil in the pan and when it is warm use a spatula to drop the toasts in and brown on both sides.

TRAMEZZINI ALLE ACCIUGHE

Anchovy Tramezzini

Anchovy butter *(p54)*
24 slices sandwich bread
24 anchovy fillets
7 oz mozzarella

Mash the butter and anchovy together to make the anchovy butter. Spread the anchovy butter on all the slices of bread. On 12 of them put 2 whole anchovy fillets and a slice of mozzarella. Close the sandwiches and press lightly together.

TRAMEZZINI ARLECCHINO

Harlequin Tramezzini

24 slices sandwich bread
Mayonnaise
Lettuce
7 oz cooked chicken breast
2 tomatoes
3 hard-boiled eggs
Gruyère
Ham
Salt
Pepper

Lightly toast the bread. Spread half the slices with a spoon of mayonnaise, some finely chopped lettuce, a few slices of boiled or roasted chicken, a couple of slices of tomato, a few rounds of hard-boiled egg, Gruyère, and ham. Season with salt, pepper, a little more mayonnaise. Close the sandwiches and press lightly together.

LITTLE PASTRIES & PLATES

TO MAKE PIE DOUGH

Mound the flour on your work surface and make a well in the centre. Chop the butter in small pieces and put it in the well with a few tablespoons of water and a pinch of salt. Combine, without working too much, to form a ball with the dough. Let it rest for at least 15 minutes. Then roll out the dough thinly, about ⅛ inch thick. Use a pastry cutter to shape the dough and lay in the mold.

TO LINE THE MOLDS

You can make little boats, trays, or shells for your butters and creams. You can also buy premade cups and shapes, which is convenient, and they are easy to make at home.

Having prepared the necessary dough, roll it out thinly on a floured surface and with the pastry cutters cut out as many disks as there are moulds you have chosen for the various preparations. It is important that the pastry cutters, whether smooth or wavy, round or oval, overhang the moulds, so that they can be easily lined up to the brim without you having to pull the pastry with your hands.

TO BAKE THE CASINGS

When the shells are first baked and then filled with the mixture, whether hot or cold, if you were to expose them to the oven as they are, the pastry would deform. To avoid this, after lining the moulds, pierce the bottom of the pastry with a small knife and fill the casings with uncooked beans before placing the casings in the pre-heated oven. When they are cooked (they should be very light in colour), remove first the beans and then the casings, very carefully so as not to damage them. This is known as blind baking.

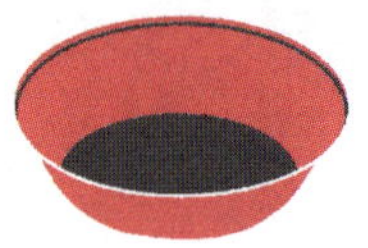

ACCIUGHE IN ROTELLINE

Anchovy Wheels

12 salted anchovies
2 oz tinned tuna in olive oil
Parsley
2 tbsp butter
1 lemon
Pepper

This recipe needs large salted anchovies. Wash them under running water to free them from the brine, divide them into two fillets, remove the spine and other small bones, and finally rinse them again.

Finely chop the tuna and some parsley, then place them in a bowl and mix with the butter. Season with a few drops of lemon juice and, if you want, a pinch of pepper.

Spread a portion of the tuna butter on each anchovy fillet and then roll all the fillets on themselves to get 24 wheels. Place on a large appetizer plate and garnish with a few slices of lemon.

BARCHETTE AL GORGONZOLA

Gorgonzola Boats

5½ tbsp butter
3½ oz Gorgonzola
1 tbsp minced onion
2 tbsp cream
Paprika

Pie dough:
1⅔ cups flour, 9 tbsp butter, 5 to 6 tbsp water

Make pie dough with the flour, butter and water. Form into boat shapes and blind-bake. Soften the butter at room temperature in a bowl. Work it with a wooden spoon.

Mix in the Gorgonzola, onion, a pinch of paprika, and lastly the cream. Put it into a pastry bag and decorate the inside of the pastry boats shortly before serving.

BARCHETTE CON CREMA DI TONNO

Tuna Boats

3½ oz tinned tuna in olive oil
3½ oz fresh soft cheese
2 tbsp cream
1 hard-boiled egg

Pie dough:
1⅔ cups flour, 9 tbsp butter, 5-6 tbsp water

Make pie dough with the flour, butter and water. Form into boat shapes and blind-bake.

Mash the tuna and cheese with the cream. Fill the little pastry boats and garnish with strips of egg white and mashed yolk.

ADA SAYS: *Barchette are small preparations of pastry shell baked in oval moulds. They are filled with fish or crustaceans and mixed with sauces such as mayonnaise and hollandaise. The casings can be bought ready-made; should you wish to make them yourself, you will find the recipe opposite.*

BARCHETTE CON GAMBERETTI

Shrimp Boats

48 shrimp
10 oz spinach
1½ tbsp butter
9 tbsp grated Parmesan
Salt

Pie dough:
1⅔ cups flour, 9 tbsp butter, 5-6 tbsp water

White sauce:
1½ tbsp butter, 3 tbsp flour, 7 tbsp milk

Make pie dough *(p64)* using the amounts listed here. Form into 24 boat shapes and blind-bake to a pale colour.

Wash the shrimp and put them in a pan of water. Simmer until they change colour, then drain and shell them.

Wash and boil the spinach until it collapses. Drain, chop it coarsely and add the butter and salt.

Prepare a white sauce *(p16)* with the butter, flour, and milk listed here. Layer each boat with spinach, then 2 shrimp each and finally the white sauce, which must be quite thick. Sprinkle each boat with the grated Parmesan. Put them in a hot oven or under a broiler to just colour the Parmesan and serve with a golden crust.

CARCIOFINI ALLA MARINARA

Artichoke and Smoked Fish Roe

Smoked fish roe
Mayonnaise
Milk
12 cooked artichoke hearts

Make a little sauce by dicing smoked fish roe and folding it with a little mayonnaise and a splash of milk. Fill the cooked artichoke hearts with this mixture.

CARCIOFINI RIPIENI DI ACCIUGHE

Artichoke with Anchovies and Capers

12 anchovies
Capers
12 cooked artichoke hearts
Butter

Using a large knife, mince the anchovies with the capers. Use this mixture to cover the artichoke hearts and finish with a little butter.

CARCIOFINI RIPIENI DI CAVIALE

Artichokes with Caviar

12 cooked artichoke hearts
Caviar
Butter

Choose some not too small artichoke hearts. Fill them a little with caviar and close the opening with a little butter.

CETRIOLI ALLA RUSSA

Creamed Cucumbers

Cucumber
Olive oil
Vinegar
Parsley
Cream
Salt
Pepper

Clean the cucumbers and cut them into thin finger-sized slices. Collect these slices in a small salad bowl and sprinkle them with a little fine salt, which will let them leach out any water they contain. After 30 minutes, take a few slices at a time, squeeze them gently and spread them over a kitchen towel to dry out.

Arrange the slices in saucers, season them with very little salt, pepper, oil, vinegar, and chopped parsley, adding a spoonful or two of cream. Refrigerate for at least 1 hour, so that the cucumbers can be served very cold.

CETRIOLI FARCITI

Stuffed Cucumbers

6 medium cucumbers
7 oz walnuts
12 basil leaves
1 cup mayonnaise
Worcestershire sauce
Roasted red pepper in olive oil
Salt
White pepper

Wash the cucumbers, dry them, peel them, halve lengthwise, then cut each half crosswise. Scrape out the seeds with a spoon leaving a thick furrow down the middle.

Choose 24 small walnuts for garnish and chop the rest with the basil. Mix this in a bowl with the mayonnaise, a few drops of Worcestershire sauce, and a pinch of white pepper. Fill the cucumbers with this mixture, decorate each of them with a walnut, a basil leaf, and a small strip of roasted red pepper.

COZZE ALLA MAIONESE

Mussels with Mayonnaise

2¼ lb mussels
1 onion
Parsley
White wine
Cream
1 lemon
Mustard
Pepper
Mayonnaise, store-bought

Scrape the mussels and pull off any beards, rinse several times and put them in a wide and low saucepan with ¾ of a chopped onion, stems of parsley, and a good pinch of coarsely ground pepper. Put the lid on the saucepan and bring it to a boil over moderate heat, shaking occasionally. No oil or water is needed because the mussels have their own liquid as they open.

When the mussels are all open, take off the heat and allow to cool. Take off and discard the empty half of the shells and keep those with mussels. Leave the liquid from the mussels in the saucepan for a while and, when the sandy part has settled, decant it very carefully.

Put a glass of white wine in a new saucepan with the rest of the chopped onion and let the wine boil until it is reduced by two-thirds. Add half a glass of the mussel broth and let it boil again until all the liquid is reduced to less than half a glass. Pass this reduced liquid through a sieve. Add a spoonful of cream and let it cool completely.

Whip a little mayonnaise into the cream and mussel liquor. Complete with a little lemon juice, a little bit of mustard, and a spoonful of chopped parsley. Pour this on the mussels.

COZZE IN SALSA PICCANTE

Spicy Mussels

2¼ lb mussels
Olive oil
1 clove garlic
5 anchovies
1 cup white wine
Vinegar
Parsley
Cayenne pepper

Scrape the mussels, open them while still raw with a knife, wash them in salted water and let drain.

In a little oil, lightly fry a clove of garlic. Take it out as soon as it browns and add the mussels. Wash and chop the anchovies and add them to the pan. Add the white wine and as much vinegar as you like, depending on how sharp you like it. Reduce. Finish the sauce with a good spoonful of chopped parsley and a pinch of cayenne pepper.

Pour the mussels into a bowl and infuse for 2 or 3 days in the frige. Serve with their sauce.

OLIVE FARCITE

Stuffed Olives

12 large olives
1 tsp capers
2 cornichons
Parsley
2 anchovy fillets
1 hard-boiled egg yolk
Olive oil

Pit the olives by taking a small thin knife and cutting the pulp off the olive, turning it in a spiral around the pit into a ribbon of one piece. Recompose it so it takes on the shape of the olive again. Soak them in a bowl with lightly salted water to prevent them from blackening until you are ready to use them. You can also buy them already pitted.

Finely chop the capers, cornichons, parsley, anchovy fillets, and the egg yolk. Blend with a spoonful of oil to make a paste and use this to fill each olive.

OLIVE PER ACCOMPAGNAMENTO DI COCKTAIL

Olives for Cocktails

24 olives
12 thin slices prosciutto

Pit the olives, as above—or buy them already pitted. Divide each prosciutto slice, which must be very thin, in half and wind around the olives and hold them together with a toothpick. Put the olives in a pan and bake in a very hot oven until the prosciutto is slightly transparent. Let them drain, but serve very hot.

OSTRICHE ALLA VENEZIANA

Venetian Oysters

12 oysters
1 lemon
Cayenne pepper
Caviar
To garnish: lemon slices, parsley

Open the oysters with a strong, small knife and wash them in salted water. Put them back in the concave shell, season with lemon juice and cayenne pepper. Border them with the caviar and cover them with the other shell. Place them in an oval dish on a base of crushed and decorated ice with sprigs of parsley and lemon slices.

ADA SAYS: *Oysters should be served in their own shells. After opening, it is a good precaution to remove them from the shell and wash them lightly in salted water to get rid of any impurities and any shell that might have broken on them. Season with lemon juice and a little pepper and place them on the plate or better over an ice block. Decorate the plate with lemon wedges.*

POMODORI FARCITI

Stuffed Tomatoes

6 green tomatoes
3 hard-boiled eggs
3½ oz tinned tuna in olive oil
Capers
Parsley
Mayonnaise
Pepper

Choose rather green tomatoes. Wash them well. Cut off the top cap and scoop out the seeds with a spoon, then place them upside down in a bowl so they drain well.

Cut the eggs into cubes. Cut the tuna into pieces. Mix together the eggs and tuna in a bowl and season with a good pinch of black pepper, a spoonful of capers, and a spoon of chopped parsley.

Blend this mixture with mayonnaise, then fill up the tomatoes. Cover the tomatoes with their caps and place them in the fridge until time to serve.

SCAMPI COCKTAIL

Shrimp Cocktail

4½ lb shrimp
Olive oil
Green lettuce
1 lemon
Salt
Pepper

Mayonnaise:
3 egg yolks, 2 cups olive oil, vinegar or lemon juice, Cognac, 2 tsp mustard, 2 tbsp ketchup

Wash and rinse the shrimp and cook for 3 minutes in lightly salted boiling water. Drain, shell them, season with oil, salt, and pepper, and leave them in this marinade for about 1 hour.

Prepare a thick mayonnaise *(p19)* using the ingredient amounts listed here and dilute with half a glass of Cognac, the mustard, and ketchup.

Carefully wash the lettuce leaves and dry them. Shred them finely and season with a little of the mayonnaise. Arrange them in crystal cups. Put the shrimp with a little mayonnaise on top and keep in the fridge until you are ready. Serve with lemon slices.

UOVA ALLA CREMA DI PROSCIUTTO

Eggs with Ham

6 eggs
3½ oz ham
1½ tbsp butter
1 loaf of bread
Salt

White sauce:
3 tbsp flour, 1½ tbsp butter,
1 cup milk

Boil the eggs by putting them in a saucepan with cold water and counting 7 minutes from the moment the water boils. Then rinse them in cold water, peel them, and cut them into disks.

Prepare the white sauce *(p16)* using ingredient amounts listed here. Make a cream with the ham, chopped very small, the butter, and 2 tablespoons white sauce.

Cut your bread into crostini slices of equal sizes. Butter them and put a slice of egg on top. Pipe or spoon the ham cream on to the egg so it rises like a pyramid.

UOVA CON GAMBERETTI

Eggs with Shrimp

6 hard-boiled eggs
2 or 3 anchovies
3½ tbsp butter
24 cooked shrimp
Optional: Marsala

Peel the eggs. Cut a small cap at the bottom and a larger cap in the upper part of the egg, to make small barrels that will stand upright, but from which you can extricate the yolk without breaking the egg white.

Carefully wash, bone, and chop the anchovies. Put them in a bowl with the yolks and mash with the butter and a splash of Marsala, if using. Put this mixture in a pastry bag, or use a spoon, to fill the cavity in the eggs so the top looks like a rose. Around the edge of each egg put 4 shelled shrimp in a crown, arranging them one resting on the other. Refrigerate until ready to serve.

UOVA CON SALSA MAIONESE

Eggs with Mayonnaise

6 hard-boiled eggs
3 anchovies
3½ tbsp butter
Mayonnaise

Peel the eggs, halve lengthwise, and separate the whites from the yolks. Wash, bone, and finely chop the anchovies. Mix the anchovies with the yolks and butter.

Spoon this paste back into the egg whites. Arrange on a plate and cover each egg with a teaspoon of mayonnaise.

UOVA CON TONNO

Eggs with Tuna

6 hard-boiled eggs
3½ oz tinned tuna in olive oil
6 anchovy fillets
Olive oil
1 lemon
Cornichons
Pepper

Peel the eggs, halve lengthwise, and separate the whites from the yolks. Put the whites, cut-side up, in a dish where they can be well aligned.

Finely chop the tuna and anchovy fillets in a bowl. Add the yolks and mash well. Add oil and the juice of a lemon and season with a pinch of pepper. Fill the whites with this puree and garnish the eggs with slices of cornichon.

CHOUX & PUFF PASTRIES

TO MAKE CHOUX PASTRY

To make choux pastry, the porportions for two eggs will be: **½ cup of water, 3½ tbsp of butter and 9½ tbsp of flour** - *but in some recipes, the exact amounts will differ.*

Put the water in a saucepan with the butter and salt. Once it boils, remove from the heat and add the flour. Stir with a wooden spoon and return to the heat. The flour, butter and water will form a paste. You need to stir constantly. Very soon the dough will form a ball and it will come off from the sides of the saucepan. When you hear a slight noise, like frying, the paste will be ready. Take off the heat and let cool.

When cool, add one egg at a time working energetically with a wooden spoon. Wait for the first egg to be completely amalgamated before adding the second. The dough should be velvety and will make some bubbles here and there.

TO MAKE PUFF PASTRY

To make puff pastry, **for 3 cups of flour plus 3 tablespoons, allow 7 tablespoons of butter.** *Mound the flour on a work surface and make a well in the middle. Pour in a few tablespoons water and a pinch of salt. Mix well with a spatula and then knead with your hands until you get a smooth, elastic dough. It is important that the dough be the same consistency as the butter. If the dough is harder than the butter, soften it by adding more water; if it is softer than butter, soften the butter by manipulating it in a wet and well squeezed towel.*

Let the dough rest. Flour the work surface and use a wooden rolling pin to roll out the dough into a square ⅓ inch thick. Cut the butter into small pieces and place in the centre of the square.

Close the four sides of the square so that the butter is enclosed perfectly and, being careful not to let the butter come out, roll out the dough into a rectangle ⅓ inch thick.

Fold the rectangle of dough into three and turn the folded dough and roll again to flatten it. Fold it again into three and let it rest for 10 minutes. Repeat this operation three times, that is: turn the dough, flatten it, and fold it again letting it rest for at least 10 minutes each time. If you plan to keep the dough for later, then leave it folded and roll it out when you want to use it.

CAROLINE

Carolines

MAKES 12

3½ tbsp butter
9½ tbsp flour
2 eggs

Prepare a choux pastry *(p71)* using half a cup of water, butter, flour, and eggs listed here. Spoon it into a piping bag with a ⅓ inch plain tip and pipe out sticks 2 inches long onto a buttered baking sheet. Do not place them too close together as they swell up and could stick together. Bake in a hot oven for 10 to 15 minutes, then take them out and let cool. Use scissors to cut inside each Caroline and make space for a filling with a flavored butter, perhaps of anchovies, or ham, or strips of chicken with mayonnaise, as you like.

ADA SAYS: *Petits pâtés are small preparations made with puff pastry: they are filled with delicate fillings.*

PETITS PÂTÉS CON CREMA DI FEGATINI

Cream Pies with Chicken Livers

MAKES 24

2 tbsp grated Parmesan
Dried mushrooms
3½ tbsp butter
3½ oz chicken livers
2 tbsp Marsala
Puff pastry, homemade *(p71)* or store-bought
1 egg
Salt
Pepper

White sauce:
1½ tbsp butter, 3 tbsp flour, 1 cup milk

Make the white sauce *(p16)* using the butter, flour and milk listed here and while still warm, add in the Parmesan. Let half an ounce of dried mushrooms soak in cold water for 20 minutes, then wash and cook them in a saucepan with a little water, half the butter, and a pinch of salt.

Wash the chicken livers, remove the gall and any traces of green. Cut the livers into two or three pieces. Put the rest of the butter in a skillet and as soon as it dissolves add the livers. Season with salt and pepper. The livers cook quickly, so keep a close eye. When they are almost cooked, pour the Marsala into the pan. Finally, chop the mushrooms and chicken livers and add them to the white sauce.

Have ready the puff pastry and roll out. After all the folds have been made, use a 2-inch round pastry cutter to cut an even number of 24 disks. Put a teaspoon of the mushroom and liver mix in the middle of half of them, then top off with the other half and paint with the beaten egg to get a good colour. Bake in a very hot oven for 10 minutes.

PETITS PÂTÉS CON CREMA DI FORMAGGI

Cheese Cream Pies

2 tbsp butter
Milk
9 tbsp grated Parmesan
7 tbsp grated Gruyère
Puff pastry, homemade *(p71)* or store-bought
1 egg
Salt

Melt the butter in small pieces in a small saucepan. Add half a glass of milk. Grate the cheeses into the milk. Keep the heat moderate, mixing well so it is quite thick.

Prepare the puff pastry and roll it out to a thickness of about ⅛ inch. Use a 2 inch round pastry cutter to cut an even number of disks. Place half of them on a plate and put a teaspoon of the cheese mix inside. Top with the other halves and wash the outside with a beaten egg so they colour. Bake for 10 minutes.

PETITS PÂTÉS CON FUNGHETTI

Mushroom Pies

7 oz mushrooms
Olive oil
Garlic
Parsley
Puff pastry, homemade *(p71)* or store-bought
2 oz ham
2 tbsp cream
1 egg
Salt
Pepper

Scrape and check the mushrooms. Rinse them and slice them thinly. Fry them in a little oil with a clove of garlic. Season with a pinch of salt and a handful of chopped parsley.

Prepare the puff pastry and roll it out to a thickness of about ⅛ inch thick. Use a 2 inch round pastry cutter to cut an even number of disks. Place half of them on a plate and put 1 teaspoon of the ham and mushrooms inside.

Bake in a hot oven for 10 minutes.

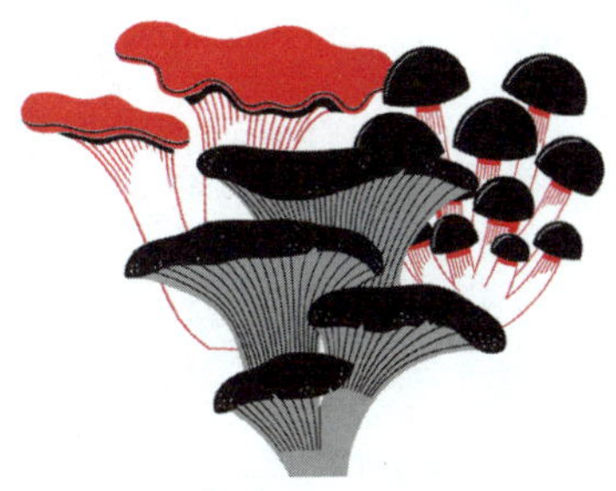

PETITS PÂTÉS CON SPUMETTA DI PROSCIUTTO

Ham Pies

MAKES 24
2 tbsp grated Parmesan
2 tbsp cream
3½ oz ham
3½ tbsp butter
Puff pastry, homemade *(p71)* or store-bought
1 egg
Salt
Optional: black truffle

White sauce:
1½ tbsp butter, 3 tbsp flour, 1 cup milk

Make the white sauce *(p16)* using the butter, flour and milk listed here and while still warm, grate in the Parmesan and add the cream. Chop the ham, add it to the butter and add to the white sauce. Mix well.

Prepare a puff pastry and roll it out to a thickness of about ⅛ inch thick. Use a 2-inch round pastry cutter to cut an even number of disks.

Place half of them on a baking tray slightly moistened with water and in the middle of each disk place 1 teaspoon of the prepared mixture and, if you like, a sliver of black truffle. Lightly moisten the borders of the disks with beaten egg and place another pastry disk on top. Coat the surface with beaten egg. Bake in a hot oven for 10 minutes.

RAMEQUINS ALL' ANTICA

Traditional Choux Buns

MAKES 35

1 tbsp chopped ham
1 tbsp grated Parmesan
Nutmeg
Abundant oil for frying
Salt
Pepper

Choux pastry:
½ cup water, 3½ tbsp butter,
9½ tbsp flour, 2 eggs

Make the choux pastry *(p71)* using the water, butter, flour and eggs listed here and add the ham, Parmesan, and a trifle of nutmeg. Stir one last time, cover and rest in a cool place. Heat the oil in a fryer or a deep pan. Pinch out little pieces of dough about the size of a hazelnut and when the oil is just lukewarm, drop pieces into the pan. Not too many at one time, you have to work in batches.

Fry at first over moderate heat, then, as the buns swell, increase the heat by shaking the pan in a circular direction. When they are a beautiful blond colour, lift out with a slotted spoon. Let the oil cool a little and then start again. The buns should be very light, empty, and tasty.

◆ ADA SAYS: *Ramequins are small balls of choux pastry into which little pieces of prosciutto, Gruyère, sliced or grated are stuffed; they are fried in abundant oil.*

RAMEQUINS MODERNI

Modern Choux Buns

MAKES 35

3½ oz Gruyère
1 egg
Salt

Choux pastry:
½ cup water, 5½ tbsp butter,
1 cup flour, 2 eggs

Make the choux pastry *(p71)* using the water, butter, flour and eggs listed here. When you have a dough, mix in the Gruyère, which should be half grated and half sliced. Put the mixture in a pastry bag with a plain tip.

Grease a baking sheet lightly and press the dough out into walnut-size buttons in rows with a little distance from each other.

Brush with beaten egg and put them in a warm oven until they are swollen, dry, and golden.

RUSTICI AL FORMAGGIO

Cheese Rustica

1 egg
3½ tbsp butter
9 tbsp grated Parmesan
7 tbsp grated Gruyère
Milk
Salt

Puff pastry:
1 cup + 3 tbsp flour, 7 tbsp butter

Prepare the puff pastry *(p71)* using the flour and butter listed here and roll it out to a thickness of about ⅛ inch. Use a 2-inch round pastry cutter to cut an even number of disks. Lightly wet a baking sheet with water and arrrange the disks; brush them with the beaten egg and cook them in a moderate heat oven.

As soon as they are cooked and turn a light blond colour, remove the pan from the oven and let them cool. Leave the oven on.

Cream the butter in a bowl and mix in the grated Parmesan and Gruyère and add a few drops of milk. Use a large knife to spread the cheese mix on half the disks and top with the others. Put them back in the warm oven for 5 minutes.

HOT APPETIZERS

BARCHETTE ALLA MARINARA

Fishing Boats

24 mussels
24 clams
Olive oil
24 shrimp
7 oz mushrooms
Parsley
Breadcrumbs
Salt
White pepper

White sauce:
3 tbsp flour, 1½ tbsp butter, 7 tbsp milk

Pie dough:
1⅔ cups flour, 9 tbsp butter

Scrape and wash the mussels and clams, clean thoroughly, then let them open in a pan with a spoon of oil, giving them the odd shake. As soon as they are all open, remove them from the shells and keep the liquid from the pan.

Boil the shrimp until they change colour, then lift out, shell them and cut into 2 or 3 pieces. Clean the mushrooms, cut them into thin slices, and sauté them with a little oil, salt, and parsley.

Prepare the white sauce *(p16)* using the flour, butter, and milk listed here. Add the sieved liquor from the shellfish and finish with a good pinch of white pepper.

Mix the mussels, clams, and shrimp in a bowl with the mushrooms and add a spoonful or two of the white sauce and chopped parsley. Make pie dough *(p64)* using the flour and butter listed here. Form into boat shapes and blind-bake. Fill the pastry boats with this mix, smoothing them well with the blade of a knife; then on each boat spread a little more white sauce.

Warm some oil in a pan and add an abundant handful of fine, grated breadcrumbs. Stir until the bread has colored and crisped. Then cover the boats with the fried breadcrumbs.

Warm for about 10 minutes in a hot oven. Arrange on a plate and serve immediately.

CASSOLETTES DI FORMAGGIO

Cheese Casserole

MAKES 12

4½ oz Gruyère
5 eggs
Salt
Pepper
Nutmeg

White sauce:
6 tbsp flour, 3½ tbsp butter, 2 cups milk

Prepare the white sauce *(p16)* using the flour, butter, and milk listed here. While still warm, season with salt, pepper, and nutmeg and grate in the Gruyère.

Separate the eggs and set the yolks aside. Beat the whites to firm peaks. Folding gently, add the whipped egg whites to the Gruyère sauce and then, one at a time, add the yolks.

Grease 12 ramekins or cassolettes (porcelain cups the size of espresso cups) generously and fill three-quarters full with the egg white mixture, because, yes, they are going to rise. Bake in a hot oven for 15 minutes.

CESTINI CON LA FONTINA

Fontina Crescents

1 egg
1 egg yolk
3½ tbsp grated Parmesan
Milk
3½ oz Fontina

Pie dough:
1⅔ cups flour, 9 tbsp butter,
5-6 tbsp water

This recipe is unusual in that the pastry cases are baked together with the filling.

Put the egg and egg yolk in a bowl. Beat in Parmesan with a fork and add, little by little, a glass of cold milk to make a liquid cream.

Have ready the pie dough *(p64)* using the ingredient amounts listed here. Line up in butter crescents. Put a few cubes of Fontina in each pastry mold with a spoon each of the prepared cream. Place the baskets on a baking sheet and bake in a hot oven for 15 minutes, until the cream is cooked and bubbling and the baskets acquire a beautiful golden colour.

CESTINI CON PROSCIUTTO COTTO

Ham Baskets

MAKES 24

Butter
Milk
1 egg
1 egg yolk
3 tbsp grated Parmesan
3½ oz ham
Salt

Pie dough:
1⅔ cups flour, 9 tbsp butterr,
5-6 tbsp water

Make the pie dough *(p64)* using the ingredient amounts listed here. Roll out the pastry to a thickness of about ⅛ inch thick. Butter the mold and line with the pastry.

Pour a glass of milk into a bowl, add a whole egg and the extra yolk, add in the Parmesan. Whisk everything together. Pour the cream into their pastry cases. Chop the ham small and scatter equally around the cases. Place the baskets on a baking sheet and bake in a warm oven at moderate heat for 15 minutes, until the cream is set and the baskets golden. Serve very hot.

ADA SAYS: *Baskets are round shells of puff pastry or shortcrust pastry dough baked in the oven in round moulds; they are filled with meat, poultry, cheese or vegetables, bound by sauces such as white sauce or gravy.*

CESTINI FANTASIA

Cheese Baskets

MAKES 24

10 oz spinach
1½ tbsp butter
3½ tbsp grated Gruyère
3½ tbsp grated Parmesan
Nutmeg
Salt

Pie dough:
1⅔ cups flour, 9 tbsp butterr,
5-6 tbsp water

White sauce:
7 tbsp butter, ¾ cup flour,
4¼ cups milk

Make the pie dough *(p64)* using the ingredient amounts listed here. Roll out the pastry to about ⅛ inch thick and lightly line buttered moulds.

Wash the spinach and boil in salted water until it collapses. Drain, squeeze out all the water, and chop. Return the spinach to the pan, add the butter, and swirl together. In the same pan add a glass of white sauce *(p16)* that you made with the butter, flour and milk. Stir in the Gruyère and Parmesan mixing all the while. Finish with a little nutmeg.

Fill the moulds with the spinach cream. Bake in a hot oven for 15 minutes, until the cream has settled and the baskets are gold. Serve hot.

MOZZARELLA IN SALSA DI TONNO

Mozzarella with Tuna Sauce

1 oz dried mushrooms
Olive oil
1 clove garlic
1 lb tomatoes
7 oz tinned tuna in olive oil
1 lb 5 oz mozzarella
Flour
Butter
Salt

Soak the dried mushrooms in water and clean them by changing the water several times. Warm some oil in a pan with the clove of garlic and take out the garlic once it starts to brown.

Chop the mushrooms and tomatoes and add to the oil. Season with a pinch of salt and let them cook. When the sauce is dense, add the tuna and simmer for a few more minutes.

Cut the mozzarella into slices ⅓ inch thick, lightly dust them in flour. Warm some butter in a pan, add the mozzarella, and cook on a high heat. Remove as soon as the cheese starts to melt. Pour the hot tuna sauce over the mozzarella. Serve immediately.

MOZZARELLA SU GALLETTE DI PATATE

Mozzarella on Potato Crackers

1 lb potatoes
1½ tbsp butter
1 egg
1 tbsp grated Parmesan
5 oz mozzarella
Nutmeg
Salt
Pepper

Peel the potatoes, cut them into wedges, and boil them in salted water. When they are cooked, drain them, put them back in the saucepan over low heat, so they dry completely.

Use a wooden spoon to break them down so they are almost puréed, then add the butter, salt, pepper, and nutmeg. Take off the heat and add the egg and the Parmesan.

Make small walnut-size balls with the mixture. Flatten them to the shape of crackers and place on a baking sheet with a slice of mozzarella on each. Bake in a preheated oven for about 10 minutes until they are golden and the cheese is melting. Serve immediately.

PARMIGIANO IN BUDINO

Parmesan Flan

2 cups grated Parmesan
7 oz Gruyère
3 tbsp tomato passata
2 eggs
2 egg yolks
Flour
Butter
Salt
Pepper

White sauce:
7 tbsp butter, ¾ cup flour,
4¼ cups milk

Make a white sauce *(p16)* using the butter, flour, and milk listed here until it is smooth and without lumps, then season with salt and pepper. Take off the heat and add the grated Parmesan, diced Gruyère cheese, tomato passata, the whole eggs, and egg yolks.

Mix everything together, then pour into a 1-quart pudding mold, buttered and dusted with flour. Place the mold in a bowl or dish with hot water and transfer everything into the oven so that the flan can cook in a bain-marie without the water boiling.

After about 1 hour, when the flan has thickened, remove it from the water, let it rest for a few minutes, then turn it upside down on a plate and serve.

PROSCIUTTO COTTO IN CHENELLE

Ham Quenelles

9 tbsp butter
1 egg
1 egg yolk
10 oz ham
Breadcrumbs
Flour
Salt

In a bowl, work the butter with a wooden spoon until it is soft and smooth, then add the whole egg and when well mixed add the extra egg yolk.

Chop the ham and add it to the butter, then add ¾ cup breadcrumbs and a spoonful of flour and mix well.

Bring a saucepan of water to a boil, then lower the heat. Test a small ball of the mixture. If you find it too soft, then add a little flour, if you find it too hard, add some more breadcrumbs.

When you have the right consistency start making the quenelles, using a small wet spoon and the blade of a knife dampened in hot water.

Make small egg-shaped quenelles, and dip each in the hot, but not boiling, water directly from the teaspoon. Keep going until you finish the mixture and leave for another 5 to 6 minutes in the water, then take them out with a slotted spoon and place on a serving dish. Sprinkle with a melted knob of butter and serve.

PROSCIUTTO COTTO IN SPUMETTE

Ham Mousse

1 lb 5 oz ham
2 egg whites
Cream
Butter
Grated Parmesan
Pepper

Chop the ham finely and slowly add the egg whites. When the mixture looks like a fine paste, refrigerate for a couple of hours.

Add 2 glasses of cream a little at a time and gently combine with a wooden spoon. Add a pinch of pepper and salt if you think the ham is not already salty enough. Leave the mixture in the fridge for another hour.

Bring a large saucepan of water to a boil, then lower the heat to a minimum. Use a tablespoon and take a spoonful of the mixture, smooth it with the blade of a knife to give it the shape of an egg, and immerse in the hot water. You will see that the ham will come off immediately. Dry the spoon and repeat this operation until you finish the mixture.

Let these mousses float for about 20 minutes, then scoop them out with a slotted spoon, and arrange them in the serving dish. Sprinkle with a little melted butter and some grated Parmesan and serve.

RICOTTA AL GRATIN

Ricotta Gratin

Flour
1 egg
10 oz ricotta
Milk
3½ oz grated Parmesan
Parsley
1½ tbsp diced ham
1½ tbsp chopped salami
2 tbsp butter
Salt

Preheat the oven to high heat before you start.

In a bowl, mix ¾ cup flour and the egg with a wooden spoon. Add the ricotta cheese and half glass of milk, mixing everything until it has reached a smooth consistency. Season with a pinch of salt. Add the grated Parmesan, chopped parsley, the diced ham, and salami.

Butter a baking pan. Pour in the ricotta mix. Bake in a hot oven for 20 minutes. When the gratin is compact and slightly golden, take out of the oven and serve immediately from the pan.

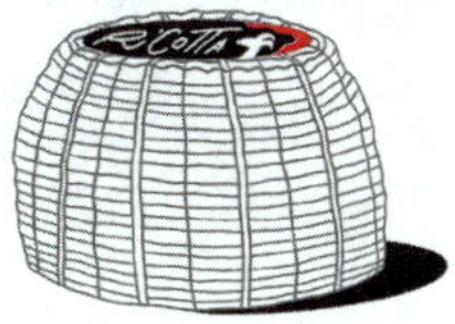

VOL-AU-VENTS

TO MAKE VOL-AU-VENTS

Vol-au-vents appear complex but are, in reality, quite simple: a puff pastry shell that contains a filling of various kinds. You can make the cases yourself or use store-bought. The timing is important. Your vol-au-vents will take only 10 minutes in the oven and you only add the sauce when they are warm and ready to serve.

Roll the puff pastry on a floured surface to about ⅓ inch thick. Use a 2½-inch round cutter to cut out the disks, moistening the cutter each time in lukewarm water. Brush the tops with egg diluted with a little water, being careful not to let the egg yolk drip on the sides, otherwise they will not rise.

Now using a 1½-inch round pastry cutter, make a light incision in the top of the dough without going too far to make the lids. Moisten a baking sheet and line up the disks. Bake in a warm oven at a good heat until they are golden and crisp. Take them out and set aside.

Use the handle of a teaspoon to empty the inside of the casings to make a place for the filling; there should be space for a spoonful. They will be heated in the oven for about 10 minutes before filling with their sauce. Serve very hot.

BOUCHÉES CON FUNGHETTI E CREMA DI LATTE

Vol-au-Vents with Mushroom Cream

MAKES 24

7 oz mushrooms
3½ tbsp butter
2 tbsp cream
Madeira or Marsala
Salt
Pepper

Puff pastry:
1 cup + 3 tbsp flour, 7 tbsp butter

Make the puff pastry *(p71)* using the ingredient amounts listed here, or use 8 ounces frozen. Cut into vol-au-vent shapes *(as above)*.

Clean, wash quickly, and dry the mushrooms. Cut them into pieces. Put half of the butter in a pan. As soon as it is hot, add the mushrooms. Cook over high heat, season with salt and pepper. As the water from the mushrooms evaporates, add the cream. Let this sauce thicken, stirring with care, then remove from the heat, pour in a dash of Madeira or Marsala and the rest of the butter. Mushrooms should be coated in the sauce. Bake the pastries, fill them, cover with the lids, and serve hot.

◆ ADA SAYS: *Bouchées are little discs of puff pastry, half an inch thick, with a diameter of about 2 inches and a hollowed-out center for its filling—it then gets covered with more puff pastry dough. They are baked in the oven and always contain a filling. They are very similar to petits pâtés.*

BOUCHÉES CON GLI SCAMPI

Vol-au-Vents with Langoustine

1 carrot
1 onion
1 celery stalk
Parsley
7 oz langoustines
Butter
1 tbsp flour
1 egg yolk
Salt
6 to 8 vol-au-vent cases *(opp. page)*

In a saucepan, simmer the carrot, onion, celery, and parsley for half an hour.

Clean the langoustines and cook them in the boiling broth for about 5 minutes. As soon as they are cooked, strain the broth and shell the langoustines. Cut them into small pieces and place them in a bowl.

Melt a little butter over moderate heat, add the flour and let it brown lightly stirring until it has a nice golden colour, then add a glass of the langoustine broth. Let the sauce cook and thicken over very low heat for about 15 minutes. At the end of cooking, check the salt.

Take the sauce off the heat and add the egg yolk a little at a time, and pour it into the bowl with the langoustines.

Heat the vol-au-vents pastry for 10 minutes, then fill them with the langoustines and sauce, cover with the lids and serve hot.

VOL-AU-VENT CON FEGATINI

Vol-au-Vents with Livers

6 medium artichokes
1 lemon
Olive oil
1 lb 5 oz chicken livers
Butter
5 oz prosciutto
Parsley
6 to 8 vol-au-vent cases *(opp. page)*
Salt
Pepper

Clean the artichokes, removing all the hard leaves and chokes, cut them into wedges. As you work put them in a bowl with water to which you have added a pinch of salt and a little lemon juice.

Put a little oil in a pan, remove the artichokes from the water, dry them and put them to cook over medium heat. Season with salt, and if they tend to dry out too much during cooking, sprinkle them with a little more water. The important thing is that the artichokes, when fully cooked, remain soft.

Now prepare the livers, carefully remove the gall and any greenish traces, and cut them, according to their size, into two or more pieces. Put a pan with some butter on the heat, add the livers, season with salt and pepper, and let them cook quickly. Before removing them from the heat, add the prosciutto cut into strips. Pour everything into the pan with the artichokes. Stir, keeping the pan on the heat for another minute or two. Add a spoonful of chopped parsley and squeeze a little lemon juice on the sauce.

Warm the vol-au-vent pastry in a light oven for about 10 minutes, then pour the prepared filling in, cover it with its lid, and serve immediately.

ADA SAYS: *If the artichokes are big, it is easier to boil them at first and then cut out the hearts.*

VOL-AU-VENT CON FINANZIERA

Vol-au-Vents with Finanziera Sauce

Breadcrumbs
Milk
1 lb 5 oz ground beef
1 egg
4 tbsp grated Parmesan
Nutmeg
9 tbsp butter
White wine
Olive oil
1 onion
1 lb 5 oz sausages
7 tbsp tomato paste
1¾ oz dried mushrooms
1 cup flour
2 cups broth
Madeira or Marsala
3 egg yolks
7 oz chicken livers
6 to 8 vol-au-vent cases *(p80)*
Salt
Pepper
Optional: small white truffle

The filling is a bit complicated because it is composed of a combination of chicken livers, meatballs, sausages, mushrooms, and truffles, all tied up with an exquisite sauce.

Wet a large handful of breadcrumbs with half a glass of milk, squeeze well with your hands and mix it with the ground beef; when the mixture is smooth, mix in the beaten egg, 2 tablespoons of the grated Parmesan, a pinch of salt, and a little nutmeg. Knead a little more and then form very small even-sized balls. Lightly flour the meatballs, then sprinkle with more breadcrumbs.

In a rather large pan, melt half of the butter and cook the meatballs over moderate heat, adding a little white wine if necessary. As soon as they are cooked, remove them from the heat and keep them warm in the same pan.

Add half a glass of oil and the finely chopped onion to a saucepan and let brown. Add the sausages, pierced with a fork, and brown them lightly; put the tomato paste diluted with 1 cup of water in the saucepan. If necessary, add a little salt, not much because the sausages are highly flavored, and cook over moderate heat for about 30 minutes.

Meanwhile, wash the mushrooms very carefully, put them in a bowl with cold water, and once softened, cut them into two or three pieces.

As soon as the sausages are cooked, remove them from the saucepan, cut them into pieces, and place them in the pan with the meatballs. In the same saucepan where the sausages were cooked, add the mushrooms, and a little water if necessary, and cook over medium heat.

Meanwhile, melt the remaining 4½ tablespoons butter in a saucepan over moderate heat and mix in the flour. As soon as the mixture is golden, gradually pour in the broth, stirring constantly. Let the sauce cook for about 15 minutes.

Add a glass of Madeira or Marsala wine and let the sauce reduce on the heat for a little longer because it must be quite thick. Remove from the heat and mix in the egg yolks diluted with a spoonful of milk and, stirring gently, add 2 tablespoons of grated Parmesan.

Finally prepare the livers. Clean them well, cut them into pieces, and brown them in a pan with a little butter, a pinch of salt, and a little pepper. When they are cooked, finish them with a spoonful of Madeira or Marsala.

Once all the elements are cooked, add the sauce with mushrooms and livers to the pan with the meatballs and sausages.

Heat the vol-au-vent pastry in a moderate oven for about 10 minutes and in the meantime, if needed, heat the sauce, but do not let it boil. Pour the sauce into the vol-au-vents. Cover with the lids and serve immediately.

ADA SAYS: *If you want, after having carefully cleaned it, you can add slices of a small white truffle which will communicate an extraordinary fragrance.*

VOL-AU-VENT CON FUNGHETTI

Vol-au-Vents with Mushrooms

1 lb 5 oz mushrooms
5 tbsp butter
White wine
Flour
7 tbsp cream
6 to 8 vol-au-vent cases *(p80)*
Salt
Pepper

Lightly wash the mushrooms, dry them carefully, trim the stems, then cut them into wedges and put them to cook in a pan with 2 tablespoons of butter, a pinch of salt and pepper. Let them develop flavor, then add a little wine and cook over moderate heat for about 10 minutes.

Then remove the mushrooms and in the same pan add 1 teaspoon of flour that you will have mixed with a nut of butter. Stir and after a while sprinkle with a little more wine. Cook the sauce, stirring it for a few minutes, then bind it with the cream, which you will pour in a little at a time, stirring constantly with a wooden spoon and keeping at a moderate heat. Return the mushrooms to the pan and finish cooking everything together.

Heat the vol-au-vent pastry in a moderate oven for about 10 minutes, put them on a serving plate, pour the prepared mushrooms in, and put the lids on. Bring to the table immediately.

VOL-AU-VENT CON GAMBERI

Vol-au-Vents with Shrimp

3 carrots
1 celery stalk
1 onion
Parsley
Bay leaf
2 tbsp butter
24 shrimp
4¼ cups white wine
10 oz mushrooms
Olive oil
4 egg yolks
Milk
Black truffle
6 to 8 vol-au-vent cases *(p80)*
Salt

White sauce:
3½ tbsp butter, 6 tbsp flour,
2 cups milk

Coarsely chop the carrots, celery, onion, and a sprig of parsley. Add them to a saucepan with a bay leaf and the butter and cook until browned. As soon as the aromatics have browned, add the shrimp, wet them with the wine, and let them boil for 10 minutes, then remove the saucepan from the heat.

Clean the mushrooms, wash them quickly, dry them, cut the stems into strips, leaving the caps whole. In a pan, gently heat a glass of oil. Add the mushrooms, raise the heat, and halfway through cooking, about 10 minutes in all, salt them and if their vegetable water has dried too much, pour into the pan a finger of wine. Once the mushrooms are cooked, remove them from the heat and keep them warm.

Prepare a white sauce *(p16)* with the butter, flour, and the milk listed here. Let it cook for 15 minutes, add salt and remove from the heat.

Remove the shrimp from their shells carefully so as not to spoil them. Add the shrimp, finely chopped parsley, egg yolks diluted with a few tablespoons of milk, mushrooms, truffles cut into thin slices to the warm white sauce and mix to distribute well.

Heat the vol-au-vent pastry in a moderate oven for about 10 minutes, place them on a serving dish, pour the filling into them, and cover them with their lids.

VOL-AU-VENT CON PISELLI

Vol-au-Vents with Peas

2 egg yolks
1 small onion
7 tbsp butter
1 lb 10 oz shelled peas
Broth
2 oz prosciutto
1 cup grated Parmesan
Nutmeg
6 to 8 vol-au-vent cases *(p80)*
Salt
Pepper

White sauce:
3½ tbsp butter, 6 tbsp flour,
2 cups milk

First make a white sauce *(p16)* with the butter, flour and milk listed here. Thicken well and pour it into a bowl. As soon as it has cooled down, add the egg yolks, stirring gently with a wooden spoon to mix them well.

Now prepare the peas: Put the finely chopped onion and all of the butter in a saucepan and simmer slowly to allow the onion to cook without turning brown. Add the peas to the saucepan, let them flavor while stirring, then season with salt and pepper and add the amount of boiling broth or water necessary to cover them. At this point, bring the cooking to very high heat, stirring occasionally and add the prosciutto cut into strips. They will cook in 15 minutes.

Stir the peas into the sauce mixture, add the grated Parmesan, and heat everything without boiling.

In the meantime, heat the vol-au-vents in a moderate oven for about 10 minutes, pour the prepared peas into them, cover it with their lids and serve.

VOL-AU-VENT CON TORTELLINI

Vol-au-Vents with Tortellini

1 whole chicken
Herbs, for broth
1½ tbsp butter
2 tbsp flour
Cream
Parmesan
2¼ lb tortellini
6 to 8 vol-au-vent cases *(p80)*
Salt

In a large pot, combine the chicken, some herbs and aromatics, and not too much lightly salted water. Once the chicken is cooked, you don't want to end up with more than 6 or 7 ladles of broth. Bring to a simmer and cook until the dark meat is cooked through.

Once the chicken is cooked, remove it, let it cool a little, then remove the breast with a knife and set aside. Bone and mince the meat of the wings, legs, and carcass. Strain the broth.

Put the butter in a saucepan and when it has melted add the flour. Cook, stirring, for 2 minutes and then pour in the strained chicken broth. Cook slowly to get a sauce of the right consistency, then off the heat, add the minced chicken and a half a glass of cream.

In large pot of boiling water, cook the tortellini to al dente. Drain, season with butter and Parmesan. Fold the tortellini into the sauce. Cut the chicken breasts into strips and add them, too. Transfer to an ovenproof dish. Add another two or three spoonfuls of broth, sprinkle abundant grated Parmesan on the tortellini, arrange here and there a few more pieces of butter and put the dish in the oven for about 10 minutes so that the tortellini can take on all the flavors.

Ten minutes before going to the table, put the vol-au-vents in a warm oven to heat, then place them on a serving dish, pour in the tortellini, put the lids on the vol-au-vents, and serve immediately.

"Soups are easy to prepare and are popular thanks to their tastiness and the cheerfulness they inspire."

Together with pasta, minestra is the most common way of starting an Italian family meal. The basic element, common to almost all minestre, is broth. Undoubtedly, the best is meat broth; then there are broths prepared with bouillon cubes or bouillon base; vegetable broth, which is much in demand in the diets of children and convalescents; plus fish broth and chicken broth. To accompany the broth, minestre usually include—besides the usual vegetables—grains such as rice, pasta, spelt, and barley. Minestre are very brothy in contrast to other soups. In Lombardy they are prepared with the addition of rice, while in Veneto and Emilia-Romagna with cappelletti or different variations of small pasta.

Minestrone is somewhere between a soup and a minestra. It is considered a full meal as it is always a rich and filling dish and can contain legumes, vegetables, grains, or pasta.

Minestrone soups are perhaps the most well-known of Italian soups and recipes obey precise rules. For perfect success, one must bear in mind two points. First, always start with the elements that take longer to cook and leave those requiring a shorter time until later. The second point concerns the quantities of aromatics; these should neither be too abundant nor too scarce—the balance must be just right.

Italian soups, on the other hand, very rarely include pasta or rice, but are always served with bread or crostini. They are dense and filling and, like minestrone, can form the basis of a full meal. In many households, especially for evening meals and during the colder months, soups are served because they are easy to prepare and are popular thanks to their tastiness and the cheerfulness they inspire.

Cream soups are built on broths and stocks and other elements such as meat, poultry, vegetables, and legumes, which are all mixed together with rice, creams, or variations on white sauces or veloutés.

There are as many fish soups, also called *brodetti* and *cacciucchi*, as there are seaside towns living off fishing, but their preparations do not differ significantly. Even if you have only Atlantic or Pacific fish, the recipes will still work.

Italian fish soups are a dish much sought after by gourmets, and they must be prepared with the utmost care. For a good fish soup, you need the perfect union of a series of elements. First of all, a good variety of fish is needed. The most suitable saltwater fish are eel, lobster, squid, mullet, sea cicada, cod, dogfish, small breed (baraccola), octopus, John Dory, bream, scorpion fish, cuttlefish, and red mullet. Then, the seasoning for fish soup must be in the right proportions and the cooking precise. Finally, the bread should be either toasted or fried in oil or butter and added at the last second.

BRODI E ZUPPE

3 BROTHS & SOUPS

BROTHS

CLARIFYING A BROTH

Clarifying a broth is always advisable. It makes sure the broth is perfectly clear.

Take 2 egg whites for each 1 quart of broth. *Beat them a little in a bowl. Add a ladle of broth, just warm. Beat everything together. Then pour the whites into the broth in the pot and whisk vigorously. Bring the pot to a boil without stopping whisking. As the broth boils, all the impurities will be caught in the clouds of egg white and underneath will be beautifully clear. Take it off the heat and let it cool for 10 minutes. Then line a sieve with a wet cloth or cheesecloth and pour the broth through into a new pan. It should be crystal clear.*

THICKENING A BROTH

Thickening a broth makes it denser, which can also significantly increase its nutritional value. Dissolve half a spoonful of cream of rice, oatmeal, or legume flour in 1 cup cold broth. This also adds extra nutrition. Pour your mix into the simmering broth and stir to get rid of any lumps.

BRODO DI CARNE

Meat Broth

MAKES 2 QUARTS

1 lb 5 oz beef
1 celery stalk
1 onion
Whole clove
1 carrot
2 or 3 tomatoes
Salt

In a pot, combine the meat and salted cold water (scant 2 teaspoon per 1 quart). Warm over moderate heat so the temperature rises slowly. After 30 minutes of simmering, add the aromatics—celery, onion, clove, carrot, and tomatoes. Continue simmering, covered.

Finally, after 3 hours or more of slow simmering, the broth will be ready. Let cool and skim off any fat on the surface. This operation will be easier if the broth is cold, because then the fat solidifies. Then strain through a sieve lined with a wet cloth or cheesecloth.

ADA SAYS: *To make good broth, you need to choose your meat carefully. Most recipes tell you to skim your broth, but if the meat is fresh, boneless, and not in huge quantities, and if you keep a very moderate heat, any foam or scum that forms is nothing but albumin, and will slowly be reabsorbed without the broth getting cloudy.*

BRODO DI PESCE

Fish Broth

MAKES 2 QUARTS

1 lb 10 oz mixed fresh fish (bream, scorpion fish, cod, gurnard, etc.)
1 onion
1 carrot
1 celery stalk
Parsley
Rosemary
Bay leaf
Salt
Peppercorns

Carefully clean the fish. Wash it and cook in a pot with 2½ quarts of water. Coarsely chop your vegetables as you go and add the herbs and 1 tablespoon of salt. Add the peppercorns at the end.

Cover the pot and set over very moderate heat, once it starts to bubble, simmer for 30 minutes. Watch over the cooking. A tumultuous boil would harm the broth making the taste too strong and making it cloudy. Strain through a sieve lined with cheesecloth.

See pages 121-129 for fish soup recipes.

BRODO DI POLLO

Chicken Broth

MAKES 2 QUARTS

4½ lb chicken
Salt
2 carrots
1 onion
1 celery stalk
Parsley

Put the chicken in a pot with about 3½ quarts cold salted water and let the temperature rise slowly. After simmering for about 30 minutes, add the scraped and washed carrots, the peeled onion, a washed and scraped celery stalk, and a bunch of parsley.

The chicken should cook for about 1 hour over moderate heat and in a covered pot.

Remove the chicken from the pot, place the broth in the fridge, and when the fat has congealed, lift it off with a slotted spoon. Strain the broth through a colander lined with dampened cheesecloth.

ADA SAYS: *For an older bird—a gallina (stewing hen)—it is generally customary to skim the broth in the first stage of cooking, before adding the vegetables; in all, it might cook longer for about 2 hours over moderate heat and with the pot covered.*

BRODO RAPIDO

Quick Broth

MAKES 1½ QUARTS

3 beef or chicken bouillon cubes or 2 tsp bouillon base
2 tbsp grated Parmesan
1 tbsp Marsala
1 tsp butter

We recommend a few small touches to improve the taste of this quick broth. Put the bouillon cubes or bouillon base into a pot with 1½ quarts water and when the water has come to a boil, add the grated Parmesan.

Stir vigorously so that the Parmesan spreads evenly through the liquid and does not thicken in any part of the pot. Finally add the Marsala wine and, if you wish, the butter off the heat.

BRODO VEGETALE

Vegetable Broth

MAKES 2 QUARTS

3 medium potatoes
7 oz Swiss chard or spinach
2 onions
3 carrots
1 small celery stalk
4 tomatoes
Grated Parmesan
Butter
Salt

Pour 3 quarts of water into a pot. Peel the potatoes but leave them whole. Wash your vegetables. Chop the onions, carrots, and celery into pieces. Then your tomatoes.

Salt the water generously. Cover and let it boil gently for 2 hours. Strain the broth through a sieve lined with cheesecloth. Finish at the table with grated Parmesan and butter.

CONSOMMÉ

Consommé

MAKES 1 QUART

6½ cups meat broth *(p88)*
10 oz lean beef
1 carrot
1 celery stalk
1 egg white
Optional: dry port

The basis for this consommé is a good meat broth, already clarified, made without tomatoes.

To the beef broth, add fresh lean and chopped beef and more aromatics like carrots and celery. Beat your egg whites in a little broth to the side and then add to the pot.

Bring everything to the boil. Boil for 1 hour. Pass through a sieve lined with dampened cheesecloth. Before serving in little cups, add a glass of dry port and warm through.

Broths with Accompaniments

BRODO CON CHENELLE DI PATATE

Broth with Potato Dumplings

1 lb potatoes
4 tsp butter
2 tbsp grated Parmesan
2 egg yolks
Nutmeg
6½ cups meat broth *(p88)*
Olive oil
Salt

Peel and chop the potatoes. Boil them in lightly salted water. When they are cooked, drain off the water, let them sit a little while still warm, so they release their moisture. Mash them in the pan, off the heat, with the butter, grated Parmesan, egg yolks, and a little nutmeg. Let cool.

Take out hazelnut-size pieces of the mash with a teaspoon and fry a few at a time in hot oil. When they have taken a nice light golden color, arrange them on a plate and serve with a hot broth.

BRODO CON GNOCCHETTI AL PROSCIUTTO

Meat Broth with Ham Gnocchetti

3½ tbsp butter
9½ tbsp flour
2 eggs
5 tbsp grated Parmesan
1¾ oz ham
Nutmeg
6½ cups meat broth *(p88)*
Salt

Put ⅔ cup of water in a saucepan, with a pinch of salt and the butter. Bring to a boil, then remove from the heat and add the flour. Stir with a wooden spoon.

Put back on the heat and keep stirring to get a smooth dough. When it starts boiling again, take the pan off the heat and keep stirring. Then put the pan back on the heat and, still stirring, make sure the dough is smooth. When it comes away from the sides and forms a ball, remove from the heat and let cool.

When the dough is completely cold, mix in one egg, and when this has absorbed, mix in a second one, then knead vigorously until it becomes elastic. Finish by mixing in the grated Parmesan, the chopped ham, and the nutmeg.

Bring your meat broth to a simmer and turn the heat right down. Use a teaspoon to fashion the gnocchetti out of the dough and let the small balls fall into the broth, with the help of a second teaspoon.

The gnocchetti will go straight to the bottom but then they will come back to the surface. Let them boil for a few minutes until they are firm, then ladle the broth into bowls and serve.

BRODO CON GNOCCHETTI DI POLENTA

Meat Broth with Polenta Gnocchetti

2 cups milk
1½ cups polenta
1½ tbsp butter
Grated Parmesan
2 eggs
6½ cups meat broth *(p88)*
Salt

Put the milk in a saucepan, season with a pinch of salt, and bring to a boil. Scatter the polenta, like rain, into the milk, stirring all the time. Let it boil and stir continuously.

Once the polenta is cooked and has taken shape, remove from the heat and add the butter and a few spoons of grated Parmesan. Beat your eggs, as for an omelet, and add to the mix. Give a good stir and let cool.

Pour your broth into a large saucepan and, as soon as it starts simmering, take small portions of the polenta mix with the tip of a teaspoon and, with the help of another teaspoon, drop peanut-size pieces of the polenta mix into the broth. They will fall to the bottom of the pan and float back up.

Let them simmer in the broth for 5 minutes, then pour the soup into the bowls, and finish with more Parmesan.

BRODO CON PALLOTTOLINE DI SPINACI

Beef Broth with Spinach Parcels

1 lb spinach
3½ tbsp butter
2 egg yolks
Grated Parmesan
Flour
1 egg
Breadcrumbs
6½ cups beef broth *(p88)*
Salt

Wash the spinach well. While the leaves are still wet, heat in a pan until they wilt (just a minute or two) then take off the heat and drain, squeezing the leaves to remove all the water. Pass them through a food mill or use scissors to chop.

Add some butter to a pan along with the spinach and, stirring, let it cook over moderate heat for 10 minutes to cook off the moisture and take on flavor. Take off the heat, let cool, and then mix in the egg yolks and a few spoonfuls of Parmesan.

Spread this mixture on a lightly buttered work surface. Let it cool. Then pinch out little balls the size of hazelnuts. Dust them lightly with flour, then roll them in beaten egg, and finally breadcrumbs.

Fry a few at a time in extra butter so they take on a beautiful golden color. Lift out with a slotted spoon and drain on paper towels. Serve the broth very hot with the spinach parcels in a vegetable dish to the side.

BRODO CON PASTA REALE

Broth with Choux Buns

3½ tbsp butter
9½ tbsp flour
2 eggs
6½ cups meat broth *(p88)*
Salt

In a pan, combine 7 tbsp water, the butter, and a pinch of salt and set over heat. As soon as the water boils, take off the heat and pour the flour in, all in one go. Stir and put the pan back on the heat for 2 or 3 minutes until the dough is homogenous and doesn't stick to the spoon or the pan.

Let the dough cool and mix in the eggs one at a time. Knead until velvety. Use a piping bag with a ⅓-inch plain round tip. Butter an sheet pan and make well-spaced lines of little balls, the size of hazelnuts, on the pan.

Bake in a hot oven for a few minutes until they have taken a nice light golden color. Remove from the oven and let them cool. Drop a handful in the hot broth just before serving.

◈ **ADA SAYS:** *They can keep for a few days in a sealed glass jar.*

BRODO CON PASTA REALE RIPIENA

Broth with Stuffed Choux Buns

6½ cups meat broth *(p88)*
Choux pastry buns *(opp. page)*
3½ oz ham
1 egg yolk
9 tbsp grated Parmesan
Nutmeg
Salt

Have good meat broth ready. Make your choux pastry and bake the buns as directed in the previous recipe. For the filling, chop the ham and mix it in a bowl with the egg, grated Parmesan, and a little grated nutmeg.

Make a small incision with scissors on one side of each choux bun and carefully insert a little stuffing with the tip of a knife.

When ready to serve, distribute the choux balls in bowls and pour the boiling broth over them immediately.

BRODO CON QUADRATINI DI SEMOLINO

Broth with Semolina Squares

1 quart milk
1 cup + 1 tbsp semolina
9 tbsp grated Parmesan
Nutmeg
3½ tbsp butter
2 eggs
1 egg yolk
6½ cups meat broth *(p88)*
Salt

Boil the milk, lightly salted, and sprinkle in the semolina. Keep stirring until cooked, then take off the heat and season with grated Parmesan, a grating of nutmeg, butter, the whole eggs, and egg yolk. Mix well.

Grease 1-quart baking dish, pour in the mix, smooth it with a knife, and bake in a moderate oven until firm. Then remove from the oven, let it cool, turn it over, and cut into squares.

Have your broth ready. Spread the squares in bowls and pour the hot broth over them.

BRODO CON ROYALE ALLA BOLOGNESE

Bolognese Broth

1 cup flour
2 whole eggs
6 tbsp grated Parmesan
Nutmeg
4 tbsp butter
6½ cups meat broth *(p88)*
Salt
Optional: finely diced vegetables or peas

Mix the flour, eggs, and the grated Parmesan in a small bowl with a pinch of salt, and a grating of nutmeg. Cut the butter into cubes and mix in.

Take a dampened paper towel, squeeze it dry, and put the dough in the middle. Tie the cloth so it makes a ball.

Prepare and bring your broth to a boil. Put the ball in the meat broth and let it cook for about two hours. Then take the bundle out, remove the wrapping, and let it cool. Cut it first into ⅓-inch-thick slices and then into ⅓-inch cubes. Bring the broth back to a boil, add the squares, and simmer for 10 minutes. You can also add diced vegetables or peas, as you like.

BRODO CON ROYALE DI GALLINA

Royal Chicken Broth

7 oz cooked chicken breast
1 egg
9 tbsp grated Parmesan
Nutmeg
6½ cups chicken broth *(p89)*
Salt

Cream sauce:
3 tbsp flour, 1½ tbsp butter, ½ cup broth

Chop the chicken. Mince twice.

Make a cream sauce *(p17)* using the ingredient amounts listed here. Take off the heat and let cool before mixing in the egg, grated Parmesan, and a grating of nutmeg.

Lastly fold in the minced chicken and blend well. Grease a 2-cup rectangular baking dish, pour in the mixture, and cook in a bain-marie for about 20 minutes.

When the mixture is firm, remove from the bain-marie, turn it out of the dish, and let it cool. Cut into equal cubes, for each bowl and cover with hot chicken broth.

BRODO CON ROYALE DI RICOTTA

Meat Broth with Ricotta Dumplings

10 oz ricotta
9 tbsp grated Parmesan
2 eggs
1 egg yolk
Lemon
Nutmeg
Butter
10½ cups meat broth *(p88)*
Salt

Sieve the ricotta into a bowl and, stirring with a wooden spoon, grate in the Parmesan, the whole eggs, egg yolk, and a bit of grated lemon zest, a pinch of salt, and a little nutmeg.

Butter a small smooth 2-cup mold or a small pan. Line it with parchment paper and also grease the top part of the paper. Pour the ricotta mix into the mold and bake in a bain-marie until the mixture has firmed up, about 20 minutes.

Remove the mold from the heat and let it sit for a few minutes. Then turn it out, gently remove the paper, and let cool completely. Cut into cubes. Put a few in each bowl and top with the boiling broth.

BRODO CON ROYALE SEMPLICE

Broth with Egg

6½ cups meat broth *(p88)*
1 whole egg
2 egg yolks
Butter

Have your broth ready. Break the whole egg into a bowl and add the extra yolks. Beat them, as for an omelet. Pour in, little by little, a glass of warm broth.

Pass this mixture through a sieve into another bowl; if you see that a little foam has formed, remove it. Butter 2-cup baking pan, pour in the egg mix, and cook in a bain-marie for 30 minutes, until it forms a cream. Let it cool. Turn the cream out onto a towel and cut into slices ⅓ inch thick and then the other way into ¾-inch squares. Place a few cubes in each bowl, pour the broth over them, and serve.

ADA SAYS: *Always keep the temperature of the water in the bain-marie very hot but below boiling point otherwise instead of thickening the cream will break up.*

CONSOMMÉ CON LE CRÊPES SALATE

Consommé with Savory Crêpes

6½ cups consommé *(p90)*
1 cup flour
2 eggs
Milk
4 tbsp butter
Salt

While the consommé is cooking, prepare the crêpes.

In a bowl, mound the flour in the shape of a volcano and put the eggs and a pinch of salt in the center. Mix with a wooden spoon to break the eggs so they slowly absorb the flour and then pour in a glass of milk a little at a time. Pour in small amounts, always stirring.

Melt the butter in an 8-inch skillet. When the butter has melted, pour in 2 spoons of the egg mixture and move it all in the same direction so it spreads on the bottom in a thin and uniform layer. The crêpe will begin to take shape. Shake the pan to shift it from the bottom. When it has taken on color, flip it over. Let the other side color and then slide the crêpe into a dish.

When all the crêpes have been made, cut them into ¼-inch-wide strips and cut the strips into 1½-inch lengths. Arrange a little of these crêpe strips in each bowl and pour in the boiling broth just before serving.

CREAM SOUPS

CREMA ALLA MADRILENA

Beef Consommé with Carrots and Tomato Cream

1½ quarts consommé *(p90)*
5 oz carrots
3 tbsp instant tapioca
2 tbsp tomato passata
3 egg yolks
3 tbsp grated Parmesan
3½ tbsp butter, cut small
7 tbsp milk or cream

Prepare a good consommé in advance.

Make a purée with the carrots: To do that, peel them, remove the woody central part, cut into pieces, boil, and then mash or blend.

Bring your consommé to a simmer and sprinkle in the tapioca. Let it cook for 5 minutes, then add the carrot purée. Warm the passata with a little butter and add to the broth. Stir and continue cooking for another 5 minutes.

Break the egg yolks into a soup tureen and mix with the grated Parmesan, the butter cut in small pieces and the milk or cream. Stir in a little of the hot broth with a wooden spoon so it blends well, then add the rest of the broth to serve.

CREMA ALLA PASTINA

Cream of Pastina

1½ quarts meat broth *(p88)* or chicken broth *(p89)*
2 tsp rice flour
3 tbsp bead-shaped pastina
3½ tbsp butter
3 egg yolks
9 tbsp grated Parmesan

Pastina are tiny beads of pasta often served to the sick.

Prepare a good beef or chicken broth.

Take half a bowl of cold broth to dissolve the rice flour. Bring the rest of the broth to a boil and pour in the bead-shaped pastina and allow it to cook.

Then add the rice flour from the other bowl. Stir often.

Meanwhile, put the chopped butter, egg yolks, and grated Parmesan into the soup tureen. Stir with a wooden spoon to mix well, then dissolve everything with 2 or 3 tablespoons of boiling broth.

When the pastina is cooked, pour the cream into the soup tureen (stirring constantly) and serve immediately.

CREMA DI ASPARAGI

Cream of Asparagus

2 quarts chicken broth *(p89)*
9 tbsp cream of rice
1 lb asparagus
9 tbsp grated Parmesan
Salt

Prepare a chicken broth. Make sure it is well degreased—cool in the fridge and skim off the fat.

Put the broth on the stove but before it gets too hot, remove about a glassful to help dissolve the cream of rice so you get a runny, lump-free slurry.

As soon as the remaining broth comes to a boil, slowly drop the rice slurry into the mix and stir with a wooden spoon. Let it come to a boil again, cover the pot, and simmer gently for about 20 minutes.

While it is cooking, scrape the asparagus, trim and cut into small pieces crosswise. Boil in lightly salted water. When cooked, combine the asparagus and the broth and serve with grated Parmesan on the side.

CREMA DI CARCIOFI

Cream of Artichoke

3 artichokes
1½ quarts meat broth *(p88)*
Lemon
3 tbsp rice starch
3½ tbsp butter
2 egg yolks
9 tbsp grated Parmesan
Salt

Prepare a good meat broth.

Remove all the leaves and choke from the artichokes. Keep only the heart and stems, wipe with lemon and keep in acidulated water so they keep their color. When ready, boil them in salted water until soft, then drain and mash them or blend, adding a ladle of broth to mix them well.

Bring the broth to a boil. Take another ladle of broth to dissolve the rice starch and add to the pot when it starts to simmer, stirring frequently, for about 10 minutes. Toward the end of the cooking time, add the artichoke purée and continue boiling for a few more minutes.

When you are ready to serve, mix the butter (chopped small), the egg yolks, and Parmesan in a soup tureen. Stir well and pour in the boiling artichoke purée. Serve immediately so that it arrives hot at the table.

CREMA DI FUNGHETTI

Cream of Mushroom

9 oz mushrooms
3½ tbsp butter
Lemon
1 cup breadcrumbs
7 tbsp cream of rice
Salt
Pepper

Scrape off any dirt on the mushrooms, wash them quickly, dry them, and cut them into thin slices. Cook 2 ounces of these mushrooms with butter in a small skillet over high heat, adding salt and a few drops of lemon juice after a few minutes. As soon as the mushrooms are cooked, set them aside and cover with wax paper to prevent them from turning black.

Put 2 quarts of cold water, the breadcrumbs, and the remaining mushrooms in a pot and cook over low heat for 1 hour. After this time, remove the pot from the heat and put the contents through a food mill or use a blender. Spoon off a little of the liquid to mix with the cream of rice and return everything to the same pot. Add the reserved sautéed mushrooms. Season with salt and pepper.

Put the saucepan back on the heat and bring to a boil for a few minutes. Divide the soup among bowls and serve piping hot.

CREMA DI GALLINA

Cream of Chicken

2 quarts beef broth *(p88)*
1 chicken
Rice
3 eggs yolks
7 tbsp cream
Butter
Grated Parmesan

When the beef broth has been boiling for about 1 hour, add a young and well-fleshed chicken to the same pot and let it cook thoroughly for about 2½ hours.

Take the chicken out and let cool. Then remove the skin and separate the bones from the meat. Keep the chicken breast aside and cut into neat strips.

Boil ½ cup of rice in a saucepan with 2 cups of the broth and, when it is very hot, drain the rice (keeping the broth) and let cool. Finely chop the dark meat from the chicken and mix in with the rice, reducing everything to a fine paste. Dissolve this paste with the reserved cooking broth from the rice.

Ten minutes before serving, return the chicken and rice paste to a saucepan and dilute it with the original meat broth. Add as much broth as you need to have a sufficiently thick liquid. Stir with a wooden spoon to dissolve the purée well. Bring back up to a boil.

Beat the egg yolks in a bowl with the cream. Add a slice of butter and a few spoonfuls of Parmesan. Take a ladle of the hot chicken and rice broth and pour slowly over the egg yolks, stirring with a spoon. When the mixture has absorbed well, add it, in small quantities, to the rest of the broth, stirring so that everything is well combined. To serve, divide in the chicken breast strips among bowls and pour in the hot soup.

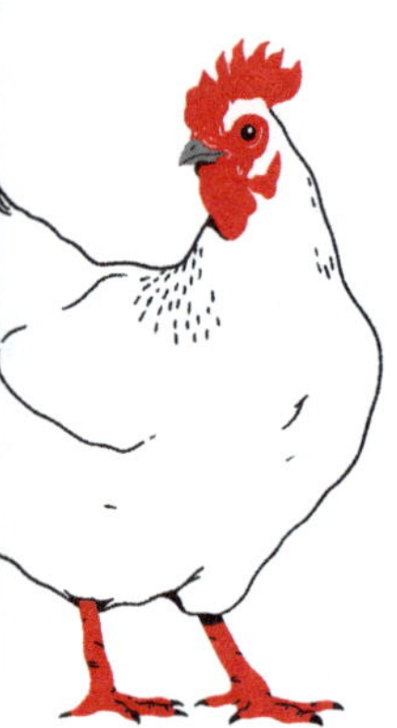

CREMA DI ORZO

Cream of Barley

2 tbsp cream of barley
2 quarts beef broth *(p88)*
2 oz dried mushrooms
7 tbsp cream
Breadcrumbs
Grated Parmesan

Put the cream of barley in a bowl and dilute it little by little with a ladle of cold broth, so that you have a loose, lump-free slurry.

Put the broth on the stove and, as soon as it comes to a boil, slowly drop in the barley slurry, stirring with a wooden spoon. When it comes to a boil again, add the dried mushrooms, which you have washed in cold water to remove all traces of dirt, but without soaking them. Cover the pot and let it boil very gently for about 20 minutes, stirring from time to time. Add more broth if you need.

Strain into a second saucepan. Take out the mushrooms. They have done their work as aromatics (and can go for another recipe). Warm the broth through for a moment and then, off the heat, finish with the cream. Give it a good stir and bring to the table. Serve with fried breadcrumbs to the side and a bowl of grated Parmesan.

CREMA DI PISELLI

Cream of Pea

1 lb 10 oz peas
7 tbsp tomato passata
Grated Parmesan
Salt

White sauce:
9½ tbsp flour, 5 tbsp butter,
3 cups milk

Make up a very loose white sauce *(p16)* using the ingredient amounts listed here. Season with a pinch of salt and let it cook slowly, stirring frequently with a wooden spoon.

Boil the peas in 3 cups of lightly salted water and then mash or blend them along with their cooking water. Pour the purée into the white sauce. Then add the tomato passata.

When the soup is thick enough, remove from the heat, season with grated Parmesan and divide among bowls.

CREMA DI POMODORO

Cream of Tomato

1 lb tomatoes
1 bay leaf
2 garlic cloves, peeled
Onion
Basil, a few leaves
1 tsp sugar
9 tbsp grated Parmesan
Salt

White sauce:
7 tbsp butter, 9½ tbsp flour,
4 cups milk

Rinse the tomatoes, cut them into pieces, and put them in a pan with a bay leaf, ½ a garlic, onion, fresh basil, sugar, and salt. Cook for about 10 minutes, then take out the bay leaf and purée everything. Return to the pan to keep warm.

Make a white sauce *(p16)* with the ingredient amounts listed here. Season it with a pinch of salt and let it thicken, always stirring with a wooden spoon, so that it is smooth and velvety.

Finally pour it into the pan with the tomatoes. Stir well and divide among bowls. Bring to the table with the grated Parmesan served on the side.

CREMA DI PROSCIUTTO

Cream of Ham

7 oz ham
10½ tbsp butter
9 tbsp cream of rice
2 quarts meat broth *(p88)*
3 egg yolks
9 tbsp grated Parmesan
Cream
Bread cubes, to fry
Salt

Finely chop the ham and mix it with 1 tablespoon of melted butter. Stir the cream of rice into 1 cup of cold broth to make a slurry. Bring the rest of the broth to a simmer and slowly stir in the slurry. Reduce the heat and let boil for 5 minutes, stirring constantly.

In another bowl, add about one-third of the butter, chopped small, the egg yolks, a good handful of Parmesan, and ½ a glass of cream. Take a ladle of boiling broth and slowly dissolve the cheese and eggs, stirring with a wooden spoon. Add another couple of ladles of broth and stir again.

Put everything back into the saucepan and keep warm for 4 or 5 minutes, but do not let the cream boil again.

Cut some cubes of bread off a loaf and fry with the rest of the butter. Pour the soup into bowls and top with the croutons. Serve immediately.

CREMA DI SPINACI

Cream of Spinach

2¼ lb spinach
7 tbsp milk
Butter
Bread cubes, to fry
Salt

Cream sauce:
1½ tbsp butter, 3 tbsp flour, 3 cups vegetable broth

Clean and wash the spinach in water, blanch it in a small amount of lightly salted boiling water and when wilted, drain, squeeze well, chop, and mash to a purée.

Prepare a cream sauce *(p17)* using the ingredient amounts listed here. As soon as the sauce is finished, add the spinach, mixing it in well, then loosen the soup with the milk.

When it is time to serve, before pouring the soup into the soup tureen, stir in a small piece of butter and a few cubes of bread fried in butter and serve.

MINESTRE

MINESTRA AL LATTE

Milk Soup

10 oz egg pasta squares
6½ cups milk
6 egg yolks
Grated Parmesan
Salt

Cook the pasta in boiling salted water. In a second pan, bring the milk to a boil.

Put the egg yolks in a bowl with a handful of grated Parmesan. Pour the hot milk into the eggs, stirring vigorously with a whisk to stop the eggs cooking. Pour everything back into the milk pan. Drain the pasta squares, add them to the milk, and let them cook for a couple of minutes, but not boil. Divide the soup among bowls and serve.

MINESTRA DI CAPPELLETTI ALLA ROMANA

Roman Chicken Soup with Cappelletti

3 quarts chicken broth *(p89)*
2 oz ham
1 lb pork tenderloin
2 oz mortadella
3½ oz turkey or chicken breast
1 egg
Nutmeg
Grated Parmesan
Marsala
Salt
Pepper

Fresh pasta:
2½ cups flour, 3 eggs

Chop all the meats—the ham, the pork, the mortadella, the turkey or chicken breast—as finely as possible.

To make the stuffing, combine the chopped meats, egg, salt, pepper, a little nutmeg, the grated Parmesan in a large bowl and add a glass of Marsala.

Make the fresh pasta *(p170)* with the eggs and flour—or you can use store-bought—and when it is ready, roll out thinly on the work surface. Use a 2-inch round cutter (or a small glass) to cut out some disks before the pasta dries out.

Start filling the disks with a little of the stuffing—about the size of a hazelnut—in the middle of the disk, then fold it back on itself to enclose the filling. Press around with your fingers and then bring the two corners together and overlap them, pressing them with your finger and thus giving the pasta the shape of a small hat, a *cappelletto*.

Dust a tray with flour and line up your cappelletti in rows. Bring your broth to a simmer. Drop the cappelletti into the broth and simmer for 10 minutes.

MINESTRA DI CAPPELLETTI DI MIRANDOLA

Modena Soup with Cappelletti

7 oz guanciale (cured pork cheek)
4½ cups fine breadcrumbs
2 eggs
4⅓ cups grated Parmesan
Nutmeg
6½ cups meat broth *(p88)*
Salt

Fresh pasta:
4 cups flour, 4 eggs

The filling has to rest overnight, so prepare ahead. Cut the guanciale into pieces and let it melt in a pan. Put some breadcrumbs in a bowl and ladle in the fat from the guanciale working with a wooden spoon. It is best not to put all the breadcrumbs in at once because the fat absorbs less or more, so work in batches. When the mixture has cooled, add the eggs and knead everything with your hands. Add the grated Parmesan and a little nutmeg and salt. Put in the fridge overnight to firm up.

The next day, make fresh pasta *(p170)* using the ingredients listed here—or you can use store-bought—and cut it into 2½-inch squares.

In the middle of each square put a hazelnut-sized lump of the crumb and cheese mix, then fold over and overlap the two opposite corners of the square to obtain a triangle, press around with your fingers to secure. If the pasta is fresh, the two parts will stick with the simple finger pressure; if the pasta is too dry, just brush the corners with a little water. Finally, raise the apex of the triangle with the fingers and unite the other two ends of the triangle, overlapping them and pressing them with your fingers to close them. You will get a kind of pointed cappelletto, which is characteristic. Cook the cappelletti in the broth for 10 minutes.

MINESTRA DI CECI

Chickpea Soup

1 lb dried chickpeas (or 2¼ lb fresh)
Parsley
Rosemary
1 garlic clove
Pig's trotter
1 celery stalk
1 large carrot
1 onion
Bread, to toast
Salt

Soak the dried chickpeas for more than 12 hours.

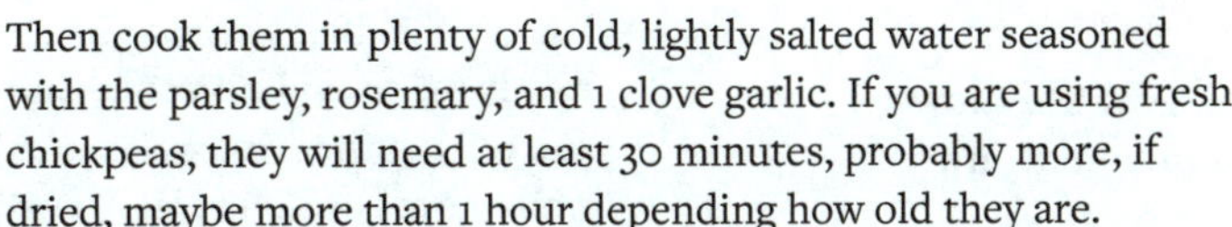

Then cook them in plenty of cold, lightly salted water seasoned with the parsley, rosemary, and 1 clove garlic. If you are using fresh chickpeas, they will need at least 30 minutes, probably more, if dried, maybe more than 1 hour depending how old they are.

Separately put the trotter in cold water with some salt, celery, carrot, and onion. Simmer and cook until the meat comes off the bones. Then chop the meat in large cubes. Sieve the trotter broth, pour it into a saucepan, and add the pieces of trotter, the diced carrot, and the drained chickpeas.

If the soup is too thick, dilute with the cooking water from the chickpeas. Boil for a few minutes. Toast some bread and divide among bowls, then ladle the soup over it.

MINESTRA DI CODA DI BUE

Oxtail Soup

2¼ lb oxtail
Flour
Butter
3½ oz prosciutto
Abundant aromatics (bay leaf, peppercorns)
2 carrots
1 large turnip
1 onion
3 or 4 celery stalks
Leek
Sugar
6 tbsp instant tapioca
Salt
Peppercorns
Optional: dry Marsala

Rinse the oxtail and cut it into pieces along the joints. Dust them in flour and fry with the prosciutto in butter to color.

When they are well browned, take them out and put them in a big soup pot with the prosciutto and cover with cold water. Bring to a boil and then season generously with whatever aromatics you have in the kitchen, but especially bay and peppercorns. Cover and simmer for 4 hours or more—you could also use a pressure cooker.

Dice the carrots, taking out the woody core, chop the turnip, the onion, the celery, and the white and light-green parts of the leek. Mix these vegetables together and season with salt and a pinch of sugar.

Stew the vegetables in 1 tablespoon of butter in a covered pan without any water. When they are almost cooked, moisten with a little broth from the oxtail and keep warm.

When the oxtail is ready, take out and keep warm in a little broth. Strain the rest of the broth thoroughly and degrease, then bring it back to a boil and add the tapioca. Cook for 10 minutes, then add the prepared vegetables and turn off the heat.

Pick the meat off the oxtail bones and cut away any fat or gristle. Cut them into regular shapes and return to the soup. Finish with half a glass of dry Marsala. The meat can also be served separately.

MINESTRA DI ORTAGGI E SALSICCE

Vegetable and Sausage Soup

1 large turnip
2 carrots
1 celery stalk
Cabbage
3½ oz lardo
2 sausages
5 oz lean salami (like Fabriano)
6½ cups meat broth *(p88)*
Butter
12 slices bread
Grated Parmesan
Optional: fresh or dried white beans or peas

Peel the turnip, carrots, and celery. Take any discolored outer leaves off half of a cabbage. Put these vegetables in a pot with lightly salted boiling water, simmer for a minute or two, then drain and refresh them in cold water. You can also add fresh or dried white beans or a handful of shelled peas at this stage.

Don't chop the vegetables. Put them in a saucepan, add the lardo, sausages, and salami in one piece. Cover with a ladle or two of broth, cover, and cook gently for 3 hours. Add more broth if you need.

Butter the bread, sprinkle with grated Parmesan, and bake or broil for a few minutes to brown.

When the vegetables and sausages are ready, take them out of the pot with a slotted spoon and chop the vegetables roughly. Slice the sausages and dice the salami and lardo.

Take a Dutch oven that can also serve as a serving dish and place some of the slices of bread in the bottom, then add a layer of vegetables, and then a few slices of sausage, salami, and lardo. Sprinkle with grated Parmesan and keep making layers in the same order until you finish up the ingredients.

Pour one or two ladles of the broth over, cover, and let sit for 15 minutes so the bread absorbs the broth and the vegetables are almost dry. When it's time, serve with the broth separately.

MINESTRA DI PASSATELLI

Passatelli Soup

6 tbsp fine breadcrumbs
Grated Parmesan
2 tbsp flour
Nutmeg
4 eggs
6½ cups meat broth *(p88)*
Salt
Pepper

Pour the breadcrumbs on a work surface and mix with a little Parmesan, flour, nutmeg, salt. and pepper. Add the eggs, as if you are making fresh pasta. The dough should be quite soft.

In the meantime, bring the broth to a boil.

Place the dough in a passatelli maker if you have one (or a potato ricer) and press the dough through the holes into the broth, cutting the strands off at about 1½ inches with the tip of a small knife. Keep going until you have cooked all the pasta.

Reduce the heat to the low simmer and let boil for 4 or 5 minutes. Mix the soup and add a little more grated Parmesan before serving.

ADA SAYS: *To make passatelli, you will either need the special "ferro da passatelli," a perforated metal disk with two handles on the side used to press the dough through, or you could also use a potato ricer, which works on the same principle.*

MINESTRA DI PASTA ALL'UOVO GRATTUGIATA

Soup with Grated Egg Pasta

2½ cups flour
3 eggs
6½ cups chicken broth *(p89)*
Grated Parmesan
Salt

Knead the flour, eggs and a pinch of salt into a dough. Shape into a ball and let it rest.

Grate the dough on a cheese grater and spread it on a work surface to dry.

Bring the broth to a simmer and as it boils, drop in the grated pasta. Cook for a few minutes and give it a good stir. Finish with grated Parmesan and serve.

MINESTRA DI PASTA E BROCCOLO

Pasta and Broccoli Soup

5 oz fresh pork skin
2 oz lardo or fatty prosciutto
1 garlic clove
Lard or oil
1 tbsp tomato paste
1 head broccoli
10 oz spaghetti or small macaroni
Grated Parmesan
Salt
Pepper

Scrape the pork skins well and put them in a pot of boiling water. Drain, remove the skins, cut them into small pieces, and boil them once more until almost cooked, about 1½ hours.

Finely chop the lardo and garlic and put this in a saucepan with half a spoon of lard or oil. Fry a little and add the tomato paste. Season with salt and pepper, then ladle a couple of spoons of water over this mix.

Rinse and cut the broccoli into florets and add these to the lardo and garlic. Cover and cook, stirring from time to time, until the broccoli is about half done. Pour in the cooking liquid from the pork skins. If you need more, add some water but it should stay a bit dry.

Break the spaghetti into short pieces and add to the boiling liquid in the saucepan. When the pasta is cooked, pour the soup into separate bowls and garnish with some grated Parmesan.

MINESTRA DI PASTA E CECI

Chickpea Soup with Cannolicchi

1 lb dried chickpeas
Baking soda (⅛ tsp for 1 qt water)
Rosemary
2 garlic cloves
3 anchovies
Olive oil
1 tsp tomato paste
10 oz cannolicchi pasta
Salt
Pepper

Soak the chickpeas in water for 12 hours or at least overnight. Then simmer in lightly salted water with the baking soda and rosemary until tender 1 to 1½ hours, depending how old they are.

Chop the garlic. Wash and bone the anchovies and cut up small. Put both in a skillet with a glass of olive oil and sauté. Add the tomato paste and a little water. Cook a little and then add to the chickpeas. Discard the rosemary and bring back to a boil.

As soon as the water boils, add the cannolicchi and cook until al dente. Season with pepper and serve.

MINESTRA DI PASTA E FAGIOLI ALLA VENETA

Venetian Bean and Pasta Soup

10 oz dried borlotti beans
5 oz lardo
Parsley
Garlic
1 celery stalk
1 carrot
10 oz cannolicchi pasta
Salt
Pepper

Soak the beans in cold water for 12 hours. Drain.

In a large saucepan, combine 3 quarts salted water, the lardo, chopped parsley, chopped garlic, the celery, carrot, and the beans. Cook over moderate heat until tender, 1½ hours—it depends on the quality of the beans.

To complete the dish, remove some of the beans from the pot and put them through a food mill or a blender. Return those to the pan and turn up the heat. When it boils, add the pasta and cook to al dente. Check the seasoning and add, if necessary, salt and pepper.

MINESTRA DI QUADRUCCI CON PISELLI

Pasta and Pea Soup

1 onion
1 celery stalk
Parsley
3½ oz guanciale (cured pork cheek)
3½ tbsp butter
2¼ lb fresh peas (or 10 oz frozen peas)
6½ cups meat broth *(p88)*
10 oz square egg pasta
Salt

Chop the onion, celery, parsley, and guanciale and brown in a pan with the butter.

Shell the peas. When the onion and herbs are well colored, add the peas. If you are using frozen, blanch for a few minutes first in boiling water.

Sauté everything for a few minutes, stirring carefully, then add the broth. Let it boil until the peas are cooked. Add the pasta squares and cook for 2 or 3 minutes. It should not be too soupy.

MINESTRA DI RISO E CAVOLFIORE

Rice and Cauliflower Soup

1 lb 5 oz cauliflower
3½ tbsp butter
2 tbsp olive oil
1½ cups rice
2 quarts vegetable broth *(p90)*
Grated Parmesan
Salt
Pepper

Clean and wash the cauliflower. Remove the core and any hard outer leaves. Chop up small and fry with half the butter and the olive oil in a wide skillet. Let it brown slowly. Season with salt and pepper and add 2 tablespoons or more of broth, cover, and cook for 10 minutes.

Bring the rest of the broth to a simmer in a saucepan. Add the rice and fried cauliflower. Mix well and let it cook for 10 minutes, then add the grated Parmesan and the rest of the butter. Keep stirring until the rice is cooked.

MINESTRA DI RISO E CICORIA

Rice and Bitter Greens Soup

2¼ lb bitter greens, like escarole
3½ oz lardo or guanciale
1 onion
Garlic
Parsley
1 celery stalk
1 carrot
Olive oil
1 tbsp tomato paste
1¾ cups rice
Salt
Pepper

Wash the escarole in plenty of water and then boil it until it is cooked. Drain and chop coarsely.

Dice the lardo and finely chop the onion, garlic, parsley, celery, and carrot. Sauté everything in a bit of oil. As soon as it starts to brown, add the tomato paste, and dilute with 4 cups of water. Season with salt and pepper.

Cook for 10 minutes, then add the drained escarole and let it take on flavor. Lastly add the rice and let it cook through. The soup will be quite thick.

MINESTRA DI RISO E FAGIOLI

Rice and Bean Soup

1½ cups dried beans
Olive oil
1 onion
1 celery stalk
1 lb tomatoes
1 chili
1¾ cups rice
Salt

Soak the beans in cold water for 12 hours. Boil them in 3 quarts of lightly salted water for about 1½ hours and keep them warm in their water.

Put half a glass of oil in a pan. Finely chop your onion and celery and, when the oil is hot, add them. Wash the tomatoes—blanch them in boiling water to release the skins—peel, scoop out the seeds, and chop the flesh only. As your celery and onion start to color, add the tomatoes, and a chopped chili. Let sweat for about 10 minutes.

Bring the beans back to a boil. Pour the tomato and vegetables into the bean pot and then add the rice. Stir occasionally until the rice is cooked through. This soup should be quite thick.

MINESTRA DI RISO E INDIVIA AL POMODORO

Rice and Endive Soup with Tomatoes

2¼ lb curly endive or escarole
1 onion
Olive oil
3½ oz lardo or guanciale
Garlic
Parsley
1 celery stalk
1 carrot
10 fresh tomatoes
1¾ cups rice
Salt
Pepper

Clean the endive, wash it well, and put it to drain.

Chop your onion and put in a pan with some oil. Dice the lardo and add to the pan. Finely chop the garlic, parsley, celery, and carrot and fry for a few minutes.

Blanch, peel, seed, and chop the tomatoes. Add the tomatoes to the pan. Season with salt. Cook for 10 minutes.

Chop the greens, add to the pan and let them sweat for a few minutes. Give it a grind of pepper. Then cover everything with 4 cups of salted water.

When the greens are cooked, in a couple of minutes, add the rice and let it cook through. The soup should be quite thick.

MINESTRA DI RISO E LENTICCHIE

Rice and Lentil Soup

12 oz dried lentils
2 onions
3½ oz lardo or guanciale
Garlic
1 celery stalk
Parsley
Olive oil
10 tomatoes (or 16 oz canned tomatoes)
1¼ cups rice
Salt

Pick over the lentils for any stones or other impurities and soak them in cold water for 12 hours. Get rid of any that rise up to the surface.

Drain and add the lentils to a pot with 6½ cups water, one of the onions, the celery, and a little salt and simmer over low heat for about 15 minutes.

Dice the lardo, the remaining onion, garlic, celery, and parsley and sauté with a little oil in a pan. Blanch, peel, seed and chop the fresh tomatoes (or use the canned tomatoes). Add the tomatoes and cook for 10 minutes.

Then add the lentils with half of their cooking water. When the lentils have mixed well with the other flavors, add the rice and let it cook. Be careful not to overcook it. If necessary, add a little more of the lentil cooking water; the soup should be quite thick.

❖ ADA SAYS: *Many dried lentils will not need soaking and you can skip this part.*

MINESTRA DI RISO E LUGANIGA

Rice, Fennel, and Sausage Soup

7 oz luganega sausage (flavored with fennel)
5 oz turnips
3½ oz prosciutto fat
3½ tbsp butter
1 small onion
1 cup rice
2 quarts broth
Parsley
Grated Parmesan
Salt

Put the luganega sausage in boiling water for 10 minutes. Take out and when cool enough to handle, peel off the casings and break into pieces. Rinse and dice the turnips. Cook them in boiling salted water for a few minutes.

Chop the prosciutto fat and melt with half the butter in a saucepan. Dice the onion and add to the fat and oil to brown. When the onion is glistening, add the pieces of sausage and the diced turnip. Let them cook together for a moment or two, then cover with some broth and keep stirring with a wooden spoon. Season with salt, then top up with the rest of the broth and put the rice in to cook when it comes to a boil again.

Cook the rice for 20 minutes or so, then complete the soup with the rest of the butter, a spoonful of chopped parsley, and grated Parmesan. Give a last good stir and serve.

MINESTRA DI RISO E PATATE

Rice and Potato Soup

1 onion
1 tbsp lard
3½ oz guanciale or lardo
Garlic
Parsley
1 tsp tomato paste
5 to 6 potatoes
1½ cups rice
Grated Parmesan
Salt
Pepper

Cut the onion into thin slices and fry in the lard in a saucepan. Dice the guanciale and garlic, chop the parsley, and add to the mix. Dissolve the tomato paste in 4 cups of water and add to the pan.

Peel and dice the potatoes, rinse them well, and when the sauce in the pan is boiling, add the rice and the diced potatoes, season with salt and pepper, and when everything is cooked, complete with a little grated Parmesan.

MINESTRA DI RISO E ZUCCHINE

Rice and Zucchini Soup

6 zucchini
3½ oz lardo
1 onion
Garlic
Parsley
1 celery stalk
1 carrot
Olive oil
10 tomatoes
2¼ cups rice
Basil
Salt
Pepper

Rinse the zucchini, trim the ends, slice lengthwise, and then dice and set aside.

Dice the lardo, onion, garlic, parsley, celery, and carrot and fry in a little oil. Seed the tomatoes and chop them, then add to the pan. Cook for about 10 minutes. Add the diced zucchini. Give them a moment before seasoning with salt and pepper and let them take on flavor.

Add 4 cups of water, cover, and bring to a boil. Add the rice as soon as it reaches the boil. Once it is cooked through, add the chopped basil.

MINESTRA DI SEMOLINO

Semolina Soup

2 quarts broth
9 tbsp semolina
3½ tbsp butter
Grated Parmesan

Put the broth in a pot and when it come to a boil pour in a rain of semolina—if you throw it in one go it will clump up, be lumpy, unsightly, and not cook evenly.

Cook for 10 minutes, stirring occasionally, and finally season with the butter and grated Parmesan.

MINESTRA DI SEMOLINO E ASPARAGI

Semolina and Asparagus Soup

2¼ lb asparagus
6 tbsp semolina
3½ tbsp butter
Grated Parmesan
Salt

Wash the asparagus and, if necessary, peel the stalks or break off the bottoms that may have dried out. Boil in salted water. When they are cooked, cut off the tips, and blend the rest into a purée with a food mill or blender.

In a saucepan, bring 6 cups of lightly salted water to a boil. Let the semolina rain in. Cook for a few minutes, then add the asparagus purée and let it simmer for another 10 minutes. Take the saucepan off the heat, season with butter and Parmesan, pour into bowls, and garnish with the asparagus tips.

MINESTRA DI TAPIOCA

Tapioca Soup

2 quarts broth
3.5 oz instant tapioca
Optional: 2 egg yolks, cream
Salt

Pour the broth into a pot. When it reaches the boil, pour in the tapioca. Stir and cook for about 15 minutes. Add a little salt if necessary, and ladle into a soup tureen.

To make it more interesting, mix one or two egg yolks with a little cream and put these at the bottom of the tureen before pouring in the soup. You can also finish the soup with a little sugar and a perfume of lemon, cinnamon, or vanilla.

STRACCIATELLE

STRACCIATELLA

Stracciatella

3 eggs
3 tbsp semolina
3 tbsp grated Parmesan
6½ cups meat broth *(p88)*
Salt

Stracciatella means little rags and is similar to a 15th century recipe called zanzarelli.

Break the eggs into a bowl and add a pinch of salt, the semolina and Parmesan. Pour a ladle of cold broth into the bowl little by little and use a fork or a small whisk to dissolve everything.

In a saucepan, bring the rest of the broth to a boil. Drizzle the whisked egg into the liquid, stirring with a fork. Let it boil gently for 4 or 5 minutes, always shaking the pan.

You will achieve a stracciatella with light flakes.

STRACCIATELLA ALLA ROMANA

Stracciatella Roman Style

6½ cups beef broth *(p88)*
Lamb shoulder or breast
6 egg yolks
Lemon
Thin slices of bread
Fresh marjoram
Grated Parmesan
Salt

Make a beef broth, adding into the pot—and this is a must—a piece of lamb's shoulder or breast.

Break the egg yolks into a bowl, thin them with the juice of a lemon, and beat with a wooden spoon.

Put the beaten eggs in a large saucepan, off the heat, and slowly pour in the boiling broth, stirring continuously with a wooden spoon. When you have poured all the broth you need into the saucepan, put it back on the stove over low heat, and stirring all the time, and let it thicken slightly.

Toast the bread and arrange 3 or 4 slices at the bottom of a bowl. Pour the soup into the bowl and serve with Parmesan on the side Traditionally it is served with fresh marjoram leaves.

ADA SAYS: *This traditional recipe, also known as brodetto, is the starting point of the Roman Easter lunch.*

STRACCIATELLA DI UOVA FILATE

Egg String Stracciatella

3 eggs
Nutmeg
6½ tbsp flour
6½ cups broth
Grated Parmesan
Salt

Put the eggs in a bowl, season with a pinch of salt and a grating of nutmeg. Sieve in the flour and whisk vigorously with a fork or spoon so the flour and eggs are mixed perfectly. Continue for 3 or 4 minutes until the mixture is velvet and elastic. This kind of batter must have the consistency of a thick cream, and detach itself rather slowly, in a continuous link, from the fork. If it is not the right consistency, it will collapse into pieces when it hits the hot broth.

Bring the broth to a boil and then reduce the heat so it is barely bubbling.

Roll a sheet of parchment paper into a tight cone, with the pointed end closed. (Or use a piping bag.) Transfer the egg mix into it and close up the bag well. When it's time, snip off the pointed end so you have a pin hole out of which the egg mix can escape. You want the egg to come out in a regular thread, and let this continuous thread fall into the broth. Move the cone around so that the thread never falls onto itself, and continue like this until you have squeezed all the contents out of the paper.

As soon as the egg touches the broth, it solidifies and forms a sort of light and long string, hence the name. Serve with grated Parmesan on the side.

STRACCIATELLA GUARNITA

Stracciatella with Peas

1 lb fresh peas in the pod
2 tbsp butter
6½ cups good meat broth *(p88)*
1 tsp potato starch
3 eggs
Grated Parmesan
Salt

Shell the peas and cook them for a few minutes in butter, salt, and a little water.

Bring the broth to a boil. As it is heating, dissolve the potato starch in a little warm broth and return it to the main pot of broth.

Beat the eggs in a bowl and season with Parmesan. Drop this mixture of eggs and Parmesan into the boiling broth and whisk the liquid with a fork so that the stracciatella make small lumps. Let it boil for a few more minutes, add the peas, and serve immediately.

STRACCIATELLA VERDE

Green Stracciatella

1 lb Swiss chard
3 eggs
9 tbsp grated Parmesan
6½ cups broth
Salt

Clean the Swiss chard, rinse it, boil, and drain it. When it cools down, squeeze it between your hands to get all of the water out and shape it into a ball the size of an apple.

Finely chop and blend the Swiss chard and put the purée in a bowl. Season with salt, the eggs, and Parmesan and whisk in some cold broth.

Bring the broth to a boil. Add the Swiss chard/egg mixture whisking all the time. Simmer for a few minutes and the green flakes will reappear. Serve Parmesan on the side.

MINESTRONE

MINESTRONE AGLI ORTAGGI

Vegetable Minestrone

1 lb fresh white beans in the pod, or canned
1 lb cabbage
4 potatoes
2 carrots
1 celery stalk
10 oz pasta or 1¼ cups rice
7 oz lardo
2 garlic cloves
Basil
Parsley
1 cup grated Parmesan
Salt
Pepper

Shell the beans and cook them in a pan with slightly salted boiled water—calculate about 2½ quarts of water. After about 20 minutes, add the cabbage cut into strips, peeled potatoes, carrots chopped in cubes, and some finely chopped white stalks of celery.

Keep boiling for about 40 minutes, adding the pasta or rice at an appropriate time for them to cook through.

Chop the lardo with the garlic, a few leaves of basil and parsley. Mix in grated Parmesan and loosen with a few spoonfuls of the cooking broth. Pour this mix into the minestrone to develop flavor for a few minutes and complete with a grind of pepper.

MINESTRONE ALLA FIORENTINA

Minestrone Florentine

2 cups dried white beans
3½ oz prosciutto
1 onion
3 garlic cloves
Olive oil
1 lb cabbage
1 celery stalk
1 leek
10½ cups broth
2 tbsp tomato paste
Rosemary
Toasted black bread slices
Salt
Pepper

Soak the dried beans in cold water for 12 hours with a pinch of baking soda.

Coarsely chop the prosciutto, the onion, and a clove of garlic and fry in a deep pan with two fingers of oil.

Cut the leaves of the cabbage, the celery, and leek into strips and, as soon as the mixture is browned, add to the pan, reduce the heat and let the flavor develop, stirring occasionally.

When the vegetables are slightly wilted, add the amount of water or broth needed to cook the beans—1¼ cups for every ½ cup of beans—and add the tomato paste. Put the beans, as above, or drained from a tin in the pan, add salt, cover the pot, and simmer over moderate heat. A minimum of two hours and a half will be necessary, as certain qualities of beans require longer cooking times.

Meanwhile prepare the soffritto, which is the element that characterizes a Florentine minestrone. Put a glass of oil, 2 cloves of garlic, 2 or 3 sprigs of rosemary in a saucepan and cook over a lively heat. As soon as the garlic browns, sieve the infused oil into a bowl (discard the solids).

When the beans have reached the right cooking point, blend with a food mill or blender and add the bean purée back to the rest of the bean liquid in the pot.

Finally, pour the infused oil into the pan and let the minestrone simmer over moderate heat for 15 minutes to allow it to absorb the aromatic seasoning well. It is customary to lay large slices of toasted black bread in the bowls before pouring the minestrone.

MINESTRONE ALLA GENOVESE

Minestrone Genovese

10 oz dried white beans
1 lb cabbage
2 potatoes
2 eggplants
2 zucchini
Fresh peas, shelled
7 oz green beans
Olive oil
9 oz short pasta or 1¼ cups rice
Salt
Pepper

Pesto:
2 cloves garlic, basil leaves, 6 tbsp grated pecorino or Parmesan, a few tablespoons oil

Soak the dried beans in cold water for 12 hours with a pinch of baking soda. Place in a large pot with 2 quarts of cold salted water and cook, covered, over moderate heat with the pan covered for about 2 hours.

When the beans have about 30 minutes left, chop the vegetables or cut the potatoes, eggplants, and zucchini into cubes according to their nature and ⅔ cup of shelled fresh peas. Add to the pot with a few tablespoons of oil, salt, and pepper. Cook for another 45 minutes, so that it is neither too abundant nor too thin: The minestrone should be fairly thick.

Adjust the timing for when to add the short pasta or the rice, as they have different cooking times.

Meanwhile, prepare the pesto that is the hallmark of this minestrone. Pound the garlic, 2 handfuls of basil, and a little salt in a stone mortar. Add the pecorino while grinding and when everything is well blended, loosen with oil and mix with a spoon until you get a cream. (If you want to use a blender, start by putting half a glass of oil in the blender jar and gradually adding the other ingredients.)

Thin the pesto with a little broth from the minestrone. About 3 minutes before the minestrone is done, gently stir in the pesto. Then remove from the heat and serve.

MINESTRONE ALLA MILANESE

Minestrone Milanese

2 tbsp tomato paste
10½ cups broth
1½ cups dried white beans, soaked
1 small celery stalk
2 carrots
2 potatoes
2 zucchini
7 oz peeled fresh fava beans
7 oz shelled fresh peas
1 lb cabbage
1⅓ cups rice
3½ oz lardo
Parsley
Garlic
Sage
Grated Parmesan
Salt

In a large pot stir the tomato paste into the broth or cold salted water. First add the beans (which have already been soaked)—and then all the other elements, starting with those for which cooking times are longer—carrot and the celery, and then potatoes, then zucchini, fresh fava beans, peas, and last, the cabbage, midribs removed, cut into fettuccine lengths.

The total time for cooking this minestrone will be about 2 hours, so calculate when you need to add the rice.

When the minestrone is done, add more water or broth if necessary, and add a mixture of chopped lardo, parsley, garlic, and a little sage. Check the seasoning and finish the minestrone with a few spoonfuls of grated Parmesan.

MINESTRONE ALLA MILANESE ESTIVO

Summer Minestrone Milanese

3½ oz lardo
1 onion
1 leek
10 oz shelled fresh fava beans
4 tomatoes
1 celery stalk
2 carrots
2 zucchini
10 oz shelled fresh peas
3½ oz pancetta
Cabbage
4 bouillon cubes
1¼ cups rice
Parsley
Garlic
Sage
Grated Parmesan

Chop the lardo and put it in a saucepan with the onion and leek. Let it brown and add all the seasonal vegetables that you can find—fresh fava beans, peeled and diced tomatoes, celery, carrots, zucchini, and peas. Add to these elements half of the pancetta. Let it flavor for a few minutes and then add 2 quarts of boiling water in which you have melted the bouillon cubes. Boil for 1 hour, adding more water if necessary, and then add the washed cabbage chopped into strips with midribs removed.

For the final stage, add the rice and cook for the necessary time. A minute before taking it off the heat, add a mixture of parsley, a little garlic, and a little sage. Complete with abundant Parmesan.

Serve immediately to stop the rice overcooking. Dice the remaining pancetta into small cubes and distribute them in each bowl.

MINESTRONE AL LARDO

Minestrone with Lardo

14 oz shelled fresh beans
4 potatoes
4 carrots
2 heads bitter greens
1 celery stalk
3 tomatoes
10 oz cannolicchi pasta
3½ oz lardo
Garlic
Basil
Parsley
Grated Parmesan
Salt

Put the beans in a pan with 2½ quarts of water and when they are cooked, add the diced potatoes, diced carrots, rinsed and chopped greens, some celery, tomatoes (peeled, seeded, and chopped), and salt. Boil slowly. Then add the cannolicchi.

Chop the lardo with the garlic, basil, and parsley and add them to the pan as soon as the pasta is cooked. Finish with grated Parmesan and serve immediately.

MINESTRONE DEL FATTORE

Farmhouse Minestrone

3½ tbsp butter
1 onion
Celery stalk
1 small carrot
Garlic
3 bouillon cubes
2 oz fatty prosciutto
5 tomatoes
Parsley
5 potatoes
4 zucchini
10 oz cannolicchi pasta
2 yellow peppers of Naples
Grated Parmesan
Basil
Fried bread cubes
Salt

In a saucepan, heat the butter, a little finely chopped onion, ½ a chopped celery, a chopped carrot, and, if you wish, a pinch of crushed garlic. Cook slowly and when they begin to turn golden, add the prosciutto cut into slices. Cook a minute or two more and then add peeled, seeded, and chopped tomatoes, and a spoonful of chopped parsley.

When the tomatoes are cooked, which will happen in a few minutes, pour 6 cups of water with the bouillon cubes into the pan, and as soon as the water boils, add the diced potatoes and zucchini, as well as the cannolicchi.

Scorch the peppers over a flame or in the oven, turning them often, to char the skins without letting the peppers themselves cook too much. Rub the skin gently with your fingers, rinse them, remove the stems and seeds, cut them into strips and add them to the minestrone.

When everything is cooked, remove the pan from the heat and season the minestrone with a few tablespoons of grated Parmesan and a few shredded leaves of fresh basil. Stir, cover the pan, and let it stew for another 5 minutes. After this time, serve in bowls and. at the last moment, add the cubes of fried bread.

MINESTRONE DI FAGIOLI FRESCHI

Fresh Bean Minestrone

1 lb shelled fresh white beans
3 zucchini
3 potatoes
3 carrots
5 tbsp butter
1 onion
3 tomatoes
2 eggs
Grated Parmesan
Salt

You can make this with canned white beans but it will not be as good.

Boil the fresh beans in 6 cups of salted water. Wash and peel the zucchini, potatoes, and carrots and cut them into cubes. Place half the butter in a saucepan and sauté the finely sliced onion.

When the onion has reached a nice golden color, add the tomatoes — peeled, seeded, and chopped — the zucchini, carrots, and potatoes. Cook everything for a few minutes and then add lots of warm water. Let it boil slowly and at the end of the cooking, add the drained boiled beans.

Now prepare an omelet, which is the characteristic of this dish. Beat the eggs in a bowl, season with a pinch of salt and grated Parmesan. Pour into a rather large pan where the remaining butter is melting. Run the eggs all over the bottom of the pan, so that the omelet is wide and thin; then turn it out onto a work surface and cut it into squares. Combine the omelet squares with the minestrone. Give a good stir and serve.

MINESTRONE DI LATTUGHE RIPIENE

Minestrone with Stuffed Lettuce Parcels

8 large lettuce leaves
Butter
Bay leaf
10 oz lean veal, thinly sliced
3½ oz sweetbreads
2 oz veal udder
Dried mushrooms
Marjoram
Garlic
Grated Parmesan
2 eggs
1 egg yolk
2 quarts broth
Salt

Choose the big leaves of the lettuce keeping the heart for other uses, rinse them and blanch them in salted water just long enough to soften them up and put them in a dish to cool.

In a pan with a little butter, some salt, and half a bay leaf, sauté the slices of veal. Meanwhile, boil the sweetbreads in lightly salted water, then add them to the pan with the meat let them flavor for a little. Remove the pan from the heat. Boil and finely chop the veal udder and mix it in the pan until evenly combined.

On the side, reconstitute ½ oz dried mushrooms in cold water then mix with a little garlic and add this mixture to the meats. Finish with salt, a generous spoonful of grated Parmesan, the whole eggs, and egg yolk. Mix everything to a cream.

Spread 2 lettuce leaves on your left palm if they are large, 3 and even 4 if small, crush the midribs well, otherwise they will not wrap well. Put a good spoonful of the meat mix inside and wrap it well in the leaves, taking care to seal well so that they do not open when boiling. To be absolutely safe, you can tie the leaves with a string; but if they have been well wrapped and the midribs crushed, the filling will not come out.

Put the broth in a low, wide pan and when it boils, drop in the lettuce packages one by one in a single layer. They must be well covered with broth.

Let it boil slowly for 20 minutes without stirring. Then put 1 or 2 in each bowl according to their size, add the broth and finish the soup with grated Parmesan.

ADA SAYS: *This Genoese preparation is traditionally served on Easter Day. Historically, the stuffing was also made with brains, cooked alongside the sweetbreads.*

MINESTRONE DI ORZO E INDIVIA

Barley and Bitter Greens Minestrone

1⅔ cups pearl barley
3½ oz prosciutto
7 tbsp butter
2¼ lb bitter greens, such as curly endive
1 onion
1 carrot
1 potato
1 celery stalk
Salt
Pepper

Soak the barley for about 2 hours. Dice the prosciutto and fry it in a large pan with half the butter. Add the barley, cook for a few minutes and then pour in 6 cups lightly salted water and well-cleaned bitter greens, washed and coarsely cut.

Boil for about 30 minutes, then add the other vegetables cut into very small pieces. Continue cooking for another 30 minutes. Finish the minestrone with the remaining butter.

ADA SAYS: *Look for pearl barley that cooks in about 1 hour, rather than bigger sizes that can take at least 3 hours.*

MINESTRONE DI ZUCCA GIALLA

Yellow Pumpkin Minestrone

Olive oil
1 onion
Garlic
2 oz pancetta
6 potatoes
1 lb yellow pumpkin
10 oz small cannolicchi pasta
Grated Parmesan
Salt
Pepper

Put some oil, a finely chopped onion, a small piece of crushed garlic, and the diced pancetta in a pan and fry over moderate heat, adding a spoonful of water from time to time to allow the onion to cook without burning.

When the onion is cooked, add the peeled potatoes cut into cubes and the yellow pumpkin cut into cubes. Let season a little, stirring with a wooden spoon. Add salt and pepper and 6 cups water. As soon as the water boils, add the cannolicchi, cover, and continue cooking, stirring occasionally.

The soup should be neither too thick, nor too soupy and if it gets too dry, add a little bit more water while it is cooking. The pumpkin, potatoes, and pasta must finish cooking at the same time. Let the minestrone rest a little and complete with ⅓ cup grated Parmesan.

MINESTRONE PRIMAVERILE

Spring Minestrone

1 carrot
2 potatoes
4 artichoke hearts
1 small cauliflower
1 cup shelled peas
10½ tbsp butter
1½ cups rice
Bouillon cube
Salt

Cut the carrot, potatoes, and artichoke hearts into cubes, and the cauliflower into florets. Rinse all the vegetables and put them in a large pan along with the peas and a good tablespoon of butter. Season with a little salt. Cook over a lively heat, adding a few tablespoons of water from time to time.

Melt another tablespoon of butter in a casserole and add the rice and a generous 2 cups of boiling broth made with a bouillon cube. Give a good stir, let return to a boil again, cover, and put it in a preheated oven for 20 minutes.

After this time, remove the Dutch oven from the oven, add the rice to the vegetables, and finish the minestrone with the rest of the melted butter.

FISH SOUPS

BRODETTO DELL'ALTO ADRIATICO

North Adriatic Brodetto

4½ lb assorted seafood
Olive oil
2 leeks
Celery
Garlic
6 cuttlefish
Vinegar
2 onions
Cinnamon
Bay leaf
Parsley
Bread slices
Salt
Pepper

The most typical varieties of fish here are: cuttlefish, essential as they give a characteristic tone to the preparation, small shark or swordfish, cod, sole, mullet, and mantis shrimp.

Carefully gut the fish, scaling them if necessary. Remove the heads, which you will need for the broth. Wash the fish under running water and cut into pieces.

Put a little oil in a large pot, add the chopped leeks, abundant celery, and a few cloves of garlic, and brown over high heat. Add the fish heads and the well cleaned cuttlefish, still whole, which are the hardest to cook. Brown a little, then wet with a few spoonfuls of vinegar and when the vinegar has evaporated, pour plenty of water into the pan to cover the heads and the cuttlefish fully, and let it boil for 30 minutes.

Take out the cuttlefish and put them aside. Strain the broth in a sieve and pressing on the heads well with a wooden spoon to extract all the flavor. Set the broth aside.

Clean the pan, slice half an onion and brown it in abundant oil, until it has taken on a dark blond color. Then add the pieces of fish. Increase the heat, season with salt, pepper, a small piece of cinnamon, a bay leaf, and plenty of roughly cut parsley. When the fish has browned a few minutes over high heat, add the broth, the cuttlefish, and finish the cooking over high heat.

Align some slices of bread in the bowls (in this case it should not be toasted) and pour the fish over it with its broth.

BRODETTO DI ANCONA

Ancona Brodetto

4½ lb assorted seafood
Olive oil
1 onion
Garlic
Parsley
1 lb tomatoes
Vinegar
Whole wheat bread
Salt
Pepper

Carefully gut the fish, scaling them if necessary, and remove the heads. Wash the fish under running water and cut into large pieces (unless small enough to leave whole).

Prepare a good sauce: Put plenty of oil in a pan with a chopped onion. When the onion is golden, add a little garlic and chopped parsley, tomatoes (peeled and chopped), salt, and pepper. Let the tomato cook down and thicken the sauce a little.

Add the various fish in order of size: the largest pieces first, then a few minutes later, the other fish. When it comes to a boil, add a little vinegar, which gives the dish its characteristic flavor.

Cook slowly in the uncovered saucepan, so that the sharp smell of vinegar can evaporate, and continue cooking for no more than 15 minutes, beyond which the fish would lose its aroma. Have ready some untoasted whole wheat bread—this is characteristic.

ADA SAYS: *The brodetto all'anconetana is typical of the Adriatic coast from Ancona to Rimini. Typical fish are sole, mullet, mackerel, scorpion fish, sea bass, turbot, small shark, eel, cuttlefish, shrimp.*

BRODETTO DI FANO

Fano Brodetto

4½ lb assorted seafood
Onion
1 carrot
1 celery stalk
Parsley
Bay leaf
Olive oil
Garlic
White wine
1 lb tomatoes
Toasted bread slices
Salt
Pepper

Carefully gut the fish, scaling them if necessary. Remove the heads, which you will need for the broth. Wash the fish under running water and cut into pieces.

Put the fish heads in a pot of water seasoned with the onion, carrot, celery, parsley, and half a bay leaf. Let it boil for about 20 minutes and then strain.

Put enough oil in a saucepan, a little chopped onion, and a chopped clove of garlic. Brown to a light gold, add chopped parsley, and immediately after the baby squid. Season with a good pinch of pepper and, as soon as the moisture of the squids evaporates almost completely, splash in a glass of white wine. Let the wine evaporate, add the tomatoes, let simmer for 5 minutes and add the prepared fish broth. Increase the heat to a lively boil, skim any impurities that rise to the surface, let it reduce a little, and then add the pieces of shark—which has been skinned and cut into chunks—and all the other fish in pieces, except the cod and the mullet.

Give it 5 minutes, then slip in the cod and mullet; return to a boil and remove from the heat. Put the toasted slices of bread in the bowls, pour the broth over them, and place the fish on the soaked slices of bread.

❖ ADA SAYS: *The most suitable fish are mullet, cod, ray, medium-size baby squid, scorpion fish, small shark, and lobster.*

BRODETTO DI PORTO RECANATI

Port Recanati Brodetto

4½ lb assorted fish and mantis shrimp
1¾ lb cuttlefish
1 onion
Olive oil
Saffron
White wine
Toasted bread slices
Salt
Pepper

Carefully gut the fish, scaling them if necessary, and remove the heads. Cut the larger ones into pieces of 2 to 3 ounces. Open the cuttlefish, remove the ink sac, rinse, and, after having pounded them, if necessary to tenderize, divide them in pieces of the right size.

Finely chop an onion and place it in a large saucepan with oil. When the onion has taken a nice golden hue, add the cuttlefish and simmer over moderate heat. Add the saffron to the saucepan to give an intense yellow color.

When the cuttlefish is well impregnated with saffron, season with salt and pepper, add enough water to cover and let them cook slowly for about 1 hour, until completely cooked.

Just before serving the brodetto, arrange a layer of shrimp on the bottom of a large pan. Put the cooked cuttlefish and the fish with the sturdier meats over them, then add a layer of the fish with the more delicate meat, covering all with the sauce from the pan.

Once everything is in the pan, add some salt (if necessary) and pour water and white wine in equal parts, making sure that the liquid almost reaches the level of the fish but not more.

Cook at a brisk simmer for a few minutes without worries because if the fish is fresh it does not break up. Carefully remove the shrimp and place them on the serving dish. This brodetto is served with lots of sauce and with toasted bread slices to the side.

BRODETTO DI SAN BENEDETTO

St. Benedict's Brodetto

4½ lb assorted fish and seafood
1 lb mussels
1 lb clams
Olive oil
2 onions or garlic
Vinegar
Red chili pepper
1 lb tomatoes
1 tbsp tomato paste
White wine
Toasted bread slices
Salt

For this characteristic brodetto, the most suitable fish to use are capone, angler, John Dory, mullet, and shrimp. You can also add cuttlefish, squid, and octopus.

Carefully gut the fish, scaling them if necessary, and remove the heads (save for the broth). Remove the bladder and the eyes from the cuttlefish, squid, and octopus and cut them into strips

Place half a glass of oil in a pan, add a chopped onion and sauté over high heat. Add the fish heads and brown them a little, then moisten with a few spoonfuls of vinegar and when the vinegar has evaporated, pour plenty of water into the pan to cover the heads. Boil for 30 minutes.

Now wash the mussels, scrape them with a small knife, remove the beards, then carefully rewash them several times. Also wash the clams very carefully and put them with the mussels in a large pan with a little oil. Let them cook, shaking them around to be sure they are all cooked. Empty the pan carefully into a sieve set over a bowl to catch the cooking liquid. Throw away the empty shells. Keep the mussels and clams in their own cooking liquid.

In a pan, heat some oil and sauté the onion *or* garlic cut into thin slices (but never use garlic *and* onion together for this broth). When the onion or garlic is fried, add some chili, a little salt, the chopped tomatoes, and the tomato paste. Dilute the sauce with the broth from the heads of the fish and from the clams and mussels and add the cuttlefish, the small squids, and octopuses, in order to cook together with the sauce.

Place the shrimp in a Dutch oven, season with the sauce and then make a second and possibly a third layer of seafood, always interspersing them with the sauce, and adding the mussels and the prepared clams. Add a glass of white wine, put the pan over very moderate heat, cover, and cook for about 20 minutes, shaking the pan occasionally, but never stirring. Accompany the brodetto with slices of toasted bread.

BRODETTO IN BIANCO

White Brodetto

1 lb mussels
1 lb clams
Olive oil
Parsley
1 onion
1 lb 5 oz small squids
1 lb 5 oz cuttlefish
2¼ lb shark
Celery stalks
Garlic
Vinegar
Bay leaf
Bread slices
Salt
Peppercorns
Optional: Fish broth

Clean, scrape, and rinse the clams and mussels in plenty of water, then put them in a large pan with a little oil, a few tufts of parsley, a chopped onion, and a few coarsely broken peppercorns. Warm up and as soon as the shellfish are open, remove them from the shells, collecting them in a bowl.

Let the liquid they have produced rest for a while, and then carefully decant it into a small saucepan making sure that there are no traces of sand.

Remove the bladder and the eyes from the squid and cuttlefish and cut them into strips. Wash and scale the shark and cut it into pieces that are not too big.

Fry some celery in a large pan with plenty of oil, 4 or 5 cloves of garlic, which you will remove as soon as they brown. At this point add the cuttlefish to the pan, brown them, moisten with half a glass of vinegar and, when this evaporates, cover them with a fish broth, if you have it, or cover with hot water

The cuttlefish should boil for 30 minutes; then remove them from the cooking liquid.

In another very large pan, heat plenty of oil and add the squid, browning them slightly. Add the shark, season with salt, pepper, bay, and coarsely chopped parsley. Increase the heat and fry for a few minutes, then add the cuttlefish broth and the liquid from the mussels and clams. Add the cuttlefish and finish cooking over high heat for about 30 minutes.

Put slices of bread in the bowls, pour the soup over them, and garnish with the mussels and clams.

CACCIUCCO ALLA LIVORNESE

Fish Stew Livornese

Olive oil
Garlic
Red chilis
4½ lb assorted seafood, including shrimp, cuttlefish, and octopus
Wine
1 lb tomatoes
Toasted bread slices
Salt

Typically this is made with eel, small shark, scorpion fish and weevers, cleaned and cut into pieces.

Put two glasses of oil in a pan with plenty of chopped garlic and red chilis. As soon as the oil begins to brown, add the cuttlefish and octopus, cut into strips, and let them cook, covered, for about 30 minutes, adding a little boiling water if necessary.

Pour in a glass of wine, wait for it to evaporate, then add the chopped tomatoes and 2 cups of water. Add a pinch of salt and cook for a few minutes, then add the other fish cut into pieces and simmer until completely cooked, about 20 minutes.

Prepare a dish with slices of toasted bread rubbed with garlic and pour the fish over it with its broth.

CACCIUCCO RAFFINATO

Refined Fish Stew

4½ lb assorted seafood including: eel, squid, gurnard, shrimp, hake, scorpion fish, mullet, John Dory, octopus, lobster
Olive oil
1 onion
1 celery stalk
1 carrot
Parsley
Garlic
Chili pepper
Bay leaf
1 lb tomatoes
Red wine
Toasted bread slices
Salt
Pepper

Carefully gut the fish, scaling them if necessary, and remove the heads (reserve for the broth). Wash under running water. Cut the bigger fish into large pieces, keeping the other fish whole. Remove the bladder and the eyes of the cuttlefish and octopus.

Put half a glass of oil in a saucepan and sauté the chopped onion, a celery stalk, a carrot, parsley, garlic, chili, and a bay leaf. Add the fish heads to these vegetables and warm through. As soon as everything is lightly browned, add a glass of red wine and continue cooking slowly, until the wine has almost all evaporated. At this point, add the chopped tomatoes. Add 2 cups of water and let it boil for 30 minutes.

Remove the garlic and the bay leaves and blend all the ingredients you have cooked into a good sauce. Transfer to a bowl and set aside.

Put half a glass of oil in another large, low saucepan and cook the octopus, cuttlefish, and squid, cut into rather small pieces. Pour the sauce into the saucepan and cook slowly for 15 minutes.

At this point, add the lobster cut into pieces, the shrimp, and the eel and, after another 5 minutes of boiling, any remaining more delicate fish.

Let it cook for another 10 minutes, check the sauce for seasoning, adding salt if necessary, and finally pour the fish with its broth into a bowl with slices of toasted bread.

ZUPPA DI BACCALÀ ALL'ITALIANA

Italian Salt Cod Soup

2¼ lb salt cod, already soaked
Olive oil
2 onions
2 garlic cloves
1 celery stalk
Bay leaf
Parsley
1 tbsp tomato paste
White wine
4 potatoes
Toasted bread slices
Garlic
Salt
Pepper

Peel the salt cod and cut it into square pieces. Put half a glass of oil in a pan with thinly sliced onions and garlic (which you can mince, giving more flavor to the soup, or leave whole and remove when it is just browned). Cook slowly, without the onion getting too dark, and then add a stalk of sliced celery and a bouquet of ½ bay leaf and a few parsley stems, tied together with a little bit of string. When the herbs are browned, add the tomato paste, let it cook, and then add a glass of white wine. Add the potatoes cut into wedges or slices (not too thin) and 4 cups of water.

When the potatoes are almost cooked, remove the aromatic bouquet and place the salt cod in the pan, adding another half a glass of oil. Reduce the heat, cover, and let it cook slowly over moderate heat for 15 minutes.

When everything is cooked, finish the soup with a couple of spoonfuls of chopped parsley and a strong grind of pepper. Prepare some toasted slices of bread lightly rubbed with garlic in a dish, and on this bread pour the salt cod, potatoes, and sauce. Let it stew for a moment and bring it to the table.

ZUPPA DI BACCALÀ ALLA MARSIGLIESE

Salt Cod Soup Marseille Style

2¼ lb salt cod, already soaked
Leek
1 celery stalk
2 garlic cloves
Lemon
Saffron
Olive oil
White wine
Parsley
Bay leaf
4 medium potatoes
Toasted bread slices
Salt

Peel the cod well, carefully slice it, and cut it into square pieces.

Put a bit of leek in a large low sauté pan with sliced celery, garlic, a strips of lemon zest, the saffron, a glass of oil, a glass of white wine, and peeled potatoes cut into large slices. Add a small bunch of parsley stems tied with a bit of string together with a bay leaf. Add enough water to cover the potatoes. If you wish you can add broth or a bouillon cube. Put the saucepan over high heat and boil.

When the potatoes are almost cooked, add the salt cod, reduce the heat, and let the cooking proceed rather slowly. After about 15 minutes, when the soup is cooked, finish it with plenty of chopped parsley.

Prepare slices of toasted bread in a bowl, pour the soup over it, and bring to the table.

ZUPPA DI COZZE

Mussel Soup

4½ lb mussels
Olive oil
Garlic
1 tbsp tomato paste
White wine
Toasted bread slices
Optional: chili

Wash the mussels, scrape them with a small knife, remove any beard from them, then repeatedly wash them with great care.

Add oil and a clove of garlic to a pan; when the garlic browns, throw it away, and add the tomato paste and a chili if you wish.

After 2 or 3 minutes, add the mussels and a glass or more of white wine to cover the mussels. Cook them over high heat, occasionally shaking the pan until they are all open.

Toast some slices of bread, rub them with a little garlic, arrange them on a plate, and pour on the mussels with their sauce.

ZUPPA DI GAMBERI

Shrimp Soup

1 small onion
1 carrot
Bay leaf
Parsley
2 tbsp butter
30 shrimps, including heads
2 cups fish broth *(p89)*
White wine
3 tbsp rice
Cayenne pepper
Optional: bread cubes fried in butter

Shrimp butter:
head and shells of shrimp;
10½ tbsp butter

Put the chopped onion and carrot in a saucepan over a low heat, with a small bay leaf, a little parsley, and the butter and cook slowly.

When they are cooked, add the well washed shrimp and a couple of spoonfuls of boiling fish broth and cook the shrimp, shaking them as often as possible until they are turn pink. Pour in a glass of white wine, cover the saucepan, and continue cooking gently for another 15 minutes, shaking from time to time. Then remove the shrimp, peel them - do not throw away the shells or the heads - and put them in another small bowl with a few spoonfuls of their broth. Finely chop and keep the cooked vegetables and herbs.

Boil the rice in a saucepan with a little fish broth and continue cooking until it is almost a mush. Add the cooked vegetables from the shrimp pan, loosen the mixture with a few spoonfuls of broth, and pass it through a sieve into a small saucepan. Add the shrimp cooking liquid and keep everything warm until you have prepared the special shrimp butter.

Put the shrimp shells and heads in a pan with the butter. Warm through to melt the butter while crushing the shells with the back of a spoon. Strain through a sieve lined with a cheesecloth into a small bowl.

When the broth is hot, first pour a small amount into the bowl with the shrimp butter, stirring with a wooden spoon. Then pour in the remaining broth, add the reserved cooked shrimp and, if you want, a pinch of cayenne pepper, as this soup should be slightly spicy. You can serve separately a plate of bread cubes fried in butter.

ZUPPA DI PESCE ALLA GENOVESE

Fish Soup Genovese

4½ lb assorted seafood
1 lb mussels
Olive oil
Onion
1 celery stalk
Garlic
Parsley
Bay leaf
White wine
6 anchovy fillets
Bread slices, fried in oil
Salt
Pepper

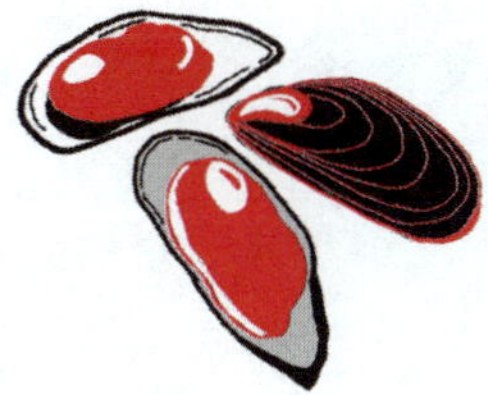

This recipe must include gelatinous fish, such as conger, sole, turbot, moray eel; rock fish, such as redfish, or gurnard, greenfinch, mullet, etc.; some molluscs, such as octopus or cuttlefish and some shellfish, usually mussels.

Carefully gut the fish, scaling them if necessary, and remove the heads. Wash under running water. Cut the fish into large pieces, then separate the firmer ones from the more delicate ones.

Remove the bladder and the eyes from the cuttlefish and squid and cut them into strips. Wash the mussels, scrape them with a small knife, remove any beard, then wash them again several times.

In a pan, put a glass and half of oil and cook the cuttlefish and squid, adding ½ a finely chopped onion, salt and pepper, and a piece of celery stalk, some parsley, and a bay leaf. Let the cuttlefish cook for about 30 minutes, adding a little water if necessary; then add a glass of white wine. Let the wine evaporate and add the chopped anchovy fillets and the firmer fish. Let them take on flavor and then cover with hot water.

After simmering for 5 minutes, add the more delicate fish, check if the quantity of water is still enough to cover and let cook for a maximum of 8 to 10 minutes.

Put the mussels in a large pan with a little oil and let them cook. When the mussels are all open, shell them and let their liquid rest a little. Decant it carefully and strain the broth through a sieve. Add the mussels to the rest of the fish and add a few spoonfuls of their broth.

Put some oil in a pan with a clove of finely chopped garlic. Set over heat and, as soon as the garlic begins to brown, add a spoonful of chopped parsley. Immediately remove the pan from the heat, and pour the sauce into the pan with the fish.

Check that it is well seasoned and pour the soup into a bowl where you have put a few slices of bread fried in oil.

ZUPPA DI PESCE ALLA MARSIGLIESE (BOUILLABAISSE)

Bouillabaisse

4½ lb assorted seafood
Olive oil
10 oz onions
3 garlic cloves
Parsley
Sprig fresh fennel
Bay leaf
Orange zest
10 oz tomatoes
Saffron
5 tbsp butter
Toasted bread slices
Salt
Pepper

For this famous dish from Marseilles, the typical fish are rockfish, which give the soup its characteristic flavor, and at least five or six other varieties including: conger eel, moray eel, John Dory, mullet, scorpion fish, cod, and a small lobster (essential).

Clean the fish carefully and take off the heads. Cut the claws off the lobster, put it on a cutting board with the back-side up and, holding it steady with your hand, split the tail in two with a well sharpened knife, then turn the lobster and open the head and torso, taking care that this second cut joins exactly with the first. Then remove the intestines and divide the tail meat into 5 or 6 pieces.

Put a glass of oil in a rather large saucepan and brown the onion. Add the chopped garlic and parsley, fennel, bay leaf, and a strip of orange zest. Cook for awhile, then peel, seed and chop the tomatoes, then add them to the pan. Let everything cook slowly.

When the tomatoes are cooked, remove the saucepan from the heat and layer in the raw lobster, the firmer-fleshed fish, and finally the seafood with more delicate flesh, all cut into pieces. Pour some boiling water into the saucepan just to cover the fish and set over high heat. As soon as the liquid boils, add another glass of oil, salt, saffron, and abundant pepper. Let boil for about 20 minutes, always over high heat, and then add the butter, mixing it in well.

Take out the fish, arrange on a plate, and pour the cooking broth, through a sieve, into another rather deep dish, in which you will have put some slices of freshly toasted bread. Serve the two plates at the same time. The fish can be garnished with parsley.

ZUPPA DI PESCE DELLE COSTE LAZIALI

Fish Soup Lazio Style

4½ lb assorted seafood
Onion
1 celery stalk
1 carrot
Parsley
Garlic
Olive oil
3 anchovies
Chili pepper
Dry red wine
5 tomatoes
Toasted bread slices
Salt

Generally used for this delicious and fragrant soup are cod, swordfish or shark, sea bass, croaker, sea bream, moray eel, conger eel, John Dory, scorpion fish, mullet, cuttlefish, and lobster.

Carefully gut the fish, scaling them if necessary, and remove the heads (reserve for the broth). Wash under running water and cut into pieces.

Put the heads—if they are large you will cut them in two pieces—in a saucepan with enough water and add half an onion, a stalk of celery, a piece of carrot, a few sprigs of parsley, and a little salt. Boil gently for about 20 minutes. Then strain the broth through a sieve and set aside.

Chop a clove of garlic, a nice sprig of parsley, the anchovies (washed and boned), and a piece of chili pepper and sauté. When everything is very soft, deglaze with a glass of red wine.

Pour a glass of oil into a pan in which the fish can cook in a single layer and set it over the heat. As soon as the oil is hot, add the garlic/chili mixture and cook over high heat for a few minutes, until the wine has evaporated. Then add the tomatoes (peeled, seeded, and chopped), remembering that the tomato must not predominate, but only be an accessory. Let the tomatoes cook for a while and then add the cuttlefish.

Cover the pot, reduce the heat, and wait for the cuttlefish to be perfectly cooked; from time to time add a few spoonfuls of some prepared fish broth. Twenty minutes before serving, add the broth to the cooked cuttlefish. Turn up the heat and when the broth boils, add the firmer fish and the lobster. If the broth does not completely cover the pieces of fish, add some boiling water. After about 10 minutes, add the more tender fish, and after checking the seasoning let it boil for 10 minutes.

Toast some slices of bread and arrange in a large rather deep dish. Remove the pan from the heat and wet the bread with fish broth. Arrange the fish on the bread, sprinkle it with some chopped parsley, and immediately bring to the table.

ZUPPA DI PESCE DEI PESCATORI PROVENZALI

Provençal Fish Soup

4½ lb assorted fish
1 large onion
Tomato
Bay leaf
Sprig of fennel
Parsley
1 celery stalk
Potatoes
Bread slices
Olive oil
Salt
Pepper

Quick aïoli:
5 to 6 garlic cloves, 1 egg yolk, 1 glass olive oil, salt

Put the various fish in a saucepan with a thinly sliced onion, a chopped tomato, bay leaf, fennel, parsley, celery, and a few potatoes, peeled and cut into wedges. Cover with water, add salt, and cook over high heat for 20 minutes.

Meanwhile, make a quick aïoli *(p29)* using the ingredient amounts listed here. This characteristic Provençal sauce can be made with a hand blender or with mortar and pestle. If you use a hand blender, put the egg yolk in a tall glass, add the oil a little at a time, as with making a mayonnaise, and, at the end, add the chopped garlic and salt. If you use a mortar, finely grind the garlic cloves with the pestle, add the salt and the egg yolk and, finally, emulsify the sauce like a mayonnaise by slowly pouring in the oil.

Prepare slices of bread on a plate, wet them abundantly with oil, season with a lot of pepper, and pour over the prepared broth. Then put the fish in another dish, serving at the same time as the aïoli.

ADA SAYS: *A specialty of the fishing families of the south of France; the name in Provençal—aïgo-saou—means salt water. Tasty and simple.*

ZUPPA DI PESCE SAN PIETRO

St. Peter's Fish Soup

3 lb 5 oz John Dory
Dried mushrooms
4 tbsp olive oil
3½ tbsp butter
1 onion
1 carrot
Parsley
1 celery stalk
White wine
2 tbsp flour
2 egg yolks
Lemon
Fried croutons
Salt
Pepper

Clean the John Dory well, rinse it thoroughly, and, with a sharp knife, fillet it by detaching the fleshy part from the rib cage. Set the fillets aside and cut the head and fish frame into pieces.

To make the fish broth. Soak ½ oz dried mushrooms in cold water to reconstitute. In a saucepan, combine a little oil, 1 tablespoon of the butter, the chopped onion, carrot, parsley, and celery, and soaked mushrooms. Set over heat and as soon as the vegetables are golden, add the fish head and fish frame and once these are browned too, sprinkle everything with 6 cups of water and a glass of white wine. Season with salt and pepper and cook at a high simmer.

After 30 minutes, put the remaining butter in another saucepan and, when the butter has melted, add the flour, stir and let it cook slowly for 4 or 5 minutes, always stirring.

Then strain in the broth, stirring well. Return to the heat and boil for 1 hour over low heat, skimming any foam or other impurities that will rise to the surface. The broth is now ready.

As serving time approaches, skin the fillets and cut them into many square pieces of a couple of fingers on each side. Put them in a saucepan pan with a little white wine and let them stew, covered, for a few minutes. As soon as they are cooked, remove them from the heat and keep them hot.

When it's time to serve, put the egg yolks in a bowl, beat them with a fork, add a little lemon juice and season with a spoonful of chopped parsley. Gradually pour the fish broth into the eggs, stirring to mix everything well. Divide the squares of cooked fish among bowls, adding fried bread cubes, or, more simply, toasted croutons. Finish each bowl with the broth and have it brought to the table.

ZUPPA DI PESCE SENZA SPINE

Boneless Fish Soup

1 lb mussels
1 lb clams
Olive oil
1 lb shrimp
3 whole soles
2¼ lb monkfish
Vinegar
Parsley
2 onions
Bay leaf
1 lb squid or cuttlefish
2¼ lb ripe tomatoes
2 garlic cloves
Bread slices, fried in oil
Salt
Pepper

Wash the mussels, scrape them with a small knife, remove any beards, then wash them again several times with great care. Wash the clams several times too. In a large pan put both the mussels and clams with a little oil and let them cook. As soon as they are open, take off the heat and when cool enough to handle, shell them and transfer them to a bowl. Carefully decant their cooking liquid into the bowl, taking care to leave the sandy part in the pan.

Shell the shrimp. Fillet the sole, saving the heads and fish frames. Debone and cut the monkfish into pieces, saving the head.

Now prepare a fish broth: Pour 2 quarts of water into a pan and half a glass of vinegar, the heads of the sole and monkfish, very little salt, a few sprigs of parsley, an onion, and ½ a bay leaf. Let this broth boil for about 20 minutes. Strain it and keep it hot.

Put some oil and a small chopped onion in a large pan. Fry a little and add the squid (or cuttlefish) and let them cook covered for about 30 minutes, adding, if necessary, a few spoonfuls of the fish broth. Add the tomatoes (peeled and seeded) to the pan and let them cook for a few minutes. Arrange in a single layer the fish fillets, shrimp, mussels and clams with their liquid, and sprinkle everything with hot fish broth. Finely chop and add the garlic, a little more salt, plenty of pepper, and let it cook over a lively heat for another 5 minutes. Serve on slices of bread fried in oil.

ZUPPA DI SCAMPI

Langoustine Soup

3 lb 5 oz langoustines
2 oz cornichons
Garlic
Anchovy
Parsley
White wine
Olive oil
1 tbsp tomato paste
Toasted bread slices
Salt
Pepper

Rinse the langoustines and dip them into a saucepan containing lightly salted boiling water. Cook them for 5 minutes, then drain them, separate the tails from the shells and heads and peel them.

Put the shells and the claws in a mortar and crush them well. Transfer the mixture to a saucepan and add 6 cups of water. Season with a pinch of salt and boil the shellfish broth until reduced to two-thirds. Strain in a sieve set over a bowl, pressing well on the solids so that you get as much of the essence of the crustaceans as possible.

Meanwhile, prepare a pesto by mincing the cornichon together with half a clove of garlic, the anchovy—washed and boned—and the parsley. Moisten with a glass of white wine.

In a saucepan, sauté 4 tablespoons of oil with a clove of garlic. As soon as this is heated but not colored, remove the garlic and add the pesto to the pan. Stir and add the tomato paste diluted with a spoonful of water.

Add the langoustine tails to this aromatic base and after a few minutes moisten them with a little strained shellfish broth. Cook for a few minutes, season with salt and pepper, and finally distribute the soup in the bowls where you have arranged some slices of toasted bread.

ZUPPA DI TELLINE

Cockle Soup

4½ lb wedge cockles (telline)
Oil
Garlic
10 oz tomatoes
Pepper
Parsley
Toasted bread slices

Telline (wedge cockles), the somewhat poor cousins of clams, have their admirers because of the goodness of their meat. Like other clams, they live in the sand and are harvested with a rake. They need special care to remove that troublesome sand.

Wash the cockles in water, and let them soak under running water or in a bowl with water and coarse salt for at least 1 hour, then drain.

Put a little oil in a skillet with a clove of garlic, which you will remove as soon as it has browned. Then peel, seed and chop the tomatoes and cook for about 10 minutes. Add the cockles, cover the pan, and let cook until all the shells are open.

Prepare some slices of toasted bread in each bowl and, before distributing the cockles with their broth into the bowls, add plenty of pepper and a spoonful of chopped parsley.

ADA SAYS: *Clams live in both salt and fresh water, whereas cockles only live in saltwater. Telline are smooth shelled, sometimes called arselle in Italian or in English they are also known as wedge cockles.*

ZUPPA DI VONGOLE

Clam Soup

4½ lb clams
10 oz tomatoes
Basil leaves
Olive oil
2 garlic cloves
Parsley
Chili
12 slices sandwich bread
Salt
Pepper

Wash the clams several times, leave them in a basin with water and coarse salt for about 1 hour, then drain.

Cut the tomatoes into small pieces and put them to cook in a pan without water but with a few basil leaves and a pinch of salt. Stir them from time to time with a wooden spoon, and when they collapse, after about 15 minutes, purée them in a food mill or a blender.

Cover the bottom of a large pan with oil, then add the garlic cloves, some chopped parsley, and basil leaves. Cook the herbs, then add the clams and cook them over high heat for a few minutes, stirring them so that every clam can feel the heat equally. Add the prepared tomato, some pepper, and some chili. Cook a few more minutes over high heat, then lower the heat and cover the pan.

Fry the slices of bread in abundant oil until golden and then place them in a large serving dish with high sides. Take the clams off the heat and pour them over the fried bread. Bring to the table immediately.

ZUPPA DI VONGOLE RAFFINATA

Refined Clam Soup

Potato starch
6½ cups fish broth *(p89)*
4½ lb clams
Olive oil
2 oz mushrooms
3½ tbsp butter
Crustless bread, fried in butter
3 egg yolks
Cream or milk
Salt

Dissolve a spoonful of potato starch in two fingers of cold water. Bring the broth to a boil and slowly pour in the potato starch slurry, stirring with a wooden spoon. Do not add the starch all at once, but a little at a time, just until you reach the desired consistency, which should be light.

Rinse the clams thoroughly and several times and put them in a pan with a little oil. Cover the pan and shake them as often as possible until they open. Then remove them from the shells and set aside. Let the cooking liquid settle and decant into another bowl, leaving any sand behind, and then add to the broth.

Wash the mushrooms quickly and cut into thick julienne. Cook them with a little butter and a little broth. When they are cooked, add them to the clams to the side.

Cut a few slices of crustless bread into sticks and fry them in butter, or lightly brown them in the oven. Put the egg yolks in a bowl, with two fingers of cream, and butter. Slowly pour the boiling broth over the eggs, little by little, stirring with a whisk.

Divide the clams among bowls and add mushrooms and bread sticks. Finish with broth and serve.

CLASSIC SOUPS

ZUPPA ACQUACOTTA

Acquacotta

2¼ lb tomatoes
4 onions
Wild mint leaves
Olive oil
Bread slices
Grated Parmesan
Salt
Pepper

Peel and seed the tomatoes and put them on to sauté with very little water until they thicken a little. At this point add the thinly sliced onions, the mint, and a little salt and cook for 30 minutes.

While the sauce is cooking, take some bread and cut it into slices and distribute among bowls. Pour 1 tablespoon of oil into each bowl and season with a pinch of salt and pepper.

When the tomato sauce is ready and piping hot, pour it into the bowls and sprinkle over some grated Parmesan.

ADA SAYS: *The acquacotta—literally cooked water—belongs to Umbrian cuisine and is an easy to make first-course dish, especially suitable for a family lunch.*

ZUPPA ALLA PAVESE

Pavese Soup

6½ cups broth
12 slices bread
Butter, for frying
1 cup grated Parmesan
12 eggs
Salt

Prepare a good broth. Toast the slices of bread or fry them in butter until golden.

Put 2 slices of bread in each bowl, break 2 eggs over them, season with grated Parmesan and a pinch of salt. Pour the boiling broth into the bowls, slowly on one side so that the eggs do not break. The heat of the broth will cook the eggs.

ADA SAYS: *If you prefer to have well-cooked eggs, poach them and lay them with a scoop on the slices of bread, being careful not to break them. Season the eggs with the Parmesan and cover with boiling broth.*

ZUPPA DI CAVOLO E SALSICCE

Cabbage and Sausage Soup

1 lb cabbage
2 oz fresh pork skin
2 sausages
1 slice lardo
Parsley
Garlic
Meat bouillon paste
Toasted bread slices
Grated Parmesan
Salt
Pepper

Trim the cabbage, remove the tough leaves, rinse the soft leaves, drain, and slice thinly.

Scrape the pork skins, put them in a small saucepan with cold water, and boil for 3 or 4 minutes. Drain and rinse them carefully in plenty of cold water to eliminate any trace of rancidity and make them very clean. Cut them into strips and set aside.

Remove the sausage casings. In a saucepan, combine the slice of lardo, the sausages, some sprigs of parsley, and a clove of garlic very thinly sliced. Set over heat and lightly brown. Then add the cabbage and the strips of pork skin. Season with salt, pepper, and the bouillon base diluted in 2 quarts of water and let it cook slowly for more than 1 hour.

When the cabbage and the pork skin are cooked, divide the slices of toasted bread among bowls, cover them with cabbage soup and a sprinkle of grated Parmesan.

ZUPPA DI CIPOLLE ALLA FRANCESE

French Onion Soup

4 medium onions
7 tbsp butter
2 tbsp flour
7 oz bread
Grated Parmesan
Grated Gruyère
Salt
Pepper
Optional: bouillon cubes or beef broth *(p88)*

Thinly slice the onions and place them in a saucepan with the butter. When the onions begin to brown slightly, add the flour. Cook for a minute or two, then add 2 quarts of water or, if you want to make the soup tastier, you can add bouillon cubes or beef broth. Season with salt and pepper and boil slowly for 30 minutes.

Cut the bread into slices and toast them to a golden color. In an ovenproof pan, make a layer of toasts, sprinkle with plenty of grated Parmesan and a little Gruyère cheese, and mix together, adding, if you like, a few pieces of butter, and continue to alternate layers of bread and cheese, ending with a thick layer of cheese and pepper. Slowly pour the onion broth through a sieve into the pan, letting the bread soak for a few minutes. Put in a preheated oven until the top layer is nicely golden.

ZUPPA DI CIPOLLE E UOVA

Egg and Onion Soup

10½ tbsp butter
2 onions
2 tbsp flour
4 egg yolks
Grated Parmesan
Toasted bread

Melt 2 or 3 tablespoons of butter in a Dutch oven and add the onion cut into very thin slices. Let the onion cook slowly, adding some water if necessary, and when it is cooked, stir in the flour.

In a pot, bring 6 cups salted water to a boil. Add a ladle of the water to the Dutch oven, and then add the remaining water in two or three batches. Cover and let it simmer for 30 minutes.

Put the egg yolks, the remaining butter, and the grated Parmesan in a soup terrine. Strain the onion broth through a sieve. Use a wooden spoon and some broth to blend the eggs, a few tablespoons of Parmesan, and the butter. Then slowly add the rest of the broth. Give one last stir and bring to the table, serving the slices of toasted bread on the side.

ZUPPA DI FAGIOLI

White Bean Soup

1 lb dried white beans
Olive oil
Sage
Garlic
Toasted bread slices
Salt
Pepper

Soak the dried beans for 12 hours or, even better, overnight. Put them in a saucepan with 2 tablespoons of oil, the sage, whole cloves of garlic, and cold water - but not too much - and no salt.

Bring the pot to a boil. Reduce the heat to a simmer, cover, and cook slowly until the water has been almost completely absorbed. It will take about 3 hours.

When they are almost done, add salt. Remove the garlic and spread them on the toast. Finish the soup with a little oil and plenty of pepper.

ZUPPA DI FAGIOLI E BIETOLE

Bean and Chard Soup

14 oz dried cannellini beans
2¼ lb Swiss chard
Olive oil
Toasted bread slices
Salt
Pepper

Battuto:
3½ oz lardo or guanciale, onion, celery stalk, carrot, garlic, parsley

Soak the beans for 12 hours or, ideally, overnight. Put them in a pot with cold water and boil them until they are completely cooked—about 2 hours.

Cook the Swiss chard, well cleaned and rinsed, in a saucepan with lightly salted boiling water and then drain.

Make the *battuto*: Chop together the lardo, onion, celery, carrot, garlic, and parsley. Add to a saucepan along with some oil and sauté. When the ingredients are colored, douse them with two glasses of water. Now, add the beans and the Swiss chard and let them develop flavor. Place a few slices of toasted bread in each bowl and then pour in the soup.

ZUPPA DI FAVE CON LE COTICHE

Fava Bean Soup with Pork Skins

1¾ lb dried peeled fava beans
10 oz fresh pork skins
3½ oz fatty prosciutto
Parsley
Marjoram
Toasted bread slices
2 onions
1 tsp tomato paste
Salt

Soak the dried beans in water for at least a day, then drain and place them in a saucepan, cover with cold water, add salt, and cook for about 1 hour.

Scrape and rinse the pork skins, boil them for a few minutes, then wash them again and cut them into pieces about 1¼ inches long.

Put the fatty prosciutto, parsley, and marjoram in a saucepan and let it heat up. Add the chopped onions. When the onions have taken on a light golden color, put the tomato paste in the pan. Let the tomato cook for about 10 minutes, then add the pork skins and moisten everything with a little water.

Once the pork is cooked, after 1 hour or more, drain the beans, add them to the saucepan and let everything season together over moderate heat for 15 minutes. Place the slices of lightly toasted bread on top of each bowl and distribute the soup.

ZUPPA DI FUNGHETTI

Mushroom Soup

1 lb cultivated mushrooms, button or bigger
3½ tbsp butter
1 cup fine dried breadcrumbs
7 tbsp cream of rice
Lemon
Salt
Pepper

Clean the mushrooms, wash them quickly in acidulated water, dry them, and cut them into thin slices. Cook about 20 percent of these mushrooms with the butter in a skillet over high heat, adding salt and a little lemon juice after a few minutes of cooking. As soon as the mushrooms are cooked, set them aside, covered with a sheet of was paper so they don't turn black.

In a pot, combine 6 cups cold water, the breadcrumbs, and the remaining mushrooms and cook over a light heat for 1 hour.

Remove the pan from the heat and purée the contents in a food mill or a blender. Return the purée to the same pot.

Stir the cream of rice with a little water in a bowl and pour it into the pot. Add the reserved cooked mushrooms, season with salt and pepper, put the pot back over heat, and let it boil for a few minutes. Pour the soup into bowls and serve hot.

ZUPPA DI PATATE

Potato Soup

2¼ lb potatoes
1 onion
Garlic
Parsley
1 celery stalk
1 carrot
2 tbsp butter
Milk
Fried bread cubes
Salt
Pepper

Peel and chop the potatoes, place them in a saucepan, cover them with water, and cook until tender. Scoop them out, purée them, and return to the same water in which they were boiled.

Chop the onion, a small piece of garlic, a few parsley leaves, a stalk of celery, and a carrot. Place this mixture in a small pan with butter, season with salt and pepper, and when it is cooked add it to the potatoes in their water.

Check the thickness of the soup and, if it is too thick, dilute it with milk. When it is time to serve, put fried bread cubes in the bowls and then pour over the soup.

ZUPPA DI POMODORI

Tomato Soup with Parmesan Crostini

6 large tomatoes
3½ oz onion
1 tbsp butter
1 tbsp flour
Parsley
6½ cups vegetable broth *(p90)*
Cream
Salt
Pepper

White sauce:
1½ tbsp butter, 5 tbsp flour, ¾ cup milk

Parmesan crostini:
bread loaf, butter, cream, ¼ cup grated Parmesan

Peel, seed and coarsely cut the tomatoes. Thinly slice the onion and cook it gently in a saucepan with the butter until done without being brown. Sprinkle the flour on the onions and stir, letting it just brown. Add the tomatoes and the chopped parsley. Season with salt and pepper and let the tomatoes cook over a very low heat, stirring often. Add the most of the broth, keeping some aside, and cook gently for about 30 minutes.

Pass everything through a very fine sieve or use a blender. Return it to the pot and set it over the heat for a few minutes, adding a few more spoonfuls of broth if the soup is too thick. Put a glass of cream and the rest of the broth in the pot.

Make a thick white sauce *(p16)* using the ingredient amounts listed here. When it is ready, add a little cream and a few spoonfuls of the grated Parmesan.

To make the Parmesan crostini, cut round slices of bread ⅓ inch thick and fry them in butter. Put some of the Parmesan sauce on each slice of bread and sprinkle with more Parmesan and some melted butter. Put these crostini in a hot oven for a few minutes, until they are lightly browned.

Serve the soup with the Parmesan crostini on the side.

ZUPPA DI ZUCCHINE

Zucchini Soup

6 large zucchini
2 tbsp lard
6½ cups vegetable broth *(p90)* or bouillon cube
6 eggs
Grated Parmesan
Parsley
Basil
Toasted bread
Salt
Pepper

Wash and cut the zucchini into cubes and put them in a pan with the lard, salt, and pepper. After frying them for a few minutes and before they start to brown, add enough broth to cover them. Cover the pan and finish cooking.

When ready to serve, beat the eggs with a few spoonfuls of grated Parmesan, a little chopped parsley and basil and pour all over the zucchini. Stir, reduce the heat, and cook for 2 or 3 minutes more to warm through.

Pour over a few slices of toasted bread in bowls.

ZUPPA SANTÉ

Santé Soup

4 potatoes
3 carrots
1 lb cabbage
1 onion
1 leek
2 celery stalks
10 oz lettuce or bitter greens
3½ tbsp butter
Grated Parmesan
2 quarts vegetable broth *(p90)*
Diced bread or toasted slices
Butter, for frying
Salt
Pepper
Optional: shelled peas

Clean the potatoes and carrots and cut them in small strips, removing the central woodiness of the carrots. Parboil a small cabbage and run the leaves under cold water, drain them and cut into thin strips. Thinly slice the onion, leek, and celery along with a little lettuce or greens and put everything in a saucepan with the butter and a pinch of salt. You can also add a few spoonfuls of shelled peas.

Set the saucepan over low heat, cover, and let the vegetables stew slowly for 30 minutes. Remember that they only need to wilt in the butter.

After 30 minutes, add the broth and let it boil gently over very low heat for another 30 minutes.

Garnish the soup with diced bread fried in butter, or with slices of toasted bread and grated Parmesan served separately.

ZUPPA SPAGNOLA FREDDA

Gazpacho

2 tomatoes
2 green bell peppers
Garlic
2 cucumbers
Olive oil
2 tbsp vinegar
Crackers
Salt
Pepper
Optional: poached eggs

Roast and seed the bell peppers. Cube the tomatoes, green peppers, onions, garlic, and cucumbers. Put everything in a large bowl and season with a glass of oil, vinegar, salt, and pepper. Place the bowl in the fridge.

When it is cold, add some crushed crackers, stir and serve. You can also add poached eggs.

"Everyone knows how to cook pasta. Not everyone knows how to cook it properly."

The plate of pasta with which the majority of Italians begin their meals is not only a delicacy, but also an energy food, rich in carbohydrates and made nutritionally complete by the fats from the toppings. The many varieties of pasta, and the even more numerous toppings, provide a vast field to explore. Here, we provide recipes for the most popular pasta dishes.

Dried pasta is a term used to differentiate it from fresh egg pasta. It is made with durum wheat flour or, better still, with durum wheat semolina, mixed with water in a process that has now become completely mechanized. Some of the dried pasta shapes in the recipes are interchangeable, but in most cases the shape has been chosen to best retain the sauce.

Fresh egg pasta, excellent when served in the usual way as tagliatelle, is perhaps at its most delicious when it contains one of the fillings that give life to famous first courses such as tortellini, agnolotti, and ravioli. Tortellini are shaped like a ring and are one of the best known and tastiest gastronomic specialties—the pride of Emilian cuisine. Agnolotti consist of a filling of minced meat enclosed in a shell of egg pasta, in various shapes. There are many ways to prepare the filling, for which you can use beef, veal, pork, or chicken mixed with egg yolks and ricotta.

Rice is available commercially in many different types: long-grain rice is suitable for soups and stews; medium-grain for pancakes and croquettes; short-grain for risotto and broths; some harder varieties are recommended for rice salads.

Gnocchi was one of the first original pasta types brought to the table, back then composed simply of flour and water. But with the appearance of the potato, gnocchi got a vigorous boost. Gnocchi are prepared from flour, potatoes, polenta, semolina, and spinach and take on very varied shapes and sizes. It is difficult to give exact amounts of flour because some varieties absorb more, others less. Generally however, ¾ cup flour is needed for every 1 pound of potatoes. Gnocchi is an easy dish, although not quick to prepare.

Polenta, or cornmeal, comes as yellow or white and even blue and should be cooked in salted water. The white, usually found around Venice, is often ground finer, while the yellow tends to be sweeter and have more vitamins. As such, it is more often used for pastries. Yellow polenta tends to be favored outside of Italy. Both yellow and white varieties are very nutritious and easy to digest.

PASTA, RISO, GNOCCHI E POLENTA

PASTA, RICE, GNOCCHI & POLENTA

4

TYPES OF PASTA

Every type of pasta has a purpose and often a sauce to match. Of course many are interchangeable. The differences are minimal, for example, ***cannolicchi*** *is a tight coiled spiral whereas* ***fusilli*** *are open spirals that allow the sauce to coat a greater area inside. Some say there are 350 shapes of pasta, others say 650. Some are just smaller variations as in* ***lasagnette*** *or* ***maccheroncini.***

Spaghetti *is now universal but lesser known are* ***bavette,*** *which are narrower; and* ***bucatini*** *which are thicker but also have a hole through the middle, and* ***trenette*** *has a little ridge to one side.* ***Tonnarelli*** *are almost square tubes like spaghetti appreciated for being a little rougher at the edges so better for sauces. Each has its own destiny.*

Shells like ***conchiglie,*** *and tubes like* ***rigatoni*** *or* ***maccheroni*** *offer more collaboration with their sauces, while flat sheets like lasagnette let the sauce cover the whole surface and on both sides.*

Egg pastas can be bought dried or fresh or can be made at home. The proportions for ***pappardelle*** *for example are 3 ½ cups flour and 4 eggs to make enough for 6 people. Pappardelle should be cut 2 fingers wide, or more, but* ***fettuccine*** *should only be a finger wide and* ***tagliatelle*** *half of that.*

Stuffed egg pastas are rightly among the most famous and reputed when they have a filling that has been specially designed to suit their shape. ***Tortellini*** *are shaped like a ring and are one of the best known and tastiest gastronomic specialties – the pride of Emilian cuisine.* ***Agnolotti*** *consist of a filling of minced meat enclosed in a shell of egg pasta, in various shapes. There are many ways to prepare the fillings for these pasta shapes for which you can use beef, veal, pork or chicken mixed with egg yolks and ricotta.*

Most pastas are cooked in boiling water, though some pasta dishes, to make the best use of the sauces, require the use of an oven.

DRIED PASTA

TO COOK AND PREPARE DRIED PASTA

There are a series of steps that have to be done carefully and need your undivided attention.

The water must be carefully measured. The calculation is easy: **10 cups of water for every 1 pound of pasta.**

The pan must have high, rounded sides and be large enough to provide enough space for the pasta to move around comfortably and thus avoid the gummy texture of pasta cooked in insufficient water. The pan must also have a lid that fits perfectly.

Add the salt as soon as the water starts to boil. **There should be about 1 tablespoon for each quart of water.**

The pasta must be added to the boiling water at just the right moment, when the water starts a rolling boil. Spread out the pasta in the boiling water – note that some shapes of pasta, like fettuccine, have a tendency to cling together, so stir well with the utmost care, using, if possible, a special wooden fork.

As soon as the water comes back to a boil, reduce the heat so the pasta can cook gently. It is not possible to determine with mathematical exactitude how long it will take because it depends on how the pasta has been made, its thickness, and the quality of flour, all of which can vary.

It is important to ensure the pasta does not overcook and to remove it from the heat as soon as it reaches the point that cooks call "al dente," which is when the pasta has lost its stiffness but still offers a certain resistance as you bite into it.

It is a good idea to prepare everything you will need to add to the pasta in advance. It is also particularly useful to have a warm serving dish on hand as well as sauce and grated cheese.

When all the various components are in place, take the pan off the heat as soon as the pasta is ready. Pour in a glass of cold water to stop the water from boiling further. Quickly drain the pasta, reserving a bit of the cooking water in case the pasta seems too dry before you season it, or you can use it to dilute the sauce if it seems too thick.

As soon as you have drained the pasta, turn it into the serving dish and immediately toss with the prepared sauce or seasoning.

BAVETTE ALLA TRASTEVERINA

Bavette Trastevere Style

Olive oil
3 garlic cloves
7 anchovy fillets
1 (35 oz) can peeled tomatoes (or a jar of tomato paste)
5 oz tinned tuna in olive oil
1 lb fresh mushrooms (or porcini)
2 tbsp butter
1 tbsp parsley
1 lb 5 oz bavette pasta
Salt
Pepper

Heat half a glass of oil with a clove of garlic which you remove as soon as the oil is hot. Fillet and cut 3 of the anchovies into small pieces, add to the pan. As soon as they have lightly browned, add the tomatoes. Flake the tuna and add to the sauce as it thickens. Season with a pinch of salt and plenty of pepper.

Carefully clean the mushrooms and slice finely. Heat another half glass of oil and fry the remaining 2 garlic cloves until they just start to color. Add the mushrooms, season, and turn the heat up high.

Finely mash the remaining 4 anchovies with the blade of a knife and blend with the butter. When all traces of moisture have evaporated from the mushrooms, add the anchovy butter and, once melted, a good tablespoon of chopped parsley.

In the meantime, cook the pasta in plenty of lightly salted boiling water until al dente. Drain and toss with the tomato and tuna sauce, scatter with the mushrooms, and serve straight away.

BAVETTE CON FAVE FRESCHE

Bavette with Fresh Fava Beans

3 lb 5 oz fresh fava beans
2 cipollini onions
Olive oil
1 lb 5 oz bavette pasta
Grated Parmesan
Salt

Shell the favas, then peel them and place in a bowl.

Heat the finely chopped onions in the oil. When they turn golden, add the beans, moistening with a ladle of hot water. Lightly salt, turn up the heat, and cook until the water has evaporated.

Cook the pasta in lightly salted boiling water, taking care not to overcook. Drain, toss with the beans, and sprinkle generously with ⅓ cup grated Parmesan.

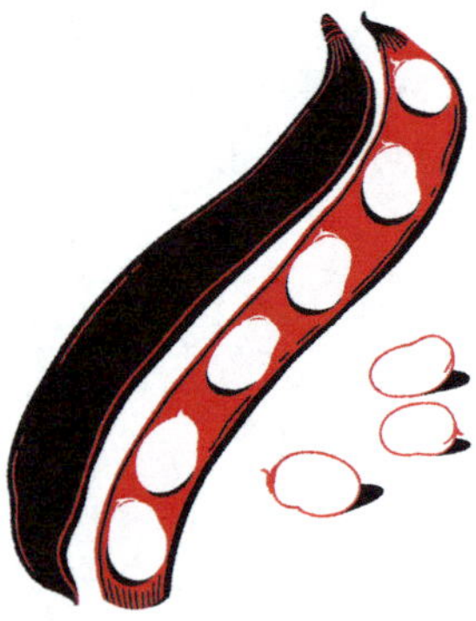

BAVETTE IN SALSA D'UOVO

Bavette in Egg Sauce

3 egg yolks
4 anchovy fillets
5 oz mozzarella
1 lb 5 oz bavette pasta
7 tbsp butter
Salt

Place the egg yolks in a bowl with the filleted chopped anchovies and mozzarella cut into cubes. Mix carefully.

Cook the pasta in lightly salted boiling water until al dente, and as soon as it is ready, drain and turn into a pan of melted butter.

Over low heat, stirring constantly, incorporate the egg mixture into the pasta and allow the flavor to diffuse for a few minutes, moistening with a few spoonfuls of the pasta cooking water. When the mozzarella begins to melt and the eggs start to become creamy, turn out onto a serving dish.

BUCATINI ALL'AMATRICIANA

Bucatini Amatriciana

1 onion
3½ oz guanciale
1 tbsp lard
2¼ lb tomatoes
1 lb 5 oz bucatini
1 cup grated pecorino
Salt
Pepper

Chop the onion with the guanciale and heat in a pan with the lard. When the onions start to lightly brown, add the tomatoes (peeled, seeded, and chopped). Season with salt and plenty of pepper—be restrained with the salt because the guanciale is already salted—and turn the heat up high for a few minutes, until the tomatoes are cooked but not breaking up.

Cook the bucatini in plenty of lightly salted boiling water and, as soon as it is ready, toss with the sauce and grated pecorino.

ADA SAYS: *This recipe is a Roman classic, a speciality of many of the city's trattorias.*

BUCATINI CON COZZE E VONGOLE

Bucatini with Mussels and Clams

3 lb 5 oz mussels
Olive oil
2¼ lb clams
2 oz dried mushrooms
Parsley
1 lb 5 oz bucatini
Chili flakes
Salt

Wash the mussels and scrape with a small knife, removing any beard. Heat them in a large skillet with a little oil, shaking the pan as you cook them. When they have all opened—diskard any that remain closed—remove the empty half shell and place the mussels in a bowl. Allow the pan liquid to stand for a short time, then strain and pour back over the mussels.

Wash the clams and heat them in the same way as the mussels. When they have opened—diskard any that remain closed—remove the empty side of the shell and add the clams to the mussels along with the strained liquid from the pan.

Soak the mushrooms in cold water to reconstitute; rinse and cook them in a small pan with 2 tablespoons of oil, a few splashes of water, and a pinch of salt. Finish with chopped parsley.

Cook the pasta in plenty of lightly salted boiling water, drain, and toss with half a glass of oil. Arrange on a large platter and cover the pasta with the mussels and clams in their side of the shells, their juice, and the mushrooms. Sprinkle the dish with parsley sprigs and chili flakes.

BUCATINI CON GAMBERI E CALAMARETTI

Bucatini with Shrimp and Baby Squid

2¼ lb mussels
1 lb clams
Olive oil
10 oz baby squid or cuttlefish
Parsley
Sage
White wine
6 tomatoes
10 oz mushrooms
Garlic
1 carrot
Onion
3½ tbsp butter
7 oz shrimp
Cognac
1 lb 5 oz bucatini
Salt
Pepper
Optional: cayenne

Scrape the mussels well, remove any beard, and rinse both the mussels and clams. Heat them with a little oil in a covered pan over moderate heat, shaking the pan from time to time until they open—diskard any that remain closed. Remove the mussels and clams from their shells and place them in a small bowl. Strain the juices and slowly pour over the clams and mussels, diskarding any sediment left in the bottom of the pan.

Remove the ink sacs and eyes from the squid or cuttlefish and wash in plenty of running water. If they seem too big, cut into smaller pieces. Heat half a glass of oil in a saucepan and, when nice and hot, add a generous tablespoon of chopped parsley and a sage leaf quickly followed by the squid or cuttlefish. Fry briefly, pour in half a glass of white wine and as soon as it has evaporated, add the tomatoes (peeled, seeded, and chopped). Sauté the tomatoes briefly to bring out their flavor, then moisten with some of the mussel and clam juice. Cover the pan and gently cook the squid or cuttlefish.

Slice and fry the mushrooms with a dash of oil, salt, and pepper. When the moisture has evaporated, add a chopped clove of garlic. Cook a little longer and then mix with the squid or cuttlefish, which should, by now, be perfectly cooked. Add the mussels and clams and keep the pan warm.

Very gently fry a little carrot and the onion, both finely chopped, in the butter. Add the well washed shrimp and increase the heat, stirring and shaking the pan. As soon as they are cooked, this will only take a few minutes, pour in half a glass of Cognac, flambé and wait for the flame to die down. Shell the shrimp and add to the seafood sauce. Diskard the shells.

Break the bucatini into pieces about 4 inches long and cook in plenty of boiling, salted water. Drain and place in a bowl. Toss with half the prepared sauce, mix in a good pinch of pepper or, if you prefer, a little cayenne.

Arrange the pasta on a serving dish, cover with the other half of the sauce, and sprinkle with chopped parsley before serving immediately.

CANNOLICCHI AL BASILICO

Cannolicchi with Basil

2½ oz fatty prosciutto
Parsley
Garlic
1 tbsp lard
2¼ lb beefsteak tomatoes
1 lb 5 oz cannolicchi pasta
9 tbsp grated Parmesan
Basil
Salt
Pepper

Chop the prosciutto finely with a little parsley and a garlic clove. Lightly fry in the lard, then add the tomatoes—peeled, seeded, and chopped. Turn up the heat and season with salt and pepper. When the tomatoes are almost cooked, which shouldn't take long, cook the pasta in lightly salted boiling water. If the sauce seems a little thick you can dilute, while the pasta is still cooking, with a few spoonfuls of the pasta water.

Drain, turn into a dish, and toss with the prepared sauce, grated Parmesan, and a handful of shredded fresh basil.

CANNOLICCHI CON FAGIOLI FRESCHI

Cannolicchi with Fresh White Beans

2¼ lb fresh white beans in their pods, or 15 oz canned beans
1 celery stalk
3½ oz prosciutto
Parsley
Basil
Olive oil
4¼ cups tomato passata
1 lb medium cannolicchi
Salt

Shell the beans and place in a saucepan with plenty of cold water and a chopped celery stalk, but don't add salt. Bring slowly to a boil, cover, reduce the heat. and cook over low heat for about 30 minutes. Only salt lightly once the beans are cooked, then let stand in their warm cooking broth.

Chop the prosciutto with a few parsley sprigs and basil leaves. Fry briefly in 2 tablespoons of oil until the fat melts and then add the passata. Season with salt and cook until the sauce thickens. Drain the beans, add to the sauce, and simmer over very low heat for a few minutes.

About 30 minutes before serving, cook the pasta in boiling salted water until just shy, drain, and add to the bean sauce stirring from time to time so the pasta integrates well with the sauce. Then, place over moderate heat for 5 or 6 minutes, and finish with some shredded basil leaves and pour into a serving dish. The beans and pasta should not be too wet but should be coated with quite a thick sauce. There is no need for cheese.

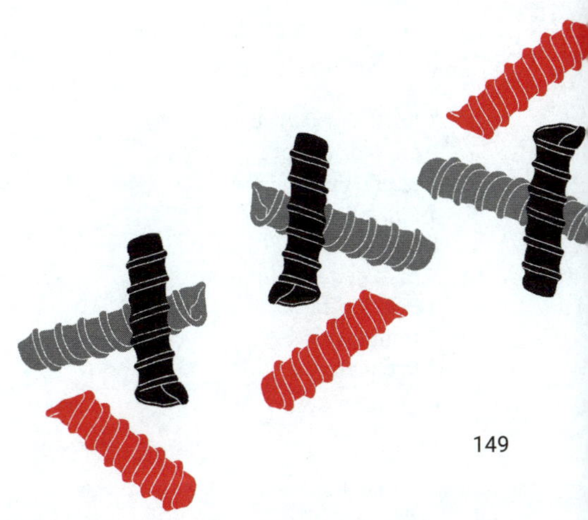

CONCHIGLIE AL MASCARPONE E FUNGHI

Conchiglie with Mascarpone and Mushrooms

1 oz dried mushrooms
3½ tbsp butter
1 lb fresh mushrooms
Olive oil
Garlic
Parsley
5 oz mascarpone
1 lb 5 oz conchiglie
9 tbsp grated Parmesan
Salt
Pepper

Soak the dried mushrooms for about 15 minutes in cold water, then carefully rinse and cut into pieces—diskarding any earthy bits. Cook gently in a small pan with half of the butter, half a glass of water, and a pinch of salt for about 20 minutes.

Carefully wipe the fresh mushrooms clean, wash quickly, break off the stems, and slice very finely. Heat a glass of oil and a garlic clove in a large skillet and as soon as the garlic starts to color remove it and add the fresh mushrooms. Cook over medium-high heat for a few minutes. Season with salt, pepper, and a handful of chopped parsley. Mix the mascarpone with both the fresh and dried mushrooms and the rest of the softened butter.

Cook the pasta in plenty of boiling salted water until al dente, drain and toss with the sauce. Sprinkle with grated Parmesan.

CONCHIGLIE CON GAMBERONI

Conchiglie with Shrimp

Olive oil
1 lb tomatoes
2 garlic cloves
Red chili
12 shrimp
1 lb 5 oz conchiglie
Parsley
Salt

In a large pan, place half a glass of oil, the tomatoes—peeled, seeded and chopped—garlic cloves, a little red chili, and a pinch of salt. Cover and cook over medium-high heat for about 10 minutes, stirring 2 or 3 times.

Meticulously wash the shrimp, add to the pan, and sauté for a few more minutes.

Cook the pasta in plenty of boiling salted water, drain and transfer to a round serving dish. Toss with the shrimp and sauce and scatter with plenty of chopped parsley.

CONCHIGLIE CON RICOTTA E SPINACI

Conchiglie with Ricotta and Spinach

1 lb 10 oz fresh spinach (or 16 oz frozen)
3½ tbsp butter
1 cup milk
2 egg yolks
9 tbsp grated Parmesan
14 oz ricotta
5 tomatoes
1 lb conchiglie
Salt

Carefully wash and boil the spinach in a little salted water, drain well, squeeze to get rid of excess water and shred.

Melt the butter in a saucepan, then add the spinach and leave for a few minutes to absorb the flavor. Pour the milk into a bowl and add the egg yolks, grated Parmesan, and ricotta. Carefully mix, then combine with the spinach. Finally add a pinch of salt.

Peel, seed, and slice the tomatoes. Cook the pasta in boiling salted water until al dente, drain, and toss with the spinach sauce. Garnish with the strips of tomato.

CONCHIGLIONI RAFFINATI

Refined Conchiglioni

10 oz porcini mushrooms
3½ oz ham
Olive oil
White wine
2 fresh artichoke hearts
1 lb 5 oz conchiglioni
3½ tbsp butter
Basil
Lemon
Salt
Pepper

Clean the mushrooms and separate the stems from the caps. Scrape and trim the stems, wash quickly, dry carefully, and cut into thin slices. Meticulously clean the caps using the tip of a small knife. Wipe with a kitchen towel to remove any traces of soil. Dice the ham and porcini caps and season with salt and pepper. Fry the caps and stalks in oil, adding a glass of white wine. Finely slice the artichoke hearts, rub with lemon juice, and add to the mix.

Cook the pasta in plenty of lightly salted boiling water until al dente. Drain and toss with the butter, mushrooms, artichoke hearts, and ham. Scatter with chopped basil, mix with care so as not to break up the porcini caps, and serve warm with a squeeze of lemon.

FETTUCCINE ALLA CREMA

Fettuccine in Cream Sauce

7 tbsp butter
2 cups cream
3 egg yolks
1 cup grated Parmesan
Nutmeg
1 lb 5 oz fettuccine
Salt

Soften the butter with the cream in a bowl and add the egg yolks, half the grated Parmesan, and a dusting of nutmeg. Mix carefully until the ingredients have thoroughly blended into the cream.

Cook the pasta in boiling salted water, taking care not to overcook it. Drain, place in a dish, mix gently with the sauce, and finally grate in the remaining Parmesan.

FETTUCCINE CON PROSCIUTTO E FUNGHETTI

Fettuccine with Ham and Mushrooms

10 oz button mushrooms
3½ oz ham
10½ tbsp butter
Basil
1 lb 5 oz fettuccine
Grated Parmesan
Salt

Wash the mushrooms and dry in a kitchen towel. Break off the stems and slice thinly. Cut the ham into strips. Heat ⅔ of the butter in a skillet and as soon as it melts, add the mushrooms and fry for about 10 minutes. Add the ham and 3 or 4 shredded basil leaves. Stir, sprinkle in a tiny touch of salt, and quickly take the pan off the heat.

Cook the pasta in plenty of boiling salted water until al dente. Drain, add to the prepared sauce along with the remaining butter and heaps of grated Parmesan.

FUSILLI ALLEGRIA

Fusilli Allegria

3½ oz chicken livers
2 tbsp butter
3 tbsp olive oil
1 shallot
16 oz canned tomatoes
10 oz ground turkey
2 tbsp dry Marsala
Parsley
1 lb 5 oz fusilli
Grated Parmesan
Salt
Pepper

Prepare the chicken livers: With a small, sharp knife, remove any greenish spots of gall and cut each liver into two or three parts. In a pan, melt the butter, oil, and a chopped shallot. Sauté for a few minutes, then add the tomatoes. Lower the heat and cook on a medium heat for about 20 minutes. Add the turkey, stir carefully, bring to a boil, and cook for a few minutes over high heat. Add the chicken livers, season with a pinch of salt and pepper, and add the Marsala. When the wine evaporates, stir in the chopped parsley.

Cook the pasta in plenty of lightly salted boiling water until al dente. Drain, toss with the sauce, sprinkle with grated Parmesan, and serve right away.

LASAGNETTE CON SPINACI E FUNGHI

Lasagnette with Spinach and Mushrooms

1 lb spinach
10½ tbsp butter
1 oz dried mushrooms
1 lb 5 oz lasagnette
9 tbsp grated Parmesan
Salt

Carefully wash and clean the spinach, then cook in a little water. Drain, squeeze well, and roughly chop. Soften in a skillet with a knob of butter.

Soak the mushrooms in cold water to revive for 20 minutes, clean well, and cook in a small saucepan with another knob of butter, salt, and a splash of water before chopping into small pieces.

Cook the pasta in lightly salted boiling water. Drain and toss with the remaining butter, the spinach, and mushrooms and sprinkle with grated Parmesan.

ADA SAYS: *This tasty dish is made with lasagnette, which are dried pasta strips a couple of fingers wide with wavy edges.*

LASAGNETTE DEL LUCCHESE

Lasagnette Lucca Style

Tomato sauce with dried mushrooms *(p39)*
1 lb spinach
7 oz ricotta
Nutmeg
Cinnamon
1 lb 5 oz lasagnette
2 tbsp olive oil or butter
1 cup grated Parmesan
Salt

Make a tomato sauce with dried mushrooms, substituting 4 cups passata for the fresh tomatoes if desired.

Wash the spinach and boil in a small amount of water. Drain and squeeze dry until it is the size of a small orange. Chop finely and place in a small bowl with the ricotta. Mix well until it becomes a creamy paste and season with a dusting of nutmeg, cinnamon, and a pinch of salt. Stir the spinach and ricotta into the tomato sauce, heat, and bring to a boil.

Cook the pasta in plenty of lightly salted boiling water, drain and toss with the olive oil or butter, the spinach/ricotta sauce, and plenty of grated Parmesan.

MACCHERONCINI CON LE POLPETTINE

Maccheroncini with Little Meatballs

Beef and tomato sauce *(p35)*
5 oz breadcrumbs
Milk
2 oz beef marrow
5½ tbsp butter
9 tbsp grated Parmesan
2 eggs
Flour
14 oz maccheroncini
Salt

Make a good beef and tomato sauce as directed. When it's thick and full of flavor and the meat is thoroughly cooked, remove the meat, let cool, chop finely, and set aside.

Soak the breadcrumbs in a little milk, squeeze with your hands, then heat the paste in a pan, stirring until it dries out and becomes thick and supple. Let cool.

Mince the cooked meat, beef marrow, and breadcrumbs together, place in a bowl, and beat in, a little at a time, 2 tablespoons melted butter, 2 tablespoons grated Parmesan, and the eggs until everything is thoroughly blended.

Dust your hands with flour, pinch off pieces of the meat mixture about the size of a small walnut and roll into balls. Arrange each one close, but not too close, together in a large, lightly buttered pan.

Pour enough sauce over the meatballs to submerge them, cover the pan, and heat gently until the sauce is hot but not boiling. Cook for 10 minutes and then test by prodding a meatball with a finger to see if it is nice and firm.

Cook the pasta in plenty of boiling salted water. When ready, drain and toss with some of the sauce and 2 tablespoons Parmesan. Arrange in a large dish and top with the meatballs, generous amounts of the remaining sauce, and sprinkle with the rest of the Parmesan. Serve right away.

MACCHERONCINI CON LE SARDE AL FORNO

Maccheroncini with Baked Sardines and Wild Fennel

Wild fennel
2 onions
Olive oil
1 lb fresh sardines
5 or 6 anchovy fillets
Saffron
6 tbsp pine nuts
5 tbsp currants
1½ lb maccheroncini
Salt
Pepper

The indispensable ingredient in this recipe is wild fennel, collected from the countryside. Pick carefully over the fennel and wash and boil only the most tender part. Drain and chop the fennel but reserve the cooking water.

Chop the onions and fry in a glass of oil until they take on a beautiful golden color. Carefully clean and bone half the sardines and add to the pan, crushing and mixing them vigorously with a wooden spoon to reduce them to a pulp. After the sardines, add the anchovies, washed, and boned with a few more drops of oil.

Keeping the pan over heat, add the chopped fennel, a pinch of saffron, salt, pepper, pine nuts, and currants - soaked in cold water and drained. If the mixture seems too thick, dilute it with some of the fennel cooking water. Cover the pan and keep warm.

Remove the backbone ("butterfly") from the remaining sardines without separating the two fillets from each other. Rinse, dry, and lightly sear on both sides in a skillet with a little oil and salt. Add the reserved fennel water to a large pan of water and bring to the boil.

Cook the pasta and as soon as it is just shy of al dente—not too done, because it is to go in the oven—drain, turn into a dish, and toss with half the prepared sauce. In a large baking dish, arrange a layer of pasta topped with a layer of the cooked sardines and a little of the sauce. Repeat until it is all used up. Cover and put in a preheated moderate oven and bake for 20 minutes. This dish can be eaten hot or cold: either way it will be exquisite.

ADA SAYS: *Pasta with sardines is a distinctive dish found mostly in Sicily.*

MACCHERONCINI E BROCCOLO ALLA SICILIANA

Maccheroncini and Broccoli Sicilian Style

Broccoli (or purple sprouting broccoli)
Oil for frying
1 lb 5 oz maccheroncini
1 cup grated pecorino
Salt

Peel off the leaves and divide the broccoli into florets. Parboil in lightly salted water, drain, and fry in a generous amount of oil.

Cook the pasta in plenty of lightly salted boiling water until al dente. Drain and toss with all or some of the frying oil, as you prefer, and with 2 tablespoons of the pecorino.

Oil a large baking dish, sprinkle another 2 tablespoons of the cheese over the bottom, and top with the pasta followed by the fried broccoli. Sprinkle the rest of the pecorino and bake in a preheated hot oven for about 10 minutes.

MACCHERONI AI QUATTRO FORMAGGI

Macaroni with Four Cheeses

3½ oz mozzarella
3½ oz Edam
3½ oz Gruyère
7 oz grated Parmesan
13 tbsp butter
1 lb 5 oz macaroni
Salt

As you see, the preparation is very easy but you have to pay attention to all the details: Make sure the butter is very hot but doesn't foam; the pasta is drained and tossed very quickly just before serving; the dish should be good and hot but not to the extent that the different cheeses melt into each other.

Cut the mozzarella, Edam, Gruyère, and half the Parmesan into fine slices the size of thick matches. The remainder of the Parmesan should be grated to serve later.

Extremely carefully melt the butter in a double boiler over high heat; it needs to be very hot but not foaming.

In the meantime, cook the pasta in plenty of boiling salted water until just a little past al dente. Drain well, toss with the slivers of cheese, and half the melted butter.

Put the cooked pasta in a large dish that retains the heat well, scatter with the remaining Parmesan, and drizzle with the rest of the butter.

ADA SAYS: *Four different cheeses form the basis for this recipe; but for the best result it is absolutely essential that they retain their individual character when the dish is served.*

MACCHERONI AI QUATTRO FORMAGGI FILANTI

Macaroni with Four String Cheeses

3½ oz Gruyère
3½ oz Edam
3½ oz provolone
3½ oz Fontina
1 lb 5 oz macaroni
Salt
Optional: grated Parmesan

Cream sauce:
3½ tbsp butter, ¼ cup flour,
2 cups beef broth or bouillon cube

Prepare a cream sauce *(p17)* using the ingredient amounts listed here.

Cut the four cheeses into strips not much bigger and not much longer than thick matches, mix them into the sauce, then take the pan off the stove, stirring carefully all the time.

Cook the pasta in plenty of boiling salted water until al dente, drain, toss with the sauce, and, if you wish, some grated Parmesan. Serve immediately while still really hot.

ADA SAYS: *In this recipe, the cheeses, enveloped in a creamy sauce, stretch and become very stringy when heated which explains the Italian name of the dish.*

MACCHERONI AL GRATIN

Macaroni Gratin

1 lb 5 oz macaroni
7 tbsp butter
Grated Parmesan
Breadcrumbs
Salt

White sauce:
3½ tbsp butter, 6½ tbsp flour,
4 cups milk

Prepare a white sauce *(p16)* with the ingredient amounts listed here.

Break the macaroni into small pieces and cook in plenty of boiling salted water. Drain and mix with the sauce, a lump of butter, and a fistful of grated Parmesan.

Butter a baking dish and pour in the pasta and its sauce. Mix the finely chopped breadcrumbs with more grated Parmesan and strew over the top. Dot with small pieces of butter and bake in a preheated oven for 10 minutes. Serve from the baking dish.

MACCHERONI CON MOZZARELLA

Macaroni with Mozzarella

2¼ lb tomatoes
1 onion
1 carrot
1 celery stalk
Basil
Oil for frying
2 eggplants
1 lb 5 oz macaroni
1 cup grated provolone
7 oz mozzarella
Salt
Pepper

Cut up the tomatoes and fry with the chopped onion, carrot, celery, basil and salt. Cook for 30 minutes, then pass all the vegetables through a food mill or purée in a blender.

Heat the oil in a saucepan and add the vegetable purée with a little salt and pepper. Cook until the sauce thickens.

Peel the eggplants, slice into rounds about ⅓ inch thick, and fry, a few at a time, in very hot oil.

Cook the pasta in plenty of lightly salted boiling water, drain, and toss with half the tomato sauce and the grated provolone.

In a baking dish, arrange layers of the dressed pasta, fried eggplant, and small slices of mozzarella. Finally pour over the remaining tomato sauce and bake in preheated hot oven for a few minutes to allow the pasta to simmer and the mozzarella to melt.

MACCHERONI CON RICOTTA

Macaroni with Ricotta

1 lb beef or pork joint
1 onion
1 celery stalk
1 carrot
Olive oil
Red wine
1¼ cups tomato passata
1 lb ricotta
7 oz provola soft cheese
1 lb 5 oz macaroni
9 tbsp grated Parmesan
Salt

First make your sauce: Roll and tie the beef or pork and arrange in a Dutch oven with the finely chopped onion, celery, and carrot. Drizzle with oil and place on the stove. Gently sauté the meat and wilt the vegetables. When the latter are almost done and the meat has acquired a beautiful brown color, season with a little salt and gradually pour over a glass of wine. When this evaporates, add the passata and slowly bring to the boil.

Once the meat is cooked, the sauce should be well reduced. Skim off the surface fat. Having prepared this sauce, turn your attention to the other ingredients: The ricotta, Neapolitan provola, and the meat from the sauce. Put the ricotta in a bowl and dilute with a few tablespoons of hot water until it becomes creamy. Add the chopped cooked meat and cubed provola.

Cook the pasta in lightly salted boiling water, drain and mix in a dish with some of the sauce and grated Parmesan.

At this point, in a baking dish, arrange alternating layers of pasta, ricotta, provola and meat. Pour over the remaining sauce and bake in a preheated moderate oven for about 10 minutes. Once it is simmering, place the dish on a tray and serve.

MACCHERONI IN INSALATA

Macaroni Salad

2¼ lb tomatoes
Basil
1 celery stalk
Garlic
Olive oil
Oregano
1 lb 5 oz macaroni
Salt
Pepper

Cut the tomatoes—without peeling or seeding—into pieces and place in a bowl. Add a bunch of finely chopped basil, celery, and garlic and dress the salad with oil, salt, pepper, and a good pinch of oregano. Toss gently and let stand for around 30 minutes.

Cook the pasta in plenty of salted boiling water until al dente. Drain and quickly rinse in cold water and drain again. Turn into a dish, mix well with the tomato salad, and let stand for a short while before serving, so the flavors mingle.

ADA SAYS: *This simple, delicious cold pasta salad is especially good in hot weather. The tomatoes must be very ripe.*

MACCHERONI IN SALSA DI FUNGHI

Macaroni in Wild Mushroom Sauce

2 oz dried mushrooms
7 tbsp butter
2 oz prosciutto
1 lb 5 oz maccheroni
Grated Parmesan
Salt

Soak the dried mushrooms in cold water. When they have reconstituted, rinse them again, squeeze and place in a small pan with half the butter and the chopped prosciutto, including the fat. When the fat melts, add enough warm water to cover the mushrooms. Salt very lightly and cook gently, adding a little extra water as the water evaporates. When the mushrooms are cooked, chop them with the little liquid left in the pan; if the sauce is too thick, add a drop more water. Pour this sauce into a pan and heat through. Finally stir in the rest of the butter, a piece at a time.

Cook the pasta in plenty of lightly salted boiling water until al dente. Drain and place in a large saucepan. Cover the pasta with the sauce and grated Parmesan, and mix together with a wooden spoon for a few minutes. When the pasta is bathed in the sauce, pour into a serving dish and serve hot.

ORECCHIETTE ALLA PUGLIESE

Orecchiette Pugliese

1 lb broccoli rabe
Olive oil
Garlic
1 lb 5 oz orecchiette
Salt
Pepper

Trim and chop the broccoli rabe. Heat a little oil in a pan with a garlic clove. Take the garlic out as soon as it starts to color. Add the broccoli rabe, season, and cook slowly over moderate heat, stirring from time to time. Moisten, if you think necessary, with a few tablespoons of water. Keep the pan covered so the steam does not escape or the greens will not cook properly and will lose their characteristic flavor.

Cook the orecchiette in plenty of salted boiling water. As soon as you drain the pasta, add to the pan containing the broccoli rabe and stir for a few minutes. Serve immediately.

PENNE ALL'ARRABBIATA

Penne Arrabbiata

3½ oz prosciutto
1 onion
Olive oil
4¼ cups tomato passata
1 red chili
1 lb 5 oz penne
1 cup grated pecorino
Salt

Chop the onion and prosciutto and fry in a pan with some olive oil. As soon as the onion starts to turn golden, pour in the passata. Salt very lightly and cook over low heat for about 30 minutes.

Chop the chili pepper into small pieces, mash with a fork, and, at the last moment, stir into the sauce.

Cook the pasta in plenty of salted boiling water until al dente. Drain, toss with the sauce, and sprinkle with grated pecorino.

PENNE ALLA VODKA

Penne with Vodka

Olive oil
Garlic
2¼ lb fresh tomatoes or canned
9 tbsp grated Parmesan
2 tbsp butter
1 cup cream
1 lb 5 oz penne rigate
Vodka
1 red chili
Basil
Salt

In a pan, heat half a glass of oil and a garlic clove. As soon as the garlic starts to turn golden diskard and add the fresh tomatoes (peeled, seeded, and chopped) or canned tomatoes. Season moderately, cover, and cook over low heat for about 30 minutes.

Grate the Parmesan into a small pan, add the softened butter and the cream and mix thoroughly.

Cook the penne in plenty of salted boiling water until al dente and drain. While the pasta cooks, bring the tomato sauce to a boil and add half a glass of vodka. Let it evaporate and at the last moment stir in the chili pepper chopped into small pieces.

Drain the penne well and add to the tomato sauce. Simmer for a few minutes and then pour into a serving bowl and carefully stir in the cheese and cream. Serve immediately.

PENNETTE PRIMAVERA

Spring Pennette Salad

3 carrots
1⅓ cups fresh peas
2 celery stalks
20 black olives, pitted
5 oz Gruyère
1¼ cups canned corn kernels
Olive oil
1 lb 5 oz pennette
Salt
Pepper

Peel the carrots. Boil for about 30 minutes in lightly salted water. Drain and cut into rounds.

Boil the peas for about 10 minutes in plenty of lightly salted water. Keep the heat high so the peas retain their green color, then drain and place in a bowl. Cut the celery into fine strips, slice the olives, and cube the Gruyère and add to the bowl. Finally add the well-drained corn and toss everything with a little oil.

Cook the pasta in plenty of salted boiling water until al dente, drain, and cool under running water. Drain again and add to the serving bowl. If necessary, add more oil. Mix the salad carefully.

RIGATONI ALLA RUCOLA

Rigatoni Salad with Arugula

1 lb 5 oz tomatoes
Olive oil
3 baby zucchini
14 oz mozzarella
Arugula
Basil
Oregano
1 lb 5 oz rigatoni
Salt
Pepper

Blanch, peel, seed, and cut the tomatoes into broad strips and place in a bowl with 2 tablespoons of oil.

Boil the zucchini for a few minutes in salted water. Cut into matchsticks and add to the tomatoes along with the diced mozzarella, plentiful shredded arugula and basil. Season with a pinch of oregano, salt, and pepper. Carefully mix and let stand for a couple of hours to absorb the flavors.

Cook the pasta in plenty of salted boiling water, drain and cool under running water. Drain again carefully. Add the rigatoni to the prepared salad and mix well.

RIGATONI CON LE ZUCCHINE

Rigatoni with Zucchini

2¼ lb zucchini
Olive oil
3½ tbsp butter
Parsley
2 eggs
1 cup grated Parmesan
1 lb 5 oz rigatoni
Salt
Pepper

Trim the ends of the zucchini, cut in quarters lengthwise, then cut each of these pieces into four. Heat 3 tablespoons of oil and the butter in a large pan and add the zucchini. Season with a good pinch of salt, cover the pan, and cook over medium heat for about 15 minutes before sprinkling with chopped parsley.

Whisk the eggs as if you were making a frittata, season with a pinch of salt, black pepper, and 2 tablespoons of grated Parmesan. Stir into the zucchini.

Cook the pasta in plenty of salted boiling water until al dente, drain and turn into a dish. Little by little, add the zucchini mixture, mixing very carefully so the eggs become creamy without curdling. Add the remaining Parmesan and serve immediately.

RIGATONI CON SALSICCE E UOVA

Rigatoni with Sausage and Eggs

10½ tbsp butter
Olive oil
6 fresh sausages
Beef broth *(p88)*
1 lb 5 oz rigatoni
Grated Parmesan
4 eggs
Salt

Heat ⅓ of the butter and 1 tablespoon of oil in a small pan over medium heat. Remove the sausages from their casings, crush them with a wooden spoon and as soon as the fat is hot, add them to the pan. Let them cook very gently so the sausage meat does not dry out, moistening from time to time with a few spoonfuls of broth or water.

Cook the pasta in lightly salted boiling water until only half-cooked. Drain and place in a Dutch oven. Toss with the sausage meat and continue to slowly cook covered over medium heat, occasionally adding a few ladles of more broth or water. The lid will help the pasta to thoroughly absorb the flavor of the sausage.

Still on the stove, once the pasta is cooked, add the remaining butter and plenty of Parmesan.

Mix well and take the dish off the heat. Beat the eggs, as if you were making a frittata, and pour them quickly onto the pasta, mixing very gently but thoroughly so the egg penetrates into the center of the dish. Cover again and keep the pan warm—but not directly over heat—for a few minutes while the eggs thicken. Take the pasta to the table.

SPAGHETTI AL GORGONZOLA

Spaghetti Gorgonzola

3½ tbsp butter
5 oz Gorgonzola
1 cup cream
9 tbsp grated Parmesan
1 lb 5 oz spaghetti
Salt

Place the butter and roughly diced Gorgonzola in a serving dish and use a wooden spatula to blend them thoroughly together. Mix in the cream and then the grated Parmesan.

Cook the pasta in plenty of lightly salted boiling water until al dente. Drain and turn into the dish with the cheese sauce. Carefully toss and serve as hot as possible.

SPAGHETTI ALLA CARBONARA

Spaghetti Carbonara

3 eggs
9 tbsp grated Parmesan or pecorino
7 oz pancetta
2 tbsp butter
Olive oil
1 lb 5 oz spaghetti
Salt
Peppercorns

Beat the eggs in a bowl, as if for a frittata, add the grated Parmesan or pecorino and coarsely ground peppercorns and mix well.

Cube the pancetta and sauté in a skillet with the butter and oil. Fry well and then add to the eggs, whisking with a fork and making sure the eggs do not curdle. The sauce should be creamy.

Cook the pasta in plenty of lightly salted boiling water until al dente. Drain and pour into a serving dish with the eggs. Stir and serve straight away.

SPAGHETTI ALLA CARBONARA DI MAGRO

Vegetarian Spaghetti Carbonara

3 eggs
1 cup grated Parmesan
1 cup grated Gruyère
Milk
Olive oil
1 lb 5 oz spaghetti
Salt
Pepper

Whisk the eggs in a serving bowl, as if you were making a frittata. Add the grated Parmesan, Gruyère, ¼ cup of milk, ¼ cup of olive oil, and a pinch of salt and pepper. Mix well together.

Cook the pasta in plenty of lightly salted boiling water until al dente. Drain and turn into the serving bowl. Toss well and send promptly to the table.

SPAGHETTI ALLE ERBE

Spaghetti with Herbs

1 onion
Olive oil
2 tbsp butter
Basil
Parsley
Mint
3½ tbsp pine nuts
Cream
1 lb 5 oz spaghetti
Grated pecorino
Grated Parmesan
Salt

Finely chop the onion and very gently fry with half a glass of oil and the butter for about 20 minutes. The onion should stay quite pale; add, if necessary, a splash of water. Season with a pinch of salt.

For best results, use a blender or processor to blend a handful of basil leaves, some sprigs of parsley, a few mint leaves, the pine nuts, a glass of oil, and a pinch of salt until well combined. Stir this into the onions and add ¾ cup of cream. Simmer, without boiling, over a very low flame.

Cook the spaghetti in plenty of lightly salted boiling water until al dente. Drain and toss with the herb and pine nut sauce and strew with the grated pecorino and Parmesan. Serve immediately.

SPAGHETTI AL NERO DI SEPPIE

Spaghetti with Squid Ink

1 lb 5 oz small cuttlefish
2 garlic cloves
Olive oil
White wine
2 tbsp tomato paste
1 lb 5 oz spaghetti
Parsley
Salt
Pepper

Carefully clean the cuttlefish, removing the eyes and bone. The body tube should be cut open to ensure the two sacs remain intact. One contains the black ink and the other a dark yellow liquid. These give the dish its flavor, so take care not to break them as they should open during the cooking.

Use a pan large enough to also hold the spaghetti. Gently fry the garlic in half a glass of oil. As soon as it begins to color, add the cuttlefish, still keeping the heat low. Once they begin to brown, pour in a glass of white wine, let it evaporate, and add the tomato paste diluted in a little water. Season, cover the pan, and cook over very low heat for about 15 minutes.

In the meantime, cook the spaghetti in plenty of lightly salted boiling water until al dente. Drain and toss for a few minutes in the pan with the cuttlefish. Sprinkle with parsley.

SPAGHETTI CON AGLIO E OLIO

Spaghetti Aglio e Olio

1 lb 5 oz spaghetti
2 garlic cloves
1 chili
Olive oil
Parsley
Salt

Cook the spaghetti in plenty of lightly salted boiling water until al dente.

Meanwhile, fry the whole garlic and the chili in a small pan with a glass of oil. When the garlic starts to turn golden, remove it from the pan.

As soon as the spaghetti is cooked, drain and toss with the hot oil and, finally, chopped parsley. Serve immediately.

SPAGHETTI CON AGLIO E POMODORO

Spaghetti with Garlic and Tomatoes

2 garlic cloves
Olive oil
2¼ lb tomatoes
1 lb 5 oz spaghetti
Salt
Optional: grated pecorino

Peel the garlic and fry gently in half a glass of oil. As soon as it starts to color, remove it and add the tomatoes—peeled, seeded, and chopped. Salt and simmer for 20 minutes.

Cook the spaghetti in plenty of lightly salted boiling water until al dente. Drain and toss with the tomatoes and serve right away adding, if you wish, a little grated pecorino.

SPAGHETTI CON AGLIO, OLIO E ACCIUGHE

Spaghetti with Garlic, Oil, and Anchovy

2 garlic cloves
Olive oil
4 fresh anchovy fillets
1 lb 5 oz spaghetti
Parsley
Salt
Pepper

Lightly fry the garlic in a glass of oil. When it starts to turn golden, remove from the pan. Add the anchovies—boned and cut into pieces—take the pan off the heat, and crush the anchovies with a fork.

Cook the spaghetti in plenty of boiling salted water until al dente. Drain and toss the spaghetti with this sauce. Season with pepper and parsley and serve very hot.

SPAGHETTI CON CACIO E PEPE

Spaghetti Cacio e Pepe

1 lb 5 oz spaghetti
Olive oil
1 cup grated pecorino
Salt
Pepper

Cook the spaghetti in plenty of boiling salted water to which you have added a spoonful of oil.

As soon as it is cooked, drain, but not completely, leave a little water to melt the grated pecorino as you add it and prevent it clogging up the pasta. Toss with plenty of ground pepper and serve very hot.

SPAGHETTI CON CAPPERI E OLIVE

Spaghetti with Capers and Olives

1 lb 5 oz spaghetti
2 garlic cloves
Parsley
Olive oil
8 oz Gaeta olives, pitted
Capers
1 cup grated pecorino
Salt

Cook the spaghetti in plenty of boiling salted water until al dente and drain well.

Brown 2 whole garlic cloves and chopped parsley in a large skillet with a glass of oil. Add the sliced olives and a handful of chopped capers and continue to fry over low heat for a few minutes. Take out the garlic cloves.

At this point, turn the spaghetti into the skillet and mix for a few minutes so the flavor of the sauce is absorbed by the pasta. Sprinkle with grated pecorino and serve.

SPAGHETTI CON CARNE E ORTAGGI

Spaghetti with Meat and Vegetables

4 yellow bell peppers
1 lb eggplant
1 celery stalk
1 carrot
Parsley
3½ oz lean prosciutto
3½ tbsp butter
3½ oz ground meat
1 lb tomatoes
1 lb 5 oz spaghetti
1 cup grated Parmesan
Salt

Roast the bell peppers in a hot oven, turning them frequently to char the skin without overcooking the flesh. When the peppers are blackened, take them out, cool slightly, and rub them gently to take off the skin, rinse, remove the stem and seeds, and cut into strips.

Cut the eggplant in half, remove any seeds, and cut into strips like the pepper. Trim the celery and cut into batons. Peel the carrot, remove any woody inner parts, and chop finely along with a few sprigs of parsley. Cube the prosciutto.

Gently melt the butter and add all the chopped vegetables, the ground meat, and prosciutto. Lightly sauté them all over low heat until they take on a beautiful golden color. At this point, add the tomatoes (peeled, seeded, and chopped). Cover the pan and let cook over moderate heat for 30 minutes.

Cook the spaghetti in plenty of lightly salted boiling water until just al dente. Drain and turn into a serving dish. Toss with the sauce and sprinkle with grated Parmesan.

SPAGHETTI CON CONDIMENTO CRUDO

Spaghetti with Raw Tomato Sauce

2¼ lb tomatoes
Olive oil
Basil
Garlic
1 lb 5 oz spaghetti
Salt
Pepper

Seed and slice the tomatoes. Place in a bowl with a glass of oil, a few basil leaves, a clove of crushed garlic, and salt and pepper. Let marinate for about 1 hour.

Cook the spaghetti in plenty of lightly salted boiling water until al dente. Drain and toss with the raw tomato sauce.

SPAGHETTI CON FUNGHI

Spaghetti with Mushrooms

10 oz mushrooms
Olive oil
Parsley
Lemon
1 lb 5 oz spaghetti
Salt
Pepper

Carefully clean the mushrooms, rinse quickly, break off the stems, and cut into very thin slices. Cook them quickly in a pan with a little oil—it will only take a few minutes—then season with salt, pepper, a good spoonful of chopped parsley, and, off the heat, a few drops of lemon juice.

Cook the spaghetti in plenty of lightly salted boiling water until al dente. Drain and toss with oil, pepper, the mushrooms, and some more drops of lemon juice. Mix well and serve at once.

SPAGHETTI CON TELLINE

Spaghetti with Wedge Clams

3 lb 5 oz telline (wedge clams)
Olive oil
2 garlic cloves
Parsley
1 lb 5 oz spaghetti
Salt
Pepper
Optional: tomato sauce

Thoroughly wash the clams and let soak for a few hours or, better still, longer, in sea water or salted water to get rid of any sand.

Add enough oil to cover the bottom of a large pan and lightly fry a clove of garlic. As soon as it starts to color, remove and add the clams. Sauté and shake the pan over high heat for a few minutes so they are all heated through. As soon as they open, take the pan off the heat and cool for a few minutes. Shell the clams—diskarding any that have not opened—and place in a bowl with the chopped parsley and a little oil. Set aside the cooking liquid in the pan and let settle, then strain well.

Cook the spaghetti in plenty of lightly salted boiling water until al dente. Drain and toss with the clams and their cooking liquid.

ADA SAYS: *If you wish, you can make a tomato sauce and heat the clams in this before tossing with the spaghetti.*

SPAGHETTI CON TONNO

Spaghetti with Tuna

Olive oil
1 garlic clove
3 fresh anchovies
2¼ lb tomatoes
7 oz tinned tuna in olive oil
Oregano
1 lb 5 oz spaghetti
Salt
Pepper
Optional: dried mushrooms

Warm half a glass of oil in a pan with a clove of garlic and when the oil is hot, remove the garlic. Add the anchovies (boned and chopped) and as soon as they have lightly browned, add the tomatoes - peeled, seeded, and chopped.

When the sauce has thickened sufficiently, after about 20 minutes, flake the tuna into the pan. Season with a little salt, plenty of pepper, and a pinch of oregano and simmer for another few minutes.

Cook the spaghetti in plenty of boiling salted water until al dente. Drain, toss with the sauce, and serve straight away.

ADA SAYS: *You might also add some dried mushrooms—reconstituted in water and fried in oil—to this recipe.*

SPAGHETTI DEL PESCATORE

Fisherman's Spaghetti

2¼ lb clams and mussels
Olive oil
Garlic
1 lb shrimp
1 lb tomatoes
Chili
Parsley
1 lb 5 oz spaghetti
Salt

Scrape, wash, and rinse the clams and mussels in plenty of water. Heat 2 tablespoons of oil in a large skillet with the garlic. When it begins to color, add the mussels, cover, and cook for a few minutes over high heat, shaking the pan from time to time so they are heated through.

When they open—diskard any that are closed—take them out of the pan and set aside. Repeat the procedure with the clams. Set the pan to one side and carefully strain off the cooking liquid into a bowl. Shell the mussels and clams and moisten them with a little of their cooking liquid.

Rinse the shrimp and place in a pan of slightly salted cold water. Bring to a boil and cook for 3 minutes. Drain and shell the shrimp and add them to the mussels and clams.

Fry a garlic clove in 2 tablespoons of oil and remove when it starts to color. Add the tomatoes (peeled, seeded, and chopped). Season with salt and a little chili, and cook for about 20 minutes. Add the shellfish and their cooking liquid.

Cook the spaghetti in plenty of lightly salted boiling water until al dente. Drain and toss with the sauce, scattered with chopped parsley. Serve right away.

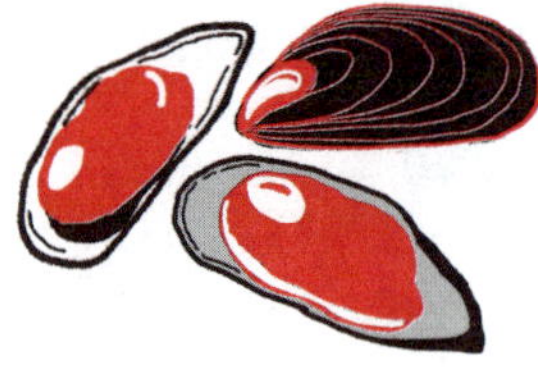

SPAGHETTINI AL CAVIALE

Spaghettini with Caviar

7 tbsp butter
4 tsp cream
2 oz caviar
1 lb 5 oz spaghettini
Salt

Gently heat the butter until it starts to melt. Before it browns, stir in the cream and caviar. Let stand for 30 minutes.

Cook the spaghettini in plenty of boiling salted water until al dente. Drain well and combine with the sauce. Mix carefully and serve at once.

SPAGHETTINI CON CARCIOFI E FUNGHETTI

Spaghettini with Artichokes and Mushrooms

3 artichoke hearts
Lemon
1 lb button mushrooms
1 garlic clove
7 tbsp butter
Parsley
White wine
1 cup meat broth or a bouillon cube
1 lb 5 oz spaghettini
9 tbsp grated Parmesan
Salt
Pepper

Cut the artichoke hearts into strips and rub with lemon juice. Quickly wash the mushrooms and carefully dry and clean them. Break off the stems and cut the mushrooms into fine slices.

Fry the garlic clove in butter and as soon as the butter melts remove the garlic. Add the artichoke hearts and mushrooms to the pan along with some chopped parsley. Lightly season with salt and pepper. Briefly sauté the vegetables uncovered over high heat. Stir in the wine a little at a time, and when this has evaporated, add some hot meat broth. Cover the pan, lower the heat, and cook for about 10 minutes; check the flavor and keep the sauce warm.

Cook the spaghettini in plenty of lightly salted boiling water until barely al dente and drain. Pour the sauce into a large skillet and mix in the pasta. Cook over medium heat for a few minutes so the flavors mingle. Sprinkle with grated Parmesan and serve at once.

SPAGHETTINI CON UOVA

Spaghettini with Eggs

6 eggs
10½ tbsp butter
1 lb spaghettini
2 oz grated Gruyère
2 oz grated Edam
9 oz mozzarella
Milk
Grated Parmesan
Salt

Poach the eggs. Melt ⅔ of the butter.

Break the spaghettini into small pieces about 5 inches long and cook in lightly salted boiling water. Drain, add to a bowl, and toss with the melted butter, grated Gruyère, and Edam.

Turn the pasta into an ovenproof dish, cover with sliced mozzarella, mositen with half a glass of milk, and sprinkle with Parmesan.

Bake the pasta in a preheated, moderately hot oven for a few minutes. As soon as you take the dish from the oven, top with the poached eggs and drizzle with the rest of the melted butter.

TORTIGLIONI ALLA RICOTTA

Tortiglioni with Ricotta

3½ tbsp butter
10 oz ricotta
1 cup cream
7 oz ham
1 lb 5 oz tortiglioni
1 cup grated Parmesan
Salt
White pepper

Tortiglioni are similar to rigatoni but narrower with deeper ridges.

Soften the butter to room temperature. Place in a bowl with the ricotta and cream and mix carefully until thoroughly blended. Finally add the ham, cut into strips.

Cook the tortiglioni in plenty of boiling salted water until al dente. Drain and turn into the bowl with the prepared sauce. Toss carefully and sprinkle with grated Parmesan and ground white pepper.

TORTIGLIONI CON FORMAGGIO

Tortiglioni with Goat Cheese

6 tomatoes
4 green and yellow bell peppers
1 cucumber
1 onion
10 oz goat cheese
3½ oz black olives, pitted
Olive oil
Oregano
1 lb 5 oz tortiglioni
Salt
Pepper

Chop the tomatoes into small pieces. Cut the peppers in half, remove the seeds, stem, and membranes and slice into fine strips. Peel the cucumber and onion and cut them also into fine strips. Place the prepared vegetables in a bowl and gently toss with the goat cheese cut into cubes and the black olives. Season with a glass of oil, salt, pepper, and oregano.

Cook the tortiglioni in plenty of boiling water until al dente. Drain and cool under running water before carefully draining again. Add the pasta to the bowl and mix well. If necessary add some more oil.

TORTIGLIONI CON PEPERONI E MELANZANE

Tortiglioni with Peppers and Eggplant

2 yellow bell peppers
Eggplant
1 celery heart
1 carrot
Parsley
Olive oil
1 lb tomatoes
1 lb 5 oz tortiglioni
1 cup grated Parmesan
Salt

Roast the peppers, turning frequently so the outer skin blackens without cooking the flesh too much. When the peppers are charred cool and gently rub off the skin, rinse, and remove the stem and seeds. Cut into strips. Slice a small eggplant in half and cut into strips as you have done with the peppers. Trim the celery heart (the white part) and cut into fine batons. Peel the carrot, removing any woody parts, and finely chop together with parsley.

Lightly heat the oil in a pan and add all the prepared vegetables. Sauté slowly until they take on a beautiful golden color. Pour the tomatoes — peeled, seeded, and chopped — into the pan. Cover and cook over medium heat for about 20 minutes. Keep a careful watch and add a little boiling water if necessary, and a touch of salt.

Cook the pasta in plenty of lightly salted boiling water until al dente. Drain, turn into a bowl, and toss with the sauce. Sprinkle with grated Parmesan.

TRENETTE CON PESTO

Trenette with Pesto

Pesto Genovese *(p49)*
1 potato
2 oz green beans
1 lb 5 oz trenette pasta
1 cup grated Parmesan
2 tbsp butter
Basil
Pine nuts
Salt

First, make the pesto with basil and pine nuts. Peel and slice the potato, chop the beans, and put both of them in a large pan of lightly salted cold water. Bring to a boil and add the pasta. The potato, beans, and trenette should all be ready at the same time. Drain and toss with the grated Parmesan and the pesto; if the latter seems too thick, dilute with a few spoons of the pasta cooking water. Arrange on a platter and garnish with some basil leaves and pine nuts.

VERMICELLI AL SALMONE

Vermicelli with Salmon

9 tbsp butter
3½ oz mascarpone
9 oz smoked salmon
1 lb 5 oz vermicelli
Salt
Optional: cream

If you want to make this dish lighter, instead of the mascarpone you can use cream.

Place the butter and mascarpone in a bowl and let soften at room temperature.

Finely chop half of the smoked salmon and roughly cut the other half into larger pieces, then add both to the bowl. Mix carefully to combine all the ingredients well.

Cook the vermicelli in plenty of lightly salted boiling water until al dente. Drain and toss with the smoked salmon sauce and, if necessary, thin with a little of the pasta cooking water.
Serve immediately.

FRESH EGG PASTA

TO MAKE EGG PASTA BY HAND

First of all, bear in mind the following formula: **1 egg for every ¾ cup of flour.**

Sift the flour onto a work surface, making a well into which you crack the eggs. Add a pinch of salt, then whisk the eggs with a fork as if you were making a frittata. Making circular movements, gradually draw in a little more flour from the inside edge on each turn. When the eggs and flour are completely incorporated, put the fork aside and begin to work the dough with your hands. Knead vigorously so the flour and egg amalgamate well and the dough becomes completely smooth. When a few beads of moisture appear on the surface, stop kneading; the dough is now just at the right stage.

Form the dough into a ball and put aside to rest under an upside down bowl for 30 minutes. Take the dough ball, divide in two, and press down on each one with the palm of your hand on the work surface so they broaden and flatten out. Now, use a rolling pin to press down on the dough so it wraps itself around the pin. Try to roll the sheet of pasta as thinly as possible, sprinkling as you go with a thin dusting of flour; the pasta will naturally take on a circular form. In order to make the pasta even finer, repeat several times; each time the repetition stretches the pasta thinner and wider. You have to turn it around and over in such a way that it stretches out in all directions while still keeping its round shape.

When the pasta is sufficiently thin, sprinkle with a little flour and fold it several times on itself. Then with a sharp knife, cut it in strips of varying widths, depending on how you are going to use it. Loosen the strands, lightly running them through your fingers, then when they have untangled, leave them to dry on a tray on a cloth lightly sprinkled with flour and cover with another cloth.

TO MAKE EGG PASTA WITH A MACHINE

Sift the flour onto a work surface making a well in the center into which you crack the eggs. Add a pinch of salt, then whisk the eggs thoroughly with a fork and very slowly draw in the flour to form a dough ball. Break off pieces of dough and begin to pass them through the rollers (first through the larger ones, then the narrower ones), making sure to flour each piece every time. When these long strips of pasta are sufficiently thin, cut them into the required shape.

TO MAKE GREEN EGG PASTA

Some regional dishes are made with egg pasta colored green with spinach. Remember that for six people, use the following proportions: **6 eggs, a scant 5 cups flour, and 1 pound spinach.**

Wash and cook 1 pound of spinach, vigorously squeeze with your hands to get rid of all the water, and pass through a food mill or purée in a blender. Make a well in a scant 5 cups flour and break in the eggs; add salt and also the spinach. Knead as usual, but roll the dough into medium-thin sheets. These will naturally take a little longer to dry because of the extra moisture from the spinach.

These fresh egg pastas are especially good with the sauces that you will find in Chapter One but these are time consuming and will need to be prepared ahead of time. Every time a sauce from that chapter is mentioned, we will cross reference it as well as list the ingredients by each recipe so you can be prepared.

FETTUCCINE ALLA CIOCIARA

Fettuccine Ciociara Style

Beef and tomato sauce *(p35)*
1 lb 5 oz fettuccine
Olive oil
9 tbsp grated Parmesan
Salt
Pepper

To make fettuccine as they do in Ciociara, southeast of Rome, the recipe has to be followed scrupulously. You must pay particular attention to the seasoning in order to end up with a really tasty result and a sauce that coats the pasta well. In Ciociara, the fettuccine is traditionally mixed with the sauce on a special wooden board.

Ahead of time, prepare the beef and tomato sauce as directed.

Use store-bought fettuccine or make the egg pasta *(opposite page)*, kneading well until the dough is firm. Cook the fettuccine in plenty of boiling salted water adding 1 tablespoon of oil.

Almost as soon as the water has come back to a boil, instead of draining the pasta, scoop the fettuccine from the pan with a large slotted spoon and carefully spread out on a wooden board before mixing with plenty of sauce and Parmesan.

Finally, delicately and carefully, lift up a small quantity of pasta with two forks so the strands absorb the sauce and arrange them, one after the other, on a large oval platter.

FETTUCCINE ALLA ROMANA

Fettuccine Roman Style

1 lb 5 oz fettuccine
Ragu Bolognese *(p32)*
Olive oil or lard
Grated Parmesan
Salt
Pepper
Optional: 1 oz dried mushrooms, chicken livers or giblets

Use store-bought fettuccine or make the egg pasta *(opposite page)* and cut into ribbons barely ⅓ inch wide. Ahead of time, make a good Bolognese ragu as directed, and add the optional dried mushrooms.

Briefly cook the fettuccine in plenty of boiling salted water to which you have added 1 tablespoon of oil. Drain and toss with the sauce and sprinkle with grated Parmesan.

ADA SAYS: *If you wish, you can add some chicken livers and giblets in the sauce.*

FETTUCCINE ALLA ZUAVA

Fettuccine Zuava

Chicken broth *(p89)*
5 oz prosciutto
3½ oz tongue, or ham
Black truffle
1 lb 5 oz fettuccine
Olive oil
Butter
1 cup cream
Grated Parmesan
Salt

Cream sauce:
⅓ cup flour, 3 tbsp butter, 4 cups chicken broth

For the cream sauce, first make a chicken broth, but omit the tomato. Make the cream sauce *(p17)* with that chicken broth and the flour and butter amounts listed here. Pass the sauce through a sieve, return to the pan, and keep warm.

A few minutes before cooking the pasta, cut the prosciutto and tongue, or ham, into pieces. Shave the truffle into fine slivers, and stir them all into the hot sauce.

Cook the fettuccine in plenty of boiling salted water with a spoonful of oil until just al dente. Drain and turn into a bowl and toss with melted butter, the cream and grated Parmesan. Serve the fettuccine with the cream sauce poured into a sauce boat so everyone can help themselves.

FETTUCCINE AL RAGÙ

Fettuccine Ragu

1 lb 5 oz fettuccine
Olive oil
Grated Parmesan
Salt
Pepper

Tomato ragu:
2¼ lb tomatoes, 10 oz lean beef, glass red wine, 3½ tbsp butter, 4 tbsp olive oil, basil

Use store-bought fettuccine or make egg pasta *(p170)* and cut into ribbons barely ⅓ inch wide to make fettuccine.

Ahead of time, make the tomato ragu *(p32)* using the ingredient amounts listed here.

Briefly cook the fettuccine in plenty of boiling salted water adding a spoonful of oil. Drain, toss with the ragù, and sprinkle with grated Parmesan.

FETTUCCINE CON MASCARPONE

Fettuccine with Mascarpone

1 lb 5 oz fettuccine
Olive oil
5 oz mascarpone
2 egg yolks
3½ oz ham
9 tbsp grated Parmesan
Salt

Briefly cook the fettuccine in plenty of lightly salted boiling water adding a spoonful of oil. Soften the mascarpone in a bowl with a few spoons of hot water. Carefully mix in the egg yolks with a wooden spoon, then add the ham cut into fine strips plus half the grated Parmesan.

As soon as the fettuccine is cooked, remove from the heat and drain. Add to the ham and mascarpone sauce, toss well so the sauce permeates the pasta, then turn it into a heated serving dish. Sprinkle with the remaining Parmesan and serve immediately while still very hot.

FETTUCCINE CON PISELLI

Fettuccine with Peas

1 onion
10½ tbsp butter
12 oz fresh or frozen peas
Milk
3½ oz prosciutto
1 lb 5 oz fettuccine
Olive oil
1 cup grated Parmesan
Salt
Pepper

Sauté a tablespoon of finely chopped onion in 2 tbsp of butter over very low heat. Without letting the onion brown, add the peas, salt, pepper, and a few spoons of milk or hot water.

Increase the heat and bring to a brisk boil, stirring from time to time, then lower and simmer for about 20 minutes. Just before you take the pan off the heat, add the prosciutto cut into strips.

Cook the egg fettuccine in plenty of boiling salted water adding a spoonful of oil. Drain and toss with the remaining butter, Parmesan, and the peas.

FETTUCCINE CON PROSCIUTTO E FUNGHETTI (AL CARTOCCIO)

Baked Fettuccine with Prosciutto and Button Mushrooms

1 lb button mushrooms
Olive oil
White wine
3½ oz prosciutto
1 lb 5 oz fettuccine
2 oz grated Gruyère
9 tbsp grated Parmesan
7 tbsp butter
Salt
Pepper

Break off the mushroom stems, wash quickly, dry, and cut into thin slices. Warm half a glass of oil in a skillet and add the mushrooms. Cook over high heat for 5 minutes, sprinkle with white wine and salt and take the pan off the heat when the wine evaporates. Cut the prosciutto in strips and add to the mushrooms.

Cook the fettuccine in plenty of boiling, salted water adding a spoonful of oil. When the water returns to a boil after adding the pasta, cook for 2 minutes, then drain and carefully mix with the butter, grated cheeses, mushrooms, and prosciutto. Lightly butter a sheet of foil and place on a sheet pan. Arrange the fettuccine on this, cover with another sheet of foil closing the two edges together to make a parcel.

Cook in a preheated oven for 10 minutes. Take the pasta out of the oven, open the parcel and turn the fettuccine into a serving dish, give it a gentle stir, and serve right away.

◆ **ADA SAYS:** *This dish can also be made in two stages with the foil parcel set aside for a few hours before heating in the oven. If doing that, the pasta should be rinsed in cold water after it is drained.*

LASAGNETTE ALLA CACCIATORA COL POLLO

Hunter's Lasagnette with Chicken

1 lb 5 oz lasagnette
2¼ lb tomatoes
Olive oil
3½ tbsp butter
1 onion
Garlic
3½ oz pancetta
3 chicken breasts
Wine
9 tbsp grated Parmesan
Parsley
Basil
Salt
Pepper

Use store-bought lasagnette or make the egg pasta *(p170)* and cut into ribbons 1¼ inches wide to make lasagnette. Blanch, peel, and carefully seed the tomatoes. Slice and set aside.

Gently heat half a glass of oil, the butter, finely chopped onion, and a garlic clove. When the onion is cooked but before it colors, take out the garlic clove and add the pancetta cut into fine strips, then the chicken cut into pieces. Turn up the heat and sauté until they take on a lovely dark blond color.

Moisten the chicken with half a glass of wine. When it starts to evaporate, add the tomatoes. Cover the pan and cook over medium heat for about 20 minutes, stirring occasionally and adding a few spoons of water if the sauce seems to be drying out. Take out a few pieces of chicken for decoration.

Cook the lasagnette in plenty of boiling salted water adding a spoonful of oil. Do not overcook. Toss the pasta with the chicken sauce and lots of grated Parmesan. Top with the chicken cut into portions and a tablespoon of parsley and basil chopped together.

LASAGNETTE ALLA GENOVESE

Lasagnette Genoa Style

1 lb 5 oz lasagnette
Basil
2 garlic cloves
Olive oil
1 cup grated pecorino or Parmesan
Salt

Use store-bought lasagnette or make the egg pasta *(p170)* and cut into ribbons 1¼ inches wide to make lasagnette.

Now prepare a pesto: Blend a handful of basil with the garlic, half a glass of oil, grated pecorino or Parmesan, and a pinch of salt.

Cook the pasta in plenty of lightly salted boiling water with a spoonful of oil until al dente. Drain and toss with the pesto diluted with a few spoons of the pasta cooking water and serve right away.

LASAGNETTE ALLA PIEMONTESE

Lasagnette Piedmont Style

1 lb 5 oz lasagnette
Olive oil
10½ tbsp butter
1 cup grated Parmesan
Nutmeg
White truffle
Salt
Pepper

Meat sauce:
10 oz beef, 3½ oz lardons of fat and lean prosciutto, half glass dry wine, onion, carrot, celery, stock

Make the meat sauce *(p34)* using the ingredient amounts listed here.

Cook the pasta in plenty of boiling salted water with a spoonful of oil until al dente. Drain and place in a dish with the butter, the Parmesan, a pinch of pepper, a grating of nutmeg, and the meat sauce. Toss well, add a shaving of white truffle and let the lasagnette stand for a short while to mingle the flavors.

PAPPARDELLE ALLA LEPRE

Pappardelle with Hare

1 lb 5 oz hare
3½ tbsp butter
Olive oil
Flour
Wine
2 cups broth
1 lb 5 oz pappardelle
Grated Parmesan
Salt
Pepper

Battuto:
2 oz pancetta, ½ onion, ½ celery stalk

The hare can either be served with the pasta or as a separate dish.

Use the saddle, loin, or the leg—without the bones—of the hare and chop into pieces.

Heat the butter and half a glass of oil and make a battuto of pancetta, onion, and celery. Fry a little and then add the hare seasoned with salt and pepper. When it is browned, sprinkle with a tablespoon of flour and moisten with two glasses of wine. As soon as this evaporates, add the broth, cover, and lower the heat. The hare will take between 1½ and 2 hours to cook; add more broth or water as necessary. When cooked, the sauce should have just the right consistency.

Cook the pasta in plenty of boiling salted water with a spoonful of oil until al dente. Drain and toss with the Parmesan and the sauce.

PAPPARDELLE CON FUNGHI IN BESCIAMELLA

Pappardelle with Mushrooms

1 lb mushrooms
Olive oil
7 tbsp butter
9 tbsp grated Parmesan
1 lb 5 oz pappardelle
Salt
Pepper

White sauce:
6½ tbsp flour, 3½ tbsp butter, 3 cups milk

Scrape and break off the mushroom stems, wash quickly, dry carefully, and cut into fine slices. Gently heat 4 tablespoons of oil and 1 tablespoon of butter. Add the mushrooms and raise the heat high to fry the mushrooms for about 10 minutes. Season with salt and pepper.

Make a white sauce *(p16)* with the ingredient amounts listed here. Carefully mix in the mushrooms.

Cook the pappardelle in plenty of boiling salted water with a spoonful of oil until al dente. Drain and toss with the remaining butter and grated Parmesan. Arrange the pasta on a serving plate and pour over the prepared sauce. Serve at once.

PAPPARDELLE CON L'ANATRA

Pappardelle with Duck

1 small duck
Olive oil
Onion
Garlic
1 carrot
1 celery stalk
Parsley
Bay leaf
White wine
Tomato paste
2 cups broth
1 lb 5 oz pappardelle
9 tbsp grated Parmesan
Salt
Pepper

Clean the duck and cut into even portions. Add a little oil to a large saucepan and add half an onion, a tiny bit of garlic, a carrot, celery stalk, and some parsley all finely chopped plus a bay leaf. Place the pieces of duck on these aromatics. Season with salt and pepper and sauté until the duck is browned.

Moisten with half a glass of wine. When it evaporates, add a little bit of tomato paste and let this briefly cook. Add the broth, reduce the heat, cover the pan, and cook very slowly for about 1½ hours. If necessary add extra broth.

When the duck is cooked, take it out of the sauce and keep hot. Strain the sauce, skim off the fat, and place in another dish. Keep warm.

Cook the pappardelle in plenty of salted boiling water with a tablespoon of oil until al dente. Drain and dress with the duck sauce and grated Parmesan. Arrange on a serving platter with the pieces of duck on top of the pasta.

TAGLIATELLE ALLA BOLOGNESE

Tagliatelle Bolognese

Ragu Bolognese *(p32)*
1 lb 5 oz tagliatelle
Cream
Grated Parmesan
Salt
Pepper
Optional: white truffle

Have ready a good ragu.

Use store-bought pasta or make egg pasta *(p170)* and when it is almost completely dried, sprinkle with flour, roll up, and cut into strips ¼ inch wide to make tagliatelle. Spread out the tagliatelle and place on a lightly floured cloth to finish drying.

Cook the tagliatelle in plenty of lightly salted boiling water with a spoonful of oil until al dente. Drain and toss with the ragu along with a few spoons of cream and plenty of grated Parmesan. Finish, if you wish, with a few slivers of white truffle.

ADA SAYS: *You can serve it at once but it is better to wait a little, with the dish covered and kept warm, to allow the flavor to permeate the pasta and sauce. This sauce also is often found with green tagliatelle made with spinach.*

TAGLIATELLE ALLA BOLOGNESE VERDI

Green Tagliatelle Bolognese

Ragu Bolognese *(p32)*
3 tbsp cream of milk
Grated Parmesan
1 tbsp olive oil
Salt
Pepper
Optional: white truffle

Green egg pasta:
2¼ lb spinach, 5¾ cups flour, 6 eggs

Make the ragu as directed.

Make a green egg pasta *(p170)* using the ingredient amounts listed here. Roll it out into sheets, not too thin, and place them to dry on a lightly floured cloth. As the spinach imparts a little moisture to the dough, it will take a little longer for it to dry.

When you see that the dough is dry, dust it lightly with flour, roll it up, and cut it into strips ¼ inch wide.

Boil the pasta in plenty of lightly salted boiling water with a tablespoon of oil until al dente. Drain and dress with the ragu, adding a few spoonfuls of cream and grated Parmesan cheese.

You can serve them immediately, or better to let them sit awhile in the bowl, covered and warm, so that they can rest.

ADA SAYS: *You can top the pasta with a few slices of white truffle.*

TAGLIATELLE ALLA GENOVESE VERDI

Genoa Green Tagliatelle

Porcini sauce *(p46)*
Olive oil
1 onion
1 garlic clove
3½ oz sausage
Veal sweetbread
3½ oz boiled spinach
3½ oz boiled borage
9 tbsp grated Parmesan
1 lb 5 oz tagliatelle
3½ tbsp butter
Salt
Pepper

Egg pasta:
4¾ cups flour, 6 eggs

Genoese tagliatelle differ from other types of green tagliatelle because instead of the usual vegetables—spinach or chard—a mixture of spinach, borage, sausage, sweetbreads, and herbs is added to the egg pasta. In this recipe, you will make your own pasta dough. Proceed as follows:

Make the porcini sauce as directed.

Put a little oil in a pan, a small piece of chopped onion, a clove of garlic, the fresh sausages—casings removed and chopped—and a small raw veal sweetbread cut into small pieces.

Cook slowly, season with salt, pepper. When everything is cooked, add a handful of spinach and as many boiled and well-squeezed borage leaves, to flavor and stew for a few minutes, stirring, and then chop everything until you get a very fine mixture, almost a paste.

For the egg pasta: Put the flour on the table arranged in a heap and place the eggs, a handful of grated cheese and the prepared mixture in the middle. Mix everything by pulling one or more into sheets that you will cut out into tagliatelle.

Boil them in plenty of boiling salted water with a tablespoon of oil until al dente. Drain and season with grated Parmesan, butter and the porcini sauce.

TAGLIATELLE AL PETTO DI POLLO

Tagliatelle with Chicken

5 oz roasted or boiled chicken breast
5 oz tongue or cooked ham
1 lb tomatoes
Olive oil
1 lb 5 oz green tagliatelle
3½ tbsp butter
9 tbsp grated Parmesan
Salt
Optional: black truffle

Cut the chicken and the tongue or cooked ham into sticks. Peel and seed the tomatoes and cut them into wedges. Cook them for a few moments in a pan with a little oil, then season with a pinch of salt.

Cook the tagliatelle in plenty of boiling salted water with a tablespoon of oil until al dente. Drain and toss with the butter, half the grated Parmesan, and tomato wedges.

Arrange in an oven dish, shape them into a dome, and decorate with the chicken and tongue or ham sticks. Sprinkle with the remaining grated Parmesan. If you want, cover the dome with slices of black truffle. Put the dish in a preheated oven at a rather lively heat for a few minutes and send to the table.

TAGLIATELLE CON LE NOCI

Tagliatelle with Walnuts

12 walnuts
7 tbsp butter
1 lb 5 oz tagliatelle
Olive oil
Grated Parmesan
Salt
White pepper

Shell the walnuts and coarsely chop, leaving some whole. Fry with half the butter, salt, and white pepper.

Boil the tagliatelle in plenty of lightly salted boiling water with a tablespoon of oil until al dente. Drain and season with the sauce diluted with a few spoonfuls of the cooking water from the pasta and plenty of grated Parmesan cheese. Sprinkle with ground white pepper.

TAGLIATELLE IN SALSA D'UOVO

Tagliatelle with Egg, Anchovy, and Mozzarella

3 eggs
6 anchovy fillets
5 oz mozzarella
1 lb 5 oz egg tagliatelle
7 tbsp butter
Olive oil
Salt

Put 3 egg yolks in a bowl. Wash, bone and cut the anchovies into pieces. Cut the mozzarella into cubes. Mix carefully.

Cook the pasta in plenty of boiling salted water with a tablespoon of oil until al dente. Drain and put them in a large pan with the melted butter.

Over low heat, stirring constantly, add the egg yolks, anchovies, and mozzarella. Heat everything, adding a few spoonfuls of the pasta cooking water. When the mozzarella begins to melt and the eggs to set, pour into a serving dish

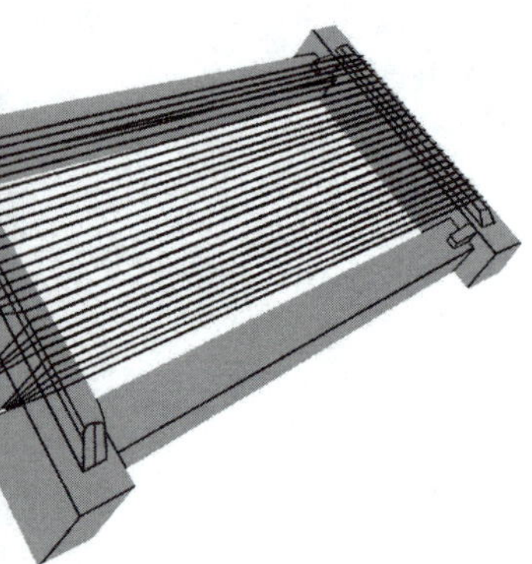

TONNARELLI ALLA CHITARRA

Tonnarelli Chitarra Abruzzese

10 oz pancetta
Olive oil
1 lb peeled tomatoes
1 cup grated pecorino and Parmesan
Salt
Pepper

Chitarra pasta:
4 cups + 6 tbsp flour, 6 eggs

For the preparation of this typical egg pasta you need the so-called chitarra, *which in English means "guitar", a traditional Abruzzese instrument made up of a wooden frame strung with very thin metal wires, which is used to cut the sheet of pasta into square-edged strands.*

Place the flour on the pastry board giving it the shape of a fountain, place the eggs in the center and knead with regular movements, working for a long time and letting the dough rest a couple of times for 15 minutes. The processing must last at least 45 minutes for the dough to be very consistent.

Cut the pancetta into small cubes and fry in oil until it has a nice golden color, then add the tomatoes and cook for another 20 minutes. Be careful when you add salt because the pancetta could be salty.

On a floured pastry board, roll the dough out with a rolling pin, keeping it a scant 1/16 inch thick. Cut the dough into rectangles no bigger than the chitarra, then place each rectangle on it, press a rolling pin over the dough so that the strands fall down through the wires.

Cook the pasta in abundant boiling salted water with a tablespoon of oil until al dente. Drain and season with the prepared sauce, grated pecorino and Parmesan.

TONNARELLI ALLA CREMA DI LATTE

Tonnarelli with Cream

10½ tbsp butter
3½ oz tongue or salami
3½ oz ham
3½ oz prosciutto
2 cups cream
1 lb 5 oz egg tonnarelli
9 tbsp grated Parmesan
Salt
Pepper

Put the butter in a pan and add the tongue or salami, ham, and prosciutto, all cut into small pieces. Let them brown for a few minutes, then add half the cream.

Boil the tonnarelli in abundant lightly salted boiling water with a tablespoon of oil until about three quarters cooked. Drain and put them in the pan with the meats and butter. Finish with the remaining cream, the grated Parmesan, and a pinch of pepper. Cook the tonnarelli until they are flavored, then immediately send them to the table.

TONNARELLI ALLE VONGOLE

Tonnarelli with Clams and Pesto

Genoa-style pesto *(p49)*
4½ lb clams
Olive oil
1 lb 5 oz egg tonnarelli
Salt
Pepper

Make the pesto as directed, but using the blender method.

Wash the clams thoroughly and put them in a rather large pan in which you have heated up a spoonful of oil. Cook for a few minutes over high heat, covered, making them jump from time to time so that everyone can feel the heat equally. When the clams are all open, remove the pan from the heat. Shell half the clams and transfer them in a bowl; keep the other half in a different bowl. Decant the cooking liquid and add it to the shelled clams, being careful not to include any sand or grit.

Boil the tonnarelli in abundant boiling salted water with a tablespoon of oil until al dente. Drain and toss with the pesto, the clams, and finally add the clams with their shells. Stir quickly and serve immediately.

TONNARELLI ALLO SFIZIO DI MARE

Tonnarelli with Shellfish

10 oz small octopus
10 oz small squid
2 medium cuttlefish
Olive oil
Garlic
Red chili
Prosecco
1 lb tomatoes
1 lb 5 oz egg tonnarelli
Salt

Clean the octopus (removing the ink sac, the skin, and the eyes) and cut them into small pieces. Rinse the pieces until they become very white and let them drain.

Clean the squid, take off the skin and fins, detach the tentacles from the body and extract the cartilaginous pen inside. Cut everything into small pieces.

Peel the cuttlefish, remove the bone, taking care not to damage the casing; cut the bag with a pair of scissors so that it opens like a book, set aside the bladder with the black ink, because you will need the other one containing a yellow liquid later. Remove the eyes and mouth.

Put a little oil with a clove of garlic and a small piece of chili in a large pan, set the saucepan over heat and as soon as the garlic is golden, remove both the garlic and the chili. Add the octopus and cook for a few minutes over high heat, then pour half a glass of white wine, preferably prosecco, into the saucepan and let it evaporate. Add the baby squid and the two cuttlefish including the yellow liquid and after a few minutes the chopped tomatoes.

Cover, reduce the heat, and cook slowly for about 1 hour, stirring occasionally and topping up with a few spoonfuls of water if the sauce gets too dry. When almost cooked, put the cuttlefish ink in the sauce. Salt lightly, mix carefully so that the black can be well blended.

Boil the tonnarelli in abundant boiling salted water with a tablespoon of oil until al dente. Drain and toss with the prepared sauce and serve immediately.

Stuffed Egg Pasta

AGNOLOTTI CLASSICI

Classic Agnolotti

10 oz slices beef, veal, or pork
Butter
1 lb cooked spinach
Grated Parmesan
1 egg yolk
2 oz prosciutto
2 oz salami
Marsala
Nutmeg
Salt
Pepper

Egg pasta:
4¾ cups flour, 4 eggs, 1 egg white

Cook the slices of pork, beef or veal in a pan with a little butter. Chop the meat, put it in a bowl with the spinach—washed, boiled, squeezed well, and chopped—a spoonful of grated Parmesan, an egg yolk, the prosciutto and salami (both diced), the Marsala, a pinch of salt and of pepper, and a trifle of grated nutmeg. Mix all these ingredients well with a wooden spoon and set aside.

Make the egg pasta *(p170)* with the flour, whole eggs, egg white, listed here and a spoonful of water. With this dough you roll two thin sheets, which you will not dry out.

On one of these sheets, use a teaspoon to place balls of the meat mixture, as big as a hazelnut, about two fingers apart, taking care to line them up to make cutting them out easier. Cover with the other sheet and use your fingers to press around the balls of the mixture. If the dough is fresh, the two sheets will stick together with the simple pressure of your fingers; if the pasta is too dry, brush only the lower sheet with a little water to make the agnolotti remain tightly closed.

At this point, with a sharp knife, or better with a wheeled pastry cutter, divide the agnolotti and then put them to dry on lightly floured cloths.

Boil the agnolotti in plenty of salted boiling water with a tablespoon of oil for about 10 minutes. Drain well to prevent the filling from diluting.

Season with butter and Parmesan. Cover them and let them stew for a moment before serving so they can gain flavor.

ADA SAYS: *A variation is to serve these agnolotti with a beef and tomato sauce.*

AGNOLOTTI SARDI

Agnolotti Sardinian Style

2 oz pancetta
1¾ lb beef
7 tbsp butter
1 carrot
1 onion
1 celery stalk
5 oz pork loin
White wine
9 oz Savoy cabbage
2½ oz mortadella
Breadcrumbs
Milk
2 eggs
Grated Parmesan
Salt
Pepper

Egg pasta:
4¾ cups flour, 4 eggs, salt

Use the quantity of meat indicated, even if it seems excessive, so that the sauce is tastier. Half the meat is used for stuffing the agnolotti, the rest you can save for preparations such as meatballs.

First, prepare the lardons: Cut the pancetta into strips, roll the strips in some salt, and then with a special needle or a small knife lard the beef, which you then tie to keep it in shape. Melt the butter in a pan, add the beef, brown it well, turning it from time to time. Season with salt and pepper. Add the vegetables—carrot, onion, and celery all cut into pieces—and the pork loin, pour in three glasses of wine, cover the pan, and cook over very low heat for 2½ hours.

Boil the Savoy cabbage for 10 minutes and chop it, then put it in the pan with the meat sauce and the mortadella. In a bowl, combine a handful of breadcrumbs soaked in milk and well squeezed, the eggs, and ⅓ cup of grated Parmesan. If the mixture is too dry you can moisten it with a few spoonfuls of the meat sauce.

Make the egg pasta *(p170)* with the flour, eggs, a pinch of salt and a few spoonfuls of water. Roll out two rather thin sheets with a rolling pin. Fill and cut the agnolotti as in the recipe for Classic Agnolotti (*previous page*).

Cook the agnolotti in plenty of boiling salted water with a tablespoon of oil. Drain them well and dress them with the meat sauce, suitably passed through a sieve and hot. Sprinkle with grated pecorino.

CANNELLONI ALLA BESCIAMELLA

Cannelloni with Beef and Tomatoes

Olive oil
3 tbsp butter
1 onion
2 oz prosciutto
Bay leaf
14 oz ground beef
Flour
10 oz tomatoes
Nutmeg
Breadcrumbs
Milk
1 egg
9 tbsp grated Parmesan
Salt
Pepper

Make a strong, well worked egg pasta *(p170)* with the ingredient amounts listed here. With a rolling pin, roll it out on the floured table into thin sheets and cut out many 3 × 4-inch rectangles.

Working in batches, boil the pasta in plenty of lightly salted boiling water with a few spoonfuls of oil. Scoop them out with a slotted spoon and transfer them to a large bowl of cold water.

Once cooled, spread the pasta out on kitchen towels without overlapping them so that they can dry.

Prepare the filling: In 2 tablespoons of butter, brown the chopped onion with the prosciutto. Add the bay leaf and then the ground beef and when this is flavored, mix in 1 tablespoon of flour and the tomatoes - peeled, seeded, and chopped. Season with salt, pepper, and nutmeg and cook slowly for 45 minutes. Take out the bay leaf.

Pass the filling through the food mill or purée in a blender. Add a

Egg pasta:
2½ cups flour, 3 eggs

White sauce:
6½ tbsp flour, 3½ tbsp butter,
2 cups milk

handful of breadcrumbs soaked in milk and well squeezed, the egg, and the Parmesan. Stir until evenly combined

Put a little of the prepared mixture on each rectangle of dough and roll them up to make cannelloni. Make up a white sauce *(p16)* using the ingredient amounts listed here.

Generously grease a baking pan. Arrange the cannelloni on top, cover them with the white sauce, grated Parmesan and butter. Put the pan in the oven at moderate heat for about 15 minutes, so that the cannelloni can brown and flavor.

CANNELLONI ALL'ETRUSCA

Cannelloni Etruscan Style

12 oz package lasagna sheets
10 oz mushrooms
3½ tbsp butter
3½ oz Gruyère
3½ oz cooked ham
9 tbsp grated Parmesan
Olive oil
Salt

Egg pasta:
2½ cups flour, 3 eggs

White sauce:
6½ tbsp flour, 3½ tbsp butter,
2 cups milk

Use store-bought lasagna sheets or make the egg pasta *(p170)* using the ingredients listed here and roll out as described in Cannelloni with Beef and Tomatoes *(opposite page)*.

Prepare a rather thick white sauce *(p16)* with the ingredients listed here, holding back a little milk for thinning the sauce later. Take about ⅔ of the sauce and put it in a bowl. When it is almost cold, mix in a handful of grated Parmesan.

Wash the mushrooms, cut thinly, and cook with a little butter, salt, and a few spoonfuls of water. Add to the white sauce. Distribute half a spoonful of this filling in each of the cannelloni rectangles, roll them up on themselves and arrange them in a single layer in a well-greased baking dish. Cut the Gruyère into very thin cubes and spread them on the cannelloni, along with the ham cut into small pieces.

Dilute the rest of the white sauce with the reserved milk and stir it well over heat. Cover the cannelloni with this sauce and finish with a sprinkling of grated Parmesan. Put the pan in a preheated oven for about 15 minutes, until the top of the sauce has slightly colored.

CANNELLONI CON MAIALE ALLA PROVENZALE

Cannelloni Provençal

1 oz dried mushrooms
1 onion
1 carrot
1 celery stalk
Parsley
8½ tbsp butter
1 lb 5 oz ground pork
Marsala
2 cups tomato passata
2 oz prosciutto
2¼ lb spinach
9 tbsp grated Parmesan
Nutmeg
1 egg
Olive oil
12 oz cannelloni
Salt
Pepper

Soak the mushrooms in cold water to reconstitute. Finely chop the onion, carrot, celery, and parsley.

Fry the vegetables in a saucepan with 2 tablespoons of butter. As they brown, add the ground pork and the mushrooms. Season with salt and pepper and allow everything to turn a dark blond color.

Then pour in 2 glasses of Marsala, let it reduce a little, and add the tomato passata. Cover the saucepan, reduce the heat, and cook slowly for 1 hour. If necessary, add a little water.

When the sauce has thickened, remove from the heat, take out the meat and mushrooms and place them in a bowl. Add coarsely chopped prosciutto and spinach and season with a couple of spoonfuls of grated Parmesan, 2 spoonfuls of the sauce from the saucepan, a trifle of nutmeg, and a whole egg. Mix well.

Place a large pan on the heat with plenty of lightly salted water to which you have added a few tablespoons of oil. When it boils add a few squares of pasta at a time. Scoop them up with a slotted spoon and spread them on kitchen towels to dry.

Spread a little of the meat mixture on each one, roll them up on themselves, and line them up in a single layer on the bottom of a large baking dish.

Season with the remaining sauce, sprinkle abundantly with grated Parmesan, add the remaining pieces of butter and place the pan in a preheated moderate oven.

CANNELLONI RIPIENI DI RICOTTA E SALSICCE

Cannelloni with Ricotta and Sausage

1 lb ricotta
9 tbsp grated Parmesan
1 egg
3 sausages
Tomato sauce *(p37)*, or canned tomato sauce
Olive oil
Butter
Salt
Pepper

Egg pasta:
2½ cups flour, 3 eggs

Make an egg pasta *(p170)* with the ingredient amounts listed here. Roll it into a ball and let it rest covered with a towel.

Drain the ricotta, transfer to a bowl, season with a good pinch of salt, a few spoonfuls of grated Parmesan, and a beaten egg and mix everything with a wooden spoon.

Put the sausages in a pan, prick them, cover them with water and simmer them. When the water is used up, let the sausages brown for a few minutes in their own fat. Then peel off the casings, chop them, and add them to the ricotta mix.

Have ready a tomato sauce made as directed or use 1¼ cups canned tomato sauce.

Roll out the dough with a wooden rolling pin to a scant ⅛ inch thick and cut it out into 2¾- to 3-inch squares.

Bring a large shallow pan filled with plenty of lightly salted water, to which you have added a few spoonfuls of oil, to a boil. When the water boils, add a few squares at a time. When they rise to the surface, pull them up with a slotted spoon and spread them out on damp kitchen towels to drain.

When they are all cooked, place a spoonful of filling in the center and wrap each square on itself, turning it into small cannelloni.

Grease an baking pan, line up the cannelloni in a single layer and pour over all the prepared sauce. Sprinkle with grated Parmesan and here and there some peanuts of butter. A few minutes before presenting this delicious first course, place the pan in a preheated oven, allow the cannelloni to flavor for about 15 minutes, then send it to the table.

CROSETTI ALLA SICILIANA

Sicilian Crosetti

1 lb fine semolina
1 egg yolk
Butter
Beef and tomato sauce *(p35)*
9 tbsp grated Parmesan
Nutmeg
Flour
Milk
Olive oil
Salt

Crosetti are like cannelloni but are made with semolina.

Put the semolina, egg yolk, a knob of butter, and a pinch of salt on the work surface and mix them with lukewarm water, as much as you need to have a dough of the right consistency. With flour-dusted hands, knead the dough firmly so as to mix the semolina well.

Once the dough is ready, cut it into 4 equal pieces that you will roll into a ball. Cover with a large overturned bowl and let rest for 15 minutes.

Prepare a good, abundant, thick, and tasty beef and tomato sauce as directed. Remove the meat from the sauce and let it cool. Then chop it and mix in a couple of spoonfuls of grated Parmesan and a trifle of nutmeg. This is the filling for the pasta. Reserve the meat sauce, too.

Roll out the pieces of dough, one at a time, on the lightly floured work surface and from each piece cut out 3 × 4¾-inch rectangles. Bring a wide pan of water to a boil. Add the rectangles of pasta a few at a time and cook them for 2 or 3 minutes, then scoop them out with a slotted spoon, rinsed under cold water, drain well, and spread them on kitchen towels to drain.

Distribute a little of the meat filling on each piece of pasta and on the filling put a little of the very thick meat sauce. Then roll up the various pieces to form many cannelloni. Grease a baking pan with butter and line up the crosetti in a single layer.

Add a little milk and grated cheese to the sauce. Pour plenty of sauce over everything, and finish with plenty of grated cheese and a little melted butter. Put the pan in a preheated oven of moderate heat for about 10 minutes and when the crosetti are well flavored, have them brought to the table.

RAVIOLI ALLA GENOVESE

Ravioli Genovese

1 lb lean beef
Olive oil
Suet
1 onion
Garlic
Rosemary
Red wine
4½ lb tomatoes
3½ oz sausage
2 oz lamb brains
2 oz sweetbreads
Borage
Bitter greens
9 tbsp grated Parmesan
Salt

Homemade curd:
1 glass milk, 1 tsp lemon juice, cream

Egg pasta:
4¾ cups flour, 2 eggs, pinch of salt

The traditional ravioli filling is made up of a little of the meat that was used to make the sauce, abundant vegetables, an orange-sized bunch of borage, and the same of boiled bitter greens—no spinach!—brains, sweetbreads, sausage, eggs, grated Parmesan, some seasoning, and the homemade curd—not ricotta! In the filling, the greens must represent about double the other components.

Make the egg pasta *(p170)* using the ingredients listed here along with enough water to create a very soft dough. Cover with a towel and let it rest.

Prepare the sauce according to the Genoese tradition: Brown the lean beef in a pan with some oil and a little minced suet. When it is browned, add salt, a little onion, a little garlic, and a few sprigs of rosemary. Let it brown for a few more minutes and then pour in two fingers of red wine. When the wine has evaporated, add the tomatoes (peeled, seeded, and chopped). Let it simmer slowly for a couple of hours or more, until the meat is well cooked and the sauce thickened.

You can easily make curd at home: a glass of milk gives 2 good spoonful of curd. In a small saucepan, gently heat the milk and add the lemon juice. Mix well, heat a little more, almost until it boils. Remove the pan from the heat and cover it. The milk will coagulate quickly. Pour into a cheesecloth-lined sieve and let the whey drain. To this well- drained curd, add about 6 tablespoons cream.

In a pan, put a little chopped onion, garlic, and a little oil. Fry lightly and then add the sausage meat—casings removed—and then the brains and sweetbreads. If using veal sweetbreads, blanch them first. Sauté and finally add the boiled greens. Season with salt and then chop everything. Transfer this mixture to a bowl, add half the minced meat (from the sauce), the egg, grated Parmesan, and the curd and mix thoroughly to obtain a perfect amalgam of all the ingredients.

Divide the dough into 2 equal parts and roll out two rather thin sheets. Place one of these sheets on the counter and, a short distance from each other, line up some filling: of a size depending on how large you want the ravioli to be. Cover the pasta sheet with the second sheet and with your fingers press around each filling to close it well. Then cut and separate. A few minutes before serving, submerge the ravioli in plenty of boiling salted water and boil them for 4 or 5 minutes, supervising cooking so they don't overcook. Drain the ravioli well and season them, in layers, with the prepared sauce and plenty of Parmesan.

ADA SAYS: *The best fat to use is from around the lamb's kidney, called suet, in which case you may want to add the kidney—minced finely—to the stuffing too.*

RAVIOLI CON LA RICOTTA (AL BURRO E SALVIA)

Ravioli with Ricotta, Butter, and Sage

14 oz ricotta
1 egg
Grated Parmesan
14 tbsp butter
Sage
Salt

Egg pasta:
3¼ cups flour, 4 eggs, 2 tbsp water

Make a sturdy egg pasta *(p170)* with the ingredient amounts listed here. Roll it out into two thin sheets.

In a bowl, loosen the ricotta with a wooden spoon. Add the egg, a couple of spoonfuls of grated Parmesan, and a pinch of salt. Put this mixture in a pastry bag with a plain ⅓-inch tip (or you can use a teaspoon). Pipe out the ricotta mixture into dollops the size of a walnut on one of the pasta sheets, arrange them in a straight line and at a distance of a couple of fingers from each other. Cover them with the other pasta sheet and press your fingers around them, make the two sheets stick together perfectly. With a special wheel cutter, or sharp knife, divide the ravioli so that they are many triangles.

Melt the butter in a pan with a handful of sage leaves, fry until they become hazelnut in color.

Cook the ravioli in plenty of lightly salted boiling water with a tablespoon of oil until al dente. Scoop them up with a slotted spoon, wait for them to drain well, then transfer to a large dish and toss with the butter and grated Parmesan. Cover the plate and wait a few minutes before serving the ravioli so that they have time to flavor.

ROTOLO DI PASTA AL SUGO

Pasta Roll with Tomato and Spinach

Tomato and basil sauce *(p38)*
4½ lb spinach
3½ oz ham
12 oz egg pasta
9 tbsp grated Parmesan
Salt
Pepper

Egg pasta:
2½ cups flour, 3 eggs

Prepare a good tomato and basil sauce. Wash and boil the spinach in very little water, drain, squeeze thoroughly, and finely mince. Chop the ham and add it to the spinach.

Make egg pasta *(p170)* with the ingredients listed here and roll into a thin sheet or buy store-bought fresh lasagna sheets. Take care not to let the fresh pasta sheets dry out. Place the spinach and ham mixture on a single layer. Then roll the dough on itself, forming a large sausage. Put the roll of dough in a clean kitchen towel, wrap it up, and tie it at both ends and in the center. Then immerse it in a saucepan containing slightly salted boiling water and let it cook for about 20 minutes.

Pull it up from the water, gently unwind it from the towel and slice it like a salami. Arrange the slices in a large buttered baking dish, and season with the tomato sauce and grated Parmesan.

ADA SAYS: *You can prepare this ahead and when ready to serve, warm the dish in a preheated oven for a few minutes.*

ROTOLO DI PASTA CON RICOTTA E SPINACI

Pasta Roll with Ricotta and Spinach

12 oz egg pasta
2¼ lb spinach
2 tbsp butter
12 oz ricotta
Nutmeg
Grated Parmesan
Salt
Pepper
To serve: 10 tbsp butter, 1⅔ cups grated Parmesan

Egg pasta:
2½ cups flour, 3 eggs

Make egg pasta *(p170)* with the ingredients listed here and roll into a thin square sheet or buy store-bought fresh lasagna sheets.

Clean and wash the spinach carefully, then boil it in a little salted water. When still very al dente, drain, chop, and season with the butter. Then place in a bowl, add the ricotta, a pinch of nutmeg, grated Parmesan, 2 pinches of pepper, and a little salt. Mix everything well until you have a sufficiently smooth mixture.

Set the pasta on a floured work surface. Cover it with the ricotta mix and roll it in the shape of a salami. Wrap the roll in a clean kitchen towel, which you will tie at both ends and in the center, and place in a saucepan with plenty of salted water, letting it simmer for about 30 minutes.

Once the roll has been removed from the water, gently release it from the wrapper; let it cool, cut it into not too thin slices and season with melted butter and ⅓ cup of grated Parmesan.

TORTELLINI ALLA BESCIAMELLA

Tortellini with White Sauce

Nutmeg
1 egg yolk
3 tbsp cream
3½ tbsp butter
2¼ lb tortellini
3½ oz grated Parmesan
Salt
Pepper

White sauce:
⅓ cup flour, 3½ tbsp butter, 2 cups milk

Prepare a loose white sauce *(p16)* with the ingredients listed here. As soon as it is ready, remove the saucepan from the heat and gently stir in the salt, pepper, a pinch of nutmeg, egg yolk, cream, and butter.

Cook the tortellini in plenty of boiling salted water until al dente, about 20 minutes. Drain and toss with the sauce. Toss gently, sprinkle with grated Parmesan, and serve hot.

TORTELLINI ALLA BOLOGNESE CON RAGÙ

Tortellini with Ragu Bolognese

Ragu Bolognese *(p32)*
Olive oil
3½ oz ground pork
2 oz turkey breast
2 oz ground veal
1 oz lean ham
2 oz mortadella
2 oz calf's brain
Lamb brain
2 egg yolks
1 cup grated Parmesan
Nutmeg
1 lb store-bought tortellini
Salt
Pepper

Egg pasta:
4 cups flour, 5 eggs, 2 egg shells water

Prepare the ragu as directed.

For the filling: Put the oil in a saucepan, when it is hot, add the ground pork, turkey, and veal. Let it brown and then add the ham, mortadella, the calf's brains and half a lamb brain. Cook a little longer and then chop everything thoroughly together or use a food processor.

Add the egg yolks, grated Parmesan, salt, pepper, and a little nutmeg. Mix everything well.

Use 1 pound store-bought egg pasta or make your own egg pasta *(p170)* using the ingredient amounts listed here. Roll it out thin enough and cut out disks with a 1½-inch round pastry cutter. Put a little filling on each disk.

Holding the disk in your hands, fold one half over the other, making sure that the two halves do not match exactly, but that the half that remains above stays a little further back than the one that remains below.

Press with your fingers on the edge so that the two parts close well, then raise the edge itself and bring the two ends over each other, closing the tortellino on the tip of the middle finger of the left hand and thus obtaining the traditional ring shape.

Once all the tortellini are made, place them on a lightly floured cloth and let them rest for a few hours. Boil the tortellini in plenty of boiling salted water with a tablespoon of oil until al dente, about 15 minutes. Drain well to prevent the sauce from diluting too much.

Serve with the prepared ragu and sprinkle with grated Parmesan.

ADA SAYS: *Tortellini, if made well in advance, become a little dry and break easily during cooking. To avoid this inconvenience, soak the dry tortellini for about 10 minutes in cold water; then take them out of the water with a slotted spoon and put them in a pot with warm and suitably salted water, which you can quickly bring to a boil.*

TORTELLINI AL PETTO DI POLLO

Chicken Tortellini

1 chicken
1 onion
Whole clove
1 carrot
Parsley
Cream
1 lb 10 oz tortellini
7 tbsp butter
9 tbsp grated Parmesan
Salt

Cream sauce:
3½ tbsp butter, 6½ tbsp flour, 2 cups chicken broth

Clean the chicken, tie it, and put it in a tight fitting saucepan. Cover it with a quart of water and put it on the stove. As the water heats up, skim it and when it reaches a boil, season with salt, the onion in which you have stuck the clove, carrot, and parsley. Cover the saucepan, reduce the heat, and simmer slowly for 45 minutes, until the chicken is well cooked.

When the chicken is cooked, remove it, let it cool a little, then remove the two breasts with a knife and set them aside. Carefully debone the rest of the chicken and chop the meat finely.

Prepare a cream sauce *(p17)* with the ingredients listed here. Cook slowly to get a sauce of the right consistency. Then, off the heat, add the chicken pieces and ¾ cup of cream.

Boil the tortellini in abundant boiling salted water, drain and then season with butter and grated Parmesan and with the warm sauce.

Transfer to an oven pan and mix in the chicken breast cut into strips. Add another two or three spoonfuls of broth, sprinkle plenty of grated Parmesan on the tortellini, arrange here and there a few more pieces of butter, and put the pan in a preheated oven for about 10 minutes, so that the tortellini can flavor well.

TORTELLONI BOLOGNESI

Tortelloni Bolognese

1 lb ricotta
1 cup grated Parmesan
Parsley
Nutmeg
1 lb egg pasta
7 tbsp butter
Salt
Pepper

Egg pasta:
2½ cups flour, 3 eggs

Put the ricotta in a bowl and add half the grated Parmesan, finely chopped parsley, salt, pepper and nutmeg. Mix everything with a wooden spoon.

Make egg pasta *(p170)* with the ingredients listed here and, if necessary, a few tbsp of water or use store-bought sheets of fresh pasta. Roll out the dough rather thinly.

With a 2¾-inch round pastry cutter, cut the dough into disks. In the middle of each disk, place a large hazelnut of the Ricotta mixture and close them, giving them the shape of a large tortellino. As you finish the tortelloni, line them up on a tray with a lightly floured towel. Then cook them in plenty of boiling salted water until al dente. Dress them with butter and Parmesan.

ADA SAYS: *These are also very good with a creamy tomato sauce.*

BAKED PASTA

TO PREPARE AND COOK LASAGNA

Lasagna are strips of pasta of various widths, which are already freely available in grocery stores, or can be made at home. Lasagna requires two successive stages of cooking: one boiling and one cooking in the oven. Boil in salted water with a few spoonfuls of oil, in a large pot a few pieces at a time. As the lasagna noodles reach the right doneness, they should be carefully removed with a large slotted spoon, one at a time. Carefully, so as not to break them, drain them well and place them on a damp cloth. After this preliminary treatment, the lasagna noodles should be arranged in layers in a pan, alternating them with the sauce. The cooking in the oven is the crowning glory of the preparation. It takes place at a moderate heat, and can last from 10 minutes to 30 minutes or more. For these recipes, you can use the sauces from chapter one.

LASAGNE ALLA MODENESE VERDI

Green Lasagna Modena Style

Beef and tomato sauce *(p35)*
Olive oil
3½ tbsp butter
Grated Parmesan
Salt

Green egg pasta:
4¾ cups flour, 3 eggs, 7 oz boiled spinach

White sauce:
6½ tbsp flour, 3½ tbsp butter, 2 cups milk

Make green egg pasta *(p170)* using the ingredients listed here or use store-bought fresh lasagna. Roll out the dough into 1 or 2 sheets that are not too thin. With a small knife divide the sheets into 4-inch squares. Put a wide pan on the heat with lightly salted water with a tablespoon of oil and when the water boils, cook the lasagna sheets a few at a time.

Place them, one at a time, on a damp cloth, letting them cool.

Have ready a good beef and tomato sauce. Make a white sauce *(p16)* with the ingredients listed here.

Butter a suitable baking dish, make a first layer of lasagna. Dress with the beef and tomato sauce and plenty of Parmesan; and continue to arrange the lasagna in layers, always alternating them with sauce and cheese. On the last layer, in addition to the sauce, pour over the white sauce spreading it with a spatula so that it completely covers the entire top. Sprinkle with grated Parmesan and put bits of butter here and there.

Put the pan in a moderate oven for about 20 minutes so that the lasagna flavors well and the top gets a nice golden crust. Serve straight from the baking dish.

ADA SAYS: *You can enrich and make the lasagna more substantial by adding extra sauce at the table.*

LASAGNE ALLA NAPOLETANA

Neapolitan Lasagna

Olive oil
1 lb ricotta
2 eggs
1 cup grated Parmesan
Butter
1 lb mozzarella
Salt
Pepper

Egg pasta:
4¾ cups flour, 5 eggs

Sausage and mushroom ragu:
10 oz ground beef, 4 sausages, 1 oz dried mushrooms, 2 tbsp tomato paste, 9 oz peeled tomatoes, dry red wine, onion, celery, carrot, parsley, olive oil

Make the egg pasta *(p170)* with the ingredient amounts listed here and if necessary a few spoonfuls of water or use store-bought fresh lasagna sheets. Roll out the dough on a floured surface into thin sheets and cut out 4-inch squares.

Bring a large pot of lightly salted water to a boil with the addition of a few tablespoons of oil. As soon as the water boils, immerse 5 or 6 squares of pasta at a time and cook a few minutes. Scoop them out with a slotted spoon and line them up on a damp kitchen cloth.

Prepare a sausage and mushroom ragu *(p33)* using the ingredient amounts listed here.

Drain the ricotta through a sieve, transfer to a bowl, and add the eggs, plenty of grated Parmesan, salt, and pepper and mix everything with a wooden spoon.

Butter a fairly large baking dish. Take the lasagna sheets one by one, cover the bottom, placing them one next to the other. Make a first layer of lasagna sheets, spread a little of the prepared ricotta. Put here and there a few slices of mozzarella and a few spoonfuls of ragu. Make a second layer of sheets and season it like the previous one. Continue like this until the last layer, which must be lasagna sheets. On this last layer put plenty of grated Parmesan and lastly make a layer, complete and united, of very thin slices of mozzarella. Finish by spreading the remaining sauce on the mozzarella.

Put the dish in a very moderate oven and let it simmer for about 45 minutes. Immediately send the lasagna to the table and serve straight from the baking dish.

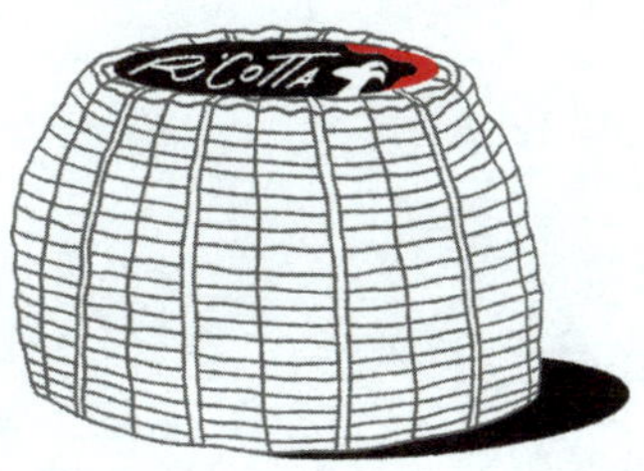

LASAGNE AL POMODORO

Tomato Lasagna

2¼ lb tomatoes
1 lb lean beef
3½ tbsp butter
Olive oil
Basil
Nutmeg
1 lb fresh lasagna sheets
9 tbsp grated Parmesan
7 oz mozzarella
Salt

Blanch, peel, seed, and chop the tomatoes. Chop the beef and put it in a saucepan with the butter and 4 tablespoons of oil. Brown it over high heat, then add the tomatoes. Season with salt, basil, and a trifle of nutmeg and cook over high heat for about 1 hour.

Put a large wide pan on the heat with plenty of lightly salted water with a few tablespoons of oil. As soon as the water boils, immerse 5 or 6 sheets of pasta at a time and cook for a few minutes. Lift them out with a slotted spoon and line them up on a damp kitchen towel.

Take an ovenproof pan; on the bottom make a layer of sauce, make a layer of lasagna sheets over the sauce; pour more sauce, sprinkle with grated Parmesan and garnish with slices of mozzarella. Continue to make layers of sauce, lasagna, Parmesan, and mozzarella, finishing with a ladle of sauce. Place the pan in the oven for about 20 minutes, then place it on a serving plate and send to the table.

LASAGNE CON FUNGHI

Mushroom Lasagna

1 lb fresh lasagna sheets
2 oz dried mushrooms
7 oz lean beef
Onion
1 carrot
Celery stalk
Parsley
7 tbsp butter
Milk
3½ oz prosciutto
1 cup grated Parmesan
Salt

Put a large wide pan on the heat with plenty of lightly salted water with the addition of a few tablespoons of oil. As soon as the water boils, immerse 4 or 6 sheets of pasta at a time. After a few minutes, scoop them out with a slotted spoon and line them up on a damp kitchen towel.

Clean the dried mushrooms and set aside in some cold salted water to reconstitute. Dice the lean beef, half an onion, a carrot, half a celery stalk, and parsley. Sauté everything with a knob of butter and, when they are well browned, sprinkle them with a few spoonfuls of milk. Add the dried and drained mushrooms. Wet with enough water, reduce the heat, and cook slowly until the mushrooms are completely cooked.

Cut the prosciutto into strips and grate the Parmesan. Butter a large shallow ovenproof pan and cover the bottom with a layer of lasagna sheets, on this layer put a few spoonfuls of the meat and mushroom sauce, and add a few strips of prosciutto. Put here and there a few pieces of butter and sprinkle with Parmesan. Make a second layer, and then a third and a fourth, alternating the pasta with sauce and ending with a layer of pasta, on which you will pour plenty of melted butter and grated Parmesan. Put the dish in a preheated oven with a good heat for about 20 minutes so that the sauce can perfume the pasta well, which will take a nice light gold color on the surface.

LASAGNE CON RICOTTA

Lasagna with Ricotta

Parsley
1 cup grated Parmesan
1 lb ricotta
Olive oil
Butter
Salt

Egg pasta:
4¾ cups flour, 5 eggs, 3 tbsp water, salt (or store-bought)

White sauce:
¾ cup flour, 7 tbsp butter, 4 cups milk

Make the egg pasta *(p170)* with the ingredients listed here and a pinch of salt, or use store-bought. Roll it out thinly with a rolling pin. From the pasta sheet, cut out 4-inch squares.

Make a white sauce *(p16)* with the ingredients listed here. Let it thicken a little making sure to get it smooth and well worked, then season with a pinch of salt, chopped parsley, and half of the grated Parmesan. While the sauce is still hot, stir in the ricotta, stirring vigorously.

When you have prepared the sauce, boil the squares of pasta a few at a time in lightly salted water with the addition of a tablespoon of oil. As soon as they come back to the surface, scoop them out with a slotted spoon and let them drain on a damp kitchen towel.

Generously butter a pan, cover the bottom with the pasta squares and spread a layer of the ricotta mix on top, sprinkle with grated Parmesan. Continue to make layers of noodles, ricotta, and grated Parmesan, finishing with the Parmesan. Put the pan in a hot oven for about 20 minutes, then send it to the table.

LASAGNE DI CARNEVALE

Carnival Lasagna

1 lb fresh lasagna sheets
1 onion
10 oz lean beef
Olive oil
2¼ lb tomatoes
Parsley
2 eggs
1 cup grated Parmesan
Flour
1 lb mozzarella
Butter
1 carrot
Salt
Pepper

Boil the lasagna sheets a few at a time in lightly salted water with the addition of a tablespoon of oil. As soon as they come back to the surface, scoop them out with a slotted spoon and let them drain on a damp kitchen towel.

Prepare the sauce: Finely slice an onion and brown it with the beef in half a glass of oil. As soon as it has taken a nice baked brown color, add the salt, pepper, and the tomatoes (peeled, seeded, and chopped). Cook for 1 hour. If the sauce reduces too much, add a few tablespoons of water or broth.

Remove the meat from the sauce and chop finely. Put the chopped meat in a bowl, add chopped parsley, the eggs, and half the grated Parmesan. Mix this mixture well and form some meatballs. Dip them in flour and fry them in hot oil.

Butter a baking dish, cover the bottom with a layer of lasagna squares, then diced mozzarella, grated Parmesan, some fried meatballs, and a little sauce. Then make more layers the same way. The last layer must be lasagna and on it put the remaining grated Parmesan and the remaining sauce. Place the pan in a preheated moderate oven for about 20 minutes, then send it to the table and serve straight from the baking dish.

MILLE FOGLIE DI PASTA ALL'UOVO

Pasta of a Thousand Leaves

Olive oil
Beef and tomato sauce *(p35)*
3½ oz sweetbreads
Butter
2 oz chicken giblets
1 oz dried mushrooms
Grated Parmesan
Salt
Pepper
Optional: truffle

Egg pasta:
4¾ cups flour, 6 eggs (or 1 lb 5 oz store-bought egg pasta)

Meatballs:
5½ oz lean ground beef, 2 tbsp butter, a large walnut of breadcrumbs, flour, lard or oil for frying

Well ahead, prepare a good beef and tomato sauce as directed.

If not using store-bought, prepare the egg pasta *(p170)* with the ingredient amounts listed here, keeping it very firm and working it vigorously. Divide this dough into 8 equal pieces and roll out each piece with a rolling pin, making sure to keep the dough in a round and rather thick shape. When you have rolled out all the dough, let it dry.

Put a large wide pan with water, a tablespoon of oil and salt on the heat and, when the water boils, take one sheet at a time and proceed gently to dip it into the boiling water. Cook for only a few minutes to keep the pasta quite firm and then, carefully, using two large slotted spoons, scoop up the cooked sheet and lay it flat on a damp kitchen towel. Cook all the other sheets one at a time.

The sauce will now be enriched with various elements: meatballs, sweetbreads, chicken giblet, truffles, and mushrooms.

Prepare the meatballs: Mix the beef with a small piece of butter and the breadcrumbs soaked in water and then squeezed dry. Season the flour with salt and pepper and make some very small meatballs, no bigger than a hazelnut, which you will toss in flour and fry in lard or oil, taking care not to let them dry out.

Prepare the sweetbreads: Soak them in fresh water for some time, drain, put them in a saucepan, cover with water, and bring them to a boil. Let them cool in their cooking water. When they are cool, free them from any skin, cut them into small pieces, and cook with a little butter in a small pan for about 10 minutes.

Prepare the giblets: Clean them very well, wash them, and cut them into small pieces, and sauté them with a little butter.

Soak the mushrooms in cold water for about 20 minutes, wash them, cut them into pieces, and cook them in a pan with half a glass of oil. Cover the pan and let it cook for a long time adding, if the pan gets dry, a little water.

When the various ingredients are ready, add them to the meat and tomato sauce.

Butter a baking dish, a little larger than the sheets of pasta, and sprinkle the bottom with a ladle of sauce. Put down the first sheet and spread more sauce on it, sprinkle over grated Parmesan and continue like this alternating disks of pasta, sauce, and grated Parmesan. You can also put, if you like, a few pieces of butter and a few slices of truffles.

Put the dish in a warm oven at a very light heat for about 20 minutes. Remove the pan from the oven and let everything settle for a few minutes. Then cut into equal servings, put each on a plate, and have it brought to the table.

RIGATONI AL FORNO

Baked Rigatoni

Tomato sauce *(p37)*
3½ oz mozzarella
3½ oz ham
2 oz grated Gruyère
9 tbsp grated Parmesan
1 lb 5 oz rigatoni
3½ tbsp butter
Salt
Pepper

White sauce:
2 tbsp butter, 3 tbsp flour, 1 cup milk

Make a tomato sauce as directed and let it thicken well. Then prepare a white sauce *(p16)* using the butter, flour, and milk amounts listed.

Cut the mozzarella and ham into small pieces, grate the Gruyère and Parmesan, and as soon as the tomato sauce is cooked, add them to the pan and pour the white sauce into the pan, stirring gently to mix the various ingredients well. Keep the sauce warm.

Boil the rigatoni in plenty of lightly salted boiling water until al dente. Drain them and toss with the sauce.

Butter a round baking pan, arrange the rigatoni, and put it in a preheated oven for about 20 minutes.

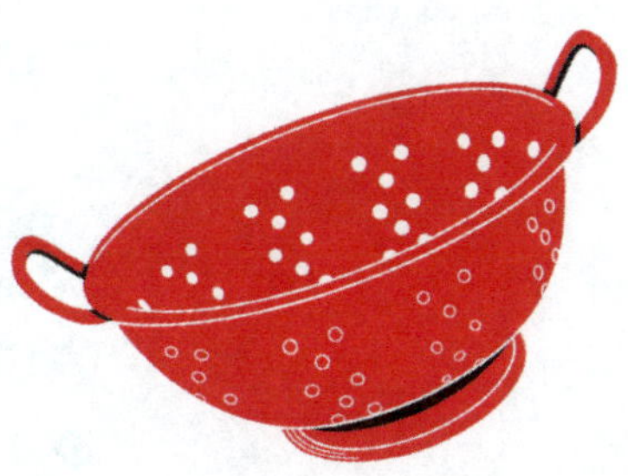

RIGATONI AL GRATIN CON ASPARAGI

Rigatoni Gratin with Asparagus

2¼ lb asparagus
2 eggs
9 tbsp grated Parmesan
Basil
Bouillon cube
14 oz rigatoni
Butter
3½ oz ham
Breadcrumbs
5 oz Fontina
Salt
Pepper

White sauce:
6½ tbsp flour, 3½ tbsp butter, 1 cup milk

Peel the asparagus, rinse them well, cut them all to the same length, tie them into bunches, and boil them in plenty of lightly salted boiling water for about 15 minutes. Remove them from the pan—do not throw the water away—run them under cold water to set the color, drain well, and cut the stalks into small pieces while keeping the tips intact.

Separate the eggs. Whip the egg whites until stiff peaks form. Make a white sauce *(p16)* using the ingredient amounts listed here. Season with salt and pepper, remove from the heat, add the Parmesan, and a few chopped basil leaves. Let cool, then add the egg yolks one at a time and finally the whipped egg whites. Fold carefully and lightly, so as not to deflate the whites.

Now pour the asparagus cooking water into a larger pot, add 8 cups of water and a bouillon cube, bring it back to a boil and boil the rigatoni in this water, keeping them very al dente.

Drain, toss with a tablespoon of butter cut into small pieces, the ham cut into strips, and the asparagus pieces (but not the tips). Butter a round mold with a center tube and sprinkle it with breadcrumbs. On the bottom, distribute 2 spoonfuls of the prepared sauce, ⅓ of the rigatoni pressed down to compact, cover them with a few slices of Fontina and over these put a little sauce. Repeat this operation until all the ingredients are used up. Finish with the sauce covered with the last slices of Fontina. Put the mold in a preheated oven for about 20 minutes. Invert the mold onto a serving dish, place the asparagus tips in the center, drizzle with melted butter, and sprinkle with grated Parmesan. Serve immediately.

TAGLIATELLE ALLA CREMA

Tagliatelle with Cream

1 cup grated Parmesan
6½ tbsp flour
3 cups milk
7 tbsp butter
Nutmeg
3 eggs
1 lb 5 oz tagliatelle
Salt

Put ½ the Parmesan in a saucepan with the flour and wet everything well with the cold milk. Season with a pinch of salt, a small piece of butter, a trifle of nutmeg and bring the pan to the heat. Always stirring with a wooden spoon, let the mixture thicken, then remove it from the heat and add the rest of the butter and remaining Parmesan and finally, when the mix has cooled a little, the egg yolks.

Whip the egg whites to a firm snow and, stirring gently, add them to the rest. Boil the pasta in slightly salted water with the addition of 2 tablespoons of oil; make sure it does not cook too much, drain. Season with the sauce.

Butter a baking dish, pour in the tagliatelle and place them in a preheated oven of moderate heat for 15 minutes or a little more. Then place the pan on a plate and send it to the table.

ADA SAYS: *Even though there is no cream in this recipe, the sauce is creamy enough.*

Timbales & Pasticci

BUCATINI E PICCIONI IN PASTICCIO

Bucatini and Pigeon Pasticcio

3 squab
8½ tbsp butter
2 oz prosciutto
Onion
1 carrot
1 celery stalk
Flour
Marsala
Bouillon cube
10 oz bucatini
9 tbsp grated Parmesan
1 egg
Salt

Pie dough:
2½ cups flour, 14 tbsp butter, 6 tbsp water

White sauce:
2 tbsp butter, ¼ cup flour, 1¼ cups milk

Make a pie dough *(p275)* using the ingredient amounts listed here. Let it rest for at least 30 minutes. Also make a white sauce *(p16)* with the butter, flour, and milk listed here and keep warm.

Choose 3 young squab, fat and well-fleshed, clean them carefully then break each pigeon into 4 serving pieces, rinse the pieces and dry them.

Put a spoonful of butter in a saucepan, the prosciutto, ½ an onion, a piece of carrot, and a celery stalk, all chopped rather finely. Let everything brown a little and then add the squab, which you will season with salt and pepper. When they have taken a nice dark color, sprinkle with ½ a spoonful of flour, mix and sprinkle with a finger of Marsala. When the wine has evaporated, cover the squab with water in which you have dissolved half a bouillon cube. Cover the saucepan and continue cooking slowly for 30 minutes or so, until the squab are cooked and the sauce sufficiently thickened.

Break the bucatini into 4-inch pieces, boil them in plenty of boiling salted water and rather al dente. Drain and transfer to a bowl.

Remove the squab from the saucepan and season the dough with the pigeon juices, 2 tablespoons of butter, and plenty of grated Parmesan cheese.

Lightly butter a shallow pan about 10 inches in diameter. Divide the pie dough into two pieces, one slightly larger than the other. Roll out the smaller piece and line the bottom of the pan.

Place almost all the bucatini in the pan—leaving a space of a couple of fingers around—and adjust the 12 pieces of squab on the bucatini. Cover with the remaining bucatini and sprinkle a fairly liquid and slightly warm white sauce over everything. Spread it well with a spatula so that it can penetrate into the far corners. Finally roll out the larger piece of dough and cover the entire pie with it. Press the edges with your fingers so that they fit perfectly, and with a small knife trim off any excess dough, giving the pie a regular shape. Brush the surface of the pie with a beaten egg and place it in a preheated moderate oven for a good 30 minutes so that the pie take on a good color. Serve it hot.

ADA SAYS: *You can use the squab giblets to enrich the sauce, but first they must be seared in butter and then poached in a little broth or water.*

CAPELLINI IN TIMBALLO

Timbale of Angel Hair Pasta

10 oz capellini (angel hair pasta)
7 tbsp butter
Grated Parmesan
1 egg
Breadcrumbs
7 oz mozzarella
3½ oz prosciutto
Optional: tomato passata, butter, salt

Boil the pasta in plenty of lightly salted boiling water until al dente. Drain, but not too much, and toss with plenty of butter, grated Parmesan, and the egg (beaten as for an omelet).

Butter a 6½-cup mold, throw in the breadcrumbs and, turning the mold in all directions, make the crumbs stick all over. Then turn it upside down, beating it lightly to release the excess.

Arrange ½ the capellini in the mold, put the mozzarella and prosciutto cut into small pieces in the middle, fill the mold with the remaining capellini, press lightly so that they fill everywhere, sprinkle the surface with a few more breadcrumbs, and pieces of butter and put in a hot oven with good heat, for about 20 minutes, to give time for the timbale to set. Remove the mold from the oven, let it rest for a few minutes, then turn it out and send to the table.

ADA SAYS: *You can also accompany this with a light tomato sauce of passata cooked with a little butter and salt and placed in a gravy boat to the side.*

MACCHERONI IN PASTICCIO

Macaroni Pasticcio

2 sausages
2 eggs
Flour
Olive oil
1 lb fresh mushrooms
1 lb macaroni
1 cup grated Parmesan
1 cup powdered sugar

Cream sauce:
3 egg yolks, 9½ tbsp flour, 2 cups milk, 6 tbsp sugar

Pie dough:
3¼ cups flour, 14 tbsp butter, 4 egg yolks, ¾ cup sugar, cinnamon

Meat sauce:
1 lb lean beef, 7 oz lean fat or ham for larding, half glass white wine, garlic, parsley, onion, carrot, celery, olive oil

Prepare a generous amount of meat sauce *(p34)* using the ingredient amounts listed here. Degrease it carefully.

Chop the meat from the sauce and transfer it to a bowl. Add the sausages (boiled and crumbled), an egg, and a spoonful of grated Parmesan. Mix well with your hands, then divide into very small meatballs. Flour them on both sides and fry them in plenty of oil.

Wash and dry the mushrooms, trim the stems, and cut into thin slices. Heat some oil in a pan, throw in the mushrooms, and cook over high heat for a few minutes, then season with salt and pepper and add them to the meat sauce.

Prepare the cream sauce *(p17)* using the eggs, flour, milk, and sugar listed here. Also make up a pie dough *(p275)* with ingredients listed here.

Break the macaroni into short pieces and cook in boiling salted water until al dente. Drain, toss with the sauce, and let them cool.

Lightly grease a shallow pan of about 12 inches in diameter. Divide the pie dough into 2 pieces, one larger than the other. Roll out the smaller piece and use it to line the pan. Add a layer of macaroni, leaving a free space of a couple of fingers around the macaroni. Arrange the meatballs so that they are all over the place. Cover with the remaining macaroni, making sure to give them the shape of a dome and pour the cream over, spreading it well with a spatula and making sure it fills all the gaps.

Roll out the second piece of dough into a round big enough to cover the whole pie. Set the dough on top and trim off the excess dough, but save the scraps. With the leftover dough, make a bead around or some other small decoration to your taste.

Wash the entire surface of the pie with beaten egg, cook it in a preheated moderate oven for about 45 minutes.

When it comes out of the oven, sprinkle it generously with powdered sugar.

◈ ADA SAYS: *Although excellent hot, the macaroni pasticcio is best served cold.*

PENNETTE IN PICCOLI PASTICCI

Pennette Pasticci

Tomato sauce *(p37)*
2 oz dried mushrooms
10 oz ground beef
2 eggs
1 cup grated Parmesan
Breadcrumbs
Milk
Parsley
Flour
Oil for frying
Butter
1 lb pennette
3½ oz mozzarella
Salt

Puff pastry:
1⅔ cups flour, 14 tbsp butter

You need 12 small round molds of 2½ inches in diameter.

Make a tomato sauce as directed and blend with the dried mushrooms (soaked and chopped).

Prepare the meatballs: In a bowl, combine the ground beef, 1 egg (beaten as for an omelet), half of the grated Parmesan, a fistful of breadcrumbs the size of a large apple (soaked in milk and squeezed), chopped parsley and a pinch of salt. Mix the ingredients well until you get a smooth mix. With floured hands shape small balls. Dip them in flour, fry them in hot oil, and add them to the tomato sauce. Let them both cook over low heat in a covered pan for about 10 minutes.

Prepare the puff pastry *(p275)* or you can use about 1 pound store-bought. Divide it into two pieces one larger than the other. Roll out the larger part of the dough on a floured surface, divide it into 12 equal parts, and line the molds so that the dough slightly overhangs the edge. Butter and breadcrumb the insides.

Boil the pennette in plenty of boiling salted water until al dente Drain and toss with the tomato sauce, the diced mozzarella, and the remaining grated Parmesan and let cool.

Fill the molds with the pasta mixture, press them well, then roll out the remaining pastry, forming 12 lids and cover the molds with them. Brush the lids with an egg yolk beaten with a little water.

Bake the pastries in a preheated moderate oven for about 30 minutes. Serve the pastries in their molds or tipped out onto a serving plate. They can be eaten both hot and lukewarm.

TORTELLINI IN PASTICCIO CON RAGÙ

Tortellini Pasticcio with Ragu

1 lb 10 oz tortellini
Prosciutto ragu *(p34)*
12 cups meat broth *(p88)* or 1 bouillon cube
5½ tbsp butter
2 tbsp breadcrumbs
1¾ cups grated Parmesan
1 egg yolk
Salt
Pepper

Egg pasta:
4¾ cups flour, 5 eggs, 2 egg shells of water

Pie dough:
2 cups flour, 12 tbsp butter, 2 egg yolks, 6 tbsp sugar, salt

Make the egg pasta *(p170)* for the tortellini using the ingredients listed here or use store-bought.

Prepare the prosciutto ragu as directed.

In the meantime, make the pie dough *(p275)* for the outer casing of the pie: Place the flour well mixed with the sugar on a work surface. Make a well in the center and add 2 egg yolks, the softened butter, and a pinch of salt. Quickly mix the ingredients, kneading them with your hands, then form into a ball, wrap in wax paper, and let it rest for 1 hour in the fridge.

Meanwhile, heat the broth—or lightly salted water—in a saucepan over the heat. When it starts boiling, add the tortellini and cook for 15 minutes. Drain and let them cool a little to lukewarm.

Divide the tart dough into 2 parts, one almost double the other. Roll out the larger part of the dough with a rolling pin into a disk big enough to cover the bottom and sides of a pie plate, which should be buttered and sprinkled with breadcrumbs first.

Arrange a layer of tortellini in the pie shell, season with a few spoonfuls of ragu, some butter, and plenty of grated Parmesan. Proceed in this way alternating layers of tortellini and layers of sauce, butter, and cheese until all the ingredients are used up. Roll out the smaller piece of dough into a disk and place on top of everything so that it perfectly covers the tortellini and rejoins the rim of the pie plate. Pinch the edges together so that everything is well enclosed.

Beat the egg yolk and brush the surface of the dough and put in a preheated moderate oven for 40 minutes. Carefully remove the pie from the mold and serve hot.

VERMICELLI IN TIMBALLO

Timbale of Vermicelli and Sardines

1 lb 5 oz vermicelli
Olive oil
Garlic
Parsley
10 oz fresh sardines
1 lb tomatoes
1 oz dried mushrooms
3 anchovies
Capers
3½ oz Gaeta olives
Breadcrumbs
Salt
Pepper

Boil the vermicelli in plenty of lightly salted water until al dente. Drain, toss with a little oil in which you have sautéed a clove of garlic. Add chopped parsley, a pinch of pepper, and let cool.

Fillet the fresh sardines, rinse them, dry them, and line them up in a pan greased with oil. Season them with a pinch of salt and let them sear on the heat.

Wash, blanch, peel, and seed the tomatoes and cut them into wedges. Cook them in a pan with 2 tablespoons of oil, over high heat so that the wedges do not come apart.

Soak the mushrooms in cold water and when they are reconstituted, cook them with a little oil, water, and a pinch of salt.

Fillet the anchovies, wash the capers, and pit the Gaeta olives.

Grease a round baking dish with oil and put in half the vermicelli, flattening them in a regular layer. Arrange half the tomato wedges on this layer of vermicelli and arrange the sardines, anchovy fillets, capers, olives, and mushrooms on top. Put the other half of the tomato wedges on top and cover with the remaining vermicelli, arranging them in a dome.

Scatter abundant breadcrumbs on this dome, so as to coat it completely and then finish with a very light drizzle of oil that you drip over everything. Put in a preheated moderate oven, until the bread has made a nice golden crust.

VINCISGRASSI IN TIMBALLO

Vincisgrassi Timbale

1 oz dried mushrooms
1 onion
Chicken broth
Tomato passata
Cinnamon
1 oz chicken livers
2 oz lamb sweetbreads
9 tbsp grated Parmesan
Black truffle
Salt
Pepper

Vincisgrassi:
2 cups flour, ¾ cup + 2 tbsp semolina, 7 tbsp butter, Marsala, 3 eggs

Thick white sauce:
1¾ tbsp butter, ¼ cup flour, ¾ cup + 1½ tbsp milk

Thinner white sauce:
3½ tbsp butter, 6½ tbsp flour, 2 cups milk

Vincisgrassi are similar to lasagna and are an exquisite pasta of the Marche region.

You can buy lasagna sheets, very similar to vincisgrassi, or make your own: Put the flour and semolina in a mount on a work surface. Make a well in the center and add a tablespoon of butter, half a glass of Marsala, and the eggs. Knead everything working the dough very well and then roll it out with a rolling pin into one or two thin sheets. Divide the sheets into rectangles measuring 4 × 6 inches. Cook the sheets one at a time in a large pot lightly salted boiling water with a tablespoon of oil. As the rectangles are cooked, place them on a damp kitchen towel so that they do not stick.

Soak the dried mushrooms. Put 2 tablespoons of butter with the thinly sliced onion in a saucepan. Cook the onion slowly and then add the dried mushrooms. Add a little broth, possibly chicken, and let the mushrooms cook. Add ¾ cup of tomato passata, season with salt, pepper, and a pinch of ground cinnamon and cook for about 20 minutes.

Make a fairly thick white sauce *(p16)* with the butter, flour and milk listed here.

When the tomato in the saucepan is cooked, add the white sauce and some more broth to dilute the sauce until it reaches the right density.

Blanch the livers in the remaining butter. Boil the sweetbreads and then cut them into pieces of about 2 inches in length.

Grease a pan of sufficient width with butter and line up a layer of pasta rectangles that you will coat with part of the sauce. On top of this, add plenty of grated Parmesan, a few cubes of liver, a few strips of sweetbread, a few slices of black truffle, and small pieces of butter. Continue making layers in this fashion until all the vincisgrassi are used up. Let sit for at least 6 hours, or overnight.

After this long rest, make another thinner white sauce with the ingredients listed here; if it gets too thick, add a little more milk. Pour it over the vincisgrassi spreading it well with a spatula and then put the dish into a rather hot oven until the sauce has a slight golden color. It will take about 30 minutes.

Put a tablespoon of butter in a pan and let it melt. When the vincisgrassi comes out of the oven, sprinkle the surface with melted butter and have them brought to the table immediately, because vincisgrassi should be eaten very hot.

RICE

TO COOK RICE

The most common and simplest way to cook rice is boiling. Use a fairly large saucepan and add a quantity of water from 3 to 4 times greater than the volume of the rice. So for 1 cup of rice you should add 3 to 4 cups of water. It takes 15 to 25 minutes to cook the rice, bearing in mind that the better the quality of the rice, the longer the cooking time.

It is not possible to establish, absolutely, how long it takes for the rice to reach the right cooking point; the time depends on the type and quality of the rice, on the tastes of the cook, on the needs of the various preparations. Some require undercooked rice; others normally cooked rice; others, finally, very well cooked. Usually the broth, the oil, butter, or the sauce will be boiling hot before the rice is added.

COOKING METHODS FOR RICE

COOKING IN BROTH

Bring the stock to a boil and pour in the rice. Stir, reduce the heat as soon as it comes to the boil, and slowly cook the rice, which must not remain too al dente.

COOKING IN SAUCES AND GRAVIES

The sauce and gravy must be quite liquid. Bring to a boil and pour in the rice; stir thoroughly to coat it well in the sauce and, once the boiling has resumed, cook the rice over very moderate heat, stirring occasionally. At the end of cooking, the rice should be al dente and almost dry. Before removing from the heat, check whether salt is needed.

COOKING IN FAT

Put the fat of your choice – butter, oil, lard, suet – into a saucepan, with or without seasoning, depending on the dish you wish to prepare, and when the fat has melted, pour in the rice, stirring continuously with a wooden spoon so that it absorbs the fat well, takes on a little flavor without coloring, but remains in separate grains. Boiling water or broth is then poured in a little at a time so that the rice is gradually cooked through, which must be al dente, keeping the heat always fairly strong.

COOKING IN MILK

Milk, in ½ of the quantity recommended for water, is brought to a boil and when it starts to boil, the rice is poured in and cooked, stirring from time to time so that it doesn't stick, adding more milk as the rice swells. Season with salt and continue until almost cooked.

RISO AL LATTE

Rice with Milk

7⅓ cups milk
2½ cups rice
Salt
Optional: grated Parmesan

Bring half the milk to a boil and as soon as it boils, pour in the rice and cook, stirring occasionally so it doesn't stick and adding, as the rice swells, the rest of the milk, while still hot. Season with a little salt and continue cooking, remembering that this rice must remain rather loose, and not as dry as, say, the usual risotto.

ADA SAYS: *This rice is delicious in its simplicity. If you want, you can add a few spoons of grated Parmesan at the last minute.*

RISO ALLA VALTELLINESE

Rice Valtellinese

3½ oz shelled fresh or ⅓ cup canned borlotti beans
1 celery stalk
10 oz cabbage
2½ cups rice
9 tbsp grated Parmesan
Sage
10 tbsp butter
Salt

Boil the borlotti beans in cold water to which you have added a celery stalk, and keep them warm in their water.

Remove the hard cabbage midribs and blanch the leaves for a few minutes in a pot of lightly salted boiling water. Drain them, then cut them into thin slices like fettuccine.

Boil the rice and the cabbage in a saucepan with plenty of boiling salted water. A few minutes before the end of cooking, add the well-drained and warmed beans. Let them flavor for a few moments and then drain off all the water and season with plenty of grated Parmesan. Fry some sage leaves in butter and pour both over the rice. Stir and serve.

RISO ARROSTO ALLA GENOVESE

Roasted Rice Genovese

8½ cups meat broth
3½ tbsp butter
Onion
7 oz fresh sausages
3½ oz shelled fresh peas
2 artichoke hearts
7 oz mushrooms
2½ cups rice
9 tbsp grated Parmesan
Salt

Have a good meat broth *(p88)* ready.

Put the butter, ½ a chopped onion, the fresh sausages (casings removed and chopped) in the pan and let them brown slowly. Add the peas, 2 very tender artichoke hearts cut in small pieces, and the well cleaned mushrooms cut into slices. Cover and cook over low heat, adding a little broth as needed.

Boil the rice in salted water for 5 minutes, drain and add it to the prepared sauce. Add enough broth to cook the rice. Grate in some Parmesan, mix, and put everything into an ovenproof pan.

Place in a preheated oven and cook until the rice is dry and has a large golden crust on the surface.

RISO CON L'ANITRA

Rice with Duck

Whole duckling
2 oz lard
1 onion
1 carrot
1 celery stalk
Parsley
Olive oil
White wine
Bouillon cube
2½ cups rice
3½ tbsp butter
9 tbsp grated Parmesan
Salt
Pepper

Carefully clean the duck, singe the feathers, cut off the head neck, and wing tips, then wash and dry it.

In a Dutch oven large enough so the duck can fit easily, place a mixture of lard, onion, carrot, celery, and parsley. Lay the duck on this bed of aromatic herbs, wiping everything with oil. Brown over medium heat, season with salt and pepper, and when the vegetables are wilted and the duck has taken on a beautiful golden color, add the white wine. As soon as this has evaporated, cover the duck with hot water or broth, in which you have dissolved half a bouillon cube, cover, and continue cooking over medium heat.

When the duck is cooked, after about 1 hour, and the liquid is fairly reduced, remove from the heat and keep it warm.

20 minutes before serving, cook the rice in lightly salted boiling water. Cut the duck into pieces and strain the cooking liquid through a sieve (discard the vegetables).

When the rice is cooked, drain it well, season with the butter and grated Parmesan, then spread it out on a serving plate, placing the pieces of duck on top. Sprinkle everything with the still boiling cooking liquid and send to the table.

RISO E PISELLI ALLA VENEZIA (RISI E BISI)

Rice and Peas Venetian Style

6½ cups meat broth or beef bouillon cube
Olive oil
3½ tbsp butter
1 oz ham or lard
Spring onion
Parsley
3 lb 5 oz fresh peas, shelled
2½ cups rice
Salt
Pepper

Have a good meat broth *(p88)* ready or you can use a bouillon cube.

In a saucepan, warm the oil and ½ the butter, then add the ham or lard, a spring onion and plenty of finely chopped parsley. Brown lightly, then pour the shelled peas into the pan, and when they are flavored, pour over a ladle of boiling broth—or water in which you will have diluted a bouillon cube—and bring up to almost a boil; then add the rice, cover with the remaining broth, and let it cook for 15 to 20 minutes.

RISO FREDDO ALLA MARINARA

Chilled Rice with Shrimp and Peppers

1½ cups rice
Lemon
1 lb shrimp
Olive oil
3 yellow and red bell peppers
3½ oz tuna in olive oil
3½ oz mushrooms in olive oil
Salt
Optional: cornichons, olives, diced lobster

Boil the rice in lightly salted boiling water and flavored with a few slices of lemon, keeping it rather al dente. Drain, rinse under cold water so that it does not overcook, spread on a clean cloth to dry.

Carefully wash the shrimp, boil them in lightly salted boiling water for about 5 minutes, then peel them, removing the heads and tails. Season with a little oil, a few drops of lemon juice, and a little salt.

Put the peppers in the oven until the skins are charred. Cool and carefully remove the skins, core and seed the peppers, and cut them into small squares. Simply season them with a little oil.

Arrange the rice on a serving dish, top with the tuna that you have chopped, mushrooms in oil, add the peppers and finally the shrimp. Season with a little salt and drizzle with oil.

ADA SAYS: *This cold rice can be made richer by adding diced lobster, sweet olives or cornichons.*

RISO GRATINATO

Rice Gratin

2½ cups rice
7 tbsp butter
3½ oz ham
1 egg yolk
Nutmeg
9 tbsp grated Parmesan
Salt
Pepper

White sauce:
6½ tbsp flour, 3½ tbsp butter, 2 cups milk

Cook the rice in boiling salted water and, when it has almost reached the right point, drain it and pour into a saucepan. Add the butter and the diced ham and mix thoroughly to let the rice absorb the sauce.

While the rice is cooking, prepare a white sauce *(p16)* with the ingredient amounts listed here. When the sauce is ready, stir in the egg yolk, a little nutmeg. and grated Parmesan. Add the sauce to the rice and give everything a good mix.

Grease a baking dish, put the rice in, smooth the surface, and put in a hot oven for a few minutes. When the rice has browned, place it on a serving plate and send it to the table.

RISO GRATINATO AI FRUTTI DI MARE

Shellfish Rice Gratin

1 carrot
2 onions
1 celery stalk
Parsley
White wine
10 oz shrimp
1 lb clams
1 lb mussels
Olive oil
Garlic
10 oz mushrooms
Flour
2½ cups rice
7 tbsp butter
Salt
Pepper

Put a carrot, an onion, a celery stalk, parsley, and ½ a glass of white wine in a saucepan with lightly salted cold water. Bring to a boil and as soon as it starts to boil, add the well washed shrimp. Let the shrimp simmer for 4 to 5 minutes, then drain, peel, and cut them into small pieces.

Carefully wash the clams in several changes of water, scrubbing them clean. Wash the mussels well and put both put in a pan with a little oil and a clove of garlic. Let them cook over high heat making them jump so that each one can feel the heat equally. When they are open, let cool until you can handle them, then shell them and put them in a bowl and cover with a little of their strained cooking liquid. Discard any that stay closed.

Remove the stems from the mushrooms, wash them quickly, and cut them into slices. Finely chop an onion, brown it with half a glass of oil and let it cook for about 10 minutes. Add the mushrooms and cook over high heat for about 10 minutes. Season with salt and pepper and sprinkle with a spoonful of flour and mix well. When the flour is well blended, add the white wine and ½ as much of the cooking liquid from the mussels and shrimp. Mix carefully until the sauce is well thickened.

Boil the rice in lightly salted boiling water, keeping it al dente. Drain it, season with the butter cut into small pieces, add the sauce with the mushrooms and seafood. Grease a baking pan, pour in the rice with its sauce and seafood and brown it in a preheated oven for about 10 minutes.

RISO IN BUDINO

Savory Rice Pudding

1 lb tomatoes
1 onion
1 celery stalk
Bay leaf
1 carrot
Olive oil
2½ cups rice
4 tbsp grated Parmesan
2 eggs
Salt
Optional: other vegetables to taste

White sauce:
3 tbsp flour, 2 tbsp butter, 1 cup milk

Wash the tomatoes, chop them, put them in a pan with the onion, celery, bay leaf, carrot, 4 tablespoons of oil, and salt. Cook the tomato until it is well reduced, then let it cool.

Make a white sauce *(p16)* with the ingredient amounts listed here. When it is ready, add it to the tomato sauce.

Boil the rice in lightly salted boiling water until very al dente. Drain and then add it to the sauce. Stir in the grated Parmesan and beaten eggs—well beaten as for an omelet—until well combined.

Butter a 4½-cup pudding mold with a central tube. Pour in the mixture, taking care that it does not reach the edge of the container. Tap the mold so there are no gaps and put to cook in a bain-marie in the oven or on the stove for about 20 minutes. When the pudding has risen up, turn it upside down on a plate, and send it to the table garnished with vegetables to taste.

RISO IN CAGNONE

Rice with Anchovies

Olive oil
1 onion
Parsley
6 anchovy fillets
2½ cups rice
7 tbsp butter
Salt
Optional: tomatoes, cut into wedges

A very old winter dish from the shepherds of Piedmont and Lombardy, typically made with cheese but this is a variation.

Put ½ a glass of oil and a finely chopped onion in a saucepan and cook for about 15 minutes, adding a little water if necessary to prevent it from browning too much. Add a handful of chopped parsley and the anchovies—washed, boned and chopped. Reduce the heat and mash the anchovies well to reduce them to a pulp. If you want, you can add some tomato wedges here.

Boil the rice in plenty of lightly salted boiling water until al dente. Drain and toss with the butter. Pour the sauce over the rice and serve immediately.

RISO IN TIMBALLO ALLA NAPOLETANA (SARTÙ)

Neapolitan Rice Timbale

Neapolitan meat sauce *(p36)* or tomato sauce *(p37)*
5 oz lean beef
14 tbsp butter
Fresh breadcrumbs
Milk
Flour
Oil or lard, for frying
1 oz dried mushrooms
4 cups meat broth *(p88)* or bouillon cubes
5 oz chicken giblets
2 sausages
2¼ cups rice
2 cups grated Parmesan
2 eggs
1 lb fresh peas
Nutmeg
1 egg yolk
Breadcrumbs
Salt
Pepper
Optional: 7 oz mozzarella, 2 oz ham

Tomato sauce:
2¼ lb tomatoes, 2 oz minced ham fat, onion, basil, butter

White sauce:
6½ tbsp flour, 3½ tbsp butter, 2 cups milk

First, prepare either a good Neapolitan-style meat sauce or a tomato sauce with a little ham added. Keep in mind that in both cases the sauce must be very thick.

Chop the lean beef and mix it with a small piece of butter and the fresh breadcrumbs soaked in milk and then squeezed. Season with salt and pepper and make some very small meatballs, no bigger than a hazelnut, which you will dip in flour and fry in oil or lard, taking care not to let them dry up.

Soak the dried mushrooms in cold water for 15 minutes and after cleaning them, cook them with a little butter and a few spoonfuls of broth or water, salt, and pepper.

Wash, clean and then cut the chicken giblets into not so small pieces and cook them with a little butter. Cook the sausages in a pan and then cut into slices.

When the sauce is done, set aside a few spoonfuls and then pour the rice into the saucepan and cook in the sauce, like a risotto, gradually adding the broth. Not too much, then season it with 3 or 4 spoonfuls of grated Parmesan and the whole eggs, checking its flavor at the same time. Pour this risotto-style mix onto a plate and wait for it to cool.

In another saucepan, combine the meatballs, mushrooms, sausages, giblets, and peas. Toss with the reserved sauce so that they can be flavored.

Make a white sauce *(p16)* with the ingredient amounts listed here and as soon as it thickens, remove it from the heat, season with salt, a little nutmeg, and stir in the egg yolk.

1 hour before serving, begin the construction of the timbale. Generously butter the inside of a 1½-quart round pudding mold, without a central tube and sprinkle it with very fine dried breadcrumbs. Turn the mold in all directions so that the crumbs sticks everywhere and then overturn it to let any excess fall out.

With the help of a spoon, arrange the risotto on the bottom and around the sides, leaving four or five spoonfuls aside. Press with the spoon to make the rice stick well to the walls and to the bottom, leaving a space in the middle like a box.

Put the prepared filling of meatballs, mushrooms, giblets, and peas in this gap, sandwiching it with the diced mozzarella and the white sauce. Add a generous spoonful of grated Parmesan and small pieces of butter, the size of hazelnuts, to the filling. Use the reserved risotto to cover the filling. Spread the rice with a spatula, sprinkle it with breadcrumbs, and place a few more pieces of butter on top. Put the timbale in a preheated moderate oven and leave it for a good 30 minues so that the breadcrumbs on top have time to make a nice golden crust.

Then take the timbale out, but do not turn it out of the mold immediately. Wait about 10 minutes for it to settle, and do not play tricks when it is overturned. With extra caution, gently pass the blade of a knife between the mold and the timbale inside to detach it and then turn it upside down onto a round plate. Send it to the table to be served hot and stringy.

ADA SAYS: *In spring it is excellent to serve the peas with ham or prosciutto: Shell the peas and cook them in a saucepan with 3½ tablespoons of butter, a pinch of salt, and a glass of water. Cook the peas for about 10 minutes over high heat, then before removing them from the heat, add 2 ounces of ham cut into strips and let flavor for a few minutes. Also cut the mozzarella into cubes.*

RISO IN TIMBALLO CON POLPETTINE

Rice Timbale with Meatballs

8½ cups meat broth or bouillon cubes
1 oz dried mushrooms
10½ tbsp butter
Garlic
Cognac
10 oz ground beef
5 eggs
Breadcrumbs
Milk
1 cup grated Parmesan
10 oz minced ham
Nutmeg
Flour
1 onion
2½ cups rice
Breadcrumbs
7 oz mozzarella
Salt

Make a meat broth *(p88)* or use bouillon cubes.

Soak the dried mushrooms in cold water for 15 minutes, then wash them, squeeze them, and cut them. Sauté with 3 tablespoons of butter and a clove of garlic, sprinkle with a small glass of Cognac and when this has evaporated, cover them with a little broth to complete the cooking.

In a bowl, mix the ground beef, 2 egg yolks, the fresh breadcrumbs soaked in milk and squeezed dry, 3 tablespoons of grated Parmesan, the minced cooked ham, salt, and a little nutmeg. Make meatballs as big as a walnut, flour them, and cook them in butter to brown well.

Now prepare the rice: Put 2 tablespoons of butter and a chopped onion in a pan, cook the onion over low heat until it becomes translucent, then add the rice and, stirring, let it absorb the sauce. Pour two ladles of boiling broth, moderate the heat, and as soon as the broth has been absorbed, wet the rice with more broth, continuing until the rice is cooked to al dente, about 15 minutes.

Remove the pan from the heat, stir in 3 whole eggs, a little grated Parmesan, and a tablespoon of butter, mix carefully, spread the rice on a large plate to cool.

Butter a tall, narrow 2-quart timbale mold and sprinkle with dried breadcrumbs. Line the bottom and sides with rice but hold a little aside. Fill the mold in layers: with meatballs, mushrooms, slices of mozzarella, grated Parmesan, and flakes of butter. Finally, cover with the reserved rice, sprinkle with dried breadcrumbs, pour a few tablespoons of melted butter over and then put the timbale in a preheated moderate oven for about 30 minutes.

Risotto

RISOTTO AI SETTE SAPORI

Risotto with Seven Flavors

2 oz dried mushrooms
7 tbsp butter
3½ oz prosciutto
3½ oz Gruyère
3½ oz mascarpone
1 cup milk
1 onion
2½ cups rice
4 cups broth or bouillon cubes
1 cup grated Parmesan
Salt

Soak the mushrooms in cold water, rinse, and clean them well, then put them in a saucepan with 2 tablespoons of butter and enough water to cover them. When they are cooked, drain and finely chop them.

Mix them in a bowl with the minced prosciutto, Gruyère cut into sticks, mascarpone, and the milk, mixing everything well.

Chop the onion and put it in an ovenproof saucepan with 2 tablespoons of butter, lightly brown the onion, wetting it several times with water, a spoon at a time. Add the rice and the boiling broth, return to a boil, cover and transfer to the preheated oven, leaving it there for 20 minutes.

Remove the pan from the oven. Stir more butter and half the grated Parmesan into the risotto and pour it into a serving dish. Arrange the mushroom, prosciutto, and cheese mix over the risotto. Finish with the remaining Parmesan and send promptly to the table.

RISOTTO ALLA BESCIAMELLA CON CARCIOFI

Artichoke Risotto

4 artichokes
Lemon
7 tbsp butter
1 onion
2½ cups rice
2 oz Parmesan
6½ cups broth or bouillon cubes
Salt

White sauce:
3 tbsp flour, 2 tbsp butter,
1 cup milk

Remove the outer leaves from the artichokes, cut out and diskard the hairy chokes, rub them with the lemon, and cut them into wedges. Submerge them in a pot of lightly salted boiling water and cook them through. Drain and put in a pan with a knob of butter and let them flavor for a few minutes.

Slice the onion and put it in a new pan with 2 tablespoons of butter letting it lightly brown. Add the rice, season with a pinch of salt and cook the rice, wetting it with ladles of hot broth, mixing it often with a wooden spoon.

Prepare a white sauce *(p16)* with ingredient amounts listed here and and when it is ready, remove from the heat and stir in the grated Parmesan.

As soon as the risotto is cooked, after about 20 minutes, top it with the remaining butter and more grated Parmesan and pour it into the serving dish.

Arrange the artichoke wedges on the risotto with their butter, pour the warm white sauce over everything and bring immediately to the table.

RISOTTO ALLA FREGOLI

Chicken Liver Risotto

6½ cups meat broth *(p88)*
5 oz chicken livers
1 oz dried mushrooms
14 tbsp butter
Onion
2 oz prosciutto
White wine
Marsala
2½ cups rice
9 oz shelled fresh peas
1 oz black truffle
1⅔ cups grated Parmesan
Salt
White pepper

Meat sauce:
10 oz beef, 3½ oz lardons of fat and lean prosciutto, half glass dry wine, onion, carrot, celery stalk

Well ahead of time, make a good meat broth as directed and some meat sauce *(p34)* using the ingredient amounts listed here.

Wash the livers, carefully remove the gall and any small part that may have been in contact with the gall that has turned green.

Soak the dried mushrooms in cold water for about 20 minutes. Put a saucepan on the heat with half the butter and half an onion cut thinly. Add the chicken livers, the prosciutto cut into strips, and mushrooms and cook over a moderate heat so that everything can brown gently, but without taking an excessive color.

Then pour in half a glass of white wine and half a glass of Marsala, add the rice, peas, and diced black truffle. Stir well so the alcohol in the wine evaporates. Then wet the rice with the broth and the meat sauce, season with salt and a pinch of white pepper and let the rice cook slowly for about 20 minutes. Finish with the other half of the butter and grated Parmesan. Give one last stir, pour the rice onto a plate and bring it immediately on the table.

RISOTTO ALLA MILANESE

Risotto Milanese

1 onion
5½ tbsp butter
Bone marrow
2½ cups rice
8½ cups meat broth *(p88)* made without tomatoes
Saffron
9 tbsp grated Parmesan
Salt
Pepper

Cut the onion into thin slices, then sauté with a spoonful of butter and an egg-size amount of well-chopped bone marrow. Cook slowly without letting it color and then add the rice.

Stir with a wooden spoon so that the rice soaks well into the fat and it does not stick, and then gradually wet with a few ladles of boiling broth. Season with salt and a pinch of pepper and cook with vivacity, always adding more boiling broth as the rice swells.

Halfway through cooking, dissolve a pinch of saffron into the saucepan. Let the risotto finish cooking, then season with the rest of the butter and grated Parmesan and send promptly to the table.

RISOTTO ALLA SBIRRAGLIA

Chicken Risotto

Whole chicken
10 oz beef trimmings (perhaps from meat broth)
2 onions
1 celery stalk
1 small carrot
2 oz pork belly or sausage meat
Celery heart
3½ tbsp butter
White wine
1 tomato
2½ cups rice
9 tbsp grated Parmesan
Salt

An exquisite preparation of Venetian cuisine.

Clean and bone a chicken carefully, cutting all the meat in small pieces. With the chicken bones, beef trimmings, an onion, a stalk of celery, and a carrot, prepare 2 quarts of broth.

Put a chopped onion and the minced pork belly in a saucepan with a knob of butter. Add the carrot and the heart of celery. Let them brown slowly and then add the pieces of chicken.

Continue cooking, covered and stirring from time to time, until the chicken has browned. Wet with a glass of white wine and let it evaporate almost completely. Then add a nice tomato, well ripe, peeled and seeded. Let the tomato cook a little and then add the rice. Ladle the hot chicken bone broth in a little at a time.

About 5 minutes before the end of the cooking, add the remaining butter and grated Parmesan. When the rice has reached the right point of cooking, after about 20 minutes, remove the celery and carrot from the pan and divide the risotto into the bowls.

RISOTTO ALLA TURCA

Turkish Risotto

2 red bell peppers
13 tbsp butter
Onion
2½ cups rice
Saffron
4 chicken livers
2 oz prosciutto
6 ripe tomatoes
Olive oil
Salt

Put the peppers in the oven, turning them often to toast the outside skin without overcooking them inside. When the skins have blackened, cool slightly, then remove the skin, rubbing them between your fingers, rinse them, remove the stems and seeds, and cut them into strips. Put the strips in a saucepan with a little butter and lightly season.

Put more than ½ the butter over heat in an ovenproof pan and add half a thinly sliced onion. Cook slowly, wetting it from time to time with a few spoons of water so that it does not color, and when it is cooked, add the rice.

Stir with a wooden spoon so the rice gets drenched in the seasoning and after a minute or two wet it with a generous 4 cups of boiling water. Season with a pinch of salt and the saffron dissolved in a little boiling water. Stir once, cover, and put it immediately in a hot oven. Leave, without stirring anymore, for exactly 20 minutes.

Clean the chicken livers. Carefully remove the gall, wash and cut them into cubes, brown them in a pan with a tablespoon of butter, season with a pinch of salt, then add the prosciutto, cut into strips. The livers cook quickly, so in a few minutes they will be ready.

Wash and cut the tomatoes into strips and cook them quickly over a very strong heat in a pan with a little oil.

After 20 minutes, remove the pan from the oven, scatter some butter in small pieces, and stir into the rice. Transfer to a plate. On top of the rice, arrange the prosciutto, livers, tomatoes, and peppers.

RISOTTO ALLA VALENCIANA (PAELLA ALLA VALENCIANA)

Paella

6½ cups meat broth *(p88)*
Olive oil
4½ oz lean pork
4½ oz veal shank meat
4½ oz baby squid
Garlic
1 onion
Bay leaf
4½ oz tomatoes or 1 tbsp tomato paste
Sugar
3½ oz chorizo
4½ oz sausages
4½ oz clams
6 shrimp
2 red bell peppers
Fresh peas
2½ cups rice
Saffron
Salt

Have ready a good meat broth.

Heat a glass of oil in a pan and when it is hot add the lean pork and the veal shank, cut into small cubes. Let them brown well then scoop up with a slotted spoon and add them to the pot with the broth.

Clean the squid, remove the internal pen-shaped cartilage, also remove the eyes and mouth, wash them thoroughly and cut the body into rings, shred the tentacles, and put them to cook in the same oil as the meat. As soon as they are cooked, put them in the broth. Still in the same oil, put a half clove of well chopped garlic, a chopped onion, and a bay leaf and let them color. Add the tomatoes (peeled, seeded, and chopped), season with salt and a little sugar and when the tomato is well cooked, add it to the broth pot. Also add the chorizo (whole).

Set the pot of broth on the stove and cook for 30 minutes, then remove the chorizo. Let the broth boil for another 30 minutes. Let the chorizo cool, then peel it and cut it into pieces.

Prick the sausages, put them in a small pan with ½ a glass of boiling water, in a strong oven for 5 minutes. Take them out and let cool. Pour the water with the fat into the broth pot. When the sausages are cool, cut them into slices.

Thoroughly wash the clams in several changes of water, put them in a pan with a little oil, heat them until they are all open, then shell them. Strain the cooking liquid and add it to the broth. Wash the shrimp well, boil for 5 minutes in lightly salted water, then shell and cut into cubes. Roast the peppers, peel them, and cut them into slivers. Boil ½ cup of fresh peas for 10 minutes in lightly salted water. Drain and cold-shock in cold water.

When the broth in the pot has boiled for 1 hour, take a large Dutch oven and heat some oil and the rice. Let it soak a little, stirring with a wooden spoon, then pour in the broth with all it contains. Add the peas, peppers, sausage, chorizo, clams, and shrimp and stir again.

Complete with a sauce made by pounding half a clove of garlic in a mortar, a teaspoon of saffron, ½ teaspoon of salt and dissolving everything with a spoonful of cold water.

Cover the pan and put in a preheated oven for 15 minutes, then turn off the oven, leaving everything to rest for another 5 minutes.

RISOTTO CON CARCIOFI E PISELLI

Risotto with Artichokes and Peas

2¼ lb fresh peas in the pod or 10 oz frozen
3 carrots
6 baby artichokes
Lemon
4 bouillon cubes
Olive oil
Butter
2 oz smoked bacon
1 onion
2 celery stalks
2½ cups rice
1 cup grated Parmesan
Salt

Shell the fresh peas. Peel the carrots, trim the ends, and cut them into slices. Remove the harder outer leaves from the artichokes, trim and using a small knife cut out the choke and rub with lemon. Cut into thin slices.

Prepare 2 quarts of broth with the bouillon cubes and keep warm.

In a large wide saucepan, put a glass of oil, 2 tablespoons of butter, the bacon diced, and the chopped onion and celery. Season with a little salt and when the fats have melted, add the peas and the artichokes and let them cook very slowly for a good 30 minutes, adding a ladle of broth if necessary. Finally add the rice.

Sweat the rice in the vegetables, then pour the boiling broth in a little at a time and, always stirring, and bring it to a boil.

To finish, pour the rice into a serving dish, sprinkle with grated Parmesan and serve immediately.

RISOTTO CON COZZE E VONGOLE

Risotto with Mussels and Clams

8½ cups fish broth *(p89)*
2¼ lb clams
2¼ lb mussels
Olive oil
Garlic
1 chili
5 tbsp butter
1 onion
2½ cups rice
Salt

Have ready a good fish broth ahead of time.

Wash the clams in several changes of water. Wash, scrub, and remove the beards from the mussels.

In a large pan with ½ a glass of oil, a whole clove of garlic, and a small chili, put the clams on to cook, covered, shaking the pan from time to time so that they all warm equally. When they are all open, take them out of the pan and put the mussels into the same pan and repeat the same operation.

When the mussels open, remove from their shells, put them in a bowl, and cover them with the cooking liquid, which should be left to stand for some time and then strained in a sieve.

In a large saucepan, put 2 tablespoons of butter, ½ a glass of oil, and brown a finely chopped onion. Add the rice, leave it soak in the sauce, then wet with the fish broth and bring it to a simmer. After about 15 minutes, add the mussels and clams to the risotto with their cooking liquid. Finish the risotto with the remaining butter, pour it into a serving dish, and serve immediately.

RISOTTO CON I GAMBERETTI

Shrimp Risotto

8½ cups fish broth *(p89)*
8 oz butter
1 onion
1 carrot
Parsley
Bay leaf
2¼ lb shrimp
Cognac
2½ cups rice
White wine
Salt
Pepper
Optional: grated Parmesan

Shrimp butter:
7 oz shrimp, 7 tbsp butter

Have ready a good fish broth.

Put a saucepan on the heat with 2 tablespoons of butter, half an onion, a carrot, a few sprigs of parsley, and a small bay leaf. Sauté, and add the washed shrimp and brown everything together for about 10 minutes, stirring occasionally. Halfway through, add a glass of Cognac and let it evaporate.

When the shrimp are cooked, peel them.

Make the shrimp butter: Boil the other 7 ounces of shrimp for 3 minutes starting them in cold lightly salted water. As soon as they are cooked, peel them. Put the shells to the side, they will help flavor your butter. Add the shrimp to a saucepan with the aromatics and the shells, add the 7 tablespoons of butter, put on the stove, and let it melt and stir the butter for a few minutes. Then strain the butter and let cool.

Put a finger of oil in a rather large saucepan, with 5 tablespoons of butter and a little chopped onion. Let the onion brown, then add the rice and let it soak, stirring. Wet it with a glass of white wine. As soon as the wine evaporates, wet the rice with the fish broth, season it with pepper, and let it cook. When the rice is almost cooked, add the shrimp and then off the heat stir in the prepared shrimp butter, which will give an exquisite perfume and a nice pink color. Give again a stir, pour into a plate, and bring to the table.

ADA SAYS: *The addition of grated Parmesan is optional, but highly recommended.*

RISOTTO CON LO SPUMANTE

Risotto with Sparkling Wine

8½ cups meat broth *(p88)* or bouillon cubes
7 tbsp butter
Olive oil
1 onion
2½ cups rice
Sparkling wine
9 tbsp grated Parmesan
Salt

Make a good meat broth as directed or use bouillon cubes.

In a large saucepan, combine 2 tablespoons of butter and ½ a glass of oil and brown the finely chopped onion. Add the rice, leave it to soak in the sauce, then add 2 glasses of sparkling wine, stirring until it has evaporated. Wet with the meat broth and cook the rice rather al dente. Finish with the remaining butter and the Parmesan.

RISOTTO CON SALSICCE

Risotto with Sausages

1 oz dried mushrooms
Onion
7 tbsp butter
4 sausages
9 oz tomatoes
2½ cups rice
Grated Parmesan
Salt

Put the mushrooms to soak for 20 minutes in cold water. Slice ½ an onion very thinly, put it in a saucepan with ½ of the butter and let it cook slowly without becoming too brown.

Then remove the casings from the sausages and chop and finely dice the mushrooms. Add both to the onion. Lightly brown the sausages and then add the tomatoes in pieces. Cover and let it cook slowly, wetting, if necessary, with a little water. If needed, add a pinch of salt.

When the mushrooms are cooked, add the rice, let them soak for a moment, stirring, and then simmer it with lightly salted boiling water or, if you have it, some broth.

Finish with the remaining butter and grated Parmesan.

RISOTTO CON SCAMPI

Risotto with Langoustines

8½ cups fish broth *(p89)*
4½ lb langoustine, or
 jumbo shrimp
Olive oil
5½ tbsp butter
1 onion
Cognac or Marsala
2½ cups rice
9 tbsp grated Parmesan
Salt
Pepper

Prepare a good fish broth ahead of time.

Wash and shell the langoustines and keep them aside in a bowl. Put a finger of oil and 2 tablespoons of butter in a saucepan. Slice the onion thinly and slowly brown the onion. Add the langoustine and cook rather slowly. Season with salt and pepper and sprinkle with a small glass of Marsala or Cognac.

Add the rice and cook step by step with the fish broth. When the rice is cooked, complete with the rest of the butter and grated Parmesan. Give a final stir and pour into a serving dish.

RISOTTO CON SEPPIE

Risotto with Cuttlefish

8½ cups fish broth *(p89)*
1 lb medium cuttlefish
Olive oil
Onion
Garlic
White wine
2 tbsp tomato paste
2½ cups rice
Salt
Optional: chili

Prepare a good fish broth ahead of time.

Cuttlefish contain a small sac with black ink inside, and another at the top with a dark yellow liquid, which serves to give more flavor to the dish. After removing the skin from the cuttlefish, remove the central bone, open them and clean them well without damaging the ink sacks, remove the mouth and eyes, cut the tentacles into small pieces, and cut the cuttlefish into thin strips. Wash everything until the cuttlefish are very white.

Put a little oil in a saucepan with half a finely chopped onion and a small piece of crushed garlic. Let them sauté to a light color then, add the cuttlefish, season with salt and pepper, and let them brown for a moment. Sprinkle them with a glass of white wine. When the wine has evaporated, add the tomato paste.

Let cook a little while stirring, then pour a couple of ladles of broth or water into the saucepan, cover, reduce the heat and let it finish cooking the cuttlefish slowly, slowly, perhaps for as long as 1 hour. You can do this ahead of time.

Then add the rice to the cuttlefish saucepan, let it flavor stirring slightly, wet it with boiling broth or water, add the black and yellow inks and continue to turn the rice from time to time so as not to let it stick, adding more boiling broth or water until completely cooked, which will take about 20 minutes.

RISOTTO CON TONNO

Risotto with Tuna

8½ cups fish broth *(p89)*
1 onion
3½ tbsp butter
2½ cups rice
7 oz tuna
Salt
Optional: 2 hard-boiled eggs, parsley, capers

Cream sauce:
3½ tbsp butter, 6½ tbsp flour, 2 cups fish broth

Prepare a good fish broth ahead of time.

Cut the onion into thin slices and sweat gently with the butter, often wetting it with spoonfuls of water, and when it is almost done add the rice, soak it in the sauce, then add, a little at a time, the fish broth or slightly warm, salted water. Stir from time to time to keep it from sticking.

Make a cream sauce *(p17)* with the ingredients listed here. Let it thicken, then stir in the minced tuna.

When the risotto is cooked, arrange it on a plate and pour over the tuna sauce. Finish, if you like, with hard-boiled eggs cut into rounds, chopped parsley, and a handful of capers.

RISOTTO CON UOVA IN SORPRESA

Risotto with Egg Surprise

6 eggs
8½ cups meat broth *(p88)* or bouillon cubes
3½ oz ham
9 tbsp grated Parmesan
2 cups rice
10½ tbsp butter
1 onion
10 oz fresh mushrooms
White or black truffle
Salt

White sauce:
2 tbsp flour, 1 tbsp butter, 2 cups milk

Boil the eggs, peel, halve them, and separate the whites and yolks.

Prepare a thick white sauce *(p16)* using the ingredient amounts listed here and let it cool. Prepare a meat broth as directed or use bouillon cubes.

Chop the ham and add it to the white sauce plus a good spoon of grated Parmesan. Use this to fill the egg white halves and join them together again. Keep them warm in a low oven. (Set the yolks aside.)

Prepare the risotto with the rice, 2 tablespoons of butter, and a chopped onion, wetting it with the broth.

Wash and cook the mushrooms separately in 1 tablespoon of butter. When the rice is cooked, season with more butter and grated Parmesan and mix in the mushrooms. Arrange the rice on the plate and surround it with the eggs.

Force the egg yolks through a sieve with the back of a spoon and sprinkle over the risotto. Complete with slices of white or black truffle and sprinkle everything with the remaining butter, browned to a light gold color.

RISOTTO IN CIAMBELLA CON FEGATINI

Risotto Mold with Livers

8½ cups meat broth *(p88)* or bouillon cubes
7 oz chicken livers
7 tbsp butter
Sage
3½ oz prosciutto
1 onion
2½ cups rice
White wine
Saffron
Breadcrumbs
Marsala
Salt
Pepper

Have ready a good meat broth as directed or use bouillon cubes.

Wash the livers, carefully remove the gall and divide each liver into two parts. Melt a tablespoon of butter in a small saucepan, add the livers, season with salt and pepper and a pinch of chopped fresh sage leaves. Add the prosciuito cut in very thin strips. The livers cook quickly and in no time they will be ready. Keep them warm.

Chop the onion finely and brown slowly in a large pan with 2 tablespoons of butter. Add the rice, mix well, add half a glass of wine and the saffron dissolved in ½ cup broth. Continue cooking the rice, gradually adding boiling broth and keep it al dente.

Butter a ring mold with a central tube, sprinkle it with breadcrumbs, fill with the prepared risotto, press, and trim well. Put the mold in a preheated oven for about 10 minutes, then turn it out onto a round serving dish with high sides.

Remove the livers from the pan and place them in the center of the rice ring. Put the pan with its juices back over heat, pour in ½ a glass of Marsala, stir, let the wine evaporate, add a few pieces of butter, stir quickly and pour this sauce over the livers.
Serve immediately.

RISOTTO IN CIAMBELLA TRICOLORE

Risotto in Three Colors

8½ cups meat broth *(p88)* or bouillon cubes
14 oz ground beef
1 egg
2 small boiled potatoes
9 tbsp grated Parmesan
Breadcrumbs
12 tbsp butter
Olive oil
1 cup tomato passata
Basil
Parsley
1 oz dried mushrooms
2 oz mascarpone
1 lb spinach
1 onion
2 cups rice
White wine
Saffron
Salt
Pepper

Have ready a meat broth as directed or use bouillon cubes.

Prepare the meatballs: Put the meat in a bowl, mix well with the egg, mashed potatoes, and 1 tablespoon of Parmesan. Mix everything and season with a pinch of salt and fashion into very small round meatballs.

Dip the meatballs in breadcrumbs and fry them in a pan with 2 tablespons of butter and half a glass of oil. Let them brown on all sides, then add the tomato passata and chopped basil and parsley. Cook for about 10 minutes, salt lightly, and mix carefully without breaking them.

Soak the dried mushrooms in cold water for 15 minutes, wash them carefully, remove the earthy parts, and cut them into small pieces. Put the mushrooms to cook in a pan with 1 tablespoon of butter, add a few spoons of their soaking water, well strained, and cook for about 15 minutes. Add salt and the mascarpone and mix with care.

Wash the spinach in several changes of water. Boil it in a little lightly salted boiling water. Drain, squeeze well to extract the water, and finally chop them on a cutting board. Season them in a pan with 1 tablespoon of butter, salt, and pepper and sprinkle with a handful of grated Parmesan.

Fry a chopped onion in a large saucepan with 2 tablespoons of butter and ½ a glass of oil without letting it brown, if necessary add a few ladles of hot water. Add the rice, stir it well to coat with the fat, then wet with ½ a glass of white wine. Add the boiling broth gradually.

Remove the rice from the heat when it is still very al dente, divide it into three equal parts. Mix the first with the spinach, the second with mushrooms and mascarpone, and the third with the saffron dissolved in a two fingers of broth.

Carefully grease a ring mold with a central tube, sprinkle with breadcrumbs, arrange, without mixing them, the three risottos: green, yellow, and white. Press well, then put the mold in a preheated moderate oven for about 10 minutes.

Turn out the rice onto a round serving dish with high sides. Arrange in the center the hot meatballs in tomato sauce and serve immediately.

RISOTTO PAESANO

Farmhouse Risotto

7 oz dried white beans, or canned
2 oz pork skin
14 oz cabbage
2 celery stalks
1 carrot
6 tomatoes
8½ cups meat broth *(p88)* or bouillon cubes
1 onion
3½ tbsp butter
2½ oz pancetta
2½ cups rice
Red wine
Salt
Pepper

The first thing to do ahead of time is to soak the dried beans for 12 hours. Otherwise, you can use canned which saves time.

Blanch the pork skin in boiling water, then cut into strips.

Wash the vegetables, chop the cabbage leaves, cut the celery into small pieces, so too the carrot and tomatoes. Put everything in a pot, add the well-drained beans, the pork skin, and the broth. Cover the pot and let it cook slowly for 2 hours.

Chop the onion and brown in a saucepan with the butter and the pancetta, over low heat. Add the rice, let it flavor mixing with care, then pour in ½ a glass of wine and let it evaporate. Continue cooking the rice gradually, pouring in the broth with the cooked vegetables and beans and stirring occasionally.

RISOTTO PRIMAVERA

Springtime Risotto

8½ cups vegetable broth *(p90)*
2¼ lb fresh peas in the pod or 10 oz frozen
3 artichoke hearts
1 lb tomatoes
7 oz green beans
10 oz potatoes
Small head lettuce
3 carrots
1 lb asparagus
2 celery stalks
1 onion
Parsley
Basil
Olive oil
3½ tbsp butter
1½ cups rice
1 cup grated Parmesan
Salt

Prepare the vegetable broth as directed and keep it warm.

Shell the fresh peas, clean the vegetables—artichokes, tomatoes, green beans, potatoes, lettuce, and carrots—and cut into small pieces. Use only the green tips of the asparagus.

Chop the celery and onion, and separately the parsley and basil.

Sauté the onion and celery with a glass of oil and butter, season with a little salt, add the prepared vegetables, leave them to stew for 30 minutes, pouring on a ladle of broth if necessary, and finally add the rice. Let the rice soak up the flavor of the vegetables, then pour, a little at a time the boiling broth and mix the rice carefully.

When the risotto is almost cooked, add the chopped parsley and basil. Then place the risotto on a serving dish and season with grated Parmesan.

GNOCCHI

GNOCCHI ALLA GENOVESE

Gnocchi Genovese

4½ lb potatoes
3¼ cups flour
Pesto Genovese *(p49)*
9 tbsp grated Parmesan
Salt

Boil the potatoes, peel them, mash them, let them cool and mix with the sifted flour. Divide into finger lengths and cut into small pieces about ¾ inch long.

Quickly roll each piece on the floured work surface, making a small dimple on each with your fingertip, and line them up side by side on a floured cloth.

Then prepare the pesto as directed.

Put a pan with salted water on the heat. When the water boils, drop in a few gnocchi at a time and as soon as they come back to the surface, scoop them out with a slotted spoon and let them drain well. Arrange them in layers in a tureen. Season each layer with the pesto diluted with a little of the cooking water from the gnocchi, plenty of grated Parmesan. Send to the table immediately.

GNOCCHI ALLA PATATA PIEMONTESE

Gnocchi Piedmont Style

4½ lb potatoes
13 tbsp butter
3¼ cups flour
2 eggs
Garlic
1 cup grated Parmesan
Salt

Peel the potatoes, cut them into wedges, and put them on the heat in a large pan with cold water and a pinch of salt. When they are cooked, drain and purée. Return the purée to the saucepan.

Place the pan back on the heat, mix with a wooden spoon and season with 1 tablespoon of butter. Remove from the heat and when it has cooled, pour in the flour, letting it fall like rain, then add the eggs. Stir and work well. The dough must be elastic.

Put a large pan on the heat with plenty of water, lightly salt, and bring it to a boil.

Then take small portions of the gnocchi dough in a teaspoon and with the help of another teaspoon drop them, a few at a time, into the boiling water. Let them boil for a few minutes and when the gnocchi come back to the surface, scoop them up with a slotted spoon. Drain well and arrange them in layers on a serving dish. Onto each layer, pour the butter—which you have browned with cloves of garlic—and sprinkle with grated Parmesan.

GNOCCHI DI PATATE ALLA ROMANA

Gnocchi Roman Style

Tomato ragu *(p32)*
4½ lb baking potatoes
3¼ cups flour
Olive oil
1 cup grated Parmesan
Salt

Have ready a tomato ragu in good time.

Boil the potatoes, peel them, mash them, and let them cool a little. When they are cooled, mix the potatoes well with the flour and oil and cut into finger lengths on a floured surface. Cut again into pieces about ¾ inch long and shape as described in Gnocchi Genovese *(p227)*.

Put a large pan of salted water on the heat. When it boils, drop in a few gnocchi at a time and as soon as they come back to the surface, take them out with a slotted spoon, let them drain, and arrange them in layers in a soup bowl. Season each layer with plenty of tomato ragu and grated Parmesan.

GNOCCHI DI PATATE CON POMODORO E FONTINA

Potato Gnocchi with Tomato and Fontina

Tomato sauce *(p37)*
4½ lb potatoes
3¼ cups flour
2 eggs
7 oz Fontina
3½ tbsp butter
9 tbsp grated Parmesan
Salt

Have ready a good tomato sauce.

Boil the potatoes, peel them, mash them, and let them cool a little. When they are cool, mix them with the flour and eggs. Cut into finger lengths and then cut across to get pieces about ¾ inch long and shape as described in Gnocchi Genovese *(p227)*.

Put on the heat a large pan with plenty of lightly salted water. When it boils, add just a few gnocchi at a time. When they come back to the surface, remove with a slotted spoon, let them drain, and arrange them on a serving plate. Season with a layer of sliced Fontina, the butter browned in a pan, and the grated Parmesan.

Serve the tomato sauce in a gravy boat to the side.

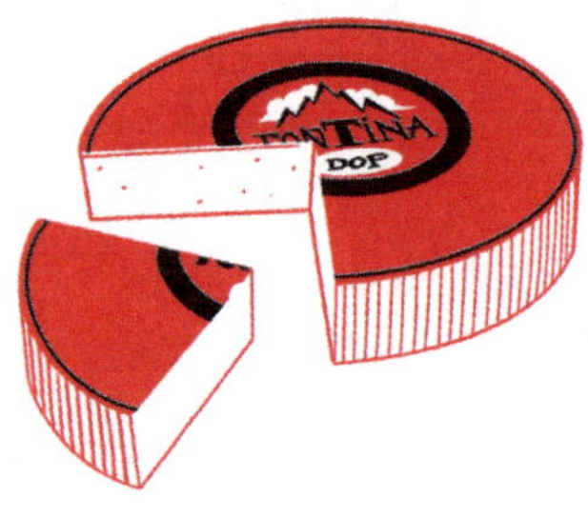

GNOCCHI DI PATATE CON SPINACI

Spinach Gnocchi

Tomato sauce *(p37)*
4½ lb potatoes
2¼ lb spinach
2 egg yolks
Nutmeg
9 tbsp grated Parmesan
1⅔ cups flour
3½ tbsp butter
Salt

Prepare a good tomato sauce.

Peel the potatoes, boil, and mash while they are still hot. Wash and boil the spinach, then squeeze dry and mix with the potatoes. Add the egg yolks, a little nutmeg, a pinch of salt, a spoonful or two of grated Parmesan. Add the flour to the dough and mix until you get a well-worked dough but still fluffy. Roll out on a floured surface into finger lengths and cut into pieces about ¾ inch long.

Drop a few gnocchi at a time into lightly salted boiling water. As soon as they come to the surface, take them out with a slotted spoon, let them drain, arrange them delicately in layers on a plate, seasoning each layer with a few pieces of butter, tomato sauce, and grated Parmesan.

GNOCCHI DI POLENTA

Polenta Gnocchi

3½ cups polenta
Butter
9 tbsp grated Parmesan
Salt

Sausage and mushroom ragu:
10 oz ground beef, 3 sausages, 1 oz dried mushrooms, wine, olive oil, onion, celery

Make a good sausage and mushroom ragu *(p33)* using the ingredients listed here.

Put a saucepan with 1½ quarts of salted water on the stove. When it is about to boil, let the polenta fall in as if it is raining. With the other hand, with a wooden spoon, stir so that you do not get any lumps. Make sure that the polenta, in addition to being quite thick, is well cooked. It will take a good hour of cooking.

Moisten a work surface with water and pour the polenta on, spreading it out, with a wet offset spatula, to a thickness of ⅜ inch or so. When the polenta is cold, cut it into small diamond shapes of a couple of fingers to each side.

Butter an ovenproof dish well. On the bottom arrange a layer of gnocchi and season with a little ragu and grated Parmesan. Make another layer and so on, starting each new layer of gnocchi a little further back from the previous layer. Pour on this kind of dome more ragu and Parmesan and arrange here and there the little pieces of butter. Put the dish in a preheated oven of strong heat for a good 15 minutes until the gnocchi have a golden and crunchy crust. Keep back a part of the sauce to be poured hot over the polenta when it comes out of the oven.

GNOCCHI DI SEMOLINO

Semolina Gnocchi

4 cups milk
1½ cups semolina
2 egg yolks
9 tbsp grated Parmesan
7 tbsp butter
Salt

Put the milk on the heat in a saucepan and when it boils, pour in slowly, slowly, like rain, the semolina, stirring continuously with a wooden spoon so that no lumps are formed. Soon it will thicken. Work the mixture with energy, continually detaching it from the bottom and from the sides of the saucepan and cook for about 10 minutes.

Remove the saucepan from the heat and season with a good pinch of salt and stir in the egg yolks, a handful of grated Parmesan, and ½ of the butter. Stir again and then pour the semolina out onto a wet work surface. Wet a large offset spatula and flatten the semolina to ⅜ inch thick. Leave it set for 1 hour. When the semolina is completely cold and congealed, cut it into squares or into diamonds of about 1½ inches on each side.

In an ovenproof dish, make a first layer of semolina gnocchi, well smeared with butter. Strew over a little grated Parmesan and make a second layer, continuing like this 3 or 4 times and arranging the second layer a little behind the first, the third a little further back from the second, so that the preparation is stepped and forms a type of small dome.

When you have arranged all the gnocchi, sprinkle them generously with grated Parmesan and sprinkle with the rest of the melted butter. Put the dish in a hot oven for 15 minutes and serve when the gnocchi have become slightly golden.

GNOCCHI CON SPINACI E RICOTTA

Spinach Gnocchi with Ricotta

4½ lb spinach
1 lb ricotta
5 tbsp grated Parmesan
3 egg yolks
Flour
5 tbsp butter
Salt

Clean and wash the spinach with great care, then boil in a little, lightly salted water. Drain, squeeze well to extract the water, and chop.

Put the ricotta in a bowl and work with a wooden spoon to loosen it well. Add the spinach, a pinch of salt, the grated Parmesan, and egg yolks. Mix everything so that the various elements are perfectly blended.

Put on the heat a large pan with plenty of lightly salted water. When the water boils, lower the heat to low, so that the boil is barely noticeable.

One at a time, take half spoonfuls of the prepared mixture and place them on a floured work surface. Roll them in flour trying, with all delicacy, to give them a regular shape with your hands, similar to that of a pigeon egg. As the gnocchi are ready, add them to the boiling water. You will see that they will soon come to the surface. Leave them alone like this for 3 or 4 minutes, then scoop them up with a slotted spoon. Let them drain and arrange them on a plate. When they are all done, brown the butter in a pan and as soon as it colors, pour over the gnocchi. Sprinkle with grated Parmesan. Serve hot.

GNOCCHI DI FARINA ALLA TEDESCA

Gnocchi German Style

1 onion
7 tbsp butter
9 oz crustless white bread
7 oz prosciutto
4 cups milk
1⅔ cups flour
Saffron
5 egg yolks
6½ cups broth or bouillon cubes
Salt

Chop a little onion, put it on the heat in a saucepan with the butter and bread cut into small cubes, brown, and add the diced prosciutto and brown lightly. Slowly pour in warm milk and leave it for about 10 minutes, so that all the milk is completely absorbed. Add the flour, salt, saffron, and the egg yolks and mix to form a paste that you will spread on the kitchen table.

When cooled, fashion to make the gnocchi of the size you like best. Cook them in the broth for about 20 minutes. Serve them in the broth.

GNOCCHI DI FARINA GIGANTI

Giant Gnocchi

Tomato sauce *(p37)*
2 cups flour
7 oz ricotta
1 egg yolk
9 tbsp grated Parmesan
2 oz ham
3½ oz mozzarella
7 tbsp butter
Salt

Have a good tomato sauce ready.

Bring a saucepan of water and a pinch of salt to to a boil. As soon as it boils, remove from the heat and throw in, all in one go, the 2 cups flour. Stir quickly with a wooden spoon to incorporate; then put the pan back on the heat and, still stirring, cook for 4 or 5 minutes, making sure the dough does not stick.

Turn this dough out onto a floured work surface, spread it out and knead. When the dough is well worked and smooth, fashion it into a ball, dust with flour, and cover with a towel. Let it rest for a good 15 minutes.

Put the ricotta in a bowl, mash with a wooden spoon or pass it through a sieve. Add the egg yolk, a spoonful of grated Parmesan, diced ham, and a few cubes of mozzarella and mix everything together.

Divide the gnocchi dough into pieces the size of a large turkey egg. Spread each piece on the palm of your hand and in the center put a part of the prepared filling. Enclose the filling by shaping the dough into an egg again. Flour your hands often, so that the dough does not stick.

Arrange the gnocchi on a floured work surface.

Bring plenty of salted water to a boil in a rather large pan. When it boils, gently add the gnocchi, one at a time. As they come back to the surface, take them out of the water with a slotted spoon and place them on a cloth to drain.

Butter an oven dish, arrange the gnocchi lined up in one layer and coat generously with tomato sauce and grated Parmesan, and dotting here and there the little pieces of butter. Put the pan in a preheated oven of light heat for 30 minutes so that the gnocchi have time to get a good flavor.

POLENTA

TO COOK POLENTA

It is difficult to provide exact quantities of water and polenta because one quality of polenta will absorb more water than another. For six people the quantities are, with a certain approximation: **12 cups water, 3½ cups polenta, salt.**

Set a pot of water and salt on the heat and when the water is about to boil, with one hand begin to drop the polenta into the pot, letting it fall like rain, while with the other hand mix with a wooden spoon until cooked, so that no lumps form.

As you can see, the preparation is very simple, but you have to proceed with a little attention to obtain a smooth and velvety mixture. The polenta is done when, as you stir, it easily comes away from the sides of the pot. It will take about 45 minutes.

Most polenta today is sold precooked, which also produces excellent results. If using precooked, follow the instructions for length of cooking on the packet.

POLENTA CON BRODO

Polenta with Broth

8½ cups meat broth *(p88)*
1⅓ cups polenta
9 tbsp grated Parmesan
Salt

Have ready a good meat broth and bring to a boil.

Drop the polenta into the boiling broth like rain; give it a good stir and cook gently for about 15 minutes, stirring occasionally.

Put the cooked polenta in a bowl and bring to the table, serving grated Parmesan on the side.

POLENTA CON BACCALÀ ALLA VICENTINA

Polenta with Salt Cod Vicenza Style

1¾ lb soaked salt cod
Flour
Cinnamon
7 tbsp grated Parmesan
Olive oil
1 onion
Garlic
4 anchovies
Parsley
White wine
3 cups milk
2 tbsp butter
3½ cups white polenta
Salt
Pepper

First, clean your pre-soaked cod which needs to be skinned and then cut into large pieces. Take a large sheet pan and without greasing it, place in a single layer lightly floured pieces of salt cod, seasoned with salt, pepper, and a little cinnamon and generously sprinkled with grated Parmesan.

Pour the oil into a saucepan, fry a little onion and some minced garlic, and when the onion is slightly golden add the anchovies—boned and cut into small pieces. With a wooden spoon mix them until they dissolve in the sauté. Add the chopped parsley and later a glass of white wine. Let the wine reduce almost entirely, add the milk and complete the sauce with the necessary butter.

Pour this sauce into the sheet pan with the cod, then cover it and put in the oven until all the liquid has dried up and the cod is cooked. This is going to take about 30 minutes.

In the meantime, cook the polenta *(p233)*. When cooked, pour the polenta onto a wooden cutting board so that it forms a crown and place the cod in the middle.

POLENTA CON COSTARELLE DI MAIALE

Polenta with Pork Ribs

3½ cups polenta
3½ oz guanciale
1 onion
1 carrot
1 celery stalk
Parsley
Olive oil
2¼ lb pork ribs
2 cups tomato passata
9 tbsp grated Parmesan
Salt

Cook the polenta *(p233)* and keep it warm in a bain-marie until ready to go to the table.

Chop the guanciale, onion, carrot, celery, and parsley. Put the mixture in a saucepan with oil. Brown, then add the pork ribs cut into not too large pieces and fry. Add the tomato passata, a pinch of salt, cover, and cook gently.

When the sauce has thickened, remove from the heat and put the pork ribs in a bowl. Remove the bones. Cut the meat into tiny pieces and put them back on the heat in the saucepan with the aromatics.

Distribute the polenta into bowls, pour the thick pork and tomato sauce over each, and sprinkle with grated Parmesan.

POLENTA CON GLI UCCELLINI SCAPPATI

Polenta with Veal and Chicken Livers

3½ oz lardo
12 slices veal (2 oz each)
6 chicken livers
7 tbsp butter
Sage
6 slices polenta, precooked
Salt
Pepper

Cut the lardo into cubes and blanch in boiling water for 5 minutes. Pound the veal slices to make them thinner and well flattened. Season with salt and pepper. Put on each of them a cube of lardo and roll up in the manner of sausages.

Remove the gall from the livers, cut them into 4 pieces, and cook them in a pan with a knob of butter and a pinch of salt and pepper.

Take six skewers and, alternating, add lardo, livers, rolled veal sausages, and sage. Arrange the skewers on a sheet pan in which you have already melted half the butter. Sprinkle with salt and pepper and cook in the oven.

Fry the polenta slices in the rest of the butter until they are golden and arrange them on the serving plate. Pull the meats off the skewers and arrange them, still hot and with their cooking juice, on top of the polenta.

POLENTA CON MOZZARELLA E ACCIUGHE

Polenta with Mozzarella and Anchovies

3½ cups polenta
Olive oil
10 oz mozzarella
35 oz canned tomatoes
2 oz anchovy fillets
2 tbsp butter
Salt
Pepper

Cook the polenta *(p233)*, keeping it rather thick. Remove it from the heat and pour it out onto a large well greased sheet pan.

When it is cool, scatter it with diced mozzarella. Place here and there the pieces of washed and boned anchovies and butter. Pour over the canned tomatoes and, finally, sprinkle with a little salt and a pinch of pepper.

Add a little more oil and put the pan in a preheated oven, of moderate heat, for about 15 minutes.

POLENTA CON SALSICCE

Polenta with Sausages

3½ cups polenta
Olive oil
Garlic
12 sausages
White wine
35 oz canned tomatoes
1 cup grated Parmesan
Salt

Battuto:
1 onion, 1 celery stalk, 1 carrot, parsley, 3½ oz guanciale

Cook the polenta *(p233)* and leave it warm in a bain-marie, until it's time to go to the table.

Put some oil and a garlic clove in a saucepan, and remove the garlic when it turns golden. Prick the sausages, place them in the saucepan and cook just long enough to sear. Remove them and add a battuto—which is diced onion, celery, carrot, parsley, and guanciale. Brown the battuto, then return the sausages to the saucepan and after a few minutes add a glass of wine. As soon as this has evaporated, add the canned tomatoes, season with a little salt, cover, and cook for about 15 minutes, supervising the cooking, so the sausages do not fall apart.

Distribute the polenta among bowls, cover with plenty of sauce, place in the center of each bowl two sausages and scatter everything with plenty of grated Parmesan.

POLENTA E FONTINA IN TORTA

Polenta and Fontina Pie

3½ cups polenta
Butter
9 oz Fontina cheese
Salt
Pepper

Cook the polenta *(p233)* and when it is firm and easily detaches from the sides of the pan, pour it into a rectangular container that's been moistened with water. Let the polenta rest and cool completely.

Then, turn it out onto a slightly wet work surface and divide it with a knife in wide and thin slices, about ¼ inch thick.

Generously butter a round deep pan about 8 inches in diameter. Make a regular layer of slices of polenta, and on these put some slices of Fontina cheese. Season the cheese with a pinch of pepper and continue to alternate layers of polenta and slices of cheese, so that the last layer is polenta. Put a few pieces of butter here and there and bake in a preheated oven for 20 minutes, until the polenta has a golden crust.

Remove the pan from the oven, invert the cake onto a plate, and serve warm and melting.

POLENTA IN BUDINO

Polenta Pudding

3½ cups polenta
7 tbsp butter
2 oz dried mushrooms
4 cups tomato passata
Breadcrumbs
Milk
1 lb ground beef
1 egg
9 tbsp grated Parmesan
Nutmeg
3½ oz mortadella
Flour
Oil for frying
Salt

Cook the polenta *(p233)*, keeping it rather thick. When the polenta is ready, butter a ring mold with a central tube. Pour in the polenta and put the mold to simmer in a bain-marie for about 30 minutes.

Thoroughly clean the mushrooms, soak them in cold water, wash them in more water. Then, put them to cook with 1 tablespoon of butter, a few spoons of water, and a pinch of salt. In another saucepan, prepare a good sauce with the tomato passata and 1 tablespoon of butter.

Soak a good handful of breadcrumbs in milk and squeeze well. Then knead everything plus the ground beef with your hands in a bowl. Add the egg, 1 tablespoon of butter, the grated Parmesan, a grating of nutmeg, and minced or cubed mortadella. Stir again and then shape some small meatballs with this mixture. Dredge them in flour and fry in very hot oil. Add the meatballs to the mushrooms, stirring gently.

When it's time to serve, turn out the polenta pudding onto a plate and pour the sauce of meatballs and mushrooms into the center.

POLENTA IN MIGLIACCIO

Polenta with Sausages and Mozzarella

14 oz sausages
3½ cups polenta
Grated Parmesan
10 oz mozzarella
7 tbsp butter
Salt
Pepper

Prick the sausages, place them in a pan, cover them with water, and bring them to a boil. Cook the sausages until the water is evaporated, then let them brown in their own fat. Finally, remove them from the pan, pull off the casings, and cut them into slices.

Cook the polenta *(p233)* and when it is thick and pulling away frm the sides of the saucepan, remove it from the heat. Season with the fatty juice of the sausages and plenty of grated Parmesan, then turn it out into a wet terrine and let it cool. When it is cool, it will be easy to turn upside down onto the table and cut it into regular slices.

Grease a baking pan and begin to make a layer of polenta slices. Cover this layer with slices of mozzarella and slices of sausages, a little grated Parmesan, pieces of butter, and a pinch of pepper. Continue to make layers of polenta and mozzarella, sausage, Parmesan, and bits of butter, ending with one layer of polenta, on which you will still put small pieces of butter.

Put the pan in a preheated oven of high heat for 30 minutes, until the polenta has a golden crust. Serve hot.

POLENTA IN TIMBALLO

Polenta Timbale

3½ cups polenta
3½ tbsp butter
1 oz dried mushrooms
2 sausages
3½ oz lean ground beef
Olive oil
7 oz mozzarella
Salt

White sauce:
3 tbsp flour, 2 tbsp butter, 1 cup milk

Cook the polenta *(p233)*. When the polenta is cooked, season it with a piece of butter and pour it into a well buttered mold, to cool.

Meanwhile, prepare the filling. Soak the mushrooms in cold water; as soon as they are ready, clean them, rinse them, and place them in a pan to cook with 1 tablespoon of butter, some water, and salt.

In another pan, cook the sausages and the ground beef with a little oil and salt. Then chop everything into small pieces. Combine the mushrooms, meats, and slices of mozzarella in a bowl.

Finally make a white sauce *(p16)* with the ingredients listed here. Let it thicken, season with a pinch of salt, and pour it into the bowl with the filling.

When the polenta is cold, leave it in the mold, take a small pointed knife and, sinking the blade into the polenta, remove some of it from the center to make a box. Into this box, pour the filling and then close the box by putting the polenta you have taken out back. Place a few peanut sized pieces of butter on the surface and bake in a preheated oven at a lively heat. After 30 minutes it will have firmed up. Let it rest for a few minutes, then invert onto a plate and send it to the table.

POLENTA PASTICCIATA IN FORNO

Baked Polenta

3½ cups polenta
2 sausages
10 oz lean ground beef
7 tbsp butter
Wine
9 oz canned tomatoes
7 oz Gruyère
3½ oz prosciutto
9 tbsp grated Parmesan
Salt

Battuto:
3½ oz guanciale, 1 carrot, 1 onion, 1 celery stalk

Cook the polenta *(p233)*, keeping it thick. Pour it out onto a slightly wet work surface, spreading it out ⅜ inch thick and let it cool.

Prepare the ragu: Remove the sausage casings, chop them together with the beef and put the mixture to brown in a pan with half the butter. When the meat has taken a nice color, add a battuto of diced guanciale, carrot, onion, and celery and sauté it for a few minutes. Add a glass of wine and let it evaporate Add the canned tomatoes, diluted with water, and a pinch of salt and cook over moderate heat.

Cut the Gruyère and the prosciutto into very thin slices. Grease a baking pan and make a layer of polenta: Season this first layer with half of the sauce, sprinkle it with grated Parmesan and slices of Gruyère and pieces of prosciutto. Make a second layer of polenta, season it with the rest of the sauce and the Parmesan and sprinkle it with the other half of the Gruyère and the prosciutto. Make a third and final layer of polenta, on which you will put some pieces of butter here and there, scattering it with grated Parmesan. Put the pan in a preheated oven of lively heat for about 30 minutes.

POLENTA PASTICCIATA IN TERRINA

Baked Polenta with Veal and Chicken Livers

2 oz dried mushrooms
Olive oil
1 carrot
1 onion
1 celery stalk
Parsley
3½ oz guanciale
10 oz veal slices
White wine
9 oz canned tomatoes
7 tbsp butter
3 chicken livers
3½ cups polenta
1 cup grated Parmesan
Salt

Clean the mushrooms, soak them in cold water to revive, and wash them well.

Put a few spoonfuls of oil in a saucepan and mix in a chopped carrot, onion, celery, parsley, and the guanciale. Then add the veal slices cut into small pieces and let them brown. Add a glass of wine and, when it has evaporated, add the canned tomatoes and cook over moderate heat for about 15 minutes. Add the mushrooms and finish cooking for another 15 minutes.

In another saucepan with 1 tablespoon of butter, cook the chicken livers for a few minutes, season with a pinch of salt and set aside.

Cook the polenta *(p233)*, but keep it rather loose. In a baking pan, make a layer of polenta. On it put a layer of veal slices and mushrooms with their thick sauce and season with grated Parmesan. Make another layer of polenta, sprinkle it with a few tablespoons of melted butter, scatter on plenty of grated Parmesan and add the chicken livers. Cover with another layer of polenta, veal and mushrooms with their sauce, and season with grated Parmesan. Finish with a layer of polenta, which you finish with melted butter and season with grated Parmesan.

Put the pan in a preheated oven of high heat for about 30 minutes. Let it rest for a few minutes, then invert it onto a serving dish and send it to the table.

"Fritto Misto alla Milanese is one of the glories of Italian gastronomy."

Fried foods must always be served very hot and so should be made at the last moment. It is almost impossible to prepare good fries when you have guests and do not have a helper.

It is best to work in relays. The oil or fat must remain hot to seal the foods quickly without saturating. To serve, fried foods should simply be sprinkled with fine salt and surrounded by lemon slices.

Fritti Misti are the pride of regional cuisines, and they are all equally good. All feature a mix of meat, fish, vegetables as well as some of the fried preparations that feature in this chapter.

One main difference between regions is the frying medium – for Milan it will be clarified butter but in Rome, traditionally, it was always strutto (lard) and nowadays it is oil.

The *Fritto Misto alla Milanese*, not wrongly considered one of the glories of Italian gastronomy, might include: artichoke, cauliflower, veal cutlets, potato croquettes, ox heart, calves' liver, thin slices of fried veal, kidneys, sweetbreads and zucchini. It is traditional to put a large piece of butter in a small frying pan and, when it has taken on a light hazelnut hue, sprinkle it over the fried food. Finally put a spoonful of meat sauce – without tomato – or mayonnaise, perhaps mixed with a little ketchup on the side.

The *Fritto Misto all'Emiliana* might include artichokes, cauliflower purée, sweetbreads, lamb's brain, liver, veal chops, breast of chicken or turkey rolled in breadcrumbs and fried, chicken nuggets and tomatoes.

The *Fritto Misto alla Napoletana* will obviously include fish, but also local specialities like panzarotti, boiled eggs, supplì and perhaps zucchini flowers. *Mostaccioli* are small, well-bound mixes, usually cut into diamonds, then browned, breaded and fried. They originate from the street food of Naples.

The *Fritto Misto alla Romana* will include artichokes, cauliflower, zucchini, breaded lamb chops, calf liver, sweetbreads and other offal, supplì, and even fried apples.

Croquettes of all kinds, from sweetbreads to Fontina, are typical in most *Fritti Misti*; certain other preparations have become associated with particular regions. In Emilia, it might be expected to include *stecchi* or chicken croquettes. Another speciality for the Emilia-Romagna region is *fagottini*, handmade disks of dough in the centre of which is a prepared mixture perhaps of ricotta and sausage. In Rome, there will nearly always be *pane dorato* and rice croquettes like *supplì*. In Naples, mozzarella will usually feature.

After frying all the elements, they should be presented separately but side by side on a large oval serving plate and are usually served with lemon wedges.

FRITTURE

5

FRIED DISHES

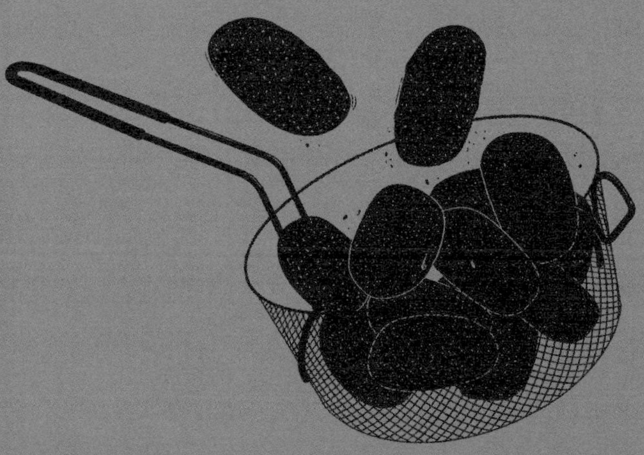

BATTERS

TO FRY

All foods can be fried. The most used fats for frying are olive and seed oils, lard and clarified butter. The butter must be clarified, melted over moderate heat (preferably in a bain-marie) for about 10 minutes until it has become as clear as olive oil and the casein has formed whitish deposits on the bottom of the pan. As soon as the butter has completely clarified, it is allowed to rest and then decanted through a fine cloth before use. In general, foods for frying must be the same size as much as possible, so that they cook at the same time. Typically, food is dipped first in flour, then briefly through beaten egg, sometimes through breadcrumbs, drained immediately and then dropped into very hot oil or lard. To make things more interesting, you can make up a special batter mixing the flour or another liquid instead of water—milk, oil, wine, beer, etc—or you might use whole eggs or just the whipped whites.

TO MAKE BATTER

Despite its simplicity, making a batter nevertheless requires special care. The batter should be prepared at least 1 hour before use. The batter needs to rest to let the ingredients combine. In a bowl large enough to contain all the pieces to be fried, mix together all the ingredients as indicated below. After putting the flour in the bowl, it is useful to work it with a wooden spoon to create a well in the centre into which the ingredients, according to the recipe, can be mixed in with circular movements. The liquid must be poured in slowly and if using water or milk, it is good if they are lukewarm. The movements to make the flour absorb the liquid should be slow and the batter must not be overworked. It should never be beaten or whipped with a spoon or it will become elastic and heavy. The batter should have a creamy appearance. If it is too liquid, the crust will be insufficient; if the batter is too dense, the crust will be too heavy.

SIMPLE BATTER
1 cup all-purpose flour; 2 tbsp olive oil; 1 glass warm water; salt

SPECIAL BATTER
1 cup all-purpose flour; 1 tbsp olive oil; 1 egg yolk; 1 glass warm milk or water; 2 whipped egg whites; 1 tbsp grated Parmesan; salt

WINE BATTER
1 cup all-purpose flour; 1 tbsp olive oil; 2 whipped egg whites; 1 tsp active dry yeast; 1 glass white wine (to dissolve the yeast); salt

FRITTI MISTI

REGIONAL SPECIALTIES

PANZAROTTI – ***Naples:*** *Make a dough (p264) and let it rest for half an hour. Then roll it out and fold it a couple of times as is done for puff pastry. Finally, divide it into many small squares; in the middle of which you place a spoonful of filling composed of diced ham, or tomato and mozzarella mixed with beaten eggs, grated Parmesan, nutmeg and chopped parsley. Fold the squares in on themselves, moistening the rim of each with beaten egg. Finally, dip the panzarotti in beaten egg and fry them, a few at a time, in oil that is not too hot.*

For other regional specialties see fried fish (p245), croquettes & fagottini (p246), mostaccioli (p253), mozzarella (p254), skewers (p256), and arancini & supplì (p259).

MEAT

CHOPS – *veal, lamb, pork, or chicken or turkey breast.*

Emilia-Romagna: *Flatten the meat with a mallet or the side of a knife and fry in a knob of butter, then season with salt and grated Parmesan. Leave to cool under a light weight. When cold, glaze with a thick white sauce (p16) bound with egg. On top of the sauce rest a slice of ham or mortadella. When the sauce is well chilled, the chops are breaded, browned in a pan, then breaded again and fried in butter or oil over high heat.*

Rome: *Flatten the chops, dip them in lightly beaten egg then in breadcrumbs and fry them over a moderate heat.*

CALVES' LIVER – *There are three ways to cook liver, but in all cases the liver must spend very little time in the pan because otherwise it may harden.*

Florence, Milan: To fry in butter: *Cut the liver into slices, dip through flour and fry.*

Emilia-Romagna: *As above and finish with chopped parsley and lemon juice.*

Rome: To fry in oil: *Wipe the liver slices through flour, beaten egg, and fry them in plenty of boiling oil.*

STRIPS OF VEAL – ***Florence, Milan:*** *Flatten some strips of veal with a meat mallet, then flour them and beat them between your hands to knock off any loose flour. In a pan, melt some butter, and before it takes on a golden colour, dip in the slices and cook on both sides. Finish with some lemon juice and finely chopped parsley.*

SWEETBREADS – *Soak the sweetbreads in fresh water to remove any blood, then place them in a small saucepan, cover with water, and bring to a boil, then turn off the heat and leave them to cool in the same water. Dry them, free them of any casings and cut into pieces, large or small.*

Florence, Naples, Rome: To fry in oil: *Dip the sweetbreads in beaten egg and fry them to a light blond colour.*

Milan: To fry in hot butter: *Dip the sweetbreads in flour and beaten egg, and fry them until they have turned a light blond colour.*

VEAL KIDNEYS – ***Florence, Milan:*** *Divide the kidneys into two pieces. Cut each of these two pieces obtained into two long slices. In a small pan, heat some butter, dip in the slices of kidney, and season with salt and pepper. The cooking should be quick and over high heat to prevent the kidneys from hardening.*

VEGETABLES

ARTICHOKES – *Strip off the first tough leaves and cut them with a sharp knife so that they are cone-shaped; scrape and shorten their stems and divide them into four wedges. Soak them in water acidulated with lemon juice.*

Florence, Milan, Naples, Rome: To fry in oil*: Dry the artichokes in a clean dishcloth, pass them in flour, then in beaten egg and fry them in boiling oil.*

Emilia-Romagna: To fry in batter*: Mash the artichokes until soft, then wipe in a thick special batter (p242) and fry them in a hot pan with boiling oil.*

CAULIFLOWERS – *Divide the cauliflowers in florets, boil in lightly salted water and drain.*

Rome: To fry in oil*: Pass the cauliflowers in a simple batter (p242) and fry in very hot oil.*

Florence, Milan: To fry in butter*: Flour the cauliflower, dip in beaten egg and fry in butter.*

Emilia-Romagna: To fry with special batter *(p647).*

TOMATOES – ***Emilia-Romagna:*** *Cut the tomatoes into horizontal slices, freed from their seeds and water. Dip them in a simple batter (p242) and fry them in oil over a fairly high heat until they have taken on a nice golden colour and have become crispy.*

ZUCCHINI – ***Florence, Milan, Naples, Rome:*** *Wash the zucchini, trim off the ends, then cut lengthwise so as to make many rather thin slices. Place the zucchini slices in a bowl and sprinkle with salt, leaving them for some time. At the time of cooking, take a few slices at a time, squeeze them between your hands, flour them and fry them in plenty of hot oil. To fry zucchini flowers (p702).*

FISH

Prepare five bowls and in each put enough flour to cover your fish. You need separate bowls for each fish, ready to fry.

MULLETS – *Clean and wash small mullets, dry them, and put them in a bowl with the flour.*

ANCHOVIES – *Remove the head from the anchovies, open them in two but without dividing them completely, remove the bone, close them back together, and put them in a bowl with flour.*

SQUID – *Cut the tentacles from the squid and extract the cartilaginous pen inside. Empty the sack, remove the outer skin and side fins. Cut the body crosswise into rings ½ inch high. Clean the tentacles and divide them according to their size into two or three pieces; cut the skinned fins into strips. Rinse, dry, and put the baby squid in a bowl with the flour.*

LANGOUSTINES AND SHRIMP – *Carefully wash the langoustines, dry them, and put them in a bowl with the flour.*

Before frying, tap each fish fillet to knock off any excess flour. In a large pan with plenty of boiling oil, fry the fish, one after the other, until golden and crunchy. Serve with lemon slices and chopped parsley.

FRIED FISH

BACCALÀ FRITTO ALLA LIVORNESE

Fried Salt Cod Livornese

2¼ lb soaked salt cod
Oil for frying
Garlic
All-purpose flour
Parsley
Salt
Optional: 2¼ lb tomatoes for sauce *(p37)*

Buy the cod already soaked. Peel and divide it into small pieces and dry them on a napkin. Flavor the warming oil with the garlic. Flour the cod and fry them to a beautiful golden colour and crunch. Arrange them on a plate. Cover with chopped parsley.

ADA SAYS: *These croquettes go very well with a thick tomato sauce.*

BACCALÀ FRITTO ALLA ROMANA

Fried Salt Cod Roman Style

12 soaked salt cod fillets
Lard or oil for frying
Salt

Batter:
1½ tbsp butter, 1 cup all-purpose flour, 1 tbsp active-dry yeast

Buy the fillets already soaked and reconstituted. Cut into suitable shapes. Mix a very smooth, lump-free batter *(opposite page)* with the ingredients listed here. Melt the butter in a pan without coloring and mix with the flour, a little water, and active-dry yeast. Let it sit for at least an hour.

Dry the fillets, then dip them in the batter soaking them well, then fry them in a pan with plenty of boiling oil or fine lard until they are crunchy and golden. Sprinkle with salt, and serve very hot.

FRITTELLE DI ACCIUGHE E TONNO

Anchovy and Tuna Fritters

12 anchovies
Parsley
14 oz tinned tuna in olive oil
Oil for frying
Salt

Batter:
2 glasses warm water, 4 tbsp olive oil, 2 cups all-purpose flour

Wash the anchovies well, bone, and divide them into fillets. Line them up on a plate, and season with oil and chopped parsley. Drain the tuna, and divide into cubes about a generous ½ inch on each side.

Prepare a rather thick batter with the warm water, oil, and flour.

A few minutes before going to the table, take a piece of diced tuna, wrap it inside a couple of anchovy fillets, dip everything in the batter, and then in a pan with hot oil. Fry over a high heat and as soon as they have turned a nice golden colour, remove them, drain, arrange on a serving dish, and serve hot.

CROQUETTES & FAGOTTINI

Croquettes

All recipes make about 20 croquettes

CROCCHETTE DI ANIMELLE

Sweetbread Croquettes

10 oz lamb sweetbreads
1½ tbsp butter
2 eggs
3½ oz sliced ham
All-purpose flour
Breadcrumbs
Oil for frying
Salt
Pepper

White sauce:
1½ tbsp butter, 3 tbsp all-purpose flour, ¾ cup milk, egg yolk

Put the lamb sweetbreads in fresh water for a while, then dry them and sear them in a pan with butter. In all they will not have to stay on the heat more than 2 or 3 minutes. As soon as they colour on one side, turn them, season with salt and pepper, lift out, and let them cool.

Prepare a thick white sauce *(p16)* with the butter, flour, and milk. Cook it well so that it is firm and consistent, season with a pinch of salt, and finish, off the heat, with an egg yolk.

Chop the sweetbreads and the ham and add them to the warm sauce, stir, and leave to cool. When the mix is cold, divide it into equal pieces. Roll the pieces in the flour, giving them the shape of corks. Wipe each croquette through the beaten egg and breadcrumbs, trying to keep them the same size and a regular shape. Fry them immediately in plenty of very hot oil and as they turn golden remove them with a slotted spoon, drain, and arrange them in a pyramid shape on a plate and have them brought to the table.

CROCCHETTE DI CREMA DI FORMAGGIO

Cheese Cream Croquettes

9½ tbsp all-purpose flour
2¼ tbsp semolina
2 egg yolks
Nutmeg
Sugar
Milk
9 tbsp grated Parmesan
5 tbsp butter
1¾ oz Gruyère
1 egg
Breadcrumbs
Lard or oil for frying
Salt
White pepper
Optional: white truffle

Put the flour, semolina, and egg yolks in a saucepan, add a grating of nutmeg, sufficient salt, a pinch of white pepper, and a pinch of sugar. Dilute with 2 glasses of milk and, when the mixture is smooth, put it on the heat to cook. When it is very velvety, remove from the heat and season with grated Parmesan and butter. Stir and cool a little.

When the mixture has lost some of its heat so the cheese will not melt immediately, add the Gruyère cut into cubes and, if you like, a small white truffle, well cleaned and cut into cubes or small sticks. Stir again to mix everything well and then pour the mixture on the kitchen table, greased with butter.

Flatten the mix with the blade of a knife, giving it the thickness of about a finger, and let it cool completely. When it is very cold, divide it into rectangles or rather into small rhombuses. Take one croquette at a time, lifting it with the blade of a knife, dip it in the flour, in the beaten egg, or just the whipped whites, and in the breadcrumbs. When you have it all breaded, rectify the shape with the blade of a knife.

Fry them in plenty of hot oil or lard. As soon as they are golden, remove them with a slotted spoon, let them drain, and then arrange them on a plate and have them brought to the table.

CROCCHETTE DI CREMA DOLCE

Sweet Cream Croquettes

5 eggs
1 cup sugar
2 cups all-purpose flour
3 cups milk
Lemon peel
Breadcrumbs
Oil for frying
Vanilla sugar

Put 4 eggs and the sugar in a saucepan, mix a little, add the flour, and dilute with the milk, adding the lemon peel grated or even cut into a thin ribbon, removing it later when the cream is cooked. Cook for about a quarter of an hour, so that the cream is well cooked, smooth and elastic.

Pour the mixture on the kitchen table or on to a large plate, flatten it to the height of an inch, and let it cool. When it turns cold, cut out some squares or diamonds. These cream squares will be your croquettes. Prepare a bowl of breadcrumbs and another bowl with a beaten egg. Pass the croquettes first in the breadcrumbs, then in the beaten egg, and then again in the breadcrumbs.

Fry the croquettes in plenty of hot oil and remove as they turn gold; drain, then arrange them in a serving dish, sprinkle with vanilla sugar, and send them to the table.

CROCCHETTE DI FORMAGGIO

Cheese Croquettes

2 cups grated Gruyère
1¼ cups grated Parmesan
4 egg whites
Breadcrumbs
Lard or oil for frying

Whip the egg whites firmly to a snow and slowly add the 2 finely grated cheeses, a little at a time, mixed together first, until you have a rather compact paste.

Roll pieces the size of a large walnut in fine breadcrumbs. When you have shaped all the croquettes, fry them in plenty of oil or lard in a very hot pan; and as soon as they are a beautiful golden colour, drain them, arrange them on a serving dish, and have them brought immediately to the table.

CROCCHETTE DI MOZZARELLA

Mozzarella Croquettes

1 lb mozzarella
All-purpose flour
1 egg
Oil for frying
Salt

Grate the mozzarella into a bowl. Take a handful and knead it until it becomes like a dough. Then add a spoonful of flour, egg, and a pinch of salt and continue to knead, always in the bowl, until everything is amalgamated and you have a soft paste.

Make small croquettes, the size of a large walnut, pass them in flour, and fry them in rather hot oil until they are a nice light golden colour.

CROCCHETTE DI PATATE

Potato Croquettes

2¼ lb baking potatoes
3½ tbsp butter
3 egg yolks
All-purpose flour
2 eggs
Breadcrumbs
Oil for frying
Salt
White pepper
Nutmeg

Peel the potatoes, cut them into wedges, and place them in a saucepan with cold water. When they are cooked, drain and leave them for a few minutes on a very low flame so all the moisture evaporates. Then pass them through a sieve and collect the purée in a saucepan, add the butter, put back on the heat, and, stirring, let the potato paste dry. When it becomes smooth and consistent, remove from the heat, season with salt, white pepper, and a little nutmeg, and add the egg yolks.

On a lightly floured table take small portions and shape them into croquettes. Then pass them through the beaten eggs, then the breadcrumbs, and fry in a pan with plenty of hot oil.

CROCCHETTE DI POLENTA E FORMAGGIO

Polenta and Fontina Croquettes

Polenta
Milk
2 egg yolks
5¼ oz Fontina
3½ oz Gruyère
All-purpose flour
1 egg
Breadcrumbs
Oil for frying
Salt
White pepper

Cook ¾ cup of polenta in lightly salted water. Spread it out on a large plate or on the kitchen table, slightly wet with water, to a thickness of just under ½ inch and let it cool completely. Then divide it into many small cubes of less than ½ inch on each side.

Put a couple of fingers of milk in a saucepan, along with 2 egg yolks, and Fontina and Gruyère cheese, both cut into cubes. Put the saucepan on very low heat, season with salt and white pepper, and, stirring with a wooden spoon, melt the cheese, but absolutely do not let it boil. When the cheese has melted, add the cubes of polenta, and stir promptly. Spread the mixture on the kitchen table with some water, making it about ½ inch deep. Let it cool and then divide into small diamonds of just over 1 inch on each side.

Gently remove all the pieces from the kitchen table with the blade of a knife, wipe them through the flour, then the beaten egg, and lastly the breadcrumbs, then fry them in plenty of hot oil. When they turn just golden, remove them with a slotted spoon, let them drain, and then arrange them on a serving dish and have them brought to the table very hot.

CROCCHETTE DI POLLO

Chicken Croquettes

14 oz cooked chicken breast
1 tbsp grated Parmesan
2 egg yolks
All-purpose flour
2 eggs
Breadcrumbs
Oil for frying
Lemon wedges
Optional: tongue, ham, black truffle, parsley, mushrooms

Prepare a white sauce *(p16)* with the butter, flour, and milk; work it well to make it very dense and rather elastic. Season with salt and nutmeg and then, off the heat, add the chopped chicken breast, the Parmesan, and the egg yolks. Stir to mix everything and then pour the mixture out on to the kitchen table, smoothing it out a little. Let it cool completely.

Take small portions of the mixture, each with a piece of chicken, and shape them into croquettes using a little flour. Then pass them through 2 beaten eggs and breadcrumbs. Make sure they come out in a nice shape. They must be regular cylinders of 2½ inches long and an inch or so in diameter.

White sauce:
7 tbsp butter, 1 cup all-purpose flour, 3 cups milk, salt, nutmeg

Fry with plenty of oil at a high heat; as they turn a beautiful blond colour, remove them, let them drain, and then arrange them on a plate, surrounded with lemon wedges.

ADA SAYS: *Fry a few at a time, because they will succeed better. In the mixture with the chicken, you could also add diced tongue or ham, diced truffle, chopped parsley, chopped cooked mushrooms, etc. for variety.*

CROCCHETTE DI SEMOLINO

Semolina Croquettes

2 cups milk
Semolina
Lemon peel
Sugar
3½ tbsp butter
2 egg yolks
Breadcrumbs
Lard or oil for frying
Salt

Put the milk in a small saucepan on the heat and, when it boils, gradually pour in ¾ cup of fine semolina, stirring continuously with a wooden spoon, so that lumps do not form. Add a pinch of salt and a piece of thinly sliced lemon peel. Cook for about 10 minutes, always stirring. When cooked, remove the lemon peel and season, off the heat, with a tablespoon of sugar, butter, and the egg yolks. Combine well and pour into a large dish, roll it out, and leave to cool.

With this mixture, shape small croquettes, pass them through breadcrumbs, and fry them in plenty of hot oil until just golden. Remove with a slotted spoon, let them drain, then arrange on a plate and bring them to the table very hot.

CROCCHETTE DI SPINACI

Spinach Croquettes

2¼ lb spinach
2 egg yolks
9 tbsp grated Parmesan
All-purpose flour
1 egg
Breadcrumbs
Oil for frying
Salt

White sauce:
3½ tbsp butter, ⅓ cup all-purpose flour, 1 cup milk, nutmeg

Make a thick white sauce *(p16)* with the butter, flour, and milk. Season with salt and a little nutmeg, and leave to cool.

Clean, wash, and lightly boil the spinach in a little salty water. Drain, squeeze well to extract the water, and chop. Incorporate the spinach into the white sauce, add the egg yolks and the grated Parmesan, and mix well.

Take a spoonful at a time of the mixture, form some croquettes, which you will dip first in the flour, then in the beaten egg, and then in the breadcrumbs.

Fry them in plenty of hot oil or lard and when just golden remove with a slotted spoon. Let them drain, then arrange them on a plate and bring to the table very hot.

CROCCHETTE DI TONNO

Tuna Croquettes

10½ oz tinned tuna in olive oil
Parsley
All-purpose flour
1 egg
Breadcrumbs
Lard or oil for frying
Pepper

White sauce:
3½ tbsp butter, 9½ tbsp all-purpose flour, 1¼ cups milk

To make the white sauce, put the butter in a small saucepan and, when it has melted, add the flour. Cook for a couple of minutes and then dilute with milk, always mixing with a wooden spoon so that lumps do not form. Cook over moderate heat to get a dense sauce.

Let the sauce cool a little then add the finely chopped tuna, a pinch of pepper, and a spoonful of chopped parsley. No salt. Mix well with a spoon and when all the ingredients are ready, turn the mixture upside down on a lightly floured kitchen table and let it get completely cold.

Then sprinkle the dough with a little flour and, rolling it on the table with your hands, make a long sausage that you will cut into four pieces.

Take one piece at a time and, always using the flour, thin it so that it is a little thicker than your middle finger, cutting it into five croquettes. Delicately, one by one, sift the croquettes through the beaten egg, then the breadcrumbs. Make sure to give the croquettes a regular shape. Fry them in plenty of very hot oil or lard.

CROCCHETTE DI VITELLO

Veal Croquettes

14 oz roast or boiled veal
1¾ oz prosciutto
9 tbsp grated Parmesan
3 eggs
Breadcrumbs
Oil for frying
Salt
Pepper
Nutmeg

White sauce:
3½ tbsp butter, ⅓ cup all-purpose flour, 1 cup milk

Finely chop the veal and the prosciutto and mix into a white sauce *(p16)* made with the butter, flour, and milk. Season with salt, pepper, and nutmeg, a few spoonfuls of grated Parmesan, and 2 whole eggs, stirring for 10 minutes until the sauce is very elastic. Pour this mixture on to the kitchen table or on a large plate, roll it out, and let it cool.

Then make some croquettes in whatever shape you like—round, pear-shaped, squared, etc.—and slide them through the breadcrumbs, then the beaten egg, and then again in the breadcrumbs. Fry the croquettes in plenty of hot oil.

CROCCHETTE LIEVITATE

Yeast Croquettes

2 cups all-purpose flour
2¼ tbsp active-dry yeast
1 potato
Sugar
1 egg yolk
1 tbsp butter
1 tbsp lard
Oil or lard for frying
Salt
Pepper

Place the flour on the table in a heap. Make a well in the middle. Dissolve the yeast in a cup with two fingers of barely warm water and wet the flour. Add a large mashed potato, a tablespoon of sugar, a good pinch of salt, pepper, an egg yolk, a tablespoon of butter, and the same of lard. Mix all these ingredients with four tablespoons of warm water. Work the dough a little and place it in a bowl sprinkled with flour, cover, and leave in a sheltered place.

After a couple of hours, when the dough has risen, bring it to a floured table and, delicately, without handling it too much, shape long, finger-sized lengths, which you cut into pieces of about 1½ inches long.

Give the croquettes a good shape and fry them in hot oil or lard. As they swell and turn gold, lift out, arrange on a serving dish, and immediately send them hot to the table.

Fagottini

FAGOTTINI CON MOZZARELLA E ACCIUGHE

Fagottini with Mozzarella and Anchovies

10½ oz mozzarella
5 anchovies
Parsley
Lard or oil for frying
Salt
Optional: thick tomato sauce with garlic and basil *(p28)*

Bread dough:
3⅓ cup all-purpose flour,
1 tbsp active-dry yeast, salt

Place the flour on the table in a heap and put the yeast in a well in the middle after it has dissolved in a little warm water. Add a pinch of salt. Add a glass of warm water and knead the flour; adjust so that the dough is rather soft. Work it vigorously and when it is well elastic, make a ball, put it in a bowl sprinkled with flour, cover, and let it rise for a couple of hours until it has swollen well.

Turn the leavened dough on the floured kitchen table, divide it into many equal pieces, each about the thickness of an egg, then enlarge them by pulling them with your hands, to make some thin disks.

Put the diced mozzarella on a plate, along with the anchovies (washed, boned, and cut into small pieces), chopped parsley, and a pinch of salt. Distribute this filling in the centre of each disk. Fold each disk in two, closing the filling inside and pressing with your fingers on the edges so that they unite well.

When you have packed all the bundles, put a pan on the heat with plenty of oil or lard and when it is hot, fry them, a few at a time, until they are firm, swollen, and a beautiful blond colour. They only need a few seconds, the time to colour.

ADA SAYS: *A long stay in the pan or too little frying would make the fagottini heavy. They should be served very hot. They are excellent on their own, but can also be accompanied with a thick tomato sauce garnished with basil.*

FAGOTTINI CON MOZZARELLA E FUNGHI

Fagottini with Mozzarella and Mushrooms

1¾ oz dried mushrooms
Olive oil
10½ oz mozzarella
6 fresh tomatoes
Basil
Oil for frying
Salt

Bread dough:
3⅓ cup all-purpose flour, 1 tbsp active-dry yeast, salt

Arrange the flour on the kitchen table. Dissolve the yeast in a little warm water, the oil, and a pinch of salt. Mix the flour and yeast by adding a glass of lukewarm water; work and beat the dough with one hand until it becomes elastic and soft and will detach in one piece from the board; then cover it and let it rise in a sheltered place.

Soak the mushrooms in cold water. When they are revived, rinse them and put them in a saucepan with a few spoonfuls of oil and a pinch of salt. Cover them with warm water until the water has all been used up. Then remove them from the saucepan, chop, and put them in a bowl with the diced mozzarella. Wash the tomatoes, blanch, remove the skin and seeds, chop them and cook over high heat, with a spoonful of oil, salt, and fresh, torn basil. When the tomatoes are ready, cool and add them to the bowl with the mushrooms and mozzarella.

Divide the leavened dough into small pieces; flatten each piece by spreading it out with your hands until it turns into a disk. In the centre of the disk put some of the prepared mixture, then fold the dough on itself to close the filling, pressing on the edges so they stick together. When you have prepared all the bundles in this way, dip them, a few at a time, in plenty of boiling oil until golden, puffy, and light. Place them on a serving plate and send them to the table.

FAGOTTINI CON RICOTTA E SALSICCE

Fagottini with Ricotta and Sausages

5 sausages
8 oz ricotta
2 tbsp grated Parmesan
Oil for frying
Salt

Bread dough:
3⅓ cup all-purpose flour, 1 tbsp active-dry yeast, salt

Arrange the flour on the kitchen table. Dissolve the yeast in a little warm water and a pinch of salt and pour into the centre well of the flour. Mix the flour by adding a glass of warm water; work the dough well and put it in a bowl, sprinkle it with flour and let it rise in a sheltered place.

Prick the sausages here and there, place them in a pan, cover them with water, and cook. When the water has all evaporated, leave for a few moments to let the sausages brown in their fat. Then peel them and cut them into slices. Sieve the ricotta, collect it in a bowl, and season with salt and grated Parmesan; then add the slices of sausage and give a good stir.

When the dough has risen, turn it over on the floured table, divide it into equal pieces, the size of an egg, which you will expand, pulling them with your hands, and fashion thin disks. In the centre of each disk put 1 or 2 spoonfuls of the filling and fold the disk in two to lock up. Press the edges with your fingers so that they join well. When you have packed all the bundles, put a pan on the heat with plenty of oil and when it is hot, fry them a few at a time until they are firm, swollen, and a beautiful blond colour. Set them on a serving plate and send them to the table.

MOSTACCIOLI

MOSTACCIOLI AL PROSCIUTTO

Ham Mostaccioli

2 eggs
All-purpose flour
1 cup milk
1 cup grated Parmesan
3½ oz ham
Breadcrumbs
Oil for frying
Salt

Separate your eggs, keeping back the whites for later. Put the egg yolks, ⅓ cup of flour, a pinch of salt, and milk in a pan, and, always stirring with a wooden spoon, warm over moderate heat for a quarter of an hour until it becomes very thick. Take off the heat and season with grated Parmesan and the ham cut into strips.

Wet the kitchen table with water, pour over the mixture, roll it out to a thickness of ½ inch, and let it cool.

When the mixture is cold, use the blade of a wet knife to divide it into many small diamonds. Wipe each in the flour, in the lightly beaten egg whites, in the breadcrumbs, and fry.

ADA SAYS: *Mostaccioli are typically found in Naples and are part of the Christmas tradition.*

MOSTACCIOLI DI POLENTA

Polenta Mostaccioli

1⅓ lb polenta
Lard or oil for frying
Salt

Prepare the polenta, keeping back enough for the frying, and when it easily detaches from the sides of the saucepan, pour it on a slightly wet table, flatten it to the thickness of a finger, and let it cool completely.

When it is cold, cut it into small diamonds. Dip these diamonds in the leftover polenta and fry them in boiling oil or lard until golden and crunchy.

MOSTACCIOLI DI SEMOLINO

Semolina Mostaccioli

7 tbsp butter
All-purpose flour
3½ oz semolina
4½ cups milk
9 tbsp grated Parmesan
2 egg yolks
Parsley
Breadcrumbs
Oil for frying
Salt

Put the butter in a saucepan. When it melts add 2 spoonfuls of flour and the semolina, dissolving everything with boiling milk. Stir the mixture with a wooden spoon for about half an hour, so it becomes a very thick cream.

Take it off the heat, season with grated Parmesan, 2 egg yolks, chopped parsley, and a pinch of salt. Pour the mixture on the slightly wet kitchen table, spread it out ½ inch thick and let it cool; finally cut it out in many small diamonds.

Wipe the mostaccioli through the flour, through the whipped egg whites, and through the breadcrumbs. Fry a few at a time in hot oil until they are golden and crunchy.

MOZZARELLA

MOZZARELLA FRITTA

Fried Mozzarella

10½ oz mozzarella
All-purpose flour
2 eggs
Breadcrumbs
Oil for frying

Cut the mozzarella into slices, not so large but rather thick. Flour them, pass them through the beaten eggs, in the breadcrumbs, and then again in the beaten eggs and in breadcrumbs again. Fry in boiling oil and, as soon as the breading has become blond, remove from the pan, adjust it in a serving dish, and immediately send to the table.

ADA SAYS: *The same technique works for pane dorato— square slices of bread about 2½ inches wide, a finger thick, wiped quickly through water or milk, then given an egg wash and then fried.*

MOZZARELLA IN CARROZZA

Fried Mozzarella Sandwich

1 loaf of bread
1 lb mozzarella
All-purpose flour
2 eggs
Oil or lard for frying
Salt

Remove all the crust from some cassette bread, cut the slices into squares of about 1½ inches; also prepare some mozzarella slices of the same size as the bread.

Place each slice of cheese between 2 slices of bread and, by hand, dip them in the flour to prevent the mozzarella from liquefying and coming out when you put it into the frying pan later. We repeat: the flouring should only be done around the crusts and not all over the bread.

After you have prepared all the slices, put a little lukewarm water in a bowl and wet only the floured part of each piece, gradually placing the pieces in a fairly large dish, where they can be placed in a single layer without touching each other.

Beat 2 eggs in a bowl, add a pinch of salt, and use them to coat the bread and line up in the large dish. Leave for a little while—an hour or more—to allow the bread to absorb all the beaten egg.

A few minutes before the meal, take the pads one at a time and slide them into the frying pan where the lard or oil will be boiling hot. Fry and serve.

PANE DORATO CON ACCIUGHE

Fried Mozzarella with Anchovy

2 loaves of bread
1 lb mozzarella
6 anchovy fillets
Oil for frying
All-purpose flour
2 eggs
Pepper

From the 2 loaves of bread cut 24 slices at ½ inch thick. On one half of these slices arrange a slice of mozzarella, and half an anchovy divided into two pieces, season with a pinch of pepper, and cover with another slice of bread.

Put a pan with enough oil on the stove. Prepare another bowl with a little water, another with flour, and another bowl with 2 beaten eggs as for an omelet. When the oil is very hot, dip the slices, for a moment, in the prepared water, pass them through the flour, and then through the beaten eggs and put them in the hot oil.

When they are gilded on one side, turn them over. When you have them all fried, arrange them on a plate and serve hot.

ADA SAYS: *This preparation is very simple and really tasty for a snack.*

PANE DORATO CON MOZZARELLA

Fried Mozzarella and Ham Sandwich

1 loaf of bread
1 lb mozzarella
3½ oz ham
All-purpose flour
Milk
2 eggs
Lard or oil for frying
Salt

Cut large fat rectangle slices from a loaf of bread, remove the crusts, and open the slice in two without separating the two parts.

Inside, put a slice of mozzarella and a slice of ham. Lightly flour the opening and the outsides, dip them for a moment in a little warm milk, and line them up in a large dish. Brush them with beaten egg. Leave them like this for at least an hour, so they become well impregnated with the egg.

Then fry them, a few at a time, in hot oil or lard. When they are a beautiful golden colour, remove them, let them drain, salt them lightly, and arrange them on a serving dish. Serve them very hot.

SKEWERS

All recipes make 12 skewers

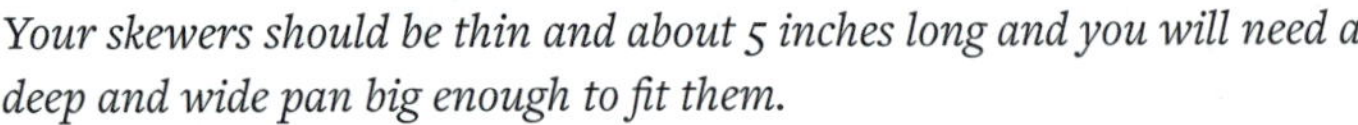

SPIEDINI ALLA NAPOLETANA

Neapolitan Skewers

2 eggplants
24 small unripe tomatoes
1 loaf of bread
8 oz mozzarella
Milk
All-purpose flour
2 eggs
Oil for frying

Your skewers should be thin and about 5 inches long and you will need a deep and wide pan big enough to fit them.

Peel the eggplants, cut them into slices of ½ inch and fry them in a pan with plenty of oil, without flour, until they have taken a beautiful light gold colour. Then remove them from the pan, let them drain, and sprinkle them lightly with salt.

Peel the tomatoes, cut the top cap, empty them of their juice and seeds, and put them to dry upside down on a plate. Cut the fried eggplant slices into equal squares.

Cut ½ inch-thick bread squares from the loaf of bread and pieces of mozzarella of the same shape and size.

Start by skewering a square of bread, 1 of mozzarella, 1 of eggplant, a tomato, etc. until you have filled the skewer, and ending with a square of bread. Be careful to leave the two ends of the skewers free to be able to handle them more easily later.

When you have finished, dip 1 skewer at a time in the milk, then pass through the flour, through the beaten eggs, and put in the pan to fry with plenty of oil. Fry the skewers to a beautiful golden colour and, when you have fried them all, arrange them on a serving dish and serve them hot.

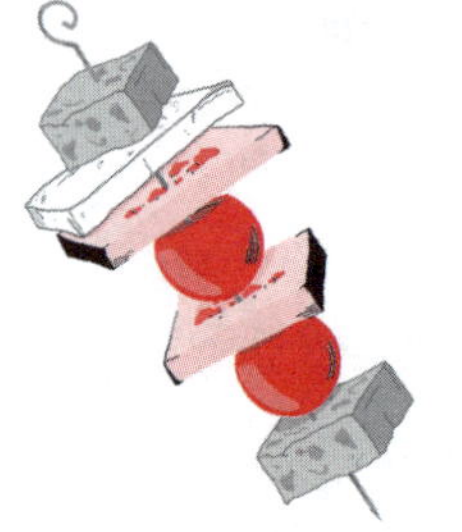

SPIEDINI ALLA PETRONIANA

Petronian Skewers

10½ oz veal or pork in a single slice
1½ tbsp butter
3½ oz Gruyère
3½ oz mortadella
Bread
Milk
All-purpose flour
2 eggs
Breadcrumbs
Oil for frying
Salt

Roll out the slice of meat and sauté with a little butter and a pinch of salt. Let it cool and cut it into squares of ½ inch. Prepare an equal number of squares of Gruyère, mortadella, kept a little thicker than usual, and of the white part of a loaf of bread. Take 12 rather long skewers and, alternating them, fix the squares of meat, cheese, mortadella, and bread, leaving space at both ends of about ½ inch.

Dip them one at a time in a little warm milk, then pass them through the flour, in beaten eggs, and finally in breadcrumbs. Bread them carefully, using the blade of a knife to help shape them neatly. When they are all ready, fry them in a lot of hot oil until they have taken on a beautiful golden colour.

ADA SAYS: *This is a recipe from Bologna; St. Petronio is the patron saint of that city.*

SPIEDINI DI SEMOLINO

Semolina Skewers

4½ oz semolina
2 cups milk
4 tbsp grated Parmesan
3 eggs
3½ oz Gruyère
All-purpose flour
Breadcrumbs
Oil for frying
Salt

Sprinkle the semolina into the boiling milk. Mix well with a wooden spoon and let it thicken, working the mixture well until it detaches from the sides of the pan. After about 10 minutes, remove the pan from the heat, season with salt, grated Parmesan, and an egg yolk. Mix everything, then pour the semolina on to a wet kitchen table. Smooth it out with wet hands or with the blade of a knife and let it cool.

With a round pastry cutter of 1 inch in diameter, divide the semolina into many disks. Cut the Gruyère into disks or squares.

Take 12 wooden skewers and add alternating disks of semolina and disks of Gruyère, leaving the skewer protruding at the ends. Wipe through the flour, through the beaten eggs, through the breadcrumbs, and finally fry in plenty of very hot oil until they are a beautiful golden colour. Arrange the skewers on a serving dish and send them to the table very hot.

STECCHI ALLA BOLOGNESE

Skewers Bolognese

7 oz of meat—chicken, turkey, veal, or pork, in one piece
1½ tbsp butter
White wine
Nutmeg
1¾ oz sweetbreads
1¾ oz chicken livers
1¾ oz ham
1¾ oz mortadella
1¾ oz Emmenthal
Breadcrumbs
2 eggs
Oil for frying
Salt

White sauce:
3½ tbsp butter, ⅓ cup all-purpose flour, 1 cup milk

Prepare a white sauce *(p16)* with the butter, flour, and milk so it is dense, well seasoned, and elastic. Leave to cool.

Cut the meat into cubes of about ½ inch and fry them in a saucepan with butter, salt, and nutmeg. After about a quarter of an hour deglaze with half a glass of white wine, reduce so as to have a very thick sauce. At this point remove the saucepan from the heat.

Prepare the sweetbreads and chicken livers, simmered and cut into cubes the same size as the meats. Also cut the ham, mortadella, and Emmenthal cheese.

Put everything in the saucepan where you have cooked the meats and mix so that all the different pieces can be veiled with a little of the sauce in the pan.

Put a piece of each ingredient on a skewer, pressing them well against each other. Wipe them through the white sauce so they are well clotted. Then slide through the breadcrumbs, then the beaten eggs, and fry them in plenty of hot oil.

STECCHI ALLA GENOVESE

Skewers Genovese

7 oz chicken livers
7 oz lamb sweetbreads
Butter
Broth
10½ oz fresh mushrooms
9 tbsp grated Parmesan
2 egg yolks
1¾ oz ham or tongue
Parsley
Black truffle
All-purpose flour
2 eggs
Breadcrumbs
Oil for frying
Salt

White sauce:
3½ tbsp butter, ⅓ cup all-purpose flour, 1 cup milk

Cook the chicken livers and sweetbreads separately in a small saucepan in butter. Cut the mushrooms into pieces and cook in the same butter with a little broth or water.

Take thin wooden skewers, about 5 inches long, and alternate the liver, sweetbread, and mushrooms.

Prepare a thick white sauce *(p16)* with the ingredients listed here and, when smooth, add the grated Parmesan, 2 egg yolks, the ground ham or tongue, a pinch of parsley, and a piece of black truffle in tiny cubes. Wipe the garnished skewers through this sauce so that they are well coated, and line them up on the kitchen table.

Prepare 1 bowl with the flour, another with 2 beaten eggs and a third bowl with breadcrumbs. When the sauce is cold and set, gently take the skewers one by one, wipe them first through the flour, then through the beaten eggs, back through the breadcrumbs, and, finally, fry in plenty of boiling oil.

ARANCINI & SUPPLÌ

All recipes make about 20 portions

ARANCINI

Arancini

14 oz rice
3½ tbsp butter
9 tbsp grated Parmesan
2 large whole eggs
Breadcrumbs
Oil or lard for frying
Salt
Filling: 3½ oz mozzarella, ¾ oz ham, 1¾ oz chicken livers, ¾ oz dried mushrooms

Beef and tomato sauce:
2¼ lb beef shin, onion, lard, or olive oil, 1¾ oz fat, pancetta, 2¼ lb tomatoes (or 4 cups passata), red wine, garlic clove, salt, and pepper

For the success of this recipe keep in mind that the rice must be well cooked—at the end of cooking it should be dry and have absorbed all the gravy; the exact quantity of sauce cannot be given because the power of rice absorption varies according to rice quality. Arancini are usually made from leftover risotto so, in that case, the rice will already be sauced.

Have ready a beef and tomato sauce *(p35)* using the ingredients listed below.

Start cooking the rice in only half of the sauce. Add the rest of the sauce, always hot, a little at a time until the rice is completely cooked. As soon as the rice is cooked, remove it from the heat, season with butter, grated Parmesan, and the eggs, beaten as for an omelet, then pour it into a large plate, flatten it, and let it cool.

In the meantime prepare the filling, which can vary depending on tastes and customs, but whose elements must be prepared separately. Only the mozzarella is expected. Cut the mozzarella and ham into cubes and chop in 1 or 2 slices of the meat from the sauce. Dried mushrooms must be revived in cold water and put in a small saucepan with the rest of the butter and a pinch of salt, covered with water, and left to cook for about 15 minutes, until the water has dried, then they are chopped and put in a bowl. Livers must be cleaned and washed with particular care and cooked quickly otherwise they harden; cook them in butter.

Get ready! Join all the various filling elements in a bowl and mix well, keeping aside diced mozzarella.

Now begin to pack the arancini: take a good spoonful of rice and place it in the palm of your left hand; put a little of the filling in the centre of the rice, adding 2 or 3 diced mozzarella pieces. Make sure to close the filling in the rice, giving it the shape of a big croquette. Then roll in breadcrumbs, so the crumbs cover it perfectly.

When you have prepared all the arancini, fry them immediately in plenty of oil or boil in lard, until they become blond and crunchy. Serve them hot.

◆ **ADA SAYS:** *Arancini and supplì are similar but arancini are typically associated with Sicily whereas supplì are associated with Rome.*

SUPPLÌ DI RISO IN BIANCO

White Rice Supplì

1 onion
7 tbsp butter
14 oz rice
6⅓ cups meat broth *(p88)* or bouillon cube
3 tbsp grated Parmesan
2 eggs
Breadcrumbs
Lard or oil for frying
Salt
Optional: 3½ oz mozzarella

This recipe differs from the previous in that the rice should be cooked in broth instead of gravy; either a good homemade meat broth without tomato or a bouillon cube.

Cut the onion into thin slices; put it in a saucepan with half the butter and cook slowly without taking colour and then pour in the rice and season with a little salt. Mix with a wooden spoon so that the rice is well soaked in the butter and does not stick; then gradually pour in the boiling broth over a high heat, always adding more boiling broth as and when the rice swells.

As soon as the rice is well cooked, season it with the remaining butter, the grated Parmesan, and eggs, beaten as for an omelet. Pour everything onto a large flat plate or board, flatten it, and let it cool.

Now begin to pack the supplì: take a good spoonful of rice giving it the shape of a large elongated croquette, and add a few breadcrumbs to help you. In the centre you can put a few cubes of mozzarella and close it up well inside the rice.

Roll the supplì in breadcrumbs so that the breading is perfect. When you have prepared all the supplì, fry them in plenty of oil or hot lard until they have become blond and crunchy. Serve hot.

SUPPLÌ A ROVESCIO

Inside out Supplì

1¼ lb ground beef
1 loaf of bread
4 tbsp butter
3 eggs
Cooked risotto rice (with or without sauce)
All-purpose flour
Breadcrumbs
Oil for frying
Salt
Pepper
Nutmeg

Have ready ⅓ cup of a cold leftover risotto seasoned with butter and Parmesan or with a meat sauce.

Dip the white part of a loaf of bread in water and squeeze dry. Shred it and add to the beef along with 2 tablespoons of butter, salt, and a pinch of pepper, and mix to a fine paste.

Beat an egg, as if making an omelet, and add to the paste. Roll out the paste and divide into 12 pieces, more or less the size of an egg. With slightly wet hands, gently knead the pieces and align them in front of you. Roll them out to a smooth piece, which must be about ¼ inch thick and about 4 inches in diameter.

Put a small scoop of rice, as big as a walnut, in the middle of the meat, roll the meat on itself, and enclose it inside the filling; fold the two ends of the roll in with your right hand so as to give the roll the shape of a croquette.

Pass the supplì in the flour, then in the beaten eggs, in which you will have grated a pinch of nutmeg, and finally in breadcrumbs. Heat plenty of oil in a pan and dip a few at a time, cooking over moderate heat until they have taken on a rather dark golden colour. Arrange them on a serving dish and immediately send to

SUPPLÌ DI POLENTA

Polenta Supplì

3½ oz polenta
11¾ oz Gruyère and Fontina
All-purpose flour
2 eggs
Breadcrumbs
Oil for frying
Salt

If you are using a modern packet of polenta, follow the instructions on the label. Otherwise, put water in a saucepan, season with salt, and bring it to a boil. Let the polenta fall in it like rain, stirring all the time. After three quarters of an hour, the polenta will be thick and it will detach from the bottom and sides of the pan. Take off the heat.

With a wet spoon take a spoonful of polenta and let it fall on a wet kitchen table. Try to give it the shape of an egg and in the centre of each egg, place a slice of Gruyère and Fontina. Prepare all the supplì in this way; let them cool.

When you are ready, flour them, pass them through beaten eggs, then through breadcrumbs, and then fry them a few at a time, in hot oil. Finally, arrange them on a serving dish and immediately send them to the table.

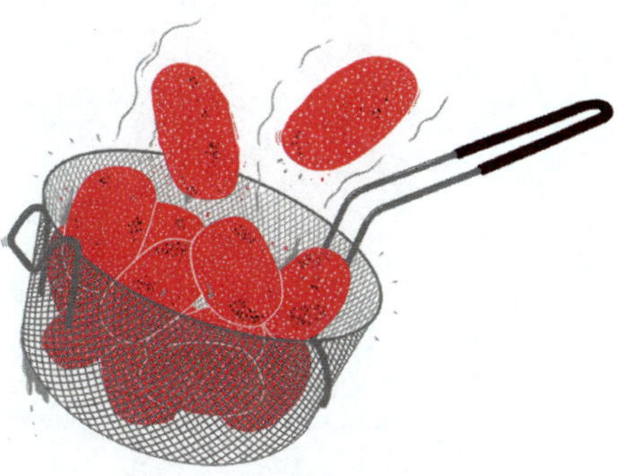

"Dough is nothing to be afraid of—it presents no particular difficulties and is easily accomplished at a well-floured kitchen table."

Pizzas and calzones are always associated with Naples. Typically calzones are baked in the oven, unlike panzerrotti, which are similar but are fried. Panzerotti are usually more associated with the region of Apulia.

The dough for a pizza or calzone is nothing to be afraid of—it presents no particular difficulties and is easily accomplished at a well-floured kitchen table. The mixes for bread and pizza are straightforward, but it is important to let the dough rest and recover from the kneading and the rolling pin before thinking about the filling. For variations there are also potato and yeast doughs, which, if you follow the instructions, are equally easy to manage. More challenging is puff pastry. We offer you the best approach to make your own puff pastry, but in truth you can find very good ready-made pastry, both fresh and frozen, in the stores these days, which can work almost as well and will save a lot of time.

Calzone is an exquisite specialty. Presented in its largest form it is "calzone" and in smaller forms as "calzoncelli." Like the pizzas and pies in this chapter, they all benefit from being made at home. The dough is always more interesting when it is made in your kitchen.

The traditional Neapolitan calzone is filled with ham, mortadella or salami, mozzarella, parsley and basil, and Parmesan. No tomato.

Calzones cook easily in the oven, but remember to turn the oven up before you start working so it is ready and at least a medium heat. Calzones will bake in 20 minutes, calzoncelli in less.

Pizza may take as long as 20 minutes in a domestic oven but if you are fortunate enough to have a wood-fired oven, then half that time will probably be enough. Pies on the other hand will need around 30 minutes. The pastry should be pricked with a fork or a knitting needle to allow the steam to escape. These little pies should also be allowed a few moments to rest when they come out of the oven and before taking them out of their tray or mold.

There are specially milled flours graded for pizza and pies, usually marked as 00. The designation means that the flour has been milled very slowly and will be very finely ground.

CALZONI, PIZZE E TORTE SALATE

6 PIZZAS, CALZONES & PIES

PIZZAS

TO MAKE PIZZA DOUGH

For calzoni and pizzas, the different doughs tend to be seasoned according to the uses and customs of the different regions. Ususally it is important to have a very hot oven.

For 1 pizza, use the following ratios: **2 cups 00 flour, 1 tbsp of active dry yeast, salt, and 1 glass of warm water.** *Place the sifted flour in a heap, crumble the dry yeast and salt in a jug with the warm water, leave for a few minutes, then slowly add to the flour. Work the dough vigorously until very smooth, elastic, and relatively soft, then make a ball and put in a bowl with a little flour on the bottom. Cover with a cloth. The dough will rise in 2 hours. Then you knead again before using.*

PIZZA ALLA NAPOLETANA

Neapolitan Pizza

Pizza dough *(as above)*
1¾ oz anchovies
5¼ oz mozzarella
10½ oz tomatoes
Olive oil or lard
Oregano
Salt
Pepper

Prepare your pizza dough, then roll it out to about 10 inches across.

Divide the washed and boned anchovies into fillets and cut the mozzarella into cubes. Wash the tomatoes, remove the skin and seeds, and chop. Arrange the anchovies, diced mozzarella, and tomatoes on the pizza. Sprinkle plenty of salt and pepper on everything and finish with a strong pinch of oregano and a little more oil. Cook the pizza in a preheated oven for about 20 minutes until the edges are dotted with bubbles that tend to scorch.

PIZZA ALLA NAPOLETANA CAPRICCIOSA

Neapolitan Pizza Capricciosa

Pizza dough *(as above)*
7 oz fresh mushrooms
Garlic
Olive oil
White wine
2 eggs
Tomato passata
1¾ oz mozzarella
8 anchovy fillets
3½ oz tinned tuna in olive oil
1¾ oz prosciutto
Salt
Pepper

Prepare your pizza dough. Trim the mushrooms, wash them quickly, dry them very carefully, and cut them into slices lengthwise. Put the garlic and enough oil in a pan to cover the bottom and, when the garlic is golden, remove it and add the mushrooms, season with salt and pepper, and let them cook over a high heat for a few minutes; then pour over half a glass of white wine, a little at a time, let it evaporate, and cook the mushrooms for about 10 minutes.

Boil the eggs, let them cool, and cut them into wedges. Turn on the oven.

When the dough has risen, turn it over on the kitchen table, knead it a little longer, flatten it into a circular disk, and place it in a greased tray. Trace four sections on the pizza with a small knife and cover each one with the tomato passata. Finely chop the mozzarella and put it only in two sections, drain a drizzle of oil over the dough, and place in the hot oven for about 15 minutes. Meanwhile, chop the anchovy fillets and the tuna. Remove the pizza from the oven and put the mushrooms on one side of the mozzarella and the anchovies and eggs on the other, in the other two spaces put the prosciutto and the tuna. Leave another 5 minutes in the oven and then serve immediately.

PIZZA ALLA NAPOLETANA CON FUNGHI E MOZZARELLA

Neapolitan Pizza with Mozzarella and Mushrooms

Pizza dough *(opp. page)*
1¾ oz dried mushrooms
1½ tbsp butter
5¼ oz mozzarella
1 lb ripe tomatoes
Olive oil
10 Gaeta olives, pitted
Basil
Salt
Pepper

This recipe can also be done with provola cheese.

Prepare your pizza dough. Soak the dried mushrooms in cold water for 20 minutes, wash them thoroughly, and cook them for about a quarter of an hour on a low heat with butter, a pinch of salt, and a few spoonfuls of water.

Dice the mozzarella. Wash, blanch, peel, and deseed the tomatoes, then cut them into slices. When the dough has risen, turn it over on the kitchen table, knead it a little longer, flatten it into a circular disk, and place it in a greased tray. Arrange on top the mozzarella, mushrooms, the tomato slices, and the olives. Season everything with a pinch of salt and pepper and a few basil leaves.

Put the pizza in the oven and let it cook for about 20 minutes.

PIZZA ALLA NAPOLETANA CON UOVA E FUNGHETTI

Neapolitan Pizza with Egg and Mushrooms

Pizza dough *(opp. page)*
10½ oz mushrooms
Olive oil
3 eggs
Salt
Pepper

Put the oven on to high and prepare your pizza dough.

Clean the mushrooms, wash them quickly, cut them into slices, and put them to cook in a pan with a little oil and a pinch of salt. While the mushrooms are cooking, boil the eggs, and, when they are boiled, shell them and cut them into cubes.

When your dough has risen, turn it over on the kitchen table, knead it a little longer, flatten it into a circular disk, and place it in a greased tray. On the dough, pour the prepared mushrooms, diced eggs, and sprinkle with a little salt and pepper. Pour over a little oil and put the tray in the hot oven for 20 minutes.

PIZZA ALLA NAPOLETANA CON VONGOLE

Neapolitan Pizza with Clams

Pizza dough *(p264)*
2¼ lb clams
2 garlic cloves
Olive oil or lard
10½ oz ripe tomatoes
Oregano
Parsley
Salt
Pepper

Prepare your pizza dough.

Wash the clams several times with great care. Put the garlic cloves and as much oil as needed in a large pan to cover the bottom, and as soon as the garlic has colored, add the clams and cook them for a few minutes over high heat, making them jump until they are cooked. When they are all open, shell them and collect them in a cup. Sieve the cooking liquid.

Wash and blanch the tomatoes and remove the skin and seeds. Then, cut them into slices. Turn up the oven to high.

When your dough has risen, turn it over on the kitchen table, knead it a little longer, and flatten it into a circular disk. Drain a drizzle of oil on the pizza so that all the dough is evenly greased; arrange the sliced tomatoes on top, season with salt and pepper, drizzle more oil over it, sprinkle a pinch of oregano, and place the pizza in the very hot oven for about 20 minutes.

As soon as the pizza is well cooked and crunchy—that is when the edges are dotted with bubbles that tend to scorch—remove it from the oven and arrange the clams and chopped parsley on top.

PIZZA ALLA NAPOLETANA DI FARINA E PATATE

Neapolitan Pizza with Flour and Potatoes

1⅔ cups 00 flour
1¾ tbsp active dry yeast
7 oz boiled potatoes
3½ tbsp butter
2 eggs
3½ oz prosciutto
3½ oz smoked provolone
Salt

Put a quarter of the flour in a cup, crumble in the active dry yeast, and with a teaspoon dissolve with a little tepid water, to obtain a very soft dough, like a thick batter. Cover the cup and put it in a sheltered place.

Put the rest of the flour on the kitchen table; in the center place a good pinch of salt, the boiled potatoes, peeled and mashed, the butter, and the whole eggs. As soon as the yeast in the cup has doubled in volume, pour it into the middle of the flour and knead, working the dough well. Then add the prosciutto in pieces and the smoked provolone in cubes. Knead a little more.

Grease with lard or butter a tray with high sides and a diameter of about 7 inches, lay in the dough, and let it rise.

When it has doubled in volume, put the pizza in a very hot oven and cook for about 20 minutes.

PIZZA ALLA NAPOLETANA MARGHERITA

Neapolitan Pizza Margherita

Pizza dough *(p264)*
1 lb ripe tomatoes
9 oz mozzarella
Olive oil
Grated Parmesan
Basil
Salt
Pepper

Turn up the oven to a good heat. Wash, peel, and deseed the tomatoes, then cut them into slices. Dice the mozzarella.

Prepare your pizza dough. When the dough has risen, turn it on the floured table, roll it out with your hands or with a rolling pin into a sheet ¼ inch thick.

Put the dough on a baking sheet, lightly greased with oil, or if you prefer in two baking pans with a diameter of about 10 inches each, previously greased. Roll out the dough again with your fingers and tap on it with your hands.

Drizzle some oil on the dough, arrange the tomato fillets, mozzarella, ½ cup of grated Parmesan, washed and dried basil leaves, and season everything with a pinch of salt and pepper. Put the pizza in the oven and let it cook for about 20 minutes until the edges are dotted with bubbles that tend to scorch.

ADA SAYS: *This simple and tasty pizza, famous all over the world, is named for Queen Margherita of Savoy, to whom it was dedicated during her stay in Naples in 1889.*

PIZZA CON CIPOLLE

Pizza with Onions

Pizza dough *(p264)*
2½ lb onions
7 oz leek, white part only
3 garlic cloves
Bay leaf
Parsley
Thyme
Olive oil
10 anchovies
3½ oz black olives, pitted
Lard
Salt
Pepper

Prepare your pizza dough. Clean the onions and the leek, remove the hard parts, chop them as finely as possible, and sweat in a saucepan over very low heat, adding the garlic cloves, whole, but slightly crushed, the herbs—the bay, parsley, and thyme, tied together so that it is possible to remove them later, and a little oil. Cooking these herbs is essential. The onion, leek, and garlic must cook very slowly, with the pan covered, stewing without taking color. They must almost unravel without becoming a purée: if they color they would have another taste. Add a little water from time to time if necessary. It takes about an hour. Finally, season with a little salt and pepper.

Turn up the oven to high. When the dough has risen, turn it on the floured table, roll it out with your hands or with a rolling pin into a sheet ¼ inch thick. Then prick the entire surface of the dough with the teeth of a fork.

Remove the garlic cloves and the bundle of herbs from the pan and pour the onions with oil onto the dough, spreading everything in one layer. On this layer, arrange the washed, boned, and cut anchovies. Scatter here and there the black olives and coarse ground pepper. Put the pizza in the oven letting it cook for about 20 minutes until the edges are well cooked and crunchy.

PIZZA CON FORMAGGI

Three Cheese Pizza

3½ oz smoked pancetta
Milk
3½ oz Parmesan
3½ oz Fontina
3½ oz Gruyère
All-purpose flour
1¾ oz ham
2 eggs
Olive oil
Butter
Salt

Pizza dough:
2 cups 00 flour, 1 tbsp active dry yeast, 1 glass warm milk, pancetta fat

Divide the pancetta into pieces and warm in a pan. Sift the flour into a heap and pour the fat from the pancetta into the center, add a pinch of salt, and the active dry yeast. Dissolve everything with a small glass of warm milk, knead the dough vigorously, and then put it in a sheltered place to let it rise.

In the meantime, divide the Parmesan, Fontina, and Gruyère into tiny pieces, or an equal quantity of other cheeses, and put them in a saucepan with 2 spoons of flour, 2 glasses of milk, and a pinch of pepper. Bring the saucepan over the heat and, always stirring with a wooden spoon, melt the mixture. Remove from the heat and add the pancetta, the ham cut into pieces, and the egg yolks. Beat the whites to a firm snow and gently add them to the mixture. Turn the oven to high.

When the dough has risen, turn it on the floured table, roll it out with your hands or with a rolling pin into a sheet ¼ inch thick. Then prick the entire surface of the dough with the teeth of a fork.

Now pour the prepared cheese mixture over the pizza, and distribute it with the blade of a knife. Sprinkle with grated Parmesan, put some small pieces of butter here and there, place the pizza in the oven, and cook over moderate heat for about 20 minutes so that the dough can cook and the cheeses swell and firm up. This pizza can be eaten hot or cold.

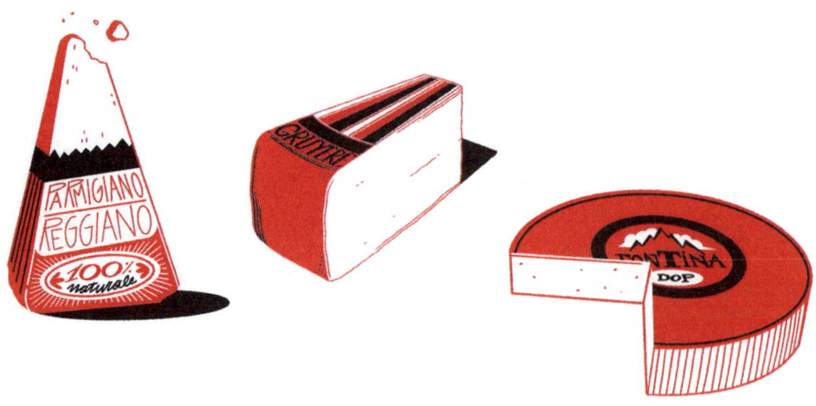

PIZZA CON SPEZZATINO

Pizza with Veal and Potatoes

2 cups 00 flour
Olive oil
1 onion
9 oz lean ground pork
9 oz lean ground veal
9 oz chicken breast
All-purpose flour
1 cup white wine
Bouillon cube
10½ oz ripe tomatoes
10½ oz peas
10½ oz mushrooms
12¼ oz potatoes
Salt
Pepper

Place the sifted flour in a heap and into the center pour four tablespoons of oil, a glass of water, and a pinch of salt. Knead vigorously until you get a dough of the right consistency, collect it in a bowl sprinkled with flour, cover, and place in the refrigerator for about half an hour.

Finely chop an onion. Color it in a saucepan with half a glass of oil; then add the pork and the veal; let it all brown, stirring occasionally. After a few minutes, add the diced chicken breast. When all the meats have reached a nice blond color, add a spoon of flour, a glass of white wine, and 2 cups of broth made with the bouillon cube. When boiling resumes, add the coarsely chopped tomatoes. Cover the saucepan, reduce the heat, and leave to cook slowly.

After about half an hour, add the shelled peas and the mushrooms, washed quickly and cut into slices. Continue cooking over very low heat for another half hour, stirring occasionally.

With a small knife, scrape the skins off the potatoes and throw them into a bowl of cold water. Drain and dry them.

In a pan with a lid, pour half a glass of oil and, when hot, add the potatoes, cover, decrease the heat, and let them brown in their steam. Occasionally shake the pan but without lifting the lid. After about half an hour the potatoes will be cooked, sprinkle them with salt, and leave them to flavor for a few minutes.

On a lightly floured kitchen board, roll out the dough so that it turns out very thin. Grease and flour a flan mold, cover it completely with the dough letting it overhang slightly. Pour the stew in. Put the mold in a preheated oven of moderate heat for about half an hour.

Place the mold on a serving dish, open the circle, and put the potatoes around the stew. Let the pizza cool for a few minutes before serving.

PIZZA DI PATATE

Potato Pizza

1 lb 5 oz baking potatoes
2½ cups 00 flour
Olive oil or lard
10½ oz mozzarella
Grated Parmesan
Oregano
6 fresh tomatoes
Salt
Pepper

Boil the potatoes, peel and mash them, and let them absorb the flour and a good pinch of salt. Turn the oven up to high.

Turn out this dough on a floured table and with the help of a rolling pin, roll it out to ¼ inch thick.

Grease an oven pan with oil or lard, place the potato dough on top and spread over the diced mozzarella, ¼ cup of grated Parmesan, a pinch of pepper, a spoonful of oregano, and a few fresh tomato fillets, without the skin and seeds. Drizzle a little oil over everything and bake the pizza in the oven in a rather lively heat for about 20 minutes.

PIZZA RITORTA CON PROSCIUTTO

Pizza and Prosciutto Twists

4 cups 00 flour
3 tbsp active dry yeast
7 oz lard
7 oz pork skins or pancetta
6 eggs
10½ oz prosciutto
Olive oil
Salt
Pepper

Put the flour on the kitchen table, arranging it in a fountain; in the center add the active dry yeast, a spoon of lard, a spoonful of crushed pork skins, salt, and pepper, and dissolve everything with two glasses of warm water to get a rather soft dough. Work it well and when it is elastic and velvety put it in a bowl and let it rise in a sheltered place.

Boil the eggs, shell them, divide them into wedges, and add them to the prosciutto, cut into cubes, and the remaining pork skins.

When the dough has risen, turn it over on the floured table, flatten it with your hands, and shape it into a rectangle. On this rectangle of dough spread plenty of lard. Fold the dough on itself as if it was a towel and roll it out slightly, sprinkling it with pepper. Finally, roll it out in a rectangle and put it on a baking sheet greased with oil.

Spread the prepared filling on the dough—eggs, prosciutto, and crushed pork skins—raising the edges and pressing them well to close. Smear the outside with lard and put in a preheated oven of lively heat for about 20 minutes. During cooking, baste again with the lard two or three times on the outside: this will allow the pizza to remain soft and flaky. It can be served hot or warm.

Pizzette

PIZZETTE ALLA NAPOLETANA

Neapolitan Pizzette

MAKES 18

Pizza dough *(p264)*
2¼ lb ripe tomatoes
Lard or oil for frying
Garlic
Oregano
Salt

Since these little pizzas cook very fast and should be served very hot, it would be better to work as a pair. One person to fry and the other to roll the dough.

Prepare your pizza dough and let rest in the fridge.

Now, prepare a thick tomato sauce: Blanch the tomatoes, remove the skin, and cut them into big pieces. Put them in a pan with a glass of oil and two cloves of garlic. The cooking must be done over high heat for about 10 minutes so that the tomatoes do not come apart too much. Season them with salt and pepper and finally flavor them with a pinch of oregano.

Turn the dough on to the floured table. Take small pieces, the size of an egg, spread them out by pulling them with your hands, and make some thin pizzas that you will fry immediately in a pan with very hot oil or lard. These pizzas should be in the pan for only a few seconds and, as soon as they are colored on one side, they must be turned to the other. Then remove the pizzas from the pan, arrange them on a large plate placing a generous spoonful of tomato on each, and send them to the table immediately.

PIZZETTE ALLA NAPOLETANA GUARNITE

Pizzette with Mozzarella and Anchovy

MAKES 18

Pizza dough *(p264)*
2¼ lb tomatoes
Oil for frying
5¼ oz mozzarella
6 anchovies
Oregano
Salt
Pepper

Prepare your pizza dough and let it rest in the fridge.

Dip the tomatoes in boiling water for a moment, peel them, deprive them of seeds, cut them into slices, and cook them in a pan with oil, over high heat, so that the slices remain whole. Season with salt and pepper and set aside.

Dice the mozzarella. Rinse, bone, and chop the anchovies and collect everything in one bowl, adding a strong pinch of oregano. When the dough is well risen, beat it lightly with the palm of your hand to deflate it.

Take the dough and make some small pizzas as on the previous page. Put a pan with plenty of oil on the stove. With floured hands take a piece of dough at a time, turn it between your fingers, pulling and thinning it so as to make a disk as wide and thin as possible, then promptly drop it into the very hot pan. These pizzas should be in the pan only for a few seconds. Remove the pizzas from the pan, arrange them on a plate, and put on top of each a spoonful of the mix of tomato, mozzarella, and anchovy.

CALZONES

CALZONCELLI ALLA NAPOLETANA

Neapolitan Calzoncelli

MAKES 12

3½ oz mozzarella
1¾ oz salami or mortadella
1¾ oz prosciutto
Oil or lard
Parsley
Basil
Grated Parmesan
1 egg
Salt
Pepper
Optional: raw tomato sauce *(p37)*

Pizza dough:
2 cups 00 flour, 1 tbsp active dry yeast, 1 glass water, ½ tbsp lard

An exquisite specialty made with the same dough as for pizza.

Heat the oven well because it must be very hot when you put the calzone in.

Cut the mozzarella and the mortadella or salami into cubes, and the prosciutto into slices.

Prepare your pizza dough *(p264)*. Then, turn the well risen dough upside down on the floured table, knead it some more, and divide it into 12 pieces. Roll it out into rather thin disks, thin it again, so that it is a disk of about 4 inches in diameter and ¼ inch thick. Add some lard to the dough and a pinch of salt.

Spread the cubes of mozzarella and slices of prosciutto and mortadella or salami on each disk, and season with a little salt and a good pinch of pepper, ½ cup of grated Parmesan, and a beaten egg. Then fold the disks in half, so as to close the filling inside.

Press with your fingers so that they remain tightly closed. Fry the calzoncelli in a pan in oil or lard, a few at a time, until golden.

When the calzone is cooked, put it in an oval dish. To make it even tastier, dress with a raw tomato sauce.

CALZONE ALLA NAPOLETANA

Neapolitan Calzone

Pizza dough *(p264)*
10½ oz mozzarella
7 oz prosciutto or salami
Olive oil or lard
Salt
Pepper
Optional: tomato sauce (made with 1 lb tomato passata, half glass olive oil, 1 onion, celery, 1 carrot, basil)

Prepare your pizza dough.

Heat the oven well because it must be very hot when you put the calzone in.

Cut the mozzarella into cubes and the prosciutto or salami into slices. Leave to the side.

Turn the well risen dough upside down on the floured table, knead it some more, roll it out into a rather thin disk, thin it again, so that it is a disk of about 14 inches in diameter and ¼ inch thick.

Grease the dough with oil or lard and then on one half spread the cubes of mozzarella and slices of prosciutto or salami, and season with a little salt and a good pinch of pepper; then fold the disk in half, so as to close the filling inside.

Press with your fingers so that the calzone remains tightly closed, grease it with a little more oil or lard and bake.

It takes about 10 minutes in a wood oven and probably twice as much in a modern domestic oven.

When the calzone is cooked, put it in an oval dish. To make it even tastier, dress with a very thick tomato sauce *(p37)*.

CALZONE ALLA NAPOLETANA CON SALSICCE E PROVOLA

Calzone with Sausages and Provolone

6 sausages
10½ oz provola
Basil
3 tbsp grated Parmesan
Oil for frying
Salt
Pepper

Pizza dough:
2 cups 00 flour, 1 tbsp active dry yeast, 1 glass water, 2 oz lard

Prick the sausages here and there with a fork and put them in a pan, covering them with cold water. Let them cook until the water evaporates, let them brown for a little longer, turning them as often as necessary so that they can color well on all sides. When cooked, peel and cut into slices, to which you will add the provolone cut into cubes and a handful of basil leaves, and season with grated Parmesan.

Prepare your pizza dough *(p264)* and incorporate the lard into the dough at the same time as the yeast. When the dough has risen well, turn it over on the lightly floured kitchen table, knock it back, and roll it out to about 12 inches in diameter. On half of this disk spread the filling, leaving around a free edge of a couple of fingers. Fold the disk back on itself and press the edges with your fingers so that they fit together. Then dip the calzone in plenty of boiling oil and let it fry on both sides. Finally, place it on the plate and serve hot.

PIES

TO MAKE PIE DOUGH

Place the flour in a heap on the kitchen table and in a well in the center, put the softened butter cut into small pieces, the iced water, and a pinch of salt. Mix the ingredients without working them too much, form a ball of dough, and rest in a cool place for at least half an hour.

TO MAKE PUFF PASTRY DOUGH

Heap the flour on the kitchen table, make a well in the center and add the water and a pinch of salt. Mix with your fingers. Gradually take the flour from the inside and knead, but without too much work, until you get a dough that is neither too hard nor too soft and very smooth. Make a ball, cover with a towel, and rest for 20 minutes. With the butter, which must be pliable but not too soft, make a mashed loaf. If the butter is too hard, work it a little in a wet towel. The butter and the dough must have the same consistency.

After 20 minutes, take the dough and with a wooden rolling pin make a square shape, about 4 inches on each side, without stretching it too much. In the middle of this put the butter and then fold the four sides of the dough on the butter, crossing them to enclose it. Lightly place the rolling pin on this square to close the dough and rest for another five minutes in the fridge. Now start the lamination process. Roll out the dough into a rectangle, stretching it in front of you so that it is three times longer than it is wide, and spreading it out ½ inch thick. Place in front of you the wide side of the strip instead of the long, as it was before, and fold the two ends toward the center, covering one with the other. You will now have a kind of three-sheet book. Then lay out the dough in a rectangle in front of you like the first time and fold again in three. You will have given the dough two turns. After these first two laps, rest the dough in the fridge for 10 minutes and then do another two laps. Another 10 minutes of rest, and then give two final laps.

Always sprinkle the dough and the table with a thin layer of flour during these operations. The lamination has the purpose of uniformly distributing the butter in the dough. The rest, every two turns, is necessary for the dough to lose the elasticity that it acquires by working it with a rolling pin. If you do not let the dough rest, it will be too elastic and during cooking the pastry can shrink. If you need to wait before using the puff pastry, it is fine to leave it folded and spread it out just before use.

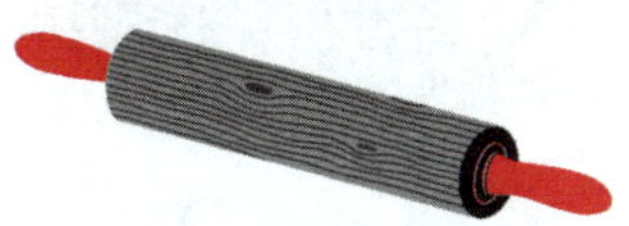

TORTA CALABRESE

Calabrian Pie

1 cup olive oil or 3½ oz lard
2¼ lb tomatoes
7 oz tinned tuna in olive oil
1¾ oz anchovies
2½ oz Gaeta olives, pitted
1½ tbsp capers
Salt
Pepper

Pizza dough:
5 cups 00 flour, 2 tbsp active dry yeast, 1 glass water

Prepare your pizza dough *(p264)* with the ingredients listed here. When the dough has risen, add the lard or a glass of oil, a pinch of pepper, and salt, and work the dough a little. When it has absorbed the seasoning, divide it into two unequal parts, flatten the bigger part, and line a previously greased baking tray with high sides and a diameter of about 12 inches.

Peel and remove the seeds from the tomatoes, cut them into pieces, and cook over a lively heat, in a pan with a few spoonfuls of oil. Season with a little salt, and, when they are cooked, but not collapsed, remove and leave them to cool.

Chop the tuna; bone the anchovies, wash them, and cut them into pieces; divide the olives in half. Add everything to the cooked tomatoes, also adding the salted capers not in vinegar. Mix with a wooden spoon and pour this sauce on the dough in the tray.

Roll out the remaining dough, apply it over the first, pressing the edges so that they stick and close the filling well. Grease the surface of the pie with a little bit of lard or oil. Place the pie in a preheated oven on high heat for about half an hour, until the dough has taken on a beautiful golden color.

ADA SAYS: *This recipe is excellent both hot and cold.*

TORTA DI PATATE ALLA FINANZIERA

Potato Pie

2¼ lb potatoes
Grated Parmesan
3 eggs
13½ tbsp butter
Breadcrumbs
1 oz dried mushrooms
3 sausages
4 chicken livers
1¾ oz prosciutto
Sage
All-purpose flour
2 tbsp tomato purée
Salt
Pepper

Boil the potatoes in lightly salted water, drain, peel, and mash them so that you get a smooth purée; mix in with ½ cup of grated Parmesan, an egg yolk, a pinch of salt, and some butter. Take a smooth cake mold, without the hole in the middle, butter it generously, sprinkle the inside with very fine breadcrumbs, and turn it upside down to drop off the superfluous. Beat an egg like an omelet, pour it into the mold, and, turning in all directions, make the egg wet the breadcrumbs. Then repeat with more crumbs to create a solid and crunchy crust.

Now take small portions of the mashed potatoes, arrange them and flatten them inside the mold, lining everything and building a kind of box a couple of inches thick, and leave an empty space in the center. Do this with great care so as not to remove any breading.

Now prepare the filling: Soak the dried mushrooms in cold water, clean them, rinse them, and put them to cook in a saucepan with a little butter or oil, salt, and a few spoonfuls of water. Prick the sausages with a needle and put them to cook in a pan, covering them with cold water.

When the water has all evaporated, let them brown in their fat, turning them from time to time so that they can be well colored on every side.

Wash the livers and with a sharp knife remove all the parts of the gall with greenish spots, and divide each liver into two or three parts. Put a knob of butter in a pan and when hot add the livers; season with salt and pepper and a few chopped sage leaves. Immediately, add the prosciutto cut into strips. The livers cook immediately, so in no time they will be ready.

Cut the sausages into slices, the livers into cubes, chop the mushrooms small, and put everything together in a small saucepan with a little butter. Sprinkle with half a spoon of flour, let it brown for a moment, and then add two spoons of tomato purée cooked separately with a knob of butter. Let everything boil, to get a very thick sauce. Hard boil 1 egg and cut into cubes and add to the filling.

Put this filling inside the prepared potato box, add two or three pieces of butter, and cover with a little more potato purée. Press slowly with your fingers all around so that this lid blends well with the other potatoes, sprinkle on a few breadcrumbs, top with a few pieces of butter, and put the pie in a preheated oven of moderate heat for around 45 minutes. Then remove it from the oven, let the pie rest for about 10 minutes, and then turn it out on a serving dish.

TORTA PASQUALINA ALLA GENOVESE

Easter Pie Genovese

4⅓ cups all-purpose flour
Olive oil
1 oz dried mushrooms
1 lb boiled and squeezed swiss chard
3 spring onions
Garlic
Parsley
7 eggs
Milk curdled with lemon juice (or 10½ oz ricotta)
1 cup grated Parmesan
7 tbsp milk
Butter
Salt
Pepper

The number of sheets is not fixed, but they should never be fewer than 10 to 12. There is a herb filling on which the curdled milk and 7 eggs are poured, all enclosed in multiple sheets of dough, as thin as paper, so as to give the idea of a pastry.

Place the flour on the kitchen table in a heap and put a pinch of salt and half a spoonful of oil in the center—no more. Dissolve the flour with water until you have a very soft dough, which you will work for a long time to make it gain elasticity. Once the dough is made, cover it with a wet and squeezed-out cloth, then with a second dry cloth, then let it rest for 15 minutes.

Soak the dried mushrooms for half an hour in cold water. Cut the stems out of the chard, rinse the leaves, and put them to boil in a little slightly salted boiling water; then drain them, rinse them in fresh water, squeeze them well, and mince them.

Put half a glass of oil in a pan with plenty of chopped spring onion. When the onion is a little browned, add the chopped dried mushrooms, a ground clove of garlic, and chopped parsley. Cover the pan and cook over moderate heat until the mushrooms are completely cooked, adding, if necessary, very little water. Remove the pan from the heat, add the chopped chard, salt, pepper and a beaten egg.

Add the juice of a lemon to the curdled milk and bring to boil. This liquid must be half the volume of the vegetable mixture. Collect it in a cloth bag—which should hang—and let it drain well; then put it in a bowl and season with a little oil, salt, pepper, 2 beaten eggs, 2 tablespoons of grated Parmesan, a little milk, and a few spoonfuls of flour, so that it results in a mixture of a certain consistency, neither too soft nor too hard.

If you don't like the slightly pungent taste of this liquid, you can replace the curdled milk with ricotta, well dissolved with a wooden spoon, half a glass of milk, a good spoonful of flour, 2 more tablespoons of grated Parmesan, two eggs, salt, and pepper. Mix everything well, making sure that the mixture is not too soft, in which case add a little more flour.

Divide the dough into 10 equal pieces and sprinkle them with flour. Choose a pan with very low edges, with a diameter of about 12 inches, and oil the bottom. Take a piece of dough and, after having spread a veil of flour on the table, flatten it with a wooden roller to a certain thickness. Then—it will be good to do this with two people—pass two hands under the dough, and, moving them appropriately, gently stretch the dough until it reaches a minimum thickness like that of tissue paper.

Place this first sheet in the pan, letting it overhang. Gently grease this first sheet with oil. With the same system, make another 3 sheets, always placing them on top of each other and oiling them. Once the fourth sheet is placed, spread the chard mixture into the pan and flatten it with the blade of a knife so as to make a regular layer, leaving a small free space all around. Pour the curdled milk mixture or ricotta over the chard and smooth out this too with a knife in a regular layer.

Now make four dimples in the cake with a spoon; in each of these dimples, slide a fresh egg, and season each egg with salt, pepper, and a slice of butter.

Then continue to roll out the sheets of dough, always pulling them as thinly as possible—and above all without tearing them—and oil them. If the lower sheets are less thin, it is not crucial, the important thing is that the maximum thinness is reached in the upper sheets.

Once the last sheet is put on, which should not be oiled, cut around the dough that surrounds it, leaving only a couple of fingers. Gradually roll the extra dough on itself to make a decorative cord, which you can use to line the inner edge of the pan and then mark with the prongs of a fork and grease with oil.

Once the cake is packaged, put it in a preheated oven of moderate heat and leave it for about half an hour until it takes on a nice golden color. It is served cold.

ADA SAYS: *It is customary, when putting down the last two sheets, to put some air in them so that during cooking the dough can swell. It is an optional embellishment and is done like this: using a straw, blow air underneath the penultimate sheet, leave the air inside, and take out the straw. The operation is repeated also for the last sheet.*

TORTA RUSTICA ALLA NAPOLETANA

Rustic Neapolitan Pie

10½ oz mozzarella
5¼ oz prosciutto
1 lb ripe tomatoes
Olive oil
Basil
Grated Parmesan
1 egg yolk
Salt
Pepper

Pizza dough:
5 cups 00 flour, 2 tbsp active dry yeast, 1 glass water

Prepare your pizza dough *(p264)* with the ingredients listed here. Cut the mozzarella into thin slices and the prosciutto into strips and put them in a bowl. Turn up the oven.

Dip the tomatoes for a minute or two in boiling water, remove the skin and the seeds, and cut them into fillets. Put a pan on the heat with a little oil, and, when the oil is steaming, throw in the tomatoes and let them blanch over very strong heat so that they can cook without falling apart. They must not be too mixed, otherwise they fall apart and instead of tomato slices you get a mush.

Lightly flour the table, lay out the dough, and divide it into two unequal parts. Flatten the larger part with a rolling pin. Grease a pan with a diameter of about 8 inches and put the flattened dough on the bottom, forming a sort of bowl slightly raised at the edges.

On the dough arrange half the slices of mozzarella and on these, spread the cooked tomato. Season with salt and pepper and a spoon or two of chopped fresh basil. Line up the strips of prosciutto on the tomato and finish with a second layer of mozzarella. Complete the filling by sprinkling everything with ¼ cup of grated Parmesan.

Take the remaining dough, roll it out with a rolling pin to form a disk, and cover the pie with this; press slowly with your fingers until the dough matches well. Wipe the surface with the beaten egg yolk. Put the pie in a preheated oven and let it cook for about half an hour at a good but not excessive heat.

TORTA RUSTICA CON CARCIOFI

Rustic Artichoke Pie

Puff pastry, homemade *(p275)* or 1 lb freshly packaged puff pastry
12 artichokes
1 lemon
All-purpose flour
Oil for frying
Butter
10½ oz ham
7 oz Fontina
1 egg yolk
Salt

Have your puff pastry well rested and ready in the fridge.

Then prepare your filling: Remove the harder outer leaves from the artichokes, shorten the stem a little while keeping the tender part; scraping and cutting some filaments, turn the choke out with a small knife and trim the top. Then cut the artichokes into wedges and keep them in a bowl of water acidulated with lemon juice. When they are all prepared, drain the artichokes, dry them, dip them in flour, and fry them in a pan with plenty of oil, over moderate heat, until they are well cooked. Salt them lightly.

Divide the puff pastry into two unequal parts and flatten the larger part on the floured board. Completely line a previously buttered and floured 12 inch diameter baking tray with high edges, so that it slightly overlaps the edge. Arrange in the tray half the slices of ham, the slices of Fontina, and all the artichokes, leveling them well with the blade of a knife, and cover them with the remaining ham. Now roll out the other piece of dough and cover the pie, matching the edges by pressing slowly with your fingers to close it perfectly. With a small knife cut the excess part of the dough and with it make decorations on the pie. Wipe the surface of the pie with a beaten egg yolk and make a few small holes with a toothpick so that it does not swell when cooking. Put the pie in a preheated oven of moderate heat for about half an hour. When cooked, remove from the oven, let it rest for about 10 minutes and then turn it out onto a serving dish.

TORTA RUSTICA CON CARNE E FUNGHETTI

Rustic Meat and Mushroom Pie

Puff pastry, homemade *(p275)* or 1 lb freshly packaged puff pastry
10½ oz mushrooms
Butter
White wine
1 onion
2¾ oz smoked pancetta
14 oz ground veal
1 egg yolk
Salt
Pepper

White sauce:
⅓ cup all-purpose flour, 3½ tbsp butter, 1⅔ cups milk

Have your puff pastry well rested and ready in the fridge or buy it ready-made. If frozen, let it thaw at room temperature.

With a small knife, trim the stems of the mushrooms, wash them quickly, dry them, and cut them into slices lengthwise. In a large pan, melt a knob of butter, add the mushrooms, cook them over medium heat until they have absorbed the water, add salt and pepper, and pour half a glass of wine into the pan a little at a time; let them cook for about 10 minutes, then remove them from the heat and let them cool.

Melt another knob of butter in a saucepan, add the chopped onion and smoked bacon, and cook over moderate heat for a few minutes, stirring occasionally to keep the onion from browning. Now place the ground veal in the saucepan, add salt and pepper, mix carefully, and cook for about 10 minutes.

Prepare a white sauce *(p16)* with the flour, butter, and milk, keeping it rather thick. Add to the meat and the mushrooms, mix well, and let it cool.

Divide the puff pastry into two unequal pieces, roll out the largest part on the floured board, and line a previously buttered and floured high-sided baking pan with a diameter of about 12 inches, so that the dough slightly overlaps the edge. Fill the pan with the prepared mixture and level the surface well with the blade of a knife.

Now roll out the other piece of dough and cover the pie, matching the edges well, pressing slowly with your fingers to close it completely. With a small knife cut the excess part of the dough and make decorations on the pie.

Brush the pie surface with a beaten egg yolk and make a few small holes with a toothpick so that it does not swell during cooking. Put the pie in a preheated oven of moderate heat for about half an hour. When cooked, remove the pan from the oven, let it rest for about 10 minutes, and then turn it out onto a serving dish.

TORTA RUSTICA CON GROVIERA

Rustic Gruyère Pie

10½ oz Gruyère
1 cup grated Parmesan
2 eggs
Salt

Pie dough:
1⅔ cups all-purpose flour,
18 tbsp (9 oz) butter

White sauce:
5 tbsp butter, 9½ tbsp all-purpose flour, 2 cups milk

Have your pie dough *(p275)* well rested and ready in the fridge.

Make a white sauce *(p16)* with the butter, flour, and milk. Turn on the oven. Add the Gruyère, cut into very small cubes, and the grated Parmesan. Continue to keep the saucepan on the heat and, always stirring, melt the cheeses. Let it cool. Put in an egg yolk and mix carefully.

Divide the pie dough into two unequal parts. Roll out the largest part thinly. Cover with this sheet a high-sided oven pan with a diameter of 8 inches, so that the dough slightly exceeds the edge; prick the bottom with the teeth of a fork. Lay in the Gruyère sauce, leveling the surface with the blade of a knife. Now roll out the remaining dough, cover the pie with your fingers pressed around it, making the edges fit well together so as to completely enclose the cheese filling. With a small knife, make decorations as you like.

Wash the surface of the pie with a beaten egg yolk, put it in a hot oven, and let it cook for about half an hour over medium heat. If the dough starts to brown, cover it with aluminum foil. After the set cooking time has elapsed, remove from the oven. Let it cool a bit and then turn it out.

TORTA RUSTICA CON INDIVIA

Rustic Escarole Pie

2 to 3 bunches escarole or other bitter greens
Olive oil
Garlic
Capers
5 anchovies
1¾ oz Gaeta olives, pitted
Raisins
Salt
Pepper

Pizza dough:
5⅔ cups 00 flour, 3 tbsp active dry yeast, 2 large tbsp lard

Sift the flour on to the kitchen table, mix it with the lard, a pinch of salt, a strong pinch of pepper, the crumbled active dry yeast, and a glass of just warm water: more or less, however much is needed to achieve a rather soft dough.

Work it vigorously and when it is elastic and velvety, collect it in a bowl, cover it, and let it rise for a couple of hours in a sheltered place until it has doubled its volume.

Meanwhile, prepare the filling: Clean, wash thoroughly, drain, and boil the escarole, and, when cooked, drain well, squeeze it with your hands, and put it to flavor in a pan with half a glass of oil, a clove of garlic, salt, and pepper. As soon as the vegetables are well flavored, remove the garlic and pour it on to a plate to cool.

When the dough has risen well, turn it out on to a lightly floured table, beat it with your hands to deflate it, and divide it into 2 equal parts. Spread one half on a pan lightly greased with oil or lard, and place the greens on the dough, spreading it up to a couple of fingers from the edge, which must remain free. On the vegetables sprinkle a handful of capers, the anchovies—washed boned, and cut into small pieces—the Gaeta olives, and the raisins soaked in water for about 15 minutes.

Cover with the other half of the dough, press around to make the two disks match, and with a small knife level the edge of the pie by removing the superfluous dough, from which you can make decorations as you like. Put in a preheated oven of moderate heat for about half an hour and serve it warm or cold.

TORTA RUSTICA CON PATATE

Rustic Potato Pie

2¼ lb potatoes
7 tbsp butter
Grated Parmesan
2 eggs
3½ oz mozzarella
3½ oz Gruyère
3½ oz ham
Basil
Breadcrumbs
4 black olives, pitted
Salt
Pepper
Nutmeg

Wash the potatoes, boil them, and as soon as they are cooked, peel them, and mash them to reduce them to a purée. Season this purée while it is still hot with half the butter, two tablespoons of grated Parmesan, the eggs, salt, pepper, and nutmeg. Knead everything well and let it cool.

Prepare the filling: Cut the mozzarella and Gruyère into cubes and put in a bowl, keeping back a few cubes of mozzarella. Cut the ham into small cubes and season everything with ½ cup of grated Parmesan and a few leaves of chopped fresh basil. Turn on the oven.

Butter an oven pan of about 8 inches in diameter and make the breadcrumbs stick on the butter by turning the pan in all directions, then turning it over to remove any superfluous crumbs.

Divide the potato pastry in half, take the first half and place it gently on the bottom and around the sides of the pan to form a box. Place the filling in the center and cover with the other half of the purée. With a fork, trace a few intersecting lines on the surface of the purée, sprinkle it with more breadcrumbs, putting a few pieces of butter here and there. Bake the pie in a hot oven at moderate heat for about half an hour to give the bread a golden hue; take it out of the oven, let it rest for at least 5 minutes, take it out of the mold, and then decorate it with a flower made up of mozzarella petals, olives, and basil stems.

TORTA RUSTICA CON PATATE ALLA CUMANA

Rustic Potato Pie Cuma Style

2¼ lb potatoes
4 tbsp butter
Grated Parmesan
2 eggs
3½ oz salami
7 oz smoked provolone
Parsley
Breadcrumbs
3 hard-boiled eggs
Salt
Pepper

Preheat the oven. Boil the potatoes in lightly salted cold water, drain, peel, and mash them in a potato masher so that you get a smooth and lump-free purée. Put the purée in a large bowl, season with half the butter, ½ cup of grated Parmesan, eggs, salt, and pepper; stir vigorously with a wooden spoon and when they are well incorporated add the salami and smoked provolone cut into small pieces, and the chopped parsley. Turn on the oven.

Butter an oven pan of about 8 inches in diameter and splash the breadcrumbs on the butter by turning the pan in all directions, then turning it over to remove any that do not stick.

Arrange half of the potato mixture on the bottom of the pan and on this spread the hard-boiled eggs cut into slices. Cover with the other half of the mixture, sprinkle with more breadcrumbs, and spread over a few flakes of butter.

Bake the pie in a medium hot oven for about half an hour to give the pie a golden hue. Remove from the oven, let it rest for at least five minutes before turning it out on to a serving dish.

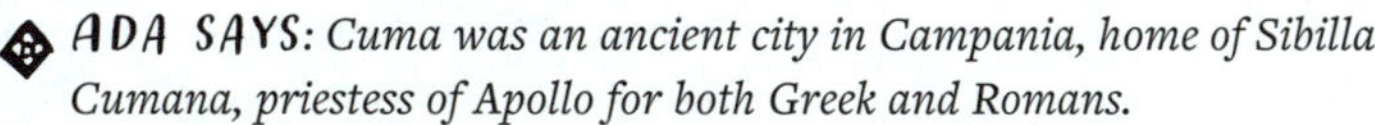

ADA SAYS: *Cuma was an ancient city in Campania, home of Sibilla Cumana, priestess of Apollo for both Greek and Romans.*

TORTA RUSTICA CON POLLO

Rustic Chicken Pie

Chicken
1 carrot
1 onion
1 celery stalk
Puff pastry, homemade *(p275)* or store-bought
1 oz dried mushrooms
2 tbsp butter
3½ oz ham
1 egg yolk
Salt

White sauce:
3½ tbsp butter, ⅓ cup all-purpose flour, 2 cups milk

Clean the chicken, empty it, flame it, and wash it thoroughly. Fill a pan with slightly salted water and bring the water to a boil. Add the herbs—carrot, onion, celery—and finally the chicken, bring to the boil again, then reduce the heat and let it simmer gently. Pay attention to the cooking, and when the chicken is at the right point, after about an hour, remove it from the broth and let it cool.

Have the puff pastry ready, either homemade or store bought.

With the butter, flour, and milk, prepare a white sauce *(p16)*. Soak the dried mushrooms in cold water, wash them thoroughly, cut them into pieces, and cook them with the butter, adding a little water and salt.

Remove the skin from the chicken, bone it, set the breast aside, and chop the rest of the meat. Add the meat to the white sauce and mix carefully. Turn on the oven.

Divide the dough into two unequal parts; roll out the largest part with a thickness of about ¼ inch and cover a high-sided oven pan with a diameter of 8 inches, so that the dough slightly extends beyond the edge. With the teeth of a fork prick the bottom. Put the filling on the dough—first the white sauce with chicken, the slices of ham, the mushrooms, the chicken breast cut into strips, and pour over the cooking liquid from the mushrooms. Now roll out the remaining dough, moisten the edge of the pan with a little water, place the dough on top, and press your fingers around it, matching the edges well, so as to completely enclose the filling. With a small knife, take away the surplus dough and make decorations on the pie.

Brush the surface of the pie with a beaten egg yolk, and make four or five small holes with a toothpick so that it does not swell when cooking. Put in a preheated oven and let it cook for about half an hour over moderate heat.

Remove it from the oven, let it cool a bit, and then turn it out.

ADA SAYS: *If the dough starts to brown too much, cover it with aluminum foil.*

TORTA RUSTICA CON POLPETTI

Rustic Octopus Pie

Puff pastry, homemade *(p275)* or 1 lb freshly packaged puff pastry
2¼ lb small octopuses
Olive oil
Garlic
1 lb ripe tomatoes
3½ oz Gaeta olives, pitted
1 egg yolk
Salt
Pepper

Have your puff pastry ready or buy it ready-made.

Clean the octopuses and divide them into pieces. Rinse the pieces until they become very white and let them drain. Put a little oil and garlic in a saucepan, and, as soon as the garlic is golden, remove it. Cut the tomatoes into strips, removing the seeds as you go, and add to the pan. Season with salt and pepper. Let the tomato cook and then add the octopuses and the Gaeta olives.

Cover, reduce the heat, and cook slowly for about an hour until the octopuses are completely cooked, adding a few spoonfuls of water during cooking if the sauce is drying too much. Turn on the oven to moderate heat.

Divide the puff pastry into two unequal pieces, roll out the larger part on the floured board, and with it line a high-sided baking pan with a diameter of about 8 inches so that the dough extends beyond the edge.

Fill the pan with the octopus and tomatoes and with the blade of a knife even out the mixture. Now roll out the other piece of dough and cover the pie, matching the edges well, pressing slowly with your fingers to close it completely. Cut the excess part of the dough with a small knife and make decorations. Wash the surface of the cake with a beaten egg yolk and make four or five small holes in it with a toothpick so that it does not swell when cooked. Put the pie in the preheated oven and cook for about half an hour over moderate heat. When it is cooked, remove from the oven and let it cool before removing from the mold.

TORTA RUSTICA CON PROSCIUTTO E SALAME

Rustic Ham and Salami Pie

Lard or olive oil
2 sausages
9 oz ricotta
Milk
3 eggs
3½ oz mozzarella
1¾ oz ham
1¾ oz salami
1½ tbsp butter
Salt
Pepper

Pizza dough:
5 cups 00 flour, 2 tbsp active dry yeast, 1 glass water

Prepare your pizza dough *(p264)* with the ingredients listed here.

When the dough has risen, deflate it, reshuffle it on the table, and divide it in two unequal pieces. Using a little flour, roll out the larger piece with the rolling pin giving it the thickness of your thumb. Grease a pan with rather high edges with a thin layer of lard or oil and line the dough on it.

Sear the sausages in a pan, then skin them and cut them into pieces. Put the ricotta in a bowl and mash it with a wooden ladle, slowly adding half a glass of milk; season with salt and pepper and then add the egg yolks, one at a time, always stirring, then add the diced mozzarella, ham, and salami, cut into small pieces, and the sausages. Whip the egg whites and gently mix them with the ricotta. Pour the mixture on the dough, leveling it with the blade of a knife.

Now roll out the smaller piece of dough making a disk for a lid. Match the two edges, pressing all around with your fingers and fold them on themselves so as to make a bead of dough that you will notch lightly with a fork. The pie does not have to completely fill the pan because in the oven the dough grows and reaches the brim. Arrange on the pie a few pieces of butter or lard and pass it in a preheated oven of lively heat for 30 minutes.

The heat must be at first lively and then it must be gradually decreased so that the pie can cook well on the inside without getting too colored on the outside. When it begins to color lightly, cover it with a sheet of aluminum foil.

When cooked, remove the pan from the oven, let the pie rest for about 10 minutes, and then turn it out onto a serving dish.

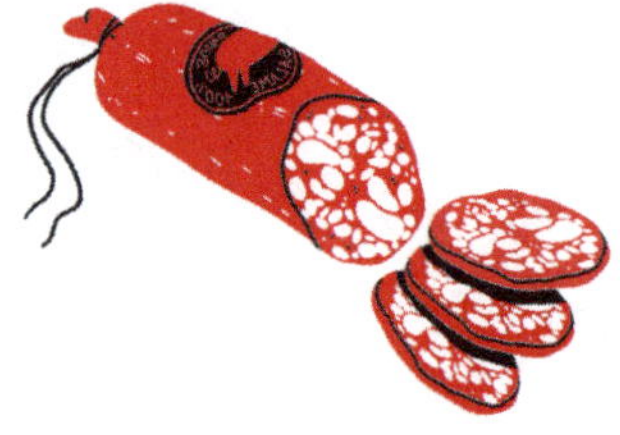

TORTA RUSTICA CON RICOTTA E SPINACI

Rustic Spinach and Ricotta Pie

Puff pastry, homemade *(p275)* or store-bought
10½ oz ricotta
3 eggs
Grated Parmesan
2¼ lb spinach (or 14 oz frozen spinach)
3½ tbsp butter
Salt

Have your puff pastry ready, either homemade or store bought.

Put the ricotta, two whole eggs, and ½ cup of grated Parmesan in a bowl and mix everything carefully using a wooden spoon. Clean the spinach, wash in many waters and drain. Boil a few minutes in salted water and as soon as it is cooked, drain it thoroughly and squeeze well to extract the water, then chop coarsely. Let the spinach flavor with the butter, adding a little salt if necessary. Now add the spinach to the ricotta and mix well. Turn on the oven.

Divide the puff pastry into two unequal pieces and roll out the larger side on a floured table; with it line a high-sided baking sheet with a diameter of about 8 inches, so that the dough slightly overhangs the edges; prick the bottom with the teeth of a fork.

Put the ricotta and spinach mixture into the dough and spread it well with the blade of a knife. Now roll out the other piece of dough, and cover the pie with it, matching the edges well by pressing slowly with your fingers to close it perfectly. Cut the surplus part of the dough with a small knife and make decorations with it.

Brush the surface with a beaten egg yolk and with a toothpick make four or five small holes, so that while cooking it won't swell. Put the pie in a hot oven and let it cook for about half an hour over moderate heat.

Remove the pie from the oven, let it cool, and then turn it out on to a serving dish.

TORTA RUSTICA CON RICOTTA E SALSICCE

Rustic Ricotta and Sausage Pie

Puff pastry, homemade *(p275)* or store-bought
Lard or oil
1 lb ricotta
Milk
3 eggs
Grated Parmesan
3½ oz mozzarella
1¾ oz prosciutto
3 sausages
Salt
Pepper

Have your puff pastry ready, either homemade or store bought. Divide the dough into two unequal parts and with the help of a little flour, roll out the largest piece with a rolling pin giving it the thickness of 1 inch. Grease a pan with rather high edges with a thin layer of lard or oil and line the dough in it. Turn on the oven to a lively heat.

Put the ricotta in a bowl and blend it with a wooden spoon, slowly adding half a glass of milk; season with salt and pepper and then add the egg yolks one at a time, always stirring, so that they are well incorporated. Add ½ cup of grated Parmesan.

Whip the egg whites to a snow and mix them gently with the ricotta, finishing the mixture with diced mozzarella, prosciutto, and sausages cut into slices. Stir and pour the mixture into the pastry tray, leveling it with the blade of a knife.

Take the remaining piece of dough, roll it out with a rolling pin in the shape of a disk, and with this cover the pie; press slowly with your fingers until the dough fits well and with a toothpick make four or five small holes so that it does not swell when cooking. The pie does not have to fill the pan completely, because in the oven the dough grows and reaches the brim.

Arrange a few pieces of lard on top and put in a preheated oven, leaving it to cook for about half an hour. The heat must be at first lively and then it must be reduced so that the pie can cook inside without getting too colored on the outside. When it is ready, take the pie out of the oven, let it cool a bit, and then turn it out onto a serving dish.

Quiche

QUICHE LORRAINE

Quiche Lorraine

7 oz bacon
4 eggs
4 tsp heavy cream
4 tsp milk
3½ tbsp butter
Salt

Pie dough:
1⅔ cups 00 flour, 14 tbsp (7 oz) butter, 1 egg yolk, salt

Quiche, a specialty of French cuisine, is basically savory pizza to be served lukewarm or cold, filled with different egg-based preparations.

Arrange the flour on the kitchen table. Cut the butter into small pieces with the egg yolk and a pinch of salt. Knead everything, adding a few spoonfuls of water, until a smooth dough of the right consistency is obtained. Don't work it too hard, and as soon as it is ready, let it rest between two floured towels, keeping it in the fridge.

Trim the skin off the bacon slices, dip them for a minute in boiling water, pull them up, and put them apart.

Break two whole eggs and two yolks into a bowl, beat them as per an omelet, season with a pinch of salt, and then warm them with the cream and the milk.

Butter a mold of about 12 inches in diameter; roll out the dough ¼ inch thick, and line the mold so that the dough overflows slightly. Pass a pastry cutter on the edge of the mold, and prick the bottom with a fork.

Line up the bacon on the bottom and pour the egg mixture over the slices and cream. Complete by adding more butter, cut into small pieces, that you scatter on the creamy mixture. Put the quiche in a preheated oven of moderate heat for about 40 minutes, until well cooked. Then remove it from the oven, and wait a few minutes before removing the mold so that the quiche can cool down a little.

"Eggs contain essential amino acids and are one of the most nutritionally complete of all foods."

The frittata, Italy's best-known egg dish, is not, in fact, merely a translation of the French word *omelette*. The two are similar, but different. An omelet is just eggs, perhaps with a filling, usually already cooked. In the frittata and its variations, the ingredients are a part of the cooking process. Smaller frittatine are a variation that are easy to prepare in batches and sure to succeed. They are a mix of eggs and flour, with a filling that has already been chopped and cooked.

Eggs contain essential amino acids and are one of the most nutritionally complete of all foods. However, eggs are prone to deteriorating with some ease and their nutritional value decreases as they lose their freshness. You can check the freshness by placing an egg in front of a flame, candle, or an electric light bulb. The interior should appear transparent and fluid—even minimal cloudiness indicates deterioration.

A few hours after an egg is laid, a small air chamber appears at the wider and rounded end due to the penetration of air through the shell, which, being porous, allows such entry. As the days go by, this chamber increases in volume. In contrast, older eggs tend to "*slosh*," so to speak.

If you immerse the egg in water, it will take, depending on how old it is, different positions. Fresh eggs lie perfectly horizontal on the bottom of the container. Eight-day-old eggs rise to one side, forming an angle of 45 degrees. Those of three weeks form an angle of 75 degrees, arranging themselves almost vertically.

When you break a fresh egg, the inner surface of the shell appears white and pink. The egg white is transparent, not at all cloudy, and it should not spread excessively, instead remaining supported around the yolk, which, in turn, should be surrounded by albumen and not stick in any way to the shell.

UOVA

7 EGGS

FRITTATE & FRITTATINE

TO MAKE A FRITTATA

A frittata is prepared with eggs, Parmesan, a little milk, salt, and pepper. You can then add vegetables, cheeses, or simply aromatic herbs. In the frittata eggs are beaten not too evenly, just enough time to mix them a little. Just mix them a little with a fork to combine the yolks and egg whites.

An essential requirement for making a good frittata or any variation is a nonstick pan. Firstly, warm the fat which can be butter, lard, or oil. Then slide in the beaten eggs, stir promptly with a wooden spoon, and, just as the frittata begins to thicken, shake the pan a little to move well the underside of the frittata. Then turn it upside down with the help of a plate or a lid of the same diameter as the pan (this operation is best done over the sink) and cook it on the other side. All this should be done over a lively fire so the frittata remains soft inside without becoming soaked in fat. Another way to obtain an excellent frittata is to cook it in a preheated oven.

TO MAKE FRITTATINE

Melt the flour with milk, to get a rather thick, smooth batter without lumps. Pour the eggs into the batter, season with salt and pepper, and whip well.

Put a pan of about 6 inches in diameter on the fire with a lump of butter or a few drops of oil. When the butter or oil is hot, pour a spoonful or two of the mixture into the pan, shaking in all directions to let it flow and spread over the entire bottom. As soon as the frittatina is sufficiently hardened, slide it onto the kitchen table. Put a little butter or oil back into the pan and continue to make thin frittatine until all the mixture is used up.

FRITTATA CON ACCIUGHE

Frittata with Anchovies

6 eggs
Milk
12 bread slices
6 anchovies
3½ oz mozzarella
3½ tbsp butter
Salt
Pepper

Generously grease an oven pan of about 6 inches diameter.

Break the eggs into a bowl, salt them lightly, and beat them with a fork and dilute with a glass of milk. Quickly dip half of the slices of bread in the beaten eggs and arrange them on the bottom of the pan to cover perfectly.

On this layer of eggy bread, place the washed, boned, and chopped anchovy fillets, and a few slices of mozzarella. Season with a pinch of pepper, put around three or four pieces of butter, the size of hazelnuts, and then make a second layer of slices of bread, dipping them in the egg like the previous ones. Beware: Put the slices very close to each other so as not to leave any empty spaces.

On top of everything, drop what is left of the beaten eggs and milk. Leave to rest for about 10 minutes to give the bread time to completely absorb the egg. Arrange here and there a few lumps more of butter and place the pan in a preheated medium oven for about 10 minutes, until the bread has a light golden crust.

You can turn this frittata upside down on a serving dish or send it straight away to the table in the same pan.

FRITTATA CON BASILICO

Frittata with Basil

6 eggs
1¾ oz grated Parmesan
Basil
Olive oil or butter
Salt
Pepper

Beat the eggs in a bowl, season with salt and pepper and the grated Parmesan, a bunch of basil leaves, washed and shredded, and mix to distribute the seasoning well.

Put a little oil or butter in the pan and when the fat is hot, pour in the eggs and make the frittata *(opposite page)* leaving it rather soft inside.

FRITTATA CON CIPOLLE

Frittata with Onions

2 onions
Olive oil
6 eggs
1¾ oz guanciale
Salt
Pepper

Coarsely chop the onions on the cutting board, put them in a pan with a glass of oil, over moderate heat, and brown them slowly so that they can cook without excessively coloring; if necessary add some water.

Beat the eggs in a bowl, add the guanciale, chopped in small pieces, season with salt and pepper, and, when the onions are well cooked and lightly brown, pour the eggs into the pan, mix well and make the frittata *(opposite page)* leaving it rather soft inside.

FRITTATA CON CIPOLLE, GUANCIALE E POMODORI

Frittata with Onion, Guanciale, and Tomatoes

2 onions
Olive oil
3½ oz guanciale
5 to 6 tomatoes
6 eggs
Salt
Pepper

Coarsely chop the onions on the cutting board, put them in a pan with a glass of oil, over moderate heat, and brown them slowly so that they can cook without becoming excessively colored; if necessary add some water.

When the onion has colored, add the diced guanciale, and immediately after, the peeled and chopped tomatoes, having taken out the seeds. Revive the fire so that the tomatoes cook, without falling apart, for 10 minutes.

Beat the eggs in a bowl, season with salt and pepper, and, when the tomato is well cooked, pour the eggs into the pan, mix thoroughly, and quickly make the frittata, which must remain rather soft.

FRITTATA CON DADINI DI PATATE

Frittata with Potatoes

3 medium-sized potatoes
Butter
6 eggs
Milk
1¾ oz grated Gruyère
Salt

Peel and dice the potatoes, put them in a pan with a little butter, add salt, and cook slowly. Beat the eggs in a bowl, add salt, a tablespoon of milk, and the grated Gruyère.

Pour the eggs into the pan with the potatoes and mix well. But cook the frittata quickly *(p294)* so that the inside remains quite moist.

FRITTATA CON FIORI DI ZUCCA

Frittata with Zucchini Flowers

6 zucchini flowers
Olive oil
6 eggs
2 tbsp grated Parmesan
Parsley
Salt
Pepper

Trim the stem of the flowers, remove the filaments, and also remove the pistil that is the base of the flower. Open the flowers a little to clean them, rinse, and dry them in a cloth.

Warm some oil in the pan and add the flowers. Cover and cook over moderate heat until they are very reduced in volume and tender. Season with a little salt and pepper and set aside.

When ready to serve, break the eggs into a bowl, season with a little salt, pepper, grated Parmesan, and chopped parsley. Put the pan with the fried zucchini flowers back on the heat and make your frittata quickly.

FRITTATA CON FIORI DI ZUCCA GUARNITI

Frittata with Stuffed Zucchini Flowers

6 zucchini flowers
Oil for frying
6 eggs
Grated Parmesan
Parsley
Nutmeg
Salt
Pepper

Stuffing:
1¾ oz mozzarella, 3 anchovies

Batter:
1 cup all-purpose flour,
2 tbsp olive oil

The important thing here is that there are enough eggs to completely submerge the zucchini flowers.

Trim the stem of the flowers, free them from any filament and pistil toward the base of the flower, put them in a basin with fresh water, rinse, and dry them. Open the flowers a little and fill each with a small garnish of diced mozzarella and small pieces of anchovy.

Pass the flowers through a rather light batter of just flour and oil and fry them in plenty of hot oil to make them crunchy and give them a beautiful color.

Break the eggs into a bowl, beat them lightly, season with salt, pepper, a little nutmeg, ½ cup grated Parmesan, and a little chopped parsley. Put a fairly large pan on the heat with a little oil. When hot, pour the beaten eggs into the pan and immediately after the zucchini flowers, aligning them in a single layer. As soon as the frittata has hardened on the underside, turn it over, and leave it to finish cooking, but do not overcook. It must be soft.

FRITTATA CON FORMAGGI FILANTI

Frittata with Parmesan and Gruyère

6 eggs
1 cup grated Parmesan
1¾ oz Gruyère
3½ tbsp butter
Salt
Pepper

Beat the eggs, season with a little salt and a pinch of pepper, and finally add the grated Parmesan and diced Gruyère. Put a pan with the butter on the stove.

Make the frittata *(p294)* so it is golden and stringy inside.

FRITTATA CON MACCHERONI

Frittata with Macaroni

12 oz cooked macaroni
 or other pasta
4 to 5 eggs
Parsley
Grated Parmesan
Olive oil or lard
Salt
Pepper

Have ready a good plate of macaroni, already cooked, perhaps even leftovers, seasoned with sauce or with butter and grated Parmesan.

Beat the eggs in a bowl and season with salt, pepper, and chopped parsley. Add the macaroni mixing well. Season with a good handful of grated Parmesan and give a last stir.

Put a pan on the heat with a little oil or lard and when the fat is hot pour the macaroni and eggs into the pan, and, on a fairly moderate heat, make the frittata *(p294)*.

ADA SAYS: *A moderate heat is recommended so that the macaroni has time to heat up well and the frittata has a nice golden crust on both sides.*

FRITTATA CON MELANZANE E ZUCCHINE

Frittata with Eggplant and Zucchini

1 eggplant
2 zucchini
Olive oil
Parsley
6 eggs
Oregano
Grated Parmesan
Salt

Wash and cut the eggplant into small cubes without peeling. Dice also the zucchini. Put both in a pan, add some oil, parsley, a little salt, and cook through.

Beat the eggs in a bowl, season with salt, pepper, a pinch of oregano, and ½ cup of grated Parmesan. When the eggplant and zucchini are cooked to the right point, pour in the beaten eggs, mix thoroughly, and make the frittata *(p294)* keeping it round and rather flat.

FRITTATA CON POMODORI E ZUCCHINE

Frittata with Tomatoes and Zucchini

2¼ lb zucchini
Celery
Olive oil or lard
6 tomatoes
6 eggs
8 tbsp grated Parmesan
Basil
Salt
Pepper
Optional: chives

This frittata must be at least 1 inch thick and be golden on the outside and very soft on the inside.

Cut the zucchini and the white part of the celery into strips and sauté in a little oil or lard. Cook a little and then add the washed, peeled, and chopped tomatoes. Season with salt and pepper.

When the zucchini, white part of celery, and tomatoes have come to the right point of cooking, break the eggs into a bowl, add the grated Parmesan, a little chopped basil, and a pinch of salt. Beat well, pour into the pan, stir, flatten, and cook gently. When cooked on one side, turn it over and cook on the other side, always slowly.

ADA SAYS: *You can decorate the edge with some zucchini wheels, toasted separately in a pan; and sprinkle with chives.*

FRITTATA CON SPINACI

Frittata with Spinach

2¼ lb spinach
Olive oil
8 tbsp grated Parmesan
Marjoram
Garlic
6 eggs
Salt
Pepper

Carefully wash and drain the spinach, cook slowly with a little oil and salt in a tightly covered pan, so the steam cannot get out. When cooked, drain well, squeeze them dry, and chop.

In another bowl, put plenty of grated Parmesan, a few marjoram leaves, half a clove of finely chopped garlic, salt, pepper, and the eggs. Mix carefully and, continuing to mix, add the spinach.

Put plenty of oil in a pan of 8 inches diameter, and, when it is slightly hot, pour in the mix, flatten it, and let it cook slowly. When the frittata is cooked on one side, turn it over and cook it on the other side, always slowly.

FRITTATA CON ZUCCHINE

Frittata with Zucchini

2¼ lb zucchini
Breadcrumbs
Milk
Grated Parmesan
Sugar
Lemon peel
6 eggs
Olive oil or butter
Salt

Wash and chop the zucchini on a cutting board, add enough salt, a few breadcrumbs soaked abundantly in milk, a little grated Parmesan, a teaspoon of sugar, and the grated zest of half a lemon. Jumble up carefully.

Beat the eggs separately; then unite everything well.

Grease a baking dish with plenty of oil or butter and sprinkle it lightly with breadcrumbs. Pour in the mixture, flatten it well, sprinkle with a few more breadcrumbs, and put the pan in a preheated oven at a moderate heat until the frittata becomes golden.

ADA SAYS: *In the same way you can prepare a frittata with any kind of vegetable. Remember, however, that while zucchini can be used raw, other vegetables may need to be simmered first, flavored in oil or butter, and then chopped finely.*

FRITTATA DI CARCIOFI AL FORNO

Frittata with Baked Artichokes

6 artichokes
Lemon juice
All-purpose flour
Oil for frying
6 eggs
Parsley
Garlic
8 tbsp grated Parmesan
Milk
Butter
Salt
Pepper

Remove the hard outer leaves from the artichokes, shorten the stem a little, and turn the choke out with a small sharp knife. Then cut the artichokes into wedges, putting them immediately into a basin of water acidulated with lemon juice. When they are ready, drain well, dry them, pass them in flour, and fry them in a pan with plenty of oil, over moderate heat, until golden and cooked.

In a bowl, beat the eggs, season them with salt and pepper. Add the chopped parsley, garlic, grated Parmesan, two spoons of milk, and, finally, the artichokes.

Butter a baking dish of about 8 inches in diameter. Pour over the mix, leveling the surface well. Put the pan in a hot oven until the frittata becomes soft and golden.

FRITTATE IN TORTINO

Frittata Flan

9½ tbsp all-purpose flour
Milk
6 eggs
Salt
Pepper
Optional: meat jelly, homemade *(p52)* or store-bought
To garnish: 2 hard-boiled eggs, capers, cornichons

Russian salad:
7 oz potatoes, 7 oz carrots, 7 oz green beans, 7 oz shelled or frozen peas, 7 oz capers, 5 cornichons, olive oil, 1 tbsp meat jelly

Mayonnaise:
2 egg yolks, 1 cup olive oil, lemon juice or vinegar

Put the flour in a bowl and slowly add half a glass of milk, stirring with a wooden spoon, to obtain a smooth batter without lumps. Add to this mixture one egg at a time, season with salt and pepper, carefully whip everything to mix the eggs into the batter.

Grease a pan of about 10 inches in diameter, let it heat well, pour half of the mixture in and make a large and thin omelet. Lift out and repeat with the other half of the mixture to make a second omelet; let the two omelets cool separately.

Prepare the Russian salad: boil the potatoes and once cooked, peel them, while still hot, and let them cool; boil separately all the other vegetables and let them cool. Cut the carrots, beans, and potatoes into small pieces and put them in a bowl together with the peas; season with oil, salt, and vinegar, add the chopped cornichons and capers. Make a mayonnaise with the eggs and oil, and, if you like, a tablespoon of meat jelly. Mix the mayonnaise into the vegetables well.

Place one omelet in the bottom of a round serving dish. Spread out the Russian salad on top, trying to cover the shape; place the second omelet on top. With the help of a spatula, even out the edges and cover the surface with the remaining mayonnaise to cover entirely. Put the dish in the fridge and before serving decorate with slices of hard-boiled eggs, cornichons, and capers.

◈ ADA SAYS: *You can finish the decoration with a nice rope of chopped gelatin if you like.*

FRITTATINE DI PATATE

Potato Frittatine

1 lb 5 oz baking potatoes
4 eggs
Grated Parmesan
2 tbsp breadcrumbs
Cream or milk
Oil for frying
Salt
Pepper
Nutmeg

Peel the potatoes, rinse them, dry them, and then grate them as if they were cheese. Put this pulp in a colander, wash with water, and then let it drain well. Put it in a towel and, bringing the ends together, squeeze all the moisture out.

Put the grated, dried potatoes in a bowl with the eggs, 2 tablespoons of grated Parmesan, the breadcrumbs, salt, pepper, a trifle of nutmeg, and 2 tablespoons of cream or milk, and mix everything.

Put a little oil in a pan of 6 inches in diameter and when it is hot pour a spoonful of the mixture into the pan; shake the pan in all directions so that the mixture spreads and becomes thinner and covers the whole base. When colored on one side, turn it over and finish cooking the other side. Continue like this making small frittatinis until all of the mixture is used up.

◈ ADA SAYS: *From time to time, remember to give a small stir to the egg mixture to stop it from breaking up.*

FRITTATINE IN MILLE FOGLIE

Frittatine Millefeuille

9½ tbsp all-purpose flour
Milk
6 eggs
7 tbsp butter
1½ oz prosciutto
1 onion
1 lb tomato passata
Grated Parmesan
Salt
Optional: basil

Put the flour in to bowl and slowly wet it with half a glass of milk; beat the eggs separately with a little salt, then add to the flour and milk, stirring constantly, and finally complete with a tablespoon of just warm, melted butter.

Put a pan of 6 inches in diameter on the fire, melt a knob of butter, and pour in a couple of spoonfuls of the egg mix. Shake the pan, spreading the mixture all over to cover the bottom. As soon as the frittatina is firm on one side, turn it over. Then slide it onto a plate. Continue to make these frittatine until the mixture is used up, stirring occasionally and settling, greasing the pan with a little butter each time.

When you have made all the frittatine, prepare a rather dense tomato sauce. First brown a mixture of fatty prosciutto and a little onion in a pan with a little butter, add the tomato passata, let it flavor slowly, season with a little salt and a little pepper, and sprinkle with enough water, allowing it to cook well and thicken.

Take a lightly greased baking dish and spread with the frittatina, a little sauce, and sprinkle with Parmesan. Place a second frittatina on the first, season it in the same way, and continue like this until the end of the frittatine, finishing with a hearty layer of sauce and more Parmesan.

Put the prepared pan in a preheated oven, of moderate heat, for 10 minutes.

ADA SAYS: *In summer you can also sandwich the frittatine with a few washed, dried, and chopped fresh basil leaves.*

FRITTATINE IN TRIPPA ALLA ROMANA

Frittatine Roman Style

9½ tbsp all-purpose flour
Milk
6 eggs
Lard or oil for frying
Grated Parmesan
Mint
Salt
Pepper

Tomato sauce:
2¼ lb tomatoes, olive oil, garlic

Have a good tomato sauce *(p37)* ready made with the tomatoes, oil, and garlic.

Then prepare the frittatine: Put the flour in a bowl with half a glass of milk; stir well to make sure that the batter is smooth and without lumps. Break in the eggs, season with salt and pepper, and beat everything as for an omelet. Then make your frittatina as above, using oil rather than butter.

When the frittatine are ready, put them on a plate; then cut them into strips of about ½ inch. Warm them in the tomato sauce for a few seconds. Tip the strips on to a plate and season with grated Parmesan and a few leaves of mint.

ADA SAYS: *Roman mint, mentuccia romana, is commonly known as lesser calamint. It has a delicate flavor of mint and oregano.*

FRITTATINE RIPIENE A FANTASIA

Frittatine Fantasy

MAKES 15

9½ tbsp all-purpose flour
Milk
9 eggs
Breadcrumbs
Butter or oil to fry
Salt
Pepper
Filling to taste: diced mozzarella with either diced ham or anchovy fillets or cooked chicken or veal

Put 3 tablespoons of flour in a bowl, and slowly moisten with the milk, to form a pretty dense batter, smooth and without lumps.

Break 6 eggs, season with salt and pepper, and beat them well and mix in with the batter.

Put a pan about 6 inches in diameter on the fire with a lump of butter or a few drops of oil; when the fats are hot, pour a spoonful or two of the mixture into the pan and, stirring in all directions, let the mixture flow and spread everywhere across the bottom.

Once all the frittatine are made, place a small filling in the center of each one of your choice, which can be made up of diced mozzarella and ham; mozzarella and anchovy fillets; mozzarella, ham, and slices of tomato, blanched separately in a pan and left to cool; mozzarella and diced cooked chicken or veal.

Moisten the edge of the frittatine with beaten egg, fold them in two on themselves enclosing their stuffing. Pass them one at a time through the beaten eggs and then breadcrumbs and fry them in a rather hot pan until they are a beautiful gold.

Then arrange on a serving dish and send them to the table hot.

ADA SAYS: *You can make egg-only frittatine, that is, without the batter; but you have to use more eggs.*

FRITTATINE RIPIENE DI CARNE E FUNGHI

Frittatine Stuffed with Meat and Mushrooms

1 oz dried mushrooms
Butter
6 eggs
3½ oz cooked veal or chicken
1¾ oz ham
Grated Parmesan
Salt

White sauce:
3½ tbsp butter, ¼ cup all-purpose flour, 2 cups milk

Batter:
9½ tbsp all-purpose flour, half glass milk

These frittatine need good quality meat which will be enhanced by the mushrooms and ham.

First, make a fairly thin white sauce *(p16)* with the butter, flour, and milk, which must be fairly liquid.

Put the mushrooms in cold water to revive, then wash them, cut them into pieces, and cook them in a pan with a spoonful of butter, a little water, and salt. As soon as the mushrooms are cooked, after about 10 minutes, put them in a bowl and add the diced veal or chicken and the diced ham. Mix everything well with a few spoonfuls of white sauce and finish with a little grated Parmesan.

Put three tablespoons of flour in a bowl, and dissolve slowly with half a glass of milk, so that you get a pretty dense batter, very smooth and without lumps. Break the eggs, season with salt and pepper, whip them, and then work into the batter to amalgamate well.

Put a pan about 6 inches in diameter on the fire with a nut of butter or a few drops of oil and make your frittatine.

Put a little of the filling on each frittatine, roll them up, and arrange them in a buttered baking pan. Cover with the white sauce, sprinkle with more Parmesan, and put them in a preheated oven, for about 10 minutes, until slightly colored.

FRITTATINE RIPIENE DI RICOTTA E SPINACI

Frittatine Stuffed with Spinach and Ricotta

1 lb 5 oz spinach
1½ tbsp butter
7 oz ricotta
Milk
Grated Parmesan
9½ tbsp all-purpose flour
6 eggs
Lard or olive oil
Salt
Optional: tomato and basil sauce *(p38)*

Clean and wash the spinach with great care, then boil it in a little salted water. Drain, squeeze well to extract all the water, chop, and put them to flavor for a few minutes in a saucepan with the butter, then leave them to cool.

Put the ricotta in a bowl, pour in a spoonful or two of milk, and mix with a wooden spoon. Add a pinch of salt and ½ cup of grated Parmesan. Add the spinach to the ricotta, mixing carefully.

Put the flour in another bowl, with a little milk to form a very soupy batter, add the eggs, season with salt, and whisk everything together.

A few minutes before going to the table, heat a knob of lard or a few drops of oil in a 6 inch pan. When hot, pour in a spoonful of the prepared egg mix. Move the pan in all directions to spread all over the bottom, and as soon as the frittatine forms, put one spoonful of the ricotta and spinach mixture in the middle and roll it up enclosing the stuffing. Slide on to a plate and repeat the operation to finish all the egg mixture but each time greasing the pan anew with a few drops of oil.

You can serve these frittatine plain, or with a tomato and basil sauce.

OMELETS

TO MAKE AN OMELET

An omelet should be folded into an oval. It is preferably cooked with butter—around 1 tbsp per egg.

Heat the butter well in the pan, add the eggs which have been sufficiently beaten and seasoned with a little salt—you can even add a little bit of cream. Mix well with a wooden spoon until they start to set. Shake the pan to release the lower part and, when it is properly clotted, lift the handle of the pan and slide the omelet toward the opposite side. Then bring the two edges quickly back toward the center to assume the characteristic oval shape.

With a brush dipped in melted butter, wash the bottom of the frying pan and overturn on to a long plate, then brush again to polish with the hot butter. The result is a simple omelet, which can be accompanied by a garnish, filled, or veiled with some appropriate sauce.

OMELETTE CON ASPARAGI E CARCIOFI

Omelet with Asparagus and Artichokes

- 10½ oz asparagus
- 3 tender artichoke hearts
- 3½ tbsp butter
- 6 eggs
- Salt
- Optional: black truffle

Scrape the stems of the asparagus, rinse them well, and cut them all to the same length. Boil in lightly salted boiling water and as soon as they are cooked, but not too much, cut off the tips and divide the rest into logs.

Cut the artichoke hearts into cubes and cook slowly in the butter. When the hearts are cooked, add them to the pan with the asparagus and let them flavor slowly, too.

Break the eggs into a bowl, beat them, season with salt, and sauté in a pan with a little butter. When folding the omelet, place the filling in the center, close it, and pass it into a serving dish.

ADA SAYS: *You can also add a black truffle, cut into rather thick slices, just heated in butter.*

OMELETTE CON PROVOLA

Omelet with Provola

2 tomatoes
Olive oil
4 tbsp grated Parmesan
Basil
5¼ oz smoked provola
6 eggs
3½ tbsp butter
Salt

Peel the tomatoes, remove the seeds, chop, and put them in a pan with a tablespoon of oil. Season with a pinch of salt and cook for a few minutes over high heat, then pour the tomato on to a plate and add the grated Parmesan, a bit of chopped basil, and diced provola.

Break the eggs into a bowl, beat them, and season with a little salt. Melt the butter in a pan of 10 inches in diameter, pour in the eggs, and make the omelet, shaking the pan from time to time so that it detaches from the bottom. When the omelet has thickened enough, put the filling in the center, fold the omelet on itself, turn it over into a serving dish, and send immediately on the table. This preparation must be enjoyed hot.

ADA SAYS: *Provola are small variations of provolone, both of which originate near Vesuvius and can be smoked or fresh.*

OMELETTE RIPIENA DI SPUMA

Chilled Omelet with Cream and Jelly

6 eggs
Grated Parmesan
5¼ oz ham
3½ tbsp butter
4 tbsp whipped cream
5¼ oz cooked chicken
 or turkey breast
1¾ oz tongue
Port
Parsley
Salt
Pepper
Optional: truffle

Thick white sauce:
2 tbsp all-purpose flour, 1 tbsp butter, half glass milk

This preparation is very suitable for an elegant breakfast.

Break three whole eggs into a bowl, season with a handful of grated Parmesan, a pinch of salt and pepper, and make a wide, thin omelet, for which you need a pan of around 12 inches in diameter. As soon as it is cooked, slide the omelet on to the kitchen table and let it cool. Now make a second identical omelet and set aside to cool.

Prepare the filling: Carefully chop the ham, mix it with a spoonful of the cold and thick white sauce *(p16)* and a tablespoon of softened butter. You can strain it through a sieve to get a finer purée, recommended, but not necessary. Finish with two spoonfuls of whipped cream but without sugar.

Then the same for the chicken: Chop the meats finely, mix with white sauce, work with softened or melted butter, and finish with whipped cream.

Now spread the ham mousse over one omelet, and top off with chopped tongue. Cover with the second omelet and spread that with the chicken or turkey, garnished with sliced truffle if possible. Gently roll up the two overlapping omelets, so as to make a large sausage, which you wrap in a sheet of aluminum foil. Put it in the fridge to chill for a few hours.

Then unroll the omelet from the aluminum foil and with a sharp knife cut slices about 1 inch thick. Place these slices in a beautiful order, in steps, on an oval plate, and garnish with a meat jus flavored with 2 or 3 tablespoons of port and topped with sprigs of parsley. Keep in the fridge until ready to serve.

POACHED EGGS

TO POACH EGGS

Poaching eggs is simple to describe, but more difficult to perform. Simple because the eggs are boiled in boiling water; difficult because the eggs can break and because the cooking time is difficult to determine. It is important to cook a few eggs at a time. An indispensable requirement to have good poached eggs is their absolute freshness.

Put a rather large pan of slightly salted water on the fire and add a few drops of vinegar to acidulate. The vinegar is essential because it helps the whites to set. Keep everything on a very low heat so that the water only hints that soon it may boil. Break the egg into a saucer and bring the saucer to the surface of the water and pour in the egg at the point where it boils; reduce the heat a little more so that the temperature is kept slightly below 212°F degrees and leave the egg so for about 3 minutes, making sure that the solidification of the whites is sufficient to enclose the yolk but not excessive. Then lift it up with a slotted spoon, place it on a plate, and trim any loose bits giving the egg a more correct shape. If the eggs are not to be sent to the table immediately, it will be good to keep them warm in slightly salted, lukewarm water.

UOVA AFFOGATE CON BURRO D'ACCIUGHE

Poached Eggs with Anchovy Butter

6 eggs
Anchovy butter *(p54)*
Parsley
Salt

Poach the eggs *(as above)*, drain them, trim, and arrange them in the serving dish.

Make your anchovy butter. Pour over the eggs and garnish with some chopped parsley.

UOVA AFFOGATE CON FUNGHI E CROSTINI

Poached Eggs with Mushrooms and Croutons

1 oz dried mushrooms
4 tbsp butter
9 oz tomato passata
6 eggs
6 bread slices
1¾ oz ham
Parsley
Salt
Pepper

Soak the mushrooms in water and then sauté in a tablespoon of butter. In another pan put some more butter and as it melts add the passata, season with salt and pepper, and let it simmer for a few minutes to thicken.

Poach the eggs *(as above)* and drain. Fry the bread slices in butter and place an egg on each one on a round plate, arranged like a crown, and surround with the tomato passata sauce. Top the eggs with the mushrooms, slices of ham, and chopped parsley.

UOVA AFFOGATE CON POMODORO E MOZZARELLA

Poached Eggs with Tomato and Mozzarella

6 large ripe tomatoes
6 eggs
Olive oil
7 oz mozzarella
3½ oz ham
Grated Parmesan
Salt
Pepper
Nutmeg

White sauce:
¼ cup all-purpose flour, 3½ tbsp butter, 1¼ cups milk, 1 egg yolk

Poach your eggs *(p307)*.

Choose tomatoes of similar shape and size, big enough to fit your eggs inside, remove the tops, drain the juice and seeds, season with oil, salt, and pepper and cook them on the wire rack in the oven without letting them fall apart.

Take them out of the oven and arrange in a baking dish and cover each with a slice of mozzarella, then a slice of ham, and on top add the poached egg.

Prepare a not-too-thick white sauce *(p16)* with the butter, flour, and milk, season with a pinch of salt, and finish with an egg yolk and ¼ cup of grated Parmesan. With this sauce, veil the eggs and put the dish in a hot oven for a few minutes: enough time to melt the mozzarella and lightly brown the sauce.

UOVA AFFOGATE CON PUNTE DI ASPARAGI

Poached Eggs with Asparagus Tips

2¼ lb asparagus
Milk
Cornstarch
4 tsp butter
Grated Parmesan
6 eggs
Salt
Optional: 6 fried croutons

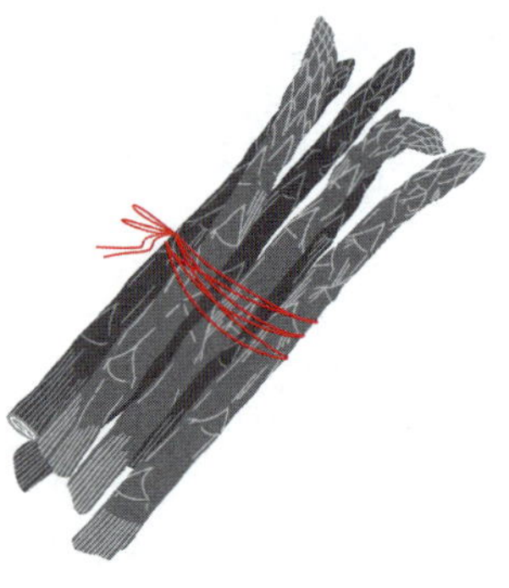

Poach your eggs *(p307)*.

Scrape the stems of the asparagus, rinse them well, and cut them to the same lengths. Boil in lightly salted boiling water, and when they are cooked, with a small knife cut off the tips, which you will keep warm in a little warm water.

Chop the rest and pass through a sieve or blend. Put this purée in a pan with half a glass of milk, a teaspoon of starch, and the butter, and season with a pinch of salt, 1 tablespoon of grated Parmesan, and let everything thicken slightly.

Arrange the eggs on a plate. Pour over a little sauce and garnish with the asparagus tips and some more grated Parmesan.

ADA SAYS: *To present this preparation in a more complete way, prepare some croutons fried in butter and place each egg on a crouton.*

BAKED EGGS

TO BAKE EGGS

Generously grease a sheet pan or baking dish, break the eggs, put salt on the whites and not on the yolks. Heat a little butter and pour a teaspoon of this boiling butter on each egg.

Put the tray in a preheated oven at a high heat, making sure that the eggs receive more heat on the upper part. As soon as the eggs are slightly set, remove them and send them to the table in the same pan.

UOVA AL PIATTO CON BURRO D'ACCIUGHE

Baked Eggs with Anchovy Butter

6 eggs
3 anchovies
5¼ oz mozzarella
Salt
Pepper

Anchovy butter:
3½ tbsp butter, 2 to 3 anchovies

Grease a sheet pan or dish, break the eggs, season with salt and pepper, and arrange some anchovy fillets and very thin slices of mozzarella cheese on top.

Put in a very lively oven for a few minutes until the eggs set, remove the tray from the oven.

Make an anchovy butter *(p54)* by boning and chopping the anchovy into small pieces, add to the melted butter, and mash with a wooden spoon. Pour this sauce over the eggs.

UOVA AL PIATTO CON PATATE

Baked Eggs with Potatoes

Butter
6 potatoes
3½ oz mozzarella
6 eggs
Grated Parmesan
Salt
Pepper

Generously grease a baking dish with butter. Line the bottom with a layer of boiled and peeled potatoes cut into slices. Arrange slices of mozzarella on the potatoes, and break the eggs on top. Season with salt, pepper, and ¼ cup of grated Parmesan. Place little pieces of butter here and there.

Put the pan in a preheated, lively oven for a few minutes and, as soon as the eggs are slightly set and the mozzarella starting to melt, send them to the table in the same pan.

UOVA AL PIATTO CON PATATE DUCHESSE

Baked Eggs with Duchess Potatoes

2¼ lb baking potatoes
6 eggs
7 tbsp butter
1 egg yolk
4 eggs
Grated Parmesan
Butter
Salt

Prepare some duchess potatoes, mixing boiled potatoes with the eggs and butter, and using a pastry bag with a spike nozzle ½ inch in diameter, make a cord around a buttered baking dish. Then do six more cords from the center of the plate so you will have a wheel.

Beat your extra egg yolk and brush it over the potatoes. Put in the oven for a few minutes. When the potatoes have taken a light gold tint, remove from the oven.

Now break the rest of your eggs on to the warm potatoes. Season with salt, a small piece of butter, and a little grated Parmesan. Put back in the oven until the whites have set.

UOVA AL PIATTO CON POMODORI E ZUCCHINE

Baked Eggs with Tomatoes and Zucchini

6 zucchini
Olive oil
3 tomatoes
6 eggs
Butter
Salt

Rinse the zucchini, divide them into pieces, and put them in a pan with half a glass of oil; cook them slowly and sprinkle with salt.

Remove the skin and seeds from the tomatoes, divide into slices, and cook over high heat in a separate pan with oil and salt, taking care not to mix them too often so as not to break them.

When the vegetables are ready, put them together and arrange them in a regular layer in a greased sheet pan or baking dish. Break the eggs over the vegetables, sprinkle with salt, put some tiny pieces of butter here and there, and place in a hot lively oven until the eggs set.

UOVA AL PIATTO NEI NIDI DI SPINACI

Eggs Baked in Spinach Nests

2¼ lb spinach
Olive oil
7 tbsp butter
Grated Parmesan
1 egg yolk
3 tbsp flour
6 eggs
3 tomatoes
Salt

Clean the spinach, rinse, and boil in very little salted water; drain, squeeze them in your hands, and chop them on the cutting board.

Put the oil and a tablespoon of butter in a pan, heat, add the chopped spinach and a pinch of salt, and let them season for a few minutes. Then, take off the heat, and season with a few spoons of grated Parmesan and an egg yolk.

Mix well, divide the mixture into equal portions, and, with the help of floured hands, form them into bases, in the center of which you will make a large dimple so that they look like nests. Line up the spinach nests on a greased sheet pan and in each nest break an egg.

Season with a pinch of salt and with one or two fresh tomato slices and a spoon of grated Parmesan. Sprinkle them with melted butter and put the pan in a preheated oven for a few minutes. When the egg white has set, remove from the oven and send them to the table as they are.

FRIED EGGS

TO FRY EGGS

Put a small pan on the stove with plenty of oil; when the oil is hot and slightly steamy, break the egg into a saucer, season with a pinch of salt, and slide it into the pan. If there is not enough oil you have to keep the pan slightly tilted to make sure all the egg is completely submerged.

UOVA FRITTE AL BACON

Fried Eggs with Bacon

Olive oil
6 eggs
12 slices bacon
Butter
Salt

In a pan with plenty of oil, fry one egg at a time. Break the egg into a saucer and then slide it gently into the hot oil. Season immediately with a pinch of salt, spoon a little oil on the egg yolk to be sure it is well wrapped up in its white. Take out with a slotted spoon or spatula. Drain.

Put the bacon slices in another pan with a little oil or butter, over moderate heat, until they become slightly transparent and crumpled. Place the bacon slices in a serving dish and on every two slices place a fried egg. Serve immediately.

UOVA FRITTE ALL'AMERICANA

Fried Eggs American Style

3½ tbsp butter
1 carrot
1 onion
Parsley
Bay leaf
1 lb tomatoes, peeled and canned
1¾ oz ham
Oil for frying
6 eggs
6 slices prosciutto
Salt
Pepper

Put a spoonful of butter in a small saucepan with a finely chopped carrot and an onion and cook gently without coloring too much. When the vegetables are lightly browned, add a bouquet of herbs composed of a few parsley stalks and a small leaf of bay tied together; add the peeled tomatoes, season with salt and plenty of pepper, and cook slowly for about 20 minutes. Then remove the herbs, and keep warm.

Cut the ham into cubes. Then put a pan with plenty of oil on the fire and, one at a time, fry the eggs. Season immediately with a little salt and add a little ham on the yolk. As soon as the egg is cooked, take out with a spatula or slotted spoon and drain.

Put a little oil in another pan for the prosciutto, in slices cut a little thick, about the size of a playing card. Pour the hot tomato sauce into a serving dish; on the sauce place the slices of prosciutto, and on each slice place an egg. Garnish with chopped parsley. Serve immediately.

ADA SAYS: *For more elegance, you can use a smooth pastry cutter of 2 or 3 inches in diameter, and cut around the white fringes to make the eggs perfectly rounded.*

UOVA FRITTE ALLA MOZZARELLA E BURRO D'ACCIUGHE

Fried Eggs with Mozzarella and Anchovy Butter

6 bread slices
Butter
9 oz mozzarella
3 anchovies
6 eggs
Pepper

Anchovy butter:
3½ tbsp butter, 3 anchovies

Use a smooth round pastry cutter of 3 inches in diameter to make neat disks from the bread slices; fry them on one side with a little butter, and then arrange them, fried part upward, in a greased ovenproof pan.

On each disk of bread put a slice of mozzarella of the same size and a good ½ inch thick; and on the mozzarella put some anchovy fillets. Finish with a pinch of pepper and put the croutons in an oven at a moderate heat.

Prepare the anchovy butter *(p54)* with the ingredients listed here.

Fry the eggs and as soon as the croutons are ready, place a fried egg on each, and drain a little anchovy butter on top.

UOVA FRITTE ALLA TURCA

Fried Eggs Turkish Style

1 cup all-purpose flour
Oil for frying
5 oz Gruyère
6 eggs
Salt

Put the flour on the kitchen table and make a well in the middle, add a pinch of salt, 2 tablespoons of oil, and 6 tablespoons of water. Knead well to obtain a smooth and soft dough.

Divide the dough into equal pieces, roll them out and give each one the shape of a square of 5 inches each side. Grate the Gruyère cheese and divide it into portions, placing it in the center of each square. In each nest put a raw egg, and a pinch of salt. Then take the 4 corners of each square, raise them, and fold them up over the egg, to enclose it perfectly.

Put a pan with plenty of oil on the heat and when it is hot, dip the bundles in, one at a time, upside down. Deep fry for a few minutes, then turn them over, and, when they are gold, remove them from the pan, drain, and serve immediately.

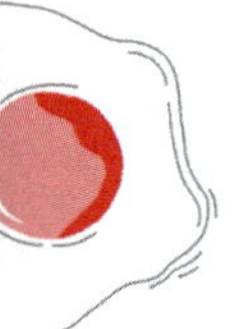
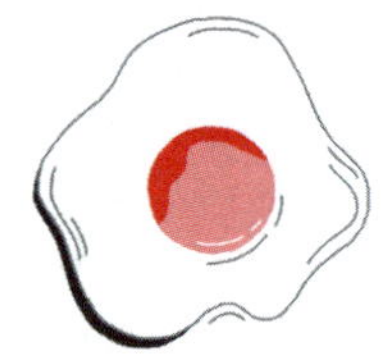

BOILED EGGS

TO BOIL EGGS

Put the eggs in cold water, turn on the heat, and, after it bubbles, boil them for 3 minutes. Then put them in cold water, so it is easier to handle and peel them. Shell carefully and leave in lukewarm water until needed. The whites, if cooked to the right point, must be clotted but not hardened and the yolk must remain runny and retain the same color as before cooking.

TO HARD-BOIL EGGS

There are two ways to hard boil an egg. In the first, put the eggs in a pan, cover with cold water, let them cook 5 minutes from when the water has started to boil, then pass them in cold water and shell them. Or place the eggs in a pan, cover them with cold water; as soon as the water has boiled, turn off the fire, leave the eggs in the water until completely cooled, then shell them.

UOVA MOLLETTE CON CARCIOFI E PISELLI

Boiled Eggs with Artichokes and Peas

6 eggs
6 bread slices
Olive oil
6 artichokes, or hearts
Lemon
1 onion
2¼ lb peas
1 bouillon cube
Milk
Grated Parmesan
Salt

Put the eggs in a saucepan with cold water, bring it to the heat, and after it boils, cook for 3 minutes. Remove and drain, dip in cold water, then shell them, and leave them covered in warm water.

With a 2 inch-diameter pasta cutter, cut disks out of the slices of bread. Then with a smaller cutter, that is 1 inch in diameter, remove the center of each disk so that you have rings. Fry these rings in hot oil, then arrange them in a crown on a plate.

Remove the eggs from the water, dry them, and place each egg upright on the bread ring.

If whole, peel the artichokes, remove the chokes, rub them with lemon juice, cut them into wedges, rinse them with acidulated water using the lemon juice, and place them in a saucepan with 3 spoons of oil and a few spoons of water. Season with a pinch of salt and cook. Cut the onion into slices and put it in another pan with 3 spoons of oil. When the onion has wilted, add the shelled peas, season with a pinch of salt, sprinkle with a few spoons of water, crumble in a bouillon cube, and let them cook over a lively heat.

When the artichokes and peas are cooked, combine the two vegetables into one saucepan. Mix 2 tablespoons of warm milk, a pinch of salt, and ⅓ cup of grated Parmesan, then pour over the vegetables. Finally, pour the sauce on the center of the plate with the eggs and fried croutons.

UOVA SODE ALLA AURORA

Aurora Eggs

6 eggs
Butter

White sauce:
1½ tbsp butter, 3 tbsp all-purpose flour, ¾ cup milk

Hard-boil and shell the eggs *(p313)*, split them in two, and separate the whites from the yolks. Cut the egg whites into regular cubes and add them to a white sauce *(p16)* made with the butter, flour, and milk. Pour this mixture into a greased baking dish. Then dice the yolks or force them through a sieve with the back of a wooden spoon, and scatter them over.

Sprinkle everything with a few spoons of melted butter and place in a preheated oven for 5 or 6 minutes. Send immediately to the table and serve very hot.

UOVA SODE ALLA MONACHINA

Monachina Style Eggs

6 eggs
10½ oz ricotta
Grated Parmesan
All-purpose flour
1 egg
Breadcrumbs
Lard or oil for frying
Salt
Pepper
Nutmeg

Hard-boil the eggs *(p313)*, and, after having shelled them, cut them in two and divide the white from the yolk. Mix the yolks with the ricotta, ¼ cup of grated Parmesan, salt, pepper, and a trifle of nutmeg.

Cover half the whites with this mix, not just in the hole in the center but across all the sides. Stick the other part of the white back over it to create a new egg.

Carefully take these eggs, flour them, dip them in the beaten egg, pass them through breadcrumbs, and fry them with plenty of hot oil or lard, until they have taken on a beautiful golden color. Arrange on a plate and serve hot.

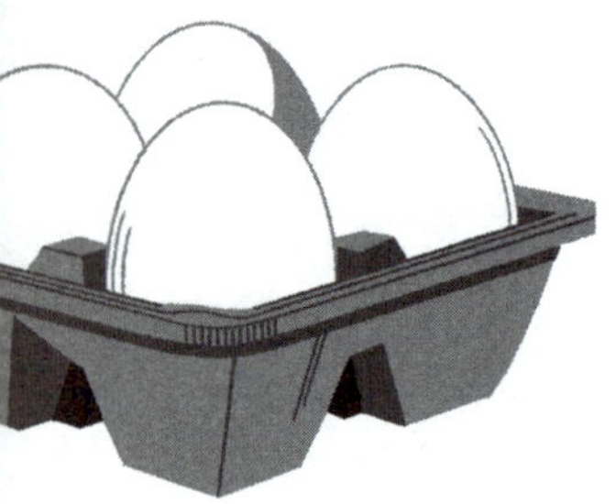

UOVA SODE CON TONNO E MAIONESE

Hard-Boiled Eggs with Tuna and Mayonnaise

6 eggs
3½ oz tinned tuna in olive oil
6 anchovy fillets
Capers
Parsley

Mayonnaise:
1 egg yolk, 1 glass olive oil,
1 tsp vinegar or lemon juice

Boil and shell the eggs *(p313)*, divide them in two, and separate the whites from the yolks. Chop the tuna in oil, the anchovies, the washed capers, and the parsley leaves. Put this mince in a bowl and mix in the egg yolks, diluting with a little oil to make it creamy.

Refill the egg whites with the filling and decorate with a mayonnaise, homemade *(p19)* or bottled.

UOVA SODE E PROSCIUTTO IN MAIONESE

Filled Eggs with Mayonnaise

10½ oz potatoes
10½ oz carrots
10½ oz shelled or frozen peas
Butter
Gelatin
6 hard-boiled eggs
5¼ oz ham
Salt

Mayonnaise:
2 egg yolks, 1 glass olive oil,
1 tsp lemon juice or vinegar

Boil the potatoes, peel them, and cut them into cubes. Do the same with the carrots. Cook the peas with a little butter, a pinch of salt, and a few spoonfuls of water.

Prepare a mayonnaise *(p19)* with two egg yolks, the oil, and a teaspoon of lemon juice or vinegar. It must be rather thick. Or you can use ready-made.

Gather the vegetables and pour the mayonnaise over them, mixing carefully. Now prepare 2 cups of gelatin as per the packet instructions and before it sets, pour a little into a round mold, so as to completely veil the bottom and the sides.

Cut the hard-boiled eggs into slices and arrange with the gelatin. When the first layer of gelatin has hardened, fill with the vegetable mayonnaise, level it off with a knife, and finish by covering with ham. Pour in the rest of the gelatin and put it in the fridge for 2 hours. When you take the mold out of the fridge, place it on a towel soaked in hot water, and, immediately, but with delicacy, turn the preparation upside down on to a serving dish.

UOVA SODE IN FAGOTTINI

Fried Egg Parcels

MAKES 20

1¼ cups all-purpose flour
2 tbsp lard
4 eggs
Parsley
Oil for frying
Salt
Nutmeg

White sauce:
2½ tbsp all-purpose flour, 4 tsp butter, half glass milk

With the flour, 4 tablespoons of water, a pinch of salt, and the lard make a well-worked dough. Shape it into a ball and let it rest for half an hour, covered with a towel.

Hard-boil 3 eggs *(p313)*, then place them in cold water, shell them, and chop.

Prepare a very thick white sauce *(p16)* with the flour, butter, and milk, and season with salt and a little nutmeg. Off the heat, add the chopped eggs and a pinch of chopped parsley. Mix everything well and let it cool.

Roll out the dough thinly and with the tip of a small knife divide it into vertical strips about 2 inches wide, then cut into rectangles. Gather the scraps, roll them out, and make more rectangles.

In the middle of each rectangle, place half a spoonful of the sauce. Wet the edges of the rectangles with a beaten egg and then fold them on themselves, pressing with the fingers to close up the filling well.

Deep fry a few at a time in plenty of oil and over a fairly moderate heat, so that the dough takes on a nice light gold color and becomes light and swells. Arrange them on a plate and have them brought to the table.

UOVA SODE PICCANTI

Pickled Eggs with Chili

6 eggs
Vinegar
Spring onion
Chili
Garlic clove
Rosemary
Salt
Black pepper

Boil and shell the eggs and put them in an airtight jar. Put 2 glasses of vinegar in a small pan, adding coarsely ground black pepper, a few slices of spring onion, a piece of chili, a pinch of salt, a clove of garlic, and a small sprig of rosemary. Bring to the boil, which you will keep slow and regular for 10 minutes, after which pour the boiling vinegar over the eggs in such a way that covers them completely. Let it cool, then close the jar tightly and wait at least 3 days before serving.

UOVA SODE TONNÉ

Boiled Eggs with Tuna

3½ oz tinned tuna in olive oil
1 onion
3 anchovies
White wine
6 eggs
Crustless white bread
Olive oil
1 lemon
Cornichons
Parsley
Pepper

Chop the tuna in oil and onion on a cutting board and put in a small pan. Rinse and bone the anchovies and cut them into small pieces. Add them and a glass of wine to the pan. Cover and cook for half an hour.

Hard-boil the eggs *(p313)*, shell them, split them in two, and place on a plate where they can be well aligned with the cut part facing up.

When the sauce is ready, dip about 2 tablespoons of the white part of a loaf bread in the milk and squeeze dry. Mix in with the tuna and anchovies and use a sieve to force it all through the holes with the back of a wooden spoon. Collect the sauce, which will be very dense, in a small bowl, dilute it with half a glass of oil and the juice of a lemon, and finish with a pinch of pepper and a tablespoon of sliced cornichons.

Put a spoon of tuna sauce on each half egg, making sure to give it a rounded shape.

Arrange the eggs on the plate and decorate with parsley.

SCRAMBLED EGGS

TO SCRAMBLE EGGS

Break the necessary number of eggs into a bowl, beat them lightly, season with a pinch of salt and pour them into a well buttered saucepan. Put the pan in a larger bowl with boiling water and with a whisk work the eggs until they thicken. At this point remove the pan from the bain-marie, season with cream or milk and flavor with diced ham, or tongue, or truffles, warmed in butter, and mix with a wooden spoon, adding also a few pieces more of butter.

UOVA RAPPRESE AI CARDI

Scrambled Eggs with Cardoons

2 lb cardoons
3 tbsp flour
7 tbsp butter
6 eggs
Grated Parmesan
Salt

Clean, cut, and boil the cardoons then drain and dry. Then flour them and arrange them in a pan, in which you have melted some butter. Season them with a little salt, put them on the stove, and brown on both sides.

When the cardoons have taken on a nice golden color, break into a bowl all the eggs, beat them as if for an omelet, season with a little salt and ½ cup of grated Parmesan, and pour into the pan with the cardoons. Let it cook, without stirring, and when the eggs thicken between the leaves, remove the container from the heat and send promptly to the table, without decanting.

UOVA RAPPRESE CON FEGATINI DI POLLO

Scrambled Eggs with Chicken Livers and Asparagus

10½ oz chicken livers
7 oz butter
Sage
Marsala
1 lb asparagus
6 eggs
2 tbsp cream
Salt
Pepper

First prepare the livers; use a sharp knife to cut out the gall and any greenish parts, wash the livers, and divide each one in 2 or 3 pieces. Put half the butter in a pan and, when it is hot, add the livers, season with salt and pepper and a few freshly chopped sage leaves. The livers cook swiftly, so in no time they will be ready. A prolonged stay on the fire would have no other effect than to harden them. Take them out and put in a serving dish.

Put the pan back on the fire, add a small glass of Marsala, bring to the boil, then pour this sauce on the livers; keep them warm.

Scrape the stems of the asparagus, rinse them well, cut them all to the same length, and tie them in bunches. Boil them standing in lightly salted boiling water, but not too much, drain well, cut the tips with a small knife, and flavor with a little butter.

Now scramble the eggs, adding the cream, and then arrange them in a crown around the livers; garnish with the tips of asparagus.

UOVA RAPPRESE GUARNITE

Scrambled Eggs with Ham and Croutons

6 eggs
Cream
3½ oz ham or tongue
5½ tbsp butter
Salt
To serve: croutons fried in butter

First, scramble the eggs *(opposite page)*, but when taking the pan out of the bain marie, add 2 tablespoons of cream and diced ham or tongue, and mix with a wooden spoon, adding a few pieces of butter.

Pour the eggs into a serving dish and garnish with croutons cut into small triangles and fried in butter.

UOVA RAPPRESE NEI POMODORI

Scrambled Eggs in Tomatoes

6 unripe tomatoes
6 eggs
Olive oil
2 tbsp cream
Salt
To serve: croutons fried in olive oil

Choose tomatoes of equal size if possible, to match your eggs; cut the tops off and use a teaspoon to remove the seeds and juice. Line them up in a pan, sprinkle with salt, season with a drizzle of oil, and put them in the oven on a high heat for a quarter of an hour so that they cook without deforming. Fry the same number of round croutons in oil, about the size of the tomatoes.

Scramble your eggs as above, adding the cream, and fill each tomato with them and put each on a crouton. Put them on a round plate and send them to the table.

SOUFFLÉS

TO COOK SOUFFLÉS

The eggs for a soufflé must be at room temperature and should be added one at a time, always working with a wooden spoon. The white must be beaten until stiff and incorporated quite gently into the rest of the mixture. The ideal temperature to bake a soufflé is around 375°F. It is important never to open the oven while the soufflé is baking or it will collapse on you. Without opening the oven, if it does start to collapse, then your soufflé is overcooked.

SUFFLÈ AL FORMAGGIO

Cheese Soufflé

2½ cups grated Parmesan
1 cup grated Gruyère
6 eggs
1½ tbsp butter
Salt
Pepper
Nutmeg

White sauce:
3½ tbsp butter, ¼ cup all-purpose flour, 2 cups milk

Make a white sauce *(p16)* with the butter, flour, and milk, and season with salt, pepper, and nutmeg. Take the sauce off the heat. While still lukewarm, add the grated cheeses and then, one by one, the yolks, stirring for a long time. Finish the mixture with the beaten egg whites.

Pour everything into a buttered baking mold and bake in a preheated oven for about 20 minutes until it grows and becomes golden. Serve immediately.

SUFFLÈ DI CARCIOFI

Artichoke Soufflé

6 artichokes
3½ tbsp butter
4 eggs
Grated Parmesan
3½ oz Gruyère
Salt

Thick white sauce:
3½ tbsp butter, ¼ cup all-purpose flour, 3 cups milk

Remove the hard external leaves from the artichokes, removing the hairy chokes. Cut off the woody stem base. Trim the tops and cut them into wedges. Leave them in a bowl of water with a spoonful of flour.

Boil a saucepan of water and cook the artichokes, but not too much. Then drain and fry them in a pan with most of the butter, letting them flavor for a few minutes on a high heat.

Prepare a thick white sauce *(p16)* with the butter, flour, and milk. Take it off the heat and add two egg yolks, ½ cup of grated Parmesan, and the diced Gruyère. Finally, beat the four egg whites into peaks and fold them into the mix. Butter a sheet pan and arrange the artichoke wedges in one layer, then pour the prepared mixture over them, smoothing with the blade of a knife, and place the tray in a preheated oven for about 20 minutes until the soufflé has grown and taken on a golden color. Serve immediately.

SUFFLÈ DI CARDI

Cardoon Soufflé

4½ lb cardoons
Tomato purée
Grated Parmesan
2 eggs
1½ tbsp butter
Breadcrumbs
Salt
Nutmeg

White sauce:
3½ tbsp butter, ¼ cup all-purpose flour, 2 cups broth

Clean the cardoons, cut them into pieces, boil them, and drain, then blend to a purée. Make your white sauce *(p16)* by melting the butter in a saucepan, add the flour, and mix in the broth. While stirring, add 1 or 2 teaspoons of tomato purée. When the sauce has thickened, remove from the heat, season with salt, 2 tablespoons of grated Parmesan, and add the 2 egg yolks, then add everything to the cardoon purée and mix well.

Beat your egg whites into peaks and gently incorporate them and season with nutmeg. Butter a 6½-cup cake mold and sprinkle with breadcrumbs, then pour in the mixture and put in a preheated oven on moderate heat, for about 20 minutes, so the soufflé can cook and swell. Serve immediately.

SUFFLÈ DI FAGIOLINI

Green Bean Soufflé

1 lb green beans
1½ tbsp butter
Grated Parmesan
4 eggs
Salt

White sauce:
¼ cup all-purpose flour, 3½ tbsp butter, 3 cups milk

Wash and boil the green beans, drain, and leave them in a bowl of cold water until they are cold. Then drain again and fry in a pan with a little butter, to flavor them. When they are cooked, chop them finely.

Meanwhile, prepare a white sauce *(p16)* with the flour, butter, and milk. Add the beans and add ½ cup of grated Parmesan. Now beat only the egg whites until stiff, and gently combine with the green beans sauce.

Butter a 6½-cup cake mold and pour in the mixture. It should only reach two thirds or even less of the mold; smooth it with the blade of a knife and put the soufflé in the oven at a moderate heat for about 20 minutes, until it is firm and puffy. Serve immediately.

SUFFLÈ DI FETTUCCINE

Fettuccine Soufflé

Grated Gruyère
Grated Parmesan
3½ oz ham
3 eggs
7 tbsp butter
1 cup milk or cream
12 oz egg fettuccine
Salt
Pepper

Grate ½ cup of Gruyère and ½ cup of Parmesan into a bowl, add the diced ham, the egg yolks—keeping the whites aside—the diced butter, and the milk or cream and mix all the ingredients well. Turn on the oven. Start beating the egg whites until stiff.

Cook the fettuccine in boiling salted water, checking often because fettuccine cook quickly. They must be *al dente*. Drain and add them quickly to the mixture in the bowl, mixing well, then gently incorporate the egg whites.

Butter a tall sheet pan, transfer the fettuccine mix, and put them in the oven, baking on a moderate heat for about 30 minutes. Serve immediately.

SUFFLÈ DI PARMIGIANO

Parmesan Soufflé

7 tbsp butter
All-purpose flour
7 tbsp milk
2½ cups grated Parmesan
4 eggs

Melt the butter in a saucepan, then add ¾ cup of flour, mix with a wooden spoon, and, still mixing, add a glass of milk. Keep stirring until the cream thickens slightly, then add the grated Parmesan and leave it to cool.

When the mixture is cold, mix in the egg yolks one at a time, stirring all the time. Beat the whites until very firm and gently add them to the mixture.

Butter a 6½-cup cake mold, pour in the Parmesan cream, and level the surface with a knife. Bake in a preheated oven on moderate heat and leave for 20 to 25 minutes, until the soufflé has risen and is firm. Serve immediately.

SUFFLÈ DI PARMIGIANO IN TAZZINE

Parmesan Soufflé Cups

All-purpose flour
Milk
3 eggs
1 cup grated Parmesan
4 tsp butter

You can use porcelain cups or paper—muffin-style—cases to bake these; the cups must be buttered, the paper cases will need to be buttered and then left in the oven for a few minutes to dry them before pouring in the mixture, which in both cases should go halfway up the side of the containers.

Put ½ cup of flour in a saucepan off the heat and dissolve it completely with ½ cup of milk, then bring the saucepan on to the heat, and, stirring constantly, let it thicken. Let the mixture cool a little and add 2 egg yolks, the grated Parmesan, and the butter.

Beat the 3 egg whites until stiff. Take a spoonful and add it to the prepared mixture, mixing with energy to dissolve it and lighten it a little. Then add the remaining egg whites, mixing them gently.

Bake in a pre-heated oven on moderate heat for 12 to 15 minutes and serve immediately.

SUFFLÈ DI PATATE

Potato Soufflé

2¼ lb potatoes
7 tbsp butter
4 eggs
Milk or cream
Salt
Nutmeg

Peel the potatoes, cut them into wedges, and boil in a saucepan with salted water. Once cooked, drain them, put them back in the saucepan but off the heat, and mash them with a wooden spoon.

Add most of the butter, a little nutmeg, the egg yolks, and a glass of milk or cream. Beat the egg whites until stiff and add them to the potato purée, mixing gently with a spoon.

Butter a soufflé mold, or a pan, pour the purée in—it must not reach more than two thirds up the sides in height—and bake in a preheated oven on moderate heat for about 20 minutes, until the soufflé is firm. Serve immediately directly from the baking dish.

SUFFLÈ DI PESCE

Fish Soufflé

2 lb fresh cod (or 1 lb 5 oz, cooked)
6 eggs
Salt
Pepper

White sauce:
7 tbsp butter, 1 cup flour, 2½ cups milk

Make a thick white sauce *(p16)* with the butter, flour, and milk. Grease a sheet pan well, add the chopped fish, then add the egg yolks, salt, and pepper.

Beat the egg whites separately until stiff and add them slowly to the mixture, gently mixing with a wooden spoon. The mixture should not be higher than half of the dish. Put the dish in a preheated oven and bake for 30 minutes at a moderate heat for the first half and then increase the temperature for the last 15 minutes. When the soufflé looks golden and has a crispy crust, take it out of the oven and serve immediately with a sauce of your choice.

ADA SAYS: *This recipe can be served both as an intermezzo and as a normal fish main course. You can use the leftover flesh of a roasted or boiled fish. Once the fish is cooked, remove the skin and any bones with great care and chop it finely.*

SUFFLÈ DI POLLO

Chicken Soufflé

3 lb 5 oz chicken
Grated Parmesan
4 eggs
1½ tbsp butter
Salt

White sauce:
½ cup butter, 1¼ cups flour, 3 cups milk, nutmeg

Clean the chicken properly, then boil it and let it cool. Remove the skin and remove all the meat from the bones. Finely chop or blend this meat and set aside.

Now prepare the white sauce *(p16)* with the butter, flour, milk, and season with nutmeg. When it is thick enough, pour it into a bowl. Add the chopped chicken and mix well. Always stirring, add the egg yolks one at a time and 4 or 5 tablespoons of grated Parmesan. Finally, beat the egg whites until stiff and gently incorporate them into the mixture. Grease a 8½-cup cake mold or a tall baking dish with butter and pour in the mixture, which must not reach higher than ⅔ of the container. Bake in a light oven for half an hour. When the soufflé has risen and turned a golden color, take it out and serve immediately.

SUFFLÈ DI POMODORO

Tomato Soufflé

5 tbsp butter
1 onion
Basil
2¼ lb sweet and meaty tomatoes
Grated Parmesan
1¾ oz Gruyère
4 eggs
Salt
Pepper

White sauce:
7 tbsp butter, 1 cup all-purpose flour, 2 cups milk

Melt most of the butter in a pan, add a small chopped onion, and chopped basil leaves, and sweat gently. Peel the tomatoes, remove the seeds, and chop them into large pieces, then add to the pan as soon as the onion has colored, seasoning with salt and pepper. Let it all thicken until it is reduced in a sauce.

Make a white sauce *(p16)* with the butter, flour, and milk. Remove from the heat when it is smooth and season with salt, ½ cup of grated Parmesan, the Gruyère cut in small pieces, the tomato sauce, and the egg yolks, and mix everything together. Beat the egg whites until stiff and gently incorporate them to the rest.

Butter a 6½-cup cake mold and pour in the mixture. Level the surface and place it in a preheated oven at moderate heat for about half an hour. When the soufflé has passed the edge of the mold and is a nice golden color, remove it from the oven and serve immediately.

SUFFLÈ DI PROSCIUTTO COTTO

Ham Soufflé

12 oz lean ham
1 cup grated Parmesan
6 eggs
1½ tbsp butter
Salt

White sauce:
3½ tbsp butter, ¼ cup all-purpose flour, 2 cups milk

Start by making your white sauce *(p16)* with the butter, flour, and milk. Let it cook until it is quite thick and then transfer into a bowl. Finely chop the ham and add it little by little to the sauce. Add the grated Parmesan and the 6 egg yolks one at a time. Beat the egg whites until stiff and gently incorporate them into the mixture. Butter a 6½-cup cake mold. Pour in the mixture, smooth it with the blade of a knife, and bake in a moderate heat oven for 25 minutes to half an hour, until the souffle has risen and is dry.

ADA SAYS: *As an alternative to the single mold you might use porcelain cups, "cocottes," and bake them only for 10 to 12 minutes. Serve immediately.*

SUFFLÈ DI RISO CON FEGATINI

Chicken Liver and Rice Soufflé

7 oz chicken livers
1 tbsp butter
Marsala
10½ oz rice
6¼ cups meat broth *(p88)*
Grated Parmesan
4 eggs
Salt

Clean the livers well, carefully removing the gall, and cook them in a saucepan with a knob of butter, salt, and a splash of Marsala. When they are cooked, cut them into thin strips.

Boil the rice for 20 minutes in the meat broth. As soon as it is cooked, drain and season with the rest of the butter and ½ cup of grated Parmesan, then mix in the chicken livers and let it cool.

Once the rice is cold, add the egg yolks and the egg whites beaten until stiff. Butter a 6½-cup cake pan, then pour in the rice mixture. Bake in a preheated oven on moderate heat for 20 minutes. Serve immediately.

SUFFLÈ DI RISO CON GAMBERETTI

Shrimp Soufflé

10½ oz rice
6 cups fish broth *(p89)*
1 lb shrimp
4 eggs
Butter
Salt

Shrimp butter:
½ cup butter, 3½ oz cooked shrimp

Cook the rice for 20 minutes in the fish broth or salted water. Wash and boil the shrimp putting them in slightly salted cold water for three minutes, drain them, shell them, and cut them in two parts lengthwise

Make the shrimp butter *(p55)* by mashing the butter and the extra shrimp together. As soon as the rice is cooked, drain and season it with the shrimp butter, then let cool. Add the egg yolks. And only when the rice is completely cold, gently fold in the beaten egg whites and lastly the shrimp. Grease a 6½-cup cake pan and pour in the rice mixture. Bake in a preheated oven for approximately 20 minutes. Serve immediately.

SUFFLÈ DI SPINACI

Spinach Soufflé

2 lb spinach
7 tbsp butter
10½ oz ricotta
Milk
4 eggs
Grated Parmesan
Salt
Pepper
Nutmeg

Clean and wash the spinach with great care, then boil in a little salted water. Drain, squeeze dry, and finely chop. Put the spinach in a pan, on moderate heat, with the butter and a pinch of salt, and mix with a wooden spoon to dry and flavor.

Melt the ricotta in a bowl with a few spoons of milk, add the egg yolks, and season with ¼ cup of grated Parmesan, a little nutmeg, salt, and pepper. Mix well, then add the spinach, and finally gently incorporate the egg whites, beaten until stiff. Transfer the mixture into a buttered 6½-cup cake pan, and bake in a moderate oven for about 20 minutes. Serve immediately.

ADA SAYS: *This soufflé can be prepared both as an intermezzo and as a delicious vegetable side dish.*

"To cook fish you must be gentle."

Fish and seafood are as important in the diet as meat. The key thing is that they must be fresh. Frozen fish retains all the qualities of fresh and can be cooked like fresh, but it must be properly defrosted.

The freshness of fish is indicated by a shiny appearance, the hardness of the flesh, and, above all, by certain greenish reflections that they retain when they are cleaned. A red shade is a sign of deterioration. Lobsters, shrimp, and scampi can be bought and cooked alive and kept in the fridge for a few days. Do not let yourself be tempted by very big lobsters because their meat is often leathery. Shrimp should have a uniform pink color. Any blackish spots on the tail are a sign of decomposition. Shellfish should be bought live and cleaned well. For mollusks like clams and mussels, they must be washed thoroughly so there is no sand or grit left in the shells.

To cook fish you must be gentle. A tumultuous boil will not only ruin the flavor and texture, it would also irredeemably tear the flesh of the fish. The boil must be almost insensible and not too long depending on the size of the fish.

You do not want to overcook it. Boil a little fish for 5 to 10 minutes; for bigger fish allow 10 minutes for each 1 lb; and a little less for turbot and ray. For cuts of bigger fish like tuna, swordfish, shark, and sturgeon allow 13 to 14 minutes for a steak of about 1 inch thickness.

As a general rule, the point when fish is cooked to perfection is recognized by pressing a finger on its back. You will be able to feel the meat yield under gentle pressure.

Certain fish are characteristic for soups—cuttlefish give a special tone but also a small shark or swordfish, cod, sole, mullet, and shrimp. Commonly also used are eel, squid, gurnard, hake, mullet, John Dory, and lobster. Other meaty fish can also be good substitutes.

Some things to look out for with fish: John Dory bones are very good for making fish stock. Salt cod or stockfish must be soaked thoroughly before cooking. River fish are often simmered in a broth of onions, carrots, celery, parsley, and peppercorns.

Many species of fish share the Atlantic; if the type of fish called for in a recipe is unavailable in your location, consider substituting a species with a similar texture. For example, if sustainably fished shark is hard to find, substitute with an equally meaty-textured thick steak-like fish such as swordfish; for thin and flaky turbot, substitute sole or flounder. They are not the same in flavor, but still similar from a cook's perspective. Many recipes are interchangeable for different varieties of fish but freshness is non-negotiable.

PESCE E FRUTTI DI MARE

8 FISH & SEAFOOD

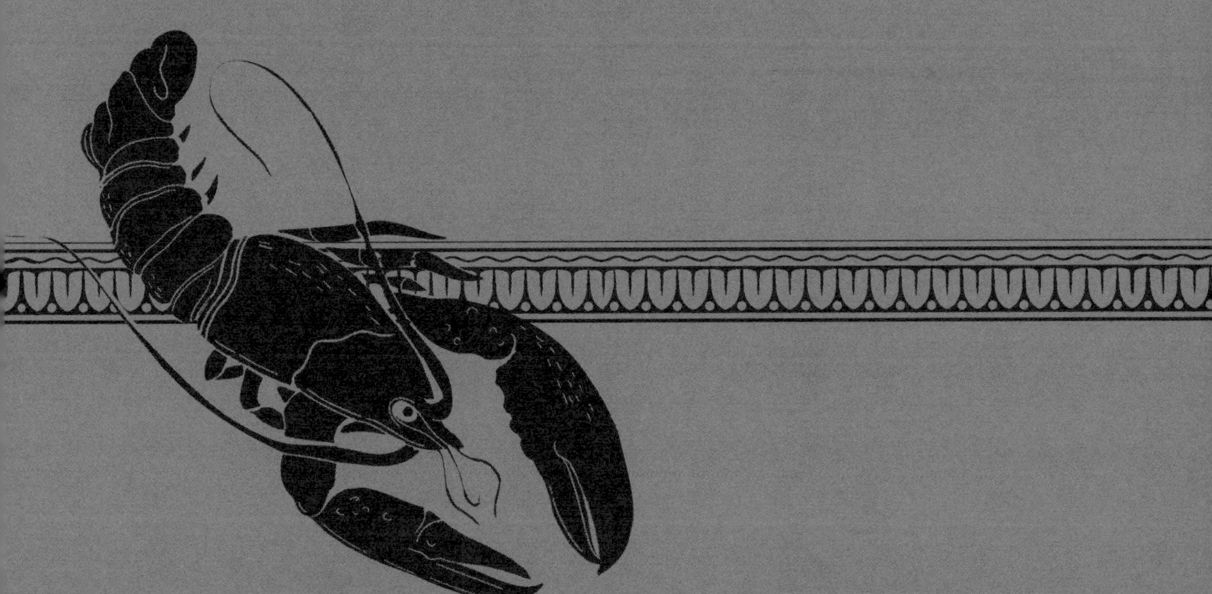

TO COOK FISH

TO ROAST

To prepare fish for roasting or the barbecue, it should be given a marinade with parsley, peppercorns, a bay leaf, and some oil and left for an hour or two before cooking. No need for lemon or salt. Alternatively, lightly flour the outside and before putting the fish in the oven or on the barbecue, warm some oil in an ovenproof dish and when it is hot, put the fish in. Turn it over immediately. Only then put the dish in the oven or on the barbecue and at intervals baste with more oil, turning it gently. With larger fish it may also be necessary to cut incisions along the back to better allow the heat to penetrate inside. Roasted fish can be served simply with a sauce of butter, salt, pepper, parsley, and lemon.

TO BRAISE

For braising in the oven, the best fish are sea bass, sea bream, and trout. Season the bottom of the pan with aromatics for underneath the fish. Brush a raised wire rack with melted butter and rub the fish with salt and pepper. Start cooking on the stove and then put the dish in a moderately hot oven, so the aromas release. After about 10 minutes, baste with a couple of glasses of white wine, turn up the heat a little, and let it continue cooking slowly for half an hour, occasionally basting again with a little of its own juices. Braising on the stovetop works for most fish, but larger fish should be cut into pieces. Put a little oil in a pan and brown a chopped onion. Add a little ground garlic and parsley, then add tomato or tomato passata and one or two boned and chopped anchovies. Season with salt and pepper. Cook for a few minutes and then wet with enough water to cover the fish. Braise slowly.

TO FRY

Butter is suitable for frying delicate fish such as sole, trout, etc. It should be clarified first though. (p242)

TO POACH

To poach a whole fish, put it in cold water with a little salt, a few peppercorns, some aromatics such as onion, carrot, parsley stalks, etc., and a half glass of vinegar. Bring the water slowly to the boil. If you want to use the fish broth for sauces or soups, substitute the vinegar with half a glass of white wine. If the fish are small, simmer the aromatics for a few minutes first, let them cool, and then drop the fish in. Fillets should go straight into the simmering water. Whichever fish you have, they should always be cooked gently over a very low heat. Any tumultuous boiling will make the fish less flavorsome and tear the skin.

SEA FISH

Anchovies

ALICI ALLA TUNISINA

Anchovies Tunisian Style

2¼ lb fresh anchovies
All-purpose flour
Oil for frying
3 large onions
2 cups white wine vinegar
Olive oil
Pine nuts
3 tbsp raisins
Salt

Remove the heads and bones from the anchovies, open them in two without splitting them completely, rinse, and dry. Flour them and deep-fry them in oil. When they are golden on both sides, remove and place them on a sheet of parchment paper and salt them lightly.

Pour some oil into a new pan and, as soon as it is hot, peel and slice the onions, and let them brown on a low heat till softened. Sprinkle vinegar over them, continuing cooking for another 3 minutes. Lay the anchovies in a bowl. Spread over some onions, a handful of pine nuts, and a spoonful of golden raisins, soaked in warm water and then squeezed dry.

Splash each layer with a few tablespoons of hot vinegar, taking care, at the end, that everything is covered with the rest of the oil. Cover and leave to rest for a day or two in a dry corner—not in the fridge.

ALICI AL LIMONE

Anchovies with Lemon

2¼ lb fresh anchovies
Breadcrumbs
Oregano
Olive oil
Lemon
Salt
Pepper

Remove the heads and bones from the anchovies, open them in two without completely splitting them, rinse, dry, and line them up in a sheet pan big enough for them to fit side by side. Sprinkle with salt.

Cover the anchovies with breadcrumbs, oregano, and a little pepper. Wash them with a little oil and the juice of a lemon.

Put the pan in a warm oven for about 20 minutes until the breadcrumbs have formed a nice golden crust.

ALICI IN TORTIERA

Anchovies Baked with Mushrooms

1¾ oz dried mushrooms
8 tbsp breadcrumbs
1 egg
9 tbsp grated Parmesan
Marjoram
2¼ lb fresh anchovies
Olive oil
Breadcrumbs
Salt
Pepper
Nutmeg

Soak the dried mushrooms in cold water for 20 minutes, rinse them, clean them carefully, chop them, and put them in a bowl. Soak the breadcrumbs in water, squeeze dry in your hands, and crumble them into the mushrooms.

Break the egg into the bowl and add the Parmesan, a little nutmeg, the marjoram, salt, and pepper; mix everything together with a wooden spoon so it blends well.

Remove the heads and bones from the anchovies, open them in two without completely splitting them, and spread a part of the prepared mixture inside. Close the anchovies back up and arrange them in a pan, where you will have poured a few spoons of oil. Sprinkle the anchovies with more breadcrumbs, pour in a little more oil, and put the pan in a warm oven for half an hour until a soft golden crust forms.

ALICI PICCANTI

Spiced Anchovies

15 anchovies preserved in salt
Olive oil
Onion
Celery
Carrot
Parsley
1 bay leaf
Chili
1¾ oz tinned tuna in olive oil
Pepper
Optional: vinegar

Choose 12 quite large, good-quality salted anchovies. The other 3 will go in the sauce. Open them, remove the bones, and rinse them. You will get 24 fillets. Roll them up on themselves and arrange on a small plate.

Put a spoon of oil in a pan, a couple of spoons of water, a little less than half a chopped onion, a piece of the heart of the celery— the central white and tender part—half a carrot, a sprig of parsley, half a bay leaf, a strong grind of pepper, and a piece of red chili. Simmer over a very low heat, occasionally replenishing with a little water, so that the mix never fries. Keep them on the heat for about half an hour.

At this point, turn up the heat and stir constantly to lose as much moisture as possible. Mash, or sieve, this together with the 3 other anchovies—washed, boned, and cut into pieces—and the tuna in oil, then collect the purée in a bowl. Mix in a few spoons of oil, stirring to blend everything, then pour it over the anchovy fillets and leave them to season for a few hours.

ADA SAYS: *You can also, if you like, flavor the sauce with a few drops of vinegar.*

Herring

ARINGHE FRESCHE IN SALSA AROMATICA

Marinated Herring in Aromatic Sauce

2¼ lb fresh herring
4½ cups white wine
2 cups wine vinegar
1 onion
2 garlic cloves
2 juniper berries
Bay leaf
Parsley
Sage
Rosemary
Chili
Salt
Peppercorns
Optional: mayonnaise

Clean the herring, wash them, dry them, and line them up in a pan.

Pour the wine and vinegar into a saucepan, add the sliced onion, cloves of garlic, juniper berries, bay leaf, stems of parsley, a few sage leaves, a sprig of rosemary, salt, pepper in grains, and a piece of chili. Turn on the heat and boil.

When the marinade has reduced to almost half, pour it, still boiling, over the herring, sieving it through a colander.

Put the pan on the stove and when everything has boiled again, remove the pan from the heat and let it cool. Serve the herring soaked with a little of the cooking broth and maybe some mayonnaise.

ARINGHE IN INSALATA

Herring Salad

1 cup rice
Olive oil
Vinegar
2 smoked herring
1 onion
1 tsp mustard
Parsley
Salt

Boil the rice in lightly salted boiling water, then drain well and, while still hot, season it with 3 tablespoons of oil and 2 tablespoons of vinegar.

Remove the head and skin from the herring, open them with a small knife, remove the central bone, set aside any roe, and finally divide into small dice, trying to remove all the smallest bones as far as possible.

When the rice is cold, mix the diced herring with it and add raw onion, chopped and rinsed thoroughly in cold water.

Place the herring roe in a small bowl and dilute it with 3 tablespoons of oil and a tablespoon of vinegar, finishing it with the mustard, and mixing everything thoroughly. Arrange the rice in a dome on a serving dish and cover it with the prepared sauce, then sprinkle with chopped parsley.

Salt Cod

BACCALÀ AL FORNO

Baked Salt Cod

2¼ lb soaked salt cod
1 lb potatoes
9 oz spring onion
Parsley
5 tomatoes
Olive oil
Salt

You can usually buy salt cod pre-soaked. If not, it needs to be soaked in a preliminary bath of fresh water, for a minimum of 18 hours, to wash out all the salt.

Peel off the skin carefully and cut it into pieces. Grease a sheet pan and add a layer of thin slices of potato on the bottom. On the potatoes sprinkle the trimmed raw spring onions and chopped parsley. Season with a pinch of salt and wet with a drizzle of oil.

Arrange the cod on the bed of potatoes and scallions with a few fresh sliced tomatoes. Make a new layer of potatoes, season again with oil and salt, and put in a preheated oven at a moderate heat for about half an hour. Place the pan on a serving plate and send to the table.

BACCALÀ AL GRATIN

Salt Cod Gratin

2¼ lb soaked salt cod
Olive oil
Parsley
Garlic
Capers
2 anchovies
Gaeta olives, pitted
Breadcrumbs
Pepper

Peel the cod and divide it into square pieces, each about a hand's width in size; fill a pan with cold water, then add the cod and heat. At the first boil, take them out with a slotted spoon and drain.

Pour a little oil into a baking dish, so as to cover the bottom, and arrange the cod, one piece next to the other, in a single layer. Season with chopped parsley, a few pieces of garlic, capers, anchovies cut into fillets, a strong pinch of pepper, and a handful of Gaeta olives. All this must be distributed evenly around the pieces of cod. Finally, cover everything with 2 handfuls of breadcrumbs.

Add some more oil on top of the breadcrumbs, then put in a preheated oven for about half an hour, until the bread has crisped up and the cod is well flavored.

BACCALÀ ALLA PIZZAIOLA

Salt Cod Pizzaiola

2¼ lb soaked salt cod
Olive oil
Breadcrumbs
1 lb tomatoes
Parsley
Oregano
Salt
Pepper

Peel and divide the cod into equal pieces and let it sit for a good half hour in rather hot water to desalt it some more. Dry the pieces and align them in a single layer in a well-oiled pan. Season with a pinch of salt and pepper.

Scatter a handful of breadcrumbs over the cod, add the peeled tomatoes, deseeded and cut into slices, and sprinkle chopped parsley and oregano over everything. Add a glass of oil and place in a preheated oven of moderate heat for about half an hour. Then arrange the cod on a plate and serve it hot.

BACCALÀ ALLA PROVENZALE

Salt Cod Provençal

2¼ lb soaked salt cod
Olive oil
Milk
Nutmeg
Fried croutons
Salt
Pepper
Optional: garlic, cream, white truffle

Skin and divide the cod into rather large pieces and put them in a pan with plenty of water. As soon as the water boils, reduce the heat to a minimum, cover, and leave for about half an hour, so that the cod can finish cooking but without boiling. Drain it, carefully remove the skin or bones, and chop.

Put half a glass of oil in a saucepan and when it is hot add the cod, working it vigorously and mashing it with a wooden spoon to reduce it to a purée. You can add a little crushed garlic. Once this is done, keeping the saucepan on very low heat, begin to add the oil, a little at a time using a spoon, always stirring so that it is incorporated into the cod. When you have added 3 or 4 spoons of oil and the mixture begins to thicken, add warm milk to bring the purée back to the right consistency; add the milk little by little and continuosly stirring. Then continue to incorporate more oil and milk until you have obtained a light purée that resembles a potato purée. You can make the preparation more refined by using a little cream.

Season with a pinch of pepper, a pinch of nutmeg, and, if necessary, a little salt, and pour into a serving dish, surrounding it with fried bread croutons.

ADA SAYS: *With this recipe you could fill vol-au-vent cases or pastry boats. In this case, you could add a little sliced white truffle.*

BACCALÀ AL LATTE

Salt Cod In Milk

2¼ lb soaked salt cod
All-purpose flour
2 onions
Olive oil
3½ tbsp butter
2 cups milk
Parsley
2½ oz black olives, pitted
Lemon
Salad leaves
Salt

Peel off the skin from the cod and divide it into pieces; dry the pieces carefully and then flour them.

Thinly slice the onions, arrange them in a pan, and put the pieces of cod on top; add the oil and the butter cut into small pieces. Place the pan on moderate heat and, as soon as the onions have begun to brown, pour over a glass of milk; cover and let the cod cook over moderate heat for about half an hour, gradually adding in the remaining milk. Check the flavor and add a little salt if necessary.

The cod, when cooked, should be almost dry; transfer it to a serving dish and sprinkle with chopped parsley; finally, decorate the plate with black olives, a lemon cut into wedges, and well-washed salad leaves.

BACCALÀ BOLLITO ALLA PORTOGHESE

Salt Cod Portuguese Style

2¼ lb soaked salt cod
2 cups milk
4 onions
Olive oil
2¼ lb potatoes
Garlic
Oregano
Nutmeg
2½ oz black olives, pitted
Parsley
Pepper
Optional: salt

Put the salt cod in boiling water, cover the container, and cook over a medium heat for about 20 minutes. After this time, let it cool a little, then peel it, divide it into pieces, and put it in another pan, covering it with boiling milk; then let it sit for about an hour.

Meanwhile, brown finely sliced onions in a pan with 4 tablespoons of oil and, as soon as they have browned, add the potatoes cut into slices. Stir and lightly brown. Then add the cod, a crushed garlic clove, pepper, oregano, and a pinch of nutmeg. Check the flavor and possibly add a pinch of salt. Mix thoroughly, then put the pan in a preheated, moderate heat oven for about 20 minutes.

Just before serving, cover the cod with the olives and chopped parsley, sending it to the table very hot.

BACCALÀ CON OLIVE VERDE

Salt Cod with Tomato and Green Olives

1 onion
Olive oil
1 cup tomato passata
2 cornichons
Capers
2½ oz green olives, pitted
Salt
Pepper
2¼ lb soaked salt cod
All-purpose flour
Olive oil
Parsley

Prepare a tomato sauce by frying some onion in oil and adding the passata, sliced cornichons, capers, olives, little or no salt, and a good pinch of pepper. The sauce must have a medium consistency.

Skin the cod, bone it if necessary, and divide it into pieces of about 2½ inches. Dry, dip them in flour, and line them up and fry in a single layer in a pan with a little oil. When the cod slices start to brown on one side, turn them over and let them brown on the other side. Then drain off almost all the oil left in the pan. Pour the tomato sauce over the pieces of cod, simmer a little; then with a spoon take some of the sauce from the bottom of the pan and spread it on top of the cod.

Finally, put the pan in a preheated oven of moderate heat for 10 minutes to allow the cod to flavor well and the sauce to thicken some more. Arrange the cod in a heated serving dish and finish with a spoonful of chopped parsley.

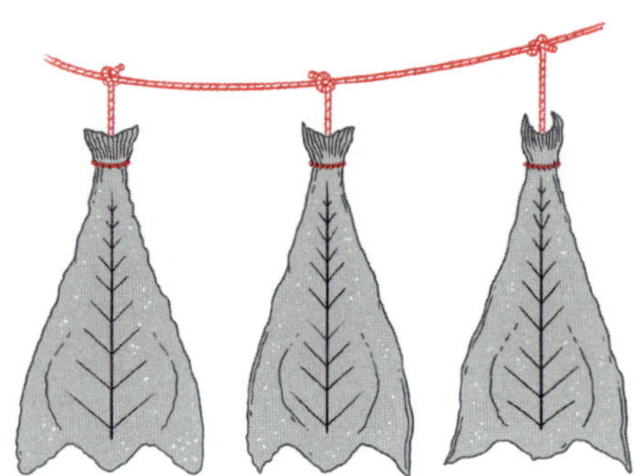

BACCALÀ CON VISCIOLE

Salt Cod with Sour Cherries

Olive oil
Onion
Garlic
10½ oz ripe tomatoes
10½ oz sour cherries
2¼ lb salt cod fillets
Pepper
Optional: salt

Chop half an onion and a clove of garlic and sweat in an oiled pan and when the onion is golden, put in the tomatoes—washed, peeled, and cut into small pieces—a little pepper, and then, after a little while, add the sour cherries along with all the juice they leached when being pitted.

Let it simmer for about 10 minutes, then lay in the cod fillets, arranging them in a single layer; cover, reduce the heat, and leave to simmer gently for another 10 minutes. Check the flavor and, if necessary, add very little salt.

ADA SAYS: *Salt cod prepared in this way is also excellent served cold.*

BACCALÀ IN FLAN

Salt Cod Flan

1 lb soaked salt cod
2 cups milk
4 potatoes
3½ tbsp butter
All-purpose flour
Grated Parmesan
Parsley
2 egg yolks
White pepper
Salt
Nutmeg

Skin the cod, divide it into small pieces in a bowl, and pour over the milk. Leave for a couple of hours.

Then pour the milk and cod into a saucepan, adding, if necessary, a little more milk or water, and cook slowly for about a quarter of an hour. Boil the potatoes, peel them, and set them aside.

When the cod is cooked, remove it from the heat with a slotted spoon and let it drain well. First chop the cod, then the potatoes, and then both together, to get a fine and well-blended mix.

Put a saucepan with the butter on the heat and, when it melts, add ¼ cup of flour. Stir, and after a few minutes, dilute with milk from cooking the cod. Continue cooking to get a smooth sauce. Remove the saucepan from the heat and add the potato and cod purée. Season with a pinch of white pepper, a little salt, a pinch of nutmeg, ¼ cup grated Parmesan, chopped parsley, and the egg yolks beaten as for an omelette. Mix well with a wooden spoon.

Generously grease a mold or a flan dish with a capacity of about 1 quart, pour the mixture in, even it out, and then cook in a bain-marie for about half an hour, until it is firm.

When the flan is ready, take it out of the water bath, let it rest for 4 or 5 minutes, and then turn it out on to a serving plate.

ADA SAYS: *You can serve simply as it is or surround with buttered mushrooms, peas, or spinach, or a gravy boat of tomato sauce finished with butter and chopped parsley.*

BACCALÀ IN PADELLA CON PEPERONI

Salt Cod with Peppers

2¼ lb soaked salt cod
6 large, fleshy green bell peppers
Olive oil
2 onions
1 lb 5 oz tomatoes
Parsley
Salt

Skin the cod and divide it into regular pieces and cover with cold water.

Roast the bell peppers in the oven. When they char, take them out, rinse them, peel off the skin, open them, remove the core and seeds, and cut them into lengths about a finger wide.

Pour half a glass of oil into a large pan, slice the onions, and fry slowly without burning. Next add to the pan the peeled tomatoes, deseeded, and cut into pieces. Cook the tomatoes and then add the bell peppers.

Remove the cod from the water, dry it, put it in the pan with the tomatoes and bell peppers, and leave it to cook over medium heat for about 20 minutes. Before sending the cod to the table, complete it with a little chopped parsley.

ADA SAYS: *You can also flour and fry the cod separately, waiting for the bell peppers to cook completely before putting them in a pan with the sauce. In this case, the cod will simply have to be warmed and flavored for a few minutes.*

BACCALÀ IN TEGLIA ALLA NAPOLETANA

Neapolitan Salt Cod

2¼ lb salt cod
All-purpose flour
Olive oil
Garlic
9 oz tomatoes, peeled
Capers
Gaeta olives, pitted
Salt
Pepper

Skin and bone the cod and cut into squares of about 4 fingers on each side. Dry these pieces in a towel, flour them, and fry them to a beautiful golden color in boiling oil.

Put a little oil in another pan and fry 2 cloves of garlic until colored, then remove. Add the blanched, peeled, and chopped, tomatoes, the capers, and a handful of olives. Add a pinch of pepper and salt and let the sauce absorb the flavors.

Arrange the cod in a single layer in a large ovenproof dish; pour over the sauce, which must be abundant, cover, and bake in the oven at a moderate heat, so that the sauce can thicken. In less than half an hour the cod will be ready. Put it in the serving dish and send it to the table immediately.

BACCALÀ IN UMIDO ALLA ROMANA

Roman Salt Cod Stew

1 onion
Olive oil
1¼ cup tomato passata
Raisins
2¼ lb soaked salt cod
Pine nuts
Salt
Pepper

Slice an onion and brown it in oil. When the onion is cooked, add the tomato passata, salt lightly, and reduce it down to the right density. Soak the raisins in warm water.

Skin, bone, and cut the salt cod into equal-sized pieces. Add them to the tomato sauce along with plenty of pepper, a handful of pine nuts, and the same amount of soaked raisins. Cook for about half an hour.

BACCALÀ RIPIENO

Stuffed Salt Cod

2¼ lb soaked salt cod in one piece
1 oz dried mushrooms
5½ tbsp butter
1 cup breadcrumbs
Milk
1 egg
9 tbsp grated Parmesan
Olive oil
Salt

Bone the cod carefully so it keeps its shape. Soak the mushrooms and, when revived, cook in a little butter and then cut into dice.

Soak the breadcrumbs in milk, squeeze, and shred into a bowl with a beaten egg, grated Parmesan, and the mushrooms, and mix everything well so it blends together.

Put the piece of cod on the kitchen table, skin-side down. Spread the sauce over with the blade of a knife, and roll the cod up lengthways, taking care that the filling stays inside. Tie it up with string.

Place the cod in an oiled pan, sprinkle with more oil, and place in a preheated oven of moderate heat. Leave to cook for about half an hour, basting it from time to time with the cooking liquid, and, if necessary, with a few spoonfuls of water.

Take the roll from the oven, free it from the string, and arrange the cod in a dish with its sauce.

Stockfish

STOCCAFISSO ALLA ANCONETANA

Stockfish Ancona Style

Olive oil
1 onion
1 carrot
Celery
Parsley
1 lb tomatoes
2¼ lb soaked stockfish
Milk
Salt
Pepper
Optional: anchovy, butter, potatoes, polenta

Stockfish is dried, unsalted fish. Usually cod. If you do not buy your stockfish already soaked, but dry, it needs to be soaked as for salt cod. Never use lukewarm water, but fresh, changing it 2 or 3 times per day for 3 or 4 days, depending on the quality and weight of the fish. Better to start the bath a few days earlier because if it is not soaked properly it will not cook well.

Put the oil in a saucepan with plenty of chopped onion. Brown the onion, then add carrot, celery, and parsley, all very finely chopped; add salt and pepper. Some also add some crushed anchovies. Sauté the vegetables and add the tomatoes. Let them cook, but not too much, and set the sauce aside.

Clean and bone the stockfish, leaving the skin on it, and cut it into big pieces. Cover the bottom of a pan with a sheet of parchment paper. On it make alternating layers of fish and sauce; pour plenty of oil over everything until it almost submerges the stockfish; then add 2 fingers of milk to cover everything well.

Let it cook very slowly for an hour and a half or 2 hours, shaking the pan from time to time but never stirring, and adjusting for salt. The milk absorbed during cooking gives it a more brilliant color and makes the fish softer. If you want you can add a little butter halfway through cooking.

You can add some potatoes, peeled and cut into pieces, so that they cook with the fish, but add them at the right time.

ADA SAYS: *This recipe is also excellent accompanied by slices of polenta.*

STOCCAFISSO ALLA MESSINESE

Stockfish Messina Style

2¼ lb soaked stockfish
1 onion
Olive oil
1 lb tomatoes
Pine nuts
Raisins
Capers
Gaeta olives, pitted
Potatoes
White wine
Salt
Pepper

Scrape and bone the fish and leave the skin on. Cut into big pieces. Fry an onion in a pan with plenty of oil, add the chopped tomatoes, cook a little, and then add the stockfish, a handful of pine nuts and the same of raisins, two tablespoons capers, a handful of olives, a few potatoes cut into large slices, a little salt, plenty of pepper, and a glass of
white wine.

Cover the pan and let it cook for about an hour and a half to 2 hours in a preheated oven at a low heat.

STOCCAFISSO ALLA VICENTINA

Stockfish Venetian Style

2¼ lb soaked stockfish
All-purpose flour
Cinnamon, ground
Grated Parmesan
Olive oil
1 onion
Garlic
4 anchovies
Parsley
White wine
3 cups milk
3½ tbsp butter
Salt
Pepper
Optional: polenta slices

Scrape and bone the stockfish, leaving the skin on, and cut it into big pieces. Take a sheet pan where the pieces can line up in a single layer and, without greasing it, arrange the lightly floured pieces of fish, seasoned with salt, pepper, and a little ground cinnamon, and sprinkled generously with grated Parmesan.

Pour a glass of oil into a pan and sauté a little diced onion and a clove of ground garlic. When the onion is lightly browned, add the anchovies—washed, boned, and cut into small pieces—and use a wooden spoon to work them into the onions. Then add the chopped parsley and immediately afterward a glass of white wine. Let the wine reduce almost completely and add enough milk to cover the pieces of stockfish. Complete the sauce with the butter.

Pour this sauce into the pan with the stockfish, cover, and put it in a preheated oven of moderate heat until all the liquid has dried—about an hour and a half, maybe 2 hours.

ADA SAYS: *This is generally served with slices of polenta.*

STOCCAFISSO IN POTACCHIO

Braised Stockfish with Tomato

2¼ lb soaked stockfish
Garlic
Rosemary
Olive oil
9 oz canned peeled tomatoes
White wine
Butter
Salt
Pepper

Scrape and bone the stockfish, leaving the skin on, and cut it into big pieces.

Fry the chopped garlic and rosemary in plenty of oil, then add the tomatoes in pieces, a little white wine, salt, and pepper.

Cover the bottom of a pan with a sheet of parchment paper, lay in the pieces of fish, and cover with the sauce. Place the pan over the heat and cook slowly until half-cooked, which will take about an hour. Add a little butter to the pan and put it in a preheated oven at a moderate heat for another hour.

When the stockfish is cooked, arrange it on a serving plate, sprinkle it with the sauce left in the pan, and send it to the table immediately.

Mullet

CEFALETTI IN GRATELLA

Grilled Baby Gray Mullets with Parsley Sauce

3 lb 5 oz baby gray mullets
Olive oil
Parsley
Oregano
Garlic
Chili
Vinegar
Salt
Peppercorns

Clean some medium-sized gray mullets without scaling them, rinse, dry, and put them in a marinade of oil, parsley, peppercorns, and oregano. Leave them for an hour or two in a cool place.

Heat up a hot grill and roast them, basting occasionally with the marinade.

Put half a clove of garlic in a pestle and mortar or a blender, add a good handful of parsley leaves, a strong pinch of oregano, and a chili. Add a few spoons of oil and a little vinegar, salt lightly, and blend for a few minutes.

When the fish are roasted to the right point, arrange them on the plate and veil them with the parsley sauce.

CEFALETTI IN SALSA

Baked Baby Gray Mullets with Anchovies

3 lb 5 oz baby gray mullets
Lemon
Oregano
Parsley
Garlic
2 anchovy fillets
6 tbsp olive oil
4 tbsp vinegar
Salt
Pepper

Clean the mullets, skin them, rinse, dry, and align in a pan, lightly greased with oil. Sprinkle them with salt, and the juice of a lemon. Put them in a preheated, moderate oven to cook.

Chop the oregano, parsley, garlic, pepper, and washed anchovies. Reduce everything to a pulp, then dilute with the oil and vinegar.

When the mullets are cooked, remove them from the oven, arrange them on a plate, pour the sauce over, and send them to the table.

CEFALO AL FORNO

Gray Mullet Baked with Lemon

3 lb 5 oz gray mullet
2 lemons
Olive oil
Parsley
Salt

Clean the mullet, scale it, take out the entrails, wash, and dry.

Line up the slices of lemon to cover the bottom of a pan and lay the fish down on top. Sprinkle with salt, pour in the oil, and chopped parsley. Bake in a moderate preheated oven for about half an hour.

Remove the fish from the oven, arrange it on a serving plate, remove the lemon slices, and pour the cooking liquid over the fish.

CEFALO CON AROMI

Baked Gray Mullet with Herbs

3 lb 5 oz gray mullet
Parsley
Bay leaves
Olive oil
All-purpose flour
Lemon
Salt
Peppercorns

After cleaning the mullet, scale it, wash it, dry it, and cover it with the herbs—parsley, a few bay leaves, peppercorns—and lightly oil everything. No garlic, lemon, or salt at this stage.

After 2 hours, lift out the fish, sprinkle with salt, add a grind of pepper, and a sprinkling of flour. In a large pan, big enough to fit the whole fish, pour enough oil to cover the entire bottom. Put the pan on the stove and, when the oil is hot, add the fish; after a few seconds, turn it over to the other side, keeping it on the heat for a few more minutes, then put the pan in a moderately hot oven.

Occasionally tilt the pan, collect the oil with a spoon, and baste the fish. After about half an hour the mullet will be cooked.

Remove from the oven, arrange it on a serving dish, pour over the little liquid left in the pan, surround it with lemon wheels, and send it to the table immediately.

CEFALO LESSO CON SALSA AROMATICA

Gray Mullet with Anchovy Sauce

3 lb 5 oz gray mullet
Vinegar
Parsley
Salt

Anchovy sauce:
½ cup breadcrumbs, vinegar, 2 salted anchovies, 1 hard-boiled egg yolk, capers, 6 pitted green olives, parsley, olive oil, lemon, pepper

Carefully clean the mullet, skin it, rinse it, put it in a fish kettle, and cover with cold water. Season the water with salt, a tablespoon of vinegar, a few stalks of parsley, and slowly simmer, always keeping the heat low and the lid on the kettle. In about half an hour the fish will be cooked.

Now prepare the anchovy sauce: Soak the breadcrumbs in a little vinegar, squeeze and chop the mix together with the anchovy pieces washed if salted, the hard-boiled egg yolk, capers, olives, parsley, and a pinch of pepper. Chop everything thoroughly, then dilute with half a glass of oil and the juice of a lemon.

Lift the mullet from the water, drain it well, and arrange it on a serving dish. Separately, serve the anchovy sauce in a gravy boat.

Grouper

CERNIA ALLA GRIGLIA

Grilled Grouper

3 lb 5 oz grouper
4 tbsp olive oil
4 tbsp breadcrumbs
Parsley
1¾ oz black olives, pitted
Garlic
Lemon
Salt
Black peppercorns

Prepare the charcoal for a barbecue, or warm the grill, to have it ready and flameless when the fish is prepared.

Gut the fish, wash it, without removing the scales, and dry it.

Prepare the stuffing: put 4 tablespoons of oil in a bowl, 4 spoons of water, and the same of breadcrumbs, a little parsley, olives, a chopped clove of garlic, some black peppercorns, and a pinch of salt. Mix thoroughly.

Stuff the belly of the fish with this mix. To facilitate the cooking of bigger fish on both sides, it is advisable to use a double-sided fish holder for grilling. The fish cooks perfectly in this way, as you can turn it from time to time without risking ruining it by breaking the skin. You can also cut oblique incisions to help the cooking of bigger fish.

In a bowl to the side put 2 tablespoons of oil and 2 of water to dampen the taste of cooked oil, seasoned with salt and lightly blended, to baste the fish from time to time.

Place the fish on the grill, and over the coals. Baste from time to time when you judge the moment to turn it over. Keep basting.

Take off the grill, put it on a serving dish, surround it with lemon wedges and parsley; serve immediately.

CERNIA IN TRANCE BRASATA

Grouper Fillets with Tomato

6 grouper fillets (5¼ oz each) fresh or frozen
All-purpose flour
1 onion
1 carrot
7 tbsp butter
White wine
1 lb canned tomatoes
Parsley
Salt
Pepper

Clean, wash, and dry the fillets, then salt, pepper, and flour them. Cut the onion and carrot into thin slices. Butter an baking dish and first put a layer of onion and carrot and then, well-aligned in a single layer, the fillets of fish. Put a small piece of butter on each, then splash with half a glass of wine. Cover with a well-buttered sheet of parchment paper and put in a warm, moderately heated oven.

Halfway through cooking, when the wine is almost completely absorbed, remove the parchment paper and add the tomatoes. Cover the pan, put it back in the oven, and cook for about half an hour in all, always at moderate heat.

When cooked, remove the fillets from the pan, line them up on a plate, add a little butter to the tomatoes in the pan, and pour them over the fish, and garnish with chopped parsley.

CERNIA IN TRANCE IN GRATELLA

Grilled Grouper Fillets with Mustard

6 grouper fillets (5¼ oz each), fresh or frozen
Olive oil
1½ tbsp butter
Mustard
Vinegar
Salt
Pepper

Clean, wash, and dry the fillets; make transverse incisions in which you can put a little oil, salt, and pepper. Oil the wire rack, heat it, line up the slices, and cook over a moderate heat for about a quarter of an hour.

Meanwhile, prepare the sauce: Melt the butter, add a teaspoon of mustard, salt and pepper diluted with a teaspoon of vinegar. Once the fillets are cooked, remove them from the grill, line them up on a serving dish, pour the sauce over, and serve hot.

Monkfish

CODA DI ROSPO AL BURRO E PREZZEMOLO

Monkfish with Parsley Butter

6 monkfish steaks (5¼ oz each)
All-purpose flour
2 eggs
Olive oil
5 tbsp butter
Lemon
For garnish: parsley, 2 hard-boiled eggs, salt

Remove the skin from the monkfish steaks, rinse, dry, and lightly dust in flour. Beat the eggs and dip the fish in them.

Pour the oil into a pan and add butter. As soon as the fat is hot, fry the steaks for 6 to 7 minutes, browning them on both sides.

When cooked, arrange the slices in a hot serving dish, add salt, and sprinkle with the juice of a lemon. Fry a little parsley in the remaining butter and pour everything on to the monkfish. Decorate with olives, slices of hard-boiled egg, and fresh parsley leaves.

CODA DI ROSPO IN UMIDO

Braised Monkfish

2¼ lb monkfish
1 oz dried mushrooms
1 onion
4 anchovy fillets
Olive oil
All-purpose flour
White wine
Parsley
Basil
1 lb canned tomatoes
Bay leaf
Oregano
Salt
Pepper

After cutting off the monkfish head, peel the skin off the tail completely, wash and dry the monkfish. Carefully wash the mushrooms and let them soak in cold water for at least a quarter of an hour.

Finely chop the onion and anchovy fillets, sauté in oil for a few minutes, using a wooden spoon to crush the anchovy into the onion.

Flour the monkfish, put it in the pan, and continue browning over a medium heat, basting it a little at a time with white wine.

Wash the parsley and basil, chop them, add them to the fish, add the tomatoes, a bay leaf, the well-drained mushrooms, a pinch of oregano, salt, and pepper. Cover the pan and let it cook over a very moderate heat for about 20 minutes. Serve immediately.

ADA SAYS: *Monkfish are usually sold by the tail, if your fishmonger has not done this, then you remove the head and take the skin off the tail.*

Red Snapper

DENTICE AL FORNO

Baked Red Snapper

3 lb 5 oz whole red snapper
Olive oil
Parsley
Bay leaves
Bread
3 lemons
Salt
Peppercorns
Tomato

Clean the snapper, peel, gut, wash, and dry it. Make 2 or 3 oblique incisions along the back so the heat can penetrate inside. Place it on a plate, marinate with oil, parsley, bay leaves, and peppercorns.

After 2 hours, lift out the fish, wipe off the aromatics, sprinkle with salt, add a pinch of pepper, and fill the belly with a handful of bread soaked in a little water and oil, seasoned with salt and pepper and chopped parsley.

Line the bottom of a pan big enough to take the whole fish with slices of lemon and lay the snapper on top.

Splash with oil, sprinkle with chopped parsley, and put it in a hot oven. Cook at a moderate heat for about 30 minutes. At intervals, baste with the cooking liquid. Turn off the oven and let the snapper stew for a few more minutes. Then remove it from the oven, arrange it on the plate, and decorate with tomato and bay leaves. Pour the cooking liquid over the fish and bring to the table.

DENTICE IN TRANCE AL FORNO

Baked Red Snapper Fillets

6 red snapper fillets (5¼ oz each)
2¼ lb potatoes
Olive oil
Spring onion
Garlic
Parsley
6 anchovy fillets
Salt
Pepper

Remove the skin and any bones from the snapper fillets, rinse, and dry them. Peel the potatoes and cut them into thin slices. Grease an oven pan with oil and place a layer of thinly cut potato slices on the bottom, season with salt and pepper, and spread a light layer of chopped fresh spring onion, a few pieces of garlic, and parsley.

On this bed, arrange the snapper fillets, seasoned with salt and pepper and some anchovy fillets. Cover the fish with more slices of potato, sprinkle with salt, season with oil, and place the pan in a warm oven at a moderate heat. After about half an hour the fish and potatoes will be cooked. You can make sure by inserting a small knife into a slice of fish and into one potato slice. Place the pan on a plate and serve without decanting.

DENTICE IN TRANCE AL FORNO CON CIPOLLINE

Baked Red Snapper Fillets with Cipollini Onions

6 red snapper fillets (5¼ oz each)
Lemon
Breadcrumbs
1 lb cipollini onions or shallots
9 oz ripe tomatoes
Olive oil
1 lb 5 oz new potatoes
White wine
Garlic
Saffron
Parsley
Salt
Pepper

Remove the skin and any bones from the snapper fillets, rinse, dry, sprinkle lightly with salt, lemon juice, and coat in breadcrumbs.

Meanwhile, slice and blanch the onions for 10 minutes in lightly boiling water. Cut the tomatoes into small pieces.

Place half a glass of oil in a saucepan and, when it is hot, color the fish fillets on both sides, then remove them and arrange them in a baking dish. In the oil left in the saucepan, sauté diced potatoes and onions for 15 minutes, add half a glass of white wine, and let it reduce by half. Then add the tomatoes, a little salt and pepper, and cook over a moderate heat for about 20 minutes.

In a bowl, crush the garlic, add half a sachet of saffron, the parsley, 4 tablespoons of oil, and 4 tablespoons of boiling water, and mix well to obtain a creamy sauce that you can spread over the fish.

Put the snapper steaks in with the cooked onions and potatoes, and bake in a warm oven for 10 minutes.

DENTICE IN TRANCE ALLA PIZZAIOLA

Red Snapper Pizzaiola

6 red snapper fillets (5¼ oz each)
Olive oil
Parsley
Bay leaf
All-purpose flour
Garlic
1 lb canned tomatoes
2 anchovies
Oregano
Salt
Peppercorns
Optional: boiled rice, butter

Remove the skin and any bones from the snapper fillets; rinse, dry, and place them on a plate. Sprinkle with oil and cover with the aromatic herbs—parsley, bay leaf, and peppercorns. After 2 hours, take the fillets out, salt, and flour them.

Cover the bottom of a pan with oil, heat it up, and lay in the fish fillets. Turn them over as soon as they have warmed up a little and continue cooking over high heat by browning them on both sides. After about a quarter of an hour the fillets will be at their right cooking point. Immediately remove them from the pan and place them on a serving dish, keeping them warm.

In the pan, add a little more oil and a whole clove of garlic. As soon as this has heated up, remove the garlic and pour in the tomatoes; season with salt and pepper and add the anchovies, washed and carefully boned, and cook on a lively heat.

When the sauce is somewhat reduced, pour over the fish slices, and sprinkle a little chopped parsley and a pinch of oregano. Garnish with a few spoons of boiled rice flavored with butter.

Whitebait

LATTERINI FRITTI

Deep-Fried Whitebait

2¼ lb whitebait or other small fish
All-purpose flour
Oil for frying
Lemon wedges
Salt

Rinse the little fish, dry them well, sprinkle them with salt, and flour them. Put them in a sieve to shake off any excess flour and fry a few at a time over a high heat for a few minutes, until they have a beautiful golden color and are crunchy. Lift out with a slotted spoon and drain on absorbent paper.

Serve very hot with wedges of lemon.

LATTERINI MARINATI

Marinated Whitebait

2¼ lb whitebait or other small fish
All-purpose flour
Oil for frying
To serve: capers, cornichons

Marinade:
2 cups white vinegar, white wine, onion, 2 cloves garlic, 2 carrots, parsley, bay, basil, marjoram, sage, salt, peppercorns

Firstly make a marinade: In a small pan warm the vinegar, a glass of white wine, half an onion, garlic, and carrots—all finely chopped, a few stalks of parsley, a bay leaf, a few leaves of basil, marjoram, sage, a few grains of pepper, a good pinch of salt, and half a glass of oil. Boil for approximately a quarter of an hour, then pour the marinade over the fish. Cover and leave to rest for at least 24 hours. If the vinegar is too strong, you can dilute it with wine, but never with water.

Rinse the fish, dry them well, sprinkle them with salt and flour. Place them in a sieve and shake off the excess flour, then throw into a pan with very hot oil a few at a time. Lift out with a slotted spoon and drain on absorbent paper. When they are cold, arrange in a bowl.

To serve, sieve the marinade to remove the herbs and replace them with some capers, cornichons cut into slices or other pickles, chopped parsley, and a few spoonfuls of oil.

ADA SAYS: *To serve as a separate course, arrange the fish on a plate and garnish with a potato salad, hard-boiled egg wedges, and lemon slices.*

Mackerel

MACCARELLO IN FILETTI ALLA MARINARA

Mackerel Fillets with Anchovy and Capers

3 mackerel fillets
Olive oil
6 anchovies
Capers
Breadcrumbs
3½ oz Gaeta olives, pitted
White wine
Salt
Pepper

Clean the mackerel with great care, remove their heads, and, with a sharp knife, flush out the backbone, and divide into fillets.

Pour plenty of oil into an oval oven pan, arrange the fillets in a single layer, and season with salt and pepper. Fillet the anchovies and divide into 2 pieces. Arrange 4 anchovy fillets on each mackerel as a large grid, together with some capers, covering everything with the breadcrumbs. Garnish with the olives, pour a good splash of white wine into the pan, add a little more oil to everything, and put in a moderately hot oven for about 20 minutes.

Cod

MERLUZZO AL FORNO

Baked Cod with Lemon

3 lb 5 oz cod
2 lemons
Olive oil
Parsley
Salt

Carefully clean the cod, gut and trim with scissors, wash, and dry it.

Line up enough slices of lemon to cover the bottom of the pan and to top the fish. Sprinkle with salt, add 5 tablespoons of oil, throw on the parsley, and put it in a preheated oven, cooking at a moderate heat for a good half an hour.

Remove the fish from the oven, arrange it on a serving dish, remove the lemon slices, and pour the cooking liquid over the cod.

MERLUZZO AL PIATTO

Cod Baked with Mushrooms

3 small cod (1 lb each)
1 onion
Olive oil
7 oz mushrooms
2 tbsp breadcrumbs
Grated Parmesan
White wine
Parsley
Lemon
Salt

Put the cod on the table with the belly in the air and make a small knife cut from head to tail, gradually widening. First, remove the entrails, then the bone, and finally the gills. In this way the cod remains whole, but open. At this point rinse, dry, and snip off all the fins with scissors.

Take an oval baking dish big enough for the fish, chop an onion, and cover the bottom of the dish with oil. Chop the mushrooms thinly and lay over the onions. Lay the cod on top. Season with a little salt and sprinkle with breadcrumbs mixed with grated Parmesan. Pour 2 fingers of white wine into the dish, so that it just covers the bottom. Add half a glass of oil and put the dish in a hot oven for 12 to 15 minutes, until the breadcrumbs are lightly browned.

Plate and serve with chopped parsley and a squeeze of lemon.

MERLUZZO IN FILETTI AL BURRO D'ACCIUGHE

Cod Steaks with Anchovy Butter

3½ oz anchovies
7 tbsp butter
Olive oil
Vinegar
6 cod fillets (9 oz each)
All-purpose flour
1 egg
Breadcrumbs
Olive oil
Parsley

To make the anchovy sauce: Put the washed, boned, and chopped anchovies in a pan with the butter, oil, and 1 tbsp of vinegar. Stir with a wooden spoon and cook in a bain-marie until the anchovies are completely melted and the sauce creamy.

Wash the cod fillets, flour them, coat them in beaten egg and breadcrumbs, and fry them until golden. Arrange them on a plate and keep them warm.

Pour the sauce over the cod fillets and garnish with some chopped parsley.

MERLUZZO IN FILETTI ALLA MAÎTRE D'HÔTEL

Cod Fillets Maître D'hôtel

6 cod fillets (9 oz each)
All-purpose flour
1 egg
Breadcrumbs
6½ tbsp butter
Parsley
Lemon
Olive oil
Salt

Wash, rinse, and dry the cod fillets, flour them, coat in beaten egg, then in breadcrumbs and put them in a pan with 2 tablespoons of butter and a few spoons of oil, and cook them on both sides, adding a pinch of salt.

Prepare the maître d'hôtel butter: mix 3½ tablespoons of softened butter well with finely chopped parsley and the juice of one lemon.

When the cod fillets are cooked, arrange them on a warm, long plate, and spread 1 tablespoon of butter on top quickly.

MERLUZZO IN FILETTI AL VINO BIANCO

Cod with White Wine

6 cod steaks (9 oz each), including the head and bones for broth
Olive oil
White wine
Salt
Pepper

Fish broth:
Cod heads and bones, 1 carrot, 1 onion, parsley, celery stalk, salt

Prepare some fish broth using the fish heads, the bones, very little water, a pinch of salt, carrot, onion, parsley, and a rib of celery. Simmer everything for 15 minutes and set aside.

A few minutes before lunch, roll up each steak lengthways so that the skin remains outside, and place the fillets so folded in a well-oiled pan. Season with salt, a little pepper, and sprinkle with a few spoons of white wine and a couple of spoonfuls of the fish broth. Cover and bring to a low simmer, so that the boil is barely noticeable. After three or four minutes, uncover the pan and, using a spoon, baste the fillets with the cooking liquid.

Cook for another three or four minutes, then arrange them on a plate, reduce the remaining liquid over a high heat, mix well, and pour on each steak.

MERLUZZO IN FILETTI GRATINATI

Cod Gratin

3 cod steaks (1 lb each)
Olive oil
6 anchovies
Parsley
Breadcrumbs
Lemon
Salt
Pepper

Lay the cod steaks skin-side down in a well-oiled ovenproof pan. Season with a pinch of salt.

Wash and bone the anchovies and put them in the blender or use a pestle and mortar to crush down well. Add a good pinch of pepper, chopped parsley, and blend everything with 4 tablespoons of oil. Spread this mix on the cod steaks, sprinkle them with breadcrumbs, a little more oil, and put the pan in the oven at a moderate heat for about 20 minutes, until the breadcrumbs have a beautiful dark gold color. Squeeze some lemon juice over the fish and bring to the table without decanting.

Hake

NASELLO RIPIENO

Stuffed Hake

3½ oz tinned tuna in olive oil
2 eggs
Parsley
2 anchovies
Lemon
2½ lb whole hake
Olive oil
White wine
Salt
Optional: mayonnaise

Finely chop the tuna, the hard-boiled eggs, parsley, and the anchovies, which should be rinsed, boned, and diluted with a few drops of lemon.

Clean and wash the hake, and, without deforming it, or removing the head or tail, take out the central bone. Fill the fish with the prepared mixture and sew the opening with needle and thread.

Put the hake in a pan, baste with a little oil, sprinkle with salt, and place in a preheated oven of moderate heat for about 20 minutes.

During cooking, baste the fish with spoonfuls of water and white wine.

ADA SAYS: *You can enjoy hake both hot and cold. If cold, accompany with mayonnaise.*

Croaker

OMBRINA AROMATIZZATA AL FORNO

Oven-Baked Croaker

3 lb 5 oz croaker
Parsley
Bay
Olive oil
All-purpose flour
Lemon
Salt
Pepper

Wash, dry, and place the croaker for a couple of hours in a bed of herbs—parsley, a few bay leaves, grains of pepper—and sprinkle lightly with oil.

After 2 hours, take the fish out and sprinkle with salt, pepper, and flour. Cover the bottom of a large pan with oil, warm on the stove, then, when the oil is hot, add the fish, and after a few minutes turn it over, keeping it on the heat for a few more minutes. Then put the pan in a preheated oven at a moderate heat.

Occasionally tilt the container, collect the oil in a spoon, and baste. After about 20 minutes remove from the oven, arrange it on the plate, pour what's left of the juices from the pan over the croaker, and surround it with lemon wheels.

OMBRINA IN TRANCE AL FORNO

Croaker Baked with Potatoes

6 croaker steaks (5¼ oz each)
2¼ lb potatoes
Olive oil
1 onion
Garlic
Parsley
Anchovies
Salt
Pepper

Take the skin off the croaker steaks and remove any bones, rinse, and dry. Peel the potatoes and cut them into very thin slices.

Oil an oven pan with half a glass of oil and place a layer of potato slices on the bottom, season with salt and pepper, and add a layer of sliced fresh onion, a few pieces of garlic, and chopped parsley. On this bed, arrange the slices of croaker, season with salt, pepper, and some anchovy fillets. Cover the fish with more potato slices, sprinkle with salt, season with oil, and place the pan in a preheated oven at moderate heat. After about half an hour the croaker and the potatoes will be cooked. Place the pan on a plate and have it brought to the table immediately without decanting.

OMBRINA IN TRANCE ALLA PIZZAIOLA

Croaker Pizzaiola

2¼ lb croaker steaks
Olive oil
Parsley
Bay leaf
All-purpose flour
Garlic
1 lb tomatoes
2 anchovies
Oregano
Salt
Pepper

Remove the skin and bones from the croaker steaks, rinse them, dry them, and put them on a plate, sprinkling them with oil and covering them with a mix of parsley, bay leaf, and peppercorns.

After 2 hours, take out the steaks and salt and flour them.

Cover the bottom of a pan with oil, heat it up, and line up the steaks. Turn them over as soon as they have felt a bit of heat and continue cooking over high heat, browning them on one side and then on the other. After about a quarter of an hour the steaks will be at their right point of cooking. Remove them from the pan and set aside to keep warm.

Put a little more oil and garlic in the pan, and, as soon as this is heated, remove the garlic and add the washed and chopped tomatoes, without their juice and seeds. Season with salt and pepper, add the washed and boned anchovies, and cook over a high heat. When the sauce is reduced, finish with a pinch of oregano and chopped parsley, and pour it over the croaker steaks.

Sea Bream

ORATA AL FORNO

Baked Sea Bream

3 lb 5 oz sea bream
2 lemons
Olive oil
Parsley
Salt

Clean the sea bream, scale, gut, wash, and dry it. Fill the bottom of a pan with lemon slices and lay more on top of the fish. Sprinkle with salt, oil, and chopped parsley, and put it in a preheated oven at a moderate heat for a good half an hour. Make sure that the cooking reaches the right point.

When cooked, the sea bream will be impregnated with a good aroma and the lemon slices will prevent the skin from sticking to the bottom of the pan. Remove the fish from the oven, arrange it on a serving dish, and pour the liquid left in the pan over the fish.

ORATA AL SALE

Sea Bream in a Salt Crust

3 lb 5 oz sea bream
4½ lb salt
Parsley
Lemon

Clean the sea bream, without scaling it, wash it thoroughly, and dry it. Sprinkle the bottom of a baking sheet big enough for the whole fish with salt; place the sea bream on top and cover it with more salt to enclose it completely.

Put the pan in a preheated oven at a high heat for about 45 minutes—calculate about 15 minutes for each 1 pound. As soon as the sea bream is cooked, remove it from the oven, free it from the salt, place it in a serving dish, garnish with parsley and lemon wedges.

ORATA BERCY

Sea Bream Bercy

3 lb 5 oz sea bream
Olive oil
Parsley
White wine
Potato starch
2 tbsp butter
Salt

After cleaning the sea bream, make 3 or 4 oblique cuts in the fattest part, parallel to each other, which will ensure better cooking. Generously oil a baking dish, big enough for the whole fish, and scatter some chopped parsley in the bottom. Lay in the fish, wet it with a glass of white wine and a little oil, and cover with oiled parchment paper.

Put it in a preheated oven at a moderate heat for half an hour. Supervise very closely to be careful that the cooking reaches the right point. During cooking, baste the fish regularly with its cooking juices.

When the fish is cooked, gently lift it up and arrange it on a serving dish. Sieve the cooking liquid through a colander and collect it in a pan. Put the pan on the stove and let it boil to reduce a little, then thicken it with a spoon of potato starch dissolved in a little cold water. Reduce the heat to the minimum, and, a piece at a time, add the butter, stirring constantly. Cover the fish with this sauce and bring to the table.

Shark

PALOMBO ALLA PIZZAIOLA

Shark Pizzaiola

6 shark steaks (5¼ oz each)
Olive oil
Parsley
Basil
Bay leaf
3 tbsp all-purpose flour
2 cloves garlic
1 lb tomatoes
2 anchovy fillets
Oregano
Salt
Peppercorns

Remove the skin and any bones from the steaks, rinse and dry them thoroughly, and place them in a bowl with 4 tablespoons of oil, chopped parsley, basil, bay leaf, and a few peppercorns. Leave to marinate for about 2 hours, turning them from time to time.

Lift out the steaks, and salt and flour them. In a pan big enough to take all the slices in one layer, put enough oil to cover the bottom, then add 2 cloves of garlic. As soon as the garlic browns, remove it and put the shark fillets in instead. Brown them on a high heat on one side and then on the other for about 10 minutes. Take them out and keep warm.

Now add the tomatoes, without skin and seeds, to the pan; season with salt and pepper, add the anchovy fillets, and let the sauce cook on a high heat until it is reduced; then pour over the steaks and sprinkle with oregano and chopped parsley.

PALOMBO IN TRANCE AL FORNO

Baked Shark Steaks

6 shark steaks (5¼ oz each)
2¼ lb potatoes
Olive oil
10½ oz spring onions
Garlic
Parsley
4 anchovy fillets
Salt
Pepper

Remove the skin and bones from the steaks, rinse, and dry thoroughly.

Peel the potatoes and cut them into thin slices. In a baking dish pour enough oil to cover the bottom; make a layer of potato slices, put a light layer of sliced spring onions on top, then a chopped clove of garlic, parsley, and pieces of anchovy fillets. Lay the steaks on this bed, season with salt and pepper and a few spoons of oil. Cover with the remaining potato slices, pour over a little more oil, and sprinkle with salt.

Place the tray in a preheated oven and cook over moderate heat for about half an hour. You can check if the cooking is done by slipping the tip of a small knife into a slice of fish and a slice of potato. Place the pan on a plate and bring to the table without decanting.

PALOMBO IN TRANCE AL VINO BIANCO

Shark in White Wine

6 shark steaks (5¼ oz each)
All-purpose flour
Olive oil
Spring onion
2 anchovies, fresh
Parsley
White wine
Broth
Salt

Take off any skin and bones from the steaks. Rinse and dry them. Lightly flour them and let them brown in a pan with a little oil for about a quarter of an hour; salt them lightly.

In a separate pan, lightly fry some finely chopped spring onions, the washed and boned anchovies, and chopped parsley in a little oil. Add a glass of wine and let it reduce almost completely, then top up with a little broth or water. Pour this sauce over the steaks and simmer lightly for a few minutes.

PALOMBO IN TRANCE CON PISELLI

Shark with Peas

6 shark steaks (5¼ oz each)
Olive oil
1 onion
Parsley
10½ oz shelled peas
1 cup tomato passata
Salt
Pepper

Take off any skin and bones on the steaks, wash, and dry them. Put a little oil in a pan, a little finely chopped onion, and chopped parsley. When the onion is golden add the shelled peas, tomato passata, and a pinch of salt.

When these are cooked, add the steaks, seasoned with salt and plenty of pepper, and simmer, very slowly, for about a quarter of an hour.

Arrange the steaks on a serving dish and pour the peas over them with the thick and tasty sauce.

PALOMBO IN TRANCE GRATINATO

Shark Gratin

6 shark steaks (5¼ oz each)
Breadcrumbs
Olive oil
Oregano
Lemon
Parsley
Salt
Pepper

Remove skin and bone from the steaks. Dip them in the finest breadcrumbs and arrange them in a single layer in a large pan in which you have poured 4 tablespoons of oil. Season with salt, pepper, and oregano, and sprinkle with a little more oil. Put the pan in a preheated oven of moderate heat for about 20 minutes.

Then place the steaks on a plate, squeeze over the juice of a lemon, and garnish with a few spoonfuls of chopped parsley. Can be served hot or cold.

John Dory

PESCE SAN PIETRO IN FILETTI AL BURRO

John Dory Fillets in Butter

All-purpose flour
6 John Dory fillets (8 oz each)
Butter
Lemon
Salt

If you have trouble finding John Dory, try substituting with red snapper, grouper or sea bass fillets.

Lightly flour the fillets, line them up in a pan, where you have melted a little butter. Cook the fillets over moderate heat on both sides, adding more butter if necessary. Arrange them on a serving dish, pour over the cooking butter, and finish with the juice of a lemon and a pinch of salt. Serve very hot.

PESCE SAN PIETRO IN FILETTI FRITTI

Deep-Fried John Dory Fillets

6 John Dory fillets (8 oz each)
All-purpose flour
1 egg
Oil for frying
Optional: breadcrumbs

Lightly flour the fillets, coat them in the beaten egg, and deep-fry them in plenty of hot oil. If you want, you can also flour them and coat them in breadcrumbs, then fry them in oil.

ADA SAYS: *You can accompany these fillets with a warm sauce, such as a Hollandaise or a fish broth with a little cream.*

PESCE SAN PIETRO IN BUDINO

John Dory Flan

2¼ lb cooked John Dory
1 cup breadcrumbs
Milk
7 tbsp butter
1 egg
Parsley
Olive oil or all-purpose flour
7 oz tomato passata
Salt
Pepper
Nutmeg

Chop the cooked fish and add the breadcrumbs, soaked in half a glass of milk and squeezed dry, and half the butter. Mix these elements well, then complete the mixture with an egg, salt, pepper, a grating of nutmeg, and chopped parsley.

Oil or butter and flour a cake mold with a hole in the middle. Place the fish mixture inside and place the mold in a bain-marie. Cook slowly for about half an hour, making sure that the water never boils. When the mixture has set, keep it warm until ready to serve.

Then turn it out and accompany with a tomato passata cooked with a tablespoon of butter, add salt, and place in a gravy boat.

ADA SAYS: *The bones of John Dory are useful for making broth for a fish soup or to thicken the sauce to accompany the fillet.*

PESCE SAN PIETRO CON CARCIOFI

John Dory with Artichokes and Potatoes

6 John Dory fillets (8 oz each)
Olive oil
Milk
All-purpose flour
1 egg
Oil for frying
3 artichoke hearts
3 potatoes
3 tbsp butter
Parsley
Salt

With a small knife, neaten the fillets, especially those of the belly. Wash, rinse and dry them. Put them in a half a glass of oil and a glass of milk mixed together, and leave for a couple of hours. Then, dry the fillets, flour them, coat them in beaten egg, and fry them in plenty of hot oil until they are golden. Season with a pinch of salt.

Cut the artichoke hearts into wedges. Coat them in flour and fry in lots of very hot oil. Peel the potatoes, cut them into small cubes, and cook them in a pan with 2 tablespoons of butter.

When serving, combine the fillets of fish, artichokes, and potatoes, add a tablespoon of butter, and cook on a high heat for a few minutes. Finish with parsley.

Swordfish

PESCE SPADA AL FORNO

Baked Swordfish

6 swordfish steaks (5¼ oz each)
2¼ lb potatoes
Olive oil
1 onion
Garlic
Parsley
3 anchovies
Salt
Pepper

Remove any skin and bones from the swordfish steaks, rinse and dry them. Peel the potatoes and cut them into very thin slices. Grease an oven pan with oil and place a layer of potatoes on the bottom, season with salt and pepper. Top with slices of onion, garlic, and some chopped parsley. Arrange the steaks on this bed, season with salt and pepper and some anchovy fillets. Cover the fish with more potato slices, sprinkle them with salt, season with oil, and place the pan in a warm oven at a moderate heat.

After about half an hour the fish and potatoes will be cooked. You can make sure they are cooked by pushing the tip of a small knife into a slice of fish and a slice of potato. Place the pan on a plate and serve without decanting.

PESCE SPADA FRITTO

Fried Swordfish

6 swordfish steaks (5¼ oz each)
Olive oil
Parsley
Lemon
All-purpose flour
1 egg
Oil for frying
Salt
Pepper

Take any skin off the swordfish, rinse, dry, and cut the steaks into regular pieces the size of dominoes. Put the pieces in a bowl, season with oil, salt, pepper, chopped parsley, and a little lemon juice and leave it for an hour or two, to let the fish absorb the flavor in the marinade.

Remove the pieces of fish, dry them slightly, coat them in flour and in a beaten egg, then fry them in plenty of hot oil until they are a beautiful blond color; season with a pinch of salt. Arrange the fish on a plate and garnish with lemon wedges.

PESCE SPADA IN TRANCE AL POMODORO

Swordfish with Tomato

6 swordfish steaks (5¼ oz each)
All-purpose flour
Olive oil
1 onion
Garlic
Celery
Bay leaf
6 tomatoes
White wine
Parsley
Capers
Salt
Pepper

Take off any skin from the swordfish steaks, rinse, dry them, flour them, and cook them in a large pan where you have warmed half a glass of oil. Brown them well on both sides, then remove them from the pan and sprinkle with salt.

Place a little more oil in the pan and the chopped onion, the crushed garlic, the chopped celery and bay leaf, and tomatoes, cut into pieces; season with a pinch of pepper and salt. Cook slowly and when the sauce is well reduced, put back the steaks and soak well in the sauce. Wet them with white wine, sprinkle with a lot of parsley and a spoonful of capers, and cook over moderate heat for about 10 more minutes. Transfer the swordfish steaks into a serving dish and send to the table.

PESCE SPADA CON I FUNGHI

Swordfish with Porcini Mushrooms

6 swordfish steaks (5¼ oz each)
Lemon
Butter
Olive oil
1 onion
1 carrot
2 cloves garlic
Anchovy
Parsley
Bay leaf
White wine
Stock cube
7 oz porcini mushrooms
All-purpose flour
1 egg
Oil for frying
Salt
Pepper

Remove any skin from the swordfish, rinse, dry, and line them up on a plate. Sprinkle them with salt and lemon juice and leave them for at least half an hour.

Put a tablespoon of butter and a finger of oil in a saucepan, add a chopped onion and finely chopped carrot, and cook slowly. When the vegetables are cooked, but not charred, add a well crushed clove of garlic. Heat the garlic without frying it too much and almost immediately after, add a chopped anchovy, a pinch of chopped parsley, and half a bay leaf; pour in half a glass of white wine. Cover and cook slowly until the wine has completely evaporated. Douse with a glass of water in which you will have melted half a stock cube. Cover the saucepan and let it simmer slowly for about 10 minutes.

Peel the porcini mushrooms, cut them into large pieces, rinse them, dry them, and cook them with half a glass of oil, a clove of garlic, and a handful of parsley. Season with a pinch of salt and pepper. When the mushrooms are cooked and have absorbed all the moisture, pour them into the casserole with the aromatics and let them absorb the flavor for a few moments.

Flour the swordfish slices, coat them in a beaten egg, fry them in hot oil, and season with a pinch of salt. Arrange these slices in a baking dish and pour the prepared mushroom sauce over them. Cover the pan and place it in the preheated oven at a moderate heat for a few minutes, then place the pan on a plate and bring to the table without decanting.

Skate

RAZZA BOLLITA AL BURRO NERO

Skate in Brown Butter

2½ lb skate wings
1 onion
Bay leaf
Vinegar
Salt
Peppercorns
Optional: skate liver

Brown butter:
7 tbsp butter, 2 tbsp vinegar, salt

Put the skate wings in a wide pan with water, a sliced onion, half a bay leaf, salt, a grind of pepper, half a glass of vinegar, and the skate's liver if you have it. Bring to a simmer, lower the heat to the minimum, and let the fish finish cooking for about 20 minutes, without boiling it again.

Take the wings out and, using the back of a knife, scrape away the black skin and the white one underneath, which should come away with ease.

Arrange on a serving dish, adding the liver cut into slices if you have it, and prepare the brown butter sauce. Put the butter in a pan, fry it until it turns a hazelnut color, and remove the pan from the heat. Reduce 2 tablespoons of vinegar and a pinch of salt in another pan by half and then pour it into the butter. Mix well and pour on the fish.

RAZZA IN SALSA DI ACCIUGHE

Skate with Anchovy Sauce

2½ lb skate
1 onion
1 carrot
Celery
1 tomato
Olive oil
6 anchovies
7 tbsp butter
Parsley
Salt

Skin the skate, clean it, and cook in water flavored with onion, carrot, celery, and tomato. Season with a pinch of salt and bring slowly to the boil. Simmer the fish for about 20 minutes, then drain, reserving the broth, and place it in a serving dish.

Put some oil in a small saucepan, wash, bone, and chop the anchovies, add the butter, and 2 or 3 spoons of the fish broth. Put the pan in a bain-marie, always stirring, mix everything, then remove the sauce from the heat and pour it hot on to the skate, completing the dish with plenty of chopped parsley.

RAZZA IN UMIDO

Steamed Skate with Tomato

2½ lb skate
Olive oil
1 onion
Garlic
Parsley
9 oz tomatoes
Salt
Pepper

Skin the skate and chop into pieces, dry them well. Put a pan on the heat with a little oil and half a chopped onion; let the onion brown and add a small piece of chopped garlic with a sprig of parsley. Just heat the garlic and add the washed and diced tomatoes, salt, and pepper. When the tomatoes are cooked, add the well-dried fish and let it cook slowly for a quarter of an hour.

Transfer the fish to a serving dish, cover it with the prepared sauce, and top it with a little chopped parsley.

Turbot

ROMBO IN FORNO

Baked Turbot

3 lb 5 oz turbot
Parsley
Bay leaves
Olive oil
All-purpose flour
Cornichons
Lemon
Salt
Pepper

Clean the turbot, wash, dry, and leave for a couple of hours in a marinade with aromatic herbs such as parsley, a few bay leaves, grains of pepper, and oil. Do not use garlic, onion, lemon, or salt.

After 2 hours, take out the fish, sprinkle with salt, add a grind of pepper, and a dusting of flour. In a large pan, big enough to fit the whole turbot, pour enough oil to cover the entire bottom. When the oil is hot, add the fish and after a few minutes, turn it over. Keep it on the heat for a few more minutes, then put the pan in the oven at a moderate heat. Occasionally tilt the pan, collect the oil with a spoon, and baste the fish.

After about 20 minutes remove the turbot from the oven, arrange it on a serving dish, pour over the liquid left in the pan, and surround it with cornichons cut in the shape of a fan, alternating with lemon wheels.

ROMBO IN FILETTI COMPOSTI

Turbot Fish Fingers

5 tbsp all-purpose flour
1 tbsp semolina
2 egg yolks
Milk
14 oz cooked turbot
Grated Parmesan
Butter
1 egg
Breadcrumbs
Oil for frying
Parsley
Lemon
Salt
Pepper
Nutmeg

Put 3 tablespoons of flour, the semolina, and the egg yolks in a pan, with salt, pepper, and nutmeg, and dissolve everything, off the heat, with 2 glasses of milk. When the mix is smooth, put it on the stove and cook it to a very thick cream.

Remove the pan from the heat and add the chopped, cooked turbot and add ¼ cup of grated Parmesan; mix and then pour this mixture on to a kitchen surface greased with butter. Flatten it with the blade of a knife, about a finger thick, and let it cool completely.

Divide the cooked fish into elongated pieces. Take the pieces one at a time, lifting them with the blade of a knife, dip them in the rest of the flour, beaten egg, and breadcrumbs, and fry them in plenty of very hot oil. Then arrange them on a plate, garnish with parsley and some lemon wedges, and have them sent to the table.

Sardines

SARDE AL FINOCCHIO

Sardines Fennel

1 large onion
Olive oil
White wine
6 tomatoes
2¼ lb sardines
Breadcrumbs
Fennel seeds
Salt
Pepper

Cut the onion into thin slices. Dip them for a moment in a pan of boiling water; after a minute or 2 drain them, put them in cold water, and drain again.

Then put the onion to brown in an oven pan with a spoonful of oil, and when it has browned, add half a glass of white wine. Reduce the wine by half and then add the peeled and chopped tomatoes. Cook for about a quarter of an hour.

Open the sardines, take off their heads and remove the bone, without detaching the 2 fillets; rinse and dry them.

When the tomato is cooked add the sardines to the pan, aligning them in a single layer. Season them with salt and pepper and cover them with breadcrumbs, mixed with crushed fennel seeds. Drizzle with oil and then put the pan in a preheated oven of moderate heat until the breadcrumbs take on a beautiful color and the sardines are cooked—about half an hour in all. Put the pan on a serving dish without decanting and send immediately to the table.

SARDE ALLA NAPOLETANA

Neapolitan Pan-Fried Sardines

2¼ lb sardines
Olive oil
Parsley
Oregano
6 tomatoes
Salt
Pepper

Open the sardines, take off their heads and remove the bone, without detaching the 2 fillets; rinse and dry them.

In a pan large enough for all the sardines to fit lined up in a single layer, pour a little oil, so that all the bottom is wet, and add the sardines. Season them with salt and pepper, plenty of chopped parsley, a strong pinch of oregano, and arrange here and there a dozen slices of tomato, from which you have removed the skin and seeds. Drizzle more oil on the sardines and put the pan on quite a high heat.

After about 10 minutes, turn them over very carefully, let them cook for another 10 minutes, then serve them hot.

SARDE FRITTE ALLA LIGURE

Fried Sardines Ligurian Style

1 oz dried mushrooms
Olive oil
1 cup breadcrumbs, plus extra for frying
Milk
4 eggs
Grated Parmesan
Garlic
Marjoram
Oregano
2¼ lb sardines
All-purpose flour
Oil for frying
Salt

Soak the mushrooms in cold water, then finely chop and cook in a little oil, water, and salt.

In a bowl, mix the breadcrumbs, dipped in milk and squeezed dry, 2 eggs, a tablespoon of grated Parmesan, the mushrooms, a very finely chopped clove of garlic, a little marjoram, and a good pinch of oregano. The mix must be quite firm.

Open the sardines, take off the heads and remove the bone, without detaching the 2 fillets; rinse them, dry them, and align them open on the kitchen board, skin-side down. Spread some of the bread-crumb mixture on each sardine and flatten it well with the blade of a knife, then close up the fillets. When you have packed all the sardines, take them one at a time, gently coat them in the flour, beaten eggs, and the extra breadcrumbs, and fry them in plenty of very hot oil.

SARDE IN TORTIERA

Baked Sardines

2¼ lb sardines
Breadcrumbs
Parsley
Olive oil
Garlic
Lemon
Salt
Pepper

Open the sardines, take off their heads and remove the bone, without separating the 2 fillets; rinse and dry them.

Mix plenty of breadcrumbs in a bowl with salt, pepper, chopped parsley, oil, a small piece of crushed garlic, and a little water, to get a dense mix.

Oil a pan and place a layer of sardines on the bottom. Spread a layer of the bread-crumb mix on top, then fish, then more breadcrumbs. Drizzle a little oil on top and bake in a hot oven for about 10 minutes until the breadcrumbs are a nice dark gold color.

Squeeze over the juice of a lemon and send to the table.

SARDE MARINATE

Marinated Sardines

2¼ lb sardines
Olive oil
Parsley
Lemon
1 loaf of bread
6 egg yolks
Vinegar
2 tbsp butter
Nutmeg
Mustard
Salt
Pepper

Clean the sardines, remove the heads, open them, and completely remove the bone without fully dividing them. Rinse carefully and reassemble them as if they were whole.

Line them up in a well-oiled pan, season with salt, pepper, parsley, and a little lemon juice, basting them with a little more oil. Bake in a preheated oven of moderate heat for about a quarter of an hour.

Prepare the toasts. Cut the slices of sandwich bread in two; fry them in oil and keep them warm. As soon as the sardines are cooked, arrange a pair on each toast, placing them in opposite directions.

Break the egg yolks into a pan with a spoon of water and vinegar, butter, a little salt, a good pinch of pepper, a grating of nutmeg, and a teaspoon of mustard. Using a whisk or a wooden spoon, scramble continuously until it is very hot and slightly thickened. Absolutely avoid boiling. Pour a little of this sauce on each toast and let it go straight on the table.

SARDE PICCANTI

Spicy Sardines

2¼ lb sardines
English mustard powder
3½ oz anchovies
Parsley
Oregano
Olive oil
Lemon
All-purpose flour
1 egg
Oil for frying
Pepper

Remove the heads of the sardines, open them on the belly side, and take out the bone, without fully dividing them. Rinse them thoroughly and dry them.

Put a teaspoon of English mustard powder in a bowl with plenty of pepper and the boned and chopped anchovies, chopped parsley, and a good pinch of oregano. Dissolve everything with a few spoons of oil and a little lemon juice.

Arrange the sardines on a large plate and spread the marinade over them. Leave them like this for at least half an hour so they have time to flavor.

A few moments before going to the table, lift out one sardine at a time, still covered in marinade, coat it in the flour and the beaten egg, and fry to a nice color in boiling oil.

When you have fried all of them, arrange them on a serving dish, and garnish with lemon wedges and a few sprigs of parsley.

Sole

SOGLIOLE ALLA MEUNIÈRE

Sole Meunière

6 sole fillets (5¼ oz each)
All-purpose flour
6 oz butter
2 lemons
Parsley
Salt

If preparing sole fillets from a whole fish, first make a straight cut in the middle of the upper part of the fish, from the head to the tail, and gradually detach the left fillet and then the right one; turn the sole and repeat, obtaining 4 fillets. Rinse and, with a meat pounder or the blade of a large knife, flatten them lightly.

Clean the sole, remove the black skin from out the underside, rinse the fillets and dry them. Coat them in flour, and fry them in butter; season with a pinch of salt.

When the soles have taken on a beautiful golden color, remove them from the pan, let them drain, and arrange them in a serving dish decorated with half slices of lemon around the edge. Squeeze a little lemon juice on the soles, sprinkle them with chopped parsley, and finish them with a little more butter, warmed in a pan until it turns a nice hazelnut color.

ADA SAYS: *To make a sole broth, thoroughly clean the heads and bones and rinse them. Then put them in a saucepan with a little onion, a few parsley stalks, a few peppercorns, water, and white wine, season with a pinch of salt, and leave to simmer slowly for about 20 minutes. Finally, sieve the broth through a colander.*

SOGLIOLE AL VINO BIANCO

Sole with White Wine

6 sole fillets (5¼ oz each)
Olive oil
7 tbsp butter
White wine
Parsley
Bay leaf
Salt
Pepper

White sauce:
1 tbsp butter, 1 tbsp all-purpose flour, 2 tbsp milk or cream, sole cooking juices

Wash the sole, dry the fillets, and arrange them in a well-oiled baking dish. Season with salt and pepper, melt the butter, and pour it over the sole, add the white wine so that it almost covers the fish, but not completely. Add the aromatics—a sprig of parsley and a bay leaf—and cover the sole with a well-greased sheet of parchment paper and then cover with the lid.

Bring the pan to a moderate heat, put it in a preheated oven for about 10 minutes. Take out the sole fillets, arrange them on a serving dish, and keep warm. Sieve the cooking juices through a colander and prepare a white sauce in the following way: In a pan, melt the butter over low heat, add the flour, and, stirring, let it cook for a few minutes, then pour a glass of the sole cooking juices into the pan and as soon as the sauce is thickened, add two tablespoons of milk or cream; check the flavor and remove the pan from the heat. Cover the sole with the white sauce *(p16)* and serve quickly.

SOGLIOLE FRITTE ALL'ITALIANA

Fried Sole Italian Style

6 sole fillets (5¼ oz each)
All-purpose flour
Oil for frying
Lemon
Salt

Carefully clean the sole fillets, remove the black skin from the underside, rinse, dry, dip them in flour, and fry them in a pan with plenty of oil, until they turn a beautiful light gold color; season them with a pinch of salt and garnish with lemon wedges. Serve immediately.

SOGLIOLE FRITTE COLBERT

Fried Sole Colbert

6 sole fillets (5¼ oz each)
2 eggs
Breadcrumbs
Oil for frying
Salt
Optional: green beans with Gruyère *(p658)*

You can accompany the fried sole with a plate of green beans with Gruyère.

Carefully clean the sole fillets, remove the black skin from the underside, open them gently on one side to take out the intestines, scrape the white skin underneath without taking it away, rinse, and dry them.

Make a maître d'hôtel butter with 3½ tbsp of softened butter, mixed with chopped parsley and the juice of a lemon.

Dip them in the eggs, beaten as for an omelette, then in the breadcrumbs, and fry them in plenty of very hot oil, a few at a time; season with a pinch of salt. Arrange the sole fillets in the serving dish. Spread the sauce over the fish.

ADA SAYS: *Jean-Baptiste Colbert was finance minister to Louis XIV in France.*

SOGLIOLE GRATINATE

Sole Gratin

6 sole fillets (5¼ oz each)
Olive oil
1 cup breadcrumbs
Oregano
Garlic
White wine
Lemon
Salt

Clean the sole, remove the black skin from the underside, wash, and dry the fillets. Lightly oil an oven pan and line up the sole in one layer. Sprinkle with salt and cover with plenty of breadcrumbs. Strew some chopped oregano leaves, a clove of garlic, and more breadcrumbs over the top, and wet with half a glass of white wine. Place in a preheated oven of moderate heat for about half an hour. Put the pan on a serving plate and send it to the table with lemon wedges.

SOGLIOLE IN FILETTI AL BURRO

Sole in Butter

6 sole fillets (5¼ oz each)
Lemon
Worcester sauce
3 tbsp all-purpose flour
7 tbsp butter
Salt
To serve: 1 lb new potatoes

Trim the sole fillets, rinse them, dry them, and place them in a dish. Season with lemon juice, ½ tsp of Worcester sauce, and a pinch of salt. Leave the fillets in this marinade for a few hours.

Remove the fillets from the marinade, flour them, and line them up in a single layer in a pan where you have melted 2 tablespoons of butter. Let them brown in the butter over a low heat and season with a pinch of salt. Place them on a serving dish and sprinkle them with lemon juice. Melt the rest of the butter in a pan and, when it is sparkling and hazelnut-colored, pour it over the fillets of sole. Serve with pan-fried new potatoes.

SOGLIOLE IN FILLETI ALLA OTERO

Sole with Baked Potato and Shrimp Sauce

6 large potatoes
6 sole fillets (5¼ oz each), with heads and bones
Olive oil
White wine
7 oz shrimp
Butter
Optional: black truffle

Sole broth:
1 onion, parsley, white wine, salt, peppercorns

White sauce:
3 tbsp butter, ¼ cup all-purpose flour, 1¼ cups milk, 1¼ cups sole broth, 1 egg yolk
¼ cup grated Parmesan

For these next two recipes, you will need the heads and bones.

Choose large, equal-sized potatoes, wash them thoroughly but do not peel. Put them in a pan, cover with cold water, and let them boil for 7 or 8 minutes, then drain them, and align them on a sheet pan in a preheated oven to bake.

When the potatoes are ready, cut off the tops and use a spoon to scoop out some of the white flesh to create little cases.

Rinse the heads and the bones of the sole fillets and put them in a pan to make a broth with a little onion, a few stalks of parsley, a few peppercorns, water, some white wine, salt, and cook slowly for about 20 minutes.

Arrange the fillets, rolled up lengthways, on an oiled baking dish, season with a little salt, and sprinkle with a few spoons of the prepared broth and with 2 spoonfuls of white wine. Cover the fillets with parchment paper, put a lid over, and bake in a preheated oven on a moderate heat for about 10 minutes.

Simmer the shrimp for 3 or 4 minutes in lightly salted water, then shell and cut into small cubes. Now prepare your white sauce *(p16)* with 2 tablespoons of butter, the flour, and equal measures of milk and sole broth. Let it thicken well, finish it with the egg yolk, another tablespoon of butter, and grated Parmesan. Mix the diced shrimp with a little of the prepared sauce and fill the potatoes up to ½ inch from the top. Place a fillet of sole on each one and coat with more sauce, spreading it regularly to cover completely.

Drain a little melted butter on to each potato and put the tray back in a preheated oven with rather strong heat for a few minutes, until the sauce turns a light golden color.

ADA SAYS: *You can also decorate each potato with a disk of black truffle.*

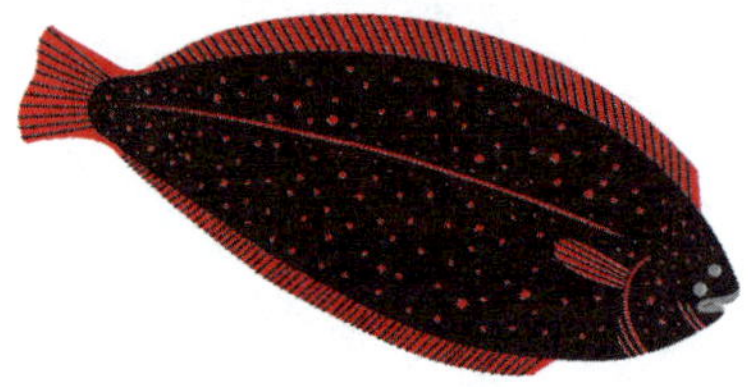

SOGLIOLE IN FILETTI PRIMAVERILI

Sole Fillets with Artichoke

3 medium-sized soles, with heads and bones
Onion
Parsley
White wine
12 artichoke hearts
Butter
Olive oil
Black truffle
Salt
Pepper

White sauce:
3 tbsp butter, ¼ cup all-purpose flour, 1¼ cups sole broth, 1¼ cups milk, 1 egg yolk, ¼ cup grated Parmesan

Divide the sole into fillets, trim them, wash them, dry them, and roll them up on themselves, keeping them in shape with string.

Rinse the heads and bones, then put them in a pan to make a broth with a little onion, a few stalks of parsley, and a few peppercorns. Sprinkle with water and white wine, season with a pinch of salt and pepper and let the broth cook slowly for about 20 minutes.

Boil the artichoke hearts until almost completely cooked and then let them finish cooking in a pan with a little butter and salt.

Put the rolled sole fillets on an oiled baking dish and cover with a little of the prepared broth. Cover with a sheet of parchment paper and a lid, placed on firmly, and put in a preheated oven of moderate heat for about 10 minutes.

Make your white sauce *(p16)* with 2 tablespoons of butter, the flour, and equal measures of broth and milk. Let it thicken well, finish with the egg yolk, another tablespoon of butter, and the grated Parmesan.

Put the artichoke hearts in a lightly buttered pan, and in the middle of each heart place a rolled sole fillet from which you have removed the string, and veil each fillet with half a spoon of sauce. If you have a truffle, grate it over and put the dish in the hot oven for a moment to brown.

SOGLIOLE MANFREDI

Sole Manfred

5 sole fillets (5¼ oz each)
1 onion
White wine
1 egg
Breadcrumbs
2 tbsp cooked tongue or ham
Butter
3 anchovies
1¾ oz ham
Bread, for croutons
Salt

Clean the sole, remove the black skin from the back; wash and dry the fillets. Put some finely chopped onion in the bottom of an ovenproof dish, lay the sole over the onion, add salt and half a glass of white wine, and cover with parchment paper. Place in a preheated oven at a high heat for 2 or 3 minutes—time to firm the meat. Remove them from the dish and let them cool.

Next coat the fillets in a beaten egg, then in breadcrumbs, into which you have added a spoonful of diced tongue and ham.

Butter a baking dish, put in the sole, and drizzle a little melted butter on top. Place in a hot oven until the fish have taken on a beautiful golden color. Finish with a little butter in which you have cooked down some anchovies and surround with fried bread cut into cubes.

ADA SAYS: *Manfred was the last king of Sicily, reigning until 1266.*

Sea Bass

SPIGOLA AL FORNO

Baked Sea Bass

3 lb 5 oz whole sea bass
Olive oil
Parsley
All-purpose flour
2¼ lb potatoes
Rosemary
3 tomatoes
Salt
Peppercorns

Clean the sea bass, gut it, wash it, and dry it. Make 2 or 3 oblique incisions on the back to help the insides cook evenly.
Place it on a plate, sprinkle it with oil, and cover with parsley and peppercorns. After 2 hours, sprinkle it with salt and flour.

Wash and peel the potatoes, cut them into thin slices, and fill the bottom of a pan big enough to take the sea bass. Season the potatoes with oil and salt, add the rosemary, and place them in a preheated oven at a moderate heat, for about half an hour.

After this time, lay the sea bass on the potatoes. Season with salt, a splash of oil, and add the chopped tomatoes. Put the pan back in the oven and cook for another half an hour. Turn off the oven and leave to stew for a few more minutes.

Then remove it from the oven, place the pan on a plate, and bring to the table without decanting.

SPIGOLA ALLA CINESE

Poached Sea Bass with Eggs

3 lb 5 oz whole sea bass
1¼ cups rice
5½ tbsp butter
3 tbsp grated Parmesan
1 egg yolk
4 eggs
Pepper
Salt

Broth:
salt, peppercorns, 1 carrot, 1 onion, stick of celery, white wine

Clean the sea bass, gut it, wash it, and dry it; then with a small knife make light engravings or slashes on both sides. Lay it in a fish kettle with cold water, a little salt, a grind of pepper, a carrot, an onion, a stick of celery, and half a glass of white wine. As soon as the water boils, lower the heat and let the fish finish cooking gently.

Cook the rice in lightly salted water and, after draining, season with 2 tablespoons of butter, grated Parmesan, and an egg yolk, and turn it out on to a buttered oven mold, a little bigger than the sea bass. Lightly press the rice into the mold with a spoon, smooth the surface, and leave the rice in the hot oven for 4 or 5 minutes until it takes the shape well. Then turn it out on to an oval serving dish. Drain the fish well and lay on top.

Hard boil 4 eggs, shell, and chop them coarsely. Warm a frying pan with the rest of the butter and when it is hot, add the chopped eggs. Season with salt and pepper, and when the eggs are hot, but not brown, pour this sauce over the sea bass to cover. Send immediately to the table.

ADA SAYS: *You can also serve the sea bass with carrots or boiled potatoes, lemon wedges, and a few parsley leaves, if you prefer.*

SPIGOLA AROMATIZZATA AL FORNO

Sea Bass Baked with Herbs

3 lb 5 oz whole sea bass
Parsley
Bay leaves
Olive oil
All-purpose flour
Lemon
Salt
Pepper

Clean the sea bass, wash and dry it, and place it for a couple of hours in a bed with aromatic herbs—a generous amount of parsley, a few bay leaves, peppercorns, etc.—and lightly sprinkle with oil. No garlic, onion, or lemon. After 2 hours, lift the fish out, salt it, and flour it.

Cover the base of a large pan, big enough to take the whole sea bass, with oil. Put the pan on the stove and, when the oil is hot, add the fish and after a few minutes turn it over, keeping it on the heat for a few more minutes; then put the pan in the oven already warmed to a moderate heat. Occasionally tilt the pan, and baste the fish. After about 20 minutes the sea bass will be cooked.

Remove it from the oven, arrange it on a serving dish, pour the liquid from the pan over the sea bass, and surround with lemon wheels.

SPIGOLA AL VAPORE

Sea Bass Steamed in White Wine

3 lb 5 oz whole sea bass
Olive oil
White wine or fish broth
7 tbsp butter
All-purpose flour
Salt

Clean the sea bass, wash and dry it, and then, with a small knife, make slight diagonal incisions, which will facilitate cooking. Salt it inside and out. Also add a little butter inside and out.

Oil a rack inside a pan or a fish kettle, lay in the fish, and cover the bottom with 2 glasses of white wine or fish broth. This liquid just needs to occupy the bottom of the pan without touching the fish. Start cooking on the stove and, when it is hot and the liquid is beginning to boil, cover the fish with a sheet of parchment paper, put the lid on the pan, and put it in a preheated oven at a moderate heat and leave for a good half hour, or more, depending on the size of the fish.

At intervals, open the oven and baste the fish with the cooking liquid. When it is cooked, slide it on to a serving dish and pour the cooking juices into a small saucepan over the heat.

Mix the butter and flour, add to the sauce from the fish, and you will see that soon it will thicken. Then remove from the heat and add a little more butter, a small piece at a time, stirring constantly. Cover the fish with this sauce and send it to the table.

SPIGOLETTE CON ACCIUGHE E FUNGHI SECCHI

Sea Bass with Anchovies and Wild Mushrooms

1 oz dried mushrooms
1 onion
2 anchovies
6 sea bass fillets
Parsley
7 tbsp butter
White wine
All-purpose flour
Lemon

Soak the dried mushrooms in cold water.

Cut an onion into thin slices. Wash and bone the anchovies. Put them all in a pan large enough to hold the sea bass with a little parsley, half the butter, and a little water, and cook over a moderate heat until the onions color. At this point, pour in a glass of white wine and simmer for a few minutes. Flour the sea bass on both sides and drop into the pan. Turn the heat down to low and cook very slowly, covered, so that the liquid does not bubble; or you can also put the pan in a preheated oven at a moderate heat, covering the fish with a sheet of parchment paper.

After about 10 minutes, remove the fish fillets from the heat, or the oven, and arrange on a serving dish.

Sieve the sauce through a colander, put it in a saucepan, and thicken it on the heat with a tablespoon of butter mixed with flour. When the sauce is a little thickened, take it off the heat and finish with a few more pieces of butter, put in a little at a time, stirring, and with a little lemon juice. With this sauce, cover the sea bass and have them brought to the table.

Tuna

TONNO FRESCO AL FORNO

Baked Tuna

6 tuna steaks (5¼ oz each)
2¼ lb potatoes
Olive oil
10½ oz spring onions
Garlic
Parsley
4 anchovy fillets
Salt
Pepper

Immerse the tuna steaks in fresh water for a few hours to drain them; then remove their skin and any bones, rinse and dry them.

Peel the potatoes and cut them into thin slices. In a large baking dish, big enough to take all the fish, pour enough oil to cover the bottom. Make a layer of potato slices, season with salt and pepper, then a layer of sliced spring onions, chopped garlic and parsley, and anchovies cut into small pieces.

On this bed, arrange the tuna steaks, season with salt and pepper and a few spoonfuls of oil, cover them with the remaining slices of potato, pour a little more oil over everything, and sprinkle with salt. Place the dish in a hot oven and cook over a moderate heat for about three quarters of an hour.

Place the baking dish on a plate and bring to the table without decanting.

TONNO FRESCO ALLA MARINARA

Tuna Baked with Olives and Capers

6 tuna steaks (5¼ oz each)
Olive oil
2 tbsp breadcrumbs
6 tomatoes
2½ oz Sicilian olives, pitted
Capers
Basil
Salt
Pepper

Immerse the tuna steaks in fresh water for a few hours to drain them; then remove their skin and any bones, rinse and dry them. Line them up in a pan with a spoonful of oil.

Sprinkle the breadcrumbs on top, along with the washed, peeled, deseeded, and sliced tomatoes, the chopped olives, some capers, the chopped basil leaves, salt, and pepper. Sprinkle everything with more spoonfuls of oil and put the pan in a warm oven on a moderate heat for a good half hour. After this time, place the pan on a serving plate and send it to the table.

TONNO FRESCO AL POMODORO

Tuna with Tomato

6 tuna steaks (5¼ oz each)
All-purpose flour
Olive oil
1 onion
Garlic
Anchovy
Parsley
White wine
1 cup tomato passata
Bay leaf
Salt
Pepper

Immerse the tuna steaks in fresh water for a few hours to drain them; then remove their skin and any bones, rinse and dry them.

Salt them lightly, flour them, and let them color in a pan with oil until light brown.

Chop half an onion and put it in another pan with a little oil and a clove of garlic. As soon as the garlic starts to change color, remove it, and, when the onion has colored, add a chopped anchovy together with plenty of parsley. Immediately add half a glass of white wine, and let it evaporate almost completely.

Add the tomato passata, let it cook for a while, season with salt and pepper, and flavor with a bay leaf. Let the sauce thicken and pour it over the tuna slices, letting it simmer quietly for about 10 minutes.

TONNO FRESCO IN CASSERUOLA

Tuna and Tomato Casserole

2¼ lb tuna (in one piece)
1 onion
Celery
1 carrot
Bay leaf
Olive oil
White wine
1 lb ripe tomatoes
1 egg yolk
Parsley
Salt

Peel the tuna, wash it, dry it, and tie it as you do with meat; then place it in a saucepan with the chopped onion, celery, carrot—all diced—a bay leaf, and 4 tablespoons of oil. Put the pan on the heat and slowly brown the fish and vegetables.

Then pour in half a glass of white wine and when the wine has evaporated, add the washed, peeled, deseeded, and sliced tomatoes; salt moderately, cover the saucepan, and let it simmer slowly.

When the tuna is cooked and the sauce is well thickened, take it off the heat and finish it with an egg yolk and chopped parsley. Give it a good stir and pour everything into a serving dish, sending immediately to the table.

TONNO SOTT'OLIO CON FUNGHI

Tuna in Oil with Mushrooms

1¾ oz dried mushrooms
Olive oil
Garlic
1 lb tomatoes, fresh or canned
1 lb tinned tuna in olive oil
Pepper

Clean and rinse the dried mushrooms and revive in cold water for about a quarter of an hour. Put a pan on the heat with a little oil and brown a clove of garlic. When it colors, remove the garlic and pour in the chopped tomatoes. Immediately afterward, add the mushrooms, which you have removed from the water and drained well. Add 2 spoons of water, cover and simmer on a moderate heat until the tomatoes and mushrooms are cooked. Then place the tuna in oil in the pan and simmer for a few minutes, until the sauce is thickened.

Finish the preparation with a pinch of pepper and arrange it on a serving dish. Do not add salt, because the tuna is already salty.

TONNO SOTT'OLIO CON PISELLI

Tuna in Oil with Peas

Olive oil
1 onion
Parsley
9 oz ripe tomatoes
3 lb 5 oz peas
14 oz tinned tuna in olive oil
Pepper

Put a pan on the heat with a little oil, a chopped onion, and a little parsley. When the onion colors, add the chopped tomatoes, and, shortly afterward, add the shelled peas and a little boiling water if necessary.

When the peas are cooked, add the tuna in oil and simmer for a few more minutes, until the sauce has reduced. Finish with a pinch of pepper, arrange on a plate, and immediately send it to the table.

TONNO SOTT'OLIO IN CROCCHETTE

Tuna Croquettes

1¾ oz dried mushrooms
1 tbsp butter
1 lb tinned tuna in olive oil
2 eggs
All-purpose flour
Breadcrumbs
Oil for frying
Nutmeg
Salt

White sauce:
3½ tbsp butter, ⅓ cup all-purpose flour, 1 cup milk

Soak the dried mushrooms in cold water, rinse them several times in fresh water so that they lose any earthy residue, and finally dice them and cook with a tablespoon of butter, a spoonful of water, and a pinch of salt.

Prepare a rather thick white sauce *(p16)* with the butter, flour, and milk. Drain off some of the oil from the tuna and mash it into the sauce. Give it a good stir, then finish with the mushrooms, an egg yolk, and a grating of nutmeg. Thoroughly mix the various elements, then tip the mixture on to a kitchen surface and let it cool.

Take a spoon to shape the mixture into croquettes. Roll each one in the flour, then in the beaten egg, and finally in the breadcrumbs. Fry the croquettes a few at a time in boiling oil and serve hot.

TONNO SOTT'OLIO IN MAIONESE

Tuna Mayonnaise

14 oz tinned tuna in olive oil
6 tbsp breadcrumbs
Grated Parmesan
3 eggs
Salt

Mayonnaise:
Egg yolk, 1 cup oil, vinegar or lemon juice

Chop the tuna and mix it in a bowl with the breadcrumbs, grated Parmesan, 2 whole eggs, and the white only of the third egg—the yolk will go in the mayonnaise. Stir the mixture well and when it is all amalgamated, give it the shape of a meatloaf.

Take a wet towel and wrap it up, closing the two ends of the towel with a string. Put everything in a saucepan, cover with water, and leave it to simmer slowly for an hour.

Take it out of the water, unwrap it, and leave to cool. Meanwhile, with the leftover egg yolk, plus another egg yolk, the oil, and a teaspoon of vinegar or lemon juice, make a mayonnaise *(p19)*.

When the tuna loaf is cold, cut it into slices about ¼ inch thick, arrange it in an oval dish, so that each slice leans on its neighbor, and cover with mayonnaise.

Red Mullet

TRIGLIE AL CARTOCCIO CON FUNGHI SECCHI

Red Mullet Parcels with Mushrooms

2 oz dried mushrooms
Garlic
Olive oil
Parsley
2 oz prosciutto
6 large red mullets
1½ tbsp butter
Salt
Pepper

Soak the dried mushrooms in cold water for a quarter of an hour, clean them well, and then chop them. In a pan, brown a clove of garlic with 2 spoons of oil; as soon as the garlic has browned, remove it, add the mushrooms and half a glass of boiling water. Season with salt, pepper, and a nice sprig of chopped parsley. After about 10 minutes, when the mushrooms are cooked, put them on a plate to cool. Chop the prosciutto and make up 12 portions. Clean the mullets, rinse, and dry them. Paint a little oil and salt on them.

Prepare 6 sheets of oven-proof parchment paper, each large enough to hold a mullet. Butter each sheet, and put inside each fish a little of the mushroom and prosciutto and roll up the mullet carefully into a parcel.

In a baking dish, large enough for all the packets to fit, pour enough oil to cover the base and line up the fish. Put in a warm oven at a moderate heat and let the mullets cook for about a quarter of an hour until the parcels have swollen; take care that the heat is moderate and the parcels do not burn. Remove the pan from the oven, place the parcels in a serving dish, and serve immediately without opening them.

ADA SAYS: *Red mullet has white, exquisite flesh, and is at its best from May to July. The biggest and tastiest mullets are those that live inshore by the rocks.*

TRIGLIE ALLA CALABRESE

Red Mullet Calabrian Style

6 large red mullets
Olive oil
Lemon
Oregano
Salt

Carefully clean the mullets, rinse, and dry them thoroughly. Cover the bottom of an oven pan with oil, line up the mullet in a single layer, season with salt, the juice of a lemon, and plenty of oregano.

Pour a little more oil on to each fish so they are greasy. Ten minutes before putting the food on the table, put the pan in a preheated oven with a lively heat and cook the mullet quickly. They should not be dry, but swimming in a liquid sauce and their own juices. Immediately send them to the table in the pan.

TRIGLIE ALLA LIVORNESE

Red Mullet Livornese Style

6 small red mullets
Olive oil
Garlic
Parsley
10 oz ripe tomatoes
All-purpose flour
1 onion
Bay leaf
Salt
Pepper
For garnish: peas with prosciutto *(p684)*

Carefully clean the mullets, wash, and dry them. Prepare a tomato sauce that should not be excessively dense, in the following way: put half a glass of oil in a pan, with a clove of garlic and a little chopped parsley, sauté slowly without letting it brown and add the chopped tomatoes; season with salt and a pinch of pepper. Simmer for about 10 minutes.

At this point prepare the side dish of peas with prosciutto: Put the butter in a pan with a spoon of finely chopped onion. Cook very slowly, so that the onion cooks without changing color, and then put in the shelled peas. Season with salt and pepper and add a few spoonfuls of broth or boiling water. Cook over a very lively heat, stirring occasionally. They will take about 10 minutes. A few minutes before removing them from the heat, add the prosciutto cut into strips.

In a pan big enough for the all the mullet to fit, heat a little oil. Flour the mullet and put them in the pan; as soon as they have felt the heat on one side, turn them over carefully. Season with finely chopped parsley, garlic, onion, a bay leaf, salt, and pepper.

After about 5 minutes, pour the tomato sauce into the pan for a few more minutes, then transfer the mullet into a serving dish, garnish with peas and prosciutto, and serve immediately.

TRIGLIE AL PIATTO

Red Mullet with Garlic and Lemon

6 large red mullets
Garlic
Parsley
Olive oil
Lemon
Butter
Salt
Pepper

Carefully clean the mullets, rinse them, dry them, line them up on the table, and sprinkle them with salt, pepper, chopped garlic, and parsley.

When it is time to cook them, lift them out of their dry marinade and arrange them on a well-oiled oven tray. Dress the fish with a little more oil, lemon juice, garlic, and melted butter.

Cover with a lid or a sheet of parchment paper and place in a warm oven at a moderate heat. After about 20 minutes, take them out, take off the lid or covering, place it on a serving plate, and send it to the table.

TRIGLIE FRITTE

Fried Red Mullet

6 small red mullets
All-purpose flour
Oil for frying
Lemon
Salt

Clean and wash the mullets, dry them, and coat them in the flour, tapping them to knock off any extra flour.

Prepare a pan with plenty of oil and when it is hot, dip the floured mullets in a few at a time. When they are golden and crunchy, lift them out and drain well, add salt, and arrange them on a serving dish, accompanied with lemon wedges.

ADA SAYS: *If the mullets are small enough, take one at a time by the tail, dip them in cold water first, and, immediately after, in very hot oil. The mullets will be more tasty and crunchy.*

TRIGLIE IN GRATELLA

Red Mullet Gratin

6 large red mullets
Lemon
Garlic
1 onion
3½ tbsp butter
6 tomatoes
White wine
Capers
Parsley
Salt
Pepper

Clean the mullets, rinse them, dry them, put them on a plate, and dress with lemon juice, salt, pepper, chopped garlic, and leave them in the marinade, in a cool place, for a couple of hours.

Chop the onion and put it in a pan with the butter, and, when it browns, add the chopped tomatoes. Season with salt, pepper, and 2 tablespoons of white wine, and leave on the stove until the sauce is reduced.

Take the mullets from their marinade, line them up on a wire rack, and grill them or put them in a preheated oven for a few minutes.

Finally, place the mullets in a serving dish, pour the sauce over them, and finish with chopped capers and chopped parsley.

TRIGLIE STUFATE AL POMODORO

Red Mullet with Tomatoes

6 red mullets
Garlic
Parsley
Olive oil
9 oz ripe tomatoes
All-purpose flour
White wine
Salt
Pepper

Carefully clean the mullets, wash them, and dry them. Peel one clove of garlic, chop it together with some parsley, and put in a pan with 4 tablespoons of oil. Braise slowly without letting it brown. Chop the tomatoes and add to the garlic and parsley; season with a pinch of pepper and salt. Simmer to reduce the sauce.

Oil an oven pan that can appear on the table, and line up the mullets side by side. Flour them lightly, brown them, turning gently, and sprinkle with salt and white wine. Let the wine evaporate and finally cover them with the tomato sauce. Put the pan in a preheated oven of moderate heat for a few minutes, then place it on a serving plate and send it to the table.

RIVER FISH

TO PREPARE RIVER FISH

River fish are usually washed with simmering hot water, well acidulated with lemon or vinegar, and, adding onion, carrot, celery, parsley, peppercorns, and abundant salt, brought to a boil again. For some very fine qualities of fish, such as trout or salmon, you can use a special broth - for 10 cups of water, slice 3 onions and 2 carrots and sauté them in a saucepan with some butter. Add celery, parsley, and a pinch of peppercorns and pour in 7 cups of water and a bottle of white wine. Salt in proportion. Simmer gently for three-quarters of an hour, sieve through a colander, and let it cool. Put the fish in the cold broth and bring slowly to a simmer.

Eel

ANGUILLA ALLO SPIEDO

Eel on a Spit

2¼ lb eel
Olive oil
Bay leaves
2 lemons
Bread
Breadcrumbs
Salt
Pepper

To skin an eel: make a circular cut at the base of the head and then hang it with a string on a grapple. Peel off the skin with your fingers around the cut, and then grab it with a cloth and pull it down from top to bottom, turning it inside out like a glove.

Skin the eel and cut it into pieces of 2½ inches. Rinse, dry, and put them in a bowl with oil, salt, pepper, a few bay leaves, and the juice from the lemons. Mix and leave them for a couple of hours to marinate. Then, take a skewer. Start with a piece of bread, then a piece of eel, alternating them with bay leaves, and finish with another piece of bread. Cook on the rotisserie or, failing this, on the barbecue or a very hot grill. When the eel begins to drain, take it away from the heat and sprinkle with breadcrumbs, turning the skewer, so that the bread sticks everywhere. Put the skewer back in place and, at intervals, repeat the breading operation 3 or 4 times. When the eel is well cooked, remove it from the spit, arrange it on a plate, and garnish with lemon wedges. It must be served very hot.

ANGUILLA ARROSTO

Roast Eel

2¼ lb eel
Olive oil
Vinegar
Bay leaf
2 tbsp breadcrumbs
Salt
Pepper

Cut the eel into pieces of 2½ inches or so. Rinse and dry them in a towel. Put these pieces in a bowl and marinate them with a glass of oil, 2 tablespoons of vinegar, a bay leaf, salt, pepper, and breadcrumbs. Mix the pieces, so that they are well covered in the sauce and leave them for a few hours.

Then, take some metal skewers and skewer 2 or 3 pieces of eel, interspersed with bay leaves. Arrange the garnished skewers in a pan. Pass the marinade through a sieve and pour it over the eels, and put them to cook in a preheated oven for about half an hour, turning them from time to time. Bring them to the table without decanting.

ADA SAYS: *In some regions of Italy, large eels called capitoni, cooked like this, form part of the Christmas celebrations.*

ANGUILLA CARPIONATA

Eel Carpionata

2¼ lb eel
Olive oil
Bay leaves
2 cups white wine vinegar
3 garlic cloves
Rosemary
Optional: whole clove
Salt
Peppercorns

Cut the eel, wash and dry it, and, without peeling the skin off, divide it into 5 or 6 pieces, throwing away the head and tail. Put these pieces into a pan with a little oil, a few bay leaves, salt, and pepper. Cook in a preheated oven at a moderate heat for about half an hour. Then take out, let them drain, and arrange them rather tightly together in a bowl.

Boil the vinegar with a pinch of salt, a few peppercorns, 2 peeled cloves of garlic, 2 or 3 bay leaves, a sprig of rosemary, and perhaps a clove. Give the vinegar a shake and then pour it hot over the eel. Cover and, from time to time, turn the pieces so that they soak up all the vinegar.

ADA SAYS: *Eel prepared in this way is very tasty and can be preserved well for a very long time.*

Carp

CARPA ALLA EBRAICA

Carp Jewish Style

14 oz onions
12 peeled almonds
Raisins
3 lb 5 oz carp
2 tsp sugar
Salt
Pepper

Carp lives in muddy fresh waters; it deteriorates quite easily and therefore must still be alive at the time of preparation. Give a hammer blow on the carp's head and immediately clean it, empty it, peel it, rub it with salt, and leave it like that for half an hour. Then wash it and divide it into pieces.

Arrange the sliced onions and chopped almonds on the bottom of a fish kettle with a good handful of soaked raisins and reform the pieces of fish back to their original shape. Cover with just enough water, not more. Add salt, pepper, and sugar. Cover and let the fish simmer for about half an hour.

Carefully lift out the fish and put the pieces in a long dish, reconstructing the shape of the fish. Sieve the fish broth through a colander, keeping back the onions which will garnish the fish. The broth will be gelatinous and will congeal to jelly. The carp is served cold, with its jelly and just the onions for accompaniment.

CARPA ALLA MARINARA

Carp in White Wine

3 lb 5 oz carp
Olive oil
1 onion
Garlic
Carrots
Parsley
1 quart white wine
3½ tbsp butter
All-purpose flour
Salt
Pepper
To serve: bread for croutons, butter for frying, 10½ oz shrimp cooked in white wine

Cut the carp into regular pieces and arrange in a bowl with a little salt, a little oil, finely chopped onion, a crushed garlic clove, a few diced carrots, a few sprigs of chopped parsley, and a pinch of pepper. Pour over the white wine and leave this marinade for about an hour.

Just before lunch, pour the fish with the wine and all the ingredients into a large saucepan and put it on the stove. The fish cooks fairly quickly, and generally, a quarter of an hour of slow simmering is enough.

As soon as the fish is ready, take it out piece by piece, placing it on a plate, drain the cooking broth through a colander, and put the liquid back on the heat to reduce a little.

Knead the butter and a scant tablespoon of flour together on the kitchen table, put them in the sauce, and mix and you will see that the sauce gradually thickens and takes on a velvety appearance.

Put the pieces of fish back in the sauce, let it heat up without boiling, and then pour everything on to a plate, surrounding it with croutons of bread fried in butter and with shrimp cooked separately in a little white wine.

Pike

LUCCIO ALLA MARINARA

Pike in Red Wine

3 lb 5 oz pike
Olive oil
1 large onion
Garlic
1 carrot
Parsley
1 quart dry red wine
3½ tbsp butter
All-purpose flour
Croutons
Salt
Pepper
To serve: bread for croutons, butter for frying, shrimp cooked in white wine

Clean the fish, wash, dry, cut it into regular small pieces, and arrange in a bowl with a little salt, half a glass of oil, finely chopped onion, crushed garlic, diced carrot, chopped parsley, and a pinch of pepper. Cover with the wine and let it sit in this marinade for about an hour.

Just before lunch, pour everything into a large pan and put it on the stove. Pike cooks fairly quickly, and generally, a quarter of an hour of slow simmer is sufficient. As soon as it is ready, take the fish out piece by piece and set aside on a plate. Drain the cooking liquid through a sieve and put it back on the fire to reduce a little. Knead the butter and flour on the table, add them to the sauce, and mix until the sauce gradually thickens and takes on a velvety appearance.

Drop the pieces of fish back into the sauce, let them heat up without boiling, and then pour everything on to a plate, surrounding it with croutons fried in butter and with shrimp cooked separately in a little white wine.

Salmon

SALMONE AL FORNO

Baked Salmon

3 lb 5 oz salmon
1 onion
Parsley
Olive oil
White wine
Salt
Pepper

Clean, wash, and dry the salmon and place it in a baking dish, covering it with chopped onion and parsley. Add salt, pepper, a few spoons of oil, and half a glass of white wine, and leave to flavor for a few hours in this marinade.

Then, bake the pan in a preheated oven and cook at a moderate heat for about three-quarters of an hour. From time to time, baste the fish with its marinade.

ADA SAYS: *You can serve it with a quick green sauce.*

SALMONE BOLLITO

Poached Salmon

3 lb 5 oz salmon
Vinegar or white wine
1 onion
1 carrot
Parsley
Celery
Bay leaf
Lemon
Salt
Peppercorns
Optional: tomato ketchup, cornichons, parsley

Mayonnaise:
2 egg yolks, ¾ cup olive oil, vinegar or lemon juice

Clean and rinse the salmon; place it in a fish kettle covered with cold water, half a glass of vinegar or white wine, a little salt, some peppercorns, and washed and coarsely chopped aromatics—onion, carrot, parsley, celery, bay leaf, etc. Bring the water to a boil slowly, let it simmer for 20 minutes, then let the salmon cool in its water.

Take it out, gently, so as not to tear it, put it in an oval dish, and remove the skin.

Make your mayonnaise *(p19)* with the eggs, oil, and a teaspoon of vinegar or lemon juice, and decorate your plate with it, along with parsley and lemon wheels.

ADA SAYS: *If you want to prepare a dish of great effect, you can divide the mayonnaise into three parts—the first part with chopped parsley, the second part with the tomato ketchup, and leave the third natural. Garnish with cornichons cut into fan shapes.*

Sturgeon

STORIONE CON FUNGHI

Sturgeon with Mushrooms

6 large sturgeon steaks
Lemon
Butter
Olive oil
1 onion
1 carrot
Garlic
Anchovy
Parsley
Bay leaf
White wine
Stock cube
2¼ lb mushrooms
All-purpose flour
1 egg
Oil for frying
Salt

The sturgeon, with its shiny scales, is highly regarded for its meat and its eggs from with which caviar is prepared. In Italy, the sturgeon is commonly found near the mouths of the Ticino and the Po rivers.

Remove the skin from the sturgeon steaks, rinse them, dry them, align them on a plate. Sprinkle with salt and lemon juice, and leave them for at least half an hour.

Put a tablespoon of butter and a finger of oil in a saucepan with a very finely chopped onion and carrot, cook slowly, and, when the vegetables are cooked, but not charred, add a piece of well-crushed garlic. Heat the garlic a little without frying it too much, and almost immediately afterward, add a chopped anchovy, a good pinch of chopped parsley, and a bay leaf. Immediately, add half a glass of white wine. Cover and cook slowly until the wine evaporates.

Then drain off a little fat and add half a glass of broth made with water and a meat stock cube. Cover again and let it simmer slowly for about 10 minutes.

Clean the mushrooms, cut them into rather large pieces, rinse them, dry them, and cook them separately with a little oil, garlic, parsley, and salt. When they are cooked and have absorbed all the moisture, add them into the sauce.

Flour the sturgeon slices, coat them in the beaten egg, and fry them to a beautiful golden color in plenty of hot oil.

Arrange these slices in a pan and pour the sauce over them. Cover and simmer over a very low heat for 5 minutes, then place the pan on a serving dish and send immediately to the table without decanting.

Trout

TROTA ALLA SAVOIARDA

Trout with Onion Butter

2½ lb whole trout
All-purpose flour
14 tbsp (7 oz) butter
Olive oil
1 lb mushrooms
Parsley
Fine breadcrumbs
1 onion
Salt
Pepper

Onion butter:
Onion, 7 tbsp butter

Trout is the most appreciated of freshwater fish.

Clean the trout, rinse, and dry. Season inside and out with a little salt and flour, and fry it in butter over a moderate heat, so that it cooks well throughout.

Put a little butter and a little oil in a pan, add well-washed, cleaned and sliced mushrooms, and season with salt, pepper, and parsley. Warm through and pour these mushrooms into an oval baking dish, spreading them all over the bottom. Place the trout on top of the mushrooms, sprinkle with melted butter, and a light layer of very fine breadcrumbs. Sprinkle over a little more butter. Put the dish in a warm oven at a moderate heat, for a few minutes to lightly brown.

Send it to the table without decanting, placing the dish on another bigger plate.

On the side, serve a gravy boat with the following simple sauce: Thinly slice an onion. Sauté half the butter, and when the butter is slightly blond, almost hazelnut, add the onion off the heat. Let it rest for a minute or 2, so that the butter can smell like onion, and then sieve through a colander and collect it in a warm gravy boat.

TROTA AL VAPORE

Steamed Trout

2½ lb whole trout
1 onion
1 carrot
Celery
Parsley
Bay leaf
7 tbsp butter for greasing
White wine
3 tbsp butter
All-purpose flour
Cream
Salt
Pepper

Clean the trout, wash it, dry it, and, if large, make diagonal incisions with a small knife—this helps the cooking. Season the fish inside and out with salt and pepper.

Chop the aromatics—an onion, a carrot, a stalk of celery, a few stalks of parsley, and half a bay leaf. Take the rack out of the fish kettle, butter well, and make a bed of the aromatics. Put the rack back and lay the trout on top. Cover the fish with well-greased parchment paper, close up the lid, and cook over a very low heat for 10 minutes, so that the aromas can release their scent without coloring. Then, pour in 2 glasses of white wine and bring it to a boil. Cover again and continue cooking over a stronger heat, but always moderate, for about half an hour, basting from time to time.

As soon as the trout is cooked, take it out and slip it on to a serving dish and keep it warm.

Now prepare the sauce: Drain the cooking juices through a sieve and into a small saucepan. Reduce the liquid to a glass. In another pan, melt a spoonful of butter, add a spoonful of flour, mixing thoroughly until butter and flour are perfectly blended; now pour in the reduced cooking juices. Simmer until the sauce is thickened, and, little by little, add half a glass of cream, stirring all the time. Remove the pan from the heat and add 2 tablespoons of butter, one piece at a time, mixing well as if you were whipping mayonnaise. Veil the trout with this sauce and send it to the table.

TROTA IN SPUMA CALDA

Trout Mousse

2 egg whites
1 lb cooked trout, no bones or skin
2 cups cream or milk
Butter
Salt
White pepper
Optional: white sauce *(p16)* or hollandaise *(p21)*

Use a fork to whip the egg whites and mix them with the trout flesh one teaspoon at a time to be sure that everything is well amalgamated. Put the bowl in the freezer for an hour. Make sure the milk or cream is cold. Take the mousse out of the freezer and, using a wooden spoon, always working gently, add a little milk or cream at a time to the cold trout and egg mix, so that everything is fully absorbed.

Butter a cake mold that has a lid and a hole in the middle, then pour in the mixture, but not too full so at least a finger is free around the rim. Cover and place the mold in a larger pan of boiling water to create a bain-marie and bake for three-quarters of an hour.

When the mousse has set, take the mold out of its bath and rest for 5 minutes. Then turn it upside down on to a serving plate. Diligently remove any liquid that spreads around the edge and bring it to the table.

ADA SAYS: *Serve with a white sauce made with fish broth, flour, and butter or a hollandaise sauce.*

TROTELLE AL BLU

Blue Trout

6 small trout
White vinegar
Parsley
1 lb new potatoes
Butter
Salt

Clean the trout and rinse them; put them in a saucepan with salt water. Strongly acidulate with vinegar: the proportion must be half water and half white vinegar. When the water boils, immerse the trout in the liquid, reduce the heat to a minimum, and let it simmer for about 10 minutes.

Arrange the trout on a serving plate, garnish with parsley and boiled new potatoes, and a gravy boat of melted butter.

ADA SAYS: *The denomination "al blu" indicates the blue color that the trout assumes in this preparation.*

TROTELLE ALLA MUGNAIA

Pan-Fried Trout in Butter

6 small trout
All-purpose flour
7 tbsp butter
Parsley
Salt
Pepper

Clean the trout, rinse them, dry them, season them inside and out with salt and pepper, and flour them.

Put a pan with 2 tablespoons of butter on a moderate heat, line the fish up in a single layer, and cook them until they have reached a nice golden color and are crunchy, then turn them. In all, they will have to cook for about 15 minutes.

Arrange the trout on a serving dish, sprinkle with finely chopped parsley, and pour the cooking juices over them.

Let the rest of the butter melt in the same pan, and, when it turns hazelnut-colored, pour it boiling over the fish and serve immediately.

TROTELLE FRITTE

Deep-Fried Trout

6 small trout
1 quart milk
All-purpose flour
Oil for frying
Parsley
Lemon
Salt
Pepper

Carefully clean the trout, wash them under running water, and put them in a bowl, covered with milk. Care must be taken that all of the trout are submerged. If necessary, add more milk or a glass of water. Leave them in this marinade for at least a couple of hours.

Now take the trout out of the milk, dry them, put a pinch of salt and a grind of pepper in each, then wipe them through the flour.

Put plenty of oil in a pan and let it heat up. Take the trout one at a time in your hands, tap them well but gently to knock off any excess flour, and place them in the boiling oil. Fry in very hot oil to obtain a nice crispy fry. Garnish with chopped parsley and lemon wedges.

CRUSTACEANS

TO COOK LOBSTERS AND OTHER CRUSTACEANS

Lobsters are prized for their meat and there are numerous recipes in international cuisine. Boiled lobsters, and other crustaceans, when they are not needed for other more complex recipes, are mostly served cold, accompanied by a salsa verde or mayonnaise or sauce derived from mayonnaise. An essential condition for these recipes to succeed is to have a fresh lobster.

Lobster

ARAGOSTA ALLA AMERICANA

Lobster American Style

1 lobster
Olive oil
1 onion
Celery
1 carrot
Garlic
Bay leaf
White wine
1 cup tomato passata
Butter
Parsley
Pepper
Salt

Put the lobster on a cutting board on its back. Cut off the claws, and, holding it steady with your hand, split the tail in two with a well-sharpened knife; then, turn the lobster over and open the head and torso, taking care that this second cut joins exactly with the first. Take out the intestines and the earthy gut and divide the tail into 5 or 6 pieces.

Put a little oil in a saucepan and fry diced onion, a little celery, a little carrot, a pinch of garlic, and a small bay leaf for a few minutes. Add the lobster tail and claws and sprinkle with a glass of white wine; add the tomato passata, a pinch of pepper, and a little salt; cover and cook for about a quarter of an hour.

Arrange the pieces of lobster on the plate. Sieve the sauce, finish it with a few pieces of butter, pour over the lobster, and top with chopped parsley.

ADA SAYS: *To simmer a live lobster, tie it to a ladle to stop it from contracting in the heat. Season the water with a carrot, an onion, a rib of celery and parsley, a little salt, and a couple of spoons of vinegar. A medium-weight lobster will cook in about 20 minutes.*

ARAGOSTA ALLA AMERICANA RAFFINATA

American Lobster with Rice and Cognac

1½ cups rice
13½ tbsp butter
1 onion
1 carrot
Parsley
Bay leaf
2¼ lb tomatoes
1 lobster, cooked
Olive oil
2 small glasses cognac
White wine
Cream
Salt
Pepper
Cayenne pepper

First, prepare the rice for the accompaniment: Boil the rice in plenty of slightly salted water, keeping it rather al dente. Drain it and wash it in cold water. Line a sheet pan with a piece of parchment paper and place in the oven to warm. On another sheet of parchment, spread out the rice on the kitchen table and cover it with the warm sheet of parchment from the oven. Leave for a few minutes to dry. Lift up the top sheet and put some butter on top of the rice and then lift the bottom sheet of parchment with the rice on it back to the sheet pan. Put the pan back in the oven at a moderate heat for a few minutes for the butter to melt and the rice to flavor well. Remove the tray from the oven, stir the rice, and pour it into a fresh bowl. Finely chop an onion and a carrot and cook them gently in butter; add a bunch of parsley and a bay leaf tied together. Wash, peel, and deseed the tomatoes; then chop them and add to the pan. Simmer for a quarter of an hour.

Cut the lobster tail into pieces, split the torso in two, and remove and set aside the coral—the eggs—and the creamy parts. Remove the legs and the earthy gut. Crack the claws and take out the meat. Pour a glass of oil into a pan and when it is steaming hot, add the lobster meats, season with salt and freshly ground pepper, and warm at a high heat, stirring with a spatula. To color the crustacean, deglaze with the cognac first and then add half a bottle of white wine and the tomato sauce. Simmer gently for 20 to 25 minutes. Carefully chop the coral and the creamy parts of the lobster and mash them to a purée. Take the lobster meats out of the pan and arrange them on the serving dish. Let the sauce reduce and bind it, using a whisk, with the coral and the creamy parts, adding a little cream. Let it cook again for a moment without boiling it anymore. Check the seasoning, adding, if you want, a pinch of cayenne pepper, and sieve the sauce. Finish it off the heat with 2 tablespoons of butter cut into small pieces.

ARAGOSTA ALLA DIAVOLA

Deviled Lobster

1 lobster, cooked
Olive oil
Parsley
Lemon
Salt
Pepper

Deviled sauce:
vinegar, chili, stock cube, 1 tsp tomato purée, 2 tbsp butter, ¼ cup all-purpose flour, French mustard, peppercorns

Split a lobster in two, lengthwise, remove the earthy gut inside, and season with salt, pepper, and oil.

Arrange it on a plate, garnish with sprigs of parsley and lemon wedges, and send it to the table accompanied by the following deviled sauce: Put half a glass of vinegar in a saucepan with a grind of pepper and a piece of chili. Let it boil until the vinegar is reduced to less than half. Then, add a glass of boiling water, in which you have dissolved half a stock cube and the tomato purée, and simmer everything slowly for about 10 minutes. Mix the butter with the flour and add it to the sauce. Cook until it thickens. The heat must be very, very low. Finish the sauce by mixing in the French mustard off the heat, then sieve through a colander and put it in a gravy boat.

ARAGOSTA ALLO SPECCHIO

Lobster in its Jelly

1 lobster
1 onion
1 carrot
Celery
Parsley
Vinegar
Black truffle
12 pastry boats, store-bought
12 mushrooms in oil
12 artichokes in oil
Salt
Pepper
To serve: cornichons, anchovy fillets, smoked salmon

Lobster jelly:
1 quart lobster broth, 2 sheets gelatin or isinglass, 2 egg whites, Marsala or white wine

Russian salad:
4 oz potatoes, 4 oz carrots, 4 oz shelled peas

Immerse the live lobster, tied to a ladle to keep it level, in a pot with slightly salted boiling water, to which you will have added the onion, carrot, a rib of celery, parsley, and 2 tablespoons of vinegar. Let it boil for about half an hour, then remove the lobster and let it cool.

With scissors or a small knife, cut out the whole tail in one piece. Clean the empty lobster shell well and set it aside.

To the shell, you will leave the legs attached, so that the lobster looks whole. With the lobster broth, prepare a lobster jelly by whisking in the soaked gelatin sheets, egg whites, and Marsala or white wine, simmer, and let it cool at room temperature but not set.

Now cut the lobster meat from the tail into regular slices of a scarce ½ inch thick and line up these slices on a plate.

Put on each slice a regular wheel of black truffle, dipped in some of the melted jelly, and then with a spoon veil the slices with the cold but not yet set jelly. Wait for the gelatin to set and then repeat the operation 2 or 3 times, so that the jelly forms a beautiful shiny layer on each slice.

Let it cool well and then tidy it with the tip of a small knife. Now, take a long oval fish plate and spread out the lobster shell, well cleaned and with the backup, so that you have the impression of seeing the lobster intact on the plate.

To make it more elegant and shiny, brush with a little more melted jelly. Under the head of the lobster, place a large tuft of parsley. Gradually add the lobster slices in order of size, always decreasing, and place them on top of each other in steps, so that with the last slice you arrive exactly at the end of the tail.

All that remains now is to finish the dish. To do this, fill a dozen small pastry boats with a variety of tasty little things such as mushrooms in oil; artichokes in oil; a Russian salad of potatoes, carrots, and peas in mayonnaise; interspersing the boats with capers, cornichons, anchovy rolls, and smoked salmon croissants. Arrange all with care, alternating colors and trying to give to the preparation a combination of vivacity and elegance, obtaining a rich bed on which to place the lobster. Lastly, cut the set jelly into rectangles or triangles around the plate.

ARAGOSTA ARCIDUCA

Lobsters in the Shell with Truffle

3 small lobsters
Black truffle
Parsley

White sauce:
1 tbsp flour, 1½ tbsp butter, 1 cup milk, mustard, marsala, salt, white pepper

Open the lobsters in two lengthwise, remove the gut, and, proceeding carefully, remove all the meat from the shell. Make sure that the shells remain whole. Use a teaspoon to take out the coral—eggs—and be sure that the entire shell is empty and clean. Keep the coral with the other meat. Cut the meat into cubes, add some slices of black truffle, and put these cubes back into the shells, spreading them a little so that they cover the tail and the head.

Make a white sauce *(p16)* with the flour, butter, and milk. Season with salt and a pinch of white pepper, and, always stirring, let it cook; then, remove it from the heat and finish it with a spoon of mustard and a splash of Marsala.

Using a spoon, drop the sauce on to the diced lobster, so that it fills the shells. Just before sending them to the table, put the lobsters on a sheet pan and put them in the oven with a good heat, so that the sauce colors.

Arrange the lobsters on a serving dish, with a few sprigs of parsley, and have them brought to the table.

ARAGOSTA ARROSTO

Roast Lobster

1 lobster
2 tbsp butter
Mustard
Parsley
Oregano
Olive oil
Breadcrumbs
Lemon
Salt
Pepper

Put the lobster on its belly on the cutting board. Holding it with the left hand, insert the knife in the middle of the back and divide it in two lengthwise.

Carefully remove the gut which goes from the end of the tail to the torso and place the 2 pieces of the tail in a small pan with the flesh side up.

Melt the butter in a pan. Mix mustard, a pinch of pepper, a little chopped parsley, oregano, and a little salt. Add a couple of tablespoons of oil and then the melted butter. Spread this mixture on the lobster and cover with some breadcrumbs. Press lightly with the blade of a knife to smooth it out, then drizzle a little more oil over everything and put the lobster in a hot oven with a rather lively heat for a quarter of an hour.

Arrange the lobsters on a plate and have them immediately brought to the table, together with a saucer of lemon wedges.

ARAGOSTA IN MAIONESE

Lobster Mayonnaise

1 lobster
Olive oil
Lemon
10½ oz green beans, fresh or frozen
10½ oz shelled peas, fresh or frozen
7 oz lettuce
1 onion
1 carrot
Celery
Parsley
Vinegar
Mayonnaise, bottled
Salt
White pepper
For garnish: 7 oz shrimp, 12 cherry tomatoes

Put the lobster on the cutting board, hold it still, and, with a sharp knife, split the tail in two; turn the lobster and, with another cut in continuation of the first, open the head and the torso. Take out the meat and remove the gut and intestine.

Cut the lobster into regular slices and season with oil, salt, lemon juice, and a pinch of white pepper.

Boil the green beans and peas separately. Carefully wash and dry the lettuce and roughly chop it. Season the vegetables and salad with a little oil, vinegar, a pinch of salt, and 2 spoons of bottled mayonnaise.

At the bottom of an oval plate, place the vegetables, level them with a spatula, and cover them with the slices of lobster. Garnish the dish with the head and the claws of the same lobster, with shrimp and cherry tomatoes. You can finish them with mounds of mayonnaise. Keep the lobster in the fridge until ready to serve.

ADA SAYS: *To garnish you may wash the shrimp thoroughly, cook them in lightly salted boiling water for 5 minutes, then peel them and toss them in a pan with oil, salt, and a few drops of lemon.*

ARAGOSTA IN MEDAGLIONI

Lobster Medallions in Jelly

1¾ lb cod
Celery
1 onion
Parsley
1 carrot
1 lobster
3½ tbsp butter
1 egg white
2 sheets gelatin or isinglass
Black truffle
Salt

White sauce:
3½ tbsp butter, 3½ tbsp all-purpose flour, 1 cup milk, salt

Clean the cod, wash it, and simmer in an abundant quart of water lightly salted and flavored with celery, onion, parsley, and carrot. As soon as the fish is cooked, take it out of the broth and leave the broth to cool. Skin and bone the cod and put it in a bowl.

Shell and cut the lobster into same size pieces as the cod.

Make a white sauce *(p16)* with the butter, flour, and milk. Season with a pinch of salt and add it to the cod. Mix well and finish with softened butter. Season with a pinch of salt and put it in the fridge.

Measure out a quart of the cold broth from the cod. Sieve and put it in a pan with an egg white and the softened sheets of isinglass or gelatin. Put the saucepan on the stove and, still whisking, bring the liquid to a boil. The egg white will clarify the broth leaving a clear liquid.

When the jelly is cool, but not yet congealed, mix 5 tablespoons in with the cod.

Put a pudding bowl of about 1½ quarts in the freezer for a few minutes to cool well. Then, pour in a few spoons of the fish jelly turning the bowl in all directions so it sticks to the bottom and the sides. Arrange the slices of lobster in the bowl at a regular distance, sandwiching them with disks of black truffle. Add a little more melted jelly and then fill with the cod. Tap the bowl to be sure there are no air bubbles, top up with more jelly, and put it in the fridge. When ready to serve, turn the bowl upside down on a round plate.

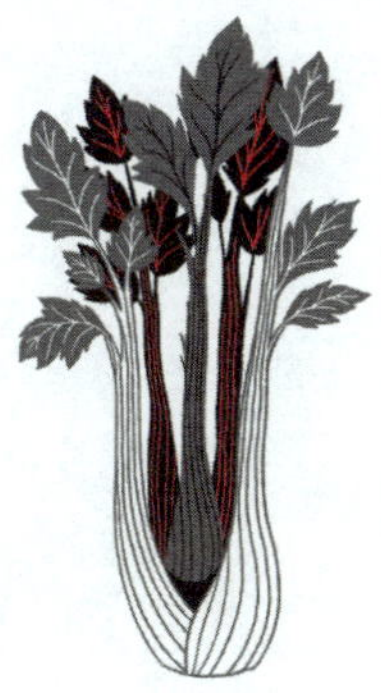

Shrimp

GAMBERETTI ALLA CREMA

Shrimp with Asparagus

4½ lb shrimp
1 cup cream
14 tbsp butter
Parsley
Salt
White pepper
2¼ lb asparagus
1 cup grated Parmesan

Carefully wash the shrimp, peel them raw, rinse, and dry. Put the shrimp in a pan and season with the cream, butter, chopped parsley, a pinch of salt, and plenty of white pepper. Place the pan over low heat and simmer for 10 minutes.

Scrape the asparagus stems, rinse them well, cut them to the same length, and tie them in bunches. Dip them in lightly salted boiling water for about 15 minutes, then drain and arrange on a plate. Cover the green part of the asparagus with grated Parmesan and drain some melted butter over. Arrange the shrimp and their sauce on top.

GAMBERETTI ALLO SPECCHIO

Glazed Shrimp

4½ lb large shrimp
Vinegar
10 cornichons
Black truffle
Salt
Pepper

Fish jelly:
1 quart fish broth, 2 gelatin sheets, 2 egg whites, Marsala or white wine

Rinse and simmer the shrimp in a pan with sufficient and slightly salted water, a large pinch of pepper, and a spoon or 2 of vinegar. In a few minutes, as they change color, you will more easily be able to slip out the flesh and take the shells off.

In the meantime, prepare the fish jelly *(p53)*: Warm the broth, melt the gelatin sheets, clarify with the egg whites over the heat, and season with the Marsala or white wine.

Pour a little freshly melted jelly into a serving dish, let it flow around, and then set it in the fridge. Arrange the shrimp in rows taking care to turn them to give them the shape of small donuts. When you have lined up the shrimp, decorate the center of each one with a thin cornichon wheel and then, proceeding carefully, slowly pour the rest of the melted but slightly thickened jelly to cover. Let it set and then decorate the edge of the plate with a cord of chopped jelly, slices of cornichon, and black truffle.

GAMBERETTI E COZZE AL PANDORATO

Shrimp and Mussels Pandorato

2¼ lb mussels
4 tbsp butter
1 onion
White wine
Parsley
All-purpose flour
10½ oz shrimp
1 loaf of bread
2 cups milk
1 egg
Oil for frying
Lemon
Salt

Scrape the mussels, wash them with water several times, and put them in a pan with half of the butter, a chopped onion, a glass of white wine, and parsley. Cook covered, and, when the mussels open, collect them in a bowl and take off their shells.

Decant the liquid leftover from cooking, put it in a pan with the rest of the butter mixed with a tablespoon of flour and thicken on the stove, stirring with a wooden spoon.

Rinse the shrimp and put them in a saucepan with lightly salted water and a few parsley stalks and boil for a few minutes. Drain them, peel the tails, and place them in the prepared sauce. Add also the mussels, keeping everything warm.

From a loaf of bread, cut ¼ inch-thick slices. Take off the crusts. Dip them in milk and beaten egg and fry them in very hot oil.

Arrange the fried slices—the *pandorato*—on a serving dish and pour over the mussel and shrimp sauce. Garnish with parsley and lemon wedges.

GAMBERETTI FRITTI

Fried Shrimp

3 lb 5 oz shrimp
All-purpose flour
2 eggs
Oil for frying
Lemon
Salt

Wash the shrimp carefully. Peel if you prefer, and gently dust them in the flour, through the beaten eggs with a pinch of salt, and fry them in a large pan with plenty of boiling oil until crispy.

Put them to drain on kitchen paper and sprinkle with salt and a few drops of lemon. Serve hot.

GAMBERETTI SU CROSTINI

Shrimp Crostini

2 carrots
1 onion
Rib of celery
4 tomatoes
Parsley
Bay leaf
3½ tbsp butter
10½ oz shrimp
White wine
1 loaf of bread
Salt

Dice the peeled carrots into tiny pieces, also the onion, celery stalk, and peeled and deseeded tomatoes; put everything in a pan with the parsley, a bay leaf, a pinch of salt and half of the butter; and bring to a simmer.

Rinse the shrimp with more water; when the vegetables are withered, put them in the saucepan; pour over a glass of white wine and continue cooking until the wine has completely evaporated; then, the shrimp and the vegetables will be cooked.

Remove the shrimp from the pan, peel, and set them aside. Put the vegetables through a sieve or blend and collect the purée in a bowl.

Cut ½ inch-thick slices from the bread and spread the purée on them, lining up the croutons on a barely buttered baking sheet. On each crouton place a few shrimp, melt the remaining butter without coloring, and drain over the crostini. Put them in a preheated oven of moderate heat for a few minutes until the slices of bread are lightly toasted.

GAMBERETTI IN COFANETTI

Shrimp in Potato Boxes

6 large potatoes
7 tbsp butter
Milk
10½ oz shrimp
1 carrot
1 onion
Tomato purée
Grated Parmesan
Salt
Nutmeg

Boil the potatoes without breaking them, and, as soon as they are cooked, drain and peel them. Then, divide them in two, lengthwise. To each half of the potato, make a cap at the bottom so they stand upright. Then, use a small knife to scrape out the flesh and make them into small boxes, your *cofanetti*.

Put the potato flesh in a saucepan with a knob of butter and half a glass of milk and mix to reduce to a smooth purée. Season with a pinch of salt and a grating of nutmeg and keep warm.

Rinse the shrimp and put them in a saucepan with the carrot, half an onion, and a pinch of salt; cover with water and boil them for a few minutes. As soon as they change color, drain them, peel them, and divide them into cubes. Mix these cubes into the potato purée, add a tablespoon of tomato purée, and ¼ cup of grated Parmesan and mix well.

Oil a baking dish, line up the potato boxes, and wipe with melted butter. In each small box, arrange the shrimp mixture, giving it a slightly rounded shape, drain a little more melted butter over, and put it in a hot oven for a few minutes. Then, place the dish on a serving plate and send it to the table.

GAMBERI LESSI

Steamed Shrimp

Vinegar
1 carrot
Celery
1 onion
Parsley
3 lb 5 oz shrimp
Olive oil
Lemon
Salt
Peppercorns

In a pan with lightly salted cold water, add a little vinegar, a few peppercorns, a carrot, a rib of celery, half an onion, and parsley, and bring to a boil. Simmer the shrimp for 5 minutes, then take off the heat, drain, and leave to cool.

When the shrimp are cold, remove the shells, put them on a serving plate, and season with oil, salt, pepper, and a little lemon juice.

ADA SAYS: *Generally, shrimp are used as a garnish but they can also make up a dish by presenting them with a side dish of asparagus, artichokes, boiled green beans, or zucchini.*

MAZZANCOLLE FRITTE

Fried Gray Shrimp

2¼ lb gray shrimp
All-purpose flour
1 egg
Oil for frying
Lemon
Parsley
Salt

With the tip of a sharp knife, cut through the back of each shrimp to the tail. With the same knife, lightly cut into the curved back of the shrimp to expose the dark vein, which you remove with the tip of the knife. In this way, the shrimp will remain whole, despite having been cleaned.

When ready to serve, gently dip the shrimp in the flour and then in the beaten egg and fry them in plenty of hot oil until they are crunchy and of a beautiful golden color. Arrange them in a pyramid on a serving dish, sprinkle with salt, and embellish with lemon wedges and chopped parsley.

Crawfish

PANNOCCHIE ARROSTO

Roast Crawfish

4½ lb whole crawfish
Breadcrumbs
Olive oil
Parsley
Salt
Pepper

Crawfish or mantis shrimp are especially tasty from September to December when they are fatter. They confer a particular scent to fish soup; but they can also be prepared alone, best plain grilled.

After rinsing thoroughly, cut the crawfish with scissors along the back and cover with a mixture of breadcrumbs, oil, parsley, salt, and pepper. Roast over a barbecue at medium heat for about 20 minutes.

PANNOCCHIE LESSATE

Poached Crawfish

4½ lb crawfish
Olive oil
Lemon
Parsley
Salt
Pepper

Rinse the crawfish and drop them into a pot of slightly salted boiling water. After about a quarter of an hour, take off the heat and let them cool in the same water.

When they are cool, drain them, peel the tails without detaching them, and arrange them in a serving dish. Dress with oil and lemon juice from the tail, abundant chopped parsley, and a pinch of pepper.

Langoustines

SCAMPI ALLA AMERICANA

Langoustines American Style

1½ cups rice
12 oz butter
4½ lb langoustines
1 onion
Celery
1 carrot
Bay leaf
Parsley
2¼ lb tomatoes
Olive oil
White wine
Salt
Pepper

Langoustines, or Dublin Bay shrimp, have an elongated shape and can be 8 inches long. They are common in the Adriatic and widespread in the rest of the Mediterranean.

First, put the rice on to cook and season with salt and a little butter.

Take the heads off the langoustines and set aside and shell the tails, removing and discarding the black vein.

Put half of the butter in a saucepan. Dice half an onion and fry with celery, carrot, bay leaf, and parsley; as they turn light brown, add skinned tomatoes, cut into pieces and deseeded. Season with salt and pepper and cook for a quarter of an hour.

In another pan, add half a glass of oil. When it is hot, add the langoustine and their heads, season with salt, and cook over high heat for 10 minutes. Then, drain off the oil and replace it with a glass of white wine. Let the wine reduce and then add the tomatoes and aromatics. Let everything simmer gently for another 10 minutes, after which you take out the langoustines.

Heat the remaining tomato sauce well and finish it off the heat with the rest of butter.

Arrange the rice in the bottom of a large serving dish. Set the heads around the edge as a crown, put the tails on the rice, pour over all the hot sauce, and send it promptly to the table.

SCAMPI ARROSTO

Roast Langoustines

6½ lb large langoustines
2 small glasses of cognac
Olive oil
Breadcrumbs
Lemon
Salt
Pepper

After rinsing the langoustines, cut them from head to tail and open them up, but be careful to leave the underlying shell intact. Put them in a bowl to marinate in the cognac.

After about an hour, take them out, place them in a baking dish, season with oil, salt, and pepper and sprinkle the breadcrumbs on top. Place in a preheated oven, making sure to shuffle them from time to time in the pan to flavor them better. After a few minutes, the langoustine are cooked.

Bring it to the table immediately and decorate the plate with lemon wedges.

SCAMPI COCKTAIL

Langoustine Cocktail

4½ lb langoustines
Olive oil
Cognac
2 tbsp mustard
2 tbsp ketchup
Green lettuce
Salt
Pepper

Mayonnaise:
3 egg yolks, 2 cups oil, vinegar or lemon

Take the heads off the langoustines, wash, and put the tails on to cook for 3 minutes in boiling water. As soon as they are cooked; shell them; season with oil, salt, and pepper; and leave them in this marinade.

Prepare a rather thick mayonnaise *(p19)* with the egg yolks, oil, and vinegar or lemon; dilute it with a glass of cognac in which you will have melted 2 tablespoons of mustard; and add 2 tablespoons of ketchup.

Wash the salad, chop it finely, dress it with a little mayonnaise, and arrange it in crystal cups. On the salad, elegantly arrange the langoustine seasoned with the mayonnaise, and put everything in the fridge until ready to serve.

SCAMPI E CALAMARETTI IN SPIEDINI

Langoustine and Squid Skewers

4½ lb langoustines
2¼ lb squid
1 yellow bell pepper
For the marinade: olive oil, parsley, bay leaf, garlic, lemon, salt, pepper

First, prepare a marinade: Put in a bowl the oil, a sprig of chopped parsley, a crumpled bay leaf, one crushed clove of garlic, the juice of half a lemon, salt, and pepper.

Then, shell the tails of the langoustines. Clean the squid, removing the tentacles, the cartilaginous pen, skin, and side fins, and rinse thoroughly. Slice both into neat squares and put both in the marinade for about an hour.

Rinse the bell pepper, remove the stalk and seeds, and cut it into regular pieces of the same size as the squid.

At this point, skewer the langoustines, squid, and peppers, alternating them as you like, and cook on the grill or barbecue.

SCAMPI IN MAIONESE

Langoustine Mayonnaise

Vinegar
1 onion
1 carrot
Celery
Parsley
4½ lb medium-sized langoustine
Olive oil
Mayonnaise, bottled
Butterhead lettuce
Salt
Pepper
To serve: 6 boiled potatoes, 6 boiled carrots

Put a pan with plenty of lightly salted water on the stove, flavor with 2 spoons of vinegar, an onion, a carrot, a rib of celery, and a sprig of parsley. As soon as the water boils, cook the well-washed langoustines, for 5 minutes; then drain and let them cool.

Remove the heads, shell the tails, and season with a little oil, a pinch of pepper, and 2 spoons of mayonnaise.

Boil the potatoes separately, with the peel, and the carrots; leave them to cool and then peel both and cut into slices.

Wash the salad leaves carefully, trying not to ruin them.

At the bottom of an oval serving dish, place the salad leaves and then the langoustine tails. Decorate with potato and carrot slices, alternating colors, and with the mayonnaise. Keep in the fridge until ready to serve.

MOLLUSKS

TO PREPARE MOLLUSKS

Nearly all mollusks require a preliminary preparation which is often done by the fishmonger. For cuttlefish, the larger, slower relative of squid be sure to ask for the inks which are a signature of some recipes. Octopus will be pounded usually on board ship or at harbor side to tenderize. Mussels, clams and oysters must be purged and washed carefully to rid them of the sand in their shells.

Squid

CALAMARETTI ALLA MARCHIGIANA

Braised Baby Squid Marche Style

2¼ lb baby squid
Olive oil
Garlic
Parsley
Anchovy
Chili or red bell pepper
White wine
Salt
For garnish: fried croutons

Squid or baby squid are similar to cuttlefish, but smaller, with the head joined to the body by a distinct neck.

Clean the squid, remove the internal pen-shaped cartilage, rinse them thoroughly without cutting the body sack, and dry them.

Put half a glass of oil in a pan with a crushed clove of garlic; as soon as the garlic turns slightly brown, add plenty of chopped parsley, and, immediately after, the baby squid. Season with salt, a chopped anchovy, and a piece of hot red pepper, or chili, or a good pinch of freshly ground pepper, and cook over high heat.

As it starts to dry, pour in a glass of white wine and allow it to evaporate completely. Add a little water, reduce the heat, cover the container, and let it finish cooking slowly, for about an hour. When they are well cooked, arrange the baby squid on a plate and surround them with fried croutons.

CALAMARETTI ALLA NAPOLETANA

Squid Neapolitan Style

Olive oil
Garlic
1 lb fresh tomatoes, or canned
2¼ lb baby squid
Pine nuts
Gaeta olives, pitted
Raisins
Bread slices
Parsley
Salt
Pepper

Put a little oil and garlic in a pan, let the garlic turn brown and remove it, and then pour in the chopped tomatoes. Season with salt and pepper, let it cook a little, and then add the cleaned and rinsed squid, a handful of pine nuts, of Gaeta olives, and raisins soaked in cold water for 10 minutes. Cover the pan, reduce the heat, and cook slowly, for about an hour, adding a few spoonfuls of water if the sauce becomes too dry.

Toast a few slices of bread. Line these up on the plate and pour the squid and sauce over. Add the chopped parsley and send it to the table.

CALAMARETTI ARROSTO

Roast Squid

1 oz dried mushrooms
6 large squid
Garlic
Oregano
Parsley
Breadcrumbs
Olive oil
Lemon
Salt
Pepper

Soak the mushrooms in cold water.

Clean the squid and rinse. Cut open the sack carefully. Take off the tentacles—remove the eye and the hard mouth—and chop with a little garlic, a pinch of oregano, a nice spoon of parsley, and abundant breadcrumbs. Chop up finely and add the revived mushrooms. Season this mixture with salt, pepper, and oil, fill the squid accordingly, and sew them together with white thread.

Align the stuffed squid in a well-oiled baking dish; season them again with a little salt, pepper, and a little more oil; and cook in a preheated oven at a moderate heat for about an hour. Send them to the table accompanied by lemon wedges.

ADA SAYS: *You can also grill or barbecue the squid but you have to oil them well and turn them often.*

CALAMARETTI E FRUTTI DI MARE

Squid with Shellfish

1 lb squid
1 onion
1 carrot
Parsley
2 bay leaves
3 cloves
Vinegar
White wine
2¼ lb mussels
2¼ lb clams
10½ oz shrimp
Olive oil
Salt
Cayenne pepper
Worcester sauce or mustard
Pepper

Clean the squid, remove the internal cartilage, and cut them out into strips. Put them in a pan with a thinly sliced onion, a carrot, chopped parsley, the bay leaves, a few peppercorns, and the cloves, and cover with a marinade of half vinegar and half white wine.

Put it on a moderate heat and let it simmer, adjusting the flame, so that the cooking is gentle. Cook for about half an hour.

Scrape and clean the mussels and clams, open them raw, and wash them in salted water. Add to the pan for a few minutes, turn off the heat, and add the chopped parsley and a pinch of cayenne pepper. Separately simmer the shrimp in salted water for 3 minutes and then peel them.

At the time of going to the table, drain the squid, clams, and mussels; arrange them on a serving dish; add the shrimp; and season with oil, salt, and pepper and a few teaspoons of Worcester sauce or a tablespoon of mustard.

CALAMARETTI FRITTI

Deep-Fried Squid

2¼ lb medium-sized baby squid
Oil for frying
All-purpose flour
Lemon
Parsley
Salt

Clean and skin the squid, remove the tentacles, and take out the cartilaginous pen inside the body. Rinse thoroughly and take off the skin from the lateral fins. Cut the body—which looks like a hood—across for rings of about ½ inch thick.

Wash the tentacles, remove the eyes and mouth, and divide them into 2 or 3 pieces. Also, skin the fins and cut them into strips. Then, rinse everything and dry.

Put a pan with plenty of hot oil on the stove—it is necessary that the oil is not too hot; otherwise, the squid will brown too much on the outside and remain raw inside; if well done, they should turn out tender on the inside, but very dry on the outside and of a very light color.

Dip the squid rings in the flour and fry them until they turn a very light gold. Fry the rings first and the fins and finally, after having floured them, the tentacles. Sprinkle a little salt over and decorate with lemon wedges and parsley.

ADA SAYS: *Watch out when frying the tentacles, which can crackle and spit, so it is best to cover the pan.*

Octopus

POLPETTI ALLA GENOVESE

Baby Octopus Genovese

1 oz dried mushrooms
3 lb 5 oz baby octopus
Olive oil
1 onion
Parsley
Garlic
Rosemary
1 cup tomato passata
Salt
For garnish: fried croutons

Put the dried mushrooms in cold water to revive. Clean the octopuses; remove and discard the dye, skin, and eyes; and chop the bodies into pieces. Rinse until they become very white and let them drain.

Warm a little oil in a pan with a chopped onion. When the onion turns golden, add chopped parsley, garlic, and rosemary; let them flavor a little; and then add the chopped mushrooms, tomato passata, and baby octopus. Cover and stew gently.

When the octopuses are well cooked, after about an hour, and the sauce is dense, pour into a serving dish, lined with croutons fried in oil.

ADA SAYS: *Around Genoa, very small octopuses are called moscardini.*

POLPETTI ALLA NAPOLETANA

Baby Octopus Neapolitan Style

3 lb 5 oz baby octopus
Olive oil
Garlic
1 lb fresh tomatoes, or canned
Pine nuts
Gaeta olives, pitted
Raisins
Bread
Parsley
Salt
Pepper

Clean the octopuses: Remove and discard the dye, the skin, the eyes, and divide the bodies into pieces. Rinse them until they become very white and let them drain.

Put a little oil and garlic in a saucepan, bring the saucepan to the fire; as soon as the garlic turns golden, take it out and add the chopped tomatoes to the pan. Season with salt and pepper. Cook for about 10 minutes and then add the octopus, a handful of pine nuts, the same amount of Gaeta olives, and soaked raisins. Cover the pan, reduce the heat, and cook slowly for an hour adding a few spoons of water if the sauce is drying out too much. Toast a few slices of bread, line these up on the plate, and pour everything over it. Add the chopped parsley and bring it to the table.

POLPETTI IN INSALATA

Baby Octopus Salad

2¼ lb baby octopus
3 garlic cloves
Olive oil
Parsley
Vinegar
6 potatoes
3 tomatoes
Salt
Pepper

Wash the octopuses thoroughly; remove and discard the eyes, skin, and the dye, and put the bodies to boil in lightly salted water for about an hour. Take them out, drain, and place them in a bowl with the whole garlic cloves, salt, pepper, half a glass of oil, parsley, and 4 tablespoons of vinegar, leaving them in the marinade all day long.

The next day, peel the potatoes, cut them into cubes, and boil them with water and salt. Then drain them, add them to the tomatoes cut into slices, and arrange them on a large plate, finishing with a few leaves of parsley. Season them with the marinade from the octopus, from which you have removed the garlic and arrange the octopus on top. Keep in the fridge. Serve very cold.

POLIPETTI IN UMIDO CON FUNGHI

Stewed Baby Octopus with Mushrooms

3 lb 5 oz baby octopus
2 anchovies
Garlic
Parsley
White wine
1 cup tomato passata
1 oz dried mushrooms
Salt
Pepper
For garnish: fried croutons

Clean the octopuses removing and discarding the dye, the skin, and the eyes, and divide the bodies into pieces. Rinse until they become very white and let them drain. Wash and bone the anchovies, chop them with a piece of garlic and a little parsley, and simmer in 2 fingers of white wine.

In a larger casserole with a lid, decant the anchovies while still hot, cook for a moment, then add the tomato passata, and, shortly after, the octopus. Season with a little salt and a good pinch of pepper, cover, and cook gently.

Soak the dried mushrooms in cold water and when they have swollen, clean them, rinse, and add them to the octopus casserole. In less than an hour, everything will be cooked.

Check if there is a need for salt and let the sauce thicken. It must be dark and fragrant. Transfer to a plate and surround with fried croutons.

POLPI IN MAIONESE

Octopus Mayonnaise

4½ lb rock octopuses
Parsley
Olive oil
Vinegar
Cauliflower
Salt
Pepper
For garnish: 7 oz Gaeta olives, pitted, 6 anchovy fillets

Mayonnaise:
2 egg yolks, ¾ cup oil, vinegar or lemon juice, mustard, 6 cornichons

For this seafood dish, characteristic of Amalfi cuisine, you should use rock octopuses, which are easily recognizable by having 2 rows of suckers on the tentacles instead of one.

After cleaning the octopuses well and removing and discarding their skin, eyes, and the dye sac, rinse the bodies thoroughly until they are very white.

Put on the fire a large pot with plenty of water, and when the water boils, add a handful of salt and then submerge the octopuses. Cover and continue cooking slowly for about an hour and a half, over moderate heat, so that they are well cooked.

Make your mayonnaise *(p19)* with the eggs, oil, and a teaspoon of vinegar or lemon juice. Season with half a teaspoon of mustard, and a generous spoon of chopped cornichons, making sure this is very dense.

Remove the pot from the heat and let the octopuses cool in the same water. When they are cold, remove them, cut them into pieces of 1 inch or 1¼ inch, and season with a good pinch of pepper, plenty of chopped parsley, oil, vinegar, and a heaped spoon of mayonnaise.

In the meantime, clean, wash, and boil a cauliflower, dividing it, as usual, into many small florets. When the cauliflower is cooked, season it in the same way as the octopus, that is with pepper, parsley, oil, vinegar, and a little mayonnaise.

Once everything has been prepared, proceed with the assembly: Arrange half the cauliflower florets as a base, and on this layer, arrange the octopuses, adding here and there some olives. Cover with the other half of the cauliflower florets, making sure to give them the shape of a dome. Cover everything with mayonnaise and decorate with a wreath of olives around the base of the dome, and some anchovy fillets tastefully placed on the dome itself.

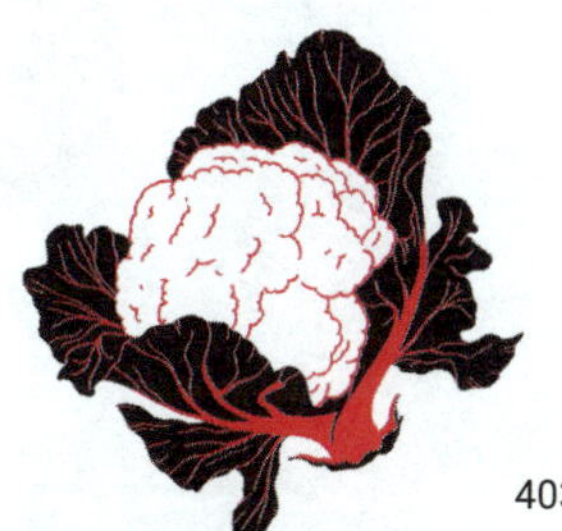

POLPO ALLA LUCIANA

Octopus Santa Lucia Style

1 large rock octopus
Chili
Parsley
3 tomatoes
Olive oil
Lemon
Salt
Pepper

Clean the octopus well, removing and discarding the dye, the eyes, and all the skin. Then beat the body, with care, to break down the hard fibers.

Wash the octopus and, without drying it, place it in a saucepan in which the octopus can occupy two-thirds of the room. Season with pepper, salt, and chili, a few sprigs of parsley, a few small chopped tomatoes, and plenty of oil. Put a lid on the pot that closes tightly. Place the pot on very low heat and let the octopus cook slowly, insensibly, for a couple of hours, and then leave it warm because this dish is best served lukewarm. You can also use a pressure cooker, in which case, adjust the time accordingly.

Don't be tempted to check anything before dinner. Then you will be surprised to see that the octopus has become a big reddish chrysanthemum, very tender, floating in an exquisite broth.

Place the pot on a plate and have it brought to the table as it is. On the table, divide the octopus into pieces and season each portion with a few spoonfuls of its broth, a little oil, and, if you like, some drops of lemon juice.

Cuttlefish

SEPPIE CON CARCIOFI

Cuttlefish with Artichokes

2¼ lb cuttlefish
Olive oil
Garlic
6 artichoke hearts
Lemon
Salt
Pepper

The first task is to skin both the head and body and take out the oblong cuttlebone taking care not to damage the casing. The sac with black dye, the so-called cuttlefish ink, must be kept aside for special preparations. The second sac containing a viscous, dark yellow liquid can also be used and will give a strong, distinct flavor to preparations.

Clean, rinse, and cut the cuttlefish into strips. Put a little oil in a pan with a clove of garlic and, just as the garlic starts to fry, throw it away. Lay the cuttlefish strips down and leave them to flavor. Season with salt and pepper; cover with water and leave them to cook slowly covered for about an hour.

Cut the artichoke hearts into wedges. Cook them in a pan with a little oil and a few spoons of water, so that they are well cooked but not too much. Season with a pinch of salt.

When the cuttlefish are cooked, bring them together with the artichokes, stir, let everything flavor for a few minutes, and then arrange them on the serving plate.

ADA SAYS: *The Roman variation of this dish uses fresh peas in the same way but the cuttlefish is cooked in white wine.*

SEPPIE IN UMIDO

Cuttlefish and Tomato Stew

2¼ lb cuttlefish
Olive oil
1 onion
Garlic
White wine
10½ oz canned tomatoes
Salt
Pepper

Clean the cuttlefish, then cut them into thin strips, cut out the tentacles, and wash everything several times until the cuttlefish become very white.

Put a little oil, half a finely chopped onion, and a small piece of crushed garlic in a pan; sauté a little and then add the cuttlefish; season with salt and pepper; let them brown a moment; and then cover with white wine. When the wine has evaporated, add the tomatoes, leave to cook a little, stirring, cover, reduce the heat, and let it finish cooking slowly for about an hour.

ADA SAYS: *Cuttlefish need a lot of cooking, so add a few spoons of water if the sauce gets too dry.*

SEPPIE RIPIENE

Stuffed Cuttlefish

6 cuttlefish
Garlic
Parsley
6 tbsp rice
3 tomatoes
3 anchovies
Olive oil
Breadcrumbs
Salt
Pepper

Clean the cuttlefish but be careful not to break the body of the fish when you take out the bone. It needs to be whole. If it breaks, sew it up with a needle and white thread.

Remove the mouth and eyes and chop or blend all the tentacles with a clove of garlic and a sprig of parsley, and season with salt and pepper.

Take one body at a time and inside put a spoon of uncooked rice, half a tomato cut into fillets, half an anchovy cut into pieces; and one part of the chopped tentacles and cuttlefish heads, adding a spoon of oil.

When you have filled all the bags, sew them with a little thread so that the filling cannot escape. Arrange the cuttlefish in a baking dish in a single layer, sprinkle them abundantly with oil and breadcrumbs, and finish them with another pinch of salt. Put the dish in a preheated oven for about an hour.

When they are cooked you will find a fragrant sauce in the dish. Transfer the cuttlefish with their sauce on to a plate, snip the sewing thread, and serve.

Mussels

COZZE ALLA MARINARA

Mussels Marinara

4½ lb mussels
2 garlic cloves
Olive oil
Parsley
Red chili
Pepper

Wash the mussels, scrape them with a small knife, remove any string or beard, and then wash again several times, with great care.

Put the garlic cloves and as much oil as needed to cover the bottom of a large pan, and, as soon as the garlic is colored, add the mussels and cook them on a high heat for a few minutes shaking them so that they jump about and all feel the heat. As soon as the mussels open, add the chopped parsley and the chili to the pan, mix well, season with a pinch of pepper, and put the mussels in a serving dish. Discard any that don't open.

Carefully pour the cooking liquid from the mussels into a pan to decant leaving any residue in the bottom, then pour it over the mussels and bring it to the table.

COZZE ALLA VILLEROY

Mussels Villeroy

2¼ lb mussels
All-purpose flour
1 egg
Breadcrumbs
Oil for frying
Salt

White sauce:
1½ tbsp all-purpose flour, 1½ tbsp butter, ⅔ cup milk, 1 egg yolk

Carefully scrape and wash the mussels; put them on the fire with a little oil and let them open, shaking from time to time. When they are all open, remove them from their shells and keep them warm in some of their own liquid. Discard any that don't open.

Make a very thick white sauce *(p16)* with the flour, butter, and milk; then add an egg yolk, mix well, and remove from the heat.

Dip the mussels one by one into the sauce and arrange them on a plate.

When the sauce has cooled and set, take a small group of mussels and wipe them through the flour, beaten egg, and breadcrumbs. When you have prepared them all, fry them in very hot oil and arrange them on a serving dish. Serve immediately.

COZZE GRATINATE

Mussels Gratin

4½ lb mussels
2 garlic cloves
Olive oil
5 tbsp breadcrumbs
Parsley
Salt
Pepper

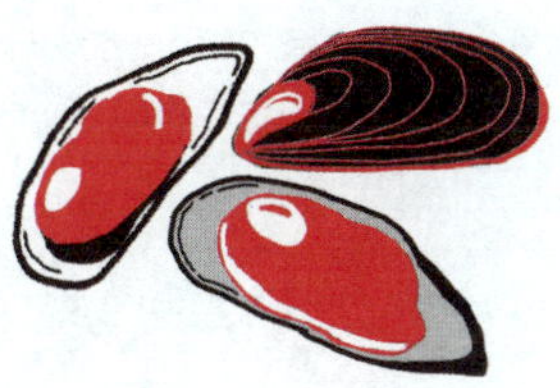

Wash and clean the mussels.

Put the garlic cloves and as much oil as needed to cover the bottom of a large pan and, as soon as the garlic is colored, add the mussels and cook them over high heat for a few minutes making them jump so they all feel the heat.

As soon as the mussels open—discard any that don't open—take them out of the pan, remove the empty half of the shell, and arrange the filled one in an oiled baking dish. Carefully pour the mussel cooking liquor into a pan. Let it settle.

Now place in a bowl the breadcrumbs, the chopped parsley, half a glass of oil, and a glass of the decanted cooking liquid; season with a pinch of salt and pepper; and mix carefully. With a teaspoon, put some of the mixture on each mussel and put the dish in a hot oven for about 10 minutes to turn brown. Bring the pan to the table without decanting.

Oysters

OSTRICHE ALLA DIAVOLA

Deviled Oysters

30 to 36 oysters
Breadcrumbs
Olive oil
Salt
Pepper or cayenne pepper
Nutmeg

White sauce:
2 tbsp butter, 2 tbsp all-purpose flour, ⅔ cup cream or milk

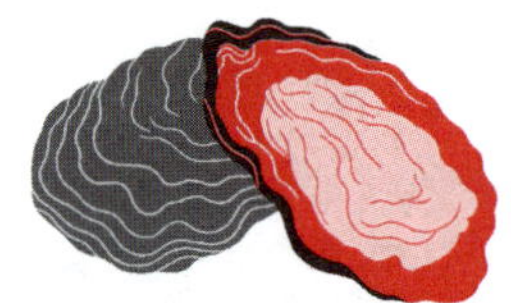

Open the oysters and collect the juice and the meat in a small pan. Throw away the flat shells and keep the concave ones. Put the pan on the fire without boiling, cover, and let the oysters simmer for a few minutes.

For the white sauce *(p16)*, put the butter in another pan, add the flour, cook for a minute or two, and then add the milk or cream, and half a glass of the oyster juices. It must be half cream and half oyster liquid.

Season with salt, nutmeg, and plenty of pepper or, if you think better, with a pinch of red cayenne pepper. Cook and thicken. Arrange a little sauce in each shell, top this with an oyster, and cover the oyster with more sauce. Finally, cover each shell with breadcrumbs fried in oil.

Arrange all the oysters on a baking dish, and, a few minutes before sending them to the table, bake them in a preheated oven at a moderate heat to warm them up.

OSTRICHE ALLA VILLEROY

Deep-Fried Oysters

30 to 36 oysters
All-purpose flour
1 egg
Breadcrumbs
Oil for frying
Salt

White sauce:
¼ cup all-purpose flour, 1½ tbsp butter, ⅔ cup milk, 1 egg yolk

Open the oysters and collect them and their juice in a pan. Simmer gently in a little salt water with their juices.

Prepare the white sauce *(p16)* with the flour, butter, and milk and make it very thick. Take off the heat and add the egg yolk.

Dip the oysters in this sauce one by one. Arrange them on a plate. When the sauce cools, it hardens in a few minutes. Take one oyster at a time, wipe it in the flour, beaten egg, and breadcrumbs, so each dressed oyster takes on the shape of a roundabout.

When you have prepared all of them, fry them in very hot oil and arrange them on a serving dish.

OSTRICHE GRATINATE

Oysters Gratin

30 to 36 oysters
Breadcrumbs
Oil for frying
9 tbsp grated Parmesan
Butter
Peppercorns

Open the oysters, throw away the flat shells and keep the concave sides.

At the last moment, put a good pinch of ground pepper in the bottom of each shell and a spoon of breadcrumbs fried in oil. Put an oyster back on the fried crumbs, sprinkle with grated Parmesan mixed with a few more breadcrumbs, not fried.

Put a piece of butter on each oyster and put them in a hot oven, with a lively heat, for about 10 minutes to brown.

Clams

VONGOLE ALLA MARINARA

Clams Marinara

4½ lb clams
2 garlic cloves
Olive oil
Parsley
Red chili
Pepper

Rinse the clams carefully and several times.

Put the garlic cloves in a large frying pan with enough oil to cover the bottom. As soon as the garlic colors, add the clams and cook them for a few minutes on high heat, giving them a good shake so they can all feel the heat equally.

As soon as all clams are open—discard any that don't open—add the chopped parsley and red chili, mix well, season with a pinch of pepper, and pour the clams into a serving dish.

◆ ADA SAYS: *You can make this recipe with many different variations of clams, such as wedge cockles (telline).*

VONGOLE E PISELLI IN INTINGOLO

Clams with Peas

1 onion
Olive oil
1 cup tomato passata
3¼ lb shelled peas
3 lb 5 oz clams
Salt
Pepper
For garnish: small triangles of fried bread

Thinly cut the onion, place it in a saucepan with 3 tablespoons of oil, brown slowly, often wetting with spoons of water, and then add the tomato passata and the peas. Season with salt and cook over a high heat, uncovered.

Rinse the clams thoroughly, place them in another pan with a little oil, cook them for a few minutes over high heat, and shake well.

As soon as the clams open, remove them from their shells and place them in a bowl with their juices.

When the peas are cooked, add the clams and a little pepper, and bring them to a boil again. Finally, pour into bowls and, if you want, surround with fried bread triangles.

"For a steak, pressing a finger in the middle should enable you to tell if the meat is perfectly cooked."

There are a number of different methods for frying, grilling, and roasting meats, depending on whether it is red meat or white meat. Red meat, after being oiled, should be placed on a hot grill grate or under the broiler so that a slightly browned crust can immediately form. This will allow the meat to retain its juices, and therefore its flavor. As soon as this crust has formed on one side, immediately turn the meat over onto the other side to allow it, too, to brown.

For a steak, pressing a finger in the middle should enable you to tell if the meat is perfectly cooked. If the meat feels elastic, it is perfectly done. If your finger sinks easily, the meat is not cooked to perfection. Beware of poking steaks or ribs with the tips of your fork when turning them. The holes made in the meat could allow the juices to escape. Instead, use a small spatula or knife blade to turn the meat.

Also, remember that meats roasted on a rack should be salted at the end of cooking, not at the start. This is because the salt, as it melts, forms a moist layer on the meat and prevents the rapid formation of a crust, which is essential.

White meats, on the other hand, should be roasted over a gentler heat and frequently based with butter during their cooking.

Abbacchio is spring lamb and *agnello*, lamb, is a few months older than spring lamb, but not old enough to be mutton. Spring lamb is very tender but has less flavor, so that justifies some of the simplicity of the early recipes in this chapter. The recipes for agnello benefit from longer cooking. In Abruzzo, it is often found as arrosticini, skewers or steaks cooked on the grill. It is also popular in South Tyrolean and Tyrolean cuisine, where it is generally stewed. For lamb, mutton, and goat, the best cuts are the leg, the saddle, and the rib chops. The poorer cuts are the shoulder, chest, and neck.

Good-quality pork should be more or less pink in color and pale. The fat should be white, greasy, and hard. All pork cuts have their merits if used appropriately—the loin for a roast, cutlets for broth and soup, etc.

CARNE

9 MEAT

VEAL

ARROSTO ALLA CASALINGA

Farmhouse Roast Veal

2 lb 10 oz veal flank
3½ oz prosciutto or pancetta
Olive oil
Garlic
White wine
1 lb tomatoes
Salt
Pepper

First of all, with a small knife, make incisions in the veal roast and insert sticks of prosciutto or pancetta. Once this is done, tie the joint up with string to keep it in shape.

Put the oil and garlic to warm in an oval Dutch oven over heat. As soon as the garlic turns gold, remove it and put the veal in to brown on all sides over high heat. Season with salt and pepper.

Pour the wine over the meat little by little and, as soon as it has all evaporated, add the tomatoes—peeled, seeded, and chopped—cover and cook over low heat for about 1½ hours adding, as the sauce reduces, a few ladles of hot water. Slice the roast and serve with its sauce.

ADA SAYS: *Flank steaks are a cut from underneath the short loin.*

ARROSTO ALLA PANNA

Roast Veal with Cream

2 lb 10 oz veal flank or bottom round
3½ oz ham
1 egg
Cognac
Marsala
2 tbsp cream
1 onion
Carrots
Olive oil
Bay leaf
White wine
Bouillon cube
Salt
Pepper

White sauce:
2 tbsp butter, ¼ cup flour, ¾ cup milk

Remove any fat, skin, or nerves from the meat. With a sharp knife make a deep horizontal incision into the meat without touching the sides. Swivel the knife to cut out a pocket in the middle.

Finely chop the trimmings you have taken out of the central pocket and also the ham. Mix together.

Prepare a very thick white sauce *(p16)* with the ingredient amounts listed here. Season with a pinch of salt and let it cool. Then add the minced meat. Stir in the egg, salt, and pepper, then put it in a bowl and stir vigorously with a wooden spoon to work in the Cognac, Marsala, and cream. Fill the pocket in the veal with this mixture and sew it up with a needle and thread; tie with string to keep it in shape.

Cut the onion into slices and the carrots into dice. Add both to a Dutch oven with a few tablespoons of oil, the meat, and a bay leaf. Let them brown gently and, when everything has taken on a nice light golden color, drain off the oil and pour in a glass of wine. Cover so that the aroma of the wine is not lost, then, as it reduces, add 3 ladles of water in which you have dissolved half a bouillon cube. Let it finish cooking over moderate heat for about 1½ hours.

Lift the roast out of the pot, cut off the string, and place on a serving dish. Strain the sauce and cover the meat with it.

ARROSTO AL LATTE

Milk Roasted Veal

1 oz dried mushrooms
3½ oz prosciutto in slices
2 lb 10 oz veal flank or bottom round
3½ tbsp butter
1 onion
Marsala
3 cups milk
Salt

Put the dried mushrooms in a small saucepan with a little cold water and leave them to soak for about 20 minutes so they reconstitute. Then rinse them several times in plenty of water to eliminate any small traces of earth. Drain them, squeeze them in your hands, and chop them on a cutting board.

Roll out the thin slices of prosciutto and wrap the veal completely. Tie the meat with string to keep it in shape and secure the slices of prosciutto.

Choose a Dutch oven in which the meat fits snugly. Melt some butter and sauté a chopped onion. When the butter is hot, add the veal. Let the meat and onion brown slowly and when both have taken a nice golden color, add the mushrooms. Baste from time to time with a few spoons of Marsala.

When all the Marsala has evaporated, season and cover with the milk and 2 cups warm water. Bring to a boil, then reduce the heat and let the meat simmer gently until the liquid has thickened and the meat is cooked through, about 1½ hours.

Then lift out the veal and cut off the string. Arrange the meat on a serving dish and cover it with the fragrant mushroom sauce.

ARROSTO IN BELLA VISTA

Roast Veal Bella Vista

2¼ lb thick veal flank
5 oz prosciutto, for larding
1 onion
Parsley
Celery
Carrot
9 tbsp butter, plus extra for serving
Marsala or white wine
Broth or a bouillon cube
Grated Parmesan
Salt
Pepper
Optional: black truffle

Duchess potatoes:
2¼ lb potatoes, 7 tbsp butter, 4 egg yolks, nutmeg

White sauce:
2 tbsp butter, ¼ cup flour, 1 glass milk

Once you have chosen a nice piece of veal, lard the meat with a few sticks of prosciutto and, if desired, with cubes of black truffle.

After this first operation, tie the meat to keep it in shape. Take a heavy-bottomed pot or Dutch and possibly oval in shape, add a finely chopped onion, a little minced parsley, minced celery, and a few slices of chopped carrot. On this bed you put the veal, add salt, 7 tablespoons of the butter, and cook with attention so that the meat and vegetables can brown without scorching.

When the meat has colored and the aromatics have turned into a golden mash, add half a glass of Marsala or white wine, and, as soon as it has evaporated, add enough broth to almost cover the meat. Simmer slowly for about 1½ hours.

While the veal is cooking, make the duchess potatoes *(p670)* using the ingredient amounts listed here and let them cool a little.

Just before the veal is ready, make up a white sauce *(p16)* with the ingredient amounts listed here.

When the veal is cooked, lift it out, strain the juices through a sieve, pressing with a wooden spoon on the vegetables to extract all the flavor. Return the sauce to the pan and let it reduce a little. To this you add the white sauce stirring well so it is incorporated. Off the heat, add another 2 tablespoons of butter, putting in one piece at a time and mixing constantly as if you were whipping up a mayonnaise.

With a sharp knife, carve the veal, trying to have equal and regular slices. Lightly butter a baking dish and arrange the veal slices on top. Pour on a few spoons of the white sauce.

Now take a pastry bag, with a ⅜ inch star tip, fill with the potato mixture, and garnish the meat with strips of potato, and surround the base of the meat with a ring of potato rosettes. Pour some melted butter over everything, sprinkle with ⅓ cup of grated Parmesan, and put the dish in a hot oven for a few minutes until the potatoes start to brown and the Parmesan starts to melt.

In the meantime, put the rest of the sauce back over very low heat and, if necessary, dilute with a little broth. Pour it steaming into a gravy boat to accompany the veal.

ARROSTO IN CASSERUOLA

Roast Veal Casserole

2 lb 10 oz veal flank
Black truffle
5 oz pancetta, for larding
Olive oil or 7 tbsp butter
Onion
Celery
Carrot
Parsley
Broth
2 tsp potato starch
Marsala
Salt
Pepper

Lard the veal flank with a few pieces of black truffle and some of pancetta. Then tie the meat to keep it in shape.

In the bottom of an oval Dutch oven—in which the veal will fit snugly—put half a glass of oil or butter, or even half oil and half butter, and a layer of coarsely chopped aromatics—onion, celery, carrot, and parsley. Lay the veal on top. Season with salt and pepper. Loosely cover with foil or parchment paper, leaving a small opening. Put the lid on, but not tightly so there is a small gap for steam to escape.

Put the dish on the heat and, as soon as the fats begin to heat up and the herbs begin to fry, immediately put everything in the oven, already preheated to moderate heat, and let the meat cook slowly for about 1½ hours.

From time to time, but not too frequently, you can turn the joint, returning each time to cover it with paper and with the lid. Always cook with a moderate heat. The meat is cooked when you can easily slip a kitchen needle into the side. Take out the veal and keep warm.

Drain off all the fat and add a couple of ladles of broth. Put back on the heat and scrape the bottom with a wooden spoon. Let it boil slowly for about 10 minutes and then sieve, pressing hard on the aromatics with a wooden spoon to extract all the sauce.

Collect this sauce in a small saucepan, boil it again and then thicken it with a teaspoon or two of potato starch dissolved in two fingers of Marsala, which you will slowly add, stirring until the sauce has reached the necessary density.

Put the veal back on a sheet pan, cut off the string, douse with a little sauce; and put it back in the oven, basting well so the sauce spreads well over the entire surface and covers the veal with a glossy coat.

Arrange the meat on a serving dish and send it to carve at the table.

ADA SAYS: *With this technique you will get a very white and tender meat.*

ARROSTO TARTUFATO

Roast Veal with Truffle

2 lb 10 oz lean veal flank
5 oz prosciutto fat for larding
Black truffle
Lard or olive oil
Salt
Pepper
To serve: braised chicory

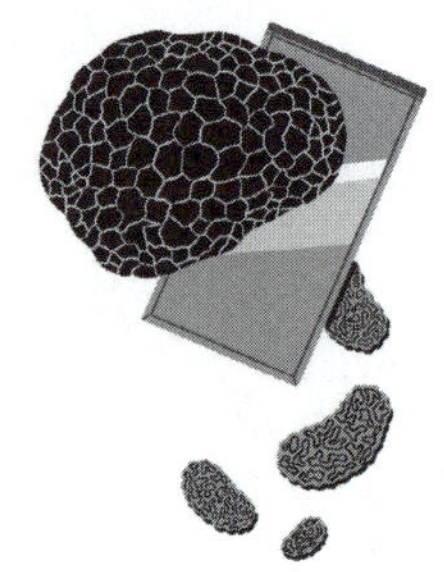

Make a few incisions in the middle of the meat with the tip of a small knife and insert some sticks of fatty prosciutto that have been rolled first in salt and pepper. Then add some matchsticks of truffle.

Tie the roast and set it in a roasting pan into which it fits snugly. Roast in a preheated oven of moderate heat for about 1½ hours. Use plenty of lard or oil, turning the veal from time to time and basting it with a few spoons of water if it starts to color too much.

To be sure it is cooked, insert a metal skewer into the meat; it must penetrate easily and the juices should run clear.

With a sharp knife, carve the veal into equal regular slices. Arrange the slices on a serving dish and surround it with braised chicory.

BISTECCHINE ALLA PETRONIANA

Petroniana Veal Steaks

6 veal steaks (4 oz each)
Flour
3½ tbsp butter
Marsala
Meat broth *(p88)* or bouillon cube
White truffle
Grated Parmesan
Salt
To serve: buttered carrots

Have some thick slices cut off of a nice piece of veal and pound them a little to even them, but not too much, because they should remain rather small and thick.

Flour the steaks on both sides. Melt some butter in a large skillet and lay the steaks in a single layer. Cook them on one side and then the other over a rather bright heat. Season with salt and, when they are lightly colored, splash them with half a glass of Marsala.

As soon as the wine evaporates, gather the steaks on one side of the pan. Pour a few spoons of broth into the pan and with a wooden spoon deglaze the cooking juices a little, so you have a sauce you can dress each steak with on both sides.

Take the pan off the heat and on each steak put some very thin slices of white truffle and plenty of grated Parmesan. On each steak, drop a spoon of broth, and the juices from the pan.

Put the pan back over moderate heat and cover. The steam from the broth will melt the Parmesan, which will make a soft pattern on the steaks.

As soon as you see that the Parmesan has melted, which happens quickly, arrange the steaks in a well heated large oval dish and garnish with buttered carrots.

BISTECCHINE ALLO ZABAIONE

Veal Steaks with Zabaglione Sauce

12 veal steaks (4 oz each)
12 slices bread
Butter
Flour
Marsala
3 egg yolks
Salt
Pepper

Make sure the steaks are tender, white, and of the same size. Pound them lightly with a wet meat mallet or with the blade of a large wet knife to weaken them a little.

Fry the bread (about ¾ inch thick) in butter to make crostini of about the same size.

Just before serving, put 3 tablespoons of butter in a skillet and when the butter melts, flour the steaks and add them to the pan. Season with salt and pepper. Take them out and arrange them on the crostini on a plate.

Deglaze the pan with a couple of spoons of water and half a glass of Marsala, so the pan is clean, and pour the liquid into a small saucepan. Let it cool a little, then whisk in the egg yolks and set the pan back over very, very low heat, constantly whisking the mixture until thickened.

When this mixture is well bound and soft, pour it over the steaks and serve immediately.

BISTECCHINE ALLO ZUCCHERO

Sugar Steaks

12 veal steaks (4 oz each)
Flour
1 egg
Breadcrumbs
3½ tbsp butter
1 to 2 tbsp sugar
1 lemon
Salt

Pound the steaks with a wet meat mallet or the blade of a large wet knife to weaken them a little.

Dredge them in the flour, then in the beaten egg, and finally in the breadcrumbs. Put them in a pan with hot melted butter and fry them to a beautiful light gold.

Season with a pinch of salt, then remove them from the pan and put in a spoon or two of sugar and let it caramelize a little. Squeeze in the juice of a lemon, mix with a wooden spoon. Put the steaks in the sauce again so that they can flavor.

Arrange them on a plate and pour the sauce over them.

ADA SAYS: *You can serve these steaks with mostarda di frutta di Cremona.*

COSTOLETTE ALLA GRIGLIA

Broiled Veal Chops

6 veal chops of equal size
7 tbsp butter
Lemon wedges
Salt
Pepper

Lightly pound the chops with a wet meat mallet, trim the bone, and season with salt and pepper. Melt the butter in a pan and drizzle half over the chops.

Preheat a grill or grill pan. Put the chops on to cook. As soon as they are browned on both sides, drizzle the rest of the butter on them and continue cooking for about 10 minutes.

Arrange the chops on a serving plate and wrap the rib bone with a strip of aluminium foil for easy handling. Serve with lemon wedges.

COSTOLETTE ALLA MODENESE

Veal Chops Modena Style

6 veal chops of equal size
2 eggs
Breadcrumbs
Butter
6 slices ham
5 oz Fontina or Gruyère
Salt

Lightly pound the veal chops with a wet meat mallet. Dredge them in the beaten eggs and then the breadcrumbs and fry in hot butter.

As soon as they are cooked, season them with a pinch of salt, place them in a single layer on a sheet pan or in a baking pan where they can arrange in a single layer. Cover each chop with a slice of ham and a thin slice of Fontina or Gruyère. Put the veal in a hot oven and as soon as the cheese melts, send immediately to the table.

COSTOLETTE ALLA PAESANA

Veal Chops Farmhouse Style

10 oz small white onions
9 tbsp butter
Broth
1 lb 5 oz potatoes
Olive oil
6 veal chops of equal size
Salt
Pepper

Peel the onions without cutting into them and cut off the roots, but not too much. As you peel them, drop them in a bowl of fresh water.

Arrange the onions in a pan with 2 tablespoons of butter and cover them with broth. Cover and cook the onions until the broth has evaporated. Note that the onions must remain white.

Peel the potatoes and cut them into wedges. In another pan, heat up half a glass of oil, add the potatoes, salt them lightly, cover and cook slowly, shaking the pan often to prevent the potatoes from sticking to the bottom. Add the onions to the pan.

Lightly pound the veal chops with a wet meat mallet and pan-fry in butter.

When they are done on both sides, season with salt and pepper and add to the same pan with the potatoes and onions and let them simmer for a few minutes. Serve immediately.

COSTOLETTE ALLA PAPILLOTE

Veal Chops en Papillote

2 oz dried mushrooms
Onion
3½ tbsp butter
White wine
6 veal chops of equal size
Olive oil
12 slices prosciutto
Salt
Pepper

En papillote, or al cartoccio, is food cooked and presented in a paper wrapper, a very simple system.

Prepare the dried mushrooms: Soak in fresh water to reconstitute, dry, clean them well, squeeze them dry, and mince them on a cutting board.

Chop a little onion—as much as a tablespoon—and lightly brown in a small pan with a small piece of butter. Then add the chopped mushrooms, splash with a finger of white wine, and, when the wine has evaporated, season with a pinch of salt and let finish cooking, basting from time to time with a few spoons of water. Make sure that at the end of cooking, which only takes a few minutes, the sauce is very dense, almost dry.

Pan-fry the chops in the rest of the butter, season with salt and pepper, and when just cooked, transfer to a plate.

Cut out 6 sheets of parchment paper large enough to contain a chop and moisten them slightly. Fold each sheet in half and with scissors cut it into a heart shape.

Grease or oil the sheet, then place in a slice of prosciutto, some of the prepared mushrooms, and a chop. On this, put a little more mushrooms and finish with another slice of ham. Bring the two parts of the sheet together and, starting from the bottom, pleat the edge proceeding gradually upwards until the chops are completely enclosed.

Put the packets on a baking sheet in an already warm oven of moderate heat, not more than 400°F, for 3 or 4 minutes to have time to warm up.

Arrange them on a plate without removing them from their paper packets and send them to the table.

COSTOLETTE ALLA VALDOSTANA

Veal Chops with Fontina

6 veal chops
5 oz Fontina
Flour
2 eggs
Breadcrumbs
Butter
Salt
Pepper
Optional: white truffle, cooked rice

With the blade of a knife, slice the meat of the chops horizontally in two without separating the two parts. Proceeding carefully, smooth out these two parts a little to make them thinner.

Cut some very thin slices of Fontina, and if possible some slices of white truffle. Slip these onto the chops. Season with a pinch of pepper and very little salt, close the chops and pound them a little with the meat mallet to close them well.

Dredge them in the flour, the beaten eggs, and breadcrumbs. Fry them slowly in a pan in butter until they are a beautiful golden color.

ADA SAYS: *You can serve these chops on rice.*

COSTOLETTE AL MOSAICO

Veal Chops with Truffle, Ham, Gruyère, and Tomato

6 veal chops
Flour
3½ tbsp butter
White wine
Broth
Black truffle
2 slices prosciutto
2 oz Gruyère
6 tomatoes
Butter
Salt
Pepper
To serve: a thick tomato sauce

Lightly pound the veal chops without deforming them, and dredge them in flour. Melt the butter in an ovenproof skillet and add the chops in a single layer. Season with salt and pepper and, as soon as they have colored on one side, turn them over. When they color on the other side, splash them with a glass of white wine. Let the wine evaporate and add a ladle of broth; turn down the heat and let them cook slowly until the sauce is well reduced and the chops are covered with a glossy, savory coating.

In the meantime, prepare a black truffle: Slice and then cut it into sticks the size of a wooden match. Then cut the prosciutto and the Gruyère into similar matchsticks.

Blanch, peel, and seed the tomatoes, and cut into chunks.

When the chops are ready, take the pan off the heat and, leaving the chops as they are, arrange on top of each one a mound of raw tomato chunks, truffle, cheese, and prosciutto.

Put a few pieces of butter on each decoration and put the dish in a preheated oven for 5 or 6 minutes to give the tomato time to cook and the cheese to melt.

Place them in a heated serving dish and serve with a thick tomato sauce seasoned with butter.

COSTOLETTE AL PREZZEMOLO

Pan-Fried Veal Chops with Parsley and Lemon Sauce

6 veal chops
3½ tbsp butter
White wine
Bouillon cube
Flour
1 lemon
Parsley
Salt
Pepper

Lightly pound the chops and then put them in a skillet and cook in butter, salt, and pepper, until completely cooked. Then put them in a serving dish and keep warm.

Deglaze the pan with half a glass of white wine and let this wine evaporate. Then add a half glass of hot water in which you have dissolved a quarter of a bouillon cube.

Reduce the sauce again, take it off the heat and finish with a scant 3 tablespoons of butter, adding a piece at a time, stirring. Stir in a little lemon juice and a good spoon of chopped parsley. Coat the chops with the sauce and send immediately to the table.

COSTOLETTE GUARNITE

Veal Chops with Tomatoes and Peppers

2¼ lb tomatoes
7 tbsp butter
1 onion
3 green, red, or yellow bell peppers
Olive oil
6 veal chops
White wine
Salt
Pepper

Blanch, peel, and seed the tomatoes, then cut into chunks. Pan-fry with 3 tablespoons of butter and season with a pinch of salt and pepper.

Cut a medium onion into thin slices and pan-fry in another pan with 2 tablespoons of butter and let it cook down slowly, until it is golden and softened.

Char the peppers in the oven or over an open flame, peel and seed them, cut into strips and pan-fry in oil and a little salt.

When the tomatoes, onions, and peppers are ready, combine them in a single container and keep them warm.

Put the veal chops in a greased skillet, brown them, season with salt and pepper, and splash in a glass of white wine. When the wine has evaporated, take out the chops and arrange them in a serving dish.

Put the tomato, pepper, and onion mixture in a saucepan. Simmer a little, then pour the sauce over the chops and send them to the table.

COSTOLETTE IN TERRINA

Veal Chop Terrine

6 veal chops
Flour
3½ tbsp butter
2¼ lb potatoes
Parsley
Olive oil
1 lb mushrooms
White truffle
Salt

Give the veal chops a nice shape, pound them lightly, sprinkle with some flour and brown them with 3 tablespoons of butter in a skillet. Season with salt and cook them through.

Cut the potatoes into thin wedges and brown in butter. Finish with a generous round of chopped parsley.

Take a terrine dish with a lid. Butter it generously and add a few drops of oil. On the bottom arrange a thick layer of mushrooms, cleaned and sliced. Season with a little salt. Arrange the chops on top and surround them with the small potato wedges. Put a few slices of white truffle on top.

Put the lid on the terrine and put it in a hot oven for 15 minutes. Then send the terrine to the table.

COTOLETTE ALLA MILANESE

Veal Milanese

2 lb veal cutlets
2 eggs
Breadcrumbs
2 tbsp butter
Lemon wedges
Salt
Nutmeg
To serve: fried potatoes

Pound the cutlets with a wet mallet to give them a beautiful shape. Season with a little salt and nutmeg. Dredge them in the beaten eggs and then the breadcrumbs, fashioning them with the palm of your hands to make a good shape.

In a skillet, melt butter over very moderate heat. Add the cutlets and brown on both sides, turning them over carefully.

Then arrange them on a plate, and serve them with a garnish of fried potatoes and lemon wedges.

ADA SAYS: *If you have to cook the cutlets in batches you should use clarified butter or you can make up for it by adding a little bit of olive oil to ordinary butter.*

COTOLETTE ALLA VIENNESE

Fried Veal Cutlets Viennese Style

6 veal cutlets
Flour
2 eggs
Breadcrumbs
Butter
6 lemon slices
6 anchovy fillets
6 green olives
Capers
2 hard-boiled eggs
Salt

Anchovy butter:
2 tbsp butter, 2 salted anchovies

Pound the cutlets with a wet meat mallet to flatten them and give them a beautiful shape.

Dredge them in flour, the beaten eggs, then breadcrumbs, compressing a little with the palm of the hand. Fry them in butter to a beautiful golden color.

Make the anchovy butter *(p54)* using the ingredient amounts listed here.

When all the cutlets are ready, arrange them on a plate, smear with anchovy butter, garnish with a lemon slice, and an anchovy fillet in which you will put a green olive. Garnish the cutlets with a mound of capers, one of egg white slices, and one of mashed boiled egg yolks.

COTOLETTE ALLA VILLEROY

Double-Fried Veal Cutlets Villeroy

6 veal cutlets
3½ tbsp butter
Grated Parmesan
4 eggs
6 slices ham or salted tongue
Flour
Breadcrumbs
Oil for deep-frying
Lemon wedges
Salt
Nutmeg
Pepper

White sauce:
¾ cup flour, 7 tbsp butter, 2 cups milk

Pound the cutlets with a wet meat mallet to flatten them and give them a beautiful shape. Pan-fry them in 3 tablespoons butter, season with a pinch of salt and a spoon of grated Parmesan. Take out and let them cool under a light weight.

Make a thick white sauce *(p16)* with the ingredient amounts listed here. Season with salt, pepper, nutmeg, grated Parmesan, and, off the heat, beat in 2 whole eggs. Put on very low heat, so that it no longer boils, but keep stirring for about 10 minutes until the sauce is very elastic and thick.

Cover the veal with a slice of ham or salted tongue and the warm sauce. Chill. Once the sauce is very cold, the cutlets will be fried again. Dredge them in flour, beaten eggs, and breadcrumbs. Deep-fry them in plenty of hot oil.

Drain well and serve very hot surrounded by lemon wedges.

CROQUETTES ALLA RUSSA

Veal Croquettes Russian Style

2¼ lb lean ground veal
2 oz crustless white bread
Milk
Onion
5 tbsp butter
2 eggs
Flour
Breadcrumbs
Olive oil
Salt
Pepper

Put the ground veal in a bowl. Soak the white bread in milk, squeeze dry, and shred in with the meat.

Thinly cut half a medium onion and very slowly pan-fry in 2 tablespoons butter. The onion needs to cook without coloring. Then add the cooked onions and all of the butter in the pan to the bowl with the ground veal. Add salt and pepper to taste and 2 egg yolks. Knead everything well with your hands to have a perfect amalgam of all the elements.

Finally, whisk 2 egg whites and fold into the mixture. Divide the mixture into equal portions. Take a piece at a time, roll it in your lightly floured hands, dredge it in the breadcrumbs, and, carefully shape it with your hands into a round croquette about ¾ inch across.

Now heat two fingers of oil in a heavy-bottomed pan with about 3 tablespoons of butter. When the fats are hot, add the croquettes in a single layer and shallow-fry slowly on one side and then the other until they are golden brown.

ADA SAYS: *These croquettes are perfectly done when the juices run clear at the prick of a fork.*

CROCCHETTE CON LA RICOTTA

Veal and Ricotta Croquettes

2¼ lb ground veal
3½ oz ham
1¼ cups ricotta
Grated Parmesan
3 eggs
Milk
Flour
Breadcrumbs
Oil for deep-frying
Salt
Pepper

Mix the ground veal, the ham (cut into small pieces), well-drained ricotta, and some grated Parmesan in a bowl.

Whisk the egg yolks with a little milk and add to the meats. Season with salt and pepper. Mix well. Then with floured hands form some croquettes, roll them in flour, then in the egg whites, and finally in the breadcrumbs.

Deep-fry them in plenty of hot oil, drain and serve immediately.

ADA SAYS: *A side dish of green beans goes well here.*

FETTINE ALLA BESCIAMELLA

Veal Strips with White Sauce

2 lb veal flank steaks, cut into strips
7 tbsp butter
5 oz Gruyère
Salt
Nutmeg
Pepper

White sauce:
¼ cup flour, 2 tbsp butter,
1 cup milk

Cut the meat into very thin slices of uniform size, if possible. Put them in a large skillet with the butter, brown them over lively heat on both sides, and season with salt and pepper.

Make the white sauce *(p16)* with the ingredient amounts listed here. Season it with a spot of salt, a grating of nutmeg, and one-third of the grated Gruyère.

Using a spatula or the blade of a knife, spread the sauce on the cooked slices of veal and top off with the rest of the Gruyère, one slice per piece of veal. Pour a few drops of melted butter on each slice and place the pan in a preheated oven at a high heat for a few minutes to melt the cheese and brown the sauce.

FETTINE ALLA BOLOGNESE

Veal Strips Bolognese

2 lb veal flank steaks, cut into strips
2 tbsp butter
7 oz ricotta
2 eggs
Nutmeg
3½ oz mortadella
Parsley
3 tbsp flour
Breadcrumbs
Oil for deep-frying
Lemon wedges
Salt
Nutmeg
Pepper

Flatten the veal steaks with a wet meat mallet and arrange them on a buttered sheet pan. Preheat the broiler to high and brown the steaks on one side, turn and brown on the other. Season with salt and pepper and remove from the oven. Arrange in a clean sheet pan and let them cool under a light weight, so that they stay flat.

When they are cooled, cut them into regular and equal strips 4 inches long and 2½ inches wide. Chop all the trimmings. Place the ricotta in a bowl, work it with a wooden spoon, season with an egg yolk, salt and nutmeg and then add the mortadella cut into cubes, chopped trimmings from the veal, and a little chopped parsley. Mix everything well.

Dredge the veal strips in this mixture so each piece is completely coated. Then dredge the strips in the flour, the beaten egg, and then breadcrumbs. Deep-fry them in very hot oil to a golden color. Arrange in a serving dish and surround with lemon wedges and immediately send them to the table.

FETTINE ALLA PIZZAIOLA

Veal Pizzaiola

2 lb veal flank steaks, cut into strips
Olive oil
2 garlic cloves
2¼ lb tomatoes
Salt
Pepper
Oregano

Flatten the steaks with a wet meat mallet and cut them into regular and equal strips. Warm a half glass of oil in a large skillet, then add 2 cloves of garlic and the veal.

Add the tomatoes—chopped into small pieces—to the veal. Season with salt, pepper, and oregano. Shallow-fry over moderate heat until the tomatoes are cooked and their sauce reduced, which will take about 20 minutes. Bring promptly to the table.

FETTINE ALL'UCCELLETTO

Genovese Veal Strips

2 lb veal flank steaks, cut into strips
3½ tbsp butter
Olive oil
Garlic
Bay leaf
1 lemon
Salt
Pepper
Optional: mushrooms

Put a little butter and ¼ cup of oil in a skillet, add a whole clove of garlic and a bay leaf. Just let everything warm up, without coloring. Season the veal steaks with salt and pepper and lay in the pan. Increase the heat and, as soon as the veal has understood the heat on one side, turn it over. In all, the slices will have to remain on the heat for only a few minutes.

Place them immediately on a serving dish, remove the garlic and bay leaf, let the cooking fat sauté a little more, the off the heat, add a few drops of lemon juice. Pour it over the veal and serve immediately. Accompany perhaps with mushrooms.

ADA SAYS: *A simple and exquisite preparation of Genoese cuisine, carried out with very white slices of veal, cut very thin and pretty small.*

FETTINE IN BUDINO

Veal Loaf

1 lb veal flank steaks, cut into strips
10 oz ground veal
7 tbsp butter
Wine
Breadcrumbs
Milk
Grated Parmesan
1 egg
Parsley
3½ oz ham
Salt
To serve: peas

Pound the veal steaks with a wet meat mallet so they are very thin. Slice into strips.

Brown the ground veal in the butter over high heat, then splash with wine and season with a pinch of salt. When the veal is cooked, mix in a bowl some bread soaked in milk and squeezed dry—as much as a big apple. Add the egg, Parmesan, and chopped parsley. Blend well.

Grease a shallow round baking pan with a diameter of about 8 inches. Line the bottom and sides with the slices of ham so it is completely covered. In the bottom, make a layer of veal strips. Then cover with a ⅜-inch layer of the ground veal mixture. Then more veal strips, more ground meat, and finish with veal strips and a few lumps of butter placed here and there. Deglaze the cooking juices with half a glass of wine.

About 30 minutes before going to the table, place the pan in a preheated oven and bake at a moderate heat. To serve, invert onto a serving dish and serve with a side dish of peas.

FETTINE IN SACCHETTI

Veal and Mozzarella Packets

18 veal steaks (2 oz each)
3½ oz prosciutto
9 oz mozzarella
Butter
Marsala
Salt
Pepper

Spread out the veal steaks on a work surface. Put on each a strip of prosciutto and a few cubes of mozzarella; season with salt and pepper. Fold each slice on itself and secure the filling with 3 toothpicks to make a little bag.

Melt a little butter in a skillet and as soon as it is hot, lay in the veal parcels in a single layer. When they color, gently turn over. When the bags are cooked, which will happen in a short time, arrange them on a plate.

Pour a little Marsala into the pan to deglaze. Working with a wooden spoon to mix the cooking juices, add a few more pieces of butter and coat the meat with this sauce.

FILETTO ALLA BOLOGNESE

Veal Tenderloin Bolognese

2 lb veal tenderloin
Flour
3½ tbsp butter
Olive oil
Marsala
Grated Parmesan
2 oz prosciutto
Meat broth *(p88)* or bouillon cube
Salt

Cut the veal into slices a finger thick and flour them.

Put the butter and a splash of oil in a shallow pan in which all the slices can fit. Set the pan over heat and when the fats have heated up, arrange the slices of meat in the pan, then cook quickly over high heat on both sides.

Season with a little salt and, when browned on both sides, pour in a glass of Marsala. When the wine has evaporated, take off the heat and immediately remove them from the pan. Pour a few spoonfuls of broth into the pan and with a wooden spoon deglaze the cooking juices.

Put the veal back in the pan and on each one spoon some grated Parmesan and a few pieces of chopped prosciutto. Spoon a few drops of broth onto each piece, and put the pan over light heat again, covering it with a lid.

The steam released from the broth will melt the Parmesan and create a creamy and fragrant coating. Arrange the preparation on a serving dish and pour on the sauce left in the pan.

FILETTO CON POMODORI

Veal Tenderloin with Tomatoes

3 round beefsteak tomatoes
6 tbsp breadcrumbs
Basil
Olive oil
6 veal tenderloin steaks
6 slices bread
White wine
3½ tbsp butter
Salt
Pepper
Optional: mashed potatoes

Slice the tomatoes in half horizontally. Use a teaspoon to take out the seeds. Put the tomato halves in an ovenproof dish, cut-side up, season with salt and pepper, cover each with a spoon of breadcrumbs, and a few shredded fresh basil leaves. Drizzle with oil. Put the dish in a preheated oven at a high heat and bake well so the tomatoes and the breadcrumbs brown, about 45 minutes.

Line the steaks up in a greased pan. Fry on both sides, add salt, and pour in a glass of wine. When they are done, arrange them on the plate.

Cut some crostini to the same size as the steaks and fry in butter. Put a steak on each one and top off with a gratinated tomato.

If you like, serve with a pyramid of mashed potato in the center.

FRICASSEA CON CARCIOFI

Fricassee of Veal with Artichokes

2¼ lb veal brisket in chunks
Olive oil
2 oz prosciutto
Onion
Parsley
Flour
White wine
6 large artichoke hearts
2 lemons
3 egg yolks
Salt

Put the veal in a Dutch oven with half a glass of oil and a mix of chopped prosciutto, onion, and parsley. Brown slowly over medium heat and, when the meat is golden, sprinkle with flour, moisten with a glass of wine, and season with salt.

Increase the heat and, when the wine has evaporated, pour in plenty of hot water to cover. Cover and braise slowly.

Cut the artichoke hearts into not very thin wedges and put them in acidulated water with the juice of a lemon.

After about 1½ hours of cooking the meat, add the drained artichokes, season with a good pinch of salt, and let cook slowly, stirring occasionally. At the end of cooking, the sauce should be nice and thick.

Put the egg yolks in a bowl, whisk in the juice of a lemon, add a spoon of chopped parsley, and pour the eggs into the sauce. Stir again, quickly remove the saucepan from the heat and keep it warm so that the eggs are creamy without breaking.

GALANTINA DI VITELLO

Veal Galantine

3½ oz mortadella
3½ oz ham
3½ oz prosciutto
1 lb lean ground veal
4 eggs
Grated Parmesan
3 tbsp pistachios
Marsala
Bouillon cube jelly *(p52)*
Salt
Nutmeg
Pepper
Optional: black truffle

Finely chop the mortadella, half of the ham, and half the prosciutto and mix with the ground veal. Beat the eggs with a fork and work those in along with a few spoonfuls of grated Parmesan, a little salt, a pinch of pepper, a trifle of nutmeg, and a few spoons of Marsala.

Cut the rest of the prosciutto and ham into cubes. Put the pistachios in hot water for 10 minutes, so they peel more easily. Add the diced ham and pistachios to the ground meat mixture and, if you like, some slices of black truffle. Mix well.

Now oil a cylindrical tin, put the mixture in, tap it a little on the table so everything fits tightly, put the lid on or cover with wax paper and tie it on with kitchen string. Immerse the tin in a tall narrow pot of boiling water so that the container stands firm, and cook in this bain-marie for about 1½ hours, making sure that the water never reaches a tumultuous boil.

Remove the cylinder from the water and let the galantine cool without turning it out. Only when the galantine is cold, turn the cylinder upside down onto a long plate. Cover with another plate and on this place a very light weight, so that the galantine is pressed but not too much and keeps its shape.

Make a bouillon cube jelly.

After a few hours, thinly slice the galantine and arrange it in a long plate with high edges; cover it with a light layer of jelly, and put the dish in the fridge until ready to serve. At the same time put any remaining jelly in the fridge so that it solidifies and you can cut it into cubes to decorate.

ADA SAYS: *For cooking the galantine you can use either a special cylindrical container, or an empty 1-quart olive oil can, from which you have removed the upper lid.*

INVOLTINI AL POMODORO

Veal and Tomato Rolls

2 lb veal flank steaks
Sage
5 oz prosciutto
Garlic
Carrot
Celery
Rosemary
Flour
Olive oil
White wine
1 lb tomatoes
Salt
Pepper
To serve: fresh salad

Use a wet meat mallet to flatten the veal steaks and arrange them on a work surface. On each one put a sage leaf, a slice of prosciutto, a slice of garlic, a carrot stick, a celery baton, and a few leaves of rosemary. Season with salt and pepper.

Roll up the slices and secure them with a wooden toothpick and lightly flour them.

Oil a pan—big enough to fit all the rolls—and warm, adding 2 cloves of garlic. As soon as the garlic browns, take it out and replace with the rolls. Brown them over high heat, add salt, pour in the wine, and let it evaporate. Add the tomatoes—peeled, seeded, and chopped—and season with a little salt and pepper. Cover the pan, let the rolls cook for about 30 minutes, then arrange them in a round serving dish and serve with a fresh salad garnish.

INVOLTINI AL PROSCIUTTO

Roast Veal and Ham Rolls with Sage

12 thin veal flank steaks
3½ oz prosciutto
Crustless white bread
Milk
Grated Parmesan
1 egg yolk
Bread for croutons
Sage
Olive oil or butter
Salt
Pepper
Nutmeg
Optional: garlic
To serve: a salad with peppers

Carve wide and thin slices from a tender piece of veal. Trim them appropriately, to give them an equal shape. Take any trimmings, a little prosciutto, the bread—dipped in milk and squeezed dry—salt, pepper, nutmeg, ⅓ cup of grated Parmesan, and, if you like, a pinch of diced garlic. Blend well and finish with an egg yolk.

Spread a little of this mix on each veal slice and then roll them up to make sausages. Take some long skewers and start with a cube of bread, then a roll of veal, then a sage leaf, another roll etc. and finish with a crust of bread.

Arrange the skewers on a baking sheet, brush them with plenty of oil or melted butter and roast in a hot oven for about 20 minutes or in a moderate oven for about 30 minutes. Serve with a salad of peppers.

INVOLTINI IN BORDURA DI PATATE

Veal Rolls with Potato

2 lb veal flank steaks
3½ oz prosciutto
Crustless white bread
Milk
Basil
8½ tbsp butter
White wine
Meat broth *(p88)* or bouillon cube
2¼ lb potatoes
2 egg yolks
Grated Parmesan
Breadcrumbs
Nutmeg
Salt

Pound the steaks and cut them into strips about 2½ inches wide. Put the chopped meat trimmings together with the chopped prosciutto in a bowl. Add the bread—soaked in milk and squeezed dry—and a handful of basil leaves. Season with a little salt and a pinch of nutmeg and mix well.

Arrange the strips on a work surface and put a part of the filling on each one, then roll them up and stick them together with toothpicks.

Melt 3 tablespoons of butter in a skillet and brown the meat rolls. Pour in some white wine and when it evaporates, add a few ladles of broth and let the meat braise and the sauce reduce for about 30 minutes.

Peel the potatoes, cut them into pieces and put them in a saucepan with lightly salted water. Boil them, then when they are cooked, drain and sieve or mash them. Put the purée back in the saucepan, season with 3 tablespoons of butter and set it over heat. Let it flavor, stirring constantly, then remove from the heat and, when it is cool, season with salt and nutmeg. Add the egg yolks and some grated Parmesan.

Grease 1-quart mold, sprinkle it with breadcrumbs, fill up with the potato purée, pressing it well. Let rest for some time, then place it in a moderate oven so that it is colored and firmed up, for about 30 minutes.

When it is ready, remove it from the oven, let it rest for a few moments, then turn the mold upside down onto a serving dish, and place the rolls in the center with their sauce.

INVOLTINI RIPIENI DI CARNE

Stuffed Veal Rolls

1 lb 5 oz flank steak
7 oz ground veal or pork
2 oz lardo
Garlic
Crustless white bread
1 egg yolk
Grated Parmesan
Butter
Flour
Broth
Salt
Pepper
Nutmeg
To serve: risotto

For this preparation you need to cut very thin slices of veal 4¾ inches long and 2½ inches wide. Spread them on a work surface and, with a small knife, cut them to equal sizes. Season with salt and pepper.

Mix the ground veal or pork with the chopped lardo, a small piece of garlic, and some bread—moistened and squeezed dry. Season with salt, pepper, a little nutmeg, the egg yolk, and a spoon of grated Parmesan. Mix well.

Distribute this filling in equal parts over each slice, smoothing it out with the blade of a knife. Roll up the slices up and then either stick two by two with a toothpick or on a long skewer separating each one with a slice of lardo.

Melt a little butter in a large pan, flour the rolls, and cook them, turning them carefully from time to time. Just as they start to brown, pour in a little broth. Cover the pan, reduce the heat, and finish cooking slowly for about 30 minutes. When cooked, the sauce must have almost all the liquid evaporated and be a shiny and savory coating.

They are served simply as they are or accompanied by a risotto.

LOMBATINE ALLA MILANESE (ROSTINI)

Veal Steaks Milanese

6 veal loin steaks
Sage
Flour
10 tbsp butter
White wine
2 cups broth
Parsley
Carrot
Onion
Celery
Rosemary
Garlic
Salt
Pepper

The steaks must have a thickness of about ¾ inch and have their tenderloin attached. Shorten the central bone, put a sage leaf at the bottom between the attachment of the loin and tenderloin and then take the upper strip of the loin and bring it around the tenderloin, holding it with a toothpick, to make it round.

Flour and put them in a skillet with plenty of hot butter and brown them on both sides, seasoning them with salt and pepper. Just as they brown, pour in a glass of white wine, turn down the heat a little, and let the liquid evaporate, turning them from time to time.

When the wine has evaporated, moisten again, little by little, with the broth and continue cooking slowly. Toward the end of cooking, add very finely chopped parsley, carrot, onion, celery, rosemary, and a hint of garlic.

Take them out of the pan and place them in a dish. Strain the sauce and dress the steaks.

LOMBATINE ALLA MODENESE

Veal Steaks Modena Style

6 veal loin steaks
Flour
1 egg
Breadcrumbs
Olive oil
2 tbsp butter
3½ oz prosciutto
5 oz Gruyère
Salt

Pound the steaks with a meat mallet to thin them a little. Dredge them in flour, beaten egg, and lastly breadcrumbs. Fry in hot oil.

Arrange the steaks in a buttered baking dish, put on each steak a slice of prosciutto and on top of this a slice of Gruyère. Put in a hot oven for a few minutes, then place on a plate and send to the table.

LOMBATINE ALLA SALVIA

Veal Steaks with Sage

14 oz potatoes
Olive oil
Garlic
6 veal loin steaks
Flour
7 tbsp butter
6 or 12 sage leaves
Salt

Wash and peel the potatoes and cut into equal, small wedges. In a large pan, heat half a glass of oil, add the potatoes, a clove of garlic, and salt. Cover. Cook slowly for about 40 minutes, taking care to stir the pan often to prevent the potatoes from sticking to the bottom.

Salt the steaks, lightly flour and fry in butter with a clove of garlic in another pan. When they are almost cooked, add one or two sage leaves for each steak and combine with the beautiful golden potatoes. Take out the garlic. Let everything flavor together, then lay up on a plate with the sage leaves and surround them with the potatoes.

Before sending them to the table, drizzle everything with a little more melted butter that has just turned the color of hazelnuts.

LOMBATINE IN INTINGOLO

Veal Steaks with Herb Sauce

6 veal loin steaks
3 tbsp flour
7 tbsp butter
White wine
Parsley
Carrot
Onion
Celery
Rosemary
Garlic
2 cups meat broth *(p88)* or bouillon cube
Salt
Pepper

Trim the steaks. Flour them. Then brown in hot butter on both sides over high heat and season with salt and pepper.

When the meat is completely brown, pour in a glass of white wine, reduce the heat, and cook slowly, turning from time to time.

Finely chop the parsley, carrot, onion, celery, rosemary, and a pinch of garlic. Add them to the steaks after the wine has evaporated and then baste, little by little with the broth, continuing to cook slowly.

When everything is ready, take out the steaks and strain the sauce, pressing well to collect all the juices. Put the veal back in the pan, cover with the sauce and heat everything again for a few minutes. Arrange the steaks with the sauce in a serving dish and send immediately to the table.

LOMBATINE PICCANTI

Veal Steaks with Peppers

6 veal loin steaks (5 oz each)
Flour
Butter
Olive oil
6 green bell peppers
Onion
Green olives, pitted
Capers
6 tomatoes
2 anchovies
Garlic
Broth
Salt
Pepper

Lightly pound the steaks, dredge them in flour, and fry in a pan with a little butter and a little oil, coloring well on both sides.

Char the peppers over a flame or in the oven. Peel, seed, and cut into strips. In a skillet, cook the peppers with very little onion, oil, and salt. When the peppers are cooked, add a handful of green olives and a spoon of capers.

In another pan, sear the tomatoes—peeled, seeded, and cut into chunks—with a little oil and salt. Add them to the peppers.

Add the anchovies—rinsed, boned, and chopped—and melt them in hot oil with a little crushed garlic. Pour this sauce in with the peppers and tomatoes, mix, and let warm.

Meanwhile, the steaks need salt and pepper, plus a few spoons of broth. Then place them on the plate, with the pepper garnish to one side.

MESSICANI DI VITELLO AL POMODORO

Veal Rolls with Tomato

12 thin slices veal (2 oz each), from flank steak
10 oz ground pork
Crustless white bread
Milk
Garlic
Parsley
Grated Parmesan
Olive oil
Carrot
Celery
Sage
White wine
2 tbsp tomato paste
2 cups broth
Salt
Pepper
Nutmeg

Spread out the veal slices.

Mix the ground pork with the white bread—soaked in milk and squeezed dry—a little chopped garlic, a little chopped parsley, salt, pepper, nutmeg, and some grated Parmesan.

Spread this filling over the slices, roll them up, and tie them with string to keep their shape.

In a large pan, heat half a glass of oil and arrange the rolls in a single layer. Let them brown on one side. While they brown, coarsely chop the carrot and celery. Put them in the pan, add a whole clove of garlic and a few sage leaves. Then turn the steaks, cover, and let cook slowly until everything has taken a beautiful gold color. Then pour in a glass of white wine and let that evaporate. Season with salt. Add the tomato paste and top up with broth from time to time cooking covered over moderate heat, overall for about 1 hour.

When they are ready, place on a serving plate and pour on the cooking sauce.

OSSOBUCO ALLA MILANESE

Osso Buco Milanese

10 tbsp butter
6 veal shanks
Flour
White wine
Parsley
Lemon zest
Garlic
Anchovy fillet
Broth
Salt
Optional: Milanese risotto *(p216)*

The osso buco is a veal shank, sawn into pieces about two fingers long, so it retains its marrow.

Generously grease a deep pan in which the shanks can be arranged in a single layer. Flour the shanks and set the pan over heat. Brown them, season with salt and pepper, and, when they are colored on one side, turn them, continuing to cook until they have a nice dark golden color. Baste with a little white wine and, when it evaporates, add some water, cover and let it finish cooking for a good hour, bearing in mind that the marrow bones must not fall apart, but should remain quite firm.

About 5 minutes before serving, mince the parsley, a small piece of lemon zest, a little garlic, and half an anchovy fillet and add to the pan. Let the osso buco boil again, turning them gently so that they can be flavored by the aromatics. Then arrange them on a plate.

Moisten the cooking juices with a few spoons of broth, stirring with a wooden spoon. Add a few pieces of butter, pour the sauce over the shanks, and send to the table surrounded, if you like, by a good Milanese risotto.

PAILLARD

Veal Paillard

6 veal steaks (7 oz each)
Olive oil
8 tbsp butter
Parsley
Salt
Pepper

Preheat a grill or grill pan. Pound the steaks to flatten them a bit, oil them lightly on both sides, put them on the grill and let cook for 3 or 4 minutes first on one side and then on the other.

Season with salt and pepper and serve with a little melted butter and a sprig of parsley.

PASTICCIO DI VITELLO

Veal and Ham Pie

1 lb 11 oz lean veal
Flour
Lemon zest
Butter
9 oz puff pastry, homemade *(p71)* or store-bought
9 oz ham
2 hard-boiled eggs
Gelatin
Salt
Pepper

This preparation consists of a puff pastry pie filled with cubes of veal and slices of ham.

Cut the veal into walnut-size cubes and put them in a bowl with salt, pepper, a spoon of flour, and the zest of a lemon.

Lightly butter a 1 quart loaf pan, 8 × 4 × 3 inches.

Roll out the puff pastry ¼ inch thick and with one part of it line the inside of the pan. Prick the pastry with the tines of a fork, then make a layer of veal cubes, on this line some slices of ham. Alternating veal and ham, fill the mold. On the last layer of ham distribute the hard-boiled eggs cut into wedges. Baste the pie with a few spoons of water and cover it with the remaining puff pastry, pressing the edges well so that they match perfectly and enclose the filling.

Make a small hole in the center to let the steam out and with the leftover pastry cuttings make some small decorations.

Put the pie in a preheated oven of moderate heat for about 1 hour, then, when it is golden, take it out of the oven and let it cool before taking it out of the pan.

Prepare 2 cups of gelatin and let it cool, but not in the fridge, because you need it to be liquid. This is to prevent the pie from crumbling when slicing. So when it is properly cold, pour a few spoons of the jelly into the hole in the middle.

PETTO FARCITO CON SALSICCE

Breast of Veal Stuffed with Sausages

2¼ lb bone-in veal breast
4 sausages
Crustless white bread
Milk
2 oz ham
1 egg
Parsley
Onion
Carrot
2 cups broth
Capers
2 cornichons
Salt
Optional: butter, flour

With a sharp knife, bone out the veal breast and slice it horizontally in half without cutting through the edges. There will be a kind of open pocket to one side.

Remove the sausage casings and place the meat in a bowl with the bread—soaked in milk and squeezed dry, about the size of an apple—the diced ham, egg, and chopped parsley and mix well. Season with a little salt.

Fill the meat pocket in the breast with the prepared mixture, sew the opening, and tie the meat up with a kitchen string.

Chop an onion and carrot and place in a Dutch oven. Put the stuffed breast on top, baste with two glasses of broth, cover, and cook slowly for 1½ hours.

When the meat is cooked, spoon off the fat on the surface and strain the cooking juices into a new pan. Add the capers and the cornichons cut into wheels. Pour everything back into the Dutch oven and, if the sauce does not seem sufficiently reduced, thicken with 1½ tablespoons of butter, mixed with flour. Bring to a boil again, then take the string off the meat, slice it, arrange it on a serving dish, and cover it with the hot sauce.

PETTO IN FRITTURA

Deep-Fried Breast of Veal with Lemon

2¼ lb thin veal breast
Onion
Carrot
Celery
Parsley
1 lemon
Flour
2 eggs
Olive oil
Lemon wedges
Salt

Poach the veal breast, thinly sliced, in a pot with hot water, flavored with the usual aromatics for the broth—onion, carrot, celery, parsley, and salt.

Let it simmer slowly until the meat is completely cooked. Then while still hot, take out the bones, then lay it on a work surface and weigh it down so it is flat.

When the meat is cold, cut it into large cubes. Put the pieces in a bowl, sprinkle with salt and drizzle with lemon juice.

After some time, flour the meat cubes, dredge them in the beaten egg and deep-fry in plenty of hot oil.

Drain well, arrange on a serving dish, sprinkle with salt and surround it with lemon wedges. Serve immediately.

PETTO IN INTINGOLO

Braised Veal with Vegetables

2¼ lb veal breast
3 zucchini
Celery
5 tomatoes
Butter
Onion
Grated Parmesan
Basil
Salt
Pepper
To serve: bread for croutons

Bone out the veal breast and cut it into squares. Cut the zucchini and celery into horseshoe shapes. Blanch, peel, seed, and chop the tomatoes.

Butter a 1½ quart baking pan. Cut the onion into slices and lay in the bottom fo then pan, then the breast pieces, the zucchini, the celery, chopped tomatoes, some grated Parmesan and chopped basil. Season with salt and pepper.

Put in a preheated oven of moderate heat for 1½ hours.

Pour everything into a plate and surround with fried croutons.

PETTO IN SALSA PICCANTE

Poached Breast of Veal with a Piquant Sauce

2¼ lb veal breast in one piece
3 eggs
2 oz sliced prosciutto
Grated Parmesan
2 oz crustless white bread
Milk
Parsley
Onion
Carrot
Celery
Salt
Pepper

Piquant sauce:
2 anchovies, capers, parsley, 6 cornichons, onion, garlic, breadcrumbs, 3 tbsp olive oil, 1 tsp vinegar

Bone out the veal breast. With a sharp knife, slice into the meat horizontally to make a large pocket without cutting through any of the edges.

In a bowl, combine the beaten eggs, the prosciutto chopped into cubes, ⅓ cup grated Parmesan, white bread—soaked in milk and squeezed dry—chopped parsley, and salt and pepper. Mix all the ingredients well. Fill the breast pocket with the mixture. Sew the opening and tie up the meat with kitchen string to keep it in shape.

Half fill a Dutch oven with water. The breast should fit neatly in it. Add the aromatics—onion, carrot, and celery—and season with salt. Bring the water to a boil and add the veal, letting it cook slowly for 1½ hours.

Meanwhile, make the piquant sauce: Dice the anchovies—rinsed and boned—some capers, parsley, the cornichons, onion, and garlic and mix in with breadcrumbs, the oil, and vinegar.

When the meat is cooked, take it out and strain the broth through a sieve. Carve the veal breast, heat it up in a pan with some of its cooking broth, pour it into a serving dish and accompany it with a gravy boat, containing the sauce.

PETTO RIPIENO AL FORNO

Roast Stuffed Breast of Veal

2¼ lb veal breast
7 tbsp butter
Fresh peas
2 boiled carrots
3 onions
2 oz crustless white bread
Grated Parmesan
2 oz prosciutto
Parsley
2 egg yolks
Nutmeg
Olive oil
White wine
Salt
Pepper

Bone out the veal breast. With a sharp knife, slice into the meat horizontally to make a large pocket without cutting through any of the edges.

In a small saucepan, melt 2 tablespoons of the butter and cook ⅓ cup of peas. Season with a pinch of salt. Slice the boiled carrots and add them to the peas. Put 3 tablespoons of butter in another pan and brown some finely chopped onion with a little water. When they are golden and almost a mush, put them in a bowl and let them cool. Then add the bread—soaked in warm water and squeezed dry—some grated Parmesan, the chopped prosciutto, the chopped parsley, the carrots, and peas. Mix in the egg yolks and season with salt and pepper and nutmeg.

Fill the veal pocket with this mix and sew up the opening and tie up the breast with string to keep it in shape. Lay it down in a Dutch oven with 2 tablespoons of butter and ¼ cup of oil. Cover and place in a preheated oven of moderate heat, letting it roast slowly for about 2 hours, basting it several times with two glasses of white wine. Then remove from the oven, untie it, and arrange on a serving dish and send it to the table.

POLPETTE AL BURRO

Veal Meatballs with Butter

2 oz crustless white bread
Milk
1 lb 5 oz lean ground veal
3 eggs
Grated Parmesan
Flour
Breadcrumbs
Butter
Salt
Pepper
Nutmeg
To serve: French fries, mashed potatoes, peas with ham, or green beans

In a pan, combine the bread and a little milk and cook over low heat, mixing with a wooden spoon to form a paste. Let cool and then work it into the ground veal.

Add 2 eggs, salt, pepper, nutmeg, and a spoon of grated Parmesan. Mix everything together well with your hands. Divide into equal portions and roll into meatballs the size of small apples.

Gently, so they do not break, flour the balls on all sides. Use a spoon to dredge them in a beaten egg and then the breadcrumbs.

Fry them in butter over moderate heat and when they color, turn them over carefully; the heat needs to be not too strong to allow the meat to cook through.

When the meatballs are cooked, arrange them in a ring on a round plate; in the middle you can put in a pyramid, French fries, mashed potatoes, peas with ham or green beans with butter.

POLPETTE AL COGNAC

Veal Meatballs Flambéed with Cognac

1 lb boiled veal
Crustless white bread
Milk
2 eggs
Grated Parmesan
Flour
3½ tbsp butter
Cognac
Salt
Pepper

Finely chop or mince the veal and mix with the bread—soaked in milk and squeezed dry. Season with salt, pepper, the eggs, and some grated Parmesan and work everything well with your hands.

Divide the meat mixture into equal portions and with floured hands form into balls the size of small apples.

Generously grease a pan big enough to fit all the meatballs, add water to cover the bottom, and bring to a boil. Drop the meatballs in. Let them firm up and thicken in the liquid.

Then place them in a serving dish with their reduced sauce. Sprinkle over a glass of Cognac and carefully light it with a long match. Promptly send them to the table.

POLPETTE CON LA SALSA VELLUTATA

Veal Meatballs with Cream Sauce

Meatballs *(p439)*
Butter
Flour
Salt
Pepper

Cream sauce:
3½ tbsp butter, 6½ tbsp flour,
4 cups broth

Make the meatball mixture and form into meatballs as described in Meatballs Flambéed with Cognac. Note that these meatballs will be cooked in the oven, not the stovetop.

After making the balls, make a cream sauce *(p17)* using the ingredient amounts listed here.

Generously grease a baking pan, pour in the sauce. Flour the meatballs and arrange in the pan in a single layer.

Put the pan in a preheated oven for about 20 minutes, until the sauce has firmed up and has formed a crust. Then remove from the oven, arrange the meatballs carefully on a serving dish, and promptly send them to the table.

POLPETTONE SCREZIATO

Meatloaf with Mushrooms and Chicken Livers

1 lb ground veal flank
2 oz crustless white bread
Milk
Grated Parmesan
2 egg yolks
3 chicken livers
1 oz dried mushrooms
Butter
2 oz ham or pickled tongue
Hard-boiled egg
Broth
Salt
Pepper

Combine the ground veal, bread—soaked in milk and squeezed dry— ⅓ cup of grated Parmesan, egg yolks, salt. and pepper. Knead until well combined.

Meanwhile, pan-fry the chicken livers briefly. Soak the dried mushrooms to reconstitute, then wash, cut them into pieces, and fry in a small saucepan with a little butter, a pinch of salt, adding a little water if needed.

Add the mushrooms to the livers, along with the ham or pickled tongue and hard-boiled egg white cut into cubes, the yolk mashed. Mix gently.

Butter a sheet of parchment paper and splash with water. Roll out the meat to a rectangle about ⅜ inch thick. Cover with the chicken liver and mushroom mix.

Now roll the meat up into a rather tight sausage. When you have it all wrapped up, wrap it with the same parchment paper and twist the paper on both sides as if wrapping a candy. Tie the ends with kitchen string and make a couple of ties around the middle of the roll.

Place the meatloaf in an oval Dutch oven into which it can fit snugly. Add enough broth to just barely come ⅓ of the way up the meatloaf. Cover tightly and place in a medium oven for 30 minutes.

After this time, carefully remove the meatloaf, unwrap it, and with a very sharp knife cut it into slices about ¾ inch thick. Arrange in a serving dish.

ROLLÈ AL FORNO CON PATATE

Roast Veal Roll with Potatoes

2 lb 10 oz thin breast of veal
Garlic
2 eggs
Olive oil
White wine
2 lb 10 oz potatoes
Rosemary
Salt
Pepper

For this recipe you need a thin breast from which you choose a large, uniform slice and ask the butcher to bone it out.

Spread the breast on a work surface and with a sharp knife trim off the skin and any fat. Pound with a wet meat mallet, then rub it with a clove of garlic, and a little salt.

Beat the eggs, season with a pinch of salt, and cook in a skillet with ¼ cup oil to make an omelet almost as wide as the slice of meat. Lay the omelet on top of the veal breast and roll it up on itself and tie it tightly with a string.

Salt the roll on the outside and put it in a baking dish with 3 tablespoons of oil and transfer to a preheat oven. Let it cook slowly for about 1½ hours, turning several times. If the pan juices gets too dry, add half a glass of white wine.

After about 1 hour, wash, peel, and cut the potatoes into small cubes and add them to the veal with a little more salt and a sprig of rosemary.

To serve, untie the breast, carve into slices, and surround with the potatoes.

ROLLÈ IN AGRODOLCE

Veal Roll with Sweet and Sour Sauce

2¼ lb veal breast
2 oz prosciutto
Parsley
Onion
Carrot
Celery
2 tbsp sugar
Vinegar
3½ tbsp butter
2 tbsp flour
Candied citrus peel
Lemon zest
Salt
Pepper

Spread the veal breast on a work surface, bone it, and pound with a wet meat mallet to flatten.

Arrange slices of prosciutto, some parsley, pepper, and salt on the meat. Roll the veal breast up on itself and tie it with a string, like a salami.

Fill a pot—in which the veal roll will fit snugly—half full of water. Add half an onion, carrot, and celery all roughly chopped and salt. Bring to a boil and only then lower the veal roll in and let simmer for 1½ hours.

When the meat is cooked, remove it from the pot and strain the broth.

In a small pan, dissolve the sugar in a little water and as soon as it has taken on a slight golden color, splash in half a glass of vinegar, mixing well.

Put the butter in the same pot where the meat was cooked, let it melt and then add the flour. Finally add a few ladles of the strained broth and stir the sauce until it is slightly thickened. Pour in the sugar and vinegar mix.

Cut the string from the veal roll and carve into slices. Add the slices to the pan and heat gently. Finish the sauce with small pieces of candied lemon or orange peel and grated lemon zest.

ROLLÈ IN CASSERUOLA

Braised Veal Roll

2 lb 10 oz thin veal breast
3½ oz ham or mortadella (enough to cover all the breast)
Sage
Olive oil
3½ tbsp butter
Red wine
Broth
Salt

For this recipe you need a large slice off the thinnest part of the breast and to have it boned.

Trim, pound, and flatten the breast on a work surface. Then arrange the slices of ham on the breast, covering it entirely. Add a few sage leaves here and there. Roll up the veal and tie it tightly with kitchen string.

Put the oil and butter in a Dutch oven over lively heat and add the meat roll. Sprinkle on a little more salt, and, watching carefully, turn the roll so it forms a brown crust on all sides.

Then pour in a glass of wine and let it evaporate. At this point lower the heat and cook gently for about 2 hours, supervising the cooking from time to time. If it looks too brown, or about to burn, add a few spoons of broth, and only if absolutely necessary, to avoid the danger of burning, some more pieces of butter.

When the roll is cooked, after about 1½ hours (check by sticking in a skewer), remove it from the heat and let cool. Once cooled, remove the string and carve it into thin slices—you cannot do this when the meat is hot. Reserve the pan juices, which you can warm up before serving and pour on by way of sauce.

ADA SAYS: *The veal breast cooked in this way does not offer any particular difficulties, but it does require attention. It is not one of those dishes that you can walk away from.*

ROLLÈ IN SALSA D'UOVO

Veal Roll with Egg Sauce

2¼ lb veal breast
Guanciale or prosciutto
Onion
1 clove
1 carrot
1 celery stalk
3½ tbsp butter
Flour
2 egg yolks
Parsley
1 lemon
Salt
Pepper

Spread the piece of veal breast on a work surface and bone it out. Pound with a wet meat mallet, then season with salt and pepper.

Trim the guanciale or prosciutto fat and spread on the breast. Then roll up the veal and tie it with string to keep it in shape.

Half fill an oval Dutch oven, in which the roll can fit snugy, with water. Add half an onion—in which you stick a clove—a carrot, parsley, a celery stalk, and salt. Bring to a boil.

When the water boils, lower the veal roll in, cover, and let it simmer slowly over a very light heat for 1½ hours, until the meat is well cooked and can be pierced easily with the point of a small knife. If, during cooking, the broth starts to evaporate, pour in a little more water, without exaggerating, however.

When the meat is cooked, remove from the pot and strain the broth.

Put 2 tablespoons of butter in another pan and as soon as it has melted, add a good spoonful of flour. Cook, stirring, and then 2 or 3 minutes later add a couple of ladles of the veal broth. Stir and cook gently for about 10 minutes, adding more broth if the sauce is too thick.

In a bowl, beat the egg yolks with a spoon of water or broth. Slowly pour the sauce over the egg yolks, stirring with a wooden ladle or better with a small whisk. Return the sauce to the saucepan where the veal was cooked. Carve the veal into slices and put back in the pot it was cooked in. Keep the pot over very weak heat so that the meat and the sauce can heat up, but without boiling.

When it is time to send the meat to the table, arrange it in an oval plate. Add a couple of spoons of chopped parsley and the juice of half a lemon to the sauce, mix, and pour over the meat. Serve hot.

ROLLÈ RIPIENO DI BESCIAMELLA E FUNGHI

Braised Breast of Veal with Mushrooms

2¼ lb thin veal breast
Milk
Basil
Sage
Parsley
Rosemary
2 oz dried mushrooms
Butter
Crustless white bread
1 egg yolk
3½ oz ham
Grated Parmesan
Salt
To serve: salad

White sauce:
2 tbsp butter, 3 tbsp flour, ¾ cup milk

Spread the veal breast on a work surface, bone it out, and flatten it with a wet meat mallet.

For the white sauce, first make an herbed milk: In a small pan, combine ¾ cup milk and a few leaves of fresh basil, sage, parsley, and rosemary and boil for a few minutes. Strain. Then make a white sauce *(p16)* using the butter and flour amounts listed here and the herbed milk. Let cool.

Reconstitute the dried mushrooms in cold water, then rinse and cook in a saucepan with 2 tablespoons butter, a ladle of water, and a pinch of salt until the water has evapoarted. Chop and fold into the cooled white sauce. Soak the bread in milk and squeeze dry so that it is the size of a small apple. Stir into the sauce, with the egg yolk, ham (diced), and ⅓ cup of Parmesan. Spread evenly over the meat.

Roll the veal breast up on itself to form a large sausage, tie with string to keep it in shape, and sew it up at both ends so the filling remains tightly closed inside.

Melt 3 tablespoons of butter in an oval Dutch oven and slowly brown the veal roll on all sides. Then sprinkle it with salt and braise over low heat, adding, if necessary, a few spoons of water during cooking. After about 1½ hours, when the roll has acquired a nice dark golden color, remove it and let it cool with a weight on it.

Then slice it and accompany it with a salad of your taste.

ADA SAYS: *Instead of braising the roll in a Dutch oven, you could also oil a baking sheet, and roast it in a preheated oven of moderate heat for 1½ hours.*

SALSICCIOTTI GIGANTI

Giant Sausages

6 veal flank steaks (5 oz each)
7 oz ground beef
6 slices mortadella
6 hard-boiled eggs
Garlic
Olive oil
White wine
Carrot
Onion
Celery
Salt

Arrange the cutlets on a work surface and spread with a little ground beef, a slice of mortadella, and a hard-boiled egg.

Roll each slice on itself and secure by tying the sausage with kitchen string.

In a pan, heat the garlic and oil and as soon as the garlic is golden remove it. Add the rolls and brown them well. Pour a glass of wine into the pan, a little at a time, and season the sausages with a little salt. Add chopped carrot, onion, and celery and let braise, covered, over low heat for about 1 hour, adding, if needed, a little wine or water.

Let the rolls cool, cut the string, halve them lengthwise, cover them with their sauce—strained or blended and slightly heated again.

ADA SAYS: *You might serve these rolls on a base of buttered spinach with a little grated Parmesan.*

SALSICCIOTTO DI VITELLO CON SPINACI

Veal Sausage with Spinach

2 lb lean veal
1 lb spinach
3 eggs
Grated Parmesan
Olive oil
Salt

A big, wide, thin slice of veal is absolutely required for this recipe so that it can be easily rolled up, like a big sausage.

First, pound the meat with a wet mallet and sprinkle it with a little salt. Clean and rinse the spinach and cook in a little lightly salted water. As soon as the leaves wilt, drain, squeeze out the water in your hands, and chop them.

At this point, beat the eggs and season with a little salt and ¼ cup of grated Parmesan. In a skillet, cook the eggs to make a wide and thin omelet roughly the same size as the slice of veal. Before the omelet sets completely, while it is still in the pan, cover it with the chopped spinach. Fold the omelet over so the spinach is completely enclosed.

Place the omelet on the slice of veal, roll it up to make a sausage and tie with string to keep everything in place.

Put the sausage in an oiled baking pan, pour in a glass of oil and put in a preheated oven of moderate heat for 1½ hours.

Remove from the oven and let it cool so you can carve very thin slices.

SALTIMBOCCA

Veal Saltimbocca

6 thin veal steaks (5 oz each)
6 sage leaves
5 oz prosciutto
7 tbsp butter
Salt
Pepper

Pound the steaks with a wet meat mallet so that they are quite thin. On each slice place a sage leaf and a slice of prosciutto and pin them together with a toothpick, as you might put a pin to keep two pieces of fabric together.

Put a skillet with about 3 tablespoons of butter on the heat. When the butter melts, add the saltimbocca prosciutto-side down—the ham contributes in part to give flavor to the meat—and season with a pinch of salt and pepper. Cook over high heat on both sides, for a few minutes, then remove from the pan, arrange them on a plate, so that the slice of prosciutto remains on top.

Deglaze the pan with a spoon or two of water, stirring the cooking juices. Add another piece of butter and as soon as this melts, pour the sauce over the saltimbocca and serve them immediately.

ADA SAYS: *The meat must be presented on the table without removing the toothpicks. It can be served plain or with a side dish of green beans, peas, artichokes, asparagus, potatoes, etc.*

SCALOPPINE AL MARSALA

Veal Scaloppine with Marsala

6 thin veal steaks (5 oz each)
Flour
10 tbsp butter
Marsala
Lemon slices
Salt
Pepper

Pound the steaks with a wet meat mallet or a moistened blade of a big knife; season with a little salt and pepper, and flour them.

In a rather large pan, melt a little butter and when the butter is hot, add the scaloppine one or two at a time. Fry them over lively heat on both sides for a few minutes; then remove them from the pan and put them on a plate. Repeat the same operation until you have cooked all the scaloppine, adding more butter each time.

When cooked, pour in half a glass of Marsala, turn up the heat for a moment, return all the scaloppine to the pan, reduce the heat and leave them to flavor for a few minutes, scraping with a wooden spoon to mix the sauce well. If necessary, add a little more Marsala.

Transfer the slices to a serving dish, garnish with lemon slices, and promptly send them to the table.

SCALOPPINE GUARNITE

Pan-Fried Veal Scaloppine with Garnish

10 oz potatoes
2 eggs
7 tbsp butter
14 oz mushrooms
Olive oil
Garlic
2 to 3 anchovy fillets
6 tomatoes
Breadcrumbs
Parsley
12 thin veal steaks (2 oz each)
Flour
Broth
Salt
Pepper
Nutmeg

This preparation requires lean and tender veal slices of a rather regular shape.

Peel the potatoes, cut them into wedges, and cook them in lightly salted water. When they are cooked, drain, return to the pan, and over low heat so that they can dry out some. Then sieve or mash with an egg yolk, about 2 tablespoons of butter, and a little nutmeg. Work the purée well over an almost nonexistent heat to have it very smooth.

Pour the potato onto a floured work surface. Divide into oval portions as large as walnuts, then flatten regularly with the help of a little flour, to make ovals 2¾ inches long, 1½ inches wide, and ¼ inch thick. Make as many potato "cutlets" as there are of veal. Arrange them on a greased sheet pan and set aside.

Clean, wash, and thinly slice the mushrooms. Cook them with oil in which you have sautéed a clove of garlic, salt, and pepper. When the mushrooms are cooked, mash 2 or 3 anchovies with 1½ tablespoons of butter and add them to the mushrooms. Stir and keep warm.

Cut the tomatoes in half horizontally. Set on a baking sheet. Top with some breadcrumbs and chopped parsley. Sprinkle with oil and season with salt. Broil or bake the tomatoes for about 30 minutes.

About 10 minutes before going to the table, brush a little beaten egg over the potato cutlets and put them in a hot oven with a lively heat until they have taken on a beautiful golden color.

Then take the scaloppine, season with salt and pepper, lightly flour them and arrange in a pan where you have heated a piece of butter. Fry over high heat so they do not toughen and as soon as they are cooked on one side, turn them over and cook them promptly on the other side. Remove the pan from the heat. Take the potato cutlets out of the oven.

At this point, take a rather large round plate and in the middle of the dish make a ring, alternating a potato cutlet and a scaloppine of veal. Put the cooking pan back on the heat, pour in a few spoons of broth, stir the cooking juices well, and pour this little sauce over the potato ring and veal slices.

Put the mushrooms in the center and the gratin tomatoes around them. Send immediately to the table.

SCALOPPINE PICCATE AL LIMONE

Veal Scaloppine with Lemon

2 lb thin veal steaks, cut into strips
Flour
2 slices prosciutto
10 tbsp butter
1 lemon
Parsley
Salt

Pound the steaks with a wet meat mallet or the side of a knife. Season with a little salt and pepper and flour them.

Cut the prosciutto into strips and sauté in a little butter. As soon as the butter is hot, add as many scaloppine as you can comfortably fit and increase the heat so they cook quickly.

As soon as the scaloppine are cooked on one side, turn over, then remove and put them on a plate. Repeat the same operation if you have more, adding more butter each time.

Pour the juice of a lemon into the pan, add a spoon of chopped parsley, and a new piece of butter. Return the cooled scaloppine to the pan, reduce the heat, and let them flavor for a few minutes, turning them from side to side so they mix well into the sauce.

Transfer to a serving dish and serve immediately to keep the scaloppine hot.

 ADA SAYS: *Only in this way will the veal be tender, juicy and not leach its juices, which would happen if the cooking was carried out over low heat.*

SPEZZATINO AL POMODORO

Veal and Tomato Stew

Olive oil
2 garlic cloves
2 lb 10 oz veal in chunks
Bay leaf
Parsley
White wine
5 or 6 tomatoes, or 9 oz canned tomatoes
Salt
Pepper

For this stew the pieces of veal must be neither too big nor too small.

Put some oil in a large saucepan, heat the garlic just slightly and when it browns, remove it and put in the veal. Sauté over high heat and brown the veal well, stirring frequently. When the veal chunks are a beautiful dark gold, season with salt and plenty of pepper, a bay leaf, and chopped parsley.

Braise for another minute or two and then baste with a glass of white wine. Let the wine evaporate completely, always over bright heat. Add the tomatoes—peeled, seeded, and cut into chunks if fresh. Let the tomato cook a little and then cover the meat with lightly salted water.

Cover, decrease the heat a lot and let the stew simmer slowly until completely cooked, that is for about 2 hours. If it gets too dry during cooking, add a little water, but without overdoing it, as the sauce must be thick.

SPEZZATINO AL MARSALA

Veal Stew with Marsala

Onion
Olive oil
2 lb 10 oz veal in chunks
Flour
Marsala
Parsley
Salt
Pepper

Chop the onion and slowly shallow-fry in oil. Then add the veal pieces and keep going to brown everything, stirring often with a wooden spoon. When the meat has acquired a nice golden color, sprinkle it with flour, pour in a glass of Marsala, and as soon it evaporates, cover the meat with hot water. Season with salt and pepper, cover, and let it simmer slowly for 2 hours.

When the meat is cooked and the sauce is sufficiently reduced, pour out onto a plate and garnish with finely chopped parsley.

SPEZZATINO CON PISELLI

Veal and Pea Stew

Olive oil
2 garlic cloves
2 lb 10 oz veal in chunks
Bay leaf
Parsley
White wine
Broth
5 to 6 tomatoes
7 tbsp butter
Onion
3 lb 5 oz fresh peas in the pod, or 1 lb frozen peas
Salt
Pepper

Warm half a glass of oil in a large pan, add the garlic and as soon as it browns, take them out and add the chunks of veal. Turn up the heat and brown the veal well, stirring it frequently. When the chunks have a nice dark gold color, season with salt and plenty of pepper, a chopped bay leaf, and chopped parsley. Let it cook for another minute or two and then baste with a glass of white wine. Let the wine evaporate completely, always over bright heat, and then add the tomatoes—peeled, seeded, and chopped. Let the tomato cook for a while and then add broth or water to cover the meat.

Cover, reduce the heat a lot and let it simmer until completely cooked, that is, for about 2 hours. If the pan gets too dry during cooking, add a little water, but without overdoing it, since the sauce must be thick.

Meanwhile, prepare the peas. Shell the peas if using fresh. Put the butter and a spoon of very finely chopped onion in a pan and sauté slowly, so that the onion cooks without coloring. Add the peas, a few spoons of broth, and season with very little salt and if you want a pinch of pepper. Cook them about halfway to tender.

About 10 minutes before removing the stew from the heat, add the peas and let them finish cooking and seasoning with the meat.

When it is ready, pour the stew with peas into a serving dish and serve immediately.

SPEZZATO MARENGO

Veal Marengo

Olive oil
2 lb 10 oz veal in chunks
1 onion
Flour
White wine
2 cups broth
6 tomatoes, or 9 oz canned tomatoes
Garlic
Bay leaf
12 spring onions
Butter
7 oz mushrooms
Bread for croutons
Parsley
Salt
Pepper

Heat half a glass of oil in a saucepan over high heat and, when it is hot, add the veal chunks. As the meat begins to brown, add a chopped onion, salt, and pepper and let it brown again until the meat has taken a nice dark gold color. Sprinkle on a scant spoonful of flour, stir in, and let the flour take on a nutty tint. Stir in a glass of white wine and the broth. When it reaches a boil again, add the tomatoes—peeled, seeded, and chopped—a crushed clove of garlic, and a chopped bay leaf. Cover, reduce the heat, and cook slowly.

Meanwhile, trim the spring onions and let them brown in butter. Remove the stems from the mushrooms, rinse, and keep ready.

After about 45 minutes add the browned spring onions and the raw mushrooms to the veal and let them all finish cooking.

When it is ready, that is, after about 2 hours from the start of cooking, let it rest for a few minutes so that the fat rises to the surface. In the meantime, fry 6 rather large triangle shaped croutons in oil.

With a spoon, remove all the fat from the surface of the sauce, pour everything onto a plate, surround it with the hot croutons, and sprinkle with finely chopped parsley.

SPIEDINI ALLA SALVIA

Veal Skewers with Sage

6 veal steaks (5 oz each), cut into strips
1 lemon
5 oz prosciutto
5 oz pancetta in slices
Red bell pepper
Yellow bell pepper
Bread
Sage
3½ tbsp butter
Salt
Pepper

Pound the cutlets with a wet mallet, cut them into strips, season with salt and pepper and a little lemon juice. On each strip, place a strip of prosciutto, roll the strips up and wrap them up with a slice of pancetta.

Wash, stem, and seed the peppers. Cut them into rectangles. Take some skewers, thread on a piece of bread, a rectangle of pepper, a sage leaf, a veal roll, a sage leaf, a slice of bread, a rectangle of pepper, and so on alternating the colors of the peppers.

Butter a baking dish well, lay the skewers on it, brush with melted butter, and put them in a preheated oven at moderate heat for about 30 minutes.

ADA SAYS: *You can serve these on a bed of rice, on which you should pour the cooking juices.*

SPIEDINI DI CARNE E PROSCIUTTO

Veal and Ham Skewers

3½ oz ham
3½ oz ground veal
2 oz crustless white bread
1 lb 5 oz veal steaks, cut into strips
Bread for croutons
Sage
Olive oil
Salt
Pepper
Nutmeg

Finely chop or mince the ham together with the ground veal. Combine in a bowl and season with a pinch of salt, pepper, and a trifle of nutmeg. Add the bread—soaked in milk and squeezed dry—and knead everything together.

Pound the cutlets with a wet mallet and spread a little of the prepared mixture over each slice. Roll the slices up. Put the rolls on skewers, alternating them with croutons of bread and sage leaves, and arrange on a sheet pan. Finally sprinkle with salt and oil and put them in a warm oven to cook for about 30 minutes.

When the rolls are cooked and the croutons are lightly toasted, remove them from the oven and send them to the table.

TIMBALLETTI DI VITELLO ALLA FINANZIERA

Veal Timbales Financier

SERVES 12

14 oz veal mince (or 9 oz veal and 5 oz turkey breast)
2 oz prosciutto
9 oz butter
4 oz crustless white bread
Milk
Grated Parmesan
5 egg yolks
7 oz chicken livers
2 sweetbreads
1 oz dried mushrooms
2 oz tongue
Bouillon base or bouillon cube
Potato starch
Marsala
Parsley
Salt
Optional: truffle, cream sauce (3½ tbsp butter, 6½ tbsp flour, 2 glasses broth, ½ cup cream)

First prepare the stuffing: Mince the veal with the prosciutto. Put this in a bowl, add 4 ounces of the butter, the white bread—soaked in milk and squeezed dry—some Parmesan, a pinch of salt, and the egg yolks. Stir until well and evenly combined. Cover it with a sheet of plastic wrap and let it rest for a couple of hours in the fridge.

While the filling is resting, prepare the financier: Put 3½ tablespoons of butter in a saucepan, chop the chicken livers and the sweetbreads and sear in the butter. When everything is ready, pour it out onto a plate.

Separately, soak the dried mushrooms in warm water, and when reconstituted, rinse and fry in 2 tablespoons of butter. When the mushrooms are cooked—after about 20 minutes—cut into small pieces. Also dice the tongue and, if you like, some truffle.

Now put 2 tablespoons of butter in a saucepan and when it melts, add half a glass of hot water, in which you have dissolved a teaspoon of bouillon base or half a bouillon cube. Boil for a minute. In a small bowl, stir ½ teaspoon potato starch into a little Marsala. Add this mixture to the sauce and cook to thicken.

When the sauce is quite thick, put the prepared financier ingredients—mushrooms and meats—in and simmer slowly until the sauce has absorbed all the liquid and the various components are almost dry but well coated in thick sauce. Add some chopped parsley.

Now butter 12 small cup-shaped molds—also called darioles or gobelotti—and line the inside with the veal stuffing and fill up with the financier.

About 45 minutes before going to the table, put the molds in a pan, pour boiling water to come almost three-quarters of the way up the molds. Cover them with a sheet of parchment paper and put the pan in a hot oven of medium heat so that the water, while maintaining itself at high temperature, never boils. It will take about 30 minutes.

When the filling is cooked and firm, remove the pan from the oven, let the timbales rest for about 10 minutes and then turn them out onto a warm plate.

ADA SAYS: *To make the recipe tastier, finish by making a cream sauce: Melt some butter in a pan and then add a small spoon of flour. Let it cook, stirring thoroughly, without letting the flour color, and then gradually add the cold broth. Stir again, reduce the heat and let it boil slowly. Cook at a bare simmer for about 30 minutes. Increase the heat and, stirring constantly, let the sauce thicken. Finish it off the heat with half a glass of cream, which you will add little by little, and always stirring. Keep this sauce warm until it is time to use it.*

TIMBALLO DI VITELLO CON I CARCIOFI

Veal and Artichoke Timbale

6 veal medallions (3½ oz each)
7 tbsp butter
6 potatoes
Lemon
4 artichoke hearts
Olive oil
Salt

Brown the veal medallions in a pan with 5½ tablespoons of butter and a pinch of salt.

Butter a baking dish. Cut the potatoes very thinly, as if you were frying them. Put half in the buttered dish with a little salt. On the potatoes arrange the veal medallions, with their cooking juices deglazed with a little water and lemon juice. On the meat place the thinly sliced artichoke hearts. Season with a pinch of salt, then make a new layer with the rest of the potatoes. Pour a little oil over everything, sprinkle on a little salt, and place the dish in a preheated oven of moderate heat for about 30 minutes.

Once baked, send the dish to the table.

TIMBALLO DI VITELLO CON IL RISO

Veal and Rice Timbale

2 onions
Olive oil
1¾ lb veal stewing steak
Flour
White wine
10 cups broth
10 tbsp butter
2¾ cups rice
Grated Parmesan
2 eggs
Breadcrumbs
Salt

Chop one of the onions and brown in a Dutch oven with oil. Then add the chunks of veal. When the meat is a nice dark golden color, sprinkle it with a little flour, season with salt and a dash of wine. As soon as the wine evaporates, pour in as much broth as needed to cover the meat. Reduce the heat and cook for about 1 hour.

Rice is very important for the preparation of the timbale. Brown a chopped onion with 3 tablespoons of butter in a saucepan. Add the rice and let it soak in the sauce, then pour in, little by little, 6 cups of boiling broth, stirring carefully.

Cook the rice to almost tender, then off the heat, immediately, season with 3 tablespoons butter and some grated Parmesan. Let the rice cool slightly, then mix in 2 beaten eggs.

Grease a 6-cup mold, sprinkle it with very fine breadcrumbs, turn the mold in all directions so that the bread sticks everywhere and then turn it over to drop out the excess. At the bottom of the mold and around the edges arrange the rice, keeping back 5 or 6 spoons. Press down with a spoon so that the rice forms a box in the middle.

Remove the veal from the Dutch oven with a slotted spoon and place it in the prepared box, seasoning with some of its sauce. Cover the box with the rice that you have kept aside, level off, and dot the top with butter. Put the timbale in a preheated oven of moderate heat for about 30 minutes.

When the timbale has set, remove it from the oven, let it rest for a few minutes, then turn it upside down onto a plate and send it to the table accompanied by the remaining hot sauce in a gravy boat.

TIMBALLO DI VITELLO CON LE PATATE

Veal and Potato Timbale

Olive oil
1 lb 5 oz potatoes
1 lb onions
1 lb 5 oz lean veal steaks, cut into strips
7 oz tomatoes
Oregano
Salt
Pepper

In a rather deep Dutch oven with a lid, pour two spoons of oil, then make a layer of potato—peeled and sliced—moisten with a drizzle of oil, and sprinkle with a little salt and pepper. Then make a layer of onion slices, drizzle over more oil and sprinkle with a little salt and pepper. Then make a layer of veal slices, pour another drizzle of oil, season with salt and pepper, and scatter on the tomatoes—peeled, seeded, and chopped. Make another layer of onions, season with a little more oil, salt and pepper, then finish with a layer of potatoes. Shred a few leaves of oregano on top with a few pieces of tomato here and there again, season with salt and pepper, and sprinkle everything with chopped oregano.

Cover the pot with a sheet of parchment paper, put the lid on, and cook over a very moderate heat for about 1 hour, shaking the pot regularly so it doesn't stick.

VITELLO IN ASPIC

Veal in Aspic

2 lb 10 oz veal flank
3½ oz salted tongue or ham
Black truffle
Butter
Onion
Celery
Carrot
Parsley
2 cups broth
Marsala
2 oz chicken livers
Bay leaf
7 oz ham
Bouillon jelly *(p52)*
Salt
Pepper

White sauce:
2 tbsp butter, ¼ cup flour, ¾ cup milk

Lard the veal with cubes of tongue or ham and black truffle—trimmed and peelings saved for later. Tie up the veal to keep its shape.

Set the veal in a Dutch oven with 3½ tablespoons of butter, a little onion, a little celery, carrot, and parsley. Sauté the meat and aromatics, and when they become golden, season with salt and pepper and then pour in the broth, cover, and cook slowly for about 2 hours.

As the broth evaporates, baste again with a large glass of Marsala and continue to cook slowly, so that the meat will breathe its perfume. When cooked, the sauce must be reduced to almost nothing, be thick, and envelop the flesh with a shiny coat.

Remove the veal and without loosening it from its bindings as yet, place it on a plate, cover it with another plate, put on this a weight and let it cool completely.

Meanwhile, clean the chicken livers and put them to cook for a few minutes in a pan with a little butter, the truffle trimmings, and a bay leaf. Cook over high heat for a few minutes, taking care that the livers do not toughen, season with salt and pepper, and baste with a spoon of Marsala. Take off the heat, let them cool and then chop them with 7 tablespoons of butter and a spoon of rather thick white sauce *(p16)* made with the ingredient amounts listed here. Blend everything and put it in the fridge.

When the veal is cold, remove the string, and slice it into rather thin slices. Spread a little of the liver purée on each slice, and on this also place a thin slice of ham, of the same width. Continue in this way to spread the various slices, interspersed with ham and gradually reassembling as if it were whole.

When you have finished all the slices, lightly press the two ends of the veal so that the various slices come together well. The veal should look as complete again as it was before being carved.

We now need a rectangular mold slightly larger than the veal. Prepare 4 cups of jelly, pour a little on the bottom of the mold and let it set in the fridge. When the jelly sets, take the recomposed veal carefully and put it in one piece in the mold, then finish filling with jelly. Put the mold in the fridge and leave it like that for about 2 hours.

When ready to serve, immerse it for a few seconds in warm water and then invert it onto a serving plate. Garnish with diced jelly.

VITELLO IN MOSAICO

Veal Baked with Truffle and Pistachios

3 tbsp pistachios
1 lb 5 oz lean veal
3½ oz tongue
3½ oz ham
Black truffle
7 oz lean pork
3½ oz anchovies
Butter
Olive oil
Salt
Pepper
Nutmeg

White sauce:
2 tbsp butter, ¼ cup flour, ¾ cup milk

Make a white sauce *(p16)* with the ingredient amounts listed here and allow to cool in the fridge.

Put the pistachios in very hot water for 10 minutes and then peel them. Cut only 14 ounces of the veal, the tongue, and ham into small cubes. Add the pistachios and some cubes of truffle.

Finely chop the rest of the veal and the pork and place in a bowl with the anchovies—rinsed, boned, and cut small. Add the cold white sauce and stir everything together. Also add the veal, tongue, ham, and pistachios. Season with salt, pepper, and nutmeg and, working with your hands, mix well.

Now butter a baking dish and fill with the mixture. Pour plenty of oil over everything, cover with a slightly moistened sheet of parchment paper, put the lid on, and put in a preheated oven of very moderate heat for about 1½ hours. If during cooking you notice that the surface of the meat is getting dry, add a little more oil and so on until completely cooked.

When it is cooked, place a wooden board on the parchment paper of the same shape and weigh it down. Let it cool like this and after a few hours, pass the blade of a knife around the inner wall, loosen the meat and invert it onto a cutting board.

Then slice it with a sharp knife and place on a serving plate, overlapping in steps, so it looks like a mosaic.

VITELLO TONNÉ

Veal with Tuna

2¼ lb veal flank
10 oz tinned tuna in olive oil
Onion
4 anchovies
2 cups white wine
Olive oil
1 lemon
Cornichons
Black olives, pitted
Capers
Salt
Pepper
Optional: mayonnaise

Pick a Dutch oven in which the meat can fit snugly. Lay in a nice piece of lean veal. Flake the tuna over it. Thinly slice an onion and add it. Wash, bone, and chop the anchovies and add them. Finally add salt and pepper and pour in the wine.

Set the pot over medium heat, cover, and cook for around 2 hours.

When the meat is cooked, take it out and put it in a terrine dish. Blend all the sauce ingredients along with a little oil and the juice of a lemon. If you want you can add to this sauce a few spoons of mayonnaise. Pour the sauce over the meat, cover the terrine, and leave it in the fridge for 24 hours so that the meat can have time to flavor well.

To serve, cut the veal into thin slices, cover with the sauce, and decorate with cornichons cut into slices, slices of black olives and capers.

ZAMPI DI VITELLO AL POMODORO

Veal Trotter with Tomato

3 veal trotters
2 onions
Carrot
Celery
Parsley
3½ tbsp butter
2 tsp tomato paste
Grated Parmesan
Cinnamon
Salt
Pepper

Scrape the trotters with a knife, singe them, and rinse them. Then put them in a pot with plenty of salted water and flavor with an onion, carrot, celery, and a little parsley. Cook at a low boil until the meat comes off the bones easily, about 2 hours.

Take the trotters out of the broth, pull the meat off the bones, and cut into small pieces.

In a saucepan, combine a chopped onion, butter, and chopped parsley. Heat over medium heat and then add the trotter pieces with a few spoons of the cooking broth. Season with salt and pepper and, when the broth is somewhat reduced, add the tomato paste. Baste again with a little broth and reduce the sauce.

Finally pour everything into a dish, season with grated Parmesan and a little cinnamon and send it to the table.

ZAMPI DI VITELLO IN FRICASSEA

Veal Trotter Fricassee

6 veal trotters
2 onions
1 carrot
1 celery stalk
Parsley
3½ tbsp butter
Bouillon cube
Potato starch
3 egg yolks
Grated Parmesan
Salt
Pepper

Scrape the trotters with a knife, singe them, and rinse them. Put them in a pot with plenty of salted water, an onion, a carrot, a celery stalk, and a little parsley. Cook at a low boil until the meat comes off the bones easily, about 2 hours.

Take the trotters out of the broth, pull the meat off the bones, and cut into small pieces.

Warm a chopped onion in butter with a little parsley. Add the trotter meat, season with salt and pepper, and let them flavor a little. Baste with a small glass of water in which you have dissolved half a bouillon cube.

Bind the sauce with some potato starch and then, off the heat, blend in the egg yolks and ⅓ cup of grated Parmesan and mix until thickened. Serve hot.

ZAMPI DI VITELLO IN GRATELLA

Grilled Veal Trotters

3 veal trotters
Onion
Carrot
3½ tbsp butter
Breadcrumbs
Salt
Pepper
Optional: tartar sauce *(p20)*

Open the trotters, take out the large central bone, singe them, scrape them, wash them, and put them in a saucepan with cold water and bring to a boil. Simmer for about 10 minutes, skimming off any foam from the surface.

Then drain, wash them again, and then put them in another pan of fresh water with salt, onion, and carrot. When they are cooked, after about a couple of hours, remove, let them cool a little, and then pull the meat off the remaining bones.

Season the meat with salt and pepper and pile them up on top of each other on a plate and weight down with a second plate on top.

When they are cold and pressed, dip them in warm butter, dredge them in breadcrumbs and brown them under the broiler set to moderate heat for 20 minutes, brushing them from time to time with melted butter. Serve with tartar sauce.

Veal Offal

ANIMELLE DI VITELLO CON PISELLI

Veal Sweetbreads with Peas

1 lb 5 oz veal sweetbreads
3½ tbsp butter
Onion
3½ oz prosciutto
Marsala
Meat broth *(p88)* or bouillon cube
Salt
Pepper
To serve: peas with prosciutto *(p684)*

Blanch the veal sweetbreads. Prepare another pan, put it on the heat with the butter, and when the butter has melted add a spoon or two of finely chopped onion and the prosciutto cut in strips. Fry a little, then put in the sweetbreads, season with salt and pepper, cover and shallow-fry slowly, turning the sweetbreads from time to time so that they color on all sides. Baste with a small glass of Marsala and then, at intervals, with a little broth or water. For cooking it will take about 15 minutes.

As soon as they are cooked, take out the sweetbreads, put them on a cutting board and cut them into slices. With a spatula, lift them onto a plate and reassemble as if whole again.

Meanwhile, put a little broth or water in the saucepan where they have been cooking and stir with a wooden spoon. Reduce the sauce, add another piece of butter, strain, and coat the sweetbreads with their sauce.

Surround with peas cooked in butter with prosciutto and onion.

ANIMELLE DI VITELLO IN MEDAGLIONI

Veal Sweetbreads with Potato

1 lb 5 oz veal sweetbreads
4 tbsp butter
Olive oil
1 onion
Flour
Marsala
Broth
1 lb potatoes (preferably Dutch)
Milk or cream
Salt

Blanch the sweetbreads. Then put them in a saucepan with 2 tablespoons of butter, oil, and a chopped onion. Sauté slowly, season with salt, sprinkle with flour and splash half a glass of Marsala. When the wine has evaporated, continue to cook the sweetbreads, bathing them often with broth or water. After about 15 minutes of cooking, cut them into slices and leave them warm soaking in their sauce.

Meanwhile, boil the potatoes, peel them, and cut into slices about ⅜ inch thick. Arrange the potato slices in a buttered baking pan, sprinkle with salt, and place a slice of sweetbread soaked in sauce on each one. Pour around a few spoons of milk or cream and place in a preheated oven for 5 minutes. Then place on a serving plate and send to the table.

ANIMELLE DI VITELLO IN SALSA

Veal Sweetbreads with Marsala Sauce

1 lb 5 oz veal sweetbreads
Pork skin
Onion
Carrot
Parsley
Bay leaf
3½ tbsp butter
Bouillon base or bouillon cube
Potato starch
2 tbsp Marsala
Salt
Peppercorns

Prepare the veal sweetbreads. Dry them on a work surface and put a light weight on them to press them down.

Scrape, blanch, and clean the pork skin and put it in a shallow Dutch oven with sliced onion, carrot, a few peppercorns, parsley, and a torn bay leaf. On this bed place the sweetbreads, pour in some melted butter, and cover with water in which you have dissolved the bouillon base or the bouillon cube. Place a sheet of parchment paper on the saucepan and then the lid and bring to a boil. At this point put the pot in a preheated oven of moderate heat for about 15 minutes, taking care, from time to time, to baste the sweetbreads with their own broth.

When the sweetbreads are cooked, put them in another saucepan. Add a ladle of water to deglaze the cooking juices and boil for a few minutes. Then strain the sauce and put it back on the heat, then thicken it with potato starch stirred into the Marsala. Stir and when the sauce seems to you to be of the right thickness remove it from the heat and pour a part of it on the sweetbreads to cover them.

Heat the sweetbreads again and put them in the oven, uncovered. Baste from time to time with the sauce and let them cook for a few minutes until the sauce has coated the sweetbreads and sets. Then place the sweetbreads on a serving dish and serve the sauce separately in a gravy boat.

FEGATO DI BUE IN SALSA AGRODOLCE

Ox Liver in Sweet and Sour Sauce

1 lb 5 oz ox liver
Flour
1 egg
Breadcrumbs
Butter
Sugar
Lemon
Salt

Cut the liver into long, thin slices, flour them, dredge them in the beaten egg, then breadcrumbs and fry them in a pan with a little butter. Season with a pinch of salt.

When the liver has taken on a nice golden tint, remove from the pan. In its place put a little more butter and sugar. Melt slowly without letting the sugar burn, and then, off the heat, squeeze in the juice of a lemon. Stir and return the liver to the pan, turning it over to soak in the sauce. Place it on a plate and immediately send it to the table.

FEGATO DI VITELLO ALL'ACETO

Calf's Liver with Vinegar

1 lb 5 oz calf's liver
3½ tbsp butter
3 tbsp vinegar
Parsley
Salt
Pepper

Cut the liver cut into small pieces. Melt the butter in a pan, add the liver, and let it brown over high heat, taking care not to overcook or it would harden. Season with salt and pepper and lastly baste it with the vinegar. Give a last stir and turn out onto a plate and garnish with parsley.

◆ ADA SAYS: *Here is a very simple preparation, easy to perform and only takes a very short time.*

FEGATO DI VITELLO ALLA FIORENTINA

Calf's Liver Florentine Style

1 lb 5 oz calf's liver
Flour
Olive oil
2 garlic cloves
Sage
Very thick tomato sauce *(p37)*
Salt
Pepper

Cut the liver into very thin slices and lightly flour them. Put two fingers of oil in a pan, adding 2 cloves of chopped garlic and 5 or 6 fresh sage leaves. When the oil is hot, put the slices down, arranging them in a single layer and, when they color on one side, turn them over and cook on the second side. Take care not to overcook.

Season with salt and pepper and then cover with lots of thick tomato sauce. Reduce the heat, let the liver just barely simmer for a few minutes, then arrange it on a plate.

FEGATO DI VITELLO ALLA MILANESE

Calf's Liver Milanese Style

1 lb 5 oz calf's liver
Parsley
Flour
2 eggs
Breadcrumbs
Butter
Lemon wedges
Salt
Pepper

Cut the liver into long slices about ¼ inch thick and arrange them on a plate. Season with salt, pepper, and a little chopped parsley and leave them to flavor for about 1 hour.

Just before serving, dredge the liver in flour, then in beaten eggs and finally the breadcrumbs.

Then put a piece of butter in a pan and fry the slices to a nice color. As soon as they are cooked, place them on a plate and garnish with lemon wedges and parsley.

FEGATO DI VITELLO ALLA VENEZIANA

Calf's Liver Venetian Style

6 onions
Olive oil
1 lb 5 oz calf's liver
Sage
Salt
Pepper
Optional: white wine

Slice the onions finely and brown in oil—for this recipe the onions must be cooked gently without coloring for at least 30 minutes, then add a little water so that the onions stew slowly.

Meanwhile, cut the liver into small pieces.

When the onions are ready, raise the heat, add a few sage leaves and the liver. Cook over high heat, so that it remains tender. If the liver is too dry, you can add a little bit of white wine.

When cooked, season the liver with salt and pepper, put it on a plate, and serve hot.

FEGATO DI VITELLO FRITTO ALLA SALVIA

Fried Calf's Liver with Sage Butter

1 lb 5 oz calf's liver
Flour
1 egg
Butter
Sage
Salt

Slice the liver into cutlets, dredge them in flour and beaten egg, then fry in a pan with butter. When they are golden, arrange them on a plate and sprinkle lightly with salt.

Have ready some fresh sage leaves to put in some fresh butter in the pan. Let them heat up and then pour the butter and sage on top of the liver.

FEGATO DI VITELLO FRITTO DORATO

Fried Breaded Calf's Liver

1 lb 5 oz calf's liver
Flour
1 egg
Olive oil
Salt

Cut the liver into wide and thin slices, flour them, dredge them in the beaten egg, and fry them in plenty of hot oil. The cooking takes place in a very short time, because the livers must be soft and delicate.

FEGATO DI VITELLO IN SALSA PICCANTE

Calf's Liver with Piquant Fennel Sauce

1 onion
2 tbsp olive oil
Garlic
Wine
Flour
1 lb 5 oz calf's liver
Fennel seeds
1 lemon
Salt
Pepper

Finely chop the onion and put it in a large pan with the oil. Brown slowly over light heat. Add a garlic clove but take it out when it has browned. Moisten the onions with some wine into which you have stirred 1 teaspoon of flour.

When the wine has evaporated, slice the liver thinly and add to the onions, increase the heat, and season with salt, pepper, and a pinch of fennel seeds.

Cook for only 3 or 4 minutes, otherwise the liver will get tough. Transfer everything onto a plate and sprinkle a few drops of lemon juice on the liver.

LINGUA DI VITELLO IN AGRODOLCE

Veal Tongue with Sweet and Sour Onions

3 lb 5 oz veal tongue
Aromatics for the broth (onion, carrot, celery, etc.)
2¼ lb small young onions
2 oz prosciutto
3½ tbsp butter
2 tbsp sugar
Vinegar
Salt
Pepper

Wash the tongue thoroughly. Put the celery, onion, and carrot in a large pot of lightly salted water and bring to a boil. As soon as it boils, add the tongue, cover, and cook over moderate heat for about 2½ hours. Remove the tongue from the broth, and take off the first and second skins. Set aside to cool. When it is cooled, carve into thin slices.

Now prepare the sweet and sour onions: Peel the onions and nick off the roots. Wash thoroughly. Prepare a mix of prosciutto in a pan with the butter and add the sugar. Melt the sugar in the fat and then add half a glass of vinegar. Put the onions in the pan, season with salt and pepper, cover, and cook over moderate heat. After about 15 minutes put the slices of tongue in the pan and let them flavor with the onions over very low heat for about 30 minutes. If the sauce reduces too much, add a little of the cooking broth from the tongue.

Arrange the slices of tongue on a serving dish and cover them with the sauce.

ADA SAYS: *The cooking broth from the tongue is excellent and should be saved to prepare soups and risottos.*

LINGUA DI VITELLO IN SALSA VERDE

Veal Tongue with Green Sauce

3 lb 5 oz veal tongue
Aromatics for the broth (onion, carrot, celery)
Green sauce *(p31)*
Salt
Pepper

Cook, cool, and slice the tongue as in Veal Tongue with Sweet and Sour Onions (*opposite page*).

While the tongue is cooling, make the green sauce.

To serve, carefully cover all the slices of tongue with the prepared sauce.

ROGNONCINI DI VITELLO AL MARSALA

Veal Kidneys with Marsala

1 lb mushrooms
Olive oil
1 lb 5 oz veal kidneys
7 tbsp butter
Flour
Marsala
Salt
Pepper

Clean and rinse the mushrooms and cook in a little oil, water, and salt.

Cut the kidneys into thin slices. Put the butter in another pan and, when it melts, add the kidneys, and let them brown over lively heat. Then sprinkle with flour and season with salt and pepper and the Marsala.

Stir over high heat for the slices to cook swiftly and the sauce to reduce. Add the mushrooms, bring back to a boil, and serve immediately.

ADA SAYS: *Veal kidneys are exquisite, do not require any preliminary preparation, and cook very quickly.*

ROGNONCINI DI VITELLO TRIFOLATI

Pan-Fried Kidneys with Anchovy

1 lb 5 oz veal kidneys
Olive oil
Garlic
Parsley
1 lemon
Salt
Pepper

Anchovy butter:
3½ tbsp butter, 2 anchovies

Choose small kidneys, free them from the fat, open them in two and slice each piece into thin slices. Put a little oil in a pan with a clove of garlic, and when it is slightly colored, remove it and add the kidneys.

Increase the heat, season with salt and pepper and just as the kidneys are cooked—they need to cook for a short time otherwise they toughen—have ready an anchovy butter *(p54)* made with the ingredient amounts listed here.

Stir and almost immediately remove the pan from the heat, finish, before pouring them into a dish, with a spoon of chopped parsley and a little lemon juice.

TRIPPA DI VITELLO ALLA MILANESE (BUSECCA)

Tripe Milanese

14 oz dried white beans
3 celery stalks
4 large potatoes
Small cabbage
4½ lb veal tripe (or precooked)
2 onions
2 cloves
4 leeks
2 carrots
5 tbsp butter
7 oz guanciale or pork belly
Bay leaf
14 oz fresh or canned tomatoes
Saffron
Sage
3½ oz lardo
Garlic
Parsley
Grated Parmesan
Bread for fried croutons
Salt
Pepper

Place the beans in a bowl of lukewarm water and soak for at least 12 hours. Drain, put them in a pot full of water, without salt, which must be added only halfway through the cooking, with a stalk of celery. Bring to a boil slowly and cook slowly for 1½ hours.

While the beans are cooking, boil the potatoes and cabbage.

If not using precooked tripe, after cleaning and rinsing the tripe, cut it into large pieces and put it in a large pot with cold water, season with salt, a celery stalk, and an onion stuck with 2 cloves. Boil for a couple of hours. Then remove it from the water and cut it into strips as regular and thin as possible.

Thinly chop the leeks, an onion, carrots, and celery and sauté in a saucepan with 3 tablespoons of butter and the chopped guanciale or pork belly, plus a bay leaf.

When they have colored, add the tomatoes—peeled, seeded, and chopped, if fresh. After about 10 minutes, add the tripe and let it flavor, adding a little salt and a pinch of saffron. Moisten with enough water and let it boil again, then simmer for another 30 minutes.

At this point, add the drained beans, drained diced potatoes, and sliced cabbage. Simmer for another 20 minutes and complete with a little sage, lardo, a clove of garlic, and parsley. Add plenty of grated Parmesan, a pinch of pepper and boil for 5 minutes. Serve with croutons fried in butter.

ADA SAYS: *While Roman tripe is preferably made with ox, the Milanese specialty of busecca must be exclusively made with veal tripe.*

BEEF

TO BOIL BEEF

To get a juicy and tasty boiled beef dish you have to soak the meat in boiling salted water. Chuck roast is recommended. The proportion of water must be about 3 quarts for every 2 pounds of meat and the proportion of salt must be 1 tablespoon for each quart of water. Once it has boiled, carefully skim off the impurities floating on top. To improve the broth, combine suitable aromatics such as celery, onion (in which you can stick a whole clove), carrot, etc. Continue to boil very slowly and cover for 3 hours or more.

When it is at the right point from a cooking point of view, put the roast in a smaller pot, cover it with a little broth, and keep it warm.

Boiled beef is usually served hot but also, as in these recipes, it can be very useful cold in different preparations. Boiled beef leaves a large part of its nutrients and its flavor in the liquid. From 2¼ pounds of raw beef you get 1½ pounds of boiled meat and about 2 quarts of broth.

TO BRAISE BEEF

For tenderloin and loin cuts there is no need to lard, because they are lean and tender enough; but for other cuts it is an excellent system to wrap the piece of meat with a few thin slices of lardo or prosciutto, tied in place with kitchen string.

*To braise a large cut, for every 1 pound of meat calculate—*1½ tablespoons of butter; 1½ tablespoons of lard; 1 ounce of onions; 1 ounce of carrots; 1 ounce of fresh pork skin or pork belly, half a glass of wine, about 1 cup broth, and salt and pepper.

The amount of cooking liquid is an approximation and can vary depending on the size and quality of the meat or even the container. Instead of broth you can use the same amount of water in which you have dissolved half a bouillon cube.

Be careful to regulate the salt, because the liquid, as it evaporates, will reduce and the flavors will be more concentrated (including the salt).

BISTECCA AI FERRI

Grilled Steak

6 sirloin steaks (5 oz each)
Olive oil
Butter
Lemon wedges
Salt

Lightly pound the steaks with a wet meat mallet, then put a few drops of oil on a plate and lay the first steak on top. Grease this with a few more drops of oil and lay on it a second steak, to which you add a few more drops of oil, and so on until you have overlapped the 6 steaks, topping with some oil on the last one. Then put them in the fridge.

When it's time to serve, preheat a grill and set a steak on it. As soon as it is cooked on one side—it takes a few minutes—turn it over and sprinkle the roasted part with a pinch of salt. After a few minutes, the steak is ready. Proceed like this for the other 5 steaks and when ready to serve, surround them with lemon wedges or spread them with tiny knobs of butter.

ADA SAYS: *If you are cooking the steaks in a pan, do not oil them. Put them in a hot pan and when they are cooked on one side, turn them over and only then lightly oil the seared part and sprinkle on a pinch of salt.*

BISTECCA ALLA ARLESIANA

Steak with Ham and Mozzarella

6 sirloin steaks (5 oz each)
Olive oil
Butter
2 eggplants or zucchini
3½ oz ham
7 oz mozzarella
Salt
To serve: crostini fried in butter, fried onion rings

Trim the steaks carefully, keeping them rather thick, and cook them in an ovenproof pan with hot oil, butter, and a pinch of salt.

As soon as the steaks are ready, put on each a nice slice of eggplant or zucchini cut lengthwise and fried in oil, without flour. On the eggplant or zucchini slice, arrange a slice of ham and cover with a thick slice of mozzarella.

Slide the steaks into a preheated oven on a rather strong heat and as soon as the mozzarella begins to melt, take the pan out. To serve, place each one on a slice of bread fried in butter and of the same size, and surround the plate with a ring of fried onion rings.

BISTECCA ALLA BRACE

Charcoal-Grilled Steak

6 rib-eye or sirloin steaks (7 oz each)
Olive oil
2 garlic cloves
Lemon
Salt
Pepper

The preparation of the steaks is simple. Pound them out lightly with a meat mallet to even them. Then prepare the marinade: Put the oil and crushed garlic in a bowl with a pinch of pepper and dip the steaks in. Let them marinate for about 2 hours, remembering to turn them from time to time.

Set up a charcoal grill and as soon as the embers are ready, put the steaks on the grill and let them cook for a few minutes on one side before turning them over on the other. When the steaks are cooked, depending on your taste—we advise you to cook them rare—salt them, arrange them on a serving dish, and decorate with lemon slices. Serve immediately.

❖ ADA SAYS: *For outdoor cooking, it is ideal to cook steaks over charcoal. It is crucial to wait until the coal has become embers before putting the steaks to cook; also you need to put each steak in a hinged grill basket so that you can turn the steak without pricking it with a fork, which would let the juices run out.*

BISTECCA ALLA FIORENTINA

Steak Florentine Style

SERVES 2

1 veal rib eye steak with tenderloin attached
Olive oil
Lemon wedges
Salt
Pepper

Put the steak on a plate, coat it well with oil and pepper, and leave it for a few minutes. Then roast it on a very hot grill—over charcoal or wood—and when cooked, drizzle with oil and salt. Serve with lemon wedges.

❖ ADA SAYS: *Among the specialties of Tuscan gastronomy, the Florentine steak has a prominent place. It is essential to use very young beef, which in Florence they call vitellone. The steak must be cut from the rib and must be about 1 inch thick. The meat must be tender and aged, i.e., not too fresh.*

BISTECCA ALLA SICILIANA

Steak Sicilian Style

Olive oil
Garlic
6 sirloin steaks (5 oz each)
Celery heart
Vinegar
6 tomatoes
3 oz Sicilian olives, pitted
6 pickled peppers
3 tbsp capers
Oregano
Salt
Pepper

Put a little oil in a pan with a clove of garlic cut into 2 or 3 pieces. Lightly brown the garlic, remove it, and add the steaks. Cook over high heat on both sides.

Cut the central heart of a bunch of celery into strips 1¼ to 1½ inches long. Rinse, dry, and fry them in the oil until they are a beautiful golden color. Then drain the oil from the pan and sprinkle a little vinegar on the fried celery.

Seed the tomatoes, cut them into chunks, and sear them separately in a pan with a little of oil. When almost cooked, add the Sicilian olives, the pickled peppers—halved, stemmed, and seeded—the fried celery, and the rinsed capers. Season with salt, pepper, and plenty of oregano.

Keep everything a few more minutes on the heat and then arrange the steaks on the plate, surrounding them with the toppings.

BISTECCA ALLA TARTARA

Steak Tartare

2 lb 10 oz beef tenderloin
12 anchovies
6 egg yolks
Onion
Parsley
3 tbsp capers
Salt
Pepper
Optional: Worcestershire sauce or mustard, cornichons, lemon slices

Finely mince the beef, season with salt and pepper, and divide it into 6 portions. Shape into steaks and place each on a plate.

On each steak make a large dimple in the center, then make a grid of anchovy fillets—rinsed and boned—and in the middle place a raw egg yolk, which will fall into the center. Around each steak arrange alternating heaps of finely chopped raw onion, chopped parsley, and capers.

ADA SAYS: *These steaks can be served with Worcestershire sauce or with mustard, cornichons, and lemon slices.*

BOLLITO ALLA PIZZAIOLA

Boiled Beef Pizzaiola

Olive oil
2¼ lb tomatoes
Garlic
Parsley
Oregano
1½ lb boiled beef *(p465)*
Salt
Pepper
Optional: broth

Oil a baking pan. On the bottom, put half of the tomatoes—peeled, seeded, and chopped—chopped garlic, chopped parsley, and a pinch of oregano.

Arrange the boiled beef, cut into regular slices, over the tomatoes and herbs in one layer and then put the remaining tomatoes, parsley, and oregano on top. Pour a little oil over everything, season with salt and pepper, add a few spoons of water or broth and place the pan in a preheated moderate oven for 30 minutes so the meat can be well stewed and flavored.

BOLLITO CARPIONATO

Marinated Boiled Beef

2 onions
Olive oil
Vinegar
Sugar
2 garlic cloves
Bay leaf
Parsley
Rosemary
Sage
White wine
Broth
1½ lb boiled beef *(p465)*
Pepper

This recipe has to be made the day before being served.

Slice the onions very thinly and fry them slowly in a pan with a finger of oil, until they are slightly golden. Then add a couple of glasses of vinegar, a teaspoon of sugar, the garlic, a bay leaf, chopped parsley, a pinch of rosemary, a leaf or two of sage, a little pepper and let everything simmer slowly over very low heat until the vinegar has almost completely evaporated. Add a glass of white wine and two glasses of broth and let cook for another 5 minutes.

Carve the boiled meat into regular slices, arrange in a bowl, and pour on the hot marinade, with all the herbs. Put the bowl in the fridge and let everything rest until the next day.

The following day, remove the beef slices from the marinade, freeing them from the herbs, and arrange them in steps on an oval plate. Around them, put little heaps of sliced cornichons,

For garnish: cornichons, green olives, pickled peppers, mushrooms in oil, artichokes in oil, boiled potatoes

green olives, pickled peppers (cut into strips), mushrooms in oil, artichokes in oil, and seasoned boiled potato slices. Tastefully alternate the various ingredients, dividing them with chopped parsley, and finally pour a drizzle of oil over everything.

BOLLITO CON PATATE

Boiled Beef with Potatoes

Onion
Celery
Carrot
Olive oil
Tomato passata
2¼ lb potatoes
1½ lb boiled beef *(p465)*
Salt
Pepper

Thinly slice the onion, celery, and carrot and put in a saucepan with a few spoons of oil. Sauté slowly and when the vegetables are a good golden color, add ¾ cup tomato passata and a pinch of pepper. Bring to a boil and then add the potatoes, peeled and cut in wedges. Boil slowly until almost completely cooked.

Cut the boiled meat into large cubes and add it to the vegetables and potatoes. Check the flavors, adding salt to taste, and make sure that the liquid is sufficient, and boil again for about 10 minutes. The sauce must be neither too thick nor too soupy.

BOLLITO IN BUDINO

Boiled Beef Pudding

1½ lb boiled beef *(p465)*
2 egg yolks
Grated Parmesan
Lemon
Salt
Pepper
Nutmeg
Optional: tomato gratin

White sauce:
¼ cup flour, 1½ tbsp butter, ¾ cup milk

Prepare a thick white sauce *(p16)* with the ingredient amounts listed here. Finely chop the cold boiled beef and add it to the white sauce still in the pan but off the heat. Stir in the egg yolks, a spoonful of grated Parmesan, salt, pepper, a grating of nutmeg, and the grated zest of half a lemon and mix everything well.

Oil and flour a round 1-quart mold. Pour the mixture in and lightly tap so that the mixture goes everywhere without any spaces.

Set the mold in a larger pan of very hot water and cook in the bain-marie for a good 30 minutes, without letting the water reach a tumultuous boil.

When you can see that the mixture has set, invert the pudding onto a round plate and serve it like this or surrounded by gratin of tomatoes.

BOLLITO IN MAIONESE

Boiled Beef with Mayonnaise

1½ lb boiled beef *(p465)*
2 hard-boiled eggs
Parsley
Capers
Cornichons
Bouillon jelly *(p52)*
Mayonnaise *(p19)*
Salt
Pepper
To serve: a salad of artichokes, green beans, potatoes, lettuce, celery, radicchio, etc.

Remove all the fat and skin from the boiled meat and cut it into cubes. Cut the hard-boiled eggs into cubes. Add the parsley, capers, and a few sliced cornichons. Season with salt and pepper, mix, and set aside.

Make up a bouillon gelatin and stir into the mayonnaise. Then mix everything together and pour into a ring mold with a central tube. Put in the fridge and let it set for at least 1 hour.

When ready to serve, dunk the bottom of the mold for a few seconds in lukewarm water and invert onto the plate. In the center you can put a vegetable salad.

BOLLITO IN MEDAGLIONI

Boiled Beef Medallions with Sage, Ham, and Mozzarella

Crustless white bread
Milk
1½ lb boiled beef *(p465)*
Grated Parmesan
1 egg
Crustless white bread
Oil for shallow-frying
3½ tbsp butter
2 oz ham
Sage
7 oz mozzarella
Salt

Take some bread—about as much as an apple—and soak in milk, then squeeze dry in your hands. Add to a bowl. Chop the beef and add to the bread. Season with ¼ cup grated Parmesan, a good pinch of salt and a beaten egg. Mix everything with your hands until you have a smooth dough and divide it into equal pieces, that you can roll in your hands, like meatballs, and then lightly squeeze to give them the shape of a disc of 2 to 2½ inches in diameter.

Cut the bread into slices of the same diameter and take off the crusts. Pour oil into a pan and when it is hot, fry the slices bread, a few at a time, and on one side only.

Arrange the fried slices in a buttered sheet pan, placing them with the fried-side up. On the bread discs, place the meat medallions, on the meat place a piece of ham, then a sage leaf, and finally a slice of mozzarella. Stick together with a toothpick so everything remains firm, dot with some butter, and put everything into a hot oven, at a good heat.

After a few minutes, when the medallions are hot and the mozzarella melting, turn onto a plate and serve.

BOLLITO IN SALSA RUSTICA

Boiled Beef with Rustic Sauce

1½ lb boiled beef *(p465)*
6 red tomatoes
2 garlic cloves
Parsley
Basil
Olive oil
Vinegar
Lemon zest
Broth
Salt
Pepper

Prepare the boiled meat in advance, then let it cool in its broth.

Make the sauce at least 5 or 6 hours in advance. Blanch and peel the tomatoes, then seed and coarsely chop them. In a bowl, combine the chopped tomatoes, diced garlic, a good handful of chopped parsley, plenty of chopped basil, salt and pepper, plenty of oil, a little vinegar, and a little bit of lemon zest. Mix everything well, cover, and refrigerate.

Cut the meat into regular slices, arrange them in a baking dish, cover them with a little boiling broth, cover, and leave them to keep warm, in a moderate oven that you have just turned off.

When ready to serve, remove the slices from the pan, arrange them on a plate, and accompany with the sauce.

BOLLITO IN TEGLIA CON ORTAGGI

Boiled Beef with Vegetables

10 oz new potatoes
Olive oil
4 carrots
Butter
1 cup fresh peas
2 oz dried mushrooms
5 oz spring onions
Celery heart
3 to 4 tomatoes
5 oz lean guanciale
Flour
White wine
Broth
1½ lb boiled beef *(p465)*
Grated Parmesan
Salt

In a pan with a little oil, cook the potatoes in their own steam so that they are well cooked and lightly browned. Clean the carrots, boil them, open them to remove any central woody core, cut them into rather large sticks 1½ to 2 inches long and season with a little butter. Cook the peas with a little butter and water. Soak the mushrooms in cold water and wash them carefully. Then cook with a little oil, salt, and water. Boil the spring onions and the celery heart and add to the rest. Quickly heat the tomatoes (peeled, seeded, and cut into chunks) in just a little oil so that they do not come apart.

Cut the guanciale into slices and then into cubes. Put them in a pan with a little oil and lightly brown. At this point, put in a heaping teaspoon of flour, mix, and splash with two fingers of white wine. Let the wine evaporate and then add a couple of glasses of broth. Let it cook for a few minutes and as soon as you see that the sauce is slightly thickened, but not too much, remove from the heat.

Generously butter a covered baking dish. Carve the beef into slices and lay in the pan. Cover with the vegetables and scatter over plenty of grated Parmesan. Make a second layer with the slices of meat and finish with another layer of vegetables and Parmesan. Pour the guanciale sauce, which must be quite liquid, over everything.

Cover and put in a preheated moderate oven for 15 minutes, until the sauce is almost dried and the meat and vegetables are well flavored. Send directly to the table in the baking dish.

BRASATO

Braised Beef

7 tbsp butter
3½ oz fresh pork skin or pork belly
3½ oz ham or prosciutto fat
3½ oz carrots
3½ oz onions
4½-pound chuck roast
Wine
1 cup broth or a bouillon cube
Salt
Pepper
Optional: potato starch

Put the butter in the Dutch oven. Coarsely chop the pork skin or pork belly, the ham or prosciutto fat, carrots, and onions. Add to the Dutch oven and brown gently. When the fat starts to smoke, add the chuck roast. Brown it well on all sides, salting every time before turning the piece. Then pour in a glass of wine in small splashes, but do not add any more until the previous one has evaporated.

Bring the broth to a boil and pour into the pan. It must be boiling so that the meat continues to cook. Cover and cook over moderate heat for about 3 hours. The meat is cooked when a skewer enters the meat with no resistance.

Once cooked, remove the meat, carve into slices, and arrange on a sheet pan. Strain the remaining broth, pressing the aromatics to extract the juices well. Baste the meat with a few spoons of broth and then place in a hot oven. As the broth reduces, repeat 2 or 3 times with more liquid, which will start to form a shiny patina on the meat. This operation can last a dozen minutes.

With the remaining liquid you can make an excellent accompanying sauce—put a tablespoon of butter in a saucepan and when it melts, add the same quantity of potato starch, mix and cook to a golden color and then pour in the meat sauce. Let it thicken gently. If, on the other hand, you want to use this meat sauce to season pasta or risotto, dilute it only with the butter, about 3 tablespoons, but not the starch.

ADA SAYS: *The purpose of this operation is to provoke, under the gentle and progressive action of the heat, the release of the meat and vegetable juices; these juices fall to the bottom and caramelize slightly, thus contributing to the flavor of a braised sauce. If the heat is too abrupt or too strong, the meat and vegetables are browned and the juices can no longer come out.*

BRASATO AL BAROLO

Braised Beef in Barolo

2¼ lb beef bottom round or chuck
1 bottle Barolo
1 onion
1 carrot
Celery
Bay leaf
Butter
2 oz ham fat
Salt
Peppercorns

Arrange the beef in an oval bowl and pour in a whole bottle of Barolo, or another red wine of the same type. Add one onion, a sliced carrot, a little minced celery, a bay leaf, a pinch of peppercorns. No salt. Leave the meat in this marinade for 24 hours, turning it every once in a while.

When you are ready to cook, take the beef out of the marinade and dry it, then tie it to keep it in shape. Put it in a saucepan with a little butter and ham fat and brown it on both sides.

Meanwhile, strain the wine from the marinade through a sieve, discard the aromatics and in another pan, reduce it by half. Then

season the meat, well browned, with a little salt and cover with the hot wine. Cover and let it finish cooking over very moderate heat for another 2 hours or more.

When the braised beef is cooked and the sauce well thickened, take it out, untie it, and arrange it in a serving dish with its well degreased sauce.

ADA SAYS: *This preparation requires an overnight marination, so you need to plan ahead. Characteristic of this exquisite preparation is that the meat ends up so falling apart that it can be served without a knife, but only with a spoon with which to cut it.*

BRASATO ALLA BRESCIANA

Braised Beef Brescia Style

2¼ lb beef bottom round or chuck
3½ oz lardo or prosciutto fat
Marjoram
Garlic
7 tbsp butter
Onion
4 tbsp lard
Red wine
Salt
Pepper

First you need to lard the meat—cut the lardo or prosciutto into about 10 pieces of the thickness and length of a little finger. Put them on a cutting board with a pinch of marjoram, a clove of diced garlic, a little salt and pepper and roll the lardons in it. With a small knife make some little incisions in the beef, open them up with your finger and insert a lardon into each one (or you can use a larding needle). Once this is done, tie it with a string.

Put the roast in a Dutch oven, season with salt and pepper, melt some butter, add half an onion chopped coarsely and the lard. Cover and brown the meat over moderate heat, taking care to turn it every 5 or 6 minutes. Turn the meat quickly and immediately cover again, since one of the characteristics of braising is to keep everything well covered and contained.

After about 30 minutes, add two glasses of red wine. Immediately cover the pot and let the meat finish cooking gently, without adding any more liquid, for at least 2 hours. In this way you will have a tasty braised beef and a thick and fragrant sauce.

ADA SAYS: *This sauce is also very useful for dressing macaroni or risotto.*

BRASATO ALLA CERTOSINA

Braised Beef Certosa Style

Butter
Olive oil
1 oz pork belly
2¼ lb beef bottom round or chuck
3 or 4 anchovies
Parsley
Broth
Salt
Pepper
Nutmeg
To serve: vegetables of your choice

Put a little butter, oil, and chopped pork belly in a Dutch oven and put over heat. When the fats are hot, add the beef, in one piece, and season with salt, pepper, and a trifle of nutmeg. Brown well and when the beef has taken on a nice dark color, add 3 or 4 anchovies (rinsed, boned, and chopped) and a good handful of parsley. Cover with boiling broth and let it simmer for at least 2 hours until the meat is well cooked and the sauce sufficiently reduced.

Finally, put the beef on a cutting board, cut it into regular slices, cover it with the well-degreased cooking sauce and surround it with vegetables.

BRASATO ALLA GENOVESE

Braised Beef Genovese

Lard
2 oz prosciutto
2 oz pork skin
Onion
Celery
Carrot
Parsley
1 oz dried mushrooms
2¼ lb beef bottom round or chuck
Red wine
Broth
Salt
Pepper
To serve: vegetables of your choice

In a Dutch oven, combine the lard, prosciutto, pork skin, plenty of minced aromatics—onion, celery, carrot, parsley—and dried mushrooms, reconstituted for about 20 minutes in cold water. Place the beef on top, add a glass of red wine, cover, and set over heat. When the wine has evaporated, put a second glass of red wine in to replace it and season with salt and pepper.

As soon as you see that the meat and vegetables have taken on a rather dark tint, cover the meat with boiling broth and let it just barely simmer for at least 2 hours until the meat is well cooked and the sauce well reduced.

Lift out the beef, put it on a cutting board, and carve into regular slices. Baste the beef with a few spoons of degreased sauce and vegetables.

ADA SAYS: *This leftover sauce is excellent with pasta.*

BRASATO ALLA PROVENZALE

Braised Beef Provençal

Lardo
Garlic
Parsley
2¼ lb beef bottom round or chuck
Red wine
3 onions
Bay leaf
3 cloves
Olive oil
2 oz pork belly
Salt
Pepper

Prepare about 10 lardons of the thickness and length of your little finger, made from a slice of lardo. On a cutting board, chop together a clove of garlic and parsley, and add a pinch of pepper. Roll the lardons in this mixture to cover them. Then insert them into the meat with a small knife or large needle. Once this is done, put the meat in a bowl, cover it with wine, a sliced onion, a crushed clove of garlic, half a bay leaf, a pinch of pepper, and a couple of cloves. No salt. Leave it for the whole night in the fridge.

The next day, remove the meat from the marinade (strain the marinade, discard the solids, and set aside). Place the meat in a Dutch oven with a little oil. Cook over bright heat so that the beef can immediately make a nice golden crust on the outside. When the meat is well browned, season with salt and pepper and keep over the heat for a few minutes.

Meanwhile, arrange on the bottom of another Dutch oven with a lid, the slices of pork belly. Then place the browned beef on top and add some chopped onions. Put the meat back over medium heat, keeping the pan covered, and when the pork starts to melt and the onions begin to fry, cover the meat with the strained marinade, adding some more if it isn't enough to cover the meat.

Cook over very low heat for at least 2 hours, until the meat is well cooked and the sauce thickens. Then, all that remains is to tilt the Dutch oven, remove the fat that will have collected on the surface with a spoon, and serve the meat with its thick and fragrant sauce.

BRASATO CON CIPOLLE

Braised Beef with Onions

5 onions
Olive oil
3½ tbsp butter
2¼ lb hanger steak or bottom round
Salt
Pepper

Peel the onions, but leave whole, make a cross cut on each without cutting them apart, and put them in a Dutch oven with half a glass of oil and butter over light heat. As soon as the onions begin to fry, add the meat and a pinch of pepper. Brown everything gently and, when the meat is nicely browned, season it with salt and, a little at a time, with up to 1 cup water.

Cook over moderate heat, stirring often and making sure to mash the onions, which will cook down to a purée.

After about 2 hours the braised meat will be cooked. Then free the beef from the string, cut it into slices, and arrange on a plate.

Remove the fat from the sauce left in the saucepan, then press this sauce together with the onions through a sieve, and cover the slices of meat with it.

BRASATO CON LATTE

Braised Beef in Milk

2¼ lb lean beef sirloin or hanger
3½ oz lardons
Olive oil
Onion
Celery
Carrot
3½ tbsp butter
4 cups milk
1 lemon
Salt

Pound the meat, lard it with the lardons, tie it to keep it in shape, and brown it in a Dutch oven with a little oil, the onion, celery, and carrot. Add the butter and let the meat acquire a nice golden color slowly while the vegetables brown.

Then salt the meat, drain off the excess fat, and cover the meat with the milk. Bring to a boil, put the Dutch oven in a preheated oven of moderate heat and cook for about 2 hours.

When the meat is cooked, strain the sauce, return it to the pot, add a little lemon juice and heat everything without bringing it to a boil.

BRASATO CON MARINATA

Braised and Marinated Beef

2¼ lb lean beef sirloin or hanger
1 onion
1 celery stalk
Carrot
Parsley
Vinegar
Red wine
Olive oil
Salt

Put the meat in a bowl, cover it with the onion, celery, carrot, and parsley and pour in half a glass of vinegar and a quarter of a glass of red wine. Cover the bowl and marinate the meat in the refrigerator for at least 12 hours.

Remove the meat from the marinade and place it in a saucepan together with some oil and the well-drained vegetables from the marinade. Sauté everything slowly and, when the meat has acquired a nice brown color, sprinkle it with salt, add another glass of wine from the marinade and, when evaporated, pour a ladle of hot water into the saucepan.

Boil gently for at least 2 hours, and if the sauce reduces too much before the meat is completely cooked, add a few more spoons of water. The sauce should be thick and fragrant.

BRASATO CON ORTAGGI

Braised Beef with Vegetables

Olive oil
2¼ lb beef bottom round
7 oz onions
Veal trotter
1 lb carrots
3½ oz pork skin
Dry wine
Celery
Parsley
Bouillon cube
Salt
Nutmeg

Heat a little oil in a pan and brown the beef. When the meat has taken on a nice golden color, remove it from the pan. Chop the onions, add them to the pan, and lightly brown.

Return the meat to the pan along with the veal trotter (cut in two), the carrots (cut into round slices), and the pork skin (blanched and cut into slices). Add half a glass of wine, half a glass of water, salt, finely chopped celery and parsley, and a little grated nutmeg.

Cover and cook gently for about 2 hours, adding, if necessary, a few ladles of hot water in which you have dissolved a quarter of a bouillon cube.

ADA SAYS: *This is an old French recipe that had its 15 minutes of fame at the beginning of the century. It still offers a pleasant variation on the way of cooking bottom round.*

BRASATO CON SALSA DI ACCIUGHE

Pressure-Cooker Braised Beef with Anchovies

2 oz ham
Sage
Lemon zest
1 celery stalk
Onion
3 cloves
2¼ lb beef, bottom round or sirloin
Olive oil
Vinegar
Anchovy paste
Parsley
1 lemon
Salt
Peppercorns

Cover the bottom of a pressure cooker with the ham slices and 4 sage leaves. Add a strip of lemon zest, a celery stalk, the uncut onion, the peppercorns, and the cloves. Finally place the meat on top of everything to keep it in shape. Season with a pinch of salt and sprinkle with half a glass of water, oil, and vinegar. Close the pressure cooker and let the meat cook at low pressure for about 1 hour.

After this time, remove it from the pot and carefully strain the cooking juices.

In a pan, melt a little anchovy paste with the cooking juices of the braised beef. Dilute this sauce with a few spoonfuls of water, season it with plenty of chopped parsley, heat it up, and then add the sliced meat.

Let it simmer and flavor for a few minutes, then remove from the heat. Finish with lemon juice and send it to the table.

CHATEAUBRIAND ALLA MAÎTRE D'HÔTEL

Chateaubriand Maître d'Hôtel

3 beef tenderloin steaks (10 oz each)
Butter
Salt

Maître d'hôtel butter:
3½ tbsp butter, parsley, lemon juice

Bring a large skillet or griddle to high heat so that the meat can sear, creating a crust that will prevent the internal juices from coming out. Add the steaks to sear on both sides.

Reduce the heat and baste regularly with butter so the meat doesn't char. Do not add salt until the meat is cooked.

A proper chateaubriand must remain slightly pink on the inside. You know the exact point of doneness when, by touching the steak with your finger, you feel that it is quite elastic.

It is usually served with this maître d'hôtel butter—softened butter mixed on a plate with the blade of a knife with chopped parsley and the juice of a lemon. The heat of the roasted meat is enough to melt the butter, which forms a tasty sauce.

Carve large slices, a couple of fingers wide, not with vertical cuts, but holding the knife tilted at an angle to the cutting board, to obtain slide cuts: This allows you to better combine the various slices and rebuild the steak as if it were still whole. The chateaubriand must be cut at the very last moment, to keep its juices.

ADA SAYS: *Chateaubriand is a very thick beef tenderloin steak weighing 10 to 14 ounces that must be pounded lightly, dipped in melted butter, and cooked on a hot grill or gridle.*

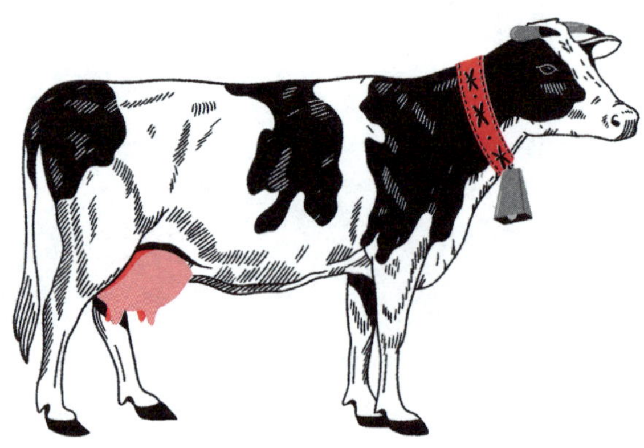

CIMA ALLA GENOVESE

Breast of Beef Genovese

1 lb thin breast of beef
Veal sweetbreads
Olive oil
Butter
Garlic
Onion
3½ oz crustless white bread
Milk
7 oz lean pork
2 oz lardo
1 egg
Grated Parmesan
Fresh peas
1 celery stalk
Carrot
Bay leaf
Salt
Pepper
To serve: cooked vegetables

This stuffed boiled beef is a particularly tasty recipe from Genoan cuisine. The real Cima alla Genovese is made with ox stomach chosen close to the breast, which, however, has very little meat on it. By using a thin piece of breast, you get more meat. Note that the broth from cooking is excellent and can be used to make excellent soups.

With a sharp knife, slice into the meat horizontally to make a large pocket without cutting through any of the edges, leaving about ¾ inch on three sides. Set aside.

Blanch the sweetbreads for a moment in boiling water, free them from their skins, and then place them in a small pan with a little oil and butter, a small piece of garlic, and a little onion. Cook slowly for a few minutes without browning the sweetbreads, then remove them from the heat and cut them into very small dice.

Soak the bread in milk, squeeze dry, and put on a cutting board with the lean pork and lardo. Chop everything finely and season with salt and pepper. In a bowl, combine the bread mixture, an egg, and a handful of grated Parmesan. Mix in the diced sweetbreads and ⅔ cup of peas.

Once the stuffing is ready, stuff the breast and press well, trying to give a round shape. With a sturdy needle and white thread, sew up the opening of the pocket, sewing also any tears that were made during the operation. Tie up 2 or 3 times to keep the shape.

Place the stuffed breast in a pot of hot water, to which you will add half an onion, the celery, a piece of carrot, and a bay leaf. After a couple of hours, put it on a plate, cover it with a second plate and weigh it down so that the insides are neatly pressed.

When it's time to eat, slice it and serve it with a plate of cooked vegetables of your choosing.

ADA SAYS: *You can also serve this with meat jelly, Russian salad, or pickled vegetables.*

COSTATA ALLA PIZZAIOLA

Rib Steak Pizzaiola

3 beef rib steaks (1 lb each)
Olive oil
3 garlic cloves
2¼ lb tomatoes
Oregano
Salt
Pepper

Pound the steaks with a meat mallet, heat a little oil in a pan and sear the steaks on both sides over high heat. When they are well browned, season them with salt, plenty of pepper, and then remove them for a moment from the pan and keep warm.

Meanwhile, chop the garlic and peel, seed, and chop the tomatoes and drain well.

Put the chopped garlic in the hot oil in the pan, and as soon as it starts to brown, add the tomatoes. Cook for 2 or 3 minutes over very strong heat, so that they do not come apart. At this point, return the meat to the pan, add a strong pinch of oregano, let the meat flavor for another minute, then arrange them on a serving plate, covering them with their thick sauce and send immediately to the table.

◆ ADA SAYS: *Having to prepare the pizzaiola steaks for several people, it is advisable to calculate a nice piece of meat of about 1 pound for every two people and then cut the meat at the table, instead of one steak per person, which, being much thinner, would not be as juicy and tasty as in the first case.*

COSTATA CON FUNGHI

Rib Steak with Mushrooms

3 lb 5 oz beef rib steak, or 2¼ lb without the bone
Onion
Carrot
Celery
Parsley
Wine
Olive oil
2 tbsp butter
Prosciutto
Meat broth *(p88)*
2 oz dried mushrooms
Salt
Pepper

Put the meat in a large container with a little onion, carrot, a little celery, a few sprigs of parsley, and add a glass of dry white or red wine. Cover and keep for a few hours in the fridge.

Then take a Dutch oven, in which the meat can fit neatly, and put in ¼ cup of oil, butter, and prosciutto cut into cubes. Also add a little chopped onion and heat the fat well and lightly color the onion.

Remove the meat from the marinade—strain the marinade and set aside. Put the meat in the pan over bright heat and quickly brown well on both sides.

When the meat is golden, season it with salt and pepper and then baste it with the strained wine from the marinade. (If you had to skip the marinating step, add a glass of wine, white or red, at this point.)

Cover the pan, reduce the heat, and let the wine evaporate completely. You will recognize the complete evaporation of the wine when the liquid in the pan begins to fry again: This is a sign that only the fat is left in the bottom. Turn the meat, making sure the juices coat everything, then baste with a couple of ladles of broth.

In the meantime, reconstitute the dried mushrooms in cold water and rinse well. Add the mushrooms to the pan. Cover again and when you have brought the sauce to a boil, reduce the heat even more and let the cooking finish very slowly, so that the meat is well cooked.

Then arrange the meat on a heated plate and put the mushroom garnish on one side.

The sauce must be degreased and must be very reduced. If need be, after removing a little fat from the surface with a spoon, let it reduce more, scraping the bottom well with a wooden spoon. With this little sauce, coat the meat.

FETTINE ALLA PIZZAIOLA

Sliced Beef Steak Pizzaiola

1 lb 5 oz sirloin steaks
Olive oil
2 garlic cloves
4 cups tomato passata
Oregano
Salt
Pepper

Pound the steaks well with a wet meat mallet so that they are not very thick but rather wide.

Put the oil and garlic cloves in a large pan and as soon as the garlic has browned, remove it and put the steaks in a single layer in the pan. Let them sauté over high heat on both sides for a few minutes, then add salt and pepper, remove them from the pan, and place them on a plate. Repeat for all the steaks.

Pour the tomato passata into the same pan, season with salt and pepper, and cook over high heat for a few minutes. Return all the steaks to the pan, cover with a lid, and cook over moderate heat for about 30 minutes.

Toward the end of cooking, sprinkle with oregano. Arrange the slices on a serving plate and send promptly to the table.

FETTINE FRITTE

Deep-Fried Beef Slices

1 lb 5 oz sirloin steak, very thinly sliced
Flour
2 eggs
Breadcrumbs
Oil for deep-frying
Salt
Nutmeg

Pound the steaks well with a wet meat mallet so that they are not very thick but rather wide.

Dredge them in flour, beating with your hands to let the excess flour fall off. Then dip the floured slices in the beaten eggs, which you will have seasoned with a pinch of salt and a trifle of nutmeg. Finally dredge in the breadcrumbs. Press them to make the breadcrumbs stick well, but knock off any excess.

Deep-fry in plenty of hot oil and cook until they are a nice dark gold color.

FETTINE FRITTE CON LA FONTINA

Fried Sirloin with Fontina

1 lb 5 oz sirloin steak, very thinly sliced
3½ oz Fontina
3½ oz ham
Flour
2 eggs
Nutmeg
Breadcrumbs
Oil for deep-frying
Salt

Pound the steaks well with the wet meat mallet so that they are thin and rather wide. Over each steak lay a thin slice of Fontina and one of ham and fold each one up like a book.

Then dredge the slices in flour, encouraging the excess flour to fall off with small strokes of your hands. Then dip the slices in the beaten eggs, which have been seasoned with a pinch of salt and a trifle of nutmeg. Finally, dredge them in the breadcrumbs. Press them to make the breadcrumbs stick well, but knock off any excess.

Finally, cook them in plenty of hot oil until they turn a beautiful gold color on both sides.

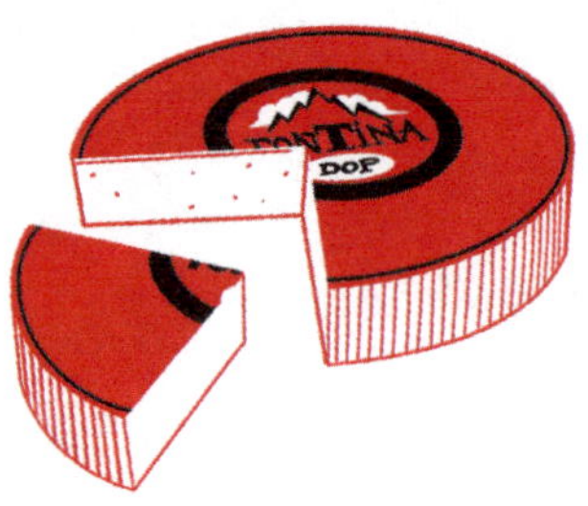

FILETTO ALLA BISMARCK

Beef Tenderloin Bismarck

10 tbsp butter
6 beef tenderloin steaks (3 to 4 oz each)
6 eggs
Salt
Pepper

Fry 3 tablespoons of butter in a pan and brown the steaks on both sides over high heat. When they are cooked, season with salt and pepper and put them on a plate.

Pour a few spoonfuls of water into the pan and with a wooden spoon mix everything so you get a little sauce that you will need in the end.

Meanwhile, put the remaining butter in another skillet, a piece at a time, let it melt and fry one egg at a time; season with a pinch of salt. As soon as the egg sets, lift it out with a slotted spatula and place it on a steak. Make one egg for each steak.

Trim the egg whites with the tip of a small knife and pour the simple sauce prepared with the cooking juices over everything.

FILETTO ALLA CACCIATORA

Hunter's Tenderloin

Olive oil
6 thick beef tenderloin medallions (5 oz each)
Marsala
Red wine
Garlic
Fennel seeds
Tomato passata
Parsley
Salt
Pepper

Put a pan on the heat with a little oil and, when the oil smokes, lay down the beef and sear over high heat on both sides. When the meat is cooked, season with salt and pepper and keep warm.

Now pour a little Marsala and red wine into the pan and use a wooden spoon to scrape up the cooking juices. When the liquid has partially evaporated, add a little diced garlic and a pinch of fennel seeds. After a minute or two, add ¾ cup tomato passata. Stir, and as soon as the sauce has become quite thick, pour it on the steaks. Finish with chopped parsley.

FILETTO ALLA CREOLA

Creole Beef Tenderloin

6 beef tenderloin steaks (3 to 4 oz each)
Butter
Onion
Flour
Broth
Olives, pitted
3 tbsp golden raisins
3 eggs
9 oz puff pastry, homemade *(p71)* or frozen
Salt
Pepper

Cook the steaks in butter over high heat for a few minutes. When they are cooked, cut them into large cubes and place them in a bowl.

Put a finely chopped onion in a pan, add 2 tablespoons of butter and cook the onion slowly without letting it brown too much. As soon as the onion is cooked, add half a spoon of flour, mix and, after a while, add half a glass of broth.

When the sauce is thick, season it with salt and plenty of pepper and add a handful of olives, raisins, 2 of the eggs, which have been hard-boiled and cut into cubes, and the beef cubes. Simmer, taking particular care that this kind of ragu be thick enough, and then pour everything into a shallow bowl to cool.

Roll out the puff pastry to a thickness of ¼ inch and cut out 6 discs of about 6 inches diameter. Distribute the prepared filling in the middle of the discs, leaving an edge of a couple of fingers, moisten this edge with a little beaten egg and fold each disc on itself. Press lightly to close the mixture well inside.

Arrange the pastries on a baking sheet, brush them with the beaten egg and bake them in a hot oven with lively heat for the time necessary for the dough to swell and acquire a nice golden color. Serve them very hot.

FILETTO ALLA PIEMONTESE

Tenderloin Piedmont Style

12 beef tenderloin tail steaks
12 slices sandwich bread
Butter
Marsala
Anchovy butter *(p54)*
White truffle
Salt
Pepper
Optional: Piedmont sauce *(p27)*
To serve: 1 lb 5 oz fresh peas, 2 oz prosciutto

Calculate two steaks per person, cut from the tail—the thinnest part—of the tenderloin about 2 inches wide and a finger thick. Wrap a string around the steaks to keep them in shape during cooking.

With a 2¾-inch round cookie cutter, cut the sandwich bread into discs. On each disc of bread, use a small knife to make a circular incision ⅜ inch from the edge and only ¼ inch deep.

After cutting the discs, fry them in butter to a beautiful golden color. During cooking the incision will open slightly, so that it will be easy, with the tip of the knife, to remove the central part and obtain a kind of round box, which you will complete by removing the inside. Keep these boxes warm.

Meanwhile, fry the steaks in a pan with hot butter over high heat. When they are cooked, season them with salt and pepper, pour a finger of Marsala into the pan and with a wooden spoon scrape the bottom of the pan to have a rather thick sauce with which you will coat the beef.

Spread the anchovy butter on the bottom of the bread boxes, also adding a few trimmings of white truffle.

In each small box, place a steak and finish by placing a slice of white truffle on each. In the middle of a round plate, arrange a pyramid of peas with prosciutto, and arrange the steaks in a ring around them in their boxes.

ADA SAYS: *You can have them served simply like this or better with a Piedmontese sauce. This sauce should be served very hot.*

FILETTO TOURNEDOS AI DADINI DI PANE

Pan-Fried Tournedos with Croutons

12 tournedos (tenderloin medallions)
Flour
7 tbsp butter
3½ oz bread for croutons
Marsala
Salt
Pepper

Sprinkle the tournedos lightly with flour. Then cook them in a pan with half of the very hot butter while keeping the heat lively. Season with salt and when the tournedos have taken on a nice brown color, remove them from the pan and arrange them on a serving dish, keeping them warm.

In the same pan, add more butter and fry the slices of bread cut into cubes. When the cubes are golden, arrange them on the plate around the tournedos. Pour a small glass of Marsala into the pan, stir with a wooden spoon to scrape up any browned bits and, as soon as this simple sauce has thickened slightly, distribute it over the meat.

FILETTO TOURNEDOS AL PROSCIUTTO

Tournedos with Prosciutto and Mushrooms

1 oz dried mushrooms
7 tbsp butter
3½ oz prosciutto
Parsley
Flour
12 tournedos (tenderloin medallions)
2 tbsp broth
1 lemon
Salt
Pepper
Optional: fried crostini

Soak the dried mushrooms in cold water for about 20 minutes, then cook them in a pan with a little butter, a little water, and salt. Take a well-proportioned pan, spread it generously with butter, and cover the bottom with a coarse mixture made with the prosciutto, mushrooms, and parsley.

Flour the tournedos lightly and arrange them in a single layer and sweat them. Turn them gently and cook them on the other side. Season with salt and pepper and finish cooking, bearing in mind that the meat must not be overcooked.

Immediately put the tournedos in a serving dish. Add another piece of butter to the pan, deglaze the bottom of the cooking with broth or water, squeeze in the juice of half a lemon and pour the sauce over the meat.

ADA SAYS: *These tournedos can also, elegantly, be served on fried round crostini.*

FILETTO TOURNEDOS FRITTO RIPIENO

Fried Tournedos with Truffle and Mozzarella

6 beef tenderloin tail steaks
3½ oz ham
White truffle
Mozzarella
Flour
2 eggs
Breadcrumbs
1½ tbsp butter
Broth
Parsley
Grated Parmesan
For garnish: artichokes and peas

Calculate one steak per person and cut from the tail—the thinnest part—of the tenderloin, about 2 inches wide and two fingers thick. Butterfly the steaks by making a horizontal cut halfway down, but do not cut all the way through, as if you were opening a book. In the middle, place a thin disk of ham, a few slices of white truffle, and a thin disk of mozzarella on top of the truffle. Close the meat and press it lightly with the palm of your hand to help it stick.

When you have prepared all the steaks, flour them, dredge them in the beaten eggs, then in the breadcrumbs and fry them slowly in some butter.

In the meantime, prepare the sauce: Put the 1½ tablespoons butter in a saucepan and when it melts, add a spoon of flour. Mix a little and then sprinkle in a small glass of broth. Cook for a few minutes to thicken, then off the heat stir in a spoon of chopped parsley and a spoon of grated Parmesan.

Pour a little sauce on each slice with a spoon and have it brought to the table immediately.

ADA SAYS: *Artichokes and peas go well with this.*

FILETTO TOURNEDOS MONACO

Tournedos Monaco

12 slices sandwich bread
Olive oil
Butter
5 oz prosciutto
9 oz pork or lamb brain
Flour
12 tournedos (tenderloin medallions)
Marsala
Salt

With a 2¾-inch round cookie cutter, cut the slices of sandwich bread into disks. Fry these crostini in oil or butter.

Also prepare 12 slices of prosciutto and 12 slices of brain. In a saucepan, combine the brain and cold water for about 10 minutes. Then drain the water, replace it with more water, and bring to a boil and let it boil for a minute. Rinse the brain under cold water, dry it, and cut into slices. Dip the slices in flour and fry them in plenty of butter. Salt them lightly.

Lightly flour the tournedos and when ready to serve, put some butter in a pan and fry over high heat, season with a little salt. Remember to keep the meat rather pink inside.

When all the meat is cooked, put another piece of butter, a tablespoon or two of water and a glass of Marsala into the pan and deglaze the pan to make a sauce.

Quickly dip the crostini in this sauce and arrange them on a long serving dish that can fit the crostini in two rows of six. On each crostini place a tournedo, pour the remaining sauce over the meat, and put a slice of ham and a slice of brain on each tournedo.

FILETTO TOURNEDOS POMONA

Tournedos Vol-au-Vents with Apple

6 apples
Honey
White wine
2 tbsp butter
Flour
12 tournedos (tenderloin medallions)
Marsala
12 small vol-au-vent cases
Bouillon cube
Salt
Pepper

Halve the apples, peel them, and then with a teaspoon dig out the core. Put the apple halves in a pan with a spoon of honey and a glass of white wine (in the absence of honey, use a couple of spoons of sugar) and let them cook. Turn them from time to time, being very careful not to let them overcook and collapse. The wine will evaporate to a large extent and at the end of cooking a very thick syrup will remain behind. Use this to baste the apples so they remain shiny. Set aside and keep warm.

Now put a piece of butter in a pan and let it heat well. Lightly flour the tournedos and cook them over rather high heat. When cooked, season with salt and pepper and sprinkle with Marsala.

Next place the vol-au-vent cases in a serving dish and place the tournedos inside. On top put half an apple upside down, that is, with the convex side at the top.

Return the pan in which the tournedos were cooked to the heat, deglaze with half a glass of water and mix the cooking juices with a wooden spoon. Add a little bouillon cube, melt it well, let it thicken a little and complete this sauce off the heat by adding the butter a piece at a time, constantly stirring. Drop a little of this sauce onto each vol-au-vent and send to the table.

FRICANDÒ

Beef Stew Catalan Style

6 hanger or round steaks (3½ oz each)
10 tbsp butter
2 oz prosciutto
6 potatoes
2 oz dried mushrooms
Olive oil
Parsley
1 lb spring onions
Nutmeg
Meat broth *(p88)*
Salt
Pepper

Pound the steaks well with a wet meat mallet. Brown them briefly in a pan with a little butter over high heat. Season with salt and pepper and set aside.

Cut the prosciutto into small strips. Peel and dice the raw potatoes. Soak the dried mushrooms in cold water, then sauté them in a pan with a little oil and parsley, then chop them. Blanch the onions for a few minutes and peel them.

Generously butter a 10-inch Dutch oven. Arrange the steaks on the bottom, cover them with the strips of ham. On the meat put the potatoes and on these the onions and mushrooms. Season with salt, pepper, and nutmeg and pour enough broth into the pan to cover everything. Put the pan in a preheated oven of moderate heat and cook for 1 hour.

FRICASSEA ALLA LUCCHESE

Fricassee Lucca Style

4 spring onions
Garlic
Parsley
Olive oil
1 lb 5 oz lean beef, diced
2 cups fresh peas
4 artichoke hearts
Sugar
Broth
Salt
Pepper
To serve: bread for croutons

Chop the onions, half a clove of garlic and some parsley sprigs. Fry in a little oil and then add the diced beef.

When the meat has browned, add the fresh peas and the artichoke hearts (cut into 8 wedges each). Season with salt, pepper, a little sugar, sprinkle with half a glass of broth or water, cover and cook slowly until completely cooked, about 1 hour.

Then place everything in a vegetable dish, surrounding it with croutons fried in oil.

ADA SAYS: *This preparation is known as "garmugia" and is an exquisite specialty of Lucca, based on meat and vegetables.*

GULYÀS

Goulash

2¼ lb beef (chuck or brisket)
1 lb onions
2 tbsp lard
Cumin seeds
Marjoram
Garlic
Flour
Meat broth *(p88)*
Salt
Pepper
Paprika
Optional: boiled potatoes

Cut all the meat into regular chunks, each the size of a large walnut. Finely chop the onions and place them in a pan with plenty of lard, a couple of spoons. Cook them slowly so they don't take color.

Then add the meat, increase the heat, and season with salt, pepper, a pinch of cumin seeds, a pinch of marjoram, half a clove of crushed garlic, and some paprika. When the meat is a little browned, sprinkle in a spoon of flour, stir and then add enough broth to completely cover the meat. Decrease the heat considerably and let it cook slowly for about 3 hours, stirring at intervals.

ADA SAYS: *Goulash is a famous Hungarian preparation based on meat, onions, and paprika. A nonnegotiable element for its success is paprika, which must be sweet, fragrant, and intensely colored. For meat, the Hungarian formula indicates chuck or brisket, but any good cut of meat is usable. A good side dish would be boiled potatoes served hot.*

GULYÀS CON CREMA DI LATTE

Goulash with Cream and Dumplings

2¼ lb beef (chuck or brisket)
Lard or olive oil
Paprika
Flour
14 oz onions
1 lb 5 oz potatoes
Meat broth *(p88)* or bouillon cube
White wine
Sour cream
Salt

Cut the meat into rather thick and finger-long squares, put them in a Dutch oven with a couple of spoons of lard or oil and, when browned a little, season with salt, a small teaspoon of paprika, and a spoonful of flour. Mix, then add the onions cut into slices and the potatoes, peeled and sliced not too thin.

Cover everything with meat broth or a dissolved bouillon cube, and add a glass of white wine and a glass of sour cream. Bring to a boil, cover, put in a preheated oven of moderate heat and let cook for about 3 hours, stirring at intervals until the meat is cooked and the sauce reduced.

For the flour dumplings: Prepare a rather thick batter of flour, water, and a little salt. Bring a saucepan of salted water to a boil. Drop in some teaspoons of batter to make many dumplings, which you will boil for a few minutes until they float back up to the surface. When they are firm, drain them, and 15 minutes before serving the meat, add them to the sauce.

INVOLTINI AL POMODORO

Beef Rolls in Tomato Sauce

10 chicken livers
7 tbsp butter
7 oz lardo
2 slices prosciutto
Parsley
Sage
1 egg
Marsala
Vinegar
2¼ lb sliced sirloin
1 cup tomato passata
Bread for crostini
Flour
Broth
Salt
Pepper

Remove the gall from the livers and also remove any greenish traces with a small knife. Brown them in a skillet with a little butter and remove them to a cutting board. To make a *battuto:* Chop the livers with a couple of slices of lardo, the prosciutto, a handful of parsley, a couple of sage leaves, salt, and pepper. Mix it with an egg, a spoon of Marsala, and a few drops of vinegar.

Flatten out the beef slices, season with a little salt and pepper, lay on a little of the *battuto*, roll them up, and skewer them together with a toothpick, sandwiching them with a slice of lardo and tying them with a few rounds of string to keep their shape during cooking.

Put a piece of butter in a pan and when it is hot, place the rolls in and fry them until they are well browned. Then add the tomato passata.

While they cook, prepare small crostini of fried bread, more or less the size of a pair of rolls. When the rolls are cooked, in 1½ hours at most, sprinkle them with a good pinch of flour and a finger of Marsala and when the liquid has almost evaporated, remove the rolls from the pan, free them from the string and the toothpicks, and place them two by two on the crostini, arranging them on a plate.

Put the pan back on the heat, deglaze the cooking juices with a ladle of broth or water, mix well and, when the sauce is slightly thickened, drizzle it on the rolls and crostini.

INVOLTINI CON FEGATINI

Beef and Chicken Liver Rolls

10 chicken livers
7 tbsp butter
7 oz lardo
2 slices prosciutto
Parsley
Sage
1 egg
Marsala
Vinegar
2¼ lb sliced beef
Bread for crostini
Flour
Broth
Salt
Pepper

Remove the gall from the livers and any greenish traces of gall also with a small knife. Brown them in a skillet with a little butter and remove them to a cutting board. To make a *battuto:* Chop the livers with a couple of slices of lardo, the prosciutto, a handful of parsley, a couple of sage leaves, salt, and pepper. Mix it with an egg, a spoon of Marsala, and a few drops of vinegar.

Flatten out the beef slices, season with a little salt and pepper. Lay on each slice some of the *battuto* and roll each slice up and skewer them in two with a toothpick, sandwiching them with a slice of lardo and tying them with a few rounds of string to keep their shape during cooking.

Put a piece of butter in a Dutch oven and when it is hot, place the rolls in and fry them until they are well browned. While they are cooking, prepare small crostini of fried bread, the size, more or less, of a pair of rolls.

When the rolls are cooked, in 1½ hours at the most, sprinkle them with a good pinch of flour and baste with a finger of Marsala. As soon as the liquid has almost evaporated, remove the rolls from the pan, free them from their string and the toothpicks, and place them two by two on the crostini, arranging them on a plate.

Put the pan back on the heat, add a ladle of broth or water, mix well, and when the sauce is slightly thickened, drop it on the rolls and crostini.

PASTICCINI DI MANZO

Beef Pastries

2½ cups flour
7 tbsp butter
4 tsp brewer's yeast
12 thin beef steaks
3½ oz prosciutto
Salt

Mound the flour on a work surface and make a well in the center. Add 2 tablespoons of butter, the brewer's yeast, and salt and dissolve everything with a scant glass of lukewarm water. Knead well, work the dough a little to make it smooth and soft, and let it rest. Pound the steaks well with a wet meat mallet so they are thin and wide. In the center of each place a slice of prosciutto, a piece of butter, and a spot of salt and roll the slice up.

Roll out the dough, cut it into 12 squares and place in each of these a meat roll. Wet the edges of the squares with water and enclose the rolls in them.

Lightly butter a baking sheet, arrange the pastries on it, not so close to each other, and bake them in a preheated oven of moderate heat for about 45 minutes, until they are colored and cooked to the right point.

ADA SAYS: *Serve them hot or cold: they are delicious both ways.*

PASTICCIO DI MANZO

Steak Pie

14 oz sirloin steaks
3½ oz prosciutto
6 large potatoes
1 oz dried mushrooms
Olive oil
Parsley
Onion
Butter
Nutmeg
Meat broth *(p88)*
Salt
Pepper

Pie dough:
1⅔ cups flour, 7 tbsp butter

Prepare a pie dough *(p275)* with the flour and butter amounts listed here, 6 tablespoons of water, and a little salt. Once the dough is made, roll it into a ball and let it rest in the fridge for 30 minutes.

Meanwhile, prepare the filling: Pound the steaks well with a wet meat mallet and then fry them in a little butter over very high heat, letting them just color on both sides. Season them with salt and set aside.

Cut the prosciutto into small slices. Peel and cut the potatoes into cubes. Soak the dried mushrooms in cold water, then when they have reconstituted, cook them in a pan with a little oil and parsley, and then chop them on a cutting board. Finally cut up half an onion and parsley.

Generously butter a baking pan. Arrange the meat in the pan, cover it with the slices of prosciutto. Make a layer of potatoes and then the onion, mushrooms, and parsley. Season with salt, pepper, and nutmeg and pour 8 or 10 spoons of broth into the pan. Dot, here and there, with 3 or 4 small pieces of butter.

Roll out the pie dough on a floured surface, giving it a thickness of about ¼ inch. Slightly moisten the rim of the pan with water and then lift the dough with both hands and place it on top of the pan. Press your fingers around so the dough sticks well at the edge. Trim with a small knife and in the middle of the pie make a round hole about ¾ inch in diameter, for the steam to come out, and then trace very light cuts—like a star—that barely affect the surface of the dough, without cutting too much.

Transfer the pie to a preheated oven of moderate heat and bake for 1 hour 15 minutes. Then have it brought to the table.

ADA SAYS: *This a characteristic dish of English cuisine.*

ROAST-BEEF AL FORNO

Roast Beef

2 lb 10 oz beef tenderloin or sirloin roast
Coarse salt
Rosemary
Olive oil
Red wine
Salt
Pepper

Turn on the oven so it is hot when you put the meat in.

With a small knife, make 3 or 4 horizontal incisions in the meat and insert a pinch of coarse salt in them. Then tie the meat to keep it in shape and in between the string and the meat put a few sprigs of rosemary.

Place a roasting pan on the heat with a little oil and as soon as it's hot, brown the meat on all sides. Season with a little more salt and pepper. Pour a glass of red wine into the pan and, immediately, put it in the oven for 30 minutes. If you want less rare beef, leave it for 40 minutes.

ADA SAYS: *This type of roast is excellent prepared the previous day, and served cold, with its little sauce heated up separately.*

ROAST-BEEF AL FORNO CON SALSA DI CAPPERI

Roast Beef with Caper Sauce

2 lb 10 oz beef tenderloin or sirloin roast
Coarse salt
Sage
Rosemary
Olive oil
Caper sauce *(p25)*
Red wine
Salt
Pepper

Cook the beef as in Roast Beef *(as above)* but add a few sage leaves between the string and the meat along with the rosemary.

While the beef is in the oven, prepare the caper sauce: Put half chopped onion in a small saucepan and cook with half the butter. When the onion is golden, add a rinsed and chopped anchovy and mash with a wooden spoon. Add the capers, chopped parsley, and a pinch of flour. Let cook for a minute or two, stirring, and then sprinkle in a finger of vinegar and half a glass of broth. Cook a little more until you have the right consistency. Finish the sauce by adding the remaining butter off the heat.

Carve the roast beef into slices and pour the warm sauce over.

ADA SAYS: *You can also add half a teaspoon of sugar to the caper sauce, but it is not necessary.*

ROAST-BEEF ALLA SPAGNOLA

Roast Beef Spanish Style

2 lb 10 oz beef tenderloin or sirloin roast
4 garlic cloves
Paprika
Red wine
Vinegar
Bay leaf
3 onions
2¼ lb canned tomatoes
3 green bell peppers
Black olives, pitted
2 oz dried mushrooms
Olive oil
Salt
Pepper

Tie the meat to keep it in shape and sprinkle it with salt, pepper, chopped garlic, and paprika. Prepare a marinade by placing the wine, vinegar, and bay leaf in a bowl. Submerge the meat in this marinade and leave it for 12 hours, taking care to turn it over from time to time.

For the second stage: Reconstitute the dried mushrooms in cold water for 15 minutes, wash, and chop. Remove the meat from the marinade; strain the marinade through a sieve and set aside.

Heat the oil in a Dutch oven, brown the meat on all sides over lively heat. Add the onions, tomatoes, chopped bell peppers, ⅔ cup olives, mushrooms, and half of the marinade.

Put the pan in a very hot oven and cook for 30 minutes if you want a rare roast beef, or a few more if you want it more cooked, supervising the cooking and basting with the remaining marinade as you go.

Strain or blend the cooking juices and serve in a gravy boat with the roast carved into slices and served on a hot serving plate.

ROAST-BEEF CON FUNGHI

Roast Beef with Mushrooms

2 lb 10 oz beef tenderloin
3½ oz dried mushrooms
7 tbsp butter
2 oz prosciutto
Salt

Roast the beef as in Roast Beef *(opposite page)* and when it comes time to serve, carve into slices and arrange on a serving plate.

Meanwhile, soak the mushrooms in cold water, rinse them, and put them in a Dutch oven with half the butter and the chopped prosciutto. Melt the fats and then add a lot of warm water to cover the mushrooms. Season with a little salt, bring to a simmer, and let cook slowly for about 30 minutes, gradually adding more water if the first batch is evaporated.

When the mushrooms are cooked, blend them with the little liquid left. If the mixture is too thick, dilute it with a little more water. Pour the sauce into a saucepan and heat it up again. Then complete by adding the rest of the butter in small pieces, stirring constantly.

Pour the hot sauce on the slices of roast beef and send immediately to the table.

ROAST-BEEF CON PATATE

Roast Beef with Potatoes

2 lb 10 oz beef tenderloin
Rosemary
1 lb potatoes
Olive oil
Salt
Pepper

Tie the meat to keep it in shape and in between the string and the meat put a few sprigs of rosemary.

Peel the potatoes, cut them into small pieces, leave them for 2 hours in cold water, then drain and dry them very carefully.

In a preheated oven, roast the meat and potatoes together, sprinkled with salt and a few pieces of rosemary, with a glass of oil. Cook it for about 30 minutes, turning the potatoes from time to time.

When they are both ready, slice the beef, arrange it on a serving dish, surround it with potatoes, and immediately send it to the table.

ROTOLO ALLA SICILIANA (FARSUMAGRU)

Beef Roll Sicilian Style

10 oz lean ground beef
Crustless white bread
Milk
6 eggs
2 egg yolks
Grated Parmesan
Nutmeg
Parsley
5 oz prosciutto
3½ oz fresh Caciocavallo
3½ oz salami
1 lb slice of beef, in one piece
Olive oil
Onion
Red wine
1¼ cups tomato passata
1 lb fresh peas
Salt
Pepper

The farsumagru is an appetizing recipe of Sicilian cuisine whose preparation consists of two elements: a large slice of meat and a filling rolled up in the meat.

In a bowl, mix the ground beef and the bread—previously soaked in milk and squeezed dry—2 whole eggs, 2 yolks, some grated Parmesan, salt, pepper, nutmeg, and a sprig of chopped parsley. Mix these ingredients well with your hands.

Cut the prosciutto into thin slices, like lardons, and also the caciocavallo and salami. Boil 4 eggs and then cut them into wedges.

Now put the large slice of meat on the table and pound it out to obtain a rectangle.

Arrange the slice of meat so that a shorter end of the rectangle is facing you. On this rectangle spread the filling, helping with slightly wet hands. Arrange the egg wedges, salami, prosciutto, and the caciocavallo parallel to the shorter side, then start rolling the meat up, forming a kind of large salami.

Carefully tie the roll to keep it in shape and place it in a Dutch oven, oval if possible, with half a glass of oil and a chopped onion. Brown gently and, as soon as the onion is golden, add some red wine. Season with a little more salt and pepper and, when the surface is well browned, add the tomato passata. Keep cooking for about 1 hour. Add the peas and resume cooking until the meat and peas have reached the right point and the sauce is well thickened.

Then remove the meat from the Dutch oven, put it on a cutting board, snip off the twine, and slice the roll into regular slices. Then arrange the slices on a serving dish, covering them with the sauce and peas, and immediately send to the table.

SALSICCIOTTI DI MANZO

Beef Sausages

2¼ lb thin-sliced beef sirloin
3½ oz lardo
Garlic
Crustless white bread
Milk
Grated Parmesan
Olive oil or butter
Flour
Salt
Pepper
Optional: broth

Season the slices of meat with salt and pepper and spread them out on a work surface. They should be rectangular, about 2½ inches wide and 4 inches long. Trim the various slices with a knife, so as to give them approximately the same shape and size.

Make a thin mixture with any trimmings removed from the steaks, together with the chopped lardo, a clove of garlic and a little white bread (previously soaked in milk and squeezed dry). Season with salt, pepper, and a spoon of grated Parmesan. Mix everything and distribute this filling over the beef slices, leveling it with the wet blade of a knife.

Roll the slices up to make "sausages" and stick each with a toothpick to hold together.

Heat a little oil or butter in a wide pan, flour the rolls and put them to cook, turning them carefully. When they reach a nice dark color, baste them with a little broth or water. Cover, reduce the heat, and finish cooking slowly for about 1 hour.

When cooked, the sauce should be almost dried out and have created a shiny flavorful coating on the rolls.

SPEZZATINO AL VINO ROSSO

Beef in Red Wine

3 lb 5 oz beef sirloin
Bay leaf
Garlic
Red wine
Onion
2 oz lardo
Olive oil
1 lb canned tomatoes
Salt
Pepper
Nutmeg

Cut the meat into chunks, put it in a bowl, season with salt, pepper, a little nutmeg, half a bay leaf, a clove of garlic, and finally 3 glasses of wine. Cover the bowl and leave in the marinade for at least 5 hours. When ready to cook, remove the meat from the marinade; strain the marinade through a sieve and set aside.

Finely chop an onion, two cloves of garlic, and the lardo and brown them gently in a Dutch oven with a few spoons of oil.

Add the well drained meat, increase the heat, and cook until well colored. Add the strained marinade and the canned tomatoes, cover, and continue braising over very low heat for about 2 hours.

SPIEDINI CON IL PANE

Beef and Bread Skewers

1 lb 5 oz beef
7 oz ham
2 tbsp butter
30 slices bread
30 sage leaves
Olive oil
Radicchio
Salt

Chop the beef and the ham into chunks, season with a little salt, mix with the softened butter, and spread on the slices of bread.

Take 6 skewers and start by sticking a slice of bread, a sage leaf, a second slice of bread and so on until you have filled the whole skewer ending with a slice of bread.

Put them on a well-oiled baking sheet, grease them with a drizzle of oil, and put them in a preheated oven of moderate heat for about 15 minutes, until the slices of bread are a beautiful golden color and the meat well cooked.

Wash the radicchio leaves, drain them well, put them on a plate and place the skewers on them, and immediately send to the table.

SPIEDINI GUARNITI

Beef and Onion Skewers

1 lb 5 oz beef tenderloin
3½ oz pancetta
12 small onions
12 small tomatoes
Olive oil
Lemon wedges
Salt
Pepper

Cut the beef into 36 pieces and the pancetta into 24 squares. Peel the onions and cut in half horizontally. Rinse the tomatoes, cut them in two like the onions, and remove the seeds.

Take 12 rather long skewers and skewer a piece of meat, then half a tomato, then a square of pancetta, and finally half an onion. Then more meat, tomato, pancetta, and onion, ending with the meat.

Arrange the skewers on a baking sheet, sprinkle with salt and pepper, drizzle with some oil, and put them in a preheated oven of moderate heat for 20 minutes. As soon as they are browned, place them on a plate and surround them with lemon wedges.

STRACCETTI

Beef Straccetti

1 lb 5 oz thin sliced sirloin
Olive oil
Red wine
Rosemary
Sage
Salt
Pepper

Straccetti are small slices of beef, very thin, that cook in a few minutes. Have the butcher cut out the strips from the sirloin.

Add the strips of beef to a large pan, with a few drops of boiling oil. As soon as the strips have taken heat, turn them over and after a few minutes splash with red wine, season with a pinch of salt and pepper, and remove them from the heat.

Put them on a serving dish, garnish with a few sage leaves or rosemary, and serve immediately.

STRACOTTO ALLA LOMBARDA

Braised Beef Lombardy Style

2 oz prosciutto
2 lb 10 oz beef sirloin roast
Olive oil
3½ tbsp butter
Red wine
2 onions
2 carrots
Celery
2 cloves
Garlic
4 cups meat broth *(p88)*
1 cup tomato passata
Salt
Pepper

Cut the prosciutto into strips and use it to lard the meat. Tie it up so it keeps its shape in cooking.

Put half a glass of oil in a suitably sized Dutch oven for the meat and add the butter. As soon as the fats are heated add the meat to brown on all sides, adding the wine a little at a time, and as soon as this evaporates, season with salt and pepper.

Now coarsely chop onions, carrots, and celery and add to the pot along with the cloves and garlic. Let flavor for a few minutes, then add the hot broth enough to completely cover the meat and, finally, the tomato passata. Cover and leave over very low heat for about 2½ hours, the time necessary to cook a well made braise.

STUFATINO ALLA FRANCESE

Beef Stew French Style

2 lb 10 oz beef chuck
5½ tbsp butter
Sugar
Flour
2 cups meat broth *(p88)*
Parsley
Bay leaves
Onion
Carrot
Celery
2 cloves
Salt
Pepper

To prepare this tasty meat dish, cut the beef into small pieces of about 2 inches each side. Put the butter in a Dutch oven, heat it up, add the meat, brown it lightly, stirring constantly. Sprinkle with salt and pepper and a light pinch of sugar, which makes the meat take a dark color.

As soon as the meat is well browned, drain the excess fat from the pan. Return to the heat, sprinkle with some flour, mix well, and add the boiling broth. Add all the herbs, chopped vegetables, and cloves. Cover and simmer over a slow heat for about 2 hours.

Then arrange on a serving plate and immediately send it to the table.

STUFATO AL FINOCCHIO

Beef and Fennel Stew

2 oz pork belly
Celery
Onion
Olive oil or butter
2 lb 10 oz beef shank
Dry wine
Flour
1 cup tomato passata
Broth
Garlic
Parsley
Fennel seeds
Salt
Pepper

Prepare a mince with the pork belly, celery, and onion and put it in a saucepan with a little oil or butter. When the fat is hot and the vegetables begin to fry, add the beef shank cut into chunks and, stirring occasionally with a wooden spoon, brown the meat and vegetables well. Season with salt and pepper and sprinkle with half a glass of dry wine that you will let evaporate almost entirely.

Then sprinkle half a spoon of flour on the meat, mix and then add the tomato passata. Let the tomato cook for a while, cover the pan, reduce the heat, and continue cooking for about 2 hours adding, if necessary, a little boiling broth.

When the meat is cooked and the sauce has thickened, finish the stew with a small mixture (a *stufato*) made with a clove of garlic, a sprig of parsley, and a few fennel seeds. Use this to season the stew, leave it for a few more minutes on the heat to flavor and then arrange it on a serving dish.

STUFATO ALLA ROMANA

Beef Stew Roman Style

Lard or olive oil
Onion
2 oz prosciutto
Garlic
2 lb 10 oz beef shank
Red wine
1 lb canned tomatoes
Salt
Pepper

Put a spoon of lard in a saucepan with a little chopped onion and, when the onion has browned, add some diced fatty prosciutto, a pinch of garlic, and immediately after the meat. Season with salt, pepper, and brown everything.

When it has taken a nice dark color, pour in a glass of wine, let it evaporate, and add the tomatoes. Cook the tomato a little and then cover, reduce the heat, and let it cook gently for a couple of hours. If the sauce dries out during cooking, add some water, but make sure that, when ready to serve, the sauce is sufficiently thickened, dark, and flavorful.

ADA SAYS: *The most characteristic side dish to go with this typically Roman dish is cardoons and celery boiled together and then added into the stew. If you do not have either available or do not like them, you can serve with zucchini, spring onions, mushrooms, separately, in side dishes.*

STUFATO AL VINO ROSSO

Beef Stew with Red Wine

2 lb 10 oz beef sirloin
Nutmeg
Bay leaf
Garlic
Red wine
Onion
Olive oil
Salt
Pepper
Optional: pork skin

Cut the meat into regular chunks as for a stew, put it in a bowl, season with salt, pepper, a little nutmeg, half a bay leaf, half a clove of garlic, and splash everything with a couple of glasses of red wine. Cover the bowl and leave the meat in the marinade, refrigerated, for at least 5 or 6 hours or if you have time in the evening, until the next day. Drain the meat into a sieve set over a bowl. Reserve the strained marinade.

Finely chop an onion and two cloves of garlic and brown them gently in a pan with a little oil. You can also add some fresh pork skins, well scraped and minced. When they have sautéed a little, drain the beef and add it to the pan over moderate heat.

After a while, increase the heat just a bit, allowing the juices from the meat to be absorbed, but keep the heat at a level that the stew can brown slowly, to a golden color. At this point, pour in the wine from the sieved marinade, cover and continue the cooking over very low heat for about 2 hours until the meat is well cooked.

Spoon off some of the fat from the surface of the little remaining sauce and spoon the stew into a serving dish.

ADA SAYS: *For this preparation you need to choose sirloin or another tender and juicy choice cut.*

TERRINA DI MANZO ALLA FRANCESE

Terrine of Beef French Style

10½ oz lardo
Bay leaves
2 lb 10 oz sirloin, sliced
Meat broth *(p88)*
3½ oz pork skin or belly
2 tsp salt
Peppercorns
Nutmeg

Cut the lardo into very thin slices. In a bowl mix the salt, 2 or 3 coarsely cracked peppercorns, a trifle of nutmeg, and a few bay leaves.

Take an ovenproof terrine dish in which you will layer the lardo, sliced meat, and seasoning mixture. There will be 5 layers of lardo and 4 layers of meat—adjust the seasoning amounts so it's evenly divided among the different layers. Start by lining the bottom with slices of lardo. Arrange a layer of beef slices on top. Continue in this way to alternate slices of lardo, slices of meat, and seasoning. The last layer must be slices of lardo.

Finally pour half a glass of good broth into the terrine and completely cover all the top with pieces of pork skin—which you will have previously scraped and rinsed several times—so that there are no gaps that would cause the meat to dry out. Close the terrine with its lid and put it in a preheated oven with very sweet heat.

Let it cook for 3 to 3½ hours, supervising it from time to time. If the liquid dries out, add one or two spoons more of the remaining broth. If between the pieces of skin some spaces open up, add some more pieces of skin.

After the necessary time, remove the terrine from the oven, drain the cooking liquid into a cup, let it cool so it can be easily degreased, and pour it back into the terrine. Lift out the pork skin and put a plate with a weight of about 8 ounces on top. Let the meat rest all night under the weight, refrigerated, and serve it the next day.

ADA SAYS: *Terrine preparations are a specialty of French cuisine. There are suitable containers of porcelain, glass, or ovenproof dishes, and with a lid. The French beef terrine is an excellent family recipe, very simple to make and above all very fast.*

TERRINA DI MANZO ALL'ITALIANA

Terrine of Beef Italian Style

2 lb 10 oz lean beef sirloin
1½ tbsp butter
1 onion
2 carrots
6 tomatoes
Bay leaves
White wine
Cognac
Marsala
Meat broth *(p88)*
Flour
Salt
Pepper

Remove some of the fat from the beef and trim it well, in order to get a very regular piece. Put the butter in a pan, let it heat well, then add the meat and brown it over high heat, turning it on all sides. In all, the meat will have to stay on the heat for 3 or 4 minutes, just the time to brown superficially. Then remove the meat from the pan, place it on a plate, and season it with salt and pepper.

Cut a medium onion and a couple of carrots into very fine slices. Peel, seed, and coarsely chop the tomatoes. Now take an ovenproof terrine, drop in the meat around which you will put the vegetables, tomatoes, and a small bay leaf. Splash the meat with half a glass of white wine, a small glass of Cognac, two fingers of Marsala, and a large ladle of excellent broth.

Then put the lid on. Make a rather soft dough, kneading a little flour on a work surface with a little water. Roll it into a rope and use the rope to seal the lid by pressing the dough into the opening all the way around.

Put the terrine in a roasting pan, pouring into the bottom of the pan a finger of cold water, and put in a preheated oven of moderate heat for about 3 hours, adding more water to the pan if necessary.

Remove the terrine from the oven, let it rest for a moment, remove the pastry rope at the edges and, without opening the dish, put it on a serving plate and promptly send it to the table.

TERRINA DI MANZO ALL'USO DI CACCIA

Terrine of Beef Hunter Style

2 lb 10 oz lean sirloin or rib eye
Onions
Carrots
Celery stalks
Parsley
Barolo or another red wine
Olive oil
Butter
Tomato paste
Broth
Partridge
Black truffle
Potato starch
Marsala
Salt
Pepper
Optional: spicy prune sauce *(p26)*

Cut the beef into small pieces. Put these in a bowl, season with salt and pepper, and on top slice a little onion, a piece of carrot, a stalk of celery, and a little parsley, then cover with red wine, preferably Barolo, but a good dry wine will do the same. Leave the pieces of meat in the marinade for about 3 hours, refrigerated. Drain the meat into a sieve set over a bowl. Reserve the strained marinade.

Then take a Dutch oven and put in a spoon of oil and one of butter, half a sliced onion, half a carrot, a stalk of celery, and some parsley. Add the meat and let it brown over rather bright heat, so that the moisture in the meat can quickly evaporate.

While the meat is browning, baste it slowly with the sieved wine from the marinade. Then add half a spoon of tomato paste, decrease the heat, and let it braise gently, adding, if necessary, a few spoons of broth. But keep in mind that the meat doesn't have to be drowned in liquid, but must braise in a confined space. Don't forget to stir the meat a few times.

When, after about 2 hours, the beef is almost cooked, put a partridge to roast in the oven. Remember that partridge, like all hunting birds, must be cooked just so, precisely, or what the French call *à point*—about 30 minutes. Let the braising of the meat and the roasting of the partridge go hand in hand.

Then assemble the braised beef in a new Dutch oven with a lid, and carve the partridge over it. Add a few cubes of black truffle and sprinkle abundantly with cooking juices, which you will finish in the following way: After you have taken the meat out, add a little more broth, scrape the bottom with a wooden spoon. Let it boil for a few minutes and strain the sauce through a sieve, collecting the juices in another pan and pressing well with a wooden spoon to extract all the juice from the vegetables. Spoon off the fat that will float to the surface, put the sauce back over heat, and thicken it lightly with a little bit of potato starch stirred into a little Marsala.

Splash this sauce on the beef and the partridge. Cover with aluminum foil and put the lid back on. Put the meats back over moderate heat and let them simmer for about 10 minutes. Then arrange on a plate and bring to the table, without opening it. A spicy prune sauce goes well with this dish.

ADA SAYS: *This recipe is very tasty, but it must be packaged with care and with attention so that the various elements are given due prominence.*

TERRINA DI MANZO CON TARTUFI

Truffled Beef Terrine

SERVES 12

10 oz beef tenderloin
1 lb 5 oz pork tenderloin
10 oz ham
Cognac
10 oz veal knuckle
14 oz mortadella
3 eggs
Black truffle
5 oz pancetta slices to cover the terrine
Salt
Pepper

Cut the beef into rather large pieces, also the pork and the ham. Put them in a bowl and season with salt, pepper, and a small glass of Cognac. Mix the pieces of meat and leave them to marinate, refrigerated, for at least 2 hours.

Meanwhile, prepare the filling: Finely chop the veal knuckle and mortadella and transfer the chopped meat to a bowl. Break the eggs and beat them as for an omelet, season with salt, and add them to the bowl. Mix everything gently, but thoroughly, until the mixture is homogeneous. Finally add the black truffle (cut into thin slices) and a small glass of Cognac. Give it a good stir again to distribute the truffle and Cognac through the filling. At this point it is important to check if you have put the right amount of salt in the filling. Take a little of the mixture, as much as a peanut, and drop it into boiling water. The mixture will cook and firm up. Taste it and if the salt is not enough add some.

When the filling is ready and the chopped meat marinated, prepare a terrine dish with a lid.

Line the bottom and sides with slices of pancetta. Pour the veal and mortadella mince into the bowl with the other meats and mix well. Pour everything into the terrine on the slices of pancetta. Finally cover everything with slices of pancetta and put the lid on.

Place the terrine in a larger pan, pouring into the bottom of this pan a finger of cold water, and put in a preheated oven of moderate heat for at least 1½ hours, adding more water to the pan if necessary. The dish will be ready when the juices bubbling out at the edges of the terrine are clear.

Then remove from the oven, remove the lid, and place a plate with a weight of about 8 ounces on the top layer of pancetta slices. If the weight were greater, the meat could be dry. This light pressure on the bowl is very important while chilling in the fridge, to ensure the dish is a certain consistency, one that will carve easily.

When it is cold, place the terrine on a serving plate without unmolding it and send it to the table.

TERRINA DI MANZO DEL GHIOTTONE

Glutton's Terrine

1 lb beef tenderloin
1 lb turkey breast
10 oz ham
7 oz tongue
7 oz fatty prosciutto
Marsala
Bouillon cube
Gelatin sheet
3½ tbsp butter
5 oz pancetta slices to cover the terrine
Salt
Pepper
Nutmeg

Cut the beef, turkey, ham, tongue, and prosciutto fat into chunks. Put them in a bowl and season with salt, pepper, and a trifle of nutmeg. Mix well, add a small glass of Marsala, and let marinate for 3 hours, refrigerated.

Meanwhile, prepare a quick jelly *(p52)* with the appropriate bouillon cube and gelatin and let it cool.

Next job is to drain the meats, keeping the marinade in another bowl. Put the butter in a Dutch oven and when it has heated add the chunks of meat and cook them over high heat, mixing them until they are dry, but not browned. Then remove the meat from the pan with a slotted spoon. Deglaze with the marinade and a small glass of Marsala and boil for a minute, so that the marinade and meat sauce can mix together, then pour this hot liquid over the meats and let cool.

Take an ovenproof terrine dish with a lid, line the bottom and the sides with slices of pancetta, and pour in the prepared meats and the marinade. Cover the meat well with a thick layer of slices of pancetta and put the lid on. Put the terrine in a larger pan and pour in a finger of cold water, and put in a preheated oven of moderate heat for at least 1½ hours, adding more water to the pan if necessary. Then remove the terrine from the oven and let it cool without removing the lid.

When the terrine feels almost cold, remove the lid and the top layer of pancetta slices and pour in half of the prepared jelly, which must be very cold, but still liquid.

The jelly penetrates between the pieces of meat and occupies the empty spaces left during the cooking and when it gets cold it sets, giving the food a nice texture and greater flavor. Place the bowl in the fridge until the gelatin has set.

ADA SAYS: *This is a dish that can be prepared even a few days in advance and kept in the fridge until ready to serve.*

UMIDO ALLA CASALINGA

Farmhouse Stew

2 lb 10 oz sirloin
Lardo
Olive oil
Garlic
Dry wine
1 onion
1 carrot
1 celery stalk
Parsley
9 oz tomatoes
Salt
Pepper

The best cut for stewed meat is the sirloin and it must be beaten on each side, with a meat mallet, to make it more tender.

Lard the meat with a dozen pieces of lardo. Tie it with string to keep its shape.

Put a little oil in a pan, add some chopped lardo, and a small piece of garlic, and as soon as this mixture is fragrant, add the meat and let it brown slowly without putting the lid on.

When the meat has taken on a nice dark color, season it with salt and pepper, splash it with half a glass of dry wine, and continue to brown until the wine has evaporated; then take off the heat and keep warm.

In the meantime, shred the onion, carrot, celery, and a little parsley. Brown them slowly in another pan until they are reduced to a dark golden slurry, giving them a slurp of water from time to time. When the aromatics are well cooked and browned, put the meat back in the pan and sauté everything for another 10 minutes, turning the meat from time to time.

Add the tomatoes (peeled, seeded, and chopped), season with a pinch of salt and pepper, and mix well. Cover and reduce the heat so that the cooking of the meat may coincide with the thickening of the sauce: which will happen in a couple of hours.

Ground Beef

BOLLITO IN BUDINO ALL'UNGHERESE

Boiled Beef Hungarian Style

1 lb sausages
1½ lb boiled ground beef
Crustless white bread
Milk
Garlic
Parsley
3 eggs
Butter
Salt
Pepper
Optional: fried marinated zucchini

Remove the sausage casings and mix with the ground beef. Add the bread (soaked in milk and squeezed dry), a little crushed garlic, chopped parsley, egg yolks, salt, and pepper. Whip the egg whites and add. Mix everything well.

Butter a pudding basin, pour in the mixture, and cook in a bain-marie for 30 minutes, ensuring that the water never reaches a tumultuous boil.

When you can see that it has set, turn out the pudding on a plate and serve it like this or surround it with fried marinated zucchini.

CROCCHETTE ALL'UVETTA E AI PINOLI

Beef Croquettes with Raisins and Pine Nuts

1 lb lean ground beef
3½ oz mortadella
Garlic
Parsley
3½ oz crustless white bread
Milk
2 eggs
Grated Parmesan
3 tbsp raisins
3 tbsp pine nuts
Breadcrumbs
Oil for deep-frying
1 lb tomatoes
Olive oil
Salt
Pepper
Nutmeg

Put the beef in a bowl. Add the chopped mortadella, garlic, parsley, and the bread (soaked in milk and squeezed dry). Season with salt and pepper, grate in a little nutmeg, then carefully mix the bread and meat.

When the mixture is compact, add the eggs, grated Parmesan, raisins (soaked in a little water), and pine nuts. Mix everything well, then make balls the size of large walnuts, and roll these in breadcrumbs.

After having breaded them, deep-fry them in abundant oil. When they are well browned, remove and keep them warm.

Chop a clove of garlic. Peel, seed, and slice the tomatoes. Put a little olive oil in a large pan, heat and add the chopped garlic. After a few minutes, add the tomatoes and cook for 2 or 3 minutes over very high heat, so that they do not come apart. Salt lightly. At this point, put the croquettes in a single layer in the pan and let them sauté for a few minutes to allow them to flavor well.

CROCCHETTE DI MANZO FRITTE

Deep-Fried Beef Croquettes

1 lb roasted or boiled beef
Grated Parmesan
2 eggs
Flour
Breadcrumbs
Oil for deep-frying
Salt
Pepper
Nutmeg

White sauce:
7 tbsp butter, ¾ cup flour,
2 cups milk

Prepare a thick white sauce *(p16)* with the ingredient amounts listed here. Remove from the heat, season with ¼ cup grated Parmesan, the egg yolks, and a little nutmeg. Chop the cooked meat, add it to the sauce, mixing everything well.

With floured hands, take small portions of the mixture and form some croquettes, roll them in flour, dredge in the beaten egg whites (left over from the yolks used for the sauce), and in the breadcrumbs.

Deep-fry in plenty of hot oil.

GRANATINE FRITTE AL BURRO

Meatballs Fried in Butter

2 oz crustless white bread
Milk
14 oz lean ground beef
2 eggs
Grated Parmesan
Flour
Breadcrumbs
Butter
Salt
Pepper
Nutmeg
To serve: French fries, or mashed potatoes, or peas with prosciutto, or beans in butter

Soak the bread in milk, squeeze, and in a saucepan over heat, stir the wet bread with a wooden spoon until it is reduced to a paste, then let it cool.

Add the cooled bread paste to the ground beef along with 1 egg, salt, pepper, nutmeg, and ⅓ cup grated Parmesan. Mix everything with your hands well, then divide into equal portions.

Take one piece at a time, place it on a floured surface, and flatten it to give it the appearance of a cutlet. Working gently, so that they do not break, flour them on both sides and, using a large spoon, coat them in the beaten egg and then in the breadcrumbs.

After you have breaded them all, give them a nice shape, use the blade of a knife, so that they are perfectly round.

Put them in a pan with a little butter and when they color on one side, carefully turn them over. The heat should not be too strong so the meat can cook well. When they are cooked, arrange them in a ring on a round plate. Serve with French fries, mashed potatoes, peas with prosciutto, or green beans with butter.

ADA SAYS: *These meatballs—granatine—are made with the classic mixture for meatballs. They are slightly crunchy on the outside, with a soft and tasty heart, scented with nutmeg.*

GRANATINE FRITTE AL POMODORO

Fried Meatballs in Tomato Sauce

14 oz lean ground beef
1 egg
Grated Parmesan
2 oz crustless white bread
Milk
Flour
Olive oil
Garlic
2¼ lb tomatoes
Oregano
Salt
Pepper

In a bowl, combine the ground beef, egg, salt, pepper, ⅓ cup grated Parmesan, and bread (soaked in milk and squeezed dry). Work everything with your hands and then divide into 12 equal portions.

Using a little flour, give each piece the shape of a flattened meatball. Flour and fry, a few at a time, in oil at moderate heat. Keep them warm.

Sauté a garlic clove with a few spoons of oil and add the tomatoes (peeled, seeded, and chopped). Season with salt and pepper and cook the tomato over high heat. When the tomato is cooked and reduced, put the meatballs on a serving plate and cover with the tomato sauce and sprinkle with a pinch of oregano.

HAMBURGER CON FORMAGGIO

Cheeseburger

1 lb 11 oz ground beef
Grated Parmesan
2 tbsp butter
2 large onions
Olive oil
5 oz Gruyère
Salt

Mix the ground beef with grated Parmesan, a pinch of salt, and softened butter. Mix everything with your hands, working it for a long time. Divide the prepared meat into 6 portions, making large meatballs with your hands. Then put them in a lightly oiled sheet pan and put them in a preheated oven for about 10 minutes, or more, according to taste.

In the meantime, rinse thickly sliced onions under fresh water, so that they lose some of their acrid taste. Fry in a tablespoon of oil and a tablespoon of water, making sure that they cook without falling apart.

When ready to, place an onion slice on each hamburger and finish with a slice of Gruyère.

Put the burgers back in the oven again for 2 or 3 minutes, so that the Gruyère can begin to melt. Serve immediately.

HAMBURGER IN FORNO

Oven-Roasted Hamburgers

1 lb 11 oz ground beef
Grated Parmesan
2 tbsp butter
7 oz potatoes
2 onions
2 oz pancetta
Olive oil
Salt

One of the secrets for the success of this recipe is that the ground meat be smooth and homogeneous.

Mix the ground beef with the Parmesan, a pinch of salt, and the softened butter. Mix everything well with your hands, working the mixture for a long time. Then divide the meat into 6 portions.

Arrange them in a lightly greased baking dish and roast in a preheated oven for about 10 minutes or more, according to taste.

Boil the potatoes, let them cool, and cut them into very small cubes. Finely chop the onions and pancetta and fry them in 3 tablespoons of oil over very low heat. When they are done and lightly browned, add the potatoes, season with a little salt, and let flavor for a few minutes.

Before serving, distribute a generous spoon of potatoes and onions over each burger and return the baking dish to the hot oven for a few minutes.

INVOLTINI DI CARNE E CAVOLO CON BESCIAMELLA

Beef and Cabbage Rolls

1 head cabbage
12 oz lean ground beef
Rice
1 egg
Grated Parmesan
7 tbsp butter
Olive oil
Meat broth *(p88)*
White sauce *(p16)*
Salt
Pepper

With a knife, trim off the lower part of the cabbage core. Then remove the harder, top leaves and use just the white and tender leaves. Wash them and dip them in boiling salted water. As soon as the water starts boiling again, drain them, rinse them under cold water, squeeze gently, and line them up on a towel.

In a bowl, combine the beef, ½ cup rice, egg, ⅓ cup Parmesan, salt, and pepper, mixing well so as to have a homogeneous mixture. Arrange one spoonful of stuffing on each cabbage leaf and, folding the leaves at the ends, form bags; then tie these rolls with a kitchen string.

Place half the butter and some oil in a large saucepan, heat the fat, then arrange the rolls not too close together, because the filling will tend to swell. Drizzle with more oil and the chopped butter and add a bit of salt. Cover the saucepan and let it simmer for 45 minutes adding, if necessary, a few spoons of boiling broth.

As soon as the rolls are cooked, take off the string, arrange them on a sheet pan lightly greased with butter, and pour one spoonful of white sauce on each of them. Transfer the pan to a preheated oven and let them brown.

PIZZA DI MANZO ALLA NAPOLETANA

Beef Pizza Neapolitan Style

2 oz crustless white bread
Milk
1 lb 5 oz lean ground beef
3 tbsp butter
1 egg
Grated Parmesan
Olive oil
10 oz mozzarella
6 tomatoes
Salt

Soak the bread in milk and squeeze thoroughly. Place the beef in a bowl, and shred the soaked bread into the bowl. Mix in half of the butter, egg, grated Parmesan, and some salt and knead everything with your hands.

Grease a shallow pan. Roll out the meat mixture to a thickness of ⅜ inch or so. On this meat "pizza," pour a drizzle of oil, dot here and there with some lumps of butter, and place in a preheated oven with moderate heat for about 30 minutes.

A few minutes before removing it from the oven, throw on the mozzarella cut into slices and the tomatoes cut into chunks. Sprinkle with salt, another drizzle of oil, and increase the heat. When the cheese begins to melt, remove the pan from the oven, place the pizza on a large plate, and immediately send it to the table.

PIZZA DI MANZO CON PROSCIUTTO

Beef Pizza with Prosciutto

3½ oz prosciutto
1 lb 5 oz lean ground beef
2 oz crustless white bread
Milk
2 egg yolks
Grated Parmesan
2 tbsp butter
Olive oil
Rosemary
Tomato passata
Salt
Pepper
Optional: garlic

Very finely chop the prosciutto. In a bowl, mix the prosciutto and ground beef. Soak the bread in milk, squeeze dry, and shred into the mix. Mix the meat and bread with your hands as thoroughly as possible. Add salt, a pinch of pepper, the egg yolks, ⅓ cup grated Parmesan, and the softened butter, still kneading as if you were making meatballs.

Once the mixture is made, grease a shallow pan with oil or butter and flatten the meat into a round about the thickness of a finger. On this mixture put abundant chopped rosemary and—if you like—some chopped garlic cloves, as the original recipe would like. Season with a little more oil or butter and put the pan in a preheated oven of moderate heat for 30 minutes, until the meat is cooked and has a nice golden-colored dark crust.

While the meat is cooking, prepare a sauce made simply with the ¾ cup tomato passata, a little butter or a little oil, and a pinch of salt. Let this sauce thicken a lot. When the meat is ready, bring it together with its sauce.

POLPETTE ALLA ROMANA

Meatballs Roman Style

1 lb 5 oz boiled beef *(p465)*
Slice of fatty prosciutto
Slice of lardo
Parsley
Crustless white bread
1 egg
Grated Parmesan
2 tbsp soaked golden raisins
2 tbsp pine nuts
Breadcrumbs
Oil or lard for deep-frying
Salt
Pepper
Nutmeg
Optional: tomato passata

Chop the boiled meat with the prosciutto fat, lardo, and a little parsley. Transfer the mixture to a bowl, season with a pinch of salt, pepper, and a trifle of nutmeg. Add some bread—as big as an apple—which you will have soaked in cold water and then squeezed. Knead everything well with your hands, trying to mix the meat as best as possible with the bread. Add the egg, 2 tablespoons of grated Parmesan, the raisins, and pine nuts. Mix it all up again and finally form many meatballs the size of small apples and slightly flatten.

Dip these meatballs in breadcrumbs and deep-fry them in plenty of oil or in lard.

ADA SAYS: *You can serve the meatballs like this, or arrange them in a pan and simmer them for a few minutes in a simple tomato sauce made by cooking passata with a little or or oil and a pinch of salt until thickened.*

POLPETTE ALLA RUSSA

Meatballs Russian Style

1 lb 5 oz lean ground beef
2 oz crustless white bread
Milk
10 tbsp butter
Flour
Onion
White wine
Paprika
Bouillon cube
Salt
Pepper
Optional: cream

In a bowl, combine the beef, bread (previously soaked in milk and squeezed dry), and half of the softened butter. Season with salt and pepper and add a little of the cream if you like. With this mixture, shape meatballs, flour them lightly, and fry them in a pan with butter. As soon as they are cooked, remove and keep them warm.

If there is too much fat, drain it, leaving only a very little and quickly brown the chopped onion in it. Then add two fingers of white wine, season with a good spoon of paprika, and add a quarter of a bouillon cube dissolved in a little hot water. Stir and let the sauce thicken, then off the heat add two spoons of cream and another piece of butter. Arrange the meatballs in a serving dish and pour on the sauce.

POLPETTONE AL LATTE

Meatloaf Braised in Milk

1 lb sausages
1 lb ground beef
Parsley
Celery
2 eggs
Grated Parmesan
Breadcrumbs
Olive oil
3½ tbsp butter
Onion
2 cups milk
Salt
Pepper

Remove the sausage casings. In a bowl, combine the sausage, ground beef, parsley, and chopped celery and mix well with your hands. Add the eggs, a few tablespoons of grated Parmesan, salt, and pepper. Form it into a large sausage shape and roll it in breadcrumbs.

In a Dutch oven in which the meatloaf can fit snugly, heat enough oil to cover the bottom, add the butter and the chopped onion, and when the fats are hot, add the meatloaf and brown it well on all sides. Carefully turn the meatloaf making sure it does not break.

Finally when it has formed a nice golden crust, add enough milk so it is almost covered. Reduce the heat, cover, and let it cook slowly for about 1 hour. At the end of cooking, the sauce should be thick and creamy.

Lift the meatloaf onto a serving dish, cover it with its own sauce, and promptly send it to the table.

POLPETTONE AL SUGO

Meatloaf with Tomato Sauce

3½ oz mortadella
1 lb 5 oz ground beef
2 oz crustless white bread
Milk
1 oz dried mushrooms
2 eggs
9 tbsp grated Parmesan
Olive oil
Garlic
Celery
Basil
Parsley
White wine
1 lb canned tomatoes
Salt
Pepper
Nutmeg

Finely chop the mortadella and mix with the ground beef. Put the white bread in a bowl and cover it with lightly salted warm milk. Soak the dried mushrooms in cold water for about 20 minutes.

In a bowl, mix the meats, the well squeezed bread, beaten eggs, grated Parmesan, a pinch of nutmeg, and salt and pepper.

Work the mixture first with a wooden spoon and then with your hands so it is well blended. Then roll it out on a floured work surface into an oval shape.

Heat some oil in an oval-shaped Dutch oven, add the meatloaf, let it brown over high heat on all sides, then add chopped garlic, celery, basil, and parsley. As soon as they have taken color, pour in a glass of white wine and when it has evaporated, add the tomatoes.

At this point, cover the Dutch oven and let the meatloaf cook over low heat for about 1 hour. When it is cooked, remove from the heat. Let it cool, cut it into slices, and place on a serving dish surrounded by its sauce, which should still be warm.

POLPETTONE CON UOVA E PROSCIUTTO

Meatloaf with Eggs and Prosciutto

3 tbsp butter
3 egg yolks
3½ oz crustless white bread
Milk
1 lb 5 oz boiled beef *(p465)*
3½ oz prosciutto
3½ oz ham
2 tbsp breadcrumbs
Broth
Melted butter
Salt
Nutmeg
Optional: shredded lettuce, 2 hard-boiled egg whites, carrot purée (2¼ lb carrot, 3½ tbsp butter, milk, ⅓ cup grated Parmesan, potato starch)

Put the butter in a bowl and stir vigorously with a wooden spoon to reduce it like a cream. Add the egg yolks, one at a time, and the bread (previously soaked in milk or water and squeezed dry). Mix well so everything is perfectly blended.

Chop the boiled beef, prosciutto, and ham. Blend in with the egg and butter mix and finish with a pinch of nutmeg and breadcrumbs. Knead well.

Spread a linen towel on a work surface and shape the mixture into a big sausage with your hands. Wrap it in the towel and tie it at both ends and in the center.

Submerge the meatloaf in an oval Dutch oven filled with hot broth, season with salt, and cook over moderate heat. It should take about 1 hour.

Finally remove it from the broth, let it rest for a few minutes underneath a light weight, and, then unwrap it, arrange it on a serving dish, and pour melted butter over it.

ADA SAYS: *If, on the other hand, you want to serve it cold, let it cool under a light weight and in the meantime prepare a carrot purée: Trim the carrots and steam or cook in boiling salted water for about*

30 minutes. Drain, let them cool a little, sieve or blend. Set the pan over heat again and stir the purée to let it dry a little. Add the butter and a little milk, then season with the grated Parmesan. If the purée is not thick enough, before removing it from the heat you can add a spoon of potato starch. Unroll the meatloaf from the towel and serve it on a bed of shredded lettuce, then surround it with the whites of two hard-boiled eggs cut into cubes, and decorate with the carrot purée.

POLPETTONE IN BAGNO MARIA

Meatloaf Cooked in a Bain-Marie

10 oz Swiss chard leaves
1 head escarole
9 oz lean ground beef
Onion
3½ oz crustless white bread
Milk
1 egg
Grated Parmesan
Butter for greasing
Salt

Mayonnaise:
1 egg yolk, half glass olive oil, vinegar

Clean, rinse, finely chop the chard and escarole and place them in a bowl with the ground beef. Add finely chopped onion, the bread (previously soaked in milk and squeezed dry), also the beaten egg, ⅓ cup of grated Parmesan, and salt. Give it a good mix with your hands.

Butter a 1-quart mold and put in the mixture, press it a little, and tap the mold to fit everything in. Set the mold in a larger pan of hot water. Place everything in a preheated oven of moderate heat. Bake for about 1 hour, until firm.

Then take the mold out of the water, let it rest a little, unmold it, and put it on a plate with a light weight on it—for example, another plate and a cup full of water. Leave it to press down until it is cold.

Make a mayonnaise *(p19)* using the ingredient amounts listed here. Slice the meatloaf into regular slices and accompany with the mayonnaise.

SALSICCIOTTI GUARNITI

Beef and Mortadella Rolls

14 oz boiled lean beef *(p465)*
2 oz crustless white bread
Milk
Grated Parmesan
3 tbsp butter
2 eggs
Olive oil
6 slices mortadella
Parsley
Broth
Flour
Marsala
Salt

Chop the boiled meat and transfer it to a bowl. Add the bread (previously soaked in milk and squeezed dry), ½ cup of grated Parmesan, half of the softened butter, and a pinch of salt. Knead all with your hands to obtain a perfect amalgam of the various elements.

Break the eggs into a bowl, season with a pinch of salt, beat them with a fork. Now, make 6 thin omelets of the same diameter as the 6 slices of mortadella. To do this, take a pan of about 6 inches in diameter, pour in some drops of oil, heat well, and then add a couple of spoonfuls of beaten egg. Immediately swirl the pan in all directions so that the egg spreads on the bottom of the pan and let it set. As soon as the omelet is firm, slide it onto a work surface and continue to make one omelet at a time.

Arrange the slices of mortadella on the work surface and spread them with the boiled meat mixture, using the blade of a knife or a spatula to spread it evenly over the entire surface. On each prepared slice place an omelet and finely chopped parsley. Roll each slice up and pin them together with toothpicks to keep them in shape.

Put a ladle of broth or water in the bottom of a pan and lay in the rolls. Let them simmer gently for a few minutes. While the rolls are heating up, knead the rest of the softened butter with a spoon of flour.

When the rolls are ready, take them out of the pan and put in the kneaded butter and flour and a splash of Marsala and mix everything with a wooden spoon to get a well-bonded sauce. Lastly, free the rolls from the toothpicks, arrange them on a plate, and pour on the sauce.

Ox & Offal

CODA DI BUE ALLA VACCINARA

Butcher's Oxtail and Cheek

3 lb 5 oz oxtail and beef cheek
3½ oz lardo
2 oz lard
Onion
Garlic
Carrot
Parsley
Red wine
1 lb canned tomatoes
8 celery stalks, from the heart
Golden raisins
Pine nuts
Salt
Pepper

For this preparation, the addition of beef cheeks is essential.

Cut the tail along its various vertebrae and the cheeks in regular pieces. Rinse everything several times. Put the meats in boiling salted water and simmer for about 1 hour. Drain and set aside.

Put the lardo and the lard in a skillet with the onion, garlic, chopped carrot, and parsley and sauté a little. Add the tail and cheeks. Season with salt and pepper, brown everything to a dark golden color, splash with a glass of wine, and when this has evaporated, add the tomatoes and some boiling water. Reduce the heat and simmer slowly, covered, for 4 hours, taking care to stir everything every now and then.

At this point, peel the celery, rinse, cut them into pieces and add them to the saucepan. Continue to cook still for another 30 minutes.

Soak the raisins. Just a few minutes before removing the saucepan from the heat, add a handful of them and the same amount of pine nuts. Pour the meats with their dressing into a semi-deep serving dish, conveniently heated, and serve immediately.

ADA SAYS: *The sauce must be dark, dense, and tasty.*

ROGNONE DI BUE IN PADELLA

Ox Kidney, Two Ways

Olive oil or lard
Ox kidney
Onion
White wine or Marsala
Tomato passata
Parsley
Salt
Pepper
To serve: fried croutons

Choose a fresh, nicely colored ox kidney. If it has a dull color and greenish stains, refuse it. Carefully rid it of any residue of fat and cut it, like a salami, into very thin slices.

Put a spoon of oil or a small amount of lard in a pan, add the kidney slices, and sauté over very high heat. After 2 or 3 minutes the kidney loses its color and turns brown. Take off the heat and transfer to a sieve set over a bowl. Let it drain for about 10 minutes, after which the kidney will have lost its impurities.

After preparing the kidney, clean the pan, add a spoonful of lard or oil, and a finely chopped half an onion and fry slowly over moderate heat. Then increase the heat, put the kidney slices in, baste with the white wine, or better still two fingers of Marsala. Add ¾ cup of tomato passata, salt, and pepper and, again over high heat, cook for another 2 or 3 minutes. Arrange everything on a plate, sprinkle with some parsley, and add some croutons fried in oil.

LAMB

ABBACCHIO AL FORNO ALLA ROMANA

Roast Spring Lamb Roman Style

3 lb 5 oz shoulder or leg lamb
Rosemary
Garlic
Lard or olive oil
2¼ lb potatoes
Red wine
Salt
Pepper

In Lazio, a suckling lamb, or spring lamb, does not weigh more than about 18 pounds.

Thoroughly wash the lamb and dry it well, nick the skin and make small incisions into which you slip a few needles of rosemary, a few pieces of garlic, and a little salt and pepper.

Put a spoon of lard or oil in a roasting pan, add the lamb, and put in a preheated oven. When the lamb is well browned, add the peeled potatoes cut in wedges. Salt the potatoes halfway through cooking. Let the lamb cook for 45 minutes, turning it from time to time. If it dries out too much, add a little water or red wine.

When the lamb is well cooked, put it on a serving dish surrounded by the potatoes and immediately bring to the table.

ABBACCHIO AL FORNO CON PATATE NOVELLE

Roast Spring Lamb with New Potatoes

3 lb 5 oz lamb loin
Olive oil
2 oz lard
Rosemary
Sage
Bay leaves
1 lb spring onions
2¼ lb small new potatoes
Salt
Pepper

Cut the lamb into pieces, wash, dry, and place in a baking dish with ¼ cup oil, the lard, a few sprigs of rosemary, some sage, bay leaves, and half of the onions cut into thin slices. Leave the other half of the onions whole.

Wash and scrub the new potatoes but leave unpeeled. Add to the dish. Season with salt and plenty of ground pepper, and put in a very hot oven. Use a spatula to turn the lamb chunks and potatoes from time to time to prevent them from sticking to the bottom, making sure the potatoes remain whole. Cook for 45 minutes until the lamb and potatoes have a nice golden color.

ABBACCHIO ALLA CACCIATORA

Hunter's Lamb

3 lb 5 oz leg of lamb
Lard
Garlic
Rosemary
Sage
Flour
Vinegar
3 anchovies
Salt
Pepper

One of the best known and most popular preparations in Roman cuisine.

Cut the lamb into small pieces of 1½ to 2 ounces each. Wash, dry, and put in a baking pan together with a spoon of lard and brown over a rather lively heat. Season with salt and plenty of pepper, and stir the lamb from time to time.

When the pieces have taken on a nice dark golden color, put in a piece of minced garlic (half a clove will be enough), a little rosemary (chopped or left whole), and a chopped sage leaf. Sauté a little more, still over high heat, and then sprinkle the lamb with half a tablespoon of flour. Stir with a wooden spoon and immediately afterwards deglaze with half a glass of vinegar diluted with half a glass of water. Mix well and use a wooden spoon to stop the meat sticking to the pan, reduce the heat a little, cover, and let it finish cooking, for about 45 minutes.

Meanwhile, wash and bone the anchovies, put them in a saucepan with one spoonful of the lamb cooking juices, and crush them with a wooden spoon.

When the lamb is cooked, pour the anchovy mash into the pan, let it flavor for a few minutes, and pour the lamb with its sauce, which must be quite thick and dark, into a serving dish.

ABBACCHIO ALLA CAMPAGNOLA

Braised Spring Lamb with Anchovy and Fennel

3 lb 5 oz bone-in leg of lamb
Olive oil
3½ tbsp butter
2 or 3 anchovies
Garlic
Fennel seeds
Vinegar
Flour
Broth
Salt
Pepper
Optional: fried crostini

Take the lamb off the bone and cut into chunks. Then wash the meat and dry it. Put a finger of oil and the butter in a large saucepan, heat up, and add the lamb to brown over high heat.

Meanwhile, prepare 2 or 3 washed and boned anchovies and a clove of garlic. Chop them so that the mince becomes like a mash. To this add a tablespoon of fennel seeds and 2 tablespoons of vinegar.

When the lamb is well browned, season with salt and pepper, and drain off some of the fat. Then add the garlic-fennel-anchovy mash, cook well and when the vinegar evaporates, sprinkle a spoonful of flour on the meat. Stir and finally add a ladle of broth or water. Let it cook for about 45 minutes, so the sauce can thicken well, then pour into a serving dish.

ADA SAYS: *You can surround the dish with a ring of crostini cut into triangles and fried.*

ABBACCHIO ALLA CASALINGA

Farmhouse Lamb

3 lb 5 oz bone-in leg of lamb
Onion
Whole Clove
1 celery stalk
Parsley
Carrot
3½ tbsp butter
Flour
1 egg yolk
Lemon
Salt
Pepper
Nutmeg

Wash the leg and put it in an oval Dutch oven in which it fits snugly. Cover with cold water and put it on the stove. The dish must be just big enough to fit all the lamb, so there is not too much water. As soon as the liquid boils, skim it carefully and then put in an onion, stuck with a clove, a stalk of celery, parsley, a carrot, and a pinch of salt. Cover and let it simmer over moderate heat until completely cooked, which will take less than an hour.

Take a smaller saucepan, melt some butter in it and add a heaped tablespoon of flour. Cook over moderate heat, stirring with a wooden spoon, and then moisten with a couple of ladles of the lamb broth. Mix well so there are no lumps and then let it cook for about 10 minutes until the sauce is velvety, without being excessively thick, in which case dilute with more broth.

Before removing from the heat, season the sauce with a pinch of pepper and a trifle of nutmeg, and then, off the heat, mix in an egg yolk and the juice of half a lemon.

Take the lamb out of the Dutch oven—take care that it must not be overcooked—arrange it in an oval dish and pour on a part of the sauce. The rest you will put it in a gravy boat.

ABBACCHIO BRODETTATO

Braised Lamb with Prosciutto and Eggs

3 lb 5 oz leg of lamb
Lard or olive oil
2 oz prosciutto
Onion
Flour
White wine
2 or 3 egg yolks
Lemon
Parsley
Salt
Pepper

Cut the lamb into pieces, wash, dry, and put in a Dutch oven with a good spoon of lard or oil. Cut the prosciutto into small pieces, chop half an onion and add both to the Dutch oven. Sauté over medium heat so the onion does not burn and the lamb does not become too colored. Season with salt and pepper.

When the meat browns, add half a spoon of flour. Stir thoroughly and, after a couple of minutes, add two fingers of white wine. When it evaporates, add enough water so the lamb is just covered, reduce the heat a little, cover, and continue cooking for about 1 hour, stirring occasionally and adding a little more water, if it dries out too much. At the end of cooking the sauce should not be too liquid.

About 10 minutes before serving, put 2 or 3 egg yolks in a bowl, dilute with the juice of a not too large lemon, and beat them a little with a fork to break them, adding a spoon of chopped parsley.

Pour the eggs over the lamb, stir and keep the pot over very low heat for 5 or 6 minutes so the eggs set without breaking up.

ABBACCHIO IN SALMÌ

Spring Lamb Braised in Red Wine

3 lb 5 oz leg or saddle of lamb
Onion
Celery
Carrots
Parsley
Bay leaf
Rosemary
Red wine
Olive oil
Salt
Pepper

Cut the lamb into regular pieces and place in a bowl with minced onion, celery, carrot, parsley, bay leaf, and rosemary and 2 glasses of wine. Leave the meat in this marinade for a few hours, refrigerated.

When it's time to cook it, drain the lamb and put in a pan with some oil. Let it brown slowly, slowly, stirring often, season with salt and pepper and a dash of the wine and marinade until it is all consumed.

When the meat is cooked, after about 1 hour, drain the sauce through a sieve and pour it over the lamb. Then heat everything up again and pour into a serving dish.

ABBACCHIO IN SALSA D'ACCIUGHE

Spring Lamb with Anchovy Sauce

3 lb 5 oz bone-in leg of lamb
Butter
Onion
Flour
White wine
Broth
2 anchovies
Parsley
Garlic
Lemon
Salt
Pepper

Rinse a leg of lamb and put it in a Dutch oven with a little butter and half a chopped onion. Season with salt and pepper and let it brown gently, until it takes on a nice dark golden color. Then sprinkle with a spoon of flour, mix well, and after a minute or two add a glass of white wine. Stir again to release the cooking juices and, when the wine evaporates, add a glass of broth. Cover and add more broth or water if needed.

When cooked, after about 1 hour, put a couple of rinsed and boned anchovies in a bowl with some parsley, a clove of garlic and a piece of lemon zest. Chop everything together and add this mixture to the pot, dissolving it well in the little sauce remaining, which must be quite dense.

Set the lamb on a plate, coating it well with the reduced sauce.

ABBACCHIO IN SPEZZATINO CON BORDURA DI PATATE

Lamb and Potato Stew

3 lb 5 oz bone-in leg of lamb
Olive oil
Onion
Carrot
Celery stalk
Flour
2¼ lb potatoes
3½ tbsp butter
2 egg yolks
Salt

Bone out a leg of lamb and cut the meat into regular chunks.

Put them in a covered pot with some oil, half a chopped onion, the carrot and celery. Sauté over moderate heat, brown slowly, and when everything has acquired a beautiful golden color, sprinkle with flour, a ladle and more of lukewarm water, and season with a good pinch of salt.

Put the lid on the pot and let it simmer slowly for about 1 hour.

Meanwhile peel the potatoes, cut them into pieces, and place them in another pot with water to cover, seasoning them with a pinch of salt. Set over heat and when the potatoes are cooked, drain them immediately and mash them while they are still hot.

Put the mash back in the pot, add the butter, and let it dry over the heat. Let them cool a little, then mix in the egg yolks until well blended.

Butter the rim of an ovenproof plate and arrange spoonfuls of the mashed potato around the edge, forming a kind of ring. Put the dish in a preheated oven of moderate heat, to firm and color.

Take the potatoes out of the oven and place the lamb with its sauce in the center of the plate.

ABBACCHIO IN SPIEDINI

Lamb Chop Skewers

3 lb 5 oz baby lamb chops
Bread
Sage
Prosciutto
Olive oil
Salt
Pepper

Bone out the chops and cut the meat into large cubes. Season with salt and pepper. Cut slices of bread into as many squares as there are lamb pieces, plus one. Then begin to skewer a first square of bread, a sage leaf, a slice of prosciutto, a piece of lamb, a slice of prosciutto, a sage leaf, and a square of bread. Continue like this until all the ingredients are used up.

Place the skewers in a baking dish, oil them generously, and cook in a preheated oven for at least 30 minutes.

When the meat is well colored and the bread has toasted, send the skewers to the table immediately, as they should be served as soon as they are done.

ABBACCHIO USO CACCIA

Braised Lamb Hunter Style

2¼ lb boneless leg of lamb
2 oz prosciutto
Sage leaves
Lemon zest
Celery
Onion
3 cloves
Olive oil
Vinegar
Anchovy
Parsley
1 lemon
Salt
Peppercorns

Tie the lamb with kitchen string to keep its shape. Choose a Dutch oven large enough to fit the lamb snugly. Cover the bottom with slices of prosciutto and 4 sage leaves. Add a piece of lemon zest, chopped celery, quartered onion, peppercorns, and cloves. Finally place the lamb on top of everything, season with a pinch of salt, add half a glass of water, and add some oil and a tablespoon of vinegar. Cover with a sheet of parchment paper and then cover with a lid and weigh the lid down with a light weight. Warm the dish over a very low heat and let the meat cook gently for 2 hours, without opening it up to see what is happening.

After this time all the liquid will almost have dried up and the meat will begin to fry. Take out the lamb and carve.

Chop the rinsed and boned anchovy together with some parsley and add this aromatic pesto to the cooking juices. Dilute with a few spoons of water, heat it up, and then return the slices of lamb. Simmer and season for a few minutes, then remove from the heat and finish with the juice of a lemon and send it to the table.

ADA SAYS: *This dish can also be served cold.*

COSCETTO DI ABBACCHIO FARCITO

Stuffed Leg of Lamb

3 lb 5 oz bone-in leg of lamb
Pearled barley
6½ tbsp butter
Onion
Olive oil
4 sausages
3½ oz calf's liver
Sage
Salt
Pepper

Put the leg on a work surface and with a sharp knife cut toward the bone, turning the meat as you go until you can remove the whole bone.

Soak ½ cup of pearled barley for at least 30 minutes in lightly salted water, then boil for an hour. Drain and let it flavor in a saucepan with a knob of butter.

Thinly chop the onion and brown gently in a Dutch oven with 3 spoons of oil and another knob of butter. When the onion is cooked, add the sausage meat (casings removed). Cook for a few minutes, turning often. Add this to the pearled barley.

Cut the calf's liver into small cubes and fry with another knob of butter, salt, and pepper. When it is cooked, add it to the rest, thus completing the filling.

Introduce the filling to the boned leg, pressing well, then sew the opening with a needle and thick thread. Put the leg in a roasting pan, season with a little salt, a few sage leaves, and a few spoons of oil. Place the pan in a preheated oven at a moderate heat. After an hour or more, remove the leg from the pan and arrange it on a serving dish.

Drain all the fat from the pan and deglaze the remaining sauce with a ladle of hot water. Place the pan on the stove and use a wooden spoon to scrape up any browned bit on the bottom of the pan. Reduce a little, then strain the sauce over the lamb and send immediately to the table.

COSTOLETTE DI ABBACCHIO ALLA VILLEROY

Lamb Chops Villeroy

12 lamb rib chops
3 tbsp butter
Marsala
2 egg yolks
Grated Parmesan
Flour
2 eggs
Breadcrumbs
Oil for deep-frying
Salt
Pepper
Optional: 2 oz ham, 2 oz mortadella, 2 oz salted tongue, 2 oz truffle

White sauce:
7 tbsp butter, ¾ cup flour,
2 cups milk

If you want to make an even finer sauce, you can mix in small cubes of ham or mortadella or salted tongue or truffle.

Put the chops with the butter and cook them over moderate heat. Season with salt and pepper and when they are cooked, deglaze with a glass of Marsala. When the Marsala has evaporated, take out the chops and cover with a sheet of parchment paper and allow them to settle. You can put a weight on them to keep them flat if you like.

Then make a white sauce *(p16)* using the ingredient amounts listed here. When the sauce is thick, take off the heat and add the egg yolks and ½ cup of grated Parmesan. Mix thoroughly.

Take one chop at a time, hold it by the bone, and dip it into the hot sauce, so that both sides are coated. Leave them on a work surface to cool. The sauce will set around them.

Just before going to the table, dredge the chops through a plate of flour, another of beaten eggs, and a third with the breadcrumbs. Tidy with the blade of a knife to give them a nice shape and, gently dip them in a pan with plenty of oil. The oil must be very hot. As the chops are already cooked, it is only a question of reheating them and fixing them to the sauce. If the oil is not hot enough the sauce will burst in the pan.

◆ ADA SAYS: *These chops are generally arranged in a ring, one leaning against the other, with a garnish in the center of cauliflower in white sauce, green beans with cheese, peas with prosciutto, or buttered spinach.*

COSTOLETTE DI ABBACCHIO A SCOTTADITO

Lamb Chops Scottadito

12 lamb rib chops
Lard or olive oil
Salt
Pepper

Scottadito chops, with the picturesque name, are a tasty Roman recipe, healthy, simple and easy to make. Scottadito literally means burned fingers. These chops should be cooked on a preheated grill or griddle.

Grease the chops with lard or oil, season with salt and pepper, and place them on preheated grill or griddle. When the chops are cooked on one side, turn them over and finish cooking. Serve as soon as they are cooked.

COSTOLETTE DI ABBACCHIO FRITTE

Deep-Fried Lamb Chops

12 lamb rib chops
2 eggs
Breadcrumbs
Oil for deep-frying
Lemon wedges
Salt

Dredge the chops in lightly salted beaten eggs and then in breadcrumbs.

Deep-fry in abundant oil over moderate heat so that the insides are cooked. Remove from the heat, let them drain well and serve very hot with wedges of lemon.

COSTOLETTE DI ABBACCHIO PICCANTI

Grilled Lamb Chops with Anchovy and Lemon Sauce

12 lamb rib chops
Oregano
Garlic
Olive oil
4 anchovies
2 tbsp parsley
1 lemon
Dijon mustard
Salt
Pepper

Put the lamb chops on a large plate, season with salt and pepper, a pinch of oregano, a few pieces of garlic, a little oil, and leave them like this for at least 1 hour.

Finely chop the washed and boned anchovies, a small piece of garlic, and cook down in two fingers of oil to obtain a purée. Add a pinch of oregano.

Pour this purée into a bowl and add the parsley, a little salt, and pepper, the juice of half lemon, and a spoon of mustard.

A few minutes before going to the table, arrange the chops on a preheated grill or griddle and, when they begin to brown, take one at a time and spread on the sauce generously, on both sides. Put them back on the grill and let them finish cooking over moderate heat.

Arrange on a plate and spread the remaining sauce over them.

◆ **ADA SAYS:** *If you don't like the taste of garlic, you can eliminate it.*

AGNELLO BOLLITO

Boiled Leg of Lamb

3 lb 5 oz bone-in leg of lamb
Onion
6 potatoes
Carrots
2 celery stalks
Salt
Optional: raw tomato sauce *(p37)*

Completely bone out the leg of lamb and tie it up to keep it in shape. Heat lightly salted water in an oval Dutch oven with an onion and when it is hot, dip the leg in and let it simmer gently. Halfway through cooking the meat, after about 30 minutes, add the peeled potatoes, peeled carrots, and celery cut in pieces. Cook on.

Lastly take the lamb out of the Dutch oven, cut off the string, carve into slices, and reassemble, surrounding it with the boiled vegetables.

ADA SAYS: *You can also accompany this lamb with a light tomato sauce made just with fresh tomatoes, oil, basil, and garlic served in a gravy boat.*

AGNELLO BRASATO

Braised Leg of Lamb

3 lb 5 oz bone-in leg of lamb
Butter
Olive oil
Onion
Carrot
Celery
Parsley
White wine
Broth
Salt
Pepper
Optional: pan-fried artichokes or peas with prosciutto

Heat a little butter and oil in a Dutch oven and when it is hot, put in the leg of lamb to brown and begin to color. Then take it out and keep it warm.

Now use the juices in the pan to sauté the roughly cut vegetables—onion, a carrot, a celery stalk. and parsley with its stems. Turn down the heat a little and slowly brown. If the vegetables threaten to scorch, pour a spoon of water over them. When the vegetables have taken on a nice dark gold tint, put the leg of lamb back in the Dutch oven with any accumulated juices and continue to brown together. Season with salt and pepper and when the lamb is well colored, add a glass of white wine. Let it cook down and top up with a second glass and a third but not until the one before has evaporated.

As the wine evaporates, start to baste the lamb with a little broth or water, about half a glass at a time, lowering the heat and keeping everything covered when you are not basting. Keep going, thus cooking gently and for a long time, for about 2 hours, turning the lamb and reducing the cooking juices well. Toward the end, give it a last good baste and cover again and leave on the stove until completely cooked. At this point the sauce must be dense and envelop the lamb in a shiny coat.

Then remove the lamb, carve it, and arrange it on a serving plate. Tilt the saucepan to one side and degrease the sauce with a spoon. If it is too thick, add a little broth or water. Then strain through a sieve into a new pan and heat well. Then, off the heat, finish it with a few pieces of butter, stirring with a wooden spoon.

Coat the lamb with this sauce and bring it to the table, serving it maybe with pan-fried artichoke hearts or peas with prosciutto.

AGNELLO IN INTINGOLO

Braised Lamb with Peas

3 lb 5 oz loin or leg of lamb
Flour
Olive oil
3½ tbsp butter
1 lb fresh peas
Bouillon cube
2 eggs
Grated Parmesan
Parsley
Salt
To serve: fried croutons

Have the lamb chopped into rather small pieces. Flour and place them in a saucepan with a few tablespoons of oil and butter. Set over heat and lightly brown the meat without coloring.

Halfway through cooking, drain off all the fat in the saucepan and add a pinch of salt and the fresh peas. Add 3 ladles of water in which you have dissolved a bouillon cube. Cover and cook for about 1 hour until the sauce is reduced.

When ready to serve, beat the eggs in a bowl, season with grated Parmesan and chopped parsley and pour into the pan off the heat. Give it a stir immediately and pour the lamb with its sauce into a serving dish surrounding it with fried croutons.

AGNELLO IN POTACCHIO ALLA MARCHIGIANA

Lamb Marche Style

Garlic
Rosemary
Olive oil
3½ lb lamb meat in cubes
White wine
1 lb canned tomatoes
Salt
Pepper

Prepare a mince of garlic and rosemary and fry it in abundant oil. When the mince has taken a dark golden color, add the lamb in cubes and brown well, finally adding salt, pepper, and a glass of white wine.

When the wine has evaporated well, add the tomatoes, then slowly cook over moderate heat, for about 2 hours.

Transfer the lamb to a serving dish and send to the table.

ADA SAYS: *This recipe of the Marche cuisine is very simple but represents a truly tasty preparation.*

AGNELLO IN SPEZZATINO AL LATTE

Lamb Cooked in Milk

3 lb 5 oz lamb chunks
2 cups milk
Salt
Pepper

Put the lamb pieces in a pan that is a snug fit. Add a half a glass of water and let it brown, adding only salt and pepper. When the water has evaporated, cover with a mix of milk and water in equal parts and continue cooking slowly for about 1½ hours, so that the liquid reduces and turns into a thick sauce.

At this point, pour everything into a serving dish and send it to the table.

AGNELLO IN SPEZZATINO CON SALSA

Shoulder of Lamb with Green Beans

3 lb 5 oz bone-in lamb shoulder
Onion
Whole clove
1 celery stalk
1 carrot
Parsley
Flour
2 tbsp butter
10 oz green beans
Fried crostini
Salt

Wash the lamb. In a pot, combine the lamb, water to cover, salt, an onion, a clove, celery, a carrot, and a sprig of parsley. Boil for about 1 hour.

When the lamb is cooked, take it out of the broth, drain it well, take the meat off the bone and place it on a work surface with a light weight on it to press it into a regular shape. Let cool. Then carve the meat.

Meanwhile, strain the broth through a sieve, pour it into another pan, boil and reduce a little. Mix some flour and butter together in a bowl, then stir it into the sauce and let it thicken slightly. Lay the pieces of lamb in the sauce, let it simmer and keep warm.

Nip off the ends of the green beans, rinse them well in fresh water, and boil them in lightly salted water. When they are cooked, drain and flavor in a pan with a little butter and a pinch of salt.

When ready to serve, make up some crostini about the same size as your lamb slices. Arrange the meat in a ring around the plate, alternating slices with fried crostini; in the center you put a dome of the boiled green beans and pour the sauce over everything.

ADA SAYS: *If there is too much sauce, pour the rest into a gravy boat and send it separately.*

BRACIOLINE DI AGNELLO CON CARCIOFI

Braised Lamb Chops with Artichokes

2 oz prosciutto
Garlic
Onion
Olive oil
12 lamb chops
White wine
6 artichoke hearts
Salt
Pepper

Chop the prosciutto, garlic, and onion and fry in a little oil. Add the chops, season with salt and pepper, cover and brown, stirring occasionally.

When the chops are browned, add half a glass of white wine and the artichokes cut into wedges. Let the wine evaporate for about 15 minutes. Finish cooking over moderate heat, then pour into a serving dish.

COSTOLETTE DI AGNELLO ALLA BOLOGNESE

Medallions of Lamb Bolognese

12 lamb rib chops
Flour
2 eggs
Breadcrumbs
Olive oil
3½ oz prosciutto
5 oz mozzarella
Salt

Remove the bones from the chops so you end up with medallions. Adjust their shape and flatten them.

Season with salt, dredge them in flour, beaten egg, and breadcrumbs. Fry in half a glass of oil. Keep cooking over fairly moderate heat so that they can cook well inside and take on a beautiful light gold color.

When cooked, arrange them on a sheet pan and on each medallion put a slice of prosciutto and a slice of mozzarella. Transfer to a hot oven. As soon as the mozzarella begins to melt, take out of the oven, arrange on a plate, and send hot to the table.

COSTOLETTE DI AGNELLO ALLA MAINTENON

Lamb Chops Maintenon

10 tbsp butter
Flour
Milk
Broth
1 oz dried mushrooms
Marsala
1 egg yolk
Garlic
12 lamb rib chops
Salt
Pepper
To serve: peas with prosciutto *(p684)* or artichoke hearts

Melt 2 tablespoons of butter in a pan and add one spoonful of flour. Cook a little while stirring, splash with half a glass of milk and half a glass of broth and, stirring constantly, thicken the sauce.

Put the dried mushrooms in cold water to reconstitute, then clean them and cook with a little butter, salt, and a few spoons of water or broth. When they are cooked, add a finger of Marsala and cook down until the mushrooms are dry. Then chop the mushrooms on a cutting board and add them to the sauce. Finish with an egg yolk and a very small amount of grated garlic.

Meanwhile, put an ovenproof pan on the heat large enough for all the chops and melt 3 tablespoons of butter. Season with salt and pepper and sear them on both sides.

Put the pan into a very hot oven for a few minutes, until the sauce creates a light golden film on the surface and the chops arrive at their proper cooking point.

Take the lamb out of the oven and arrange in a crown on a plate. You might garnish with peas with prosciutto or artichoke hearts.

ADA SAYS: *If you don't like the subtle taste of garlic, it can be done without.*

COSTOLETTE DI AGNELLO GUARNITE

Lamb Chops with Prunes and Vegetables

Prunes
12 lamb rib chops
Butter
Olive oil
Marsala
Onion
2 oz prosciutto
Bouillon cube
To serve: 4 potatoes, 2 cups fresh peas, 6 carrots, salt

First soak ⅔ cup of prunes.

Brown the chops on both sides in 2 tablespoons of butter and some oil. Add salt and half a glass of Marsala and when the wine has evaporated, cover them with a spoon of water and let them cook gently with the lid on.

Meanwhile, fry a chopped half an onion in a small saucepan with very little oil and the prosciutto cut into strips. As soon as the onion is slightly browned, deglaze with another half glass of Marsala and add the soaked pitted prunes. Dissolve the bouillon cube in a little water and add to the pan and let it boil for 30 minutes until the prunes are well cooked. Finally, sieve everything and leave the sauce to warm.

When the chops are cooked, arrange them in a ring in a serving dish and partially cover with the prune sauce.

In the center of the plate, you could serve fried potato sticks, peas and carrots equally cooked in butter, salt, and a little bit of water.

COSTOLETTE DI AGNELLO IN SALSA PICCANTE

Roast Lamb Chops with Mustard Sauce

5½ tbsp butter
Parsley
12 lamb rib chops
Breadcrumbs
Onion
Flour
Bouillon cube
3 tbsp olive oil
2 tbsp vinegar
Dijon mustard
Salt
Pepper

Melt half of the butter, pour into a bowl, and season with salt, pepper and chopped parsley. Dip the chops, slightly flattened, in this flavored butter, then dredge in breadcrumbs. Arrange them in a well-oiled baking dish and put in a preheated oven of moderate heat for about 20 minutes.

Meanwhile, finely chop the onion, put it in a saucepan with the rest of the butter, and cook gently, adding a little flour. Dilute with a glass of water in which you have dissolved half a bouillon cube, stir, and cook for a few minutes. As soon as the sauce thickens, season with the oil, vinegar, salt, pepper, and mustard. Pour the sauce into a gravy boat.

COSTOLETTE DI AGNELLO PRIMAVERILI

Deep-Fried Lamb Chops with Spring Vegetables

12 lamb rib chops
Flour
Olive oil
10 oz mushrooms
2 tbsp butter
2 egg yolks
1 egg
Breadcrumbs
Oil for deep-frying
Salt
To serve: 1 lb asparagus, 1 lb fresh peas, 2 oz prosciutto

White sauce:
¾ cup flour, 7 tbsp butter, 2 cups milk

Arrange the chops, flatten them, and clean the bones. Flour and salt them and arrange in an oiled skillet. Fry over low heat until almost fully cooked.

Then place them on a work surface and let them cool under parchment paper and a light weight.

Clean the mushrooms, rinse them, cut in slices and cook in the butter and a pinch of salt.

Make a thick white sauce *(p16)* with ingredient amounts listed here. Once thick, remove from the heat and finish with a pinch of salt and the egg yolks. Stir and add the sauce to the mushrooms.

Spread this sauce, while still hot, over the lamb chops, so it covers them all and let it cool.

Finally dredge the chops in flour, beaten egg, and breadcrumbs. Deep-fry them in oil over high heat.

Arrange them on a serving dish and garnish with asparagus tips cooked in butter *(p626)* and peas with prosciutto *(p684)*.

COSTOLETTE DI AGNELLO SOUBISE

Deep-Fried Lamb Chops with Onion Sauce (Soubise)

12 lamb rib chops
Oil or lard for deep-frying
Butter
2 onions
Flour
1 egg
Breadcrumbs
Salt
Pepper
Nutmeg

White sauce:
2 tbsp butter, ¼ cup flour, ¾ cup milk

Lightly flatten the chops, arrange them in a pan with a little oil or butter, and fry them lightly, on one side only, sprinkling them with salt.

Remove them from the pan, arrange on a work surface in a circle and cover them with a sheet of parchment paper and put a weight on top, so that the meat remains well flattened.

Prepare a very thick white sauce *(p16)* using the ingredient amounts listed here.

Then prepare a soubise: Peel and have the onions and cook in boiling water for 5 or 6 minutes so they lose all their pungency. Drain and cool, return to a pan in water to just covere along with a hazelnut-size piece of butter. When they are well cooked, remove and purée through a food mill or blend them. Transfer to a bowl, season with salt, pepper, a little bit of nutmeg, and add a couple of spoons of the white sauce.

When the sauce is cold, distribute a little over each chop, smooth it out with the blade of a knife giving it a slightly rounded shape, then gently take the chops, flour them, dredge in the beaten egg and then breadcrumbs.

When you have prepared all the chops, deep-fry them in oil or in very hot lard. Arrange the lamb chops in a ring, one on top to the other and in the center pour the remaining sauce.

ADA SAYS: *The fame of the Prince of Soubise, marshal of France—according to the Dictionary of the Accademia dei Gastronomi—had more to do with his appreciation of good food than any of his military victories. The sauce named after him is based on the common garden onion, exalted by all the ancient schools of medicine, and when used judiciously and treated with particular attention, makes a pleasant and tasty sauce.*

Lamb Offal

ANIMELLE DI ABBACCHIO AL PROSCIUTTO

Lamb Sweetbreads with Prosciutto

1 lb 5 oz lamb sweetbreads
3½ tbsp butter
2 oz prosciutto
Marsala
Salt
Pepper

Soak the sweetbreads in warm water for at least 1 hour. Then put them in a saucepan, cover with cold water, and bring the water to a boil. Then plunge the sweetbreads under cold running water, drain, dry, and take off the outside skin.

Warm some butter in a pan and, when it is hot, add the sweetbreads and fry them over high heat. As soon as they begin to brown, season with salt and pepper, add the chopped prosciutto, and cook all together for a minute or two. Then baste with a little Marsala. Once the Marsala has evaporated, remove the sweetbreads from the heat, arrange them on a plate, and have them brought to the table immediately.

ANIMELLE DI ABBACCHIO CON CARCIOFI

Lamb Sweetbreads with Artichokes

1 lb 5 oz lamb sweetbreads
6 artichoke hearts
Olive oil
3½ tbsp butter
2 oz prosciutto
Marsala
Salt
Pepper

Soak and blanch the sweetbreads as above. Cut the artichoke hearts into wedges and fry them in a little oil and salt over moderate heat, bathing them from time to time with a few spoonfuls of water, so that when fully cooked they are soft.

A few minutes before going to the table, put the butter in a small pan and, when it is hot, add the sweetbreads and fry over lively heat. As soon as they begin to brown, season with salt and pepper and add some strips of prosciutto. After a couple of minutes, add the artichokes, and baste everything with a little Marsala. As soon as the wine evaporates, arrange the sweetbreads and the artichokes on a plate and have them brought to the table immediately.

ANIMELLE DI ABBACCHIO FRITTE

Pan-Fried Sweetbreads

1 lb 5 oz lamb sweetbreads
Flour
2 eggs
Butter for frying
Lemon wedges
Parsley
Salt

Soak and blanch the sweetbreads as on page 531. If they are very large, cut them in two.

Salt them, flour them, dredge them in the beaten eggs and fry them thoroughly in foamy butter.

Arrange on a plate, finish with lemon wedges and chopped parsley and serve very hot.

SCHIENALI DI ABBACCHIO CON LA PASTELLA

Deep-Fried Sweetbreads

1 lb 5 oz lamb sweetbreads
Oil for deep-frying
Salt

Special batter:
1 cup flour, glass milk, ¼ cup grated Parmesan, olive oil, 2 eggs

Gently remove the skin from the sweetbreads without breaking them, put them in cold water in a Dutch oven and bring to a boil.

Take them out and run under cold water. Cut them into not too large pieces.

Prepare the special batter: In a bowl, stir together the flour, milk, Parmesan, 1 tablespoon oil, and a pinch of salt. Mix well and then add the two egg yolks. Whip the egg whites and fold them in. Let the batter rest for about 1 hour.

Dip the blanched sweetbreads in the batter and deep-fry in plenty of hot oil to a deep golden color. Season with salt to serve.

SCHIENALI DI ABBACCHIO FRITTI DORATI

Pan-Fried Sweetbreads in Butter

1 lb 5 oz lamb sweetbreads
Flour
2 eggs
Butter for frying
Lemon wedges
Salt

Gently remove the skin from the sweetbreads and blanch as on page 531. Cut into pieces about 2 inches long.

Flour them, dredge in beaten eggs, and fry in bubbling butter. Season with a pinch of salt. Serve hot surrounded by lemon wedges.

CORATELLA DI ABBACCHIO CON CARCIOFI

Lamb Offal with Artichokes

3 lb 5 oz lamb offal (lung, heart, liver)
10 artichoke hearts
3 lemons
Lard or olive oil
Onion
Wine
Parsley
Salt
Pepper

This typical Roman preparation would require the use of lard, but you can also use oil to cook the offal as well as to cook the artichokes.

Cut the lung, heart, and liver separately into thin slices and remove any traces of green gall from the liver.

Cut the artichoke hearts into wedges, rub them with lemon and place them to cook in a pan with a spoonful of lard over moderate heat. As they cook, so that they remain soft, wet them occasionally with a few spoons of water. Season them with salt and pepper.

When the artichokes are cooked, take a rather large pan and add a spoonful of lard and half a chopped onion. Let the onion cook just a little and then add the lung to the pan. Sauté slowly so there is no risk of it scorching. When the lung has browned, it will hiss characteristically, season it with a little salt and pepper and wet it with a finger of wine. Let the wine dry and add the heart. After a few minutes the heart will also be cooked, then add the liver. Season with a little more salt and pepper and as soon as the liver has lost its reddish color, put the artichokes in the pan as well. Turn up the heat a little and add another finger of wine, letting it finish cooking all together for a very short time.

Pour the offal on a serving plate and finish it with a spoon of chopped parsley and a few drops of lemon juice. Garnish the plate with lots of lemon wedges and send immediately to the table. Offal must be served very hot.

Mutton

CASTRATO BRACIATO ALL'ACETO

Braised Mutton with Vinegar

3 lb 5 oz mutton
Olive oil
2 onions
Garlic clove
Whole clove
Ground cinnamon
Lemon zest
Potato starch
Vinegar
Salt
Pepper
Nutmeg

Wash, dry, and cut the mutton into large pieces and put it to brown in a large pan with some oil. When it turns gold, remove from the pan. Add the sliced onions and fry in the fat.

Return the mutton to the pan and add crushed garlic, salt, pepper, a pinch of nutmeg, clove, a pinch of cinnamon, and strips of zest from a lemon. Cover everything with enough water and cook over moderate heat for a good hour until the meat is cooked and the liquid is almost consumed.

Dissolve the potato starch in two fingers of vinegar, add it to the pan, give everything a good shake, then take off the heat. Remove the lemon zest and pour into a serving dish.

CASTRATO IN SPEZZATINO ALLA FRANCESE

Braised Mutton with Carrots

3 lb 5 oz mutton
Olive oil
1 onion
1 celery stalk
Parsley
Garlic
Bay leaf
2 cloves
Red or white wine
2 tbsp tomato paste
10 carrots
Salt
Pepper

Have the butcher chop the mutton into pieces, not too big nor too small. Wash and dry them.

Put a little oil in a good-size Dutch oven with a sliced onion, chopped celery, some chopped parsley, and a clove of crushed garlic. Add the meat and start cooking over lively heat. Season with salt and pepper, half a bay leaf, and one or two cloves. Stir occasionally with a wooden spoon and, when the meat and herbs have taken on a nice dark color, add a glass of wine, white or red.

Scrape the bottom with a wooden spoon to mix the mutton and its aromatics well and wait for the wine to evaporate. Then stir in the tomato paste diluted with enough water to cover the meat. Cover the Dutch oven and reduce the heat and stew slowly. The mutton needs to cook for 1 to 1½ hours. If the water evaporates too much add some more without overdoing it.

Meanwhile, peel and dice the carrots and have them ready in a bowl of water.

When the mutton is three-quarters of the way through cooking, take the Dutch oven off the heat and tilt it toward you. You will see that the meat has given off a lot of fat, which you carefully remove with a spoon, slowly, slowly.

When you have degreased the stew, add the diced carrot, mix well. If necessary, add a little more water; cover, and let it finish cooking. The mutton should be tender and fragrant and the sauce very dense.

Heat a serving dish, pour the stew in, and send immediately to the table.

CASTRATO NELLE FOGLIE DI VITE

Mutton-Stuffed Grape Leaves with Eggs

Grape leaves
1 lb 5 oz lean ground mutton
Mint
3 tbsp rice
6 eggs
3 tbsp butter
Olive oil
Salt
Pepper

Pick tender grape leaves. Rinse them well and boil for 2 minutes. Lay them open on a work surface and trim off the stem.

Mix the ground mutton with a few mint leaves and 3 spoons of well-washed uncooked rice, 2 whole eggs, salt, and pepper. Mix everything together well.

Place half a spoon of the mix in the center of each grape leaf and roll them up.

Choose a skillet big enough to hold all the stuffed grape leaves in a single layer. Set it over heat with 3 tablespoons of butter and 2 tablespoons of oil. Let the fat warm before you arrange the stuffed leaves in a single layer and sprinkle over a very little salt. Cover and let flavor, shaking the saucepan from time to time to prevent the rolls from sticking.

After about 15 minutes, add enough water to cover, and cover the pan again and continue cooking over medium heat. When the water has almost all evaporated the rolls will be cooked.

Beat 4 eggs in a bowl, add a pinch of salt, remove the pan from the heat, pour in the eggs, and let rest in the warmth, so the eggs are creamy and not broken.

COSCETTO DI CASTRATO AL FORNO

Baked Leg of Mutton

3 lb 5 oz leg of mutton
Olive oil
Garlic
1 lb onions
1 lb potatoes
7 oz tomatoes
Parsley
Salt
Pepper

Wash and dry the mutton leg. Oil a pan and place the leg in the middle with a chopped clove of garlic, salt, and pepper.

Peel the onions, cut each one horizontally in half, and arrange around the meat. Peel the potatoes, cut them into wedges, and place them on the onions. Put slices of tomato on top. Season with salt, pepper, chopped parsley, and a few spoonfuls of oil.

Put the pan in a preheated oven of moderate heat for a good hour until the leg and its side dish are at the right cooking point.

COSCETTO DI CASTRATO ALL'INGLESE

Boiled Mutton with Mint Sauce English Style

3 lb 5 oz leg of mutton
2 onions
2 cloves
Parsley
Carrot
Celery
Mint sauce *(p26)*
Salt

Rinse and dry the mutton leg, tie it with string, and put it in a Dutch oven where it fits snugly. Cover with cold water. Season with 2 onions, in each of which you stick a clove, a few sprigs of parsley, a carrot, a couple of celery stalks, and salt. When the water boils, cover, reduce the heat, and let cook on a slow and regular simmer for a couple of hours.

While the mutton is cooking, make the mint sauce and let steep as directed, then pour the sauce into the gravy boat.

Lift the mutton out from the broth, free it from the string, arrange the meat on a dish, and send it to the table accompanying it with the mint sauce to the side.

COSCETTO DI CASTRATO IN CASSERUOLA

Mutton in a Dutch Oven

3 lb 5 oz leg of mutton
2 oz prosciutto fat
Onion
Carrot
Celery stalk
Parsley
Basil
Olive oil
Red wine
Salt
Pepper

Rinse and dry the mutton leg, lard it with the pieces of prosciutto fat and roll in a little salt and pepper. In a Dutch oven, combine the onion, carrot, celery, parsley, and basil (all minced). Set the mutton on this bed of vegetables, brush it with oil and a glass of red wine. Cover and place over heat.

When the wine has evaporated, season with salt and pepper again and brown for a few minutes. As soon as the meat and vegetables acquire a dark tint, pour in a few ladles of hot water and let barely simmer over very low heat for a couple of hours, until the meat is cooked, the vegetables done, and the sauce reduced.

Spoon some of the fat off the surface of the sauce, arrange the leg on a plate and cover with the thick aromatic sauce.

COSTOLETTE DI CASTRATO AI FUNGHI

Mutton Chops with Mushrooms

12 mutton chops
Parsley
Onion
2 oz dried mushrooms
Carrot
5 tbsp butter
6 tomatoes
Red wine
Olive oil
Salt

Arrange the mutton chops on a plate with the oil and a little chopped parsley. Soak the mushrooms.

Skin and chop the onion and carrot and put them in a pan to sauté with half of the butter and a pinch of salt. Add the chopped parsley and the tomatoes, washed, peeled, and sliced, and the reconstituted mushrooms, also chopped. Let them all cook gently, often adding a few spoons of lightly salted water.

Butter a large skillet and arrange the chops in a single layer. Put the pan on a high heat and, when the meat is browned on one side, turn it over, season it with a spot of salt and cover it with the mushroom and tomato sauce. Add a glass of wine, cover and let it cook for another half hour.

Finally arrange the chops on a serving dish and cover them with their fragrant mushroom sauce.

COSTOLETTE DI CASTRATO IN GRATELLA

Grilled Mutton Chops

12 mutton chops
1 lemon
Olive oil
Onion
Parsley
Salt
Pepper
To serve: mushrooms in oil

For this preparation it is necessary that the chops be rather thick but not too fatty.

Place the chops on a plate, squeeze the juice of a lemon over them, and season with salt, pepper, oil, a little chopped onion, and some chopped parsley. Leave them in this marinade for a couple of hours.

Preheat a grill or grill pan to high heat. Lift the chops straight from their marinade onto the grates or pan. When they are colored on one side, turn them over.

Moderate the intensity of the heat and cook more gently as you go, basting occasionally.

Then arrange on a serving dish and serve immediately with preserved mushrooms in oil as a garnish.

GOAT

CAPRETTO AL FORNO

Oven-Baked Kid with Artichoke Salad

3 lb 5 oz shoulder or leg of kid
2 oz ham
Rosemary
Lard
7 tbsp breadcrumbs
9 tbsp grated pecorino
Salt
Pepper

Artichoke salad:
6 artichoke hearts, lemon,
3 hard-boiled eggs, olive oil,
vinegar, mint

Wash the kid thoroughly and dry it well, then lard it with diced ham and sprigs of rosemary. Grease a pan with lard, lay the goat on top, and season with salt and pepper. Sprinkle with the breadcrumbs mixed with grated pecorino.

Place in a preheated oven at high heat and cook for a good hour.

In the meantime, for the artichoke salad: Boil the artichoke hearts in plenty of lightly salted boiling water, acidulated with the addition of lemon juice. Take care to keep the wedges at the right point of cooking. Drain and put them in a serving dish with the hard-boiled eggs cut into wedges. Season with salt, pepper, oil, vinegar, and mint leaves.

As soon as the kid is cooked, bring it to the table with its salad.

CAPRETTO E CARCIOFI BRODETTATI

Kid Braised with Artichokes

3 lb 5 oz leg or saddle of kid
Olive oil
2 oz prosciutto
Onion
Parsley
Flour
White wine
6 large artichoke hearts
3 egg yolks
1 lemon
Salt

Wash the kid thoroughly and dry it, put it in a Dutch oven with oil and a mix of chopped prosciutto, onion, and parsley. Brown slowly over medium heat.

When the meat is golden, sprinkle with flour, moisten with a glass of wine, and season with salt. Raise the heat and when the wine has evaporated, pour in a few ladles of hot water to cover. Cover and cook slowly for about 1 hour.

After about 30 minutes, add the artichoke hearts and cook slowly, stirring from time to time. At the end of cooking the sauce should be sufficiently thick.

Put the egg yolks in a bowl, dilute them with the juice of a lemon, mix them, add a spoon of chopped parsley, and pour the eggs into the sauce. Stir again, promptly remove the pot from the heat, and keep it warm so that the eggs are creamy without breaking.

CAPRETTO IN SPIEDINI

Kid on Skewers

3 lb 5 oz leg of kid
30 slices bread
5 oz prosciutto
Olive oil
Salad greens
Salt
Pepper

Wash and dry the leg and cut into 24 cubes. Place them in a bowl and season with salt and pepper.

Then cut 30 square slices of bread and 48 of prosciutto. Take 6 skewers and begin to skewer a square of bread, a square of prosciutto, a cube of meat, another square of prosciutto, and then again one of bread, calculating for each skewer 4 cubes of meat, 5 slices of bread, and 8 of prosciutto.

When you have filled all the skewers, place them in a well-oiled pan, drizzle a little more oil on them, and sprinkle them with salt. Place in a hot oven for about 30 minutes until they are colored and toasted.

Arrange the skewers on a plate garnished with salad greens.

CAPRETTO NEL VINO

Kid Braised in White Wine

2 oz dried mushrooms
3 lb 5 oz leg of kid
Onion
Celery
Carrot
Parsley
Sage
2 oz smoked pancetta
White wine
2 tbsp butter
Flour
Salt
Pepper

Reconstitute the dried mushrooms in cold water. Rinse the kid, then dry it.

In a Dutch oven, combine the chopped onion, celery, carrot, parsley, sage, and dried mushrooms. Cut the pancetta into small dice and season with salt and pepper. Lay the leg of kid on top and pour on 2 cups of white wine. Cover the Dutch oven with a sheet of parchment paper, put the lid on top of the paper, and cook over very low heat for about 1½ hours.

At this point, check the state of the kid and the amount of liquid left: Cook on, if the meat is not cooked, or take it out of the pot and let the liquid thicken.

Remove any fat from the surface and add the butter mixed with ½ teaspoon of flour. Let it cook for a few minutes and finally put the kid back in the Dutch oven so that it can flavor the sauce.

CAPRETTO STUFATO CON FUNGHI

Kid Stewed with Mushrooms

3 lb 5 oz leg of kid or chops
2 oz guanciale
Onion
Red wine
2 oz dried mushrooms
2¼ lb canned tomatoes
Salt
Pepper

Wash and dry the kid and cut into pieces. Put the pieces in a Dutch oven with a glass of water and brown without any seasoning, except salt and pepper. As soon as it has browned, add the diced guanciale and chopped onion and, after a few minutes, a glass of red wine.

Meanwhile, soak the dried mushrooms in cold water, then rinse them, carefully removing the earthy parts. When the wine has evaporated, add the dried mushrooms to the pan together with the tomatoes. Let it simmer slowly for about 1 hour.

CORATELLA DI CAPRETTO ALL'USO DI SARDEGNA

Goat Offal Sardinian Style

2 lb 10 oz kid's offal (lung, heart, liver, small intestine)
Sage
Olive oil
1½ tbsp lard
1 lemon
Salt
Pepper

Separate the intestines from the offal and cut it into large pieces. Slowly unravel the pieces, without breaking them, and squeeze them, passing them between the thumb and forefinger, to clean them out. Then rinse them well, dry them, and cut them in as many portions as there are skewers.

Now fill the skewers, alternating a piece of liver, one of lung, and one of heart and placing a fresh sage leaf between every two pieces.

When you have skewered all the offal, take the piece of intestine and fix one end of it to the end of each skewer using a piece of string. Once this is done, begin to wrap the offal with the intestine, in very elongated spirals. Get to the other end of the skewers, go back, thus forming a kind of offal net. Continue to wrap the intestines until the end, passing them over and over, and tie the other end with string.

Grease everything with a little oil, season with salt and pepper, and place the skewers on a wire rack over a sheet pan.

The cooking must be done at moderate heat so that the offal can cook well inside, without scorching outside. When you see that the offal is cooked, take a piece of lard and melt it in a pan and then let drizzle over the skewers.

Remove the skewers, arrange on a plate, and before sending it in, squeeze lemon juice over it.

PORK

ARISTA DI MAIALE CON L'ANANAS

Pork Loin with Prosecco and Pineapple

2¼ lb pork loin
1 pineapple
Olive oil
Garlic
Prosecco wine
Salt
Pepper

Tie the pork loin so it keeps its shape. Wash the pineapple and cut off the head and leaves. Use a small curved, very sharp knife to remove the peel, cut into slices, and cut out the central woody core. Take 4 slices and dice and keep the others back for later.

Put 2 tablespoons of oil and a clove of garlic in an ovenproof pot and set over heat. As soon as the garlic is golden, remove it and add the loin. Brown over high heat on all sides, turning it carefully, then pour in half a glass of prosecco. When the wine evaporates, season with salt and pepper and add the diced pineapple.

Put the pot in a preheated oven of moderate heat and let cook for about 1 hour. If it gets too dry, baste with more prosecco.

When cooked, remove the loin from the pot, carve into slices, not too thin, put them on a serving dish, finish with the cooking juices, and decorate with the reserved slices of pineapple.

BRACIOLINE DI MAIALE AL VINO BIANCO

Pork Chops Braised in White Wine

6 pork chops
Flour
Garlic
Rosemary
3½ tbsp butter
White wine
Salt
Pepper

First, pound the chops a little with a wet meat mallet. Even them with a small knife and dredge them in flour on both sides.

Next dice the garlic and rosemary. Melt some butter in a roasting pan, fry the rosemary and garlic, and then brown the chops a few minutes on each side. Season with salt and pepper and pour a glass of wine and another of water to cover.

Put the dish in a hot oven and cook until the liquid has reduced to a well-bound sauce. Allow about 20 minutes. This preparation should be served very hot.

BRACIOLINE DI MAIALE CON CIPOLLE

Grilled Pork Chops with Onions

6 thin pork chops
Olive oil
3 onions
Salt

Pound the chops with a wet meat mallet. Trim them. Brush with oil and salt and put them on the grill or grill pan, just to color.

Peel the onions and halve them horizontally. Put them in an ovenproof pan with a little oil, season with salt, and brown them slightly, turning them very carefully. When the onions wilt, drizzle a little more oil over them, then lay a grilled chop on top and put in a preheated oven of moderate heat for a few minutes.

Take out of the oven, gently arrange the preparation in a serving dish and send it to the table.

COSTOLETTE DI MAIALE AL FINOCCHIO

Pork Chops with Fennel and Marsala

6 pork chops
Olive oil
Marsala
Red wine
Garlic
Fennel seeds
Tomato paste
Salt
Pepper

Fry the pork chops in a pan with a little oil over moderate heat. Season with salt and pepper and let them brown well on one side and then turn over. When they are cooked, after about 20 minutes, take them out, place them in a serving dish, cover with another plate, and keep warm.

Immediately pour into the hot pan half a glass of Marsala and half a glass of red wine. Add a little chopped garlic, a pinch of fennel seeds, and a spoon of tomato paste. Stir and boil over lively heat. When the liquid has reduced by almost two-thirds and the sauce is dense, pour over the pork and bring immediately to the table.

COSTOLETTE DI MAIALE AL FORNO

Baked Pork Chops

6 pork chops
Flour
1 egg
Breadcrumbs
Olive oil
Wine
Salt
Pepper

Pound the chops and dredge them in the flour, then a beaten egg, and lastly breadcrumbs.

Arrange them in a well-oiled ovenproof dish, season with a pinch of salt and pepper, and put them in a hot oven of moderate heat for about 20 minutes.

Halfway through cooking, pour in half a glass of wine and let finish cooking.

COSTOLETTE DI MAIALE ALLA MODENESE

Pork Chops Modena Style

Sage
Rosemary
Garlic
6 pork chops
Butter
White wine
Salt
Pepper

For this recipe you need tender chops with plenty of fat around them.

Chop together the sage, rosemary, and a small piece of garlic. Season with salt and pepper and spread on a plate. Season the cutlets on both sides in this mix.

Arrange the chops in a single layer in a lightly buttered pan. Pour in enough water to almost cover and put on the stove.

When the water has evaporated and the chops begin to fry, turn them around, so they take a nice light hazelnut color. There is no need to add other fats as the pork has enough fat of its own.

When the chops are well colored, add half a glass of white wine, turn up the heat, turn them once more and, as soon as the wine dries out, put them on the plate.

COSTOLETTE DI MAIALE CON MOSTARDA

Pork Chops with Mustard

6 pork chops
Olive oil
Dry mustard
1 lemon
Parsley
Salt
Pepper

Pan-fry the chops in a little oil and a spot of salt.

Dissolve the mustard in a cup with the juice of half a lemon and season with salt and pepper. Add chopped parsley and 3 tablespoons of oil. Beat this sauce with a fork to thicken it well and dilute it again with a few more drops of lemon.

As soon as the chops are cooked, arrange them on a warm plate, pour the sauce over each chop, and immediately send to the table without letting them get cold.

COSTOLETTE DI MAIALE CON CETRIOLINI

Pork Chops with Cornichons

6 pork chops
Olive oil
Onion
Flour
White wine
Broth
Dijon mustard
Cornichons
Salt
Pepper

Season the chops with salt and pepper on both sides and fry in a little oil. As soon as they are cooked, after about 15 minutes, arrange them on a plate, cover them with another plate, and keep them warm.

Put a spoon of chopped onion in the same pan and let it brown. Add a spoon of flour, cook a little, stirring with a wooden spoon, and then deglaze with half a glass of wine and half a glass of broth or water. Leave to boil for a few minutes so the sauce thickens. Then put the chops back in this sauce and stew them over a very low heat for about 10 minutes, without letting them boil.

Take off the heat, put the chops on a serving dish and finish the sauce with a little mustard and a tablespoon of chopped cornichons. Pour the sauce over the chops and have them brought to the table.

COSTOLETTE DI MAIALE FARCITE

Deep-Fried Pork Chops with Fontina and Prosciutto

6 thick pork chops
2 oz Fontina
2 oz prosciutto or mortadella
Nutmeg
1 egg
Breadcrumbs
Oil for deep-frying
Salt
Pepper

With a sharp knife, trim off some of the fat around the chops and then butterfly the meat. To do this, place your left hand on the chop and carefully cut horizontally through the meat, going almost to the bone, so it opens like a little book.

Into this opening put thin slices of Fontina and prosciutto or mortadella. Season with nutmeg, a little salt, and a little pepper. Close the chops so that the two cut parts fit together perfectly, and then with a large, wet knife lightly pound the meat to flatten it a little and bring everything together better.

Wipe the chops in the beaten egg, taking care to wet the edges well, and then in the breadcrumbs. With the blade of a knife, press the bread well and do not neglect to seal up the opening.

Deep-fry in abundant oil over moderate heat so that they have time to cook inside and out.

COSTOLETTE DI MAIALE PICCANTI

Grilled Pork Chops with Pepper Sauce

6 pork chops
Olive oil
Parsley
Garlic
Tomato passata
6 pickled green peppers
3 anchovies
Salt
Pepper

Lightly flatten the pork chops with the side of a wet knife, and if they are too fatty, trim a little. Oil them, season with salt and pepper, and put them on to a preheated grill or grill pan for about 20 minutes.

Prepare a tasty sauce as follows: Chop the parsley with a pinch of garlic and put both in a saucepan with a little oil. When the mince has heated up, add ¾ cup tomato passata and cook for a few minutes. Core and seed the pickled peppers, chop, and add them. Rinse and bone the anchovies and add them. Top everything with a good grind of pepper.

Arrange the chops on a plate and pour the hot sauce over them.

FETTINE DI MAIALE IN AGRODOLCE

Pork Strips with Sweet and Sour Sauce

Pork skin
3 tbsp raisins
3 tbsp dried cherries
3 prunes
Candied orange peel
Olive oil
12 thin pork steaks, cut into strips
Sugar
Chocolate, grated
Vinegar
3 tbsp pine nuts
Salt

Scrape the fresh pork skins and put them in a small saucepan with cold water and boil them for 3 or 4 minutes. Drain and rinse in cold water. Then cut them into rather large pieces and put them back to cook covered, over very low heat with plenty of water until completely cooked, about 30 minutes.

Soak the raisins, dried cherries, and prunes in warm water, so they will be ready. Also chop the candied orange into small dice.

A few minutes before going to the table, warm some oil in a skillet and cook the steaks over high heat.

When the meat is cooked, take it out and keep warm and pour a little water into the same pan and, stir to pick up any pieces stuck to the bottom or sides. Add a spoon of sugar, a spoon of grated chocolate, a splash of vinegar and a pinch of salt. Make sure everything is well mixed, then add the raisins, pine nuts, sour cherries, and prunes and the little cubes of candied orange peel.

Add the pork skin in pieces to the sauce and let everything cook at a bare simmer for 3 to 4 minutes, then transfer everything to the serving plate.

FETTINE DI MAIALE IN SALSA DI CAPPERI

Pork Strips in Caper Sauce

12 thin pork steaks, cut into strips
Flour
1 tbsp butter
1 egg
Breadcrumbs
Oil for deep-frying
Salt

Caper sauce:
onion, 3½ tbsp butter, anchovy, 2 tbsp capers, parsley, flour, vinegar, broth, sugar (optional)

Make the caper sauce first: Chop half a medium-sized onion and sauté in a little butter. When the onion is golden, add a chopped anchovy, mashing it with a wooden spoon. Add a couple of spoons of chopped capers, a spoon of chopped parsley, and a pinch of flour. Cook for a minute or two, stirring, and then sprinkle with a finger of vinegar and half a glass of broth or water. Let it cook a little longer until you have a good consistency. You can also add a little sugar, which is not necessary, however. Finish the sauce by adding another small piece of butter.

Lightly pound the pork slices, flour them, and dredge them in lightly salted beaten egg and breadcrumbs. Deep-fry them in abundant oil. Season with a pinch of salt.

Arrange the slices on a plate and pour the hot caper sauce on top.

GALANTINA DI MAIALE

Pork Galantine

1 lb pork tenderloin
3½ oz prosciutto
3½ oz tongue
10 oz pancetta
3 tbsp pistachios
Black truffle
Nutmeg
Marsala
1 lb lean pork
Pork caul
Onion
Whole cloves
Celery
Carrot
Parsley
Bouillon cube jelly *(p52)*
Salt
Pepper

Cut the pork tenderloin into cubes about ¾ inch on each side, and put them in a bowl with the prosciutto, one-third of the pancetta, and the tongue (all cut into cubes).

Blanch the pistachios, which will make them easier to peel, but leave them whole and add to the meats. Cut the truffle into cubes.

Season all the ingredients with salt, pepper, some grated nutmeg and a glass of Marsala. Mix well, cover with a plate, and leave for an hour or more, so everything is well perfumed and flavored with the Marsala.

Now we need to prepare the filling: Mince the lean pork and the rest of the pancetta and season it with salt and pepper.

Then we have to deal with the caul: Cut half of the net and put it in a pan of hot water. It will soften and become like a wet handkerchief. Then roll it out on a work surface.

Use a spoon or, better, your hands to mix the mince with the cubes of meat so it is evenly distributed. Roll up into a sausage shape. Do not worry about the Marsala in the bowl: It will be incorporated in the filling and will serve to make the galantine more fragrant.

Once this is done, place it on the caul network and shape it like a large sausage. Wrap it well in the caul and use your hands to keep it in shape. Fold the two ends of the net and stitch them up. Wrap the galantine in a linen towel, twisting at both ends so it is like a large candy, and secure each end with string and a strong knot. Tie the middle with two more lengths of string. It must remain solidly packed.

Put it in a large saucepan with water, salt, and the usual aromatics—onion stuck with a few cloves, carrot, celery, parsley—and when the water reaches a boil, lower the flame as much as possible and let it cook for 1½ hours, just barely simmering.

Tke the galantine from its broth, let it rest for 5 or 6 minutes, then cut the strings and unwind from the towel. Dip this towel in cold water, rinse it a little, squeeze it, spread it on the table and wrap the galantine back in it again, tying it up as before.

This time you need to weight down the galantine to give it a good shape by covering it with a plate and a weight. The weight must not be too heavy or the mixture will dry out. Leave it alone until the next day, so that the galantine can be well pressed and neat.

Prepare a jelly with the appropriate meat bouillon cube and put it to thicken in the fridge.

The next day, remove the bindings, open the towel, cut the galantine into slices, and arrange on a rather long plate with high sides. Cover it with the jelly. You can also chop the jelly into rectangles for garnish. Keep the dish in the fridge until time to serve.

ADA SAYS: *Truffles and pistachios, as well as giving more flavor, contribute to the visual mosaic, which is one of the qualities of this preparation. You can use any leftover broth, thoroughly degreased, to make soup or minestrone.*

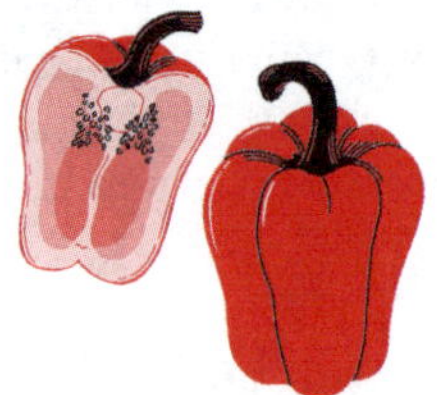

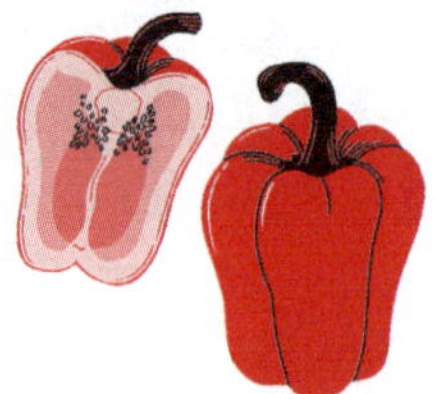

LOMBATINE DI MAIALE ALLA NAPOLETANA

Pork Steaks Neapolitan Style

2 red or yellow bell peppers
7 oz fresh mushrooms or 2 oz dried mushrooms
Garlic
Olive oil
6 thick pork loin steaks
Tomato passata
Salt
Pepper

Roast the peppers, charring the skin so it comes off more easily. Clean the fresh mushrooms and cut them into slices. If you are using dried mushrooms, soak them in cold water first until they reconstitute, about 15 minutes, and rinse thoroughly.

Fry a clove of garlic in a little oil and take it out before it colors. Sear the steaks in this oil to a beautiful golden color. Season them with salt and pepper, then remove them and keep them warm.

Put ¾ cup tomato passata in the same pan, add the peppers and mushrooms and finally the steaks again. Cover and cook slowly for about 30 minutes.

LOMBATINE DI MAIALE AL POMODORO

Pork Loin Steaks with Tomato

6 thick pork loin steaks
Olive oil
White wine
Tomato passata
Broth
Salt
Pepper

The steaks should be very thick, at least a couple of fingers; better more than less.

Put a little oil in a pan and when it is hot, add the steaks in a single layer. Season with salt and pepper. When they are well browned, drain off all the fat and deglaze with a glass of white wine. Cover and let the wine evaporate slowly, turning the steaks from time to time.

When the wine has completely evaporated, add ¾ cup tomato passata, cover, reduce the heat, and cook slowly for another 30 minutes until the sauce is well reduced and the steaks well cooked. If the sauce dries too soon, add a little broth or water.

Arrange on a serving dish, cover the steaks with the sauce, which must not be excessively abundant but very dense.

LOMBATINE DI MAIALE CON SALSA AROMATICA

Pork Steaks with Aromatic Sauce

6 pork loin steaks
5 tbsp olive oil
2 carrots
Parsley
Bay leaf
3 tbsp flour
5½ tbsp butter
Red wine
Tomato passata
Celery heart
Onion
Lemon zest
Salt
Pepper

Lightly pound the steaks, put them on a plate with some oil, salt, pepper, and a mix of chopped carrot, parsley, and a bay leaf. Cover with a plate and leave them like this for 2 hours.

After this time, remove the steaks from the marinade, dry, and flour them. Put them in a skillet big enough for them all to fit in a single layer with half of the butter and 3 spoons of oil. Sauté until they are golden brown on both sides. Then remove them from the pan and pour in a glass of wine, letting it evaporate by about three-quarters. Then add ¾ cup tomato passata, return the steaks to the pan, cover, and simmer for about 30 minutes so that the meat can flavor the sauce.

Meanwhile, cut the celery into very small cubes, the same with the carrot, onion, zest of half a lemon, and chopped parsley. Season with a little salt and put the vegetables in a pan with a little more butter, cover, and cook gently for about 30 minutes, adding a few spoons of water from time to time.

Finally, pour all the vegetables into the pan with the steaks and tomatoes.

When the meat is well cooked and the sauce lightly reduced, pour everything into a serving dish.

LOMBATINE DI MAIALE CON SALSA DI PRUGNE

Pork Steaks with Prune Sauce

Prune sauce *(p26)*
6 pork loin steaks
Olive oil
Wine
Salt
Pepper

First, prepare the prune sauce: Soak the prunes in warm water and take out the stones. Sauté half the chopped onion, chopped prosciutto and the butter, until the onion is golden. Then add half a glass of vinegar and let it evaporate by half. Now add the prunes, cover with enough water, season with a little salt and a bay leaf. Simmer slowly, covered, until the plums are very soft. When the plums are cooked, sieve everything or blend. You will get a thick and very tasty sauce to coat the pork steaks.

Pan-fry the steaks in a little oil and seasoned with salt and pepper for about 20 minutes. When they are well browned, spoon on a little wine and cook that down.

Arrange on a serving dish, coating each steak with prune sauce.

MAIALE ALLA MILANESE (BOTTAGGIO)

Pork Milanese (Bottaggio)

3½ tbsp butter
2 oz guanciale
1 onion
2 pig trotters
7 oz pork skin
Pig's head
Pork ribs
6 loin steaks
6 sausages
1 celery stalk
2 or 3 carrots
Cabbage
Salt
Pepper

Put the butter in a very large pan, add the sliced guanciale and a chopped onion, and brown. Add the trotters, the skin, a piece of pig's head, some ribs, loin steaks, and sausages. Let everything brown and then add minced celery, 2 or 3 carrots cut into sticks, salt, and pepper. When the meats are browned, cover them with water and let them cook slowly for a few hours until the various ingredients are well cooked.

About 20 minutes before serving, wash and shred a cabbage and carefully add to the meats.

Arrange the bottaggio on a serving dish and serve very hot with its cabbage.

ADA SAYS: *This succulent Milanese preparation, in which pork finds one of its most popular applications, belongs to the kind of dish that represents a complete meal. The dish can also be enriched with a few pieces of chicken and or turkey. In Milan it is called cassöla, posciandra, or bottaggio.*

MAIALE AL LATTE

Pork Loin Cooked in Milk

2 lb 10 oz pork loin
5 tbsp butter
Milk
Salt
Pepper
Optional: white truffle

To make this tasty preparation, use a good-quality cut like loin, boned and trimmed of fat, according to the Bolognese custom.

Season the loin the day before with salt and pepper and leave it like that for a night (although it can be done at the moment or after the meat has been seared).

In an oval Dutch oven in which the loin fits snugly, melt some butter and brown the loin.

Cover it almost entirely with milk, cover the Dutch oven, and cook slowly for about 2 hours.

When the loin is cooked, the milk should have thickened like cream and taken on a golden color. Remove the meat, slice it, arrange it on a plate, and pour on the sauce, which can be enriched with white truffle.

MAIALE ARROSTO

Roast Pork with Apple Sauce

2 lb 10 oz pork loin
Lard or olive oil
White wine
Salt
Pepper

Apple sauce:
4 apples, 1 lemon, salt

Tie the pork loin with string so that it does not deform when cooked. Put it in a roasting pan, in which it fits snugly, with a little lard or oil, salt, and pepper. Roast in a preheated oven of moderate heat for about 2 hours. If the meat gets too dry, baste it with a little white wine, turning it from time to time.

Accompany it with the following applesauce: Peel the apples, halve them, core, and cut them into thin slices. In a small pot, combine the apples with water to cover and cook until tender. Mash them with a wooden spoon to get a purée without lumps; or push them through a sieve, which is simpler and quicker. The sauce should be quite dense, but not excessively. If it is too thick, add more water.

When it is time to put it on the table, grate lemon zest over it, add just a little salt, and give it a shake. Off the heat, squeeze over a little lemon juice and serve the sauce lukewarm.

ADA SAYS: *The best cut for roast is, without a doubt, the loin. In this recipe all sorts of flavorings must be banished from the meat: Pork is so tasty that it doesn't need any seasoning. It is best eaten hot, but it is also very good cold, and as an alternative to apple sauce, you could accompany it with a purée of potatoes or of chestnuts.*

MAIALE ARROSTO CON CAVOLETTI DI BRUXELLES

Roast Pork with Brussels Sprouts

2 lb 10 oz pork loin
5½ tbsp butter
Olive oil
Broth
2¼ lb Brussels sprouts
Salt
Pepper

Tie the pork loin to keep it in shape and place it in a deep Dutch oven, preferably terra-cotta, with the butter and ¼ cup of oil. Brown the meat, season with salt and pepper, and continue slowly cooking, basting it with a few spoons of broth and turning it over occasionally.

Meanwhile, trim the Brussels sprouts and drop them into a pan of boiling water for 10 minutes and drain.

About 30 minutes before the meat is cooked, which should be about 2 hours in total, pour the sprouts into the pan with the meat and mix well so they are flavored in the cooking sauce.

Carve the pork and lay up the slices in a round dish with the Brussels sprouts in the middle.

MAIALE BRASATO ALLA GENOVESE

Braised Pork Loin Genovese

2 lb 10 oz pork loin
1 tbsp lard
3½ oz prosciutto
3½ oz pork skin
Onion
Celery
Parsley
Carrot
1 oz dried mushrooms
Red wine
Broth or bouillon cube
Salt
Pepper

Tie the meat to keep it in shape. Choose a Dutch oven in which it fits tightly.

Finely chop together the lard, prosciutto, pork skin, all the vegetables, including the mushrooms (first soaked in warm water to reconstitute). Place them in the Dutch oven and set the pork on top. Pour in half a glass of red wine, cover, and put it on the heat. When the wine has reduced, add the remaining wine, season the meat with salt and pepper, and let it brown well.

As soon as the meat and vegetables start to darken, add enough boiling broth to cover three-quarters of the meat. Reduce the heat to low and cook at a bare simmer for about 2 hours until the meat is well cooked and the sauce sufficiently reduced. When cooked to the right point, the tip of a small knife inserted into the meat should meet no resistance.

Once the meat is cooked, put it on a carving board, remove the string, and carve into slices. Garnish with vegetables to taste and sprinkle it with a few spoonfuls of well-degreased sauce.

ADA SAYS: *The remaining sauce is excellent for serving on pasta.*

MAIALE IN MESSICANI

Braised Pork Rolls

12 thin boneless pork loin chops
10 oz fatty pork
Crustless white bread
Milk
Garlic
Parsley
Grated Parmesan
Flour
Butter
Pork belly fat
Carrot
Celery
Sage
White wine
Tomato passata
2 cups broth
Salt
Pepper
Nutmeg

Carefully pound the pork with a wet meat mallet until very white and thin.

Chop the fatty pork meat finely and mix it with the bread—previously soaked in milk and squeezed dry—a little chopped garlic, a little chopped parsley, salt, pepper, nutmeg, and a spoon or two of grated Parmesan. Distribute this filling over the loin slices and roll them up. Dredge them in flour and arrange them in one layer in a large pan, with some melted butter and pork fat from the belly.

Let the rolls brown on one side. Meanwhile, prepare a mix of carrot and celery and add to the pan. Add also a clove of garlic and a few sage leaves.

Then turn the rolls, cover, and let brown slowly until the vegetables and the rolls have a nice gold color. Then add a little white wine and let it almost completely evaporate. Add ¾ cup tomato passata and finish cooking over moderate heat, covered. It will take an hour overall.

Lift out the rolls and place them in another pan. Add the broth to the tomato mix in the first pan. Let it boil a little, stirring well with a spoon to free up all the cooking juices, then strain through a sieve. Degrease the sauce, put it back to boil for about 10 minutes, and pour it over steaks.

ADA SAYS: *It is appropriate to accompany this excellent preparation with a side dish that fits well, for example a garnish of peas, or a purée of potatoes.*

MAIALE IN POLPETTONE CON VERDURE

Pork Meatloaf with Vegetables

1½ lb cabbage
1½ lb spinach
5 oz Swiss chard
5 oz bitter greens
1 egg
3½ oz crustless white bread
Flour
1 lb 5 oz pork
Vegetable trimmings for the broth (onion, carrot, celery, parsley)
Olive oil
1 lemon
Salt
Pepper

Clean the cabbage leaving 4 or 5 big leaves aside, which you will need later to wrap the filling. Also clean the spinach, Swiss chard, and the greens. Rinse all the vegetables in several changes of water and cut them finely.

Bring a pot of water to a boil. Add the green vegetables, leaving them there for a few minutes. Then scoop them out with a slotted spoon and gently dip the leaves in cold water so as not to break them. Drain and chop.

Gather the vegetables in a large bowl, season with salt and pepper, add the beaten egg and the breadcrumbs (soaked in water and squeezed dry), and a spoonful of flour. Mix everything with your hands.

Cut the pork into cubes and add to the mixture. Line up the large cabbage leaves on a linen towel, overlapping them. Spread the meatloaf mixture over the leaves in a large sausage shape. Wrap up in the leaves, and then in the towel. Tie the two ends with string and also tie another knot around the middle.

Warm a pan with water and the usual vegetables and aromatics—onion, carrot, celery, parsley—and lower the cabbage leaf roll in carefully. Simmer for 2 hours.

Take out of the pan and leaving it well wrapped up in the towel, put it in a cool place with a plate and a weight on top.

When the meatloaf is cold and well pressed, unwrap it from the towel, slice it, arrange it on a serving dish, drizzle with some oil and the juice of a lemon and serve.

MAIALE IN SPIEDINI

Pork Skewers

2 lb pork tenderloin
Ciabatta-style rolls
Bay leaves
3½ oz prosciutto
Olive oil
Salt
Optional: watercress

For this preparation we must use pork tenderloin, which in Rome is also called the loin.

Remove any fat on the outside of the tenderloin and cut into large cubes, weighing about 2 ounces each.

From the rolls cut as many slices as there are pieces of pork, plus keep the end crusts.

Take 3 skewers and start by sticking a slice of bread, a bay leaf, a slice of prosciutto, and a piece of tenderloin, one more a slice of prosciutto, a bay leaf, a slice of bread, and so on until the skewer is full, and finish with an end crust. Prepare the second and third skewers in the same way.

Then put them in a baking pan, brush them with oil, sprinkle with salt, and bake in the oven at a regular heat for about 45 minutes.

As soon as the meat is cooked and the bread is crisp, remove from the oven, free everything from the skewers and send them hot to the table, perhaps garnished on a bed of watercress.

MAIALE TONNÉ

Pork with Tuna

2 lb 10 oz pork loin
10 oz tinned tuna in olive oil
1 onion
4 anchovies
White wine
Olive oil
2 lemons
Cornichons
Black olives, pitted
Capers
Salt
Pepper
Optional: mayonnaise *(p19)*

Surround the loin in a pan with the mashed tuna in oil, a thinly sliced onion, the anchovies—rinsed, boned, and chopped—salt, pepper, and 2 cups of white wine. Cover and put over moderate heat, and let it simmer slowly until completely cooked, about 2 hours.

Take out the loin and keep warm in a terrine-style dish. Mash everything else left in the pan and dilute with half a glass of oil and the juice of 2 lemons. If you want you can add a few spoons of mayonnaise, homemade or store-bought.

Pour the sauce over the meat, cover, and leave it in the fridge for 24 hours so that the meat can have time to flavor well.

When ready to serve, cut the pork into thin slices, cover them with the sauce, and decorate with sliced cornichons, sliced black olives, and capers.

MAIALE USO CACCIA

Hunter's Pork

2 oz prosciutto
4 sage leaves
1 lemon
Celery
Onion
3 cloves
2 lb 10 oz pork loin
Olive oil
Vinegar
Anchovy
Parsley
Salt
Peppercorns

In a pressure cooker (or a Dutch oven in which the pork fits snugly), cover the bottom with slices of prosciutto, the sage leaves, strips of lemon zest, celery stalks, half an onion (not chopped), the cloves, and some peppercorns. Tie the pork so it stays in shape and place in the pot. Season with a pinch of salt and baste with half a glass of water, half of oil, and half of vinegar.

Cover and let the meat cook at low pressure for about 1 hour (or longer in a Dutch oven). After this time, all the liquid will have almost evaporated and the meat will begin to fry. Let it breathe, open the pot, and remove the meat immediately. Strain the cooking juices carefully.

Chop a rinsed and boned anchovy with some parsley and combine this aromatic pesto in a new pan with the pork cooking juices. Dilute with a spoon of water, let it heat up, carve the meat in slices and then add them to the mix.

Let it simmer and season for a few minutes. Remove from the heat, finish with the juice of the lemon and send to the table.

ADA SAYS: *This can also be served cold.*

PASTICCIO DI MAIALE

Pork Pie with Truffle

1¾ cups flour
2 tbsp butter, plus extra for greasing
9 oz pork tenderloin
3½ oz prosciutto
Marsala
9 oz lean pork
7 oz thinly sliced pancetta
1 egg
Bouillon cube jelly *(p52)*
Salt
Pepper
Optional: black truffle

For the pie you need a springform pan about 6 inches across.

Mound the flour on a work surface and mix it with the butter, a pinch of salt, and half a glass of warm water. Knead to a smooth dough, well worked, and of the right consistency. Roll into a ball, wrap in a towel, and let it rest for 30 minutes.

Prepare the filling: Thoroughly clean all the fat from the pork tenderloin and cut it into sticks the size and thickness of a finger. Do the same for the prosciutto. Put them in a bowl, season with a little salt, abundant pepper, and a finger of Marsala. At this point you can enrich the pie filling with a few cubes of black truffle.

Chop the lean pork very finely and also half of the pancetta. Season with salt and pepper and set aside.

Roll out half of the dough to a thickness of ¼ inch on a lightly floured surface. Grease the springform pan and line it with half of the dough. There will be a lot of excess hanging over the edges of the pan. Trim the excess and keep the trimmings to the side.

Line the bottom and sides of the springform with some of the remaining thinly sliced pancetta.

Drain the Marsala from the bowl with the loin, prosciutto, and truffle. Take some of the minced pancetta and lean pork and flatten it into the bottom of the mold to make a regular layer. On this layer make another one of the tenderloin, prosciutto, and truffle. Cover with another layer of minced meat and so on, finishing with a layer of minced pancetta and pork.

On this last layer put any remaining slices of pancetta.

With the remaining dough, make a lid and press the top and bottom together. Brush the top of the pie with a beaten egg and with a small knife make a circular hole in the middle.

Roll out a small piece of leftover pastry and with the help of two round cookie cutters, one bigger and one smaller, form a donut that you will arrange around the drilled hole. Take a strip of parchment paper, roll it up about 1¼ inches high, slip it into the hole in the pastry to stop the pie shrinking.

Finally bake the pie in a preheated oven at a moderate heat for about 1 hour. Let it cool without taking off the springform sides.

Make 2 cups of bouillon cube jelly and then put into the freezer to thicken. When the pie is cooled, pour the jelly, a little at a time, into the central hole on top.

Put the pie in the fridge for a few hours, so that the gelatin sets, and only then unmold the pie and arrange it in the serving dish.

Cut the remaining jelly into rectangles or triangles for decoration and garnish.

Sausages

SALSICCE CON FAGIOLI

Sausages with Beans

1 lb dried white beans (*cannellini*)
Baking soda
12 sausages
Olive oil
Tomato passata
Salt
Pepper

Soak the beans in cold water for 12 hours. Drain them, wash them, put them in a pot with plenty of cold water. Season with salt and a pinch of baking soda, cover, and bring to a low boil; keep the heat moderate because a tumultuous boil could damage them. Depending on the quality of the beans, they will take 2 to 3 hours to cook.

Poke the sausages here and there with a skewer and place them in a skillet. Add cold water to cover. Place the pan on the heat. As they cook, the water will evaporate, leaving the sausages to brown in their own. Turn them from time to time so that they can color well on all sides. With this method, the sausages cook beautifully without any added fat.

In the fat left over from cooking the sausages, add a little oil, and put in ¾ cup of tomato passata. Cook for about 10 minutes. Then add the beans, season with salt and pepper and cook slowly for another 10 minutes.

When the beans are flavored, put the sausages back in the pan as well to flavor before putting everything into a warm serving dish.

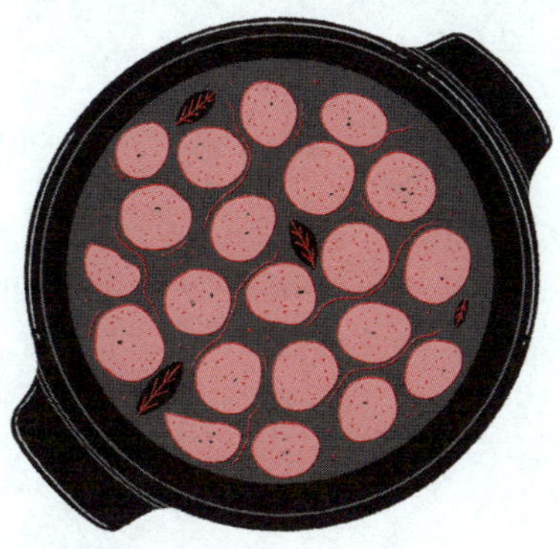

SALSICCE CON INDIVIA

Sausages with Escarole

2¼ lb escarole
12 sausages
Olive oil
Salt

Clean the escarole by trimming the base and removing all the external leaves so only the white part remains; rinse it in several waters; then boil it in lightly salted boiling water, but do not overcook it.

Drain it, refresh under cold water, then drain it again, and squeeze it in your hands to make it dry.

Cook the sausages in a pan and when they are ready, take them out and keep them warm.

In the fat left over from cooking the sausages, add a little oil, put the escarole in to flavor for a few minutes. Arrange the escarole on a serving dish and place the sausages on top.

SALSICCE CON CARDI

Sausages with Cardoons

2¼ lb cardoons
1 lemon
7 tbsp butter
12 sausages
Grated Parmesan
Salt

Clean the cardoons and cut them into pieces about 4 inches long, remove any hard bits, and rinse in water acidulated with the juice of a lemon. In a pot of lightly salted boiling water, cook the cardoons for about 1 hour. Drain and dry them.

Melt the butter in a large ovenproof pan and add the cardoons. Remove the sausage casings, break up the meat, and lay on top. Pour in a ladle of water, sprinkle with grated Parmesan, and place the pan in a preheated oven of moderate heat for 10 minutes, to cook the sausages and brown the cheese.

WÜRSTEL IN TEGAME

Frankfurters with Cabbage

2¼ lb cabbage
12 frankfurters
Olive oil
Garlic
Vinegar
Dijon mustard
Salt

Core the cabbage, remove the hardest leaves, rinse, and put the tenderest leaves to cook in lightly salted boiling water, uncovered, for about 20 minutes. When they are cooked, cut the leaves into thin ribbons about ¼ inch wide.

Prick the frankfurters and put them in a pan with water to cover with water. Cook them until the water has evaporated.

About 15 minutes before serving, fry a clove of garlic in a little oil and, when it browns, remove it and put the cabbage in its place. Cover, let it flavor for a few minutes, then add half a glass of vinegar, a pinch of salt, and, then off the heat a tablespoon of mustard. Stir with a wooden spoon so the cabbage is well coated with the sauce.

Transfer the frankfurters to the center of a serving dish, surrounding them with the prepared cabbage.

ZAMPI DI MAIALE

Pig's Trotters with Green Sauce

6 pig's trotters
Celery
Onion
Carrot
Whole clove
Green sauce *(p31)*
Salt
Peppercorns

Buy the trotters raw, scrape them, singe them, and blanch them in boiling water. Simmer in water flavored with celery, onion—stuck with some cloves—carrot, salt, and a few peppercorns.

Let them cook slowly for about 2 hours, until the meat comes off the bones easily. Serve hot with a green sauce of anchovies, parsley, capers, cornichons, breadcrumbs, garlic, and vinegar. They can also be served just as they are.

ADA SAYS: *An exquisite dish when cooked in a well-flavored broth and served hot.*

ZAMPI DI MAIALE CON BROCCOLI

Pig's Trotters with Broccoli and Sausages

6 pig's trotters
Celery
Onion
Whole clove
Carrot
3 lb 5 oz broccoli
6 sausages
Olive oil or lard
Grated Parmesan
7 oz mozzarella
2 eggs
Salt
Pepper

Clean the trotters well, then scrape them and singe them. Bring a pot of water to a boil with celery, onion (stuck with a clove), carrot, salt, and a few peppercorns. Add the trotters and simmer slowly for about 2 hours, until completely cooked.

When the trotters are nearly cooked, peel the broccoli, divide the top into florets, then boil in abundant salted water.

When the trotters are cooked, cut them in two and take out the main bones. Also prepare some sausages, cooking them slowly with a little lard or oil in a pan and basting with a few spoonfuls of water to prevent them from breaking up.

When the sausages are cooked, remove them from the pan and cut into slices, not too thin.

On the bottom of a Dutch oven, pour a ladle or two of the cooking broth from the trotters and make a layer of trotter. Arrange the broccoli on top, season with plenty of pepper, plenty of grated Parmesan, and a few slices of cooked sausage. Top everything with a layer of mozzarella slices. Pour a little more broth over everything.

Break two eggs into a bowl and beat them as if for an omelet. Stir in a few spoons of grated Parmesan and then spread this mixture on top of the mozzarella.

Place the Dutch oven in a preheated oven of moderate heat and leave it for a good 30 minutes.

Send to the table in the Dutch oven. The beaten egg will have made an appetizing golden crust on the surface and the various ingredients will have had the opportunity to harmoniously blend their characteristic flavors and aromas.

ADA SAYS: *There are those who prefer to add a greater amount of broth... to be able to dip bread into the sauce.*

ZAMPONE CON LE LENTICCHIE

Zampone with Lentils

1 lb lentils
Onion
Celery
1 zampone sausage (fully cooked)
Olive oil
2 oz fatty prosciutto
Salt

Lentils these days only need 15 or 20 minutes of cooking. But in the old days they would cook for much longer.

To cook, rinse the lentils and put them in a pot with cold water flavored with an onion and a celery stalk. Bring to a boil and cook until tender, 10 to 15 minutes. Halfway through cooking, add 2½ teaspoons of salt.

Boil the precooked zampone following the instructions on the packaging. When it is cooked, unwrap it and let it cool, because it's easier to sliced when cold. When slicing, try to keep the slices close to each other so that it remains as if it were intact.

Chop the prosciutto, onion, and celery. In a rather large pan, heat a little oil over low heat, add the prosciutto and vegetables and let brown for about 10 minutes. Add the drained lentils and add a few ladles of the zampone broth and let it boil slowly for about 10 minutes. Put the hot lentils in a serving dish, place the slices of the zampone on top, and serve immediately.

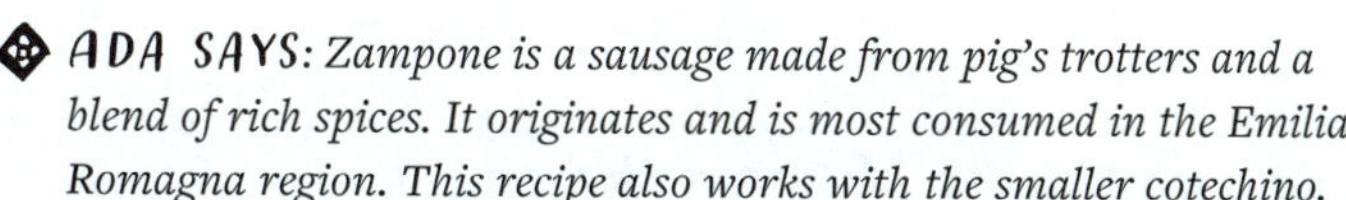

ADA SAYS: *Zampone is a sausage made from pig's trotters and a blend of rich spices. It originates and is most consumed in the Emilia-Romagna region. This recipe also works with the smaller cotechino.*

ZAMPONE CON RISO

Zampone with Rice

1 zampone sausage (fully cooked)
Butter
Onion
1½ cups rice
Grated Parmesan
Salt
Optional: bouillon cube

Boil the precooked zampone following the instructions on the packaging. When cooked, unwind it from the wrapper, set aside the cooking broth and let the sausage cool.

In a saucepan, fry a little butter with a few slices of thinly sliced onion. Add the rice, let it flavor for a moment, mixing with a wooden spoon. Then add the cooking broth from the zampone. The zampone broth will tend to be salty: in any case it is not a bad idea to taste the rice, and correct with more salt if necessary. If the cooking broth is not enough, add a few ladles of broth or a diluted bouillon cube.

When the rice is cooked, remove the pan from the heat. Use a spoon to make a large hole in the middle of the rice into which you put a few tablespoons of grated Parmesan. Cover and let it rest for a couple of minutes, then with a fork stir the rice and pour it into an oval plate, placing it to one side. Carve the zampone into slices, and arrange them alongside.

ZAMPONE CON SPINACI

Zampone with Spinach

2 lb 10 oz uncooked zampone sausage
Onion
2 celery stalks
Carrot
2¼ lb spinach
7 tbsp butter
Lemon
Grated Parmesan
Salt

Usually zampone are cooked, but for an uncooked zampone, soften it by soaking it in cold water for at least 5 hours or better all night. Drain it, prick it in several parts, wrap it in a linen towel or cheesecloth, and tie it with a string.

Put the zampone in a saucepan, cover with plenty of water, and slowly bring to a boil. At this point skim carefully, reduce the heat, add an onion cut into pieces, the celery, the carrot cut into small wheels, and continue cooking gently so the zampone does not break. After 3 hours of very slow cooking, remove the pan from the heat, take out the zampone, free it from its wrapping, and wait for it to cool before slicing.

Wash and clean the spinach with care to eliminate all traces of earth and cook over high heat with very little water and a pinch of salt. As soon as the leaves collapse, drain thoroughly. In a large baking pan, melt some butter, add the spinach, place the zampone slices on top, sprinkle with lemon juice, and some grated Parmesan and place the pan in a preheated oven of moderate heat to brown.

Ham

INVOLTINI DI PROSCIUTTO ALLO SPECCHIO

Prosciutto in Jelly with Russian Salad

Russian salad *(p725)*
Bouillon cube jelly *(p52)*
6 slices prosciutto
Mayonnaise, store-bought
12 green olives
12 black olives
Butter
6 cornichons
Pickled red peppers
Vinegar
Salt

Make the Russian salad and prepare 2 cups of bouillon cube jelly and let it cool.

Arrange the slices of prosciutto on a work surface, on each slice spread some Russian salad and then roll them up. On a round plate arrange the rolls, decorate them with black and green olives, flakes of butter, slices of pickled red pepper, and with cornichons. Pour the jelly over everything, put the dish in the fridge for the gelatin to set.

PROSCIUTTO COTTO IN BUDINO

Ham Flan

5 tbsp butter
6 tbsp flour
2 cups milk
Nutmeg
3 eggs
Grated Parmesan
1 lb ham
Salt
Pepper

Put the butter in a saucepan and when it melts, add the flour, mix with a wooden spoon, and slowly add the milk. Keep stirring and cooking this sauce until it is very thick. Season it with a little pepper, a trifle of nutmeg, and very little salt.

Remove the pan from the heat and let the sauce cool. Then mix in the egg yolks, ⅓ cup grated Parmesan, and the chopped ham. Mix thoroughly. Whip the egg whites to a soft peaks and fold them in.

Oil a 2- to 3-cup pudding mold, flour it and then turn it upside down and tap the mold to knock off any excess. Add the ham mixture. Set the mold in a larger pan with water to come halfway up the sides.

Cook the pudding for about 1 hour.

Take it out of the water, let it rest, and cool for a few minutes and then invert onto a plate and bring it to the table.

◆ ADA SAYS: *Green beans with cheese are a good garnish for this flan.*

PROSCIUTTO COTTO IN CROSTA

Ham in a Crust

9 oz homemade *(p71)* or frozen puff pastry
6 tbsp flour
4½ tbsp semolina
2 cups milk
2 eggs
5 tbsp butter
Grated Parmesan
9 oz ham
Salt

Roll out the puff pastry—thawed at room temperature if frozen. Divide into two unequal parts. Flatten the bigger part with a rolling pin to about ⅛ inch thick. Oil the inside of an 8-inch round pan. Lay the dough in the pan covering the edges well, trim it and prick the bottom with the tines of a fork.

Now make the filling: Put the flour and the fine semolina in a saucepan, mix in the cold milk, stirring well, and cook for about 10 minutes until it is a thick cream. Take off the heat, season with salt, the two egg yolks, 3 tablespoons of butter, and plenty of grated Parmesan, mixing well.

Transfer to a plate and as soon as the cream has cooled a little, pour it into the pastry shell, spreading it and leveling it with the blade of a knife. Cut the ham into strips and criss-cross them on top.

Roll out the remaining puff pastry and cut it into strips to cover the ham. Whisk the egg whites and brush over the surface. Place in a warm oven of moderate heat for about 30 minutes. Serve warm.

PROSCIUTTO FRESCO DI MAIALE AL MARSALA

Marinated Fresh Ham with Marsala

2 lb 10 oz fresh ham, one piece
Marsala
Olive oil
Pork skin
Onions
Carrots
Celery
Parsley
Broth
Potato starch
2 tbsp butter
Salt
Pepper

Buy a fresh ham, boneless and in one piece. Put it in a Dutch oven or dish where it fits snugly and pour in 2 large glasses of Marsala. Leave for one day, taking care to turn it from time to time so every part is soaked in the wine.

Reserving the marinade, drain the ham. Tie it so it keeps its shape and put it in the Dutch oven with a little oil, some washed pork skin, and a layer of chopped aromatics—onions, carrot, celery, parsley. Season with a little salt and a pinch of pepper and brown everything gently, so that the aromatics do not burn.

Now baste the ham—a spoonful every so often from the Marsala marinade and then water, not excessively, and keep cooking, turning often for about 2 hours.

Just before serving, lift out the ham, remove the string, cut it into regular slices, and arrange it around an oval plate. Use a spoon to carefully degrease the remaining sauce, dilute with some water or broth, and strain through a sieve. The sauce should amount to a large glass. Take a teaspoon of potato starch and dissolve it in a cup with two fingers of cold water. Put this, a little at a time, into the boiling sauce, stirring with a wooden spoon. As soon as you see that the sauce thickens, take off the heat and pour in another glass of Marsala and some melted butter and mix to a beautiful golden color. Put a couple of spoons of sauce on the meat and send the rest to the table in the gravy boat.

Pork Offal

CORATA DI MAIALE IN INTINGOLO

Braised Pork Offal

2¼ lb pork offal (lung, heart, liver, spleen)
Lard
Rosemary
Bay leaf
2 tbsp tomato paste
Toast
Salt
Pepper or chili
Optional: red wine

Cut the various parts of the offal into small pieces, each the size of a hazelnut. Take a saucepan, put a spoonful of lard in, and, when it is hot, put down the pieces, all together. Brown well over lively heat until it is very dark; season with plenty of salt, pepper, or with a few pieces of chili, as it must be very spicy. When it has browned, you can, but it is not necessary, baste with half a glass of red wine.

After this first part of the operation, add a sprig of rosemary, half a bay leaf, and a couple of spoons of tomato paste. Mix well, then after a few minutes, add about 4 cups of water. Cover the saucepan and continue cooking over more moderate heat, so that it can take place gently, for about 1 hour.

Meanwhile, prepare bowls with a few slices of toasted bread inside. When the meats are cooked, distribute among the bowls with its juice. This sauce should not be too thick nor too liquid. In the first case, add a little more water; in the second, boil it over high heat to obtain the quantity sufficient to wet the bread.

FEGATELLI DI MAIALE

Pork Liver with Bay

1 lb 5 oz pork liver
7 oz pork caul
Bay leaves
Bread for croutons
Lard
Salt
Pepper

Cut the liver into not too large pieces, season with salt and pepper, wrap them in a square of pork caul, and fix on a skewer or small sticks, alternating them with bay leaves and croutons. (Alternatively, skip the bread and just pin two pieces of wrapped liver together on a toothpick, with a bay leaf in the middle.)

Brush everything with melted lard and cook in a hot oven or pan for about 20 minutes.

◆ ADA SAYS: *A good rule of thumb for preparing pork caul is to fold the net back on itself and immerse it for 2 or 3 minutes in lukewarm water. Then take it out, open it on the table and cut it out. Thus, the net adapts better to the liver and breaks down less easily.*

FEGATELLI DI MAIALE ALLA PETRONIANA

Petronian Pork Liver

1 lb 5 oz pork liver
Sage
Rosemary
1 lemon
Pork caul
Slices bread
Bay leaf
Olive oil
White wine
Salt
Pepper
To serve: fried polenta

Cut the liver into chunks. Season with salt, pepper, sage, chopped rosemary, and a little lemon juice. Then wrap each piece of liver in a net of pork caul.

Take some rather long skewers and thread them as follows: a ⅜ inch-thick slice of bread, a sage leaf, a piece of liver, a leaf of sage, and another slice of bread to finish. Make all the other skewers in the same way and arrange them in a sheet pan with a little oil.

Brush the top of the skewers with oil and put them in a preheated oven for about 20 minutes. Halfway through cooking, turn the skewers to finish cooking them well.

When they are cooked, deglaze the pan with a finger of white wine. Put the livers on a plate and coat them with their cooking juices. Surround them with rectangles or diamonds of polenta deep-fried in oil.

TESTA DI MAIALE IN GALANTINA (COPPA)

Pig's Head Galantine

Pig's head
Pig's trotter
Ham hock
Onion
2 cloves
Carrot
Celery
Parsley
Lemon zest
Pistachios
Pine nuts
Salt
Pepper

Scrape half a pig's head, clean it with boiling water, add one trotter and a ham hock, and put everything in a large pot with plenty of boiling water. Season with a little salt, an onion—stuck with the cloves—a carrot, a celery stalk, and a sprig of parsley.

Let it simmer gently for 2 hours until the bones separate easily from the meat. Then take out the various meats from the pot, remove all the bones and cut the meat into small pieces, collecting them in a bowl.

Season with more salt, plenty of pepper, the grated zest of a lemon or cut into small pieces, a handful of fresh pistachios, kept for about 10 minutes in boiling water and then peeled, and a handful of pine nuts.

Mix well while still hot, then turn out onto a large strong cloth or linen and roll it tightly like a sausage and tie up the ends. Put a weight on it—an oval plate with a chopping board on top—and leave it like that refrigerated for half a day.

After that, remove the binding and serve.

COTECHINO CON CARDI

Cotechino with Cardoons

2¼ lb cotechino sausage
4½ lb cardoons
7 tbsp butter
Grated Parmesan
1 lemon

Take care when cutting the cotechino to keep the slices close to each other in such a way that it still looks as if it were whole.

Rinse the cotechino, prick it here and there, wrap it in a towel, tie it, and add it to a pan with cold water. Bring the water to a boil, then reduce to slow and regular heat and cook for about 2 hours.

As soon as the sausage is cooked, unwrap it from the towel and, while still hot, gently pull off the skin. Let it cool, then slice it.

Clean the cardoons and cut them into pieces of about 4 inches long. Rinse them in water acidulated with lemon juice. In a pot of lightly salted boiling water cook them for about a hour, then drain.

Melt the butter in a large sheet pan, add the cardoons and on these put the slices of cotechino. Sprinkle with plenty of grated Parmesan and place the pan in a moderate oven to brown for about 15 minutes.

ADA SAYS: *Cotechino is a sausage made of pork, lard, pork skin, and rich spices and originates from the Emilia-Romagna region. It is similar to, but usually smaller than, zampone.*

GINOCCHIETTI DI MAIALE IN SALSA CALDA

Ham Hock with Spinach Sauce

3 ham hocks
Bay leaves
Onion
Whole cloves
Carrot
Parsley
2¼ lb spinach
Lemon zest
Bouillon base or bouillon cube
1 lemon
1 egg yolk
Fine and coarse salt
Pepper

Scrape the ham hocks, rinse, and dry them. Then rub them with plenty of coarse salt. Put them in a bowl and cover them with more salt and a few bay leaves, leaving in the fridge for at least 2 days.

After this time, remove from the brine, and rinse them several times. Bring a large pot of water flavored with onion—stuck with cloves—carrot, clove, parsley, and salt to a boil. Add the ham hocks, lower the heat, and cook slowly for about 2 hours.

Clean and rinse the spinach, boil it in a little lightly salted water, and when the leaves collapse squeeze out the water with your hands. Blend or purée and dilute with a few spoons of the broth from the cooking, season with a pinch of pepper, a little salt, and a piece of diced lemon zest.

Heat the sauce, then finish it off the heat, with a teaspoon of bouillon base or half a bouillon cube, a few drops of lemon juice, and an egg yolk.

When the ham hocks are cooked, take them out of the broth, arrange them in a serving dish, and send them to the table accompanied by their sauce.

"Generally speaking, all birds follow the same rules in cooking."

Previously we had to butcher, pluck, and singe the pinfeathers of poultry at home. Today, most birds are sold already cleaned and plucked, which saves a lot of effort and time. It is still advisable to buy a whole bird and joint it yourself, which is a simple procedure. Also, you can save the remaining pieces of carcass to make stock.

Generally speaking, all birds follow the same rules in cooking. Pour a glass of oil over the bird and season with salt and pepper. Usually a whole bird is roasted for 25 minutes per pound. Larger older birds will often be barded before roasting, that is to say wrapped with a slice of prosciutto or lardo, which is then removed 15 minutes before the end of the cooking.

Chicken can also be poached with aromatics such as celery, onion, carrot, and parsley. You need a pot in which the chicken fits snugly. Cover the bird with lightly salted cold water and bring to a simmer. Then add the aromatics. Do not boil, rather let it simmer gently, calculating 25 minutes per pound. Check the doneness regularly and when the bird is cooked through, remove it from the stock and let it cool. Usually, it will be served with its broth.

The turkey is the largest of all poultry species, and in Italy, it is rarely cooked whole. For this reason, more emphasis is placed on recipes here for preparing turkey breast and cutlets, which are typically poached.

Ducks and geese are very tasty and nutritious, but have a fair amount of fat, making them not that easy to digest.

The adult pheasant only weighs a few pounds, and one pheasant can be enough for three or four people. In former times, pheasants were presented at the table adorned with their heads, tails, and wings, but this practice has long since been abandoned. In any case, we recommend that you always buy a female pheasant instead of a male pheasant, because female pheasants, provided they are young, are fatter, more delicate, and tastier.

Wild game has firmer flesh, less fat, and is often all dark meat. Game birds must be young and well nourished, as is true of any poultry, and fortunately most game birds tend to be young as they are hunted annually.

Of other wild animals, rabbit meat is nutritious, very digestible, and delicious, as long as the rabbit is young and the meat is fresh. Rabbit lends itself to a number of very tasty preparations.

The best months for eating hare—an excellent animal, slightly larger than a rabbit—are the winter months during which its meat reaches its maximum flavor. Hare needs to be aged for a few days before cooking. As does venison, which also nearly always needs a strong marinade.

POLLAME E SELVAGGINA

10

Poultry & Game

CHICKEN

CAPPONE ARROSTO IN FORNO

Roast Capon

4½ lb whole capon
2 oz lardo, sliced
Olive oil
Salt
Pepper

Clean the capon; wash it, dry it, and tie it to keep it in shape.

Cover the breast with slices of lardo and place the capon in a pan of the right proportions. Pour half a glass of oil over it. Season with salt and pepper and put in a preheated oven of moderate heat, calculating for the cooking about 25 minutes per pound. About 15 minutes before the end of cooking, remove the lardo and allow the breast to brown.

CAPPONE ARROSTO TARTUFATO

Roast Capon with Truffle

4½ lb whole capon
1¾ oz black truffle
Pork fat
Cognac
Marsala
Olive oil
Salt
Pepper

Clean the capon, then wash and dry it. Carefully remove all the fat and chop it.

Thoroughly rinse the truffles, cleaning them with a hard toothbrush under running water to take away all traces of dirt. With a little knife, thinly pare the skin and chop it together with the pork and capon fat.

Cut the rest of the peeled truffles into wedges and put them in a bowl with salt, pepper, a little Cognac, a little Marsala, and a little oil. Leave them in this marinade for 1 hour.

After an hour of marinating, pour the truffles with their dressing into the fats and knead everything with your hands. Fill the capon with this mixture, sew it, tie it, to keep it in shape and roast in a hot oven at a moderate heat by calculating 25 minutes per pound.

Transfer the capon to a serving dish, pour over the cooking sauce, and send it to the table.

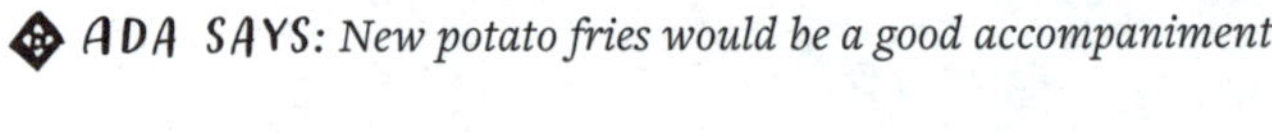

ADA SAYS: *New potato fries would be a good accompaniment.*

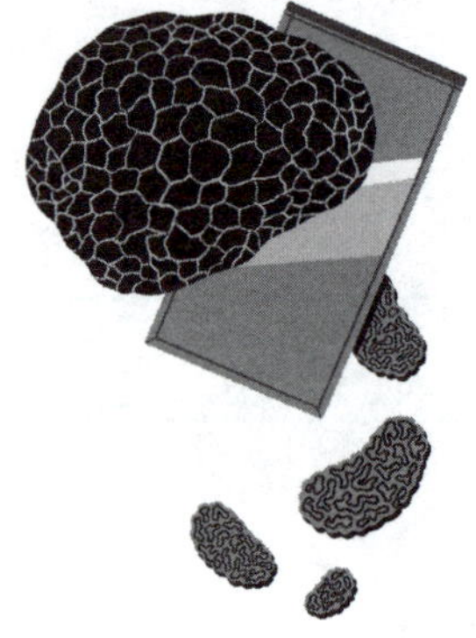

CAPPONE CON ORTAGGI

Roast Capon with Chestnuts and Brussels Sprouts

4½ lb whole capon
2 oz smoked pancetta
Olive oil
20 whole chestnuts
6 carrots
2 tbsp butter
10½ oz Brussels sprouts
White wine
Bouillon base or bouillon cube
Salt

Preheat the oven. Clean the capon, wash it, dry it, and tie it to keep it in shape. Wrap the breast with the smoked pancetta to cover and place it in a roasting pan. Pour over half a glass of oil. Season with a pinch of salt and put it in a preheated oven of moderate heat, turning it often and basting it at intervals with a few spoons of water, calculating 25 minutes per pound.

Make an incision in the skin of the chestnuts: Roast them in the oven without letting them burn and then peel. Peel the carrots, cut into cubes, and cook them with the butter, a pinch of salt, and a few spoons of water.

Remove any yellowed leaves on the outside of the Brussels sprouts, rinse and boil them in a little lightly salted water. As soon as the sprouts are cooked, add them to the carrots. Add the chestnuts and bring to a boil again.

When the capon is cooked, remove it from the pan and lay it down on the cutting board. Carve it into regular pieces.

Drain the fat from the pan and pour in half a glass of white wine and a ladle of water. With a wooden spoon, stir the cooking juices, add the bouillon base—or half a diluted bouillon cube—and, constantly stirring, let it thicken. When the sauce has taken the right consistency, arrange the pieces of capon in an roasting pan, sandwiched with the Brussels sprouts, carrots, and chestnuts. Pour the sauce over everything, place the pan in a hot oven for a few minutes, then place it on a serving plate and send it to the table.

GALLETTI ALLO SPIEDO

Roast Poussins with Anchovies

3 small poussins
Olive oil
2 garlic cloves
Rosemary
2 anchovy fillets
2 tbsp vinegar
Salt
Pepper

Clean the poussins and skewer them for easier handling. Brush with oil and season with salt and pepper.

Put half a glass of oil in a pan, the garlic, and a pinch of rosemary. As soon as the garlic is golden, take it off the heat and add a couple of anchovies, crushed and dissolved with a spoon or two of vinegar.

Oil a baking dish and put the poussins in a warm oven at moderate heat for about 30 minutes. Baste them from time to time with the prepared anchovy sauce, using the skewers to turn them.

When the birds are cooked, split them in two and arrange them on a plate. Serve with sprigs of rosemary.

GALLETTI IN GRATELLA

Broiled Poussins with Deviled Sauce

3 poussins
Butter
6 tomatoes
Parsley
Black olives, pitted
Capers
Breadcrumbs
Dijon mustard
Olive oil
Salt
Pepper

Deviled sauce:
vinegar, chili, bouillon cube, 1 tsp tomato purée, 2 tbsp butter, ¼ cup all-purpose flour, French mustard, peppercorns

Clean the poussins and then cut them in half lengthwise along the backbone. Press down on the breast to flatten and rub with a little salt and pepper and brush with melted butter.

Cut the tomatoes in half and fill with parsley, chopped olives, capers and breadcrumbs. Preheat a broiler to high and cook the poussins for about 30 minutes, broiling the tomatoes alongside.

When the poussins are almost cooked, take out and spread them with mustard and more melted butter and cover with breadcrumbs and put them back to finish cooking so the breadcrumbs take on a beautiful gold color.

Make up a deviled sauce: Put half a glass of vinegar in a saucepan with a grind of pepper and a piece of chili. Let it boil until the vinegar is reduced to less than half. Then, add a glass of boiling water, in which you have dissolved half a stock cube and the tomato purée, and simmer everything slowly for about 10 minutes. Mix the butter with the flour and add it to the sauce. Cook until it thickens. Keep the heat very, very low. Finish the sauce by mixing in the French mustard off the heat, then sieve through a colander and put it in a gravy boat.

Serve with the stuffed tomatoes.

GALLETTI RIPIENI

Braised and Stuffed Poussins

3 poussins
Nutmeg
Marsala
Olive oil
3 sausages
10½ oz veal cutlets
Bay leaf
1 egg yolk
4 tbsp butter
Salt
Pepper

This recipe requires an overnight marination, so the evening before, debone the poussins—or ask your butcher to do it—so you just have the breasts but with the wings and thighs attached.

Put the deboned poussins in a bowl and season with salt, pepper, a grating of nutmeg, and half a glass of Marsala. Marinate overnight in the fridge.

The first thing to do the next day is to prepare the stuffing: Put a little oil in a saucepan and as soon as it is hot, add the chopped sausages—casings removed. When the sausages have taken a light color add the veal, brown on both sides, then season with salt, pepper, and a small, torn bay leaf. Pour in another glass of Marsala, cover, and simmer gently over very low heat for 5 minutes.

Transfer everything into a bowl to cool. Chop the veal finely and blend well with a wooden spoon. Add the egg yolk, and 2 tablespoons of the butter. Cover with plastic wrap and put in the fridge until you are ready.

Spread the poussins out on a work surface—save the marinade for basting. Divide the filling into thirds and spread on the birds. Pull up the edges of the skin to reconstruct the chicken. With a needle and thread, sew up the birds and tie them up with a string.

About 45 minutes before going to the table, melt the rest of the butter in a pot big enough to take all three birds and brown them gently on all sides. Baste with the leftover marinade and a few more spoons of Marsala, from time to time, until the birds are completely cooked.

When they are cooked, remove the string and arrange them on a plate. Serve with a salad of watercress or with peas with ham or with sautéed mushrooms.

GALLINA ALLO SPECCHIO

Chicken and Truffle in Jelly

1 whole chicken
1 onion
1 celery stalk
1 carrot
Parsley
Marsala
3 hard-boiled eggs
7 oz ham or tongue
Black truffle
Salt

Jelly:
1 quart chicken broth, glass Marsala, 2 egg whites, 2 gelatin sheets

Clean the chicken. Fill a pot with water and bring it to a boil. Add the aromatics—onion, celery, carrot, and parsley—and some salt and then lower in the chicken. Reduce the heat and let it simmer gently for about 1½ hours.

Take out the chicken and let it cool—when it is cold it can be more easily cut up. Remove the skin, gently remove the breasts with a small knife, and set them aside; then remove all the remaining meat and chop coarsely.

Make the jelly: Degrease the broth carefully and then clarify with the Marsala and egg whites. Soak the gelatin sheets for about 10 minutes, then squeeze them with your hands and add them to the broth. Bring to a boil, then reduce to very low heat cook for about 2 minutes, constantly stirring. Remove from the heat. As it cools, pour in the Marsala, then let it cool again but not entirely, it must remain liquid.

Now you need a round, deep dish about 8 inches in diameter. Pour on the plate a few spoonfuls of still liquid jelly, mix in the minced chicken, and put in the fridge to set.

Once set, arrange the slices of ham or tongue over the first layer. Cut the breast into regular strips and set them in a radial pattern so that between one ray and the other you can still glimpse the ham. Cut the hard-boiled eggs into small wheels and arrange them and the truffle (cut into slices) on the breasts. Pour in the jelly very carefully so the various ingredients do not shift.

Put the dish in the fridge and leave it until the jelly is completely firmed up.

GALLINA DEL GHIOTTONE

Glutton's Chicken

1 medium chicken
5 oz rigatoni pasta
Grated Parmesan
Butter
Salt

White sauce:
2 tbsp flour, 2 tbsp butter, 1¼ cups milk, nutmeg

Poach the chicken as in Chicken and Truffle in Jelly recipe *(p573)*.

Prepare a rather thin white sauce *(p16)* with the butter, flour and milk listed here, plus a trifle of nutmeg.

Boil the rigatoni in plenty of lightly salted boiling water, keeping them rather al dente. Drain and toss with half of the prepared sauce and a spoon of grated Parmesan.

Take the chicken out of the pot and gently, with a very sharp small knife, slice off the breast meat (keeping it intact) and set aside. With a pair of sturdy kitchen shears, cut off whatever is left of the rib cage to create an open box. Fill this with the rigatoni in cream sauce. Put the breasts back in place to give it its original shape. Heat the remaining sauce, add a spoon of Parmesan, and spoon over the breasts and the rest of the chicken. Transfer the whole construction to a greased baking dish and put in a preheated oven at a lively heat. When the sauce is slightly browned, arrange it on a serving plate and have it brought to the table immediately.

GALLINA IN BELLA VISTA

Chicken Bella Vista

1 large chicken
Butter
Onion
1 carrot
1 celery stalk
Parsley
Bay leaf
Chicken broth or water
Lemon
Vinegar
Olive oil
Jelly *(p52)*
Salt
Pepper

In a Dutch oven, preferably oval, in which the chicken will fit neatly, add some butter, half a chopped onion, a carrot, and the celery cut into small pieces, and chopped parsley. Put the pot on the stove and when the aromatics begin to fry, add the chicken and brown slowly over medium heat, covered.

When everything has taken a very light color, season with salt, pepper, and half a chopped bay leaf. Sprinkle with two ladles of water or broth, so that this liquid reaches only halfway up the chicken. Cover, reduce the heat, and let it cook slowly, turning the chicken from time to time so that it can cook well on all sides. If necessary, add a little more broth, bearing in mind that when cooked, you will need no more than a glass of broth for the cream sauce.

While the chicken is cooking, prepare the mayonnaise *(p19)* with the ingredient amounts listed here (or use store-bought).

When the chicken is done, remove from the pot and let it cool. Strain the cooking juices and skim off the fat.

Make the cream sauce *(p17)* with the butter, flour and chicken broth. Once it has thickened, add the strained cooking juices from the chicken. Continue cooking, stirring, over rather strong heat,

Mayonnaise:
1 egg yolk, ½ cup olive oil, lemon juice

Cream sauce:
2 tbsp butter, 2 tbsp flour, ½ glass broth from the chicken

Vegetable salad:
2 potatoes, 2 carrots, 3½ oz green beans, 3½ oz zucchini, 5 or 6 cornichons, capers, olive oil, vinegar

until that you have obtained a velvety, very thick sauce. Then remove it from the heat and pour it into a cup.

Now prepare a vegetable salad: Boil all the vegetables, cut them into very small cubes, and transfer them to a salad bowl. Add cornichons (cut into thin slices) and a spoon of capers and season everything with salt, abundant pepper, oil, and vinegar. Make sure that the oil and vinegar are not excessive, but only enough to flavor the vegetables.

Remove the skin from the chicken, take off the breast and cut it into slices. Season with very little oil and a few drops of lemon juice. Remove all the remaining meat from the bones and chop finely. Add this minced meat to the velvety cream sauce and mix well.

Having prepared everything in this way, now take a smooth round 1-quart mold without a hole in the middle. Put the mold in the freezer and let it cool well. Make up 1 quart of jelly as in the Chicken and Truffle in Jelly recipe *(p573)* with the gelatin and broth from the chicken.

Then take 2 or 3 spoons of the jelly and slowly turn the mold in all the directions, let this jelly coat the whole of the inside. When a first layer is set, put in another couple of spoonfuls, so as to make a rather thick lining.

Now add the mayonnaise to the vegetable salad and also add a spoon or two of jelly. Mix everything and put a layer in the bottom of the mold.

Now take the velvety sauce, add a couple of spoons of jelly, and mix to evenly combine. Lay this on the chopped breast meat and flatten, then add a second layer of vegetable mayonnaise, another layer of breast, another of sauce until all the material is used and the mold is full. The last layer must be salad.

Once the last layer is done, strain more jelly slowly into the mold, so it fills any small gaps left. Put in the fridge and leave it like that until ready to serve. Put the remaining jelly in the fridge to set well.

When ready to serve, dip the mold for a few seconds in hot water. Carefully unmold onto a serving dish and surround with rectangles or triangles of jelly.

GALLINA IN ROSA

Braised Chicken with Tomato

3 lb 5 oz whole chicken
7 tbsp butter
White wine
Milk
Tomato passata
Salt
Pepper
To serve: new potatoes

Clean a young and plump chicken and cut it into 8 or 10 serving pieces.

Place the pieces in a saucepan, add the butter, ¾ cup of white wine, ¾ cup milk, and the same amount of tomato passata. Season with salt and pepper. Cover and cook slowly until the liquid is transformed into a tasty and thick sauce, about 1 hour.

Take out the chicken pieces, arrange them on a serving dish, cover with the sauce, and surround it with fried new potatoes.

GALLINA IN TERRINA

Chicken Terrine

1 large whole chicken
4 large chicken livers
Black truffle
Cognac
1 lb lean ground pork
9 oz pancetta
Marsala
Butter
White wine
Broth
Meat jelly *(p52)*
Salt
Pepper

The first thing to do is to debone the chicken in such a way as to keep the skin intact—or ask your butcher to do this.

Wash the chicken livers, put them in a bowl, add the truffle (peeled and cut into cubes), and season everything with salt, pepper, and a glass or two of Cognac. Cover the bowl and set it aside.

In a skillet, sauté the ground pork and minced pancetta together. Season with a little salt (pancetta being sufficiently salty), abundant pepper, and a glass of Marsala or Cognac and mix well.

Spread out the boneless chicken in front of you and smooth a layer of filling all over on the inside. Sprinkle with the chopped truffle and in the center put the chicken livers.

Carefully, rebuild the chicken, sewing the opening closed. Then wrap it completely in the slices of pancetta, and tie everything in place with kitchen string.

Butter an oval Dutch oven, put the chicken in, cover with the lid, and put in the fridge overnight, or even for a whole day, to allow the truffle to scent everything.

The next morning, put the Dutch oven on the stove and brown the chicken over a very moderate heat, so it takes a nice golden color. Baste with a glass of white wine, and when the wine evaporates, and enough broth to reach the middle of the bird. Baste again with the broth and close the Dutch oven tightly. Braise for about 1 hour 15 minutes over very moderate heat, or better in a moderate heat oven. The chicken must not cook tumultuously, but slowly, slowly, and the cooking must be gentle in the steam released in the Dutch oven.

While the chicken is cooking, prepare about 1 quart of meat jelly. When it is ready, take out the chicken and let cool. Carefully degrease the cooking juices from the Dutch oven and pour it into another container. Add the prepared jelly to it.

When the chicken is cold, untie the string, free it from the pancetta, and place it in an oval bowl in which it fits snugly. Cover it with the prepared jelly and put everything in the fridge until the sauce is well set.

Place the bowl on an oval platter and send it to the table. This chicken should be cut into slices like a galantine.

ADA SAYS: *If you don't have a Dutch oven, use another pot that closes up tightly and can go into the oven if possible.*

GALLINA NELLA PENTOLA

Chicken in a Pot

1 whole chicken, giblets reserved
1¼ cups beef broth *(p88)*
Abundant aromatics (onion, carrot, celery, parsley)
3 sausages
1 loaf of bread, no crust
Milk
Parsley
Garlic
1 egg yolk
Marsala
3½ tbsp butter
6 cooked shrimp
Salt
Pepper
Optional: black truffle

This is the traditional recipe for the famous chicken that Henry IV of France promised all his subjects.

Fill a large oval pot—in which the chicken will fit easily—with the beef broth and aromatics—onion, carrot, celery, and parsley—and let them cook slowly for about 2 hours.

In the meantime, rinse the chicken, dry it, and stuff it like this: Remove the sausage casings and put the meat in a bowl. On a cutting board, chop the liver and the heart. Add a piece of crustless bread (the size of an egg, dipped in milk and well squeezed in your hands), some parsley, a pinch of garlic (the recipe requires it, but you can also make it without), and chop everything finely. Add this mince to the sausage meat, along with an egg yolk, a spoon of Marsala, the butter, a pinch of salt, a little pepper, and, if possible, a black truffle cut into cubes. Mix well with your hand to form a smooth paste. Fill the chicken with this stuffing and truss the chicken.

Once the broth is ready, place the chicken in the pot and let it cook gently for 1 hour or more. Remove to an oval platter, surround it with a crown of parsley. Garnish with shrimp simmered in lightly salty water for a few minutes.

PETTI DI POLLO AL BURRO CON PISELLI

Chicken Breast with Peas

3 lb 5 oz fresh peas in the pod or 3½ cups shelled or frozen
10½ tbsp butter
1 onion
Sugar
Parsley
2 lb boneless, skinless chicken breast
Flour
Marsala
Salt
Pepper

Shell the peas. Put half the butter and a very finely chopped onion over very low heat, then add the peas. Let them sit for a few moments in the butter, add a few spoons of boiling water, a pinch of salt, and a little pepper. Turn up the heat and cook for 15 to 20 minutes, stirring occasionally. Toward the end of cooking add a teaspoon of sugar and chopped parsley.

Cut the chicken breasts horizontally in half to make thin cutlets and flatten them lightly with the blade of a large wet knife to give them a nice shape. Flour them lightly.

In a large skillet, heat some of the remaining butter, add the cutlets in a single layer and brown them over a high heat, on both sides. Reduce the heat and let them cook for about 10 minutes.

Now pour in half a glass of Marsala, mix carefully and let the breasts flavor for a few minutes. Pour the prepared peas into a serving dish and unite with the chicken. Serve hot.

PETTI DI POLLO FRITTI

Shallow-Fried Chicken

2 lb boneless, skinless chicken breast
Flour
2 eggs
Breadcrumbs
Butter
Lemon
Parsley
Salt
Pepper

Flatten the chicken breasts as above.

Dredge the chicken first in the flour, then the beaten eggs seasoned with salt and pepper, and lastly the breadcrumbs. Warm the butter so it bubbles and fry the cutlets on both sides, taking care not to overcook them.

Arrange the breasts in an oval serving dish and decorate with wedges of lemon and parsley.

PETTI DI POLLO IN BESCIAMELLA

Chicken Breast in White Sauce

2 lb boneless, skinless chicken breast
Flour
7 tbsp butter
Marsala
Parsley
Salt
Pepper

White sauce:
3½ tbsp butter, 6½ tbsp flour, 2 cups milk

Cut the chicken breast into cutlets as above, then pound and lightly flour them.

In a large skillet, heat up a part of the butter, add as many breasts as can fit in a single layer, let them brown over high heat on both sides. Reduce the heat and let them cook for about 10 minutes. Then pour in the Marsala, stir carefully and let them flavor for a few minutes.

Make a white sauce *(p16)* with the butter, flour and milk listed here.

Butter a baking dish, arrange the breasts inside, cover with the sauce, and put in a preheated oven for about 10 minutes. Garnish with parsley.

POLLO AL FORNO

Roast Chicken

1 whole chicken
2 oz pancetta
Olive oil
Salt
To serve: watercress

You can cook this in two ways: on a spit over an open fire or in the oven.

Put the chicken in a bowl, sprinkle with plenty of oil and generously with salt. Wrap the chicken breast with a few thin slices of pancetta held in place with kitchen string. Put it in a well warmed oven, where it will have to stay about 1 hour, according to its size and its quality. You can flip it a couple of times. When the chicken is almost cooked, remove the pancetta and let the breast color, too.

Carve it so it can be reassembled to look like it is whole and guests can help themselves with ease. Garnish the dish with watercress.

POLLO ALLA CACCIATORA

Hunter's Chicken

1 whole chicken
Olive oil
Onion
Parsley
Celery
Garlic
2 bay leaves
White wine
Salt
Pepper

Clean the chicken and cut it into serving pieces.

In a pot, put a little oil, half a chopped onion, a little parsley, a little chopped celery, and a little crushed garlic. As they start to brown and soften, add the pieces of chicken, salt, and pepper.

When the chicken begins to brown, add the bay leaves and keep going until the chicken has become a beautiful dark gold color.

At this point, baste it with half a glass of white wine, stir and, when the wine has evaporated, baste with a little water, reduce the heat, cover and let it finish cooking, for about 45 minutes.

ADA SAYS: *This preparation is among the best known, therefore we advise you to resort to it when you have a very good free-range chicken.*

POLLO ALLA CACCIATORA CON OLIVE

Braised Chicken with Olives

1 whole chicken
3 tbsp olive oil
3 garlic cloves
White wine
2 tbsp vinegar
40 Gaeta olives, pitted
2 anchovy fillets
Salt
Pepper

Cut the chicken into serving pieces.

Put the oil in a pan with the whole garlic cloves and, when it is really hot, add the chicken, season with salt and pepper, and let it brown to a beautiful dark gold color.

Only then, baste with half a glass of white wine, the vinegar, half the olives left whole. Chop the rest of the olives and the anchovies and stir into the sauce.

Wait until the wine has reduced a little and pour in a little water. As soon as the boiling resumes, reduce the heat and leave to finish cooking and the sauce to thicken for about 45 minutes.

POLLO ALLA MARENGO

Chicken Marengo

1 whole chicken
Olive oil
6 tomatoes
White wine
2 garlic cloves
Bread, for croutons
6 shrimp
3 fried eggs
Parsley
Salt

Cut the chicken into serving pieces. Place the breasts in a pan containing very hot oil—do not use butter or lard. Sear the chicken breasts over high heat and as soon as they are golden, remove them.

Add the remaining chicken pieces and when all of them have been seared, drain the oil and add the tomatoes—peeled, seeded, and chopped—a glass of white wine, and the crushed garlic cloves. Reduce a bit. Return the breasts to the pan to cook a couple more minutes.

Place the chicken and sauce into a serving dish and surround it with croutons fried in oil, shrimp cooked in white wine, and fried eggs. Garnish with chopped parsley and serve.

ADA SAYS: *This preparation belongs to classical cuisine and its origin goes back to the Battle of Marengo in 1799.*

POLLO ALLA PANNA

Chicken Braised in Milk

1 whole chicken
3½ tbsp butter
Milk
Potato starch
Cream
Salt

Choose a tender and plump chicken. Wash and dry and put it in an oval Dutch oven where it fits tightly with some butter.

Let it brown slowly without turning too much. Season with salt and when it takes on a light uniform color, baste with a glass of warm milk. Cover the Dutch oven and put it in a preheated oven of moderate heat. Leave for about 45 minutes, turning it again from time to time.

Transfer the chicken to a serving dish and keep warm. Tilt the pot, and remove the fat that has collected on the surface. Heat the sauce well and then thicken it with a little potato starch.

When the sauce is slightly thickened, lower the heat as much as possible and, in small quantities, add half a glass of cream, stirring with a spoon. Coat the chicken with a few spoons of the sauce and send the rest to the table in a sauce boat.

POLLO ALLA SALVIA

Braised Chicken with Sage

1 whole chicken
Butter
Olive oil
White wine
2 oz prosciutto
Sage
Salt
Pepper

Clean a young and plump chicken and cut it into serving pieces.

Put a spoon of butter and a spoon of oil in a pan, add the chicken pieces, season with salt and pepper, and let them brown until a rather dark gold. At this point, drain the fat and baste with a glass of white wine. Add the prosciutto in strips and a few fresh sage leaves.

Moderate the heat, cover, and let it braise slowly until the chicken is cooked and the sauce is reduced, about 45 minutes. Must be served immediately.

POLLO ARROSTO

Roast Chicken with Potatoes

1 lemon
1 whole chicken
Bouillon cube
2¼ lb potatoes
Olive oil
Rosemary
Salt

Cut the lemon in half and put inside the chicken along with the bouillon cube. Wash, peel, and cut the potatoes into slices. Cover the bottom of a Dutch oven with the potatoes. Season them with oil, salt, pepper and a few sprigs of rosemary. Place the chicken on top and put the Dutch oven in a preheated oven with good heat and cook for about 1 hour.

During cooking you can turn the chicken a couple of times and mix it in with the potatoes. It should be eaten straight out of the oven.

POLLO BRACIATO CON FUNGHI

Braised Chicken with Porcini Mushrooms

1 whole chicken
2 tbsp butter
Olive oil
1 onion
Broth
Tomato passata
1 lb porcini mushrooms
Salt
Pepper

Put the chicken in a Dutch oven in which it can fit snugly, with butter, oil and a finely chopped onion. Set the pot over light heat and slowly brown everything, basting from time to time with a ladle of broth, a little at a time.

When the meat and onion are well browned, season with a pinch of salt, a pinch of pepper, and ¾ cup of tomato passata. Cover and cook slowly for about 45 minutes. After this time, the chicken will be cooked.

Wash and cut the porcini into slices. Remove the chicken from the pot and in its place put the mushrooms. Add a little more salt and cook the mushrooms over high heat, stirring often.

Return the chicken to the Dutch oven for a few minutes. Then carve and serve surrounded by its very tasty garnish of mushrooms.

POLLO CON LE PRUGNE

Chicken with Prunes

1 whole chicken
7 tbsp butter
1 onion
Carrot
Celery
Parsley
10½ oz prunes
Salt
Pepper

Cream sauce:
1¾ tbsp butter, 3 tbsp flour,
1 cup chicken broth

Clean a plump chicken and cut it into serving pieces.

In a pan, melt the butter, and add the chopped onion, carrot, celery, and parsley and sauté for a few minutes. Add the pieces of chicken, mix carefully, and let everything brown until all the ingredients are golden. Season with salt and pepper and then cover with 6 cups of boiling water. Boil over moderate heat for 1½ hours.

Put the prunes in warm water for 1 hour, then pit them and cut them into pieces. Put them to cook in a small saucepan with a glass of water for about 10 minutes.

Make a cream sauce *(p17)* with the flour, butter, and the broth from the chicken and finally mix in the prunes.

When cooked, arrange the chicken pieces on a serving dish and cover with the sauce. Serve immediately.

POLLO CON PEPERONI

Chicken with Peppers

1 whole chicken
Olive oil
2 garlic cloves
White wine
1 lb yellow and red bell peppers
1 onion
Salt
Pepper

Clean the chicken and cut into small pieces.

In a large saucepan, heat some oil and the garlic. As soon as the garlic has browned, remove it and put the chicken in the saucepan, season with salt and pepper and let it brown over high heat until it has taken on a nice dark golden color.

Pour ½ cup of wine into the pan, let it evaporate. Then add the chopped peppers and a sliced onion. Stir occasionally and add a little water if necessary. Continue to cook until the chicken is done.

POLLO FRITTO ALLA FIORENTINA

Fried Chicken Florentine Style

1 whole chicken
Parsley
Olive oil
Lemon
Flour
2 eggs
Salt
Pepper

Clean the chicken and cut into serving pieces. Put the chicken pieces in a dish, season with salt, pepper, parsley, oil, and the juice of a lemon, and leave them to marinate for an hour or two.

Dry the chicken pieces, flour them and dredge them in the beaten eggs. Fry them in a pan with plenty of moderately hot oil for about 10 minutes, then remove, drain well, put them to dry on paper towels, sprinkle with salt, and serve hot surrounded by wedges of lemon.

ADA SAYS: *There is a similar recipe for fried chicken, Viennese style, where you dredge chicken pieces not only in flour but also breadcrumbs and then dredge them in beaten eggs and fry.*

POLLO IN CASSERUOLA

Chicken Braised in a Dutch Oven

1 whole chicken
10 tbsp butter
14 oz spring onions
2¾ cups shelled fresh peas
Marsala
Bouillon base
Salt

Put the chicken in a buttered Dutch oven in which it fits snugly. Season with a pinch of salt, cover, and set the pot over a very low heat, taking care to let it cook slowly. From time to time turn it over and baste it with a few spoons of the cooking juices, immediately covering again—it cooks better in its own steam. After about 45 minutes it will be cooked. Remove from the pot and keep it hot.

While the chicken is cooking, peel the onions and put them in boiling water for 5 minutes. Drain and arrange in a single layer in a pan with 3 tablespoons of butter. Cook over a low heat, adding a few spoons of water and a pinch of salt. Meanwhile, cook the peas over high heat, with 3 tablespoons of butter and some spoonfuls of water.

Skim off and discard all the fat from the liquid left in the pan from the chicken and dilute the remaining juices with Marsala. Add ½ teaspoon of bouilllon base, mix, bring briefly to a boil, then pour it into a saucepan and keep it warm.

Take out the chicken and lay over the peas and spring onions. Pour the hot sauce over the top and send immediately to the table.

POLLO IN INSALATA

Chicken Salad

1 whole chicken
Olive oil
1 head lettuce
3 bell peppers
2 hard-boiled eggs
3 tomatoes
Vinegar or lemon juice
Salt

Put the chicken in roasting pan, sprinkle it with oil and generously with salt. Put it immediately in a preheated oven with a good heat and roast for about 25 minutes per pound. Turn it a couple of times and baste with the cooking juices. As soon as it is cooked and cooled, pull the meat off the bones and cut into pieces.

Wash the lettuce and slice it very thinly. Roast and peel the peppers and cut them into thin strips. Cut the eggs into small pieces. Wash the tomatoes and cut them into slices.

Put the chicken pieces in a salad bowl, season with oil and vinegar or lemon juice, and add the lettuce, peppers, eggs, and tomatoes. Jumble up carefully.

POLLO IN MAIONESE

Chicken Mayonnaise

1 whole chicken
Carrot
Celery stalk
1 onion
Olive oil
Vinegar
Parsley
Salt
Pepper
Russian salad *(p725)*
Optional: broccoli

Fill a saucepan in which the chicken fits easily with water. Bring the water to a boil, add a carrot, celery, an onion, and finally the chicken. Return to a boil, then reduce the heat and let it simmer gently for about 1 hour.

When the chicken is cooked, remove it from its broth and let it cool. Pull the meat off the bones and cut it into pieces. Season with salt, pepper, oil and vinegar and a little parsley and leave it like that for a couple of hours.

Make a Russian salad with potatoes, carrots, green beans, cornichons, and capers with mayonnaise.

On the bottom of an oval plate, spread a layer of the Russian salad and top with the pieces of chicken. Cover the chicken pieces with the rest of the salad and with a spatula try to give a rounded shape. Spread mayonnaise over this dome. Keep the dish in the fridge until ready to serve. Serve perhaps with broccoli.

POLLO IN MAIONESE ALLA FRANCESE

Chicken Mayonnaise French Style

1 whole chicken
Carrot
Celery
1 onion
Olive oil
Vinegar or lemon juice
Parsley
Mustard
Green lettuce
Mayonnaise, store-bought
Salt
Pepper

Poach the chicken with the carrot, celery, and onion as above. When it is cool enough to handle, pull the meat from the bones and cut the chicken into pieces. Season with salt, pepper, oil, and vinegar and a little parsley and leave it like that for a couple of hours.

On the bottom of an oval plate, make a layer of lettuce leaves, well washed, dried, finely chopped, and seasoned with oil, vinegar, salt, and a little mustard. On this salad bed, arrange the chicken pieces and cover with the mayonnaise.

Keep the dish in the fridge until ready to serve.

POLLO IN PADELLA

Pan-fried Chicken

1 whole chicken
Olive oil
2 slices prosciutto
Garlic
White wine
6 tomatoes
Broth
Salt
Pepper

Clean the chicken and cut it into serving pieces. Put a little oil in a pan and when hot, fry the prosciutto cut into small pieces. Add the chicken and season with salt and pepper. When they have taken on a nice golden color, add a small piece of diced garlic and half a glass of white wine.

After the wine has evaporated, add the tomatoes—peeled, seeded, and chopped—and, if necessary, add a few spoons of broth.

Keep the cooking over high heat. The chicken should be ready in 45 minutes. Send it to the table immediately, making sure that the sauce is thick, dark, and there isn't too much of it.

POLLO IN PASTICCIO

Chicken Pie

1 whole chicken
12 tbsp butter
6 small veal cutlets
1 oz dried mushrooms
2 oz prosciutto
2 large potatoes
Onion
Parsley
1¼ cups flour
Broth
Salt
Pepper

Clean the chicken and cut into serving pieces. Put a pan with 2 tablespoons of butter on the stove and when the butter is hot, add the chicken pieces just to lightly brown, not to cook through. Remove the chicken pieces.

Add the veal to the same pan and cook briskly, so as to immediately brown the slices on both sides without holding them too much on heat. Set them aside.

In the meantime, soak the dried mushrooms in cold water, then rinse thoroughly. Cook the mushrooms in the leftover butter and in the same pan as the veal, adding a little water.

Cut some slices of prosciutto, the size of a domino. Peel and dice the potatoes. Chop the onion and some parsley.

To make the pie: Mound the flour on a work surface. Add 5 tablespoons of butter, about 4 spoons of water, and a pinch of salt. Mix to form a dough, shape into a disk, and let it rest in the fridge for 30 minutes.

Generously butter a baking dish about 8 inches in diameter. On the bottom of the dish, arrange the chicken pieces, interweaving them with the veal and the rectangles of prosciutto. Season with salt and pepper, but salt moderately, bearing in mind that the prosciutto is already a little salty in itself.

Arrange the diced potatoes over the meat. Add the mushrooms, onion, and finally the parsley. Add a glass of broth or water and put here and there, little pieces of butter. Now roll out the dough on a floured surface to a thickness of just ⅜ inch. Wet the rim of the baking dish, place the dough over the filling and press it on the rim so that sticks well. Trim off the surplus dough, and make a hole of about ⅜ inch in diameter in the middle so the steam can escape during cooking.

Put the finished pie in a preheated oven of moderate heat for about 45 minutes. If the pastry tends to become too brown, cover it with a sheet of aluminum foil.

When it is ready, put the dish on a plate and have it brought to the table.

POLLO IN POTACCHIO ALLA MARCHIGIANA

Braised Chicken Le Marche Style

1 whole chicken
Garlic
Rosemary
Olive oil
White wine
1 cup canned tomatoes
Bell peppers
Salt
Pepper

Clean the chicken and cut it into serving pieces. Chop the garlic and rosemary and fry them in abundant oil. When they have taken a dark blond color, lay in the chicken pieces and brown, adding salt, pepper, and a glass of white wine. When this is well evaporated, add the tomatoes, bring slowly to a moderate heat, and braise for about 45 minutes.

Arrange the chicken in a serving dish. Garnish with roast peppers.

ADA SAYS: *This recipe is typical of the Marche cuisine, well known by connoisseurs for its goodness and succulence. The recipe is very simple, it can be done quickly but its execution will earn the deserved admiration of diners.*

POLLO IN SALSA PICCANTE

Braised Chicken in a Piquant Sauce

1 whole chicken
Olive oil
1 onion
Flour
White wine
6 tomatoes or 9 oz canned tomatoes
Bouillon cube
Vinegar
Anchovy
Cornichon
Capers
Garlic
Parsley
Bread, for croutons
Salt
Pepper

Clean the chicken and cut into serving pieces. Put a pan with a little oil over moderate heat with a chopped onion. Sauté without browning too much.

Add the chicken pieces, let them brown and season with salt and abundant pepper. When the chicken has taken on a nice dark golden tint, sprinkle it with half a spoon of flour and then baste with half a glass of white wine. Let the wine evaporate well before adding the tomatoes—peeled, seeded, and chopped. Cook the tomato a little, and then cover the chicken with boiling water in which you have diluted a bouillon cube. Moderate the heat, cover, and let it finish cooking slowly for about 45 minutes. When fully cooked, the sauce can be well reduced.

Meanwhile, put half a glass of vinegar on the stove in a saucepan and let it boil until it has reduced by almost two-thirds. Chop a washed and boned anchovy, a couple of cornichons, a spoon of capers, garlic, and some parsley. Put all this in a cup and dissolve it in the boiled vinegar.

About 5 minutes before removing the chicken from the heat, add the vinegar mixture, stir, let it flavor and then pour the chicken into the dish together with its sauce, which must be very thick. You can surround the chicken with fried bread croutons.

Chicken Offal

FEGATINI DI POLLO ALLA SALVIA

Pan-Fried Chicken Livers with Sage

1 lb 5 oz chicken livers
5 tbsp butter
Sage
2 oz prosciutto
Marsala
Salt
Pepper
Optional: croutons cut in triangles, fried in oil

With a sharp knife, remove any green parts from the livers and cut each one into two or three pieces. Put 3½ tablespoons of butter in a pan and, when it is hot, add the livers, season with salt, pepper, and a few fresh, chopped sage leaves. Almost immediately add the prosciutto cut into strips. The livers cook quickly, so in no time they will be ready; a prolonged cooking would have no other effect than that of hardening the livers and the prosciutto.

Remove the pan from the heat, arrange the livers with the strips of prosciutto in a warm serving dish. Return the pan to the heat, pour in a spoon or two of Marsala, stir, let the wine evaporate a little, add another 1½ tablespoons of butter, stir quickly and pour this sauce over the livers.

Have it brought to the table immediately. If you want, you can surround the dish with triangular croutons fried in butter.

FEGATINI DI POLLO CON CARCIOFI

Chicken Livers with Artichokes

6 artichoke hearts
Lemon
Olive oil
1 lb 5 oz chicken livers
Butter
6 slices prosciutto
Parsley
Salt
Pepper
To garnish: croutons cut in triangles, fried in oil

Cut the artichoke hearts into wedges and keep them in a bowl of water acidulated with a squeeze of lemon and some salt.

Put a little oil in a pan, take the artichokes out of the water, dry them, and fry over a medium heat. Season with salt and if during cooking they tend to dry out too much, wet them with a little water. The important thing is that the artichokes, when fully cooked, should be soft.

In the meantime, prepare the livers, removing the gall and any green parts, and cut, depending on their size, into two or more pieces.

Put a pan with some butter on the heat, add the livers, season them with salt and pepper, and let them cook quickly. Before taking them off the heat, add the prosciutto cut into strips. Just heat the prosciutto through and then pour everything into the pan with the artichokes.

Stir, keeping the pan on the heat for another minute or two. Add a spoonful of chopped parsley and squeeze in a little lemon juice. Pour everything into a well heated serving dish, taking care to send it to the table immediately. You can complete the preparation by surrounding it with a crown of croutons, cut into triangles and fried in abundant hot oil.

PASTICCIO DI FEGATINI

Chicken Liver Pie

1¾ cups flour
2 tbsp butter
9 oz chicken livers
Bay leaf
Marsala or Cognac
10½ oz bacon
7 oz lean ground pork
2 eggs
Bouillon cube jelly *(p52)*
Salt
Pepper
Optional: black truffle

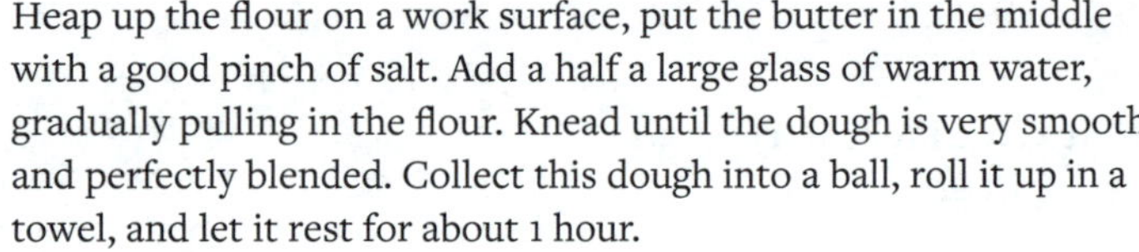

Heap up the flour on a work surface, put the butter in the middle with a good pinch of salt. Add a half a large glass of warm water, gradually pulling in the flour. Knead until the dough is very smooth and perfectly blended. Collect this dough into a ball, roll it up in a towel, and let it rest for about 1 hour.

Meanwhile, remove the gall and any green traces from the livers. If they are too big, cut them into two or three pieces, but without chopping them too much. Put them in a bowl, season with salt, pepper, and half a bay leaf and sprinkle with a little Cognac. If you want to add a black truffle, peel it, cut it out into cubes and add the trimmings to the bowl with the livers. Cover with a plate and set aside.

Now prepare the filling: Chop two-thirds of the bacon and mix in with the ground pork and if you are using them, any trimmings from the truffle. Season with salt and pepper and add an egg yolk and a little Marsala or Cognac, and mix well preferably using your hands.

Use a springform pan of about 6 inches diameter. Divide the dough in half and roll out one piece to a thickness of about ¼ inch. Line the pan with the dough.

Very thinly cut the rest of the bacon, flatten them with a meat mallet to thin them even more and line the bottom and sides of the pan over the dough. Keep three or four slices back for the top.

Place a layer of filling on the bottom, then some liver, then some truffle cubes, if you are using. Cover with another layer of filling, and so on, ending with a last layer of filling. Cover with the reserved slices of bacon.

Now roll out the remaining dough, cutting out a lid a little wider than the pan. Press the lid down on the pie and decorate with the leftover pastry trimmings. Brush a beaten egg over the top of the pie, and then with a small knife make a circular hole in the middle.

Roll out a small piece of leftover dough and make a donut to fit around the hole in the middle. Finally, take a strip of parchment paper and roll a chimney 1¼ inches high, and slip it down the hole, which will prevent the pie from shrinking.

Bake in a preheated oven at moderate heat for about 1 hour. Let it cool. After a few hours, when the pie is completely cold, make 2 cups of bouillon cube jelly. Take about 1 cup of the jelly and place it in a small pan. Put the pan in the fridge until the jelly is like oil, then pour it, a little at a time, into the central hole of the pie. This thick jelly will fill up any spaces, as well as cement the pie better and giving it even more taste.

Put the pie in the fridge for a few hours, so the jelly can set, and only then unmold it and arrange it in the serving dish. Cut the remaining jelly into rectangles or triangles to decorate.

REGAGLIE DI POLLO

Chicken Gifts

1 lb 5 oz chicken gifts (gizzards, livers, hearts)
3½ tbsp butter
1 onion
3½ oz prosciutto
Broth
Salt

Open the gizzards, without dividing completely, take out and discard the inner sacs, and rinse and boil in a little water. Prepare the livers, removing any green spots of gall, then cut them into two or three pieces.

Put the butter in a small saucepan and sauté some finely chopped onion and prosciutto. Add the gizzards, then after a while put in the hearts and finally the livers, which just need to be briefly cooked.

When all the gifts are browned, sprinkle them with 2 tablespoons of broth and leave them to flavor over very low heat.

ADA SAYS: *Chicken gifts—the regaglie—can be eaten as a main course or they can serve as a condiment for pasta dishes, fried bread, or flans.*

REGAGLIE DI POLLO ALLA FINANZIERA NEL FLAN DI CREMA

Chicken Gifts Flan Financier

10½ oz ground beef
1 cup breadcrumbs
Milk
10½ tbsp butter
5 eggs
Grated Parmesan
Nutmeg
Flour
Olive oil
1 onion
10½ oz sausages
1¼ cups tomato passata
7 oz chicken gifts (livers, gizzards, hearts, kidneys)
2 oz dried mushrooms
Salt
Pepper

White sauce:
7 tbsp butter, 7 tbsp flour, 3 cups milk

Start by preparing the meatballs: Mix the ground beef with the breadcrumbs, soaked in milk and squeezed between the hands. When the mixture is homogeneous, mix in 2 tablespoons butter, a beaten egg, ⅓ cup of grated Parmesan, a pinch of salt and a trifle of nutmeg. Knead a little longer, then, shape many small balls of equal size and flour them lightly. Put some butter in a large pan and sauté the meatballs over moderate heat. As soon as they are cooked, set them aside.

Put some oil in a skillet with a finely chopped onion and when they brown, prick the sausages and add them. Let the sausages brown slightly, then add the tomato passata and a little salt.

Cut the gizzards in half and take out the inner sacs and add the gizzards to the sausage and tomatoes. Reconstitute the mushrooms in cold water, wash, and remove any earthy residue.

After 20 minutes, remove the sausages from the saucepan and, in their place, put the mushrooms. Cover and if necessary add a ladle of water, then braise over moderate heat. When the sauce is done and the mushrooms are cooked, take out the gizzards and chop into small pieces and keep with the meatballs.

Now make the flan: Prepare a thick white sauce *(p16)* with the butter, flour and milk listed here. Season with salt and nutmeg, pour it into a bowl, and let it cool.

Once the white sauce is cool, add 4 eggs, one at a time, mixing well with a wooden spoon. Pour the mixture into a buttered flan dish and bake in a water bath for about 45 minutes, until it is firm. Remove from the water bath and let it rest for a few minutes, then turn it out onto a serving plate.

And here we are at the assembly of the financier. Cut the sausages into two or three pieces, then put them in the pan with the mushrooms and tomato. Also add in the meatballs and the gizzards. In another pan warm some butter, cut the livers into 2 or 3 pieces and gently fry for a few minutes with a pinch of salt and pepper. Then add them also to the other meats and mushrooms.

Carefully, using a small ladle, fill the center of the flan with the financier, elevating it to a dome and serve immediately.

TURKEY

TACCHINO ARROSTO IN FORNO

Roast Turkey

6 lb 10 oz young turkey
2 oz prosciutto in slices
Olive oil
Salt
Pepper
Optional: flour

Clean the turkey, rinse it, and dry it. Cover the turkey breast with thin slices of prosciutto kept in place with kitchen string. Season it with salt and pepper, put it in a roasting pan, brush with oil, and place in a preheated oven of moderate heat, calculating about 25 minutes per pound for cooking.

About 15 minutes before the end of cooking, remove the slices of prosciutto and let the breast brown.

ADA SAYS: *A little secret to give the skin a magnificent golden color and a very appetizing crunch: When you have removed the slices of prosciutto and the turkey breast has started to color, sprinkle the breast with a little flour, and then collecting a little fat from the bottom of the pan with a spoon, baste slowly on the floured breast. Close the oven and after a few minutes repeat the operation, three or four times. When you baste with the fat, do it with the utmost delicacy so as not to wash off any flour.*

TACCHINO ARROSTO RIPIENO

Roast Turkey Stuffed with Chestnuts

20 chestnuts
20 green olives
6 sausages
3½ oz pancetta
6 lb 10 oz young turkey
Flour
Optional: black truffle

Nick the skin of the chestnuts and put them to roast in the oven, so that they cook without coloring. When they are cooked, peel them. Take the pits out of the green olives and remove the casings from the sausages. Chop half of the pancetta and mix everything together. Fill the turkey with this stuffing. You can, if desired, add diced black truffle.

Once the turkey is full, sew up the skin. Finally truss the turkey, wrap the breast with thin slices of pancetta. Keep them in place with kitchen string.

Put the turkey in a preheated oven at moderate heat, calculating 25 minutes per pound. Occasionally baste the turkey with the cooking juices.

About 15 minutes before the end of cooking, remove the pancetta and let the breast brown. Place the turkey on a round platter and send it to the table whole.

TACCHINO ARROSTO TARTUFATO

Roast Turkey with Truffle

2 oz black truffle
10½ oz pork fatback
Cognac
Marsala
Olive oil
1 medium-size young turkey
Salt
Pepper

Thoroughly rinse the truffles by cleaning them with a stiff brush under water, and with a small knife, thinly peel off the skins, which you will chop along with the pork fat. Set the pork fat aside.

Cut the rest of the truffles into wedges and put them in a bowl with salt, pepper, a little Cognac, a little Marsala, and a little oil, leaving them in this marinade for 1 hour.

Pour the truffles with their marinade into the pork fat and mix everything with your hands. Fill the turkey with this mixture and sew it up. Put it to roast in a preheated oven of moderate heat calculating 25 minutes per pound.

From time to time baste the turkey with its cooking juices. Take the turkey out of the oven, place it on a round serving dish and send it to the table whole.

TACCHINO RIPIENO ALLA LOMBARDA

Stuffed Turkey Lombardy Style

14 oz ground beef
9 oz sausage meat
3 eggs
9 tbps grated Parmesan
Nutmeg
3½ oz prunes
3 apples
15 chestnuts
Pancetta
White wine
1 whole turkey breast
Olive oil
2 oz prosciutto
Sage
Rosemary
Broth
Potato starch
Salt
Pepper
Optional: giblets

In a bowl, mix the ground beef, sausage meat, 2 or 3 eggs, plenty of grated Parmesan, salt, pepper and nutmeg. Mix well. Pit the prunes, peel, core, and chop the apples, and peel the chestnuts. Mix these well. If you have the giblets, chop the liver, heart, and kidney well with a handful of large cubes of pancetta.

Add a small glass of white wine and carefully pack the turkey with this filling. Pull the skin of the neck onto the back and sew it up. With the same needle, prick it here and there and tie with string.

Generously oil a large oval Dutch oven, lay in the bottom a few slices of prosciutto, a little sage, and a little rosemary. Place the prepared turkey on this aromatic bed. Put the pot on the stove and brown the turkey to a golden color, turning it frequently so that it colors equally well on all sides. When it is well colored, drain all the fat and baste the turkey with half a glass of white wine. Moderate the heat and braise for 25 minutes per pound, basting, at intervals, with broth, a ladle at a time. Do not forget, from time to time, to take with a spoon a little of the cooking juices and pour it slowly over the turkey breast.

When the turkey is cooked, take it out of the pot, free it from the string, and arrange it on the serving dish.

Deglaze the cooking juices well and, if there is not enough, add a little broth. Strain through a sieve into a saucepan, degrease it well and, if needed, bind the sauce with a little potato starch. With a few spoonfuls of this sauce, coat the turkey breast and send out the rest in a sauce boat.

FILETTI DI TACCHINO AI FUNGHETTI

Turkey Cutlets Pan-Fried with Mushrooms

2 lb turkey breast cutlets
2 eggs
1 cup breadcrumbs
9 tbsp butter
10½ oz mushrooms
Lemon
Parsley
Bouillon base or bouillon cube
Marsala
Potato starch
Salt

Flatten the cutlets with the side of a wet knife, sprinkle with salt, and dredge in the beaten eggs and the breadcrumbs.

In a frying pan, large enough so the cutlets can fit side by side in a single layer, melt 7 tablespoons of butter. When it melts, and before it colors, lay in the turkey and pan-fry over moderate heat for about 10 minutes, taking care that they do not color too much.

Now prepare the mushrooms like this: Wash, dry and trim them and cut into thin slices. Sauté with the rest of the butter, a squeeze of a lemon, and some salt. Keep the heat rather lively for the first 5 minutes, then lower the heat and let it finish cooking for another a few minutes. Finish them with a handful of chopped parsley.

Then prepare the sauce: Dissolve the bouillon base or a bouillon cube in a glass of Marsala and add the potato starch and a pinch of salt. Pour the sauce over the turkey, simmer for a few more minutes to thicken, then arrange the cutlets in a serving dish, pour the sauce over them, and surround with the mushrooms.

FILETTI DI TACCHINO ALLA BOLOGNESE

Turkey Cutlets Bolognese

3½ tbsp butter
2 lb turkey breast cutlets
Flour
Marsala
Broth
White truffle
Grated Parmesan
Salt

Warm the butter in a large, wide pan in which the cutles will fit in in a single layer.

Pound the cutlets lightly with the side of a wet knife, to give them a beautiful shape and smooth them a little. Then lightly flour them and, as soon as the butter is hot, put them in the pan, frying them quickly on both sides over lively heat. Season with salt and, just as they slightly color, baste with a little Marsala. When it has evaporated, push the turkey to one side of the pan, pour in a few spoons of broth, scrape the bottom of the pan and turn the turkey in the juices so they are well coated with a little sauce.

Remove the pan from the heat and, working quickly, put on each cutlet very thin slices of white truffle and plenty of grated Parmesan. Splash with the broth and sauce, cover, and put back over moderate heat. The steam from the broth will melt the Parmesan, completing this fragrant preparation.

FILETTI DI TACCHINO ALLA MODENESE

Turkey Cutlets Modena Style

2 lb turkey breast cutlets
2 eggs
Breadcrumbs
Butter, for frying
3½ oz ham
5 oz Fontina or Gruyère
Salt

Pound the cutlets with the side of a wet knife to give them a good shape. Dredge them through the beaten eggs, and then the breadcrumbs and fry them in butter to a golden color. Salt them lightly.

Place them immediately in a baking dish, cover with a slice of ham and another of Fontina or Gruyère cutting the slices to have the same shape as the cutlets.

Put them immediately in a very hot oven and, as soon as the cheese melts, arrange the turkey on the plate and immediately send them to the table.

FILETTI DI TACCHINO AL PROSCIUTTO

Turkey Cutlets with Prosciutto

2 lb turkey breast cutlets
Flour
2 eggs
Breadcrumbs
Butter, for frying
6 slices prosciutto
9 tbsp grated Parmesan
1 cup tomato passata
Parsley
Salt

Pound the cutlets with the side of a wet knife, but not too much. Flour them, dredge them in the beaten eggs, and then the breadcrumbs and pan-fry them in butter, taking care not to overcook. Salt them lightly.

In the meantime, prepare 6 slices of prosciutto of the same shape as the cutlets. As soon as the cutlets are cooked, place a slice of prosciutto on each one and then a slightly domed half spoon of grated Parmesan. Line up all the cutlets in a baking dish, place on each mound of Parmesan a few very small pieces of butter and bake in a very hot oven just long enough to melt the cheese.

To serve, decorate the cutlets, at one end with a little tomato passata cooked with a little butter and on the other an equal amount of chopped parsley. Serve promptly.

FILETTI DI TACCHINO FRITTI

Turkey Cutlets Fried in Butter

2 lb turkey breast cutlets
2 eggs
Breadcrumbs
Butter, for frying
Lemon
Parsley
Salt

Pound the cutlets with a wet meat mallet so they are quite thin. Then dredge them in the beaten eggs and the breadcrumbs and fry in bubbling butter, taking care not to overcook, then add salt slightly. Arrange the cutlets in an oval serving dish and decorate with lemon wedges and parsley.

PETTO DI TACCHINO IN MAIONESE

Turkey Breast with Mayonnaise

2 lb turkey breast in one piece
1 carrot
1 onion
1 celery stalk
Russian salad *(p725)*
Salt

Simmer the turkey breast in lightly salted boiling water flavored with a carrot, an onion, and celery for about 30 minutes. Remove the turkey from its broth, leave it to cool before carving.

Make a Russian salad with potatoes, carrots, green beans, cornichons and capers mixed with a few spoons of mayonnaise.

Take an oval platter and lay the Russian salad on the bottom. Arrange the turkey slices neatly on top. On the slices of turkey spread mayonnaise using a spatula. Keep in the fridge until ready to serve.

ADA SAYS: *Before serving, you might garnish each plate with an orange salad made of lettuce, fennel, carrot, orange, and olive oil.*

PETTO DI TACCHINO IN MEDAGLIONI

Turkey Medallions with Mushrooms

2 lb turkey breast
Butter
7 oz mushrooms
Flour
Bouillon cube
Salt
Pepper

Carve the turkey breast into thin cutlets and line them up in a buttered skillet. Cook them over high heat, turning them as they cook. Remove them from the pan and let them cool with a light weight on top.

When they are cold, use a round pastry cutter with a diameter of about 2¾ inches to cut out as many discs as you can, but take care to obtain an even number because they will then have to be paired, two by two.

Chop the trimmings from the slices and transfer to a bowl. Quickly wash the mushrooms, dry them, trim the stems and cut them into small pieces. Place them in a saucepan with a knob of butter, salt, and a ladle of water and cook them until the water is completely evaporated. Chop them and add to the turkey trimmings in the bowl. Mix everything and let it cool.

On half of the turkey medallions put a layer of the sauce mix and then top off like a sandwich with another medallion.

Butter a baking dish. Lightly flour the medallion sandwiches and lay up in the dish. Dissolve the bouillon cube in some warm water and put three spoons in the dish. Pop some peanut-size bits of butter on each medallion and put the pan in the oven for a few minutes.

ADA SAYS: *Serve with a purée of potatoes or vegetables of the season.*

PETTO DI TACCHINO IN TIMBALLETTI

Turkey Timbale

10½ oz turkey breast
Vegetables for broth (carrot, onion, celery)
2 carrots
2 potatoes
1 cup shelled fresh peas
3½ tbsp butter
10½ oz puff pastry, homemade *(p275)* or frozen
1 egg
Salt

Cream sauce:
3½ tbsp butter, 6½ tbsp flour, 2 cups broth from the turkey

Simmer the turkey breast in a pan with 6½ cups lightly salted water and flavored with the usual aromatics for broth—carrot, onion, celery. Let it simmer slowly until the meat is well cooked and the broth reduced and fragrant. Then remove the turkey from the pot, remove the skin, and let it cool. Once cooled, cut it into small pieces. Strain the cooking liquid through a fine sieve. Degrease the liquid and set aside for the cream sauce.

In a separate pan, boil the carrots, potatoes, onions, and peas in lightly salted water. When the vegetables are cooked, drain them, peel the potatoes and carrots and cut them into cubes, then put them in a bowl.

Make a cream sauce *(p17)* using the ingredient amounts listed here and the reserved turkey broth. Once thickened, remove from the heat and finish with the butter in small pieces, adding one at a time and stirring constantly.

Take 6 ovenproof molds, in the shape of small glasses, that can go in the oven. On the bottom of each, place one portion of turkey breast, then a layer of the vegetables, then pour in the sauce taking care not to get any on the side of the glass.

Roll the pastry to a thickness of ¼ inch. Use a pastry cutter of about 3 inches and cut out 6 rounds. Apply a round of dough to the rim of each mold to form a lid for each timbale and press the dough so that it sticks well. Brush the lids with beaten egg, and with the tip of a small knife mark out some small decorations. Finally put the timbales in a lively oven where they should remain for about 15 minutes. Place the molds on a serving dish and send to the table.

ADA SAYS: *If using frozen puff pastry, first thaw it at room temperature for 20 minutes.*

TACCHINO IN BUDINO CON SALSA DI FUNGHI

Turkey Flan with Mushroom Sauce

14 oz turkey breast
Vegetables for broth (carrot, onion, celery)
2 eggs
5 oz ham or tongue
Butter
Flour
2 oz dried mushrooms
Salt
Pepper
Optional: black truffle

White sauce:
9½ tbsp flour, 5 tbsp butter, 2 cups milk

Put the turkey breast in lightly salted boiling water with a carrot, an onion, and a celery stalk and simmer for about 30 minutes. Remove the turkey breast from its broth, let it cool, then finely chop.

Make a thick white sauce *(p16)* with the ingredient amounts listed here. Season with a pinch of salt and pepper and let cool. Split the sauce unevenly into two bowls, one for the turkey and the other for the mushrooms. To the larger portion of sauce, add the beaten eggs. Mix well and add the minced turkey, plus diced ham or tongue, and, if you like, small pieces of truffle.

Butter and flour a 1-quart mold. Pour in the meat mixture and cook in a water bath in a very oven on very low heat, until the custard is firm.

For the mushroom sauce: soak the mushrooms in cold water, clean them, rinse them, and cook them in a small saucepan with some butter, a ladle of water, and a pinch of salt. When the mushrooms are cooked and all the water has been used up, drain and add to the second bowl of white sauce with 1½ tablespoons butter.

When everything is ready, turn the flan upside down onto the serving plate and send it to the table, accompanied by the sauce, served separately in a sauce boat.

TACCHINO SPEZZATO IN SALSA DI UOVO

Turkey Stew with Egg and Lemon

3 lb 5 oz boneless, skinless turkey in chunks
3½ tbsp butter
Olive oil
1 onion
Flour
White wine
Broth
3 egg yolks
Lemon
Parsley
Salt

In a Dutch oven, combine the turkey, butter, 4 tablespoons oil, and a chopped onion. Cook over medium heat so that the onion does not burn and the turkey does not turn too brown. As soon as it begins to color, sprinkle with flour and season with salt. Stir with a wooden spoon and after a couple of minutes baste with half a glass of white wine. When the wine has evaporated, cover with broth and continue cooking, covered, for about 1½ hours, stirring occasionally. At the end of the cooking, the sauce should not be too liquid.

A few minutes before serving, put the egg yolks in a bowl, beat in the juice of a lemon with a fork, and finish with chopped parsley. Pour the eggs over the hot turkey mixture, mix and leave the pot on an almost imperceptible flame for 5 or 6 minutes until the eggs have time to set. Then pour everything into a serving dish and immediately send to the table.

OTHER BIRDS

ALLODOLE NEL NIDO

Larks in a Nest

12 large potatoes
7 tbsp butter
12 larks (ortolans)
6 slices prosciutto
3 tbsp olive oil
Salt

Peel the potatoes and, with a sharp knife, hollow out very carefully the center not breaking the sides. Then remove a slice at the base so that they can stand upright and, still with a small knife, carve them a bit on the outside, so they look like small cups (nests).

Dip a brush in melted butter and paint inside each potato nest. Wrap a plucked and cleaned lark in prosciutto. Set the larks in the nest and keep in place with a toothpick. Baste with oil and sprinkle with salt.

Butter a baking dish and line up the nests, basting again with melted butter and oil. Put the dish in a preheated oven of moderate heat for about 45 minutes.

Arrange the nests on the serving dish and, without removing the band of prosciutto from the larks, send to the table.

ANITRA ALL'ARANCIA

Duck with Orange

1 whole duck, with giblets
Olive oil
1 onion
Sage
2 oranges
White wine
Bouillon cube
Sugar
Salt
Pepper

Cut the duck into serving pieces, rinse and dry them. Put the pieces of the duck, the heart, the liver, and the gizzard in a Dutch oven with half a glass of oil. Add the chopped onion, 3 sage leaves, and strips of orange zest from half an orange. Sauté.

Drain off all the oil, season with salt and pepper, and keep on a moderate heat to brown. When the duck is a beautiful brown, baste with half a glass of wine. Dissolve half a bouillon cube in 2 ladles of hot water and when the wine has evaporated, top up the liquid in the pan. Continue cooking slowly.

When the duck is ready, about 2 hours later, arrange it on a serving platter and keep it warm. Strain the cooking juices through a sieve and return it to the pot. If the sauce has reduced too much add a few spoons of water. Add a pinch of sugar and the oranges—peeled, seeded, and chopped. Pour over the duck.

ANITRA IN SALMÌ

Salmi of Duck

1 whole duck
2 oz pancetta
Cognac
Broth
Butter
Carrot
Onion
Bay leaf
Parsley
White wine
Flour
10 mushrooms
Black truffle
Salt
Peppercorns

Cover the duck breast with the slices of pancetta and roast the whole bird, on a spit or in the oven, for about 20 minutes, so that it is just starting to cook. Then carve the duck into 5 pieces, that is: the 2 legs, the 2 breasts with the wings attached, and the central part of the breast.

Put a splash of Cognac in a Dutch oven, flambé it, and let it burn for a moment. Add 2 tablespoons of boiling broth. Add the pieces of duck, cover them with a sheet of buttered parchment paper, so that they do not dry out, cover, and cook the duck over very moderate heat for about 1½ hours. During cooking, check that the liquid does not reduce too much, in which case just add a little water.

Chop half a carrot and a quarter of an onion. Put them in a saucepan with a little butter, a bay leaf, a few sprigs of chopped parsley, a pinch of peppercorns, and a little salt and let them soften. When they start to color, drain the fat and baste with white wine. Reduce the wine by half and then add a generous ladle of broth. Slightly thicken the sauce with a small piece of butter mixed with a little flour and let it boil slowly for about 10 minutes.

Finish this sauce off the heat, by adding a few small pieces of butter, one at a time, and stirring to combine well to give it a velvet texture.

Meanwhile sauté the mushrooms whole in a little butter with slices of truffle. Add these to the sauce and pour over the pieces of duck, reheat everything, but without letting it boil.

ADA SAYS: *This recipe also works well with goose.*

BECCACCE ARROSTO CON CROSTINI

Roast Woodcock with Crostini

6 woodcocks
6 slices lardo
Butter
Olive oil
1 loaf of bread
12 chicken livers
Bay leaf
Bouillon cube
Potato starch
Marsala
1 egg yolk
Watercress
Salt
Pepper

Woodcock are one of the best birds to cook on a spit but can also very well be roasted in the oven. They should be cooked at the last moment and served hot. So calculate the necessary time so that they do not have to wait too long for their crostini.

Pluck the woodcocks and singe the pinfeathers. Remove the giblets and discard the gizzard and the gall. Keep the heart, liver, and intestines for the crostini.

Rinse the woodcocks, dry them, season them inside with a pinch of salt. Bend the head down to one side of the bird and use the beak to pierce through both thighs to hold them in place. Then wrap each bird with a large, thin slice of lardo across the breast, securing the lardo with kitchen string. Salt the woodcocks and baste with melted butter or oil and put them in a preheated, rather bright oven, for about 30 minutes. Woodcocks do not have to cook for a long time, they should be colored externally but remain pink inside.

An operation that instead requires a little more time is their crostini: From a loaf of bread, cut out slices about ⅜ inch thick, the size of a playing card. Take an ovenproof skillet in which the crostini can fit in a single layer. Put in some butter and, when it is well melted and steaming, fry the crostini on one side to a very light blond color. When you have fried the slices of bread, remove them and leave the butter in the pan because it will still be needed.

Remove all traces of gall from the chicken livers. On a cutting board, roughly chop the chicken livers as well as the heart, liver, and intestines of the woodcock.

Melt a little butter in a saucepan, add the chicken livers and the woodcock giblets and season with salt and pepper and half a bay leaf. Fry, stirring to combine, until everything cooks, which will happen in a few minutes. Transfer to a bowl.

Now put a saucepan on the heat with a finger of water, and dissolve half a bouillon cube in the water. Put a finger of cold water in a glass and dissolve ½ teaspoon of potato starch. When it has dissolved well, gradually pour the potato starch into the broth to thicken the sauce. Mix it and, when you see that it is thickened, remove it from the heat and mix in a spoon of Marsala. Pour the sauce into the bowl with the livers and giblets, add an egg yolk, and mix well.

With a spoon divide this filling among the crostini, placing it on the fried side of the bread. Use a knife to give the filling a rounded shape, then line up the crostini in the skillet that still has the butter from the first cooking of the crostini. If this butter is not enough, add a little more.

About 10 minutes before serving, put the skillet in the oven so that the bottom of the crostini colors in turn, and at the same time the filling can firm up and color slightly.

To serve, free the woodcocks from the lardo on their breasts, arrange them in the serving dish, on the sides of which you will accommodate the croutons, garnishing with watercress.

BECCACCE FARCITE

Stuffed Roast Woodcock

6 woodcocks
2 oz pancetta
1 oz dried mushrooms
Butter
Parsley
1 egg yolk
2 oz prosciutto
White wine
Broth
1 loaf of bread
Lemon
Salt
Pepper

Pluck the woodcocks and singe the pinfeathers. Remove the giblets and discard the gizzard and the gall. Keep the heart, liver, and intestines and chop with the pancetta.

Soak the dried mushrooms in cold water for 15 minutes, then clean, rinse, and cook them in a pan with 2 tablespoons butter, a pinch of salt, and a little bit of water. When the mushrooms are cooked and dry, mince them and add this mince to the giblet/pancetta mixture and complete the stuffing with a little salt, pepper, chopped parsley, and an egg yolk.

Fill the woodcock with this stuffing and sew them up. Then wrap the breast with the slices of prosciutto, and hold everything in place with kitchen string.

Butter a baking dish and put the woodcock in to roast in a preheated oven of moderate heat for about 20 minutes, taking care to baste them, from time to time, with a little wine white and a few spoons of broth.

While the woodcocks are cooking, prepare 2 large crostini of bread, cutting a loaf of bread lengthwise. Fry them in butter.

As soon as the woodcocks are cooked, cut them in two and place them on the crostini with their stuffing. Squeeze over a little lemon juice and bring immediately to the table.

BECCACCINI AL COGNAC

Pan-Fried Snipe with Cognac

12 snipe
Butter
Cognac
Bouillon base or bouillon cube
Salt
Pepper

Gut the snipe, singe them, wash and dry, and split in two. Fry them in butter over a lively heat. Season with salt and pepper, letting them cook for about 6 minutes.

When they are just cooked, arrange them on a plate. Pour a little Cognac into the cooking pan to deglaze, stirring the juices well with a wooden spoon. Add a pinch of bouillon base or bouillon cube dissolved in just a little boiling water. Stir, then pour this little sauce over the snipe and immediately send to the table.

BECCACCINI ARROSTO

Roast Snipe

12 snipe
12 slices prosciutto
7 tbsp butter
3½ oz lardo, in slices
Sage
White wine
12 bread slices
Salt

Gut the snipe, singe them, wash and dry them. Cross the legs and bend the head to one side so you can use the beak to pierce through the thighs and hold them in place. Wrap the breasts with the prosciutto and tie in place with kitchen string.

Line the birds up in a roasting pan, add the butter, the lardo cut into cubes, and a few sage leaves. Roast in the oven for about 30 minutes, then season with salt and, when they are well browned, drain all the fat from the pan into a bowl and baste the birds with half a glass of white wine.

Use the fat that you have removed from the pan to fry the slices of bread, browning on both sides, then line them up in a serving dish and place a snipe on each slice. Pour on all the sauce left in the pan and send promptly on the table.

FAGIANO ALLA CREMA

Pheasant in Cream

2 pheasants
7 tbsp butter
1 onion
Red wine
1 cup cream
Lemon
Salt
Pepper

Pluck the pheasants, singe them, wash them, and dry them. Place them in a Dutch oven with the butter, and brown them over high heat until they have taken on a beautiful golden color. Add the finely chopped onion and season with salt and pepper.

Pour a glass of red wine into the pot and cook it to evaporate. Add the cream, reduce the heat to low, and gently simmer for about 1 hour. When cooked, the pheasants must be tender and compact.

Finish with a few drops of lemon juice, cover the pan, and have it brought to the table.

ADA SAYS: *This recipe also works well with partridge.*

FAGIANO ARROSTO AL COGNAC

Roast Pheasant with Cognac

2 young pheasants
Rosemary
Juniper berries
2 slices pancetta
1 onion
9 oz butter
Olive oil
White wine
Broth
Cognac
Salt
Pepper

Pluck the pheasants, singe them, wash them, let them drain and dry them.

Chop a few leaves of rosemary and crush a few juniper berries on a cutting board, add to them salt and pepper and rub this mix inside the pheasants. Wrap the breasts with the slices of pancetta and hold them in place with kitchen string.

Preheat the oven to moderate heat so that it is hot when the pheasants are ready.

In the meantime, coarsely chop an onion and brown it with the butter and oil in a roasting pan big enough for both birds. As the onion colors, put the pheasants in the pan, and brown them to a golden color. Baste them little by little with a glass of white wine, cover, and put in the oven at a moderate heat and roast for about 1 hour. If you see the pheasants begin to dry, pour some boiling broth into the pan, a little at a time.

When the pheasants are cooked, pour a small glass of Cognac into the pan, let it evaporate, and mix well. Remove the kitchen string and bring the pheasants to table with the pancetta.

ADA SAYS: *It is very important for the success of this dish that the pheasants be well cooked, that is when pricking them with a fork the juices run clear with no trace of blood.*

FAGIANO IN SALMÌ

Salmi of Pheasant

2 pheasants
2 pancetta slices
Cognac
Broth
Butter
1 carrot
Onion
Bay leaf
Parsley
White wine
Flour
1 lb mushrooms
Black truffle
Salt
Peppercorns

Pluck, clean, and singe the pheasants. Wrap them in the pancetta slices and roast in a preheated oven of moderate heat for about 20 minutes.

Take them out, let them cool, and then carve the meat into not very large pieces. Remove the skin.

Put a small glass of Cognac in a Dutch oven, flambé, and let it burn for a moment. Add a few spoons of hot broth. Put the pieces of pheasant in the pot, cover them with a sheet of buttered parchment paper so that they do not dry out, cover and cook over a very moderate heat for about 30 minutes. During cooking, check that the liquid does not reduce too much; if needed, add a little more water or broth.

Chop the carrot and half an onion and put them in a saucepan with a little butter, a bay leaf, a few sprigs of chopped parsley, a few peppercorns, and a little salt and let them wilt. When they color, drain off the fat and baste with a glass of white wine. Let the wine reduce by half and then add a couple of spoons of broth. Slightly thicken the sauce with a small piece of butter mixed with a little flour and let it simmer slowly for about 10 minutes more.

Finish the sauce off the heat by adding, one at a time, a few pieces of butter and stirring to combine well and give the sauce a velvet sheen.

While the pheasants are still cooking, prepare the mushrooms: Wash them quickly, scrape them, and trim the stems, and slice. Pan-fry in butter, season with salt, and cook over moderate heat for 10 minutes. Finish them with a thinly sliced small black truffle.

Arrange the pheasants in a round serving dish, cover with the sauce, very hot, and surround them with the truffled mushrooms.

ADA SAYS: *This recipe also works well with partridge.*

GALLINA FARAONA IN SALMÌ

Salmi of Roast Guinea Fowl

1 guinea fowl
2 oz pancetta slices
Cognac
2 cups broth
Butter
Carrot
Onion
Bay leaf
Parsley
White wine
Flour
10 mushrooms
Truffle
Salt
Peppercorns

Pluck, clean, and singe the guinea fowl, rinse it, dry it, wrap the breast with the pancetta and roast it in a lively oven for about 20 minutes.

Carve the guinea fowl into several not very large pieces. Remove the skin and trim them to the same size.

Put half a glass of Cognac in a skillet, flambé it and let it burn for a moment. Add 2 tablespoons of hot broth and the pieces of guinea fowl, cover with a sheet of lightly buttered parchment paper so they do not dry out. Cover and set aside to stay warm.

Chop half a carrot and a quarter of an onion; put them in a new pan with a little butter, a bay leaf, chopped parsley, a few peppercorns, and a little salt and let them color. After it has colored, drain off the fat and pour in half a glass of white wine. Let the wine reduce by half and then add a ladle of hot broth. Strain everything into a bowl, pressing well with the back of a wooden spoon to extract all the juice from the herbs.

Put this strained sauce in a small saucepan, thicken it slightly with a piece of butter mixed with a little flour and let it boil slowly for another 10 minutes, skimming off any impurities that rise to the surface.

Finish the sauce off the heat, putting in, one at a time, a few pieces of extra butter, and stirring to give it a velvet texture. Pour this sauce over the pieces of guinea fowl, and reheat everything, but without letting it get to a boil.

Sauté the mushrooms separately in a little butter, with a peeled and thinly sliced small truffle. Mix into the sauce and pour over the guinea fowl.

OCA ARROSTO IN FORNO

Roast Goose

Olive oil
1 goose, with giblets
3 onions
3 carrots
Celery
Parsley
Butter
Broth
Marsala
Flour
Salt
Pepper

Stuffing:
4 sausages, handful of pitted green olives, 10 to 15 roasted chestnuts, black truffle

Pour the oil into an oval Dutch oven in which the goose fits neatly. Coarsely chop the onions, carrots, celery, and parsley and sauté along with the goose trimmings—the neck, chopped heart, chopped gizzard, even the tips of the wings.

Prepare the stuffing more or less according to the size of the goose: Remove the sausages from the casings, add a good handful of pitted green olives, 10 to 15 peeled chestnuts (roasted in a light oven or on the grill), and finally some black truffle. Inside the goose, put a little salt, pepper, a few pieces of butter, and the prepared stuffing.

Put the goose in the Dutch oven, season with salt and pepper and let it fry a little over heat. Generously grease a sheet of parchment paper the size of the Dutch ovevn and place it on the goose, then tear off a flap so that there is a small opening to one side through which you can baste the bird and check the cooking. Cover the pot with the lid, but set it ajar so the steam can come out freely.

Heat the oven to moderate heat, put in the Dutch oven and roast for about 3 hours. At intervals, stir the vegetables and turn the goose; if they are burning, add a few spoons of water or broth. When the goose is well cooked and golden, remove it from the pot and keep it hot.

Set the Dutch oven on the stove, pour in half a glass of Marsala to deglaze and stir with a wooden spoon to get up the browned bits. As soon as the wine evaporates, pour in a little more broth or water, then strain the cooking juices and transfer to a small pan. Put the pan on the heat, add the butter mixed with a little flour and let the sauce thicken slightly.

To serve the whole goose, arrange it on a platter, coat it with a few spoons of sauce and send the rest aside in a sauce boat. Or carve it and reassemble in its original shape.

PERNICI IN CASSERUOLA

Partridge Casserole

6 partridge
3½ tbsp butter
2 tbsp olive oil
Bouillon cube
Cognac
Salt
Pepper

Pluck the partridges, singe them, gut them, wash and dry them thoroughly.

Put the partridges, butter, and oil in a Dutch oven. Set over high heat to brown. Dissolve the bouillon cube in hot water and baste the birds with it. Reduce the heat, cover, and braise for about 20 minutes. When cooked, remove the partridges from the Dutch oven and set on a serving platter. Deglaze the pot with a small glass of Cognac and bring this sauce to a boil. Pour the sauce over the partridges. Bring to the table immediately.

PICCIONE ARROSTO

Roast Squab

3 squab
3 thin pancetta slices
Olive oil
1 loaf of bread
Watercress
Salt
Pepper

Clean the squab carefully and remove the head and neck, like a chicken. Then singe them and dry them. Clip the claws and wrap the breast with the pancetta, then truss like a chicken.

Put them in a small roasting pan with oil, salt, and pepper and roast in a preheated oven for about 30 minutes.

Carve the squash in two and present them at the table on slices of sliced bread fried in oil and surrounded by watercress.

PICCIONE IN TERRINA

Braised Squab with Peppers and Mushrooms

3 squab
7 tbsp butter
Marsala
Bouillon base or bouillon cube
2 bell peppers
20 spring onions
10½ oz mushrooms
3 tbsp cream
Potato starch
Salt
Pepper

This recipe does not present any difficulty in terms of execution but you will get an exquisite stewed squab.

Clean the squab (*as above*). Carve into quarters. Put the pieces in a Dutch oven with 3½ tablespoons of butter. Brown them over light heat and, just as they color, season with a little salt and baste them with a small glass of Marsala. Cover and reduce the heat.

When the Marsala has evaporated, cover the squab with a few ladles of water in which you have dissolved the bouillon base or half a broth cube. Cook at a slow boil for about 30 minutes.

While they are cooking, prepare the vegetables: Roast the peppers, peel and cut into strips. Boil the spring onions. Wash the mushrooms and cut into thin strips.

When the squab are cooked, there will still be a lot of liquid in the Dutch oven. Take the pieces of squab out and set them aside in a warm bowl.

In the saucepan, melt and brown 3½ tablespoons of butter. Add a pinch of salt and a little pepper, boil and reduce the sauce, which you finish with the cream and 1 teaspoon potato starch.

Arrange the squab pieces in a covered baking dish, cover with the vegetables and then pour over the prepared sauce. Cover and put it in light oven for about 20 minutes. Transfer to a serving plate and send to the table.

QUAGLIE ALLO SPIEDO

Spit-Roasted Quail

12 quail
12 thin lardo slices
Sage
13 bread slices
Olive oil
Salt
Pepper

Choose plump and very fresh quails. Pluck them, singe them, gut and dry them. Bard them with the slices of lardo and the sage leaves.

The spit-roasting can take place over an open fire outdoors or indoors in a rotisserie oven, if you have one. Put a slice of bread on the spit, then a quail and so on and finish with a slice of bread. Spit-roast the quail, basting them with oil from time to time to keep them soft. Watch over the cooking because, on a high flame, they will soon be ready.

Remove the bread and quail from the spit and arrange with elegance in a serving dish.

QUAGLIE ARROSTO CON POLENTA

Roast Quail with Polenta

12 quail
12 thin lardo slices
2 cups polenta
14 tbsp butter
Salt
Pepper

Wrap the quail with the slices of lardo, holding it in place with kitchen string.

Then cook the polenta *(p233)* keeping it rather thick. As soon as it is cooked, pour it into a rectangular mold, let it cool, then turn it upside down and cut it into 12 slices. Fry the slices in butter until golden.

Take a large pan in which all the quail can fit in a single layer. Melt half of the butter and as soon as it is hot, lay down the quail and brown them until they are cooked: it will take about 20 minutes.

In a very hot dish, arrange the slices of polenta and put a quail on top and serve immediately.

QUAGLIE PICCANTI

Spicy Quail

6 quail
2 eggs
Olive oil
Breadcrumbs
Broth
Potato starch
7 tbsp butter
Lemon
Parsley
Cayenne
Garlic
Salt
Pepper

Open up the quail with a cut along the back, then thoroughly clean them, inside and out, rinse and dry them.

Press on the breastbone of each one with your hand to flatten them without deforming them. Season with salt and pepper.

Soak them in the beaten eggs with ½ tablespoon of oil. Then dredge in the breadcrumbs. Set in a pan and bake them in the oven, turning them often so that the breadcrumbs do not burn.

As soon as they are cooked, arrange them on a plate, coating them with the following sauce: Put half a glass of broth in a saucepan, then thicken slightly with 1 teaspoon potato starch dissolved in a little cold water. Remove the pan from the heat and stir in the butter, a piece at a time, whisking constantly and not adding the next piece of butter until the first is fully amalgamated. When all the butter is blended, add a few drops of lemon, a spoonful of chopped parsley, a good pinch of pepper or a pinch of cayenne, and a pinch of crushed garlic.

TORDI CON FUNGHI

Braised Thrush with Porcini

1 lb porcini mushrooms
Olive oil
Garlic
Parsley
12 thrush
Butter
2 oz prosciutto
Onion
Cognac or Marsala
Broth
Salt
Pepper

Peel the porcini mushrooms, slice, rinse and cook over high heat with oil, garlic, salt, and chopped parsley.

Pluck and singe the thrushes, remove their necks and heads. Use scissors to cut their backs and gut them, rinse, dry them. Place them on a work surface breast-side up, and press them down slightly to flatten without deforming them.

Place a little oil and butter and the chopped prosciutto in a pan. Heat, add the thrushes, season with salt and pepper and a little chopped onion and brown them on both sides over high heat. At this point, baste with a small glass of Cognac or a finger of Marsala. Let the liquid evaporate and then baste again with enough broth to just cover the birds. Turn down the heat and cook until the sauce is very reduced, about 15 minutes.

Arrange the porcini mushrooms in the middle of the plate and the thrushes on top and dress with some of the pan juices.

FURRED GAME

Rabbit & Hare

CONIGLIO AI CAPPERI

Rabbit with Capers

4½ lb rabbit legs and loin
Vinegar
Red wine
2 onions
1 celery stalk
Carrot
Olive oil
4 anchovies
Capers
Parsley
Flour
Salt
Pepper

Rinse the rabbit, dry it and put it in a bowl with the vinegar, the wine, 1 onion (cut into slices), the celery and carrot (chopped into small pieces), salt, and pepper. Let sit in the marinade for at least 12 hours.

Remove and dry the meat and reserve the marinade. Place the rabbit in a saucepan with the other onion, also cut into slices, and half a glass of oil and brown slowly. Strain the marinade and add half of it to the pan with the rabbit. Cover, and braise for about 1 hour.

Meanwhile, prepare the sauce: Bone, wash, and cut the anchovies into small pieces and heat them in a saucepan with 2 spoons of oil to dissolve them completely. When they are reduced to a paste, add ⅓ cup of capers and the chopped parsley, add the rest of the strained marinade, and thicken the sauce with a spoon of flour, dissolved in a finger of water. Boil the sauce for 30 minutes, then add it to the rabbit and simmer for another 10 minutes.

CONIGLIO ALLA CACCIATORA

Hunter's Rabbit

4½ lb whole rabbit, cut in pieces
Olive oil
Sage
1 garlic clove
Vinegar
3 anchovies
Potato starch
Capers
Salt
Pepper

Rinse the rabbit pieces, dry them, and put them in a pan with oil. Add a handful of sage leaves and the garlic and brown over high heat. Season with salt and pepper and baste with a glass of vinegar and one of water. Cover the pan and cook over moderate heat for about 1 hour. If it starts to dry out, add some spoons of hot water.

Now prepare the sauce: wash and bone the anchovies, chop and melt in the vinegar with 1 teaspoon potato starch. Add ⅓ cup of capers.

Add the caper and anchovy mixture to the rabbit. Bring to a boil again so that the sauce can thicken slightly. When it reaches the right thickness, remove the pan from the heat, arrange the pieces of rabbit in a serving dish, and send immediately to the table.

CONIGLIO ALLA CAMPAGNOLA

Rabbit Country Style

4½ lb whole rabbit, cut in pieces
Olive oil
4 garlic cloves
Rosemary
White wine
Salt
Pepper

Rinse the rabbit pieces and, without drying them, put them in a pan with the oil, garlic cloves left whole, and a rosemary sprig.

Bring the heat up to medium and when the rabbit is lightly browned, season with a pinch of salt and a little pepper. Baste with a glass and half of white wine. Stir with a wooden spoon, cover the pan, and braise slowly and let the wine reduce. Then, little by little, add some spoons of water until the meat is cooked and the sauce reduced, about 1 hour.

Remove the garlic cloves from the pan and pour the rabbit into a serving dish with its tasty sauce.

CONIGLIO ALLA LIGURE

Rabbit with Olives Ligurian Style

4½ lb whole rabbit, cut in pieces
Olive oil
3½ tbsp butter
2 garlic cloves
Rosemary
Thyme
1 onion
White wine
Broth or bouillon cube
2 oz black olives, pitted
Salt
Pepper

Cut the rabbit into pieces, wash well, and dry. Place in a pan with oil, butter, garlic, rosemary, and a pinch of thyme and brown it carefully over moderate heat.

When the rabbit pieces have taken on a nice uniform color, stir in a finely chopped onion and season with salt and pepper. Baste with some wine, increase the heat a little to let it evaporate, then reduce the heat and continue cooking gently for 1 hour, adding one or two spoons of broth if the liquid dries out too much.

A little before removing the rabbit from the heat, add the pitted black olives. Finally remove the garlic cloves from the sauce and serve the rabbit in a round serving dish.

CONIGLIO IN AGRODOLCE

Sweet and Sour Rabbit

4½ lb whole rabbit, cut in pieces
Red wine
2 onions
Cloves
Parsley
Bay leaf
Lard
Flour
Broth or bouillon cube
2 tbsp sugar
Vinegar
Raisins
Pine nuts
Salt
Peppercorns

Cut the rabbit into pieces, rinse, dry well, and put in a bowl.

In a saucepan, combine two glasses of red wine, half a chopped onion, a couple of cloves, a few sprigs of parsley, a bay leaf, and 4 or 5 whole peppercorns. Heat this marinade without letting it boil, remove it from the heat and when it is just warm, pour it over the rabbit. Leave it like this for a few hours. Remove the rabbit pieces from the marinade and strain the marinade.

Brown a chopped onion in ¼ cup of lard. Flour the rabbit pieces and add to the pan with the onion and lardo, basting from time to time with the strained marinade. When all the wine has evaporated and the rabbit pieces have taken a nice dark color, season with salt and pepper and then baste with enough hot broth—or water in which you've dissolved half a bouillon cube—to cover the pieces of rabbit. Reduce the heat, cover the saucepan, and let it cook slowly for about 1 hour.

When the rabbit is cooked, tilt the saucepan and with a spoon remove any fat that floats to the surface of the sauce. If too liquid, reduce it a little.

Separately, combine the sugar in a saucepan moistened with water and melt over heat. When the sugar has taken a light blond color, wet it with half a glass of vinegar and stir with a wooden spoon. Transfer to the saucepan with the rabbit, add a handful of raisins and a handful of pine nuts. Simmer for another 4 or 5 minutes over very weak heat. Arrange on a serving dish.

CONIGLIO IN PADELLA

Slow-Cooked Rabbit with Tomatoes

4½ lb whole rabbit, cut in pieces
Olive oil
Garlic
2 oz prosciutto
Parsley
White wine
4 or 5 tomatoes
Salt
Pepper

Wash and dry the rabbit pieces and put them in a pan with two fingers of oil. Sauté briskly, let the meat brown, then add salt, pepper, a little crushed garlic, a few cubes of prosciutto, and a spoon of chopped parsley.

When the rabbit is well browned, baste with the white wine and, once the wine has evaporated, put the tomatoes (peeled, seeded, and chopped) in the pan. Add a little water, moderate the heat, cover, and let it cook gently for about 1 hour so that the sauce can thicken well.

CONIGLIO IN SALMÌ

Salmi of Rabbit

4½ lb whole rabbit, cut in pieces
1 onion
Celery
Carrot
Parsley
Bay leaf
Rosemary
Sage
Red wine
Olive oil
Flour
Salt
Pepper

Anchovy sauce:
rabbit cooking juices, 2 anchovies, parsley, pepper, garlic, vinegar, white wine

Wash and dry the rabbit pieces and arrange in a bowl. Cover with chopped onion, a little celery, carrot, and parsley. Add half a bay leaf, a pinch of rosemary, a leaf of sage, a good pinch of pepper and sprinkle everything with a glass of red wine. Leave alone for an hour or two. Reserving the marinade, take the rabbit pieces out and pat them dry.

Put a little oil in a saucepan, heat it well, and add the pieces of rabbit. Season with salt and let them brown, then add the various herbs used in the marinade. When the rabbit is browned and dark in color, sprinkle with half a spoon of flour, stir, and after a minute or two pour in the wine from the marinade. Reduce the wine and add a ladle or two of water. Reduce the heat a little, cover, and let it finish cooking gently for about 1 hour.

As soon as the rabbit is cooked, prepare the anchovy sauce: Put the rabbit pieces in another saucepan and strain the cooking juices. Finely chop a couple of anchovies (washed and boned), a spoon of parsley, a pinch of pepper, and a little garlic. Dilute with a splash of vinegar and a little of white wine.

Pour this sauce on the rabbit, stir, put it back on the heat and keep on a very low heat, without boiling, for 5 minutes.

CONIGLIO IN SALSA D'UOVA

Rabbit in Egg Sauce

4½ lb whole rabbit, cut in pieces
3½ tbsp butter
Onion
2 oz prosciutto
Parsley
Flour
White wine
2 egg yolks
Lemon
Salt
Pepper

Wash and dry the pieces of rabbit. Put the butter in a pan and as soon as it melts add the rabbit. Sauté over rather high heat and after 2 or 3 minutes, add a little chopped onion, salt and pepper, a few slices of chopped prosciutto, and a spoon of parsley.

Sauté well and, when the rabbit has taken on a nice blond tint, sprinkle with a half spoon of flour. Stir again and then pour in half a glass of white wine. As soon as the wine has evaporated, add just enough water to cover the rabbit. Reduce the heat, put the lid on the saucepan, and let it cook until the rabbit is fully cooked and the sauce is thick and reduced, about 1 hour.

Then break two egg yolks into a bowl, squeeze over the juice of half a lemon, and add a spoon of chopped parsley and whisk well.

Take the pan of rabbit off the heat and stir in the egg mixture. Return to the heat cover, and simmer for 5 minutes. Pour into a serving dish, cover the meat with its sauce, and have it brought to the table.

LEPRE ALLA CAMPAGNOLA

Hare Country Style

1 whole hare, cut in pieces with its offal
4 cups white wine
1 onion
Celery
Carrot
Bay leaves
Rosemary
2 oz lardo
2 oz prosciutto
Bouillon cube
Olive oil
Croutons
Butter
Salt
Pepper

The night before, place the pieces of hare in a bowl and cover them with the following marinade: Boil the white wine with half an onion for 5 minutes, then add the chopped celery, carrot, a few bay leaves, rosemary, salt, and pepper and continue cooking. Turn off the heat and let cool. Once cooled, pour it over the hare. Make sure that all the pieces of hare are well covered, and refrigerate for 12 hours.

Remove the hare from the marinade and strain the marinade. In a saucepan, sauté a mix of lardo, prosciutto, and a half onion. Add the pieces of hare and brown them well. Add the strained marinade to the pan and let it evaporate. Dissolve half the bouillon cube in hot water and mix in.

Meanwhile, chop the hare offal and fry in a pan with a little oil, salt, and pepper. When they are a little browned, pour them into the saucepan with the hare and let it finish cooking for about 2 hours. Pour the tasty and easy preparation on a plate, accompanying it with croutons fried in butter.

LEPRE ALLA SANT'UBERTO

Saint Umberto's Hare

Olive oil
1 onion
1 carrot
1 celery stalk
Whole clove
Sage
Bay leaf
Rosemary
1 garlic clove
Red wine
Vinegar
1 whole hare, cut in pieces
Flour
Currant jelly
Orange zest
Salt

Saint Umberto is the patron saint of hunters.

A day ahead make the marinade: Put two or three spoons of oil in a saucepan, a chopped onion, carrot, and celery and cook over moderate heat for 15 minutes without letting the vegetables catch. Then add a clove, two sage leaves, a bay leaf, a little rosemary, and the garlic in slices. Let it cook for a couple of minutes and then pour in two glasses of red wine and two fingers of vinegar. Stir, bring to a boil, remove the pan from the heat and pour the marinade into another container to cool.

Arrange the washed and dried pieces of hare in a bowl, pour over the cooled marinade with all the aromatics and marinate overnight.

The following day, reserving the marinade and all the vegetables and herbs, remove the hare pieces and pat dry. Heat a little oil in a Dutch oven, add the hare, and fry over high heat. Season with a pinch of salt and when the hare begins to color, spoon over the herbs and vegetables from the marinade and salt slightly. When everything has taken on a rather dark tint, stir in a spoon of flour and cook for a minute or two. Then add the liquid from the marinade one spoon at a time, waiting until the first has evaporated before adding another. When you run out of wine, add water. Cover, reduce the heat, and let it cook gently, for about 2 hours. When the meat is done, remove the pieces of hare and keep warm. If there is a lot of fat on the surface, skim it off then strain the sauce into a smaller pan. Add a spoon of currant jelly and a half spoon of slivered orange zest. Once the currant jelly has melted, put the pieces of hare back into the saucepan, stir, and keep warm until ready to serve.

LEPRE IN SALMÌ

Salmi of Hare

1 whole hare, cut in pieces
1 onion
Celery
Carrot
Parsley
Bay leaf
Rosemary
Sage
Red wine
Olive oil
Flour
Salt
Pepper

Anchovy sauce:
broth from the hare, 2 anchovies, parsley, pepper, garlic, vinegar, white wine

Carefully rinse the pieces of hare, dry them and arrange them in a bowl, covering them with a chopped onion, celery, carrot, and parsley. Add half a bay leaf, a sprig of rosemary, a sage leaf, and a good pinch of pepper and cover everything with two glasses of red wine. Let the hare marinate for 12 hours.

Take the hare pieces out of the marinade and dry them. Put a little oil in a saucepan, heat it well and add the hare. Season with salt and pepper and let them brown, adding gradually the various aromatics from the marinade. When the pieces are browned and dark, dust them with half a spoon of flour, stir, and after a minute or two pour in the marinade, bit by bit. Let this cook down and then top up with a ladle or two of water, reduce the heat a little, cover, and let it finish cooking gently for about 2 hours.

When the hare is cooked, strain the cooking juices, add a little hot water if needed, and pour back over the hare.

To make the anchovy sauce: Chop a couple of washed and boned anchovies, a spoon of parsley, a pinch of pepper, and a little garlic, and dilute with a touch of vinegar and a finger of white wine. Pour this sauce over the hare, mix, and keep over very low heat, but without boiling, for 5 minutes.

Arrange the hare in a serving dish, coat it with the sauce and serve.

Venison

CAPRIOLO IN MARINATA

Marinated Roe Deer

3 lb 5 oz venison tenderloin
Onion
Garlic
Cloves
Olive oil
4 tsp vinegar
1 cup white wine
Broth
Potato starch
2 tbsp butter
Salt
Pepper

Place the venison tenderloin in a bowl with a sliced onion, chopped garlic, cloves, salt, pepper, oil, and vinegar. Cover and let the meat sit in the marinade for 3 days, taking care to turn it at least once a day.

Reserving the marinade, remove the meat from the marinade and dry it briefly. Put it in a Dutch oven with a little oil over low heat and let the meat slowly take on color. Then baste half and half with wine and broth, and with a glass from the marinade. Cover and simmer over a low heat for 2 hours.

When the meat is cooked, remove from the pot and keep it warm. Keep the pot on the heat, scrape the cooking juices with a wooden spoon, then strain through a sieve into a small saucepan. Thicken the juices with 1 teaspoon of potato starch mixed with the butter. Check the flavor of the sauce, then place it in a sauce boat and send it out with the venison.

ADA SAYS: *Roe deer is a small deer species quite common in the woods of the Alps and is sought after. Its meat is delicate and tasty, as long as it is young deer between 1 and 2½ years old. But even then, it needs a marinade to improve its flavor.*

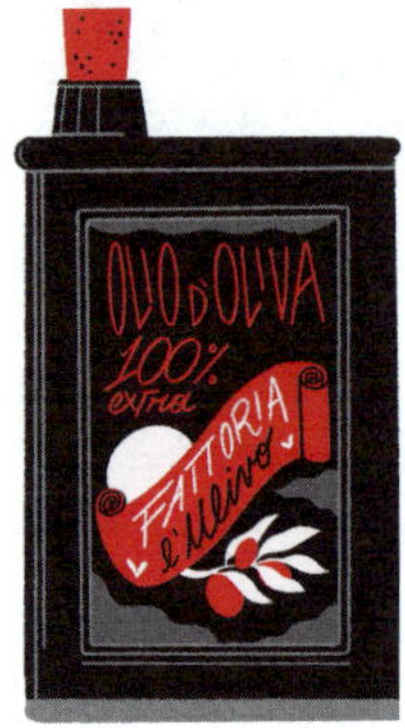

CAPRIOLO IN SALMÌ

Salmi of Venison

Leg of venison
1 onion
Celery
Carrot
Parsley
Bay leaf
Rosemary
Sage
Red wine
Olive oil
1 tbsp flour
Salt
Pepper

Rinse the leg of venison very carefully and dry it. Then arrange it in a bowl and cover it with an onion, a little celery, a carrot, and parsley, all chopped. Add half a bay leaf, a sprig of rosemary, a sage leaf, and a good pinch of pepper and douse everything with a glass of red wine. Let sit for 1 to 2 hours, then take it out of the marinade and pat it dry.

Put 4 tablespoons of oil in a Dutch oven, heat it well and add the leg. Season with salt and let it brown, gradually adding the various herbs used in the marinade (which you scoop out with a slotted spoon). When the venison is dark brown, sprinkle it with the flour, stir and after a minute or two pour in the wine from the marinade. Reduce the heat, cover, and let it finish braising gently for 2 hours, adding, if necessary, a few extra ladles of water.

When ready to serve, take out the venison and arrange it on a platter. Strain the cooking juices—add a little water if you want—and pour over the meat.

CERVO FARCITO

Stuffed Leg of Venison

Leg of venison
10½ oz prosciutto
7 oz lardo
Parsley
2 egg yolks
Pork caul
Olive oil
Red wine
3 tbsp tomato paste
Salt
Pepper

Bone out the leg of venison, leaving only the shank attached. Chop the meat scraps with the prosciutto, lardo, and parsley. Place the mince in a bowl and season with salt, pepper, and the egg yolks. Knead everything well. Use this simple filling to put inside the leg, in place of the bone. Sew the opening well and wrap the stuffed leg in a piece of pork caul netting first soaked in warm water for a few minutes.

Take an oval Dutch oven and put in the leg with a few spoons of oil. Brown slowly, adding salt and pepper, and when the meat has taken on a nice brown tint, baste it with a glass of red wine. When the wine has evaporated, add the tomato paste, dilute it with a few ladles of hot water, season again with salt and pepper and let it cook slowly for 2 hours until the meat is well cooked and the sauce somewhat reduced.

DAINO IN SALSA DI CILIEGE

Venison with Cherry Sauce

3 lb 5 oz boneless venison loin
Olive oil
1 onion
1 carrot
1 celery stalk
Parsley
2 garlic cloves
Mint
Oregano
Bay leaf
Sage
Rosemary
Red wine
Vinegar
3½ tbsp butter
Bouillon cube
1 tbsp flour
Salt

Cherry sauce:
Orange, Marsala, 5 tbsp currant jelly, cinnamon, 10 oz cherries in syrup

For this exquisite hunting preparation you will need a boneless loin of deer, more commonly called the saddle.

Carefully clean the meat, trim off any skin and fat and cut it into slices a couple of fingers thick, which you will then pound lightly with a moist meat mallet or a wide knife.

Arrange the slices in a bowl and prepare the marinade: Put a little less than half a glass of oil in a saucepan with a chopped onion, a thinly sliced carrot, chopped celery, and plenty of parsley. Cook for about 30 minutes over very moderate heat so that the vegetables do not color; adding if necessary a little water.

Add the sliced garlic and a mix of herbs to include a hint of mint and oregano, a torn bay leaf, a little sage, and a little rosemary. Stir and, just as it starts to heat up, add a glass and a half of red wine and a touch of vinegar. Let it boil undistrubed for 5 minutes and then remove from the heat and let it cool.

Pour the cooled marinade, with all the aromatics, over the venison. If the marinade was not enough to cover the meat, add some water. Cover the bowl and put it in the fridge for 3 or 4 days, turning the meat over once a day. If you are short of time, you can reduce the marination time to a day.

When ready to cook, remove the venison slices from the marinade, free them from the herbs, and dry them well. Put half of the butter and a little oil in a skillet and heat over high heat. When the fats are hot, add the meat to brown on both sides. Season with salt and braise, reducing the heat a little, and basting with a few spoonfuls of the marinade.

When the slices are cooked, after about 1 hour, arrange them on a serving dish and keep warm.

Drain some of the fat left in the pan and put it back on the heat. Strain the remaining marinade and pour into the pan. Add half a bouillon cube and let the sauce reduce by about half. Thicken it then with the rest of the butter mixed with the flour, give a last stir and return the venison to the pan. Let them soak up the sauce, over very low heat, without boiling. There should be very little sauce and it should be very little. Cover the pan and keep it warm until ready to serve.

Make a cherry sauce: With a vegetable peeler, pull off the orange zest in strips. Cut the zest into tiny slivers and put them in a small pan with a glass of sweet Marsala and the juice of the orange. Bring to a boil and cook until the liquid has reduced by half. Then add the currant jelly, a pinch of cinnamon, and when the jelly has melted, add the cherries in syrup and give it a stir.

Pour the cherries with their sauce into a small sauce boat. Serve the cherry sauce alongside the venison.

Boar

CINGHIALE IN AGRODOLCE ALLA ROMANA

Sweet and Sour Boar Roman Style

Red wine
Vinegar
3 onions
2 carrots
3 celery stalks
Parsley
5 cloves
Bay leaf
Leg of wild boar
Lardo
7 oz prosciutto
Olive oil
Salt
Peppercorns

Sweet and sour sauce:
sugar, garlic, bay leaf, vinegar, 2 tbsp grated chocolate, potato starch or flour and butter, handful of soaked raisins, handful of dried sour cherries, soaked pitted prunes, candied lemon peel, candied orange

Wild boar should always be kept in a marinade, for at least a couple of days before cooking. Some cooks take off the skin (unless it is very young), because it is always hard and not very digestible.

Put a saucepan on the stove with two glasses of wine and a little less—say half a glass—of vinegar. Add an onion, a carrot, a couple of celery stalks, and a sprig of parsley, all chopped. Add 3 cloves, a bay leaf, and a good pinch of peppercorns. Bring to a boil and then let the marinade cool.

Place the leg of wild boar in a bowl, pour over the cold marinade with all the herbs and vegetables and leave it in this aromatic bath for a couple days, taking care to turn it at least once a day.

When ready to cook, remove the boar from the marinade, dry it and tie it with a little string to keep it in shape. Pour a little oil into a Dutch oven, and when it is hot, add the leg and brown for a long time and on a rather lively heat. Season with salt and pepper, and add a couple of medium-size onions, a carrot. and a celery stalk (all chopped), a couple of cloves, half a bay leaf, strips or dice of lardo and prosciutto.

Continue to brown over high heat, turning from time to time, until the meat is a nice dark brown, then baste with a glass of red wine. Stir the cooking juices well with a wooden spoon across the bottom of the pot to deglaze, and as soon as the wine has evaporated, add enough water to cover the meat. As soon as it boils, put the lid on, reduce the heat, and let it finish cooking slowly for about 2 hours.

Remove the leg from the Dutch oven, remove the string, and put it in a smaller pan with a few spoons of sauce, cover it and keep it hot. With a spoon skim off all the fat from the surface of the cooking juices. Set this well-degreased sauce aside for the sweet and sour sauce.

Make the sweet and sour sauce: Put the sugar in a pan with crushed garlic and a bay leaf. Let the sugar melt, stirring frequently without adding water, and when it becomes light blond, wet with vinegar. The sugar will seize up a little and when it has completely melted again, add the grated chocolate. Simmer a little longer and, when the chocolate has also melted, add the degreased cooking juices from the wild boar. Stir to combine, let it heat up well and if this sauce is too loose, thicken with a little potato starch dissolved in a finger of water, or with a walnut of butter mixed with a teaspoon of flour.

When you have the right consistency, strain the sauce into another pan and add the soaked raisins, the dried sour cherries, and some soaked prunes (all cut into small pieces) and a little lemon peel and candied orange, cut into cubes.

Finally, slice the wild boar, arrange it on a serving plate and pour the sweet and sour sauce over it.

ADA SAYS: *If you prefer a currant sauce, carefully degrease the wild boar broth and, if it is too loose, thicken it with a little potato starch dissolved in two fingers of water; if it is too thick, add a little broth or water. You need enough to coat all the boar. Strain it into a second pan and put it back on the heat. Add currant jelly, pine nuts, and candied orange peel, cut into small pieces. When the jelly is well dissolved, remove the saucepan from the heat and finish with a few pieces of butter.*

CINGHIALE IN UMIDO

Boar Stew

- 1 onion
- 1 carrot
- 1 celery stalk
- Parsley
- Red wine
- Bay leaf
- Sage
- Marjoram
- Boar leg
- Olive oil
- Tomato passata
- Salt
- Pepper

Cut the onion, carrot, celery, and parsley into small pieces and place them in a pan with a glass of red wine, a bay leaf, a few sage leaves, and a little marjoram. Bring to a boil and pour over the boar leg. Cover and marinate for 24 hours, turning two or three times.

The next day take out the leg, dry it, tie with kitchen string, and place in a Dutch oven with a spoon of oil. Brown slowly, add salt and pepper, and when the meat has a nice brown tint, pour over the marinade and a glass of red wine. When the wine has evaporated, pour in ¾ cup of tomato passata, season again with salt and pepper and braise slowly for about 2 hours until the meat is cooked and the sauce reduced. Take the leg out of the pot, untie it, carve, and arrange it on an oval serving dish and pour its boiling sauce over.

"Color, brightness, and firmness are all signs of good produce."

We have a wonderful array of salad lettuces, many of which are part of the chicory family but are quite different, often just called bitter greens—escarole, endive, puntarelle, raddichio, and so forth. They are distant cousins of daisies and dandelions. They can be enjoyed fresh as salads or cooked.

Potatoes abound in carbohydrates, starches, proteins, and minerals. For gnocchi and purées choose white so-called mealy varieties, while the yellow, waxy varieties should be used for salads.

Vegetable preserves like sun-dried tomatoes or pickles are the safest and easiest preserves to make at home.

All vegetables must be fresh and preferably cooked immediately. Their colors, their brightness, and firmness are all signs of good produce.

Cultivated mushrooms, for the most part, do not require major preparation. Usually, it is enough to cut off the stems, wash them properly, dry them, and cook, as appropriate, whole or cut into slices.

Of all the wild mushrooms the porcini (boletus edulis) is the king but it can, as can others, be confused with poisonous varieties and so great care must be taken and should only be bought from trusted sources. Wild mushrooms are at their most abundant and flavorful in fall and spring.

Dried mushrooms present specific problems for the kitchen. Firstly they must be soaked for 15–20 minutes to revive before cooking in oil or butter, usually with a chopped onion. They must also be scrubbed clean of any dirt, rinsed, and quickly dried in a cloth without pressing so hard as to break them.

Truffles come in three main varieties. The white truffle, or the Alba truffle, is found from the end of August to the middle of January. The *bianchetto*, or *mazzola*, is found from early January to the end of April. The black truffle is found from September to April.

Many varieties of beans are bunched together under the name *fagioli* but might include butter beans, cannellini (the best), navy, strawberry. When they are dried for storage they must be soaked overnight and then cooked with a few aromatics such as carrot and celery for as long as 2 or 3 hours, depending on age. This also used to be the case with lentils but these days they do not need soaking and will cook in 20 minutes or so.

ORTAGGI, LEGUMI E INSALATE

11

VEGETABLES, LEGUMES & SALADS

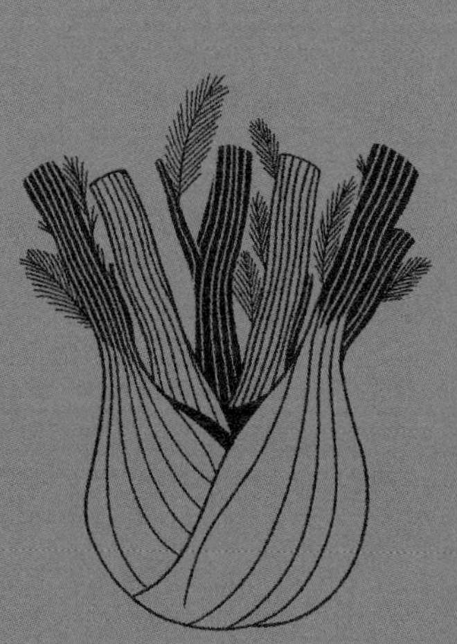

VEGETABLES

Asparagus

 **TO COOK ASPARAGUS**

Cultivated asparagus and its wild cousin must be prepared with great care, in this way: Scrape the stems, rinse them well, cut the asparagus all to the same length, and tie them in bunches. Dip in lightly boiling, very salty water, making sure not to overcook them because it is a rule that they remain al dente. When they are at the right point of cooking, pull them up and refresh in cold water to revive their color; then drain well, untie them, and arrange them on a serving dish.

ASPARAGI AL BURRO

Asparagus with Butter

2¼ lb asparagus
Grated Parmesan
7 tbsp butter
Salt

Boil the asparagus as a bundle, but not too much, drain them very well, untie them, and arrange them in an oval serving dish. Cover the green part with ½ cup grated Parmesan. Brown the butter until it turns hazelnut and dress the tips. This preparation, well accepted by all, should be brought to the table immediately.

ADA SAYS: *You can also happily just dress the asparagus with lemon and oil.*

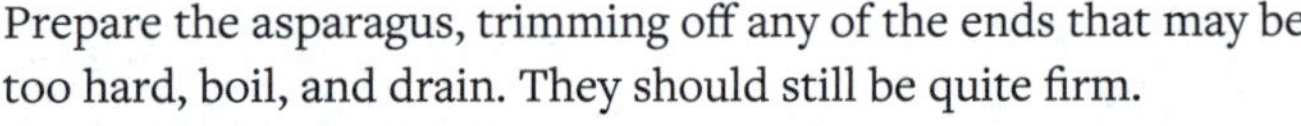

ASPARAGI AL PROSCIUTTO

Asparagus with Prosciutto

2¼ lb asparagus
5¼ oz prosciutto
10½ tbsp butter
Grated Parmesan
Salt

Prepare the asparagus, trimming off any of the ends that may be too hard, boil, and drain. They should still be quite firm.

Take 5 or 6 asparagus tips at a time, gather them in a bunch, wrap them in a long, thin slice of prosciutto, and hold in place with a toothpick. Melt two thirds of the butter in an ovenproof dish, lower the bundles in, sprinkle with ½ cup grated Parmesan, and put the pan in a preheated oven of moderate heat for a few minutes until the cheese has melted.

Once out of the oven, arrange the asparagus on a serving dish and sprinkle with the remaining melted butter.

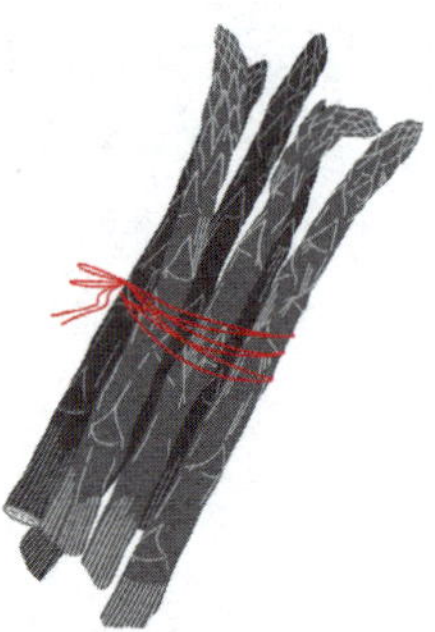

ASPARAGI CON LE UOVA

Asparagus with Eggs

2¼ lb asparagus
6 poached eggs
Grated Parmesan
Butter
Salt

Prepare the asparagus, breaking off any harder parts, at the base of the stem, trim if neccessary, and boil them in a bundle. Drain them very well. Arrange in an ovenproof dish.

Poach the eggs and place them on the tips of the asparagus, seasoning them with plenty of grated Parmesan and melted butter. Add salt and put the eggs and asparagus in a very hot oven for 1 or 2 minutes. Once out of the oven, drain a little more melted butter on the eggs and serve.

ADA SAYS: *Care must be taken that both the asparagus and the eggs are well drained, otherwise the butter will be diluted by the water and the food will be tasteless.*

ASPARAGI IN BUDINO

Asparagus Flan

2¼ lb asparagus
5 tbsp butter
3 eggs
Flour
2 oz ham
2 tsp heavy cream
Breadcrumbs
Salt

Trim and prepare the asparagus, boil in a bundle so they are almost cooked, drain, and leave to cool.

Put the butter in a bowl and mix with a wooden spoon to soften, then add, 1 at a time, the egg yolks and a pinch of salt; work for a long time so that the mixture is soft and smooth. Whisk the egg whites to a firm snow and add them, delicately, to the yolks. Drop ⅓ cup of flour into the bowl and mix slowly, and then add the diced ham and the asparagus cut into 1 or 1½ inch pieces. Finally, to make the mixture even softer, mix in some whipped cream, stirring gently.

Grease a cake mold with a capacity of 3 cups, sprinkle it with fine breadcrumbs so they stick all over and pour in the mixture. Place the mold in another container containing hot water and cook the mixture in this bain-marie for about 45 minutes until it is firm, making sure that the water in the container, while remaining warm, never boils. When the mixture has set, leave it for a few more minutes, still in a bain-marie, then turn it out and send it to the table.

ASPARAGI IN INSALATA

Asparagus Salad

2¼ lb asparagus
Olive oil
Vinegar
1 onion
Parsley
Mint
Salt
Pepper

Boil the asparagus in a bundle, and place them on a serving dish.

Put a quarter of a glass of oil in a small bowl with the vinegar, salt, and pepper, and beat everything with a small whisk or fork until the oil is blended with the vinegar. Finish the sauce with a finely chopped onion, a few sprigs of well chopped parsley, and a mint leaf.

Place the sauce in a gravy boat and send it to the table as accompaniment to the asparagus.

ASPARAGI IN SALSA GRATINATA

Asparagus Gratin

2¼ lb asparagus
7 tbsp butter
2 hard-boiled eggs
2 tbsp breadcrumbs
Parsley

Boil the asparagus and lay up ready in a plate.

Put the butter in a pan and let it fry it until it has a nice light hazelnut color. Then add the chopped hard-boiled eggs, breadcrumbs, and chopped parsley. Mix well.

Cover only the green parts of the asparagus with this sauce. Send immediately to the table.

Beets

BARBABIETOLE E CIPOLLE IN INSALATA

Beet and Onion Salad

6 white onions
Olive oil
6 baked beets
Vinegar
Basil
Salt

Remove the skin from the onions and put them in a pot of boiling water. Boil for about 10 minutes, then drain, cut them horizontally in 2, and arrange them in a well-oiled dish. Sprinkle with salt, and drain a little oil on them and place them in a warm oven with a light heat, for about an hour. In this way the onions will be wilted, tender, and very sweet.

Then arrange them on a plate, pour over the little seasoning left in the pan, and let them cool.

Take the beets and divide them into thin slices. Season with oil, salt, a little vinegar, chopped fresh basil leaves, and arrange them on the cooked onions.

ADA SAYS: *You can if you like bake fresh beets alongside the onions, but be sure they are similar in size. The skin should come off easily in your hands.*

BARBABIETOLE E CIPOLLE IN SALSA

Beet and Onion in Sauce

3 onions
4 anchovy fillets
Mustard
Vinegar
Olive oil
6 large cooked beets
Salt
Pepper

Bake the onions in the oven, then mash or blend them. Collect the purée in a bowl and add the washed, boned, and chopped anchovy fillets, a pinch of mustard, vinegar, pepper, salt, and 4 tablespoons of oil. Whip this sauce with a fork. Cut the beets into cubes and mix in and pour everything into a crystal bowl.

Broccoli & Broccoli Rabe

TO COOK THE CABBAGE FAMILY

The cabbage family - broccoli, broccoli rabe, cabbage, cauliflower, etc. - all have the defect of emitting an unpleasant odor during cooking, the more penetrating, the less the plants are fresh. The problem can be alleviated by putting a piece of bread with lemon juice or a large chunk of bread soaked in vinegar in the cooking water.

BROCCOLETTI DI RAPE A CRUDO (RAPINI)

Pan-Fried Broccoli Rabe

4½ lb broccoli rabe
Lard or olive oil
Garlic
Salt
Pepper

Remove the few harder outside leaves and rinse the broccoli rabe. Put a saucepan on the heat with a little lard or oil and a clove of garlic, which you will remove as soon as it colors.

Then add the broccoli rabe, season with salt and pepper, and sauté slowly over a medium heat for about 10 minutes, mixing from time to time and basting with a few spoons of water if they threaten to burn.

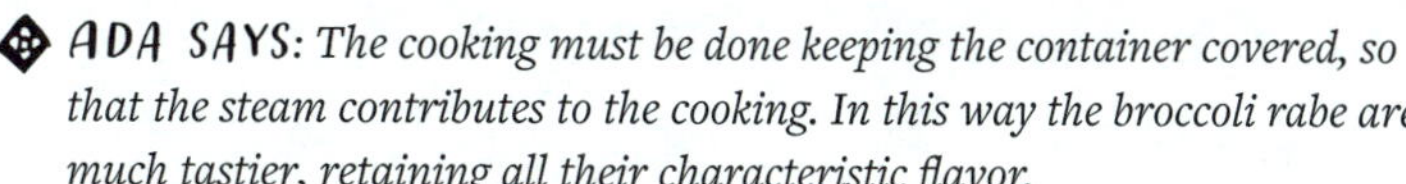

ADA SAYS: *The cooking must be done keeping the container covered, so that the steam contributes to the cooking. In this way the broccoli rabe are much tastier, retaining all their characteristic flavor.*

BROCCOLETTI DI RAPE RIPASSATI IN PADELLA

Pan-Fried Broccoli Rabe with Chili

4½ lb broccoli rabe
Lard or olive oil
Garlic
Salt
Optional: Chili (*pepperoncino*)

Remove the harder, outside broccoli leaves. Bring a pan of lightly salted water to a boil and add the broccoli rabe. When they are cooked, after about 10 minutes, drain well and squeeze dry.

Put a spoon of lard or 2 fingers of oil in a pan. Fry a clove of garlic until it browns, then take it out and discard. Add also, if you like, a piece of chili—*pepperoncino*. Then add the broccoli rabe, season with pepper, and leave a few moments to get to know each other.

BROCCOLO A CRUDO ALLA ROMANA

Broccoli Roman Style

1 large broccoli head
Olive oil
Garlic
Wine
Carrots
Lemon
Chilis
Salt

Clean the broccoli, remove the outer leaves, keeping some more tender ones; cut them into rather small pieces. Split the stems of the florets along their entire length. Keep the leaves and florets in fresh water until ready to cook.

Put a little oil in a pan, adding a couple of diced garlic cloves. Sauté lightly, without letting the garlic brown, and then put in, firstly, the broccoli leaves, season with salt and pepper, and then add the well-drained florets. Season with a little more salt and pepper and, after a little, baste with a glass of dry wine. Cover and sauté slowly for about 10 minutes, stirring from time to time carefully so as not to break the florets.

When cooked, arrange the florets on a serving dish, garnish them with raw carrot sticks, rubbed with a little lemon, and fresh chilis, and serve them as a separate vegetable dish or as a side dish for boiled or roasted meats.

BROCCOLO A CRUDO ALLA SICILIANA

Broccoli Sicilian Style

1 large broccoli head
1 large onion
2 oz Gaeta olives
3 anchovy fillets
2 oz Caciocavallo cheese
Olive oil
Red wine
Fried croutons
Salt

Caciocavallo cheese is a cheese made out of sheep's or cow's milk produced in southern Italy. For this recipe, you can also use provolone, Fontina or Gruyère.

Clean the broccoli, divide into many florets, and rinse. Thinly slice a large onion, remove the stones from the Gaeta olives, wash and bone the salted anchovy fillets, and finally chop the Caciocavallo with a knife.

Pour a little oil into an oven dish. In the bottom arrange a little onion, a few olives, a little cheese, and some anchovy fillets.

On this first layer make a very compact layer of raw broccoli florets. Season with a little salt, sprinkle with a little more oil, and continue to alternate layers until the dish is full. Pour a little more oil over everything and wet everything with a glass of red wine. Cover and put it on a very light heat for about a quarter of an hour.

Then arrange on a plate and surround with fried croutons.

ADA SAYS: *You have to adjust the heat so that when cooked the wine has just evaporated, without you ever having to mix the food during cooking.*

BROCCOLO LESSATO ALL'AGRO

Broccoli with Lemon

1 large broccoli head
Olive oil
Lemon
Salt

Clean the broccoli, remove outer leaves, and divide into many florets.

Put the necessary water and salt in a saucepan and when the boil has risen, add the leaves and florets. When they are cooked, after about a quarter of an hour, drain and toss in a serving dish with oil and lemon.

Mix them carefully without breaking them and send them to the table.

BROCCOLO RIPASSATO IN PADELLA

Broccoli with Prosciutto

1 large broccoli head
Garlic
Lard or olive oil
2 oz prosciutto
Salt
Pepper

After carefully washing and boiling the broccoli, brown a clove of garlic in a pan with a spoon of lard or oil. As soon as the garlic browns, remove it and add the cooked broccoli, season with salt and pepper, and let it flavor in the sauce over medium heat.

If the broccoli dries out too much, add a little water and then check the flavor. A few minutes before removing from the heat add the prosciutto, cut into strips. Give it a good stir and pour into a serving dish and serve hot.

Swiss Chard

BIETOLE LESSATE

Swiss Chard with Lemon

4½ lb Swiss chard
Olive oil
1 lemon
Salt

Wash the chard and rinse thoroughly to free them from any earth. Put a little lightly salted water in a saucepan, and when it boils, throw in the chard and let them boil well.

Drain them well, put them on a serving dish, and season with oil and lemon juice. After a good stir, send to the table.

BIETOLE GRATINATE

Swiss Chard and Mushroom Gratin

3 lb 5 oz Swiss chard
3 tbsp dried mushrooms
2 onions
Olive oil
Parsley
2 garlic cloves
3 eggs
Grated Parmesan
Breadcrumbs
Salt
Pepper

Remove the stalks from the chard, wash the leaves carefully, and cut them into strips. Place them in a saucepan with a little salt, without adding water. Cover and cook over a very moderate heat, taking care to stir from time to time and immediately covering the container again. In this way the chard gets enough water from their own steam. Cook, but not too much, drain, and squeeze them dry in your hands.

Soak the mushrooms to revive. Cut 2 onions into slices and cook them in a saucepan with a large glass of oil; as soon as the onion is golden, add chopped parsley, 2 cloves of garlic, and the well-washed mushrooms. And finally the chard.

Let everything flavor well and after a few minutes take the pan off the heat. Let it cool for a while, and then season with beaten eggs, a pinch of pepper, 2 spoons of grated Parmesan, a little more oil, and the necessary salt.

Oil an oven pan and sprinkle some breadcrumbs on top. Pour in the chard and onion mix, flatten it, and cover with more breadcrumbs. Put the pan in a preheated oven until the breadcrumbs have taken on a nice golden hue.

BIETOLE RIPASSATE IN PADELLA

Pan-Fried Swiss Chard with Garlic

4½ lb Swiss chard
Garlic
Olive oil
Salt

Wash the chard carefully, simmer in a little lightly salted boiling water, and when they are cooked let them drain well and squeeze them dry carefully.

Brown the garlic in a pan with some oil. When the garlic begins to brown, pour the chard into the pan. Season with salt, stirring with a wooden spoon, and place in a serving dish, after removing the garlic.

Artichokes

TO CHOOSE ARTICHOKES

In Italy, artichokes are sold while they are still young and small in which case they can simply be cut in half. Older, larger artichokes will more easily be handled by boiling first and removing the hairy choke and just keeping the heart.

TO BOIL ARTICHOKES

Put a pot of lightly salted water with a glass of vinegar or lemon juice over moderate heat and when it boils, add the artichokes. Cook, taking care to keep them at the right point of cooking. Place them in a bowl upside down to drain them well, then place on a serving dish. You can serve them hot or cold, removing the chokes if necessary. The hot ones can be seasoned with oil, salt, and pepper; cold with mayonnaise or more simply with oil and lemon.

CARCIOFI DI RISO

Artichokes with Rice

12 small very tender artichokes
1 lemon or vinegar
Olive oil
1 onion
3 anchovy fillets
1 cup rice
Broth
Breadcrumbs
Salt
Pepper

Prepare the artichokes in boiling acidulated water and drain and remove the choke. Make this filling: Put a little oil and half a thinly chopped onion in a pan, brown the onion, and then add 3 anchovy fillets, washed, boned, and cut into pieces. Mash them with a wooden spoon to reduce them to a pulp, and then add the rice. Season with salt and pepper, sprinkle with water or lightly salted broth, and bring it to a complete cooking.

Transfer the cooked rice to a plate and let it cool a little. Then put a spoonful in each half artichoke, making a nice rounded shape.

As you fill the artichokes, line them up in a baking tray, so that they all fit in 1 layer. When you have prepared them all, sprinkle over the breadcrumbs. Put 3 or 4 spoons of water and a spoon of oil in the pan and then drain a little more oil on each artichoke. Put the pan in a preheated oven of lively heat for about 10 minutes to allow the breadcrumbs to color.

CARCIOFI FRITTI ALLA GUIDA

Deep-Fried Artichokes Jewish Style

12 young and tender Romanescu artichokes (*cimaroli*)
1 lemon
Salt
Pepper
Abundant oil for frying

To fry these artichokes Jewish-style, they must be prepared in a special way.

You need to use a sharp knife to trim the stalks back hard, leaving about 3 fingers length. Take off all the dark green leaves so all that remains is the round heart like a flower. Add the artichokes to a bowl of cold acidulated water with some lemon juice so that they don't blacken.

Beat them lightly on the table. Season with salt and pepper.

Put plenty of oil in a pan (which in the traditional recipe would require an earthenware pot to ensure its characteristic dark gold color). Turn on the heat and arrange the artichokes stem up and so that they are not too crushed, and deep fry at a moderate heat, so that they also cook inside. Turn the artichokes from time to time, especially if the oil in the pan is not enough to cover them. Flatten them against the bottom of the pan, reviving the heat a little, so that the leaves acquire a dark gold color and crunchiness.

When the artichokes are nearly cooked, place a bowl containing cold water near the pan, dip your hand in the water, and carefully splash a little of this water on the boiling oil. This causes a crackling sound, which has the effect of completing the crunchy shell of the artichokes.

Keep them a little longer in the pan, then remove them, let drain, arrange them on a plate, and serve hot.

CARCIOFI FRITTI ALLA VILLEROY

Fried Artichokes Villeroy

12 small very tender artichokes or just the hearts
2 lemons
2 eggs
Grated Parmesan
Flour
Breadcrumbs
Salt
Pepper
Nutmeg

White sauce:
3½ tbsp butter, 3½ tbsp flour, 1 cup milk

Cut the artichoke hearts into wedges, removing the chokes, and put them in a bowl of water acidulated with lemon juice to keep fresh.

Make up a white sauce *(p16)* with the butter, flour, and milk; work with great care, and when the sauce is well thickened, take off the heat and add an egg yolk, ½ cup of grated Parmesan, salt, pepper, and a little nutmeg and let it cool.

Meanwhile, in salted water, slightly acidulated with a few drops of lemon juice, boil the artichoke wedges, but not too much. Drain them, then dip them a few at a time, in the cold sauce. Pull them up with a fork, line them up without touching on a large plate or on the kitchen table, and let them cool.

Gently take out the artichoke wedges with their clotted sauce shirt, coat them in flour, then beaten egg and breadcrumbs, and fry them in very hot oil. As the artichokes are already cooked, the frying must not have anything else to do but make a crispy crust.

Arrange the artichokes on a serving dish, surround them with lemon wedges, and serve.

CARCIOFI FRITTI CON PASTELLA

Deep-Fried Artichokes in Batter

12 small very tender artichokes or just the hearts
1 lemon
Oil for frying

Batter:
1 cup flour, olive oil, warm water, 2 egg whites, salt

Firstly, whisk up the batter with the flour, 2 tablespoons of oil, a glass of warm water, 2 beaten egg whites, and salt.

Cut the artichokes into wedges, removing the chokes, and let them macerate for some time with salt, lemon juice, and a little oil.

Then dip the artichoke wedges in the batter. Fry them in plenty of oil, of moderate heat, until they are well cooked and golden. Sprinkle them with salt.

CARCIOFI FRITTI DORATI IN FRICASSEA

Deep-Fried Artichokes Fricasse

12 small very tender artichokes or just the hearts
2 lemons
Flour
5 to 6 eggs
Oil for frying
Butter
Broth
Parsley
Salt
Pepper

Cut the artichokes into wedges, removing the chokes, and keep them in a bowl of acidulated water. Then drain, dry, and coat in the flour and then in 2 beaten eggs. Fry them in plenty of oil, of moderate heat, until they are well cooked and golden.

Heat a little butter in another pan, add the fried artichokes, sprinkle them with salt and pepper, and baste with a little broth. Leave them to flavor on a moderate heat for a few minutes.

Beat 3 or 4 eggs with a little lemon juice. Add half a spoon of chopped parsley, and pour everything into the pan with the artichokes off the heat. Stir, cover the bowl, and leave to warm through for 3 to 4 minutes, time for the eggs to set.

CARCIOFI IN MAIONESE

Artichokes with Russian Salad

6 artichokes, young
1 lemon
Russian salad *(p725)*
Salt
Pepper
Optional: carrots, sage, capers

Mayonnaise:
2 egg yolks, ¾ cup olive oil,
1 tbsp vinegar

Take off the hardest outer leaves, cut the artichokes almost in half, taking away all the upper part of the leaves and all of the choke, so the artichokes can stand up straight. With the tip of a small knife, make a little vacuum in the middle of each artichoke, rub them with lemon, and finally boil them in salted water so they are well cooked.

Meanwhile, make up a small Russian salad, of peas, potatoes, and carrots, all cut into cubes, the same size as the peas. Slice the cornichons and capers to the same size. Season the salad with salt, pepper, and a few spoonfuls of thick mayonnaise *(p19)* made from the egg yolks, oil, and vinegar.

Fill the center of the artichokes with this mixture. Set the artichoke on a bed of raw carrots cut into sticks and drizzled with lemon, some sage leaves, and capers.

CARCIOFI IN TORTA ALLA PARMIGIANA

Artichokes Parmigiana

12 small very tender artichoke or just the hearts
2 lemons
Flour
Oil for frying
2 eggs
1 onion
2 oz prosciutto
Butter
9 oz canned tomatoes or fresh, peeled
Grated Parmesan
Salt
Pepper
Optional: 4 oz mozzarella

Cut the artichokes lengthwise into many rather thin slices, removing the chokes and rubbing them with lemon juice to stop them browning, then dip them in the flour and fry them to golden in plenty of oil; or, if you want an even more refined result, after flouring, dip them in beaten eggs and deep-fry in abundant oil.

Lightly brown a chopped onion and some diced prosciutto in butter. Then add the peeled tomatoes, season with salt and pepper, and cook until the tomato in the sauce is sufficiently thickened.

Butter a baking dish with low sides or an oven pan and spread a little tomato sauce in the middle. On this sauce make a layer of fried artichokes and on the artichokes spread a little more sauce and ½ cup of grated Parmesan. Continue in this way to alternate layers of artichokes, sauce, and cheese, ending with a last layer of sauce and plenty of grated Parmesan. Put a few pieces of butter here and there again, and put the pan in a preheated oven of moderate heat for about a quarter of an hour to allow the artichokes to flavor well.

ADA SAYS: *You can also put a few slices of mozzarella between layers, if you wish.*

CARCIOFI LESSATI IN SALSA DI ACCIUGHE

Artichokes with Anchovy

12 small very tender artichokes or just the hearts
Vinegar or lemon juice
1 lemon
Broth
3½ tbsp butter
Grated Parmesan
2 hard-boiled eggs
Parsley
2 anchovy fillets
Salt

Boil the artichokes with the vinegar or lemon juice and even better than water, in broth. When cooked, drain them well, removing the chokes if necessary. Wet them with melted butter, roll them in ¼ cup grated Parmesan, and place them in an ovenproof dish.

Put the artichokes in a hot oven for a few minutes, and when they come out of the oven, baste with this sauce: Shell the hard-boiled eggs, dice them with a knife, mix in the chopped parsley, and 2 washed and boned anchovy fillets. Put the remaining butter in a saucepan on the heat and when it froths, put in the eggs, anchovy fillets, and chopped parsley. Stir and pour over the artichokes. Serve with lemon.

CARCIOFI LESSATI IN SALSA D'ORO

Artichokes with Scrambled Eggs

12 small very tender artichokes or just the hearts
Vinegar or lemon juice
1 lemon
3½ tbsp butter
6 eggs
Milk
Salt
To serve: Bread for croutons

Cut the artichokes into wedges, removing the chokes, and boil in lightly salted water with a glass of vinegar or lemon juice. Drain and keep warm.

Melt the butter over a low heat, beat the eggs as for an omelet, and pour into the pan, season with a pinch of salt. Stir until the eggs have thickened to a cream and finally dilute them with half a glass of milk, always keeping the heat very low.

Place the artichoke wedges in this egg cream sauce, heat everything, and pour the preparation on to the plate, surrounding it with triangles of bread, fried in oil, and lemon wedges.

CARCIOFI NEL TEGAME ALLA ROMANA

Braised Artichokes Roman Style

12 small very tender artichokes
2 lemons
Garlic
Mint
Olive oil
Salt
Pepper

Remove the harder outer leaves from the artichokes, cut the stem so that they can stand up straight; trim the leaves halfway down so you have a conical shape and remove the chokes. Rub the cut sides with lemon juice to stop them browning, open the leaves a little, and add salt, pepper, a few pieces of garlic, and a few leaves of mint.

Line up the artichokes in a pan, with the cut side down and stem side up. Pour in a couple of glasses of water and half a glass of oil. Season with a little more salt and cook over moderate heat keeping the container well covered.

Halfway through cooking, turn the artichokes around so they cook evenly. When they are cooked, arrange them on a plate, and baste the artichokes with their juice. Excellent both hot and cold.

CARCIOFI NEL TEGAME CON PISELLI

Artichokes with Peas

12 small very tender artichokes or just the hearts
7 tbsp butter
3 lb 5 oz peas
2 egg yolks
1 lemon
Salt
To serve: bread for croutons

Cut the artichokes into wedges, removing the chokes. Let the butter melt in a pan and season the artichokes in it, adding a pinch of salt. Then baste them with a few ladles of water and let them cook. When the artichokes are half cooked, add the shelled peas and cook everything over high heat, adding a little more salt and water.

Whisk the egg yolks with a few drops of lemon, then take the pan off the heat and add to the artichokes. Stir very carefully so as not to spoil the artichokes and peas. When the egg is slightly creamy, pour into the serving dish and serve with cubes of bread fried in oil.

CARCIOFI RIPIENI AL GRATIN

Artichoke Gratin

6 artichokes, preferably the purple-tinged Romanescu
Vinegar or 1 lemon
10 oz mushrooms
3½ tbsp butter
White wine
3½ oz ham or salted tongue
Parsley
1 lb small new potatoes
Olive oil
Salt
Pepper

White sauce:
2 tbsp butter, 2 tbsp flour, 1¼ cups milk

Simmer the artichokes in lightly salted boiling water with a glass of vinegar or lemon juice. Let them cook for about 5 minutes, then drain, remove the chokes, and dry them delicately.

Clean, and quickly wash the mushrooms, cut them into slices, and put them to cook in a pan with most of the butter; season with salt and pepper and cook over high heat. As their liquid dries out, pour half a glass of wine into the pan and let it evaporate too. In about 10 minutes the mushrooms will be ready.

Prepare a white sauce *(p16)* with the butter, flour, and milk. Fold in the mushrooms, diced salted tongue or ham, and chopped parsley. Mix carefully and fill the bottom of the artichokes with this mixture.

With a small knife, lightly scrape off the skin of the new potatoes and throw them into a basin of cold water, then drain and dry them. Put them to cook, in a single layer, in a pan (whose lid closes perfectly) with half a glass of oil. Cover, reduce the heat, and let them cook slowly in their own steam. During cooking, shake the pan several times, without uncovering it; after half an hour the potatoes will be cooked and a nice golden color, then sprinkle them with salt and let them flavor for a few more minutes.

Arrange the stuffed artichokes in a buttered baking dish and put them in a preheated oven of moderate heat until they have formed a light golden crust. Serve the artichokes surrounded with the golden potatoes.

CARCIOFI RIPIENI ALLA SICILIANA

Stuffed Artichokes Sicilian Style

12 small very tender artichokes
1 lemon
Olive oil
1 onion
Garlic
Parsley
4 tbsp breadcrumbs
7 tbsp butter
4 to 5 anchovy fillets
Salt
Pepper

Remove the harder outer leaves from the artichokes, cut the stem so they can stand upright, trim the top with scissors taking off the spiky tips, remove the chokes, and rub them with a little lemon to stop them browning. Slightly spread the leaves and season the inside with salt and pepper.

Now prepare the filling: Put half a glass of oil in a pan with a small thinly sliced onion, half a clove of crushed garlic, and a spoon of chopped parsley.

Meanwhile, toast 4 tablespoons of breadcrumbs in a pan with a little oil.

Separately, use the blade of a knife to mix the butter with the washed, boned, and chopped anchovy fillets.

When the onion is a dark blond color, add the toasted breadcrumbs, the anchovy butter, a pinch of salt, bearing in mind the anchovy fillets are already salty, and a good pinch of pepper. Mix to combine all the ingredients, and then with a spoon distribute the filling in the artichokes.

Place them in a baking dish, where they can stand in a single layer, add 2 ladles of water and a drizzle of oil. Cover and cook slowly in a preheated oven of very moderate heat for about half an hour.

CARCIOFI RIPIENI DI BESCIAMELLA

Artichokes with Prosciutto and Parmesan

12 small very tender artichokes
Vinegar
2 egg yolks
Grated Parmesan
3½ oz prosciutto slices
Salt
Pepper
Nutmeg

White sauce:
2 tbsp flour, 2 tbsp butter, ¾ cup milk

Put the artichokes in boiling salted water with a glass of vinegar and cook so they are still al dente. Finally, drain them well, remove the chokes and all of the leaves, and dry them.

Meanwhile, prepare a fairly thick white sauce *(p16)* with the flour, butter, and milk and off the heat finish with 2 egg yolks, 4 tablespoons of grated Parmesan, salt, pepper, nutmeg, and diced prosciutto. Leave to cool, and then spoon a little on each half of the artichoke.

Butter an baking dish, arrange the artichoke hearts in 1 layer, sprinkle with a little more Parmesan, a few drops of melted butter, and place in a preheated oven on a lively heat until they color.

CARCIOFI RIPIENI DI PANGRATTATO ED ACCIUGHE

Artichokes with Breadcrumbs and Anchovy fillets

12 small very tender artichokes
1 lemon
Olive oil
Breadcrumbs
Garlic
3 anchovy fillets
Parsley
Salt
Pepper

Cut the artichokes in half, removing the chokes and rubbing with lemon to stop them browning. Arrange them, cut side up, in an baking dish, with a few spoons of water and a few spoons of oil.

Fill them with a rather dense mixture of breadcrumbs, oil, a little water, a small piece of garlic, washed, boned, and chopped anchovy fillets, parsley, salt, and pepper.

Drizzle a little more oil on the artichokes, and place the pan in a preheated oven of moderate heat for about half an hour until the bread takes on a nice golden color. They can be served both hot and cold.

CARCIOFI RIPIENI DI PETTO DI POLLO

Artichokes Stuffed with Chicken Breast

12 small very tender artichokes
Vinegar or lemon
7 oz cooked chicken breast
1 egg yolk
Grated Parmesan
3½ oz prosciutto slices
2 eggs
Breadcrumbs
Oil for frying
Salt
Pepper
Nutmeg

White sauce:
2 tbsp butter, 2 tbsp flour, ¾ cup milk

For this recipe the artichokes must be prepared in a particular way.

Put the artichokes in a pan with lightly salted boiling water and a glass of vinegar or lemon juice. Let them cook for about 5 minutes. Then drain, remove the chokes, and dry them gently.

Chop the boiled or roasted chicken breast on a cutting board and then place it in a bowl, with 3 spoons of white sauce *(p16)* made with the butter, flour, and milk, plus, off the heat, an egg yolk, ¼ cup grated Parmesan, salt, pepper, a pinch of nutmeg, and the prosciutto chopped into cubes.

Fill the artichokes with this mix, flour them, brush over the beaten egg, and cover with breadcrumbs and fry them, making sure they reach the table hot.

CARCIOFI RIPIENI DI TONNO

Artichokes with Tuna

12 small very tender artichokes
3½ tbsp butter
Flour
Milk
4 oz tinned tuna in olive oil
Parsley
Breadcrumbs
White pepper

Prepare the artichoke hearts in boiling water and remove the choke. Make this filling: Melt half of the butter in a pan, add a heaped spoon of flour, mix and melt with a small glass of milk. Let it thicken, always stirring, then remove the saucepan from the heat and add the chopped tuna in oil, a spoon of chopped parsley, and a pinch of white pepper. Salt is not necessary, as the tuna is sufficiently salty.

Fill the artichokes with this mixture, smoothing the filling with the blade of a knife, sprinkle over a few breadcrumbs and then line them up in a well buttered oven tray. Put another piece of butter on each artichoke, and put the dish in a preheated oven of lively heat for a few minutes.

As soon as the bread has a golden crust, arrange the artichokes on a plate, pour the butter from the pan over them, and have them brought to the table.

Cardoons

TO PREPARE CARDOONS

Cardoons are an ancient part of the artichoke family. They are a thistle, commonly called hunchbacks or sometimes gobbi. To prepare them: Remove the tough, stringy outer leaves and divide into pieces about 4 inches long. With the tip of a small knife, remove the fluff, which comes off in long threads. Do this work quickly because the thistles blacken in contact with the knife; and as soon as a piece is prepared, rub it with half a lemon and keep it in a basin of water and half a glass of vinegar. With the same speed, remove the woody peel that covers the heart of the thistle, which is the most delicate part, rub it with the lemon as well and put it in the acidulated water.

CARDI

Cardoons

1 lemon
4½ lb cardoons
Salt

Put lightly salted water in a large pot on the heat, add the juice of half a lemon, and as soon as the water has boiled, add the carefully drained cardoons and boil again. Cook for about an hour over low heat, covered. If you don't need the cardoons right away, keep them in their cooking liquid so as not to leave them exposed to the air, or cover them with a sheet of waxed paper.

CARDI AL FORNO

Baked Cardoons

4½ lb cardoons
7 tbsp butter
1 cup grated Parmesan
Salt
Pepper
Nutmeg

Prepare and cook the cardoons as above. Butter a round baking tray for the trimmed and boiled cardoons. Sprinkle with a little nutmeg, a pinch of pepper, melted butter, and grated Parmesan cheese.

Place the pan for about half an hour in a preheated oven of moderate heat and let the edges brown. Serve them immediately without decanting.

CARDI ALLA BESCIAMELLA

Cardoons in White Sauce

4½ lb cardoons
7 tbsp butter
Grated Parmesan

White sauce:
3½ tbsp flour, 3½ tbsp butter, 2 cups milk

Make a white sauce *(p16)* with the flour, butter, and the milk. Put the trimmed and boiled cardoons, as above, into a baking dish with most of the butter and the salt. Pour over the white sauce. Season with ½ cup grated Parmesan, put a few pieces of butter here and there, and place in a preheated oven for about 15 minutes, so they can brown.

CARDI ALLA PARMIGIANA

Cardoons Parmigiana

4½ lb cardoons
Flour
2 eggs
Oil for frying
Grated Parmesan
Butter

Coat the trimmed and boiled cardoons, see opposite, in the flour, then the beaten eggs, and fry them to a beautiful golden color in plenty of oil.

When you have cooked all of them, butter an baking dish and make a layer of fried cardoons. Spread over this layer grated Parmesan and thin slices of butter. Repeat the operation until you use up all the cardoons.

Bake the pan in a preheated oven of moderate heat for about 15 minutes, so that the thistles can flavor well and the surface browns slightly.

CARDI AL PROSCIUTTO

Cardoons with Prosciutto

4½ lb cardoons
3 tbsp dried mushrooms
3½ oz prosciutto slices
3 onions
Olive oil
White wine
9 oz canned tomatoes
Parsley
Salt
Pepper

Trim and boil the cardoons, as opposite. Reconstitute the mushrooms in warm water and then wash and chop. Also chop the prosciutto.

Finely chop the onions, fry in half a glass of oil over a high heat until they are golden. Add half a glass of white wine and the tomatoes. Then add the chopped mushrooms and the prosciutto and chopped parsley. Sauté for 10 minutes.

Drain the cardoons and put them in an baking dish and pour over the sauce. Bake in a hot oven for about 10 minutes.

Carrots

CAROTE AL BURRO

Carrots with Butter

2¼ lb carrots
7 tbsp butter
Flour
Sugar
Broth
Salt
Optional: lemon and oil

Scrape the carrots, top and tail and rinse them, quarter them, take out any woody core, and cut into matchstick lengths. Keep them in fresh water until you are ready.

Melt most of the butter in a pan and add the well-drained carrots. Let them flavor a little and then season with salt, half a spoon of flour, and a strong pinch of sugar. Stir, and then baste with broth or water until the carrots are completely covered; cover and poach over a moderate heat, stirring occasionally. After about 20 minutes the carrots will be cooked.

Remove the carrots and reduce the sauce, if it is still too liquid, remove the pan from the heat and add a few more pieces of butter and send to the table.

ADA SAYS: *You can also serve the carrots with lemon and oil.*

CAROTE AL LATTE

Carrots in Milk

2¼ lb carrots
3½ tbsp butter
Milk
1 egg yolk
Salt
To serve: bread for croutons

Cut the carrots into not very thin slices and poach them in lightly boiling salted water. Leave them to cook for 5 minutes. Then drain and place them in a pan with the butter, a glass and a half of milk, and a pinch of salt.

Put the pan back on a low heat and finish cooking. When the liquid has reduced, whisk an egg yolk into a cold half glass of milk and pour over the carrots.

Reduce the heat, mix well with a wooden spoon, and wait for the egg to set without letting it boil. After 5 minutes, transfer the carrots into a serving dish and surround them with fried croutons.

CAROTE GIALLE RIPIENE

Stuffed Carrot with Tuna

6 large carrots
4 oz tinned tuna in olive oil
Loaf of bread
2 cups tomato passata
Olive oil
Vinegar
Parsley

For this recipe you will need a zucchini corer.

In a small bowl, mix the tuna, the bread, soaked in water and squeezed dry in your hands so it is about the size of an egg, add chopped parsley.

Lightly scrape the carrots. Insert the tip of the corer into one end and slowly, slowly turn round to extract the core and empty the middle. Repeat the exercise from the other end so there is space for the stuffing. Or if this is not working, slice the carrots lengthwise and take out the core so there is space for the stuffing.

Cover with the passata diluted with a little oil and vinegar so it is very loose. Bake in a low-heat oven until the sauce is thick and the carrots cooked, which may be about 45 minutes.

CAROTE GIALLE AL MARSALA

Glazed Carrots with Marsala

1 lb or 12 small carrots
3 tbsp butter
3 tbsp sugar
1 tbsp flour
6 fl oz Marsala
Parsley
Salt
Pepper

Peel and chop the carrots. Melt the butter in a pan and add the carrots, salt, pepper and sugar. Roll the carrots around so they are well covered, then add a tablespoon of flour, the Marsala or broth to cover.

Bring up to a simmer. Cover and cook for 20 – 25 minutes, checking every now and then that there is enough liquid. Top up if necessary. The sauce should be thick and the carrots tender. Serve with chopped parsley and black pepper.

CAROTE IN PURÈ

Carrot Purée

6 large carrots
10 tbsp butter
5 tbsp rice
Salt
To serve: bread for croutons

Quarter the carrots lengthwise and take away the woody inner part. Cut into slices and fry in the butter. Cook, covered, over a low heat, so they steam rather than roasting.

After about a quarter of an hour pour 1¼ quarts of water into the saucepan. When it boils, add the rice, season with salt, and cook for an hour, so that the rice and carrots are well done. Strain everything through a fine mesh sieve, blend, and collect the resulting purée in a bowl. If the purée is too thick, dilute it with a little more water and then pour it back into the saucepan to heat it. Check the salt. Complete with a few cubes of fried bread and a piece of butter.

CAROTE MARINATE

Marinated Carrots

2¼ lb carrots
2 garlic cloves
Olive oil
Vinegar
Oregano
Salt
Pepper or red chili flakes

Trim the carrots, then simmer, but keep them whole. As soon as they are cooked, drain them, quarter them, and take out the central woody core. Chop each into 2 or 3 pieces.

Put the carrots in a salad bowl with a couple of peeled garlic cloves, salt, pepper or chili, oil, plenty of vinegar, and 3 or 4 pinches of oregano. Mix everything and leave at least 1 day to give everything time to flavor well.

Cabbage

CAVOLO ALL'ACETO

Cabbage in Vinegar

1 cabbage head
Bread
Vinegar
Lard
2 oz lardo
Garlic
Sugar
Salt

Take off the hard outer cabbage leaves and discard. Keep the tender leaves that are left and put them to boil in lightly salted boiling water with some bread soaked in vinegar and cook over a high heat, uncovered, for about 20 minutes.

When they are cooked, drain, and cut them into thin ribbons about ¼ inch wide.

Put a little lard, a small piece of lardo, and a small piece of garlic in a saucepan and when the fats melt, lay down the cabbage. Let it flavor well and season with salt and a little pepper.

Then baste with half a glass of water and a half of vinegar and add half a teaspoon of sugar. Cover and simmer over moderate heat until the liquid has almost disappeared.

CAVOLO IN SALSA DI ACCIUGHE

Cabbage in Anchovy Sauce

2¼ lb cabbage
Vinegar
4 anchovy fillets
Olive oil
Salt
Pepper

Boil the cabbage leaves. Then drain and keep warm in a bowl.

Put 4 tablespoons of vinegar in a pan with the washed and boned anchovy fillets, cut into pieces. Always stirring with a wooden spoon, let the anchovy fillets melt down; then add half a glass of oil, salt and pepper and bring to a boil.

Pour the hot sauce on to the cabbage leaves and mix well. Place everything on the serving dish, so it gets to the table still hot.

Brussels Sprouts

TO COOK BRUSSELS SPROUTS

Brussels sprouts look very good in elegant preparations. To boil Brussels sprouts a certain amount of attention is needed: Put water and salt in a saucepan - 9 cups of water to 3½ tsp of salt for 1 lb of sprouts - and when it comes to a boil, add the sprouts.

Simmer uncovered - this is very important - for 10 or 15 minutes depending on the size of the sprouts. As soon as they are cooked, drain them immediately because the cooking water causes them to turn yellow.

CAVOLETTI DI BRUXELLES AL BURRO

Brussels Sprouts with Butter

1 lb 5 oz Brussels sprouts
7 tbsp butter
Parsley
Pepper
Salt

Boil the sprouts, as above, and then drain.

Warm half of the butter in a very large pan. Throw in the sprouts and leave them to flavor over high heat, moving the pan with a constant motion so that the sprouts can be mixed without the help of a fork, so as not to damage them.

After 7 or 8 minutes, when the sprouts have started to brown, remove them from the heat, add the pepper, the chopped parsley, and the rest of the butter, divided into small pieces.

Shake the pan again, add salt, and pour the sprouts into a vegetable bowl and serve hot.

CAVOLETTI DI BRUXELLES AL FORNO CON GUANCIALE

Baked Brussels Sprouts with Guanciale

1 lb 5 oz Brussels sprouts
Butter
2 oz guanciale or pork ventresca, cut in cubes
3½ oz lardo slices
Broth
Salt
Pepper
Nutmeg

Boil the sprouts, as above, then put them in a generously buttered baking tray with the guanciale or ventresca cut into cubes. Season with salt, pepper, and nutmeg. Cover with thin slices of lardo and cover completely with broth.

Put the dish in a preheated oven of moderate heat and cook for half an hour. Take a look at them at intervals and if they get too dry, add a few more spoons of broth.

When cooked, the pan should be almost dry and the sprouts well glazed. Arrange the sprouts in a vegetable dish and serve them as they are with the diced bacon and the slices of lardo from the cooking.

CAVOLETTI DI BRUXELLES FRITTI

Fried Brussels Sprouts

1 lb 5 oz Brussels sprouts
Flour
Grated Parmesan
Olive oil
2 eggs
Salt

Boil the sprouts *(opposite page)* and drain.

Make a batter with the flour and a little water, add ¼ cup grated Parmesan, a little oil, and a little salt. When you have mixed everything well, add the egg yolks and finally the whipped egg whites.

Cover the sprouts in the batter and fry them in plenty of very hot oil. Finish them with a pinch of salt. Serve immediately.

Cauliflower

TO COOK CAULIFLOWER

Using a small knife, remove the cauliflower florets 1 by 1 from the trunk or central stalk; as you remove them, shorten the stems a little. When you arrive at the center the florets will be more tender. Remove them from the stem in small groups.

Put these florets in a bowl with plenty of cold water and, if you want, add a few tablespoons of vinegar. The cauliflower must be cooked in plenty of water - 10 cups of water and 3½ tsp of salt of salt per 1 pound of cauliflower. Put the water to boil with some bread soaked in vinegar and as soon as it boils, add the florets, stem down.

Bring the water to a boil again, which must always be very strong to preserve the whiteness of the cauliflower. Do not put the lid on. Cook for about 15 minutes. As a precaution, check the cooking a little before this time because 1 minute too much is enough to ruin the florets.

As soon as the stems are tender, remove the pan from the heat and immediately pour cold water into the pan to stop them cooking. This way you will have time to drain the florets a little at a time with a slotted spoon because if you pour them all together into the strainer, you may ruin them. Arrange the florets on a serving dish and season with oil and vinegar or lemon.

CAVOLFIORE FRITTO

Fried Cauliflower

2¼ lb cauliflower
Oil for frying

Batter:
1 cup flour, water,
olive oil, 2 egg whites, salt

First prepare a batter: Put the flour in a bowl, add a glass of water, a tablespoon of oil, a pinch of salt, and mix lightly with a fork. Let the batter rest for about an hour.

Prepare the cauliflower, boiling and draining carefully, as above.

Beat the egg whites until stiff and add them to the batter. Pass the cauliflower florets through the batter and fry them in plenty of hot oil.

CAVOLFIORE LESSATO ALLA BESCIAMELLA

Cauliflower with White Sauce

2¼ lb cauliflower
Grated Parmesan
Butter
Breadcrumbs

White sauce:
⅓ cup flour, 3½ tbsp butter, 3 cups milk

Boil the cauliflower and drain carefully.

Make up a fairly liquid white sauce *(p16)* with the flour, butter, and milk and add a little grated Parmesan.

Butter an baking dish and arrange the florets inside and pour over the sauce. Top with a little more Parmesan and breadcrumbs. Arrange here and there some small pieces of butter.

Put them in a preheated oven for about 20 minutes, so they can be well gratinated.

CAVOLFIORE LESSATO ALLA NAPOLETANA

Cauliflower Neapolitan Style

2¼ lb cauliflower
Olive oil
Vinegar
3 anchovy fillets
2 oz Gaeta olives, pitted
Capers
Breadcrumbs
Salt
Pepper

Boil the cauliflower, but not too much and drain well.

Season the florets in a bowl with oil, vinegar, salt, and pepper. Add the anchovy fillets, washed, boned, and divided into fillets, also the pitted olives and a handful of capers. Mix carefully and arrange on a serving dish.

ADA SAYS: *A very common preparation in Naples for Christmas Eve.*

Onions

CIPOLLE AL FORNO

Baked Onions

2¼ lb onions
Olive oil
Parsley
Salt
Pepper

Clean the onions. Cut off the roots and tops and remove the skin. Bring a pan of water to a boil and drop the onions in and let them cook for about 10 minutes, drain well and cut them in half horizontally.

Oil an baking dish, arrange the half onions, cut side up, season with salt, pepper, and chopped parsley. Drizzle a little oil over them and bake in a preheated oven of very moderate heat for about an hour.

When they are well wilted, remove them from the oven, arrange them on a serving dish, and pour over the oil from the pan.

CIPOLLE FRITTE IN ANELLINI

Fried Onion Rings

1 lb red onions, like Tropea
Flour
Lard or oil for frying
Salt

This fried onion preparation is exquisite and goes well with zucchini fritters. Tropea onions are preferable, but not very large ones.

Peel the onions, trim them at the ends, and cut them horizontally into slices a ¼ inch thick. These slices will be composed of many concentric rings. Dip the rings in boiling water, boil them for 5 minutes, then drain and put them in a basin with fresh water.

After a few minutes, drain them again and put them to dry on a sheet of absorbent paper.

Take a few rings at a time, flour them, and fry them in plenty of oil or lard until they have a faint pale gold color. Remove them from the pan and sprinkle lightly with salt.

CIPOLLE LESSATE

Boiled Onions

2¼ lb onions
Parsley or oregano
Olive oil
Salt
Pepper

Trim and clean the onions then dip them in plenty of lightly salted boiling water and let them cook for half an hour or more depending on size. When cooked, drain them, cut them in half, arrange them on a plate, and season with a little chopped parsley or oregano, salt, pepper, and a little oil.

ADA SAYS: *These onions are excellent with boiled meat, or even alone. They are particularly good also used as a side dish for tuna in oil cut into thin slices.*

CIPOLLE RIPIENE DI CARNE

Onions Stuffed with Meat

6 red onions, like Tropea
5½ tbsp butter
2 oz breadcrumbs
3½ oz lean beef or ground veal
1 egg yolk
Parsley
Olive oil
Breadcrumbs
Salt
Pepper

Peel the onions and halve them horizontally. Put them in boiling water for about 10 minutes. Then put them in cold water, drain, and dry on a sheet of absorbent paper.

Remove 3 to 4 rings from the center of each onion to have a bowl-shaped space in the middle for the filling. Sprinkle with salt.

Take the trimmings you have just removed from the onions and chop and put them in a small saucepan with a little butter and let them cook on a very low heat without coloring; then set aside.

Put the breadcrumbs in a saucepan, with 2 fingers of water; when after a few minutes the breadcrumbs have absorbed all the water, put them on the stove, and work vigorously with a wooden spoon until they become an elastic dough and a easily detached from the spoon. Turn this upside down on a plate, flatten it a little, spread a piece of butter on top, and let it cool.

Chop the lean beef or ground veal with two thirds of the butter, already softened, the cold bread, a pinch of salt, a pinch of pepper, and an egg yolk. Add these ingredients little by little, always chopping, to obtain a very fine paste. Lastly add a good spoon of chopped parsley and the chopped onion cooked in butter.

Spoon the filling into each onion and smooth it with the blade of a knife. Oil an oven dish and line up the onions side by side, sprinkle them with a few breadcrumbs, and drain a little melted butter on each. Put in a preheated oven of very moderate heat and let the onions cook for a long time, for about an hour, so that they wilt slowly.

CIPOLLE SULLA GRATELLA

Grilled Onions

2¼ lb onions
Olive oil
Parsley
Salt
Pepper

Trim and skin the onions, then put them in boiling water to cook slowly for 10 minutes. Drain, cut them in half, and arrange them on a grill rack. Season them with a little oil, chopped parsley, salt, and pepper.

Grill for a long time on a very low heat, until you see they are well wilted. Then arrange them on the serving dish and pour a little more oil over them.

Cipollini onions

TO PREPARE CIPOLLINI

Cipollini are similar to shallots except they are much sweeter. Remove the outer skin and trim the roots, but not too much, because when cooking they could open easily. As you peel them, put them in a basin with fresh water.

During the season, after having peeled and rinsed them, you can cook them like this without doing anything else; but from October onward, that is, when the onions begin to age a little, it is a good idea to blanch them in lightly salted boiling water first, thus achieving 2 purposes: to remove a little bitterness and to facilitate cooking. There is no need for this blanching to be too long, as long as the onions boil for a few minutes.

CIPOLLINE AL FORNO

Baked Cipollini Onions

2¼ lb cipollini onions
Olive oil
Salt
Pepper
Optional: if to be eaten cold, add vinegar or lemon juice

Baked onions can be eaten both hot and cold.

Put the onions in the oven as they are, and let them brown slowly. When they are roasted, skin them as if you were peeling roasted chestnuts. Arrange the hot onions in a vegetable dish and season with oil, pepper, and salt. For onions to be eaten cold, add a few drops of oil or lemon juice.

ADA SAYS: *Cipollini are also known as summer minis, a substitute can be pearl onions or shallots.*

CIPOLLINE AL SUGO DI POMODORO

Cipollini Onions in Tomato Sauce

2¼ lb cipollini onions
Olive oil
Sugar
1¼ cups tomato passata
Salt
Pepper

Skin the onions, nick off the roots, and keep in a basin with fresh water. Then line them up in a pan in a single layer in a baking dish with a little oil. Season with a little salt, pepper, and a spoon of sugar.

Cover the onions with the tomato passata, cover the pan, and cook over medium heat, making sure that at the end of cooking, after about half an hour, the sauce is reduced and envelops the onions in a shiny coat.

CIPOLLINE AL VINO BIANCO

Cipollini Onions in White Wine

2¼ lb cipollini onions
7 tbsp butter
Flour
3 cups white wine
Salt

Trim and skin the onions. Let the butter melt in a large pan and add the onions; season with a little salt, sprinkle with a little flour, and brown them slightly, stirring carefully.

Then baste with 3 cups of white wine, put the lid on the pan, and cook slowly, letting the liquid evaporate and condense. When the onions are cooked, pour them into a serving dish and send them to the table.

CIPOLLINE CON PISELLI

Cipollini Onions with Peas

3½ tbsp butter
1 onion
1 lb cipollini onions
3 lb 5 oz peas in the shell (or 1 lb 5 oz shelled)
Broth
2 oz prosciutto
Parsley
Salt
Pepper

Put the butter and a spoon of finely chopped onion in a good sized saucepan. Cook slowly, so the onion cooks without browning; if necessary, add a little water. Peel the cipollini and add them along with the shelled peas. Season with salt and pepper and add a few spoons of boiling broth.

Let them cook slowly for half an hour, stirring several times. A few minutes before removing the saucepan from the heat, add the prosciutto cut into strips and the chopped parsley. Pour everything into a round serving dish and serve hot.

ADA SAYS: *You may also use pearl or baby onions for this recipe.*

CIPOLLINE GLASSATE BIANCHE

Glazed Cipollini Onions

2¼ lb cipollini onions
5½ tbsp butter
Vegetable broth
Salt

Skin the cipollini onions and arrange them in a pan, in a single layer. Add a nice piece of butter and cover with broth.

Cover and cook until all the broth has evaporated and reduced to a thick sauce. Then turn them over carefully so that they are evenly coated with sauce and arrange them on the plate. These onions must remain white.

ADA SAYS: *For a darker glaze you can add a teaspoon of sugar to the cooking and a few spoons of beef or chicken broth at the end to color.*

CIPOLLINE IN AGRODOLCE

Sweet and Sour Cipollini Onions

2¼ lb cipollini onions
2 oz prosciutto fat
Lard or butter
Sugar
Vinegar
Salt
Pepper

Trim and skin the cipollini onions. Dice a small piece of prosciutto fat and put it in a pan with the lard or 2 tablespoons of butter. Heat and then add 2 spoons of sugar. Dissolve the sugar in the fat, stirring, and then add half a glass of vinegar.

Put the onions in the pan, season with salt and a little pepper, cover and cook for about half an hour over moderate heat.

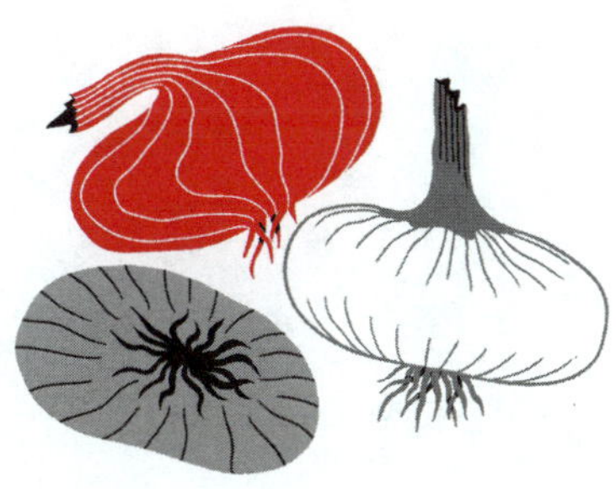

Fennel

FINOCCHI ALLA BESCIAMELLA

Fennel with White Sauce

2¼ lb fennel
Butter
Breadcrumbs
Salt

White sauce:
3½ tbsp butter, 3 cups milk,
⅓ cup flour, salt, nutmeg

Remove the hardest outside leaves of the fennel. Cut the rest into wedges, rinse them, and put them in boiling salted water. Drain them and leave them aside.

Prepare a fairly liquid white sauce *(p16)* with the butter, flour, milk, salt, and nutmeg.

Butter an baking dish, put the fennel in, and cover everything with the sauce. Sprinkle a few breadcrumbs over everything, put a few pieces of butter here and there and cook for about 20 minutes in a preheated oven, until the sauce and breadcrumbs are slightly colored.

FINOCCHI AL POMODORO

Fennel with Tomato

2¼ lb fennel
Flour
Olive oil
Salt
Pepper

Tomato sauce:
1 onion, 1 carrot, celery, basil, olive oil, fresh tomatoes (or use canned)

Remove the harder outer layers from the fennel, cut the rest into slices, and rinse them several times.

Prepare a tomato sauce *(p28)* sweating the diced aromatics—onion, carrot, celery, basil—in 2 tablespoons of oil and sauté slowly then add the chopped tomatoes.

Meanwhile, bring a pan of lightly salted water to a boil and blanch the fennel slices for a few minutes.

Let them drain well, then coat each slice in the flour and line them up in a frying pan with a little oil. Brown gently and turn them over so they are well colored before you pour in the tomato sauce. Bring the dish to a boil then arrange on a serving dish.

FINOCCHIO IN TEGAME

Pan-Fried Fennel

2¼ lb fennel
Garlic clove
Olive oil
Salt

Remove the hard outer layers from the fennel, cut them into quarters and rinse them. Drain and put them in a pan in which you have sautéed a clove of garlic in a little oil. Leave them to flavor for about 10 minutes, season with salt, then baste with a little water, cover, and let them finish cooking gently for about half an hour until they are tender and the sauce has reduced.

Mushrooms

TO DRY MUSHROOMS

The best mushrooms to dry are porcini. They must be cleaned with the utmost care, removing every small trace of earth, their green beard, and all the parts even slightly affected by worms.

Cut them into rather large slices, as they dry up a lot in volume, place them on wooden boards, and expose them to the sun, turning them over at intervals of 5 or 6 hours. After the first sunny day they will decrease a lot and become light. You can then, gradually, gather them in a single table and let them dry well. When they are dry, store them in gauze bags, keeping them hanging in the air. When you want to use them, you will only have to soak them in cold water.

FUNGHETTI COLTIVATI AL PREZZEMOLO

Pan-Fried Mushrooms with Parsley

1 lb 5 oz mushrooms
Olive oil
Garlic
Parsley
Salt

Quickly wash the mushrooms, scrape and trim the stems, and divide them into thin slices. Put 6 tablespoons of oil in a pan with a chopped clove of garlic and then add the mushrooms. Season with salt and pepper. Fry over a high heat, stirring occasionally. In about 10 minutes the mushrooms will be ready. Remove the pan from the heat and finish with plenty of finely chopped parsley.

FUNGHETTI COLTIVATI CON CREMA

Mushrooms in Cream

1 lb 5 oz mushrooms
Olive oil
3½ tbsp butter
1 onion
7 tbsp heavy cream
Salt
Pepper

Quickly wash the mushrooms, scrape and trim the stems, and divide them into thin slices.

Put a saucepan on the heat with 3 tablespoons of oil and a little butter, and add a little chopped onion. Sweat gently without letting the onions color. Then add the sliced mushrooms, season with a little salt and a good pinch of pepper, and let them flavor over a very moderate heat.

When they are cooked, which will happen in a short time, pour in the cream, stir, and let the cream slowly be absorbed.

ADA SAYS: *Mushrooms prepared in this way make a rich and elegant garnish for veal, chicken, and poached eggs.*

FUNGHI A FUNGHETTO

Porcini with Garlic

2¼ lb porcini mushrooms
Olive oil
Oregano
Garlic
Salt
Pepper

Porcini must be firm and not too big.

Clean and cut them into thin slices of about ¼ inch.

Put a little oil in a pan, and when it is hot, add the mushrooms, season with salt and pepper. When the porcini are cooked and all the moisture has dried, add a strong pinch of oregano and plenty of diced garlic. Stir, leave to flavor for a moment, and serve.

FUNGHI AL FORNO

Baked Porcini

2¼ lb porcini mushrooms
Breadcrumbs
Parsley
Mint
Garlic
Olive oil
Salt
Pepper

Choose rather large and firm porcini, and use only the caps, keeping the stems for other uses. Quickly wash the tops, dry them with a towel, trim them with the tip of a small knife to completely remove all traces of earth.

Prepare some breadcrumbs, in which you will mix chopped parsley, a pinch of mint, and a trifle of minced garlic; fill the mushroom caps with this mixture from the inside.

Oil the mushrooms, season with salt and pepper, carefully roll them in the breadcrumbs, and line them up in an oiled pan. Drain a little more oil on the mushrooms and then cook them in a preheated oven for about 10 minutes, turning them from time to time.

ADA SAYS: *If breadcrumbs are not to your taste, you can omit them, after having seasoned the porcini just with garlic, oil, parsley, salt, and pepper.*

FUNGHI ALLA LIGURE

Porcini Ligurian Style

2¼ lb porcini mushrooms
Olive oil
2 garlic cloves
2 tbsp tomato purée
Oregano
Salt
Pepper

Wash and cut the porcini into thin slices. In a pan, possibly of terracotta, pour the oil, 1 clove of diced garlic and 1 whole garlic clove. Add the tomato purée, a pinch of oregano, and cook, stirring everything, over low heat, for a few minutes; then add the slices of mushrooms, season with salt and pepper, stir again, raise the heat slightly, and reduce it after 5 minutes.

Continue cooking for another 10 minutes, taking care to serve the excellent preparation immediately.

FUNGHI AL TEGAME

Porcini with Anchovy and Tomato

2¼ lb porcini
Olive oil
3 anchovy fillets
2 garlic cloves
6 tomatoes
Mint
Salt
Pepper
To serve: bread for croutons

Clean and cut the mushrooms into large slices, rinse, and dry them.

Put a little oil in a pan with the rinsed and boned anchovy fillets. Let the fish collapse, then add the mushrooms, 1 or 2 whole cloves of garlic, the seeded tomatoes, a pinch of mint, salt, and pepper. Cover the pan and cook over a rather bright heat, stirring them from time to time for about 10 minutes. Then remove the garlic cloves, pour the mushrooms on the plate, and surround them with fried croutons.

ADA SAYS: *The porcini had its own traditional pan—the tegame—which is the low-sided, twin-handled pan with a lid originally in terracota but now found in all kinds of metals, and widely used for other dishes as well.*

FUNGHI BRODETTATI

Porcini Braised in White Wine

2¼ lb baby porcini
5½ tbsp butter
Flour
White wine
Mushroom broth or stock cube
2 egg yolks
1 lemon
Parsley
To serve: bread for croutons

Clean and cut the mushrooms into slices, rinse, and dry them.

Put half of the butter in a pan and when it is hot add the mushrooms; season with salt and pepper and cook over high heat until all traces of humidity are gone. Sprinkle with a spoon of flour, then with half a glass of white wine. Stir and when the wine has evaporated, add a glass of boiling mushroom broth or a mushroom stock cube. Stir and cook for about a quarter of an hour.

When the sauce has well thickened, remove the pan from the heat and pour the egg yolks whipped with the juice of a lemon over the mushrooms. Add a spoon of chopped parsley and the rest of the butter. Mix, cover, and leave it warm for another 5 minutes, so that the eggs can set

Then pour the mushrooms into a serving dish and surround them with triangles of bread, fried in butter.

FUNGHI FRITTI DORATI

Fried Baby Porcini

1¾ lb baby porcini, preferably ovoli
Flour
2 eggs
Olive oil or lard
Salt
To serve: lemon wedges

The triumph of the young egg-shaped porcini is frying, in which it develops all its qualities of flavor and aroma. Choose well-closed and firm porcini ovoli.

Cut the mushrooms into wedges, pass them through the flour, then the beaten eggs, and fry them over moderate heat in abundant oil or lard, so that they can cook completely evenly in the inside and take a nice light gold color on the outside.

When the mushrooms are at the right point, arrange them on a serving dish, add salt, and garnish with lemon wedges.

FUNGHI FRITTI RIPIENI

Deep-Fried Stuffed Porcini

12 porcini mushrooms of similar size
Lard or oil for frying
7 oz ground veal
Parsley
Grated Parmesan
Flour
2 eggs
Breadcrumbs
Lemon wedges
Salt

White sauce:
2 tbsp butter, 2 tbsp flour, ¾ cup milk

Remove the mushroom caps from the stems, clean them without breaking them, wash them quickly, and set them aside.

Choose some of the best stems, clean them carefully, wash them, cut them into small pieces, and cook them in a saucepan with a little oil.

Make up a thick white sauce *(p16)* with the butter, flour, and milk.

Cook the ground veal in a pan with a little oil and salt, then add the cooked stems, a good spoon of thick white sauce, chopped parsley, and a spoon of grated Parmesan.

Pair the caps 2 by 2, putting a part of the prepared filling in the middle, sticking them together, then dust with flour, wipe through the beaten eggs, then the breadcrumbs, and deep fry over a moderate heat in plenty of oil or lard, so the mushrooms cook inside.

When they are a beautiful golden color, arrange them on a plate, add salt, garnish with sprigs of parsley, and lemon wedges.

FUNGHI RIPIENI AL FORNO

Baked Stuffed Porcini

13 porcini mushrooms
Olive oil
1 onion
Garlic
2 anchovy fillets
Parsley
Bread
Breadcrumbs
1 egg
1 lemon
Salt
Pepper

Choose a dozen beautiful porcini mushrooms, possibly all of an average size of about 2 inches in diameter. You will also need another large mushroom for the filling.

Remove the stems, clean the caps with great care, wash them, dry them lightly, and place them in a pan with a little oil for 5 minutes in a moderate oven, so that they lose moisture.

Carefully clean and wash the stems and chop them, adding the extra mushroom kept aside.

Put a saucepan on the stove with a little oil, a chopped onion, and a piece of garlic, 2 anchovy fillets, washed, boned, and chopped and a spoon of chopped parsley. Sauté a moment, add the chopped mushroom stems, season with salt and pepper, and sear over high heat for 5 minutes.

Remove the saucepan from the heat. Soak the bread, about the size of an egg, in water, squeeze dry, and shred into the mushroom mix. Add a whole egg and combine to have a smooth mixture. Fill the inside of the porcini. Sprinkle over ½ cup of breadcrumbs and arrange in an oven dish with a few spoons of oil. Drop a very light drizzle of oil on each mushroom, and give them about 20 minutes in an already hot oven at a lively heat, so that the bread has time to brown.

When the mushrooms come out of the oven, squeeze a little lemon juice over them and have them brought to the table.

FUNGHI TRIFOLATI

Sautéed Porcini

2¼ lb porcini mushrooms
Olive oil
3 garlic cloves
1½ tbsp butter
5 anchovy fillets
Parsley
1 lemon
Salt
Pepper
To serve: bread for croutons

Clean the mushrooms, cut them into slices, rinse thoroughly, and dry.

Put a pan on the heat with a little oil and 3 whole garlic cloves, which you remove as soon as they color. Transfer the mushrooms to the pan, season with salt and pepper, and cook over a bright flame.

Mash a knob of butter with the washed and boned anchovy fillets and, when all traces of liquid have disappeared from the mushrooms, add to the pan.

Keep the pan on the stove a little longer, to let the butter melt and heat the anchovy fillets, add a good spoon of chopped parsley, remove the pan from the heat, squeeze over a few drops of lemon juice, and pour into a serving dish, surrounding them with croutons fried in butter or oil.

Chicories

INDIVIA ALLA ROMANA

Endive Roman Style

2¼ lb endive
Olive oil
2 to 3 garlic cloves
3 to 4 anchovy fillets
4 tomatoes
Salt
Pepper

When buying endive salad leaves (indivia, from the family cichorium, not Belgian), you need to pay close attention to freshness. The so-called endive head must appear compact, with hard, clear leaves, without spots, and with a very white interior.

Clean the endive, cut off the root, and remove all the outer leaves so that only the white part remains; rinse in several changes of water; then boil it in lightly salted boiling water, without, however, cooking it too much, drain it, and refresh in cold water.

Put the oil in a pan with the garlic, and as soon as the garlic starts to turn brown, remove it and put 3 or 4 washed and boned anchovy fillets, cut into small pieces, in the pan. Fry a little, mash the anchovy fillets with a wooden spoon, then add the tomatoes in pieces, without skin or seeds.

When the tomato is cooked, put the endive in the pan, after squeezing it dry in your hands; season with salt and pepper, and leave it to flavor over moderate heat for a quarter of an hour.

INDIVIA BRACIATA

Braised Endive

2¼ lb endive
Olive oil
Garlic
Basil or Roman mint
2 oz black olives
3 tbsp pine nuts
Salt

Clean the endive removing the harder outer leaves; and then rinse well to completely eliminate the earth.

Place them upright next to each other in a saucepan, with the oil, garlic and a few leaves of basil or field mint (mentuccia), the pitted olives, and a little salt. Cover and put on a low heat for about half an hour.

Finally, add a handful of pine nuts. Can be served alone, or with boiled or roast meats.

INDIVIA DEL BELGIO ALLA BESCIAMELLA

Belgian Endive with White Sauce

1¾ lb Belgian endive
6 tbsp butter
1 lemon
Salt

White sauce:
2 tbsp butter, 2 tbsp flour, 7 tbsp heavy cream

Unlike indivia in the previous two recipes, the Belgian version is force grown to keep its leaves white or yellow and the shape of a torpedo.

Take a small head of very white endive, clean by trimming off the base and removing any soft or discolored outer leaves. Rinse, drain, and line up in a saucepan, side by side. Add a couple of glasses of water, two thirds of the butter, a pinch of salt, and the juice of half a lemon. Cover and quickly bring the water to a boil. Then reduce the heat and continue cooking gently for a good half hour.

Make up a white sauce *(p16)* with the butter, flour, and cream, and lastly add the rest of the butter, 1 piece at a time, working with a wooden spoon.

When the endives are cooked and still hot, transfer to a baking dish and cover with the white sauce. Put them in a preheated oven of lively heat for a few minutes and serve without decanting.

INDIVIA DEL BELGIO ALLA PARMIGIANA

Belgian Endive Parmigiana

1¾ lb Belgian endive
10½ tbsp butter
Grated Parmesan
Breadcrumbs
Parsley
1 boiled egg

Clean the endive, rinse it, and dip in lightly salted boiling water; let it cook to the right point, then remove, and drain well; cut each head in half lengthwise and line them up in an oven dish.

Pour over a third of the butter, melted, add ½ cup grated Parmesan, and place the dish in a preheated oven of high heat for a few minutes to melt the cheese.

Meanwhile, melt the rest of the butter in another pan and brown a spoon of breadcrumbs. Remove from the heat and finish the sauce with chopped parsley and the chopped hard-boiled egg.

When the endive comes out of the oven, pour the sauce over, put the pan on a plate, and have it brought to the table promptly.

Eggplant

MELANZANE ALLA PARMIGIANA

Eggplant Parmigiana

6 long eggplants
Olive oil
2 tbsp butter
Grated Parmesan
Basil
10 oz mozzarella
Salt

Tomato sauce:
2¼ lb fresh tomatoes, 1 onion, 1 carrot, celery, basil, olive oil

Wash and dry the eggplants, remove the stems, peel them, cut them into thin slices lengthwise, and fry them immediately in oil without flour; season with a pinch of salt.

Prepare a tomato sauce *(p28)* in good time sweating down the onion, celery, and carrot in oil, then adding the tomatoes and a little basil. Or you can use canned sauce.

Butter an oven dish, and when all the eggplants are fried, start by setting up a layer of eggplant. Season with the tomato sauce, ½ cup grated Parmesan, in which you have mixed a few leaves of shredded fresh basil, and a few slices of mozzarella. Continue in this way to arrange the eggplants in layers, and finish with the sauce.

Put them in a hot oven of moderate heat, for about a quarter of an hour to flavor.

ADA SAYS: *Some recommend putting the eggplants in salt for a few hours, then rinsing and drying them; but, in our opinion, these preliminary operations are useless. Only one thing is important: Choose very fresh eggplants, the best are from Naples.*

MELANZANE ALLA PARMIGIANA IN BIANCO

Eggplant Parmigiana, White Variation

6 eggplants
Olive oil
4 tbsp butter
Grated Parmesan
10 oz mozzarella
Salt

Prepare and fry the eggplants, then butter a low-sided baking dish and lay the eggplants down in layers, interspersing each layer with plenty of grated Parmesan, a few pieces of butter, and slices of mozzarella. Finish with a layer of eggplant and a final sprinkling of grated cheese.

Place pieces of butter here and there again and put the eggplants in a preheated oven for about a quarter of an hour so that they flavor. Serve very hot and stringy.

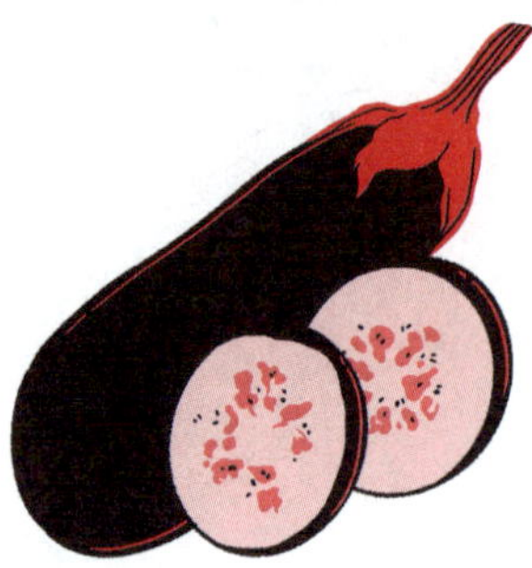

MELANZANE ALLA SICILIANA (CAPONATA)

Eggplant Sicilian Style (Caponata)

4 eggplants
Oil for frying
2 to 3 celery hearts
Onions
Vinegar
Sugar
Tomato passata
2 tbsp capers
Sicilian olives
3½ oz bottarga
Parsley
10 oz baby octopus
Flour
For decoration: 1 hard-boiled egg, shrimp, lobster claws,
Optional: small cooked lobster, swordfish steak

San Bernardo sauce:
olive oil, 3½ oz almonds, 3 slices bread, 3 anchovy fillets, 1 orange, sugar, grated chocolate, vinegar

Wash and dry the eggplants, remove the stems, peel them, cut them into slices and then dice and fry them in hot oil, without flour, until they have a nice golden color; season with a pinch of salt.

Carefully rinse 2 or 3 celery hearts, that is the whiter and more tender central parts, remove the stalks, cut them into sticks, and fry them in hot oil, without flour.

Sauté a chopped onion in a little oil and as soon as the onion starts to color—it must remain almost white—pour in the vinegar, sugar, and a good spoon of tomato passata. Stir and cook over medium heat.

When the tomato is cooked, add the capers, the pitted olives, and the bottarga, cut into very thin slices. Then add a good spoonful of parsley, the eggplants, and fried celery.

Aside, prepare the octopus and possibly a small lobster. Divide the octopuses according to their tentacles, lightly flour them, and fry them in abundant boiling oil. Remove the tail meat from the lobster and cut it into slices. If you wish separately, you can add 3 slices of swordfish fried in oil Add these ingredients to the saucepan, stir, and let everything cook for a few minutes, over a low heat. Then pour everything on to a plate and let it cool completely.

Then arrange the caponata in the serving dish, giving it a slight dome shape, and smooth it well with a spatula.

Prepare a San Bernardo sauce: In a frying pan with very little oil, toast the peeled almonds until they have taken on a rather dark brown color and put 3 slices of bread in the oven, so that they are well toasted. Chop the almonds and bread together, adding the washed, boned, and chopped anchovy fillets, and the juice of 1 orange.

When everything is reduced to a very fine paste, put in a small saucepan, add a spoon of sugar, a generous spoon of grated chocolate, 2 fingers of vinegar, and a finger of water. Melt everything over medium heat and when the sauce has thickened, strain through a fine mesh sieve and completely cover the caponata, smoothing it with the blade of a knife.

You can decorate the caponata with hard-boiled egg wedges, boiled shrimp, and the shelled lobster claws.

MELANZANE ALLA SIRACUSANA (CAPONATINA)

Eggplant Syracuse Style (Caponatina)

6 eggplants
Olive oil
Celery
Sugar
Grated chocolate
Vinegar
Capers
Sicilian green olives, pitted
Salt
Pepper

Wash and dry the eggplants, remove the stems, cut them into slices and then into cubes, without removing the skin. Fry them in hot oil, without flour, until they have a nice golden color; season with a pinch of salt.

Choose the white and tender central stalks of celery, cut them into sticks a couple of fingers long. Fry the celery in the same pan, without flour, until crispy.

Combine the eggplants and celery, drain a little of the frying oil and add a spoon of sugar, a spoon of grated chocolate, a touch of vinegar, a spoon of capers, and a few pitted green Sicilian olives. Mix everything, season with salt and pepper, leave to flavor a little on the heat, and then pour into the plate.

ADA SAYS: *This preparation is an excellent side dish for roasted meats or fish.*

MELANZANE ARROSTITE

Roast Eggplants

6 eggplants
Olive oil
Garlic
Salt
Pepper

Wash and dry the eggplants, remove the stems, cut them in 2 without peeling them, and make cross-linked incisions in the white part with a small knife. Arrange them in an oven pan lightly greased with oil, placing them on the skin side, season with salt, pepper, oil, very little garlic, and let them cook gently in a preheated oven of moderate heat for about half an hour.

MELANZANE FRITTE

Deep-Fried Eggplants

6 eggplants
Flour
Eggs
Oil for frying
Salt

Wash and dry the eggplants, remove the stems, peel them, cut them into not very large pieces, flour them, wipe them through the beaten eggs, and fry them in plenty of very hot oil; season with a pinch of salt.

ADA SAYS: *Made in this way, the eggplants closely resemble fried ovoli porcini mushrooms.*

MELANZANE FRITTE CON LA PASTELLA

Deep-Fried Eggplants in Wine Batter

6 eggplants
Oil for frying
Salt

Batter:
1¼ cups flour, 1 egg yolk, 7 tbsp white wine, salt

Wash and dry the eggplants, remove the stems, peel them, and cut them lengthwise into slices.

Make a rather thick, lump-free batter with the flour, egg yolk, wine, a pinch of salt, and a few spoons of water. Whisk the egg white to a snow and fold it into the batter.

Dip the eggplant slices in this special batter, so they are all wrapped up, and fry them a few at a time in abundant oil of moderate heat. Arrange the eggplants on a serving dish, season with a pinch of salt, and send them to the table very hot.

MELANZANE IN BUDINO CON CARNE

Eggplant Flan with Beef

3 eggplants
Flour
Oil for frying
7 oz ground beef
Butter
Grated Parmesan
2 eggs
Milk
Salt

Wash and dry the eggplants, peel them, and divide them into long slices ¼ inch thick. Flour them and fry them in plenty of very hot oil; season with a pinch of salt.

Pan fry the ground beef with a little oil and salt.

Butter a cake mold: Line up some slices of the fried eggplant, cover with ¼ cup grated Parmesan, a layer of beef, and cover the meat with more eggplant and Parmesan.

Beat the eggs, add 2 spoons of milk and salt, and pour into the mold. Put the mold in a preheated oven of moderate heat and when it is firm, after about half an hour, take it out and drizzle a few spoons of melted butter on top, seasoned with a pinch of salt.

MELANZANE IN POLPETTE

Deep-Fried Eggplant Balls

6 eggplants
2 garlic cloves
Parsley
Loaf of bread
Milk
2 eggs
Dried marjoram
Flour
Oil for frying
Salt
Pepper

Wash the eggplants, dip them for a few minutes in lightly salted boiling water, then drain and peel them.

Chop the eggplant pulp with the garlic cloves and parsley and place in a bowl. Soak the white of a loaf of bread in milk, squeeze dry, and shred into the eggplant mix. Add the eggs, a pinch of dried marjoram, salt, and pepper. Fashion this dough into balls.

Flour the balls and fry in abundant oil over a rather moderate heat. Arrange the balls on a serving dish and serve hot.

MELANZANE IN TIMBALLO CON PROSCIUTTO

Eggplant and Prosciutto Timbale

4 eggplants
4 tbsp flour
Oil for frying
Bouillon or stock cube
Grated Parmesan
3½ oz prosciutto
7 tbsp butter
Salt

Wash and dry the eggplants, remove the stems, peel them, and cut them into round slices ¼ inch thick.

In a bowl put the flour and a pinch of salt and dissolve with a ladle of cold water, stirring with a fork to obtain a dense and elastic batter.

Wipe the eggplant slices through the batter and fry them in plenty of very hot oil; season with a pinch of salt.

When you have fried all the eggplants, arrange them in layers in a buttered baking dish, alternating the layers with ⅔ cup grated Parmesan and slivers of prosciutto. Finish with a layer of Parmesan and a small knob of butter.

Meanwhile, in a small saucepan, put the meat extract or use a stock cube, a pinch of salt, a knob of butter, and melt everything with a ladle of hot water. Boil the sauce then pour over the timbale.

Put the dish in a preheated oven of moderate heat for about 10 minutes, then place it on a serving plate and send it to the table.

MELANZANE RIPIENE ALLA NAPOLETANA

Neapolitan Stuffed Eggplants

6 eggplants
Olive oil
6 tomatoes
3 red bell peppers
6 tbsp breadcrumbs
Parsley
Oregano
2 anchovy fillets
2 oz capers
3½ oz Gaeta olives
10 oz mozzarella
3½ tbsp butter
Salt
Pepper

Wash and dry the eggplants, remove the stem, and cut them in 2 lengthwise without peeling them. With a small knife extract the pulp so that each eggplant remains almost in the shape of a boat, and season with salt, 3 spoons of oil, and a pinch of pepper.

Blanch the tomatoes into boiling water, peel them, remove the seeds, and cut them into strips.

Then roast the bell peppers *(p677)*. Remove their skins, rinse them, remove the seeds, and cut them into thin fillets.

Put the breadcrumbs, chopped parsley, a little oregano, the washed and boned anchovy fillets cut into small pieces, the capers, and the pitted olives cut into small pieces in a bowl. Season everything with salt and 3 spoons of oil, mixing well. Fill each half eggplant with this mixture, leveling it well with the blade of the knife. On top of each half lay a few tomato slices and a few pepper slices.

Pour a little oil into an oven dish and line up the eggplants in a single layer. Drizzle a little oil on each one, and cook in a moderate heat oven for an hour.

Five minutes before removing the eggplants from the oven, put a slice of mozzarella and a piece of butter on each one. Bake again, increasing the heat a little, then send to the table.

MELANZANE RIPIENE DI CARNE

Eggplant Stuffed with Meat

6 eggplants
1 onion
Olive oil
Garlic
7 oz lean ground beef
Basil
Saffron
Broth
1 cup tomato passata
Mint
Salt
Pepper or cayenne

Wash and dry the eggplants, remove the stem, and divide them in half by length without peeling them. With a small knife, empty the flesh, leaving a thickness of about ½ inch so you have 12 small boats that you sprinkle with salt and oil.

Chop the flesh you have taken out of the eggplant and keep ready.

Sauté over a low heat a chopped onion in some oil and when it turns slightly brown, add a clove of diced garlic, and as soon as the garlic has heated up, add the ground beef, and brown over a cheerful heat.

As soon as the meat has browned, season it with salt, plenty of pepper, or even a pinch of cayenne, 2 or 3 torn basil leaves, a sachet of saffron, and the flesh from the eggplants.

Stir, wet with 2 fingers of broth or water, reduce the heat, and let it cook slowly, covered, for about 10 minutes.

Fill the eggplant halves with this mixture, leveling the filling with the blade of a knife. Oil an baking dish and line up the filled eggplants in a single layer. Drop a little more oil on the eggplants and then bake them in a preheated oven of moderate heat for three quarters of an hour, even an hour.

Then remove them from the oven and, before sending them to the table, spread a layer of thick tomato sauce on each eggplant, made with oil, tomato passata, salt, and finished with chopped mint leaves. Arrange the eggplants on a serving dish and serve them hot.

MELANZANE USO FUNGHI

Eggplant Mushroom Style

6 eggplants
Olive oil
Garlic
Oregano
Salt
Pepper

Wash and dry the eggplants, remove the stems, and cut them into wedges without peeling them. Remove some of the internal pulp if the seeds are very developed, and cut into diagonal pieces.

Put 4 tablespoons of oil in a pan, fry a piece of garlic, and remove before it colors and replace with the eggplant, season with salt, pepper, and a pinch of oregano. Cook slowly.

ADA SAYS: *You can serve them like this, or you can add a few pieces, halfway through cooking, of tomato, skinless, and seedless.*

Potatoes

PATATE AL FORNO ALLA PARMIGIANA

Baked Potatoes Parmigiana

2¼ lb yellow baking potatoes
7 tbsp butter
Stock cube
Grated Parmesan
Salt

Wash the potatoes, peel them, cut them into very small cubes, and cook them in butter, without frying them too much. As soon as they are cooked, season with a quarter of a stock cube dissolved in half a glass of hot water. Mix them, arrange them in an oven dish, sprinkle with ¼ cup grated Parmesan, a few knobs of butter, and pass them for about 10 minutes in a preheated oven of lively heat, so that the Parmesan can melt.

PATATE AL FORNO CON MOZZARELLA

Baked Potatoes with Mozzarella

2¼ lb potatoes
7 tbsp butter
5¼ oz mozzarella
1 cup milk
Salt

Wash the potatoes, peel them, and cut them into very thin slices; then arrange them in a colander, sprinkle with salt, mix them with your hands, and cover them with a weight to help them dry. Leave them for about an hour, then pull them up and dry them in a towel.

Butter a baking dish and make a layer of potato slices in the bottom; on this arrange a few slices of mozzarella and a few knobs of butter. Continue with another layer of potatoes, then add more Mozzarella and butter, and cover everything with a last layer of potatoes. Pour the milk over the potatoes and place the dish in a preheated oven of moderate heat, letting it cook until the milk has evaporated and the potatoes are well cooked. Then place the pan on a plate and send to the table.

PATATE AL FORNO IN SORPRESA

Baked Potato Surprise

2¼ lb potatoes
7 tbsp butter
Flour
1 cup milk
2 eggs
3½ oz Gruyère
Salt
White pepper
Nutmeg

Choose medium-sized potatoes, possibly all the same size, wash them, put them to boil or cook them in the oven, and when they are cooked, peel them and split them in half lengthwise.

With a teaspoon, extract a little flesh from the middle of each potato, leaving about ½ inch thick around the sides. Match up the potatoes for later with their other halves.

Now prepare the filling: Melt half of the butter and add 2 spoons of flour, cook for a minute or 2, stirring, dilute with the milk. Season with salt and white pepper and a trifle of nutmeg and, always stirring, let the mixture thicken well.

When it is like a thick cream, remove from the heat and let it cool. Then add a whole egg and a yolk and finally the Gruyère cut into cubes.

Use a teaspoon to fill the half potatoes with this mix and reassemble them, each with its own half, to get the whole potato back in shape.

Place the reassembled potatoes in a lightly buttered pan, and brush with melted butter and lightly salt each one. Put them in a preheated oven of moderate heat for about 20 minutes until they become slightly blond. Then arrange them on a plate, sprinkle them with the remaining melted butter, and serve hot.

PATATE AL FORNO IN VESTE DA CAMERA

Baked Potatoes in their Jackets, Two Ways

2¼ lb potatoes
Butter
Salt

In the first way, choose nice potatoes, large and as regular as possible, wash them thoroughly, and then put them in a saucepan covering them with water, to which you will add a good pinch of salt. When the potatoes have boiled for 7 or 8 minutes, drain them, align them on a hot oven rack with a lively heat, and let them finish baking for about half an hour. It goes without saying that these potatoes should not be peeled.

In the second way, after having carefully washed the potatoes, without peeling them, wrap them, 1 by 1, in a sheet of aluminum foil, and put them in a preheated oven of high heat for about three quarters of an hour, then free them from the baking foil.

When the potatoes are cooked, either way, send them to the table accompanied by a saucer of butter and salt.

PATATE DUCHESSE

Duchess Potatoes

2¼ lb baking potatoes
7 tbsp butter
4 egg yolks
1 egg
Salt
Pepper
Nutmeg

Duchess style potatoes are a mix of boiled eggs and potatoes reduced to purée, widely used for croquettes and as a side dish for meat and fish. Diligence in drying the purée is the cornerstone of the operation.

Wash the large and mealy potatoes, peel them, cut them into wedges, rinse them, and put them on the heat in a saucepan covering them with cold salty water. Cover and cook the potatoes over high heat; when the flesh yields under the pressure of the fork, drain and place in a light oven to dry them out completely. Then mash or blend and add the butter; season with salt, white pepper, and a little nutmeg. Then put the saucepan on the stove, and, stirring, let the purée dry some more.

Stir it continuously with a wooden spoon until it becomes smooth and consistent. Then remove from the heat, let it cool a little and add 4 egg yolks, 1 at a time, mixing thoroughly.

To prepare a border of duchess potatoes: Place the mixture in a pastry bag with a star tip and scallop the inner edge of a baking dish with a garland of small stars. Lightly brush with a beaten egg and brown in a preheated oven at a moderate heat for about a quarter of an hour.

ADA SAYS: *This potato wreath makes a nice decoration for other preparations you put inside such as meat stews or vegetables.*

PATATE DUCHESSE IN CROCCHETTE

Duchess Potato Croquettes

2¼ lb duchess potatoes
Flour
2 eggs
Breadcrumbs
Oil for frying

Carefully prepare the duchess potatoes *(as above)*. Place the mixture in a piping bag, fitted with a round tip and pipe torch shapes 3 inches long and 1-inch thick, gently fashioning them on a floured table. When you have shaped them all, lightly brush them with beaten egg and sprinkle with breadcrumbs.

Put plenty of oil in a pan and when it is hot, fry the croquettes until golden. Then remove them from the pan, drain, and immediately send them to the table.

ADA SAYS: *Duchess potatoes can also be baked in the oven.*

PATATE DUCHESSE IN CROCCHETTE CON RICOTTA

Duchess Potato Croquettes with Ricotta

2¼ lb duchess potatoes
Grated Parmesan
5¼ oz ricotta
Parsley
2 hard-boiled eggs
Flour
2 egg whites
Breadcrumbs
Butter and oil for frying

Prepare the duchess potatoes *(opposite page)* and while still hot, add ¼ cup grated Parmesan, ricotta, chopped parsley, and the hard-boiled eggs chopped into small pieces. Mix carefully and pour on to a plate, and leave to cool.

Then lightly flour the kitchen table, and with floured hands fashion into croquettes. Coat each in the flour, beaten egg whites, and breadcrumbs, and cook them in a pan with butter and a few spoonfuls of oil, until golden brown.

PATATE DUCHESSE IN SCODELLINE RIPIENE

Duchess Potatoes with Beef and Tomato

2¼ lb duchess potatoes
Breadcrumbs
Lard or oil for frying
2 oz prosciutto
7 oz lean ground beef
Loaf of bread or a boiled potato
Milk
3 hard-boiled eggs
7 tbsp butter
9 oz canned tomatoes
Salt
Pepper
Nutmeg

Prepare the duchess potatoes *(opposite page)*, then take a good spoonful at a time, roll it with your hands in the breadcrumbs, make it into a ball, mash it gently on the table, and then with your fingers push a little in the middle in order to have a round bowl. Repeat until you have used up all the potatoes.

Fry these bowls in oil or lard, take them up gracefully from the pan, drain well, arrange them in a crown on a plate, and pour into each one some of this sauce: Chop the prosciutto and mix with the ground beef, and then mix in the white of a loaf of bread soaked in milk and squeezed dry, or a little extra potato. Season with salt, pepper, nutmeg. With floured hands, shape many meatballs, as big as hazelnuts, which you will fry in oil or lard.

Cut the hard-boiled eggs into cubes. Let the butter melt in a pan, add the tomatoes and salt, and let the sauce thicken. Pour in the meatballs and hard-boiled eggs, heat without boiling, and with a spoon distribute the sauce in the potato bowls.

PATATE DUCHESSE VARIATE ALLA DAUPHINE

Dauphin Potatoes

2¼ lb duchess potatoes *(p670)*
Flour
Egg
Breadcrumbs
Oil for frying

Choux pastry:
½ cup water, 3½ tbsp butter, ⅔ cup flour, 2 eggs, salt

Dauphin potatoes are a nice derivation of duchess potatoes, to which a little sugar-free choux pastry (p71) is added.

Prepare the duchess potatoes. Then, with the water, butter, and flour, a pinch of salt, and the 2 whole eggs, prepare the choux pastry in this way: Put the water, the butter cut into small pieces, and the salt in a small saucepan and have the flour ready. Stir to melt the butter well, and as soon as the liquid comes to a boil, pull the pan back and throw the flour in 1 fell swoop. Mix well and then put the container back on the heat, always stirring. Soon the dough will collect in a ball, which will detach from the sides. Work this well with a spoon and after a few minutes, when you hear it make a slight noise, as if it were frying, remove from the heat and let the dough lose most of its heat.

When it is almost cold, add the eggs, one at a time stirring vigorously, and not putting the second egg in until the first is completely blended. Once this is done, continue to work the dough well with the spoon until the dough is velvety and will tear here and there, even making bubbles.

Add to the duchess potatoes and mix the 2 compounds with a spoon, thus obtaining the mixture of the dauphin potatoes.

With these potatoes you can shape croquettes far superior to common croquettes: either round, the size of a large walnut, or in the shape of a real croquette, that is, like a cork, which must be floured or, better, floured, passed through beaten egg and then in breadcrumbs and fried in plenty of hot oil. Drain and serve immediately.

ADA SAYS: *Dauphin potatoes are used to garnish both meat and fish. The internal mixture does not remain empty after cooking, as in choux, but it is light and tasty.*

PATATE DUCHESSE IN CASSOLETTES

Dauphin Potatoes with Chicken Livers

2¼ lb dauphin potatoes
3½ tbsp butter
3 tbsp dried mushrooms
7 oz chicken livers
Sage
1 egg
3 tbsp prosciutto
Salt

Prepare the dauphin potato dough *(opposite page)*. Butter small ovenproof ramekins—cassolettes—and line them with a layer of dauphin potatoes ¼ inch thick.

Soak the dried mushrooms to revive. Then chop and cook in a little butter. Sear the chicken livers briefly with sage. Mix together.

Cover the base of the ramekins with a layer of dough, add the chicken livers and mushrooms, then close up with more dough, brush the surface with beaten egg, and put in a preheated oven at a lively heat for about a quarter of an hour, to allow the potatoes to develop a little and lightly color. Garnish with strips of prosciutto.

Remove from the oven, arrange on a plate, and send to the table.

❖ ADA SAYS: *Another filling you might try is peas and prosciutto cooked in broth with some scallions.*

PATATE FRITTE

Fried Potatoes

1 lb potatoes
Oil for frying
Salt

These crunchy fries are universally known, but not everyone knows how to make them perfectly.

After washing and peeling the potatoes, cut them into very thin slices. When you have cut the number you need, collect them on a plate, sprinkle them with salt, mix them gently, and tilt the plate with a spoon underneath so they drain well. Leave the potatoes like this for about an hour.

Then take a few at a time, squeeze them gently in your hands, and dip them, 1 by 1, into the pan with plenty of very hot oil. Fry a few at a time, and as soon as they have become a nice blond color, remove them from the pan, sprinkle them with salt, and serve hot.

❖ ADA SAYS: *You can also make straw potatoes in the same way by cutting the potatoes into long slices ⅛ inch thick, which you will then cut into thin strips; to obtain many sticks the length and thickness of a wooden match, you can also use a mandolin for this. These potatoes are an excellent garnish for steak.*

PATATE IN BUDINO

Potato Flan

2¼ lb potatoes
7 tbsp butter
Grated Parmesan
2 eggs
3½ oz mozzarella
3½ oz Gruyère
4 slices prosciutto
Basil
Fine breadcrumbs
Salt
Pepper
Nutmeg

Wash the potatoes, boil them, and, as soon as they are cooked, peel them, and mash to reduce them to a purée. Season while still hot with 4 tablespoons of butter, 2 heaped spoons of grated Parmesan, the eggs, salt, pepper, and nutmeg. Stir everything well and let it cool.

Dice the mozzarella and Gruyère and mix in a bowl with the proscutto, also cut small, and season everything with a little grated Parmesan, salt, pepper, and a few torn leaves of fresh basil.

Butter a cake pan, without a hole in the middle, of about 3 cups capacity, and add some very fine breadcrumbs, turning the mold in all directions and then turning it upside down to remove the excess.

Take a little of the potato mixture at a time, and gently place it on the bottom and around the sides of the mold, to form a box. Place the cheese filling in the middle, and cover with a little more potato mixture. Sprinkle the top with a few more breadcrumbs, adding a few pieces of butter here and there as well.

Bake in a preheated oven of moderate heat for about three quarters of an hour, to give the bread a golden hue. When you take it out of the oven, let it rest for at least 5 minutes, then take it out of the pan and bring to the table.

PATATE IN PURÈ

Potato Purée

2¼ lb potatoes
7 tbsp butter
Milk
1 egg yolk
Grated Parmesan
Salt

Wash and peel the potatoes and cut them into small pieces. Put them to boil in slightly salted cold water; as soon as they are cooked, strain through a fine mesh sieve or blend or mash them and collect the purée in a saucepan. Bring the pan over the heat and, keep stirring with a wooden spoon, let the purée dry, a bit. Add the butter and as much milk as is necessary to give lightness to the purée, which you will work well to make it very soft. Finally, season with an egg yolk and a spoon of grated Parmesan.

PATATE IN TEGAME (RÖSTI)

Pan-Fried Potatoes (Rösti)

2¼ lb potatoes
3½ oz lard
2 onions
Salt

Wash the potatoes, boil them in lightly salted cold water, peel them while still hot, and cut them into thin slices.

In a large frying pan, with low sides and with a lid, melt the lard, then add the potatoes, salt them lightly, cover them with the lid, and let them brown over high heat for about 10 minutes.

While the potatoes are frying, cut the 2 onions into very thin slices.

Use a plate to turn the potatoes as if they were an omelet, add more lard to the pan, put the potato slices back into the pan and put the onion slices on top, put the lid back on, and let them braise for another 10 minutes.

Turn the potatoes and onions again, as if you were turning an omelet, adding more lard; this time the onion slices will be in contact with the pan, so brown them for about 10 minutes more, then pour everything into a serving dish and serve immediately.

PATATE IN TEGAME ALLA PIZZAIOLA

Pan-Fried Potatoes Pizzaiola

2¼ lb potatoes
Olive oil
Garlic
6 tomatoes
Oregano
Salt
Pepper

Wash the potatoes, boil them, peel them, and cut them into slices or wedges.

Put 3 to 4 tablespoons of oil in a pan with the garlic, which you take out as soon as it browns. Wash and peel the tomatoes, take out the seeds, chop, and sauté over a rather high heat, season with salt, pepper, and a good pinch of oregano. Add the potatoes to flavor in the sauce for a few minutes.

PATATE IN TEGAME AL PROSCIUTTO

Pan-Fried Potatoes with Prosciutto

2¼ lb non-floury potatoes
Olive oil
3½ oz prosciutto
1 large onion
Garlic
6 tomatoes
Parsley
Basil
Salt

Wash the potatoes, boil them, peel them while still hot, and cut them into slices.

Put a little oil in a pan and the roughly chopped prosciutto. Just heat the oil and then add the thinly sliced onion. When the onion begins to brown, add 2 diced cloves of garlic. Brown a little more while you blanch, skin, seed, and chop the tomatoes and add them to the pan. Let the tomato cook a little, add the sliced potatoes, and season with salt, pepper, plenty of chopped basil and parsley. Stir, cover, reduce the heat, and cook slowly for a few more minutes.

PATATE IN TIMBALLO CON SALSICCE

Potato and Sausage Bake

2¼ lb potatoes
3½ tbsp butter
3 sausages
Grated Parmesan
Salt

Wash and peel the potatoes and cut them into slices, not too thin, nor too thick. Generously butter a baking dish and place a layer of potatoes on the bottom. Put the sliced and skinned sausages on the potatoes; add salt, a few knobs of butter, grated Parmesan, and cover with another layer of potatoes on which you put a few more knobs of butter and a pinch of salt.

Put the pan in a preheated oven of moderate heat and let the potatoes cook slowly until a nice golden crust has formed on the surface.

ADA SAYS: *This bake can be prepared long before the meal and reheated on the spot.*

PATATE LESSE IN INSALATA CON TONNO

Potato and Tuna Salad

1 lb potatoes
Olive oil
Vinegar
Celery
7 oz tinned tuna in olive oil
7 tbsp butter
1 lemon
6 anchovy fillets
2 unripe tomatoes
2 hard-boiled eggs
Salt
Pepper
Optional: mayonnaise *(p19)*

Wash the potatoes, boil them, peel them, cut them into cubes, and season with 4 tablespoons of oil, vinegar, salt, and pepper.

Remove the outer leaves from the celery, so that only the white part remains, rinse, cut into sticks, and add to the potatoes. Give it a good stir and arrange the salad on a plate in the shape of a cone.

Chop the tuna together with the butter and a few drops of lemon. Mix it well with a wooden spoon, then spread it over the potatoes to complete the cone.

Garnish with anchovy fillets rolled up in rings and rounds of tomato and hard-boiled egg. To make the preparation more elegant, you can decorate it with a ribbon of mayonnaise.

PATATINE NOVELLE IN TEGAME

Pan-Fried New Potatoes

2¼ lb baby new potatoes
Olive oil
Rosemary
Salt

Choose some small new potatoes, possibly all of the same thickness, and with a small knife lightly scrape off any skin. Keep them in a bowl of cold water, then drain and dry them.

In a frying pan, with a lid that closes perfectly, pour half a glass of oil to cover the whole of the bottom. Heat it up and then arrange the potatoes in a single layer, add a stalk of rosemary, cover, reduce the heat, and let the potatoes brown and cook slowly in their own steam.

After about half an hour the potatoes will be cooked and a beautiful golden color. Then sprinkle them with salt, let them flavor for a few more minutes, and serve.

ADA SAYS: *During cooking, shake the pan several times, taking the handle with your right hand and holding the lid with the other so as not to reveal the potatoes or let their steam out.*

Bell Peppers

TO SKIN PEPPERS

Bake the peppers in the oven until the skin wrinkles and blackens. Or you can scorch on an open flame. Then you can easily rub the skin off in your hands when cool. Or, more secure, is to seal the hot peppers in a plastic bag for 15 to 20 minutes and then the skins will come off more easily.

PEPERONATA

Peperonata

2¼ lb bell peppers
1 lb tomatoes
1 lb onions
Olive oil
Vinegar
Salt

Rinse the peppers, remove the stem and seeds, and cut them into thin strips. Remove the skin and seeds from the tomatoes and add them to the peppers. Remove the outer skin from the onions, cut them, and add them to the other vegetables.

Use a large frying pan, one on which the lid closes perfectly, season with a few tablespoons of oil and salt, and add all the vegetables, cover, and bring it to a moderate heat. Cook slowly, always with the container covered.

After about an hour of this slow and regular simmer, the peperonata will be almost at the right cooking point. Then pour in a glass of vinegar and boil for a few more minutes. When the sauce has reduced, pour everything into a serving dish.

ADA SAYS: *This appetizing preparation can be served both hot and cold. It is very suitable to accompany hot and cold roasted meats.*

PEPERONI AL GRATIN

Peppers Gratin

2¼ lb bell peppers
Olive oil
3 tbsp capers
3½ oz Gaeta olives
Breadcrumbs
3 anchovy fillets
Salt
Pepper

Scorch the peppers over an open flame or roast in the oven to blacken the skin. Then rub them gently with your fingers, remove the thin outside skin, rinse, remove the stem and seeds, and cut them into strips.

Season them in a dish with oil, capers, pitted Gaeta olives, a handful of breadcrumbs, the chopped anchovy fillets, salt, and pepper.

Oil a baking dish and put everything in, sprinkle with more breadcrumbs, and a drizzle of oil. Place the pan in a preheated oven of light heat and brown slowly. You can serve them both hot and cold.

PEPERONI ALLA ROMANA

Peppers Roman Style

2¼ lb sweet green bell peppers
Lard or olive oil
1 onion
5 to 6 tomatoes
Salt

Scorch and skin the peppers and cut into strips. Put a tablespoon of lard or half a glass of oil and half a finely chopped onion in a pan. When the onion is cooked and has taken on a slight yellowish tint, add the skinned and seedless chopped tomatoes to the pan. Cook for a few minutes, and then pour in the peppers, season with a little salt. Cover and continue cooking over moderate heat for another quarter of an hour or more, until the peppers are tender and tasty.

ADA SAYS: *If the sauce is too thin and the peppers start to stick, baste them with a few spoons of water.*

PEPERONI COL GUANCIALE

Peppers with Guanciale

2¼ lb bell peppers
Olive oil
1 onion
10 tomatoes
7 oz guanciale
Salt
Pepper

Scorch and skin the peppers and cut into strips. Put a very little oil in a rather large frying pan; slice the onion thinly and sauté with 2 spoons of water so it cooks without catching. When the onion has dried and turned blond, peel and deseed the tomatoes, slice and mix in with the onion.

When the tomato is cooked, add the peppers, season with salt and pepper, and moderate the heat to flavor everything well. After about a quarter of an hour, chop the guanciale into large thin slices and mix in with the rest, stir, and continue cooking over moderate heat for a few more minutes, until the guanciale is well heated and has taken on an almost transparent appearance.

If the guinciale has given out too much fat, remove some of it with a spoon, tilting the pan. Then pour the peppers into a serving dish and serve immediately hot.

PEPERONI CONDITI

Marinated Peppers

2¼ lb bell peppers
Olive oil
Garlic
Parsley
Salt
Pepper

Scorch and skin the peppers. Cut them into long strips about the width of a finger. Line up on a plate and season with oil, salt, and pepper.

You can add a few cloves of garlic cut into small pieces and garnish with parsley.

PEPERONI IMBOTTITI

Stuffed Peppers

6 sweet yellow bell peppers
6 eggplants to match
Olive oil
3 to 4 tbsp tomato purée
3½ oz Gaeta olives, pitted
2 oz salted capers
Salt

Skin the peppers, but leave them whole, taking care not to damage them, so the peppers will be like bags, which you then dry on absorbent paper.

Rinse the eggplants, dry them, remove the stems, and cut them into cubes, keeping the peel on. Fry a few at a time, in a pan with hot oil, without flour, then take them out and deglaze the pan with the tomato purée, a few spoons of water, and a pinch of salt.

When the tomato sauce is ready, add it to the fried eggplant and season everything with the pitted olives and the capers.

Mix everything and fill the peppers, which you line up, upright, in an oven dish, making sure that the filling does not come out. Pour about a quarter of a glass of oil over the peppers and place the pan in a preheated oven of moderate heat, so that the peppers can finish cooking slowly and gain flavor. It is preferable to serve this preparation completely cold.

PEPERONI IN FRITTURA

Fried Peppers

1 lb yellow bell peppers
Flour
1 egg
Lard or oil for frying
Salt
Pepper

Scorch and skin the peppers, remove the seeds and cut them into long strips, the width of a finger. Line up these strips on a plate and season with salt and pepper.

When ready to go to the table, lightly dry the pepper fillets, coat them in flour, then beaten egg, and fry them a few at a time, in oil or lard, but very hot. This can be served alone and can also be used to accompany roasted meats.

PEPERONI IN SALSA D'UOVO

Peppers with Eggs

2¼ lb yellow or sweet red bell peppers
5 meaty tomatoes
Olive oil
5 eggs
Butter
Salt
Bread for croutons

Scorch and skin the peppers and cut into thin strips.

Skin and seed the tomatoes and sauté in a little oil over a high heat so that they do not fall apart too much. After some time, add the peppers, season with salt, and leave to flavor well.

Break the eggs into a bowl, beat them as if for an omelet, add a pinch of salt, and pour them into the pan. Make sure that the heat now is not too strong, and with a wooden spoon, or rather, with a small whisk, scramble the eggs, tomatoes, and peppers so that the eggs remain creamy. Add a few pieces of butter, mix again, and pass the peppers on a plate, surrounding them with fried croutons.

PEPERONI RIPIENI ALLA MARINARA

Peppers Stuffed with Squid or Octopus

9 yellow bell peppers
Olive oil
1 large eggplant
Flour
Oil for frying
Garlic
6 tbsp breadcrumbs
6 tomatoes
3 small octopuses or squid
2 tbsp tomato purée
Capers
2 oz Gaeta olives, pitted
Parsley
Salt

Choose peppers of regular shape, rather large, and, essential, very fresh. Of these, 3 will be used for the filling.

Remove the stem from the peppers by making a circular cut around the head with a small knife, and then empty the peppers of their seeds.

Now time to think about the filling: Take 3 peppers, wash them, cut them into strips, and season them in a pan with a little oil and salt.

Skin the eggplant, cut into ½ inch cubes, rinse them, flour them, and fry them in hot oil. When these cubes have taken on a nice golden color, remove from the pan.

Put a couple of spoons of oil in a new pan—you can use the oil from the eggplants, and fry a clove of garlic. Remove it as soon as it starts to brown and swirl 6 spoons of breadcrumbs into the oil. Stir with a wooden spoon, until the bread is well soaked in oil and lightly toasted, then remove to a plate.

Dip the tomatoes in boiling water for a moment to be able to peel them more easily, cut them into wedges, and carefully remove the seeds. Bring a pan of oil to a boil and add the tomatoes, season with a pinch of salt, and cook over a very high heat for a few minutes.

Carefully wash and divide the small octopuses or baby squid into small pieces, flour them, and fry them in boiling oil.

Finally, prepare a tomato sauce with the purée, a little oil, garlic, and salt. This sauce must be sufficiently thick, and as a quantity about 2 tablespoons.

Once all the ingredients have been prepared, collect in a bowl the pepper fillets, the tomato fillets, the eggplant cubes, the fried bread, and the octopus or squid. Add a spoon of capers and a handful of pitted and halved Gaeta olives. Also add a ladle of tomato sauce and some chopped parsley. Mix all these ingredients and then, with a spoon, fill the 6 peppers.

Pour a couple of spoonfuls of oil, half of the remaining tomato sauce, diluted with a few spoons of water, into a baking dish of proportionate size, and place in the peppers, 1 next to the other. Sprinkle each abundantly with oil and finally pour the remaining tomato sauce over, spreading it a little all over. Put the casserole in a preheated oven of very moderate heat for about an hour. The peppers must cook very slowly.

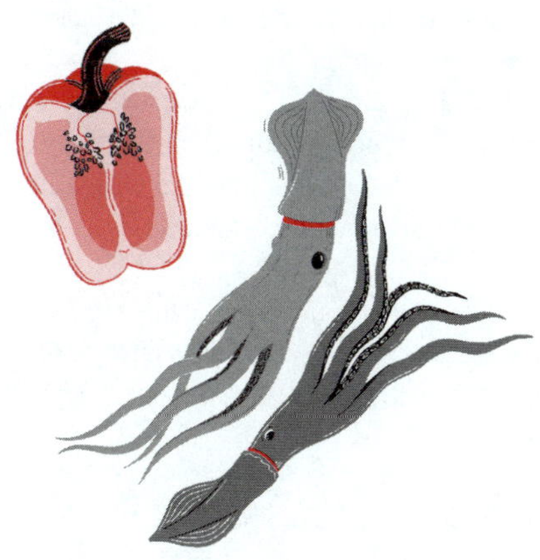

PEPERONI RIPIENI ALLA NAPOLETANA

Stuffed Peppers Neapolitan Style

6 yellow bell peppers
Olive oil
12 tbsp breadcrumbs
3 tbsp raisins, soaked
30 Gaeta olives, pitted
6 anchovy fillets
Parsley
Basil
3 tbsp capers
Salt
Pepper

Tomato sauce:
1 onion, celery, 1 carrot, olive oil, 1 lb canned tomatoes, basil, salt

For this preparation you have to choose beautiful Neapolitan yellow bell peppers, which are very sweet.

Remove the stem from the peppers with a small knife, making a circular cut around the head and then empty the peppers of the seeds; rinse them again and line them up on a plate. The finished peppers must have the appearance of bags.

Prepare a thick tomato sauce in good time: Sauté the chopped onion, celery, and carrot in 2 tablespoons of oil, then simmer the tomatoes, covered, and season with torn basil and salt. Or you can use a canned sauce.

Now to prepare the stuffing: Put a pan with about a glass of oil on the heat, and, when it is hot, add the breadcrumbs. Stirring with a wooden spoon, lightly toast the bread, which you then pour into a bowl. To the toast add the soaked raisins, the pitted olives, the washed, boned, and chopped anchovy fillets, some chopped parsley, a few basil leaves, and the capers. Mix everything well and if too dry, add a little more oil. Fill the peppers with this mix.

When you have filled them all, take an oven dish big enough for all the peppers to fit side by side; pour a little oil on the bottom, arrange the peppers, proceeding gracefully so that the filling does not come out. Finally, sprinkle the peppers with a little more oil and put a spoon of prepared tomato sauce on each of them. Put in a preheated oven of moderate heat and simmer for a long time—about an hour. These peppers can be served both hot and cold.

PEPERONI RIPIENI DI FUNGHI

Peppers Stuffed with Mushrooms

6 yellow bell peppers
1 lb mushrooms
Olive oil
Garlic
Breadcrumbs
Milk
2 eggs
Grated Parmesan
Salt
Pepper

Prepare the peppers as above. Be careful to remove the stem from the top of the pepper not to damage the bags, and place them on the absorbent kitchen paper to dry.

Quickly wash the mushrooms, scrape, and trim the stem, cut them into small pieces, and put them to cook in a pan with a little oil, a clove of garlic, and a pinch of salt and pepper.

When the mushrooms are cooked and their sauce very well reduced, chop them together with breadcrumbs previously soaked in milk and squeezed. Mix in the eggs, salt, pepper, and ½ cup grated Parmesan.

With this mixture, well blended, fill the peppers. Put them in an oven dish, side by side, with a drizzle of oil, place in a preheated oven of moderate heat for about an hour. After this time, remove the pan from the oven, place on a serving plate, and send to the table.

PEPERONI RIPIENI DI PESCE E DI RISO

Peppers Stuffed with Fish and Rice

6 bell peppers
7 oz swordfish
Tomato passata
Olive oil
Basil
1 cup rice
3½ tbsp butter
Salt

Remove the stems and seeds of the peppers without washing them.

Cut the fish into small slices and line them up in a pan where you have already prepared a simple tomato sauce with ¾ cup tomato passata, a spoonful of oil, salt, and basil. Cook for a few minutes, making sure that the sauce thickens a lot.

Boil the rice in lightly salted boiling water, which you will dress, after draining, with the butter. Add the diced fish to the rice and fill the peppers with this mixture. Arrange them straight in a baking dish in which they fit tightly, baste with a few spoons of oil, add salt, and place them in a preheated oven with light heat for about an hour.

After this time, remove the pan from the oven, place it on top of a serving dish, and send it to the table.

Peas

PISELLI ALLA FRANCESE

Peas French Style

10 tbsp butter
3 lb 5 oz peas in the pod (or 1 lb 5 oz shelled)
Sugar
Lettuce
Parsley
2 to 3 scallions
Flour
Salt

Melt two thirds of the butter in a pan, add the shelled peas, salt, a teaspoon of sugar, and mix everything so as to have a compact mass. Put the pan in the fridge for about 20 minutes, only then put it on the heat with a glass of water, a heart of lettuce, tied with a thread so that the leaves do not come off, a bunch of parsley, and 2 or 3 scallions. Cover and simmer the peas gently over very low heat until completely cooked.

When serving, remove the lettuce, parsley, and onions; then mix the rest of the butter with a tablespoon of flour aside and then put it in the saucepan to thicken the peas. Leave on the heat for a moment, stir, and pour into a serving dish.

PISELLI ALL'INGLESE

Peas English Style

3 lb 5 oz peas in the pod (or 1 lb 5 oz shelled)
7 tbsp butter
Salt

Shell the peas and put them to boil in plenty of lightly salted boiling water. Cook over high heat, so that the peas stay very green.

As soon as they are cooked, drain them and immediately send them to the table, accompanying them with a plate of butter wheels or shells; or, put the butter on top of the peas so that they appear on the table with a covering of butter.

PISELLI ALLA PANCETTA AFFUMICATA

Peas with Smoked Pancetta

3½ oz smoked pancetta
3 lb 5 oz peas in the pod (or 1 lb 5 oz shelled)
1 onion
Sugar
2 tbsp butter
Bread for croutons
Salt

Cut the pancetta into cubes and place it in a pan with a few spoons of water, so that it can warm up without frying too much.

Shell the peas, thinly slice the onion, and add both to the pan. Season with very little salt and a pinch of sugar and baste with a few ladles of hot water.

Cook over a high heat, uncovered, and at the end of cooking, mix the butter with the peas, off the heat.

Pour the peas on to the plate and garnish with fried or toasted croutons.

PISELLI ALL'USO SARDO

Peas Sardinian Style

3 lb 5 oz peas in the pod (or 1 lb 5 oz shelled)
Olive oil
1 onion
6 eggs
Grated Parmesan
Loaf of bread
7 tbsp milk
2 tbsp butter
Salt

Shell the peas and put them in a saucepan with half a glass of oil, sliced onion, and a little water; season with a pinch of salt and cook over a high heat and with the lid on.

Break the eggs into a bowl, season them with salt and some grated Parmesan, and beat them as in an omelet. Soak the white of the loaf of bread in milk. When it is soaked, squeeze it and add it to the beaten eggs. Finally, add the cooked and well-drained peas, and mix everything well.

Butter a dish of about 8 inches in diameter, pour in the mixture of eggs and peas, and put in a preheated oven of moderate heat for half an hour until firm and transformed into a tasty cake.

Then turn it upside down on the plate and send it hot to the table.

PISELLI AL PROSCIUTTO

Peas with Prosciutto

7 tbsp butter
1 onion
3 lb 5 oz peas in the pod, or 1 lb 5 oz shelled)
Broth
3 oz prosciutto
Salt

Put the butter and a spoonful of finely chopped onion in a saucepan. Cook slowly until the onion cooks without turning brown, and then add the shelled peas. Season with salt and pepper, and add a few spoons of broth or boiling water. At this point, bring the cooking to a very high heat, stirring occasionally. They should be ready in about 10 minutes.

A few minutes before removing from the heat, add a couple of spoons of prosciutto cut into strips.

Tomatoes

TO SKIN AND SEED A TOMATO

Plunge a tomato in boiling water for 10 seconds. The skin will open up and be easy to peel. For neat pieces, cut into quarters, remove the seeds with the tip of a knife - which can go for other preparations like vinaigrette - and slice the flesh only.

POMODORI COL RISO

Tomatoes with Rice

12 large tomatoes
1¾ cups rice
Olive oil
Parsley
Basil
Mint
Sugar
Garlic
Salt
Pepper
Optional: potatoes

Wash the tomatoes, remove the tops with a horizontal cut that will serve as a lid. Use a teaspoon to take out the pulp and juice and put them in a bowl. In the same bowl, add the rice and season with 2 spoons of oil, a little chopped parsley, a few leaves of basil and mint, a pinch of sugar, a little salt and pepper, and a few cloves of garlic left whole so they can be removed later. Let the rice soak in this sauce for about half an hour.

Line up the tomato shells in a well-oiled oven dish in which they can stand side by side, cut side up. Fill with the rice mix, and top with their lids. Sprinkle with a little salt and more oil and bake them in a preheated oven of moderate heat for about an hour. Between 1 tomato and the next, you can put washed and peeled potato wedges sprinkled with salt.

ADA SAYS: *Stuffed tomatoes with rice can be prepared a few hours in advance because, perhaps, they are better cold than hot.*

POMODORI CON INSALATA RUSSA

Tomatoes with Russian Salad

6 tomatoes
Mustard, prepared or dry
Vinegar
Russian salad *(p725)*
Parsley
Salt
Pepper

Mayonnaise:
1 egg yolk, half glass olive oil

Choose 6 nice tomatoes that are not too ripe and of medium size, wash them thoroughly, and then remove the top cap from each one. With a spoon, empty the seeds and put them in the fridge while you proceed to the other preparations.

Make a mayonnaise *(p19)* with the egg yolk and oil and finish it with a teaspoon of mustard or dry mustard dissolved in a little vinegar.

Prepare a small Russian salad with the potatoes, carrots, and green beans and add some mayonnaise.

Arrange the tomatoes on a serving dish, fill them with the Russian salad, finish them with the remaining mayonnaise, and cover them with their caps. You can garnish the dish with parsley leaves. Keep in the fridge until ready to serve.

POMODORI FARCITI

Stuffed Tomatoes

6 tomatoes
3 hard-boiled eggs
3½ oz tinned tuna in olive oil
Parsley
Capers
Salt
Pepper

Mayonnaise:
1 egg yolk, half glass olive oil, vinegar, salt

Choose tomatoes, which must not be very ripe, wash them well, and remove the top caps. With a spoon, empty them of the seeds.

Make up a mayonnaise *(p19)* with the egg yolk, oil, a splash of vinegar, and salt.

Shell the hard-boiled eggs and cut them into cubes. Put them in a bowl with the tuna, chopped parsley, capers, and a pinch of pepper. Blend this mixture with the mayonnaise and fill the prepared tomatoes. Put the caps back on the tomatoes, arrange them on a serving dish, and keep them in the fridge until ready to serve.

POMODORI GRATINATI

Tomatoes Gratin

12 tomatoes
Olive oil
7 oz black olives
Capers
Parsley
Breadcrumbs
Salt
Pepper

Rinse the tomatoes, divide them in 2 with a horizontal cut, and take out the seeds and juice with a teaspoon.

Oil a large pan and place the half tomatoes side by side in a single layer, with the cut side up. On each half tomato, arrange a few pitted olives and a few capers, season with salt and a little pepper, and sprinkle a little finely chopped parsley on top.

Then cover with the breadcrumbs, and slowly drain a little oil on each tomato. Put in a preheated oven at moderate heat for about half an hour.

POMODORI IN PADELLA

Pan-fried Tomatoes

1 lb 5 oz large ripe tomatoes
Olive oil
Parsley
Basil or mint
Salt
Pepper

Rinse the tomatoes, cut them horizontally in 2, empty the seeds and put them in a single layer, with the cut side up, in a large dish with 2 to 3 tablespoons of oil. Season with salt, pepper, chopped parsley, and basil, or even a few leaves of field mint—*mentuccia*—and let them cook well first on 1 side and then, turning them carefully with a small spoon, let them cook on the other side as well. In a few minutes the tomatoes will be dry and cooked.

POMODORI IN PASTICCIO

Tomato Crostata

6 large ripe tomatoes
3½ oz tinned tuna in olive oil
2 to 3 anchovy fillets
Parsley
Basil
Loaf of bread
Garlic
Oregano
14 tbsp butter
1⅔ cups flour
Salt
Pepper
Optional: 1 egg, beaten, to wash

Choose 6 large tomatoes, fleshy and ripe, dip them for a few moments in boiling water to be able to peel them more easily, then remove the top caps with a knife and carefully empty the seeds from the tomatoes using a teaspoon. Season with salt and a pinch of pepper and set aside.

Chop the tuna in oil, the anchovy fillets, washed and boned, a little parsley, a few basil leaves, a large egg-sized wedge of bread soaked and squeezed dry, a little garlic, if you like, a pinch of oregano, and a quarter of the butter. Blend well to a paste and use this to fill the tomatoes.

With the flour, half of the butter, a pinch of salt, and about 4 spoons of water, prepare a dough. Split into 2 and roll out. Butter a 10 inch pan and spread out the dough, arrange the stuffed tomatoes gracefully, making sure to leave an edge of a couple of fingers around them. Drain plenty of melted butter on the tomatoes.

Once this is done, roll out the other piece of dough and cover the tomatoes. Press around with your fingers so that the upper and lower sides stick together perfectly, and then with the tip of a small knife, even the edge so it is regular. Finally, make a small hole in the middle of the pie, and optionally, gild everything with a few brushes of beaten egg.

Put the pie in a preheated oven of moderate heat and let it cook for about three quarters of an hour. If the dough starts to brown too much, cover with a sheet of parchment paper and continue cooking, always at moderate heat.

After it is cooked, slide the pie into a serving dish and surround it with a few sprigs of parsley. It can be served both hot and cold.

POMODORI RIPIENI DI CAPPERI E ACCIUGHE

Tomatoes Stuffed with Capers and Anchovies

12 ripe tomatoes
Olive oil
1 onion
4 anchovy fillets
Parsley
Capers
Breadcrumbs
Salt
Pepper
Nutmeg

Choose rather large and ripe tomatoes, wash them, and remove their upper caps with a horizontal cut, empty the seeds, and place them upside down in a bowl to drain well.

Put half a glass of oil in a pan with a chopped onion and cook gently without letting the onion brown. Then remove from the heat and add 4 anchovy fillets, washed and boned and cut into small pieces, a spoon of chopped parsley, a generous helping of capers, and 2 or 3 spoons of breadcrumbs; mix everything together, and complete it with a little salt and very little nutmeg. Fill the tomatoes with this mixture.

Then brown some more breadcrumbs in a pan with a little oil, and spread them on the tomatoes. Arrange the tomatoes in an oiled baking dish, pour a little more oil over them. Put them in a preheated oven at moderate heat for about half an hour.

POMODORI RIPIENI DI CARNE

Tomatoes Stuffed with Meat

12 tomatoes
Loaf of bread
10 oz ground meat
Milk
4 tsp butter
1 egg
Grated Parmesan
Olive oil
Salt
Nutmeg

Rinse the tomatoes, remove the upper caps, empty them of the water and seeds, and place them upside down in a bowl to drain.

Meanwhile, take half as much white of bread as there is ground meat, dip it in the milk, and squeeze dry. Shred it into the mince, add the butter, egg, ¼ cup grated Parmesan, a little nutmeg, and a pinch of salt. Mix everything well.

Then fill the tomato shells with the mixture. Oil an sheet pan, line up the tomatoes, and drizzle with oil. Finally, put the pan in a preheated oven of moderate heat, leaving it to cook for about an hour.

POMODORI RIPIENI DI CIPOLLE

Tomatoes Stuffed with Onion

12 large not too ripe tomatoes
2¼ lb onions
Olive oil
2 tbsp capers
3½ oz black olives
Parsley
Salt

Rinse the tomatoes, divide them in half horizontally, empty out the juice and seeds so you have 24 bowls. Sprinkle with salt and place on a plate upside down for about half an hour.

Cut the onions into thin slices and place them in a pan with 6 spoons of oil and a pinch of salt. Cook slowly, slowly, adding a little water to prevent the onions from burning. When the onions have wilted, pour them on to a plate and let them cool.

Then fill the tomato halves with the cooked onions, smooth the surface with the blade of a knife and decorate with some capers, some pitted olives, and chopped parsley. Drizzle with oil and place them in the fridge until ready to serve.

POMODORI RIPIENI DI FRUTTI DI MARE

Tomatoes with Seafood

12 tomatoes
4½ lb mussels, shell on
4½ lb clams, shell on
Breadcrumbs
Garlic
Olive oil
Parsley
Red chili flakes
Salt
Pepper

Rinse the tomatoes, remove the top caps, which you will keep aside, empty the pulp and seeds, and place them upside down in a bowl for about half an hour to dry.

Wash the mussels in running water, scrape them with a small knife, remove any string, then wash them again several times, with great care. Also rinse the clams in several changes of water.

Put 2 cloves of garlic and enough oil to cover the bottom of a large frying pan, and, as soon as the garlic colors, add the mussels and cook them over high heat for a few minutes, shaking them so they all feel the heat equally. As soon as they open, pour them into a large bowl and cook the clams in the same pan, following the same system. Discard any that don't open.

When the clams are all open, remove them from the heat, pour them into a large bowl, then shell both the mussels and the clams, collecting them in a single container. Keep back a little of the cooking juices for later.

Season the shellfish with a handful of chopped parsley, a little red chili flakes, a grind of pepper, a few spoons of breadcrumbs, and a little oil. Fill the tomatoes with this mixture and cover them with their caps. Oil an oven tray and line up the tomatoes; pour over a little of the cooking juices from the mussels and clams, and put in a preheated oven of moderate heat for about half an hour until the tomatoes are a little withered.

ADA SAYS: *They can be served both hot and at room temperature.*

POMODORI RIPIENI DI FUNGHI

Tomatoes Stuffed with Mushrooms

12 not too ripe tomatoes
1 lb mushrooms
Olive oil
Garlic
1 loaf bread
Milk
2 eggs
Grated Parmesan
Salt
Pepper

Rinse the tomatoes, remove the top caps, empty the juice and seeds, and place them upside down on a bowl to dry.

Quickly wash the mushrooms, scrape them, trim their stems, cut them into small pieces ,and cook them in a pan with a little oil, a clove of garlic, and a pinch of salt and pepper. When the mushrooms are cooked and their sauce very well reduced, chop them together with the white of the bread, previously soaked in milk and squeezed out.

Season with the eggs, salt, pepper, and ½ cup grated Parmesan, then fill the prepared tomatoes with this mixture.

Pour a few spoonfuls of oil into a baking dish, line up the tomatoes, and drizzle with more oil. Finally, put the dish in a preheated oven of moderate heat, cook for about half an hour.

POMODORI RIPIENI DI PISELLI

Tomatoes with Peas

12 large ripe tomatoes
1 onion
Olive oil
12 oz shelled peas
Meat broth or stock cube
Grated Parmesan
Salt

White sauce:
1½ tbsp flour, 1½ tbsp butter, 1 cup milk

Cut the tomatoes horizontally, remove the seeds and also some of the pulp, which you drain and keep aside. Turn the tomatoes over in a bowl to drain as well.

In a frying pan, brown the onion with the oil and add the tomato pulp. At this point, pour the peas into the pan, let them flavor, and baste with a few ladles of hot broth.

Make a white sauce *(p16)* with the flour, butter, and milk listed here, and, when it is ready, add the peas, mixing well to obtain a smooth filling for the tomatoes. Fill the tomatoes with this mixture.

Now place the stuffed tomatoes in a baking dish lightly greased with butter, sprinkle them with ½ cup grated Parmesan, and put them in a preheated oven for about half an hour.

POMODORI RIPIENI DI TONNO

Tomatoes with Tuna

12 tomatoes
9 oz tinned tuna in olive oil
Capers
Parsley
Olive oil
Salt
Pepper

Rinse the tomatoes, remove the caps that will serve as lids, empty them of juice and seeds, and place them upside down in a bowl to dry.

Chop the tuna and mix in with a spoonful of capers and parsley. Oil a baking dish, arrange the tomatoes in a single layer and put a spoonful of the tuna mixture in each. Drop just a drizzle of oil on each tomato and season with salt and pepper, if you like.

Cover the tomatoes with their caps, baste them with more oil, and put them in a preheated oven at moderate heat for about half an hour.

Leeks

PORRI ALLA CREMA DI LATTE

Leeks in Cream

8 leeks
Butter
Broth
1 cup heavy cream
Salt

Clean the leeks, remove the outer leaves, cut off the roots, cut off the tough green leaves, leaving only the white part, rinse them, dip them in boiling water, and let them cook almost until half cooked—7 or 8 minutes. This helps to sweeten them by making them lose their slight bitterness.

Then cut them in half lengthwise, and align them possibly in a single layer, in a buttered pan. Baste the leeks with a little broth, cover, and let them finish cooking. Toward the end, add the cream and allow to absorb slowly. Then place them in a serving dish.

PORRI IN FLAN

Leek Flan

2¼ lb leeks
3½ tbsp butter
3½ oz pancetta
Flour
2 cups milk
1 egg
Salt
Pepper
Nutmeg

Flan:
1⅔ cups flour, 7 tbsp butter, salt

An exquisite preparation, which can be served as a dish in itself, or as a fine side dish for roasted or grilled meat.

For the flan, put the flour, the butter, and a pinch of salt on the kitchen table and mix everything with about half a glass of water. Make a ball of the dough and let it rest.

Clean the leeks, remove the outer leaves, cut the roots off, and remove the green leaves leaving only the white part. Slice them crosswise, rinse them, and dip them in a pot with plenty of lightly salted boiling water. Let them boil for 5 minutes, and then drain.

Now put the butter and the chopped pancetta in a frying pan. Melt the butter and let the pancetta become slightly transparent. Then add the leeks, and over a very moderate heat, let them sauté for a good quarter of an hour, without letting them brown.

Sprinkle a heaped spoon of flour over the leeks and then gradually pour over boiling milk, which you add in small quantities, a bit at a time. Season with salt, pepper, and nutmeg. When the milk boils again, reduce the heat, cover, and let it finish cooking with an insensitive simmer for about half an hour. Then pour out the leeks on to a plate and let them cool completely.

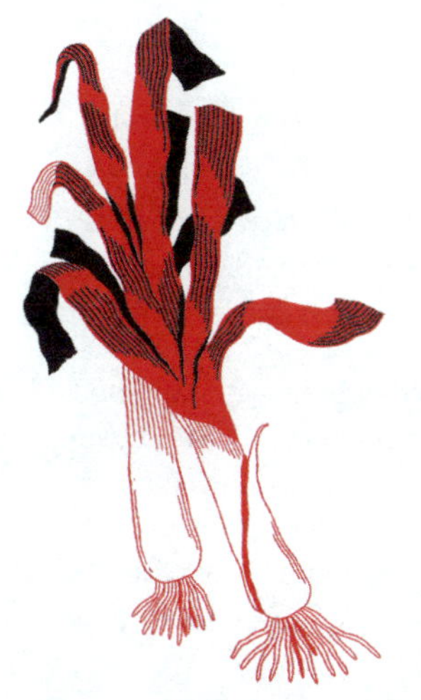

Roll out the dough for the flan to a thickness of ⅛ inch and line an 8 inch circular flan dish. Pass a wooden roller over the edge of the flan, to remove the superfluous dough. Then pour the cold leeks into the dish. Line them up with the blade of a knife. With the leftover dough make a rather tight lattice work with strips of dough ½ inch wide and arranged in a lozenge, like for a tart. Brush with the beaten egg and put the flan in a preheated oven of lively heat for about half an hour. After this time, remove it from the oven, and slide the flan into a serving dish.

PORRI IN PADELLA

Pan-Fried Leeks

12 leeks
Olive oil
Salt

This is the simplest way to cook leeks.

Clean the leeks, remove the outer leaves, cut off the roots, remove the green leaves leaving only the white part. Then rinse them, and dip them into a pot with plenty of lightly salted boiling water.

Let them boil for a quarter of an hour and then drain and place them in a pan in which you have heated up a little oil. Season with a pinch of salt and let them flavor for a few minutes.

Turnips

RAPE ALLO ZUCCHERO

Turnip with Sugar

2¼ lb turnips
3½ tbsp butter
Sugar
Flour
Broth or water
Salt

Peel and cut the turnips into thin slices. Melt a little butter in a pan, add the turnips, season with salt, a little sugar, and a little flour.

Baste them with a little broth or water, enough to cover, and cook them over moderate heat. At the end of cooking the sauce must be so reduced that it covers the turnips with a glossy and tasty veil.

Celery

SEDANI AL FORNO

Baked Celery

2¼ lb celery
1 onion
Prosciutto
5½ tbsp butter
Broth or stock cube
2 oz Gruyère
Salt
Pepper

When purchasing celery, choose the clumps that have fresh ribs and intact leaves, without reddish veins.

Open the celery up to the heart, from which you will take the white stalk; discard the harder outer ribs and the leaves, and cut the whiter ribs into pieces of about 4 inches long. Scrape and put them in fresh water and wash them thoroughly to get rid of all traces of earth.

Plunge them into plenty of lightly salted boiling water and boil them for a few minutes, then drain, put them in cold water, and dry. Chop the onion and the prosciutto and sweat in a knob of butter. When the onion is cooked, add the celery and let them flavor together. Season with salt and pepper and baste with a ladle of water in which you have dissolved a stock cube. Cover, reduce the heat, and let it finish cooking.

When the celery is cooked, after about 10 minutes, arrange them in a baking dish, sprinkle over some grated Gruyère, then the rest of the butter, and place the dish in a hot oven for a few minutes. Remove from the oven, place the dish on a tray and send to the table.

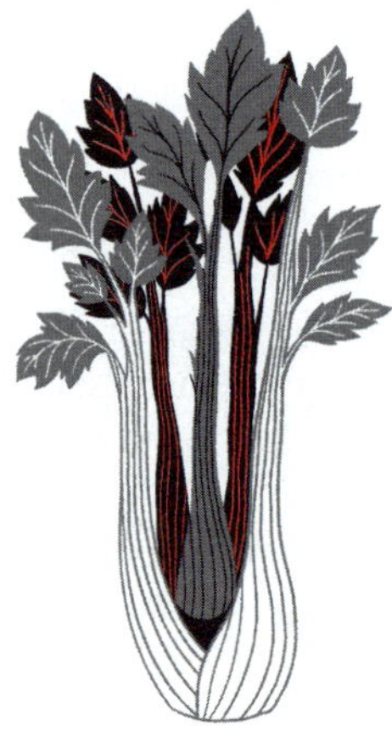

SEDANI ALLA PARMIGIANA

Celery Parmigiana

2¼ lb small young celery
Broth
2 oz prosciutto
1 onion
Clove
Grated Parmesan
Butter

For this preparation you don't need very large celery, but white and very fresh.

These preliminary operations are important: Remove some outer stalks from the celery, trim the stem, cut the leaves, leaving the stalks about 6 inches long, and rinse them thoroughly. Put a pot of water on the stove, and when it boils, throw in the celery. As soon as the water boils again, drain the celery and put it in a bowl with plenty of cold water. Wash them again, slightly spreading the ribs, but without detaching them, and finally pass the celery under the tap to remove any earth.

Chop and tie the celery into bunches of 2 or 3 pieces and line them up in a large and low saucepan. Cover with broth, add a few slices of prosciutto, a small onion, a clove, and a little salt. Cover the saucepan and let it boil slowly for about 10 minutes until completely cooked.

When the celery is cooked, remove from the pan, drain them well, untie them, and arrange them on a plate and season with plenty of grated Parmesan and melted, frothing butter.

Spinach

 **TO COOK SPINACH**

Spinach cooks very quickly. Just wet from washing, it goes straight in the pan until it collapses, maybe 1 or 2 minutes. Then, importantly, it must be squeezed dry before using in a recipe.

SPINACI A CRUDO

Braised Spinach

4½ lb spinach
1 onion
3½ tbsp butter
Olive oil
2 oz pancetta
Garlic
Grated Parmesan
Salt
Pepper
Optional: bread for croutons

Clean the spinach and rinse several times to remove the earth.

Then sauté a chopped onion in the butter, plus a few spoons of oil, the pancetta, cut into small pieces, and a little garlic. When it is well colored, add the spinach.

Cover the casserole, reduce the heat, and let the spinach cook in its own water. As soon as this has completely evaporated, season, off the heat, with grated Parmesan, salt, and pepper, and arrange them on a serving dish, surrounding them, if you wish, with small triangles of fried bread.

SPINACI AL BURRO

Spinach with Butter

4½ lb spinach
7 tbsp butter
Grated Parmesan
Salt
Pepper
Nutmeg

Clean and wash the spinach with great care, then boil it in a little lightly salted water. Drain, squeeze well to extract all the water, and put to flavor in a pan with plenty of butter, salt, pepper, and nutmeg.

Before pouring them into a serving dish, add ¼ cup grated Parmesan off the heat and give a final stir.

SPINACI AL GRATIN

Spinach Gratin

4½ lb spinach
7 tbsp butter
Grated Parmesan
Salt
Pepper

Clean and wash the spinach, with great care, then boil it in a little lightly salted water. Drain, squeeze well to extract all the water, and chop on the cutting board.

Then flavor in a pan with butter, salt, and pepper and, off the heat, finish with a spoon of Parmesan and cool on a plate.

About 10 minutes before going to the table, butter an oven dish and lay in the chopped spinach. Put a few pieces of butter here and there, and generously sprinkle with more Parmesan. Put the dish in a preheated oven, and, as soon as the cheese melts, the spinach will be au gratin, serve it.

SPINACI ALLA ROMANA

Spinach Roman Style

4½ lb spinach
Raisins
Lard
Pine nuts
Salt
Pepper

Wash and blanch the spinach, drain, and squeeze dry. Soak the raisins in warm water.

Melt 2 tablespoons of lard in a pan and add the spinach, salt, and pepper. Then add the pine nuts and soaked raisins. Mix well and arrange on a serving plate.

SPINACI CON ACCIUGHE

Spinach with Anchovy fillets

4½ lb spinach
7 tbsp butter
3 to 4 anchovy fillets
Garlic
Salt
Pepper
To serve: bread for croutons

Wash and blanch the spinach and squeeze dry.

Just before going to the table, put the butter in a frying pan and let it fry until it becomes blond. Then add the spinach, season with salt, pepper, and a few washed, boned, and chopped anchovy fillets together with a small piece of garlic. Leave to flavor a little and arrange the spinach on the plate. Garnish with fried croutons.

SPINACI CON PARMIGIANO E UOVA

Spinach with Parmesan and Eggs

4½ lb spinach
Butter
2 eggs
Grated Parmesan
Salt
Nutmeg
To serve: bread for croutons

Wash and blanch the spinach, squeeze dry, and chop on the cutting board.

Then put the spinach in a pan with a little butter, let it flavor, season with a little salt and a little nutmeg. Reduce the heat and pour a couple of beaten eggs into the pan as for an omelet. Stir immediately, and add a few spoons of grated Parmesan. Stir again, cover, let it rest for a few minutes on the heat.

Fry your croutons and arrange the spinach in the middle.

SPINACI CON PROSCIUTTO E GROVIERA

Spinach with Prosciutto and Gruyère

4½ lb spinach
7 tbsp butter
Milk
3½ oz prosciutto
3½ oz Gruyère
Grated Parmesan
Salt

Wash and boil the spinach, squeeze dry, and chop on the cutting board.

Melt half of the butter in a pan, then add the spinach, a glass of milk, a pinch of salt, and cook for a few minutes, over a high heat. Butter a baking dish and pour in the spinach. Cut the prosciutto and the Gruyère into thin sticks and place them around the spinach. Sprinkle with ½ cup Parmesan, place here and there with knobs of butter, and place the container in a preheated oven of high heat for a few minutes.

When the cheese begins to melt, place the pan on a serving plate and send immediately to the table.

SPINACI IN BUDINO

Spinach Flan

4½ lb spinach
7 tbsp butter
2 eggs
1 egg yolk
Grated Parmesan
Flour
Salt

White sauce:
2 tbsp flour, 2 tbsp butter, 1 cup milk, salt, nutmeg

Tomato sauce:
1 lb tomatoes, 1 onion, celery, carrot, basil, olive oil, 3 tbsp dried mushrooms

This is one of the preparations best suited to spinach.

Wash and blanch the spinach, squeeze dry, and chop very finely. Sauté over moderate heat with half of the butter, and mix to dry. Then season with a little salt and pour them on to a plate.

Make up a white sauce *(p16)* with the flour, butter, and milk listed here which should be thick and rather elastic. Season it with salt and nutmeg and pour it into a bowl. We need half as much sauce as we have spinach.

When the sauce is lukewarm, pour in the spinach and mix carefully. Break 2 eggs and a yolk in a bowl, and beat these eggs as for an omelet. Then add them, a spoon or 2 at a time, to the spinach mixture, always stirring. When you have incorporated all the eggs, add a couple of spoons of grated Parmesan.

Butter a cake mold with a hole in the middle, with a capacity of 4 cups, flour it, and then turn the mold upside down to let the excess flour fall out. Put the spinach mixture into the mold, and then immerse it almost to the brim in a container containing boiling water. Cook the flan in the water bath over very low heat for about an hour, making sure that the water never boils. If the pudding struggles to harden, which should not happen if the sauce has been done well, you can, three quarters of the way through cooking, carefully lift the whole bain-marie into a moderate oven.

While it is cooking prepare a good tomato sauce *(p28)* with the dried mushrooms, and the usual aromatics.

When touching the mixture in the mold, it should be firm. Take the mold out of the water and let the it rest for at least 5 minutes. Then turn it out on a serving plate.

Pour the well thickened tomato sauce in the middle and around the spinach mold.

SPINACI IN CROSTINI

Spinach Crostini

4½ lb spinach
7 tbsp butter
Pine nuts
Salt
Nutmeg
To serve: bread for croutons

Wash and blanch the spinach, squeeze dry, and chop. Put it in a pan with a little butter, let them flavor, and season with a little salt and a little nutmeg.

In the meantime, fry some medium-sized croutons in butter. Arrange them in a serving dish and on each of them place a spoonful of spinach just removed from the heat. Garnish with whole and chopped pine nuts so as to compose like a flower and send promptly to the table.

SPINACI IN SFORMATO CON FUNGHI

Spinach and Mushroom Flan

4½ lb spinach
7 tbsp butter
1 lb ricotta
Grated Parmesan
4 eggs
Flour
1¾ lb mushrooms
White wine
Salt
Pepper
Nutmeg

Wash and blanch the spinach, squeeze dry, and chop. Melt half of the butter in a pan, add the spinach, mix with a wooden spoon, and leave them to flavor over a moderate heat for a few minutes.

Blend the ricotta in a bowl with a few spoons of water, ¼ cup grated Parmesan, the 4 egg yolks, a touch of nutmeg, and salt and pepper. Mix well, then add the spinach and finally the egg whites whipped to a firm snow.

Butter and flour a mold, with a hole in the center, of capacity of 4 cups, pour the mixture in, and bake in a preheated oven of moderate heat for half an hour until it has swollen and firmed on the outside.

While the flan is in the oven, prepare the mushrooms: Trim the stems, wash them quickly, so as not to let them absorb the water, dry them carefully, then cut them into slices lengthwise. Melt the rest of the butter in a frying pan, big enough so the mushrooms can fit in a single layer. Add the mushrooms, season with salt and pepper, and let them cook over a very low heat until all the liquid evaporates. Then pour half a glass of white wine into the pan a little at a time, letting it evaporate too. When the mushrooms are cooked correctly, keep them warm.

By this time, the flan will be ready: Remove it from the oven and lay it into a serving dish, making sure it keeps its shape. Arrange a part of the mushrooms in the center in a crown, and the rest all around.

Truffles

TO CHOOSE TRUFFLES

Choose some nice truffles whose scent is neither too strong nor too garlicky, because this scent could hide a chemical reaction. Pay attention also to the lumps of earth that increase the weight of the truffle.

Carefully clean the truffles with water and a toothbrush to remove any earthy residue, then cut them into very thin slices.

The white (Alba) truffle is yellowish-gray in color with white veins inside. Its volume varies greatly and its weight ranges from a few ounces to nearly 2 pounds. It has exquisite flavor and extraordinary fragrance. It does not usually want cooking. Grate the white truffle on foods cooked with butter, on cold and lightly cooked meats, on fried eggs, and also on mushrooms in salads but without lemon.

The black truffle is wrinkled on the outside and purplish-black on the inside with characteristic white veins. It has a subtle, persistent, exquisite scent. Especially fine specimens are found in Norcia and Spoleto in Italy. The black, and other truffles, need the heat to bring out the flavor and should be incorporated in your cooking.

The bianchetto truffle is yellowish-white with whitish veins inside. It has a decent fragrance, but mostly a light garlicky taste, which means it is less valued.

You must consume the truffle as soon as possible and in the meantime keep it wrapped in a cloth or in a sheet of newspaper in the vegetable compartment of the fridge. Do not keep the truffle in rice, as it was once done, because the rice dehydrates it.

TARTUFI BIANCHI ALLA PARMIGIANA

White Truffles with Parmesan

1½ tbsp butter
White truffles
Grated Parmesan
1 lemon

Put the butter in a small pan, and when it has melted and colored add the sliced truffles. As soon as they are hot—they must not fry—remove the pan from the heat and sprinkle with ¼ cup grated Parmesan, adding a few drops of lemon.

TARTUFI BIANCHI ALLA PIEMONTESE

White Truffles Piedmont Style

White truffles
Parmesan
Olive oil
Lemon wedges
Salt
Pepper

Carefully clean the truffles with water and a toothbrush to remove any earthy residue, then cut them into thin slices.

In a pan with a lid, make alternating layers of thinly sliced white truffles and Parmesan, putting salt, pepper, and oil on top of each layer; put the pan on the heat for 10 minutes, covering with the lid. Serve with lemon wedges.

TARTUFI NERI ALLA PROVENZALE

Black Truffles Provençal

Black truffles
Lard
White wine
Garlic
Olive oil
1 lemon

Carefully clean and scrub with a toothbrush and slice the truffles.

Warm the sliced truffles in a pan with a few slices of lard, half a glass of white wine, and a clove of garlic. Take off the heat after a few minutes and add a drizzle of oil. Serve hot with the addition of a few drops of lemon juice.

TARTUFI NERI IN SALSA

Black Truffle Sauce

Black truffles
Garlic
3 anchovy fillets
Olive oil
1 lemon

Wash and clean the truffles well; chop them with a clove of garlic and the washed and boned anchovy fillets.

Heat gently in a pan for 10 minutes with a drizzle of oil, then add a little lemon juice.

ADA SAYS: *With this sauce, delicious croutons are made, or white fish, legumes, game, etc. are garnished. This sauce is also used to dress spaghetti, without adding any other seasoning.*

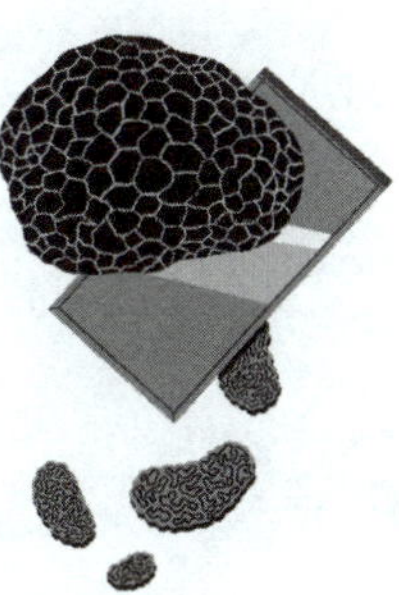

Jerusalem Artichokes

TOPINAMBUR FRITTI E TRIFOLATI

Jerusalem Artichokes, Two Ways

1¾ lb Jerusalem artichokes
Oil for frying
2 garlic cloves
Broth or stock cube
Bay leaf
Parsley
Salt
Pepper

Batter:
⅓ cup flour, 7 tbsp white wine, 2 tbsp butter or margarine, 2 egg whites, salt

This recipe consists of two distinct preparations: Fried Jerusalem artichokes with batter and sautéed Jerusalem artichokes. The two preparations should be brought to the table at the same time.

First of all, with the flour, wine, salt, and melted butter, prepare a batter and leave it to rest for at least an hour.

Meanwhile, devote your attention to the Jerusalem artichokes to be sautéed—take half the artichokes, wash them, and cut them into slices. In a pan, heat 4 spoons of oil and 2 cloves of garlic, and as soon as the oil is hot add the artichoke slices, season with salt and pepper. As soon as they are flavored, add half a glass of hot broth to the pan, add a bay leaf, and continue cooking very slowly for 5 minutes, garnishing them at the end with plenty of chopped parsley.

Now wash the rest of the artichokes, blanch them al dente for 5 minutes in lightly salted boiling water, then drain, and when they are cold, cut them into slices that are not too thin.

Whip the egg whites to a snow and fold into the resting batter. Wipe the artichoke slices through the batter and fry them in plenty of hot oil, and, when they are golden, drain them on absorbent paper.

ADA SAYS: *Jerusalem artichoke is a species of sunflower, native to Canada, but also cultivated in Europe, of which the irregular and gnarled tubers of the size of a potato are eaten, which are very nutritious and whose taste is similar to that of the true artichoke.*

TOPINAMBUR IN SALSA VERDE

Jerusalem Artichokes in Green Sauce

2¼ lb Jerusalem artichokes
Olive oil
Salt

Green sauce:
loaf of bread, milk, 2 anchovy fillets, parsley, capers, 6 cornichons, olive oil, vinegar, salt, pepper

Scrape the artichokes, cut them into pieces, rinse, and boil them in slightly salted boiling water for 5 minutes. Then let them cool with a little oil.

Make up a green sauce *(p31)* with the ingredients listed here; soak the white of the bread in milk and squeeze dry, mash it up with the chopped anchovy fillets, parsley, capers, cornichons, oil, a splash of vinegar, salt, and pepper.

Cover the artichokes with the sauce.

Pumpkin

ZUCCA ALLA CACCIATORA

Hunter's Pumpkin

2¼ lb yellow pumpkin
Olive oil
Garlic
Rosemary
Salt
Pepper

Peel the pumpkin, remove the seeds, and cut it into small, rather thin rectangular slices.

Put half a glass of oil in a pan with a couple of garlic cloves, and when the garlic begins to fry, remove them and replace with the pumpkin pieces. Season with salt, pepper, and a good pinch of rosemary.

Stir occasionally but gently so as not to break the pumpkin too much, which will be ready in just over a quarter of an hour.

ZUCCA FRITTA ALLA SICILIANA

Fried Pumpkin Sicilian Style

2¼ lb pumpkin
Oil for frying
Vinegar
Sugar
Mint
Salt
Optional: garlic

Peel the pumpkin, remove the seeds, and cut it into thin slices that you will divide into rectangular pieces, like playing cards, and that you will fry in a pan with plenty of hot oil without flour.

When the pumpkin slices are cooked, drain almost all the oil, leaving only a little. Put the pan back on the heat and baste the pumpkin with a little vinegar. Add salt, a pinch of sugar, and a few chopped mint leaves. Let it flavor a little longer. It is optional to add a little chopped garlic.

ZUCCA FRITTA CON PASTELLA

Deep-Fried Pumpkin in Batter

2¼ lb yellow pumpkin
Lard or oil for frying
Salt

Batter:
Water, 1 cup flour, 2 tbsp olive oil, salt

Peel the pumpkin, remove the seeds, and cut it into very thin slices, which you will divide into rectangular pieces, like playing cards.

Wipe the pieces in a simple batter *(p242)* made with water, flour, oil and a little salt, and fry them in plenty of hot oil or in lard. Serve immediately.

ZUCCA LESSATA

Pumpkin with Horseradish

2¼ lb yellow pumpkin
Olive oil
Vinegar
Horseradish root
Salt

Peel the pumpkin, remove the seeds, and cut it into slices that are not too large. Place a pot of water on the heat and when it boils, add the pumpkin slices and cook for 20 minutes.

When they are cooked, drain them, put them in a salad bowl, and season with oil and salt. You can simply add a few spoonfuls of vinegar, but if you want to prepare a tastier dish: Take a horseradish root, wash it thoroughly, dry it, and then grate. This very spicy condiment will add flavor to the pumpkin.

Zucchini

FIORI DI ZUCCA FRITTI

Fried Zucchini Flowers

1 lb 5 oz zucchini flowers
Oil for frying
Salt

Batter:
1 cup flour, 2 tbsp olive oil, 1 glass warm water

Zucchini flowers must be very fresh and not very open.

Prepare the batter with flour, oil, and warm water at least one hour before frying the flowers.

Spike the stem of the flowers a little, free them from some filament and pistil, wash, and dry them.

Then dip them in the batter and fry them in a pan with plenty of hot oil. Salt them lightly.

FIORI DI ZUCCA FRITTI RIPIENI

Stuffed Zucchini Flowers, Three Ways

Breadcrumbs
Parsley
6 anchovy fillets
1 lb 5 oz zucchini flowers
Oil for frying
Salt
Pepper
Optional: mozzarella, prosciutto, flour, 1 egg

Batter:
1 cup flour, 2 tbsp olive oil, 1 glass warm water

Firstly, prepare the batter with the flour, oil, and warm water at least an hour before frying.

Make a stuffing of breadcrumbs, oil, chopped parsley, chopped anchovy, and pepper.

Or with mozzarella and prosciutto.

Or with mozzarella and chopped anchovy.

Gently remove the pistil from the zucchini flowers and fill them with the mixture.

When all the zucchini flowers are ready, dip them in the batter, or you can also just dust with flour and wipe through a beaten egg, and fry them in hot oil. Salt them lightly.

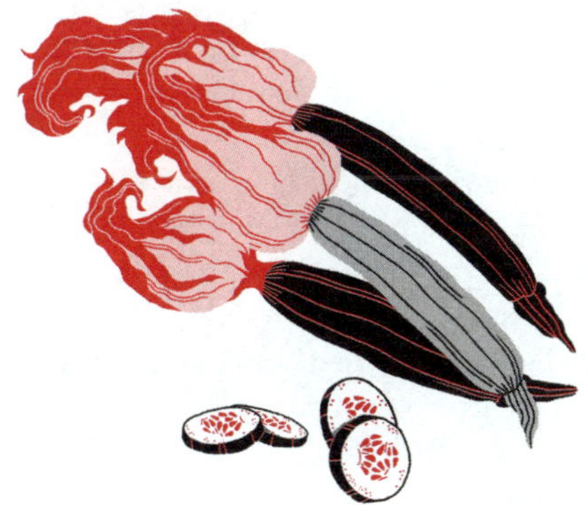

FIORI DI ZUCCA IN PADELLA

Pan-Fried Zucchini Flowers

1 lb 5 oz zucchini flowers
Garlic
Olive oil
Salt
Pepper

Trim the stalks of the flowers a little, free them of some filament, and the pistil, wash, and dry them.

Brown a clove of garlic in a pan with half a glass of oil, remove the garlic, and put the flowers down. Season with salt and pepper and cook covered, over moderate heat, for about 10 minutes, moving them, carefully, from time to time, with a wooden spoon.

ZUCCHINE ALLA GENOVESE

Zucchini Genovese

2¼ lb medium-sized zucchini
Olive oil
Garlic
Parsley
Oregano
Salt
Pepper

Zucchini must be used not long after they have been removed from the plant, when the seeds are very small and the flesh firm.

Wash the zucchini, trim the ends, dry them, and cut them into sticks as long as your little finger, discarding some of the inner part that contains the seeds.

Put them in a pan with plenty of oil and cook over high heat. Season with salt, and when they are almost cooked, add a clove of diced garlic with some parsley, a good pinch of oregano, and a little pepper.

Keep on the heat for a few more minutes and then let them be brought to the table.

ZUCCHINE AL TEGAME

Zucchini with Tomato

2¼ lb zucchini
1 onion
Olive oil
1 lb tomatoes
Salt
Pepper

Wash the zucchini, trim the ends, dry them, cut them into 4 wedges lengthwise, and then divide these wedges into 2 or 3 pieces.

Brown a little onion with a finger of oil, and then add the peeled and chopped tomatoes. Finally, add the zucchini and season with salt and pepper.

Cook over very light heat, so that they can flavor well, basting from time to time with a little water if the sauce is too thick. But be careful not to add too much water, as, when cooked, the vegetables must remain almost dry.

ZUCCHINE FARCITE ALLA LIGURE

Zucchini Ligurian Style

12 medium-sized zucchini
Dried mushrooms
Olive oil
2 oz bread
Oregano
2 eggs
Grated Parmesan
2 oz prosciutto, sliced
Salt
Pepper

White sauce:
2 tbsp butter, 2 tbsp flour, 1 cup milk

Choose equal sized zucchini, rinse them, and dry them. Make a white sauce *(p16)* with the butter, flour, and milk listed here and leave to cool.

Using a long thin vegetable peeler, pierce the ends of the zucchini and hollow out the centers, keeping the flesh back for the filling.

Bring a pan of water to a boil and blanch the zucchini for 2 or 3 minutes, but no more than this. Then put them in cold water, and dry them.

Then divide them in half lengthwise to make two small boats.

Soak ½ ounce of dried mushrooms and when they have revived sauté in a little oil.

Soak the bread and squeeze dry and mix with the zucchini pulp that you took from the center, salt, pepper, a little oregano, and fold into the cold white sauce.

Then add an egg yolk and ¼ cup grated Parmesan. Cut the prosciutto and mushrooms into tiny cubes. Stir to combine everything, and put in a pastry bag with a smooth nozzle ½ inch opening. Before filling the zucchini, it is good to grease them lightly with oil and sprinkle them with a little salt. Fill the halves, making a large bead in the middle. Brush this filling with a beaten egg.

Put the finished zucchini in a well-oiled oven dish and in a preheated oven of moderate heat for half an hour, until they have a nice golden crust.

ZUCCHINE FARCITE DI CARNE

Zucchini with Beef

10 oz lean beef
1 onion
1 carrot
Celery
Grated Parmesan
Parsley
Basil
12 medium-sized zucchini
Olive oil
Breadcrumbs
3½ tbsp butter
Salt

Brown sauce:
2 tbsp butter, ¼ cup flour,
1 cup broth from meat

Put the lean beef to boil in lightly salted boiling water with an onion, a carrot, and a rib of celery. When after about an hour the meat is cooked, chop it thoroughly. Prepare a brown sauce with the butter, flour, and the broth from the meat. When the sauce is thick and without lumps, add the ground meat. Season with ¼ cup grated Parmesan, chopped parsley, torn basil, and mix thoroughly.

Rinse the zucchini, check the ends, dry them, cut them in half, and use the vegetable peeler to gouge out some of the flesh from the middle.

Cut them in half lengthwise to get small boats and blanch for 10 minutes in boiling water, then remove them and refresh in cold water to revive their color. Drain well and line them up in an oiled dish.

Spread the meat mixture on to the zucchini boats, smooth the surface with the blade of a knife, and sprinkle a few breadcrumbs and a small piece of butter on each boat.

When it is time to send to the table, put the dish in a preheated oven of lively heat for about 20 minutes, and, as soon as the breadcrumbs have browned, remove from the oven and arrange them on a plate.

ADA SAYS: *This dish can also be served cold.*

ZUCCHINE FARCITE DI RISO E PROSCIUTTO

Zucchini with Rice and Ham

1 cup rice
3½ tbsp butter
Grated Parmesan
2 oz prosciutto
12 medium-sized zucchini
3½ oz mozzarella
Salt

Cook the rice in lightly salted water, drain, and season with half of the butter, 2 spoons of grated Parmesan, and the prosciutto cut into small pieces.

Prepare the zucchini: halved into boats and blanched for 10 minutes, then fill with the rice, level the surface with the blade of a knife, and place a thin slice of mozzarella on each piece. Drain a little more melted butter over everything and place the dish in a preheated oven with a lively heat for about 20 minutes.

ZUCCHINE FRITTE DORATE

Fried Zucchini

2¼ lb zucchini
Flour
2 eggs
Oil for frying
Salt

Wash the zucchini, trim the ends, dry them, and cut them into sticks as long as your little finger, discarding some of the inner part that contains the seeds.

When it is time to fry, take the sticks a few at a time, sprinkle them in flour, toss them for a moment, then strain through a fine mesh sieve to remove the unnecessary flour, pass them through the beaten eggs, and fry them, not too many at a time, over moderate heat in plenty of oil.

When they are cooked and have a nice golden color, drain them, sprinkle them lightly with salt, and send them to the table.

ZUCCHINE FRITTE GRATINATE

Fried Zucchini Gratin

2¼ lb zucchini
Flour
Oil for frying
Butter
Grated Parmesan
Meat broth, without tomato *(p88)*
Breadcrumbs
Salt

Prepare the zucchini and cut into sticks. Collect them on a plate, sprinkle them with salt, and, placing the plate on a slope (put a spoon underneath), leave them to rest for about an hour, so that their juices can drain.

Then take a few at a time, squeeze them gently, flour them, and fry them to a golden color in plenty of hot oil.

When you have fried them all, melt a little butter in a pan. Add the zucchini steaks, a few spoons of grated Parmesan, a little meat broth, and let them flavor a little, stirring gently.

Generously butter an oven dish, pour in the mixture, add a little more meat broth, and sprinkle with Parmesan and breadcrumbs. Arrange here and there some small pieces of butter and put the dish in a hot oven with rather strong heat to brown the bread until it takes a light golden tint.

ZUCCHINE FRITTE IN FILETTI

Fried Zucchini Fillets

2¼ lb zucchini
Flour
Oil for frying
Lemon wedges
Salt

Wash the zucchini, check the ends, cut them lengthwise into thin slices, and divide into sticks discarding some of the inner part that contains the seeds. Put them on a plate, sprinkle with salt, and leave them like this for an hour or more. The dish must be on a slope so the juices can drain.

When it is time to fry, take a few at a time, squeeze them gently in your hands, flour them, shake off any unnecessary flour, and fry a batch at a time in plenty of hot oil.

As the fillets are fried, take them out, drain, sprinkle them with salt, and arrange them in a serving dish. Surround with lemon wedges and send them to the table very hot.

ZUCHINE FRITTE IN TIMBALLO

Zucchini Timbale

2¼ lb zucchini
Oil for frying
10 oz tomatoes
5¼ oz mozzarella
3 anchovy fillets
Olive oil
Basil
Salt

Wash and dry the zucchini, cut them obliquely into slices about ¼ inch thick. Put them on a plate, at an angle, sprinkle with salt, and leave them like this for an hour or more to drain.

When it is time to fry, take them a few at a time, squeeze them gently in your hands, and fry them in a pan with hot oil. When you have fried all of them, place them in an oven dish.

Peel the tomatoes and remove the seeds, divide them into fillets, and cook them over high heat in a pan with a little oil from the zucchini, after which pour them into the oven dish with the fried zucchini, and arrange the Mozzarella in slices on top. Wash and bone the anchovy fillets and cut into small pieces and position them around. Season with a little salt, oil, and garnish with fresh basil.

Put the dish in a hot oven and as soon as the Mozzarella begins to melt, remove from the oven, place the dish on a plate, and send it to the table.

ZUCCHINE FRITTE MARINATE (ALLA SCAPECE)

Marinated Fried Zucchini

2¼ lb zucchini
Oil for frying
Garlic
Basil
Parsley
1 cup vinegar
Salt
Pepper

Wash the zucchini, trim the ends, dry them, and cut them on an angle into slices about ¼ inch thick.

Fry the slices, a few at a time, in a pan with boiling oil, without flour, making them take on a dark gold color. Then arrange them in layers in a bowl, or, better yet, in a tureen, placing on each layer a little chopped garlic, a few leaves of fresh basil, and plenty of chopped parsley.

When you have arranged all the slices, boil the vinegar to cover, adding a pinch of salt and a pinch of pepper. As soon as the vinegar boils, pour it over the zucchini and cover the dish with its lid. Allow the zucchini to flavor well before serving.

ADA SAYS: *These tasty zucchini can be kept for a few days and can be served alone or to accompany boiled meat or grilled steaks.*

ZUCCHINE RIPIENE DI CARNE ALLA ROMANA

Zucchini Roman Style

12 small zucchini
7 oz lean beef
1 egg
Grated Parmesan
Loaf of bread
Prosciutto
1 onion
2 tbsp lard or butter
Parsley
2 tbsp prosciutto fat
2 cups tomato passata
Salt
Pepper

For this preparation, which belongs to Roman cuisine, small and very fresh zucchini are needed.

Wash the zucchini, trim the ends, dry them, and hollow out the centers with a thin vegetable peeler to make room for the stuffing. When you have emptied them all, prepare the filling: Chop the lean beef, collect it in a bowl, and add the whole egg and ½ cup grated Parmesan. Soak some of the white of the bread, about the size of a large egg, in water, squeeze dry, and shred into the mix. Add some diced prosciutto, salt, and pepper. Mix everything well and fill the zucchini.

Sauté a finely chopped onion in the lard or butter in a baking dish big enough so the zucchini fit in a single layer. Add a little chopped parsley and the prosciutto fat. When everything has taken a blond color, add the tomato passata, season with salt and pepper, and when the sauce has boiled a few minutes, place the zucchini in the pan. Bring it to a boil again, then cover and put in a preheated oven at very moderate heat for about an hour.

The sauce at the beginning must be rather liquid, so as to almost cover the zucchini. If it reduces too soon, add boiling water during the cooking.

ADA SAYS: *For this dish to be successful, the zucchini must be well cooked, without however being overdone, and the sauce must be abundant, dense, and tasty.*

ZUCCHINE RIPIENE DI TONNO

Zucchini Stuffed with Tuna

12 zucchini
Loaf of bread
Olive oil
Parsley
3½ oz tinned tuna in olive oil
Salt
Pepper

Tomato sauce:
1 lb fresh tomatoes, 1 onion, stalk of celery, 1 carrot, basil

Wash the zucchini, trim the ends, dry them, and use a long thin vegetable peeler to hollow out the central core to make room for the filling.

Soak the white of the bread and squeeze it dry and working with a wooden spoon put it in a pan on the stove so it is very dry. Take off the heat and in a bowl mix with a spoon of oil, a little chopped parsley, a pinch of salt and pepper, and the chopped tuna. Mix everything well and fill the zucchini with this mixture.

Prepare a tomato sauce *(p28)*, with the ingredients listed here, in a baking dish. It does not have to be very thick, because while cooking, it will thicken by itself. Lay in the zucchini. Bake in a preheated oven of moderate heat for about an hour. If the sauce dries too soon, add a little boiling water.

ADA SAYS: *Instead of cooking the zucchini in the sauce, you can cook them in a pan in which you have sautéed a little onion in oil. In this case, the zucchini should be browned over a very low heat and bathed from time to time with a few spoons of water, as they must wilt, but not brown.*

LEGUMES

Chickpeas

TO COOK CHICKPEAS

Canned chickpeas are already cooked, but if they are dried, you leave the chickpeas to soak in fresh water overnight, then put them to cook in plenty of cold water in which you have added ¼ tsp of baking soda for every 5 cups of water. When the water has boiled, add a handful of salt. Continue cooking for about half an hour. When the chickpeas are cooked, keep them warm, leaving them to soak in their cooking water.

CECI ALLA MARINARA

Marinated Chickpeas

Olive oil
4 anchovy fillets
Parsley
1 lb dried chickpeas, or canned
Salt
Pepper

Prepare the chickpeas as above or use canned, washed, and drained. Warm the oil in a pan, then over a very light heat blend in the washed and boned anchovy fillets. Add a strong pinch of pepper and a spoon of chopped parsley.

Drain the chickpeas and collect them in a serving dish, where you will dress them with the anchovy and parsley sauce, mixing them so that they flavor well. Serve hot.

CECI AL POMODORO

Chickpeas with Tomato

1 lb dried chickpeas, or canned
1 onion
Garlic
Olive oil
4 oz pancetta
1 lb tomatoes
Salt

Prepare the chickpeas as above or use canned, washed and drained.

Sauté a finely chopped onion and half a clove of garlic in a pan with a few tablespoons of oil. When the onion is a beautiful golden color, add the pancetta cut into small pieces and the washed tomatoes, skin and seeds removed.

Season with a pinch of salt and cook for a few minutes. At this point, drain the chickpeas, let them drain for a few seconds, then turn them into the tomato saucepan. Leave on the stove for about 15 minutes so that the chickpeas flavor the sauce and then pour them into a serving dish.

CECI IN PURÈ

Chickpea Purée

1 lb dried chickpeas
1 cup olive oil
1 lemon
Parsley
Salt

When the chickpeas are cooked, let them drain for a long time; then strain through a fine mesh sieve and blend—by hand or in a food mill—and collect the purée in a bowl.

Work the purée for a long time with a wooden spoon adding the oil a bit at a time and a few drops of lemon. When you have finished all the oil and the purée is well worked and swollen, put it on a plate and sprinkle plenty of chopped parsley over it.

Beans

TO COOK BEANS

Beans are, among all plant foods, the tastiest and richest in nutrients. Canned beans are cooked and just need to be drained and rinsed. Dried beans must undergo a preliminary treatment: They must be rinsed and soaked in cold water for 12 hours. Then drained, placed in a pot with plenty of suitably salted cold water, covered, and boiled, taking care that the heat is moderate because a turbulent boil could damage them. A pinch of baking soda can be added during boiling to facilitate the cooking.

There are a large number of varieties of dried beans - many different varieties are still called fagioli - and therefore we can only indicate the average duration of cooking: from 2 to 3 hours also depending on age. The best are cannolini but butter beans and white beans are also useful.

Cooking fresh beans, of course, is simpler: they are cooked, more or less depending on their variety, for about 45 minutes in a pot with plenty of boiling water, without a lid.

FAGIOLI ALLA MAÎTRE D'HÔTEL

Beans Maître D'hôtel

1 lb 5 oz dried beans
3½ tbsp butter
Parsley
1 lemon
Salt
Pepper

Keep the beans warm in their cooking water, see opposite.

Put the butter in a saucepan and as soon as it melts, drain the beans and immediately put the beans in the saucepan. Season with salt, pepper, and a spoon of chopped parsley.

Mix the beans so that they can be well flavored; remove the saucepan from the heat, squeeze over a little lemon juice, stir again, and pour into a vegetable bowl. They should be served immediately, hot.

FAGIOLI ALLA PANCETTA

Beans with Pancetta

1 lb 5 oz dried beans
3½ oz pancetta
Olive oil or lard
Vinegar
Parsley
Salt
Pepper

Keep the beans warm in their cooking water, see opposite.

Slice and dice the pancetta, and lightly heat the cubes in a pan with a little oil or lard, so that they fry slightly and lose some fat. At this point, pour a little vinegar into the pan, let it boil once, and immediately remove the pan from the heat.

Drain the beans and collect them in a salad bowl. Season with salt, plenty of pepper, ground at the last moment, a spoon of chopped parsley, and the diced pancetta and vinegar. Stir and bring to the table.

FAGIOLI ALL'USO TOSCANO

Tuscan Beans

10 to 14 oz fresh or dried white beans
Olive oil
Sage
2 garlic cloves
Salt
Pepper

Contrary to what is commonly practiced, to cook white beans in the Tuscan style, dried beans should not be soaked beforehand, nor should the water be changed in the first phase of cooking, since any suspension of boiling inevitably causes the beans to harden. This way of cooking the beans is the pride of Tuscan cuisine. The beans used mostly are white ones (cannolini). For the cooking of the beans, according to the authentic recipe, a tall flask is used instead of a pot.

This amount of beans will fit into a large terracotta flask. Be warned not to completely fill the flask. Put the beans in, add a spoonful of oil, 2 sage leaves, 2 cloves of garlic, and not too much water. Salt should not be put in at all.

Hang the flask over the embers of the fire, in the corner of the fireplace leaving it open so that the steam can escape freely. In this way the beans absorb the oil and aromatics. Dry beans will take about 3 hours of very slow cooking; less for shelled fresh beans. When the beans have almost reached the end of cooking, add the salt. The beans prepared in this way are then seasoned with a little more oil and pepper.

FAGIOLI AL PARMIGIANO IN PURÈ

Purée of Beans and Parmesan

1 lb 5 oz dried beans
1 onion
Celery
Parsley
1 carrot
Grated Parmesan
Butter
Salt

Soak the dried beans *(p710)* and then put them on to boil for about 2 hours with the onion, celery, parsley, carrot, and salt. When the beans are cooked, mash them with all the cooking vegetables, collect the purée in a bowl, and season with 5 spoonfuls of grated Parmesan.

Butter an baking dish, pour the purée in, smooth the surface with the blade of a knife, put some butter here and there, and bake at a lively heat. Brown the purée lightly, then place the pan on a plate and send to the table.

FAGIOLI CON LE COTICHE

Pork and Beans

1 lb 5 oz dried white beans
5¼ oz pork skin (*cotenne*)
2 oz prosciutto fat
Garlic
Parsley
Lard
1 onion
2 cups tomato passata
Salt
Pepper

Soak *(p710)* and boil the beans and keep them warm in their cooking water.

Scrape the pork skin, then put it in cold water and boil for 3 or 4 minutes; then drain and rinse in cold water to clean. Then cut into rather large pieces and put them back to cook in a covered container over very low heat with plenty of water until soft. When the beans and pork skin are cooked, chop the prosciutto fat, garlic, and parsley on the chopping board and put this mixture in a pan with the lard and the finely chopped onion. Sauté and when everything has a nice golden color, add the tomato passata, salt, and pepper and let the sauce cook for about half an hour. Then add the drained beans and pork skin, mix, and cook for half an hour on very moderate heat.

FAGIOLI FRESCHI ALL'UCCELLETTO

Fresh Beans All'Uccelletto

2¼ lb fresh beans
Olive oil
Garlic
Sage
1 lb canned tomatoes
Salt
Pepper

Shell the beans, put them in a pan with cold water and a pinch of salt, and cook them until they are almost completely cooked, about 40 minutes.

Put a little oil in a pan, add a couple of garlic cloves and as soon as the garlic has colored, throw it away. Add the drained beans, season with salt, pepper, and a few sage leaves. Stir, add the peeled tomatoes, and let it boil for 20 minutes.

FAGIOLI FRESCHI AL POMODORO

Fresh Beans with Tomato

2¼ lb fresh beans
Lard
2 oz prosciutto fat
1 onion
Celery
Parsley
1 lb ripe tomatoes
Salt
Pepper

Excellent to accompany boiled and braised meats.

Shell the beans, put them in a pan with cold water, a pinch of salt, and cook them until they are almost completely cooked, about 40 minutes.

In a casserole, melt a spoon of lard and make a *battuto* chopping together the prosciutto fat, a little onion, a rib of celery, and a nice sprig of parsley. When it browns, wash and purée the tomatoes then add them to the saucepan, season with salt and pepper, and cook over moderate heat.

When the sauce is sufficiently reduced, drain the beans and put them to flavor in the casserole, thus completing their cooking and ensuring that the sauce is thickened. Check the flavor of the beans, and then pour them into a vegetable bowl.

Green Beans

TO COOK GREEN BEANS

The pods of young beans - green beans - lend themselves to a large number of preparations and are tender and sweet.

For cooking, trim off the ends, rinse, and drop them in boiling water. Cook over a high heat uncovered. When they are finished cooking, immerse them in fresh water, renewing it often until the green beans have cooled. This cooking system will give your beans a nice green color.

Especially at the end of the season, green beans can have the annoying drawback of developing an inedible string beside the pod. In that case, leave them as they are and give them a brief boil. Then the strings will come off completely.

FAGIOLINI A CORALLO

Green Beans with Tomato

1 lb 5 oz flat or green beans or snow peas
1 onion
Lard
1 lb fresh tomatoes, or canned
Parsley
Salt
Pepper

Trim off the ends of the green beans and rinse them. Brown the chopped onion in a pan with a spoon of lard and add the chopped tomatoes without skins or seeds, or a can of peeled tomatoes. Cook the tomato a little and then put the green beans down and season with salt and pepper.

Cover the pan and continue cooking over very moderate heat for about half an hour, adding a few spoons of water from time to time. Finish with chopped parsley.

FAGIOLINI A CORALLO DEL FATTORE

Green Beans with Tuna and Anchovy

Vinegar
Basil
Parsley
1 onion
Garlic
3½ oz tinned tuna in olive oil
1 lb 5 oz green beans
6 anchovy fillets
Olive oil
Pepper
Salt

Put a small glass of vinegar and very finely chopped basil and parsley in a salad bowl. Finely chop a small fresh onion, collect it in a strip of towel, dip the towel for a moment in water, and then squeeze the onion dry and add to the vinegar, with a clove of crushed garlic. Now chop the tuna in oil and add it to the rest.

Boil the beans, drain them, and put them in the salad bowl while still hot, mix well, and complete with the anchovy fillets, washed, boned, and cut into fillets.

Cover the salad bowl and leave the beans to flavor for at least 4 hours, mixing them at long intervals. When ready to go to the table, season with a little oil, a good pinch of pepper, and a little salt.

FAGIOLINI AL FORMAGGIO

Green Beans with Gruyère

1 lb 5 oz green beans
7 tbsp butter
1 onion
7 oz grated Gruyère
Salt

Remove the ends of the green beans, rinse them, and put them in lightly salted boiling water. Cook them over a high heat, uncovered, and as soon as they are cooked, drain, immerse them in fresh water, renewing it often until the green beans have cooled.

In a large pan, melt the butter, add the onion cut into rings, and cook slowly, basting with a few spoonfuls of water. When the onion has cooked, drain the beans and add them to the onion so that they can gain flavor. Then arrange everything—still warm—on a serving dish and sprinkle over grated Gruyère. Serve immediately.

ADA SAYS: *A variation is to finish the cooking with some butter and strips of prosciutto.*

FAGIOLINI IN BUDINO

Green Bean Flan

1 lb 5 oz green beans
7 tbsp butter
3 eggs
Grated Parmesan
Breadcrumbs
Salt
Nutmeg

White sauce:
3½ tbsp butter, 3½ tbsp flour,
1 cup milk

Trim the green beans at both ends, rinse, and put them in lightly salted boiling water over a high heat, uncovered. Drain and chop them coarsely to take 2 or 3 pieces from each bean.

Then, sauté the beans with a little butter, season with salt, and leave them to flavor for a few minutes.

In the meantime, make up a white sauce *(p16)* with the butter, flour, and milk. When it is smooth and thick, season with a pinch of salt, a trifle of nutmeg, and off the heat add the beaten eggs and 1 or 2 spoons of grated Parmesan. Pour this sauce into the pan with the beans and mix with a wooden spoon.

Generously butter a smooth round mold with a capacity of about 3 cups, and throw in around a handful of breadcrumbs, turning the mold, so they cover all the inside. Then turn the mold upside down to knock off the superfluous breadcrumbs.

Pour the beans and sauce into the mold, flatten the surface, and sprinkle a few more breadcrumbs on top. Arrange a few pieces of butter here and there, and put the flan in a preheated oven for about three quarters of an hour, so that the inside can firm up and the outside has a nice golden and crunchy crust.

After this time, remove the mold from the oven and wait 3 or 4 minutes before turning it out. Then turn it upside down on a round plate and have it brought to the table.

FAGIOLINI IN TIMBALLO CON POLPETTINE

Timbale of Green Beans with Meatballs

Breadcrumbs
Milk
3½ oz chicken livers
5 tbsp butter or lard
3 tbsp dried mushrooms
Grated Parmesan
1 lb green beans
Salt
Pepper
Nutmeg

Meatballs:
5¼ oz lean ground beef, ½ cup breadcrumbs, 1 egg, ¼ cup grated Parmesan, milk, flour, lard or oil

White sauce:
2 tbsp butter, ¼ cup flour, 1¼ cups milk

Wet the breadcrumbs with a little milk, put them in a small pan over a very moderate heat, mix with a wooden spoon until reduced to a paste, and leave to cool.

In a bowl, make the meatballs *(p507)*—*granatine*—combine the beef with the breadcrumbs, season with the egg, ¼ cup grated Parmesan, salt, pepper, and a little nutmeg. Mix, then divide into many tiny meatballs, flour them and fry them in hot lard or oil.

Blanch the chicken livers in some butter, and cut into 2 or 3 pieces.

Finally, revive the dried mushrooms in cold water, then clean them carefully, squeeze them, cut them, and cook them with one third of the butter, salt, and a few spoons of water.

Make up a fairly liquid white sauce *(p16)* with the butter, flour, and milk and finish it with a pinch of salt and a spoon of grated Parmesan. Pour the meatballs, mushrooms, and livers into the sauce and set aside.

Boil the green beans and as soon as they are cooked, drain, and put them in a pan with the rest of the butter, to flavor. Pour a little more than half of the beans into a low-sided baking dish. Pour the meatballs and their sauce in the middle and cover with the remaining green beans, making sure to give the timbale the rounded shape of a dome.

Sprinkle a few breadcrumbs on the dome, put a few pieces of butter here and there again, and give the timbale about 10 minutes in an already hot oven with a lively heat so that the bread can be slightly crusted and browned.

Fava Beans

FAVE AL GUANCIALE

Fava Beans with Guanciale

6½ lb older, large fava beans
1 onion
2 oz guanciale
Lard or olive oil
Broth
Salt
Pepper

Shell the beans, plunge them in plenty of boiling salted water. Cook a few minutes, then drain. Take off the outside skins.

Brown a thinly sliced onion and the diced guanciale in a spoon of lard, or half a glass of oil, over low heat. Add the fava beans, season with salt and pepper, baste with a little broth or water, and cook over high heat, until well cooked. Depending on the quality of the beans, the cooking time can vary from three quarters of an hour to an hour and a half.

FAVE ALLA MAÎTRE D'HÔTEL

Fava Beans Maître D'hôtel

6½ lb fava beans
10½ tbsp butter
Parsley
Salt

Shell the beans, plunge them in plenty of boiling salted water. Cook a few minutes, then drain. Take off the outside skins.

Melt the butter in a saucepan and flavor the beans in it, stirring them constantly, but gently. After about 10 minutes, take off the heat, turn into a serving dish, and cover with plenty of chopped parsley.

FAVE IN PURÈ

Fava Bean Purée

6½ lb fava beans
Cream
12 tbs butter
Salt
To serve: bread for croutons

Shell the beans, plunge them into boiling salted water for a few minutes. Then drain and take off the outside skin.

At this point, blend them and put the purée back into the saucepan. Bring the saucepan over the heat and heat it up, adding ¾ cup heavy cream a little at a time. After about 10 minutes, add the butter, mix with a wooden spoon so that it blends well. Finally, turn out into a serving dish garnished with fried croutons.

ADA SAYS: *An excellent side dish for fried or poached eggs, white meats, and boiled vegetables especially chicory or puntarelle.*

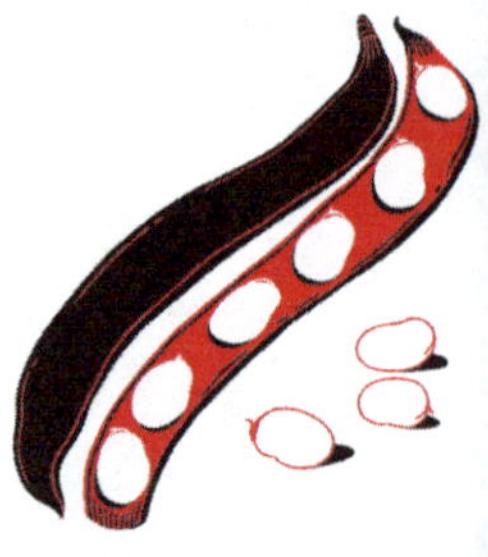

Lentils

LENTICCHIE IN PURÈ

Lentil Purée

1 lb lentils
Celery
1 carrot
1 onion
Garlic
1 cup olive oil
Parsley
Salt

Put the lentils to boil with aromatics of celery, carrot, onion, and garlic. Cook the lentils till soft, about twenty minutes, then pick out any aromatics you have used.

Blend and collect the lentil purée in a bowl. Work the purée for a long time with a wooden spoon adding a spoon of oil 1 at a time, they will soak up quite a lot of oil. When you have finished all the oil and the purée is well worked and swollen, put it on a serving dish and sprinkle over plenty of chopped parsley.

ADA SAYS: *Modern lentils do not usually need long cooking, they will ususally cook in 20 minutes. They can be served as a dish as is or as a side dish with cotechino, zampone, or duck.*

LENTICCHIE RIPASSATE IN PADELLA

Lentils in a Pan

1 lb lentils
Celery
Parsley
1 carrot
Olive oil
Garlic
1 onion
2 oz guanciale
Salt
Pepper

Cook the lentils and then drain and take out the aromatics, as above.

Pour a glass of oil into a pan and add a clove of garlic to brown, then remove it. In its place put the finely chopped onion and the diced guanciale. Fry to a golden color, then pour the lentils into the pan and leave them to flavor for a few minutes, adding a pinch of pepper if you like.

SALADS

INSALATA A COLORI

Colorful Salad

7 oz red radicchio
Head curly endive
Head escarole
1 orange
Fennel
Radishes
Olive oil
Mustard
Salt

Clean, rinse, and cut the radicchio, endive, and escarole—or any other colorful, seasonal chicories of your choice. Carefully wash and peel an orange and cut it into thin slices, removing the seeds. No white pith should remain. Also wash the fennel and cut it into slices. Wash the radishes but leave whole.

Arrange everything in a salad bowl, keeping them separate from each other so that the salad is, as its name states, bright and colorful. Dress with salt, oil, and, if you like mustard diluted with a little oil.

INSALATA ALL'ARANCIA

Orange Salad

2 heads lettuce
Fennel
2 carrots
Olive oil
Orange
Salt
Pepper

Carefully wash and drain the lettuce leaves and the fennel. Thinly cut the lettuce heads, cut the fennel into small sticks, add a few wheels of raw carrot, well cleaned, and finely chopped.

Season with oil, salt, and pepper and arrange the salad in a bowl. Cover with the orange slices, as above, which give a particular flavor to this preparation.

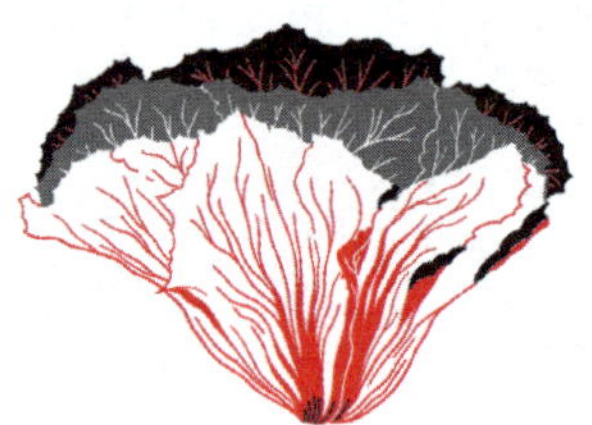

INSALATA AMERICANA

American Salad

3 waxy, salad potatoes
2 hard-boiled eggs
1 onion
Celery
6 tomatoes
Mustard
Olive oil
Vinegar
Salt

Boil and peel the potatoes and hard-boiled eggs; cut both into thin slices. Also slice an onion into rings, raw or boiled. Wash and slice the white inner stalks of the celery. Peel the raw tomatoes, preferably not too ripe, and cut them into very thin slices.

Put everything into the salad bowl, except the hard-boiled eggs.

Dress with salt, oil, vinegar, a little mustard, and lastly cover with the slices of egg.

INSALATA ANDALUSA

Andalusian Salad

2 salad potatoes
White wine
2 sweet red chilis
2 tomatoes
1½ tbsp capers
Olive oil
Vinegar
Mustard
Rice
3½ oz green olives, pitted
Salt
Pepper

Boil the potatoes, peel them, cut them into cubes, and marinate them for half an hour with a glass of white wine. Then, drain and mix with the sweet chili cut into strips, the tomatoes cut into slices, and the capers. Season with oil, vinegar, salt, pepper, and a little mustard.

To the mixture add ½ cup of rice boiled in lightly salted water, drained and left to cool.

Arrange the salad in a dome, and decorate with some spare slices of tomato, fillets of sweet chili, and pitted green olives.

INSALATA ARLECCHINO

Harlequin Salad

Smoked herring
3 to 4 cornichons
Gaeta olives, pitted
2 hard-boiled eggs
3 boiled potatoes
2 cooked beets
French mustard
1 lemon
Salt
Pepper

Peel and fillet a nice smoked herring and cut it into cubes. Cut 3 or 4 cornichons into small wheels, a handful of Gaeta olives, and slice the hard-boiled eggs, boiled potatoes, and the beets.

Collect everything in a glass salad bowl and season with a little salt, plenty of pepper, a teaspoon of French mustard, and lemon juice. Stir and bring to the table.

INSALATA BELGA

Belgian Salad

2 heads Belgian endive
7 oz carrots
Anchovy paste in a tube
Fennel
5½ oz sweetcorn, canned
Balsamic vinegar
Olive oil
Salt

The Belgian endive is a very white and slightly bitter salad. Not to be confused with more leafy varieties of so-called chicories.

Clean and rinse the endive, fennel and carrots and drain them well; cut them into very thin slices. In a bowl, put a heaped teaspoon of anchovy paste, dissolve it with a little balsamic vinegar, add the oil and very little salt. Beat with a fork to emulsify the ingredients and dress the prepared vegetables. Lastly drain the liquid from the corn and mix in well.

INSALATA CON GAMBERETTI

Shrimp Salad

10 oz shrimp tails
2 boiled potatoes
1 head lettuce
Capers
4 anchovy fillets
Olive oil
Vinegar
Mayonnaise, store-bought
Mustard
Salt

Poach the shrimp in salted boiling water for 5 minutes. Drain. As soon as they are cold, peel them and cut them into thirds.

In a crystal bowl, arrange a layer of boiled potatoes in slices, then make a rather higher layer of well washed and finely cut lettuce.

Season with a handful of capers, small pieces of anchovy, a little oil, a little vinegar, and a pinch of salt. Finish with a layer of shrimp and drizzle over a little mayonnaise mixed with the mustard.

INSALATA CON SALSA MAIONESE

Celery, Apple, and Fennel Salad

Celery
Fennel
1 head escarole
1 apple
Mayonnaise, store-bought
Salt

Wash and divide the inner stalks of the celery and a large fennel into sticks, and finely chop a few leaves of white escarole. Rinse the vegetables, drain them, and arrange them in a crystal bowl.

Add a washed apple, divided into sticks, and a little salt. Give it a good stir and dress with the mayonnaise.

INSALATA CON SALSA WORCESTER

Fennel and Carrot Salad

Fennel
2 carrots
Celery
1 head escarole
1 apple
Ketchup
Worcester sauce
1 lemon
Olive oil
Salt
Pepper

Mayonnaise:
1 egg yolk, 7 tbsp olive oil,
7 tbsp vinegar

Wash and cut the fennel and carrots into sticks the size of matches; then, take only the very white central part from a celery and cut it too into sticks.

Wash and thinly cut a head of white escarole. Place these vegetables in a glass salad bowl and season with salt, pepper, oil, and lemon juice, leaving them for half an hour.

Then, add an apple washed and also divided into sticks. Prepare a mayonnaise *(p19)* with an egg yolk, half a glass of oil, and vinegar, keeping it rather thick. Add 2 tablespoons of ketchup and a few drops of Worcester sauce. Blend well. Spoon the sauce on to the salad and serve immediately.

INSALATA DI CAVOLO CRUDO

Raw Cabbage Salad

White savoy cabbage
Red chili
1 white onion
2 stalks celery
Sugar
Mustard
1 lemon
White vinegar
Green peppercorns
Salt

Peel the cabbage, cut it into strips, rinse, and dry, then put in a salad bowl together with a teaspoon of finely chopped red chili, the white onion, and celery.

Make the dressing in another bowl: Put 1½ spoons of sugar, 1 teaspoon of mustard, 2 spoons of lemon juice, 2 teaspoons of white vinegar, 6 green peppercorns, and a pinch of salt; mix everything well with a fork—this is the secret to the success of the preparation.

Finally, pour the sauce into the salad bowl with the cabbage, onion, and celery and mix well again.

INSALATA DI CETRIOLI

Cucumber and Parsley Salad

1 lb 5 oz cucumber
Olive oil
Vinegar
Parsley
Salt
Pepper

Peel the cucumbers and cut into very thin slices. Collect the slices in a small salad bowl and sprinkle with a little fine salt, to deprive them of their watery juices.

After half an hour, take a few slices at a time, squeeze them gently and spread them on a napkin or kitchen paper, which you roll up slowly to dry well.

After a while, remove the slices from the napkin, arrange them in a salad bowl, season with very little salt, pepper, oil, vinegar, and chopped parsley, and send to the table.

INSALATA DI CRESCIONE ALLO YOGHURT

Watercress Salad with Yogurt

2¼ lb watercress
1 red bell pepper
Celery
3 ripe tomatoes
1 cucumber
1 cup yogurt
Olive oil
Salt

Clean the watercress, free it from the hardest leaves and stems, wash, drain, and cut coarsely on the cutting board. Put the cress into a salad bowl.

Wash the red bell pepper and cut into strips. Wash the celery and cut into small pieces. Wash the tomatoes, remove the seeds, and cut them into wedges. Peel and thinly slice the cucumber. Mix everything with the watercress.

Pour the yogurt over everything, and add 2 tablespoons of oil and salt moderately. Mix carefully.

INSALATA DI FARRO

Spelt Salad

7 oz spelt (*farro*)
1 cup Parmesan
Arugula
Olive oil
Balsamic vinegar
Salt

Leave the spelt to soak for at least half an hour, then rinse it several times and cook in a pot with plenty of lightly salted cold water for about half an hour over a very moderate heat.

Once the farro is cooked, drain it, put it in a salad bowl, season with flakes of Parmesan, well washed and dried arugula, oil, balsamic vinegar, and a pinch of salt.

INSALATA DI INDIVIA

Bitter Leaf Salad

1 head endive
2 oranges
6 walnuts
3½ oz Gruyère
Olive oil
Salt
Pepper

Clean the endive, nicking off the base and removing all the outer leaves, so that only the whiter parts remain; then cut it thinly; rinse it several times, let it drain well, and arrange it in a salad bowl.

Season the salad with the zest of an orange, without the white part, and with slices from the orange. Then add the chopped walnuts, diced Gruyère, oil, salt, and pepper, and the juice of another orange. Give it a good stir and send to the table.

INSALATA DI LATTUGA ALLA CASALINGA

Farmhouse Salad

3½ oz sourdough bread
1 head lettuce
2 green tomatoes
1 onion
Olives
Capers
Basil
Parsley
2 eggs
Olive oil
Vinegar
Salt
Pepper

Divide the bread into cubes and put them in a bowl and sprinkle over a little water. Leave the bread cubes in the water for a good half hour. Wash the lettuce and tomatoes thoroughly. Then add thinly sliced onion, the chopped lettuce leaves, the seeded and chopped tomatoes, a few pitted olives, a few capers, a few basil leaves, and chopped parsley.

Boil the eggs for 5 minutes, shell them, divide them into cubes, and add them to the rest. Season with oil, vinegar, salt, pepper, and then serve.

INSALATA DI LATTUGA GUARNITA

Rice and Ham Salad

Rice
Lemon slices
2 oz ham
Olive oil
1 head lettuce
3 tomatoes, not too ripe
2 hard-boiled eggs
Salt
Pepper

Boil ½ cup of rice in lightly salted water flavored with a few slices of lemon, keeping it rather *al dente*. Drain it, pass it under cold water to stop the cooking, and place it in a colander to drain.

Cut the ham into tiny pieces and add to the rice, season with 3 tablespoons of oil and pepper, and mix everything well.

Cover the bottom of the salad bowl with the rinsed lettuce leaves. In the center of the bowl, arrange the seasoned rice in a cone and surround it with the washed tomatoes cut into small wheels, alternating them with hard-boiled eggs also cut into small rounds. Season with a little salt and a drizzle of oil.

INSALATA DI OVOLI CRUDI

Raw Salad of Mushrooms

2 lb baby porcini, preferably ovoli
Olive oil
2 lemons
Parmesan
Salt
White pepper

Quickly wash the mushrooms, rub them with a towel, dry, slice them thinly, and collect them in a salad bowl.

Put a glass of oil, the juice of 2 lemons, and a pinch of salt in another bowl and whisk with a fork for a few minutes.

Season the mushrooms with a grind of white pepper, pour over the sauce, mix gently, and you will obtain a tasty preparation. To enrich the taste, shave in some Parmesan in thick flakes.

INSALATA DI PUNTARELLE

Puntarelle Salad

1 lb puntarelle
4 anchovy fillets
Garlic
Olive oil
White vinegar
Salt

Remove all the big, hard leaves from the puntarelle and keep them aside; use only the tips inside and the tender paler leaves. Take off the hard stem with a sharp knife and then cut everything into very thin slices, like streamers. Put them in fresh water for at least 1 hour; after this time the leaves will have all curled up forming rings.

Wash and bone the anchovy fillets, cut them into small pieces, put them in a small bowl, add some chopped garlic, season with the oil, vinegar, and salt, and mix well. Drain the puntarelle rings well, put them in a salad bowl, and season with the prepared sauce.

ADA SAYS: *Any leaves that you have removed because they are too hard to eat raw, are excellent boiled and seasoned with a little oil or sautéed in a pan.*

INSALATA DI SCAROLE E RADICCHIO

Salad of Escarole and Radicchio

1 lb escarole
1 lb radicchio
Olive oil
Balsamic vinegar
1 orange
Salt

Rinse the escarole and cut out only the whiter leaves. Rinse and cut the radicchio. Mix the 2 salads together, arrange them in a crystal salad bowl, and season with salt, oil, and a little balsamic vinegar.

Now, peel an orange, cut it into horizontal slices; with a knife flip out all the seeds, and make a crown of these slices on top of the salad.

INSALATA DI SEDANI

Celery Salad

3 stalks celery
Olive oil
2 hard-boiled eggs
3½ oz black olives, pitted
Salt
Pepper
English mustard, powdered
Vinegar

Thoroughly rinse the inner white stalks of the celery, to remove every little trace of earth. Then cut them thinly and put in a bowl with a few spoons of oil. Leave to macerate for at least an hour.

After this time, add the hard-boiled eggs cut into thin slices and the pitted black olives. Season everything with a pinch of salt, a little pepper, and a teaspoon of mustard dissolved with 2 spoons of vinegar. Give it a good stir and serve.

INSALATA DI SPINACI CRUDI

Raw Spinach Salad

1 lb spinach
Olive oil
Anchovy paste
Balsamic vinegar
Parmesan
5½ oz corn, canned
Salt

For this salad choose very fresh spinach, with very green leaves, not too big and only small, stiff stems.

Clean the spinach, washing with great care, in several waters, discarding all the damaged or too large leaves, assigning them to another use; drain the rest, dry in a cloth, and put them in a salad bowl.

Season with oil, a little anchovy paste, diluted with a spoon of balsamic vinegar and very little salt; finish them with Parmesan in flakes and sweetcorn.

ADA SAYS: *You can replace the anchovy paste with diced smoked ham if you prefer.*

INSALATA FANTASIA

Fantasy Salad

Celery
Fennel
3½ oz Gruyère
2 heads Belgian endive
Artichokes, jarred and marinated
Mushrooms, jarred and marinated
Boiled eggs
2 anchovy fillets
Capers
Olive oil
Wine vinegar
Cherry tomatoes
Baby corn on the cob
Salt
To serve: Bread for croutons
Optional: mayonnaise

Wash and cut the inner white stalks of a celery and the central part of the fennel into sticks and also cut the Gruyère into sticks. Wash and thinly cut the Belgian endive heads and combine all the vegetables in a salad bowl.

Complete with 2 or 3 artichokes, some mushrooms in oil, the whites of the hard-boiled eggs cut thinly, the anchovy fillets, and a pinch of capers; season with salt, oil, a little wine vinegar and, if you like, a little store-bought mayonnaise.

Decorate with whole boiled egg yolks, well washed cherry tomatoes, a few small corn cobs, and a handful of bread croutons fried in oil.

ADA SAYS: *This fantasy salad can be enriched, to your taste, according to the time of year with all the seasonal varieties.*

INSALATA RUSSA

Russian Salad

10 oz salad potatoes
10 oz fresh or frozen peas
7 oz green beans
7 oz carrots
Olive oil
Cornichons
Capers
Wine vinegar
Salt
For garnish: 2 hard-boiled eggs, 3 to 4 tinned anchovy fillets, capers, English mustard

Mayonnaise:
3 egg yolks, 1¼ cups olive oil, vinegar or lemon juice

First make the mayonnaise *(p19)* with the egg yolks, oil, and vinegar or juice of a lemon.

Boil the potatoes with all the peel; once cooked, peel them and let them cool. Clean and then boil all the other vegetables separately and leave to cool.

When all the vegetables are ready, cut them into equal-sized cubes, and put them in a bowl, season with oil, salt, and vinegar. Add some chopped cornichons and a few capers, a few tablespoons of mayonnaise, and, if desired, even a little English mustard.

Arrange the salad in a dome-shape on a plate and cover with mayonnaise and decorate to your taste with eggs, anchovy fillets, capers, and so forth.

ADA SAYS: *Can be an excellent filling for artichokes.*

PESCE IN INSALATA CON MAIONESE

Fish Salad

2¼ lb mixed white fish
1 carrot
1 onion
Celery
Parsley
White wine
Lettuce
Vinegar
Lemon
Olive oil
Salt
Pepper
For decoration: 2 hard-boiled eggs, 6 anchovy fillets, lettuce heart, cornichons, black olives, capers,

Mayonnaise:
2 egg yolks, ¾ cup olive oil, lemon juice or vinegar

Russian salad:
10 oz potatoes, 7 oz carrots, 7 oz green beans, 10 oz shelled fresh or frozen peas, 6 cornichons, capers

Clean and wash the fish well; then simmer in a large pan with a little lightly salted water in which you will have added a carrot, an onion, a stick of celery, a sprig of parsley, and half a glass of white wine. Bring it to the boil and adjust the cooking time depending on the thickness of the fish—about 10 minutes for every 1 pound. As soon as the fish is cooked, remove it from the broth, peel, bone it, and let it cool, then cut it into fillets and season with a little oil and salt and lemon juice.

Now prepare a mayonnaise *(p19)* with the egg yolks, the oil, and a teaspoon of lemon juice or vinegar, or you can use store-bought mayonnaise.

For the Russian salad: Boil the potatoes in their skins and once cooked, peel them and let them cool; boil all the other vegetables separately and let them cool. Dice the carrots, potatoes, and green beans; put everything in a bowl, add the peas, the cornichons cut into equally small pieces, and capers. Season with a little oil, a pinch of salt, and a few spoons of the prepared or purchased mayonnaise. Mix well.

In the bottom of an oval dish, first put a layer of lettuce, washed, dried, and cut into thin strips, then a layer of fish fillets, finished with the salad. Try to give the salad a regular shape, elongated like a fish. Cover everything, with the help of a spatula, with the remaining mayonnaise. Keep the dish in the fridge until ready to serve.

PICKLES

CAROTE IN VITERBO

Viterbo Carrots

5¼ to 7oz sun-dried purple carrots
4 cups vinegar
Candied citron peel
Raisins
Pine nuts
Chocolate

Preserving liquid:
4 cups vinegar, 2½ cups sugar,
1 tsp anise seed, cinnamon

For this preparation, we use elongated shaped vegetables—beets, carrots, parsnips, etc.—cut into strips and left to dry, which were a feature of the region around Viterbo, north of Lazio.

Soak the dried carrots in vinegar in a large container. As they absorb the vinegar, they grow in volume; take them out and do the same again until they will not absorb anymore.

Then prepare the following aromatic pickling bath: Put 4 cups of vinegar, sugar, aniseed, and a cinnamon stick the size of your little finger in an earthenware pan. Let it boil for a quarter of an hour, remove from the heat, and let it cool.

Remove the carrots from the vinegar, let them drain, and then place them in a large glass jar, with a little diced candied citrus peel, a few raisins, some pine nuts, and a little grated chocolate.

Fill the jar with the aromatic vinegar, without removing the aniseed, and if that is not enough, top it up with common vinegar. Close the jar tightly by applying the lid and a piece of parchment paper, and wait at least two weeks before serving.

CAPPERI SOTT'ACETO

Pickled Capers

Capers
Vinegar
Salt

Put the capers, just picked, in a strong solution of water and salt, in the proportion of 7 oz salt per 4 cups of water. Leave them in this solution for 24 hours; then let them drain well and scatter them on mats or kitchen towels to dry out in the sun completely. When they are completely dry, put them back in the same container, cover them with vinegar, and leave them to soak for a day. Drain them again, then, arrange them in glass jars, and cover them with more boiled and cooled vinegar.

CAPPERI SOTTO SALE

Capers in Salt

Capers
Salt

After keeping the capers for 24 hours in the saline solution, as above, and letting them dry, take glass jars and make a layer of salt in the bottom, then a layer of capers and so on, until the jars are filled. Keep in mind that the last layer must be salt. Close the jars with parchment paper tied with string.

CARCIOFINI SOTT'OLIO

Artichokes in Oil

Lemons
Artichoke hearts
White wine
Vinegar
Bay leaf
Cloves
Peppercorns
Olive oil

Squeeze plenty of lemon juice into a bowl and soak the artichokes in this juice as you prepare them. If they are fresh, all the leaves must be trimmed off leaving only the heart.

When you have prepared them all, put them to boil in white wine, acidulated with a little vinegar and flavored with a bay leaf, cloves, peppercorns, and a few slices of lemon. With a good white wine, you will have the ideal bath.

When the artichokes are cooked, but not too much, remove them from the bath, put them to drain on a large fine mesh sieve. Cover them with a folded cloth, so there is no contact with the air which would blacken them.

When they are very dry, arrange them in glass jars, where you will also put a few pieces of bay and a few peppercorns. Then cover them with oil and leave them like this for 3 or 4 days. After this time, the artichokes will have absorbed a lot of oil and those in the upper part may be uncovered. Top up with more oil up to a finger above the artichokes, and only then close the jars with the lid, apply a piece of parchment paper over the lid and tie it tightly. The parchment should be wet so when it dries it can smooth out.

By preparing the artichokes in this way, the artichokes can be kept for a very long time.

ADA SAYS: *Water harms the conservation of artichokes; it must therefore be absolutely banned at any stage of preparation.*

CAVOLO ACIDO

Pickled Cabbage (Sauerkraut)

Cabbage
Salt

The preparation of pickled cabbage—in German sauerkraut; in French choucroute—is very simple.

Cut the cabbages into strips like fettuccine, either by hand or with a special machine, and then place in a wooden barrel with interposed layers of salt. They are left to macerate like this for some time, until fermentation takes place with its characteristic smell. If buying these cabbages from the places of production enclosed in barrels, they must be cooked.

ADA SAYS: *If buying these cabbages from the places of production enclosed in barrels, they must be cooked.*

CAVOLO ACIDO COTTURA CON PANCETTA

Pickled Cabbage with Pancetta

Sauerkraut *(opposite page)*
1 onion
1 carrot
Pancetta
Peppercorns
Juniper berries
Goose fat or pork lard
Broth
White wine
Butter

Put the *sauerkraut*, in proportionate quantities to your needs, in cold water and rinse for a long time to remove the salt. Then squeeze them in your hands and put them in a casserole with a whole onion, a carrot, and a nice piece of smoked pancetta. Also add a gauze bag of peppercorns and a few juniper berries.

Season with a few spoons of goose fat or pork lard. Sprinkle with enough broth to almost cover the cabbage, add a glass of white wine, cover, and let it cook slowly for 4 or 5 hours. If the broth is very fatty, do without the goose fat or lard. The cabbages must gradually remain dry.

When cooked, remove the bag with the pepper and juniper, and also remove the onion and carrot. Slice the pancetta and serve it with the cabbage and some butter.

ADA SAYS: *Suitable both alone, as well as to accompany beef or pork, especially smoked goose sausage, etc.*

CETRIOLINI SOTT'ACETO

Cucumbers in Vinegar (Cornichons)

Small cucumbers
Vinegar
Tarragon
Salt
Pepper
Optional: garlic

Take some small cucumbers, place them on a rough kitchen cloth, sprinkle with salt, fold the cloth, and rub—rubbing will lose some of the roughness of their skin. Then spread them out on a cloth and let them dry for a few hours in the open air.

Boil the vinegar: Arrange the cucumbers in a bowl and when the vinegar has boiled, pour it over them. It goes without saying that the vinegar must be in such proportions that it can completely cover the cucumbers. Leave it alone until the next day.

You will find that the cucumbers have turned a rather unsympathetic greenish yellow color. Don't worry about it; drain the vinegar and put it to boil again. As soon as the vinegar is about to boil, put the cucumbers back in it, which will help partially regain their green color. After boiling, take off the heat, and distribute the cucumbers in one or more glass jars. Add a few peppercorns, a few cloves of garlic, optional, and a few leaves of tarragon to each jar, cover with vinegar, and then, when the jars are cold, close them with the lid. Wait at least a week before starting to consume them.

CIPOLLINE SOTT'ACETO

Pickled Onions

2¼ lb small onions
4 cups vinegar
Garlic
Cinnamon stick
Bay leaf
Peppercorns
Clove
Olive oil
Salt

Skin the onions, preferably small and of the same size, and blanch for a minute in boiling water, in which you have added a pinch of salt.

Put 2 cups of vinegar, a clove of garlic, a piece of cinnamon, half a bay leaf, a few peppercorns, a clove, and a pinch of salt in a saucepan. Add the blanched onions, and cook for 10 minutes.

Drain and arrange them in a glass jar. Now boil some more fresh vinegar and let it cool. Pour this cold vinegar over the onions, add a bay leaf, a piece of cinnamon, and a little oil, which spreading on the surface of the vinegar will ensure better conservation. Make sure that the onions remain well submerged in the liquid, then close the glass jars with their lids and keep them in the pantry.

FUNGHI SOTT'ACETO

Pickled Ovoli Porcini

Baby porcini or cremini mushrooms, preferably ovoli
White vinegar
Peppercorns
Cinnamon stick
2 garlic cloves
Bay leaves
4 to 5 cloves
Salt

The best mushrooms for this preparation are ovoli, baby porcini, which must be very fresh, firm, and completely closed.

Remove the deteriorated parts and the outer skin, clean them with a towel, then cut them into large wedges.

Put a saucepan with enough white vinegar and plenty of salt on the stove. As soon as the vinegar boils, add the mushrooms and boil them for 5 minutes. After this time, remove the pot from the heat, add a few peppercorns, a piece of cinnamon, 2 cloves of garlic, a couple of bay leaves, and 4 or 5 cloves. Cover the pot and leave everything to rest for half an hour.

Then drain all the vinegar, which you can use for other purposes, but which is no longer needed for this preparation. Lift out the garlic and the bay leaves but keep the pepper, cinnamon, and cloves. Put the mushrooms and their spices in a glass jar and cover with a new fresh cold vinegar. Close the jar and store in the pantry.

OLIVE DI GAETA

Olives of Gaeta

11 lb Gaeta olives
Coarse salt
10½ quarts of water

You need a taller rather than wide container, preferably earthenware. Put 11 pounds of olives in this container and cover them with water. The amount of water needed will be about 5 quarts. In any case, take into account the water you will use so you remember exactly the amount later. Leave the olives like this and after 4 days drain the water and put as much salt on the olives as there were quarts of water. Assuming you have used 5 quarts, you will need 1 pound of salt. Mix well and leave the olives in salt for 24 hours.

After 24 hours, pour the same amount of water on the olives that you used in the beginning to cover them again. Take the container to the pantry and don't worry about the olives any more for 40 days.

After the set time has elapsed, the olives are ready and all you have to do is arrange them in jars, then cover them with a cold brine of boiled water and salt in equal proportions. This brine ensures the preservation of the olives and enhances their taste.

OLIVE VERDI ALLA SICILIANA

Green Sicilian Olives

Green olives
Fennel seeds and sprigs
Salt

Choose some beautiful green olives, let them dry for a couple of days in the sun, then immerse them in plenty of strongly salted water flavored with fennel seeds. Arrange some sprigs of wild fennel on top of the jar to keep the olives submerged. Leave them like this for a few days before using them.

PEPERONCINI SOTT'ACETO

Chili Peppers in Vinegar

Chilis
Vinegar
Salt

Cut the ends of the chili peppers with scissors, spread them out on baskets or trays, and expose them for a couple of days to the sun, so that the moisture they contain can evaporate as much as possible.

Then arrange them in earthenware jars, and pour boiling vinegar over them in which you have put plenty of salt. Let them stand for about 40 days.

Then drain the vinegar, which in contact with the vegetable water of the peppers will be very diluted, and replace it with more unboiled fresh vinegar, so that it completely covers the peppers.

Then put the lids on the jars. The peppers will be ready for use after a couple of months.

PEPERONI SOTT'OLIO

Peppers in Oil

Bell peppers
Vinegar
Olive oil
Salt

Choose beautiful peppers with intact and spotless surfaces. Remove the stem and internal seeds and divide them into strips that you will leave to dry in the sun for a few hours.

Then put them in an earthenware pot, cover them with vinegar, add a little salt, and boil for a quarter of an hour. After this time, drain the vinegar, and line up the pepper strips on a cloth to dry them well.

After 24 hours, place them in earthenware or glass jars completely submerging them with olive oil.

Tomato Preserves

POMODORI A PEZZI O PELATI

Tomato Passata

2 lb of fleshy tomatoes

Choose fleshy tomatoes for sauce, wash them, peel them, cut them into wedges, remove the seeds, and collect them in a bowl. Prepare airtight jars of 3 cups (1½ pints), each jar will fit about 2 pounds of tomatoes, well washed and dried.

Introduce the tomato wedges into the jars, distribute the liquid part left in the bowl in each jar. Close the jars, wrap them in kitchen towels, and put them straight in to a large pot with cold water, which must reach up to the neck of the jars. Tomatoes must be cooked immediately because they ferment easily.

Bring the water slowly to the boil and let it simmer for at least an hour. Let the jars cool in the same water, then take them out, dry them, and store them in a cool place. When you want to use them, all you have to do is season the tomatoes over high heat for a few minutes with a little oil or butter and season them with salt, pepper, and a handful of basil or parsley.

POMODORI SECCHI

Sun-Dried Tomatoes

Fleshy tomatoes
Basil leaves
Salt

Choose fleshy tomatoes, wash, and dry them thoroughly. Break them in half without separating them, cover the inside with abundant salt, line them up on boards or racks, and place them in the sun for at least a dozen days, taking care to turn them over from time to time, and collect them and take them inside at home during the night.

When the tomatoes are dry, close them up by putting a basil leaf in each of them. Expose the closed tomatoes to the sun for another day or for a few hours in the oven at a very light heat and then arrange them in jars covered with oil, or wrapped tightly in parchment paper.

ADA SAYS: *During the winter, when you want to use dried tomatoes, you just have to soak them in a little warm water, which you can then use to cook them, or you can use them in their dry state for broth, soups, and as an appetizer.*

"All your skills must be expressed their upmost in this most complex, yet enjoyable area of cooking."

We have finally arrived at one of the most important chapters in cooking—desserts. Compared to the previous sections, this is almost a college course in itself. All of your skills learned so far, from following the working order in a recipe to an absolute respect for process, must be expressed to their utmost in this complex, yet enjoyable, area of cooking. And sometimes you will need inventiveness and imagination to understand and solve difficult preparations.

These dessert recipes are laid out in a progressive order to help you develop your skills as you go along. The chapter begins with "Sugar Basics"—the preparations and techniques that will underpin the recipes.

This is followed by puddings, which get their name from the special mold in which different cooking and pastry preparations are cooked. Hot puddings are preferably served with an accompanying sauce. Cold puddings, on the other hand, are served alone and represent the first step towards frozen desserts.

Soufflés, which require greater skill, are a warm and extremely delicate preparation made from a basic mixture of egg whites, whipped into peaks, and then baked. The egg whites, under heat, increase in volume, and it is this characteristic that distinguishes soufflés from puddings.

This chapter also includes frozen desserts. Parfaits are relatively easy to handle and are tasty and light desserts. The various Bavarois — charlottes and mousselines—do not have substantial differences in technique. They all have cream as their main basic element and milk, coffee, or fruit purée as a complementary element.

Ice cream is an umbrella term that encompasses several preparations with clearly different characteristics. Real ice creams are milk and egg-based creams with the addition of elements, such as chocolate, almonds, and vanilla, However, variously sweetened fruit purées are also entitled to the name.

FRUTTA & DOLCI

12

FRUIT & DESSERTS

SUGAR BASICS

TO CARAMELIZE SUGAR

Sugar goes through various stages when it is heated – the small thread, the soft and hardball, crack and caramel. As you continue cooking, the sugar begins to take on an increasingly intense yellow-brown color, until it becomes eventually completely black and steaming, turning into burnt sugar or caramel (320°F to 365°F). When testing sugar, it is prudent to immerse your fingers in cold water before repeating this operation and plunge them back into the water as soon as the sugar has stuck to your fingers. Safer and surer is to use a thermometer.

To cook the sugar, a small saucepan with a concave bottom is recommended. Add 1 cup of sugar and sprinkle with a little water, enough to moisten it and make a paste. Then add 1 tablespoon of glucose and set the saucepan over the heat. As soon as the sugar comes to a boil, skim and continue cooking on a rather lively heat.

After a few minutes of boiling, dip the wooden spoon in the sugar and squeeze a little between your index finger and thumb. If it is not very resistant, the cooking is said to have reached the point of a small thread.

After a few minutes, by repeating the operation, the sugar will offer more resistance and will make a characteristic noise when breaking, or cracking.

Then it will thicken slightly so that it can be rolled up like a soft ball, After a while and some more cooking, the ball will harden and become a hard ball.

Finally, the sugar will no longer congeal into a ball, but will spread out into a thin sheet, which as the heat increases, will become harder until it breaks sharply like a glass.

thread = 230°F-234°F
soft ball = 234°F-241°F
hard ball = 250°F-266°F
soft crack = 270°F-289°F

TO SPIN SUGAR

Put 1 cup of sugar in a small saucepan and sprinkle over a few drops of water to make a paste, adding very little glucose. Let the sugar melt and begin to boil. When it has reached the caramel grade (338°F), the sugar is ready to be spun.

Place 2 sticks on the kitchen table at a distance of about 16 inches from each other, leaving them about 20 inches from the table and holding them steady with 2 weights. Dip a fork in the caramelized sugar, and when the sugar begins to pour, shake the fork quite quickly back and forth between the sticks. In this way, very long and light threads will form which you will collect on the 2 parallel sticks, forming a net. For the sugar to flow well, it must be allowed to cool a little, but without waiting too long. Spun sugar is generally used as garnish. For a better appearance, you can add a few drops of food coloring.

PRESERVED FRUIT

TO PRESERVE FRUIT

There are excellent products on the market now based on pectin, a natural gelling agent from apples, that reduce the cooking time of jellies and jams to a minimum, while keeping the taste of fruit intact. You can also buy sugar jam where pectin is already added.

The cooking of jams is not regulated by a fixed time, but passes through two distinct phases – evaporation and cooking proper. In the first phase, boiling has no other purpose than to evaporate the water the fruit contains: here, therefore, the fire can be bright.

In the second phase we enter the true amalgam of fruit with sugar, and it will be prudent to decrease the strength of the fire a little. As the foam forms on the surface, it will be better to remove it because, being albuminous material, it would disturb the clarity of the setting. If you, at the beginning of cooking, immerse a slotted spoon in the boiling gelatin and lift it out, you will see that the liquid falls back in quick drops. But as cooking progresses, renewing the experiment, which must be done often, you will notice that these drops detach less quickly and end up gathering on the lower edge of the spoon, from which they separate in more voluminous masses and at rather longer intervals of time.

At this point, which the French call the nappe, the spoon remains almost enveloped in a veil of fruit, indicating the precise and infallible degree of the right point of cooking of all jams and jellies.

The jars to be used must be made of glass, and have a screw or spring lid. In order to be hermetically sealed, they must be very clean, dry, and warm.

To preserve the jam you can follow two procedures. In the first, pour the ready-made jam, still hot, into the jars, close them tightly, overturn them once or twice and let them cool. In the second, pour the jam that has lost some of its heat into the jars, and wait until it is completely cold. Then place on each jar, in contact with the jam, a disk of white parchment paper soaked in pure alcohol, and then close the jar with its lid.

TO CARAMELIZE FRUIT

This preparation requires skewers 4 to 5 inches long. Thread the fruit to be caramelized onto these skewers: 3 to 4 large grapes, an orange or mandarin segment, pitted cherries, peach segments, and whichever other fruit you'd like.

*Prepare the caramelized sugar (*opposite page*) and, holding the skewer at one end, dip the fruit in it. Leave to drip and then place the skewers around the rim of a metal colander, pinning the end of the skewer into one of the holes in the colander. If there are any smears, cut them off with scissors before the sugar is cold. When the caramelized fruit is cold, arrange the skewers on a serving plate; you can decorate the plate with some chocolates.*

ALBICOCCHE IN CONFETTURA

Apricot Jam

Apricots
Sugar

Wash and split the apricots in 2, remove the stone and if they are very ripe, mash and collect the pulp in a bowl. Otherwise, put them in a saucepan with a little water and cook them before sieving or mashing them. Weigh the apricots and match with a similar weight in sugar. Put both in a saucepan on the stove and cook until the right condensation is obtained.

The exact cooking point is reached when dipping a slotted spoon in the jam and lifting it up, the mixture comes off slowly in large drops. The setting point is 221°F on a thermometer.

When the jam is ready, pour it, still hot, into jars; close them, turn them over once or twice and let them cool.

ALBICOCCHE IN POLPA

Apricot Purée

2¼ lb apricots

Carefully wash the apricots, split them in half, remove the stones, mash them, and collect the pulp in well-cleaned and sterilized champagne bottles. Fill them up to the beginning of the neck, leaving a gap of at least 4 fingers, plug them and tie the cap solidly in a cross. Then wrap them in some dish cloths, place them straight in a pot and pour cold water over, which must reach up to the neck of the bottles. Bring the water gently to a boil, boil the bottles for an hour and let them cool in the same water. Then take them out of the pot, close them with sealing wax and keep them in a cool place. When, during the winter, you need a little jam, all you have to do is open a bottle, weigh the pulp, add as much sugar and cook. And if you want to make an excellent fruit ice cream, you can use this purée.

ARANCE IN CONFETTURA

Oranges in Jam

4½ lb oranges
4½ lb sugar
Vanilla sugar
2 tsp cognac
Optional: vanilla extract or vanilla sugar

Lightly prick the oranges with a pin, the peel only without piercing the inner pulp, and soak them in running water or renew it often, for 2 or 3 days. Remove the 2 caps of the peel, upper and lower, from the oranges, and cut these into very thin sticks; the rest of each orange divide into thin slices and diskard the seeds.

Place the oranges and the slivers from the cut caps in a saucepan and boil slowly for 3 or 4 hours. After this time, add the sugar and cook again—always stirring with a wooden spoon—for another hour, until you see that the jam has reached the right point of density.

Then remove from the heat, perfume it with vanilla sugar, or simply with a dash of vanilla, and add the cognac. When the jam is ready, pour it still hot into the jars; close them, turn them over once or twice and let them cool.

ARANCE IN GELATINA

Orange Jelly

12 oranges
Sugar (6 tbsp per glass of orange juice)

Use thin-skinned oranges that are the ripest and therefore juiciest.

Cut the oranges in half and squeeze the juice into a bowl. Pass the juice through a muslin and collect it in a large saucepan. Add the sugar to the juice and place the pan on the stove, stirring with a wooden spoon to facilitate the melting of the sugar. Carefully remove the yellowish foam that will form as soon as the jelly has reached boiling: foam that would harm the clarity of the jelly itself. Cook over a bright flame. The orange juice contains a good amount of water, which must evaporate to achieve the necessary condensation. We recommend that you supervise the saucepan and keep ready to lift it or temporarily remove it from the heat, because the orange juice, when boiling, often tries to overflow. Gradually the boiling will become calmer and cooking will approach the precise point. This cooking point is easily recognized, when the jelly no longer flows as if it were water, but will have acquired a little consistency and will leave a light trace on the spoon. You can drop a little on a plate and observe if these drops become firm as it cools.

When the jelly is ready, pour it still hot in to the jars; close them, turn them upside down once or twice and let them cool.

CASTAGNE IN CONFETTURA

Chestnut Jam

MAKES 2 JARS

1 lb 2 oz chestnuts, or vacuum-sealed in a packet
Salt
Milk
1½ cups sugar
Vanilla
Pure alcohol, vodka, or grappa

Choose large, full, rounded and very shiny chestnuts, brown in color, without spots or cuts. Knick the shell, boil, and then immerse them again in a pot with boiling water with the addition of a pinch of salt. When the chestnuts are cooked, drain them, remove the skin and after having cleaned them all, put them in a saucepan, wet them with half a glass of milk and break them with a wooden spoon to reduce them to a paste. This paste must be very stiff: for this purpose you will leave it to dry well on the fire, working it a lot with a spoon and when it is well dry you sieve it.

Now put the sugar on the heat in a small saucepan, moisten it with a little water and as soon as the sugar has reached a degree of cooking, pour it immediately, in a continuous stream, on the chestnut paste, while stirring with the other hand to quickly mix the sugar and the mass. The jam will seem rather runny, but when it gets cold it will return to the right density. When you have added all the sugar, stir a little more to smooth the jam. Finish with a dash of vanilla and pour it into the jars, just lukewarm. When the jam is completely cold, cover it with a disk of parchment paper soaked in pure alcohol and then close the jar with its lid.

ADA SAYS: *If you cannot find pure alcohol, then clear vodka or grappa will be successful too but remember, they are not as strong.*

CILIEGE IN CONFETTURA

Cherry Jam

2¼ lb cherries
3¾ cups sugar

Choose a quantity of very juicy cherries, wash them thoroughly and remove the stem and then the stone. When you have pitted them all, weigh them and for each 2 and a quarter pounds of fruit calculate between 3½ and 3¾ cups of sugar. Put the sugar in the pan, pour in a glass of water, melt and then put it on the stove and let it boil for 3 or 4 minutes, skimming it thoroughly. Then pour the cherries into the pan and cook over a rather lively fire.

Skim the jam and mix it and when you see that the cherries have shriveled and the syrup veils the spoon, remove the jam from the heat, pour it still hot into the jars; close them, turn them upside down once or twice and let them cool.

CILIEGE SOTT'ACETO

Cherries in Vinegar

Cherries
Thyme
Cinammon stick
Cloves
Vinegar

Choose firm and fleshy cherries, wash them thoroughly and trim the stems. Arrange them in a bowl with a sprig of thyme, a piece of cinnamon, and a clove or 2. Boil some vinegar and pour it boiling over the cherries until they are covered. Cover the container and leave it for 3 or 4 days.

Then drain the vinegar into the saucepan and let it boil for a few more minutes, and leave to cool. Meanwhile, place the cherries in a glass jar and when the vinegar is completely cold, pour it over the cherries and close the jar.

CILIEGE SOTTO SPRITO

Cherries in Spirit

Cherries
Clove
Cinammon
Sugar
Pure alcohol, vodka, or grappa
Optional: Alchermes liqueur

It is good to keep the cherries in cylindrical glass jars, with a capacity of one or 2 quarts.

Wash, dry, and spread the cherries on a tablecloth and leave them in the air for a day; then, cut the stems in half with scissors, arrange them in glass jars, where you will also put 4 or 5 cloves, a piece of cinnamon. and a little sugar, allowing a full spoon for a quart.

Cover the cherries with pure alcohol, close the jar and then tie a piece of parchment around the rim of the jar. Take the cherries to the pantry, and wait to use for a couple of months.

Cherries in alcohol are generally served accompanied with a little of their flavored liquid. If you like them less alcoholic, you can replace one part of the alcohol, about a quarter, with sugar syrup. Some also recommend diluting with Alchermes liqueur.

COTOGNATA

Quince in Squares

2¼ lb quinces
2¼ lb sugar
Olive oil

Wash and boil the whole quinces, without peeling them and, as soon as they are cooked, but not too much, peel and sieve them. Collect the pulp in a bowl and dry in a water bath so it loses all its moisture.

Weigh as much sugar as the weight of the puréed quince. Put the sugar in a saucepan, moisten it with a little water, and bring up to the right texture, then pour it over the quince pulp, stir, let it cook a little longer still in a bain-marie, and then pour this paste into a mold lined with lightly oiled parchment paper. Let it rest until the next day, and then turn out.

COTOGNE IN GELATINA

Quince Jelly

Quinces
Sugar
1 lemon
Pure alcohol, vodka, or grappa

Wash and cut the quinces into pieces without peeling them, cover them with water, put them on moderate heat, and let them boil slowly until the mass is undone. At this point, turn them out with their liquid on a muslin-lined sieve and collect the liquid in a saucepan. Weigh this liquid and add an equal weight of sugar.

Let it thicken on the heat and when the jelly veils the spoon and comes off rather slowly in large drops, remove from the heat, squeeze over a little lemon juice, not too much, and then pour it into well-washed, dry glass jars.

Close them tightly, turn them upside down once or twice and let them cool. When it is cold, cover with a paper disk soaked in pure alcohol and close the jar.

COTOGNE IN CONFETTURA

Quince Jam

1 lb 2 oz quinces
1¼ cups sugar

Wash and boil the quinces whole, which is preferable, or in wedges, but without peeling them, and as soon as they are cooked, but not crushed, remove them from the water, peel them, and mash them.

Collect all the pulp, weigh it, add an equal weight of sugar and cook over moderate heat, stirring constantly, until the jam has reached the right degree (221°F on a thermometer). Once the jam is finished, you can, according to your taste, flavor it with a few drops of lemon juice. Then pour it, still hot, into the jars, close them, turn them over once or twice, and let them cool.

FICHI IN CONFETTURA

Fig Jam

1 lb 2 oz figs
1¼ cups sugar
Optional: ground cinnamon

Peel the figs and weigh them. Calculate a weight of sugar as equal to half that of the figs. Put the sugar in a saucepan and dissolve it with a little water, to have a syrup that is not too liquid. When this syrup starts to boil, add the figs and set the cooking over a moderate heat, stirring often with a wooden spoon, until the jam is well condensed. When the jam is ready, pour it, still hot, into the jars, close them, turn them over once or twice. and let them cool.

ADA SAYS: *If you like, you can flavor the jam with a little ground cinnamon during cooking.*

FICHI SECCHI

Dried Figs

Ripe figs

Figs must be harvested when ripe. Do not peel the figs but open them in 2 with your hands vertically, from the bottom up, so as not to separate them, but leaving them held together by the stem. Once this is done, place them in the sun on cane racks, so that the inner part of the fig is the one that remains exposed to the sun. After a day, turn them over and put them back in the sun, and repeat this operation for many days, until the figs have assumed that special consistency that characterizes this preparation. In August, and in very hot countries, it will take about 6 days. In the evening it is good to remove the racks to the house, to prevent sudden rain from getting them wet. When they are ready, close them, press them with your fingers to join them well, and thread them on wooden or cane skewers.

After that you can proceed to sterilize: Collect all the figs skewered on the skewers, tie the ends of the skewers together, and dip them for a moment in boiling water. Let them drain a little and then put them back in the sun for another half day. Or, on the other hand, you can put the figs in the oven, on large plates, and pass them in an already hot oven with very light heat for at least an hour, until they have lost all moisture.

FICHI SECCHI AL CIOCCOLATO

Dried Figs with Chocolate

Dried figs
Almonds
Candied citron
Dark chocolate
Powdered sugar

Dry the figs in the sun without disinfecting them *(opposite page)*. Stuff them with almonds lightly toasted in the oven, and a few pieces of candied citron strips. Close up with your fingers and bake them in a preheated oven of moderate heat.

As soon as they begin to take on a beautiful golden color, remove them from the oven and while still very hot, roll them in a mixture of grated chocolate and powdered sugar. Or dip the hot figs in a saucepan in which you have melted dark chocolate in a bain-marie. Figs in chocolate are kept in wooden or tin boxes.

FRAGOLE IN CONFETTURA

Strawberry Jam

2¼ lb strawberries
1 quart white wine
Lemon
3½ cups sugar

Carefully wash the strawberries in a little white wine, drain and put them to dry in a pan over a normal heat, with the addition of the juice of a lemon, for about 10 minutes. Now add the sugar, mix so that the sugar blends perfectly with the strawberries and cook the jam over a very low heat, stirring and skimming it from time to time, for about 2 hours, until the strawberries are completely crushed and the syrup veils the wooden spoon. Pour the jam, still boiling, into well washed and dried glass jars; close the jars hermetically with their lid, turn them upside down once or twice and let them cool.

MELE IN CONFETTURA

Apple Jam

2¼ lb apples
4 cups sugar

Wash and core the apples and boil them with the peel. When they are well cooked, let them drain well, and then sieve them. Weigh the pulp and for each 2 and a quarter pounds, calculate 4 cups of sugar. Put the pulp and sugar in a saucepan, place it on the stove and bring the jam to the boil, stirring constantly. After the jam has boiled, give it another 4 or 5 minutes, then remove it from the heat. When the jam is ready, pour it, still hot, into the jars; close them, turn them over once or twice, and let them cool.

MORE IN GELATINA

Blackberry Jelly

2¼ lb blackberries
4 cups sugar

Rinse the blackberries in fresh water and then put them on the stove with a glass of water for every 2 and a quarter pounds of fruit. Let them boil for a quarter of an hour, mixing and crushing them with a wooden spoon, and then turn them out into a sieve, collecting the juice in a bowl. Measure the juice and for each quart calculate 4 cups of sugar.

Put sugar and juice in a saucepan and boil, carefully skimming: When this has thickened so as to veil the spoon and fall back in slow and heavy drops, the jelly will be made. Pour it still hot into the jars; close them, turn them upside down once or twice, and let them cool.

PESCHE INTERE ALLO SCIROPPO

Whole Peaches in Syrup

Hard peaches
1¼ quarts pure alcohol, vodka, or grappa
Optional: vanilla bean

Sugar syrup:
3 parts water to one part sugar

The preferred peaches are those with hard flesh. The peel can be removed or left on. Preserved peaches are generally left whole.

Choose peaches without bruises, and prick them here and there with a long pin up to the stone. Then arrange them in a wide pan, aligning them in a single layer, and cover them with a boiling sugar syrup *(p736)*, made with 3 parts of water and one of sugar. Cover the container and let the peaches soak for 24 hours.

Then place them in well-washed and dried glass jars and cover them with a solution made with 2 parts of 85% pure alcohol and one part of syrup. This mixture can be flavored with a vanilla bean, split lengthwise, which you can also leave in the jar. Close the jars tightly.

PESCHE SOTTO SPIRITO

Peaches in Spirit

3¼ lb peaches
3½ cups sugar
2 cups pure alcohol, vodka or grappa
Rum

Peel the peaches, split them in half, and remove the stone. Then plunge them into boiling water and cook for a few minutes. As soon as they are cooked, pull them up with a perforated spoon, and let them drain and cool.

Then place them in a wide pan in which they can be aligned in a single layer and cover them with a boiling syrup made up of sugar and water, about one third to two thirds. Let it stay like this until the next day, then remove the peaches from the liquid, and boil the liquid for 2 minutes with the another half cup of sugar. Pour this new boiling syrup over the peaches and let it sit for 2 days.

At this point, put the peaches in a glass jar with of a couple of quarts capacity. Then mix half a quart of the peach syrup to half a quart of 90% alcohol and 2 small glasses of rum. Stir and pour over the peaches. Close the jar hermetically, pouring a little paraffin on to the opening and then secure the lid with a parchment paper disk tied tightly to the rim of the jar. This paper will need to be slightly moistened so that it will dry tightly. It is necessary to wait a couple of months before consuming.

PRUGNE IN CONFETTURA

Plum Jam

1 lb 2 oz plums
1 cup sugar
1 lemon

Carefully wash the plums and remove the stones, then weigh them and add half their weight in sugar. Put in a saucepan and cook over high heat with the juice of one lemon, stirring constantly, because the plums easily stick to the pan. Let it cook until the fruit becomes transparent, that is from 30 to 40 minutes. When the jam is ready, pour it, still hot, into the jars; close, turn them over once or twice, and let them cool.

ADA SAYS: *For this jam it is advisable to use Greengage plums.*

PRUGNE SECCHE

Dried Prunes

Ripe plums

Choose large plums that have reached maturity, but are not over ripe. Put a saucepan with water on the heat and when it boils, immerse the plums, leaving them there for a few minutes, until they come to the surface and their skin is cracked. Pull them up with a slotted spoon and arrange them on wooden boards in the sun. When they dry on one side, turn them over and leave them like this for a few days, until they are completely dry. Take the plums indoors in the evening, so that the humidity of the night does not delay the drying process. You can pass the prunes in a preheated oven with very light heat for at least an hour, until they have lost all moisture. Then wrap in a small bag and keep them.

RIBES IN GELATINA

Currant Jelly

Currants
Sugar

Wash and purée the currants. collecting the juice in a bowl. Weigh the juice and add the same weight of sugar; pour everything into a pan and put it on the stove. Stir with a wooden spoon to facilitate the melting of the sugar, and remove the foam that gradually comes to the surface. When the jelly no longer flows like water and the spoon is veiled, remove from the heat. When the jelly is ready, pour it still hot in jars; close them, turn them upside down once or twice, and let them cool.

UVA NATALIZIA

Christmas Grapes

2¼ lb grapes

To store fresh grapes to be displayed on the Christmas table, it is necessary to have a rather dark, well-ventilated and dry room.

Pull from one wall to the other some large strings, well stretched, on which you will hang the grapes. The clusters must be just ripe and chosen with great care, they must not have any specks or small lesions to the skin. Not only that, but even when the bunches, with all perfectly healthy grapes, have been hung, they must be subjected to constant surveillance, to remove, if necessary, those grapes that, despite the care, tend to spoil.

The bunches of grapes, detached from the plant, must not be washed; even cleaning them with a soft cloth, which some recommend, is not recommendable. It is much better, for the success of conservation, that the berries are touched as little as possible, to prevent external contacts from causing damage. The grapes, preserved in this way, can be kept for several months, even till spring.

ADA SAYS: *Naturally, farmers have the easier task: the bunches can be hung as soon as they are picked from the plant.*

UVA SOTTO SPIRITO

Grapes in Spirit

Large, fleshy grapes
1 cinnamon stick
¾ cup sugar
10 cloves
1 oz mace
Wild flowers
1 quart alcohol
Optional: vanilla extract

To put grapes in alcohol, it will be better to use large and fleshy grapes. Choose the best, detaching them one by one with scissors from the bunch, without however removing the small stalk. Get yourself a glass jar that can hold all the grapes, and put them in. Add the cinnamon stick, 2 inches long, the sugar, the cloves, the mace, which is the outer shell of the nutmeg, and maybe a pinch of wild flowers. On these pour a quart of alcohol and shake until the sugar is dissolved. To give more perfume to the preparation, you can also add a little vanilla. Pour everything into the kilner jar; close it with its lid, and tie a piece of parchment paper over it. This paper will need to be slightly moistened so that it will dry tightly. Leave the grapes to rest for at least 2 months.

VISCIOLE IN CONFETTURA

Sour Cherry Jam

2¼ lb sour cherries
3½ cups sugar

Wash the sour cherries, and dry them, first removing the stem, and then the pit. When you have pitted them all, weigh them and for each pound of fruit, calculate 3 quarters of the weight of sugar. Put the sugar in the pan, pour a glass of water on to it, let it melt, and then put it on the stove and let it boil for 3 or 4 minutes, skimming it thoroughly. Then put the sour cherries into the pan and cook over a rather lively fire. Skim the jam and mix it and when you see that the sour cherries have shriveled and the syrup veils the spoon, remove the jam from the heat. When the jam is ready, pour it still hot into the jars; close them, turn them over once or twice, and let them cool.

VISCIOLE IN CONFETTURA E SCIROPPO DI VISCIOLE

Sour Cherry Jam and Syrup

4½ lb ripe sour cherries
6½ cups powdered sugar
6¾ lb sugar

Wash, dry, and remove the stalk and stones from the sour cherries. Put the sour cherries in a suitable pan, cover them with powdered sugar, and leave them for 10 or 12 hours.

After this time, set the pan to the heat and let the sour cherries boil for 20 minutes. Then pour everything into a colander, and set over a bowl to collect the juice.

Put the drained sour cherries back into the pan, cover with sugar, and boil for 40 minutes. Put this hot jam in glass jars, well washed and dried; close them, turn them upside down once or twice and let them cool.

Now measure the juice obtained from the sour cherries and add the same volume of sugar to it; set the syrup over heat on the stove and let it boil for half an hour, skimming it carefully. When it is cold, bottle it.

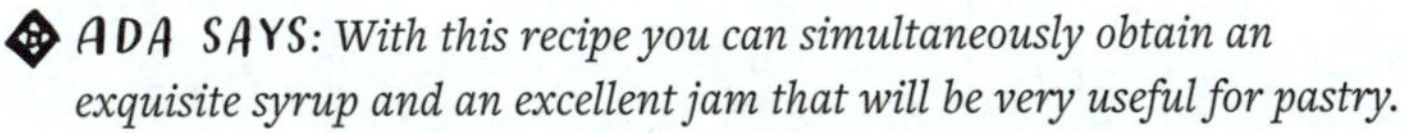

ADA SAYS: *With this recipe you can simultaneously obtain an exquisite syrup and an excellent jam that will be very useful for pastry.*

FILLINGS & ICINGS

TO WHIP EGG WHITES

Put the egg whites in a bowl, keep it a little tilted and, with a whisk, beat the whites in a rhythmic manner. You will get a faster result using a blender.

The whites are at the right point when, lifting a part of them with the whisk, a small cone is formed whose tip remains very straight – like snowy peaks. After having whipped the whites, if you need to incorporate them into a cake mixture, mix them in using a wooden spoon with the greatest delicacy so as not to spoil them. Egg whites give lightness to preparations.

TO FILL A CAKE

All cakes – sponge, genoise, Margherita, etc. – can be filled and decorated. To do this, use the blade of a long knife, split the cake into 2 disks and place them on the table with the insides facing up. Pour a couple of glasses of liqueur and a glass of water into a cup and wet the 2 disks with this slightly diluted liqueur. On the lower disk, spread some jam or cream – chocolate, butter, custard, etc. Reassemble the cake as if it were whole and spread over and around the jam or cream.

TO MAKE ICING

Icings are usually sugar-based coatings used to embellish and decorate desserts. To make a basic water icing, mix powdered sugar in a bowl with apricot jelly, which has the function of giving it a sheen, and melt it with very little water, mixing with a wooden spoon.

Work the icing for a few minutes to blend well. Put the water in carefully otherwise you will be forced to add more icing sugar. You need to obtain the right density, which, lifted with a spoon, descends in a rather dense ribbon. The water icing can be scented with a few drops of liqueur of your choice, and colored with harmless food colorings.

TO COAT A CAKE

To coat a cake, first spread it with a little hot apricot jelly, then pour over the icing, still warm, trying to level the layer with the blade of a knife. Let the superfluous icing drain off and put the coated cake for a moment in an oven with barely noticeable heat, to dry more quickly and make it even shinier.

To make a coffee icing, use coffee in place of water. To make a liqueur icing, mix in a tablespoon. If the liqueur used is maraschino, or another colorless liqueur, and you want to obtain a very white ice, omit the jam.

TO MAKE FONDANT

To make fondant, the following ration is required: **For 1 ¼ cups sugar, use 1 tablespoon of glucose.** *Put the sugar, glucose, and a little water in a small saucepan to make the paste. Stir with a wooden spoon and put on the heat. Cook the sugar, up to a thread (230°F), then sprinkle a little water on it and pour it out on to a wet kitchen table splashed with water. Sprinkle a little more water on the fondant and let it cool a little. Take a sturdy wooden or metal spatula and start working the sugar, pushing it in front of you and then overturning it towards the center. Work the sugar well, always swiping with the spatula on the table and always bringing the sugar back to the center. Do this work on both sides, refining it with a certain force. As the sugar receives this kind of spatula massage, it bleaches and becomes harder, more elastic and white. Continue patiently and the hard and elastic mass will suddenly become very white and will spread placidly on the table into a white mass, which is the fondant.*

Collect the fondant with the spatula and knead it well with slightly wet hands, working it as if it were egg pasta dough. Make it into a ball, put it in a bowl and cover it with a wet and squeezed-out dish towel. It will keep for a long time provided you always keep the towel moist to prevent it from making a crust.

TO COAT WITH FONDANT

The above amount of fondant is required to coat a cake of 8 inches in diameter. Place the cake to be coated on the kitchen table and spread it with apricot jelly (p750)*, which makes the fondant flow better and gives a greater shine. Then pour the fondant on the cake, spread it all over the cake, and let it fall along the sides and cover it completely. To facilitate this operation, use a pastry spatula or the blade of a long knife, which you will quickly pass from one end of the cake to the other. If any point remains uncovered, promptly cover it by bringing back some of the fondant that will have spread around the cake.*

As soon as you see that the fondant begins to thicken slightly, insert the blade of a large knife under the coated cake, lift it, freeing it from smudges, and place it on another part of the table, letting the fondant dry completely. This happens in a few minutes.

If the fondant is not totally smooth, put the cake in a moderate oven for a few minutes, and the heat will even it out. Leftover fondant, as long as it does not contain crumbs, can be reused. However, a word of warning: if it is heated several times, it will lose its original lustre. Fondant can be colored with food coloring or scented with a few drops of essence.

GELATINA ALL'ALBICOCCA

Apricot Jelly

⅓ cup apricot jam
1 cup powdered sugar

Apricot jam and icing sugar, in equal proportions, are useful to make a cream or fondant stick better to cakes, or also to coat cakes garnished with candied fruit.

Put a little apricot jam in a small saucepan and an equal amount of powdered sugar. Cook a little until a small thread forms. Take a small portion between your thumb and forefinger to check. Cooking makes this jelly transparent and more compact and it should be spread while hot.

GHIACCIA COTTA AL CIOCCOLATO

Chocolate Icing

3½ oz dark chocolate
¾ cup powdered sugar

Grate the chocolate into a small pan, wetting it with a little warm water. Put the saucepan over a very low heat, or in a bain-marie, so that the chocolate melts gradually.

Put the sugar in another saucepan, wet it with a little water, to make a paste, mix it carefully at first and then let it cook until a small thread forms between the thumb and forefinger, wet your finger first *(p736)*. This is the first degree of cooking of sugar (212°F) and is reached quickly; so be careful not to pass it.

Put the bain-marie containing the chocolate on the table and drop in the boiling sugar syrup, little by little, and mix carefully as if whipping mayonnaise. Once all the sugar has been added, work the chocolate for a little longer and if it has become too thick, before coating the cake, heat it slightly on a very low heat until it becomes fluid again.

GHIACCIA REALE

Royal Icing

3⅔ cups powdered sugar
2 egg whites
Lemon juice
Potato starch

Put the sugar and the egg whites in a bowl and work them vigorously with a wooden spoon or with an electric beater, until the mixture is elastic, well whipped, very white, and very stiff. A few drops of lemon juice will facilitate and speed up the processing, and even a little potato starch can be mixed in. For decoration, the royal icing is enclosed in a small pastry bag, or a syringe, and released in a thin thread.

ADA SAYS: *A mixture of egg white and powdered sugar is called royal icing. Royal icing, which was once used a lot in confectionery preparations and also to coat cakes, is now used for the coating of some special sweets and some kinds of petits-fours and finds a wider use in decoration, especially to embellish cakes already coated with fondant, like Easter cakes.*

CREAMS & SAUCES

CREMA AL BURRO

Buttercream

10½ tbsp butter
4 tbsp powdered sugar
Optional: coffee or liqueur

Pastry cream:
1 egg yolk, scant ¼ cup sugar, scant ¼ cup all-purpose flour, 3 tbsp milk

Make a pastry cream *(p752)* using the ingredient amounts listed here. Then take the butter and put it in a bowl and, if necessary, especially in winter, let it soften by putting it in a wet and wrung-out napkin and working it with your hands; then whip it with a wooden spoon until it is as soft as cream. Then add the powdered sugar, mixing it in a little at a time, and immediately afterwards the cold pastry cream. You can vary the taste by adding half a cup of cold coffee or a glass of liqueur.

CREMA BIANCA

White Cream

7 tbsp butter
¾ cup powdered sugar
1 egg white
Vanilla extract

Put the butter in a bowl, whip it to a cream, and add the sugar. When the butter and sugar are well blended, gently add the egg white whipped to stiff peaks. Perfume this soft cream with vanilla.

CREMA DI MANDORLE (FRANGIPANE)

Almond Cream (Frangipane)

⅔ cup almonds
¾ cup powdered sugar
1 egg
3½ tbsp butter
Rum

Put the shelled almonds in a saucepan with cold water and bring to the boil. Remove the saucepan from the heat, and then one by one, take off the skins and keep them in a bowl with fresh water.

When you have them all peeled, dry them with a towel and let them dry in the oven at a very moderate heat—they must not color. Then crush them in a pestle and mortar with the sugar or you can use a blender to make a flour.

Sieve the almond flour into a bowl and add the egg: Mix with a wooden spoon to blend everything well and, always stirring, add the melted butter, in 2 or 3 additions. Stir again until the mixture is well whipped and finish it with a glass of rum.

CREMA INGLESE

Crème Anglaise

5 egg yolks
¾ cup sugar
2 cups milk
Optional: lemon or orange peel, vanilla extract, light cream

Put the egg yolks and sugar in a pan and work the eggs for a long time with a wooden spoon or a whisk, until they become swollen and foamy. Put the milk on the heat and bring it almost to a boil. When it is near boiling, pour it in small quantities, over the whipped eggs, working vigorously with a whisk or spoon. When you have added all the milk, place the custard on the heat and, always stirring, cook it, bringing it close to boiling, but taking care not to let it boil or it would separate irredeemably. When you see that the custard is slightly thickened and can cover the back of a spoon, take it off the heat.

Pour it into a bowl and leave it to cool, stirring it from time to time. This cream can be flavored with a little lemon or scraped orange peel, or with a touch of vanilla.

ADA SAYS: *This preparation acquires even more finesse by replacing some of the milk with the same amount of cream, but off the heat.*

CREMA INGLESE AL CIOCCOLATO

Chocolate Crème Anglaise

4 egg yolks
4 heaped tbsp sugar
1 tsp potato starch
Milk
4 tbsp grated chocolate

Put the egg yolks, sugar, and potato starch in a small saucepan, mix with a wooden spoon until the eggs swell and become foamy, then dilute with 2 glasses of almost boiling milk. Put the pan back on the heat and, always stirring, cook the cream until it is slightly thickened and coats the spoon, being careful not to let it boil. To this cream, add the grated chocolate, dissolved separately in a little warm milk. Mix in with great care, and then remove it from the heat.

CREMA PASTICCIERA

Pastry Cream

¾ cup powdered sugar
3 egg yolks
½ cup all-purpose flour
Lemon zest
Vanilla extract
2 cups milk
Optional: 2 tbsp butter, chocolate, Marsala

Put the sugar and egg yolks in a saucepan. Stir with a wooden spoon until the eggs have become swollen and foamy; then add the flour, and a little grated lemon zest, or a touch of vanilla. Put the milk on the heat and when it is almost boiling pour it, in small quantities, over the eggs, flour, and sugar, whisking all the while.

When you have added all the milk, put the saucepan back on the heat, stirring constantly with a wooden spoon. You will soon see that the cream will gradually thicken. Continue to mix it all the time and, once it has boiled, let the cream simmer for 5 minutes so that it loses the taste of raw flour.

Then remove it from the heat, and, if you like, add the butter, which gives it a greater finesse. Stir again and while the cream is cooling, remember to mix it from time to time to stop any skin from forming on the surface.

◆ ADA SAYS: *To make a chocolate cream, before removing it from the heat, add chocolate that you have melted in a bain-marie, and mix well. It should be scented with a few drops of vanilla. If it is too thick, dilute it with a little more milk, which you add, in small quantities, stirring. To make zabaglione, add a glass of Marsala instead of chocolate.*

CREMA PRINCE

Chocolate Cream

3½ oz dark chocolate
½ cup milk or light cream

This simple cream is used to fill cakes and small sweet pastries.

Chop or grate the chocolate into a small saucepan, wetting it with the milk or cream. Keep the saucepan over a very low heat to melt the chocolate, stirring with a wooden spoon. When the chocolate is perfectly melted, pour it into a bowl and let it cool. Then whip it again vigorously with a small whisk, until the cream is light. Working it lightens it a little. Kept in the refrigerator, it hardens significantly.

SALSA CALDA AL FALERNO

Hot Falerno (Wine) Sauce

1 quart red Falerno or other rich red wine
7 oz sweet grapes, perhaps Malaga
Rum
10½ oz quince jelly
⅔ cup shelled pistachios
7 oz assorted candied fruit, mainly cherries
Cherry brandy

Put the red Falerno wine in a saucepan and let it evaporate by almost two-thirds. While it is cooking, open and seed the grapes and macerate in the rum. Then add to the grapes, the quince jelly, the pistachios, and the assorted candied fruit, with a prevalence of candied cherries, all chopped and diced. Stir and complete the sauce off the heat by adding a small glass of cherry brandy.

◆ ADA SAYS: *Many desserts should be accompanied by a sweet sauce. Among the most complex and tastiest are the special wine sauces. This hot Falerno sauce is excellent, for example, to accompany hot baba. Falerno is an ancient wine from the region of Campania known to the Romans and now classified with a protected status.*

SALSA CALDA AL VINO ROSSO

Hot Red Wine Sauce

3 cups red wine
Strawberry jam
⅔ cup raisins
⅓ cup pine nuts
2½ oz candied orange peel
Maraschino liqueur
Potato starch

Put the red wine in a saucepan and boil it until it evaporates by about two-thirds. While the wine boils, sieve the strawberry jam. When the wine has reduced, remove from the heat and add the softened jam, the raisins, well washed in hot water and left to swell a little in clean hot water, the pine nuts, the candied orange peel, cut into small pieces, and a small glass of maraschino. Put the saucepan back on the heat and when the liquid boils, add in a teaspoon of potato starch that you have dissolved separately with a little cold water, and mix with a wooden spoon until the sauce has reached a light density. Stop when the sauce is sufficiently thick.

ADA SAYS: *This sauce is excellent served hot with fritters and baba.*

SALSA CALDA SIRACUSANA

Hot Siracusan Sauce

2 cups wine, preferably Syracuse Muscat Zibibbo
2 cloves
Cinnamon stick
6 egg yolks

Put the wine, cloves, and a piece of cinnamon on the heat in a saucepan, and let it boil until the wine has evaporated by half. Then pass the wine through a muslin sieve, collecting it in a bowl, and let it cool completely.

Break the egg yolks into a small saucepan, blend them with the cold wine, and then put the saucepan in a bain-marie and whip the mixture with a whisk until there is a kind of light eggnog.

ZABAIONE

Zabaglione

1 egg yolk
1 tbsp sugar
Marsala or white wine
Optional: vanilla extract or the seeds from a vanilla bean, grated orange zest or lemon

The zabaglione is cooked in a bain-marie; for each egg yolk you need a tablespoon of sugar and 2 tablespoons of Marsala or white wine.

Put all the ingredients together in a heat-proof bowl, and set over a saucepan with a finger of boiling water. Put it on the heat and begin to whisk the eggs. Due to the action of the heat and the whisk, the egg first becomes frothy; then it mounts and finally sets into a soft and light mass.

Zabaglione can be flavored with vanilla, grated orange zest, or lemon.

TOPPINGS

TO MAKE CRUMBLE

To crumble chocolate, scrape a bar of dark chocolate with a sharp knife, then keep it in a glass jar with a lid to decorate cakes and bonbons.

For almond crumble, put shelled almonds in a saucepan with cold water and bring almost to the boil. This makes it easy to remove the skin. Then wash them in cold water, dry them, cut them into filets or crush them into grains, and put, for a few minutes, in a moderate oven until they are dry and slightly browned.

To skin hazelnuts, put them in a moderate oven until they are lightly toasted. Then turn them out on a sieve and swipe them with your hand on the meshes of the sieve so the toasted skins come off quickly. Then chop them coarsely.

Put shelled pistachios in a saucepan with cold water, adding a pinch of salt to the water that sets and preserves the green color of the nut, and bring the water almost to boiling point. Rub off the skins and rinse them in cold water, dry them, cut them into filets or chop them into grains, which you will put in a moderate oven for a few minutes until they are completely dry.

CANDITURA DELLE SCORZETTE D'ARANCIA

Candied Orange Peel

Oranges
Sugar syrup *(p736)*
Sugar

Cut the oranges into 4 wedges, take off the peel and put the wedges in a basin of water for 2 or 3 days so they lose all their bitterness.

Boil a saucepan of water and cook the peels for about a quarter of an hour, until you can scratch them easily with a toothpick, without over-cooking. Put them back in fresh water, drain and arrange them in a new pan.

Prepare the sugar syrup with the sugar and glucose, boil it until small thread and pour it over the orange peels. Cover the container and put it away until the next day.

The next day, drain the syrup back into the saucepan. Refresh the syrup with more sugar, bring to a boil and pour it back, still hot, over the orange skins. Repeat the operation every day for 3 days.

Store the candied orange peels in a glass jar and cover them completely with syrup. They keep well for some time.

MARZAPANE (PASTA DI MANDORLE)

Marzipan (Almond Paste)

Shelled almonds
Sugar
1 egg

Put shelled almonds in a small saucepan, cover them with water and put them on the stove, making the water almost boil. Remove from the heat and when the water has lost some of its heat, take off the skins. Dry them in a towel. Crush them with sugar and a beaten egg in small quantities to make a smooth and very fine paste.

PASTA DI NOCCIOLE

Hazelnut Paste

Hazelnuts
Sugar

Toast the hazelnuts in the oven, rub them on a sieve with your hands and let the toasted skins pop off; then chop or crush them coarsely.

Put the sugar in a saucepan and melt it, without adding any water. When it has completely melted, add the chopped hazelnuts and mix thoroughly to make a single mass that you pour out on to the kitchen table and leave to cool. Then put the mixture in the blender and blend for a long time until the hazelnuts become oily and you get a thick and fragrant cream.

ADA SAYS: *If you stir the sugar too much while it melts, it will crystalize irredeemably.*

MANDORLE PRALINATE

Candied Almonds

MAKES 10½ OZ

1 cup sugar
3 cups shelled almonds
Gum arabic
Optional: extra sugar

Moisten half of the sugar with a little water and cook to a soft ball (234°F). Then add the almonds with all their skins. With a wooden spoon begin to mix the sugar, it will turn golden and it will eventually congeal into many whitish particles and have a grain that veils the almonds.

Transfer everything on to the kitchen table. Carefully clean the pan and add the rest of the sugar, which you will cook again up to a soft ball. Put the almonds back in and repeat the same operation as before.

Naturally this time the quantity of sugar that will settle on the almonds will be greater. That might be enough, but if you want very sweet almonds you have to repeat the operation a third and last time with another ½ cup of sugar.

To finish, dissolve a little gum arabic in a very little water, preferably in a bain-marie, and pass the almonds through the gum solution and dry on a sieve. If you want a brownish colour, you will need to add a few drops of burnt sugar—caramel—to the gum arabic solution.

MANDORLE SALATE

Salted Almonds

Almonds
1 egg white
Fine salt

Put the almonds in cold water and bring to a boil slowly. As soon as the water is about to boil, remove the pan from the heat, let it cool and skin the almonds. After drying them in a cool oven (130°F), put in a light oven and shuffle them often, turning with a spatula, to let them brown slightly. Then remove them from the oven, collect them on a plate, and let them cool.

When they are cold, sprinkle with a little freshly broken egg white, mix with a fork, and then mix them with your hands so that they are all covered with a very light layer of egg white. Then sprinkle the almonds with a fair amount of fine salt. Mix them so that they are covered with the salt all over and then spread them again on a tray in the oven, with a barely noticeable heat to dry.

PUDDINGS

BUDINO DI BURRO E CANDITI

Butter and Candied Fruit Pudding

3½ oz assorted candied fruit, like cherries and orange
Kirsch or maraschino liqueur
3 egg yolks
½ cup sugar
14 tbsp butter

Divide the candied fruit into regular cubes, place them in a bowl, pour half a glass of liqueur over them, and leave them in the marinade.

Place the egg yolks in a bowl together with the sugar and mix them for a long time with a wooden spoon or with a small whisk. When the egg yolks are well whipped, add a small glass of maraschino liqueur. Now put the softened butter in another bowl and, always mixing with a wooden spoon, reduce it to a soft and fluffy cream. Then add the egg yolks, little by little, and complete with the diced candied fruit.

Line a rectangular mold with a capacity of about one quart with parchment paper. Pour the sweet mixture in, tap the mold so it fills up properly, level the surface with a knife, and put in the fridge until it sets. Unmold, remove the paper, and divide it into slices.

ADA SAYS: *This dessert can be made without using the oven.*

BUDINO DI CASTAGNE

Chestnut Pudding

10½ oz chestnuts
2 tbsp powdered sugar
2 tbsp butter, plus extra to grease
2 eggs

Peel the chestnuts, boil them, remove the inner skin and, finally, work them through a sieve. Collect the chestnuts in a saucepan, put it on the heat, add the sugar and the softened butter, and mix with a wooden spoon, so as to dry the purée well.

Remove the pan from the heat and bind the mixture with the egg yolks. Separately, whip the whites very firmly into a snow and gently add them to the mixture.

Grease a mold with a capacity of one quart. Spoon the mixture in and cook in a bain-marie for 3-quarters of an hour, until the pudding is firm. Then overturn it on to a serving plate and send it to the table.

BUDINO DI CILIEGE

Cherry Pudding

1 lb 2 oz cherries
1¼ cups breadcrumbs
Rum
3 eggs
¾ cup powdered sugar
1 lemon
Butter for greasing

Wash the cherries, remove the stems and pits and have them ready. Also macerate the breadcrumbs in half a glass of rum so they are well-soaked. Whip 2 egg whites to a firm snow.

Put 2 egg yolks and one whole egg in a bowl with the sugar, the grated zest of one lemon, and the juice of half a lemon. Begin to whip the eggs with the sugar and work them for quite a long time to get a velvet and swollen mixture.

When the eggs are whipped, add the breadcrumbs and finally add the 2 whipped whites up to a very firm snow. Butter a one-quart pudding mold. Fill the mold up to 2 fingers deep with this mixture. Lay some cherries on top, cover with more filling, then more cherries and finally finish with a layer of the egg mixture, sugar, and breadcrumbs. Put the mold in a preheated oven of moderate heat for an hour, until the pudding is firm. Then remove it from the oven, let it rest for 10 minutes, and then turn it out onto a round serving dish. Can be served hot or cold.

BUDINO DI CIOCCOLATO

Chocolate Pudding

3 cups milk
5½ oz chocolate
⅓ cup sugar
Vanilla extract
3 eggs
Butter for greasing

Put a glass of milk in a pan and, over a very low heat, melt the chocolate, already broken into small pieces or, better, grated.

In another pan, boil the remaining milk, then add the melted chocolate and the sugar and simmer over a very low heat for about 10 minutes, stirring with a wooden spoon because it must not stick. Remove the pan from the heat, perfume with a few drops of vanilla and transfer to a bowl. Let this mixture cool.

Then finally finish it with the eggs, beaten as for an omelette. Stir to mix everything and pour into a buttered and sugared one-quart-and-a-half pudding mold. Cook in a bain-marie for an hour or more. When the pudding is well set, remove it from the heat, let it rest for 5 minutes, and then turn it out on to a round serving dish and decorate.

BUDINO DI CIOCCOLATO ALLE MANDORLE

Chocolate Pudding with Almonds

2 cups milk
⅓ cup sugar
2½ oz chocolate
⅓ cup almonds
3½ oz hard cookies or rusks
3 eggs
2 egg yolks
Butter for greasing

Put the milk, sugar, and grated chocolate on the heat in a small pan and bring everything to a boil to dissolve well. Then remove the saucepan from the heat.

Meanwhile, blanch and skin the almonds and, after having dried them well, blend them, a few at a time, with the cookies or rusks. You can also use a food processor. Once you have finished blending the almonds and cookies together, add them to the chocolate saucepan; mix and leave to cool.

When the mixture is cold, add 5 egg yolks, one by one, stirring with a wooden spoon, and when they have blended, add 3 whites whipped to stiff peaks.

Butter a one-and-a-half-quart mold with a central hole and sprinkle with sugar. Transfer in the chocolate mixture and bake in a bain-marie, in a preheated oven of moderate heat, for about an hour.

Let it cook for a few more minutes to ensure perfect cohesion of the mixture, then, after removing the mold from the oven, wait at least 10 minutes before turning out the cake. This pudding is very delicate and should be served lukewarm.

BUDINO DI FRUTTA

Fruit Pudding

1 lb 2 oz fresh fruit
Rum
2 tbsp sugar
3½ oz ladyfingers or sponge cake
Almond oil
Jam

Crème Bavaroise:
2 cups milk, 5 egg yolks, 1 cup vanilla sugar, 2 gelatin sheets

First, prepare your Crème Bavaroise *(p777)* using the ingredient amounts listed here.

Then wash and dice the fruit, put it all in a bowl with a glass of rum and the sugar and leave it for half an hour. Cut the ladyfingers or sponge cake into small pieces and place a finger-high layer in a lightly greased mold wiped with almond oil. On this layer, sow a few pieces of diced fruit, a few teaspoons of jam, and a little Crème Bavaroise. Alternate layers of cookies, diced fruit, and cream, and finish by pouring the remaining cream into the mold. Leave in the fridge for 2 or 3 hours.

BUDINO DI MELE

Apple Pudding

1 lb 2 oz apples
3 tbsp sugar
Ground cinnamon
2 tbsp butter
4 tbsp breadcrumbs
¼ cup raisins
3 egg whites
Butter for greasing

Wash and peel the apples, cut them into wedges, and put them in a pan, covering them with a little water. Cook the apples until they are done; then sieve, put them back on the heat, and let them dry. Add the sugar and, always stirring with a wooden spoon, let the apple purée thicken.

Then turn the apple purée out into a bowl, season with the ground cinnamon and butter, and finally mix in the breadcrumbs and raisins that you have previously soaked in warm water. When the apple mixture is completely cold, gently mix in 3 egg whites whipped to firm snow.

Butter a one-quart mold, pour the apple mixture in, tap the mold so that it fills completely, and place in a preheated oven of moderate heat for about 40 minutes. When the apple pudding has hardened, turn it upside down on a plate and serve hot.

ADA SAYS: *We recommend Reinette or Annurca apples or other crisp, sweet apples.*

BUDINO DI PESCHE

Peach Pudding

8 peaches
White wine
3 tbsp sugar
3 egg whites

Wash, blanch, peel, pit and then cook the peaches in a glass of white wine and the sugar. Blend them and let the mixture dry on the heat to get a purée that is sufficiently dense.

When cold, gently add 3 egg whites beaten to a firm snow. Pour it all into a smooth buttered mold and cook in a bain-marie, without letting the water boil. After about a quarter of an hour, turn out and serve it hot.

BUDINO DIPLOMATICO CALDO

Hot Diplomat Pudding

¼ cup raisins
2 oz candied orange peel
Rum
7 oz sponge cake
Butter for greasing
Marsala
3 eggs
1 egg yolk
½ cup sugar
2 cups milk
4 tbsp apricot jelly

Soak the raisins in warm water, squeeze them lightly, and put them in a small bowl together with the diced candied orange peel. Splash over a glass of rum, stir it, and leave for a while.

Cut the sponge cake into cubes. Abundantly butter a smooth mold with a hole in the middle of the capacity of one quart and a half. Start by putting a couple of cubes of sponge cake in the bottom of the mold, and on them lay a few raisins and candied peel.

Have ready, in a cup, half a glass of Marsala diluted with the same amount of water. With a spoon, drop a little on the first layer of sponge cake, raisins, and fruit. Make a second layer of sponge cake, raisins, and orange and sprinkle this too with a spoonful of diluted Marsala, and so on, until you have used all the sponge cake, all the raisins, and all the oranges. Press lightly on the sponge, so that the mixture reaches 3 fingers from the edge of the mold, because when cooking, the pudding grows a little and if the mold were filled any higher the mixture would overflow.

After garnishing the mold, put 3 whole eggs and a yolk and the sugar in a bowl. Work with a wooden spoon to dissolve everything well, and then dilute with the cold milk, which you add a spoonful at a time, always stirring.

Spoon this liquid cream into the mold. Add a few spoons at a time, waiting until the previous one has been absorbed before adding more. Proceed in this way until the cream slowly reaches the top of the mold.

As soon as all the cream has been absorbed, place the mold in a bain-marie filled with boiling water and put both in a preheated oven of moderate heat, leaving the pudding to cook for about an hour. When it is firm, remove the mold from the bain-marie and let the pudding rest for about 10 minutes. Then turn it out of the mold and send it to the table, accompanying it with some apricot jelly warmed through in a pan.

ADA SAYS: *If you pour in the cream all at once, the top half of the sponge would float and the bottom get too soggy.*

BUDINO DI PRUGNE

Prune Pudding

1 lb 2 oz dried plums (prunes)
2 heaped tbsps powdered sugar
Lemon peel
2 gelatin sheets
Olive oil for greasing
1 cup heavy cream

Wash the prunes and place them in a saucepan with the powdered sugar, 4 glasses of water, and thinly sliced lemon peel without a trace of the white part. Let it boil slowly for an hour, then lift out the stones and mash the pulp and the remaining juice.

Collect the purée in a bowl and add the gelatin sheets, soaked in cold water, squeezed in your hands, and melted in a saucepan with a couple of spoons of boiling water. Stir and pour everything into an oiled half-quart pudding mold. Put the mold in the fridge. Whip the cream and when the mold has set, arrange on top in a pyramid shape.

BUDINO DI RICOTTA

Ricotta Pudding

3 tbsp semolina
1 lb 5 oz ricotta
4 tbsp powdered sugar
2 eggs
Candied citron and orange
Handful raisins
Rum
Butter for greasing
Handful breadcrumbs
Vanilla sugar

Boil a generous glass of water in a small saucepan and slowly drop in the semolina, stirring with a wooden spoon so that no lumps form. The mixture will soon become very thick. Keep it on the stove for a couple of minutes, always stirring, and then pour it on to a plate, flatten it and let it cool.

Purée the ricotta or work it carefully in a bowl with a wooden spoon to dissolve it well. Add the powdered sugar, one whole egg, one yolk, one spoonful of candied citron and orange, one spoon of raisins soaked in warm water, and a glass of rum. Mix everything, add the cold semolina, and lastly the egg white whipped to a snow.

Butter a smooth (not ridged) one-and-a-half quart mold. Throw in a handful of breadcrumbs, and turn the mold in all directions so that the bread sticks everywhere, then turn it over to drop off the extra. Pour in the ricotta mixture, making sure that it reaches only two-thirds of the way up because it grows a little during cooking. Put the pudding in the oven at moderate heat for about an hour, until it becomes a beautiful golden color. Then take it out of the oven, let it rest for about 10 minutes, take it out of the mold, and when it is cold, sugar it with vanilla sugar. This pudding can also be served warm, but it is preferable cold.

DESSERTS WITH FRUIT & NUTS

ALBICOCCHE COLBERT

Apricots Colbert

2¼ lb apricots
¾ cup sugar
5½ oz short-grain white rice
2½ cups milk
Vanilla bean, split
All-purpose flour
1 egg
Breadcrumbs
Oil for frying
Butter for greasing
Jam
Salt

Open the apricots without breaking them entirely, remove the stone and simmer them for 5 or 6 minutes in a little water to which you have added a few spoons of sugar. Check that they do not fall apart, then remove them from the syrup, which you will keep aside, and drain.

Put the rice in a saucepan and cover it with cold water. Let it boil for 2 minutes; then drain the water and replace it with boiling milk flavored with a vanilla bean. When the rice has boiled again, put the saucepan on very low heat, add a pinch of salt and the rest of the sugar, cover the saucepan and let it boil very slowly for about 20 minutes without stirring the rice. When the rice is cooked, pour it into a bowl to cool completely.

Open the apricots and in the middle of each, instead of the stone, put a spoonful of sweet rice. Close them up, sprinkle them in flour, dip them in beaten egg and then breadcrumbs and fry them in oil.

After filling the apricots, transfer the remaining rice into a small smooth, buttered mold with a hole in the middle and press it lightly so that it fills all the corners. Let the rice rest for about half an hour and then turn it out into the middle of a serving dish. Arrange the prepared apricots in a pyramid shape in the middle and, before sending to the table, pour over everything a little sauce. Make this from the syrup in which the apricots were cooked, in which you will dilute a spoonful of jam to your liking.

ALBICOCCHE IN BORDURA DI PASTA DOLCE

Apricot Mold

2 eggs
½ cup sugar
1⅓ cups plain flour
2 tsp active dry yeast
Lemon
4 tbsp milk
9 tbsp butter, plus extra for greasing
Breadcrumbs
1 lb 2 oz apricots
Powdered sugar
Marsala

Break the eggs into a bowl, both yolks and whites, add the sugar and beat for a long time using a whisk or an electric beater. When the mixture is well whipped and soft, add the flour into which you have mixed the yeast. Scent the mixture with the grated lemon peel and dilute it with the milk and butter melted in a saucepan. Mix everything with a wooden spoon.

Grease a one-and-a-half quart mold with a hole in the middle, smooth or fluted. Sprinkle it with very fine breadcrumbs and turn it upside down to throw away anything that does not stick. Pour the mixture into the mold and cook it in a preheated oven of moderate heat for about half an hour. After this time, turn the cake upside down on a wire rack and let it cool.

In the meantime, split the apricots, remove the stones, and place them in a bowl, concave side up. Sprinkle with powdered sugar and a small glass of Marsala. Put them in the fridge and when you are ready to present the dessert, pour them, with all their juices, into the middle of the cake. To enrich this nice, tasty and elegant preparation, you can add any fruit that the summer can offer you – peaches, plums, cherries, etc.

ANANAS ALLA CREOLA

Creole Pineapple

10½ oz short-grain white rice
1 quart milk
Vanilla
2 tbsp butter, plus more butter as needed
Salt
¾ cup sugar
3 egg yolks
Pineapple, canned
8 bananas
Rum
Apricot jam

Put the rice in a saucepan, covering it with cold water. Let the rice boil for 2 or 3 minutes. Then drain it, wash in cold water and put it back to cook, this time with the milk. Spice the milk with vanilla, and add the butter and salt as well. After another 10 minutes of cooking, sweeten the rice with most of the sugar. Cover the saucepan, put it on a very low heat and let it finish cooking without stirring for about 20 minutes.

Once the rice is cooked, mix in the egg yolks one at a time with a fork. Butter a smooth, bordered mold with the capacity of an abundant quart. Put the rice in, pressing it lightly so that it takes the shape of the mold well.

Open the pineapple can and divide each slice in 2. Place the half slices in a pan aligning them, cover them with half of the syrup from the can and let them warm through. Peel the bananas, cut them into slices and place them in a bowl, sprinkling them with a little more sugar and a few glasses of rum.

When ready to serve, turn out the rice border on to a round serving dish and arrange the half slices of pineapple on the rice, in steps. In the center of the rice, place the sliced bananas. lifting them into a slight pyramid.

Put a few spoonfuls of apricot jam in the rest of the pineapple syrup to make a warm sauce of the right density, which you can finish with the rum left over from the banana marinade. Pour this hot sauce over the bananas and pineapple slices and serve.

ADA SAYS: *This excellent sweet dish can be served just warm or left to cool.*

BANANE ALLA FIAMMA

Bananas Flambé

6 bananas
Powdered sugar
Cognac or rum
All-purpose flour
2 eggs
Oil for frying

Peel the bananas, arrange them in a bowl and leave them in a marinade of sugar and cognac or rum for a couple of hours. Then drain them, wipe them in flour, then beaten eggs and fry them in plenty of hot oil. Let them drain well, arrange them in a metal dish and sprinkle abundantly with powdered sugar.

Heat a skewer and, placing it on the sugar, draw a pattern of your choice on the bananas, for example a herringbone. Sprinkle the bananas with rum or cognac, bring them to the table, set the liqueur on fire, and serve immediately.

BANANE IN FRITTURA DOLCE

Sweet Fried Bananas

6 bananas
Powdered sugar
Lemon juice
Orange peel
Rum
Simple batter *(p242)*
Oil for frying

Peel the bananas and divide them in half, lengthwise. Arrange in a bowl, sprinkle them with sugar, add a few drops of lemon juice, a little grated orange peel and 2 small glasses of rum. Leave the bananas like this for some time, possibly for a few hours, so that they can flavor well.

Make a simple batter with plain flour, water and oil and keep in a cool place for at least an hour.

Just before sending the bananas to the table, remove them from the marinade, drain them, coat them in the batter and fry them in plenty of hot oil. Remove them from the pan when they are slightly blond. Then arrange them on a plate with a napkin, sift over powdered sugar and serve hot.

BARCHETTE ALLE FRAGOLE

Pastry Boats For Wild Strawberries

Flour for dusting
Butter for greasing
¾ cup dried beans
1 lb 2 oz wild strawberries
2 cups white wine
Port
Currant jelly
1¾ cups sweetened whipped cream
Lemon zest

Prepare the shortcrust pastry *(p784)* in good time using the ingredient amounts listed here. Mix everything quickly, without adding even the smallest amount of water. Collect the dough in a ball and let it rest for about half an hour covered with plastic wrap.

With a rolling pin, roll out a rather thin dough on a floured table and fashion into the shape of small boats. If you have boat-shaped molds, you can use them. Butter each one and fit with parchment paper. Fill the boats with dried beans, to prevent the dough from rising excessively, and bake them in a moderate heat oven for about 20 minutes.

Empty the boats of their beans, unmold them and keep them aside. The boats can be prepared one or 2 days in advance, or you can buy them packaged from a baker.

Take the wild strawberries, wash them in a little white wine, drain and let them flavor for about 10 minutes with a glass of port.

Shortcrust pastry:
1⅓ cups all-purpose flour, ½ cup sugar, 7 tbsp butter, 2 egg yolks, zest of ½ lemon, pinch salt or use store-bought boat-shaped pastries

Spread the boats with a little currant jelly, fill them with a little whipped cream, and then decorate with wild strawberries and lemon zest.

CASTAGNACCIO RAFFINATO

Refined Chestnut Cake

3¾ cups chestnut flour
1½ cups milk
Salt
2 tbsp sugar
Rosemary
Orange peel
Handful pine nuts
Handful soaked raisins
½ cup walnuts
Olive oil
2 tbsp butter

Pour the chestnut flour into a bowl and add the milk, little by little, mixing carefully. The dough must be very soft, so if necessary, add a little water. Add a pinch of salt, sugar, rosemary, orange peel cut into strips, pine nuts, soaked raisins, and chopped walnuts. Season everything with 2 tablespoons of oil. Mix the ingredients well, then pour into a round baking pan lightly greased with oil. The castagnaccio must have a thickness of about ¾ inch. Put a few flakes of butter on top. Put the castagnaccio in a preheated oven of moderate heat for about an hour, until a dark crust forms on the surface.

CROCCANTE

Almond Crunch

2 cups almonds
2½ cups powdered sugar
Lemon
Olive oil

Put the shelled almonds in a pan with cold water, bring them almost to the boil, take off the heat, and drain. One by one, remove the skins, and put them into a bowl with fresh water. When you have peeled them all, dry them with a towel and cut them into strips or crush them into pieces about the size of large grains of rice. Let them dry on an open towel or in a light oven, avoiding them taking on any colour.

Put the sugar in a saucepan, squeeze over the juice of a lemon, then put it on a moderate heat and let it melt gently, mixing it slowly. When the sugar has dissolved, pour in the chopped almonds and stir continuously with a wooden spoon, so the almonds soak up all the sugar.

When the almonds and sugar have taken on a nice dark blond color, remove from the heat, and pour the mixture on to an oiled baking sheet. With thc help of a potato masher, flatten the mixture to a thickness of quarter of an inch, and then with the blade of a knife draw deep lines across it to divide it into rectangles or rhombuses, so you can break it neatly when the crunch is cold. Keep cool.

FRUTTA IN BORDURA DI RISO DOLCE

Fruit with Sweet Rice

¾ cup pudding rice
1 quart milk
Salt
Sugar
2 tbsp butter
Vanilla extract
2¼ lb various fruits—peaches, pears, apples
Rum
Apricot jam
Handful soaked raisins
Candied orange peel
Candied cherries
Grapes
2 egg yolks
Butter for greasing

Cook the rice in the milk. Add a little salt, 5 spoons of sugar, butter, and a little vanilla.

While the rice is cooking, peel and cut 3 or 4 peaches, some pears, some apples, etc. As each fruit does not need the same cooking time, cook each one separately in a saucepan with a little water and sugar. When they are cooked, but not too much, drain and combine the light syrups in which they have cooked in a saucepan, add a few spoonfuls of sugar, let it thicken on the heat, then reduce the heat, and add a small glass of rum and a spoonful of apricot jam.

Return the cooked fruit to this hot, thick syrup, add a handful of soaked raisins, a few cubes of candied orange peel, some candied cherries and some nice fresh grapes; cover and let it rest.

In the meantime, the rice will have cooked. Mix in a couple of egg yolks off the heat.

Then butter a smooth mold, with a capacity of about 3 cups, with a hole in the center. Spoon the rice in, tap the mold a little on a cloth so that it is well filled, level the rice and press it down with a spoon. Cover the mold and leave it for 10 minutes so that the rice can take the shape of the mold well. Then turn it over on a round plate, remove the mold, place the fruit in a pyramid shape in the middle, and pour over all the syrup, which must be very thick.

MELE ALLA CASTELLANA

Castellana Apples

6 apples, like Reinette
Butter
Sugar
Candied fruit
Apricot jam
1 oz biscotti
1 oz amaretti *(p848)*

Pastry cream:
⅓ cup sugar, 3 egg yolks, ⅓ cup all-purpose flour, 2 cups milk, lemon juice

If you cannot find Reinette apples, choose another firm-textured baking apple such as Golden Russet or Granny Smith.

Prepare a pastry cream *(p752)* using the ingredient amounts listed here.

Peel the apples, remove the core, arrange them in a buttered pan, sprinkle them with sugar, add a spoonful of water to the pan and cook them in a hot oven for about 20 minutes, just so that their cooking is not complete, but 3 quarters finished. Then fill the core of each one with a few pieces of candied fruit mixed with a little apricot jam and cover the apples entirely with the rather thin pastry cream. Crush a few cookies and amaretti and scatter the crumbs over the cream. Place here and there a few pieces of butter and bake the apples until brown in the oven, for 5 or 6 minutes. Serve them hot.

MELE IN SORPRESA

Apple Surprise

6 apples
Jam
Butter for greasing
1 egg
Vanilla sugar

Shortcrust pastry:
1⅔ cups all-purpose flour, 9 tbsp butter, ⅔ cup sugar, 2 egg yolks, lemon peel, salt

Make the shortcrust pastry *(p784)* using the ingredient amounts listed here. Let the dough rest for half an hour, then divide it into 6 equal parts, which you roll, one at a time, on a floured table, into 6 large squares.

Wash and peel the apples and remove the core, and place them, one by one, in the middle of a square of dough. Fill the center of the apple with jam to your liking and, raising the 4 corners of the square, wrap the fruit. Cut off the superfluous dough. Use your fingers try to make sure that the dough adheres well to the apple, wrapping it perfectly. Reshuffle the scraps of dough and flatten them again, and you can make some small decorations. A grooved dough cutter of 2 inches in diameter can make a spiked disk for the tip of the apple.

Align the apples on a baking sheet lightly greased with butter. Brush each one with a little beaten egg and put them in a moderate oven for about an hour, so that they can cook and brown. Arrange them on a plate with a towel and sprinkle with vanilla sugar. You can serve them both hot and cold.

MONTEBIANCO

Montebianco

2¼ lb chestnuts
Salt
Milk
5 tbsp sugar
8 small meringues, store-bought
2 cups whipped cream
Optional: vanilla bean, split

Knick the skin of the chestnuts and put them to boil in cold water with a pinch of salt. When they are cooked, remove the skins, put them in a saucepan, cover them with milk and put them back on the heat adding, if you like, a vanilla bean. Mash the chestnuts with a wooden spoon, and when you have obtained a smooth and sustained purée, add the sugar. Use a potato ricer to mash the purée so that it comes out of the holes in the form of many small vermicelli.

When you have a fair amount, arrange them, with the tip of a small knife, on the plate, trying to get a conical shape. Surround each cone with the meringues, cover with lightly sweetened whipped cream, and with the blade of a knife shape it all around. giving the dish the appearance of a sharp mountain covered with snow.

PANFORTE

Panforte

⅔ cup almonds
⅔ cup hazelnuts
¼ cup cocoa powder
2 tbsp ground cinnamon
⅓ cup all-purpose flour
3½ oz candied orange peel
3½ oz candied pumpkin or melon
3½ oz candied citron peel
½ cup sugar
1 cup honey
Edible rice paper (communion wafers)
Powdered sugar
Optional: pepper or other spices

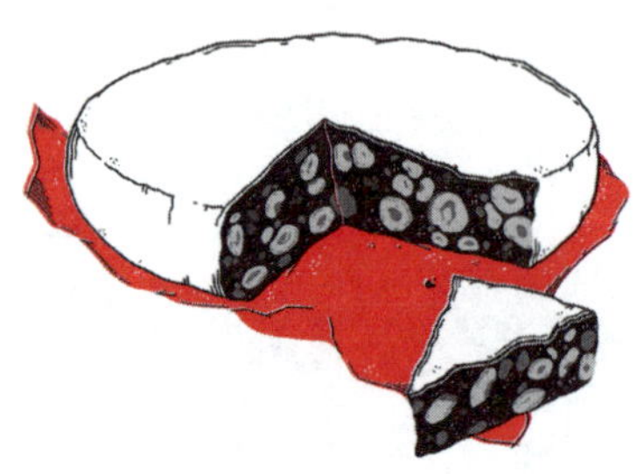

Blanch the almonds in boiling water, skin them and let them dry. Toast the hazelnuts lightly in the oven, then rub off their skins. Mix both with the cocoa powder, the cinnamon, and the flour. Cut the candied orange peel, pumpkin or melon, and citron peel into strips and mix in with the nuts.

Melt the sugar and honey in a saucepan over a low heat, stirring. Continue stirring constantly, until taking a little of the mixture, with wet fingers, and dipping your fingers in cold water, you will get a rather consistent ball. At this point, pour all the prepared nuts and fruits into the saucepan. Stir to combine everything.

Butter the sides of an 8 inch spring form pan. Line the circle, the sides, and edges with the rice paper. Pour the nut and fruit mixture in, and level it with the blade of a knife. It must be about ½ inch high.

Bake in a preheated oven with a very light heat so that the panforte does not brown. After half an hour, remove from the oven, let the cake cool, and then unclasp the ring around the cake. Sprinkle with powdered sugar mixed with a lot of ground cinnamon.

ADA SAYS: *You can also finish with a little pepper or spice.*

PERE AL MARASCHINO

Pears in Maraschino

10 pears
3½ tbsp butter
5 tbsp sugar
Maraschino liqueur
Handful raisins
½ cup all-purpose flour
1 egg

Wash and peel the pears and cut them into wedges, removing the seeds. Grease the bottom of an ovenproof pan with a diameter of about 6 inches and arrange the pear wedges around in a circle. Sprinkle over 4 spoons of sugar and a couple of spoons of water, 2 small glasses of maraschino liqueur and some raisins soaked for about 10 minutes in warm water. Mix everything and wait for the sugar to melt.

Put the flour, a spoon of sugar, one tablespoon of butter and a spoon of water on the kitchen table, and mix everything together, then let it rest for about 10 minutes. Roll out this dough into a rather thick disk so that you can cover the pan. Wet the inner edge of the pan with a little beaten egg. Lay out the disk of dough over the pan and press gently with your fingers so that the dough sticks well to the edge. Trim the dough, brush the pastry with beaten egg, and then place in a larger pan containing a finger of cold water. Bake in a preheated oven of moderate heat for about half an hour, until the pastry is well coloured. Let it cool a little, then place the pan on a serving dish and bring it to the table.

ADA SAYS: *Spadona are a typical variety of pears from Central Italy which work well here. Some subtitutes: Comice or Conference pears.*

PERE MARGHERITA

Margherita Pears

6 medium-size pears
Sugar
Vanilla
3½ oz sponge cake
Pastry cream *(p752)*
Rum

Zabaglione:
1 egg, 1 tbsp sugar, 2 tbsp Marsala

Wash and peel the pears and use a peeler or small knife to core them from underneath, removing the core and seeds. Cook the pears in a light vanilla syrup, made with water, a little sugar and a touch of vanilla. When they are cooked, remove them from the syrup and fill the inside with a thick pastry cream and half a glass of rum.

Cut out 2 inch disks of sponge cake, about ½ inches thick. Make as many as there are pears, set them on a serving dish and sprinkle them lightly with more rum. On each sponge place a pear. Whip up a zabaglione *(p754)* using the ingredient amounts listed here and cover everything.

PESCHE ALLA CREMA

Peaches with Maraschino Cream

6 soft peaches
Vanilla bean, split
Maraschino liqueur
1 cup single cream
Powdered sugar

Sugar syrup:
2 cups sugar, 3 cups water

Dip the peaches for a moment in boiling water so it is easier to peel the skin. Prepare a sugar syrup *(p736)* using the ingredient amounts listed here, perfume it with vanilla and let it boil. As soon as it boils, remove from the heat and dip the peaches in to the syrup, so they are submerged in a single layer. Cover, let the syrup cool and then put everything in the fridge.

Add a small glass of maraschino to the cream and chill in the fridge. At the time of serving, pull up the peaches without spoiling them, drain them and arrange them in a crystal bowl that you might place in a larger bowl containing crushed ice. Add a little maraschino cream to the peaches, then sprinkle them with plenty of powdered sugar. Send the remaining cream to the table in a gravy boat.

PESCHE ALLA IMPERATRICE

Empress Peaches

½ cup pudding rice
3 cups milk
Salt
5 tbsp sugar
2 egg yolks
Vanilla extract
3 big peaches
2 tbsp currant or raspberry jelly
Optional: shelled pistachios

Simmer the rice with 2 cups of milk. When the rice has cooked, season it, off the heat and still in the same saucepan, with a pinch of salt and 3 tablespoons of sugar. Arrange the finished rice in a crystal bowl, level it with the blade of a knife and put it in the fridge.

In the meantime, prepare a cream in the following way: Put the egg yolks in a pan and beat them with 2 full spoonfuls of sugar. Dilute the eggs and sugar with a small glass of milk, put the saucepan on the stove and, always stirring, let the cream thicken a little, but do not let it boil, or it will separate. Then flavor this cream with vanilla—a bean or a drop of extract. Add the cream to the rice, mixing it with a fork.

Now, take 3 large peaches, wash them, peel them, open them in 2, remove the stone and let them cook just barely in a syrup made with one part sugar to 4 parts water and a few drops of vanilla extract. When the peaches are well syruped, remove them, let them cool and arrange them on the rice, putting everything back in the fridge. Boil the syrup left over from cooking the peaches, and when it is very thick, add a couple of spoons of currant or raspberry jelly. Stir. Keep the sauce in the fridge too and when it is time to serve, pour over the peaches and rice and garnish, if you like, with chopped pistachios.

PESCHE ALLA PIEMONTESE

Piedmontese Peaches

7 medium-size peaches
2 tbsp sugar
2 tbsp butter
5 amaretti *(p848)*
1 egg yolk
Butter for greasing

Rinse the peaches, dry them, split them in 2 without peeling them, and remove the stones. Dice one peach completely, but with the others just dig out some flesh from inside, put the flesh a bowl and mash. If the peaches are tender, just mash with a fork; if they are hard, chop them on the cutting board.

Add the sugar, butter, crushed amaretti cookies and egg yolk. Stir, and then fill the 6 peaches with this mixture, giving them a nice shape with the blade of a knife. Butter a pan in which the peaches can stand in a single layer, and place the pan in a preheated oven of moderate heat for about an hour. Serve hot or cold.

PESCHE ALLO ZABAIONE

Peaches Zabaglione

6 peaches
Sugar
Peach liqueur
12 candied cherries

Sponge cake:
¼ cup all-purpose flour, 2 tbsp sugar, 1 egg, vanilla

Zabaglione:
1 egg yolk, 2 tbsp Marsala, 1 tbsp sugar

Make a sponge cake *(p810)* with the flour, sugar and egg or use store-bought.

Wash, dry, and split the peaches in 2, remove the stones, peel them and put them in a hot syrup made with a little water, sugar and a little liqueur. Keep them on a very low heat for some time without letting them fall apart.

From the sponge cake, cut round platforms for each peach half about a finger high. Place them in a crown shape on a crystal plate. Drizzle over a teaspoon of the syrup from the peaches and place on each a half peach. Inside each peach place a candied cherry.

Be ready to whip up the zabaglione *(p754)* with the egg yolk, Marsala and sugar. Pour a little zabaglione on each half peach and bring to the table immediately.

PESCHE IN BORDURA DI PASTA DOLCE

Peaches in Sweet Pastry

1 lb 2 oz yellow peaches
2 tbsp honey
9 tbsp butter, plus extra for greasing
Salt
1 lemon
2 eggs
1 cup all-purpose flour
Milk
1 tsp baking soda
3½ oz dark chocolate

Rinse the peaches, skin them and remove the stone. Cut into quarters and line them up in a pan. Add a spoon of honey, about half a glass of water, and simmer them on the heat.

Meanwhile, prepare the pastry: Put the butter in a bowl and work it with a wooden spoon to reduce it to a well-whipped cream. Then add a spoon of honey, salt, grated lemon peel, and the egg yolks. Continue to mix and add the flour by spoonfuls, diluting with half a glass of milk. Finally, add the 2 egg whites whipped to a snow and the baking soda. Put it in a buttered, bordered mold of one quart and immediately place in a preheated oven of moderate heat, for about half an hour. Then, take the cake out of the oven, turn it upside down on a plate and in the center arrange the peaches.

Cover everything with this chocolate sauce: Grate the chocolate into pieces and place in a small heatproof bowl. Wet it with a few spoonfuls of milk and then set over a saucepan filled with an inch of water. Melt the chocolate over a low heat, stirring over the bain-marie with a spoon or whisking until it has completely melted. Then pour over the peaches and serve.

TORRONE

Nougat

¾ cup honey
2 egg whites
1 cup sugar
3¼ cups blanched almonds
1½ cups blanched hazelnuts
Candied orange or citron
Lemon
Edible rice paper (communion wafers)

Put the honey in a rather large saucepan, placing this in another larger pan of boiling water over a moderate heat. Stir with a wooden spoon. This is the most boring operation, since cooking in a bain-marie is slow, about an hour and a half.

After the honey has cooked for an hour, whip the egg whites up to a firm snow. Test the density of the honey, which should be close to caramelizing, then add the whipped egg whites, a little at a time, always stirring. The mass will swell and become white and foamy.

Cook the sugar, just moistened with water, which, when cooked over direct heat and not in a bain-marie like the honey, is much quicker. When the sugar has caramelized as well, pour it slowly, while stirring constantly, into the saucepan with the honey and egg whites. It is advisable, when the honey is almost finished cooking, to start caramelizing the sugar so it can be added to the honey right after stirring in the egg whites. Never tire of mixing; and since the whites necessarily dilute the mixture, continue cooking for a little longer. You will see that the white mass shrinks and hardens. Try rolling a little of the mixture in cold water between your fingers. When it is very hard, without however having reached caramelization, mix in the skinned almonds and the hazelnuts, a tablespoon of candied fruit in pieces and the zest of a lemon. Stir quickly because the mass tends to harden. Make sure that the almonds and hazelnuts are distributed well.

The nougat is cooked: You will notice it from the scent that rises from the pan. Put some edible paper on the kitchen table, and pour the nougat over it, trying to get a rectangular shape, using a wide blade of the knife. You will need to get a rectangle about 8 inches by 6, and a couple of fingers high. Lay some more wafers on top and press the nougat with a light weight. Leave it like this for a quarter of an hour and then cut the nougat into long pieces, which you will wrap in parchment paper to preserve them better.

ADA SAYS: *It is always preferable to cook honey in a water bath; the work is longer, but the result is far superior.*

TORRONE TENERO AL CIOCCOLATO

Soft Chocolate Nougat

Nougat *(p774)*
¾ cup honey
3¾ cups hazelnuts
6½ oz dark chocolate
1½ cups sugar
2 egg whites
Edible rice paper, communion wafers

First, make your nougat. While the honey is coming up to caramelization, put the hazelnuts in the oven to toast and then rub off the skins. Put the dark chocolate in a small saucepan over a very low heat, melting it with half a glass of sugar syrup, made with 3 tablespoons of sugar to 2 tablespoons of water, and work it with a spoon to have it smooth and the density of a cream. If it is too thick, add a few more drops of water.

After adding the sugar to the honey and egg whites, add the warm chocolate and nuts. Stir to mix everything well, and remove from the heat. The nougat is ready. Finish on the kitchen table with the rice paper and leave for 15 minutes under a weight before cutting.

TORTA ALLO ZIBIBBO

Grape Cake

FOR 6 TO 8 PEOPLE

1⅔ cups all-purpose flour
1 tbsp baking powder
Salt
8½ tbsp butter, plus extra for greasing
½ cup sugar
4 eggs
⅔ cup golden raisins
4¼ oz grape jelly
2 oz candied citron
2 to 3 tbsp beer

First, sift the flour with the baking powder and a pinch of salt. Then in a bowl, work the butter with the sugar first, then the eggs, adding them one at a time alternating with spoonfuls of flour. When all are well blended, add the raisins, grape jelly, and candied peel, mix carefully, and pour in the beer, adjusting the quantity according to the density of the dough, which must be compact but not hard. Mix carefully and work the preparation for a few more minutes.

Butter a smooth baking pan, line it with parchment paper, and pour in the mixture. Put the pan in a preheated oven of moderate heat and bake for about an hour, taking care to reduce the heat again after the first half hour.

ADA SAYS: *This cake is simple to make and does not require too much time or special care. It can be used at the end of lunch and for picnics and snacks for children. The best grape jelly to use is Muscat, known as zibibbo in Sicily, which is an ancient grape reportedly enjoyed by Cleopatra.*

TORTA DI MIRTILLI

Blueberry Cake

7 eggs
1 cup sugar
1 lb blueberries, fresh or frozen
10½ oz ladyfingers
Butter for greasing
Vanilla extract
½ cup whipped cream, slightly sweetened

Break the eggs, and separate the whites from the yolks. Beat the yolks with the sugar until they become very frothy. Wash the blueberries and add them to the beaten eggs, and fold with the crushed ladyfingers. Add a few drops of vanilla. Mix everything with great care because this is one of the secrets of the success of the preparation. You need a well-buttered, round-shaped pan to pour everything in.

Whip the egg whites until stiff, but not very firm, and spoon them on to the dough. Bake in a preheated oven at moderate heat for about 40 minutes. Then let it cool and decorate with splashes of sweetened whipped cream.

EGG DESSERTS

ARISTOCRATICO DI UOVA ALLA NEVE

Aristocrat Meringue

4 eggs
4 tbsp powdered sugar
Vanilla
¾ cup sugar
¾ cup milk
Light cream

Separate the egg whites and yolks. Whip the whites to a snow, and then, mixing gently, sprinkle in the powdered sugar, scented with a touch of vanilla.

Grease a smooth or large fluted one-quart pudding mold. Sprinkle with powdered sugar. Pour in the egg whites. Tap the mold lightly so that they cover the base and level the surface with the blade of a knife. Cook in a bain-marie for about 20 minutes, until the whites are firm.

Put the egg yolks in another non-stick pan, and add the sugar. Mix the eggs and sugar together and then dissolve in a glass of boiling milk, which you add in small quantities, always stirring. Set the saucepan over the heat and continuously working the cream with a wooden spoon, let it thicken a little, but make sure that it does not boil because that would make it separate.

Take the egg whites out of the bain-marie and let them rest for 5 minutes. Lift out and dress with a little cream, sending the rest of the cream to the table in a gravy boat.

CREMA A BAGNOMARIA

Cream Bain-Marie

2 eggs
4 egg yolks
½ cup sugar
2 cups milk
Lemon zest or vanilla extract
Butter for greasing

Break the whole eggs and 4 yolks into a bowl. Beat them with the sugar and dilute with the warm milk, flavored with the zest of lemon or a few drops of vanilla. Pour the milk over the eggs, one spoonful at a time, stirring with a wooden spoon or whisk. Sieve the cream, carefully remove the foam that has formed, and pour the mixture into a smooth, greased mold with a capacity of one quart. Put the mold in a larger bowl full of very hot water—the water must reach a couple of fingers from the rim—and cook on the stove, or rather in an already hot oven of moderate heat. The water, while remaining very hot, should never boil. The cream should cook for about an hour.

When you see that it has set, remove it from the bain-marie, let it rest for about 10 minutes, and then turn it out into a serving dish. The cream can be served lukewarm, but it is preferable cold.

CREMA AL CARAMELLO

Crème Caramel

2 eggs
4 egg yolks
½ cup sugar
2 cups milk
4 tbsp powdered sugar
Vanilla bean or zest of lemon

Make a bain-marie cream *(p776)* with your eggs, sugar, and warm milk and sieve.

Put the powdered sugar in another saucepan, moisten with a little water so that it remains just dripping, and let it cook. As soon as you see the sugar take on a dark blond, caramel color, remove it from the heat and pour it into a mold. Turn the mold quickly so that the sugar can veil the bottom and the sides. Wait for it to cool.

Now pour the cream mixture into the mold and put it in a larger pan full of very hot water—the water must reach a couple of fingers from the edge—and cook in the oven. The cream should cook for about an hour.

When you see that the cream has set, remove it from the bain-marie, let it cool, and put it in the fridge. Crème caramel should be eaten cold. When it is time to bring it to the table, take it out of the mold by inverting onto a serving plate.

ADA SAYS: *While the water in a bain-marie remains very hot, it should never boil; if necessary you can put a few ice cubes in the water to cool it down.*

CREMA BAVARESE

Crème Bavaroise

2 cups milk
Vanilla bean
1 cup sugar
5 egg yolks
2 gelatin sheets

Put the milk in a small saucepan on the stove with a vanilla bean—split lengthways—and bring the milk gently to a boil.

In another saucepan, put the sugar and egg yolks; stir a little with a wooden spoon and then gradually pour the boiling milk into the saucepan, stirring constantly to dissolve the eggs and sugar well. Set the saucepan back over the heat and, without ever stopping stirring, let the mixture start to simmer gently, but be careful not to let it boil, or the eggs separate.

As soon as you see that the cream veils the back of the spoon a little, remove the saucepan from the heat, and add the gelatin sheets—kept in fresh water for 15 minutes and then squeezed in your hands. Stir with a spoon to mix them well and then pour the cream into a bowl to cool, not forgetting to mix it again, from time to time, so as not to have a film on the surface.

CRÊPES ALLA CREMA

Cream Crêpes

MAKES 24

1⅓ cups all-purpose flour
2 whole eggs
1 egg yolk
Salt
Sugar
2 cups milk
Cognac
Butter
Candied citron

Pastry cream:
½ cup sugar, 3 egg yolks, ½ cup all-purpose flour, 2 cups milk, lemon zest

Place the flour in a bowl in a heap, and place the 2 whole eggs and the extra yolk, a pinch of salt, and a pinch of sugar in the middle. With a wooden spoon, mix the eggs with the flour, slowly blending them with the cold milk, which you add little by little. When the mixture is well incorporated, smooth, and without lumps, top it with a spoonful of cognac and let it rest for at least half an hour.

Take a frying pan of 7 inches in diameter, heat it on the stove and then, with a brush lightly dipped in a little melted butter, lightly grease the bottom. Then pour a spoon of the prepared mixture into the pan, in a quantity that, by shaking the pan in all directions, the mixture can just cover the bottom. Let the crêpe brown, shaking the pan from time to time, and, as soon as the underside is colored, turn it over. As soon as it is also colored on the other side, remove it, and with the same system make all the other crêpes promptly.

Prepare a pastry cream *(p752)* in a bain-marie with the sugar, egg yolks, flour, warm milk, and a zest of lemon. When all the crêpes are ready, put a spoonful of the cream on each, then fold them in 2 and arrange them in a fan shape on a round dish that can go in the oven. Sprinkle with sugar, and a few moments before serving, cook them in a preheated oven of moderate heat to melt the sugar. Decorate with the candied citron cut into very thin strips and serve immediately.

CRÊPES ALLE FRAGOLE

Strawberry Crêpes

Crêpes
Strawberry jam
Cognac
Powdered sugar
Strawberries
Lemon

Make the crêpes as above, then spread a spoonful of strawberry jam on each, previously melted with a little cognac. Fold over and arrange in an ovenproof dish and sprinkle with powdered sugar. A few moments before serving, heat them in a preheated oven over moderate heat to melt the sugar. Then decorate with the strawberries washed in water and lemon juice.

CRÊPES SUZETTE

Crêpes Suzette

Crêpes
7 tbsp butter
½ cup sugar
Curaçao
Powdered sugar
Orange

Prepare the crêpes as above and keep them on a plate to stay warm.

Put the butter in a bowl and whip it with a wooden spoon and, when it is soft, add an equal amount of sugar, stirring constantly. Complete this buttercream with a glass of curaçao and powdered sugar flavored with a squeeze of orange. Spread the crêpes with this mixture, fold them in four, sugar them again, and send them immediately to the table.

FRITTATA DELL'IMPERATORE (KAISERSCHMARRN)

Emperor's Frittata

4 eggs
Salt
5 tbsp sugar
1 lemon
Butter
1 tbsp candied orange or fruits in syrup
2 egg whites
Apricot jam

Break the eggs into a bowl, season with salt, a spoon of sugar, and the zest of a lemon, and whisk everything together. Put a knob of butter in a pan and when the butter is hot, pour in the eggs. As soon as the omelet is firm on both sides, take it off the heat and add a teaspoon of candied orange peel, or fruit kept in syrup, perhaps whole cherries, sour cherries, peaches, or apricots, all cut into cubes.

Put the pan back on the heat, fold the omelet in such a way as to give it an elongated shape and, without overcooking it, turn it over into a lightly buttered oval oven dish.

Whip the 2 egg whites to a firm snow; then sieve 3 full spoons of powdered sugar over them slowly, stirring lightly with a wooden spoon. Spread the omelet with a little apricot jam and cover it with a little of the egg whites.

Put the remaining egg whites in a pastry bag with a smooth round nozzle of quarter of an inch in diameter, and pipe over the omelet. Then sieve another spoonful of powdered sugar over the omelet. Cook in a preheated oven of very light heat for about 10 minutes, until the meringue has dried and has taken on a slightly pale gold tint.

FRITTATA DOLCE

Sweet Frittata

4 eggs
¼ cup sugar
Lemon zest or vanilla pod
Salt
All-purpose flour
2 tbsp butter
4 tbsp jam
Powdered sugar

Separate the whites from the egg yolks and put them in 2 bowls. To the yolks add the sugar and whip them with a spoon; then add the zest of half a lemon or the seeds from a vanilla pod, a trifle of salt and sieve over the flour like rain.

Whip the egg whites to a firm snow and add them, a little at a time, stirring gently. Melt the butter in a round baking pan of about 10 inches in diameter. As soon as the butter is hot, remove the pan from the heat, pour in the egg mixture, and put it in a preheated oven of moderate heat. After a quarter of an hour, the omelet must be firm and well swollen. Spread it quickly with jam, fold it in 2, enclosing the jam inside, then slide it on to an oval dish and sugar it abundantly with powdered sugar. It should be served immediately.

MERINGHE

Meringue

MAKES 12

2 egg whites
½ cup sugar
Butter
All-purpose flour
1¾ cups whipped cream

Put the egg whites in a saucepan and beat them with a whisk, with a rhythmic and rather energetic motion, until they become very stiff. Do not get tired of whipping the whites, because success depends on this. You can use an electric mixer.

When the whites are whipped, drop 2 not-very-full spoonfuls of sugar for each egg white – 1½ oz per egg – into the bowl, and mix very lightly with a wooden spoon.

Spread a thin layer of butter on a baking tray and let a little flour fall over it from a sieve. Tap to remove the superfluous flour and then, with a soft brush, lightly take away some of the flour, so just a thin layer remains. Put the meringue mixture in a pastry bag with a round nozzle and, pressing on the pocket, let a little out on to the tray, giving it the shape of a rather small egg. To have a good result it is necessary to hold the bag horizontally and rest the nozzle on the plate. In this way, after a few tests, the meringues will have a good shape.

When you have piped all the meringues, sprinkle them well with sugar and then, tilting the tray, gently knock off the superfluous sugar. Leave the meringues to rest for about 10 minutes. When the sugar has melted and the meringues appear slightly shiny, move the plate into a moderate oven. The meringues must not undergo real cooking, but only dry and not color.

After half an hour or more, and when you feel that they are dry and you can see that they have taken on a slightly blond tint, remove them from the oven. Take them off the tray with the blade of a flexible knife, turn them over and put them back in the lukewarm oven with the heat turned off.

To serve, spread a spoonful of whipped cream on the flat part of each one and couple them so you have large eggs filled with cream. They must be filled when you are ready to serve, otherwise they tend to get damp.

ADA SAYS: *The oven should be moderate, which is to say 356°F/325°F - gas 3 or 4.*

MOUSSELINE MIMÌ

Mousseline Mimì

6 egg whites
3 cups powdered sugar
Optional: Crème anglaise (1 egg yolk, 1 tbsp sugar, 1 tsp potato starch, ¾ cup milk, vanilla)

Put the egg whites in a bowl, whisk them to a firm snow, and then add 3 quarters of the powdered sugar, stirring gently with a wooden spoon.

Put the remaining sugar in a small pan; moisten with a spoonful of water and caramelize it until it is a dark blond colour.

Lightly heat a pudding mold with a capacity of about one quart. Pour the caramelized sugar in, and turn the mold in all directions to make sure the sugar covers the entire inside. Leave to cool.

Then pour in the egg whites and sugar, noting that it reaches just 2 thirds up the sides. Lightly tap the mold on the table so everything is covered and bake in a bain-marie. The water must be very hot, but never enough to declare a boil. Cook until the meringue is firm. Then remove from the oven and let it cool.

Only then do you turn out the soft pudding, on which the caramelized sugar will form a tasty sauce.

❖ **ADA SAYS:** *You can also accompany this dessert with crème anglaise (p752) made like this: Beat the egg yolk with the sugar and potato starch in a saucepan, dissolve with the milk, and let everything set over a very light heat, stirring constantly with a wooden spoon. Then flavor this cream with a little vanilla, and, when it is cold, serve it separately in a gravy boat.*

OMELETTE ALLA MARMELLATA

Jam Omelet

FOR 6 PEOPLE

9 eggs
Salt
1 lemon
10½ tbsp butter
Apricot jam
Rum

Beat the eggs in a bowl with a little salt and a little grated lemon peel. Put the butter on the stove in a pan and when it melts pour in the eggs. As soon as the omelet is somewhat firm on both sides, promptly put the apricot jam in the middle. Fold the omelet, leave it to finish cooking, and then pour it on to a metal serving plate. Pour 3 small glasses of rum over the omelet and set the liqueur on fire.

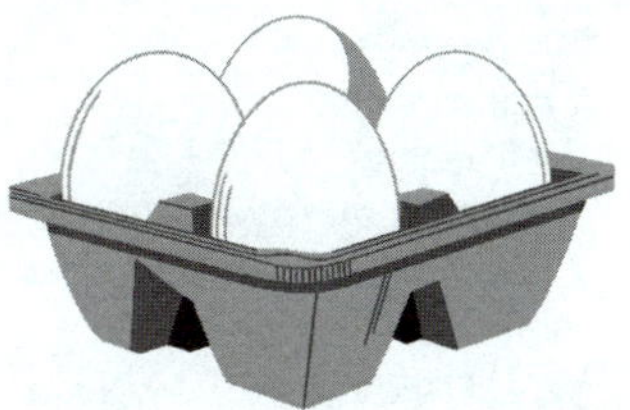

OMELETTE AL RUM

Rum Omelet

5 eggs
5 tbsp sugar
5 tbsp rum
Butter
Powdered sugar

Divide the whites and yolks into separate bowls. Add the sugar to the yolks and work them until they are well whipped. Then whip the whites to a snow and fold into the yolks along with the rum. Mix gently to combine everything.

Grease an oval oven dish, sprinkle with powdered sugar, and spoon in the prepared mixture, giving it a rounded oval shape. Smooth the mixture with the blade of a knife, and with the tip of the knife make a small cavity in the middle, which, by decreasing the thickness a little, facilitates the cooking. Bake in a preheated oven of moderate heat for 25 to 30 minutes.

Five minutes before removing the omelet from the oven, sprinkle it with powdered sugar, which when melted, will cover the omelet with a light caramelized layer. Pour some more rum into the center of the omelet and, after setting it on fire, have it brought to the table immediately.

PUDDING RÊVE

Zabaglione Pudding

8 eggs
2 egg yolks
1¼ cups sugar
9 tbsp butter
½ cup all-purpose flour
Vanilla extract
Butter for greasing

Zabaglione:
2 egg yolks, white wine, cognac, 3 tbsp sugar

Whip the 8 egg yolks in a bowl with ¾ cup of the sugar. Add the melted butter, just warm and not hot, because otherwise it would spoil the whipped eggs. Stir to mix with the eggs and fold the sifted flour on to the mixture. Whip the whites to a very firm snow and mix them with great delicacy, finishing with a touch of vanilla.

Abundantly butter a smooth pudding tray, with a hole in the middle and a couple of quarts capacity. Fold in the mixture of eggs, butter and flour, bearing in mind that it should not reach more than two-thirds high. Cook in a bain-marie for a good half hour.

When the pudding has set, remove it from the water bath, let it rest for 5 minutes and then turn it out. Separately, serve a zabaglione *(p754)* using the ingredient amounts listed here.

TORTA BIANCA

White Cake

10 egg whites
1 cup sugar
Vanilla extract
1½ cups potato starch
7 tbsp butter, plus extra for greasing
Vanilla sugar
Optional: fruit jam

Put 4 egg whites in a bowl, with the sugar and a little vanilla, and beat vigorously and with a rhythmic motion with a whisk or electric mixer. Work the mixture until you have obtained a soft and swollen mass.

Whip the other 6 egg whites in another bowl without adding any sugar, and beat them until they are well supported. If using the same whisk, wash it well between operations. When the 6 whites are worked to the point, add them to the bowl with the first batch with the sugar, and mix with a large metal spoon with great

delicacy. Then add the potato starch, which you will rain down from a sieve, always mixing lightly with a spoon; lastly the butter, which you have melted in a pan at very low heat.

When the butter has also been absorbed, grease a pan with a diameter of about 8 inches, sprinkle it with sugar and pour in the prepared mixture. Bake in a moderate heat oven for about 3 quarters of an hour.

When it has colored, touch it in the center with a finger and feel if it is firm, then remove it from the oven, turn it out of the mold and let it cool. When the cake is cold, place it on a plate and sprinkle with vanilla sugar.

ADA SAYS: *You can fill the cake with a fruit jam of your taste.*

TORTA DI MANDORLE

Almond Cake

3¾ cups almonds
1 cup sugar
2⅓ cups all-purpose flour
Lemon zest
6 eggs
Butter for greasing
3 cloves
Ground cinnamon

This almond cake is simple to make, healthy, appetizing, and tasty. It can be used at the end of lunch and for picnics: it will be well received by adults and children alike.

Put the almonds in a bowl filled with boiling water for a few minutes, then peel them and place them for 5 minutes to dry on a baking sheet, in a preheated oven at very moderate heat.

Take them out and blend half of them with half the sugar to obtain a fine and soft dough.

Put the flour in the middle of the kitchen table and add the blended almonds, the grated zest of a lemon, and 5 egg whites; knead the dough until it is fairly firm. Divide in half. Roll out with a rolling pin so you have 2 disks of dough the diameter of the pan. Grease the pan and place a first disk on the bottom.

Blend the remaining almonds and sugar, a whole egg and the 5 yolks, cloves and a pinch of cinnamon. Arrange this cream in the pan, level it with a well-moistened knife, and cover it with the other disk of dough. Bake in a preheated oven of moderate heat for about 40 minutes.

ADA SAYS: *During the last 10 minutes it is advisable to cover the surface of the cake with a sheet of aluminum foil so as not to let it brown too much.*

PASTRY DESSERTS

Pastry Doughs

PASTA FROLLA

Sweet Shortcrust Pastry

⅔ cup all-purpose flour
¼ cup sugar
3½ tbsp butter
1 egg yolk
Lemon zest
Salt

Put the sifted flour on the kitchen table and, in the middle, pour in the sugar, the butter in pieces, the egg yolk, the grated lemon zest, and a pinch of salt. Knead everything quickly without adding even the smallest amount of water, as the dough mixes very well. Collect it in a ball, leave it to rest for about half an hour in the fridge, covered with plastic wrap, and then it is ready. The proportions must be maintained between the various elements.

ADA SAYS: *Shortcrust requires little time for its preparation and can give rise to some tasty recipes.*

PASTA FROLLA ALLA ROMANA

Roman Short Pastry

1⅓ cups all-purpose flour
½ cup sugar
3½ oz lard, or half lard and half butter
1 egg
Lemon zest or ground cinnamon

Make a well with the sifted flour and put in the middle the sugar, the lard or, if you do not like the fatty taste of the lard, half lard and half butter, the whole egg and the lemon zest or a pinch of ground cinnamon. Knead without adding water, collect the dough in a ball, and let it rest for about half an hour in the fridge covered with a towel.

PASTA FROLLA SENZA UOVA

Short Pastry Without Eggs

11 tbsp butter
⅓ cup sugar
¾ cup all-purpose flour
1 cup potato starch
Lemon zest

First mix the butter with the sugar and a little grated lemon zest using your hands and a wide blade of a knife. Then blend the plain flour and the potato starch and work it. In the beginning, especially in winter, it will seem to crumble; but slowly, continuing to carefully combine the various ingredients, you will get a perfect dough. Make it into a ball and let it rest for about half an hour in the fridge covered with cling film.

ADA SAYS: *You can use this egg-free shortcrust pastry for all uses of the common shortcrust pastry. It is a very useful recipe.*

PASTA RAPIDA NON LIEVITATA

Non-Leavened Quick Pastry

3 eggs
3 tbsp sugar
3 tbsp all-purpose flour
Butter for greasing

In some preparations it is not necessary for the dough to rise and rest. It can be used straight away. Among the main preparations are cookies and strudel.

Put the egg yolks in a bowl with the sugar and work the mixture until it is well whipped and appears light and fluffy. Then sift over the flour and, finally, gently add 3 egg whites, whipped to a snow.

Grease a sheet of parchment paper cut into a square of about 10 inches and spread the mixture over in a regular layer. Place the sheet on the hot plate of the oven and cook on a high heat. After a few minutes the pastry will be cooked, then turn it over on the kitchen table, remove the parchment paper and let it cool.

ADA SAYS: *Without fear of denial, we can say that quick, unleavened dough is the easiest pastry to make.*

Pastry Desserts

CAKE ALLA FRUTTA

Fruit Cake

1¼ oz dried zibibbo or other dried grapes
1¼ oz dried figs
1¼ oz dates, pitted
¼ cup almonds
1¼ oz candied citron
1¼ oz candied orange peel
Rum
10 tbsp butter, plus extra for greasing
2 eggs
⅓ cup sugar
1 cup all-purpose flour
Butter for greasing

Deseed the grapes and chop with the dried figs, dates, almonds, peeled the usual way, the citron peel and orange peel, and collect everything in a bowl. Pour a small glass of rum over the fruit, cover and leave to macerate for 2 or 3 hours, preferably longer.

Put the butter in a bowl, in winter it will be better to soften it a little, and whisk it for a long time with a wooden spoon until it becomes creamy. Then, still working, add the egg yolks, putting one in at a time, and after the egg yolks the sugar. Continue to work a little more until you have a well-assembled mixture. Aside, now beat the egg whites and mount them to a firm snow. Mixing gently, add the whites to the whipped butter, then add the fruit mixture, and finally sieve over the flour, slowly dropping it like rain, always mixing with great delicacy.

Abbundantly butter a cake pan, with a capacity of about one and a half quarts, pour the mixture in, beat on the table a little so it spreads regularly and level it with the blade of a knife. However, take care not to overfill the pan, but leave the dough a little below the edges. Cook the cake in a preheated oven of moderate heat, leaving it to bake for an abundant hour, until dipping a large needle into the cake, the needle will come out completely clean and dry.

CICERCHIATA

Cicerchiata

2 eggs
3 tbsp sugar
Olive oil
1⅓ cups all-purpose flour
Honey
Almonds
Sugar
Ground cinnamon

Mix the eggs, sugar, and 4 tablespoons of oil with as much flour as it will take to have a soft dough. Once the dough is made, take a little at a time and shape into small balls, the size of a chickpea. Fry them in plenty of oil, making them take on a light golden color.

Warm the honey in a saucepan until it caramelizes. Check it is ready by dropping a few drops into a bowl with water, it must harden immediately. At this point, add the pieces of fried dough to the saucepan and mix everything gently with a wooden spoon.

Transfer to a wet plate, and with your hands also wet with water, give the cake the shape of a large donut, which you will garnish with toasted almond slices, sugar, and ground cinnamon.

ADA SAYS: *These are traditionally served at Christmas.*

CROSTATA ALLA FRUTTA FRESCA

Fresh Fruit Tart

Butter for greasing
Pastry cream *(p752)*
Flour
¾ cup dried beans
7 oz blueberries
7 oz strawberries
7 oz cherries
4 plums
2 citron or limes
7 oz kumquats
Optional: apricot jam or jelly

Shortcrust pastry:
1⅓ cups all-purpose flour, 7 tbsp butter, 2 egg yolks, ½ cup sugar, lemon, salt

Make your shortcrust pastry *(p784)* using the ingredients listed here, and chill in the fridge. In the meantime, make a pastry cream. Set it aside and wait for it to cool, stirring it from time to time.

Roll out the shortcrust pastry on a lightly floured surface. Lightly grease and flour a 12 inch cake pan with low edges. Roll out the shortcrust pastry and fit it in the pan. Prick the dough with a fork; cover it with a sheet of parchment paper, and put the dried beans on top so that the dough does not rise while cooking. Put the pan in a preheated oven of moderate heat and bake for about half an hour.

Remove from the oven, let it cool, remove the beans and the sheet of parchment paper and turn it out on to a suitably sized dessert plate.

Start the decoration now: Spread the tart with a layer of pastry cream. Wash and dry the fruit, cut the plums and citron or limes into slices and decorate the tart as you like. The tart can be enriched with all those fruit varieties that the season offers.

ADA SAYS: *To give more shine to the fruit, brush it with a veil of apricot jam dissolved in warm water and passed through a sieve or with jelly.*

CROSTATA DI CONFETTURA

Jam Tart

SERVES 12

Flour for dusting
Butter for greasing
Sour cherry or other jam
1 egg

Shortcrust pastry:
3 egg yolks, 2 cups all-purpose flour ¾ cup sugar, 10½ tbsp butter, 1 lemon, salt

Have your shortcrust pastry *(p784)* ready. After resting the pastry in the fridge, take out and divide in half. On a lightly floured surface, roll one part into a disk. Butter and flour a very low baking pan of about 12 inches in diameter. Lay in the first disk. Open a jar of jam of any kind of fruit, sour cherry is commonly used, and pour the jam over, spreading it up to 2 fingers from the edge.

Roll out the rest of the pastry on a floured table and make finger-wide strips, or cylinders, with which you will criss cross the jam. Wash the edge and the netting with a beaten egg and bake in a preheated oven of moderate heat for about half an hour.

CROSTATA DI CREMA

Cream Tart

Shortcrust pastry *(p784)*
Pastry cream *(p752)*
Butter for greasing
1 egg
Powdered sugar

While your shortcrust pastry is resting in the fridge, make up a pastry cream and set aside and wait for it to cool, stirring from time to time to prevent it from forming any skin on the surface.

When the cream is cold, take the shortcrust pastry and cut it into 2 equal parts. Butter and flour a low baking pan of about 12 inches in diameter. Roll out and lay in one piece of dough as a base.

Pour the cream on to the pastry, spreading it with the blade of a knife up to 2 fingers from the edge. Take the rest of the dough you have set aside and roll it out on the floured table. Using a wheeled pastry cutter, make finger-wide ribbons, which you place like a grid on the cream. Brush the surface with a beaten egg. Bake in a moderate heat oven for about half an hour; then finally sprinkle it with powdered sugar.

CROSTATA DI FRAGOLA

Strawberry Tart

Shortcrust pastry *(p784)*
¾ cup dried beans
Strawberry jam
7 oz strawberries
10½ oz wild strawberries
Lemon juice
2 kiwi fruit
Fruit jelly

Carefully grease and flour a 10 inch diameter cake pan. Take the pastry out of the fridge and with a rolling pin, roll out on the floured table and cover the bottom of the pan with it. Prick the dough all over with a fork; cover it with a sheet of parchment paper, and put some dried beans on top so that it does not rise while cooking. Place the pan in the preheated oven and let it cook for about half an hour at moderate heat.

Remove from the oven, take out the dried beans and the parchment paper, and let cool. Now proceed to finish the tart: Spread the pastry with a thin layer of strawberry jam; wash the strawberries and wild strawberries in water and lemon juice and let them drain; peel and slice the kiwis. Decorate the tart with this fruit. To give a greater shine to the fruit, brush it with a transparent jelly, either homemade apricot *(p750)* or store bought.

CROSTATA DI RICOTTA

Ricotta Tart

1¼ cups ricotta
4 eggs
¼ cup sugar
Ground cinnamon
3 tbsp candied orange
Butter for greasing
Vanilla sugar

Shortcrust pastry made without eggs:
11 tbsp butter, ⅓ cup sugar, ¾ cup all-purpose flour, 1 cup potato starch

Pastry cream:
¼ cup sugar, 2 egg yolks, ¼ cup all-purpose flour, 1 cup milk, lemon zest

Make your shortcrust pastry *(p784)* using the ingredient amounts listed here and without any eggs and rest it in the fridge. Prepare the pastry cream *(p752)* using the ingredient amounts listed here. Set it aside while waiting for it to cool, stirring it from time to time.

Work the ricotta, 3 egg yolks, sugar, and cinnamon in a bowl with a wooden spoon. When the ricotta has softened, add the cold cream, candied citron and orange peel, cut into small pieces, and 3 egg whites whipped to a firm snow. Blend everything gracefully.

Divide the shortcrust pastry into 2 unequal pieces and roll out the largest piece on a floured table to a thickness of less than ¼ inch with a rolling pin. Lightly butter a pan of 8 inches in diameter, or rather a flan circle of the same diameter, and line it with the dough to form a kind of box. Pour the ricotta mixture into this box, level it with a the blade of a knife, and using the rest of the dough, make strips like ribbons, which you will arrange in a criss-cross over the ricotta. With the blade of a knife, smooth around the tart, wash it with a little beaten egg and put in a preheated oven of moderate heat for a good half hour. When the tart is at the right point, take it out of the mold, arrange it on a plate and sprinkle it abundantly with vanilla sugar.

FLAN AI CANDITI

Candied Flan

Shortcrust pastry *(p784)*
7 oz candied fruit, possibly to include apricots, pears, almonds, citron and orange peel
Rum or cognac
Butter for greasing
Flour for dusting
7 oz sponge cake, homemade *(p810)* or store bought
Liqueur, to taste
Cherry jam
¼ cup raisins
Vanilla
For decoration: citron or candied orange peel, powdered sugar, salt

Almond cream:
⅔ cup peeled almonds, 5½ tbsp butter, 2 egg yolks, ½ cup sugar

Prepare the shortcrust pastry and let it rest in the fridge. Blend the skinned almonds to a flour. Macerate the candied fruit with the cognac or rum for half an hour.

Line a greased and floured cake pan with the prepared dough, pressing slowly with your fingers so that the dough sticks well and forms a box. Run the rolling pin round the edge of the pan, to trim off any excess. Cut the sponge cake into thin slices and with half of them make a layer on the pastry and splash abundantly with a liqueur of your choice. Then cover them with a layer of jam, preferably cherry, and on the jam place half the raisins and the macerated chopped candied fruit.

Cover the candied fruit with the other half of the sponge cake, sprinkling this second layer with more liqueur as well.

Prepare the cream by placing the butter, egg yolks, and sugar in a bowl. Add the blended almond flour. Whip everything with a wooden spoon and when the mixture is smooth and soft, add a little vanilla, the egg whites whipped to a firm snow, the rest of the raisins, and the diced citron or orange peel, mixing so that each element blends perfectly. Cover the flan with half of this cream, smoothing it with a wide knife blade. Bake this delicious cake in a preheated oven of moderate heat for about 40 minutes. When it is cooked, slip it out onto a dessert plate, cover it with the remaining cream, decorate it with the citron peel, candied orange, and raisins. It is preferably eaten cold.

FLAN AL CIOCCOLATO

Chocolate Flan

Shortcrust pastry *(p784)*
Candied flan *(opp. page)*

Chocolate cream:
½ cup sugar, 2 egg yolks, vanilla, ¼ cup all-purpose flour, 3½ oz chocolate, 2 glasses milk, 3½ tbsp butter

Follow the recipe above except the cream filling is different: Prepare the cream by putting the sugar, egg yolks, a little vanilla, flour, and grated chocolate in a saucepan; mix everything with a wooden spoon and dissolve with milk. Put the saucepan on the stove and let the cream thicken well. When it is ready, mix in the butter off the heat. Let it cool and add the egg whites whipped to firm snow to the mixture. Pour into the pan and bake for 40 minutes.

FLAN DI RISO

Rice Flan

Dried beans
Butter for greasing
3 cups milk
¾ cup pudding rice
Salt
⅓ cup sugar
3 tbsp butter
3½ oz candied fruit
2 eggs
Sweet liqueur
Apricot jam

Shortcrust pastry made without eggs:
1 cup all-purpose flour, 5½ tbsp butter, ⅓ cup sugar, vanilla

Make your shortcrust pastry dough *(p784)* using the ingredient amounts listed here and without eggs. Roll out and bake with parchment paper and dried beans for half an hour in a greased cake pan. Let it cool.

To make the filling: Place the milk on the heat, and when it boils, add the rice and a few grains of salt. When the rice is cooked, but not too much, take it off the heat and season with the sugar, butter, chopped candied fruit, egg yolks, and a glass of sweet liqueur. Mix lightly with a fork and finally add, gently, the whites whipped to a snow. Transfer this mixture on to the shortcrust pastry, flatten it with the blade of a knife, and bake the flan again in a very moderate heat oven for about a quarter of an hour.

Then remove from the oven, let it cool completely, then slide the flan on to the serving plate. Spread the apricot jam on the flan and, if you like, decorate it with candied fruit.

GÂTEAU ALL'ARANCIA

Candied Orange Cake

6 oz candied orange peel *(p755)*
Rum
9 tbsp butter
½ cup sugar
3 eggs
Orange
⅔ cup all-purpose flour
⅔ cup potato starch

Macerate the candied orange peel in 2 small glasses of rum for half an hour. Whip the butter with the sugar in a bowl. After having worked the mixture well, add 3 eggs, one at a time. Then add the zest of an orange and the macerated candied orange peel. Then mix in the flour and potato starch.

Pour the mixture into a baking pan with high sides and lined with buttered paper, bake in a preheated oven at high heat and send it to the table without removing the paper.

ADA SAYS: *You can trim the edges of the paper with scissors to make star shapes.*

PASTIERA NAPOLETANA

Neapolitan Easter Pie

MAKES 12

9 oz cooked wheat (*grano cotto*)
2 cups milk
Salt
1 lemon
Sugar
Ground cinnamon
2 cups ricotta
1¾ cups sugar
6 eggs
2 tbsp orange blossom water
3½ oz candied citron peel
3½ oz candied pumpkin
Butter or lard
Powdered sugar

Shortcrust pastry:
2 cups all-purpose flour, 10½ tbsp butter or lard, ¾ cup sugar, 3 egg yolks

Make up a shortcrust pastry *(p784)* using the ingredients listed here without working the ingredients too much; let it rest in the fridge for about half an hour wrapped in plastic wrap.

Put the *grano cotto* in a saucepan and cook for about a quarter of an hour in cold water. Then drain the water and replace it with boiling milk. Add a pinch of salt, thinly sliced lemon peel without any traces of white, a teaspoon of sugar, and a pinch of ground cinnamon. Cover and cook slowly, until the milk is completely absorbed. Then pour the wheat on to a plate, remove the lemon peel, and let it cool.

Put the ricotta in a bowl and work it a little with a wooden spoon; then add the sugar and, one at a time, 6 egg yolks, always stirring. Add a good pinch of cinnamon, the zest of a lemon, the orange flower water, the citron peel, and the candied pumpkin, cut into cubes, and finally the wheat. Stir to mix all these ingredients well and finish the compound by adding the egg whites whipped separately to a firm snow, which you combine very gently.

Take a cake pan of about 10 inches in diameter, not too low, and grease it with a veil of lard or butter. Bring the shortcrust pastry to the table and divide it into 2 significantly unequal pieces with a knife. Flatten the largest piece with the rolling pin, making a disk, and with this disk line the inside of the pan. Trim off the edges with a small knife. Pour the ricotta mixture into the lined pan, smoothing it out slightly with the blade of a knife. With the smaller piece of dough make strips a couple of fingers wide, which you will arrange in a grid on the ricotta mix. Bake the pie in a moderate heat oven for about 3 quarters of an hour, until it has taken on a beautiful golden color. Leave it to cool in the pan, then invert with a plate, so that it remains with the mesh side up, and sugar it abundantly with powdered sugar.

PASTICCIO DI GNOCCHI ALLA CREMA

Gnocchi Cream Pie

MAKES 12

½ cup all-purpose flour
½ cup sugar
2 tsp guar gum powder
2 tsp potato starch
Salt
Ground cinnamon
5 egg yolks
2 cups milk
3½ tbsp butter, plus extra for greasing
1 egg
Powdered sugar

Shortcrust pastry made without eggs:
2 cups all-purpose flour, 10½ tbsp butter, ¾ cup sugar, lemon zest

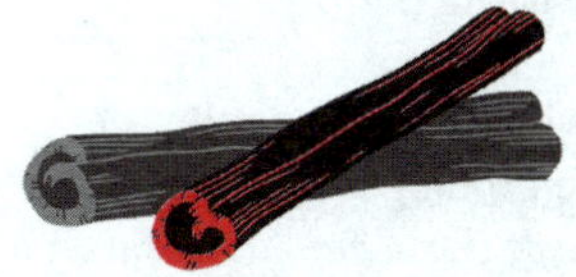

Prepare a shortcrust pastry *(p784)* using the ingredient amounts listed here and without working the ingredients too much; let it rest in the fridge for about half an hour wrapped in plastic wrap.

Put the flour, and an equal amount of sugar with the guar powder and potato starch, a pinch of salt, a strong pinch of ground cinnamon, and egg yolks in a saucepan. Blend everything with the cold milk, preferably using a whisk. Put the saucepan on the stove and, still stirring, let the mixture heat up. When you see that it begins to thicken, add the butter, remove the whisk, and continue to mix quite vigorously with a wooden spoon. Soon the mixture will thicken a lot. Continue to work vigorously with the spoon and when it detaches from the sides of the saucepan, remove the mixture from the heat and pour it out on to a wet kitchen table. Flatten it with a wide wet knife blade, to half an inch thick, and when it has lost most of its heat, level it well, so as to smooth it out evenly. If the mixture has been well executed, as soon as it is cold it will be well set. Then divide it into strips about an inch wide, and cut into small dumplings with oblique cuts at a distance of about an inch from each other.

Divide the shortcrust pastry into 2 unequal pieces so that the smallest is one third of the size. Roll out the smallest piece into a rather thin disk, place it on the lightly greased baking sheet and trim it to 12 inches in diameter with a small knife. Add a layer of dumplings on the dough, leaving around a free edge of a couple of fingers; then make a second, starting a little further back and continue in this way to make increasingly narrow layers, so as to arrange like gnocchi in the shape of a dome.

When you have arranged all the filling, roll out the largest piece of shortcrust pastry, flattening it to a thickness of less than an eighth of an inch, to obtain a disk that can completely cover the pie. Brush the entire edge of the lower disk of dough with beaten egg. Then wrap the larger sheet around the rolling pin and unroll it over the filling. Press with your fingers around the edges so that the 2 disks stick together, and then with the tip of a small knife cut off the superfluous dough giving the pie a nice round shape. Brush the whole dome of the pie with beaten egg. Knead the leftover dough, roll it out again and make, using as a model a coffee saucer, a round disk of about 4 inches that you will apply in the middle of the pie. Model it with your fingertips to give it a regular shape and then engrave it with the handle of a fork, making many small impressions at a distance of about an inch from each other. Brush with beaten egg and bake the finished pie in a preheated oven of moderate heat for about 40 minutes, until the shortcrust pastry has taken on a not too dark golden color. Then remove the pie from the oven, let it cool a little and then slide it carefully on to a large serving dish. Sprinkle it with powdered sugar and eat warm.

ROCCIATA DI ASSISI

Assisi Roll

1⅔ cups all-purpose flour
19 tbsp sugar
Olive oil
Salt
2 oz dried zibibbo or sable grapes
⅓ cup raisins
¾ cup shelled walnuts
½ cup prunes, pitted
½ cup dried figs
⅔ cup hazelnuts
2 apples
⅔ cup almonds
Marsala
Powdered sugar

Mix the sifted flour with half a spoonful of sugar, 4 tablespoons of oil, a pinch of salt, and water in proportion, trying to obtain a rather soft dough. Let it rest for a while and then roll it out as thinly as possible.

On the thin dough arrange a mixture of dried grapes, raisins soaked in warm water, walnuts, prunes, dried figs, hazelnuts, sliced apples and almonds, all coarsely chopped and mixed with a lot of sugar, half a glass of Marsala and a little oil.

Roll the dough on itself, forming a long roll that you will place in a pan greased with oil, arranging it in a spiral or serpentine shape. Oil the top of the cake and cook in a preheated oven of moderate heat for about half an hour. When it is well cooked, remove it from the oven and sprinkle generously with powdered sugar.

STRUDEL DI MELE

Apple Strudel

1⅔ cups all-purpose flour
1 egg
Salt
Sugar
17½ tbsp butter
2¼ lb apples
Fine breadcrumbs
Handful raisins
Handful almonds
Lemon zest
Apricot jam
Powdered sugar

Put the flour on the kitchen table in a heap and put an egg, a pinch of salt and half a spoonful of sugar in the middle.

Put 2 tablespoons of butter and half a glass of water in a saucepan over a very low heat, so that the butter can melt and the water heat up, but not excessively, and pour the water and the melted butter over the flour, and work the dough vigorously for a sufficient time. It must be smooth and soft and not stick to the fingers.

Once the dough reaches the right point, knead it vigorously, and for quite a long time, against the table, to give it elasticity; then roll it into a small loaf, and put it in a corner of the lightly floured table.

Now prepare the filling: Peel the apples, split them in 2, remove the core, and cut them into very thin slices.

Separately, in a pan, brown 2 tablespoons of very fine breadcrumbs in the same quantity of butter. Soak your raisins in warm water.

Put the dough on a lightly floured cloth on a table and roll it out as thin as possible with a floured wooden rolling pin. If, due to the irregular pressure of the roller, the edge of the sheet has an uneven thickness, it will be better to cut this part away. When you have spread it well, brush with melted butter to moisten. Then, flour your hands and put them under the dough and begin to spread it, pulling it lightly, until it is as thin as possible and uniform, without tearing. Roll it out with your hands as thin as possible, gently moisten it some more with melted butter, and arrange the sliced apples on top. Sprinkle the fried breadcrumbs on top, and add, to taste, a few spoonfuls of soaked raisins, some peeled and thinly sliced almonds, a little lemon zest, and some teaspoons of jam placed here and there. Complete with plenty of powdered sugar, which you will sprinkle all over the place.

Lift a flap of the floured cloth and slowly roll the strudel on itself, without ever touching it with your hands. It should be like a long sausage. Then squeeze this sausage at both ends to seal the filling well and prevent it from coming out.

Grease a baking sheet and, again with the help of the floured cloth, slide the strudel on to it, gradually giving it a twisted shape. Brush the strudle with more melted butter, applying it lightly, and cook in a preheated medium hot oven for about an hour.

After this time, remove it from the oven, sprinkle with powdered sugar, and cut it into pieces.

ADA SAYS: *The strudel is a Tyrolean dessert and consists of a pastry shell that contains a fruit filling. According to the seasons, it can also be made with many other kinds of fruit, not just apples—pitted cherries or pears and peaches, peeled and cut into thin slices, like the apples here.*

TORTA ALLA VIENNESE

Viennese Cake (Sacher Torte)

½ cup almonds, shelled
⅔ cup sugar
5 tbsp butter, plus extra for greasing
4 eggs
2½ oz chocolate
¼ cup all-purpose flour
Lemon peel
Apricot jam
Apricot jelly *(p750)*

Chocolate icing:
3½ oz dark chocolate,
½ cup sugar

Put the shelled almonds in a saucepan with cold water, bring them almost to a boil, remove the saucepan from the heat and then, one by one, remove the skins, passing them gradually into a bowl with fresh water. When you have peeled them all, dry them with a towel and let them dry more in the oven at very moderate heat; they must not color. Then crush or blend them with a third of a cup of sugar, putting them in a little at a time. You can also use a food processor. Gradually pass this almond flour through a sieve.

Put the butter in a bowl, in winter it will be better to soften it first, and whip with a wooden spoon until creamy. Gradually add the same weight of sugar, always stirring; then the egg yolks, one at a time. Always continue to beat with a wooden spoon, adding from time to time a spoonful of the prepared almond flour, until it is all used up.

Grate the chocolate into a small bowl over a pan of hot water over very low heat and, without adding any water, stir to melt it perfectly. When it is just lukewarm, add it to the mixture, a little at a time and always stirring with a wooden spoon. Whip the egg whites to a firm snow and gently add them to the mixture. Finish by adding a little plain flour. Cut the peel of half a lemon with a small knife, chop it into very small pieces, and stir into the mixture.

Butter and flour a cake pan of 8 inches in diameter, pour in the mixture and, immediately, put the cake in a preheated oven of moderate heat, and leave it for about 40 minutes. This cake doesn't have to be very tall.

When it is cooked, take it out and let it cool, then divide it into 2 disks which you will spread, internally, with apricot jam. Then reassemble the cake, spread it with hot apricot jelly and cover with a shiny layer of chocolate icing *(p750)* using the ingredient amounts listed here.

TORTA DEL PARADISO

Paradise Cake

1 lb butter
2½ cups sugar
5 eggs
6 egg yolks
1⅔ cups all-purpose flour
2 cups potato starch
2 lemons
Powdered sugar

Put the butter in a bowl and work it for a long time with a wooden spoon so it is a soft cream. Then, gradually, add the sugar, without ever stopping to mix, and then the eggs and the yolks, beaten together, as if for an omelet. The eggs should be added slowly, by spoonfuls, not adding any more until the first ones are well blended. Finally, add the flour and potato starch mixed together and then the zest of the lemons. Do not work the dough too energetically but try to mix with the greatest lightness.

Grease a large 12½ inch diameter pan, sprinkle it with potato starch and pour in the mixture, which must reach two-thirds up the sides. Bake in a preheated oven of moderate heat for an hour and then generously sift over with powdered sugar. It is good to wait a couple of days before serving.

TORTA DI CIOCCOLATO

Chocolate Cake

10½ oz dark chocolate
7 tbsp butter, plus extra for greasing
⅓ cup all-purpose flour
½ cup sugar
5 eggs
Orange
Milk
Salt
Powdered sugar

In a bain-marie, melt the dark chocolate with the softened butter. As soon as it has melted, remove from the heat and add the sifted flour, sugar, egg yolks, one at a time, the zest of an orange, half a glass of milk and a pinch of salt. Mix thoroughly, then, finally, add the egg whites whipped to a firm snow, very gently so as not to dismantle the mixture.

Butter a round cake pan, with a diameter of about 10 inches, fold the mixture in and bake in a preheated oven at a moderate heat for about half an hour. When the cake has cooked, take it out and let it cool on a wire rack, then slide it on to a serving dish and sprinkle it, generously, with powdered sugar.

DESSERTS WITH YEAST

TO WORK WITH ACTIVE DRY YEAST

With active dry yeast there are no difficulties – just prepare the dough well, mixing the yeast in well and, without wasting time, put it in the oven. Active dry yeast is available in sachets. Half an ounce is enough for one pound of flour. You can mix it separately on a large sheet of paper together with the flour to be used and, after having mixed it well, sieve. In this way, the yeast mixes with the flour, ensuring maximum leavening in the oven. Do not let the finished preparation wait too long before putting it in the oven because the humidity can make the active dry yeast ferment, little by little, preventing it from carrying out its action during cooking.

TO WORK WITH FRESH YEAST

Dough with fresh yeast is far more challenging. In its handling, fresh yeast must be added to the main ingredients such as eggs, sugar, and flour. In these preparations the difficulty lies not so much in forming the dough, as in obtaining the precise leavening. Sometimes a draft of air is enough, or the choice of an insufficiently sheltered place to put the dough to rest, preventing the leavening process from taking place.

BOMBA AL MASCARPONE

Marscapone Bombs

MAKES 6

Liqueur
1¼ cups mascarpone
1¼ cups powdered sugar
Dark chocolate
Milk
¼ cup hazelnuts
¼ cup powdered sugar
Candied cherries
Candied orange
Optional: pastry cream (1 egg yolk, ¼ cup all-purpose flour, 2 tbsp sugar, ½ cup milk)

Baba dough:
1¼ cups all-purpose flour, 9 tbsp butter, ¾ oz fresh yeast, 3 eggs, salt, sugar

Have ready your baba dough *(p808)* using the ingredients listed here, then split into 2 disks, half an inch high. Lightly wet one part with a small glass of fairly strong liqueur. Line the bottom of a mold with the wet part inside.

Cut out one or more rectangular strips from the remaining baba and line the sides of the mold with them, also wetting these with a small glass of liqueur. Trim with a small knife to fit.

Put the mascarpone in a bowl, and whip with a wooden spoon until it becomes a very fine and soft cream. Then add the powdered sugar and the liqueur, and continue to whisk for a little longer.

Then divide it into 3 unequal parts: one very abundant part, one less so, and one quite small. Add a tablespoon of chocolate melted with half a glass of milk to the smallest part. To the larger part make up this mixture with the hazelnuts: Toast the nuts in the oven, skin them, and coarsely chop them. Melt the sugar in a small saucepan over moderate heat and when it has dissolved, add the crushed hazelnuts, mix well with a wooden spoon, and blend this paste while still hot, for a long time, until the mixture is like a melted cream. Put the plain mascarpone in the bottom of the mold, so that it reaches one third up the side and reserve a small amount, which you will use later. Flatten this layer with the blade of a knife and on this first layer spread a layer of chocolate mascarpone, which should be no more than 3 quarters of an inch. On this layer, fit 4 or 5 candied cherries and a few cubes of candied orange peel. Spread out this second layer as well and fill the mold with hazelnut mascarpone. After flattening this last layer as well, place the second baba disk on top, to close the cake.

Place a sheet of parchment paper on top, close the mold and put it in the fridge. Leave the cake alone for a couple of hours and then turn it out.

Blend the rest of the plain mascarpone with a spoon and spread thinly over the cake. Complete with a generous sprinkling of powdered sugar, which falling on the mascarpone layer will form an elegant crust. Arrange the dessert on a serving plate.

ADA SAYS: *If the cake has to be kept for a while, you can make it last longer by adding, when whipping the mascarpone, a little thick and cold cream, made with an egg yolk, flour, sugar, and milk.*

BOSSOLÀ DI BRESCIA

Brescia Donuts

1¼ cups strong bread flour
1 oz fresh yeast
3 eggs
Salt
3½ tbsp butter, plus extra for greasing
⅓ cup sugar
Vanilla extract
Sugar

Place 1 cup of flour on the table and in the center crumble in the yeast, then add 2 whole eggs, a pinch of salt, and a little water and begin to knead. Then add the softened butter divided into small pieces and the sugar, gradually absorbing all the ingredients into the dough, and finally the vanilla. Work the dough vigorously until it is very soft, so it gains elasticity, and, when it is velvet, cover it with a towel and let it rise for about an hour, until it has doubled in volume.

When the dough has risen, deflate it, beating it with your hand, turn it over on the table and gradually add the rest of the flour, if necessary, to bring it to the consistency of a very soft bread dough. Once the flour has been incorporated, work the dough again vigorously, and then make a donut shape that you will place in a low-sided buttered pan, and let it rise again until it is well increased in volume and is soft to the touch. It will take 2 to 3 hours.

Once the dough has risen, brush it very lightly with beaten egg and sprinkle abundant grains of sugar over it. Bake in a preheated oven of moderate, but always good heat, for a good half hour. Once removed from the oven, leave it to cool on a wire rack.

BOSTON PIE

Boston Pie

Butter for greasing
½ cup unsweetened cocoa powder
2 tbsp butter
1 cup sugar

Pastry dough:
1⅔ cups all-purpose flour, 1 cup sugar, salt, ½ oz active dry yeast, 7 tbsp butter, vanilla extract, ¾ cup milk, 1 egg

Cream:
⅔ cup sugar, ⅓ cup all-purpose flour, salt, 2 cups milk, 1 egg, 2 tbsp butter, vanilla extract

For the dough: Place the flour, sugar, a pinch of salt, the active dry yeast, the butter, very soft but not melted, and the vanilla in a bowl and mix everything with the cold milk. Stir vigorously and add an egg. Continue to mix until well blended.

Butter and flour 2 large low-sided trays with a diameter of about 12 inches and pour the mixture into both; half in one and half in the other. Place the 2 large trays in a preheated oven of moderate heat and cook for about half an hour. When cooked, remove them from the trays and let them cool on wire racks.

For the cream: Put the sugar, flour, and a pinch of salt in a saucepan and dissolve everything with the milk. Place the saucepan over a very light heat and, always stirring with a wooden spoon, warm the mixture for 3 or 4 minutes, then remove it from the heat and pour a few spoonfuls into a bowl where you will have beaten an egg as for an omelet. Give it a good stir and pour back into the first pan. Bring the heat up again, still low, and, always stirring, continue cooking for about a quarter of an hour. When the mixture is smooth and velvet, remove it from the heat and add the butter and vanilla. Pour the cream into a bowl and, always stirring with a wooden spoon, let it cool.

Put one of the cakes on a round serving dish, pour over the cream, and spread with the blade of a knife over the entire surface. Set the other cake on top and press lightly with your hands so that it sticks well.

To finish, place the cocoa and butter in a saucepan on a very light flame and as soon as the butter has melted, add 3 or 4 tablespoons of boiling water and the sugar. Remove the saucepan from the heat and always keeping it warm, beat the mixture until it is soft, blended and fluid. Then pour it on the cake and make sure that it covers it all, even on the sides. Leave to cool.

ADA SAYS: *Boston pie is an exquisite American pie.*

CAKE AL CIOCCOLATO

Chocolate Cake (Gluten Free)

7 tbsp butter
½ cup sugar
3 eggs
1 cup cocoa powder
¾ cup potato starch
½ oz active dry yeast

Put the butter in a bowl and whip it with a wooden spoon until it is soft and fluffy. When the butter is well whipped, add the sugar, and, when the sugar has also blended, add the egg yolks, again one at a time. Always keep stirring and then sift the cocoa and potato starch with the active dry yeast. Whip the egg whites to a firm snow and add them gently to the mixture.

Bake the cake in a rectangular mold with a capacity of one and a half quarts, or in a pan that must be buttered but not floured. Bake in a preheated oven of moderate heat for 3 quarters of an hour.

CAKE DI UVA PASSA

Raisin Cake

10½ tbsp butter, plus extra for greasing
¾ cup sugar
2 eggs
2 egg yolks
1¼ cups all-purpose flour
½ cup raisins
3¼ oz candied peel
¼ oz active dry yeast
Optional: rum

This cake is of English origin. For the best results, keep the raisins and candied fruits in a small glass of rum for a few hours beforehand.

Whip the butter in a bowl with a wooden spoon. Gradually add the sugar, eggs, yolks, flour, raisins, candied fruit, and finally the yeast.

Grease a cake pan with a capacity of about one and a half quarts and pour the dough in, being careful that it does not reach the brim, and place in a moderate heat oven for an abundant hour.

Remove the cake from the mold and let it cool on a wire rack.

ADA SAYS: *To test the right degree of cooking, place a finger on top: if under the pressure of your finger it makes a slight noise, as if it were frying, it means that it still contains moisture.*

CAKE PREZIOSA

Preziosa Cake

9 tbsp butter
⅔ cup sugar
3 eggs
Lemon juice
Maraschino liqueur
1⅔ cups all-purpose flour
Handful raisins
Candied citron or orange
¼ oz active dry yeast
Butter for greasing

Put the butter in a bowl and start whipping it with a wooden spoon. When it has become like a cream, add the sugar, work again, and add the egg yolks, one at a time. When these too have amalgamated, squeeze the juice of half a lemon into the mass and also add a tablespoon of maraschino or other liqueur of your choice, as long as it is not anisette.

Then work the flour into the mixture, mix well, add the egg whites that you have whipped to a firm snow, and finally add the raisins soaked in warm water and a tablespoon of diced candied citron or orange. The raisins and candied fruit must be floured first. Finish with the active dry yeast and mix a little more.

Grease a rectangular baking pan with a capacity of about one and a half quarts, place the mixture in, and bake in a preheated oven at a moderate temperature for 3 quarters of an hour.

ADA SAYS: *We always made this sweet, simple, and elegant cake at the magazine* Preziosa, *which is always very dear to me because it reminds me of past times in peaceful activity editing the magazine.*

GÂTEAU DI MANDORLE

Almond Gâteau

5 tbsp butter, plus extra for greasing
3 eggs
¾ cup sugar
5 tbsp milk
1¼ cups all-purpose flour
¼ oz active dry yeast
1 cup peeled almonds

Put the butter in a bowl, whip it with a wooden spoon, add the egg yolks, one at a time and, when blended, add the sugar. Continuing to whisk, add the milk, one spoonful at a time. Finally, add the egg whites beaten to a firm snow. Put the flour and yeast in a sieve and let it rain into the bowl, while slowly, slowly, and with great delicacy, mixing it in. Finally add the peeled and crushed almonds. Give a last stir.

Butter a quart cake pan with high sides, and without a hole in the middle. Pour the mixture in and bake in a moderate oven for over half an hour. When it is cooked, and it has taken on a nice dark gold color, turn it out on a wire rack and let it cool.

KUGELHUPF

Kugelhupf

- 2 cups all-purpose flour
- ¾ oz fresh yeast
- 10½ tbsp butter, plus extra for greasing
- ¼ cup sugar
- 2 egg yolks
- 2 eggs
- Milk
- Salt
- 2½ tbsp raisins
- 1 oz candied citron peel
- Lemon zest
- ⅔ cup almonds

Take a quarter of the flour and put in a large cup. Crumble over the yeast and add a little lukewarm water. Cover the cup and leave to rise in a sheltered place for about a quarter of an hour to double.

Put the butter, which must be soft even in winter, in a very large bowl and whip it with a wooden spoon, so as to make it soft and fluffy. Add the sugar and after a while add an egg yolk; mix and then add 2 or 3 spoonfuls of the flour; then, always stirring, another egg yolk, then another 2 or 3 spoonfuls of flour, and finally the 2 whole eggs, always alternating them with a little flour. As you work the dough, also add, in small quantities, half a glass of warm milk. Also add the salt and finally the yeasted flour, which must have doubled its volume.

Then remove the spoon and, using your hands, knead the dough. When it is elastic and shiny and comes off in one piece from the bowl, complete with the raisins soaked in warm water, the citron peel cut into strips, and the lemon zest. Work a little more, then cover the bowl with a folded towel and put it to rise again in a sheltered place for a couple of hours.

Generously butter a large fluted cake pan with a capacity of 2 quarts and a hole in the middle. Cover the entire inside with crushed almonds, turning the pan in all directions so they stick to the layer of butter.

After 2 hours, take the dough and beat it with the palm of your hand again, and then let it fall, in pieces, back into the bowl. It should reach half way up. Put the dough back in a sheltered place and let it rise again. Then bake the cake in a preheated oven of regular heat, and leave for 20 to 25 minutes, more or less according to the strength of the oven; and when the dough is golden brown, remove from the oven, let it rest for a few minutes and then turn out the cake. It is eaten cold and slightly sugary. It stays fresh for some time.

PANDORO ALLA CREMA

Cream Pandoro

2 cups strong bread flour
¼ oz yeast
⅓ cup sugar
2 eggs
3 egg yolks
6 oz butter
Vanilla extract
Powdered sugar
Optional: cream

Crème anglaise:
6 egg yolks, ¾ cup sugar, 2 cups milk, half vanilla bean, liqueur

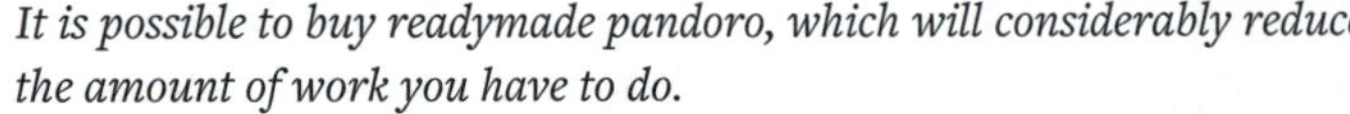

It is possible to buy readymade pandoro, which will considerably reduce the amount of work you have to do.

Put a spoonful of flour in a cup, crumble the yeast in, and dissolve everything with a spoonful of just warm water. The result must be a very soft dough. Leave to rise for about 20 minutes, until it has more than doubled its volume.

Now put in a bowl half a cup of flour, a spoonful of sugar, an egg and a yolk. and a teaspoon of butter, just melted. Add the yeast from the cup, and knead the new dough for 4 or 5 minutes in the same bowl, to combine all the elements well. Cover the bowl and put it in a sheltered place for an hour, until this new dough has doubled its volume.

At this point, put a cup of flour, 2 more spoonfuls of sugar, one tablespoon melted butter, an egg, 2 yolks, a touch of vanilla, and a pinch of salt on the kitchen table. Add the yeast and work all the ingredients with your hands, vigorously beating the dough, which is rather soft, to make it elastic and light. Beat this dough for about 10 minutes, until it comes off in one piece from the table and your hands.

Then add another third cup of flour and gradually incorporate it into the dough, removing it well from the table with the blade of a knife. The dough must become like that of a very soft bread dough, and it will no longer stick to your hands or to the table. Work the dough for a few more minutes, pressing it with the palm of your hand, rolling it, and handling it; and when you see that it is well worked, make a ball and place it in another bowl, on the bottom of which you will sprinkle a little flour. Cover the bowl and let it rise again for about 3 hours.

Then turn the dough over on the lightly floured table, deflate it with small strokes of the hand, and fold it several times on itself, smoothing it with your hand. Then roll it out in the shape of a square and in the middle put 10 tablespoons of butter divided into small pieces. Return the 4 corners of the square towards the center, so as to close the butter well. When you have closed the butter well, roll out the dough slightly, and then fold it in 3, as is done for puff pastry; roll it out again lightly, fold it in 3, then let it rest for about 20 minutes.

After 20 minutes, roll out the dough again, fold it back, and roll it out again, giving the dough 2 more turns. Fold it again and let it rest for another 20 minutes. The pandoro is thus finished.

You will now have to slightly reshuffle the dough on the table, trying, with the hollow of your hand, to make it rotate on itself. Do all this lightly and without too much pressure, because the dough is delicate. During the various manipulations, if necessary, use a little flour. When you have rolled the dough well, put it in a greased and sugared baking pan. Put the pan in a sheltered place, and wait for the dough to rise to the edge. Then bake the pandoro in a moderate heat oven, and after a quarter of an hour reduce the heat a little so that the pandoro can also cook in the middle, without becoming too brown.

When, after about half an hour, the pandoro is well cooked, dipping a long kitchen needle in so it will come out very clean, turn it out of the tin on a wire rack and let it cool.

Now prepare the crème anglaise *(p752)*: Put the egg yolks and sugar in a small saucepan; whisk the eggs for a long time, until they become swollen and frothy. Place the milk, flavored with half a bean of vanilla, on the stove and bring it to almost boil; when it is very near boiling, remove the vanilla, and pour the milk in small quantities over the whipped eggs, working vigorously. Once all the milk has been added, put the cream on the heat again and, always stirring, cook it, bringing it close to boiling, but taking care not to let the boil rise because in this case the cream would separate irremediably. When you see that the cream is slightly thickened and it veils the spoon, remove it from the heat, pour it into a bowl, and let it cool, stirring it from time to time, so that it does not form a skin on the surface.

Cut the pandoro sideways, obtaining 4 disks and moisten them lightly with liqueur. Arrange the pandoro base disk, sprinkled with powdered sugar, on a dessert plate, cover it with a layer of cream, cover with the second disk, turned so that the tips do not match, and continue like this until having reassembled the whole pandoro. Drain the remaining cream over the whole pandoro and complete with a decoration of your choice.

ADA SAYS: *You can replace a part of the milk with the same amount of cream that, however, must be added off the heat.*

PANE DOLCE DI NOCI

Sweet Walnut Bread

3⅓ cups strong bread flour
¼ oz active dry yeast
½ cup sugar
1 egg
1½ cups milk
Salt
1 cup shelled walnuts
Butter for greasing

Sift the flour and mix with the yeast. Then, add the sugar and egg and dilute with the milk. Add a pinch of salt and the well-chopped walnuts. Stir again and pour into a greased rectangular baking pan. Bake in a preheated oven of moderate heat for about 3 quarters of an hour. Serve cold, thinly sliced and spread with fresh butter.

PINZA ALLA BERTOLDESE

Bologna Christmas Cake

3⅓ cups strong bread flour
1¾ oz fresh yeast
1 cup jam
½ cup almonds
½ cup hazelnuts or walnuts
¼ cup cocoa
Dried zibibbino or sable grapes, macerated in rum
⅓ cup dried figs
5 tbsp butter
Lemon peel
Olive oil for greasing
Honey dissolved in rum

Put ⅔ of a cup of flour in a small bowl, crumble the yeast in the middle, and dissolve everything with a few spoonfuls of just lukewarm water to have a dough. Cover the bowl and put it in a sheltered place for about a quarter of an hour, until the dough doubles in volume.

Arrange the rest of the flour on the table, put the yeast mix in the middle, and mix with a little warm water, until you have a dough a little softer than bread dough. Work it vigorously, put it in a bowl, cover it with a towel, and let it rise for another couple of hours.

After this time, deflate it by beating it with your hands, put it back on the table, add a fruit jam to taste, the peeled almonds cut in half, the hazelnuts or chopped walnuts, the cocoa, the grapes macerated in a little rum, dried figs cut into strips, butter, and the peel of a lemon, without any white part, cut into strips. Knead everything together making a large donut and place it in a rather large pan, lightly greased with oil. Let it rise for 2 to 3 hours.

Then bake the cake in a preheated oven with good heat for an hour. Once the cake has been removed from the oven, brush with hot honey diluted with a little rum.

PIZZA PASQUALE PALOMBELLA

Palombella Easter Pizza

4⅔ cups all-purpose flour
1 oz fresh yeast
6 eggs
14 tbsp butter, plus extra for greasing
1¼ cups sugar
Lemon peel
Ground cinnamon

Sift the flour and crumble in the yeast, the eggs, the butter, cut into small pieces, the sugar, the grated lemon peel, and a pinch of cinnamon in the middle. Mix everything thoroughly, let the flour absorb everything, then knead strongly with your hands until it comes off in one piece.

Butter a pan 12 inches in diameter and about 4 inches high. Put the dough in and let it rise in a sheltered place for a few hours. When it is well developed, bake it in a preheated oven of rather moderate heat for about 40 minutes.

PIZZA PASQUALE RICRESCUITA

Pizza Pasquale

6⅓ cups strong bread flour
8 eggs
Ground cinnamon
1⅓ cups ricotta
Salt
2 lemons
1¾ oz fresh yeast
Lard for greasing

Sift the flour on the table and in the middle put the eggs, a pinch of cinnamon, ricotta, a pinch of salt, the zest of the lemons, and crumble over the yeast. Knead with your hands. When the dough has become elastic, velvet, and comes off the table in one piece, distribute it in one or more pans greased with lard. The dough should reach less than half the height of the pans. Leave to rise for about 10 hours in a sheltered place and then bake in a preheated oven of moderate heat for about 40 minutes.

STIACCIATA ALLA FIORENTINA

Florentine Stiacciata

3⅓ cups strong bread flour
1 oz fresh yeast
2 eggs
Salt
⅔ cup sugar
1 orange
10½ tbsp lard or butter, plus extra for greasing
Powdered sugar

Put the flour in a bowl. Crumble the yeast into 1¼ cups of just lukewarm water, dissolve, and then gradually incorporate with the flour. Work the dough with your hands until it becomes elastic and comes off in one piece from the bowl; then cover the bowl with a towel and let the dough rise, keeping it in a sheltered place for about an hour, and let it double in volume.

When the dough has risen well, deflate it with your hand and add the eggs, salt, sugar, and grated orange peel. The dough will soften a lot. Still keeping it in the bowl, begin to work it with your hands, beating it vigorously so it regains its elasticity. After about 10 minutes of work, when the dough comes off in one piece from the bowl, add the lard or butter; and work it some more to mix everything well.

Grease a pan of about 12 inches in diameter and put the finished mixture in the bottom. Cover it and wait for the dough to rise again. It will take from an hour and a half to 2 hours.

Bake in a hot oven and let it take on a beautiful golden color. It will take about half an hour. When it is cooked, take out and let it cool and dry on a wire rack. Then put it on a plate and sprinkle with powdered sugar. The stiacciata must not be very high—less than one and a half inches only.

TORTA AL COCCO

Coconut Cake

⅔ cup all-purpose flour
2 cups coconut flour
1 cup sugar
3 eggs
Yogurt
Port
6 tbsp butter, plus extra for greasing
½ oz active dry yeast
Milk
Powdered sugar

Put the 2 flours, sugar, 3 egg yolks, small jar of yogurt, small glass of port, and softened butter in a bowl. Mix all the ingredients thoroughly. Whip the egg whites to a firm snow and add them very gently into the mixture. Dissolve the yeast in a glass of slightly sweetened milk, and then mix in.

Transfer everything to a well-buttered cake pan with high sides and bake in a preheated oven of moderate heat for about half an hour, until it has taken on a beautiful golden color. When it is cooked, take it out of the tray and put on a wire rack to cool, then sprinkle with powdered sugar.

TORTA BILBOLBUL

Bilbolbul Cake

1⅔ cups all-purpose flour
1 cup sugar
1 cup cocoa powder
¾ oz active dry yeast
Orange peel
Ground cinnamon
1 tsp baking powder
1 cup milk
Butter for greasing
Fine breadcrumbs

Butter a cake pan with high sides, about 8 inches in diameter, and then sprinkle with very fine breadcrumbs. Take care to turn the pan in all directions, so that the crumbs cover the pan well, and then turn it over to knock off any loose crumbs.

Put the flour, sugar, cocoa powder, yeast, zest of orange peel, half a teaspoon of ground cinnamon, and baking powder in a bowl; dilute with milk and mix with a wooden spoon until smooth and velvet, like a cream. Without working the dough too much, pour it into the prepared pan.

Put the pan in a rather hot oven and bake for half an hour. It should not be very hard, so take it out of the oven without letting it dry too much, and while it retains a certain softness. Turn out on a wire rack.

ADA SAYS: *Bilbolbul was a cartoon character in the 1930s.*

TORTA DI MELE

Apple Cake

6 golden delicious apples
Rum
⅔ cup raisins
2 eggs
1 egg yolk
1¼ cups sugar
1 lemon
1⅔ cups all-purpose flour
½ oz active dry yeast
Milk
Butter for greasing
Breadcrumbs
Ground cinnamon

Wash, peel, and cut the apples into thin slices and put them to macerate in a little rum together with the raisins.

Break the eggs, separating the whites from the yolks. Put the 3 yolks in a bowl, add 1 cup of sugar, and work until soft and well whipped. Now add the grated lemon zest, then slowly the sifted flour, mixed with the yeast, a glass of milk, and the whites whipped to stiff peaks. Mix the ingredients gently.

Butter a round cake pan. Sprinkle it with breadcrumbs, then add the batter. Cover it with the drained apple slices. Sprinkle the apples with a pinch of cinnamon, raisins, and the rest of the sugar. Put the cake in a preheated oven of moderate heat for about half an hour. Halfway through cooking, cover the pan with a sheet of parchment paper. Let the cake cool and turn it out on a serving dish.

TORTA MERINGATA

Meringue Cake

7 tbsp butter, plus extra for greasing
⅔ cup sugar
2 eggs
⅔ cup all-purpose flour
¼ oz active dry yeast
⅓ cup almonds
1 egg white
1 tbsp sugar
Apricot jam
Powdered sugar

Whip the butter in a bowl and, always stirring with a wooden spoon, until creamy. Add all but a spoon of the sugar and, when blended, add the egg yolks, one at a time. Then add the active dry yeast to the flour and sift both over the cream. Finally, mix in the 2 egg whites beaten to a firm snow, but mix them slowly so as not to dismantle the mixture.

Grease and flour a pan with a diameter of about 8 inches, pour in the soft mixture and place in a preheated oven of moderate heat.

Meanwhile, skin and crush the almonds. Beat an egg white to a very firm snow. Blend in a spoon of sugar and the crushed almonds. When the cake is slightly firm, take it out of the oven for a few moments. Spread it with apricot jam and place the meringue and almond mix on the jam, spreading it with the blade of a knife, then place the cake back in the oven for about half an hour, reducing the heat, so that the meringue can dry without coloring too much. Then remove the cake and leave to cool. When it is time to send it to the table, sprinkle abundantly with powdered sugar.

TORTA PASQUALE CASALINGA

Farmhouse Easter Cake

1 oz fresh yeast
2⅓ cups all-purpose flour
3 eggs
2 tbsp butter, plus butter for greasing
Salt
1 orange
1 lemon
Ground cinnamon
½ cup sugar
Optional: candied orange peel

Dissolve the yeast in a cup with 2 fingers of just lukewarm water, and mix with a teaspoon, add the flour to get a rather soft dough. Cover the cup and put it in a sheltered place for 20 minutes until the yeast has doubled in volume.

Sift the flour and blend in the eggs, butter, a pinch of salt, the zest of orange and lemon and a pinch of cinnamon on the kitchen table. Mix everything well and then add the leavened dough. Beat the dough energetically on the table, until it becomes elastic and velvet. Then add the sugar and knead the dough a little more.

Grease a cake pan with a diameter of 8 inches, arrange the dough inside, and leave it to rise for 3 or 4 hours in a sheltered place.

When the dough has reached the edge of the pan, put the cake in a hot oven. The heat must first be quite strong; however, as cooking progresses, decrease the intensity a little, so that the cake can cook well inside without browning too much on the outside. The required cooking time is about 3 quarters of an hour.

ADA SAYS: *You can enrich the cake with a spoonful of candied orange peel cut into strips that you will try to distribute evenly in the dough after adding the sugar, if you like.*

Baba

TO MAKE A BABA

The success here is entirely entrusted to the energy with which the pastry is beaten.

The following proportions make 6 babas: **1¼ cups strong bread flour, ¾oz fresh yeast, 3 eggs, 9 tablespoons butter, sugar and salt to taste.**

Sift the flour. Take ⅓ of the flour to whisk in a bowl with the yeast and about 2 fingers of just warm water, so as to have a rather soft dough. Cover and put it in a sheltered place, but away from any heat.

After about a quarter of an hour the yeast will have doubled in size; pour it into a bowl where you will have put the rest of the flour, salt, eggs, and butter. Knead everything with your hands, then work the dough vigorously, lifting it with your fingers and beating it vigorously against the sides of the bowl.

After 5 or 6 minutes, the dough should be smooth, velvet, and elastic, and it should come off in one piece. Then add sugar to taste, and work a little more.

Butter a rather tall mold with a hole in the middle and a capacity of about 1½ quarts. Take the dough, in small portions, and drop it in. In all it should take up just over a third of the space. Put it in a sheltered place and let it rise. Make sure there are no drafts or any excessive heat sources nearby.

After an hour and a half the dough will have risen to the edge of the mold. Then bake the baba, keeping it for about 20 minutes in a well-heated oven, until it has a nice golden color. To make sure it is cooked, you can dip a long needle into the cake and see if any raw dough still sticks to it. Turn out the baba and pour over a spoonful of boiling rum syrup prepared as follows.

TO COAT A BABA

Put 4 tablespoons of powdered sugar in a bowl, moisten it with a little water, and mix with a teaspoon, adding more water gradually, until you have a rather runny cream. Do not put in more water than is strictly necessary, so as not to be forced to add any more sugar.

To finish, add a tablespoon of rum and a little apricot jelly (p750)*. Spoon on top of the cake and let it flow on the rounded surface and down the sides. Put the cake in the oven for a very short time so that the icing dries more quickly and takes on a shine. Baba can also be served hot, and in this case it is served with a hot red wine sauce* (p754)*.*

BABÀ ALLA CREMA

Cream Baba

Baba *(opp. page)*
3 eggs
3 tbsp sugar
Vanilla extract
10 oz mascarpone

When your baba is baked and cooled, then prepare this cream: Beat the egg yolks and the sugar and a little vanilla until they become a soft and frothy cream. Stir in the mascarpone softened at room temperature, continuing to mix.

Finally, add the whipped egg whites very gently. Fill the baba with this cream. You can use the remaining cream as garnish.

BABÀ ALLA FRUTTA

Baba with Fruit

Baba *(opp. page)*
4 tbsp sugar
Rum or kirsch
Fruits in season
1¾ cups whipped cream
Optional: crushed almonds

When your baba is baked and cooled, take it out of the mold while still hot. Dress it with this syrup: Boil 4 spoonfuls of sugar in a little water for a couple of minutes and then add 2 small glasses of rum or kirsch, off the heat.

Wash and cut the fruit into pieces, mix with the whipped cream and place on top of the baba.

ADA SAYS: *This baba can be enriched with crushed almonds, scattered in the greased mold before adding the dough and baking.*

SPONGE & GENOISE CAKES

Genoise and sponge cake are similar in all their quantities and differ only in the processing of the eggs, used hot in the first and cold in the second. **For each egg, allow 2½ tablespoons of sugar and 3 tablespoons of all-purpose flour.** *A sponge differs because it is worked cold, and the egg whites and yolks are whipped separately.*

TO MAKE GENOISE CAKE

The following amounts are required to make a genoise cake: **⅔ cup sugar, 4 eggs, lemon zest, ⅔ cup all purpose flour, and butter for greasing.**

Put the sugar in a saucepan and break the eggs over the sugar, adding a little lemon zest, gently scraped, so as not to get any of the white part. Place the saucepan on a light heat, and keeping it tilted to one side, beat the eggs and sugar vigorously with a whisk until soft and swollen. When the mixture is at the right point and has reached a slight heat, remove the pan from the heat but continue to beat until the mass is cold. It must have increased in volume a lot and make ribbons; that is, by lifting a little and letting it fall it must form a continuous ribbon, without interruptions. Remove the whisk and take a wooden spoon. Slowly drop the sifted flour on to the whipped eggs and use the wooden spoon to lightly blend the flour into the mixture.

Grease a cake pan with a diameter of about 10 inches, sprinkle it with flour, turn it over and tap it lightly to drop off the superfluous flour. Pour the mixture in, and place in a preheated oven of moderate heat for about 40 minutes.

TO MAKE SPONGE CAKE

The following amounts are required to make a sponge cake: **4 eggs, 1 cup powdered sugar, ⅔ cup all purpose flour, vanilla extract, lemon or orange zest, and butter for greasing.**

Separate the egg whites and yolks from the eggs. Put the egg yolks and the sugar in a bowl, and work vigorously with a wooden spoon until the mixture is well whipped, light, and swollen. Whip the remaining egg whites by beating them well with a whisk, until they are a firm snow. Gently add the egg whites to the yolks and then pour the sifted flour over everything. You can flavor the sponge cake with a little vanilla extract or with a little grated lemon or orange zest.

Butter and flour a pan with rather high edges and a diameter of about 10 inches. Pour in the mixture and put the pan in a preheated oven of moderate heat for about 40 minutes. Then turn out the sponge cake on a wire rack, and let it cool.

BOCCA DI DAMA

Flourless Almond Sponge Cake

7 eggs
3 egg yolks
1½ cups sugar
1 cup all-purpose flour
Lemon
Ground cinnamon
2½ oz candied orange
Butter for greasing

Almond paste:
¼ cup almonds, 2½ tbsp sugar, 1 egg

You can buy ready-skinned almonds, or to do it yourself: Shell and skin the almonds and dry them well. Blend them together with the sugar and a beaten egg, which you add in small quantities, in order to have a smooth and very fine paste.

Now prepare the dessert: Put the eggs, yolks, and sugar in a saucepan over a very low heat, and tilting the pan to one side, whisk the eggs and sugar. When the mixture is hot, but not too hot, remove the saucepan from the heat and continue to beat vigorously until you have a well swollen mass. Remove the whisk and add the almond paste, the flour, which you rain in from a sieve, the zest of a lemon, and a pinch of cinnamon, mixing everything delicately with a wooden spoon; and finally add the candied orange peel, cut into small pieces.

Butter and flour a baking pan, with a diameter of 10 inches and 3 high, and pour in the mixture, which should reach no more than 2 thirds of the pan. Bake in a preheated oven of moderate heat for about 40 minutes.

CASSATA ALLA SICILIANA

Cassata Sicilian Style

1½ cups ricotta
1 cup sugar
Vanilla extract
1¾ oz chocolate
3½ oz candied fruit
Sponge cake, store bought or homemade as opposite
1 cup vanilla sugar
Optional: maraschino liqueur or another sweet liqueur

Work the ricotta and season with the sugar and a little vanilla; work it well with a wooden spoon, to melt it and whip it like a cream. It would be advisable, but strictly not necessary, to add a little sweet and white liqueur, such as maraschino here.

When you have a soft cream, season it with pieces of chocolate and a few spoonfuls of candied fruit cut into cubes. Take a small baking pan and line the bottom and the inside with parchment paper. Cut the sponge cake into slices, and line the entire bottom. Add a little ricotta cream to the rest of the slices to line the insides. You will have thus obtained a kind of box, in which you will pour the ricotta cream. With the blade of a knife smooth the surface, then cover it with more slices of sponge cake, to close the cake.

Put the tin in the fridge, so the cream can harden a little. Then take a plate, place it on the baking sheet, turn everything upside down and turn out the cassata, removing the paper adhering to the sponge. Sprinkle generously with vanilla sugar.

ADA SAYS: *This is a well-known dessert, not to be confused with the ice cream of the same name.*

GÂTEAU CON CREMA AL CAFFÈ

Mocha Cream Cake

Butter for greasing
Maraschino liqueur
10½ tbsp butter
4 tbsp powdered sugar
Strong coffee
⅔ cup almonds

Genoise cake:
4 eggs, ⅔ cup sugar, ⅔ cup all-purpose flour, vanilla extract

Pastry cream:
1 egg yolk, 1 tbsp sugar, 3 tbsp all-purpose flour, 3 tbsp milk

This dessert is quite easy to make and gives excellent results.

Using the ingredient amounts listed here, prepare a Genoise cake *(p810)*. Bake it in a greased and floured baking pan, 8 inches in diameter and with sufficiently high sides. Then turn it out on a wire rack and let it cool.

When it is cold, cut it in 2 horizontally. Wet the insides with a little maraschino liqueur diluted with a very little water.

Prepare the following coffee cream: Put the butter in a bowl, whip it with a wooden spoon and then add, a little at a time, the powdered sugar, and a spoonful of cold pastry cream *(p752)* made using the ingredient amounts listed here. Then add half a cup of very strong, very cold coffee. Spread a quarter part of this cream on one part of the cake, and top with the other part to recompose its original shape. Take almost all of the remaining cream, leaving behind a spoonful, and spread it with the blade of a knife on the top of the cake and on the outside edges.

Peel the almonds, cut them into strips or crush into grains, and let them dry in a warm oven until they take on a very light blond color. With these almonds coat the edge of the cake.

Put the rest of the cream in a small pastry bag, with a spout of quarter of an inch, and pressing on the pocket make a crown of small stars on the edge of the cake.

GÂTEAU DIPLOMATICO

Diplomatic Cake

Puff pastry, homemade *(p820)* or store bought
Alchermes liqueur
Rum
Powdered sugar

Genoise cake:
5 eggs, ¾ cup sugar, ¾ cup all-purpose flour

Pastry cream:
3 egg yolks, ¼ cup plain flour, ¾ cup plain sugar, lemon zest, 2 cups milk

Make a puff pastry or buy it fresh packaged. Roll it out a quarter of an inch thick and with a small knife cut out a first round disk with a diameter of 12 inches. Put this disk on a baking sheet, prick it all over, and bake it in the oven at already a rather lively heat.

Gather the remaining dough and then roll out a new cutting to obtain another disk of the same diameter as the first, which you will prick and bake as soon as you remove the first from the oven.

Prepare a Genoise cake *(p810)* using the ingredient amounts listed here and bake it in a pan with a diameter of 10 inches. Also, prepare a not excessively thick pastry cream *(p752)* using the ingredient amounts listed here.

With a sharp knife, split the Genoise cake in 2, place one of the puff pastry disks on top and splash a little Alchermes and rum over it and spread it with the cream. Cover with the other Genoise cake disk, sprinkle this too with alchermes and rum and cover again with cream, using all the remaining cream. And finally close the cake with the second puff pastry disk, which must be the most beautiful of the 2. Press lightly and then, with a sharp knife, trim around the edges. Sprinkle with powdered sugar, and place it in a large serving dish.

PAN DI SPAGNA FARCITO

Chocolate Sponge Cake

Liqueur
Butter for greasing
Optional: whipped cream

Sponge cake:
5 eggs, ¾ cup sugar, ¾ cup all-purpose flour, lemon or orange, vanilla

Chocolate crème anglaise:
4 egg yolks, 4 tbsp sugar, 1 tbsp potato starch, 2 tbsp milk, 1¾ oz dark chocolate

Prepare a sponge cake *(p810)* with the ingredients listed here. As soon as it is cooked, take it out of the tin, put it on a wire rack and let it cool.

Meanwhile, prepare the crème anglaise: Put the egg yolks, sugar, and potato starch in a saucepan, mix with a wooden spoon until the eggs swell and foam, then dilute with boiling milk. Put the pan on the heat and stir continuously to slightly thicken the cream. Be careful not to let it boil. To this cream, add the grated dark chocolate, previously dissolved in a little milk. Mix carefully and remove from the heat; leave to cool, stirring occasionally.

With the blade of a long knife, divide the sponge cake into 2 disks. Place them face side up. Pour 2 glasses of liqueur and a glass of water into a cup and wet the insides of the cakes.

On the lower disk spread half of the prepared chocolate cream, then recompose the cake, as if it were whole, and spread over and around the remaining chocolate cream. On top, decorate with whipped cream.

TORTA ALL'ALBICOCCA

Apricot Genoise

1 cup almonds
Liqueur
3 tbsp sugar
Jar of apricot jam
To garnish: candied fruit

Genoise cake:
4 eggs, ⅔ cup sugar, ⅔ cup all-purpose flour

Firstly, put the shelled almonds in a small saucepan with cold water, bring them almost to a boil, remove the saucepan from the heat and then, one by one, remove the skins and keep them in a bowl with fresh water. When you have peeled them all, dry them in a towel and cut them into slices or crush into grains. Then spread on a baking sheet and bake at moderate heat, until they are dry and have taken a very light blond color.

Make your genoise cake *(p810)*. Divide it in two with a horizontal cut and wet the 2 disks with 2 small glasses of liqueur, of your choice, diluted with a little water. Sieve a jar of apricot jam. Spread a little on the larger disk and cover it with the other disk, to recompose the whole cake. Put the rest of the jam in a saucepan, add 2 or 3 spoons of sugar, and cook the sugar and jam for a few minutes, until a small thread forms between your fingers. Then pour this hot jelly on the cake, and spread it with the blade of a knife, covering all the cake. Scatter the almonds on top and around the edges and decorate with candied cherries, some candied orange filets, or other candied fruit as you like. When you have finished, slide it on to a serving dish.

TORTA ALLA CREMA DI CASTAGNE

Chestnut Cream Cake

Maraschino liqueur
7 tbsp butter
1¾ cups whipped cream
Vanilla extract

Genoise cake:
⅓ cup all-purpose flour, ½ cup potato starch, ⅔ cup sugar, 4 eggs

Chestnut cream:
1 lb 2 oz chestnuts, ¾ cup milk, 4 tbsp sugar

Have ready a Genoise sponge *(p810)*, and using the ingredients listed here, or use store bought. Divide it in 2 with a horizontal cut and wet each of the 2 disks with a sweet liqueur, for example maraschino.

To make the chestnut cream: Boil the chestnuts, peel them, remove the skins, and sieve them. Collect the chestnut purée in a saucepan and melt it on the stove with a glass of milk with a little dissolved sugar. Work the purée well to make it very smooth, then pour it out on to a plate and let it cool.

Whip the butter in a bowl with a wooden spoon until it is soft and fluffy; add, little by little, the purée of chestnuts, always working with the spoon, and finally incorporating the whipped cream with great delicacy. Perfume with a touch of vanilla; in this way, you will obtain a fine and tasty chestnut cream.

Spread a part of this cream on the lower disk of the cake; cover with the other disk, recomposing the cake, then spread it and garnish it on the outside with the remaining cream.

ZUPPA INGLESE

Trifle

1 egg white
¾ cup sugar
Alchermes liqueur
Rum
Candied peel
Powdered sugar

Sponge cake:
⅔ cup all-purpose flour, ⅔ cup sugar, 4 eggs, vanilla

Pastry cream:
3 egg yolks, ½ cup sugar, ⅓ cup all-purpose flour, 2 cups milk

Prepare a sponge cake *(p810)* using the ingredients listed here, or buy one. Make a pastry cream *(p752)* using the ingredient amounts listed here. Pour it into a bowl and let it cool a little, stirring it from time to time.

Whip the egg white to a snow and make sure it is very stiff and firm. Sieve the sugar over and mix slowly with a metal spoon.

Cut the sponge cake into slices a quarter inch thick. Line them up in 2 separate dishes and wet one half with Alchermes and the other half with rum. Spread the bottom of a baking pan with a diameter of about 12 inches with 2 or 3 spoonfuls of the custard. Then make a layer with the Alchermes sponge cake covering the entire bottom, and on this layer pour more custard in the middle, arranging it in a dome. You can add chopped candied fruit to decorate, if you like. Arrange the slices of sponge cake dipped in rum on the custard, keeping the shape of a light dome, and finally pour over the whipped egg whites, which you spread with the blade of a knife, so as to completely coat the cake. Sprinkle with powdered sugar, wait a few minutes, and then place the cake in an already hot oven of very light heat for about 20 minutes, so that the meringue can dry and take on a light-blond color. This trifle is served cold.

ADA SAYS: *To cover the cake, instead of the whipped egg whites, you can, alternatively, use 2 cups of sweetened whipped cream.*

Savoys, Madeleines & Margheritas

GÂTEAU MARGHERITA

Margherita Cake

6 eggs
1½ cups powdered sugar
1½ cups potato starch
7 tbsp butter
Lemon zest
Vanilla sugar

Put the egg yolks and the powdered sugar in a bowl, and work the mixture until it is well whipped and appears light and fluffy. Whip the whites to a firm snow, and then mix into the eggs, adding them slowly with a wooden spoon. Then gently, gently pour in the potato starch and drain over freshly melted butter and a little grated lemon zest, which will impart a pleasant aroma.

Grease a tray with a diameter of about 10 inches, sprinkle it with potato starch, turn it over and beat it lightly to drop off the superfluous starch. Pour in the mixture and immediately bake in a preheated oven with moderate heat for about half an hour. When it has cooked, take it out of the tin and let it dry and cool on a pastry rack. Then sprinkle with vanilla sugar.

PASTA MADDALENA

Madeleine Cake

4 eggs
2 yolks
¾ cup sugar
⅔ cup all-purpose flour
1¼ cups potato starch
3½ tbsp butter, plus extra for greasing
Lemon zest

Put the eggs, the yolks, and the sugar in a bowl and whisk everything. Put the bowl over a saucepan with an inch of water set over on very low heat. Holding the container tilted, continue to beat until the mixture has become lukewarm. Be careful not to heat too much or the eggs will separate, and the success of the preparation would be compromised.

Remove from the heat and continue beating until the eggs are cold and well whipped. Then blend the flour and the starch together and sift, dropping them like rain from a sieve. Finally, pour in the just warm butter. Complete with the addition of the lemon zest and give a last light stir.

Grease and flour a tin of about 10 inches in diameter, put the mixture in, and bake in a preheated oven of moderate heat for 3 quarters of an hour.

ADA SAYS: *An alternative is to prepare a chocolate cream with grated chocolate, sugar, egg yolks, all-purpose flour, milk, and a touch of vanilla. Cut the* Maddalena *cake into 2 disks, fill them with the cream, put the cake back together, and sprinkle with powdered sugar.*

PASTA SAVOIARDA

Savoy Cake

5 eggs
1¼ cups sugar
⅔ cup potato starch
⅓ cup all-purpose flour
Lemon or orange zest or vanilla extract
Butter for greasing

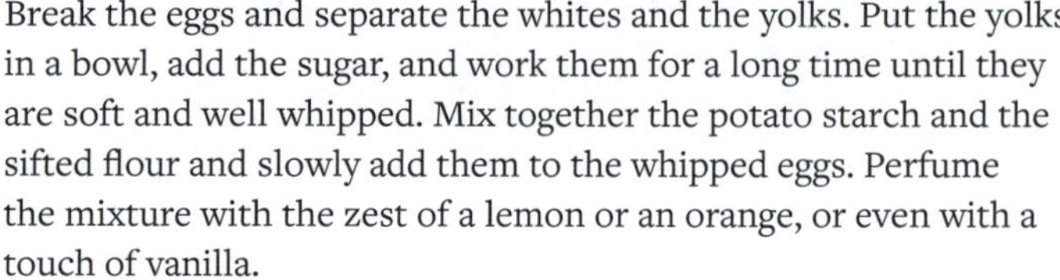

Break the eggs and separate the whites and the yolks. Put the yolks in a bowl, add the sugar, and work them for a long time until they are soft and well whipped. Mix together the potato starch and the sifted flour and slowly add them to the whipped eggs. Perfume the mixture with the zest of a lemon or an orange, or even with a touch of vanilla.

Whip the 5 whites to a firm snow and mix them with great delicacy into the mixture. Butter and sprinkle a little potato starch into a tall mold with a capacity of one and a half quarts. Pour in the mixture but do not fill it right to the top or it will spill over. Bake in a preheated oven of moderate heat for about 3 quarters of an hour.

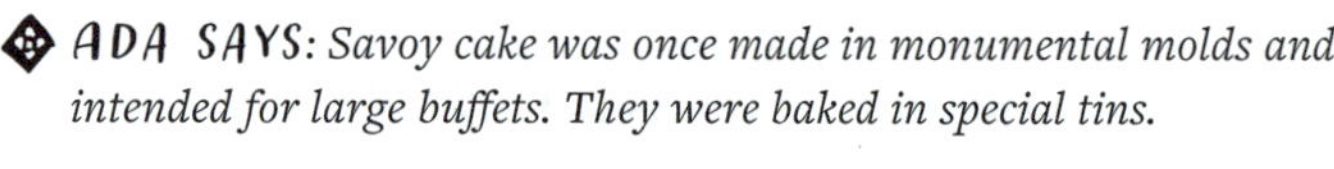

ADA SAYS: *Savoy cake was once made in monumental molds and intended for large buffets. They were baked in special tins.*

TORTA MARGHERITA

Margherita Cake with Marscapone

Margherita cake *(p815)*
3 eggs
⅓ cup sugar
1 cup mascarpone
Liqueur
Optional: chocolate chips

Have ready your Margherita cake, and make this cream to fill: Put the egg yolks in a bowl, add the sugar, and work them until they are soft and well whipped. Add the mascarpone, kept at room temperature, a little at a time, mixing carefully, and a glass of liqueur. Whip the egg whites to a firm snow and add them to the mixture with great delicacy so as not to disassemble them.

Divide the cake in 2 with a horizontal cut and spread one of the 2 disks with the mascarpone cream. Cover the cake with the other disk, then spread it and garnish it on the outside with the remaining cream. You can decorate it with chocolate chips.

Choux Pastry

TO MAKE CHOUX PASTRY

The following amounts are required to make choux pastry: **3 ½ tablespoons of butter, ½ cup water, salt, ½ cup flour, 2 eggs.**

Put the butter, water, and a pinch of salt in a small saucepan and place on the stove. Meanwhile, have the flour near you, already weighed. As soon as the water boils, take the saucepan from the heat and suddenly pour the flour into it; mix with a wooden spoon and put it back on the heat. Soon the dough will form a ball, which will come off the spoon and the sides of the saucepan. Let it cook for another 2 or 3 minutes, always stirring it, and when it makes a very slight noise, as if it were frying, remove it from the heat and turn it upside down on a plate. Let it cool, then put it back in the pan, which will also be cold, and add the eggs, one at a time, not adding the second if the first is not well blended. Continue to work the dough vigorously with the spoon, until it is velvety. It will bubble here and there and, if stirred slowly, it will tear. At this point the choux is ready to be used.

BIGNÈ IN TORTA

Choux Beignets

MAKES 70

Powdered sugar
Lemon zest
Olive oil or lard
Vanilla sugar
Optional: 10½ oz candied cherries or 7 oz sugar violets

Choux pastry:
1 cup all-purpose flour, 7 tbsp butter, 4 eggs, 1 cup water

Spun sugar:
1¼ cups sugar, 1 tsp glucose

Make the choux pastry *(as above)*, using the ingredients listed here. When the dough is velvety smooth and bubbles here and there, add a teaspoon of powdered sugar and the zest of a lemon. Work a little more to combine these last ingredients, and let the dough rest covered for a while in a cool place.

Heat a pan with plenty of oil, or lard, and when the liquid is just warm, drop some pieces of dough the size of large hazelnuts, into the pan making sure to give them a rounded shape. You can use 2 teaspoons: one for the dough, the other to drop the dough into the pan. Fry first on moderate heat; then, as the beignets swell, increase the heat, shaking the pan in a circular motion. If there is enough liquid, the beignets will turn on their own, doing the most graceful somersaults. As soon as they are a nice blond color, remove them, let the pan cool a little, and start the operation again, making sure not to put too many beignets in at a time.

To decorate, make some spun sugar *(p736)*. In a small saucepan, prepare some spun sugar boiled with a little water and glucose. Once the sugar has reached the right point, place the pan next to you resting it on a folded cloth, take one beignet at a time with your fingers and quickly dip one part in the sugar, applying it immediately along the outer edge of a round serving dish, remembering that the beignets should be placed sideways, with the rounded part facing outwards. Make a whole crown of beignets, always dipping them in sugar. On this first crown make another one slightly smaller and so on until you have a complete pyramid.

Finish the cake, if you like, with spun sugar and decorate it with candied cherries and sugar violets.

PROFITEROLES

Profiteroles

MAKES ABOUT 70

Vanilla extract
Marsala
Cocoa powder
1¼ cups sugar
Glucose
Optional: rum, whipped cream, hazelnut paste (2 tbsp sugar, ¼ cup toasted hazelnuts)

Choux pastry:
1 cup water, 1 cup all-purpose flour, 7 tbsp butter, 4 eggs, salt

Pastry cream:
3 cups milk, ⅔ cup all-purpose flour, 4 egg yolks, ⅓ cup sugar

Make your choux pastry *(p817)* using the ingredients listed here. Pipe the dough in a pastry bag with a smooth nozzle of half an inch and let walnut-sized balls come out on to the baking sheet, placing them a little apart from each other. The oven must be very hot and the choux should not cook for more than 10 to 15 minutes and must be empty, light, and of a beautiful golden color.

Once all the choux have been made, prepare the pastry cream filling *(p752)* using the ingredient amounts listed here. Immediately pour it into a bowl and let it cool, stirring it from time to time to prevent it from forming a skin. You can divide the cream into 3 bowls, adding a touch of vanilla to one bowl and thus forming a vanilla cream; to another a spoonful of Marsala; to the third a spoonful of chocolate powder, dissolved in hot cream, thus obtaining a chocolate cream.

Small choux can also be filled only or partially with whipped cream. Any leftovers can go for decoration. Fill the choux buns by first making a side cut with scissors and then stuff them using a pastry bag with a smooth nozzle quarter of an inch wide and filling them with the cream.

If making the hazelnut paste: Melt the sugar in a saucepan over moderate heat without adding water. As soon as the sugar has melted, add the skinned hazelnuts, coarsely boil, and mix. When the sugar and hazelnuts are warm, blend them until you get an oily and fragrant paste.

SAINT-HONORÉ

Saint-Honoré

10½ oz puff pastry, homemade *(p820)* or store bought
Butter for greasing
½ cup sugar
Glucose
Optional: candied cherries

Choux pastry:
3½ tbsp butter, ½ cup all-purpose flour, 2 eggs, ½ cup water, salt

Pastry cream:
2 egg yolks, ¾ cup sugar, 1 cup all-purpose flour, 1 quart milk, lemon zest or vanilla, 2 gelatin sheets, cognac, Marsala, 2 oz chocolate (or 1 quart whipped cream)

Make up a puff pastry or use store-bought. Roll it out to ½ inch thick, making sure to give it a round shape. Place a round lid of 10 inches in diameter on the dough, as a model, and remove the superfluous dough with a small knife, but not cutting it flush with the lid, but leaving a generous finger around it. Wrap the disk on the rolling pin and lay it on a baking sheet lightly greased with butter. Then use the tines of a fork to prick it well all over, reaching as far as touching the plate. Put it in a preheated oven and cook over a fairly high heat for about a quarter of an hour; then remove and let it cool. Place the lid, the one you used as a model, back on the disk and with the tip of the knife follow the edge exactly, removing the excess dough. This is your base.

Prepare a choux pastry *(p817)* using the ingredient amounts listed here. Put the choux paste in a pastry bag with a smooth round nozzle measuring half an inch. Butter the baking sheet and release balls of choux dough as big as nuts on to the plate. Arrange at a distance of a few fingers from each other, so that as they grow they don't stick together. Put in the oven at a good heat. In the oven the choux grows, swells, and takes on a beautiful golden color. In all, they should not remain in the oven for more than a quarter of an hour. Before removing them from the oven, make sure that the dough is firm and the choux is dry, otherwise you would run the risk of seeing them deflate as they cool. Put the choux on a wire rack and let them cool completely. When they are cold, make an incision on one side with scissors, one inch long, for the filling.

For the filling, for which you will use a pastry bag with a small nozzle, you can use a white cream *(p751)*, a zabaglione *(p754)* or a chocolate cream *(p753)* or just sweetened whipped cream. You can flavor the whipped cream with vanilla or zest of lemon or even finish it with a little Marsala or cognac. You can also divide the cream into 2 parts. One part vanilla, lemon, Marsala, or cognac; in the other part, 2 ounces of grated dark chocolate, melted at very low heat with a few drops of water or milk. The chocolate cream can be flavored with a touch of vanilla.

Now, put the sugar in a small saucepan, wet it with a couple of spoons of water, add a teaspoon of glucose, and cook until caramel in color. Make sure that the cooking is well achieved and that the sugar breaks cleanly, since there is nothing less pleasant than a caramel sugar that sticks to the teeth. When the sugar is well cooked, remove the saucepan from the heat, and bring everything close to you.

Take one choux at a time, with your fingers, dip it partly in the caramelized sugar, take it out, and place it on the edge of the puff pastry disk. Immediately take the second choux, repeat the operation, and place it next to the first, and so on until you have made the crown. Once all the choux are attached, you can embellish them by placing half a candied cherry on each of them, which will easily stick to the sugar, thus giving a pleasant note to the preparation. Fill the central void with the remaining cream, putting it down in large spoonfuls, one next to the other, to obtain a surface with large undulations. If you have prepared 2 types of cream, fill the choux pastry half with plain cream and half with chocolate cream. Even with the whipped cream, the choux is filled first, and the rest is put in large spoonfuls in the center of the cake. Once the cake is finished, gently lift it and place on a serving plate.

◆ **ADA SAYS:** *St. Honoré is a patron saint of bakers. The cream to garnish the cake must be in abundant quantity, and it is advisable to add a couple of gelatin sheets, previously soaked in cold water and then dissolved in a trifle of hot water, which help the consistency.*

Brioche & Puff Pastry

TO MAKE BRIOCHE

The following amounts are required to make brioche: **1⅓ cups strong bread flour, ¼ oz active dry yeast, 2 eggs, 2 tablespoons sugar, 9 tablespoons butter, plus more for greasing, and salt.**

Put ⅔ of a cup of flour in a bowl and add the yeast previously dissolved in 2 fingers of warm water. Mix the yeast and flour so that the result is a dough of the right consistency that can collect into a ball. With a knife, make 2 cross incisions on the ball, wrap in a towel, and leave to rise in a sheltered place for 10 to 15 minutes.

Arrange the remaining flour on the table, put the eggs, sugar, and salt in the middle and mix everything. Work the dough vigorously on the table, lifting it and beating it hard with one hand, until it forms a homogeneous whole and comes off in one piece from the table and from your hands.

Meanwhile, in a quarter of an hour or 20 minutes, the yeast ball will have doubled its volume; take it, crush it in your hands and pull it out to make a small pizza about 4 inches in diameter, which you will put on top of the mixture of flour, eggs, sugar, and salt. By pressing and working with your fingers and hands, make the 2 pastries mix to form a single whole.

Work a little more, and lastly add the butter, which, in winter, must be softened a little with your hands. Add the butter to the dough, always beating and working a small knob at a time. You will have to make it absorb, so always beating and working with your hands, until you obtain an elastic, velvety dough, which will come off the table in one piece. This last part will not require more than 10 minutes of work.

Then put the dough in a bowl and take care to cover it immediately and take it to a sheltered place. After an hour and a half, when the dough has begun to rise, depress it again with the palm of your hand to temporarily stop it rising. Once this is done, cover the bowl with its lid, and place it in the fridge for another 6 or 7 hours. This apparent anomaly of leavening in the fridge gives excellent results.

Once the set time has elapsed, you will find that the dough has risen considerably and appears in a swollen mass. Turn it over on a lightly floured kitchen table, tap it lightly with your open hand to deflate it, and fold it back on itself 2 or 3 times, without kneading it, but smoothing it with small strokes with the palm of your hand. Then roll the dough into a ball and place it in a smooth, straight, and high-walled mold, slightly buttered, with such a capacity that the dough reaches just up to the middle.

Let it rise in a sheltered place and when the dough has reached the edge, lightly brown by brushing it with a beaten egg and bake it in a high heat oven for about 20 minutes.

TO MAKE PUFF PASTRY

The following amounts are required to make puff pastry: **⅔ cup strong bread flour, 3 tablespoons water, salt, 7 tablespoons butter.**

Sift the flour and arrange it in a heap. Put the water and a pinch of salt in the middle and mix with your fingers. Gradually take the flour from the inside, knead, but without working too much, until you get a dough that is neither too hard nor too soft, and very smooth. Make it into a ball, cover it with a towel. and let it rest for about 20 minutes. After 20 minutes, take the dough and with the rolling pin give it a square shape, but without spreading it too much, about 4 inches per side. In the middle of this square, place the butter in a piece that you will have softened by working in a napkin. Then bring the 4 sides of the dough over the butter so the edges meet, enclosing the butter. Lightly place the rolling pin on this square to close the dough well and let it rest for another 5 minutes.

Then we begin to perform the so-called work of the turns. Roll out the dough into a rectangular strip again, stretching it in front of you, so that it is 3 times longer than it is wide, making sure to roll it out to an equal thickness of about ½ inch. Halve the strip in front of you, wide instead of long, and fold the 2 ends towards the center, covering one with the other. You will have thus obtained a kind of 3-sheet book. Then roll out the dough again in a rectangle in front of you like the first time. Bring it back horizontal and fold it again in 3. You will have given the dough 2 turns.

After these first 2 rounds, let it rest in the fridge for 10 minutes and then do another 2 rounds, exactly the same way. Another 10 minutes of rest and then give the last 2 and final laps. During the operation of the turns, always lightly dust the dough and the table with a veil of flour. After the 6 prescribed rounds, the dough is ready and you can roll it out. Remember that whenever a dessert is made with puff pastry, it is good to wait about 10 minutes before putting it in the oven.

TO MAKE SIMPLIFIED PUFF PASTRY

For simplified puff pastry, allow: **10 tablespoons of flour for 7 tablespoons of butter.**

Blend the flour with the butter. The dough should not be worked with your hands, because the butter would soften too much, but with a spatula or a wide knife blade. When the butter has completely absorbed the flour and regained its compactness, flatten it into a square shape as high as a finger. Then put in another 6 tablespoons of flour, which you will have mixed on the table with a little water and a pinch of salt, to make a very soft dough, which sticks to the fingers. Give this soft dough a round shape and enclose in it the butter, as for common puff pastry.

Without waiting, roll out the dough into one rectangular strip that you will then place in front of you, wide side nearest to you. Lift one of the shorter sides of the strip, and fold it over the middle of the strip. Do the same for the left side, and then fold the dough again so it is folded in half on itself. In this way, you will have a kind of book made up of 4 sheets instead of 3. The rest of the operations are the same as those of the common puff pastry: only the dough always folds in 4 instead of 3, and only 4 turns are given instead of 6, and always in a row, without letting the dough rest between one turn and the other. In about 10 minutes, the puff pastry will be ready to be cut out and baked.

BRIOCHES PICCOLE

Small Brioches

Butter for greasing
1 egg

Brioche dough:
1⅓ cups strong bread flour, 9 tbsp butter, 2 tbsp sugar, ¼ oz fresh yeast, 2 eggs, salt

Make the brioche dough *(p821)* using the ingredients listed here, and when it has well risen, turn it over on to a lightly floured kitchen table, depress it lightly with your open hand to deflate it, and fold it on itself 2 or 3 times without kneading it, but smoothing it out with small strokes with the palm of the hand.

Once this is done, always dusting the table with flour, lightly roll out 4 fifths of the dough to make a large torch shape with a diameter of about 2 inches, which you will cut with a knife into pieces like a large walnut, about 3 quarters of an ounce in weight. Roll the rest of the dough with your hands and cut it into smaller pieces the size of a hazelnut.

Line up the smaller nuts of dough on the table and grease them very lightly with butter. Take one large piece of dough at a time, roll it into a ball, and place one in each mould. With your index finger, slightly wet with water, make a hole in the middle of each ball of dough. Roll up the small pieces of dough, giving them the shape of tiny pears, and insert the tips of these pears into the hole, so that the round part remains outside.

After about half an hour, with a brush dipped in beaten egg, wash the brioches and put them in a hot oven giving them 5 or 6 minutes of cooking, until they have a nice dark gold colour.

GÂTEAU FRANGIPANE

Frangipane Cake

14 oz puff pastry, homemade (*p820*) or store bought
Butter for greasing
1 egg
Powdered sugar

Almond cream:
⅔ cup almonds, ½ cup sugar, 1 egg, 3½ tbsp butter, rum

Roll out the puff pastry to a thickness of ¼ of an inch. Place a 7 inch spring form pan on a baking sheet and lightly butter the inside of the circle and the sides. With a part of the dough, line the inside of the circle and the edges to have a round box. With the tip of a small knife, make a few small holes in the bottom and adjust the edges of the flan well.

Then prepare the almond cream: Peel the almonds, let them dry in a warm oven without letting them brown; then blend them with sugar and sieve. Put the prepared almond flour in a bowl and add the egg; mix with a wooden spoon, and, always stirring, finally add the melted butter in 2 or 3 goes. Stir again until the mixture is well whipped and finish it with a glass of rum.

Now pour this cream into the puff pastry box, spreading it evenly with the blade of a knife. With the remaining dough, cut 6 strips of about 3 quarters of an inch wide, which you will place on top of the gâteau, in a special X-shaped weave. Lastly, lightly brush the puff pastry with a little beaten egg and then bake in a preheated oven of moderate heat for about half an hour.

Five minutes before removing from the oven, sprinkle it abundantly with powdered sugar, and put it back in the oven immediately. The sugar, when melting, will form a light caramelized layer on the cake, giving it greater elegance. When the cake is cooked, remove it from the oven without turning it out immediately, but letting it cool a little. When it is still warm, remove the circle from the flan, lift the cake. and slide it on to a wire rack so that it can cool. Then place it on a serving dish.

MILLEFOGLIE ALLA CREMA

Cream Millefeuille

1¼ lb puff pastry, homemade *(p820)* or store bought
Cognac or Marsala
⅔ cup shelled almonds
Powdered sugar
Optional: 20ml whipped cream, candied cherries

Pastry cream:
3 egg yolks, 3 oz sugar, 2½ oz flour, 2 cups milk

Prepare a puff pastry or buy it fresh packaged. Roll it out and make 5 disks. Sprinkle the baking sheet lightly with water and bake the puff pastry disks in a preheated oven.

Using the ingredient amounts listed here, make a pastry cream *(p752)* and pour it into a bowl. Add a small glass of Marsala or cognac and leave to cool, stirring the cream from time to time to stop any skin forming.

Shell and skin the almonds in the usual way, dry them in a towel, and cut them into slices or crush into grains. Then spread these almonds on a baking sheet and bake them at moderate heat, until they are dry and have a very light blond color.

Put a disk of puff pastry on the table and spread a quarter part of the pastry cream on top. Overlap a second disk, spread it with cream and so on until you have overlapped 4 disks and have all 4 spread with cream. Then take the last disk and close the mille feuille, but be careful to place this disk upside down, so that the flat part of it remains upside. Spread a little of the cream left aside around the edges of the millefeuille and scatter the almonds over. Then sprinkle the powdered sugar abundantly over the top, so as to make it completely white. Place the finished millefeuille on a dessert plate.

ADA SAYS: *The millefeuille can also be finished by spreading a layer of whipped cream on the upper disk and placing a crown of candied cherries around it. Or, less work is just to spread the pastry with jam.*

SFOGLIATA DI RICOTTA

Ricotta Sfogliata

3 tbsp raisins
Candied orange
Rum
1¼ cups ricotta
¾ cup sugar
Vanilla extract
7 oz puff pastry, homemade *(p820)* or store bought
1 egg
Powdered sugar

Crème anglaise:
1 egg yolk, 2 tbsp sugar, ¾ cup milk

For best results, half an hour before making the dessert, place the raisins and the diced candied fruits in a cup and sprinkle them with rum. Then sieve the ricotta and season with the sugar, the raisins, a tablespoon of candied orange peel, cut into cubes, and a touch of vanilla.

Prepare a crème anglaise *(p752)* using the ingredient amounts listed here and add it to the ricotta, with a little rum from macerating the fruits. Roll out the puff pastry to a thickness of quarter of an inch and make a disk 8 inches in diameter. Knead the scraps and make another disk a little thinner and of the same diameter. Put this on the baking sheet.

On this disk, spread the ricotta mixture, leaving a free edge of about an inch around the sides. Wet the edge with beaten egg. Cover with the other disk. Press slowly with your fingers so the 2 disks fit together and then, with a small knife, equalize the 2 disks. Lightly brush the pastry with beaten egg and put it in a hot oven for about 20 minutes.

Five minutes before taking out of the oven, sprinkle it abundantly with powdered sugar, to create a light caramelized layer.

SWEET SOUFFLÉS

SUFFLÈ AL CIOCCOLATO

Chocolate Soufflé

2 cups milk
½ cup sugar
½ cup all-purpose flour
⅔ cup cocoa powder
Butter
3 egg yolks
4 egg whites
Optional: whipped cream

Boil one and a half cups of the milk in a saucepan with the sugar. In a separate bowl, mix the flour with the rest of the cold milk until you obtain a sticky dough. When the milk in the saucepan boils, combine it, bit by bit with the flour and milk. Leave it to cook, mixing for a couple of minutes, then take off the heat adding in the sifted cocoa powder, and a knob of butter. When the mixture is almost completely cool, top it off with the egg yolks.

Separately, whip the egg whites into stiff peaks, and then gently add them to the rest. Strain the mixture into a one quart soufflé mold, that has already been buttered and sprinkled with sugar, and cook in a preheated oven at a moderate heat for half an hour. Serve with whipped cream if desired

SUFFLÈ AL RUM

Rum Soufflé

All-purpose flour
¾ cup milk
½ cup sugar
Butter
3 egg yolks
4 egg whites
Ladyfingers
Rum
Powdered sugar

Stir together a generous tablespoonful of flour in a cup with some cold milk until you have a runny batter. Warm a pan with the rest of the milk and half the sugar and as it reaches the boiling point combine, bit by bit, with the flour and milk, mixing well until there are no lumps. Continue to cook for a couple of minutes, always mixing, until it thickens, then take off the heat and add a knob of butter. Leave it to cool a little and then add the egg yolks, one at a time.

Whip the egg whites into stiff peaks. When the mixture is almost completely cold, add a tablespoon of the whipped egg white at a time and mix carefully into the batter.

Butter a soufflé mold of one and a half quart capacity. Add in a couple of spoons of sugar, turning over to ensure it sticks everywhere. Turn upside down to tap off any excess.

Dice or crush the ladyfingers and sprinkle them generously with a glass of rum. Pour a layer of the egg mixture into the mold, then the diced cookies, and then alternate between the mixture and cookies. At the end the mix should only reach halfway up the mold.

Bake the soufflé in a preheated oven of moderate heat for about half an hour. In the oven, the mixture grows and rises to the brim of the mold, so it is good to decrease the heat a little towards the end of baking. Five minutes before taking the soufflé out of the oven, dust the surface with powdered sugar, which will melt and form a light caramelized layer on the soufflé. As soon as the soufflé is cooked, place on a serving plate and send immediately to the table.

SUFFLÈ DI ALBICOCCHE

Apricot Soufflé

1 lb 2 oz apricots
2 cups sugar
Vanilla extract
⅓ cup almonds
8 egg whites
Butter to grease
Powdered sugar

Wash and split the apricots in half, remove the stones and, if they are very ripe, mash them, collecting the pulp in a bowl. Otherwise, put them in a saucepan with a little water and let them cook a bit before mashing.

Cook the apricot purée with the sugar. Flavor with vanilla and cook until they form a dense jam, then leave to cool.

Shell and peel the almonds and dry in a cloth without putting them in the oven. Crush them or chop into flakes. Whip the egg whites to stiff peaks and add to the apricot jam, combining carefully with a wooden spoon.

Butter a soufflé mold generously, then scatter the almond dust around and also a dusting of powdered sugar. Pour the apricot mixture and whipped egg whites into the mold and bake in a preheated oven at moderate heat for more than half an hour, until, that is, the soufflé is well puffed. Have it brought to the table immediately.

SUFFLÈ DI CASTAGNE

Chestnut Soufflé

1 lb 2 oz chestnuts
5½ tbsp butter
1 tbsp sweetened cocoa powder
Sugar
Vanilla extract
4 egg whites
Powdered sugar

Knick the skins and put the chestnuts in a pot with plenty of water. Bring to a boil and when they are cooked, remove their skins, and work them to a purée. Collect the purée in a small saucepan, add 4 tablespoons of butter, a tablespoon of cocoa powder, 2 tablespoons of sugar, and mix with a wooden spoon while drying everything over the heat. Lastly, flavor with a splash of vanilla. Turn into a bowl and leave it to cool.

Whip the egg whites into stiff peaks and delicately add into the chestnut mixture, taking care to mix, nice and slowly so as not to deflate the eggs.

Butter a quart soufflé mold and coat with sugar. Add the chestnut mixture, smooth it out with the blade of a knife, and bake in a hot oven for about half an hour.

When the soufflé has swelled up and risen to the surface, take out of the oven, place the mold on a plate with a cloth on it. Dust the top with powdered sugar and send it to the table before it deflates.

SUFFLÈ DI CREMA E BANANE

Cream and Banana Soufflé

3 bananas
¾ cup sugar
Rum
4 eggs
⅓ cup all-purpose flour
½ cup milk
2 tbsp butter
Vanilla extract
⅓ cup almonds
Powdered sugar

Peel the bananas, cut them into thin, slanted slices, and place them in a bowl with 2 tablespoons of the sugar, a shot of rum or other liqueur, and let them absorb the flavor for a little while.

In a small saucepan, mix ⅔ of a cup of sugar with 4 egg yolks with a wooden spoon and then add the flour. Slowly dampen with the milk, then the butter, and a touch of vanilla and set it over the heat, continuously stirring, until it is a thick cream. Leave it to cool and then whip 2 egg whites into stiff peaks and add carefully to the cream.

Shell and skin the almonds, dry in a cloth and thinly slice. Butter a quart soufflé mold. Pour in a first layer of cream, on top of this make a layer of slices of banana, and repeat 3 or 4 times, finishing—about half the way up—with a layer of cream. Scatter the almonds on top.

Place in a preheated oven of moderate heat for a quarter of an hour. Open the oven and generously dust the soufflé, which will have gently increased in volume, with powdered sugar. Close the oven and leave to cook for another 5 or 6 minutes, time for the soufflé to rise completely and for the sugar to caramelize. Serve immediately.

SUFFLÈ DI FRAGOLE

Strawberry Soufflé

1 lb 2 oz strawberries
White wine
½ cup sugar
4 egg whites
Butter for greasing
Optional: 1 cup light cream, powdered sugar, vanilla extract

Thoroughly clean the strawberries, wash them with the wine and mash them, then add sugar to the resulting purée. Whip the egg whites to stiff peaks and delicately fold them into to the strawberry purée.

Butter a quart soufflé mold and sprinkle with sugar. Pour the strawberry mixture in up to 2 thirds of the mold, smooth it with the blade of a knife, and put it in a preheated oven of light heat for about 20 minutes. When the soufflé has risen, place it promptly on a plate without removing it from the mold and have it sent immediately to the table. On the side, you can serve the cream, heated in a bain-marie, sweetened with sugar, and finished with a touch of vanilla.

CHILLED DESSERTS

BAVARESE ALLA VAINIGLIA

Vanilla Bavarois

Vanilla bean
2 cups milk
1 cup sugar
5 egg yolks
2 gelatin sheets
¾ cup sweetened whipped cream
Sweet almond oil
Optional: sugar, chocolate, pine nuts to decorate

Split the vanilla bean in half lengthwise and add it with the milk to a small saucepan. Bring it gently to the boil, then turn off the heat and let it rest.

Put the sugar and the 5 egg yolks in another pan; stir a little with a wooden spoon and then gradually pour over the milk, stirring constantly to melt the eggs and sugar well. Set the pan back over the heat, and without ever stopping stirring, let the mixture warm up, but be careful not to let it boil, or the eggs will curdle. As soon as you see that the cream veils the spoon a little, remove from the heat, and add the gelatin, kept in cold water for a few minutes and then squeezed in your hands, so it dissolves immediately. Stir with a spoon to mix well and then pour the cream into a bowl, not forgetting to mix it again, from time to time, so as not to let any skin form on the surface. It is a good idea to sieve the cream into the bowl.

When the cream has cooled, put it in the fridge for a while and when the cream is cold, as soon as you see that it has begun to thicken, gently add the whipped cream.

Grease a 1 quart mold with sweet almond oil and then keep it upside down for a few minutes so that the excess oil can drain free. Now pour the prepared mixture in and put in the fridge for a couple of hours. When serving, turn out the Crème Bavaroise on a plate and garnish with sugar, grated chocolate, and pine nuts.

BAVARESE DI CIOCCOLATO

Chocolate Bavarois

Crème Bavaroise *(as above)*
½ cup cocoa

This Bavarois differs from the vanilla recipe above only in that it has cocoa, which you put in the same boiling cream, adjusting as follows: Once the vanilla cream is made, divide it into 2 equal parts: one half you will leave as it is, and to the other half you will add the cocoa. Let it cool, add a little whipped cream to the vanilla Crème Bavaroise and use it to half fill a mold. Chill in the fridge for half an hour to set, and only then add the cocoa cream. Leave in the fridge for another hour and a half, and then turn out on to a serving plate.

BAVARESE DI FRAGOLE

Strawberry Bavarois

7 oz strawberries
1 lb 2 oz wild strawberries
2 lemons
1½ cups powdered sugar
2 gelatin sheets
2 cups milk
Sweetened whipped cream
Sweet almond oil
1 orange

Wash the strawberries and wild strawberries in water acidulated with the juice of a lemon. Keep a few back for decoration. Then push them through a sieve to collect a purée in a bowl—or you can use a blender. Grate over the zest of a lemon, being careful to grate only the yellow part. Squeeze over the juice of half a lemon and sweeten with powdered sugar.

Put the gelatin sheets in cold water and after about 10 minutes, when they are softened, squeeze them with your hands and arrange them in a saucepan with the milk. Set the saucepan over a very low flame and let the jelly liquefy. Then pour it over the strawberry purée. Mix everything and let the bowl cool in the fridge.

When you see the mixture has begun to thicken, slowly mix in the whipped cream. Take a pudding mold, grease it lightly with sweet almond oil, then turn it over, and let it drain for a few minutes. Spoon in the strawberry mousse and tap it lightly on a cloth so there are no gaps. Now put it back in the fridge until it has set well. Turn out on a dessert plate, decorate with more strawberries, and half slices of oranges and lemons.

BISCUIT AL CAFFÈ

Coffee Cups

1 egg
5 egg yolks
1 cup sugar
Strong coffee
6 gelatin sheets
1 cup sweetened whipped cream

Put one whole egg and 5 egg yolks, the sugar, and 3 tablespoons of very strong and cold coffee in a small bowl. We insist on this point, because if the coffee is not strong and aromatic, the sweet will be tasteless. The aroma of the coffee must predominate.

Set the bowl over a larger saucepan of hot water on a very low heat with an average temperature between 120°F and 140°F degrees. Whisk the mixture vigorously, at least for a quarter of an hour, and when it is well whipped, remove it from the hot water and continue to beat it until it is completely cold, at least for another quarter of an hour.

In the meantime, you will have softened the gelatin sheets in cold water. When they are soft, remove, squeeze them in your hands and put them in a saucepan over very low heat to melt. Set aside to cool—this jelly must be almost cold and well diluted before pouring slowly into the egg and coffee mixture, while stirring with a wooden spoon. When it is well blended, complete the preparation with the whipped cream.

Distribute the mixture into cups, smoothing the surface with the blade of a knife, then put them in the fridge for about an hour.

BISCUIT AL CIOCCOLATO

Chocolate Cups

3 egg yolks
3 tbsp sugar
2 tbsp potato starch
2 cups milk
½ cup cocoa powder
1 cup whipped cream
Optional: candied cherries, almonds, hazelnuts

Put the egg yolks in a saucepan with the sugar and potato starch, mix them with a wooden spoon, and dilute with 1½ cup of cold milk. Set the pan over a light heat and, constantly stirring, let it thicken and cook. Stir the cocoa powder into the remaining milk. When the egg mixture begins to thicken, add the cocoa mixture and and continue stirring for a few more minutes. Then remove from the heat, pour into a bowl and let it cool completely, stirring often with a spoon. At the end, gently add the whipped cream.

Spoon into a glass cup and keep it in the fridge until ready. Decorate with candied cherries divided in half, or with chopped hazelnuts or almonds.

BISCUIT AL LIMONE

Lemon Cups

3 eggs
3 tbsp sugar
Lemon peel
Potato starch
Lemon juice
¾ cup sweetened whipped cream
Pistachios

Beat the egg yolks in a saucepan. To another saucepan, add ¾ cup of water, the sugar, and thinly sliced lemon peel (use only the yellow skin). Set over medium heat and bring to a boil. Once it boils, remove the pan from the heat, cover, and let it cool completely.

When the syrup is cold, pour it over the beaten egg yolks, add a teaspoon of potato starch, and the juice of half a lemon. Set the pan back over a low heat and, always stirring with a wooden spoon, let the cream thicken slightly. Then pour it into a bowl and let it cool, stirring often.

In another bowl whip the whites to a very firm snow. Gently, fold in the egg whites so as not to disassemble them. Also add the whipped cream to make the mixture even softer. When the mixture is well blended, distribute it in cups, garnishing with a pinch of pistachio nuts and place in the fridge.

BISCUIT ALLO ZABAIONE

Zabaglione Cups

3 eggs
6 tbsp Marsala
3 tbsp sugar
2 cups whipped cream
Optional: cookies

Put 3 egg yolks, the Marsala wine, and sugar in a small saucepan. Set the saucepan over a very low heat and whisk energetically, but without bringing it to the boil. Remove the saucepan from the heat and let the mixture cool while continuing to beat it with the whisk.

When it is cold, mix in 2 egg whites whipped to stiff peaks, and finally the whipped cream using a wooden spoon. Distribute this mixture into the cups and put them in the fridge for about an hour, so they can be served very cold. They can be accompanied by cookies.

CHARLOTTE CLASSICA

Classic Charlotte

3 egg yolks
⅓ cup sugar
1 cup milk
4 gelatin sheets
Vanilla extract
1 cup sweetened whipped cream
3½ oz ladyfingers

Beat the egg yolks and sugar a little in a pan to mix them and then spoon over the boiling milk, one spoonful at a time, always stirring.

Soften the gelatin sheets for a quarter of an hour in cold water, and put the saucepan on a very moderate heat, beating with a whisk. Always heat the mixture by whipping it, and bring it almost to the boil, but making sure it does not boil, or the eggs would fall apart and the mixture would be wasted.

When it is hot, remove the saucepan from the heat, add a touch of vanilla, and continue beating with the whisk until completely cold. Put the whipped cream in a bowl and gradually mix the sweetened egg mixture with it, mixing everything very lightly with a wooden spoon. Pour this mixture into a mold lined with parchment paper and surrounded by ladyfingers. Leave in the fridge for a couple of hours. Then turn it upside down on a serving plate, remove the paper, and send to the table.

CHARLOTTE DI CASTAGNE

Chestnut Charlotte

Apricot jam
Chocolate
Marron glacé

Chestnut cream:
1 lb 2 oz chestnuts, ¾ cup milk, vanilla extract, 5 tbsp sugar

Crème Bavaroise:
1 cup sugar, 5 egg yolks, 2 cups milk, vanilla extract, 2 gelatin sheets, ¾ cup sweetened whipped cream

This delicious dessert, with a beautiful effect, can be served instead of ice cream. It consists of 2 essential parts: a chestnut cream coating and a filling of Crème Bavaroise with vanilla.

For the chestnut cream: Knick the chestnuts and put them to boil. When they are cooked, remove the inner skins, put them in a saucepan, wet them with the milk, and season with a little vanilla. Mash the chestnuts with a wooden spoon to reduce them to a purée, and work this well, making it dry well, so that it is very substantial. Then add the sugar, stir again, and pour the purée into a bowl to cool.

Now prepare the Crème Bavaroise *(p777)* using the ingredients listed here: Put the sugar in a pan and, with a wooden spoon, add the egg yolks. Then dilute with the milk, which you will gradually pour in, stirring constantly, to blend the eggs and sugar well. Also add a touch of vanilla. Put the pan on the stove and bring to a gentle simmer being careful not to let it boil. When you see that the mixture is very hot and has slightly thickened, enough to veil the wooden spoon, immediately remove the saucepan from the heat and add the gelatin, previously soaked in cold water and squeezed in your hands. Stir a little to combine it well and then pour this cream through a sieve into a bowl. When the Bavarois is cold and begins to thicken, add the sweetened whipped cream.

Take a charlotte mold with a capacity of about one and a half quarts; place a disk of parchment paper on the bottom and a long strip of paper around it, so as to completely line the mold. Now take the chestnut mixture and, proceeding carefully, arrange it slowly, and a little at a time, on the bottom and around the wall of the mold, to make a box. Into this box pour the Crème Bavaroise. Cover with a sheet of parchment paper and put it in the fridge for a couple of hours to allow the charlotte to set well.

When ready to serve, turn out on a serving plate and after removing the paper, spread it with apricot jam and sprinkle with grated chocolate. Tidy and finish by putting a marron glacé in the middle.

CHARLOTTE DI CREMA

Cream Charlotte

MAKES 12

7 oz sponge cake
Jam
2 oz dark chocolate
Milk
Sweet liqueur
Optional: sweetened whipped cream, candied fruit

Pastry cream:
1 quart milk, 6 egg yolks, 1 cup sugar, ⅔ cup all-purpose flour

Line the inside of a charlotte mold with a generous capacity of one quart with parchment paper. Then line the bottom and the sides with slices of sponge cake, keeping the slices sticking to each other with a little jam. Then make up the pastry cream *(p752)* using the ingredient amounts listed here. Put half of it into the prepared mold, without leaving it too cold. On this cream, place a layer of slices of sponge cake and lightly tap the mold so there are no gaps.

In the meantime, you will have melted the dark chocolate over very low heat with a spoonful of milk. Add this chocolate to the remaining cream, which will therefore become a chocolate custard. With it, finish filling the mold, ending with another layer of sponge cake slices. Let it cool and then put in the fridge.

After a couple of hours, unmold the cake, remove the paper, and sprinkle it abundantly with a sweet liqueur. You can serve it like this, or make it more elegant by coating it with slightly sweetened whipped cream and candied fruit.

CHARLOTTE DI FRAGOLA

Strawberry Charlotte

SERVES 6 TO 8

3 egg yolks
⅓ cup sugar
1 cup milk
4 gelatin sheets
1 cup sweetened whipped cream
1 lb 2 oz strawberries
Lemon juice
Sweet liqueur
9 oz ladyfingers
Optional: whipped cream, strawberries, blackberries

Put the egg yolks in a pan with the sugar, work them a little, and then pour over the boiling milk, a spoonful at a time, always stirring. Soften the gelatin and squeeze and whisk into the mix over a very moderate heat. Bring to a simmer, being careful not to let it boil because you would waste everything.

Remove the pan from the heat and continue stirring until it is completely cold, stirring gently with a wooden spoon. As soon as it is quite thick, drop it slowly into a bowl in which you have put the whipped cream. Gently mix together.

Carefully wash the strawberries in water and lemon juice and let them macerate for about half an hour in a little sweet liqueur.

Take a charlotte mold of about one and a half quarts, line it with parchment paper, as big as the bottom of the mold, without buttering the mold or paper; then with a strip of the same paper as high as the mold, complete the lining of the interior. With some ladyfingers, rounded part downwards, cover the bottom of the mold. Also cover the inner walls by placing the ladyfingers upright next to each other and with the convex part against the wall. Pour in a little of the cream and over this make a layer of well-drained strawberries. Continue to alternate layers of cream and strawberries until the whole mold is filled. Put in the fridge for a couple of hours, then turn out on a cake plate, remove the paper, and decorate with whipped cream, strawberries, and blackberries.

CREMA AL CIOCCOLATO NELLE COPPE

Chocolate Cream in Cups

½ cup potato starch
3 cups milk
5 tbsp butter
⅓ cup sugar
½ cup cocoa powder
Optional: almond biscottini

Melt the potato starch in some cold milk in a small saucepan. When it has melted, add the butter, sugar, cocoa powder, and set the pan over the heat. Stir with a wooden spoon until the cream has well thickened.

Slightly wet crystal bowls with water, drain, and then pour in the cream. Leave to cool. Serve simply or with almond biscottini.

CREMA AL MASCARPONE NELLE TAZZE

Mascarpone Cream in Cups

4 egg yolks
½ cup sugar
Maraschino liqueur or rum
⅔ cup mascarpone
Optional: almond biscottini

Whip the egg yolks with the sugar in a bowl, and splash with 2 small glasses of rum or maraschino. Put the mascarpone in another bowl and work it for a long time with a wooden spoon to make it very soft. Gradually add the whipped eggs to the mascarpone, mixing them lightly together.

Distribute the mixture into the cups and leave to cool in the fridge. Serve with almond biscottini.

CREMA E BANANE NELLE COPPE

Cream and Banana in Cups

3 bananas
Sugar
Rum
2 egg yolks
1 tsp potato starch
¾ cup milk
Small meringues
To serve: 2 to 3 tbsp whipped cream

Peel the bananas, cut them into slices, and place on a plate with a spoonful of sugar and a little rum, leaving them to flavor for a time that can vary from half an hour to an hour.

Then prepare the following cream: Put the egg yolks, 2 spoons of sugar, and potato starch in a small saucepan. Dissolve everything with the milk, put the saucepan over the heat and, always stirring, slightly thicken the cream, which must be of a consistency less than that of a custard. Let the cream cool and then mix in 2 or 3 tablespoons whipped cream. In this way the cream will acquire a greater lightness.

Divide the banana slices in the bottom of 6 bowls, adding the little syrup that will have formed on the plate. Divide the cream into the bowls and, with the blade of a knife, smooth the surface. Once this is done, put the bowls in the fridge so that they can cool.

These cups are finished by surrounding with a ring of cream and in the middle 8 small meringues the size of walnuts, stacked like a small pyramid.

CREMA MALAKOFF

Crème Malakoff

MAKES 12

Apple
Pear
2 bananas
Pineapple
Fresh or canned peaches
2 tbsp sugar
Liqueur
Marsala
2 cups sweetened whipped cream
7 oz sponge cake, homemade or shop bought
Optional: lemon peel, candied orange, candied fruit

Pastry cream:
3 egg yolks, 3 tbsp sugar, 2 tbsp all-purpose flour, 2 cups milk, vanilla extract

Make a pastry cream *(p752)* using the ingredient amounts listed here. When it has thickened, finish it with a touch of vanilla and let it cool, mixing it from time to time.

Now prepare a fruit salad: Cut into cubes or slices an apple, a pear, a couple of bananas, a few slices of pineapple, and, if you like, even some fresh peaches or canned in syrup, and put them to macerate with a couple of spoons of sugar and a few glasses of liqueur, preferably maraschino or kirsch. You can add a few zests of lemon peel or candied orange to the fresh fruit, or other candied fruit of your choice.

Splash the cold pastry cream with a small glass of Marsala and mix lightly with a couple of spoons of whipped cream. Put a little bit of this cream in the bottom of a crystal bowl of suitable diameter, and on this cream make a first layer of sponge cake cut into slices and sprinkled with the same quality of liqueur you have used to macerate the fruit salad. On this layer of sponge cake spread another layer of cream, and on the cream make a layer of fruit. Continue like this until all the ingredients are used up, ending with a layer of sponge cake on which you will pour over the liqueur in which the fruit has macerated. With the remaining cream, make a small dome on the cake, which you can decorate as you like with some candied fruit and a little bit of the same cream, kept aside and piped through a pastry bag.

Once the dessert is finished, put it in the fridge for at least a couple of hours. Then place the crystal bowl on a serving dish.

ADA SAYS: *This is a dessert of the ancient cuisine, a kind of refined trifle that can be served instead of ice cream.*

GELATINA DI MANDARINO NELLA BUCCIA

Tangerine Jelly in Their Skins

7 tangerines
Lemon juice
Lemon peel
3 gelatin sheets
1 cup sugar
2 egg whites

Choose 6 large tangerines, very fresh and with intact peel, and with a sharp knife take away a cap at the top. Through this opening, with a teaspoon, you can begin to break the internal wedges so that you can extract them slowly without damaging the shell.

When you have emptied all the segments, blend them, and collect all the juice in a bowl. Also squeeze in the juice of a 7th tangerine and half a lemon. Finally, pass everything through muslin or a sieve.

Cut the peel of the 7th tangerine into strips, and completely remove the white part and keep it aside. You will also, subtly, remove the peel of the half a lemon and set this aside as well.

Soak the gelatin sheets in cold water and let them soften. Place the sugar and 1½ cups of water in a small saucepan, add the lemon peel and that of the 7th tangerine, and just heat the water. When the sugar is well dissolved, remove from the heat and let the syrup cool.

In a bowl, beat 2 egg whites until stiff peaks form and then, a little at a time, add the syrup, always whisking, to obtain a frothy liquid. Also leave the lemon peel and the shredded mandarin peel in this liquid, which will perfume the syrup even more. Finally, add the gelatin squeezed with your hands to remove extra water, and put everything in a small saucepan over moderate heat.

Still whisking, bring the liquid to a boil, then remove from the heat, cover it and let it stand without stirring for about 10 minutes. After this time, sieve the liquid and when it is almost cold, add the tangerine juice that was prepared at the beginning.

Wait until the gelatin mixture is completely cold, and when it takes on an oily appearance, spoon it into the shells of the tangerines, putting the lid on each peel so that the tangerine is whole again. You can wet the cut part with a few drops of gelatin, which will close the tangerine even better when it takes hold. As you have finished the tangerines, arrange on a serving dish and then place in the fridge.

MOUSSELINE DI BANANE

Banana Mousseline

⅓ cup sugar
4 egg yolks
1 tsp potato starch
1 cup milk
4 bananas
Rum
¾ cup sweetened whipped cream
¼ cup peeled pistachios

Put the sugar, egg yolks, and potato starch in a saucepan and dissolve everything, little by little, with the warm milk. Set the saucepan over the heat, stirring constantly and without letting the cream boil. When this has sufficiently thickened and veils the spoon, remove it from the heat and pour it into a container, leaving it to cool.

Purée the bananas and collect the purée in a bowl. When the cream is cold, put it in the fridge for a while and, as soon as you see that it begins to thicken, mix in the banana purée, 2 small glasses of rum, and the slightly sweetened whipped cream, which you should add slowly. Transfer this mixture into a crystal bowl and cover the surface with pistachios, cut into halves. Put in the fridge for at least an hour. This very quick mousseline must not be turned out of the mold, but served in the same crystal bowl in which it is prepared.

MOUSSELINE DI FRAGOLE

Strawberry Mousseline

3 egg whites
¾ cup sugar
10½ oz strawberries
Lemon juice
Cognac
Orange liqueur or curaçao
2 tbsp powdered sugar
2 cups whipped cream
Butter
Optional: small meringues, chocolate chips

Whisk the egg whites to a very hard snow by hand or use an electric blender. Put the sugar in a small pan, splash with a little water to obtain a runny paste, and cook to a strong bubble, or a rather hard ball *(p736)*. Then take the pan off the heat immediately, and drop the sugar slowly over the egg whites, in a thin stream, along the side of the pan with one hand, while with the other you shake circularly with a whisk to mix the sugar with the whites. When you have combined all the sugar, beat the meringue a little more with the whisk, which should be a soft, very white and rather voluminous mass.

Clean and wash the strawberries, purée them, then add the lemon juice, a small glass of cognac and orange liqueur or curaçao. Mix this strawberry purée into the meringue, also adding the powdered sugar.

Put the whipped cream into a bowl, setting aside a little bit for later as garnish, and slowly drop the strawberry and meringue mixture in, stirring gently. Transfer to a one quart mold and cover with a paper disk, sealed with a cord of butter. Leave in the fridge for 2 hours.

Then turn out the mousseline on a dessert plate, and decorate it with little meringues, chocolate chips, and the extra whipped cream.

MOUSSELINE DI MELE

Apple Mousseline

2¼ lb cooking apples
Lemon zest
½ cup sugar
1¼ cups sweetened whipped cream
Cookies

Peel the apples, remove the cores, and cut into slices; place them on the heat in a pan with 2 glasses of water, the zest of the lemon and the sugar. Cook until the apples have completely collapsed and all the liquid is consumed. Then sieve and collect the purée in a bowl, leaving it to cool.

When the apple purée is very cold, add the sweetened whipped cream and mix carefully, but lightly so as not to dismantle it. Transfer to a crystal bowl and place it in the fridge. When ready to serve, place the bowl on a serving plate, accompanying the mousseline with cookies of your choice.

ICE CREAM

TO MAKE ICE CREAM

These cold preparations have a first operation in common: the thickening of the compound through the action of the cold, which can take place either by using an ice cream maker or by using the freezer.

If using a freezer, 2 warnings must not be neglected. The mixture put in the ice trays is usually mixed with a small wooden ladle to prevent the formation of icicles and to allow, instead, its uniform thickening into a soft and velvet cream.

The second warning is that to obtain a good ice cream it is essential to respect the quantities; an ice cream that is too "lean", that is, low in sugar, is bland and grainy. An ice cream that is too "fat", that is overabundant with sugar, has a hard time freezing. To get the right consistency, it helps to have a lid. The time required for ice cream to harden in the freezer is at least 2 hours.

To unmold the ice cream is not too difficult an operation but one that requires a certain delicacy. You can quickly dip the frozen mold in warm water or, better still, rub the mold with a cloth dipped in boiling water and wrung out. Then remove the lid, turn the mold upside down and shake it slightly to release the ice cream.

CASSATA ALLA SICILIANA

Sicilian Cassata

2 cups milk
¾ cup sugar
5 egg yolks
Vanilla extract
1 cup sweetened whipped cream
2 oz candied fruit
2 oz praline almonds

Cassata is made up of 2 parts: the casing of ice cream, and the filling consisting of cream with the addition of pieces of candied fruit and praline almonds.

With the milk, sugar, egg yolks, and vanilla make an ice cream, as follows: Put the egg yolks and sugar in a small pan and work the mixture for a long time until it becomes swollen and frothy. Put the milk in another saucepan on the stove and bring it almost to boiling point, but do not let it reach a boil. Pour the hot milk, in small quantities, on to the whipped egg yolks, always working vigorously with a whisk, and do not add any more milk until the previous quantity has been absorbed. After you have added all the milk, put the cream mixture on the stove and, always stirring, bring it almost to the boil, but making sure it does not actually reach a boil. As soon as the cream has slightly thickened, remove it from the heat, perfume it with a splash of vanilla, pour it into a bowl, and let it cool, stirring occasionally.

Put the cold cream into a pan in the freezer; leave it like this for about 2 hours, stirring with a small wooden spatula every half hour. At the same time, put an empty 3-quarter quart mold or tray into the freezer to cool alongside the cream.

When the frozen cream is ready, quickly pour the cream into the cold mold, distributing it on the bottom and on the sides of the mold, so as to leave a space in the middle where you will put the whipped cream, a few pieces of candied fruit, and some chopped praline almonds. Tap the mold lightly to make sure everywhere is full, level the surface, put a disk of parchment paper on top, and then close the mold. Put in the freezer for at least 2 hours. After this time, dip it in warm water and turn out the ice cream.

ADA SAYS: *You can use an ice cream maker; the proportions are the same.*

GELATO ALLA PANNA

Cream Ice Cream

1 cup sugar
Vanilla extract
2 cups unsweetened whipped cream

Put half a glass of water and the sugar over the heat in a pan. Melt the sugar well and perfume with a touch of vanilla and let it cool. Gently add the whipped cream. Then mold and freeze for at least 2 hours.

GELATO DI CIOCCOLATO

Chocolate Ice Cream

½ cup potato starch
2 cups milk
3½ tbsp butter
¼ cup sugar
½ cup cocoa powder
1 cup cream

Melt the potato starch in a small pan with the cold milk, and when it has dissolved, add the butter, sugar, and cocoa powder. Set the saucepan over heat and, always stirring with a wooden spoon, let the cream thicken.

Remove from the heat and pour into a bowl, add the cream, and let it cool. Place in the freezer for 2 hours.

Transfer the mixture to a mold and return it to the freezer for at least another 2 hours.

GELATO DI CREMA CON FRAGOLE IN COPPA

Strawberry Ice Cream in Cups

10½ oz strawberries
¾ cup powdered sugar
2 oranges
Ice cream *(p839)*
1 cup whipped cream

Wash and clean the strawberries, then place them in a bowl, sprinkle with powdered sugar and the juice of 2 oranges; then place them in the fridge.

Prepare an ice cream. When the cream has frozen, arrange it in cups, leveling the surface. In the middle, group the strawberries and around the ice cream, use a piping bag with a star nozzle to make a border using whipped cream.

GELATO DI NOCCIOLA

Hazelnut Ice Cream

½ cup shelled hazelnuts
1¼ cups sugar
Lemon juice
Butter for greasing
1 quart milk
Vanilla extract, or bean
6 egg yolks
Cream

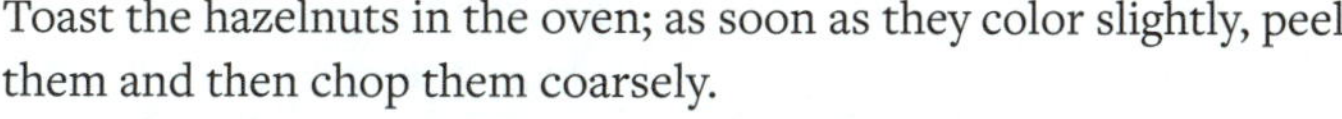

Toast the hazelnuts in the oven; as soon as they color slightly, peel them and then chop them coarsely.

In a small pan, place ¼ cup of sugar and a few drops of lemon juice. and set over the heat. When the sugar has completely melted and is well colored, add the chopped hazelnuts; stir and cook until the mass has taken on a nice brown color. Then pour the hazelnut paste on to a lightly buttered kitchen table and let it cool. Then blend into a smooth and fragrant paste. Bring the milk to a boil and perfume it with a touch of vanilla, or with a vanilla bean, split lengthwise.

Beat the egg yolks with 1 cup of sugar and when the yolks are well whipped, add all the boiling milk, little by little. Put the saucepan over heat and, always stirring with a wooden spoon, let the cream thicken slightly, without boiling it. When the cream veils the spoon, remove it from the heat and stir in the hazelnut paste. Transfer the mixture into a bowl and let it cool, stirring often.

When the hazelnut cream is completely cold, add a little cream. Freeze for at least 2 hours.

ADA SAYS: *You can sieve the mixture, but then you will remove the nuts.*

TORTA GELATA DI CREMA E CIOCCOLATO

Ice Cream and Chocolate Cake

2 egg yolks
⅓ cup sugar
1½ cups milk
1 cup light cream
Vanilla extract
3 tbsp potato starch
2 tbsp butter
3½ oz dark chocolate

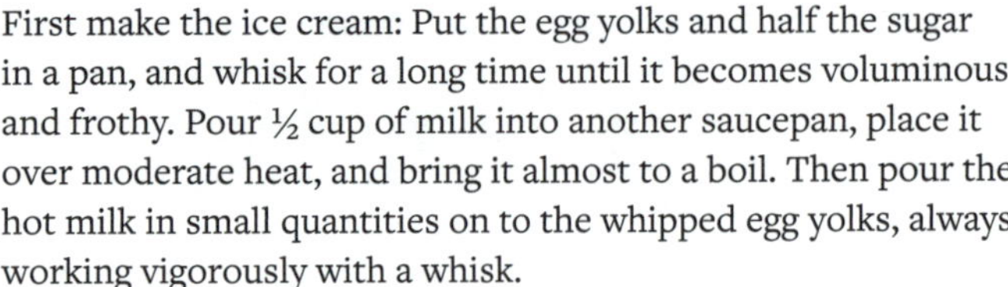

First make the ice cream: Put the egg yolks and half the sugar in a pan, and whisk for a long time until it becomes voluminous and frothy. Pour ½ cup of milk into another saucepan, place it over moderate heat, and bring it almost to a boil. Then pour the hot milk in small quantities on to the whipped egg yolks, always working vigorously with a whisk.

After you have added all the milk, put some of the cream over the heat, and always stirring, bring it almost to a boil. When the cream has slightly thickened, take off the heat, add another ¼ cup of milk and a touch of vanilla and pour into the bowl with the eggs and sugar mix. Blend and leave to cool completely.

Meanwhile, blend the potato starch in a small saucepan with the cold milk, and when it has melted, add the butter, sugar, and chocolate. Set the saucepan over heat and, always stirring with a wooden spoon, melt the chocolate and thicken the mixture well.

Take off the heat, pour the mixture into another bowl, add the rest of the cream, and let it cool.

Then take 2 cold containers that can go into the freezer—one for the cream and one for the chocolate mixture. Fill them and put back to freeze for 2 hours, mixing with a small wooden spatula every half hour. Before removing the containers, put a 3 cup mold in the freezer to cool as well.

When the 2 creams are ready, remove the mold from the freezer, line with sheets of parchment paper and pour the chocolate mixture in so that it covers the entire bottom and presents a smooth surface. On top of the chocolate mixture pour the plain ice cream, press it lightly, level the surface and cover it with another sheet of parchment paper. Close the mold and put it back in the freezer for at least 2 hours, then dip the mold in warm water and gently remove the frozen cake from the mold.

Granita

GRANITA DI ALBICOCCHE

Apricot Granita

1¼ cups sugar
1 lb 2 oz apricots
Vanilla extract
Lemon juice

Put a pan with the sugar and one cup of water over heat and bring to the boil, stirring once or twice.

Wash, halve and pit the apricots, and cut them into small pieces without peeling them and put them in the syrup. Cook over medium heat for about half an hour without a lid. Cool and then sieve the mixture, adding a touch of vanilla and the juice of one lemon.

Pour the mixture into a cold container that can go into the freezer, kept in the fridge, and put back into the freezer, leaving it there for about 2 hours, and mixing with a small wooden spatula in the container itself about every half hour. Then distribute the granita into crystal bowls and serve.

GRANITA DI ARANCE

Orange Granita

1 lb 2 oz oranges
1¾ cups sugar
1 lemon

First juice your oranges, reserving the peel. Put 2 cups of water in a small saucepan with the sugar and the peel of the oranges cut very thin, without the white pith. Boil for a few minutes, remove the saucepan from the heat, and let the syrup rest.

When it is completely cold, remove the peel and add the orange juice and lemon juice, mixing everything together.

Pour the mixture into a cold container that can go into the freezer and let the granita freeze and solidify for at least 2 hours, stirring with a spatula every half hour in the container itself. Serve in crystal bowls.

GRANITA DI CAFFÈ CON PANNA

Coffee Granita

¾ cup sugar
4 cups coffee
Whipped cream

Heat 2 cups of water and the sugar together until dissolved. Then prepare a rather strong coffee and add it to the syrup. Transfer to a bowl and leave to cool.

Pour the mixture into a cold, even freezing, container that can go into the freezer and let the granita freeze and solidify for at least 2 hours, stirring with a spatula every half hour in the container itself.

Serve in crystal bowls with 2 spoonfuls of whipped cream.

GRANITA DI FRAGOLE DI BOSCO

Wild Strawberry Granita

2½ cups sugar
10½ oz wild strawberries
1 lemon
1 orange

Heat 2 cups of water and the sugar until it is dissolved. Transfer into a bowl and let it cool.

Carefully wash the strawberries and put them through a fine sieve, collecting the strawberry juice in another bowl. When the syrup is cold, add the juice of the lemon and orange. Pour the mixture into a cold container and freeze for about 2 hours, stirring with a spatula every half hour.

GRANITA DI LIMONE

Lemon Granita

2½ cups sugar
2 cups water
5 lemons

Heat 2 cups of water and the sugar until it is dissolved. Transfer into a bowl and let it cool. When the syrup is cold, add the juice of 5 lemons and the zest from one lemon. Then freeze and stir every half hour for at least 2 hours.

GRANITA DI PESCHE

Peach Granita

1½ cups sugar
2 cups water
1 lb 2 oz peaches
Vanilla extract
1 lemon

Make your sugar syrup, as above, bearing in mind that the quantities are slightly different, and leave to cool. Wash, halve and pit the peaches. Cut into small pieces without peeling them and put them in the syrup. Cook over medium heat for about half an hour without a lid. Cool and then purée the mixture, adding a touch of vanilla and the juice of one lemon. Freeze for 2 hours.

GRANITA DI VISCIOLE

Sour Cherry Granita

1 lb 2 oz sour cherries
1½ cups sugar
2 cups water
1 lemon

Wash the sour cherries and remove the pits and mash them, collecting the juice in a bowl or easier, blend them in a food processor. Make your syrup with the sugar and water and when it is cold, add to the cherries. Squeeze over the juice of a lemon. Pour out into a cold container and freeze, stirring every half an hour.

Sherbet

SPUMA GELATA DI ALBICOCCHE

Apricot Sherbet

7 oz ripe apricots
2 cups sweetened whipped cream
1 cup powdered sugar

Wash and purée the pitted apricots, collect the purée in a bowl, and slowly add the whipped cream and powdered sugar, which you drop like rain, mixing with great delicacy.

Take a cold container, pour in the mixture, and return it to the freezer, leaving it there for about 2 hours and stirring with a small wooden spatula every half hour. Transfer the foam into crystal bowls, leveling the surface with the blade of a knife.

SPUMA GELATA DI BANANE

Banana Sherbet

3 bananas
2 tbsp lemon juice
2 tbsp orange juice
½ cup sugar
3 eggs
3 gelatin sheets
Sweetened whipped cream

Peel the bananas and mash them with a fork in a bowl. Then add the lemon and orange juices, ¼ cup of the sugar and the egg yolks.

Soak the gelatin in cold water for about a quarter of an hour; then squeeze in your hands, and put it in a pan with 2 tablespoons of water and melt over medium heat. Pour the bananas into the gelatin water and place the pan inside a second pan of warm, not boiling, water to create a bain-marie. Keep the heat on, stirring all the time and and making sure that the water never comes to a boil. When the cream has thickened, pour it into a bowl. Whip the egg whites to a very firm snow, add the remaining sugar, and gently add them to the prepared cream.

Take a cold container that can go into the freezer. Pour the mixture into it and put the filled container back into the freezer. Leave it there for about 2 hours, stirring with a small wooden spatula in the container itself every half hour. Remove the sherbet from the container, distribute in the crystal bowls, and garnish with whipped cream.

SPUMA GELATA DI CIOCCOLATO

Chocolate Sherbet

Milk
4½ oz dark chocolate
⅔ cup sugar
2 cups whipped cream
Vanilla extract

Put a small pan on the heat with a small glass of milk and when it is hot add the grated chocolate. Place the saucepan over very low heat, cover it and let the chocolate soften for about 10 minutes. When the chocolate has softened, mix it well with a wooden spoon.

In another pan, add the sugar with half a glass of water. Set over heat and stir until the sugar has completely dissolved, preventing the syrup from boiling. Pour the syrup into the chocolate mixture and, with a small whisk, combine. Let them cool, remembering from time to time to work the mixture a little with the whisk, to prevent it from getting a skin on the surface.

When this mixture is cold, continue to work it with a whisk. Then remove the whisk and add the cream very gently, using a wooden spoon, and complete with a touch of vanilla. Pour the mixture into a tray and freeze for about 2 hours, stirring with a spatula every half hour.

SPUMA GELATA DI CREMA E FRAGOLE

Strawberry and Cream Sherbet

4 egg yolks
¾ cup sugar
2 cups whipped cream
Vanilla extract
1 lb 2 oz strawberries
Lemon juice

Put the egg yolks and ½ cup of sugar in a bowl. Immerse the bowl in a larger container containing cold water, and place both over moderate heat, working the mixture vigorously with a whisk until it is well whipped. Heat until the mixture is warm to the touch, then remove from the heat and continue beating for a long time until the mixture is cold, soft, and fluffy. Do not get tired of beating because the success is ensured by the careful processing of the eggs.

When the mixture is cold and well whipped, place it in a bowl, slowly add the whipped cream, perfume it with a touch of vanilla, and place the bowl in the fridge to set.

Clean and rinse the strawberries in water acidulated with lemon, and purée them. Put the purée in a bowl, season it with a few drops of lemon and ¼ cup of sugar and put it in the fridge too.

When both are almost set, add a layer of egg foam to the bottom of a 1 quart soufflé mold and smooth it well with the blade of a knife. Make another layer of strawberry purée on this layer; then continue to alternate layers until the whole mold is filled. Then put the mold in the freezer and let it freeze for at least 2 hours.

SPUMA GELATA DI FRAGOLE

Strawberry Sherbet with Blackberries

1 lb 2 oz strawberries
1½ lemons
2 cups whipped cream
1 cup powdered sugar
7 oz blackberries
¼ cup white wine
Colored sugar grains
Small meringues

Wash the strawberries in water acidulated with the juice of one lemon. Purée or blend them and collect this purée in a bowl, adding the juice of another half a lemon. Then add the whipped cream, keeping aside a little for decoration later, and the powdered sugar, which you drop as a shower from a sieve, mixing delicately so as not to collapse the cream, folding that is, from top to bottom and not with a rounded movement.

Take a cold container from the freezer, pour in the mixture, and put it to freeze for at least 2 hours, stirring with a small wooden spatula about every half hour to avoid excessive hardening.

Carefully wash the blackberries in white wine, drain, and put them in the fridge so that they are cold at the time of use. Remove the foam from the freezer, unmold it on a plate by placing the container for a moment in boiling water, then decorate with blackberries and whipped cream, with colored sugar grains and very small meringues.

SPUMA GELATA DI PESCHE

Peach Sherbet

2¼ lb soft peaches
Lemon juice
¾ cup sugar
Maraschino liqueur
3 gelatin sheets
½ cup whipped cream

Wash, peel, and pit the peaches, purée or blend, and mix with the juice of a lemon, the sugar, and a glass of maraschino.

Soak the gelatin, then squeeze and warm with 2 tablespoons of water over a medium heat to dissolve. Pour into the peaches, mixing well: finally, add the whipped cream, taking care to mix it well into the purée.

Pour into a cold container and freeze for 2 hours, stirring every half an hour. Finally, pour into cold cups and smooth out the surface with a warm blade.

SPUMA GELATA DI ZABAIONE

Zabaglione Sherbet

2 eggs
1 egg yolk
6 tbsp Marsala
3 tbsp sugar
1 cup whipped cream
Chocolate

Separate the eggs and put the 3 egg yolks, the Marsala, and sugar in a small saucepan. Warm over a very low heat and beat the mixture vigorously with a whisk until it is well whipped and has consistency. Take off the heat and let the mixture cool while continuing to beat it with the whisk.

Let it cool while you whip the egg whites to a firm snow. Blend in the whites and finally the whipped cream, stirring very gently with a wooden spoon.

Fold into a cold container and freeze for 2 hours, mixing with a small wooden spatula every half hour. Then take out of the freezer, distribute in crystal bowls and decorate with grated chocolate.

COOKIES & SWEET TREATS

AMARETTI

Amaretti

MAKES 24

½ cup almonds
1 cup sugar
2 egg whites
All-purpose flour
Butter for greasing
Powdered sugar

Shell the almonds and put them in a saucepan with cold water, bring to a boil, drain, skin them and drop into a bowl of cold water. Drain and let them dry in the oven over very moderate heat without coloring. Then crush them in the mortar, or chop them in the food processor, with a generous half a cup of sugar; then sieve them so you have a flour.

Whip the egg whites to a firm snow in a bowl and spoon carefully over the rest of the sugar. When the sugar has been absorbed in to the egg whites, mix in the almond flour.

Put the mixture in a pastry bag with a smooth nozzle. Butter and flour a baking sheet and place on it, a little distant from each other, portions of the mixture, as large as small walnuts, which you will crush lightly. Sprinkle them with powdered sugar and let them rest for many hours.

Finally, bake the amaretti in a preheated oven of moderate heat, where they will expand and swell, remaining empty inside.

BAICOLI DI VENEZIA

Venetian Dry Cookies

1½ cups all-purpose flour
2 tbsp active dry yeast
Butter
1 tbsp sugar
1 tbsp orange flower water
Salt

Wafer-thin, these oval cookies are named after small mullet fish, the baicoli. They can be stored for a long time.

Prepare a little ball of dough by placing a few tablespoons of flour on the table, making a small hollow center in the middle and crumbling the yeast into it. Dissolve the yeast in a few tablespoons of water and knead the yeast and flour together to form a fairly firm loaf. Roll it into a ball and make two cross-shaped cuts on top. Wrap it in a towel and place it in a warm place to rise.

After about half an hour, the dough ball should have doubled in volume. Place the rest of the flour, a knob of butter, a scant tablespoon of sugar, the yeast loaf, a good pinch of salt, six tablespoons of water and the orange blossom water on the table.

Knead well into a dough and then divide into two parts. Shape each part into a roll about 10 inches long, making sure it is nice and even, then place the two rolls on a baking tray, leaving a little space between them. Cover with a folded tea towel and leave to rise.

When they have risen – which will take a good hour – bake them in a hot oven just long enough to set the loaves without allowing a crust to form. This prevents a tough outer layer, making it easier to slice thinly later. They should look like two soft loaves of ordinary bread.

After a few hours, when the loaves have completely cooled, use a very sharp knife to cut very thin and slightly slanted slices, so that each slice is three inches wide. Carefully lay the slices on a baking tray so that they do not break, and bake them until they are a light golden brown, turning them over as necessary.

BISCOTTI AGLI ANICI

Anise Seed Cookies

MAKES 20

1⅔ cups all-purpose flour
½ cup sugar
3½ tbsp butter, plus extra for greasing
1 egg
Salt
¼ oz anise seeds
2 tsp active dry yeast
Milk

Place the flour on the table. Add the sugar, the butter, egg, a pinch of salt, the anise seeds, and the yeast, and mix with a few spoons of milk to obtain a paste that is not too hard, nor too soft.

With your hands, shape the dough into a large 12 inch long roll and place it on a greased and floured baking sheet. Bake in a preheated oven at moderate heat for about 20 minutes, then remove it from the oven, let it cool and slice it, about ½ inch thick.

Align them in a single layer back on the baking sheet and toast in the oven on both sides so that they are light, crunchy, and of a beautiful golden color.

BISCOTTI AI PINOLI

Pine Nut Cookies

MAKES 40

2 tbsp sugar
4 eggs
Lemon
1½ cups all-purpose flour
Butter for greasing
⅓ cup pine nuts
Powdered sugar

Put the sugar and 4 whole eggs in a saucepan. Whisk the eggs over a very low heat until the mixture is lukewarm. Take off the heat and continue to whisk until the eggs are cold and have become very frothy. Then add the zest of a lemon and let the flour fall slowly into it, mixing it gently.

Butter the baking sheet, lightly flour it, and then tap to remove any excess flour. Put the mixture in a pastry bag with a smooth round nozzle with a ½ an inch opening and let the dough fall out on to the pan, a little distance between each other. If one pan is not enough, make a second one.

Scatter the cookies with the pine nuts, and then sprinkle with powdered sugar. Let them rest for a few minutes, and when the sugar has dissolved, bake in a preheated oven of moderate heat for about half an hour, until they have a nice golden color.

BISCOTTI ALLE MANDORLE

Almond Cookies

MAKES 40

6 eggs
¾ cup sugar
1 cup all-purpose flour
⅓ cup shelled almonds
Salt
2 tbsp raisins
2 tbsp candied citron
¼ oz active dry yeast
Orange
Butter for greasing

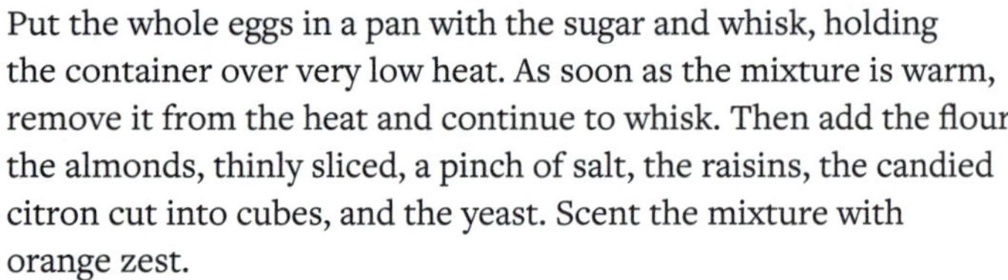

Put the whole eggs in a pan with the sugar and whisk, holding the container over very low heat. As soon as the mixture is warm, remove it from the heat and continue to whisk. Then add the flour, the almonds, thinly sliced, a pinch of salt, the raisins, the candied citron cut into cubes, and the yeast. Scent the mixture with orange zest.

Put the mixture in a pastry bag with a smooth nozzle of ½ an inch, and pipe a long roll on to a greased and floured baking tray. Make a second roll, and finally a third above the first 2. Repeat the operation to get long loaves that you will immediately bake in a preheated oven of moderate heat.

When the loaves are cooked and lightly blond, let them cool, and cut them into diagonal slices of ½ inch thick. Align them on the baking sheet and put them back to bake, for about 10 minutes.

BISCOTTI SALATI

Cumin Cookies

MAKES 30

1⅓ cups all-purpose flour
7 tbsp butter, plus extra for greasing
½ cup milk
1 tbsp salt
Cumin seeds

Rub the flour into the butter, and then add the milk and salt. No sugar. Make a ball of the dough and let it rest for half an hour in the fridge.

Then roll it out ¼ of an inch thick, and with a smooth round pastry cutter measuring 2 inches in diameter, cut some small rounds. Collect the scraps, press together, and roll them out again to make more rounds. Repeat until you have used up all the dough.

Put these cookies on a baking sheet greased with a thin layer of butter, brush with a little milk, and then sprinkle them with a pinch of salt and a strong pinch of cumin seeds. Bake in a preheated oven at a rather lively heat. As soon as the cookies are slightly colored, remove them and let them cool on a wire rack.

◆ ADA SAYS: *These cookies will keep quite a long time in a tin box. Serve them with tea or beer.*

BISCOTTI SAVOIARDI

Savoy Cookies

MAKES 40

3 eggs
⅓ cup sugar
½ cup all-purpose flour
Salt
Butter for greasing
2 tbsp sugar
2 tbsp powdered sugar

Put 3 egg yolks and the sugar in a bowl, and whisk with a wooden spoon until they are soft and foamy and bubble here and there. Then mix in the flour and a pinch of salt.

Whip the 3 egg whites to a very firm snow. Take a spoonful of these whites and add to the yolks and sugar, stirring vigorously. Then add the remaining whites, mixing with great delicacy, incorporating them into the yolks.

When everything is well blended, butter the baking sheet, sprinkle it with flour, and then tap the plate to knock off any excess flour. Once this is done, gently remove a little more flour with a brush, so that only a thin layer remains.

Put the egg and flour mixture in a pastry bag with a smooth round nozzle measuring ½ an inch in diameter and pipe to release sticks 3½ to 4 inches long on to the baking sheet, at a certain distance from each other.

Take a couple of spoonfuls of sugar and mix with the powdered sugar. Thoroughly sprinkle the cookies with this sugar. Leave it like this for about 10 minutes and when you see that the sugar has completely dissolved, repeat the sugaring operation.

Wait another 2 or 3 minutes and then bake in a preheated oven of moderate heat until they become light gold. Remove, using the blade of a knife, and put them to cool on a wire rack.

BISCOTTINI AL MIELE

Honey Cookies

MAKES 50

2 cups all-purpose flour
¼ cup honey
2 tbsp butter
1 egg
Pinch salt
½ cup milk
¾ oz active dry yeast

Place the flour in a heap. Melt the honey in a pan, add the butter, the egg, beaten as if for an omelet, a pinch of salt, and the milk in which you have diluted the yeast. Add to the flour and knead well, then roll out the dough into a thin sheet. Use a pastry cutter to cut as many cookies of the shape you prefer.

Lightly dust a large baking sheet with flour, line up the cookies, brush with milk to polish them, and place them in a preheated oven of moderate heat for a few minutes, until they have taken on a light blond color.

BISCOTTO ARROTOLATO

Rolled Cookies

3 eggs
3 tbsp sugar
3 tbsp all-purpose flour
Salt
Butter for greasing
Apricot jam
Powdered sugar
Optional: crushed almonds, chocolate custard (4 egg yolks, 4 tbsp sugar, 1 tsp potato starch, 1½ cups milk, 4 tbsp grated chocolate), candied fruit

Separate the egg whites and yolks. Put the egg yolks in a bowl with the sugar and whip them with a wooden spoon; then mix in carefully the sifted flour and a pinch of salt and let it rest for a while. There is no need to work a lot.

The egg whites must be whisked to a very firm snow and slowly added to the yolks, stirring gently so that they do not fall apart.

Butter a sheet of parchment paper, 10 inches square, and roll out the mixture so as to make a regular layer of scarcely ¼ of an inch deep. Place the sheet on the baking pan and bake in a preheated oven at a very high heat. As soon as the cake is almost cooked, which will happen in a few minutes, turn it over on a cloth, remove the paper, quickly spread the cake with apricot jam, roll it up on itself, rather tightly, and put it back for a few minutes in the oven. Remove from the oven and let it cool. Trim the ends, a little crosswise, arrange on a plate, and sprinkle with powdered sugar.

ADA SAYS: *To make more elegant, spread on the outside as well a little jam and then roll it in chopped almonds, or spread it on the outside with a chocolate custard made using the ingredient amounts listed here. You can also decorate with a few pieces of candied fruit.*

BISCOTTO ARROTOLATO ALLA CREMA BIANCA

Rolled Cookies with White Cream

Rolled biscuit dough *(as above)*
White cream *(p751)*
Crushed almonds
Alchermes liqueur

Make the rolled biscuit dough as above, but the filling here is different. Make a white cream.

Splash the top of the dough with Alchermes liqueur, place the cream on top, and spread it over the entire surface of the square, leaving a small amount to finish the cake on the outside. Roll the dough on itself, thus forming the cake, which you will hold tightly with your hands to keep in shape. Line up the 2 ends with a knife, spread the rolled cake with the cream left aside and complete it with a sprinkling of crushed almonds. Let the cake rest for a few hours in the fridge and finally divide it into cookie slices with a very sharp knife.

ADA SAYS: *Alchermes is an old tonic of herbs and spices favored in Tuscany, Emilia-Romagna, and Sicily.*

BOCCONOTTI DI RICOTTA

Ricotta Bocconotti

MAKES 24

2¼ cups ricotta
¾ cup sugar
4 eggs
Ground cinnamon
2 oz candied orange peel
Butter for greasing

Shortcrust pastry:
2 cups all-purpose flour, ¾ cup sugar, 10½ tbsp butter, 3 egg yolks, ground cinnamon, salt

Prepare a shortcrust pastry *(p784)* using the ingredient amounts listed here. Roll it into a ball and let it rest for half an hour in a sheltered place. Then divide the dough into 2 parts and roll out one rather thinly, to a thickness of ⅛ of an inch.

Put the ricotta, the sugar, 3 eggs, a teaspoon of cinnamon, and the diced orange peel in a bowl. Mix thoroughly. On the rolled out part of the dough, line up piles of mixture at a certain distance from each other. Wet the empty spaces with a little beaten egg, roll out the other piece of dough and cover the piles with this. Press gently with your fingers between one pile and the other to make the 2 pieces stick together; then with a knife or a spiked wheel, separate the bocconotti.

Line them up in a lightly greased baking sheet, wash with beaten egg, and bake them in a preheated oven of moderate heat for about half an hour. They are eaten cold.

ADA SAYS: *In the packaging of the bocconotti you can also follow a more hasty procedure—roll out the first sheet directly on to the baking sheet, arrange the ricotta mix on it, cover with the other sheet and bake without separating the bocconotti, which are only cut when baked and still very hot. Bocconotti must not have a strictly regular shape.*

Donuts & Fritters

CIAMBELLE ALLE MANDORLE

Baked Almond Donuts

MAKES 50

⅔ cup almonds
3 cups all-purpose flour
7 tbsp butter
¾ cup sugar
½ cup potato starch
2 eggs
1 egg yolk
Lemon zest
⅛ oz baking soda
½ oz active dry yeast
1½ tbsp milk
Oil for greasing

Shell and skin the almonds, or buy them ready to go. Dry them with a towel and cut them into strips.

Put the flour on the table in a heap and make a well, in the vacuum place the butter cut into small pieces, the sugar, potato starch, a whole egg and an extra yolk, the zest of a lemon, the baking soda, yeast, and the milk. Quickly mix everything, and form regular-sized donuts. Brush them with beaten egg, sprinkle them with almonds, and bake them in a preheated oven of moderate heat for about 20 minutes on a baking sheet greased with oil.

CIAMBELLE AL VINO

Baked Wine Donuts

MAKES 36

3⅓ cups all-purpose flour
¾ cup olive oil
½ cup sugar
¾ cup wine
Oil for greasing

Put the flour in a heap and add the oil, sugar, and a glass of light wine, white or red, in the well in the middle. You need a paste that is neither too hard nor too soft. Make it into a ball, let it rest for a few minutes, and then divide it into 4 or 5 pieces.

Take one piece at a time and stretch it over a lightly floured board to make a roll the width of your thumb. Cut this into pieces of about 8 inches and make a donut out of each one, pressing the ends together so that they do not then open. Proceed in the same way until all are used up.

Line up the donuts on a lightly oiled baking sheet, sprinkle them with sugar, and bake them for about 20 minutes in a preheated oven at a good heat.

CIAMBELLE DI QUARESIMA

Lenten Donuts

MAKES 36

3⅓ cups all-purpose flour
2 tbsp sugar
1 tbsp anise seeds
Salt
½ cup white wine
¾ oz fresh yeast
Olive oil

Place the flour on the kitchen table in a heap. In the middle put the sugar, a spoonful of anise seeds, a pinch of salt, half a glass of white wine, and the yeast dissolved in a small glass of just warm water. Knead everything and work the dough a little, which should be quite soft. Make it into a ball and put it to rise in a sheltered place for about an hour.

Then turn it out on the kitchen table, sprinkled with flour. Beat it lightly with your hands and then make a sausage that you will cut into 4 parts. Take one piece at a time, roll it on the table with your hands to obtain a long rope the thickness of a little finger, and cut out pieces 6 to 8 inches long. Fold these into a donut shape, pressing on the center.

Now put a large, low pan of water on the heat. As soon as the water boils, lower the heat, so that the boiling remains imperceptible.

Then take a few donuts at a time and dip them into the water. They will fall to the bottom of the container, but after a few seconds they will rise to the surface. Then lift them out with a perforated spoon and place them on a napkin, aligning them next to each other. When all the donuts have boiled, place them on a baking sheet and give them about a quarter of an hour in a rather bright oven. They must take on a dark gold color and become light.

FRAPPE

Fritters

MAKES 1 LB 2 OZ

3⅓ cups all-purpose flour
2 tbsp lard or butter
1 egg
2 egg yolks
Powdered sugar
Salt
½ cup white wine
Lard or oil for frying

Make a mound with the flour and place in the middle the lard, the egg, the egg yolks, a spoonful of sugar, and a pinch of salt, and mix everything with the white wine to obtain a dough, like everyday egg pasta. Let this dough rest for some time and then roll it out very thinly, on a lightly floured table. Use a knife or a serrated pastry cutter to create ribbons of your choice, long or short, simple or knot-shaped, which you will fry a beautiful light gold color in abundant oil or lard.

After frying the fritters, arrange them in a pyramid shape on a plate with a towel and sprinkle them abundantly with powdered sugar. Usually they are served cold, but they can also be served hot.

ADA SAYS: *These little sweets are traditional preparations, especially on Shrove Tuesday or Maundy Thursday. If you want to serve a sauce as an accompaniment to the frappe, we recommend hot red wine sauce* *(p754)* *or cold zabaglione* *(p754)**.*

FRITTELLE DI RICOTTA

Ricotta Fritters

MAKES ABOUT 20

⅔ cup breadcrumbs
Milk
1 cup ricotta
¼ cup sugar
2 egg yolks
Orange
All-purpose flour
1 egg
Lard or oil for frying
Powdered sugar

Soak the breadcrumbs in milk, and squeeze dry. Work the ricotta in a bowl with a wooden spoon to blend it well. Then add the breadcrumbs, the sugar, 2 egg yolks, and the zest of an orange. Stir to bring everything together.

Take ½ a tablespoon of this mixture, roll it in the flour, and then in the beaten egg, and finally fry in lard or oil. Since the mixture is very soft, you will have to flour each one very carefully. When they are light gold, remove them from the pan, let them drain, and then arrange them on a serving dish, sprinkling them with powdered sugar. They are also good cold, but it is preferable to serve them hot.

FRITTELLE DI RISO

Rice Fritters

MAKES ABOUT 80

1⅓ cups all-purpose flour
Salt
½ oz fresh yeast
1 cup rice
¼ cup sugar
Ground cinnamon
Lemon
Oil for frying
Powdered sugar

In a bowl, put the flour, and a good pinch of salt, crumble in the fresh yeast, and dilute everything with a large glass of warm water. Stir with a spoon, until this thick batter is smooth, without lumps, and elastic. Cover it with a lid and place the bowl in a sheltered place, so that the dough can rise.

In a saucepan with a quart of lightly salted boiling water, boil the rice, cooking it for a long time, not less than half an hour. Drain it, season it with 2 spoonfuls of sugar, a teaspoon of cinnamon, the zest of lemon, and pour it into a bowl and let the rice lose some of its heat.

When it is lukewarm, add it to the dough, which in the meantime should have doubled in volume. Stir vigorously and don't get tired until dough and rice are well blended. Place the bowl again in a sheltered place and let the mixture rise for at least 2 more hours.

Pour plenty of oil into a pan and let it heat up strongly. Take a little of the dough with a teaspoon and, with the help of another teaspoon, shape a ball. Drop the ball into the hot pan. Fry a few balls at a time: They will swell a little and become light; let them brown, turn them over gently, then remove them from the pan and let them drain. Place them in a pyramid on a serving dish, sprinkle with powdered sugar, and serve hot.

FRITTELLE DI SAN GIUSEPPE

San Joseph Fritters

MAKES ABOUT 12

1½ cups all-purpose flour
¼ oz fresh yeast
Salt
Oil for frying
Sugar

Put ½ a cup of flour on the table and arrange it in a heap. Dissolve the yeast in 2 fingers of just warm water and pour in the middle. Knead to a dough of the right consistency. Make a ball and put it in a bowl that you will cover and keep in a sheltered place for about an hour and a half.

After this time, transfer to a larger bowl, with one cup of flour and a pinch of salt. With a small glass of warm water, gradually dissolve, and work the dough with one hand for about 20 minutes, always beating vigorously until it becomes velvet, elastic, and comes off in one piece from the bowl and from your hand. Cover the bowl and leave the dough to rest for 4 hours, keeping it in a sheltered place so that it can rise again.

At this point, put plenty of oil in a pan and heat well. Then, with your fingers slightly wet with water, take pieces of dough the size of large walnuts. Place the 2 thumbs in the middle of each ball of dough and pushing under with the 2 index fingers and the 2 middle fingers, spread the dough gracefully so as to have a donut the diameter of a saucer, because when they are in the pan, the frittelle shrink. Then dip it in boiling oil. When you have fried them all golden and crispy, arrange them on a serving dish, sprinkle them with sugar, and serve hot.

ADA SAYS: *St. Joseph's day is celebrated on March 19th each year.*

KRAPFEN

Krapfen

MAKES ABOUT 30

1 lb 2 oz potatoes
1 oz fresh yeast
Milk
3⅓ cups all-purpose flour
2 tbsp sugar
2 eggs
Butter
Salt
Apricot jam
Oil for frying
Powdered sugar

Boil the potatoes in their skins, drain them, peel them while still hot, and mash them with a potato masher. Dissolve the yeast in a little warm milk. Arrange the flour on the kitchen table in a heap and put the mashed potatoes, the yeast mixture, sugar, the eggs, softened butter, and a pinch of salt in the well, and dissolve everything with as much milk as it will take to obtain a rather soft paste. Work the dough vigorously and then collect it in a bowl, placing it in a warm place so that it can rise.

When the dough has more than doubled its volume, turn it over on the floured table and beat it with your hands to deflate it. Then roll it out to the height of ½ inch and with a round and smooth dough cutter, cut some disks, also using the scraps, which you will knead and roll out again until all the dough is used up. Try to get an even number of disks. You can choose to your liking, or according to your needs, the diameter of the disks to obtain larger or smaller cakes.

On one side smear a little apricot jam or another fruit jam if you prefer. Slightly moisten the edges and cover with another disk. Arrange in a tray covered with a floured towel, cover them with another towel and leave them to rest in a sheltered place for a while.

When they begin to rise again, take them, delicately, one at a time and fry them in a pan with high sides where there is plenty of hot oil. Fry a few at a time, turning them as soon as they color; and when they are a beautiful golden color, remove them, let them drain, arrange them on a dessert plate and sprinkle them with plenty of powdered sugar.

KRAPFEN ALLA CREMA

Cream Krapfen

MAKES ABOUT 30

Krapfen dough *(p857)*
Oil for frying
Powdered sugar

Pastry cream:
1 cup milk, vanilla bean, 2 egg yolks, 3 tbsp sugar, ¼ cup all-purpose flour

Make your Krapfen. While the dough is rising, prepare the pastry cream using the ingredients listed here. Boil the milk with a vanilla bean. In another saucepan, mix the egg yolks with the sugar, add the flour, and pour in the warm milk, from which you have removed the vanilla bean. Mix thoroughly. Put the pan on the heat and, always stirring, thicken the cream for a few minutes. Let the cream cool, stirring it from time to time so that a skin does not form on the surface.

Take your Krapfen disks and on one half of these disks place a little of the prepared cream. Then, slightly moisten the edges of the disks with a little milk and cover them with the disk without cream. Place on a floured tray, cover them with a towel, and leave them in a sheltered place for about half an hour.

When they begin to rise again, take them gently, one at a time, and fry them in a high-sided pan with plenty of boiling oil. Cook a few at a time, turning them as soon as they color. When they are a nice golden color, remove them, drain well, arrange them on a dessert plate, and sprinkle them with plenty of powdered sugar.

MARITOZZI AL BURRO

Maritozzi

MAKES 12

1 oz fresh yeast
1⅓ cups all-purpose flour
1 egg
3½ tbsp butter, plus extra for greasing
Salt
3 tbsp sugar
1 tbsp pine nuts
3 to 4 tbsp raisins
Candied orange peel
Optional: vanilla extract

Dissolve the yeast in a cup with a little bit of just warm water. Add a third of a cup of flour, and add a little more water, if necessary, to make a soft dough, which you will mix with a teaspoon. Cover and place in a sheltered place.

After a quarter of an hour this yeast will have doubled in volume. Put one cup of flour on the kitchen table, make a well in the middle, and pour in the yeast, an egg, the butter, a pinch of salt, and one or 2 tablespoons of warm water, as much as is needed to have a pretty dough. Work this dough vigorously on the table, beating it with your hands, and when it comes off easily from the fingers and the table, add 2 spoonfuls of sugar. Work the dough a little longer, roll it in the flour, make it into a soft ball, and place it in a floured bowl. Cover and put in a sheltered place.

After an hour, when the dough has begun to swell, turn it over on the floured table and add a spoon of pine nuts, 3 or 4 spoons of raisins soaked in warm water, and a spoon of candied orange peel cut into strips. Work a little with your hands to distribute, then shape a large cylinder with the dough, from which you will cut out 12 pieces that you will roll, one by one, on the table, giving them an oval shape.

Place these pieces on to a lightly buttered plate, at a great distance from each other, and then flatten them with your fingers so that you have small, low, and oval sandwiches. Set the plate aside to let the Maritozzi rise again for a couple of hours, until they are well swollen.

Meanwhile, preheat the oven and make sure it is very hot. When the Maritozzi have risen, put them in the oven. They should cook in 6 or 7 minutes at most and turn a dark gold color. A longer stay in the oven would produce a crust, taking away the characteristic softness. As soon as they are cooked, take them out and with a brush wipe over each one a thick syrup, made with a spoon of sugar dissolved in very little water, putting them back in the warm oven for an instant to let the sugar dry. In the syrup you can add a trifle of vanilla.

Sweet Treats

BONBONS AL CAFFÈ

Coffee Bonbons

MAKES 25

⅔ cup hazelnuts or almonds
3½ oz dark chocolate
½ cup sugar
2 tbsp butter
Coffee
Powdered sugar

Put the shelled hazelnuts or almonds in a saucepan with cold water, bring to the boil, drain, remove the skins and keep in a bowl with cold water. Dry them with a towel, without letting them dry in the oven, and crush them in the mortar; or use an processor.

Grate the chocolate and add the sugar and the chopped hazelnuts or almonds. Mix everything and blend with the butter and a small tablespoon of very strong and cold coffee. Try to obtain a smooth mixture, working it on the kitchen table with a blade of a large knife, so as not to heat it too much with your hands.

Sprinkle the table with powdered sugar and working quickly with your hands, form a roll, from which you cut out pieces as large as a cherry. Quickly roll these bonbons to give them a regular shape and turn them over in the rest of the sugar to coat them and give them a good appearance.

BONBONS ALL'ARANCIA

Orange Bonbons

MAKES 25

3½ oz orange peel
½ cup sugar
Powdered sugar

Buy some nice oranges, untreated, wash them carefully, and peel them with a very sharp knife, trying not to take any of the white pith. Immerse the orange peels in cold water and leave them for 2 days, often renewing the water, so that they lose their bitter taste.

After 2 days, put them in cold water and cook until they are very soft, then drain, squeeze, and sieve them. Weigh the pulp obtained and add the same weight of sugar.

Put the orange purée and sugar in a saucepan and, stirring constantly, cook over medium heat until a very thick jam is obtained. Transfer to a plate and let it cool.

When the jam is cold, make balls the size of a small walnut. Roll these bonbons in powdered sugar and then arrange them in pleated paper cups.

BONBONS DI CASTAGNE AL CIOCCOLATO

Chocolate and Chestnut Bonbons

MAKES 25

7 oz chestnuts or ready peeled packet
Salt
¾ cup milk
2 tbsp butter
1 tbsp sugar
Vanilla
2½ oz grated chocolate

If they are not already peeled, knick the skin of the chestnuts and cook them in lightly salted water. When they are cooked, take off the inner skins and put them in a saucepan with the milk and butter, boiling them again and breaking them with a spoon to reduce them to purée.

Add a spoonful of sugar and a little vanilla and shape this dough into balls as big as cherries, then roll them in grated chocolate, so that this sticks well and covers them.

BONBONS DI CASTAGNE ALLE MANDORLE

Chestnut Bonbons with Almonds

MAKES 50

⅓ cup almonds
9 oz chestnuts
2½ oz dark chocolate
2 tbsp butter
1 tbsp sugar
Liqueur of your choice

Skin the almonds, dry them, chop them into grains, and put the grains in a preheated oven at very moderate heat until dry and slightly golden.

Boil and peel the chestnuts, then blend them. Grate the chocolate in, add the butter, a spoonful of sugar, and a teaspoon of liqueur and mix well. As soon as the dough is amalgamated, take a piece at a time and fashion into small nuts.

Roll the bonbons in the chopped almonds and arrange them in pleated paper cups.

BONBONS DI FRAGOLE

Strawberry Bonbons

MAKES 30

30 strawberries
2 cups white wine
2 tbsp sugar
Curaçao
9 oz dark chocolate
Orange peel
9 oz cooking chocolate (couverture)

Choose strawberries, possibly all of the same size, with firm flesh. Do not remove the stalks, wash them gently in a little white wine, drain, put them in a bowl, and sprinkle them with sugar. Splash them with a little liqueur, leaving them to macerate for a couple of hours.

After 2 hours, remove the strawberries from the marinade, let them drain, and line them up on a towel where they can dry.

Melt the dark chocolate in a bain-marie without diluting it with milk or water and, when it is just warm, perfume it with a little grated orange zest. Immerse the strawberries one by one in this dark chocolate, coat them well and, pulling them up with a two-pronged fork, let them drain, then align them on a sheet of wax paper.

When the dark chocolate is dry, grate the cooking chocolate into a medium bowl set over a saucepan of simmering water over low heat to create a bain-marie, take care not to heat it too much. As soon as it melts, remove the saucepan from the bain-marie and work the chocolate well with a wooden spoon, until it is completely cold and set. Put the pan back into the bain-marie over less than lukewarm water and, as soon as the chocolate shows a sign of melting, remove it from the heat and continue to mash it with the spoon, working it a little longer. By dipping a finger in melted chocolate, you should not feel the sensation of heat.

Put the strawberries into this chocolate, pull them up with the same 2-pronged fork, let them drain and align them again on a sheet of wax paper to dry. Let the bonbons rest for a few hours; the humidity of the strawberry melts the dark chocolate, which will remain trapped in the chocolate coating.

BONBONS DI NOCI

Walnut Bonbons

MAKES 25

¾ cup walnuts, plus 25 halves for decoration
½ cup sugar
3 tbsp strong brewed coffee
Ground coffee
Liqueur

Shell the walnuts. Set aside 25 half kernels in good condition, and blend the rest.

Calculate the same weight of sugar as walnuts. Put the walnut mix on the table and add to it 3 spoonfuls of very strong coffee, a pinch of ground coffee, a pinch of sugar, and a few drops of liqueur. Knead everything together into small balls and roll into leftover sugar.

On each bonbon press one of the walnut halves. Place the bonbons in the pleated paper cups.

CANNOLI

Cannoli

MAKES 25

1 cup all-purpose flour
Lard or back fat (*strutto*)
Salt
1 tsp sugar
Marsala or wine
Olive oil for frying
Candied fruit
Vanilla sugar

Cream:
2¼ cups ricotta, 1¼ cups sugar, orange flower water, chocolate, candied fruit or pistachios

Put the flour, lard, a pinch of salt, and a teaspoon of sugar on the table and mix with a little Marsala or red or white wine, so as to have a rather hard dough. Collect it in the shape of a ball and let it rest for about an hour, covered with a towel.

Roll it out rather thinly, ⅛ of an inch, no more, and make 12 squares of about 4 inches on each side. Place on each square, in the direction of the diagonal, a cannoli horn or a tube of an equivalent diameter. Wrap two points of the pastry square around the tube and fry in plenty of oil.

The casing must be fried to a rather dark blond color. They must be crunchy. It is good to fry one or two at a time, being careful not to break them. When the casings are well colored, remove them from the pan, let them cool a little, carefully remove them from their tubes, and let them finish cooling. Repeat with the remaining dough squares.

Now put the ricotta in a bowl and add the sugar. Give it a little stir and then, one or 2 spoonfuls at a time, sieve to obtain a very delicate cream, which you can flavor with a little orange blossom water. To this cream you can add a few shavings of chocolate, a few pieces of candied pumpkin, or chopped pistachios, or candied orange peel, to your taste.

Fill the cannoli tubes using a spoon or a pastry bag with a smooth round nozzle and a large opening. Then, wiping the blade of a knife over the 2 openings, level the cream well. Finally, place a piece of candied fruit on each of the 2 ends, inserting it into the cream. Arrange the cannoli on a tray and sprinkle them abundantly with vanilla sugar.

CANNONCINI

Cannoncini

MAKES 24

10½ oz puff pastry, homemade *(p820)* or packaged
1 egg
Butter for greasing
Powdered sugar
Pastry cream *(p752)*

Roll out the fresh puff pastry in a rectangle, ⅛ of an inch thick, square the dough and cut out strips of ¾ of an inch wide and 6 inches long. Brush the left sides with a beaten egg, but without reaching the ends.

Roll your cannoli tube, or equivalent, under the first strip, at one end. With your fingers, close the end, which you then turn along the spiral, so that each new ring of the spiral itself overlaps, and then sticks, on the egg-brushed part. At the end, having already twisted the entire strip in a spiral, attach the end by pressing with your fingers.

Arrange the cannoncini on a baking sheet lightly veiled with butter, brush them with the beaten egg and bake them in a hot oven with strong heat. When the cannoncini are almost cooked, which will happen in a few minutes, take out the baking sheet for a moment, sprinkle the cannoncini with powdered sugar and bake again for a few minutes. Take the cannoncini out of the oven, let them cool a little, then free them from the cannoli mold and fill them using a pastry bag filled with a pastry cream.

CAVALLUCCI DI SIENA

Siena Cavallucci

MAKES 30

1 cup all-purpose flour
1 oz candied orange peel
Anise seed
Ground cinnamon
½ cup walnuts
¾ cup sugar
1 egg white
Butter for greasing

Put the flour, candied orange peel, minutely chopped with a knife, a teaspoon of chopped anise seeds, and a heaped teaspoon of cinnamon in a bowl. Then, on the table, chop the walnuts with a knife, which you will add to the rest.

Now put the sugar in a small saucepan with half a glass of water, and let the sugar soften well so that it becomes a paste. Put the saucepan on the stove and cook the sugar to a hard ball *(p736)*. As soon as it has reached this degree, pour all the prepared ingredients into the saucepan all at once, remove it from the heat, and mix vigorously, combining everything well.

Turn this thick dough on to the lightly floured table, let it cool a little and then with your hands wet with egg white, kneading it to make a smooth mass. Roll it out with a rolling pin to just ½ an inch thick and make small squares of about 1½ inches on each side, which you will gradually line up on the baking sheet that has been lightly greased with butter and scattered with flour. Bake in a preheated oven with a very light heat for a good half hour, so that they can dry without coloring.

CIALDONI

Waffle Cones

9 tbsp butter, plus extra for greasing
6 eggs
¼ cup vanilla sugar
Active dry yeast
1⅓ cups all-purpose flour
1 cup sweetened whipped cream

The packaging of the wafers requires the use of a special waffle iron.

Put the melted butter in a bowl and whip with a wooden spoon until it just begins to thicken. Then add 6 egg yolks with the vanilla sugar, one at a time. When the eggs are well combined, add a pinch of yeast and the flour. Mix and complete with the 6 whipped whites and sweetened whipped cream, which you will gently add to the rest.

Heat the waffle iron, open it, and pour in a scant spoonful of the mixture. Close the waffle maker, put it back on the heat, first on one side, then on the other, and after a few minutes, when the waffle has taken on a nice light gold color, open the waffle maker, remove the waffle and without waiting for it to cool, roll it around a stick. Do this last operation promptly, otherwise the dough, cooling and drying, will break. The waffle iron must be lightly greased with butter and the anointing must be repeated from time to time.

CIAMBELLONE

Ciambellone

14 tbsp butter
1 cup sugar
7 eggs
5 cups all-purpose flour
Baking powder
Salt
Milk
5 tbsp yogurt
¼ cup raisins
2 oz grated chocolate
⅓ cup almonds
1 oz active dry yeast
Powdered sugar

Soften the butter, cut into small pieces, and put them in a bowl with the sugar, the whole eggs, and the sifted flour mixed with the baking powder and a pinch of salt. Also add the milk and the yogurt. Work everything with the mixer, until the mixture is soft and well blended.

Soak the raisins in cold water, grate the chocolate and shell, skin and chop the almonds. Add all 3 to the mix. Grease and flour a high-sided mold, pour the mixture in, leveling the surface with a wooden spoon and place it in a preheated oven at a moderate temperature for about an hour. Before unmolding, let the ciambellone rest for about 10 minutes, out of the oven, so they get cold, then place on a serving dish and cover with powdered sugar.

CIOCCOLATINI ALLE MANDORLE

Chocolate Almonds

MAKES 30

⅔ cup peeled almonds
1 cup cocoa powder
2 tbsp liqueur of your choice
Powdered sugar

Crush the peeled almonds and mix with the cocoa powder and a splash of liqueur. Work the mixture well to obtain a soft dough and add, if necessary, a little water. With this chocolate paste, make balls, like small nuts, and roll them in powdered sugar.

DATTERI E NOCI CON PASTA DI MANDORLE

Date and Walnut Bonbons

MAKES 40

⅔ cup almonds
½ cup sugar
3½ oz spinach
Maraschino liqueur
40 dates or walnuts
Optional: ¾ cup sugar

Boil and skin the almonds and dry them in the oven. Then pound or blend them with the sugar. Blend a few almonds and a little sugar at a time, and make sure that the almonds do not give up any oil; then pass the flour obtained through a sieve.

Now we need to make a green color. Wash and dry well and chop a handful of raw spinach leaves, put them in a towel, and squeeze hard. A greenish liquid will come out. Collect it in a small cup. Put on the heat and at the first boil you will see that the liquid has decomposed. Then sieve it. The watery part will go away, and a green substance will remain on the sieve, which is the required color.

Mix this green with the sugared almond flour, and if you see that the dough is struggling to form, add a few drops of water or better some maraschino liqueur.

If using dates: Cut the dates lengthwise on one side and, without splitting them completely, remove the pit. Open the dates and in the opening put a little almond paste, making sure to arrange it evenly so that between the two lips—let's say—of the date you can see a nice strip of green almond paste.

If using walnuts: Shell the walnuts without damaging them and cut them into two with a small knife. Between one side and the other, place a little almond paste and reconstruct the walnut. Let them dry and then you can serve them like this.

Melt the sugar in a small saucepan, until it caramelizes. Then remove the saucepan from the heat and presto presto, but very carefully because you could burn yourself, using a special fork dip the prepared fruits one by one in to this sugar. If the sugar has been cooked well it will dry out immediately, forming a shiny and crisp coverage.

ADA SAYS: *If you want, you can caramelize the walnuts.*

DIPLOMATICI PICCOLI

Little Diplomats

MAKES 25

7 oz puff pastry, homemade *(p820)* or store bought
Butter for greasing
Pastry cream *(p752)*
Sponge cake, homemade *(p810)* or store bought
Alchermes liqueur
Powdered sugar

You can buy packaged fresh puff pastry, ready for use, make it yourself, or buy frozen puff pastry and let it thaw at room temperature. Divide it into two equal pieces and roll them out into 2 very thin squares, prick them with a fork, and bake them on a well-greased and floured baking sheet, in a preheated oven at moderate heat, for about an hour or as directed on the packet.

Make up the pastry cream using egg yolks, sugar, flour, milk and lemon zest. It should not be excessively thick. Let it cool, stirring it from time to time so that it does not form a skin.

Put a little pastry cream on one of the 2 cooled squares, make a layer of slices of sponge cake wetted with a little Alchermes liqueur, spread with more cream, and finish with the other square of pastry. Line up the sides of the square, and then with a very sharp pointed knife, divide it into many squares of about 3 fingers on each side. In order to cut the various squares well, the puff pastry must not be overcooked and therefore not too crunchy. Dust the little diplomats generously with powdered sugar and arrange them on a tray.

LINGUE DELLE SUOCERE

Mother-In-Law's Tongues

1 cup sugar
Vanilla extract
1⅓ cups all-purpose flour
¾ cup milk or cream
2 egg whites
Butter for greasing

Put the sugar, perfumed with a splash of vanilla, and the flour in a bowl and add the milk or cream until you get a thick cream. Whip the egg whites to a very firm snow and gently add them to the rest. Put the mixture in a pastry bag, with a smooth ½ inch nozzle, and pipe 5 inch long ropes on a greased and floured baking sheet. Bake them in an already hot oven of very light heat, as if they were meringues, until they are firm and slightly colored.

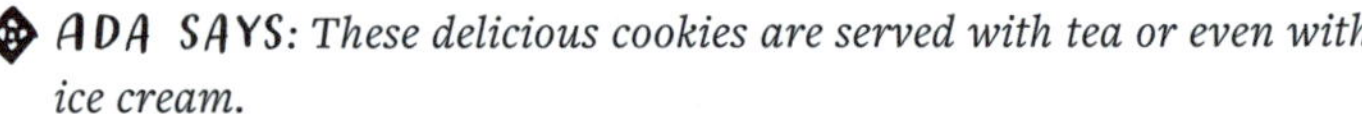
ADA SAYS: *These delicious cookies are served with tea or even with ice cream.*

LINGUE DI GATTO

Cat's Tongues

7 tbsp butter
4 tbsp powdered sugar
4 tbsp all-purpose flour
Lemon zest
2 egg whites

Whip the butter in a bowl with a wooden spoon. Add the powdered sugar, then, always working, the flour, the zest of a little lemon, and finally the egg whites. Stir to mix everything well, but do not work the whites too much because there is no need.

Put this mixture in a pastry bag with a smooth nozzle ¼ of an inch in diameter, or in a foil. Lightly butter the baking sheet and, pressing on the pocket, pipe the mixture to about the thickness of a pencil and a length of about 4 inches, making sure that they are not too close to each other because when they cook they flatten, and then they would stick together. Bake in a very hot oven for a few minutes, until they are slightly golden at the edges, and still white in the middle. Remove from the oven and let them cool.

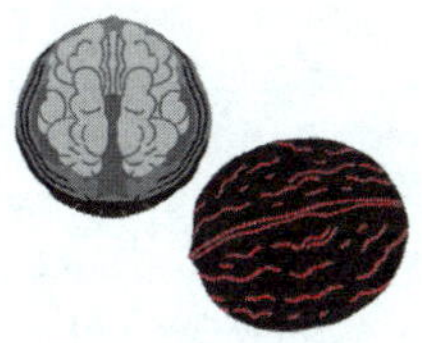
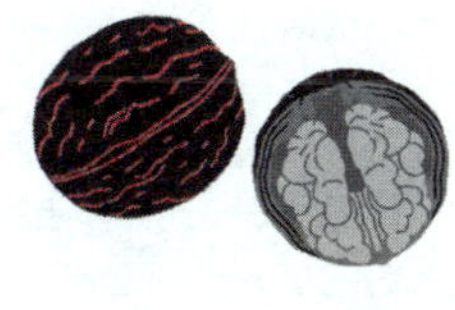
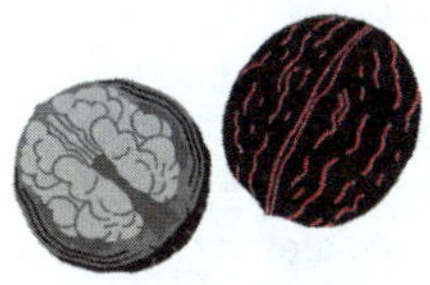

MOSTACCIOLI DI NOCI

Walnut Mostaccioli

MAKES 18

2 cups walnuts
⅓ cup honey
2 egg whites
Pepper
Ground cinnamon
1 cup all-purpose flour

Chop the walnuts with a knife to a very fine grain, place them in a bowl, and add the honey, 2 egg whites, a pinch of finely ground pepper, and a little cinnamon. Knead everything and mix in the flour on the table, until it becomes a rather consistent dough, which, however, you will not have to work too much.

Roll out this dough to ¼ inch thick and cut it into sticks that you line up on the baking sheet. Bake them in a preheated oven of light heat for about 20 minutes. Wait until they are cool and firm before removing them from the sheet.

NOCCIOLINI

Baked Hazelnuts

MAKES 50

1 cup shelled hazelnuts
½ cup sugar
¾ cup all-purpose flour
1 cup potato starch
1 egg
2 egg yolks
9 tbsp butter
Lemon zest
Powdered sugar
Butter for greasing

Toast the hazelnuts in a light oven. Then, after having skinned them, chop them with the sugar, so you have a kind of flour. To this hazelnut flour, add the all-purpose flour, potato starch, a whole egg and 2 egg yolks, the softened butter, and the zest of a lemon.

Mix everything, turn onto a kitchen table, and divide it into many pellets the size of large hazelnuts. Sprinkle with powdered sugar, line them up on a lightly greased baking sheet, and bake them in a preheated oven with light heat for about 20 minutes.

PASTICCETTI DI GNOCCHI

Gnocchi Pastries

MAKES 24

½ cup all-purpose flour
⅓ cup sugar
2 tsp cornstarch
2 tsp potato starch
Salt
Ground cinnamon
5 egg yolks
2 cups milk
3½ tbsp butter
1 egg
Powdered sugar

Shortcrust pastry:
2 cups all-purpose flour, 10½ tbsp butter, ¾ cup sugar, 3 egg yolks, lemon zest

Make a shortcrust pastry *(p784)* using the ingredient amounts listed here. Do not overwork it. Let it rest for about half an hour covered with a towel.

Now prepare the sweet gnocchi mixture: Put the flour, sugar, 2 teaspoons of cornstarch and 2 teaspoons of potato starch, a pinch of salt, a strong pinch of ground cinnamon, and 5 egg yolks in a pan. Blend everything with the cold milk, preferably using a whisk. Put the saucepan on the stove and, still stirring with the whisk, let the mixture heat up. When you see that it begins to thicken, add the butter, remove the whisk, and continue to mix quite vigorously with a wooden spoon. Soon the mixture will thicken a lot. Continue to work it vigorously with the spoon to make it gain flexibility and when you see that it tends to detach from the sides of the saucepan, remove it from the heat, and pour it on to the kitchen table, slightly wet with water.

Wet the blade of a large knife with water and smooth it out to a thickness of ½ inch. Once the cream is cool, level it with wet hands to smooth it out evenly. If the mixture has been well executed, as soon as it is cold it will set well.

Then divide it into strips an inch wide, which you will then cut into very small rhombus-shaped dumplings with oblique cuts a distance of an inch from each other.

Roll out the shortcrust pastry into a rather thin sheet and create 2 disks: the smallest with a diameter of 4 inches, the largest 6 inches. Arrange a layer of dumplings on the smaller disk, leaving a free edge of half an inch all around. On the first layer make a second one starting a little more inside, and a third one even further in, so that it takes the shape of a dome. Brush the edge with beaten egg and cover the dumplings with the corresponding larger disk. Press with your fingers around the edges so that the overlapping disks stick together, and with a small knife trim the superfluous dough, giving the pastry a nice round shape.

Knead the shortcrust pastry scraps and make as many ropes as there are pastries, and arrange around the edge of each pastry. Make many small footprints on the cords half an inch apart and gild with beaten egg. Arrange on a greased baking sheet, a little distant from each other, and lift the sheet in to a preheated oven of moderate heat for about 40 minutes, until the shortcrust pastry has taken on a nice color, not too dark gold. Then remove the gnocchi from the oven, let them cool, and sprinkle them with powdered sugar.

PASTICCINI ALL'ARANCIA

Orange Pasticcini

MAKES 20

7 tbsp butter
3 tbsp powdered sugar
2 egg yolks
Orange
Curaçao
7 oz sponge cake, homemade *(p810)* or shop bought
⅓ cup almonds

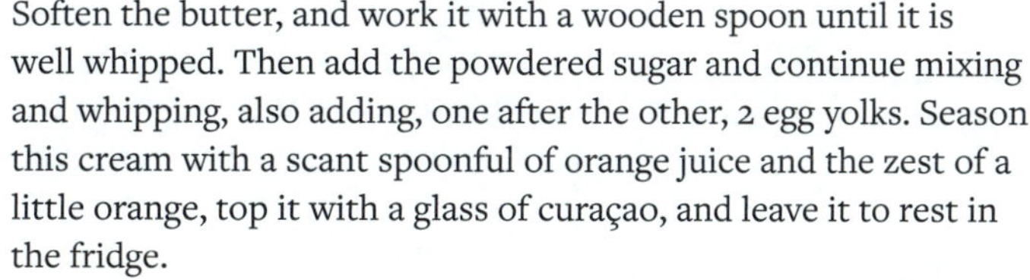

Soften the butter, and work it with a wooden spoon until it is well whipped. Then add the powdered sugar and continue mixing and whipping, also adding, one after the other, 2 egg yolks. Season this cream with a scant spoonful of orange juice and the zest of a little orange, top it with a glass of curaçao, and leave it to rest in the fridge.

Cut the sponge cake into slices ½ an inch thick and then, with a round or oval pastry cutter, cut out into medium-sized disks or ovals. On these spread a generous layer of the cream, making sure to give it a slightly rounded shape. Sprinkle some almond slices on the cream, and finish the pastries by sprinkling them with more powdered sugar.

PASTINE ALL'UVETTA

Raisin Pastine

MAKES 40

¼ cup raisins
7 tbsp butter, plus extra for greasing
½ cup sugar
1 egg white
⅔ cup all-purpose flour

First, soak the raisins in warm water. Then work the butter with the sugar in a bowl and when the mixture has become like a cream, add an egg white; stir again and add the flour. Butter the baking sheet. Then gently form balls the size of a walnut with your hands. Place them on the baking sheet a little distant from each other. Put 2 or 3 raisins in the middle of each ball. Put the sheet in a preheated oven of moderate heat for about 20 minutes. In the oven the balls will flatten and take the shape of disks, the rim of which will take on a dark-blond color.

PASTINE PLUM CAKE

Black Raisin Pastries with Rum

MAKES 80

4 tbsp butter
¼ cup sugar
2 eggs
¼ cup black raisins
Rum
Candied orange peel
Lemon zest
½ cup all-purpose flour

Work the butter in a bowl; mix it with a wooden spoon, whipping it until it becomes soft and creamy, add the sugar, and continue stirring. When the sugar has been absorbed, add an egg yolk. Keep mixing and after a couple of minutes, add a second egg yolk. You will keep the whites of these 2 eggs aside.

In the meantime, you will have put the well-cleaned black raisins in a cup and washed them with a little rum. Also prepare a spoonful of candied orange peel cut into tiny cubes. When the 2 egg yolks are blended, pour the raisins with all the rum, and a tablespoon of diced candied orange peel into the mixture, also adding the zest of a lemon. Stir again and then, a little at a time, add the flour. Finally, whip the egg whites to a firm snow and put them in the bowl, gently combining them with the rest.

When everything is ready, butter the baking pans. You will need at least 3 pans. Put the mixture in a pastry bag with a smooth nozzle with a ½ inch opening and pipe and release balls the size of a small walnut on the pans, placing them a little distant from each other so they don't stick. Put the first pan in a preheated oven of moderate heat. In the oven, the balls flatten and take a round shape. When they have become light blond, with slightly more colored edges, remove the pan, lift off the pasties with a spatula, and put them to dry. Then bake the other pastries. Can be served both hot and cold.

PETIT FOURS DI PASTA DI MANDORLE

Almond Petit Fours

MAKES 2¼ LB

3 cups shelled almonds
2½ cups sugar
2 cups powdered sugar
5 egg whites
Lemon zest
Butter for greasing
Candied fruit

To prepare the almond flour: Put the shelled almonds in a pan and cover them with water that you will heat until almost boiling. Then peel the almonds, keeping them in fresh water, and when you have peeled them all, drain them, spread them on the baking pan to dry completely in a very moderate heat. The almonds should not be colored, but simply dry.

Finely chop a handful of almonds together with a little sugar. Put them through a sieve until you have finished them all. Then add the powdered sugar. Put everything on the kitchen table, and mix with 5 egg whites and the zest of a lemon, to obtain a dough that, without being very hard, has a certain consistency and holds up.

Put this dense almond paste in the pastry bag fitted with a spiked nozzle ½ inch in diameter. Lightly butter the baking sheet and then pipe the paste to make little pastries and decorate each one with a candied fruit. Let them rest all night on the sheet and the following day, bake them in a very hot oven until they have golden edges.

PINOCCATE

Pinoccate

MAKES 24

1 cup almonds
1¼ cups sugar
2 egg whites
Butter for greasing
Pine nuts

Peel the almonds, dry them with a towel, and without letting them dry in the oven, crush them or chop them with sugar, adding a little bit of freshly beaten egg white from time to time, just to break it. Continue to pound or mince until you have obtained a smooth paste of the right consistency.

Put this dough in a pastry bag with a smooth nozzle ½ inch in diameter. Lightly butter a baking sheet and pipe out some small balls, the size of a rather large walnut. Sprinkle some pine nuts on each ball and let the pinoccate rest for several hours to make a crust. Then bake them in a hot oven for about 10 minutes, until they are golden.

PRINCIPESSINE

Little Princesses

MAKES 40

¾ cup all-purpose flour
Salt
7 tbsp butter, plus extra for greasing
Milk or cream
Powdered sugar

Knead the flour, a pinch of salt, and the butter on the kitchen table, and to make the dough smoother, add a spoon of milk or cream. It should be smooth and similar to shortcrust pastry. Make it into a ball, let it rest for a few minutes, and then roll it out into a rectangle. Fold it in 3 as if you were making a puff pastry. Roll it out again and fold it up; and do so 4 times.

Once this is done, let the dough rest for about 10 minutes, and then roll it out into a rectangular sheet with a thickness of less than ¼ of an inch. With a corrugated round pastry cutter measuring 2 inches in diameter, cut spiked disks that align on a lightly buttered baking sheet. Mix the scraps and make some more to use up all the dough. Put the sheet in a preheated oven of moderate heat until they are a very light blond color. In the oven, these pastries grow a little and become like puff pastries.

Now prepare the kitchen table with a few spoons of powdered sugar. Remove the sheet from the oven and lifting the princesses with the blade of a knife, gently run them though the powdered sugar on both sides. Then place them on a wire rack to let them cool.

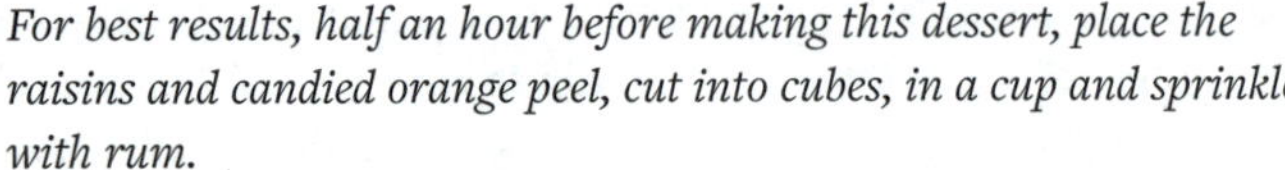

SFOGLIATELLE DOLCI DI RICOTTA

Sweet Ricotta Sfogliatelle

1 tbsp raisins
1 tbsp candied orange peel
2 tbsp rum
1 cup ricotta
½ cup sugar
9 oz puff pastry, homemade *(p820)* or packaged
7 tbsp butter
Powdered sugar

Pastry cream:
1 egg yolk, 2 tbsp sugar, 2 tbsp all-purpose flour, ¾ cup milk, vanilla

For best results, half an hour before making this dessert, place the raisins and candied orange peel, cut into cubes, in a cup and sprinkle with rum.

Work the ricotta in a bowl with a wooden ladle and season with the sugar, then add the raisins and candied orange peel.

Prepare the pastry cream: Put the egg yolk with the sugar in a pan, mix with a wooden spoon, add the flour. Heat the milk with the vanilla and when it is almost boiling pour it over the egg, sugar, and flour, mixing thoroughly. Set the pan back over the heat, continuing to stir; you will see that soon the cream will thicken. Let it boil slowly, for a few minutes, so that it can lose the flavor of flour. Add the ricotta cream, also adding the rum that was used to macerate the raisins and candied fruit.

Roll out the puff pastry as thinly and evenly as possible. Make 4 strips, each about 4 inches wide; brush them abundantly with melted butter, then overlap them and put them in the fridge. After about half an hour, when the butter has hardened, roll up the strips and cut the roll into slices. With a rolling pin spread out each slice, giving it an oval shape. On the middle of each oval put a scant spoonful of cream and Ricotta, leaving the edge free. Fold the oval in 2, pressing with your fingers to make the edges fit and adhere well. Repeat this operation for all the ovals.

Arrange the sfogliatelle on a well-greased baking sheet, brush them with butter and cook them in a hot oven for a quarter of an hour; then turn the oven down a little for 20 minutes, and finally, lower the heat again to low and bake 5 or 6 minutes at low heat. Take the sfogliatelle out of the oven and sprinkle them abundantly with powdered sugar, place them on a dessert plate, and let them cool.

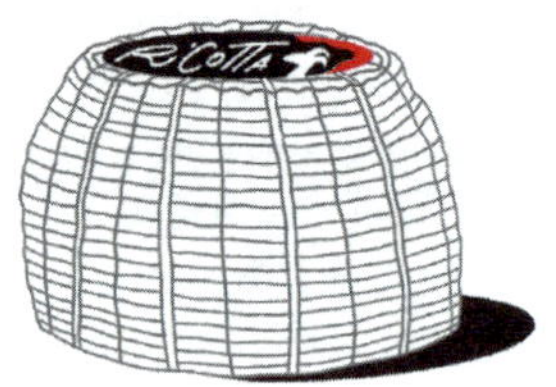

SOSPIRI

Sospiri

MAKES 50

5 eggs
½ cup sugar
⅔ cup all-purpose flour
Salt
Jam or pastry cream *(p752)*
Liqueur of your choice
Fondant *(p749)*
Apricot jam

Break the eggs, putting the yolks in a bowl and the whites in a small saucepan. Add the sugar to the yolks and work them with a wooden spoon. Then mix in the flour and salt. Do not work for too long.

What needs to be done perfectly is to beat the whites, until they are very strong. When they are ready, pour them into the bowl together with the yolks and sugar, and with a wooden spoon, slowly, slowly, mix them. Put the finished dough in a pastry bag, with a smooth round nozzle with a diameter of ½ inch. Close the pocket at the top and pipe some bullets the size of a large walnut, collecting them, well aligned, at a certain distance from each other, on parchment paper-lined baking sheets. Bake in a preheated oven of rather brilliant heat.

As soon as they are cooked and blond, carefully remove from the paper and use a small knife to empty them a little on the flat side, the one that was in contact with the paper. Put in this small void a little pastry cream or jam, and then couple the cakes two by two, so that the two flat parts remain in the middle.

After having them all coupled, with a sharp knife trim them in the lower part so that they stand straight. Then splash with the liqueur of your choice, diluted with a little water, and line them up on the table in front of you.

Prepare the fondant: Take the sugar and glucose, melt them in a saucepan, let them cool slightly, working them with a spatula, and dilute them a little. This dilution can be done either with a few drops of lukewarm water or milk, or with a little liqueur, if you want to flavor the fondant. It must be like a not too thick cream.

Brush the sospiri with a slight haze of apricot jam; then, holding them with the tip of a small knife or a fork, dip them into the fondant, let them drain, and align them on a wire rack, waiting for the fondant to dry.

ADA SAYS: *Fondant can also be colored, with food colors—pink, pale green, yellow, etc. The color should be added in very small quantities when the fondant is already dissolved. Keep the fondant warm throughout the icing process. Instead of using liqueur you can, after diluting the fondant with a very little warm water, add a few drops of essence: strawberry, if you are going to color the fondant in pink; lemon, if you will leave the fondant in white; pineapple or orange, if you are going to color the fondant in yellow, etc. Use only the necessary amount of fondant, as fondant that has been heated several times loses its characteristic sheen.*

SPIRALI

Spirals

MAKES 20

1⅔ cups all-purpose flour
¼ oz fresh yeast
1 egg
9 tbsp butter
3 tbsp sugar
2 tbsp chopped almonds
Raisins
To serve: thick syrup (½ cup water, 1 cup sugar)

These belong to the old school of pastry, and are known under various denominations.

In a cup, put a third of a cup of flour and crumble in the yeast. Dissolve with a little warm water. Let it rise. After about a quarter of an hour the yeast will have doubled in volume. Then place the remaining flour in a heap and place an egg in the well, 2 tablepoons of butter cut in pieces, the sugar, the yeast mixture, and very little warm water, as much as you need to have a rather soft dough. Work it well, place it in a rather large bowl, and let it rise for at least a couple of hours in a sheltered place.

When the dough has risen, overturn it on a lightly floured table and deflate it in small strokes, folding it several times on itself. Then roll it out into a square and in the middle place the remaining butter in small pieces. Fold the 4 corners of the square toward the center to enclose the butter inside, and then fold the dough in 4. Roll out the dough and fold it again in 4. Let it rest for about 10 minutes in the fridge and then roll it out again, giving it 2 more turns.

Let it rest for another 10 minutes and then roll out the dough again into a rectangle that is up to 10 inches high and 14 inches long. The thickness should be about ¼ of an inch. Strew a couple of spoonfuls of sugar, a couple of spoonfuls of peeled and chopped almonds, and a handful of raisins soaked in warm water. Then roll the dough into the longer side of the rectangle, so as to make a kind of salami that will have a diameter of about 2 and a half inches. Cut out many slices of half an inch, and line them up on the baking sheet, a little distant from each other. Put the sheet in a sheltered place and let it rise for an hour. Then put them in a rather hot oven, and when they are baked to a dark gold, brush them with a warm, rather thick sugar syrup.

SPUMETTE MANDORLATE ALLA VANIGLIA

Almond and Vanilla Spumette

MAKES 15

1 egg white
1 cup powdered sugar
Lemon juice
Vanilla
1 cup almonds, peeled and crushed
Butter for greasing
All-purpose flour

Work the egg white with the powdered sugar in a bowl, whipping the mixture until you have a very white mass, rather swollen, and with the consistency of a very thick cream. From time to time you will add a few drops of lemon juice to facilitate the operation. When the white is well whipped, add a touch of vanilla and the crushed almonds. Mix well.

Then butter and lightly plain flour the baking sheet. With a teaspoon, take a quantity of the mixture, the volume of a walnut, and with another teaspoon detach this mixture and let it fall on the sheet. Keep the mounds rather high and a little distant from each other so that they do not stick together. When you have put all the mixture down, put the sheet in an already hot oven with very light heat for about 20 minutes or more, until the spumette are well firmed, increased in volume, and have taken a very slight color, then score them with the blade of a knife and let them cool on a wire rack.

STRUFFOLI ALLA NAPOLETANA

Neapolitan Struffoli

MAKES 10

3⅓ cups all-purpose flour
8 eggs
2 egg yolks
Lard or olive oil
1 tsp sugar
Salt
Lemon zest
¾ cup honey
3 oranges
2½ oz candied orange peel
2½ oz candied citron peel

Arrange the flour on the kitchen table in a heap and place the eggs and the yolks, 4 tablespoons lard, sugar, a pinch of salt, and the zest of half a lemon in the middle, and mix everything as if it were the usual egg pasta. Roll out the dough rather thick, and cut into sticks the size of a macaroni. With diagonal cuts, divide these sticks into many very small mostaccioli (small, smooth penne), which you will fry in lard or oil, a few at a time, until they have taken on a light gold color.

Melt the honey in a saucepan, add the grated peel of 3 oranges, the fried struffoli, and finally the orange peel and the citron peel cut into very small squares. With a wooden spoon, mix slowly and very carefully, without crushing the pieces of dough, and continue to mix until all the honey is absorbed. At this point, pour the mixture on to a round plate, with your hands slightly wet with water, give this mass a conical shape, and let it cool.

TARTUFI AL CIOCCOLATO

Chocolate Truffles

MAKES 35

Butter for greasing
Cocoa powder

Choux pastry:
½ cup all-purpose flour, 3½ tbsp butter, 2 eggs, salt, sugar

Chocolate cream:
3 egg yolks, ½ cup sugar, 2 cups milk, 2 oz dark chocolate

Using the ingredient amounts listed here, prepare a choux pastry *(p817)*. Put it in the pastry bag with a smooth nozzle ½ an inch in diameter, close the pocket, and pipe choux the size of a walnut on a lightly buttered baking sheet. Bake them in a very hot oven for about 10 minutes, and when they are cooked and cold, fill them with chocolate cream *(p753)* made using the ingredient amounts listed here.

Fill all the choux, spread them with a trifle of the same chocolate cream, and then roll them in the cocoa powder, so that they take on the appearance of large truffles.

TEGOLINE

Tegoline Cookies

8 tbsp butter, plus extra for greasing
1 cup sugar
2 eggs
2 egg whites
⅓ cup chopped almonds
3½ oz candied orange peel
Orange flower water
¾ cup all-purpose flour
Oil for greasing

These cookies are very afraid of humidity: therefore, to keep them, you will have to put them in a tin box, where they will keep for a long time.

In a bowl, whip the butter with a wooden spoon until it becomes creamy, add the sugar and work the mixture to make it soft. Then put 2 eggs and 2 egg whites in the bowl, the almonds with their skins, the candied orange peel cut into tiny cubes, and a tablespoon of orange flower water. Finally, incorporate the flour and mix gently. Take a pastry bag, fix it with a smooth nozzle and place the dough in, which must be very fluid and light.

Grease and flour one or more baking sheets and drop the mixture into many balls very far from each other. Then lift the sheet with your hands and place it back on the board, giving it a strong blow. Blowing will cause the balls to widen and flatten, and take the form of disks of 2 inches in diameter. Put in the oven and bake them in an already hot oven with very lively heat, and when they have taken a slight brown color, but they are not yet firm, detach them and remove them from the sheet with the blade of a knife, and, still very hot, place them on the rolling pin, lightly greased with oil. Fold them with your hands to make the tiles take the shape of the roller and let them cool on the roller itself. They will immediately firm up and take on the slightly curved humpback shape. For this operation to be successful, you will not have to remove the sheet from the oven, but keep it at the door and work promptly.

TIRAMISÙ

Tiramisu

2 cups bitter coffee
6 eggs
7 tbsp sugar
2 cups marscapone
10½ oz ladyfingers
Unsweetened cocoa
Coffee beans

Make the coffee, strong and bitter, and let it cool. Break the eggs, separating the whites from the yolks. Put the yolks in a bowl, add the sugar, and beat until they are soft and well whipped. Add the mascarpone, kept at room temperature, a little at a time, mixing carefully. Whip the egg whites to a firm snow, and add them to the mixture with great delicacy so as not to disassemble them.

Take a rectangular dish with high sides and start preparing the tiramisú: Arrange the ladyfingers, or other cookies of your choice, on the bottom, wet them with the coffee, and cover them with the prepared cream. Make a second layer of ladyfingers, coffee, and cream, and then a third. Finish by covering everything with the cream. Place the tiramisú in the fridge covered with plastic wrap and when serving, sprinkle it with cocoa and decorate it with coffee beans.

VENTAGLI

Fans

MAKES 30

7 oz puff pastry, homemade (*p820*) or store-bought
Powdered sugar

Using the ingredient amounts listed here, make a puff pastry or buy it fresh packaged and lay it out on the lightly floured table, giving it the shape of a rectangle. Fold it so that the 2 shorter sides of the rectangle come together in the center, matching. Fold the dough one more time, bringing the same sides over each other so as to obtain a long and narrow strip of 4 sheets. With a knife, cut many strips of ½ an inch in width, neither more nor less, as if they were spaghetti, but without letting them open.

Butter the baking sheet and arrange the strands. Bake them in the oven with good heat. In the oven the dough expands and the fans open, and from narrow and high as they were, they become low and wide. They must not remain in the oven for too long: a few moments before removing them you can sprinkle them with powdered sugar, which melting will caramelize a layer on the fans.

FRUIT

ANANAS A SORPRESA

Pineapple Surprise

Pineapple
Pear
Apple
Banana
Grapes
Rum
2 tbsp sugar

Carefully cut off the cap with the tuft of the pineapple. With a small curved knife with a serrated edge, carve out the pineapple from the shell, without damaging the shell, in which it is to be served. Remove the woody part from the pineapple's center and cut the flesh into squares and place them in a bowl with the peeled and sliced pear, apple and banana and a well-washed bunch of grapes; pour over a few glasses of rum and season with sugar.

Fill the pineapple with the fruit mix, replace the cap, with its crown, and keep in the fridge until ready to serve.

ANANAS FARCITO

Pineapple with Kirsch

Pineapple
Sugar
Kirsch or maraschino liqueur
10½ oz strawberries
Lemon
Whipped cream
Candied citron

Cut the pineapple in half lengthwise and with a very sharp knife remove all the flesh, including the woody core in the center, and keep the 2 shells aside.

Cut the flesh into cubes and macerate with ½ cup of sugar and a glass of kirsch for three-quarters of an hour.

Quickly wash the strawberries, remove the stems and place most of them in a bowl with the lemon juice. Drain and keep the best for decoration. Add the rest to the pineapple and pour everything back into the pineapple shells.

Garnish with whipped cream, the best strawberries kept aside, the candied citron and keep in the fridge until ready to serve.

ANANAS RIPIENO

Pineapple with Kiwi and Pomegranate

Pineapple
Sugar
Maraschino liqueur
3 kiwi
Lemon
Pomegranate

Cut the pineapple in half lengthwise and with a very sharp small knife remove all the flesh, removing the woody part in the center and keeping the 2 shells aside.

Cut the pineapple into cubes and infuse with ½ cup of sugar and a glass of maraschino liqueur, for about three-quarters of an hour.

Peel and slice the kiwis and place them in a bowl with the lemon juice, then add the slices to the pineapple cubes. Put both back into the pineapple shells and garnish with ripe pomegranate seeds.

ARANCE AL MARASCHINO

Oranges with Maraschino

6 oranges
7 oz sugar lumps
Maraschino liqueur

For garnish: cherries in syrup

Wash and cut the oranges into slices sideways without peeling them. Place these slices in a crystal bowl, and crumble the sugar cubes over them, which you have first rubbed on an orange peel so that they remain fragrant.

Add 2 glasses of maraschino liqueur and leave to infuse for an hour, placing the bowl in the fridge. Decorate the bowl with some cherries in syrup.

ARANCE E FRAGOLE

Oranges and Strawberries

6 oranges
Sugar
1 lb 2 oz strawberries
Wine
Lemon juice
Optional: kirsch

Choose 6 nice, thick-skinned oranges, wash them and then cut them a little higher than half way. Carefully remove the wedges, peel them, cut them in half and season with a little sugar in a bowl.

Wash the strawberries in wine and water, remove the stems and add them to the orange wedges in the bowl. Season with lemon juice and, if necessary, more sugar.

Put the 6 orange shells in a moderate oven for a few minutes. Before going to the table, arrange the shells on a serving dish, fill with strawberries and orange wedges and, if you like, a few drops of kirsch.

AVOCADOS CON ANANAS E POMPELMO

Avocado with Pineapple and Grapefruit

3 avocados
4 slices pineapple
Grapefruit
Almonds
Sugar
Brandy
6 tbsp whipped cream

Split the avocados in half. Pit, peel, and cut them into cubes. Set aside the shells. Cut the pineapple slices into cubes, put both in a bowl and add the peeled grapefruit also cut into cubes.

Put ⅓ cup of shelled almonds in a small saucepan with cold water, bring them almost to the boil, drain and remove the skins, then chop them coarsely and add them to the bowl. Season with ¼ cup of sugar and a small glass of brandy. Let everything macerate for an hour in the fridge.

Put the fruit mixture back in the avocado skins and garnish with the whipped cream.

BANANA ALLA PANNA

Banana and Rum Cream

6 bananas
Rum
Whipped cream

Put the peeled bananas in a bowl, sprinkle them with a glass of rum, and leave them in the marinade for a couple of hours, turning them from time to time so that they are well flavoured.

Fill a pastry bag with whipped cream proportional to the size of the bananas and cover each banana with a string of whipped cream.

CACHI AL COGNAC

Persimmon in Cognac

6 persimmon
6 tbsp sugar
2 tbsp vanilla sugar
6 tbsp cognac

Choose 6 beautiful persimmons, healthy and ripe, wash them gently and dry them. Cut them in half horizontally and remove the stones. Season with the 2 kinds of sugar and with the cognac. Leave to infuse for an hour in the fridge.

ADA SAYS: *For vanilla sugar, you steep the sugar with a fresh vanilla pod or you can just flip out the seeds from the pod. Keep in an air-tight jar.*

CASTAGNE ARROSTITE

Roasted Chestnuts

2¼ lb chestnuts

Clean the chestnuts with a slightly damp cloth. Then with a very sharp pointed knife make an incision in the rounded part. When you have engraved them all, arrange them in the roasting pan, cover them with a damp cloth and place them in a very low heated oven, shaking them from time to time, so they do not burn.

When they are cooked, after about 3 quarters of an hour, put them on a serving dish and send them to the table very hot.

CASTAGNE ARROSTITE ALLA FIAMMA

Flambéed Roasted Chestnuts

1 lb 5 oz chestnuts
1¼ cups sugar
Rum

Roast the chestnuts (see above), but when they are ready, let them cool and carefully peel them.

Put the sugar and a glass of water in a small saucepan. Let it boil and immediately warm the peeled chestnuts in this syrup, keeping them on the fire until the syrup is almost completely absorbed.

Then pour the chestnuts into a rather deep dish, pour in a couple of glasses of rum and set the rum on fire, stirring the chestnuts with a spoon until the flame goes out. Then send them to the table very hot in the same dish.

CASTAGNE LESSATE IN PURÈ

Chestnut Purée

2¼ lb chestnuts
Salt
Bay leaves
Milk
3½ tbsp butter
Sugar

Knick the skin of the chestnuts and put them to cook in plenty of cold water to which you have added a pinch of salt and 2 bay leaves. When they are cooked, peel and remove the second skin and put them to cook again in a saucepan with a little milk and butter for about 10 minutes.

Mash them and then work them with a wooden spoon to have a smooth purée. Season with a pinch of salt, sugar, and use as a base for desserts.

CASTAGNE LESSATE IN SUFFLÈ

Boiled Chestnuts in Soufflé

2¼ lb chestnut purée
½ cup chicken broth
Salt
3½ tbsp butter
2 egg whites
Bay leaf

Make a chestnut purée (opposite page), then wet with the broth, season with a pinch of salt, and a knob of butter. Work the purée well with a wooden ladle over the fire until it becomes smooth and has absorbed all the broth. It should have the consistency of an ordinary potato purée, that is, neither too hard nor too soft.

Transfer to a bowl and let it cool. In the meantime, whip the egg whites into a snow, and when they are firm, fold them carefully into the cold chestnut purée.

Grease a soufflé mold and fill it, but be sure not to reach higher than 2 thirds of the mold, as the mixture swells up a when cooked.

Put the mold in a preheated oven of moderate heat for about 20 minutes and then serve the soufflé without making it wait.

COCOMERO AL RUM

Watermelon with Rum

Watermelon
Sugar
Rum

Remove the top cap from the watermelon and with the help of a sharp knife and empty it out leaving only the white part and the shell. Turn the watermelon shell over to remove any water that may have formed during the operation and sprinkle the inside with ½ cup of sugar.

Put the flesh in a salad bowl, remove the seeds and superfluous water, then cut into cubes. Put the watermelon flesh back in its place, sprinkle it with the remaining sugar and with rum. Finally, place the watermelon in the fridge, leaving it there until ready to serve.

FICHI

Sweet Figs

2¼ lb figs
To serve: sugar or cream

Peel the figs very gently so that they do not spoil and arrange them in a glass bowl. Then put them in the fridge until ready to serve, remembering that the figs must be very cold. You can present them simply like this, or, if you want, sprinkle them with sugar or with cream.

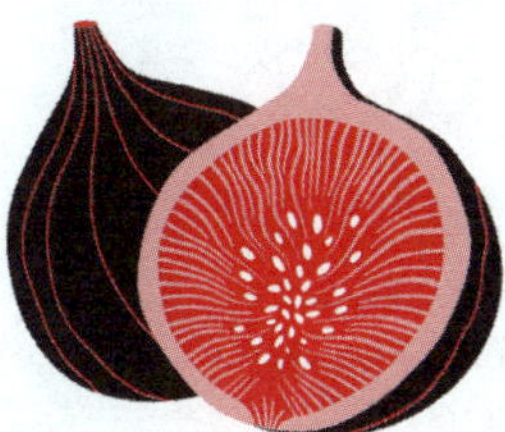

FRAGOLE CARMEN

Strawberries Carmen

10½ oz strawberries
2 cups white wine
Orange
1 lemon
Orange peel
1¾ cups sweetened whipped cream
1 lb 2 oz wild strawberries

Carefully wash the strawberries in a little white wine, drain them, and set aside any that are crushed or that seem too ripe. Arrange the others in a crystal bowl, sprinkle with orange juice and put them in the fridge. Sieve or blend the other strawberries, and immediately squeeze the juice of half a lemon over them.

Add to this purée a thin piece of orange peel without the white part, that you have set aside, cut into strips, and put this in the fridge as well.

When you go to the table, fold the strawberry purée into the whipped cream, being very careful not to let the cream separate, mixing it from top to bottom and not with a rotating motion. Then pour this pink cream over the strawberries and decorate the bowl with whole or halved wild strawberries, previously washed in a little white wine and well drained.

FRAGOLE CONDITE

Strawberries with Rum or Maraschino

2¼ lb strawberries
White wine
Sugar
Lemon
Rum or maraschino liqueur

Choose the strawberries carefully and wash them in white wine. Repeat the operation at least twice to free them from any traces of earth. Then place them in a glass bowl, sprinkle with sugar and lemon juice, or with a glass of rum, or half a glass of maraschino liqueur. Place the bowl in the fridge until ready to serve.

FRAGOLE CON YOGURT

Strawberries with Yogurt

2¼ lb strawberries
1 cup yogurt
1 cup sugar
2 oranges

Carefully wash the strawberries, mash them and add them to the yogurt, then add the sugar and mix.

Season with the juice of 2 oranges and immediately put in the fridge. They must be served very cold. At the time of use, share in crystal bowls.

MELE AL FORNO

Baked Apples

2¼ lb apples
Butter for greasing
Sugar
Wine

Rinse the apples, dry them and core them without peeling. Then put them in a lightly buttered oven pan, and sprinkle with sugar. Add a few spoons of white wine and put in a moderate oven for about half an hour until the apples are cooked and the wine has dried up.

MELE COTTE COL VINO

Pan-Fried Apples with Wine

2¼ lb apples
Lemon
Wine
Sugar
Butter

Peel the apples, cut them into wedges, remove all the seeds and keep them in a bowl with water and lemon juice so that they do not blacken. Slice them thinly and put them in a pan with a glass of wine, sugar and a small knob of butter. Cook on high heat, stirring occasionally, and when the apples are cooked, arrange them on a serving dish and send them to the table hot.

MELE COTTE RIPIENE

Stuffed Baked Apples

6 apples, like Reinette or Golden Russet
Butter for greasing
⅔ cup raisins
White wine
1 oz candied citron
4 tbsp butter
½ cup sugar

Rinse the apples, dry them, core them without peeling and place them in a buttered oven dish. Wash the raisins and let them revive in half a glass of white wine. Fill the void of the apples with raisins, close the holes with a disk of candied citron, put a piece of butter on the apples and sprinkle them with sugar. Add a few more spoons of white wine to the dish, and place in a moderate heat oven for half an hour, until the apples are cooked and the wine dried. Send them to the table in the same container.

ADA SAYS: *Citron is a very thick-skinned lemon, one of the original varieties.*

MELE FRITTE

Apple Fritters

1 cup all-purpose flour
2 tbsp olive oil
¾ cup lukewarm water
2 whipped egg whites
Salt
6 apples
2 tbsp powdered sugar
Cognac or rum
Lemon peel
Lard or oil for frying

First, make up the batter with the flour, oil, water, whipped egg whites, and salt at least an hour ahead.

Peel the apples and remove the core with a small knife. Then cut them transversely into slices of about a ¼ inch, to get many doughnut crescents. Put the cut apples in a bowl, sprinkle them with a spoon or 2 of powdered sugar, a small glass of cognac or rum and a grating of lemon peel. Let them stand like this for an hour, turning them over a couple of times so that they all have to time to flavor.

A few minutes before going to the table, take the apples out of the marinade, let them drain, dip them in the batter and fry them in oil or lard until they have a nice golden color. Before sending them to the table, if you want to serve them as a sweet dish, sprinkle them with a little sugar.

ADA SAYS: *This recipe is very well appreciated by children, but in that case remember to leave out the cognac or rum.*

MELONE RIPIENO

Melon with Peaches and Rum

Melon
2 peaches
2 pears
Sugar
Rum or maraschino liqueur

Cut the upper part of the melon with a knife to obtain a kind of box with its lid. With a spoon, remove all the seeds and filaments from the inside and then, again with the spoon, detach and take out the flesh, up to the white part. Remove any seeds and cut the flesh into cubes. Dice a couple of peaches and peeled pears.

Sprinkle the inside of the melon with a little sugar, sprinkle the diced fruit that you have mixed together rather abundantly with sugar and fill the melon with these. Pour a glass of rum or maraschino inside, replace the melon lid, close the opening and then put the melon in the fridge for 2 hours. Place it on a plate with a towel and send it to the table.

ADA SAYS: *You can add diced bananas and pineapple, jam, preferably strawberry, and other fruit that the season can offer you.*

MELONI E FRAGOLE

Melon with Strawberries

3 small melons (cantaloupe or Charentais)
2 peaches
1 orange
1 lemon
4 tbsp sugar
7 oz strawberries
Optional: 2 tbsp kirsch

Cut the melons horizontally and remove the seeds and filaments and cut the flesh into cubes. Wash, peel, and slice the peaches.

Put the fruit in a bowl, and season with the squeezed juice from the orange and lemon, add the sugar and the well-washed strawberries and if you like, the kirsch. Place the bowl in the fridge for a couple of hours and before going to the table, fill the emptied melon shells with the fruit.

PERE COTTE ALLA CREMA DI LATTE

Poached Pears with Cream

12 pears
½ cup sugar
½ cup light cream

Wash and peel the pears, trim the stem and empty them from underneath by removing the core with a peeler. Place them in a pan with the sugar and cover with water. Set the pan over a light heat, cover and cook for a few minutes after boiling, then remove the pears from the heat and let them cool. Finally, place them on a serving dish and cover with the cream.

PESCHE CON YOGURT

Peaches with Yogurt

2¼ lb yellow peaches
1 cup sugar
1 cup yogurt
Lemon zest

Wash, core, and chop the peaches, then season with the sugar. Add the yogurt and flavor the mixture with grated lemon peel. Refrigerate until ready for use.

POMPELMO ALL'ARANCIA

Grapefruit with Blood Orange

2 blood oranges
2 white grapefruits
2 pink grapefruits
1 kiwi
3½ oz sugar
Cherries in syrup
Lemon peel

Wash and peel the oranges, grapefruits, and the kiwi. Cut the fruit into regular slices and arrange them in a round or oval serving dish, alternating the various colors. Sprinkle with sugar and decorate with cherries and strips of lemon peel.

UVA IN COPPA

Grapes in a Cup

1 melon
2¼ lb black grapes
2 egg whites
1 cup sugar

Cut the melon horizontally and remove the seeds and filaments with a spoon, take out the pulp and cut it into cubes.

Wash the grapes thoroughly. Beat the egg whites in a bowl and dip in them, for a few minutes, half of the grapes, then remove them and roll them in sugar. Now prepare the cup. alternating the grapes with sugar, those without sugar and the diced melon.

VISCIOLE IN CAMICIA

Sour Cherries in Their Shirts

2¼ lb sour or ordinary cherries
2 egg whites
Powdered sugar

Carefully wash the cherries, dry them, and shorten the stems, leaving a piece an inch long. Beat the egg whites in a bowl and dip in the cherries. Take one cherry at a time and holding it by the stem, roll it in the powdered sugar so it is well covered. Then arrange the cherries in a pyramid shape on a round plate.

Fruit Salads

COCOMERO FARCITO

Watermelon Salad

½ cup raisins
Watermelon
4 apricots
4 peaches
2 pears
3 bananas
Lemon
Orange
Maraschino liqueur
6 tbsp sugar

First soak the raisins in warm water for half an hour and then drain. Wash the watermelon and remove the upper cap using a very sharp knife, and if possible making sure that the incision is made in a zig-zag pattern. With a spoon empty the watermelon and place the pulp in a salad bowl. Deprive the pulp of seeds and superfluous water, then cut it into chunks, as large as nuts.

Carefully wash the apricots, peaches, and pears, pit and cut them into pieces. Also peel and slice the bananas. Season all the fruit with the juice of a lemon and orange, 2 small glasses of maraschino liqueur and the sugar. Gently mix and fill the watermelon with the mixture.

Place the prepared watermelon in the fridge and leave it for a couple of hours.

FRUTTA MERINGATA

Fruit Meringue

2 soft peaches
2 pears
1 cup sugar
Almonds
Handful raisins
3½ oz sponge cake
Liqueur
Apricot jam
Optional: candied orange peel
3 egg whites
1¼ cups powdered sugar
Candied cherries

Peel the peaches and pears, cut them into slices and cook them for a few minutes in a dense sugar syrup *(p736)*. Peel a few almonds and put a handful of raisins in 2 fingers of hot water.

Make a layer of slices of sponge cake on the bottom of an oven dish, and sprinkle them with a little of the syrup in which the fruit has cooked and a small glass of liqueur. Now open a small jar of apricot jam and pour the contents into a bowl. To this jam, mix the cooked fruit, almonds, raisins and, if you like, a few cubes of candied orange peel and a little more liqueur. Place all this in a light dome on the sponge cake.

Whisk 3 egg whites to a snow. When they have risen, drop the powdered sugar on top, stirring gently. Cover the fruit with this meringue forming a nice cone, which you will decorate with some candied cherries or pieces of candied fruit, and some of the same meringue kept aside and placed in a foil. Drop a little more powdered sugar on everything and bake a preheated oven of moderate heat, to dry the meringue and let it take on a very light blond-light colour. This preparation can be served hot or cold.

MACEDONIA ALLO SPUMANTE

Sparkling Fruit Salad

2 bananas
1 grapefruit
6 slices pineapple
2 bunches green grapes
16 candied cherries
Cognac
4 tbsp sugar
2 cups dry sparkling wine

Peel and slice the bananas and grapefruit and dice the pineapple slices; add the well-washed grapes, the candied cherries, a glass of cognac, and sprinkle with sugar. Put the fruit in the fridge for a couple of hours.

When serving, arrange the fruit salad in bowls and pour the ice-cold sparkling wine on top.

MACEDONIA DI FRUTTA

Fruit Salad

¾ cup walnuts, almonds, pistachios
2 bananas
2 apples
2 pears
7 oz cherries
2 oranges
½ cup sugar
Maraschino liqueur
To serve: 1¾ cups whipped cream or ice cream

You can enrich the fruit salad by adding all the fruits the season can offer you.

Steep the walnuts, almonds and pistachios in boiling water for 10 minutes, so they are easier to peel. Wash and chop all the fruit—deseeding and pitting as needed—and add the juice from the oranges. Divide into small bowls and keep them in the fridge for a couple of hours.

When ready to serve, garnish with lightly sweetened whipped cream or ice cream.

MACEDONIA DI NOCE DI COCCO

Coconut Salad

1 pineapple
Apple
Orange
1 coconut
Grappa or whisky
1¾ cups sweetened whipped cream

Peel the pineapple, remove the woody core, and cut the pulp into squares. Put the pulp in a bowl, add the apple and orange, already peeled and cut into squares.

Cut the coconut into 2 parts—place a screwdriver on the coconut where you want to break it, and tap with a hammer to open. With a sharp knife remove the pulp and cut it into very thin slices and add them to the bowl. Season with a small glass of grappa or whisky.

Before going to the table, garnish everything with lightly sweetened whipped cream.

RECIPE FINDER & INDEX

RECIPE FINDER

1 SAUCES

White Sauces
basic white sauce....16
white sauce with onions....16
spicy white sauce....16

Cream Sauces
cream sauce....17
mushroom cream sauce....17
double cream sauce....17
cream sauce with eggs....18
creamy tomato sauce....18

Egg Sauces
mayonnaise....19
mustard and cornichon mayonnaise....19
anchovy mayonnaise....20
garlic mayonnaise....20
quick whole-egg mayonnaise....20
tartar sauce....20
quick tartar sauce....21
green mayonnaise....21
hollandaise sauce....21
orange hollandaise....22
cream hollandaise....22
simple cream hollandaise....22
light hollandaise....22

Classic Sauces
gorgonzola sauce....23
amatriciana sauce....23
carbonara sauce....23
drover's sauce....24
spicy bread sauce....24
mustard sauce....24
spicy anchovy sauce....25
pickled onion sauce....25
caper sauce....25
mint sauce....26
spicy prune sauce....26
spicy hard-boiled egg sauce....26
spicy tomato sauce....26
horseradish sauce with cream....27
piedmont sauce....27
traditional tomato sauce....28
almond and chocolate sauce....28

Quick Sauces
quick garlic sauce....29
quick anchovy sauce....29
quick anchovy and egg sauce....29
quick egg and mustard sauce....30
quick lemon sauce....30
quick caper sauce....30
quick tuna and anchovy sauce....31
quick spicy green sauce....31

Ragus
ragu bolognese....32
tomato ragu....32
sausage and mushroom ragu....33
dried mushroom ragu....33
almond ragu....33
prosciutto ragu....34
meat sauce....34
beef and red wine sauce....35
beef and tomato sauce....35
neapolitan meat sauce....36
meat and mushroom sauce....36

Tomato Sauces
tomato sauce with seven flavors....37
tomato sauce....37
raw tomato sauce....37
tomato and basil sauce....38
pizzaiola sauce....38
arrabbiata sauce....38
tomato sauce with mushrooms....38
tomato sauce with dried mushrooms....39
tomato sauce with herbs....39
tomato sauce with peppers and eggplant....40
tomato sauce with sausages....40
tomato sauce with tuna and mushrooms....41
spicy tomato sauce with cipollini onions....41
refined tomato sauce....41

Fish Sauces
shellfish sauce....42
spicy squid sauce....42
refined shellfish marinara sauce....42
sardine sauce....43
fish sauce....43

Special Sauces
bagna cauda....44
brown butter sauce....44
sauce for the pope....44
walnut sauce....45
mascarpone sauce....45
ham and pea sauce....45
mushroom sauce....46
mushroom and spinach sauce....46
porcini sauce genoa style....46
cream of wild mushrooms....47
ricotta sauce....47
ricotta and spinach sauce....47
ricotta and sausage sauce....48
sausage and egg sauce....48
watercress purée....48
pesto genovese....49
spicy pesto....49

2 APPETIZERS

Jellies, Butters & Creams
meat jelly....52
fish jelly....53
country style butter....53
montpellier butter....54
anchovy butter....54
tarragon butter....54
shrimp butter....55
sardine butter....55
white fish cream....55
chicken cream....55
ham cream....56
truffle cream....56
gorgonzola cream....56
parmesan cream....56

Bruschetta, Canapés & Crostini
classic bruschetta....57
tomato bruschetta....57
harlequin canapés....57
anchovy canapés....57
shrimp canapés....58
ham and jelly canapés....58
neapolitan crostini....58
chicken liver crostini....59
pork liver crostini....59
ricotta and sausage crostini....60
pepper galettes....60

Sandwiches
harlequin sandwiches....61
prosciutto or tongue sandwiches....61
sandwiches with anchovies and ham....61
horseradish tartine....62
harlequin toast....62
grilled chicken frittata sandwiches....62
anchovy tramezzini....63
harlequin tramezzini....63

Little Pastries & Plates
anchovy wheels....65
gorgonzola boats....65
tuna boats....65
shrimp boats....66
artichoke and smoked fish roe....66
artichoke with anchovies and capers....66
artichokes with caviar....66
creamed cucumbers....67
stuffed cucumbers....67
mussels with mayonnaise....67
spicy mussels....68
stuffed olives....68
olives for cocktails....68
venetian oysters....69
stuffed tomatoes....69
shrimp cocktail....69
eggs with ham....70
eggs with shrimp....70
eggs with mayonnaise....70
eggs with tuna....70

Choux & Puff Pastries
carolines....72
cream pies with chicken livers....72
cheese cream pies....72
mushroom pies....73
ham pies....73
traditional choux buns....74
modern choux buns....74
cheese rustica....74

Hot Appetizers
fishing boats....75
cheese casserole....75
fontina crescents....76
ham baskets....76
cheese baskets....76
mozzarella with tuna sauce....77
mozzarella on potato crackers....77
parmesan flan....78
ham quenelles....78
ham mousse....79
ricotta gratin....79

Vol-au-Vents
vol-au-vents with mushroom cream....80
vol-au-vents with langoustine....81

vol-au-vents with livers........81
vol-au-vents with finanziera sauce........82
vol-au-vents with mushrooms........83
vol-au-vents with shrimp........84
vol-au-vents with peas........85
vol-au-vents with tortellini........85

3 BROTHS & SOUPS

Broths

meat broth........88
fish broth........89
chicken broth........89
quick broth........89
vegetable broth........90
consommé........90
broth with potato dumplings........90
meat broth with ham gnocchetti........91
meat broth with polenta gnocchetti........91
beef broth with spinach parcels........92
broth with choux buns........92
broth with stuffed buns........93
broth with semolina squares........93
bolognese broth........93
royal chicken broth........94
meat broth with ricotta dumplings........94
broth with egg........95
consommé with savory crêpes........95

Cream Soups

cream of pastina........96
cream of asparagus........97
cream of artichoke........97
cream of mushroom........98
cream of chicken........98
cream of barley........99
cream of pea........99
cream of tomato........100
cream of ham........101
cream of spinach........101

Minestre

milk soup........102
roman chicken soup with cappelletti........102
modena soup with cappelletti........103
chickpea soup........103
oxtail soup........104
vegetable and sausage soup........104
passatelli soup........105
soup with grated egg pasta........106
pasta and broccoli soup........106
chickpea soup with cannolicchi........107
venetian bean and pasta soup........107
pasta and pea soup........107
rice and cauliflower soup........108
rice and bitter greens soup........108
rice and bean soup........108
rice and endive soup with tomatoes........109
rice and lentil soup........109
rice, fennel, and sausage soup........110
rice and potato soup........110
rice and zucchini soup........110
semolina soup........111
semolina and asparagus soup........111
tapioca soup........111

Stracciatelle

stracciatella........112
stracciatella roman style........112
egg string stracciatella........113
stracciatella with peas........113
green stracciatella........113

Minestrone

vegetable minestrone........114
florentine minestrone........115
minestrone genovese........116
minestrone milanese........116
summer minestrone milanese........117
minestrone with lardo........117
farmhouse minestrone........118
fresh bean minestrone........118
minestrone with stuffed lettuce parcels........119
barley and bitter greens minestrone........120
yellow pumpkin minestrone........120
spring minestrone........120

Fish Soups

north adriatic brodetto........121
ancona brodetto........122
fano brodetto........122
port recanati brodetto........123
st. benedict's brodetto........124
white brodetto........125
fish stew livornese........126
refined fish stew........126
italian salt cod soup........127
salt cod soup marseille style........127
mussel soup........128
shrimp soup........128
fish soup genovese........129
bouillabaisse........130
fish soup lazio style........131
provençal fish soup........132
st. peter's fish soup........132
boneless fish soup........133
langoustine soup........134
cockle soup........134
clam soup........135
refined clam soup........135

Classic Soups

acquacotta........136
pavese soup........136
cabbage and sausage soup........137
french onion soup........137
egg and onion soup........138
white bean soup........138
bean and chard soup........138
fava bean soup with pork skin........139
mushroom soup........139
potato soup........140
tomato soup with parmesan crostini........140
zucchini soup........141
santé soup........141
gazpacho........141

4 PASTA, RICE, GNOCCHI & POLENTA

Dried Pasta

bavette trastevere style........146
bavette with fresh fava beans........146
bavette in egg sauce........147
bucatini amatriciana........147
bucatini with mussels and clams........147
bucatini with shrimp and baby squid........148
cannolicchi with basil........149
cannolicchi with fresh white beans........149
conchiglie with mascarpone and mushrooms........150
conchiglie with shrimp........150
conchiglie with ricotta and spinach........150
refined conchiglioni........151
fettuccine in cream sauce........151
fettuccine with ham and mushrooms........151
fusilli allegria........152
lasagnette with spinach and mushrooms........152
lasagnette lucca style........153
maccheroncini with little meatballs........153
maccheroncini with baked sardines and wild fennel........154
maccheroncini and broccoli sicilian style........154
macaroni with four cheeses........155
macaroni with four string cheeses........155
macaroni gratin........156
macaroni with mozzarella........156
macaroni with ricotta........157
macaroni salad........157
macaroni in wild mushroom sauce........158
orecchiette pugliese........158
penne arrabbiata........158
penne with vodka........159
spring pennette salad........159
rigatoni salad with arugula........160
rigatoni with zucchini........160
rigatoni with sausage and eggs........161
spaghetti with gorgonzola........161
spaghetti carbonara........161
vegetarian spaghetti carbonara........162
spaghetti with herbs........162
spaghetti with squid ink........162
spaghetti aglio e olio........163
spaghetti with garlic and tomatoes........163
spaghetti with garlic, oil, and anchovy........163
spaghetti cacio e pepe........164
spaghetti with capers and olives........164
spaghetti with meat and vegetables........164
spaghetti with raw tomato sauce........165
spaghetti with mushrooms........165
spaghetti with wedge clams........165
spaghetti with tuna........166
fisherman's spaghetti........166
spaghettini with caviar........167
spaghettini with artichokes and mushrooms........167
spaghettini with eggs........167
tortiglioni with ricotta........168
tortiglioni with goat cheese........168
tortiglioni with peppers and eggplant........168
trenette with pesto........169
vermicelli with salmon........169

Fresh Egg Pasta

fettuccine ciociara style........171
fettuccine roman style........171
refined fettuccine........172
fettuccine ragu........172
fettuccine with mascarpone........172
fettuccine with peas........173
baked fettuccine with prosciutto and button mushrooms........173
hunter's lasagnette with chicken........174
lasagnette genovese........174
lasagnette piedmont style........175
pappardelle with hare........175
pappardelle with mushrooms........176
pappardelle with duck........176
tagliatelle bolognese........177
green tagliatelle bolognese........177
genoa green tagliatelle........178
tagliatelle with chicken........179

tagliatelle with walnuts 179
tagliatelle with egg, anchovy, and mozzarella 179
tonnarelli chitarra abruzzese 180
tonnarelli with cream 181
tonnarelli with clams and pesto 181
tonnarelli with shellfish 182
classic agnolotti 183
agnolotti sardinian style 184
cannelloni with beef and tomatoes 184
cannelloni etruscan style 185
cannelloni provençal 186
cannelloni with ricotta and sausage 187
sicilian crosetti 188
ravioli genovese 189
ravioli with ricotta, butter, and sage 190
pasta roll with tomato and spinach 190
pasta roll with ricotta and spinach 191
tortellini with white sauce 191
tortellini bolognese 192
chicken tortellini 193
tortelloni bolognese 193

Baked Pasta
green lasagna modena style 194
neapolitan lasagna 195
tomato lasagna 196
mushroom lasagna 196
lasagna with ricotta 197
carnival lasagna 197
pasta of a thousand leaves 198
baked rigatoni 199
rigatoni gratin with asparagus 200
tagliatelle with cream 200
bucatini and pigeon in pasticcio 201
timbale of angel hair pasta 202
macaroni pasticcio 202
pennette pasticci 203
tortellini pie with ragu 204
timbale of vermicelli and sardines 205
vincisgrassi timbale 206

Rice
rice with milk 208
rice valtellinese 208
roasted rice genovese 208
rice with duck 209
rice and peas venetian style (risi e bisi) 209
chilled rice with shrimp and peppers 210
rice gratin 210
shellfish rice gratin 211
savory rice pudding 211
rice with anchovies 212
neapolitan rice timbale (sartù) 212
rice timbale with meatballs 214
risotto with seven flavors 215
artichoke risotto 215
chicken liver risotto 216
risotto milanese 216
chicken risotto 217
turkish risotto 218
paella 219
risotto with artichokes and peas 220
risotto with mussels and clams 220
shrimp risotto 221
risotto with sparkling wine 221
risotto with sausages 222
risotto with langoustines 222
risotto with cuttlefish 223
risotto with tuna 223
risotto with egg surprise 224
risotto mold with livers 224
risotto in three colors 225
farmhouse risotto 226
springtime risotto 226

Gnocchi
gnocchi genovese 227
gnocchi piedmont style 227
gnocchi roman style 228
potato gnocchi with tomato and fontina 228
spinach gnocchi 229
polenta gnocchi 229
semolina gnocchi 230
spinach gnocchi with ricotta 231
german gnocchi 231
giant gnocchi 232

Polenta
polenta with broth 233
polenta with salt cod vicenza style 234
polenta with pork ribs 234
polenta with veal and chicken livers 235
polenta with mozzarella and anchovies 235
polenta with sausages 236
polenta and fontina pie 236
polenta pudding 237
polenta with sausages and mozzarella 237
polenta timbale 238
baked polenta 238
baked polenta with veal and chicken livers 239

5 FRIED DISHES
Fried Fish
fried salt cod livornese 245
fried salt cod roman style 245
anchovy and tuna fritters 245

Croquettes & Fagottini
sweetbread croquettes 246
cheese cream croquettes 246
sweet cream croquettes 247
cheese croquettes 247
mozzarella croquettes 247
potato croquettes 248
polenta and fontina croquettes 248
chicken croquettes 248
semolina croquettes 249
spinach croquettes 249
tuna croquettes 250
veal croquettes 250
yeast croquettes 251
fagottini with mozzarella and anchovies 251
fagottini with mozzarella and mushrooms 252
fagottini with ricotta and sausages 252

Mostaccioli
ham mostaccioli 253
polenta mostaccioli 253
semolina mostaccioli 253

Mozzarella
fried mozzarella 254
fried mozzarella sandwich 254
fried mozzarella with anchovy 255
fried mozzarella and ham sandwich 255

Skewers
neapolitan skewers 256
petronian style skewers 257
semolina skewers 257
skewers bolognese 258
skewers genovese 258

Arancini & Supplì
arancini 259
white rice supplì 260
inside out supplì 260
polenta supplì 261

6 PIZZAS, CALZONES & PIES
Pizzas
neapolitan pizza 264
neapolitan capricciosa pizza 264
neapolitan pizza with mozzarella and mushrooms 265
neapolitan pizza with egg and mushrooms 265
neapolitan pizza with clams 266
neapolitan pizza with flour and potatoes 266
neapolitan pizza margherita 267
pizza with onions 267
three cheese pizza 268
pizza with veal and potatoes 269
potato pizza 270
pizza and prosciutto twists 270
neapolitan pizzette 271
pizzette with mozzarella and anchovy 272

Calzones
neapolitan calzoncelli 273
neapolitan calzone 274
calzone with sausages and provolone 274

Pies
calabrian pie 276
potato pie 277
easter pie genovese 278
rustic neapolitan pie 280
rustic artichoke pie 281
meat and mushroom pie 282
rustic gruyère pie 283
rustic escarole pie 284
rustic potato pie 284
rustic potato pie cuma style 285
rustic chicken pie 286
octopus pie 287
ham and salami pie 288
spinach and ricotta pie 289
rustic ricotta and sausage pie 290
quiche lorraine 291

7 EGGS
Frittate & Frittatine
frittata with anchovies 295
frittata with basil 295
frittata with onions 295
frittata with onion, guanciale and tomatoes 296
frittata with potatoes 296
frittata with zucchini flowers 296
frittata with stuffed zucchini flowers 297
frittata with parmesan and gruyère 297
frittata with macaroni 297
frittata with eggplant and zucchini 298

frittata with tomatoes and zucchini 298
frittata with spinach 298
frittata with zucchini 299
frittata with baked artichokes 299
frittata flan 300
potato frittatine 300
frittatine millefeuille 301
frittatine roman style 302
frittatine fantasy 302
frittatine stuffed with meat and mushrooms 303
frittatine stuffed with spinach and ricotta 304

Omelets
omelet with asparagus and artichokes 305
omelet with provola 306
chilled omelet with cream and jelly 306

Poached Eggs
poached eggs with anchovy butter 307
poached eggs with mushrooms and croutons 307
poached eggs with tomato and mozzarella 308
poached eggs with asparagus tips 308

Baked Eggs
baked eggs with anchovy butter 309
baked eggs with potatoes 309
baked eggs with duchess potatoes 310
baked eggs with tomatoes and zucchini 310
eggs baked in spinach nests 310

Fried Eggs
fried eggs with bacon 311
fried eggs american style 311
fried eggs with mozzarella and anchovy butter 312
fried eggs turkish style 312

Boiled Eggs
boiled eggs with artichokes and peas 313
aurora eggs 314
monachina eggs 314
hard-boiled eggs with tuna and mayonnaise 315
filled eggs with mayonnaise 315
fried egg parcels 316
pickled eggs with chili 316
boiled eggs with tuna 317

Scrambled Eggs
scrambled eggs with cardoons 318
scrambled eggs with chicken livers and asparagus 318
scrambled eggs with ham and croutons 319
scrambled eggs in tomatoes 319

Soufflés
cheese soufflé 320
artichoke soufflé 320
cardoon soufflé 321
green bean soufflé 321
fettucine soufflé 321
parmesan soufflé 322
parmesan soufflé cups 322
potato soufflé 322
fish soufflé 323
chicken soufflé 323
tomato soufflé 324
ham soufflé 324
chicken liver and rice soufflé 324
shrimp soufflé 325
spinach soufflé 325

8 FISH

Sea Fish
anchovies tunisian style 329
anchovies with lemon 329
anchovies baked with mushrooms 330
spiced anchovies 330
marinated herring in aromatic sauce 331
herring salad 331
baked salt cod 332
salt cod gratin 332
salt cod pizzaiola 332
salt cod provençal 333
salt cod in milk 333
salt cod portuguese style 334
salt cod with tomato and green olives 334
salt cod with sour cherries 335
salt cod flan 335
salt cod with peppers 336
neapolitan salt cod 336
roman salt cod stew 337
stuffed salt cod 337
stockfish ancona style 338
stockfish messina style 339
stockfish venetian style 339
braised stockfish with tomato 340
grilled baby gray mullets with parsley sauce 340
baked baby gray mullets with anchovies 340
gray mullet baked with lemon 341
baked gray mullet with herbs 341
gray mullet with anchovy sauce 341
grilled grouper 342
grouper fillets with tomato 342
grilled grouper fillets with mustard 343
monkfish with parsley butter 343
braised monkfish 344
baked red snapper 344
baked red snapper fillets 345
baked red snapper fillets with cipollini onions 345
red snapper pizzaiola 346
deep-fried whitebait 346
marinated whitebait 347
mackerel fillets with anchovy and capers 347
baked cod with lemon 348
cod baked with mushrooms 348
cod steaks with anchovy butter 348
cod fillets maître d'hôtel 349
cod with white wine 349
cod gratin 349
stuffed hake 350
oven-baked croaker 350
croaker baked with potatoes 351
croaker pizzaiola 351
baked sea bream 352
sea bream in a salt crust 352
sea bream bercy 352
shark pizzaiola 353
baked shark steaks 353
shark in white wine 354
shark with peas 354
shark gratin 354
john dory fillets in butter 355
deep-fried john dory fillets 355
john dory flan 355
john dory with artichokes and potatoes 356
baked swordfish 356
fried swordfish 356
swordfish with tomato 357
swordfish with porcini mushrooms 357
skate in brown butter 358
skate with anchovy sauce 358
steamed skate with tomato 358
baked turbot 359
turbot fish fingers 359
sardines with fennel 360
neapolitan pan-fried sardines 360
fried sardines ligurian style 361
baked sardines 361
marinated sardines 362
fried sardines with mustard and anchovy 363
sole meunière 363
sole with white wine 364
fried sole italian style 364
fried sole colbert 364
sole gratin 365
sole in butter 365
sole with baked potato and shrimp sauce 366
sole fillets with artichoke 367
sole manfred 367
baked sea bass 368
poached sea bass with eggs 368
sea bass baked with herbs 369
sea bass steamed in white wine 369
sea bass with anchovy and wild mushrooms 370
baked tuna 370
tuna baked with olives and capers 371
tuna with tomato 371
tuna and tomato casserole 372
tuna in oil with mushrooms 372
tuna in oil with peas 373
tuna in oil croquettes 373
tuna mayonnaise 374
red mullet parcels with mushrooms 374
red mullet calabrian style 375
red mullet livornese style 375
red mullet with garlic and lemon 376
fried red mullets 376
red mullet gratin 377
red mullet with tomatoes 377

River Fish
eel on a spit 378
roast eel 378
eel carpionata 379
carp jewish style 379
carp in white wine 380
pike in red wine 380
baked salmon 381
poached salmon 381
sturgeon with mushrooms 382
trout with onion butter 383
steamed trout 384
trout mousse 384
blue trout 385
pan-fried trout in butter 385
deep-fried trout 385

Crustaceans
lobster american style 386
american lobster with rice and cognac 387
deviled lobster 387

lobster in its jelly 388
lobsters in the shell with truffle 389
roast lobster 389
lobster mayonnaise 390
lobster medallions in jelly 391
shrimp with asparagus 392
glazed shrimp 392
shrimp and mussels pandorato 393
fried shrimp 393
shrimp crostini 394
shrimp in potato boxes 394
steamed shrimp 395
fried gray shrimp 395
roast crawfish 395
poached crawfish 396
langoustines american style 396
roast langoustines 397
langoustine cocktail 397
langoustine and squid skewers 398
langoustine mayonnaise 398

Mollusks
braised baby squid marche style 399
squid neapolitan style 399
roast squid 400
squid with shellfish 400
deep-fried squid 401
baby octopus neapolitan style 401
octopus naples style 402
baby octopus salad 402
stewed baby octopus with mushrooms 402
octopus mayonnaise 403
octopus santa lucia style 404
cuttlefish with artichokes 405
cuttlefish and tomato stew 405
stuffed cuttlefish 406
mussels marinara 406
mussels villeroy 407
mussels gratin 407
deviled oysters 408
deep-fried oysters 408
oysters gratin 409
clams marinara 409
clams with peas 409

9 MEAT
Veal
farmhouse roast veal 412
roast veal with cream 412
milk roasted veal 413
roast veal bella vista 414
roast veal casserole 415
roast veal with truffle 416
petronian veal steaks 416
veal steaks with zabaglione sauce 417
sugar steaks 417
broiled veal chops 418
veal chops modena style 418
veal chops farmhouse style 418
veal chops en papillote 419
veal chops with fontina (valdostana) 420
veal chops with truffle, ham, gruyère and tomato 420
pan-fried veal chops with parsley and lemon sauce 421
veal chops with tomatoes and peppers 421
veal chop terrine 422
veal cutlets milanese 422
fried veal cutlets viennese style 423
double-fried veal cutlets villeroy 423
veal croquettes russian style 424
veal and ricotta croquettes 424
veal strips with white sauce 425
veal strips bolognese 425
veal pizzaiola 425
genovese veal strips 426
veal loaf 426
veal and mozzarella packets 427
veal tenderloin bolognese 427
veal tenderloin with tomatoes 428
fricassee of veal with artichokes 428
veal galantine 429
veal and tomato rolls 430
roast veal and ham rolls with sage 430
veal rolls with potato 431
stuffed veal rolls 432
veal steaks milanese 432
veal steaks modena style 433
veal steaks with sage 433
veal steaks with herb sauce 433
veal steaks with peppers 434
veal rolls with tomato 434
osso buco milanese 435
veal paillard 435
veal and ham pie 436
breast of veal stuffed with sausages 436
deep-fried breast of veal with lemon 437
braised veal with vegetables 437
poached breast of veal with a piquant sauce 438
roast stuffed breast of veal 438
veal meatballs with butter 439
veal meatballs flambéed with cognac 439
veal meatballs with cream sauce 440
meatloaf with mushrooms and chicken livers 440
roast veal roll with potatoes 441
veal roll with sweet and sour sauce 442
braised veal roll 442
veal roll with egg sauce 443
braised breast of veal with wild mushrooms 444
giant sausages 444
veal sausage with spinach 445
veal saltimbocca 446
veal scaloppine with marsala 446
pan-fried veal scaloppine with garnish 447
veal scaloppine with lemon 448
veal and tomato stew 448
veal stew with marsala 449
veal and pea stew 449
veal marengo 450
veal skewers with sage 450
veal and ham skewers 451
veal timbales financier 452
veal and artichoke timbale 453
timbale of veal and rice 453
veal and potato timbale 454
veal in aspic 454
veal baked with truffle and pistachios 455
veal with tuna 456
veal trotter with tomato 456
veal trotter fricassee 457
grilled veal trotters 457
veal sweetbreads with peas 458
veal sweetbreads with potato 458
veal sweetbreads with marsala sauce 459
ox liver in sweet and sour sauce 460
calf's liver with vinegar 460
calf's liver florentine style 460
calf's liver milanese style 461
calf's liver venetian style 461
fried calf's liver with sage butter 461
fried breaded calf's liver 462
calf's liver with fennel piquant sauce 462
veal tongue with sweet and sour onions 462
veal tongue with green sauce 463
veal kidneys with marsala 463
pan-fried kidneys with anchovy 463
tripe milanese 464

Beef
grilled steak 466
steak with ham and mozzarella 466
charcoal—grilled steak 466
steak florentine style 467
steak sicilian style 467
steak tartare 468
boiled beef pizzaiola 468
marinated boiled beef 468
boiled beef with potatoes 469
boiled beef pudding 469
boiled beef with mayonnaise 470
boiled beef medallions with sage, ham, and mozzarella 470
boiled beef with rustic sauce 471
boiled beef with vegetables 471
braised beef 472
braised beef in barolo 472
braised beef brescia style 473
braised beef certosa style 474
braised beef genovese 474
braised beef provençal 475
braised beef with onions 475
braised beef in milk 476
braised and marinated beef 476
braised beef with vegetables 477
pressure-cooker braised beef with anchovies 477
chateaubriand maître d'hôtel 478
breast of beef genovese 479
rib steak pizzaiola 480
rib steak with mushrooms 480
sliced beef steak pizzaiola 481
deep-fried beef slices 481
fried sirloin with fontina 482
beef tenderloin bismarck 482
hunter's tenderloin 483
creole beef tenderloin 483
tenderloin piedmont style 484
pan-fried tournedos with croutons 484
tournedos with prosciutto and wild mushrooms 485
fried tournedos with truffle and mozzarella 485
tournedos monaco 486
tournedos vol-au-vents with apple 486
beef stew catalan style 487
fricassee lucca style 487
goulash 488
goulash with cream and dumplings 488
beef rolls in tomato sauce 489
beef and chicken liver rolls 490
beef pastries 490
steak pie 491
roast beef 492
roast beef with caper sauce 492
roast beef spanish style 493
roast beef with wild mushrooms 493
roast beef with potatoes 494
beef roll sicilian style 494
beef sausages 495

beef in red wine....................495
beef and bread skewers....................496
beef and onion skewers....................496
beef straccetti....................496
braised beef lombardy style....................497
beef stew french style....................497
beef and fennel stew....................498
beef stew roman style....................498
beef stew with red wine....................499
terrine of beef french style....................500
terrine of beef italian-style....................501
terrine of beef hunter style....................502
truffled beef terrine....................503
glutton's terrine....................504
farmhouse stew....................505
boiled beef hungarian style....................505
beef croquettes with raisins and pine nuts....................506
deep-fried beef croquettes....................506
meatballs fried in butter....................507
fried meatballs in tomato sauce....................507
cheeseburger....................508
oven-roasted hamburgers....................508
beef and cabbage rolls....................509
beef pizza neapolitan style....................509
beef pizza with prosciutto....................510
meatballs roman style....................510
meatballs russian style....................511
meatloaf braised in milk....................511
meatloaf with tomato sauce....................512
meatloaf with eggs and prosciutto....................512
meatloaf cooked in a bain-marie....................513
beef and mortadella rolls....................514
butcher's oxtail and cheek....................515
ox kidney, two ways....................515

Lamb

roast spring lamb roman style....................516
roast spring lamb with new potatoes....................516
hunters' lamb....................517
braised spring lamb with anchovy and fennel....................517
farmhouse lamb....................518
braised lamb with prosciutto and eggs....................518
spring lamb braised in red wine....................519
spring lamb with anchovy sauce....................519
lamb and potato stew....................520
lamb chop skewers....................520
braised lamb hunter style....................521
stuffed leg of lamb....................522
lamb chops villeroy....................523
lamb chops scottadito....................524
deep-fried lamb chops....................524
grilled lamb chops with anchovy and lemon sauce....................524
boiled leg of lamb....................525
braised leg of lamb....................525
braised lamb with peas....................526
lamb marche style....................526
lamb cooked in milk....................526
shoulder of lamb with green beans....................527
braised lamb chops with artichokes....................527
medallions of lamb bolognese....................528
lamb chops maintenon....................528
lamb chops with prunes and vegetables....................529
roast lamb chops with mustard sauce....................529
deep-fried lamb chops with spring vegetables....................530
deep-fried lamb chops with onion sauce (soubise)....................530
lamb sweetbreads with prosciutto....................531
lamb sweetbreads with artichokes....................531
pan-fried sweetbreads....................532
deep-fried sweetbreads....................532
pan-fried sweetbreads in butter....................532
lamb offal with artichokes....................533
braised mutton with vinegar....................533
braised mutton with carrots....................534
mutton-stuffed grape leaves with eggs....................535
baked leg of mutton....................535
boiled mutton with mint sauce english style....................536
mutton in a dutch oven....................536
mutton chops with mushrooms....................537
grilled mutton chops....................537

Goat

oven-baked kid with artichoke salad....................538
kid braised with artichokes....................538
kid on skewers....................539
kid braised in white wine....................539
kid stewed with mushrooms....................540
goat offal sardinian style....................540

Pork

pork loin with prosecco and pineapple....................541
pork chops braised in white wine....................541
grilled pork chops with onions....................542
pork chops with fennel and marsala....................542
baked pork chops....................542
pork chops modena style....................543
pork chops with mustard....................543
pork chops with cornichons....................544
deep-fried pork chops with fontina and prosciutto....................544
grilled pork chops with pepper sauce....................545
pork strips with sweet and sour sauce....................545
pork strips in caper sauce....................546
pork galantine....................546
pork steaks neapolitan style....................548
pork steaks with tomato....................548
pork steaks with aromatic sauce....................549
pork steaks with prune sauce....................549
pork milanese (bottaggio)....................550
pork loin cooked in milk....................550
roast pork with apple sauce....................551
roast pork with brussels sprouts....................551
braised pork loin genovese....................552
braised pork rolls....................552
pork meatloaf with vegetables....................553
pork skewers....................554
pork with tuna....................554
hunter's pork....................555
pork pie with truffle....................556
sausages with beans....................557
sausages with escarole....................558
sausages with cardoons....................558
frankfurters with cabbage....................559
pig's trotters with green sauce....................559
pig's trotters with broccoli and sausages....................560
zampone with lentils....................561
zampone with rice....................561
zampone with spinach....................562
prosciutto in jelly with russian salad....................562
ham flan....................563
ham in a crust....................563
marinated fresh ham with marsala....................564
braised pork offal....................565
pork liver with bay....................565
petronian pork liver....................566
pig's head galantine....................566
cotechino with cardoons....................567
ham hock with spinach sauce....................567

10 POULTRY & GAME

Chicken

roast capon....................570
roast capon with truffle....................570
roast capon with chestnuts and brussels sprouts....................571
roast poussins with anchovies....................571
broiled poussins with deviled sauce....................572
braised and stuffed poussins....................572
chicken and truffle in jelly....................573
glutton's chicken....................574
chicken bella vista....................574
braised chicken with tomato....................576
chicken terrine....................576
chicken in a pot....................577
chicken breast with peas....................578
shallow-fried chicken....................578
chicken breast in white sauce....................578
roast chicken....................579
hunter's chicken....................579
braised chicken with olives....................580
chicken marengo....................580
chicken braised in milk....................581
braised chicken with sage....................581
roast chicken with potatoes....................581
braised chicken with porcini mushrooms....................582
chicken with prunes....................582
chicken with peppers....................583
fried chicken florentine style....................583
chicken braised in a dutch oven....................584
chicken salad....................584
chicken mayonnaise....................585
chicken mayonnaise french style....................585
pan-fried chicken....................586
chicken pie....................586
braised chicken le marche style....................587
braised chicken in a piquant sauce....................588
pan-fried chicken livers with sage....................588
chicken livers with artichokes....................589
chicken liver pie....................590
chicken gifts....................591
chicken gifts flan financier....................592

Turkey

roast turkey....................593
roast turkey stuffed with chestnuts....................593
roast turkey with truffle....................594
stuffed turkey lombardy style....................594
turkey cutlets pan-fried with mushrooms....................595
turkey cutlets bolognese....................595
turkey cutlets modena style....................596
turkey cutlets with prosciutto....................596
turkey cutlets fried in butter....................596
turkey breast with mayonnaise....................597
turkey medallions with mushrooms....................597
turkey timbale....................598
turkey flan with mushroom sauce....................599
turkey stew with egg and lemon....................599

Other Birds

larks in a nest....................600
duck with orange....................600
salmi of duck....................601
roast woodcock with crostini....................602

stuffed roast woodcock ... 603
pan-fried snipe with cognac ... 604
roast snipe ... 604
pheasant in cream ... 604
roast pheasant with cognac ... 605
salmi of pheasant ... 606
salmi of roast guinea fowl ... 607
roast goose ... 608
partridge casserole ... 608
roast squab ... 609
braised squab with peppers and mushrooms ... 609
spit-roasted quail ... 610
roast quail with polenta ... 610
spicy quail ... 610
braised thrush with porcini ... 611

Furred Game

rabbit with capers ... 612
hunter's rabbit ... 612
rabbit country style ... 613
rabbit with olives ligurian style ... 613
sweet and sour rabbit ... 614
slow cooked rabbit with tomatoes ... 614
salmi of rabbit ... 615
rabbit in egg sauce ... 615
hare country style ... 616
saint umberto's hare ... 616
salmi of hare ... 617
marinated roe deer ... 618
salmi of venison ... 619
stuffed leg of venison ... 619
venison with cherry sauce ... 620
sweet and sour boar roman style ... 622
boar stew ... 623

11 VEGETABLES, LEGUMES & SALADS

Vegetables

asparagus with butter ... 626
asparagus with prosciutto ... 626
asparagus with eggs ... 627
asparagus flan ... 627
asparagus salad ... 627
asparagus gratin ... 628
beet and onion salad ... 628
beet and onion in sauce ... 628
pan-fried broccoli rabe ... 629
pan-fried broccoli rabe with chili ... 629
broccoli roman style ... 630
broccoli sicilian style ... 630
broccoli with lemon ... 631
broccoli with prosciutto ... 631
swiss chard with lemon ... 631
swiss chard and mushroom gratin ... 632
pan-fried swiss chard with garlic ... 632
artichokes with rice ... 633
deep-fried artichokes jewish style ... 634
fried artichokes villeroy ... 634
deep-fried arichokes in batter ... 635
deep-fried artichokes fricasse ... 635
artichokes with russian salad ... 636
artichokes parmigiana ... 636
artichokes with anchovy ... 637
artichokes with scrambled eggs ... 637
braised artichokes roman style ... 637
artichokes with peas ... 638
artichoke gratin ... 638
stuffed artichokes sicilian style ... 639
artichokes with prosciutto and parmesan ... 639
artichokes with breadcrumbs and anchovy fillets ... 640
artichokes stuffed with chicken breast ... 640
artichokes with tuna ... 641
cardoons ... 641
baked cardoons ... 642
cardoons in white sauce ... 642
cardoons parmigiana ... 642
cardoons with prosciutto ... 643
carrots with butter ... 643
carrots in milk ... 643
stuffed carrots with tuna ... 644
glazed carrots with marsala ... 644
carrot purée ... 644
marinated carrots ... 645
cabbage in vinegar ... 645
cabbage in anchovy sauce ... 645
brussels sprouts with butter ... 646
baked brussels sprouts with guanciale ... 646
fried brussels sprouts ... 647
fried cauliflower ... 647
cauliflower with white sauce ... 648
cauliflower neapolitan style ... 648
baked onions ... 649
fried onion rings ... 649
boiled onions ... 649
onions stuffed with meat ... 650
grilled onions ... 651
baked cipollini onions ... 651
cipollini onions in tomato sauce ... 652
cipollini onions in white wine ... 652
cipollini onions with peas ... 652
glazed cipollini onions ... 653
sweet and sour cipollini onions ... 653
fennel with white sauce ... 654
fennel with tomato ... 654
pan-fried fennel ... 654
pan-fried mushrooms with parsley ... 655
mushrooms in cream ... 655
porcini with garlic ... 656
baked porcini ... 656
porcini ligurian style ... 656
porcini with anchovy and tomato ... 657
porcini braised in white wine ... 657
fried baby porcini ... 658
deep-fried stuffed porcini ... 658
baked stuffed porcini ... 659
sautéed porcini ... 659
endive roman style ... 660
braised endive ... 660
belgian endive with white sauce ... 661
belgian endive parmigiana ... 661
eggplant parmigiana ... 662
eggplant parmigiana, white variation ... 662
eggplant sicilian style (caponata) ... 663
eggplant syracuse style (caponatina) ... 664
roast eggplants ... 664
deep-fried eggplants ... 664
deep-fried eggplants in wine batter ... 665
eggplant flan with beef ... 665
deep-fried eggplant balls ... 665
eggplant and prosciutto timbale ... 666
neapolitan stuffed eggplants ... 666
eggplant stuffed with meat ... 667
eggplant mushroom style ... 667
baked potatoes parmigiana ... 668
baked potatoes with mozzarella ... 668
baked potato surprise ... 669
baked potatoes in their jackets, two ways ... 669
duchess potatoes ... 670
duchess potato croquettes ... 670
duchess potato croquettes with ricotta ... 671
duchess potatoes with beef and tomato ... 671
dauphin potatoes ... 672
dauphin potatoes with chicken livers ... 673
fried potatoes ... 673
potato flan ... 674
potato purée ... 674
pan-fried potatoes (rösti) ... 675
pan-fried potatoes pizzaiola ... 675
pan-fried potatoes with prosciutto ... 675
potato and sausage bake ... 676
potato and tuna salad ... 676
pan-fried new potatoes ... 676
peperonata ... 677
peppers gratin ... 677
peppers roman style ... 678
peppers with guanciale ... 678
marinated peppers ... 679
stuffed peppers ... 679
fried peppers ... 680
peppers with eggs ... 680
peppers stuffed with squid or octopus ... 680
stuffed peppers neapolitan style ... 682
peppers stuffed with mushrooms ... 682
peppers stuffed with fish and rice ... 683
peas french style ... 683
peas english style ... 683
peas with smoked pancetta ... 684
peas sardinian style ... 684
peas with prosciutto ... 684
tomatoes with rice ... 685
tomatoes with russian salad ... 686
stuffed tomatoes ... 686
tomatoes gratin ... 686
pan-fried tomatoes ... 687
tomato crostata ... 687
tomatoes stuffed with capers and anchovies ... 688
tomatoes stuffed with meat ... 688
tomatoes stuffed with onion ... 688
tomatoes with seafood ... 689
tomatoes stuffed with mushrooms ... 689
tomatoes with peas ... 690
tomatoes with tuna ... 690
leeks in cream ... 690
leek flan ... 691
pan-fried leeks ... 691
turnip with sugar ... 692
baked celery ... 692
celery parmigiana ... 693
braised spinach ... 693
spinach with butter ... 694
spinach gratin ... 694
spinach roman style ... 694
spinach with anchovy fillets ... 695
spinach with parmesan and eggs ... 695
spinach with prosciutto and gruyère ... 695
spinach flan ... 696
spinach crostini ... 697
spinach and mushroom flan ... 697
white truffles with parmesan ... 698
white truffles piedmont style ... 699
black truffles provençal ... 699
black truffle sauce ... 699
jerusalem artichokes, two ways ... 700
jerusalem artichokes in green sauce ... 700
hunter's pumpkin ... 701

fried pumpkin sicilian style........................ 701
deep-fried pumpkin in batter..................... 701
pumpkin with horseradish......................... 702
fried zucchini flowers................................. 702
stuffed zucchini flowers, three ways......... 702
pan-fried zucchini flowers......................... 703
zucchini genovese....................................... 703
zucchini with tomato.................................. 703
zucchini ligurian style................................ 704
zucchini with beef....................................... 705
zucchini with rice and ham........................ 705
fried zucchini... 706
fried zucchini gratin.................................... 706
fried zucchini fillets.................................... 706
zucchini timbale.. 707
marinated fried zucchini............................ 707
zucchini roman style.................................. 708
zucchini stuffed with tuna.......................... 708

Legumes

marinated chickpeas.................................. 709
chickpeas with tomato............................... 709
chickpea purée.. 710
beans maître d'hôtel................................... 710
beans with pancetta.................................... 711
tuscan beans.. 711
purée of beans and parmesan..................... 712
pork and beans.. 712
fresh beans all'uccelletto........................... 712
fresh beans with tomato............................. 713
green beans with tomato............................ 713
green beans with tuna and anchovy........... 714
green beans with gruyère........................... 714
green bean flan... 714
timbale of green beans with meatballs...... 715
fava beans with guanciale.......................... 716
fava beans maître d'hôtel............................ 716
fava bean purée.. 716
lentil purée.. 717
lentils in a pan.. 717

Salads

colorful salad... 718
orange salad.. 718
american salad.. 718
andalusian salad... 719
harlequin salad.. 719
belgian salad... 719
shrimp salad.. 720
celery, apple, and fennel salad.................. 720
fennel and carrot salad.............................. 720
raw cabbage salad....................................... 721
cucumber and parsley salad....................... 721
watercress salad with yogurt..................... 721
spelt salad.. 722
bitter leaf salad.. 722
farmhouse salad.. 722
rice and ham salad....................................... 723
raw salad of mushrooms............................ 723
puntarelle salad.. 723
salad of escarole and radicchio................. 724
celery salad.. 724
raw spinach salad....................................... 724
fantasy salad.. 725
russian salad.. 725
fish salad.. 726

Pickles

viterbo carrots.. 727
pickled capers.. 727
capers in salt.. 727
artichokes in oil... 728
pickled cabbage (sauerkraut).................... 728
pickled cabbage with pancetta.................. 729
cucumbers in vinegar (cornichons).......... 729
pickled onions... 730
pickled ovoli porcini................................... 730
olives of gaeta.. 731
green sicilian olives.................................... 731
chili peppers in vinegar.............................. 732
peppers in oil... 732
tomato passata... 733
sun dried tomatoes...................................... 733

12 **FRUIT & DESSERTS**

Preserved Fruit

apricot jam.. 738
apricot purée... 738
oranges in jam... 738
orange jelly.. 739
chestnut jam.. 739
cherry jam.. 740
cherries in vinegar....................................... 740
cherries in spirit... 740
quince in squares... 741
quince jelly... 741
quince jam.. 741
fig jam... 742
dried figs... 742
dried figs with chocolate............................. 743
strawberry jam... 743
apple jam.. 743
blackberry jelly.. 744
whole peaches in syrup............................... 744
peaches in spirit... 744
plum jam... 745
dried prunes... 745
currant jelly.. 745
christmas grapes.. 746
grapes in spirit... 746
sour cherry jam.. 747
sour cherry jam and syrup.......................... 747

Fillings & Icings

apricot jelly... 750
chocolate icing... 750
royal icing.. 750

Creams & Sauces

buttercream.. 751
white cream.. 751
almond cream (frangipane)........................ 751
crème anglaise.. 752
chocolate crème anglaise............................ 752
pastry cream... 752
chocolate cream... 753
hot falerno (wine) sauce.............................. 753
hot red wine sauce.. 754
hot siracusan sauce...................................... 754
zabaglione... 754

Toppings

candied orange peel.................................... 755
marzipan (almond paste)............................ 756
hazelnut paste.. 756
candied almonds.. 756
salted almonds... 757

Puddings

butter and candied fruit pudding.............. 758
chestnut pudding.. 758
cherry pudding... 759
chocolate pudding.. 759
almond chocolate pudding.......................... 760
fruit pudding.. 760
apple pudding... 761
peach pudding.. 761
hot diplomatic pudding............................... 762
prune pudding.. 763
ricotta pudding... 763

Desserts with Fruit

apricots colbert.. 764
apricot mold.. 764
creole pineapple.. 765
bananas flambé... 766
sweet fried bananas...................................... 766
pastry boats for wild strawberries............. 766
refined chestnut cake................................... 767
almond crunch... 767
fruit with sweet rice...................................... 768
castellana apples... 768
apple surprise.. 769
montebianco.. 769
panforte.. 770
pears in maraschino...................................... 770
margherita pears.. 771
peaches with maraschino cream.................. 771
empress peaches.. 772
piedmontese peaches.................................... 772
peaches zabaglione.. 773
peaches in sweet pastry................................. 773
nougat... 774
soft chocolate nougat..................................... 775
grape cake.. 775
blueberry cake.. 775

Egg Desserts

aristocrat meringue.. 776
cream bain-marie.. 776
crème caramel... 777
crème bavaroise.. 777
crêpes with cream... 778
strawberry crêpes.. 778
crêpes suzette.. 778
emperor's frittata (kaiser schmarren)........... 779
sweet frittata.. 779
meringue.. 780
mousseline mimì... 781
jam omelette... 781
rum omelette.. 782
zabaglione pudding... 782
white cake.. 782
almond cake... 783

Pastry Desserts

sweet shortcrust pastry................................. 784
roman short pastry.. 784
short pastry without eggs............................... 784
non-leavened quick pastry............................. 785
fruit cake.. 785
cicerchiata.. 786
fresh fruit tart.. 786
jam tart... 787
cream tart.. 787
strawberry tart.. 787
ricotta tart... 788
candied flan.. 788
chocolate flan.. 789
rice flan.. 789
candied orange cake.. 790
neapolitan easter pie.. 790

gnocchi cream pie 791
assisi roll 792
apple strudel 792
viennese cake (sacher torte) 794
paradise cake 795
chocolate cake 795

Desserts with Yeast
mascarpone bombs 796
brescia donuts 797
boston pie 798
chocolate cake (gluten free) 799
raisin cake 799
preziosa cake 800
almond gâteau 800
kugelhupf 801
pandoro filled with cream 802
sweet walnut bread 803
pinza bolognese 804
easter palombella pizza 804
easter ricresciuta pizza 804
florentine stiacciata 805
coconut cake 805
bilbolbul cake 806
apple cake 806
meringue cake 807
farmhouse easter cake 807
cream baba 809
baba with fruit 809

Sponge & Genoise Cakes
flourless almond sponge cake 811
cassata sicilian style 811
mocha cream cake 812
diplomatic cake 812
chocolate sponge cake 813
apricot genoise 813
chestnut cream cake 814
trifle 814
margherita cake 815
madeleine cake 815
savoy cake 816
margherita cake with mascarpone 816
choux beignets 817
profiteroles 818
saint-honoré 818
small brioches 822
frangipane cake 823
cream millefeuille 824
ricotta sfogliata 825

Sweet Soufflés
chocolate soufflé 826
rum soufflé 826
apricot soufflé 827
chestnut soufflé 827
cream and banana soufflé 828
strawberry soufflé 828

Chilled Desserts
vanilla bavarois 829
chocolate bavarois 829
strawberry bavarois 830
coffee cups 830
chocolate cups 831
lemon cups 831
zabaglione cups 831
classic charlotte 832
chestnut charlotte 832
cream charlotte 833
strawberry charlotte 834
chocolate cream in cups 834
mascarpone cream in cups 835
cream and banana in cups 835
crème malakoff 836
tangerine jelly in their skins 836
banana mousseline 837
strawberry mousseline 838
apple mousseline 838

Ice Cream
sicilian cassata 840
cream ice cream 840
chocolate ice cream 841
strawberry ice cream in cups 841
hazelnut ice cream 841
ice cream and chocolate cake 842
apricot granita 843
orange granita 843
coffee granita 843
wild strawberry granita 844
lemon granita 844
peach granita 844
sour cherry granita 844
apricot sherbet 845
banana sherbet 845
chocolate sherbet 846
strawberry and cream sherbet 846
strawberry sherbet with blackberries 847
peach sherbet 847
zabaglione sherbet 847

Cookies & Sweet Treats
amaretti 848
venetian dry cookies 848
anise seed cookies 849
pine nut cookies 849
almond cookies 850
cumin cookies 850
savoy cookies 851
honey cookies 851
rolled cookies 852
rolled cookies with white cream 852
ricotta bocconotti 853
baked almond donuts 853
baked wine donuts 854
lenten donuts 854
fritters 855
ricotta fritters 855
rice fritters 856
san joseph fritters 856
krapfen 857
cream krapfen 858
maritozzi 858
coffee bonbons 859
orange bonbons 860
chocolate and chestnut bonbons 860
chestnut bonbons with almonds 860
strawberry bonbons 861
walnut bonbons 861
cannoli 862
cannoncini 863
siena cavallucci 863
waffle cones 864
ciambellone 864
chocolate almonds 864
date and walnut bonbons 865
little diplomats 866
mother-in-law's tongues 866
cat's tongues 866
walnut mostaccioli 867
baked hazelnuts 867
gnocchi pastries 868
orange pasticcini 869
raisin pastine 869
black raisin pastries with rum 870
almond petit fours 870
pinoccate 871
little princesses 871
sweet ricotta sfogliatelle 872
sospiri 872
spirals 874
almond and vanilla spumette 875
neapolitan struffoli 875
chocolate truffles 876
tegoline cookies 876
tiramisu 877
fans 877

Fruit
pineapple surprise 878
pineapple with kirsch 878
pineapple with kiwi and pomegranate 878
oranges with maraschino 879
oranges and strawberries 879
avocado with pineapple and grapefruit 879
banana and rum cream 879
persimmon in cognac 880
roasted chestnuts 880
flambéed roasted chestnuts 880
chestnut purée 880
chestnut soufflé 881
watermelon with rum 881
sweet figs 881
strawberries carmen 882
strawberries with rum or maraschino 882
strawberries with yogurt 882
baked apples 882
pan-fried apples with wine 883
stuffed baked apples 883
apple fritters 883
melon with peaches and rum 884
melon with strawberries 884
poached pears with cream 884
peaches with yogurt 885
grapefruit with blood orange 885
grapes in a cup 885
sour cherries in their shirts 885
watermelon salad 886
fruit meringue 886
sparkling fruit salad 886
fruit salad 887
coconut salad 887

INDEX BY INGREDIENT

A

Acquacotta, 136
Agnolotti. *see also* **Pasta**
Agnolotti Sardinian Style, 184
Classic Agnolotti, 183
Almond
Almonds, How to shell, 751
Almond and Chocolate Sauce, 28
Almond and Vanilla Spumette, 875
Almond Cake, 783
Almond Cookies, 850
Almond Cream (Frangipane), 751
Almond Crunch, 767
Almond Gâteau, 800
Almond Petit Fours, 880
Almond Ragu, 33
Amaretti, 848
Baked Almond Donuts, 853
Candied Almonds, 756
Chestnut Bonbons with Almonds, 860
Chocolate Almonds, 864
Chocolate Pudding with Almonds, 760
Flourless Almond Sponge Cake, 811
Marzipan (Almond Paste), 756
Pinoccate, 871
Salted Almonds, 757
Amatriciana Sauce, 23
Anchovy
Anchovies Baked with Mushrooms, 330
Anchovies Tunisian Style, 329
Anchovies with Lemon, 329
Anchovy and Tuna Fritters, 245
Anchovy Butter, 54
Anchovy Canapés, 57
Anchovy Mayonnaise, 20
Anchovy Tramezzini, 63
Anchovy Wheels, 65
Artichoke with Anchovies and Capers, 66
Artichokes with Anchovy, 637
Artichokes with Breadcrumbs and Anchovy Fillets, 640
Baked Baby Gray Mullets with Anchovies, 340
Baked Eggs with Anchovy Butter, 309
Braised Spring Lamb with Anchovy and Fennel, 517
Cabbage in Anchovy Sauce, 645
Cod Steaks with Anchovy Butter, 348
Fried, stuffed pasta with Mozzarella and Anchovies, 251
Fried Eggs with Mozzarella and Anchovy Butter, 312
Fried Mozzarella with Anchovy, 255
Fried Sardines with Mustard and Anchovy, 363
Frittata with Anchovies, 295
Green Beans with Tuna and Anchovy, 714
Gray Mullet with Anchovy Sauce, 341
Grilled Lamb Chops with Anchovy and Lemon Sauce, 524
Mackerel Fillets with Anchovy and Capers, 347
Pan-Fried Kidneys with Anchovy, 463
Pizzette with Mozzarella and Anchovy, 272
Poached Eggs with Anchovy Butter, 307
Polenta with Mozzarella and Anchovies, 235
Porcini with Anchovy and Tomato, 657
Pressure-Cooker Braised Beef with Anchovies, 477
Quick Anchovy and Egg Sauce, 29
Quick Anchovy Sauce, 29
Quick Tuna and Anchovy Sauce, 31
Rice with Anchovies, 212
Roast Poussins with Anchovies, 571
Sandwiches with Anchovies and Ham, 61
Sea bass with Anchovy and Wild Mushrooms, 370
Skate with Anchovy Sauce, 358
Spaghetti with Garlic, Oil, and Anchovy, 163
Spiced Anchovies, 330
Spicy Anchovy Sauce, 25
Spinach with Anchovy Fillets, 695
Spring Lamb with Anchovy Sauce, 519
Tagliatelle with Egg, Anchovy, and Mozzarella, 179
Tomatoes Stuffed with Capers and Anchovies, 688
Anise Seed
Anise Seed Cookies, 849
Lenten Donuts, 854
Appetizers*, *52-85
To Line the Moulds, 64
To Bake the Casings, 64
Apple. *see also* **Fruit**
Apple Cake, 806
Apple Fritters, 883
Apple Jam, 743
Apple Mousseline, 838
Apple Pudding, 761
Apple Strudel, 792
Apple Surprise, 769
Baked Apples, 882
Castellana Apples, 768
Celery, Apple and Fennel Salad, 720
Pan-Fried Apples with Wine, 883
Stuffed Baked Apples, 883
Tournedos Vol-Au-Vents with Apple, 486
Apricot. *see also* **Fruit**
Apricot Genoise, 813
Apricot Granita, 843
Apricot Jam, 738
Apricot Jelly, 750
Apricot Mold, 764
Apricot Purée, 738
Apricot Sherbet, 845
Apricot Soufflé, 827
Apricots Colbert, 764
Arancini, 259
Artichoke. *see also* **Cardoon; Jerusalem artichoke**
To Boil Artichokes, 633
To Choose Artichokes, 633
Artichoke Risotto, 215
Artichoke and Smoked Fish Roe, 66
Artichoke Gratin, 638
Artichokes Parmigiana, 636
Artichoke Soufflé, 320
Artichoke with Anchovies and Capers, 66
Artichokes in Oil, 728
Artichokes Stuffed with Chicken Breast, 640
Artichokes with Anchovy, 637
Artichokes with Breadcrumbs and Anchovy Fillets, 640
Artichokes with Caviar, 66
Artichokes with Peas, 638
Artichokes with Prosciutto and Parmesan, 639
Artichokes with Rice, 633
Artichokes with Russian Salad, 636
Artichokes with Scrambled Eggs, 637
Artichokes with Tuna, 641
Boiled Eggs with Artichokes and Peas, 313
Braised Artichokes Roman Style, 637
Braised Lamb Chops with Artichokes, 527
Chicken Livers with Artichokes, 589
Cream of Artichoke, 97
Cuttlefish with Artichokes, 405
Deep-Fried Artichokes in Batter, 635
Deep-Fried Artichokes Fricasse, 635
Deep-Fried Artichokes Jewish Style, 634
Fricassee of Veal with Artichokes, 428
Fried Artichokes Villeroy, 634
Frittata with Baked Artichokes, 299
John Dory with Artichokes and Potatoes, 356
Kid Braised with Artichokes, 538
Lamb Offal with Artichokes, 533
Lamb Sweetbreads with Artichokes, 531
Omelet with Asparagus and Artichokes, 305
Oven-Baked Kid with Artichoke Salad, 538
Risotto with Artichokes and Peas, 220
Rustic Artichoke Pie, 281
Sole Fillets with Artichoke, 367
Spaghettini with Artichokes and Mushrooms, 167
Stuffed Artichokes Sicilian Style, 639
Veal and Artichoke Timbale, 453
Asparagus
To cook asparagus, 626
Asparagus Flan, 627
Asparagus Gratin, 628
Asparagus Salad, 627
Asparagus with Butter, 626
Asparagus with Eggs, 627
Asparagus with Prosciutto, 626
Cream of Asparagus, 97
Omelet with Asparagus and Artichokes, 305
Poached Eggs with Asparagus Tips, 308
Rigatoni Gratin with Asparagus, 200
Scrambled Eggs with Chicken Livers and Asparagus, 318
Semolina and Asparagus Soup, 111
Shrimp with Asparagus, 392

B

Baba, 808-809
To Coat a Baba, 808
To Make a Baba, 808
Bagna Cauda, 44
Banana. *see also* **Fruit**
Banana and Rum Cream, 879
Banana Mousseline, 837
Banana Sherbet, 845
Cream and Banana in Cups, 835
Cream and Banana Soufflé, 828
Bananas Flambé, 766
Sweet Fried Bananas, 766

Batter
To Fry, 242
To Make Batter, 242
Simple Batter, 242
Special Batter, 242
Wine Batter, 242
Deep-Fried Artichokes in Batter, 635
Deep-Fried Eggplants in Wine Batter, 665
Deep-Fried Pumpkin in Batter, 701
Bavette. *see also* **Beef**
Bavette in Egg Sauce, 147
Bavette Trastevere Style, 146
Bavette with Fresh Fava Beans, 146
Beans. *see also* **Fava beans; Green beans**
To Cook Beans, 710
Bean and Chard Soup, 138
Beans Maître D'hôtel, 710
Beans with Pancetta, 711
Cannolicchi with Fresh White Beans, 149
Fresh Bean Minestrone, 118
Fresh Beans All'uccelletto, 712
Fresh Beans with Tomato, 713
Pork and Beans, 712
Purée of Beans and Parmesan, 712
Rice and Bean Soup, 108
Sausages with Beans, 557
Tuscan Beans, 711
Venetian Bean and Pasta Soup, 107
White Bean Soup, 138
Beef. *see also* **Bavette; Ox; Steak; Tournedos**
To Boil Beef, 465
To Braise Beef, 465
Beef and Bread Skewers, 496
Beef and Cabbage Rolls, 509
Beef and Chicken Liver Rolls, 490
Beef and Fennel Stew, 498
Beef and Mortadella Rolls, 514
Beef and Onion Skewers, 496
Beef and Red Wine Sauce, 35
Beef and Tomato Sauce, 35
Beef Broth with Spinach Parcels, 92
Beef Consommé with Carrots and Tomato Cream, 96
Beef Croquettes with Raisins and Pine Nuts, 506
Beef in Red Wine, 495
Beef Pastries, 490
Beef Pizza Neapolitan Style, 509
Beef Pizza with Prosciutto, 510
Beef Pizzaiola, 468
Beef Roll Sicilian Style, 494
Beef Rolls in Tomato Sauce, 489
Beef Sausages, 495
Beef Slow Cooked in Red Wine, 499
Beef Steak Pizzaiola, 481
Beef Stew French Style, 497
Beef Stew Roman Style, 498
Beef Straccetti, 496
Beef Tenderloin Bismarck, 482
Beef Terrine Hunter Style, 502
Boiled Beef Hungarian Style, 505
Boiled Beef Medallions with Sage, Ham, and Mozzarella, 470
Boiled Beef Pizzaiola, 468
Boiled Beef Pudding, 469
Boiled Beef with Rustic Sauce, 471
Boiled Beef with Mayonnaise, 470
Boiled Beef with Potatoes, 469
Boiled Beef with Vegetables, 471
Braised and Marinated Beef, 476
Braised Beef, 472
Braised Beef Brescia Style, 473
Braised Beef Certosa Style, 474
Braised Beef Genovese, 474
Braised Beef in Barolo, 472
Braised Beef in Milk, 476
Braised Beef Lombardy Style, 497
Braised Beef Parma Style, 474
Braised Beef Provençal, 475
Braised Beef with Onions, 475
Braised Beef with Vegetables, 477
Breast of Beef Genovese, 479
Cannelloni with Beef and Tomatoes, 184
Chateaubriand Maître D'Hôtel, 478
Cheeseburger, 508
Creole Beef Tenderloin, 483
Deep-Fried Beef Croquettes, 506
Deep-Fried Beef Slices, 481
Duchess Potatoes with Beef and Tomato, 671
Eggplant Flan with Beef, 665
Fricassee Lucca Style, 487
Hunter's Tenderloin, 483
Meat and Mushroom Sauce, 36
Meat Jelly, 52
Meat Sauce, 34
Oven-Roasted Hamburgers, 508
Ragu Bolognese, 32
Marinated Boiled Beef, 468
Pressure Cooker Braised Beef with Anchovies, 477
Rib Steak with Mushrooms, 480
Roast Beef, 492
Roast Beef Spanish Style, 493
Roast Beef with Capers, 492
Roast Beef with Potatoes, 494
Roast Beef with Wild Mushrooms, 493
Tenderloin Piedmont Style, 484
Terrine of Beef French Style, 500
Terrine of Beef Italian Style, 501
Truffled Beef Terrine, 503
Zucchini with Beef, 705
Beet
Beet and Onion Salad, 628
Beet and Onion in Sauce, 628
Bell Pepper
To Skin Peppers, 677
Braised Squab with Peppers and Mushrooms, 609
Chicken with Peppers, 583
Chilled Rice with Shrimp and Peppers, 210
Fried Peppers, 680
Marinated Peppers, 679
Peperonata, 677
Peppers Gratin, 677
Peppers in Oil, 732
Peppers Roman Style, 678
Peppers Stuffed with Fish and Rice, 683
Peppers Stuffed with Mushrooms, 682
Peppers with Eggs, 680
Peppers with Guanciale, 678
Peppers Stuffed with Squid or Octopus, 680
Salt Cod with Peppers, 336
Stuffed Peppers, 679
Stuffed Peppers Neapolitan Style, 682
Tomato Sauce with Peppers and Eggplant, 40
Tortiglioni with Peppers and Eggplant, 168
Veal Chops with Tomatoes and Peppers, 421
Veal Steaks with Peppers, 434
Blackberry Jelly, 744
Blueberry Cake, 775
Bouillabaisse, 130
Boar
Boar Stew, 623
Sweet and Sour Boar Roman Style, 622
Brioche
To Make Brioche, 821
Broccoli. *see also* **Broccoli rabe**
To Cook the Cabbage Family, 629
Broccoli Roman Style, 630
Broccoli Sicilian Style, 630
Broccoli with Lemon, 631
Broccoli with Prosciutto, 631
Maccheroncini and Broccoli Sicilian Style, 154
Pasta and Broccoli Soup, 106
Pig's Trotters with Broccoli and Sausages, 560
Broccoli Rabe. *see also* **Broccoli**
To Cook the Cabbage Family, 629
Pan-Fried Broccoli Rabe, 629
Pan-Fried Broccoli Rabe with Chili, 629
Broth
To Clarify a Broth, 88
To Thicken a Broth, 88
Beef Broth with Spinach Parcels, 92
Bolognese Broth, 93
Broth with Choux Buns, 92
Broth with Egg, 95
Broth with Potato Dumplings, 90
Broth with Semolina Squares, 93
Broth with Stuffed Buns, 93
Chicken Broth, 89
Fish Broth, 89
Meat Broth, 88
Meat Broth with Ham Gnocchetti, 91
Meat Broth with Polenta Gnocchetti, 91
Meat Broth with Ricotta Dumplings, 94
Polenta with Broth, 233
Quick Broth, 89
Royal Chicken Broth, 94
Vegetable Broth, 90
Bruschetta, 57
Brussels sprouts
To Cook Brussels Sprouts, 646
Baked Brussels Sprouts with Guanciale, 646
Brussels Sprouts with Butter, 646
Fried Brussels Sprouts, 647
Roast Capon with Chestnuts and Brussels Sprouts, 571
Roast Pork with Brussels Sprouts, 551
Bucatini. *see also* **Pasta; Spaghetti**
Bucatini Amatriciana, 147
Bucatini and Pigeon Pasticcio, 201
Bucatini with Mussels and Clams, 147
Bucatini with Shrimp and Baby Squid, 148
Butter
Anchovy Butter, 54
Asparagus with Butter, 626
Baked Eggs with Anchovy Butter, 309
Brown Butter Sauce, 44
Brussels Sprouts with Butter, 646
Butter and Candied Fruit Pudding, 758
Carrots with Butter, 643
Cod Steaks with Anchovy Butter, 348
Country Style Butter, 53
Fried Calf's Liver with Sage Butter, 461
Fried Eggs with Mozzarella and Anchovy Butter, 312

Butter. (cont.)
John Dory Fillets in Butter, 355
Meatballs Fried in Butter, 507
Monkfish with Parsley Butter, 343
Montpellier Butter, 54
Pan-Fried Sweetbreads in Butter, 532
Pan-Fried Trout in Butter, 385
Poached Eggs with Anchovy Butter, 307
Ravioli with Ricotta, Butter, and Sage, 190
Sardine Butter, 55
Shrimp Butter, 55
Skate in Brown Butter, 358
Sole in Butter, 365
Spinach with Butter, 694
Tarragon Butter, 54
Trout with Onion Butter, 383
Veal Meatballs with Butter, 439

C

Cabbage
To Cook the Cabbage Family, 629
Beef and Cabbage Rolls, 509
Cabbage and Sausage Soup, 137
Cabbage in Anchovy Sauce, 645
Cabbage in Vinegar, 645
Frankfurters with Cabbage, 559
Pickled Cabbage with Pancetta, 729
Pickled Cabbage (Sauerkraut), 728
Raw Cabbage Salad, 721
Cake
To Coat a Cake, 748
To Fill a Cake, 748
To Make a Genoise Cake, 810
To Make a Sponge Cake, 810
Calf's liver
Calf's Liver Fiorentina Style, 460
Calf's Liver Milanese Style, 461
Calf's Liver Venetian Style, 461
Calf's Liver with Fennel Piquant Sauce, 462
Calf's Liver with Vinegar, 460
Fried Calf's Liver with Sage Butter, 461
Fried Breaded Calf's Liver, 462
Calzones, 273-274
Cannelloni. *see also* **Pasta**
Cannelloni Etruscan Style, 185
Cannelloni Provençal, 186
Cannelloni with Beef and Tomatoes, 184
Cannelloni with Ricotta and Sausage, 187
Cannoli, 862
Cannolicchi. *see also* **Pasta**
Cannolicchi with Basil, 149
Cannolicchi with Fresh White Beans, 149
Chickpea Soup with Cannolicchi, 107
Cappelletti. *see also* **Pasta**
Modena Soup with Cappelletti, 103
Caper
Artichoke with Anchovies and Capers, 66
Caper Sauce, 25
Capers in Salt, 727
Mackerel Fillets with Anchovy and Capers, 347
Pickled Capers, 727
Pork Strips in Caper Sauce, 546
Quick Caper Sauce, 30
Rabbit with Capers, 612
Roast Beef with Capers, 492
Spaghetti with Capers and Olives, 164
Tomatoes Stuffed with Capers and Anchovies, 688
Tuna Baked with Olives and Capers, 371
Capon. *see also* **Chicken**
Roast Capon, 570
Roast Capon with Chestnuts and Brussels Sprouts, 571
Roast Capon with Truffle, 570
Carbonara Sauce, 23
Cardoon. *see also* **Artichoke; Jerusalem artichoke**
To Cook Cardoons, 641
Baked Cardoon, 642
Cardoon Soufflé, 321
Cardoons (Artichoke Thistles), 641
Cardoons in White Sauce, 642
Cardoons Parmigiana, 642
Cardoons with Prosciutto, 643
Cotechino with Cardoons, 567
Sausages with Cardoons, 558
Scrambled Eggs with Cardoons, 318
Carp
Carp in White Wine, 380
Carp Jewish Style, 379
Carrot
Beef Consommé with Carrots and Tomato Cream, 96
Braised Mutton with Carrots, 534
Carrot Purée, 644
Carrots in Milk, 643
Carrots with Butter, 643
Fennel and Carrot Salad, 720
Glazed Carrots with Marsala, 644
Stuffed Carrot with Tuna, 644
Marinated Carrots, 645
Viterbo Carrots, 727
Cauliflower
To Cook Cauliflower, 647
To Cook the Cabbage Family, 629
Cauliflower Neapolitan Style, 648
Cauliflower with White Sauce, 648
Fried Cauliflower, 647
Rice and Cauliflower Soup, 108
Celery
Baked Celery, 692
Celery Parmigiana, 693
Celery Salad, 724
Celery, Apple and Fennel Salad, 720
Cheese. *see also* **Fontina; Gorgonzola; Gruyère; Mozzarella; Parmesan; Ricotta**
Cheese Baskets, 76
Cheese Casserole, 75
Cheese Cream Pies, 72
Cheese Croquettes, 247
Cheese Cream Croquettes, 246
Cheese Rustica, 74
Cheese Soufflé, 320
Fried Sirloin with Fontina, 482
Macaroni with Four Cheeses, 155
Macaroni with Four String Cheeses, 155
Spaghetti Cacio e Pepe, 164
Three Cheese Pizza, 268
Tortiglioni with Goat Cheese, 168
Cherry. *see also* **Fruit; Sour cherry**
Cherries in Spirit, 740
Cherries in Vinegar, 740
Cherry Jam, 740
Cherry Pudding, 759
Venison with Cherry Sauce, 620
Chestnut
Refined Chestnut Cake, 767
Boiled Chestnuts in Soufflé, 881
Chestnut Bonbons with Almonds, 860
Chestnut Charlotte, 832
Chestnut Cream Cake, 814
Chestnut Jam, 739
Chestnut Pudding, 758
Chestnut Purée, 880
Chestnut Soufflé, 827
Chocolate and Chestnut Bonbons, 860
Flambéed Roasted Chestnuts, 880
Montebianco, 769
Roast Goose, 608
Roast Turkey Stuffed with Chestnuts, 593
Roasted Chestnuts, 880
Chicken. *see also* **Capon; Poussin**
Artichokes Stuffed with Chicken Breast, 640
Braised Chicken in a Piquant Sauce, 588
Braised Chicken Le Marche Style, 587
Braised Chicken with Olives, 580
Braised Chicken with Porcini Mushrooms, 582
Braised Chicken with Sage, 581
Braised Chicken with Tomato, 576
Chicken and Truffle in Jelly, 573
Chicken Bella Vista, 574
Chicken Braised in a Dutch Oven, 584
Chicken Braised in Milk, 581
Chicken Breast in White Sauce, 578
Chicken Breast with Peas, 578
Chicken Broth, 89
Chicken Cream, 55
Chicken Croquettes, 248
Chicken Gifts, 591
Chicken Gifts Flan Financier, 592
Chicken in a Pot, 577
Chicken Marengo, 580
Chicken Mayonnaise, 585
Chicken Mayonnaise French Style, 585
Chicken Pie, 586
Chicken Risotto, 217
Chicken Salad, 584
Chicken Soufflé, 323
Chicken Terrine, 576
Chicken Tortellini, 193
Chicken with Peppers, 583
Chicken with Prunes, 582
Cream of Chicken, 98
Fried Chicken Florentine Style, 583
Grilled Chicken Frittata Sandwiches, 62
Glutton's Chicken, 574
Hunter's Chicken, 579
Hunter's Lasagnette with Chicken, 174
Pan-Fried Chicken, 586
Roast Chicken, 579
Roast Chicken with Potatoes, 581
Roman Chicken Soup with Cappelletti, 102
Royal Chicken Broth, 94
Rustic Chicken Pie, 286
Shallow-Fried Chicken, 578
Tagliatelle with Chicken, 179
Chicken liver. *see also* **Chicken**
Baked Polenta with Veal and Chicken Livers, 239
Beef and Chicken Liver Rolls, 490
Chicken Liver and Rice Soufflé, 324
Chicken Liver Crostini, 59
Chicken Liver Pie, 590
Chicken Liver Risotto, 216
Chicken Livers with Artichokes, 589
Cream Pies with Chicken Livers, 72
Dauphin Potatoes with Chicken Livers, 673

Meatloaf with Mushrooms and Chicken Livers, 440
Pan-Fried Chicken Livers with Sage, 588
Polenta with Veal and Chicken Livers, 235
Scrambled Eggs with Chicken Livers and Asparagus, 318

Chickpea
To Cook Chickpeas, 709
Chickpea Purée, 710
Chickpea Soup, 103
Chickpea Soup with Cannolicchi, 107
Chickpeas with Tomato, 709
Marinated Chickpeas, 709

Chili
Chili Peppers in Vinegar, 732
Clams with Chili, 409
Pan-Fried Broccoli Rabe with Chili, 629
Pickled Eggs with Chili, 316

Chocolate
Almond and Chocolate Sauce, 28
Chocolate Almonds, 864
Chocolate and Chestnut Bonbons, 860
Chocolate Bavarois, 829
Chocolate Cake, 795
Chocolate Cake (Gluten Free), 799
Chocolate Cream, 753
Chocolate Cream in Cups, 834
Chocolate Crème Anglaise, 752
Chocolate Cream, 753
Chocolate Cups, 831
Chocolate Flan, 789
Chocolate Ice Cream, 841
Chocolate Icing, 750
Chocolate Pudding, 759
Chocolate Pudding with Almonds, 760
Chocolate Sherbet, 846
Chocolate Soufflé, 826
Chocolate Sponge Cake, 813
Chocolate Truffles, 876
Dried Figs with Chocolate, 743
Ice Cream and Chocolate Cake, 842
Soft Chocolate Nougat, 775

Choux pastry. *see also* **Pastry**
To Make Sweetened Choux Pastry, 817
To Make Unsweetened Choux Pastry, 71
Broth with Choux Buns, 92
Broth with Stuffed Buns, 93
Choux, 817
Choux Beignets, 817
Modern Choux Buns, 74
Traditional Choux Buns, 74
Profiteroles, 818
Saint-Honoré, 818

Cipollini onion. *see also* **Onion**
To Prepare Cipollini, 651
Baked Cipollini Onions, 651
Baked Red Snapper Fillets with Cipollini Onions, 345
Cipollini Onions in Tomato Sauce, 652
Cipollini Onions in White Wine, 652
Cipollini Onions with Peas, 652
Glazed Cipollini Onions, 653
Sweet and Sour Cipollini Onions, 653
Spicy Tomato Sauce with Cipollini Onions, 41

Clam. *see also* **Shellfish**
Bucatini with Mussels and Clams, 147
Clam Soup, 135
Clams with Chili, 409
Clams with Peas, 409
Neapolitan Pizza with Clams, 266
Refined Clam Soup, 135
Risotto with Mussels and Clams, 220
Spaghetti with Wedge Clams, 165
Tonnarelli with Clams and Pesto, 181
White Brodetto, 125

Coconut
Coconut Cake, 805
Coconut Salad, 887

Cod. *see also* **Fish; Salt Cod**
Baked Cod with Lemon, 348
Cod Baked with Mushrooms, 348
Cod Fillets Maître D'hôtel, 349
Cod Gratin, 349
Cod Steaks with Anchovy Butter, 348
Cod with White Wine, 349

Coffee
Coffee Bonbons, 859
Coffee Cups, 830
Coffee Granita, 843

Conchiglie. *see also* **Pasta**
Conchiglie with Mascarpone and Mushrooms, 150
Conchiglie with Ricotta and Spinach, 150
Conchiglie with Shrimp, 150

Conchiglioni, 151

Consommé
Beef Consommé with Carrots and Tomato Cream, 96
Consommé, 90
Consommé with Savory Crêpes, 95

Crawfish. *see also* **Fish**
Poached Crawfish, 396
Roast Crawfish, 395

Cream
Almond Cream (Frangipane), 751
Banana and Rum Cream, 879
Banana Cream in Cups, 835
Basic White Sauce, 16
Cheese Cream Pies, 72
Chestnut Cream Cake, 814
Chicken Cream, 55
Chilled Omelet with Cream and Jelly, 306
Chocolate Cream, 753
Chocolate Cream in Cups, 834
Cream and Banana Soufflé, 828
Cream Baba, 809
Cream Bain-Marie, 776
Crème Bavaroise, 777
Cream Charlotte, 833
Cream Hollandaise, 22
Cream Ice Cream, 840
Cream Krapfen, 858
Cream of Artichoke, 97
Cream of Asparagus, 97
Cream of Barley, 99
Cream of Chicken, 98
Cream of Ham, 101
Cream of Mushroom, 98
Cream of Pastina, 96
Cream of Pea, 99
Cream of Spinach, 101
Cream of Tomato, 100
Cream of Wild Mushrooms, 47
Cream Pies with Chicken Livers, 72
Cream Sauce, 17
Cream Sauce with Eggs, 18
Cream Tart, 787
Creamed Cucumbers, 67
Crêpes with Cream, 778
Double Cream Sauce, 17
Fettuccine in Cream Sauce, 151
Gorgonzola Cream, 56
Goulash with Cream and Dumplings, 488
Ham Cream, 56
Horseradish Sauce with Cream, 27
Leeks in Cream, 690
Malakoff Cream, 836
Mascarpone Cream in Cups, 835
Mocha Cream Cake, 812
Mushroom Cream Sauce, 17
Mushrooms in Cream, 655
Pandoro Filled with Cream, 802
Parmesan Cream, 56
Pastry Cream, 752
Peaches with Maraschino Cream, 771
Pheasant in Cream, 604
Poached Pears with Cream, 884
Roast Veal with Cream, 412
Rolled Cookies with White Cream, 852
Simple Cream Hollandaise, 22
Strawberry and Cream Sherbet, 846
Sweet Cream Croquettes, 247
Tagliatelle with Cream, 200
Thousand Leaves with Cream, 824
Tonnarelli with Cream, 181
Truffle Cream, 56
Veal Meatballs with Cream Sauce, 440
White Cream, 751
White Fish Cream, 55

Croaker. *see also* **Fish**
Croaker Baked with Potatoes, 351
Croaker Pizzaiola, 351
Oven-Baked Croaker, 350

Crostini
Chicken Liver Crostini, 59
Neapolitan Crostini, 58
Pork Liver Crostini, 59
Ricotta and Sausage Crostini, 60
Roast Woodcock with Crostini, 602
Shrimp Crostini, 394
Spinach Crostini, 697
Tomato Soup with Parmesan Crostini, 140

Crumble
To Make Crumble, 755

Cucumber
Creamed Cucumbers, 67
Cucumber and Parsley Salad, 721
Cucumbers in Vinegar (Cornichons), 729
Stuffed Cucumbers, 67

Cumin Cookies, 850
Curd, 189
Currant Jelly, 745

Cuttlefish. *see also* **Fish; Shellfish**
Cuttlefish and Tomato Stew, 405
Cuttlefish with Artichokes, 405
Risotto with Cuttlefish, 223
Stuffed Cuttlefish, 406

D

Date and Walnut Bonbons, 865

Deer. *see also* **Venison**
Marinated Roe Deer, 618

Duchess potato. *see also* **Potato**
Baked Eggs with Duchess Potatoes, 310
Duchess Potato Croquettes, 670
Duchess Potato Croquettes with Ricotta, 671
Duchess Potatoes, 670
Duchess Potatoes with Beef and Tomato, 671

Duck
Duck with Orange, 600
Pappardelle with Duck, 176
Rice with Duck, 209
Salmi of Duck, 601

E

Eel. *see also* **Fish**
Eel Carpionata, 379
Eel on a Spit, 378
Roast Eel, 378

Egg
To Bake Eggs, 309
To Boil Eggs, 313
To Fry Eggs, 311
To Hard-Boil Eggs , 313
To Make a Frittata, 294
To Make An Omelet, 305
To Make Frittatine, 294
To Poach Eggs, 307
To Scramble Eggs, 318
To Whip Eggs Whites, 748
Artichokes with Scrambled Eggs, 637
Asparagus with Eggs, 627
Aurora Eggs, 314
Baked Eggs with Anchovy Butter, 309
Baked Eggs with Duchess Potatoes, 310
Baked Eggs with Potatoes, 309
Baked Eggs with Tomatoes and Zucchini, 310
Bavette in Egg Sauce, 147
Boiled Eggs, 313
Boiled Eggs with Artichokes and Peas, 313
Boiled Eggs with Tuna, 317
Braised Lamb with Prosciutto and Eggs, 518
Broth with Egg, 95
Chilled Omelet with Cream and Jelly, 306
Cream Sauce with Eggs, 18
Egg and Onion Soup, 138
Egg String Stracciatella, 113
Eggs Baked in Spinach Nests, 310
Eggs with Ham, 70
Eggs with Mayonnaise, 70
Eggs with Shrimp, 70
Eggs with Tuna, 70
Emperor's Frittata (Kaiser Schmarren), 788
Filled Eggs with Mayonnaise, 315
Fried Egg Parcels, 316
Fried Eggs American Style, 311
Fried Eggs Turkish Style, 312
Fried Eggs with Bacon, 311
Fried Eggs with Mozzarella and Anchovy Butter, 312
Frittata Flan, 300
Frittata with Anchovies, 295
Frittata with Baked Artichokes, 299
Frittata with Basil, 295
Frittata with Eggplant and Zucchini, 298
Frittata with Macaroni, 297
Frittata with Onion, Guanciale and Tomatoes, 296
Frittata with Onions, 295
Frittata with Parmesan and Gruyère, 297
Frittata with Potatoes, 296
Frittata with Spinach, 298
Frittata with Stuffed Zucchini Flowers, 297
Frittata with Tomatoes and Zucchini, 298
Frittata with Zucchini, 299
Frittata with Zucchini Flowers, 296
Frittatine Fantasy, 302
Frittatine Stuffed with Meat and Mushrooms, 303
Frittatine Millefeuille, 301
Frittatine Roman Style, 302
Frittatine Stuffed with Spinach and Ricotta, 304
Grilled Chicken Frittata Sandwiches, 62
Hard-Boiled Eggs with Tuna and Mayonnaise, 315
Jam Omelet, 781
Marinated Sardines, 362
Meatloaf with Eggs and Prosciutto, 512
Monachina Style Eggs, 314
Mutton-Stuffed Grape Leaves with Eggs, 535
Neapolitan Pizza with Egg and Mushrooms, 265
Omelet with Asparagus and Artichokes, 305
Omelet with Provola, 306
Peppers with Eggs, 680
Pickled Eggs with Chili, 316
Poached Eggs with Anchovy Butter, 307
Poached Eggs with Asparagus Tips, 308
Poached Eggs with Mushrooms and Croutons, 307
Poached Eggs with Tomato and Mozzarella, 308
Poached Sea Bass with Eggs, 368
Potato Frittatine, 300
Quick Anchovy and Egg Sauce, 29
Quick Egg and Mustard Sauce, 30
Quick Whole-Egg Mayonnaise, 20
Rabbit in Egg Sauce, 615
Rigatoni with Sausage and Eggs, 161
Risotto with Egg Surprise, 224
Rum Omelet, 782
Sausage and Egg Sauce, 48
Scrambled Eggs in Tomatoes, 319
Scrambled Eggs with Cardoons, 318
Scrambled Eggs with Chicken Livers and Asparagus, 318
Scrambled Eggs with Ham and Croutons, 319
Soup with Grated Egg Pasta, 106
Spaghettini with Eggs, 167
Spicy Hard-Boiled Egg Sauce, 26
Spinach with Parmesan and Eggs, 695
Sweet Frittata, 788
Tagliatelle with Egg, Anchovy, and Mozzarella, 179
Turkey Stew with Egg and Lemon, 599
Veal Roll with Egg Sauce, 443

Eggplant
Deep-Fried Eggplants, 664
Deep-Fried Eggplant Balls, 665
Deep-Fried Eggplants in Wine Batter, 665
Eggplant and Prosciutto Timbale, 666
Eggplant Flan with Beef, 665
Eggplant Mushroom Style, 667
Eggplant Parmigiana, 662
Eggplant Parmigiana, White Variation, 662
Eggplant Sicilian Style (Caponata), 663
Eggplant Stuffed with Meat, 667
Eggplant Syracuse Style (Caponatina), 664
Neapolitan Stuffed Eggplants, 666
Roast Eggplants, 664
Tomato Sauce with Peppers and Eggplant, 40
Tortiglioni with Peppers and Eggplant, 168

Endive
Belgian Endive Parmigiana, 661
Belgian Endive with White Sauce, 661
Braised Endive, 660
Endive Roman Style, 660
Rice and Endive Soup with Tomatoes, 109

Escarole
Rustic Escarole Pie, 284
Salad of Escarole and Radicchio, 724
Sausages with Escarole, 558

F

Fagottini
Fagottini with Mozzarella and Anchovies, 251
Fagottini with Mozzarella and Mushrooms, 252
Fagottini with Ricotta and Sausages, 252

Fava bean. *see also* **Bean**
Bavette with Fresh Fava Beans, 14
Fava Bean Soup with Pork Skin, 139
Fava Beans Maitre D'hotel, 716
Fava Beans Purée, 716
Fava Beans with Guanciale, 716

Fennel
Beef and Fennel Stew, 498
Braised Spring Lamb with Anchovy and Fennel, 517
Calf's Liver with Fennel Piquant Sauce, 462
Celery, Apple and Fennel Salad, 720
Fennel and Carrot Salad, 720
Fennel with Tomato, 654
Fennel with White Sauce, 654
Maccheroncini with Baked Sardines and Wild Fennel, 154
Pan-Fried Fennel, 654
Pork Chops with Fennel and Marsala, 542
Rice, Fennel, and Sausage Soup, 110
Sardines with Fennel, 360

Fettuccine. *see also* **Pasta**
Baked Fettuccine with Prosciutto and Button Mushrooms, 173
Fettuccine Ciociara Style, 171
Fettuccine in Cream Sauce, 151
Fettuccine Ragu, 172
Fettuccine Roman Style, 171
Fettuccine Soufflé, 321
Fettuccine with Ham and Mushrooms, 151
Fettuccine with Mascarpone, 172
Fettuccine with Peas, 173
Refined Fettuccine Zuava, 172

Fig. *see also* **Fruit**
Dried Figs, 742
Dried Figs with Chocolate, 743
Fig Jam, 742
Sweet Figs, 881

Fish. *see also* **Carp; Cod; Croaker; Cuttlefish; Eel; Gray mullet; Grouper; Herring; John dory; Kid; Monkfish; Red mullet; Red snapper; Salmon; Salt cod; Sardine; Sea bream; Sea bass; Shark; Skate; Sole; Stockfish; Swordfish; Trout; Tuna; Turbot**
To Braise Fish, 328
To Fry Fish, 328
To Poach Fish, 328
To Prepare River Fish, 378
To Roast Fish, 328
Artichoke and Smoked Fish Roe, 66
Ancona Brodetto, 122
Boneless Fish Soup, 133

Deep-Fried Whitebait, 346
Fano Brodetto, 122
Fish Broth, 89
Fish Jelly, 53
Fish Salad, 726
Fish Sauce, 43
Fish Soufflé, 323
Fish Soup Genovese, 129
Fish Stew Livornese, 126
Fried Fish, 252
Fish Soup Lazio Style, 131
Marinated Whitebait, 347
North Adriatic Brodetto, 121
Peppers Stuffed with Fish and Rice, 683
Port Recanati Brodetto, 123
Provençal Fish Soup, 132
Refined Fish Stew, 126
St. Benedict's Brodetto, 124
St. Peter's Fish Soup, 132
White Fish Cream, 55

Fondant
To Coat with Fondant, 749
To Make Fondant, 749

Fontina. *see also* **Cheese**
Deep-Fried Pork Chops with Fontina and Prosciutto, 544
Fontina Crescents, 76
Fried Sirloin with Fontina, 482
Polenta and Fontina Pie, 236
Polenta and Fontina Croquettes, 248
Potato Gnocchi with Tomato and Fontina, 228
Veal Chops with Fontina, 420

Fritti Misti, 243-244

Fruit. *see also* **Apple; Apricot; Banana; Cherry; Coconut; Fig; Grape; Lemon; Melon; Peach; Pear; Pineapple; Prune; Quince; Raisin; Sour cherry; Strawberry; Watermelon**
To Preserve Fruit, 737
Baba with Fruit, 809
Butter and Candied Fruit Pudding, 758
Fresh Fruit Tart, 786
Fruit Cake, 785
Fruit Meringue, 886
Fruit Pudding, 760
Fruit Salad, 887
Fruit with Sweet Rice, 768
Preserved Fruit, 737-747
Sparkling Fruit Salad, 887

Fusilli allegria, 152

G

Garlic
Garlic Mayonnaise, 20
Pan-Fried Swiss Chard with Garlic, 632
Porcini with Garlic, 656
Quick Garlic Sauce, 29
Red Mullet with Garlic and Lemon, 376
Spaghetti Aglio e Olio, 163
Spaghetti with Garlic and Tomatoes, 163
Spaghetti with Garlic, Oil, and Anchovy, 163

Gazpacho, 141

Gnocchi. *see also* **Pasta**
Giant Gnocchi, 232
German Gnocchi, 231
Gnocchi Genovese, 227
Gnocchi Pastries, 878
Gnocchi Piedmont Style, 227
Gnocchi Roman Style, 228
Polenta Gnocchi, 229
Potato Gnocchi with Tomato and Fontina, 228
Spinach Gnocchi, 229
Spinach Gnocchi with Ricotta, 231
Semolina Gnocchi, 230

Goat. *see also* **Kid**
Goat Offal Sardinian Style, 540

Goose, Roast with Chestnut and Olive Stuffing, 608

Gorgonzola. *see also* **Cheese**
Gorgonzola Boats, 65
Gorgonzola Cream, 56
Gorgonzola Sauce, 23
Spaghetti with Gorgonzola, 161

Goulash, 488
Goulash with Cream and Dumplings, 488

Grape. *see also* **Fruit**
Christmas Grapes, 746
Grape Cake, 775
Grapes in a Cup, 885
Grapes in Spirit, 746
Mutton-Stuffed Grape Leaves with Eggs, 535

Grapefruit with Blood Orange, 885

Green bean. *see also* **Bean; Fava bean**
To Cook Green Beans, 713
Green Bean Flan, 714
Green Bean Soufflé, 321
Green Beans with Gruyère, 714
Green Beans with Tomato, 713
Green Beans with Tuna and Anchovy, 714
Shoulder of Lamb with Green Beans, 527
Timbale of Green Beans with Meatballs, 715

Gray mullet. *see also* **Fish**
Baked Baby Gray Mullets with Anchovies, 340
Baked Gray Mullet with Herbs, 341
Gray Mullet Baked with Lemon, 341
Gray Mullet with Anchovy Sauce, 341
Grilled Baby Gray Mullets with Parsley Sauce, 340

Grouper. *see also* **Fish**
Grilled Grouper, 342
Grilled Grouper Fillets with Mustard, 343
Grouper Fillets with Tomato, 342

Gruyère. *see also* **Cheese**
Frittata with Parmesan and Gruyère, 297
Green Beans with Gruyère, 714
Gruyère Croquettes, 245
Rustic Gruyère Pie, 283
Spinach with Prosciutto and Gruyère, 695
Veal Chops with Truffle, Ham, Gruyère and Tomato, 420
Veal Strips with White Sauce, 425

Guinea Fowl, Salmi, 607

H

Hake, Stuffed, 350

Ham. *see also* **Pork; Prosciutto**
Boiled Beef with Sage, Ham, and Mozzarella, 470
Cream of Ham, 101
Eggs with Ham, 70
Fettuccine with Ham and Mushrooms, 151
Fried Mozzarella and Ham Sandwich, 255
Ham and Jelly Canapés, 58
Ham and Pea Sauce, 45
Ham and Salami Pie, 288
Ham Baskets, 76
Ham Cream, 56
Ham Flan, 563
Ham Hock with Spinach Sauce, 567
Ham in a Crust, 563
Ham Mostaccioli, 253
Ham Mousse, 79
Ham Pies, 73
Ham Quenelles, 78
Ham Soufflé, 324
Marinated Fresh Ham with Marsala, 564
Meat Broth with Ham Gnocchetti, 91
Rice and Ham Salad, 723
Roast Veal and Ham Rolls with Sage, 430
Sandwiches with Anchovies and Ham, 61
Scrambled Eggs with Ham and Croutons, 319
Steak with Ham and Mozzarella, 466
Veal and Ham Pie, 436
Veal and Ham Skewers, 451
Veal Chops with Truffle, Ham, Gruyère and Tomato, 420

Hare
Hare Country Style, 616
Pappardelle with Hare, 175
Salmi of Hare, 617
Saint Umberto's Hare, 616

Hazelnut
Baked Hazelnuts, 867
Hazelnut Ice Cream, 841
Hazelnut Paste, 756

Herring
Herring Salad, 331
Marinated Herring in Aromatic Sauce, 331

Horseradish
Horseradish Sauce with Cream, 27
Horseradish Tartine, 62
Pumpkin with Horseradish, 702

I

Ice cream, 839-842
To Make Ice Cream, 839

J

Jelly
To Use Jelly, 52
To Use Gelatin Bouillon, 52
Meat Jelly, 52
Fish Jelly, 53

Jerusalem artichoke. *see also* **Artichoke; Cardoon**
Jerusalem Artichokes in Green Sauce, 700
Jerusalem Artichokes, Two Ways 700

John Dory. *see also* **Fish**
Deep-Fried John Dory Fillets, 355
John Dory Fillets in Butter, 355
John Dory Flan, 355
John Dory with Artichokes and Potatoes, 356

K

Kid. *see also* **Goat**
Kid Braised in White Wine, 539
Kid Braised with Artichokes, 538
Kid on Skewers, 539
Kid Stewed with Mushrooms, 540
Oven-Baked Kid with Artichoke Salad, 538

Krapfen, 857
Kugelhupf, 801

L

Lamb. *see also* **Lamb chops; Mutton; Spring lamb**
Boiled Leg of Lamb, 525
Braised Lamb Hunter Style, 521
Braised Lamb with Peas, 526
Braised Lamb with Prosciutto and Eggs, 518
Braised Leg of Lamb, 525
Farmhouse Lamb, 518
Hunter's Lamb, 517
Lamb and Potato Stew, 520
Lamb Cooked in Milk, 526
Lamb Marche Style, 526
Lamb Offal with Artichokes, 533
Lamb Sweetbreads with Artichokes, 531
Lamb Sweetbreads with Prosciutto, 531
Medallions of Lamb Bolognese Style, 528
Shoulder of Lamb with Green Beans, 527
Stuffed Leg of Lamb, 522
Lamb chops. *see also* **Lamb**
Braised Lamb Chops with Artichokes, 527
Deep-Fried Lamb Chops, 524
Deep-Fried Lamb Chops with Onion Sauce (Soubise), 530
Deep-Fried Lamb Chops with Spring Vegetables, 530
Grilled Lamb Chops with Anchovy and Lemon Sauce, 524
Lamb Chop Skewers, 520
Lamb Chops Maintenon, 528
Lamb Chops Scottadito, 524
Lamb Chops Villeroy, 523
Lamb Chops with Prunes and Vegetables, 529
Roast Lamb Chops with Mustard Sauce, 529
Langoustine
Langoustines American Style, 396
Langoustine and Squid Skewers, 398
Langoustine Cocktail, 397
Langoustine Mayonnaise, 398
Langoustine Soup, 134
Risotto with Langoustines, 222
Roast Langoustines, 397
Vol-Au-Vents with Langoustine, 81
Larks in a Nest, 600
Lasagna. *see also* **Pasta**
To Prepare and Cook Lasagna, 194
Carnival Lasagna, 197
Green Lasagna Modena Style, 194
Lasagna with Ricotta, 197
Mushroom Lasagna, 196
Neapolitan Lasagna, 195
Tomato Lasagna, 196
Lasagnette. *see also* **Pasta**
Hunter's Lasagnette with Chicken, 174
Lasagnette Genovese, 174
Lasagnette Lucca Style, 153
Lasagnette Piedmont Style, 175
Lasagnette with Spinach and Mushrooms, 152
Leek
Leek Flan, 691
Leeks in Cream, 690
Pan-Fried Leeks, 691
Lemon. *see also* **Fruit**
Anchovies with Lemon, 329
Baked Cod with Lemon, 348
Broccoli with Lemon, 631
Deep-Fried Breast of Veal with Lemon, 437
Gray Mullet Baked with Lemon, 341
Grilled Lamb Chops with Anchovy and Lemon Sauce, 524
Lemon Cups, 831
Lemon Granita, 844
Pan-Fried Veal Chops with Parsley and Lemon Sauce, 421
Quick Lemon Sauce, 30
Red Mullet with Garlic and Lemon, 376
Swiss Chard with Lemon, 631
Turkey Stew with Egg and Lemon, 599
Veal Scaloppine with Lemon, 448
Lentil
Lentil Purée, 717
Lentils in a Pan, 717
Rice and Lentil Soup, 109
Zampone with Lentils, 561
Lobster. *see also* **Shellfish**
To Cook Lobster and Other Crustaceans, 386
American Lobster with Rice and Cognac, 387
Deviled Lobster, 387
Lobster American Style, 386
Lobster in its Jelly, 388
Lobster Mayonnaise, 390
Lobster Medallions in Jelly, 391
Lobsters in the Shell with Truffle, 389
Roast Lobster, 389

M

Macaroni. *see also* **Pasta**
Frittata with Macaroni, 297
Macaroni Gratin, 156
Macaroni in Wild Mushroom Sauce, 158
Macaroni Pasticcio, 202
Macaroni Salad, 157
Macaroni with Four Cheeses, 155
Macaroni with Four String Cheeses, 155
Macaroni with Mozzarella, 156
Macaroni with Ricotta, 157
Maccheroncini. *see also* **Macaroni; Pasta**
Maccheroncini and Broccoli Sicilian Style, 154
Maccheroncini with Baked Sardines and Wild Fennel, 154
Maccheroncini with Little Meatballs, 153
Mackerel Fillets with Anchovy and Capers, 347
Madeleine Cake, 815
Maritozzi, 858
Marzipan (Almond Paste), 756
Mascarpone
Conchiglie with Mascarpone and Mushrooms, 150
Fettuccine with Mascarpone, 172
Margherita Cake with Mascarpone, 816
Mascarpone Bombs, 796
Mascarpone Cream in Cups, 835
Mascarpone Sauce, 45
Mayonnaise
Anchovy Mayonnaise, 20
Boiled Beef with Mayonnaise, 470
Chicken Mayonnaise, 585
Chicken Mayonnaise French Style, 585
Eggs with Mayonnaise, 70
Filled Eggs with Mayonnaise, 315
Garlic Mayonnaise, 20
Green Mayonnaise, 21
Hard-Boiled Eggs with Tuna and Mayonnaise, 315
Langoustine Mayonnaise, 398
Lobster Mayonnaise, 390
Mayonnaise, 19
Mussels with Mayonnaise, 67
Mustard and Cornichon Mayonnaise, 19
Octopus Mayonnaise, 403
Quick Whole-Egg Mayonnaise, 20
Tuna Mayonnaise, 374
Turkey Breast with Mayonnaise, 597
Meatballs
Fried Meatballs in Tomato Sauce, 507
Maccheroncini with Little Meatballs, 153
Meatballs Fried in Butter, 507
Meatballs Roman Style, 510
Meatballs Russian Style, 511
Rice Timbale with Meatballs, 214
Timbale of Green Beans with Meatballs, 715
Veal Meatballs Flambéed with Cognac, 439
Veal Meatballs with Butter, 439
Veal Meatballs with Cream Sauce, 440
Meatloaf
Meatloaf Braised in Milk, 511
Meatloaf Cooked in a Bain Marie, 513
Meatloaf with Eggs and Prosciutto, 512
Meatloaf with Mushrooms and Chicken Livers, 440
Meatloaf with Tomato Sauce, 512
Pork Meatloaf with Vegetables, 553
Melon. *see also* **Fruit**
Melon with Peaches and Rum, 884
Melon with Strawberries, 884
Meringue
Aristocrat Meringue, 776
Fruit Meringue, 886
Meringue, 780
Meringue Cake, 807
Milk
Braised Beef in Milk, 476
Carrots in Milk, 643
Chicken Braised in Milk, 581
Lamb Cooked in Milk, 526
Meatloaf Braised in Milk, 511
Milk Roasted Veal, 413
Milk Soup, 102
Pork Loin Cooked in Milk, 550
Rice with Milk, 208
Salt Cod in Milk, 333
Minestrone
Barley and Bitter Greens Minestrone, 120
Farmhouse Minestrone, 118
Fresh Bean Minestrone, 118
Florentine Minestrone, 115
Minestrone Genovese, 116
Minestrone Milanese, 116
Summer Minestrone Milanese, 117
Minestrone with Lardo, 117
Minestrone with Stuffed Lettuce Parcels, 119
Spring Minestrone, 120
Vegetable Minestrone, 114
Yellow Pumpkin Minestrone, 120
Mint Sauce, 26
Monkfish
Braised Monkfish, 344
Monkfish with Parsley Butter, 343
Mozzarella. *see also* **Cheese**
Baked Potatoes with Mozzarella, 668
Boiled Beef with Sage, Ham, and Mozzarella, 470
Fagottini with Mozzarella and Anchovies, 251

Fagottini with Mozzarella and Mushrooms, 252
Fried Eggs with Mozzarella and Anchovy Butter, 312
Fried Mozzarella, 254
Fried Mozzarella and Ham Sandwich, 255
Fried Mozzarella Sandwich, 254
Fried Mozzarella with Anchovy, 255
Fried Tournedos with Truffle and Mozzarella, 485
Macaroni with Mozzarella, 156
Mozzarella Croquettes, 247
Mozzarella on Potato Crackers, 77
Mozzarella with Tuna Sauce, 77
Neapolitan Pizza with Mozzarella and Mushrooms, 265
Pizzette with Mozzarella and Anchovy, 272
Poached Eggs with Tomato and Mozzarella, 308
Polenta with Mozzarella and Anchovies, 235
Polenta with Sausages and Mozzarella, 237
Steak with Ham and Mozzarella, 466
Tagliatelle with Egg, Anchovy, and Mozzarella, 179
Veal and Mozzarella Packets, 427

Mushroom. *see also* **Porcini**
To Cook Mushrooms, 655
To Dry Mushrooms, 655
Anchovies Baked with Mushrooms, 330
Baked Fettuccine with Prosciutto and Button Mushrooms, 173
Braised Breast of Veal with Wild Mushrooms, 444
Braised Squab with Peppers and Mushrooms, 609
Cod Baked with Mushrooms, 348
Conchiglie with Mascarpone and Mushrooms, 150
Cream of Mushroom, 98
Cream of Wild Mushrooms, 47
Dried Mushroom Ragu, 33
Dried Mushrooms, 721
Eggplant Like Mushrooms, 676
Fagottini with Mozzarella and Mushrooms, 252
Fettuccine with Ham and Mushrooms, 151
Frittatine Stuffed with Meat and Mushrooms, 303
Kid Stewed with Mushrooms, 540
Lasagnette with Spinach and Mushrooms, 152
Macaroni in Wild Mushroom Sauce, 158
Meat and Mushroom Pie, 282
Meat and Mushroom Sauce, 36
Meatloaf with Mushrooms and Chicken Livers, 440
Neapolitan Pizza with Mozzarella and Mushrooms, 265
Milk Roasted Veal, 413
Mushroom and Spinach Sauce, 46
Mushroom Cream Sauce, 17
Mushroom Lasagna, 196
Mushroom Pies, 73
Mushroom Sauce, 46
Mushroom Soup, 139
Mushroom Vol-Au-Vents, 80
Mushrooms in Cream, 655
Mutton Chops with Mushrooms, 537
Neapolitan Pizza with Egg and Mushrooms, 265
Neapolitan Pizza with Mozzarella and Mushrooms, 265
Pan-Fried Mushrooms with Parsley, 655
Pappardelle with Mushrooms, 176
Poached Eggs with Mushrooms and Croutons, 307
Peppers Stuffed with Mushrooms, 682
Raw Salad of Caesar Mushrooms, 723
Red Mullet Parcels with Mushrooms, 374
Rib Steak with Mushrooms, 480
Roast Beef with Wild Mushrooms, 493
Sausage and Mushroom Ragu, 33
Sea Bass with Anchovy and Wild Mushrooms, 370
Spaghetti with Mushrooms, 165
Spaghettini with Artichokes and Mushrooms, 167
Spinach and Mushroom Flan, 697
Stewed Baby Octopus with Mushrooms, 402
Sturgeon with Mushrooms, 382
Swiss Chard and Mushroom Gratin, 632
Tomatoes Stuffed with Mushrooms, 689
Tomato Sauce with Dried Mushrooms, 39
Tomato Sauce with Mushrooms, 38
Tomato Sauce with Tuna and Mushrooms, 41
Tournedos with Prosciutto and Wild Mushrooms, 485
Tuna in Oil with Mushrooms, 372
Turkey Cutlets Pan-Fried with Mushrooms, 595
Turkey Flan with Mushroom Sauce, 599
Vol-Au-Vents with Mushrooms, 83
Vol-Au-Vents with Mushroom Cream, 80

Mussels. *see also* **Shellfish**
Bucatini with Mussels and Clams, 147
Fisherman's Mussels, 406
Mussel Soup, 128
Mussels Gratin, 407
Mussels with Mayonnaise, 67
Risotto with Mussels and Clams, 220
Shrimp and Mussels Pandorato, 393
Spicy Mussels, 68
Villeroy Mussels, 407
White Brodetto, 125

Mustard
Fried Sardines with Mustard and Anchovy, 363
Grilled Grouper Fillets with Mustard, 343
Mustard and Cornichon Mayonnaise, 19
Mustard Sauce, 24
Pork Chops with Mustard, 543
Quick Egg and Mustard Sauce, 30
Roast Lamb Chops with Mustard Sauce, 529

Mutton. *see also* **Lamb**
Baked Leg of Mutton, 535
Boiled Mutton with Mint Sauce English Style, 536
Braised Mutton with Carrots, 534
Braised Mutton with Vinegar, 533
Grilled Mutton Chops, 537
Mutton Chops with Mushrooms, 537
Mutton in a Dutch Oven, 536
Mutton-Stuffed Grape Leaves with Eggs, 535

N

Nougat, 774

O

Octopus
Baby Octopus Genoa Style, 401
Baby Octopus Salad, 402
Octopus Mayonnaise, 403
Octopus Naples Style, 402
Octopus Santa Lucia Style, 404
Octopus Pie, 287
Peppers Stuffed with Squid or Octopus, 680
Stewed Baby Octopus with Mushrooms, 402

Olives
Braised Chicken with Olives, 580
Green Sicilian Olives, 731
Olives for Cocktails, 68
Olives of Gaeta, 731
Rabbit with Olives Ligurian Style, 613
Roast Goose, 608
Salt Cod with Tomato and Green Olives, 334
Spaghetti with Capers and Olives, 164
Stuffed Olives, 68
Tuna Baked with Olives and Capers, 371

Onion. *see also* **Cipollini onion**
Baked Onions, 649
Beef and Onion Skewers, 496
Beet and Onion Salad, 628
Beet and Onion in Sauce, 628
Boiled Onions, 650
Braised Beef with Onions, 475
Deep-Fried Lamb Chops with Onion Sauce (Soubise), 530
Egg and Onion Soup, 138
French Onion Soup, 137
Fried Onion Rings, 649
Frittata with Onion, Guanciale and Tomatoes, 296
Frittata with Onions, 295
Grilled Onions, 651
Grilled Pork Chops with Onions, 542
Pickled Onion Sauce, 25
Pickled Onions, 730
Pizza with Onions, 267
Onions Stuffed with Meat, 650
Tomatoes Stuffed with Onion, 688
Trout with Onion Butter, 383
Veal Tongue with Sweet and Sour Onions, 462
White Sauce with Onions, 16

Orange. *see also* **Fruit**
Candied Orange Cake, 790
Candied Orange Peel, 755
Duck with Orange, 600
Grapefruit with Blood Orange, 885
Orange Bonbons, 860
Orange Granita, 843
Orange Hollandaise, 22
Orange Jelly, 739
Orange Pasticcini, 869
Orange Salad, 718
Oranges and Strawberries, 879
Oranges in Jam, 738
Oranges with Maraschino, 879
Orecchiette Pugliese, 158
Osso Buco Milanese, 435

Ox. *see also* **Beef**
Butcher's Oxtail and Cheek, 515
Ox Kidney, Two Ways, 515
Ox Liver in Sweet and Sour Sauce, 460
Oxtail Soup, 104

Oyster
Deep-Fried Oysters, 408
Deviled Oysters, 408
Oyster Gratin, 409
Venetian Oysters, 69

P

Pappardelle. *see also* **Pasta**
Pappardelle with Duck, 176
Pappardelle with Hare, 175
Pappardelle with Mushrooms, 176
Parmesan. *see also* **Cheese**
Artichokes with Prosciutto and Parmesan, 639
Frittata with Parmesan and Gruyère, 297
Parmesan Cream, 56
Parmesan Flan, 78
Parmesan Soufflé, 322
Parmesan Soufflé Cups, 322
Purée of Beans and Parmesan, 712
Spinach with Parmesan and Eggs, 695
Tomato Soup with Parmesan Crostini, 140
White Truffles with Parmesan, 698
Partridge Casserole, 608
Pasta. *see also* **Bucatini; Cannelloni; Cannolicchi; Cappelletti; Conchiglie; Fagottini; Gnocchi; Lasagna; Lasagnette; Macaroni; Maccheroncini; Pappardelle; Penne; Ravioli; Rigatoni; Spaghetti; Spaghettini; Tagliatelle; Tonnarelli; Tortellini; Tortiglioni**
To Cook and Prepare Dried Pasta, 145
To Make Egg Pasta By Hand, 170
To Make Egg Pasta with a Machine, 170
To Make Green Egg Pasta, 170
Pasta and Broccoli Soup, 106
Pasta and Pea Soup, 107
Pasta of a Thousand Leaves, 198
Pasta Roll with Ricotta and Spinach, 191
Pasta Roll with Tomato and Spinach, 190
Soup with Grated Egg Pasta, 106
Timbale of Angel Hair Pasta, 202
Venetian Bean and Pasta Soup, 107
Pastry. *see also* **Choux pastry**
To Make Puff Pastry Dough, 275
To Make Sweetened Puff Pastry, 820
To Make Unsweetened Puff Pastry, 71
Broth with Choux Buns, 92
Cannoncini, 863
Non-Leavened Quick Pastry, 785
Pastry Cream, 752
Pastry Boats for Wild Strawberries, 766
Peaches in Sweet Pastry, 773
Puff Pastry, 820
Roman Short Pastry, 784
Saint-Honoré, 818
Short Pastry Without Eggs, 784
Simplified Puff Pastry, 820
Sweet Shortcrust Pastry, 784
Peach. *see also* **Fruit**
Empress Peaches, 772
Melon with Peaches and Rum, 884
Peach Granita, 844
Peach Pudding, 761
Peach Sherbet, 847
Peaches in Spirit, 744
Peaches in Sweet Pastry, 773
Peaches with Maraschino Cream, 771
Peaches with Yogurt, 885
Peaches Zabaglione, 773
Piedmontese Peaches, 772
Whole Peaches in Syrup, 744
Pear. *see also* **Fruit**
Pears in Maraschino, 770
Poached Pears with Cream, 884
Margherita Pears, 771
Pea
Artichokes with Peas, 638
Boiled Eggs with Artichokes and Peas, 313
Braised Lamb with Peas, 526
Chicken Breast with Peas, 578
Cipollini Onions with Peas, 652
Clams with Peas, 409
Cream of Pea, 99
Fettuccine with Peas, 173
Ham and Pea Sauce, 45
Pasta and Pea Soup, 107
Peas English Style, 683
Peas French Style, 683
Peas Sardinian Style, 684
Peas with Prosciutto, 684
Peas with Smoked Pancetta, 684
Rice and Peas Venetian Style (Risi e Bisi), 209
Risotto with Artichokes and Peas, 220
Shark with Peas, 354
Stracciatella with Peas, 113
Tomatoes with Peas, 690
Tuna in Oil with Peas, 373
Veal and Pea Stew, 449
Veal Sweetbreads with Peas, 458
Vol-Au-Vents with Peas, 85
Penne
Penne with Vodka, 159
Penne Arrabbiata, 158
Pennette Pasticci, 203
Spring Pennette Salad, 159
Pepper Galettes, 60
Persimmon in Cognac, 742
Pesto
Pesto Genovese, 49
Spicy Pesto, 49
Tonnarelli with Clams and Pesto, 181
Trenette with Pesto, 169
Pheasant
Pheasant in Cream, 604
Roast Pheasant with Cognac, 605
Salmi of Pheasant, 606
Pies, 275-291
To Make Pie Dough, 64, 275
Pike in Red Wine, 380
Pine nut
Beef Croquettes with Raisins and Pine Nuts, 506
Pine Nut Cookies, 849
Spaghetti with Herbs, 162
Pineapple. *see also* **Fruit**
Avocado with Pineapple and Grapefruit, 739
Creole Pineapple, 765
Pineapple Surprise, 878
Pineapple with Kirsch, 878
Pineapple with Kiwi and Pomegranate, 878
Pork Loin with Prosecco and Pineapple, 541
Pizzas, 264-274
To Make Pizza Dough, 264
Pizzaiola, Sauce, 38
Pizzette, 271-272
Plum Jam, 745
Polenta
To Cook Polenta, 233
Baked Polenta, 238
Baked Polenta with Veal and Chicken Livers, 239
Meat Broth with Polenta Gnocchetti, 91
Polenta and Fontina Pie, 236
Polenta and Fontina Croquettes, 248
Polenta Gnocchi, 229
Polenta Mostaccioli, 253
Polenta Pudding, 237
Polenta Supplì, 261
Polenta Timbale, 238
Polenta with Broth, 233
Polenta with Mozzarella and Anchovies, 235
Polenta with Pork Ribs, 234
Polenta with Salt Cod Vicenza Style, 234
Polenta with Sausages, 236
Polenta with Sausages and Mozzarella, 237
Polenta with Veal and Chicken Livers, 235
Roast Quail with Polenta, 610
Porcini. *see also* **Mushroom**
Baked Porcini, 656
Baked Stuffed Porcini, 659
Braised Chicken with Porcini Mushrooms, 582
Braised Thrush with Porcini, 611
Deep-Fried Stuffed Porcini, 658
Fried Baby Porcini, 658
Pickled Ovoli Porcini, 730
Porcini Braised in White Wine, 657
Porcini Ligurian Style, 656
Porcini Sauce Genoa Style, 46
Porcini with Anchovy and Tomato, 657
Porcini with Garlic, 656
Sautéed Porcini, 659
Swordfish with Porcini Mushrooms, 357
Pork. *see also* **Ham; Pork chops; Pork steak; Prosciutto**
Braised Pork Loin Genoa Style, 552
Braised Pork Offal, 565
Braised Pork Rolls, 552
Fava Bean Soup with Pork Skin, 139
Frankfurters with Cabbage
Ham and Salami Pie, 288
Hunter's Pork, 555
Meat and Mushroom Sauce, 36
Neapolitan Meat Sauce, 36
Pig's Head Galantine, 566
Pig's Trotters with Broccoli and Sausages, 560
Pig's Trotters with Green Sauce, 559
Polenta with Pork Ribs, 234
Pork and Beans, 712
Pork Galantine, 546
Pork Liver Crostini, 59
Pork Liver Petroniana, 566
Pork Liver with Bay, 565
Pork Loin Cooked in Milk, 550
Pork Loin with Prosecco and Pineapple, 541
Pork Meatloaf with Vegetables, 553
Pork Milanese (Bottaggio), 550
Pork Pie with Truffle, 556
Pork Skewers, 554
Pork Steaks with Tomato, 548
Pork Strips in Caper Sauce, 546
Pork Strips with Sweet and Sour Sauce, 545
Pork with Tuna, 554
Roast Pork with Apple Sauce, 551
Roast Pork with Brussels Sprouts, 551

Pork chops. *see also* **Pork**
Baked Pork Chops, 542
Deep-Fried Pork Chops with Fontina and Prosciutto, 544
Grilled Pork Chops with Onions, 542
Grilled Pork Chops with Pepper Sauce, 545
Pork Chops Braised in White Wine, 541
Pork Chops Modena Style, 543
Pork Chops with Cornichons, 544
Pork Chops with Fennel and Marsala, 542
Pork Chops with Mustard, 543
Pork steak. *see also* **Pork**
Pork Steaks Neapolitan Style, 548
Pork Steaks with Aromatic Sauce, 549
Pork Steaks with Prune Sauce, 549
Potato. *see also* **Duchess potato**
Baked Eggs with Potatoes, 309
Baked Potatoes in Their Jackets, Two Ways, 669
Baked Potato Surprise, 669
Baked Potatoes Parmigiana, 668
Baked Potatoes with Mozzarella, 668
Boiled Beef with Potatoes, 469
Broth with Potato Dumplings, 90
Croaker Baked with Potatoes, 351
Dauphin Potatoes, 672
Dauphin Potatoes with Chicken Livers, 673
Fried Potatoes, 673
Frittata with Potatoes, 296
John Dory with Artichokes and Potatoes, 356
Lamb and Potato Stew, 520
Mozzarella on Potato Crackers, 77
Neapolitan Pizza with Flour and Potatoes, 266
Pan-Fried New Potatoes, 676
Pan-Fried Potatoes (Rosti), 675
Pan-Fried Potatoes Pizzaiola, 675
Pan-Fried Potatoes with Prosciutto, 675
Pizza with Veal and Potatoes, 269
Potato and Sausage Bake, 676
Potato and Tuna Salad, 676
Potato Croquettes, 248
Potato Flan, 674
Potato Frittatine, 300
Potato Gnocchi with Tomato and Fontina, 228
Potato Pie, 277
Potato Pizza, 270
Potato Purée, 674
Potato Soufflé, 322
Potato Soup, 140
Rice and Potato Soup, 110
Roast Beef with Potatoes, 494
Roast Chicken with Potatoes, 581
Roast Spring Lamb with New Potatoes, 516
Roast Veal Roll with Potatoes, 441
Rustic Potato Pie, 284
Rustic Potato Pie Cuma Style, 285
Shrimp in Potato Boxes, 394
Sole with Baked Potato and Shrimp Sauce, 366
Veal and Potato Timbale, 454
Veal Rolls with Potato, 431
Veal Sweetbreads with Potato, 458
Poussin. *see also* **Chicken**
Braised and Stuffed Poussins, 572
Broiled Poussins with Deviled Sauce, 572
Roast Poussins with Anchovies, 571
Prosciutto. *see also* **Ham; Pork**
Artichokes with Prosciutto and Parmesan, 639
Asparagus with Prosciutto, 626
Baked Fettuccine with Prosciutto and Button Mushrooms, 173
Beef Pizza with Prosciutto, 510
Braised Lamb with Prosciutto and Eggs, 518
Broccoli with Prosciutto, 631
Cardoons with Prosciutto, 643
Deep-Fried Pork Chops with Fontina and Prosciutto, 544
Eggplant and Prosciutto Timbale, 669
Lamb Sweetbreads with Prosciutto, 531
Meatloaf with Eggs and Prosciutto, 512
Pan-Fried Potatoes with Prosciutto, 675
Peas with Prosciutto, 684
Pizza and Prosciutto Twists, 270
Prosciutto in Jelly with Russian Salad, 562
Prosciutto or Tongue Sandwiches, 61
Prosciutto Ragu, 34
Spinach with Prosciutto and Gruyère, 695
Tournedos with Prosciutto and Wild Mushrooms, 485
Turkey Cutlets with Prosciutto, 596
Zucchini with Rice and Ham, 705
Prune. *see also* **Fruit**
Chicken with Prunes, 582
Dried Prunes, 745
Lamb Chops with Prunes and Vegetables, 529
Pork Steaks with Prune Sauce, 549
Prune Pudding, 763
Spicy Prune Sauce, 26
Pumpkin
Deep-Fried Pumpkin in Batter, 701
Fried Pumpkin Sicilian Style, 701
Hunter's Pumpkin, 701
Pumpkin with Horseradish, 702
Yellow Pumpkin Minestrone, 120

Q

Quail
Roast Quail with Polenta, 610
Spicy Quail, 610
Spit-Roasted Quail, 610
Quiche Lorraine, 291
Quince. *see also* **Fruit**
Quince in Squares, 741
Quince Jam, 741
Quince Jelly, 741

R

Rabbit
Hunter's Rabbit, 612
Rabbit Country Style, 613
Rabbit in Egg Sauce, 615
Rabbit with Capers, 612
Rabbit with Olives Ligurian Style, 613
Salmi of Rabbit, 615
Slow Cooked Rabbit with Tomatoes, 614
Sweet and Sour Rabbit, 614
Ragus, 32-36
Raisin. *see also* **Fruit**
Beef Croquettes with Raisins and Pine Nuts, 506
Black Raisin Pastries with Rum, 870
Raisin Cake, 799
Raisin Pastine, 869
Ravioli. *see also* **Pasta**
Ravioli Genovese, 189
Ravioli with Ricotta, Butter, and Sage, 190
Red mullet. *see also* **Fish**
Fried Red Mullets, 376
Red Mullet Calabrian Style, 375
Red Mullet Gratin, 377
Red Mullet Livornese Style, 375
Red Mullet Parcels with Mushrooms, 374
Red Mullet with Garlic and Lemon, 376
Red Mullet with Tomatoes, 377
Red snapper. *see also* **Fish**
Baked Red Snapper, 344
Baked Red Snapper Fillets, 345
Baked Red Snapper Fillets with Onions, 345
Red Snapper Pizzaiola, 346
Red wine. *see also* **Wine**
Beef and Red Wine Sauce, 35
Beef in Red Wine, 495
Beef Slow Cooked in Red Wine, 499
Hot Red Wine Sauce, 778
Pike in Red Wine, 380
Spring Lamb Braised in Red Wine, 519
Rice
Cooking Methods for Rice, 207
To Cook Rice, 207
American Lobster with Rice and Cognac, 387
Artichokes with Rice, 633
Chicken Liver and Rice Soufflé, 324
Chilled Rice with Shrimp and Peppers, 210
Fruit with Sweet Rice, 768
Paella, 219
Peppers Stuffed with Fish and Rice, 683
Rice and Bean Soup, 108
Rice and Bitter Greens Soup, 108
Rice and Cauliflower Soup, 108
Rice and Endive Soup with Tomatoes, 109
Rice and Lentil Soup, 109
Rice and Peas Venetian Style (Risi e Bisi), 209
Rice and Potato Soup, 110
Rice and Zucchini Soup, 110
Rice Flan, 789
Rice Fritters, 856
Rice Gratin, 210
Rice Timbale with Meatballs, 214
Rice Valtellinese, 208
Rice with Anchovies, 212
Rice with Duck, 209
Rice with Milk, 208
Rice, Fennel, and Sausage Soup, 110
Roasted Rice Genovese, 208
Savory Rice Pudding, 211
Shellfish Rice Gratin, 211
Timbale of Veal and Rice, 453
Tomatoes with Rice, 685
White Rice Supplí, 260
Zampone with Rice, 561
Zucchini with Rice and Ham, 705
Ricotta. *see also* **Cheese**
Cannelloni with Ricotta and Sausage, 187
Conchiglie with Ricotta and Spinach, 150
Duchess Potato Croquettes with Ricotta, 671
Fagottini with Ricotta and Sausages, 252
Frittatine Stuffed with Spinach and Ricotta, 304
Lasagna with Ricotta, 197
Macaroni with Ricotta, 157
Meat Broth with Ricotta Dumplings, 94
Pasta Roll with Ricotta and Spinach, 191
Ravioli with Ricotta, Butter, and Sage, 190
Ricotta and Sausage Sauce, 48

Ricotta. (*cont.*)
Ricotta and Sausage Crostini, 60
Ricotta and Spinach Sauce, 47
Ricotta Bocconotti, 853
Ricotta Fritters, 855
Ricotta Gratin, 79
Ricotta Pudding, 763
Ricotta Sauce, 47
Ricotta Sfogliata, 825
Ricotta Tart, 788
Rustic Ricotta and Sausage Pie, 290
Spinach and Ricotta Pie, 289
Spinach Gnocchi with Ricotta, 231
Sweet Ricotta Sfogliatelle, 872
Tortiglioni with Ricotta, 168
Veal and Ricotta Croquettes, 424

Rigatoni. *see also* **Pasta**
Baked Rigatoni, 199
Rigatoni Gratin with Asparagus, 200
Rigatoni Salad with Arugula, 160
Rigatoni with Sausage and Eggs, 161
Rigatoni with Zucchini, 160

Risotto
Artichoke Risotto, 215
Chicken Liver Risotto, 216
Chicken Risotto, 217
Farmhouse Risotto, 226
Risotto in Three Colors, 225
Risotto Milanese, 216
Risotto Mold with Livers, 224
Risotto with Artichokes and Peas, 220
Risotto with Cuttlefish, 223
Risotto with Egg Surprise, 224
Risotto with Langoustines, 222
Risotto with Mussels and Clams, 220
Risotto with Sausages, 222
Risotto with Seven Flavors, 215
Risotto with Sparkling Wine, 221
Risotto with Tuna, 223
Shrimp Risotto, 221
Springtime Risotto, 226
Turkish Risotto, 218

Rum
Banana and Rum Cream, 879
Black Raisin Pastries with Rum, 870
Melon with Peaches and Rum, 884
Rum Omelet, 782
Rum Soufflé, 826
Strawberries with Rum or Maraschino, 882
Watermelon with Rum, 881

S

Salad
American Salad, 718
Andalusian Salad, 719
Artichokes with Russian Salad, 636
Asparagus Salad, 627
Baby Octopus Salad, 402
Beet and Onion Salad, 628
Belgian Salad, 719
Bitter Leaf Salad, 722
Celery Salad, 724
Celery, Apple and Fennel Salad, 720
Chicken Salad, 584
Coconut Salad, 887
Colorful Salad, 718
Cucumber and Parsley Salad, 721
Fantasy Salad, 725
Farmhouse Salad, 722
Fennel and Carrot Salad, 720
Fish Salad, 726
Fruit Salad, 757
Harlequin Salad, 719
Herring Salad, 331
Macaroni Salad, 157
Orange Salad, 718
Oven-Baked Kid with Artichoke Salad, 538
Potato and Tuna Salad, 676
Prosciutto in Jelly with Russian Salad, 562
Puntarelle Salad, 723
Raw Cabbage Salad, 721
Raw Salad of Mushrooms, 723
Raw Spinach Salad, 724
Rice and Ham Salad, 723
Rigatoni Salad with Arugula, 160
Russian Salad, 725
Salad of Escarole and Radicchio, 724
Shrimp Salad, 720
Sparkling Fruit Salad, 887
Spelt Salad, 722
Spring Pennette Salad, 159
Tomatoes with Russian Salad, 686
Watercress Salad with Yogurt, 721
Watermelon Salad, 886

Salmon. *see also* **Fish**
Baked Salmon, 381
Poached Salmon, 381
Vermicelli with Salmon, 169

Salt cod. *see also* **Cod; Fish; Stockfish**
Baked Salt Cod, 332
Fried Salt Cod Livornese, 245
Fried Salt Cod Roman Style, 245
Italian Salt Cod Soup, 127
Polenta with Salt Cod Vicenza Style, 234
Roman Salt Cod Stew, 337
Salt Cod Flan, 335
Salt Cod Gratin, 332
Salt Cod in Milk, 333
Salt Cod Neapolitan Style, 336
Salt Cod Pizzaiola, 332
Salt Cod Portuguese Style, 334
Salt Cod Provençal, 333
Salt Cod Soup Marseille Style, 127
Salt Cod with Peppers, 336
Salt Cod with Sour Cherries, 335
Salt Cod with Tomato and Green Olives, 334
Stuffed Salt Cod, 337

Sardines. *see also* **Fish**
Baked Sardines, 361
Fried Sardines Ligurian Style, 361
Fried Sardines with Mustard and Anchovy, 363
Maccheroncini with Baked Sardines and Wild Fennel, 154
Marinated Sardines, 362
Neapolitan Pan-Fried Sardines, 360
Sardine Butter, 55
Sardine Sauce, 43
Sardines with Fennel, 360
Timbale of Vermicelli and Sardines, 205

Sauces, 14-49

Sausage
Beef Sausages, 495
Breast of Veal Stuffed with Sausages, 436
Cabbage and Sausage Soup, 137
Calzone with Sausages and Provolone, 274
Cannelloni with Ricotta and Sausage, 187
Fagottini with Ricotta and Sausages, 252
Giant Sausages, 444
Pig's Trotters with Broccoli and Sausages, 560
Polenta with Sausages, 236
Polenta with Sausages and Mozzarella, 237
Potato and Sausage Bake, 676
Rice, Fennel, and Sausage Soup, 110
Ricotta and Sausage Sauce, 48
Ricotta and Sausage Crostini, 60
Rigatoni with Sausage and Eggs, 161
Risotto with Sausages, 222
Rustic Ricotta and Sausage Pie, 290
Sausage and Egg Sauce, 48
Sausage and Mushroom Ragu, 33
Sausages with Beans, 557
Sausages with Cardoons, 558
Sausages with Escarole, 558
Tomato Sauce with Sausages, 40
Veal Sausage with Spinach, 445
Vegetable and Sausage Soup, 104

Sea bream. *see also* **Fish**
Baked Sea Bream, 352
Sea Bream Bercy, 352
Sea Bream in a Salt Crust, 352

Sea bass. *see also* **Fish**
Baked Sea Bass, 368
Poached Sea Bass with Eggs, 368
Sea Bass Baked with Herbs, 369
Sea Bass Steamed in White Wine, 369
Sea Bass with Anchovy and Wild Mushrooms, 370

Semolina
Broth with Semolina Squares, 93
Semolina and Asparagus Soup, 111
Semolina Croquettes, 249
Semolina Gnocchi, 230
Semolina Mostaccioli, 253
Semolina Skewers, 257
Semolina Soup, 111
Sicilian Crosetti, 188

Shark. *see also* **Fish**
Baked Shark Steaks, 353
Shark Gratin, 354
Shark in White Wine, 354
Shark Pizzaiola, 353
Shark with Peas, 354

Shellfish. *see also* **Clam; Crawfish; Lobster; Mussels; Octopus; Oyster; Shrimp; Squid**
To Prepare Mollusks, 399
Fishing Boats, 75
Refined Shellfish Marinara Sauce, 42
Shellfish Rice Gratin, 211
Shellfish Sauce, 42
Squid with Shellfish, 400
Tonnarelli with Shellfish, 182

Shrimp. *see also* **Shellfish**
Shrimp with Asparagus, 392
Bucatini with Shrimp and Baby Squid, 148
Chilled Rice with Shrimp and Peppers, 210
Conchiglie with Shrimp, 150
Eggs with Shrimp, 70
Fried Gray Shrimp, 395
Fried Shrimp, 393
Glazed Shrimp, 392
Shrimp and Mussels Pandorato, 393
Shrimp Boats, 66
Shrimp Butter, 55
Shrimp Canapés, 58
Shrimp Cocktail, 69
Shrimp Crostini, 394
Shrimp Risotto, 221
Shrimp Salad, 720
Shrimp Soufflé, 325

Shrimp Soup, 128
Vol-Au-Vents with Langoustine, 81
Shrimp with Asparagus, 392
Shrimp in Potato Boxes, 394
Sole with Baked Potato and Shrimp Sauce, 366
Steamed Shrimp, 395
Vol-Au-Vents with Shrimp, 84

Skate. *see also* **Fish**
Skate in Brown Butter, 358
Skate with Anchovy Sauce, 358
Steamed Skate with Tomato, 358

Snipe
Pan-Fried Snipe with Cognac, 604
Roast Snipe, 604

Sole. *see also* **Fish**
Fried Sole Colbert, 364
Fried Sole Italian Style, 364
Sole Fillets with Artichoke, 367
Sole Gratin, 365
Sole in Butter, 365
Sole Manfred, 367
Sole Meunière, 363
Sole with Baked Potato and Shrimp Sauce, 366
Sole with White Wine, 364

Sospiri, 882

Soufflés, 320-325
To Cook Soufflés, 320

Soups, 96-141

Sour cherry. *see also* **Cherry; Fruit**
Salt Cod with Sour Cherries, 335
Sour Cherries in their Shirts, 885
Sour Cherry Granita, 844
Sour Cherry Jam, 747
Sour Cherry Jam and Syrup, 747

Spaghetti. *see also* **Pasta; Spaghettini**
Fisherman's Spaghetti, 166
Spaghetti Carbonara, 161
Spaghetti with Capers and Olives, 164
Spaghetti Cacio e Pepe, 164
Spaghetti Aglio e Olio, 163
Spaghetti with Garlic and Tomatoes, 163
Spaghetti with Garlic, Oil, and Anchovy, 163
Spaghetti with Gorgonzola, 161
Spaghetti with Herbs, 162
Spaghetti with Meat and Vegetables, 164
Spaghetti with Mushrooms, 165
Spaghetti with Raw Tomato Sauce, 165
Spaghetti with Squid Ink, 162
Spaghetti with Tuna, 166
Spaghetti with Wedge Clams, 165
Vegetarian Spaghetti Carbonara, 162

Spaghettini. *see also* **Pasta; Spaghetti**
Spaghettini with Artichokes and Mushrooms, 167
Spaghettini with Caviar, 167
Spaghettini with Eggs, 167

Spinach
To Cook Spinach, 693
Beef Broth with Spinach Parcels, 92
Braised Spinach, 693
Conchiglie with Ricotta and Spinach, 150
Cream of Spinach, 101
Eggs Baked in Spinach Nests, 310
Frittata with Spinach, 298
Frittatine Stuffed with Spinach and Ricotta, 304
Ham Hock with Spinach Sauce, 567
Lasagnette with Spinach and Mushrooms, 152
Mushroom and Spinach Sauce, 46
Pasta Roll with Ricotta and Spinach, 191
Pasta Roll with Tomato and Spinach, 190
Raw Spinach Salad, 724
Ricotta and Spinach Sauce, 47
Spinach and Mushroom Flan, 697
Spinach and Ricotta Pie, 289
Spinach Croquettes, 249
Spinach Crostini, 697
Spinach Flan, 696
Spinach Gnocchi, 229
Spinach Gnocchi with Ricotta, 231
Spinach Gratin, 694
Spinach Roman Style, 694
Spinach Soufflé, 325
Spinach with Anchovy Fillets, 695
Spinach with Butter, 694
Spinach with Parmesan and Eggs, 695
Spinach with Prosciutto and Gruyère, 695
Veal Sausage with Spinach, 445
Zampone with Spinach, 562

Spring lamb. *see also* **Lamb**
Braised Spring Lamb with Anchovy and Fennel, 517
Roast Spring Lamb Roman Style, 516
Roast Spring Lamb with New Potatoes, 516
Spring Lamb Braised in Red Wine, 519
Spring Lamb with Anchovy Sauce, 519

Squab
Braised Squab with Peppers and Mushrooms, 609
Roast Squab, 609

Squid. *see also* **Shellfish**
Braised Baby Squid Marche Style, 399
Bucatini with Shrimp and Baby Squid, 148
Deep-Fried Squid, 401
Langoustine and Squid Skewers, 398
Peppers Stuffed with Squid or Octopus, 680
Roast Squid, 400
Spaghetti with Squid Ink, 162
Spicy Squid Sauce, 42
Squid Neapolitan Style, 399
Squid with Shellfish, 400

Steak. *see also* **Beef**
Beef Steak Pizzaiola, 481
Charcoal-Grilled Steak, 466
Fried Sirloin with Fontina, 482
Grilled Steak, 466
Steak Florentine Style, 467
Steak Pie, 491
Steak Rib Pizzaiola, 480
Steak Sicilian Style, 467
Steak Tartare, 468
Steak with Ham and Mozzarella, 466
Sugar Steaks, 417

Stew
Beef and Fennel Stew, 498
Beef Stew Catalan Style, 487
Beef Stew French Style, 497
Beef Stew Roman Style, 498
Cuttlefish and Tomato Stew, 405
Fish Stew Livornese, 126
Kid Stewed with Mushrooms, 540
Lamb and Potato Stew, 520
Stewed Baby Octopus with Mushrooms, 402
Turkey Stew with Egg and Lemon, 599
Veal and Pea Stew, 449
Veal and Tomato Stew, 448
Veal Stew with Marsala, 449

Stockfish. *see also* **Fish; Salt cod**
Braised Stockfish with Tomato, 340
Stockfish Ancona Style, 338
Stockfish Messina Style, 339
Stockfish Venetian Style, 339

Stracciatelle, 112-113

Strawberry. *see also* **Fruit**
Melon with Strawberries, 884
Oranges and Strawberries, 879
Pastry Boats for Wild Strawberries, 766
Strawberries Carmen, 882
Strawberries with Rum or Maraschino, 882
Strawberries with Yogurt, 882
Strawberry and Cream Sherbet, 846
Strawberry Bavarois, 830
Strawberry Bonbons, 861
Strawberry Charlotte, 834
Strawberry Crêpes, 778
Strawberry Ice Cream in Cups, 841
Strawberry Jam, 743
Strawberry Mousseline, 838
Strawberry Sherbet with Blackberries, 847
Strawberry Soufflé, 828
Strawberry Tart, 787
Wild Strawberry Granita, 844

Sturgeon with Mushrooms, 382

Sugar
To Make Icing, 748
To Make Sugar Syrups, 736
To Spin Sugar, 736
Sugar Steaks, 417
Sugar Syrups, 736
Turnips with Sugar, 692

Supplì, 260

Sweetbread
Deep-Fried Sweetbreads, 532
Lamb Sweetbreads with Artichokes, 531
Lamb Sweetbreads with Prosciutto, 531
Pan-Fried Sweetbreads, 532
Pan-Fried Sweetbreads in Butter, 532
Sweetbread Croquettes, 246
Veal Sweetbreads with Marsala Sauce, 459
Veal Sweetbreads with Peas, 458
Veal Sweetbreads with Potato, 458

Swiss Chard
Swiss Chard and Mushroom Gratin, 632
Swiss Chard with Lemon, 631

Swordfish. *see also* **Fish**
Baked Swordfish, 356
Fried Swordfish, 356
Swordfish with Porcini Mushrooms, 357
Swordfish with Tomato, 357

T

Tagliatelle. *see also* **Pasta**
Genoa Green Tagliatelle, 178
Green Tagliatelle Bolognese, 177
Tagliatelle Bolognese, 177
Tagliatelle with Chicken, 179
Tagliatelle with Cream, 200
Tagliatelle with Egg, Anchovy, and Mozzarella, 179
Tagliatelle with Walnuts, 179

Tangerine Jelly in Their Skins, 836
Tapioca Soup, 111
Tarragon Butter, 54
Thrush, Braised with Porcini, 611
Tiramisu, 877

Tomato. *see also* **Tomato sauce**
To Skin and Seed a Tomato, 685
Baked Eggs with Tomatoes and Zucchini, 310
Beef and Tomato Rolls, 489
Beef and Tomato Sauce, 35
Beef Consommé with Carrots and Tomato Cream, 96
Braised Chicken with Tomato, 576
Braised Stockfish with Tomato, 340
Calabrian Pie, 276
Cannelloni with Beef and Tomatoes, 184
Chickpeas with Tomato, 709
Cream of Tomato, 100
Cuttlefish and Tomato Stew, 405
Duchess Potatoes with Beef and Tomato, 671
Fennel with Tomato, 654
Fresh Beans with Tomato, 713
Frittata with Onion, Guanciale and Tomatoes, 296
Frittata with Tomatoes and Zucchini, 298
Green Beans with Tomato, 713
Grouper Fillets with Tomato, 342
Pan-Fried Tomatoes, 687
Pasta Roll with Tomato and Spinach, 190
Poached Eggs with Tomato and Mozzarella, 308
Porcini with Anchovy and Tomato, 657
Pork Steaks with Tomato, 548
Potato Gnocchi with Tomato and Fontina, 228
Red Mullet with Tomatoes, 377
Rice and Endive Soup with Tomatoes, 109
Salt Cod with Tomato and Green Olives, 334
Scrambled Eggs in Tomatoes, 319
Slow Cooked Rabbit with Tomatoes, 614
Spaghetti with Garlic and Tomatoes, 163
Steamed Skate with Tomato, 358
Stuffed Tomatoes, 686
Stuffed Tomatoes, 69
Sun-Dried Tomatoes, 733
Swordfish with Tomato, 357
Tomato Bruschetta, 57
Tomatoes Gratin, 686
Tomato Lasagna, 196
Tomato Passata, 733
Tomato Ragu, 32
Tomato Soufflé, 324
Tomato Soup with Parmesan Crostini, 140
Tomatoes Stuffed with Capers and Anchovies, 688
Tomatoes Stuffed with Meat, 688
Tomatoes Stuffed with Mushrooms, 689
Tomatoes Stuffed with Onion, 688
Tomatoes with Peas, 690
Tomatoes with Rice, 685
Tomatoes with Russian Salad, 686
Tomatoes with Seafood, 689
Tomatoes with Tuna, 690
Tuna and Tomato Casserole, 372
Tuna with Tomato, 371
Veal and Tomato Rolls, 430
Veal and Tomato Stew, 448
Veal Chops with Truffle, Ham, Gruyere and Tomato, 420
Veal Chops with Tomatoes and Peppers, 421
Veal Rolls with Tomato, 434
Veal Tenderloin with Tomatoes, 428
Veal Trotter with Tomato and Cinnamon, 457
Zucchini with Tomato, 704

Tomato sauce. *see also* **Tomato**
Amatriciana Sauce, 23
Arrabbiata Sauce, 38
Cipollini Onions in Tomato Sauce, 652
Creamy Tomato Sauce, 18
Fried Meatballs in Tomato Sauce, 507
Meatloaf with Tomato Sauce, 512
Penne with Vodka, 159
Penne Arrabbiata, 158
Raw Tomato Sauce, 37
Refined Tomato Sauce, 41
Spaghetti with Raw Tomato Sauce, 165
Spicy Tomato Sauce, 26
Spicy Tomato Sauce with Cipollini Onions, 41
Tomato and Basil Sauce, 38
Tomato Sauce, 37
Tomato Sauce with Dried Mushrooms, 39
Tomato Sauce with Herbs, 39
Tomato Sauce with Mushrooms, 38
Tomato Sauce with Peppers and Eggplant, 40
Tomato Sauce with Sausages, 40
Tomato Sauce with Seven Flavors, 37
Tomato Sauce with Tuna and Mushrooms, 41
Traditional Tomato Sauce, 28

Tonnarelli. *see also* **Pasta**
Tonnarelli Chitarra Abruzzese, 180
Tonnarelli with Clams and Pesto, 181
Tonnarelli with Cream, 181
Tonnarelli with Shellfish, 182

Tortellini. *see also* **Pasta**
Chicken Tortellini, 193
Tortellini Bolognese, 192
Tortellini Pie with Ragu, 204
Tortellini with White Sauce, 191
Vol-Au-Vents with Tortellini, 85

Tortelloni Bolognese, 193

Tortiglioni. *see also* **Pasta**
Tortiglioni with Peppers and Eggplant, 168
Tortiglioni with Ricotta, 168
Tortiglioni with Goat Cheese, 168

Tournedos. *see also* **Beef**
Fried Tournedos with Truffle and Mozzarella, 485
Pan-Fried Tournedos with Croutons, 484
Tournedos Monaco, 486
Tournedos Vol-Au-Vents with Apple, 486
Tournedos with Prosciutto and Wild Mushrooms, 485

Trenette with Pesto, 169
Trifle, 821
Tripe Milanese, 464

Trout. *see also* **Fish**
Blue Trout, 385
Deep-Fried Trout, 385
Pan-Fried Trout in Butter, 385
Steamed Trout, 384
Trout Mousse, 384
Trout with Onion Butter, 383

Truffle. *see also* **White truffle**
To Choose Truffles, 698
Black Truffle Provençal Style, 699
Black Truffle Sauce, 699
Chicken and Truffle in Jelly, 573
Chocolate Truffles, 876
Fried Tournedos with Truffle and Mozzarella, 485
Lobsters in the Shell with Truffle, 389
Pork Pie with Truffle, 556
Roast Capon with Truffle, 570
Roast Turkey with Truffle, 594
Roast Veal with Truffle, 416
Truffle Cream, 56
Truffled Beef Terrine, 503
Turkey Cutlets Bolognese, 595
Veal Baked with Truffle and Pistachios, 456
Veal Chops with Fontina, 420
Veal Chops with Truffle, Ham, Gruyere and Tomato, 420
White Truffles Piedmont Style, 698
White Truffles with Parmesan, 698

Tuna. *see also* **Fish**
Anchovy and Tuna Fritters, 245
Artichokes with Tuna, 641
Baked Tuna, 370
Boiled Eggs with Tuna, 317
Eggs with Tuna, 70
Hard-Boiled Eggs with Tuna and Mayonnaise, 315
Mozzarella with Tuna Sauce, 77
Quick tuna and anchovy sauce, 31
Pork with Tuna, 554
Potato and Tuna Salad, 676
Risotto with Tuna, 223
Spaghetti with Tuna, 166
Tomato Sauce with Tuna and Mushrooms, 41
Tomatoes with Tuna, 690
Tuna and Tomato Casserole, 372
Tuna Baked with Olives and Capers, 371
Tuna Boats, 65
Tuna Croquettes, 250
Tuna in Oil Croquettes, 373
Tuna in Oil with Mushrooms, 372
Tuna in Oil with Peas, 373
Tuna Mayonnaise, 374
Tuna with Tomato, 371
Veal with Tuna, 456
Zucchini Stuffed with Tuna, 708

Turbot. *see also* **Fish**
Baked Turbot, 359
Turbot Fish Fingers, 359

Turkey
Roast Turkey, 593
Roast Turkey Stuffed with Chestnuts, 593
Roast Turkey with Truffle, 594
Stuffed Turkey Lombardy Style, 594
Turkey Breast with Mayonnaise, 597
Turkey Cutlets Bolognese, 595
Turkey Cutlets Fried in Butter, 596
Turkey Cutlets Modena Style, 596
Turkey Cutlets Pan-Fried with Mushrooms, 595
Turkey Cutlets with Prosciutto, 596
Turkey Flan with Mushroom Sauce, 599
Turkey Medallions with Mushrooms, 597
Turkey Stew with Egg and Lemon, 599
Turkey Timbale, 598

Turnips with Sugar, 692

V

Vanilla
Almond and Vanilla Spumette, 875
Vanilla Bavarois, 839
Vanilla Sugar, 880

Veal. *see also* **Calf's liver; Veal chops; Veal cutlet**
Baked Polenta with Veal and Chicken Livers, 239
Fricassee of Veal with Artichokes, 428
Braised Breast of Veal with Wild Mushrooms, 444
Braised Veal Roll, 442
Braised Veal with Vegetables, 437
Breast of Veal Stuffed with Sausages, 436
Deep-Fried Breast of Veal with Lemon, 437
Farmhouse Roast Veal, 412
Genovese Veal Strips, 426
Grilled Veal Trotters, 457
Meat and Mushroom Pie, 282
Milk Roasted Veal, 413
Osso Buco Milanese, 435
Pan-Fried Veal Scaloppine with Garnish, 447
Pan-Fried Kidneys with Anchovy, 463
Petronian Veal Steaks, 416
Pizza with Veal and Potatoes, 269
Poached Breast of Veal with a Piquant Sauce, 438
Polenta with Veal and Chicken Livers, 235
Roast Stuffed Breast of Veal, 438
Roast Veal and Ham Rolls with Sage, 430
Roast Veal Bella Vista, 414
Roast Veal Casserole, 415
Roast Veal Roll with Potatoes, 441
Roast Veal with Cream, 412
Roast Veal with Truffle, 416
Veal Saltimbocca, 446
Stuffed Veal Rolls, 432
Timbale of Veal and Rice, 454
Veal and Artichoke Timbale, 453
Veal and Ham Pie, 436
Veal and Ham Skewers, 451
Veal and Mozzarella Packets, 427
Veal and Pea Stew, 449
Veal and Potato Timbale, 454
Veal and Ricotta Croquettes, 424
Veal and Tomato Rolls, 430
Veal and Tomato Stew, 448
Veal Baked with Truffle and Pistachios, 455
Veal Croquettes, 250
Veal Croquettes Russian Style, 424
Veal Galantine, 429
Veal in Aspic, 454
Veal Kidneys with Marsala, 463
Veal Loaf, 426
Veal Marengo, 450
Veal Meatballs with Butter, 439
Veal Paillard, 435
Veal Pizzaiola, 425
Veal Roll with Sweet and Sour Sauce, 442
Veal Roll with Egg Sauce, 443
Veal Rolls with Potato, 431
Veal Rolls with Tomato, 434
Veal Saltimbocca, 446
Veal Sausage with Spinach, 445
Veal Scaloppine with Lemon, 448
Veal Scaloppine with Marsala, 446
Veal Skewers with Sage, 450
Veal Steaks with Zabaglione Sauce, 417
Veal Stew with Marsala, 449
Veal Strips Bolognese, 425
Veal Strips with White Sauce, 425
Veal Sweetbreads with Marsala Sauce, 459
Veal Sweetbreads with Peas, 458
Veal Sweetbreads with Potato, 458
Veal Tenderloin Bolognese, 427
Veal Tenderloin with Tomatoes, 428
Veal Timbales Financier, 452
Veal Tongue with Green Sauce, 463
Veal Tongue with Sweet and Sour Onions, 462
Veal Trotter Fricassee, 457
Veal Trotter with Tomato, 456
Veal with Tuna, 456
Veal chops. *see also* **Veal**
Broiled Veal Chops, 418
Pan-Fried Veal Chops with Parsley and Lemon Sauce, 421
Veal Chops En Papillote, 419
Veal Chops Farmhouse Style, 418
Veal Chops Modena Style, 418
Veal Chop Terrine, 422
Veal Chops with Fontina, 420
Veal Chops with Tomatoes and Peppers, 421
Veal Chops with Truffle, Ham, Gruyère and Tomato, 420
Veal cutlet. *see also* **Veal**
Double-Fried Veal Cutlets Villeroy, 423
Fried Veal Cutlets Viennese Style, 423
Veal Cutlets Milanese, 422
Veal steak. *see also* **Veal**
Veal Steaks Milanese, 432
Veal Steaks Modena Style, 433
Veal Steaks with Herb Sauce, 433
Veal Steaks with Peppers, 434
Veal Steaks with Sage, 433
Vegetable and Sausage Soup, 104
Venison. *see also* **Deer**
Salmi of Venison, 619
Stuffed Leg of Venison, 619
Venison with Cherry Sauce, 620
Vermicelli with Salmon, 169
Viennese Cake (Sacher Torte), 794
Vol-au-vents
To Make Vol-Au-Vents, 80
Mushroom Vol-Au-Vents, 80
Tournedos Vol-Au-Vents with Apple, 486
Vol-Au-Vents with Finanziera Sauce, 82
Vol-Au-Vents with Langoustine, 81
Vol-Au-Vents with Livers, 81
Vol-Au-Vents with Mushrooms, 83
Vol-Au-Vents with Mushroom Cream, 80
Vol-Au-Vents with Peas, 85
Vol-Au-Vents with Shrimp, 84
Vol-Au-Vents with Tortellini, 85

W

Walnut
Date and Walnut Bonbons, 865
Sweet Walnut Bread, 803
Tagliatelle with Walnuts, 179
Walnut Bonbons, 861
Walnut Sauce, 45
Walnut Mostaccioli, 867
Watercress
Watercress Purée, 48
Watercress Salad with Yogurt, 721
Watermelon. *see also* **Fruit**
Watermelon Salad, 886
Watermelon with Rum, 881
White Sauce (Béchamel), 16
White truffle. *see also* **Truffle**
Veal Chops with Fontina, 420
White Truffles Piedmont Style, 698
White Truffles with Parmesan, 698
White wine. *see also* **Wine**
Carp in White Wine, 380
Cipollini Onions in White Wine, 652
Cod with White Wine, 349
Kid Braised in White Wine, 539
Porcini Braised in White Wine, 657
Pork Chops Braised in White Wine, 541
Sea bass Steamed in White Wine, 369
Shark in White Wine, 354
Sole with White Wine, 364
Wine. *see also* **Red wine; White wine**
To Make Wine Batter, 242
Baked Wine Donuts, 854
Deep-Fried Eggplants in Wine Batter, 665
Hot Falerno (Wine) Sauce, 753
Pan-Fried Apples with Wine, 883
Risotto with Sparkling Wine, 221
Woodcock
Roast Woodcock with Crostini, 602
Stuffed Roast Woodcock, 603

Y

Yeast
To Work with Active Dry Yeast, 796
To Work with Fresh Yeast, 796
Active Dry Yeast, 796
Fresh Yeast, 796
Yeast Croquettes, 251
Yeast, Desserts with, 796-809

Z

Zabaglione
Peaches Zabaglione, 754
Veal Steaks with Zabaglione Sauce, 417
Zabaglione Cups, 831
Zabaglione Pudding, 782
Zabaglione Sherbet, 847
Zampone
Zampone with Lentils, 561
Zampone with Rice, 561
Zampone with Spinach, 562
Zucchini. *see also* **Zucchini flower**
Baked Eggs with Tomatoes and Zucchini, 310
Fried Zucchini, 706
Fried Zucchini Fillets, 706
Fried Zucchini Flowers, 702
Fried Zucchini Gratin, 706
Frittata with Eggplant and Zucchini, 298
Frittata with Tomatoes and Zucchini, 298
Frittata with Stuffed Zucchini Flowers, 297
Frittata with Zucchini, 299
Marinated Fried Zucchini, 707
Pan-Fried Zucchini Flowers, 703
Rice and Zucchini Soup, 110
Rigatoni with Zucchini, 160
Stuffed Zucchini Flowers, Three Ways, 702
Zucchini Genovese, 703
Zucchini Ligurian Style, 704
Zucchini Roman Style, 708
Zucchini Soup, 141
Zucchini Stuffed with Tuna, 708
Zucchini Timbale, 707
Zucchini with Beef, 705
Zucchini with Rice and Ham, 705
Zucchini with Tomato, 704

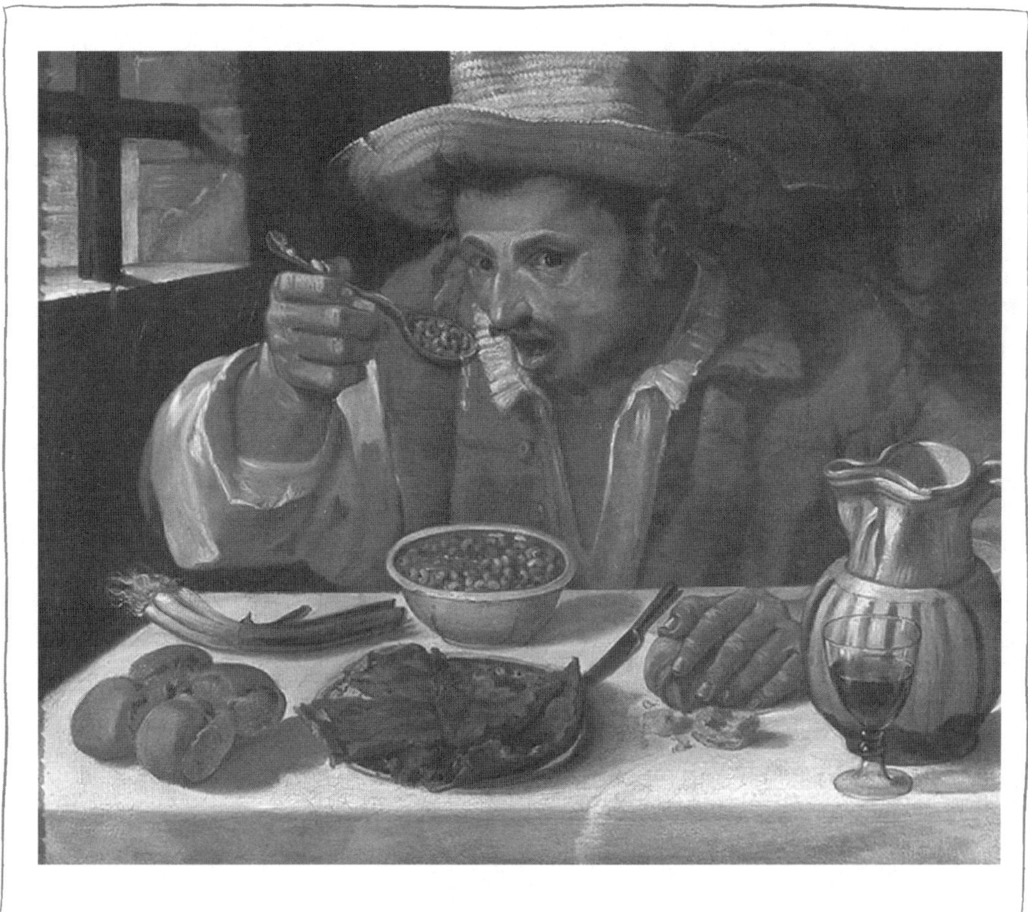

Mangiafagioli ("The Bean Eater") was painted by Annibale Carracci in Bologna in the mid-1580s. It has become identified with *The Talisman of Happiness* as it has been used on the covers of many editions published by Editore Colombo. The painting hangs in the Palazzo Colonna in Rome, Italy.

"In the same way I feel that every American kitchen should have a copy of *The Joy of Cooking*, I now believe any lover of Italian food should get this brilliant translation of *The Talisman of Happiness*, Ada Boni's nearly hundred-year-old masterpiece, finally available in English. Just as the title proclaims, *The Talisman* will bring magical powers to your kitchen, from twelve versions of minestrone soup to nineteen spaghetti recipes and enough desserts to satisfy every child on your block. *The Talisman of Happiness* is all-encompassing in a very delectable way."

—NANCY SILVERTON, award-winning chef, bestselling author, and co-owner of Mozza Restaurant Group

---

"*Il Talismano della Felicità* is an essential resource for anyone interested in Italian cooking. It's a timeless classic, filled with deep culinary wisdom and definitive recipes to turn to time and again."

—RITA SODI and JODY WILLIAMS, award-winning chefs, restaurateurs, and bestselling authors

---

"*The Talisman* is an absolute treasure that sits at the very foundation of the modern understanding of regional Italian cooking. Ada Boni, through her words and extraordinary recipes, has been a conduit for Italian food and its anthropology."

—EVAN FUNKE, chef, bestselling author, and master pasta maker